The Political Lincoln

The Political Lincoln

An Encyclopedia

Paul Finkelman
Martin J. Hershock
Editors

A Division of SAGE
Washington, D.C.

CQ Press
2300 N Street, NW, Suite 800
Washington, DC 20037

Phone: 202-729-1900; toll-free, 1-866-4CQ-PRESS (1-866-427-7737)

Web: www.cqpress.com

Copyright © 2009 by CQ Press, a division of SAGE. CQ Press is a registered trademark of Congressional Quarterly Inc.

All rights reserved. No part of this publication may be reproduced or transmitted in any form or by any means, electronic or mechanical, including photocopy, recording, or any information storage and retrieval system, without permission in writing from the publisher.

Cover design: Kimberly Glyder
Composition: Auburn Associates, Inc.

♾ The paper used in this publication exceeds the requirements of the American National Standard for Information Sciences—Permanence of Paper for Printed Library Materials, ANSI Z39.48-1992.

Printed and bound in the United States of America

12 11 10 09 08   1 2 3 4 5

ISBN: 978-0-87289-486-0

In Loving Memory of
Simon Finkelman (1921–2008) and
Stanley Hershock (1925–2008)

About the Editors

Paul Finkelman is the President William McKinley Professor of Law and Public Policy at Albany Law School and the author or editor of more than twenty books, including *Landmark Decisions of the United States Supreme Court.*

Martin J. Hershock is associate professor and department chair of history at the University of Michigan–Dearborn and the author of *The Paradox of Progress: Economic Change, Individual Enterprise, and Political Culture in Michigan.*

EDITORIAL ADVISORY BOARD

Christine Dee
Fitchburg State College

Walter Hill
National Archives and Records Administration

Harold Holzer
The Metropolitan Museum of Art

Michael Morrison
Purdue University

Contents

About the Editors	vii
Articles and Contributors	xvii
Introduction	xxxi

A TO Z ENTRIES

Abolitionism	1
Adams, Charles Francis	5
African Americans and Lincoln	8
Alabama Claims	15
American Colonization Society	18
American System	20
Anaconda Plan	22
Antietam Campaign	25
Antislavery	27
Assassination	31
Atlanta Campaign	35
Ball's Bluff, Battle of	39
Baltimore Mob	42
Banking and Monetary Policy	45
Banks, Nathaniel	47
Bates, Edward	48
Bedell, Grace	50
Bell, John	51
Benton, Thomas Hart	53
Black Hawk War	56
Black Suffrage	58
Blair, Austin	61
Blair, Francis	63
Blair, Montgomery	65
Bleeding Kansas	67

Blockade, Union Naval	71
Booth, John Wilkes	74
Border States, Lincoln and	78
Brady, Mathew	82
Breckinridge, John Cabell	84
Brooks, Preston	86
Brown, John	88
Browning, Orville	92
Buchanan, James	94
Bull Run, First Battle of (First Manassas)	97
Burial and Tomb, Lincoln's	99
Butler, Benjamin	100
Cabinet, Lincoln's	103
Cameron, Simon	106
Campaign of 1856, Presidential	109
Campaign of 1858, Lincoln's Senatorial	111
Campaign of 1860, Presidential	115
Campaign of 1864, Presidential	120
Cass, Lewis	124
Central Pacific Railroad	126
Chandler, Zachariah	127
Chase, Salmon Portland	129
Circuit Courts	133
Civil Liberties	135
Clay, Henry	139
Cleveland Convention, 1864	141
Colfax, Schuyler	145
Colonization	147
Compensated Emancipation	149
Compromise of 1850	152
Confederate States of America	154
Confiscation Acts	157
Confiscation Act, Second	160
Congress, Lincoln's Relations with	162
Conscription Act	167
Constitution and Slavery, The	170
Constitutional Law, Lincoln and	173
Constitutional Union Party	177
Contrabands	179
Cooke, Jay	182
Cooper Union Address	183
Copperheads	186
Corruption in the Federal Government	190
Crittenden Compromise	191

Curtin, Andrew Gregg	194
Davis, Jefferson	197
Declaration of Independence, Lincoln's View of	200
Democratic Conventions, 1860	203
Democratic Party	206
Democrats, Peace	209
Desertions/Presidential Pardons	211
Doughface	213
Douglas, Stephen A.	214
Douglass, Frederick	218
Draft, Military	221
Draft Riots, New York City	224
Dred Scott v. Sandford (1857)	227
Ellsworth, Elmer Ephraim	233
Emancipation Monument	234
Emancipation Proclamation	236
Everett, Edward	240
Ex parte Merryman	242
Fessenden, William Pitt	247
Fillmore, Millard	248
Florville, William	250
Foreign Relations and Diplomacy, Lincoln's	252
Fort Pickens	254
Fort Sumter	256
Forts Henry and Donelson	264
Founding Fathers, Lincoln's View of	267
Fredericksburg and Chancellorsville, Battles of	269
Free Soil Party	272
"Free Soil, Free Labor, Free Men"	274
Freeport Doctrine	277
Frémont, John C.	280
Garrison, William Lloyd	283
General War Order Number One	286
German Americans, Lincoln and	288
Gettysburg, Battle of	291
Gettysburg Address	294
Grant, Ulysses S.	297
Great Britain, Relations with	301
Great Emancipator	303
Greeley, Horace	306
Greenbacks	308
Habeas Corpus	311
Hamlin, Hannibal	315
Hampton Roads Conference	318

Hay, John	320
Herndon, William H.	324
Hicks, Thomas Holliday	327
Homestead Act	328
Honest Abe	331
House Divided Speech	332
Hunter, David	336
Iconography	339
Illinois	341
Illinois Central Railroad	344
Inaugural Address, First	346
Inaugural Address, Second	350
Income Taxes	353
Indiana	355
Indian Relations, Lincoln and	356
Inflation	358
Internal Improvements	360
Jackson, Andrew, As a Model for Lincoln	363
Jackson, Claiborne Fox	366
Johnson, Andrew	368
Joint Committee on the Conduct of the War	372
Kansas-Nebraska Act	377
Kentucky (as Lincoln's Birthplace and in the Civil War)	381
King Cotton	383
Knights of the Golden Circle	385
Know-Nothing (American) Party	388
Lawrence, Kansas	391
Lee, Robert E.	393
Legal Tender Act of 1862	396
Liberty Party	398
Life of Washington, by Parson Weems	400
Lincoln, Childhood and Youth	401
Lincoln, Young Manhood to Eve of Political Career	404
Lincoln, Legal and Early Political Career	407
Lincoln, As a National Figure, 1854–1865	410
Lincoln, Memory of	414
Lincoln, Edward Baker	417
Lincoln, Mary Todd	418
Lincoln, Nancy Hanks	422
Lincoln, Robert Todd	424
Lincoln, Sarah Bush Johnston	426
Lincoln, Thomas	428
Lincoln, Thomas "Tad"	429
Lincoln, William "Willie" Wallace	431

Lincoln-Douglas Debates	433
Lincoln Historic Sites, Preservation of	439
Lincoln in Film	444
Lincoln in Music	446
Lincoln Memorial	448
Lincoln on Currency	451
Lincoln Penny	452
Logan, Stephen T.	454
Long Walk, The	455
Magoffin, Beriah	457
Mason, James	458
McClellan, George B.	460
McLean, John	464
Mexican War	469
Missouri Compromise, The	471
Morgan's Raid	474
Mormons, Attacks on	476
Morrill, Justin Smith	478
Morrill Land Grant Act	479
Morrill Tariff	481
Morton, Oliver P.	482
National Banking Act of 1863	485
National Union Party	487
New Salem, Illinois	490
New York Tribune	492
Nicolay, John G.	495
Northwest Ordinance	497
Old Northwest	501
Order of Retaliation	503
Overland Campaign	505
Patronage, Lincoln and	509
Peoria Speech, Lincoln's	510
Personal Liberty Laws	514
Phillips, Wendell	516
Pierce, Franklin	518
Political Culture, Lincoln and	520
Political Philosophy, Lincoln's	522
Polk, James K.	526
Pomeroy Circular	529
Popular Sovereignty	531
Pottawatomie Creek Massacre	534
Prayer of Twenty Millions, The	536
Prize Cases, The (1863)	538
Proclamation Calling Militia and Convening Congress	540

Contents

Racism and Racial Thought, Lincoln and	545
Radical Republicans	549
Railroads	552
Rail-splitter Image, Lincoln's	554
Reconstruction	555
Republican Nominating Convention of 1860	559
Republican Party, The	563
Rhetoric in Lincoln's Public Speeches	566
Richmond, Lincoln's Arrival in	569
Rivers and Harbors Convention	571
Ruffin, Edmund	573
Rutledge, Ann	575
Scott, Winfield	579
Secession	581
Seward, William	585
Shenandoah Valley Campaigns of 1862 and 1864	588
Sherman, John	591
Sherman, William T.	593
Sherman's March to the Sea	597
Shields, James	599
Shiloh, Battle of	600
Sioux Uprising	603
Slave Power/Slavocracy	604
Slavery	607
Slavery in the Thirtieth Congress	611
Slidell, John	614
Soldiers' Home	616
Soldiers' Vote	618
Speed, Joshua F.	621
Spot Resolutions	623
Stamps, Postage	625
Stanton, Edwin M.	627
Stephens, Alexander Hamilton	629
Stowe, Harriet Beecher	632
Strong, George Templeton	634
Stuart, John Todd	636
Sumner, Charles	637
Taney, Roger B.	643
Taylor, Zachary	647
Temperance	649
Ten Percent Plan	651
Thanksgiving	654
Thirteenth Amendment	656

Todd Family	659
Trent Affair	661
Trumbull, Lyman	664
Union Pacific Railroad	667
U.S. Colored Troops (USCT)	669
U.S. Supreme Court, Lincoln's Appointments to	673
U.S. Supreme Court, Lincoln's View of	677
Vallandigham, Clement Laird	681
Vandalia, Illinois	685
Vicksburg Campaign	686
Virginia Plan	689
Volunteers, Ninety-Day	692
Wade, Benjamin Franklin	695
Wade-Davis Bill	696
War Democrats	700
Washington, D.C.	702
Weed, Thurlow	704
Welles, Gideon	706
Whig Party	707
Whigs, Conscience	710
Whigs, Cotton	713
Whitman, Walt	714
Whittier, John Greenleaf	716
Wide Awakes	718
Wilmot Proviso	720
Wood, Fernando	724
Yates, Richard	727
Young America	728
Zouaves	731
Index	733

Articles and Contributors

Abolitionism
JOHN W. QUIST
Shippensburg University

Adams, Charles Francis
ROBERT W. BURG
University of Wisconsin–Sheboygan

African Americans and Lincoln
MATTHEW NORMAN
Gettysburg College

Alabama Claims
JAMES M. CORNELIUS
Abraham Lincoln Presidential Library and Museum

American Colonization Society
ALLAN YAREMA
Abilene Christian University

American System
HARRY L. WATSON
University of North Carolina at Chapel Hill

Anaconda Plan
ALLAN PESKIN
Cleveland State University

Antietam Campaign
BROOKS D. SIMPSON
Arizona State University

Antislavery
JOHN WICKRE
University of North Dakota

Assassination
DAVID E. LONG
East Carolina University

Atlanta Campaign
BROOKS D. SIMPSON
Arizona State University

Ball's Bluff, Battle of
PETER SMITH
Wayne State University

Baltimore Mob
DAVID E. LONG
East Carolina University

Banking and Monetary Policy
MARK S. JOY
Jamestown College

Banks, Nathaniel
WILLIAM H. BROWN
North Carolina Office of Archives and History

Bates, Edward
DAVID E. ARTHUR
CQ Press

Bedell, Grace
SAMUEL P. WHEELER
Southern Illinois University

Bell, John
MARTIN J. HERSHOCK
University of Michigan–Dearborn

Benton, Thomas Hart
ROBERT W. BURG
University of Wisconsin–Sheboygan

Black Hawk War
KERRY A. TRASK
University of Wisconsin–Manitowoc

Black Suffrage
PAUL FINKELMAN
Albany Law School

Blair, Austin
JAMES SCHWARTZ
Eastern Illinois University

Blair, Francis
ROBERT W. BURG
University of Wisconsin–Sheboygan

Blair, Montgomery
MICHAEL T. SMITH
McNeese State University

Bleeding Kansas
NICOLE ETCHESON
Ball State University

Blockade, Union Naval
MARK THORNTON
Ludwig von Mises Institute

Booth, John Wilkes
MICHAEL W. KAUFFMAN
Owings, Maryland

Border States, Lincoln and
ROBERT S. TINKLER
California State University, Chico

Brady, Mathew
FRED BEUTTLER
Historian's Office, U.S. House of Representatives

Breckinridge, John Cabell
WILLIAM H. BROWN
North Carolina Office of Archives and History

Brooks, Preston
ALISON MANN
University of New Hampshire

Brown, John
PAUL FINKELMAN
Albany Law School

Browning, Orville
CARA L. SHELLY
Oakland University and University of Michigan–Dearborn

Buchanan, James
PAULA COCHRAN
Mifflinburg, Pennsylvania

Bull Run, First Battle of (First Manassas)
BROOKS D. SIMPSON
Arizona State University

Burial and Tomb, Lincoln's
PAULA COCHRAN
Mifflinburg, Pennsylvania

Butler, Benjamin
ANTHONY SANTORO
University of Heidelberg

Cabinet, Lincoln's
RON J. KELLER
Lincoln College

Cameron, Simon
PAULA COCHRAN
Mifflinburg, Pennsylvania

Campaign of 1856, Presidential
CHRISTINE DEE
Fitchburg State College

Campaign of 1858, Lincoln's Senatorial
BRUCE TAP
Grand Rapids, Michigan

Campaign of 1860, Presidential
CHRISTINE DEE
Fitchburg State College

Campaign of 1864, Presidential
MICHAEL GREEN
College of Southern Nevada

Cass, Lewis
WILLARD CARL KLUNDER
Wichita State University

Central Pacific Railroad
MARK S. JOY
Jamestown College

Chandler, Zachariah
JAMES SCHWARTZ
Eastern Illinois University

Chase, Salmon Portland
FREDERICK J. BLUE
Youngstown State University

Circuit Courts
JOHN A. LUPTON
The Papers of Abraham Lincoln

Civil Liberties
SAMUEL B. HOFF
Delaware State University

Clay, Henry
HARRY L. WATSON
University of North Carolina at
    Chapel Hill

Cleveland Convention, 1864
JOHN C. WAUGH
Pantego, Texas

Colfax, Schuyler
MICHAEL GREEN
College of Southern Nevada

Colonization
ALLAN YAREMA
Abilene Christian University

Compensated Emancipation
ALISON MANN
University of New Hampshire
PAUL FINKELMAN
Albany Law School

Compromise of 1850
JOHN C. WAUGH
Pantego, Texas

Confederate States of America
ALYSSA ARNELL
Florida Atlantic University

Confiscation Acts
BRADLEY SKELCHER
Delaware State University

Confiscation Act, Second
BRADLEY SKELCHER
Delaware State University

Congress, Lincoln's Relations with
DAVID E. LONG
East Carolina University

Conscription Act
IAN MICHAEL SPURGEON
Ph.D., University of Southern
　Mississippi

Constitution and Slavery, The
PAUL FINKELMAN
Albany Law School

Constitutional Law, Lincoln and
PAUL FINKELMAN
Albany Law School

Constitutional Union Party
RUSSELL McCLINTOCK
Saint John's High School
Shrewsbury, Massachusetts

Contrabands
IAN MICHAEL SPURGEON
Ph.D., University of Southern
　Mississippi

Cooke, Jay
MARK S. JOY
Jamestown College

Cooper Union Address
HAROLD HOLZER
The Metropolitan Museum of Art

Copperheads
JENNIFER L. WEBER
University of Kansas

Corruption in the Federal
　Government
MICHAEL T. SMITH
McNeese State University

Crittenden Compromise
CARA L. SHELLY
Oakland University and University of
　Michigan–Dearborn

Curtin, Andrew Gregg
J. THOMAS MURPHY
Bemidji State University

Davis, Jefferson
C. ELLEN CONNALLY
University of Akron

Declaration of Independence,
　Lincoln's View of
CHANDRA MANNING
Georgetown University

Democratic Conventions, 1860
CHRISTINE DEE
Fitchburg State College

Democratic Party
JOEL H. SILBEY
Cornell University

Democrats, Peace
JOEL H. SILBEY
Cornell University

Desertions/Presidential Pardons
SEAN A. SCOTT
Ouachita Baptist University

Doughface
CARA L. SHELLY
Oakland University and University of Michigan–Dearborn

Douglas, Stephen A.
JAMES L. HUSTON
Oklahoma State University

Douglass, Frederick
L. DIANE BARNES
Youngstown State University

Draft, Military
LINCOLN AUSTIN MULLEN
Bob Jones University

Draft Riots, New York City
G. MEHERA GERARDO
Youngstown State University

Dred Scott v. Sandford (1857)
PAUL FINKELMAN
Albany Law School

Ellsworth, Elmer Ephraim
CARA L. SHELLY
Oakland University and University of Michigan–Dearborn

Emancipation Monument (Freedman's Memorial to Abraham Lincoln)
MARCY S. SACKS
Albion College

Emancipation Proclamation
PAUL FINKELMAN
Albany Law School

Everett, Edward
ALFRED L. BROPHY
University of Alabama

Ex parte Merryman
PAUL FINKELMAN
Albany Law School

Fessenden, William Pitt
CARA L. SHELLY
Oakland University and University of Michigan–Dearborn

Fillmore, Millard
PAUL FINKELMAN
Albany Law School

Florville, William
CARA L. SHELLY
Oakland University and University of Michigan–Dearborn

Foreign Relations and Diplomacy, Lincoln's
FREDERICK J. BLUE
Youngstown State University

Fort Pickens
PETER SMITH
Wayne State University

Fort Sumter
JIM CAMPI
Civil War Preservation Trust

Forts Henry and Donelson
BROOKS D. SIMPSON
Arizona State University

Founding Fathers, Lincoln's View of
CHANDRA MANNING
Georgetown University

Fredericksburg and Chancellorsville, Battles of
BROOKS D. SIMPSON
Arizona State University

Articles and Contributors

Free Soil Party
FREDERICK J. BLUE
Youngstown State University

"Free Soil, Free Labor, Free Men"
MARCY S. SACKS
Albion College

Freeport Doctrine
JAMES L. HUSTON
Oklahoma State University

Frémont, John C.
PAUL FINKELMAN
Albany Law School

Garrison, William Lloyd
PAUL FINKELMAN
Albany Law School

General War Order Number One
ANTHONY SANTORO
University of Heidelberg

German Americans, Lincoln and
MISCHA HONECK
University of Heidelberg

Gettysburg, Battle of
CAROL REARDON
Richards Civil War Era Center
Penn State University

Gettysburg Address
CHRISTOPHER HAGER
Trinity College

Grant, Ulysses S.
BROOKS D. SIMPSON
Arizona State University

Great Britain, Relations with
JAMES M. CORNELIUS
Abraham Lincoln Presidential Library

Great Emancipator
SEAN A. SCOTT
Ouachita Baptist University

Greeley, Horace
ROBERT C. WILLIAMS
Davidson College

Greenbacks
MARK S. JOY
Jamestown College

Habeas Corpus
PAUL FINKELMAN
Albany Law School

Hamlin, Hannibal
PAULA COCHRAN
Mifflinburg, Pennsylvania

Hampton Roads Conference
CARA L. SHELLY
Oakland University and University of Michigan–Dearborn

Hay, John
MICHAEL BURLINGAME
Connecticut College

Herndon, William H.
SAMUEL P. WHEELER
Southern Illinois University

Hicks, Thomas Holliday
CARA L. SHELLY
Oakland University and University of Michigan–Dearborn

Homestead Act
MARK S. JOY
Jamestown College

Honest Abe
PAULA COCHRAN
Mifflinburg, Pennsylvania

House Divided Speech
CHRISTOPHER HAGER
Trinity College

Hunter, David
WILLIAM H. BROWN
North Carolina Office of Archives and History

Iconography
HAROLD HOLZER
The Metropolitan Museum of Art

Illinois
RON J. KELLER
Lincoln College

Illinois Central Railroad
MARK S. JOY
Jamestown College

Inaugural Address, First
RUSSELL McCLINTOCK
Saint John's High School
Shrewsbury, Massachusetts

Inaugural Address, Second
ANTHONY SANTORO
University of Heidelberg

Income Taxes
DAVID T. MITCHELL
University of South Alabama

Indiana
KEITH A. EREKSON
University of Texas at El Paso

Indian Relations, Lincoln and
SCOTT L. STABLER
Grand Valley State University

Inflation
MARK S. JOY
Jamestown College

Internal Improvements
MARK S. JOY
Jamestown College

Jackson, Andrew, As a Model for Lincoln
PAULA COCHRAN
Mifflinburg, Pennsylvania

Jackson, Claiborne Fox
IAN MICHAEL SPURGEON
Ph.D., University of Southern Mississippi

Johnson, Andrew
BROOKS D. SIMPSON
Arizona State University

Joint Committee on the Conduct of the War
BRUCE TAP
Grand Rapids, Michigan

Kansas-Nebraska Act
NICOLE ETCHESON
Ball State University

Kentucky
JACOB F. LEE
The Filson Historical Society
Louisville, Kentucky

King Cotton
ROBERT W. BURG
University of Wisconsin–Sheboygan

Knights of the Golden Circle
BRUCE TAP
Grand Rapids, Michigan

Know-Nothing (American) Party
M. PHILIP LUCAS
Cornell College

Lawrence, Kansas
NICOLE ETCHESON
Ball State University

Lee, Robert E.
BROOKS D. SIMPSON
Arizona State University

Legal Tender Act of 1862
PATRICK VAN HORN
University of Michigan–Dearborn

Liberty Party
PAUL FINKELMAN
Albany Law School

The Life of Washington, by Parson Weems
SAMUEL P. WHEELER
Southern Illinois University

Lincoln, Childhood and Youth
PAULA COCHRAN
Mifflinburg, Pennsylvania

Lincoln, Young Manhood to Eve of Political Career
CHRISTOPHER SCHNELL
The Papers of Abraham Lincoln

Lincoln, Legal and Early Political Career
JOHN A. LUPTON
The Papers of Abraham Lincoln

Lincoln, As a National Figure, 1854–1865
BRUCE TAP
Mifflinburg, Pennsylvania

Lincoln, Memory of
CHRISTOPHER BATES
University of California, Los Angeles

Lincoln, Edward Baker
CARA L. SHELLY
Oakland University and University of Michigan–Dearborn

Lincoln, Mary Todd
JASON EMERSON
Cazenovia, New York

Lincoln, Nancy Hanks
CARA L. SHELLY
Oakland University and University of Michigan–Dearborn

Lincoln, Robert Todd
PAULA COCHRAN
Mifflinburg, Pennsylvania

Lincoln, Sarah Bush Johnston
PAULA COCHRAN
Mifflinburg, Pennsylvania

Lincoln, Thomas
PAULA COCHRAN
Mifflinburg, Pennsylvania

Lincoln, Thomas "Tad"
PAULA COCHRAN
Mifflinburg, Pennsylvania

Lincoln, William "Willie" Wallace
PAULA COCHRAN
Mifflinburg, Pennsylvania

Lincoln-Douglas Debates
BRUCE TAP
Grand Rapids, Michigan

Lincoln Historic Sites, Preservation of
JIM CAMPI
Civil War Preservation Trust

Lincoln in Film
CHRISTOPHER BATES
University of California, Los Angeles

Lincoln in Music
CHRISTOPHER BATES
University of California, Los Angeles

Lincoln Memorial
KATHRYN ALLAMONG JACOB
Schlesinger Library, Radcliffe
    Institute, Harvard University

Lincoln on Currency
MARK S. JOY
Jamestown College

Lincoln Penny
CARA L. SHELLY
Oakland University and University of
    Michigan–Dearborn

Logan, Stephen T.
SAMUEL P. WHEELER
Southern Illinois University

Long Walk, The
A. JAMES FULLER
University of Indianapolis

Magoffin, Beriah
JACOB F. LEE
The Filson Historical Society
Louisville, Kentucky

Mason, James
ANTHONY SANTORO
University of Heidelberg

McClellan, George B.
BROOKS D. SIMPSON
Arizona State University

McLean, John
PAUL FINKELMAN
Albany Law School

Mexican War
PAUL FINKELMAN
Albany Law School

Missouri Compromise, The
JOHN MACAULAY
Erskine College

Morgan's Raid
KEITH A. EREKSON
University of Texas at El Paso

Mormons, Attacks on
BRYON C. ANDREASEN
Abraham Lincoln Presidential
    Library and Museum

Morrill, Justin Smith
PETER C. HOLLORAN
Worcester State College

Morrill Land Grant Act
MARK S. JOY
Jamestown College

Morrill Tariff
MARK S. JOY
Jamestown College

Morton, Oliver P.
A. JAMES FULLER
University of Indianapolis

National Banking Act of 1863
PATRICK VAN HORN
University of Michigan–Dearborn

National Union Party
GREGORY J. DEHLER
Front Range Community College

New Salem, Illinois
SAMUEL P. WHEELER
Southern Illinois University

New York Tribune
PAUL FINKELMAN
Albany Law School

Nicolay, John G.
MICHAEL BURLINGAME
Connecticut College

Northwest Ordinance
DAWN P. HUTCHINS
Florida Atlantic University

Old Northwest
CHRISTINE DEE
Fitchburg State College

Order of Retaliation
DAVID E. ARTHUR
CQ Press

Overland Campaign
BROOKS D. SIMPSON
Arizona State University

Patronage, Lincoln and
ROBERT W. BURG
University of Wisconsin–Sheboygan

Peoria Speech, Lincoln's
MATTHEW NORMAN
Gettysburg College

Personal Liberty Laws
ROBERT S. TINKLER
California State University, Chico

Phillips, Wendell
L. DIANE BARNES
Youngstown State University

Pierce, Franklin
MICHAEL A. MORRISON
Purdue University

Political Culture, Lincoln and
LAWRENCE FREDERICK KOHL
University of Alabama

Political Philosophy, Lincoln's
JOSEPH R. FORNIERI
Rochester Institute of Technology

Polk, James K.
SAM W. HAYNES
University of Texas at Arlington

Pomeroy Circular
JASON EMERSON
Cazenovia, New York

Popular Sovereignty
MICHAEL A. MORRISON
Purdue University

Pottawatomie Creek Massacre
NICOLE ETCHESON
Ball State University

Prayer of Twenty Millions, The
CARA L. SHELLY
Oakland University and University of
    Michigan–Dearborn

Prize Cases, The (1863)
MICHAEL T. CAIRES
University of Virginia

Proclamation Calling Militia and
    Convening Congress
DAVID E. LONG
East Carolina University

Racism and Racial Thought, Lincoln
    and
RUSSELL McCLINTOCK
Saint John's High School
Shrewsbury, Massachusetts

Radical Republicans
GREGORY J. DEHLER
Front Range Community College

Railroads
GREGORY J. DEHLER
Front Range Community College

Rail-splitter Image, Lincoln's
GERALD J. PROKOPOWICZ
East Carolina University

Reconstruction
WILLIAM C. HARRIS
North Carolina State University

Republican Nominating Convention
    of 1860
DAVID E. ARTHUR
CQ Press

Republican Party, The
MARTIN J. HERSHOCK
University of Michigan–Dearborn

Rhetoric in Lincoln's Public Speeches
CHRISTOPHER HAGER
Trinity College

Richmond, Lincoln's Arrival in
DAVID E. LONG
East Carolina University

Rivers and Harbors Convention
CHRISTOPHER SCHNELL
The Papers of Abraham Lincoln

Ruffin, Edmund
L. DIANE BARNES
Youngstown State University

Rutledge, Ann
SAMUEL P. WHEELER
Southern Illinois University

Scott, Winfield
ALLAN PESKIN
Cleveland State University

Secession
RUSSELL McCLINTOCK
Saint John's High School
Shrewsbury, Massachusetts

Seward, William
JOHN WICKRE
University of North Dakota

Shenandoah Valley Campaigns of
    1862 and 1864
BROOKS D. SIMPSON
Arizona State University

Sherman, John
WILLIAM H. BROWN
North Carolina Office of Archives and
    History

Sherman, William T.
BROOKS D. SIMPSON
Arizona State University

Sherman's March to the Sea
BROOKS D. SIMPSON
Arizona State University

Shields, James
LAWRENCE FREDERICK KOHL
University of Alabama

Shiloh, Battle of
BROOKS D. SIMPSON
Arizona State University

Sioux Uprising
ELEANOR L. HANNAH
University of Minnesota Duluth

Slave Power/Slavocracy
FREDERICK J. BLUE
Youngstown State University

Slavery
ALYSSA ARNELL
Florida Atlantic University

Slavery in the Thirtieth Congress
MATTHEW NORMAN
Gettysburg College

Slidell, John
PETER C. HOLLORAN
Worcester State College

Soldiers' Home
FRANK D. MILLIGAN
President Lincoln's Cottage at the Soldiers' Home
National Trust for Historic Preservation

Soldiers' Vote
MATTHEW NORMAN
Gettysburg College

Speed, Joshua F.
SAMUEL P. WHEELER
Southern Illinois University

Spot Resolutions
SAM W. HAYNES
University of Texas at Arlington

Stamps, Postage
PAUL FINKELMAN
Albany Law School

Stanton, Edwin M.
BROOKS D. SIMPSON
Arizona State University

Stephens, Alexander Hamilton
CARA L. SHELLY
Oakland University and University of Michigan–Dearborn

Stowe, Harriet Beecher
L. DIANE BARNES
Youngstown State University

Strong, George Templeton
CARA L. SHELLY
Oakland University and University of Michigan–Dearborn

Stuart, John Todd
WILLIAM C. HARRIS
North Carolina State University

Sumner, Charles
FREDERICK J. BLUE
Youngstown State University

Taney, Roger B.
ROBERT S. TINKLER
California State University, Chico

Taylor, Zachary
DAVID E. ARTHUR
CQ Press

Temperance
JOHN W. QUIST
Shippensburg University

Ten Percent Plan
BRUCE TAP
Grand Rapids, Michigan

Thanksgiving
PAULA COCHRAN
Mifflinburg, Pennsylvania

Thirteenth Amendment
BRADLEY SKELCHER
Delaware State University

Todd Family
ERIKA NUNAMAKER
Papers of Abraham Lincoln

Trent Affair
ANTHONY SANTORO
University of Heidelberg

Trumbull, Lyman
MICHAEL T. SMITH
McNeese State University

Union Pacific Railroad
MARK S. JOY
Jamestown College

U.S. Colored Troops (USCT)
JOHN DAVID SMITH
University of North Carolina at Charlotte

U.S. Supreme Court, Lincoln's Appointments to
R. OWEN WILLIAMS
Yale University

U.S. Supreme Court, Lincoln's View of
R. OWEN WILLIAMS
Yale University

Vallandigham, Clement Laird
CHRISTINE DEE
Fitchburg State College

Vandalia, Illinois
BRADLEY SKELCHER
Delaware State University

Vicksburg Campaign
BROOKS D. SIMPSON
Arizona State University

Virginia Plan
BRUCE TAP
Grand Rapids, Michigan

Volunteers, Ninety-Day
CARA L. SHELLY
Oakland University and University of Michigan–Dearborn

Wade, Benjamin Franklin
BRUCE TAP
Grand Rapids, Michigan

Wade-Davis Bill
DAVID E. LONG
East Carolina University

War Democrats
CHRISTINE DEE
Fitchburg State College

Washington, D.C.
IAN MICHAEL SPURGEON
Ph.D., University of Southern Mississippi

Weed, Thurlow
WILLIAM C. HARRIS
North Carolina State University

Welles, Gideon
CALEB KLINGLER
Eastern Michigan University

Whig Party
LAWRENCE FREDERICK KOHL
University of Alabama

Whigs, Conscience
GREGORY J. DEHLER
Front Range Community College

Whigs, Cotton
GREGORY J. DEHLER
Front Range Community College

Whitman, Walt
PETER C. HOLLORAN
Worcester State College

Whittier, John Greenleaf
L. DIANE BARNES
Youngstown State University

Wide Awakes
DAVID E. LONG
East Carolina University

Wilmot Proviso
MICHAEL A. MORRISON
Purdue University

Wood, Fernando
PETER C. HOLLORAN
Worcester State College

Yates, Richard
RON J. KELLER
Lincoln College

Young America
WILLIAM THOMAS KERRIGAN
Muskingum College

Zouaves
PETER SMITH
Wayne State University

Introduction

Abraham Lincoln is, by any popular measure, our greatest and most recognizable president. Whenever Americans are asked to rank their presidents, Lincoln comes out on top. Most professional scholars agree. This makes sense. His job was the hardest of any president's, leading the nation through four years of civil war. And he accomplished it stunningly well: winning the war, preserving the Union, and ending slavery. Lincoln comes to us like a comet streaking across our political landscape, our national history, and the core of our nation's meaning. Then, just as quickly, he was gone, the victim of an assassin's bullet. Like Moses, who led the Israelites to Canaan but was not allowed to enter the Promised Land, Lincoln had led his people to the promised land of a restored Union and led nearly four million slaves to the promised land of liberty, only to be snatched away from an admiring nation, prevented from entering the newly redeemed land of freedom.

Almost unknown in 1854, Lincoln was elected president six years later by an overwhelming electoral vote and a substantial popular plurality against three other candidates, all focusing their attention on demonizing and defeating him. They all failed, and he handily won the election even though he was not on the ballot in most of the South. He then guided the nation through the most difficult four years in its history.

Lincoln's reputation is mostly a function of the challenges he faced and the success he achieved in leading the nation. But it is also a function of his talents and skills in comparison with those of his contemporaries. That he was a towering giant surrounded by six decades of lilliputian presidents is surely a factor in his reputation. Compared to the likes of those who preceded him—Van Buren, Tyler, Taylor, Fillmore, Pierce, and Buchanan—and those who followed him—Johnson, Grant, Hayes, and Arthur—Lincoln looks even larger than his six-foot-four-inch frame.

His reputation is also enhanced by his wonderful use of language. Lincoln's Second Inaugural is one of the greatest speeches of nineteenth-century America; his poignant Gettysburg Address helped resurrect the core values of the Declaration of Independence while providing a higher meaning than even nationalism for the Civil War; and his Cooper Union Address brilliantly articulated the hopes, fears, and goals of a new political party.

Lincoln's use of language, his speeches, and his greatness are also enhanced by his humble origins. He is the embodiment of democracy and American virtue. He rose from abject poverty and was self-educated and hardworking—the "railsplitter," "Honest Abe," the ultimate self-made man who led his nation through its greatest crisis and its most horrific war.

Lincoln's place in history rests on his role as the "Great Emancipator" even more than on saving the Union. With a stroke of his pen Lincoln brought liberty to four million slaves. At least until the 1960s he was the greatest friend of civil rights to ever sit in the White House. He is the great humanitarian, the common man who brought liberty to all, martyred for his commitment to freedom. In death, and in life, he is mysterious, tragic, heroic, and somehow holy.

But there is a less positive version of the Lincoln saga. He is the man who trampled on civil liberties and stubbornly allowed hundreds of thousands of his fellow countrymen to die in a war of conquest against his own people. He is the president who stalled on emancipation, who considered colonization of blacks viable, who was slow to move toward emancipation and slower still to move toward the rights of blacks. Are these the more accurate versions of Lincoln?

The complex memories and images of Lincoln confound us: great emancipator or racist; patron of liberty or opponent of civil liberties; self-made man or overly ambitious huckster.

However one views Lincoln, anyone interested in the history of America knows he is a force to understand, a figure to come to terms with. This encyclopedia is designed to teach and educate about Lincoln, to be a resource for anyone interested in him. It is the product of scores of noted scholars and massive research. Our goal here is to understand Lincoln as a political figure, the leader of a nation, a philosopher, a lawyer, a constitutional theorist, and a commander in chief. We have focused on the political Lincoln because that is what he was all about. Others may be interested in his psychology, his family life, his private personality. But those facets interest people only because of his importance as a political figure. Thus we have provided a ready reference volume that helps students, scholars, and citizens understand the political life and challenges of our sixteenth president.

This book is the result of an enormous group effort. First, we owe a huge debt to our authors, who wrote the entries that make up the volume. A reference book of this nature requires experts to summarize concisely what they know and offer their specialized knowledge to the world. Those who wrote for this project illustrate the highest qualities of dedication to scholarship, accuracy, and the value of understanding history.

The staff at CQ Press is among the best in the nation. Our editor, Andrea Pedolsky, provided us with leadership and encouragement. Our project manager, David Arthur, is a gem. He was tireless in finding authors (himself among them),

Introduction

having materials reviewed, and keeping our project moving. Managing editor Joan Gossett ensured a seamless and timely production process. Without their leadership, we could not have brought this project to the public. Our board of advisers did what a good board does—they advised us, suggested entries and authors, and were there for consultation when we needed them. We also thank Fredd Brewer at Albany Law School, who was particularly skilled in managing our database and coordinating many of the invitations for this project.

This volume goes to press as America prepares to celebrate the bicentennial of Lincoln's birth. We hope that we can add to the debate and understanding of his significance in our history and the history of the world.

PAUL FINKELMAN
Albany, New York

MARTIN HERSHOCK
Dearborn, Michigan

A

Abolitionism

Organized opposition to slavery emerged in the eighteenth century, with American revolutionary and European Enlightenment ideals propelling that hostility. During the late eighteenth and early nineteenth centuries, the states north of Maryland, which held fewer slaves than those to the south, adopted measures that ultimately abolished slavery within their borders. Yet Southern slavery became further entrenched during the nineteenth century, spreading to the new states south of the Ohio River.

African Americans had long mobilized against slavery, but the growth of antebellum revivalism increasingly led some white Northerners to embrace immediatist abolitionism. These abolitionists hoped to end slavery by launching a moral revolution. Never members of a uniform movement, abolitionists generally agreed on the immediate ending of slavery and the recognition of African Americans' civil and political rights. They differed from the majority of white Northerners who, despite agreeing that slavery was immoral, regarded it as a problem that defied easy answers and did not require immediate elimination.

Many abolitionists exhibited the spirit of "come-outerism" and sought to separate themselves from political parties and churches they believed tainted by slavery. While Northern opposition to slavery grew during the antebellum years, few northerners despised slavery sufficiently to join an antislavery society, unite with an abolitionist church, aid fugitive slaves, or vote for the abolitionist Liberty Party. The 3 percent of Northern voters who supported the Liberty Party's 1844 presidential ticket suggests the proportion of Northern men and women who embraced a radical "come-outer" form of abolitionism. Meanwhile, other committed opponents of slavery continued to work within the national political parties and mainstream churches, and offered abolitionists moral and financial support.

Abraham Lincoln never belonged to an abolitionist society or voted for an abolitionist political party. He distrusted moral reformers' zeal and believed abolition societies to be counterproductive. As a lawyer Lincoln once represented slave owners seeking fugitive slaves; in Congress he worked closely with slaveholding politicians. Nevertheless, Lincoln opposed slavery and believed it contradicted the Declaration of Independence. He stated in 1858, "I have always hated slavery, I think as much as any abolitionist." In 1864 he described himself as "naturally anti-slavery. If slavery is not wrong, nothing is wrong. I can not remember when I did not so think, and feel."

Black residents of Washington, D.C., celebrate the fourth anniversary of Emancipation Day in the District of Columbia, on April 18, 1866. As a congressman, Abraham Lincoln urged that slavery be ended in the federal city. On April 16, 1862, as president, he signed the Compensated Emancipation Act, which abolished slavery in the capital.

Source: The Granger Collection, New York

Although Lincoln believed that Congress lacked power to interfere with slavery in the states, he backed the Wilmot Proviso. Troubled by slavery in the District of Columbia, Congressman Lincoln proposed in January 1849 that slaves there be emancipated and their owners compensated. Lincoln's overture foundered, with Southern House members fearing that the measure might encourage emancipation elsewhere and abolitionists believing that compensated emancipation legitimized slavery. Abolitionists particularly objected to Lincoln's fugitive slave provision, included to make his bill appealing to Southern politicians, which later led abolitionist Wendell Phillips to blast Lincoln as "that slave hound from Illinois."

The Kansas-Nebraska Act's passage in May 1854 allowed for slavery's legalization in federal territories where the Missouri Compromise had previously prohibited it. Later that year Lincoln publicly criticized the act in a series of speeches that challenged its author, Stephen Douglas. Douglas, Lincoln charged, treated slavery with moral indifference and refused to recognize that blacks' humanity entitled them to fundamental rights. Like the abolitionists, Lincoln defined his hostility to slavery in moral terms. Unlike the abolitionists, Lincoln opposed racial equality and felt overwhelmed by the prospect of ending slavery. On the latter point he conceded, "If all earthly power were given me, I should not know what to do."

By early 1856 Lincoln counted himself among the Republicans. Unlike the Liberty Party, the newly created Republican Party was not abolitionist, as it did not seek to end slavery in the states. Nonetheless the Republicans condemned slavery and insisted that it be absent from all federal territories. Many abolitionists, particularly former Liberty Party members, embraced the Republican Party, which encouraged Democrats and white Southerners to label the Republicans, inaccurately, as abolitionists.

Lincoln's selection as the 1860 Republican presidential nominee disappointed many abolitionists, as they favored William Seward, who they believed held stronger antislavery convictions. During that year's campaign, some abolitionists broadcast Lincoln's professed antipathy to racial equality and encouraged fellow abolitionists to vote for Gerrit Smith, of the Radical Abolition Party, or to abstain from voting altogether. Yet numerous abolitionists, recognizing that Lincoln and his party represented the rising tide of Northern antislavery sentiment, gave Lincoln their unqualified endorsement. They included Henry Stanton, Elizur Wright, and Joshua Leavitt, as well as Radical Republicans with close abolitionist ties, such as Salmon Chase, Charles Sumner, and Joshua Giddings.

Once the Civil War began, federal troops confronted thousands of escaped slaves who sought refuge behind Union lines—slaves who represented labor and potential troops. Meanwhile, abolitionists urged Lincoln to undermine the Confederacy through emancipation. Lincoln saw things differently. He believed that his oath to defend the Constitution, and the need to retain broad popular support in suppressing the rebellion, overrode his antislavery proclivities. Promising not to interfere with slavery in the states, throughout 1861 Lincoln instructed his generals to return slaves to loyal masters. He also revoked proclamations of Generals John C. Frémont (1861) and David Hunter (1862) that freed slaves in Missouri and South Carolina, respectively. Lincoln's policies in 1861 and 1862 often led abolitionists to criticize him.

Even so, the Civil War created an atmosphere favorable to emancipation. As the war continued, antislavery sentiment, as well as the number of African American fugitives from the Confederacy, increased. Abolitionists, long regarded by many Northerners as dangerous revolutionaries, suddenly found themselves in public opinion's vanguard. Lincoln, always mindful of public opinion, embraced emancipatory measures. In spring 1862 Lincoln called for federal compensation to any state adopting gradual abolition and signed bills ending slavery in the District of Columbia and the federal territories. Clearly, neither Southern slaves, nor the Congress, nor Lincoln passively awaited slavery's disintegration.

The Confederacy's continued resistance during the summer of 1862 forced Lincoln to take stronger actions against slavery, resulting in his preliminary Emancipation Proclamation of September 1862. Abolitionists offered it a mixed response. Some complained that the proclamation affected only the rebellious states, lacked protections for freedmen and freedwomen's civil rights, and did not ensure against slavery's future reintroduction. Others recognized the proclamation's limitations yet deemed it, as William Lloyd Garrison did, "an important step in the right direction, and an act of immense historic consequence." Not surprisingly conservatives, who had previously distinguished Lincoln from Radical Republicans, now lumped Lincoln with the abolitionists.

After Lincoln signed the final Emancipation Proclamation on January 1, 1863, some abolitionists distrusted his antislavery resolve and worried that he might compromise emancipation to end the war. Lincoln adhered to the proclamation and explained, in December 1863, that he would neither retract nor modify it. He also made slavery's abandonment a prerequisite for peace.

The Republican contest for the 1864 presidential nomination divided abolitionists. One wing, led by Garrison, worked for Lincoln's renomination and reelection; another wing, led by Phillips, concluded that Lincoln, by failing to seek land redistribution, black male suffrage, universal education, and protections against racial discrimination, would only shortchange African Americans. The Phillips wing prevailed in four major abolitionist societies. Some abolitionists seriously considered the insurgent candidacies of Salmon P. Chase and John C. Frémont, both of which fizzled well before that year's election. Leading abolitionists who enthusiastically campaigned for Lincoln also included Theodore Tilton, Anna Dickinson, Henry Wright, William Burleigh, and Gerrit Smith. Abolitionists who refused to endorse Lincoln included Elizabeth Cady Stanton, Susan B. Anthony, and George Cheever.

In 1864 Lincoln's commitment to ending slavery became clearer. That June, he used his influence to ensure the inclusion of an antislavery constitutional amendment in the Republican Party platform. After his reelection, Lincoln immediately lobbied for congressional passage of the Thirteenth Amendment—a step not required for Union victory but entirely consistent with his antislavery beliefs. The Thirteenth Amendment's passage so pleased Lincoln that he signed it—a constitutionally unnecessary action.

During his final two years, Lincoln endorsed proposals supportive of black citizenship, including the use of black troops, the Freedman's Bureau bill, and limited black male suffrage. Although his positions and those of abolitionists grew closer, Lincoln's commitment to building consensus, and his style of working through private actions, invariably clashed with abolitionists' ideal of fomenting social change through activism. Speaking in 1876, Frederick Douglass noted that abolitionists often viewed Lincoln as "tardy, cold, dull, and indifferent." But when measuring Lincoln in terms of public opinion, "a sentiment he was bound as a statesman to consult, he was swift, zealous, radical, and determined."

The end of slavery in 1865 led some abolitionists to abandon their cause and declare victory. Others, led by Wendell Phillips, insisted that abolitionists continue fighting for African Americans' rights. Abolitionists advocated congressional civil rights legislation and land redistribution. Many went South to establish schools for emancipated African Americans. During the early 1870s abolitionists disbanded. Those who lived more than a few years longer would learn how far short of fulfillment were their hopes of a moral revolution.

See also *Antislavery; Brown, John; Douglass, Frederick; Garrison, William Lloyd; Slavery*

—JOHN W. QUIST

BIBLIOGRAPHY

Basler, Roy P., ed. *Collected Works of Abraham Lincoln.* New Brunswick, N.J.: Rutgers University Press, 1953.

Cox, LaWanda. *Lincoln and Black Freedom: A Study in Presidential Leadership.* Columbia: University of South Carolina Press, 1982.

Guelzo, Allen C. *Lincoln's Emancipation Proclamation: The End of Slavery in America.* New York: Simon and Schuster, 2004.

McPherson, James M. *The Struggle for Equality: Abolitionists and the Negro in the Civil War and Reconstruction.* Princeton: Princeton University Press, 1964.

Oakes, James. *The Radical and Republican: Frederick Douglass, Abraham Lincoln, and the Triumph of Antislavery Politics.* New York: Norton, 2007.

Stewart, James Brewer. *Holy Warriors: The Abolitionists and American Slavery.* New York: Hill and Wang, 1996.

Vorenberg, Michael. *Final Freedom: The Civil War, the Abolition of Slavery, and the Thirteenth Amendment.* Cambridge: Cambridge University Press, 2001.

Adams, Charles Francis

The grandson of President John Adams and the son of President John Quincy Adams, Charles Francis Adams (August 18, 1807–November 21, 1886) was a two-term congressman from Massachusetts, minister to the Court of St. James during the Civil War, and a candidate for both the vice presidency in 1848 and the presidency in 1872. Like many in his family, Adams was expected to enter public service. Those expectations proved burdensome but not enough to offset the advantages inherent in his paternity. Though Adams would have to shoulder all that being an Adams entailed throughout his life, in doing so he followed the path prescribed for him creditably.

Groomed as a statesman and a historian, possessed of a reputation for probity and discretion, and connected within Republican circles, Adams nevertheless was situated poorly to serve Abraham Lincoln in 1861. Though he had campaigned throughout Wisconsin for Lincoln, Adams's choice for president had been New York senator William Seward. Seward's prominence within the party, even as Lincoln's rival for the nomination, gave him a strong claim to be in Lincoln's cabinet. Adams had no such claim, and his role, if any, in the administration was dependent on Seward's influence.

Though discussed for Treasury secretary and considered as New England's geographical contribution to the cabinet, Adams lost out to Salmon Chase and Gideon Welles. Seward next recommended Adams for a plum diplomatic mission. But Lincoln preferred John Frémont and William Dayton, the party's presidential and vice presidential candidates from 1856, as ministers (or ambassadors) to France and Great Britain. In response, Seward lobbied against Frémont's appointment and was able to persuade the president to consider Adams in his plans (thereby shifting Dayton from Great Britain to France). Adams, however, was uncertain if he wanted to be so included. Although he desired the position, his appointment resulted in marital tension and furthered a rift with Sen. Charles Sumner, who coveted the post as well.

After his confirmation by the Senate but before he traveled to London, Adams met with Lincoln. The interview was short and unsettling for Adams—the informal, rough-hewn western president dispatched the formal, polished easterner with nary a word, too busy pondering other appointments, apparently, to say more. Lincoln had left no question that it was Seward to whom Adams owed his position. Yet nothing the president said or left unsaid precluded the development of a sound working relationship with the principal members of his foreign policy team, a fact that was lost on Adams at the time and later.

Though instructions were not forthcoming immediately, Adams learned quickly that Lincoln would provide tactical directives when necessary. Upon arriving in London, Adams found that not only was much of elite society hostile to the Union, but Queen Victoria's government had already recognized the Confederacy as a belligerent. That action was in line with international law and followed from the Union blockade. Thus the administration would have to walk a fine line—keeping the British as neutral as possible, under the threat of war if Britain recognized the Confederacy, while not actually precipitating another war. Seward, in the role of saber rattler, nearly went too far, but with Sumner's advice Lincoln directed his minister to maintain the threat of war while not appearing provocative. Stepping into his role, Adams continually offset and defused with sober assurance the disquieting reports received in London from Britain's minister to the United States, Baron Richard Lyons.

Lincoln's policy was tested most severely during the *Trent* crisis, the successful denouement of which would require his team to fulfill their roles perfectly, in the winter of 1861–1862. When a British ship steaming between Cuba and St. Thomas was intercepted by the U.S. Navy, two Confederate diplomats were detained. The incident caused an international crisis by impinging on British honor. War would ultimately be averted when the Lincoln administration released the captives and paid reparations for damages. Adams, however, delivered no official apology.

The *Trent* crisis had been handled effectively, but its resolution was not enough to eliminate the tension between the Union and Great Britain. Nor could Lincoln's policy do more than seek to avoid another such crisis, while quarantining the Confederacy; prospects for rolling back the British declaration of belligerency seemed slim. Adams improved Lincoln's policy through his suggestion that the Union no longer purchase military equipment from Great Britain, hoping by this shift to achieve consistency in the U.S. argument while discouraging sales to the Confederates. Until the *Alabama* crisis in summer 1862, British neutrality was maintained, if not buttressed. But when the British government allowed the Confederacy, via a loophole in Britain's laws, to purchase rams meant to disrupt the Union blockade, the United States formally protested and again threatened war, ultimately winning reparations for damages from the British in an international tribunal (at which Adams represented the United States) ten years later.

With success on the battlefield and the Emancipation Proclamation, events swung British public opinion behind the Union, guaranteeing the success of Lincoln's policy and making Adams's role much easier. Adams's assessments were not always correct. He would criticize Lincoln's presidency in 1873, while lionizing Seward, giving Seward more credit than he deserved for the administration's policies and censuring Lincoln for being too involved in patronage. Adams also misread the level of support in the British cabinet for intervention: Earl John Russell was less friendly to the Union, while Viscount Henry Palmerston was friendlier. But Adams's assessments had been of use. More important, Lincoln's policy held, his team served him ably, and Adams followed the path Lincoln prescribed for him creditably.

See also *Seward, William*

—ROBERT W. BURG

BIBLIOGRAPHY

Adams, Charles Francis Jr. *Charles Francis Adams.* Boston: Houghton Mifflin, 1900.

Adams, Henry. *The Education of Henry Adams.* Boston: Houghton Mifflin, 1918.

Duberman, Martin B. *Charles Francis Adams, 1807–1886.* Boston: Houghton Mifflin, 1960.

Jones, Howard. *Union in Peril: The Crisis over British Intervention in the Civil War.* Chapel Hill: University of North Carolina Press, 1992.

African Americans and Lincoln

Abraham Lincoln's attitude and policies concerning African Americans were subjects of much speculation and controversy during his lifetime and remain so today. In 1836, while campaigning for reelection to the Illinois state legislature, Lincoln claimed that he was in favor of "admitting all whites to the right of suffrage, who pay taxes or bear arms, (by no means excluding females)." While this endorsement of woman suffrage was tongue-in-cheek, there is abundant evidence that Lincoln opposed suffrage for African Americans during much of his political career; he also endorsed plans to settle African Americans outside the United States. Yet at the same time, there is other evidence to suggest that these positions reflected his understanding of the political and social realities of antebellum America, rather than deeply held personal beliefs. Illustrating this is the apparent contradiction that until 1862 Lincoln believed that the national government had no constitutional power to interfere with slavery in the states, while at the same time he always opposed slavery.

The contradiction between what he *could* do about slavery and race discrimination and what he *wished he could do* is clear in his famous letter to Albert G. Hodges, a Kentucky newspaper editor. Lincoln urged Hodges and other Kentucky leaders to end slavery in their state because the federal government did not have jurisdiction to do so. Thus Lincoln wrote, "I am naturally anti-slavery. If slavery is not wrong, nothing is wrong. I can not remember when I did not so think, and feel. And yet I have never understood that the Presidency conferred upon me an unrestricted right to act officially upon this judgment and feeling."

Racism was prevalent throughout the antebellum North, yet Illinois was a particularly unwelcome place for African Americans. With its southern counties settled heavily by upland Southerners, the state erected a variety of legal barriers to discourage African Americans from moving to Illinois. Collectively known as "Black Laws," these measures prohibited African Americans from voting, holding office, serving in the state militia, intermarrying, and testifying against whites in court. Lincoln never questioned the Black Laws, and he was not above appealing to the racial prejudices of Illinois voters. In speeches made during the 1840 presidential campaign Lincoln criticized Martin Van Buren for having once supported limited franchise rights for African Americans in New York. This type of appeal played very well in a state that overwhelmingly approved a new constitution in 1848 that denied civil rights to African Americans and also gave the legislature authority to enact measures to keep African Americans from settling in the state. A new law was approved in 1853 that made it illegal for persons of African descent to settle in Illinois. Those found guilty of violating the law were

An idealized lithograph characterized African American reaction to the Preliminary Emancipation Proclamation, issued on September 22, 1862. President Lincoln announced that on January 1, 1863, all slaves held in rebellious states would "be then, thenceforward, and forever free."
Source: The Granger Collection, New York

subject to a fine, and if the fine could not be paid, the offender was sold into a temporary form of slavery. Though these laws were specific to Illinois, similar barriers could be found in Indiana, where Lincoln was raised, as well. Although he never challenged the Black Laws, Lincoln had a number of black clients, which was unusual for a lawyer in central Illinois.

As early as 1837, while in the Illinois legislature, Lincoln condemned slavery as an institution founded on "injustice and bad policy," yet he was equally critical of abolitionists, for he feared that their radical agitation posed a serious threat to national unity. Lincoln was a great admirer of Henry Clay, the "Great Compromiser," who had helped form the Whig Party. Though he was a slaveholding Kentuckian, Clay urged his state to adopt a plan for gradual emancipation that required freed slaves to be sent to Liberia, a country in West Africa that had been established under the auspices of the American Colonization Society (ACS). Lincoln also favored gradual emancipation and colonization. During his single term in the U.S. House of Representatives, he drafted a plan for gradual, compensated emancipation in Washington, D.C. In an 1852 eulogy of his hero, Clay, Lincoln praised Clay's work in behalf of the ACS and expressed his wish that after the "dangerous presence of slavery" was removed from the United States the former slaves would be returned to "their long-lost father-land."

As Lincoln rose to national political prominence in the 1850s he made it clear that he was opposed only to the extension of slavery into the territories and was not in favor of interfering with slavery in the states where it already existed. In part the reason was that he believed that slavery was entirely a state institution and that Congress had no power to touch slavery in the states. Consistent with his Whig ideology and his love of the Union, he also believed that any attempt by the national government to end slavery would lead to a constitutional catastrophe. However, Lincoln made it clear that he believed preventing the extension of slavery would lead to its end. As he noted in his 1858 "House Divided" speech, he hoped the *"opponents* of slavery, will arrest the further spread of it, and place it where the public mind shall rest in the belief that it is in the course of ultimate extinction." In making his case against the Kansas-Nebraska Act and the doctrine of popular sovereignty, Lincoln asserted that slavery violated the founding principle contained in the Declaration of Independence that "all men are created equal." Lincoln also disputed the majority opinion of the U.S. Supreme Court in the *Dred Scott* decision. Though Chief Justice Roger Taney ruled that African Americans were not citizens and could never become citizens because the founders did not intend either the Declaration of Independence or the Constitution to apply to them, Lincoln deemed this "counterfeit logic." Lincoln believed that the Declaration "contemplated the progressive improvement of all men everywhere," including African Americans.

Lincoln's defense of the rights of African Americans made him vulnerable to attacks from his political opponents. Sen. Stephen A. Douglas, Lincoln's chief rival, frequently charged that if Lincoln believed the Declaration of Independence included all men it meant that Lincoln favored the complete social and political equality of the races. The prospect of complete racial equality was highly distasteful to the vast majority of Illinoisans, and Lincoln attempted to clarify his position by making a distinction between natural rights and civil rights. Lincoln explained that just because he believed African Americans were human beings, and therefore entitled to natural rights, such as the right to enjoy the fruits of their own labor, it did not necessarily follow that he wanted to marry a black woman or have African Americans vote. Douglas's charges became more strident when Lincoln challenged him for the U.S. Senate in 1858. In what has become one of his most infamous and oft-quoted utterances, Lincoln tried to defuse Douglas's accusations when he opened their debate at Charleston with the following statement:

> *I will say then that I am not, nor ever have been in favor of bringing about in any way the social and political equality of the white and black races,—that I am not nor ever have been in favor of making voters or jurors of negroes, nor of qualifying them to hold office, nor to intermarry with white people; and I will say in addition to this that there is a physical difference between the white and black races which I believe will for ever forbid the two races living together on terms of social and political equality.*

Lincoln also upheld the constitutionality of the Fugitive Slave Act of 1850, supported the efforts of the ACS, and denounced radical abolitionists. These positions led some black abolitionists to be critical of the Republican Party's nomination of Lincoln for the presidency. H. Ford Douglas was active in the movement to repeal the Illinois Black Laws, and he stated in 1860, "I do not believe in the antislavery of Abraham Lincoln." There was some basis for Douglas's skepticism: He had traveled through Illinois in 1858 with a petition urging the legislature to repeal the law that prohibited African Americans from testifying against whites. When Douglas approached Lincoln with his petition Lincoln refused to sign. Frederick Douglass, the nation's leading African American activist, was also perplexed by the seeming contradiction between Lincoln's principled opposition to slavery and his unwillingness to support racial equality.

Douglass's disappointment was heightened when he read Lincoln's First Inaugural Address. Though Lincoln asserted that the Union was perpetual and pledged to uphold the authority of the Constitution, he also reiterated his position that the federal government had no authority to interfere with slavery in the states and claimed that his administration would enforce the Fugitive Slave Act. Douglass perceived Lincoln's inaugural as unnecessarily conciliatory toward slaveholders. When the war commenced, Douglass and other African Americans were frustrated with Lincoln's view that the war was being fought for the sole purpose of preserving the Union. African Americans were turned away from recruiting offices, and when Generals John C. Frémont and David Hunter issued emancipation proclamations for their military jurisdictions, Lincoln revoked them.

By late 1861 it was apparent that the war would last much longer than most had initially anticipated. Lincoln revived his idea of gradual, compensated emancipation, and in March 1862 he urged Congress to give financial assistance to states that enacted plans for gradual emancipation. Congress proceeded to pass a bill providing for compensated emancipation in Washington, D.C., but despite a personal appeal from Lincoln, most members of Congress from the loyal slave states rejected the president's proposal on the basis that it was too expensive, unconstitutional, and a "radical" alteration of their "social system."

After being rebuked by the Border State members of Congress, Lincoln began to draft an emancipation proclamation. As Lincoln moved toward emancipation, he grappled with the question of what would be the fate of the newly freed persons. The law that emancipated slaves in Washington, D.C., included an appropriation to assist former slaves who wished to leave the country. This provided Lincoln with an opening to promote colonization as a possible solution. In August 1862 he met with a delegation of African Americans from Washington, D.C., and urged them to be leaders in the colonization movement. Lincoln stated to the delegation: "On this broad continent, not a single man of your race is made the equal of a single man of ours....I cannot alter it if I would....It is better for us both, therefore, to be separated." While the leader of the delegation expressed a willingness to tour Northern cities and promote colonization, Lincoln's remarks infuriated Frederick Douglass and many other African Americans. Complicating Lincoln's views, he also consistently opposed forced colonization and made sure that the law ending slavery in the District of Columbia only allowed for voluntary expatriation. Lincoln's position on colonization may have in fact been a political ploy to gain the support of white conservatives who opposed emancipation.

Lincoln's December 1862 annual message recommended constitutional amendments to provide compensated emancipation and colonization at federal expense, but these proposals attracted little interest in Congress. Lincoln also explored the possibility of opening new colonies in Central America and on an island controlled by Haiti. Opposition from neighboring countries thwarted the Central American plan, and the Haitian scheme was a dismal failure that ended in 1864, when the government sent a ship to bring the surviving colonists back to the United States. By 1864 Lincoln had abandoned plans for colonization. Ultimately very few African Americans were willing to leave the country of their birth, even if the government was willing to pay for their relocation.

Lincoln's final Emancipation Proclamation not only transformed the war into what Frederick Douglass called an "abolition war," but it also called on African Americans to serve in the military. Though the proclamation applied only to the states in rebellion, because that was the only part of the nation where Lincoln had the constitutional authority to interfere with slavery, Lincoln earned widespread praise from many African Americans, including William Florville, a Haitian immigrant who had been Lincoln's barber and his client in Springfield. Florville wrote to Lincoln that he and other persons of color were very grateful for the proclamation and that he hoped that Lincoln would soon apply it to all the slave states.

Lincoln met Frederick Douglass for the first time in 1863, and Douglass came away impressed that Lincoln had treated him with kindness and respect. Douglass urged Lincoln to issue a proclamation making it clear that the government would not tolerate the unequal treatment of black soldiers who were taken prisoner. Shortly after his first meeting with Douglass, Lincoln issued a proclamation warning the rebels that any mistreatment of black prisoners would be met with retaliation. Lincoln also urged Congress to ensure that the widows and orphans of African American soldiers received the same benefits as those of white soldiers. During the summer of 1864, when Lincoln's prospects for reelection appeared uncertain, he met with Douglass to discuss a plan to facilitate the liberation of as many African Americans as possible before his term in office expired. Lincoln believed that if he lost the election, his Democratic successor would recognize the Confederacy and revoke the Emancipation Proclamation. As Lincoln's political fortunes brightened, the plan to assist African Americans in escaping from the rebel states to the North became unnecessary. Lincoln and Douglass met for the final time on March 4, 1865, after Lincoln delivered his Second Inaugural Address at the Capitol. Douglass had listened to Lincoln's speech and was so impressed that he felt compelled to attend the traditional public reception at the White House so that he could congratulate the president in person. No African American had ever attended the reception, but after a dispute with the guards, Douglass was able to gain admittance. When Lincoln caught sight of Douglass he referred to him as his "friend" and was eager to know what Douglass thought of his speech. Douglass deemed it a "sacred effort"—a far cry from his verdict regarding Lincoln's First Inaugural Address.

In March 1864 Lincoln met with a delegation of African Americans from Louisiana who presented him with a petition requesting that they be given the right to vote. Louisiana became Lincoln's model for restoring the rebel states to the Union, and the meeting with the African American delegation prompted him to write Michael Hahn, the newly elected governor, and recommend that the new state constitution include a limited provision for African American suffrage. Lincoln wrote to Hahn: "I barely suggest for your private consideration, whether some of the colored people may not be let in—as, for instance, the very intelligent, and especially those who have fought gallantly in our ranks. They would probably help, in some trying time to come, to keep the jewel of liberty within the family of freedom. But this is only a suggestion, not to the public, but to you alone."

Historians have debated whether the Hahn letter provides evidence that Lincoln's views on race had progressed since the 1850s. Lincoln's proposal for restoring the rebel states to the Union included very generous terms, as all but a select number of high-ranking Confederates were eligible for amnesty if they swore an oath of allegiance and agreed to abide by all acts and proclamations that pertained to slavery. Providing African Americans with civil rights was not a prerequisite, and Lincoln only suggested to Hahn that the constitutional convention consider allowing some African Americans to vote. Hahn showed Lincoln's letter to members of the convention, but the new constitution did not directly enfranchise any African Americans. Instead, the legislature was given authority to take action on the subject. However, the constitution did provide persons of color with some rights, including public education. Lincoln was pleased with the outcome of the convention and observed that African Americans in Louisiana would be treated more equitably than those in his own state of Illinois.

On April 11, 1865, Lincoln made a speech to a crowd gathered outside the White House. Instead of focusing his remarks on the recent news of Lee's surrender to Grant, Lincoln devoted much of his speech to the task of reconstruction and a defense of the new Louisiana government. Lincoln repeated publicly what he had privately written to Governor Hahn regarding his desire that the franchise be extended to African American veterans and also those who were "very intelligent." For the first time in U.S. history a president had publicly advocated equal rights for at least some African Americans, and it allegedly enraged one member of the audience so much that he vowed to kill Lincoln. John Wilkes Booth made good on his pledge three nights later.

In the wake of the assassination, Frederick Douglass wrote that Lincoln was "emphatically, the blackman's president." Eleven years later Douglass delivered a speech at the dedication of a monument to commemorate the Emancipation Proclamation. In his remarks, Douglass claimed that Lincoln was "preeminently the white man's President." Douglass continued to have great admiration for Lincoln, but his two statements mirror Lincoln's divided legacy on the issue of race. In the decades immediately following the Civil War many African Americans celebrated Lincoln as the "Great Emancipator." During the twentieth century some African Americans began to view Lincoln's legacy more critically. W. E. B. DuBois became skeptical of Lincoln's hallowed image, but the most sustained and influential criticism has come from Lerone Bennett, who began his assault on Lincoln's reputation with an essay titled "Was Abe Lincoln a White Supremacist?" that was published in the February 1968 issue of *Ebony*. Bennett's article provoked controversy and also prompted academic historians to examine Lincoln's views on race more carefully. Today there is no consensus on the issue, and one can only speculate whether Reconstruction would have had a more favorable outcome for African Americans if Lincoln had lived to complete his second term.

See also *Douglass, Frederick; Racism and Racial Thought, Lincoln and*

—MATTHEW NORMAN

Author's note: Numerous items pertaining to Lincoln and African Americans, including William Florville's letter of December 27, 1863; Edward M. Thomas's letter of August 16, 1862; the response of Border State members of Congress to Lincoln's proposal for compensated emancipation; and a draft of Lincoln's letter to Michael Hahn are in the Abraham Lincoln Papers at the Library of Congress, available online at http://memory.loc.gov/ammem/alhtml/malhome.html.

For other Lincoln documents, including his July 6, 1852, eulogy of Henry Clay; his June 26, 1857, speech on the *Dred Scott* decision; his statement from the September 18, 1858, debate with Douglas at Charleston; his August 14, 1862, address on colonization to the delegation of African Americans; and his final public speech of April 11, 1865, see Roy P. Basler et al., eds., *The Collected Works of Abraham Lincoln* (New Brunswick, N.J.: Rutgers University Press, 1953). Available on-line at http://quod.lib.umich.edu/l/lincoln/.

H. Ford Douglas's speech on Lincoln was published in the July 13, 1860, issue of *The Liberator*.

Frederick Douglass's reminiscences of Lincoln are in his autobiography, *Life and Times of Frederick Douglass*. I consulted the 1893 edition of this work that is available in Frederick Douglass, *Autobiographies* (New York: Library of America, 1994).

Douglass's statement about Lincoln being the "blackman's president" and the text of his 1876 address at the unveiling of the Freedmen's Monument in Washington, D.C., are in the Frederick Douglass Papers at the Library of Congress, available on-line at http://memory.loc.gov/ammem/alhtml/malhome.html.

BIBLIOGRAPHY

Bennett, Lerone. "Was Abe Lincoln a White Supremacist?" *Ebony,* February 1968, 35–42.

Blight, David W. *Frederick Douglass' Civil War: Keeping Faith in Jubilee.* Baton Rouge: Louisiana State University Press, 1989.

Cox, LaWanda. *Lincoln and Black Freedom: A Study in Presidential Leadership.* Columbia: University of South Carolina Press, 1994.

Fehrenbacher, Don E. "Only His Stepchildren: Lincoln and the Negro." *Civil War History* 20 (1974): 293–310.

Fredrickson, George M. "A Man but Not a Brother: Abraham Lincoln and Racial Equality." *Journal of Southern History* 41 (1975): 39–58.

Guelzo, Allen C. "How Abe Lincoln Lost the Black Vote: Lincoln and Emancipation in the African American Mind." *Journal of the Abraham Lincoln Association* 25 (2004): 1–22.

Harris, William C. *With Charity for All: Lincoln and the Restoration of the Union.* Lexington: University Press of Kentucky, 1997.

Oakes, James. *The Radical and the Republican: Frederick Douglass, Abraham Lincoln, and the Triumph of Antislavery Politics.* New York: Norton, 2007.

Quarles, Benjamin. *Lincoln and the Negro.* 1962. Reprint, New York: Da Capo, 1990.

Vorenberg, Michael. "Abraham Lincoln and the Politics of Black Colonization." *Journal of the Abraham Lincoln Association* 14 (1993): 23–45.

Alabama Claims

The CSS *Alabama* was one of seven British-built ships that exacted serious damage on Union shipping between 1861 and 1865. Lacking the resources to engage the U.S. Navy in combat, the Confederacy instead focused on the disruption of shipping to the United States, a practice called "commerce raiding." The *Alabama,* commanded by Raphael Semmes, sank or captured seventy ships and so became the eponym of this class of commerce raiders, which Lincoln called "piratical craft." The *Alabama* was sunk on June 19, 1864, off Cherbourg, France, by the USS *Kearsarge.* Following Lincoln's recommendation the *Kearsarge's* commander, Captain John A. Winslow, was advanced in rank and given the official thanks of Congress. Similar credits were extended to the captain of a ship that sank the CSS *Albemarle* off Plymouth, North Carolina, on October 27, 1864.

Shortly thereafter, Thomas Balch, a nongovernment attorney in Philadelphia, suggested to Lincoln the use of an international court of arbitration to settle the legal, maritime, and commercial problems resulting from the damage done by the *Alabama* and the other British-built ships. Lincoln approved of the idea and asked Balch to go to England to float the idea, but nothing came of the effort.

In 1871 the Treaty of Washington settled the Anglo-American dispute over these ships, and in 1872 an international body, the Tribunal of Arbitration—representatives of five nations, meeting in Geneva—awarded the United States 3.23 million British pounds, in gold (about $15.5 million), for direct losses caused by the *Alabama,* the *Florida,* and to a lesser degree by the *Shenandoah,* which sank much of the Pacific whaling fleet in mid-1865, before word of the war's end had reached it. All three of the ships had been built in Britain for the

Confederacy during time of war. Damages caused by several other ships were thrown out ($11.5 million of the award went to private claimants; $4 million to the U.S. government).

It has sometimes been assumed that Lincoln's own approach to claims, like that of any reconstruction policy he might have had, would have been temperate or mollifying. In his absence, Sen. Charles Sumner of Massachusetts, a state that suffered greatly from the loss of ships and goods, led the call that the U.S. government should demand official redress from Britain. Sumner, before the war one of the most outspoken friends of Britain, was joined by other maritime- and insurance-state politicians in demanding compensation not just for ships and goods lost to Confederate raiders built in Britain, but for the lengthened war effort itself. Accordingly the figure of $1.5 billion in "indirect claims" from Britain was bandied about at one time, approximating much of the entire cost of the war to the North. The very mention of such a legally hazy case soured Anglo-American relations on other fronts for several years. Politicians tended to revive the issue before elections, when Britain-hating Irish immigrant voters could be stirred to turn out by the issue.

The legal issue was complex. A maritime "right of capture" had long been seen as a form of self-defense and as fair wages of war. The Liverpool shipbuilder J. R. Laird acted within international law by building ships for the Confederacy. Fitting them out with military armor, weapons, and stores, however, could not be done in any British possession. The island of Bermuda, however, being a crown colony and not technically part of a national empire, hovered outside such a restriction, and that is partly where ships of the *Alabama* class were armed for battle. Bahamian islands were also used, a more direct infraction of law, while French and Spanish ports played a small role.

Lord Palmerston's government was generally aware of these activities and was much pressured by two men to intervene and order Laird to desist. They were U.S. minister Charles Francis Adams and the U.S. consul in Liverpool, Thomas C. Dudley, who used spies and other informers to track activity in British shipyards. Aware that Confederate agents in Britain had ordered blockade-running vessels, for weeks in 1862 they pressed Lord Russell, the foreign minister, to prevent any from sailing. Russell's own laggard action (he confessed as much in 1875), coupled with a mental breakdown by another official involved, let the *Florida* slip out to sea less than an hour before Russell's estoppel arrived. In the press, the members of Palmerston's government were made to look like conscious abettors of the Confederate cause.

Memories of Union incapacity against British-built war vessels, topped by the *Alabama*'s sinking, easily fed the flames of nationalist anger later on. Americans felt little compunction about harboring Irish terrorists in flight from crimes in England or Canada, and the public cry in large U.S. cities to Make Britain Pay grew, despite mild efforts by William H. Seward to damp them down. William Gladstone, the prime minister from 1869, who while a member of the British cabinet in 1862 had nearly lent official recognition to the government of Jefferson Davis, seems to have felt the error of the old policy. He assented to the call of Ulysses Grant's administration for an international tribunal to settle all claims outstanding from the Civil War.

The tribunal, the Joint High Commission, met in the Washington Conference in March 1871. Grant's secretary of state, Hamilton Fish, headed the five-man U.S. team. (Fish met earlier with an Anglo-Canadian businessman and swore to rule out any claim to Canadian lands.)

The Earl of Ripon and Sir Stafford Northcote headed the British delegation. Even allowing the conference to occur on foreign soil was a signal that the British were willing to concede some fault, but at no time would admission of the rightness of any "indirect claim" be brooked. So it was that on May 8, 1871, the Treaty of Washington was signed. Canadian issues figured largely. Permission for U.S. fishing vessels to enter certain Canadian waters was granted, and vice versa, and the international boundary through the San Juan Islands, in Puget Sound—contended since at least 1846—was put up for arbitration. Sir John Macdonald, Canadian prime minister and a member of the British team, was enraged; a further fraying of the Anglo-Canadian knot had occurred.

The later arbitration panel met in Geneva in mid-1872, with representatives from the United States, Britain, and three neutrals: Italy, Brazil, and Switzerland. Only now were U.S. "indirect claims" against Britain for the whole cost of pursuing the *Alabama,* and continuing the war so long, thrown out. Announcement of the award, on September 14, left the Grant administration well positioned to run for reelection in six weeks, having twisted the British lion's tail.

Militarily, the victory by the American-built *Kearsarge,* within sight of the English and French coasts, announced at last a Union naval capability that would challenge the primacy of the seas after the Civil War. The British-built *Alabama* had been, in Lincoln's words, "a vessel superior in tonnage, superior in number of guns, and superior in number of crew."

Far more important a precedent, though, was that the episode stands as the first international arbitration by a mixed panel in history. Two major powers sat, agreed, sought outside counsel, paid up, and rapidly moved toward amity.

The amity resulting from the *Alabama* settlement—a moral because legally correct victory for the United States; a penalty small enough to be forgotten in a year by the British—recast the issue of the Civil War in British eyes. As slavery disappeared from the western world in a generation, Lincoln was seen to have fought for a rightful cause, just as Anglo-American forces in the twentieth century fought back undemocratic or retrograde enemies. Absent his personal involvement in the diplomacy, Lincoln's example may be seen in a growing belief in law as society's emollient. Just as he learned executive action on the job after work as a lawyer and legislator, and as he grew into recognition of equal political rights for nonwhites, he might well have supported the unprecedented move of putting an international dispute between powers to multiparty arbitration, as before a jury of one's peers.

See also *Adams, Charles Francis*

—JAMES M. CORNELIUS

BIBLIOGRAPHY

Cook, Adrian. *The Alabama Claims: American Politics and Anglo-American Relations, 1865–1872.* Ithaca, N.Y.: Cornell University Press, 1975.

Cross, Coy F., II. *Lincoln's Man in Liverpool: Consul Dudley and the Legal Battles to Stop Confederate Warships.* DeKalb: Northern Illinois University Press, 2008.

Cushing, Caleb. *The Treaty of Washington.* New York: Harper and Brothers, 1873.

Jones, Howard. *Union in Peril: The Crisis over British Intervention in the Civil War.* Chapel Hill: University of North Carolina Press, 1992.

American Colonization Society

Robert Finley, Elias Caldwell, and Francis Scott Key created the American Colonization Society in 1816 as a Christian, humanitarian outreach to free blacks. The initial goal of the society was colonizing free American blacks to Africa. Northerners had banned the institution of slavery in their states, but many had an antipathy to the presence of free blacks enjoying equal rights. Many Southern slave owners, such as James Madison, welcomed the birth of the Colonization Society and worked with it at both state and national levels. They understood that one of the chief obstacles to emancipation was the question of the status of blacks once their bondage ended, and they hoped that the society would provide the answer to that dilemma. Henry Clay, the "Great Compromiser" and a Southern slave owner, added his stature to the organization and eventually, like Madison, took command of the movement as its national president from 1836 to 1849.

Americans from both slave and free states invested money and effort in the movement. A board of managers elected by the society's members set day-to-day policy in cooperation with a president, secretary, treasurer, recorder, and numerous vice presidents. Such eminent citizens as secretary of the Treasury William Crawford, Speaker of the House Henry Clay, William Phillips, Colonel Henry Rutgers, John Eager Howard, Samuel Smith, John C. Herbert, John Taylor, General John Mason, Andrew Jackson, Robert Ralston, and Richard Rush served as vice presidents. While slates of prestigious officers lent the society an aura of national leadership, the board and the executive secretary carried out the work.

Public support rose in the 1820s and early 1830s, and the society established local auxiliaries in Virginia, North and South Carolina, Georgia, Massachusetts, Connecticut, Rhode Island, New York, Pennsylvania, and Ohio. Under the Slave Trade Act of 1819, Congress appropriated funds for returning slaves rescued from the illegal slave trade. With the help of President James Monroe, the society used the funds to establish a colony of free blacks in Africa, which was later called Liberia.

Public support waned in the later 1830s and 1840s, at least partly because of the huge expense of transporting emigrants and resettling them in Africa. More important, free blacks overwhelmingly proved unwilling recruits to the cause of resettlement, openly opposing leaving their homeland. Colonization, moreover, provoked opposition among many radical abolitionists on grounds of racism. Firebrands such as William Lloyd Garrison denounced American Colonization Society propaganda for branding free blacks inferior and incapable of citizenship, lowering rather than elevating blacks, and serving to intensify prejudice and hatred.

Interest in the society revived in the 1850s, as the issue of slavery increasingly polarized the nation. For many throughout the republic who opposed political and economic equality for free blacks, African colonization seemed a satisfactory compromise between the extremes of either preservation of slavery or its immediate demise. Once again prominent political leaders such as Daniel Webster, Edward Everett, Stephen A. Douglas, and Millard Fillmore attended the society's meetings. President Fillmore considered recommending using federal funds for colonization in his 1852 State of the Union address, but in the end he decided against it, fearing an increase in tensions over slavery.

Although not a member of the society, the "Old Henry Clay Whig" Abraham Lincoln supported colonization. In his eulogy of Henry Clay in 1852 Lincoln spoke approvingly of Clay's involvement in the effort to colonize free blacks in Liberia: "This suggestion of the possible ultimate redemption of the African race and African continent, was made twenty-five years ago. Every succeeding year has added strength to the hope of its realization. May it indeed be realized." Lincoln delivered a speech, now lost, to the society at Springfield, Illinois, on January 4, 1855. Two years later, in another Springfield speech, Lincoln argued that if the races were to be separated this "must be effected by colonization." The future president then added, "Let us be brought to believe it is morally right, and, at the same time favorable to, or, at least not against our interest, to transfer the African to his native clime, and we shall find a way to do it, however great the task may be." In his famous series of debates with Stephen A. Douglas in 1858, Lincoln referred favorably to the Colonization Society and the emigration scheme.

On becoming president Lincoln addressed colonization and the acquisition of new territory as a possibility for Congress to consider in his annual message in 1861 and again in 1862. Then in his 1862 "Appeal to Border State Representatives to Favor Compensated Emancipation" Lincoln again touted the transport of emancipated slaves to some territory in South America where land was abundant and cheap. Addressing an audience of free blacks in the White House, Lincoln declared that even though free from slavery they would not be accepted as equals by the white majority. Lincoln then concluded that it "is better for us both, therefore to be separated." He commented on the success of Liberia, but realized that many free blacks harbored no yearnings for Africa because of the distance, and therefore suggested another possible site. "The place I am thinking about having a colony is in Central America."

While the Civil War raged, Lincoln raised the possibility of Latin American colonization with his cabinet, which explored the idea at some length. Eventually it grew apparent to Lincoln that free blacks had less interest in leaving the United States than he had thought, and his plans for colonization appeared less realistic. The Civil War's end and Lincoln's assassination doomed the colonization movement, although the American Colonization Society continued to function on a small scale as an agency for promoting African American emigration and education.

See also *Colonization*

—Allan Yarema

BIBLIOGRAPHY

Basler, Roy P., ed. *The Collected Works of Abraham Lincoln.* New Brunswick, N.J.: Rutgers University Press, 1953.

Fox, Early Lee. *The American Colonization Society, 1817–1840.* Baltimore: Johns Hopkins University Press, 1919.

Litwack, Leon F. *North of Slavery: The Negro in the Free States, 1790–1860.* Chicago: University of Chicago Press, 1961.

Staudenraus, P. J. *The African Colonization Movement, 1816–1865.* New York: Columbia University Press, 1961.

Yarema, Allan. *The American Colonization Society: An Avenue to Freedom?* Lanham, Md.: University Press of America, 2006

American System

The American System was a program for national economic development associated with Henry Clay, antebellum representative, senator, and Whig Party leader from Kentucky. In its broadest meaning, the American System included four interlocking elements: (1) a protective tariff to foster American industry, (2) a national bank to provide credit and a uniform currency, (3) a system of roads and canals ("internal improvements") to link all parts of the country, and (4) the sale of public land to raise necessary revenue. Important parts of the American System were adopted in the years following the War of 1812 but were largely overturned by Jacksonian Democrats in the 1830s. The American System remained a key objective of the Whig Party, with strong support from Abraham Lincoln during his Illinois years, and continued to inspire the economic policies of his Republican Party.

Members of the "National" wing of the Jeffersonian Republican Party began to support federal assistance to economic development in the aftermath of the War of 1812. In 1816 Congress chartered the Second Bank of the United States and adopted a modestly protective tariff. Sen. John C. Calhoun of South Carolina, then in his nationalist phase, also proposed using the bonus paid by the bank to plan a national transportation system, a measure vetoed by President James Madison on constitutional grounds. Though he first used the term "American system" in 1820 to support South American independence, Clay applied it to economic policy in an 1824 speech to the House of Representatives in support of a higher tariff. He argued that tariff protection would foster American industries and create a home market for American agriculture, reconciling diverse interests and freeing the United States from European domination.

Congress raised the tariff in 1824 and 1828, with minor modifications in 1832. This legislation aroused intense hostility from Southerners, now led by John C. Calhoun, who opposed any subsidy to manufacturing and worried that a protective tariff would rest upon broad construction of the Constitution and thus create a precedent for antislavery measures. Under Calhoun's leadership, South Carolina "nullified" the tariff in 1832 and moved to the brink of civil war. To avert the danger, Clay and Calhoun agreed to the Compromise Tariff of 1833, abandoning the principle of protectionism over a period of nine years.

Other features of the American System also suffered in the early 1830s, as Jacksonian Democrats fought to reduce the power of the federal government. President Andrew Jackson resisted internal improvements at federal expense in his veto of the Maysville Road in 1830 and vetoed the recharter of the Bank of the United States in 1832. With a federally planned and executed program of public works widely seen as unconstitutional, Clay shifted to calling for a distribution of federal revenue to the states for the purposes of internal improvements. Congress complied with the Surplus Distribution Act of 1836, but the Panic of 1837 curtailed that program.

During the years of the Second American Party System, the Whig Party consistently sought to restore the American System, and the Democrats generally resisted. Under Clay's leadership, Whigs fought for distribution, higher tariffs, and a new national bank during the John Tyler administration, but the president successfully opposed them. With federal support limited, friends of economic development turned to the states. Abraham Lincoln was a strong supporter of banks and internal improvements in the Illinois legislature. Without centralized direction, however, the growth of infrastructure suffered from local political jealousies until business institutions, especially national railroad corporations, assumed nearly full control of transportation policy in the late nineteenth century.

Lincoln's Republican Party adopted several modified aspects of the American System. Tariffs rose dramatically in the Civil War, and high tariffs remained a centerpiece of Republican economic policy until well into the twentieth century. Today economists widely believe that free trade promotes development more effectively than protectionism, but nineteenth-century data are too unreliable to make definitive judgments about the effects of antebellum tariffs. Republicans under Lincoln also established national banks to control wartime credit and currency without returning to a central bank. Republicans did not attempt to plan a national transportation network and did not fund internal improvements from the direct sale of public lands. Instead they sacrificed revenue for the sake of rapid settlement and widespread landownership. Congress passed the Homestead Act in 1862, granting 160 acres of the public domain to each actual settler. In the same year, Congress issued massive land grants to subsidize a transcontinental railroad, and subsequent administrations continued that policy.

See also *Clay, Henry*

—Harry L. Watson

BIBLIOGRAPHY

Baxter, Maurice G. *Henry Clay and the American System.* Lexington: University Press of Kentucky, 1995.

Harris, William C. *Lincoln's Rise to the Presidency.* Lawrence: University Press of Kansas, 2007.

Howe, Daniel Walker. *The Political Culture of the American Whigs.* Chicago: University of Chicago Press, 1980.

Larson, John Lauritz. *Internal Improvement: National Public Works and the Promise of Popular Government in the Early United States.* Chapel Hill: University of North Carolina Press, 2001.

Moore, Glover. *The Missouri Controversy, 1819–1821.* Lexington: University of Kentucky Press, 1953.

Remini, Robert V. *Henry Clay: Statesman for the Union.* New York: Harper and Row, 1991.

Anaconda Plan

"Anaconda" was the name popularly given to the strategic plan proposed in the early days of the Civil War by the commanding general of the Union army, Winfield Scott (1786–1866). From his long experience as a soldier, Scott was able to foresee the deadly course the war might take. He predicted a three-year struggle, requiring 300,000 men and costing $250 million. And for what? "Fifteen devastated provinces!...to be followed for generations by heavy garrisons."

Scott thought he knew a better way. From his experience as a negotiator, especially during the nullification crisis of 1831, he had learned the value of buying time to allow passions to cool and compromise to be reached. He agreed with secretary of state William Seward that Southern nationalism was a temporary enthusiasm that would subside if it were not fed by an escalating cycle of violence. Furthermore, as a Virginian, Scott thought he understood his fellow Southerners. They were bold and brave, he conceded, but also impulsive and impatient, and "they will not submit to being bored."

Scott's strategy followed from these considerations. Rather than invade the South and put down the rebellion by force, he proposed to isolate the refractory states from the rest of the world and allow their latent patriotism to overcome their transient grievances. Using the North's superior naval resources, he would blockade the South's coasts, cutting off the export of cotton and the importation

An artist's depiction of "Scott's Great Snake," or the Anaconda Plan. General Winfield Scott's plan to isolate the Confederacy with only a naval blockade was considered too passive by Republicans, whose slogan was "Forward to Richmond!" Though Scott's plan was dismissed, a naval blockade played a significant part in Lincoln's war strategy.

Source: The Granger Collection, New York

of European goods. Naval power, in the form of gunboats, would also control the great river systems of the West, especially the Ohio and Mississippi, drawing the noose even tighter. The gunboats would be supported by columns of regular soldiers who would try to avoid pitched encounters.

Scott assured President Lincoln that when Southerners "feel this pressure, not having been exasperated by attacks made upon them..., the Union spirit will assert itself..., and I will guarantee that in one year's time, all difficulties will be settled." But, as he further warned the president, if the South should be invaded by a hostile force, "You will consolidate what is now an insurrection, and make of it a rebellious government—which you may be able to put down in two or three years, but I doubt it."

The president was not convinced. Although he relied on Scott for advice on military matters, this proposed strategy was based on a dubious set of political premises, and Lincoln had harbored little respect for Scott's political savvy ever since his disastrous presidential run in 1852.

Scott himself realized that his plan faced major obstacles, chief of which was "the impatience of our patriotic and loyal Union friends." Scott's passive and seemingly inglorious strategy was at odds with the volatile, impulsive American temperament. Critics derided his program as the "Anaconda Plan," after the great snake that squeezes its prey to death.

Most of the cabinet feared that if the enlistments of the ninety-day volunteers expired without some positive military action, enlistments would dry up, bond sales falter, and morale plummet. Egged on by the daily cry of "Forward to Richmond!" in Horace Greeley's influential *New York Tribune,* they urged an immediate march on the rebel capital to end the war with one blow. Overriding the general's misgivings, they demanded an immediate advance into Virginia which, as Scott had warned, ended in a Union defeat at Bull Run (July 21, 1861).

With that, the Anaconda Plan was shelved (along with General Scott himself), to be replaced by war to the bitter end. Some aspects of Scott's plan, such as the blockade and the division of the Confederacy through control of the Mississippi River, were retained but only as elements of that total war that Scott's strategy had been designed to avoid.

See also *Blockade, Union Naval; Scott, Winfield*

—ALLAN PESKIN

BIBLIOGRAPHY

Nevins, Allan, Milton Halsey, and Thomas Strong, eds. *The Diary of George Templeton Strong.* New York: Macmillan, 1952.

Peskin, Allan. *Winfield Scott and the Profession of Arms.* Kent, Ohio: Kent State University Press, 2003.

Stone, Charles P. "Washington in 1861," *Magazine of American History* 12 (July 1884): 59–60.

Townsend, E. D. *Anecdotes of the Civil War in the United States.* 1884. Reprint, New York: Kessinger Publishing. 55–56, 260–262.

The War of the Rebellion: A Compilation of the Official Records of the Union and Confederate Armies. Series 1, vol. 51. Washington, D.C.: U.S. Government Printing Office, 1897. 369–370, 386–387.

Antietam Campaign

In the aftermath of the Confederate victory at Second Manassas (August 28–30, 1862), Robert E. Lee decided to advance the Army of Northern Virginia north across the Potomac River into Maryland. Lee reasoned that he might demoralize Northern support for the war, woo Marylanders to join the Confederacy, and influence Great Britain and France as they pondered whether to offer their services to broker a peace settlement that would recognize Confederate independence. Once in Maryland, Lee contemplated continuing north into Pennsylvania, but only after he had nullified the threat to his rear posed by the Union garrison at Harpers Ferry, Virginia.

As Lee advanced toward the Potomac, Abraham Lincoln decided to reorganize the three forces now located near Washington, D.C.: the Army of the Potomac, still under the command of George B. McClellan; the Army of Virginia, led by John Pope; and the garrison forces around Washington, as well as reinforcements arriving at the capital. Although the president suspected McClellan of failing to give Pope his total support in the weeks leading up to Pope's defeat at Second Manassas, he could not avoid evidence that Pope's performance had been abysmal and that he was unpopular with many of his soldiers. Moreover, general in chief Henry W. Halleck had come close to collapsing altogether in struggling to respond to the Confederate offensive. Against the advice of several cabinet members, including secretary of war Edwin M. Stanton and secretary of the Treasury Salmon P. Chase, Lincoln decided to place McClellan in command of the forces around Washington, including a refashioned Army of the Potomac.

Lee crossed the Potomac on September 4; a week later McClellan set out after him. Finding that the residents of western Maryland shared little of the secessionist sympathies of their eastern counterparts, Lee decided to overwhelm the Harpers Ferry garrison by first surrounding it with a multipronged offensive, while a small covering force kept an eye on McClellan. Union forces slowly pressed westward, but fortune smiled on McClellan when on September 13 several Union soldiers came across a copy of Lee's orders outlining the Harpers

Ferry operation. Armed with this information, McClellan advanced against South Mountain, a range stretching north and southwest of Frederick, Maryland, with the intent of forcing his way through the mountain's passes and falling upon portions of Lee's badly divided force. Learning of the orders mishap, Lee decided to continue moving against Harpers Ferry while ordering covering forces to defend the mountain passes. On September 14, advance Union elements battled Confederates at Turner's Gap to the north and Crampton's Gap to the south, eventually prevailing. Lee pulled his covering force back to a series of heights north and east of Sharpsburg, Maryland, located some ten miles due north of Harpers Ferry. Any Union advance would have to come across Antietam Creek, which ran north and southeast of Sharpsburg. Anticipating the fall of Harpers Ferry, Lee hoped he would have time to reunite his army before contesting McClellan's advance.

Although Union forces crossed South Mountain and approached Antietam Creek on September 15 and 16, McClellan declined to attack, believing that he was outnumbered by the Confederates. The Confederates prevailed at Harpers Ferry, surrounding and capturing some 12,419 Union soldiers on the morning of September 15, and by that afternoon, lead elements of the victorious army were on the road to Sharpsburg.

McClellan had perhaps 75,000 men in position on the morning of September 17, when he planned to attack Lee's army, estimated at between 30,000 and 35,000, with one division still at Harpers Ferry. Although in later years McClellan would claim that he planned to attack both Confederate flanks in coordinated attacks, the battle as fought followed a roughly north-to-south pattern, with the Union forces often breaking Confederate positions in bloody combat, only to find themselves checked by realigned defenders. In the afternoon, Union forces under Ambrose Burnside finally forced a Confederate position behind a bridge and pressed forward, only to encounter A. P. Hill's men, who had hurried north from Harpers Ferry to check the last Union thrust. For the day Union casualties totaled some 12,401 men, while Confederate losses reached 10,318, nearly a third of Lee's army. It was the bloodiest single day of combat in the American Civil War. McClellan declined to renew his attack on September 18, and that night Lee commenced in earnest his withdrawal back across the Potomac, checking what there was of a Union pursuit at Shepherdstown on September 19–20.

Disappointed that Lee had managed to retreat across the Potomac, Lincoln nevertheless grasped the opportunity offered by Antietam. If it was not the decisive victory he would have preferred, Antietam at least offered Lincoln something that resembled a victory, and he took advantage of it to issue the preliminary Emancipation Proclamation on September 22, 1862. The president had been waiting since July for just such a victory, so that it would not look as if the proclamation was a desperate measure issued in the wake of a string of Union defeats. Two days later the president issued a second declaration suspending the writ of habeas corpus in cases involving support of the Confederacy or resistance to raising military forces. Not everyone welcomed news of either proclamation, including McClellan: Lincoln was aware of this when he visited McClellan's headquarters at the beginning of October. By then the president was growing frustrated with the pace of McClellan's operations. Joseph Hooker, who had been wounded in the opening attacks at Antietam, had already told the president that McClellan had lost a golden opportunity by hesitating to attack and failing to follow up his successes. The following month the president finally removed McClellan in the immediate wake of the midterm elections. By giving Lincoln the victory he needed to announce his emancipation plans, the battle was far more decisive politically than it was militarily, although it did repulse the first Confederate advance across the Potomac.

See also *McClellan, George B.*

—BROOKS D. SIMPSON

BIBLIOGRAPHY

Cooling, Benjamin F. *Counter-Thrust: From the Peninsula to the Antietam.* Lincoln: University of Nebraska Press, 2007.

Gallagher, Gary W., ed. *The Antietam Campaign.* Chapel Hill: University of North Carolina Press, 1999.

Harsh, Joseph L. *Taken at the Flood: Robert E. Lee and Confederate Strategy in the Maryland Campaign of 1862.* Kent, Ohio: Kent State University Press, 1999.

McPherson, James M. *Crossroads of Freedom: Antietam.* New York: Oxford University Press, 2002.

Murfin, James V. *The Gleam of Bayonets: The Battle of Antietam and the Maryland Campaign of 1862.* Thomas Yoseloff, 1965. Reprint, Baton Rouge: Louisiana State University Press, 1982.

Sears, Stephen W. *Landscape Turned Red: The Battle of Antietam.* New York: Houghton Mifflin, 1983.

Antislavery

Starting with the Enlightenment and the development of Western liberal thought, the once rarely questioned system of slavery became the object of considerable debate. The influential ideas of John Locke that "the natural liberty of man is to be free from any superior power on earth" suggested that the enslaving of others was contrary to natural law. In the colonies that would become the United States, these ideas permeated the culture, as Americans began to rally against their own "enslavement" by the British government. Nearly all the major founders, including many of the slaveholders, expressed opposition to slavery in principle. Among the slaveholders, Patrick Henry explained his position the best, and most honestly, when in a private letter he called slavery an "abominable practice," yet suggested that his continued practice of the institution owed to "the general inconvenience of living here without them." This was a position of which Henry confessed, "I will not, I cannot justify it."

These ideals culminated first in an antislavery movement in the late eighteenth and early nineteenth centuries that led to the abolition of slavery in all of the Northern states and to thousands of private manumissions in the South. One of the first efforts by antislavery forces to affect national policy on slavery occurred in 1790 when a group of Pennsylvania Quakers presented a petition to Congress calling for the abolition of the slave trade. Yet because the Constitution protected the African slave trade until 1808, it would be eighteen more years until their cause was successful.

In 1816 the American Colonization Society was established in the quixotic belief that the best method to remove slavery was to remove all black Americans, voluntarily, to Africa to alleviate the racial tensions that were expected to result from large-scale emancipation. Four years later, slavery became the focal point of national debate when questions arose over whether Missouri would enter the Union as a free or a slave state.

It was during these early debates that the young Abraham Lincoln encountered controversy over slavery. Lincoln's father, Thomas Lincoln, was a poor farmer living in Kentucky, a slave state. Thomas Lincoln was listed among several who broke away and formed their own Baptist congregation in protest over slavery. When Lincoln's family moved to Indiana shortly afterward, Lincoln claimed years later, it "was partly on the account of slavery." As with the larger antislavery movement, the Lincolns' opposition to slavery sprang from a mixture of moral and economic considerations. As a small farmer Thomas Lincoln could not compete with the large farms that were able to use slave labor. Yet included in their opposition was the plain belief that slavery was fundamentally wrong. In an 1864 letter Abraham Lincoln stated, "I am naturally anti-slavery. If slavery is not wrong, nothing is wrong." Looking back to his earliest days he added, "I can not remember when I did not so think, and feel."

In 1837, while in the Illinois state legislature, Lincoln was one of only six representatives to vote against a resolution, in response to the growing abolitionist movement, that called "the right of property in slaves...sacred to the slaveholding States." Several weeks later Lincoln introduced his own bill, which attracted only one other supporter, stating that "the institution of slavery is founded on both injustice and bad policy" but that as to the abolitionists, their "doctrines tend rather to increase than abate its evils." As a lawyer in Illinois, Lincoln successfully argued for the freedom of blacks and, unlike most lawyers, had black clients. But he also took a least one case (which he lost) on behalf of a master trying to recover his slave. Later while serving in the U.S. Congress

Lincoln proposed a bill, which never reached the floor, to abolish slavery in the District of Columbia.

The key to understanding Lincoln's early approach to the antislavery movement can be found in his admiration of Henry Clay. For Clay, slavery was an inherited evil that needed somehow to be resolved. Lincoln was unsure how slavery "could be at once eradicated, without producing a greater evil, even to the cause of liberty itself." Like Clay, Lincoln was pessimistic about the possibility of blacks and whites living together free and equally. To free the enslaved and have them live as "underlings" was to Lincoln hardly better than slavery. Further it was believed to increase the chances of a much-feared race war. For the slaves to be freed and amalgamated into white society, Lincoln's "feelings" would "not admit of this; and if" his sentiments "would," he "well" knew "that those of the great mass of white people" would not agree to it. Though Lincoln understood the irrational characteristic of his own feelings, he understood that "whether this feeling accords with justice and sound judgment" was "not the sole question, if indeed...any part of it. A universal feeling whether well or ill founded cannot be safely disregarded." For Lincoln, society's deep-seated prejudices mandated gradual and voluntary colonization schemes as the best hope of safely eradicating slavery. Lincoln's antislavery strategy was a long-term plan that recognized the antislavery impulses of slaveholders such as Henry Clay and was patient in allowing the South to end slavery in its own way.

In January 1854 this plan was shattered. Stephen Douglas, hoping to stave off a crisis among the Southern states, introduced a bill, eventually known as the Kansas-Nebraska Act, repealing the Missouri Compromise and opening the door for slavery in Kansas. When word reached Lincoln of the developments in Washington he commented to T. Lyle Dickey, a fellow lawyer traveling with him on the Illinois legal circuit, "I tell you, Dickey, this nation cannot exist half-slave and half free." The Kansas-Nebraska Act was a dramatic turn in political events, and it had a profound influence on Lincoln's future in politics.

The antislavery movement was large and encompassing in the North. Although relatively few abolitionists desired the immediate abolition of slavery, a large coalition of Northerners hoped to prevent slavery from spreading into the territories. The motives were mixed. Some, like Lincoln, genuinely abhorred the practice of slavery on moral and philosophical grounds and sought its containment as a means to effect its ultimate abolition. Others saw slavery as an impediment to developing a strong, free-labor economy, and some opposed the introduction of slavery to new territories out of the racist desire to keep those areas entirely white.

One of the immediate consequences of the Kansas-Nebraska Act was the disintegration of the national Whig Party. Prior to 1854 the Whig Party could unite its Northern and Southern members on banks, tariffs, and internal improvements, but the introduction of the issue of slavery permanently split the two factions. The result was the eventual formation of the Republican Party, based on a "free soil" (no extension of slavery) platform. Third parties had existed before, notably the Liberty Party (1840–1848) and the Free Soil Party (1848–1852), but it was only with the formation of the Republican Party in 1854 that a major party was established with an antislavery platform.

Throughout the 1850s Lincoln was a relatively minor figure in the Republican Party. Although he had long been a respected figure in Illinois state politics, it was only in 1858, during his Senate race against Stephen Douglas, that Lincoln developed anything of a national reputation. His reputation was furthered by a series of speeches he made around the country between 1859 and 1860. Even so, by 1860 Lincoln was still a long shot to win the nomination for president. Sen. William H. Seward of New York was the favored candidate. However Seward's perceived radicalism, and Lincoln's skilled positioning, eventually won the Illinois Republican the nomination. His nomination displeased strong opponents of slavery, who thought Lincoln was weak on the issue. Eastern abolitionists had wanted Seward or Salmon Chase and saw Lincoln as a "first rate, second rate man," with no strong commitment to opposing slavery.

Once in office, Lincoln found himself navigating between both sides of the antislavery movement. William Seward surprisingly took a more conservative stance, desiring to maintain the old antislavery policies and let slavery die a natural death. Other radicals, such as secretary of the Treasury Salmon P. Chase and Massachusetts senator Charles Sumner, advocated more vigorous action on emancipation. Lincoln was initially hesitant to move quickly on emancipation. He was primarily concerned with how the Border States would receive such policies, yet he also had concerns about the legality of executive orders dealing with emancipation.

With the Union victory at Antietam in September 1862, Lincoln felt the conditions were right and was convinced that he had the legal authority to offer emancipation in the areas that were in rebellion. By January 1, 1863, Lincoln's Emancipation Proclamation became a reality. Yet legal questions remained about the proclamation, as well as about the status of slavery in the areas it did not touch. Lincoln's victory in the 1864 elections, which also brought a large increase in the Republicans' margin of control in Congress, emboldened him to make extraordinary efforts to lobby the lame duck Congress into passing the Thirteenth Amendment to the Constitution, completely abolishing slavery. By the time of Lincoln's death, that amendment was being considered in the individual states. By the end of the year it was ratified and became the law of the land.

See also *Abolitionism*

—JOHN WICKRE

BIBLIOGRAPHY

Annals of Congress, 1st Congress, 2nd Sess., 1224–1228.

Bailyn, Bernard. *The Ideological Origins of the American Revolution.* Cambridge, Mass.: Belknap Press of Harvard University Press, 1992.

Burin, Eric. *Slavery and the Peculiar Solution: A History of the American Colonization Society.* Gainesville: University of Florida Press, 2005.

Commager, Henry Steele, and Richard B. Morris, eds. *The Spirit of Seventy-Six: The Story of the American Revolution as Told by Participants.* Cambridge, Mass.: De Capo, 1995.

Foner, Eric. *Free Soil, Free Labor, Free Men: The Ideology of the Republican Party before the Civil War.* New York: Oxford University Press, 1995.

Locke, John. *Two Treatises of Government.* Edited by C.B. Macpherson. Indianapolis: Hackett, 1980.

Warren, Louis. *Lincoln's Youth: Indiana Years Seven to Twenty-One, 1816–1830.* New York: Appleton, Century, Crofts, 1959.

Assassination

On April 14, 1865, only five days after General Robert E. Lee's surrender to General Ulysses S. Grant at Appomattox, Virginia, Abraham Lincoln took his wife to Ford's Theatre in Washington to see the farcical comedy *Our American Cousin,* starring the well-known actress Laura Keene. While the Lincolns watched from the box above the stage, actor John Wilkes Booth slipped into the box and shot Lincoln in the back of the head, wounding him mortally. Nine hours later, on the morning of April 15, Abraham Lincoln died.

The nation, and particularly the nation's capital, had been experiencing a week of celebration of the end of the Civil War. The end had come rather swiftly, after Union General Grant had broken General Lee's lines outside of Petersburg and then forced his surrender at Appomattox Court House. Grant's victory at Petersburg left the Confederate defense of the capital city of Richmond untenable, and Confederate forces and the Confederate government hastily withdrew. Shortly after Union troops secured the city, Lincoln traveled to Richmond and walked through the still-smoldering ruins of the Confederate capital.

On Sunday afternoon, April 9, Lincoln arrived back in Washington just in time to receive the news of Lee's surrender at Appomattox. While enjoying the festive atmosphere in the nation's capital, the president also began attending to some of the weighty matters that loomed large with the war's end. What was to be done about Confederate leaders, especially those who had left the U.S. Army or government to serve the Confederacy? What was to be done about the newly freed slaves? And what would be the policy regarding the military occupation of the Southern states?

By Friday the president, who in the preceding months had often been afflicted with melancholia and insomnia and had all too frequently been emotionally and physically bowed down by the war, was feeling better than he had in some time. His mood reflected that throughout the day, and he informed members of his cabinet about a dream that he had had the night before, the same dream that he had previously had on the eve of momentous events (such as Gettysburg, Antietam, and Fort Sumter). He dreamt that he was on some kind of vessel, moving rapidly toward an indiscernible shore. Because he believed that the dream was somehow prophetic of great events that would occur that day, he predicted that word would probably arrive from General Sherman, in North Carolina, that Joseph Johnston's army, the last principal army in the Confederacy still in the field, had surrendered.

That same day he took his wife, Mary, on a carriage ride, talking with her about a hopeful future, what they might look forward to doing, and where they might travel. This was in contrast to his usually bleak assessment of his personal future once the war came to an end.

A group of covert Confederate operatives had formed around their leader, John Wilkes Booth, over the last year or so of the war. They were a rather motley collection of individuals except for their leader, who was the son of a well-known acting family that included Junius Booth and Edwin Booth. Lewis Powell (aka Lewis Payne), whom Booth assigned to kill secretary of state William H. Seward at his home, was a former Confederate soldier who had been captured by Union troops during the war. George Atzerodt, a German-born carriage maker, had been part of the conspiracy when it contemplated kidnapping the president, but he balked when Booth spoke of assassination. Nevertheless Atzerodt did not withdraw from the conspiracy and was ordered to go to the hotel room of Vice President Andrew Johnson and assassinate him. Atzerodt lost his nerve and was drinking in the hotel bar when he was supposed to be stalking Johnson. Booth, who had only that day read that the Lincolns would be attending Ford's Theatre that evening, knew that his connections, as a frequent and well-known actor in Washington, would gain him access to the theater, where he could get close enough to Lincoln to shoot him. Booth even bored a small hole in the door to the box where the Lincoln party would be seated, to ensure that he could gain access, and rigged the outer door to bar anybody else from entering the box.

At around eight o'clock that evening, the Lincolns departed from the White House in a carriage, which would carry them the few blocks to the theater. With them were Clara Harris, the daughter of Sen. Ira Harris of New York, and her fiancé, Major Henry Rathbone. Curiously, a number of other people who had been invited to join the Lincolns had all declined for various reasons. First among those were General Ulysses S. Grant and his wife, Julia. Mrs. Grant could not countenance being in the presence of Mary Todd Lincoln since an embarrassing episode several weeks earlier during a review of troops at Petersburg. Grant used a planned visit to their children in New Jersey as a convenient excuse. Secretary of War Stanton, who found the theater a foolish diversion, and a dangerous one as well, not only declined the invitation but also refused to allow his chief telegrapher, Thomas Eckert, to go. Lincoln encouraged Indiana representative Schuyler Colfax to join them, but he was preparing to travel to the West Coast and declined. The president almost seemed reluctant to go himself, but it had been announced in the newspapers that day. His last words to his bodyguard William Crook before leaving the White House were, "It has been advertised that we will be there, and I cannot disappoint the people." Crook had the night off, and Lincoln would not hear of his joining the party to provide security.

When the party arrived at Ford's Theatre the play had already begun. As the Lincolns entered their box, to the side of and above the stage, the players interrupted the performance to salute the president, as the orchestra struck up "Hail to the Chief," and the audience gave Lincoln a standing ovation. The play continued, as Booth returned from a final meeting with his coconspirators, at which he had assigned them their deadly responsibilities. A full-blown alcoholic at this point in his life, Booth stopped at the bar next door to Ford's to imbibe some liquid courage.

Shortly after ten o'clock Booth entered the theater and mounted the stairs to the balcony. The play was under way, and nobody would have paid any attention to Booth as he crossed behind the crowd and entered the outer door into the box where the presidential party sat. Booth was very familiar with *Our American Cousin,* and he knew just the moment in the play when he wished to strike. It was a scene in the third act when Harry Hawk, playing the lead male role, was alone on the stage and had just uttered the funniest line of the play: "Don't know the manners of good society, eh? Well, I guess I know enough to turn you inside out, old gal—you sockdologizing old man-trap." The crowd laughed loudly, but not so loudly as to cover the sound of the derringer shot that Booth fired into the back of Lincoln's head from very close range. Still, most people in the audience thought it was just part of the play until Major Rathbone jumped from his seat and attempted to grab Booth. But the assassin had a knife with him as well as the gun, and he slashed at Rathbone, badly cutting his upper arm. As Booth prepared to jump from the box to the stage, Rathbone again grabbed at him, probably influencing his leap enough to cause his spur to get caught in the Treasury flag draped from the front of the box. Booth landed awkwardly on the stage, breaking his left fibula just above the ankle. He stood up in front of the stunned audience with the knife held above his head and shouted, "Sic semper tyrannis!" the Virginia state motto, meaning "Thus be it ever to tyrants." Others in the crowd claimed he also said, "The South is avenged." He then hastened across the stage and into the alley behind the theater, where Joseph "Peanuts" Burroughs held his horse. Burroughs had been enlisted to hold the horse by Edman Spangler, a stagehand at the theater whom Booth had initially hired to hold the horse. Booth struck Burroughs in the head with the handle of his knife, mounted, and kicked Burroughs in the face before spurring the horse toward the Navy Yard, where he would meet Davy Herold and Lewis Powell.

At about the same time Booth was doing his deed at Ford's Theatre, Lewis Powell was approaching the home of William Henry Seward, the secretary of state. Seward had been recovering from a near-fatal carriage accident nine days earlier that had left him with a crushed jaw and a broken shoulder. He had been fitted with a brace to hold his jaw in place. While Davy Herold waited outside, Powell went to the front door of Seward's residence and announced that he had medicine to deliver to the secretary of state. He said the physician had instructed him to deliver it in person. The servant tried to tell him that he could not go up, but Powell was so insistent that he allowed him to pass. At the second floor landing Seward's son Fred met him and told him he could go no further, in spite of Powell's insistence that he must deliver the medicine in person. After appearing to relent and start back down the stairs, Powell suddenly turned and sprang upon Fred, attempting to shoot him in the head with a navy revolver. The gun misfired, but he struck Fred Seward's head so violently with the pistol that he was knocked out, his skull crushed in two places. Powell then charged into Secretary Seward's bedroom brandishing the broken pistol in one hand and a large knife in the other. A soldier guarding Seward, Private George Robinson, was slashed in the forehead, and then Powell rushed at the bed where the secretary lay. Fanny Seward, his wife, attempted to plead with Powell but to no avail. He plunged the knife into Seward's cheek and neck. The initial blows knocked Seward off the bed and temporarily out of Powell's reach. Seward's son Gus ran into the room and attacked the intruder, along with Private Robinson, and both of them suffered further wounds for their efforts, Gus being slashed in the forehead and right hand. Powell then ran from the room and bolted down the stairs, stabbing one more person, State Department messenger Emerick Hansell, in the back as he departed. Seward and his sons all survived, but his wife, badly shaken by the attack, would die in June 1865.

At Ford's Theatre there was a stunned silence as Lincoln's body slumped forward in his rocking chair. Mary Lincoln began screaming, and Major Rathbone began shouting, "Stop that man!" Pandemonium broke out. Charles Leale, a young army surgeon who was off duty that evening, was the first doctor to enter the presidential box. He found Lincoln in his chair being held up by Mary. The president had no pulse, and Leale thought him dead. He lowered Lincoln to the floor. By this time Charles Taft, another doctor from the audience, was literally lifted to the box from the stage and climbed over the railing. Together the doctors cut off Lincoln's collar and Leale began feeling around the unconscious man's head with his hands. He soon discovered the hole behind the left ear. He removed a blood clot, which improved Lincoln's breathing. Nevertheless, he knew it made no difference and announced that the wound was mortal. When a third doctor, Albert King, arrived they decided to move Lincoln to a house across the street from Ford's Theatre. Henry Safford, a boarder at William Peterson's boarding house, told them, "Bring him in here, bring him in here." Lincoln was carried into a first floor bedroom, where they had to lay him diagonally across the bed because he was too tall to lie straight. There he died at 7:22 a.m. on the morning of April 15, 1865. It was an Easter weekend that has ever since been referred to as "Black Easter."

See also *Booth, John Wilkes*

—DAVID E. LONG

BIBLIOGRAPHY

Kauffman, Michael W. *American Brutus: John Wilkes Booth and the Lincoln Conspiracies.* New York: Random House, 2004.

Steers, Edward, Jr. *Blood on the Moon: The Assassination of Abraham Lincoln.* Lexington: University Press of Kentucky, 2001.

Swanson, James L. *Manhunt: The Twelve Day Chase for Lincoln's Killer.* New York: HarperCollins, 2006.

Swanson, James L., and Daniel Weinberg. *Lincoln's Assassins: Their Trial and Execution.* New York: HarperCollins, 2001.

Winik, Jay. *April 1865: The Month That Saved America.* New York: HarperCollins, 2001.

Atlanta Campaign

In the spring of 1864 William T. Sherman took charge of three field armies—the Army of the Tennessee, the Army of the Cumberland, and the Army of the Ohio—totaling just under 100,000 men encamped in northwest Georgia. His objective, as set forth by the new general in chief, Ulysses S. Grant, was simple: He was to advance southward, destroy the Confederate Army of Tennessee, some 50,000 strong (with 15,000 reinforcements to arrive soon) under the command of Joseph E. Johnston, and capture Atlanta, Georgia, a key rail junction. Johnston's objective was equally simple: prevent Sherman from destroying his army or taking Atlanta.

Sherman's thrust toward Atlanta was one of the key elements of Grant's grand strategy for 1864, which featured simultaneous and coordinated offensives against the major Confederate field armies, the cities they protected, and the logistical underpinnings of the Confederacy. Pressuring the Confederates at several key places simultaneously would prevent the Confederates from taking advantage of their interior lines to shift forces from one area to another to check Union offensive operations. Sherman's task was complicated by the terrain in Georgia, which featured a series of mountain ranges running southwest to northeast, with rivers often separating them, and with but a single rail line stretching from Chattanooga to Atlanta to serve as a supply line for the advancing Union forces.

On May 7 Sherman commenced his offensive by sending James B. McPherson's Army of the Tennessee through Snake Creek Gap toward Resaca, while his other forces sought to keep the Confederates pinned. Encountering resistance, McPherson pulled back, enabling Johnston to elude being outflanked if not cut off. The opposing forces sparred north of Resaca on May 14 and 15, whereupon Sherman again slid around Johnston's flank, threatening the Confederate supply line and forcing Johnston to withdraw. Thus began the pattern of a campaign that featured several short, sharp clashes, Union flanking movements, and Confederate withdrawals, at a far lower cost in casualties than was being incurred by Grant and Lee in Virginia. Only at Kennesaw Mountain on June 27 did Sherman order a major frontal assault, which the Confederates handily repulsed.

By the middle of July, Sherman was closing in on Atlanta. Confederate president Jefferson Davis, unhappy that Johnston had been unable to keep Sherman in check and worried that the general might give up Atlanta without a fight, replaced him with John Bell Hood, who was known as an aggressive division commander. Between July 20 and July 28, Hood launched three attacks against portions of Sherman's army, but despite incurring high casualties, Hood was unable to do more than slow Sherman down. Nevertheless, by August the situation around Atlanta, to the untrained eye, resembled the situation at Richmond and Petersburg, with Union advances seemingly halted in their tracks and settling down for a long siege. The summer stalemate, coming after a spring of high hopes for a decisive Union victory, increased war weariness in the North just as the Democratic Party was preparing to journey to Chicago to nominate its presidential candidate for the fall election.

During August Sherman worked methodically to cut Atlanta off from the rest of the Confederacy to nullify its worth as a railroad junction, but he failed to inflict lasting damage on railroads leading out of the city. Hood struggled to counter Sherman's thrusts, most notably with a cavalry raid that threatened to sever the Union rail line at Dalton, but to no avail. By month's end Sherman decided to launch a major offensive that would destroy the rail links for good and compromise Confederate supply lines. At Jonesborough, he succeeded in smashing through the Confederate defenders, forcing Hood to evacuate Atlanta on the night of September 1. As the Confederates retreated, they set fire to material of military value. The following day, Sherman's army entered the city, and he telegraphed Washington, "Atlanta is ours, and fairly won."

Atlanta's fall came just days after the Democratic presidential convention had named George B. McClellan as its candidate on a platform calling for a negotiated end to the Civil War. The fall of Atlanta served as a powerful counter to notions that the Union war effort was once more a failure. Lincoln, all too aware that his chances for reelection largely hinged on the progress of Union arms, became somewhat more confident of his political prospects, although he remained skeptical until October. Confederate efforts to force Sherman to give up the city proved fruitless, although Sherman discovered that he could not bring Hood to bay. That led him to conceive of his famed March to the Sea: Grant, however, urged him to wait until after the November presidential election before commencing his campaign.

In truth, Sherman had met only one of Grant's two objectives, for the Army of Tennessee remained a dangerous fighting force in the field. Moreover, his operations in August had gone a long way toward taking Atlanta out of the war, so the actual occupation of the city in itself was not as critical as it might have seemed. If anything, holding the captured city proved something of an albatross around Sherman's neck. However, given popular attitudes that equated military success with the taking of cities, the fall of Atlanta bolstered Northern morale and enhanced Lincoln's chances for reelection, although exactly to what extent has recently been the subject of renewed discussion, with some scholars questioning whether the Union victory had all that much impact on the outcome of the election of 1864. Nevertheless, many people at the time accorded it great weight in securing Lincoln's reelection, and certainly the president appreciated it.

See also *Sherman, William T.; Sherman's March to the Sea*

—BROOKS D. SIMPSON

BIBLIOGRAPHY

Castel, Albert. *Decision in the West: The Atlanta Campaign of 1864*. Lawrence: University Press of Kansas, 1992.

McMurry, Richard. *Atlanta 1864: Last Chance for the Confederacy*. Lincoln: University of Nebraska Press, 2000.

B

Ball's Bluff, Battle of

The Battle of Ball's Bluff occurred on October 21, 1861, when Union and Confederate forces clashed outside the town of Leesburg, Virginia. Ball's Bluff was a lengthy stretch of high ground featuring a steep, in some places sheer, drop to the Potomac River, into which the Confederates pushed the Union troops, subjecting them to another stinging defeat on the heels of the Battle of Bull Run. Poor strategic planning and the Union army's lack of real combat experience could not counter the better positioned Confederate soldiers and more seasoned Confederate officers.

Congress felt the ramifications of the defeat on two fronts: First, the Senate lost a member, Edward Baker, a steadfast Lincoln supporter from Oregon, who was killed at the battle. Second, the defeat led radical Republicans in Congress to create a Joint Committee on the Conduct of the War to investigate the causes of the defeats at Bull Run and Ball's Bluff. The defeat also further strained relations between the army's new commander, General George McClellan, and President Lincoln.

The battle's roots stretched back to the Bull Run disaster. Stung by that defeat, the Army of the Potomac, now under the command of McClellan, hoped to engage Confederate forces at the town of Leesburg to bolster public support of a war that had long passed the "ninety-days" threshold. Facing intense scrutiny from the public, radical Republicans in Congress, and prominent newspaper editors such as Horace Greeley, Abraham Lincoln approved McClellan's plan to dispatch Union forces along the Potomac.

On October 21, McClellan, anxious to atone for the embarrassing "Quaker Gun" incident at Manassas, ordered General Charles P. Stone and his brigade to draw Confederate fire while Colonel Edward Baker, the senator from Oregon and close friend of President Lincoln, made his way across the Potomac into Virginia to attack the Confederate flank. The 15th Massachusetts regiment, commanded by Harvard graduate Colonel Charles Devens, had been sent across the Potomac the previous day to capture a Confederate camp. At noon on October 21, a combined force of Confederate infantry, dismounted cavalry, and artillery engaged the Massachusetts regiment in a clearing close to Ball's Bluff. Devens, believing that he would be reinforced by Baker's entire brigade, withdrew to the top of the bluff, where he again faced the Confederate onslaught. General Stone ordered the men to "hold what ground you have" and wait for Baker's reinforcements, which were slow to arrive, as the boats meant to ferry men across the Potomac only held twenty-five at a time. After crossing the Potomac, Baker moved his Pennsylvania regiment up the steep hill. With no escape route, Baker and his men faced the hill in front of them, the river below them, and constant Confederate sniper fire from the Mississippians atop the hill who, as Shelby Foote stated, "were reminded of turkey-shoots down home."

In spite of poor planning and execution, the Union assault managed to reach the top of the bluff, only to find four additional Mississippi and Virginia regiments, under the command of Lieutenant Colonel H. W. Jenifer, waiting to attack. Fierce fighting continued until the Confederates overwhelmed the beleaguered Union forces and repelled the advancing troops. Baker's regiment, now intermixed with members of the 15th Massachusetts, faced a steady barrage from their counterparts charging down the hill. The bloodied Pennsylvania and Massachusetts men retreated to the inadequate flatboats along the Potomac. Most of those fortunate enough to escape the melee soon overloaded the boats and drowned in the river. More than one-half of the 1,700 men in Baker's brigade were killed, wounded, or taken prisoner. (Among the Union's many wounded was a young lieutenant from Massachusetts named Oliver Wendell Holmes Jr.) Confederate casualties were negligible. Instead of the victory that was to assuage public uncertainty about the war, Union forces met another stunning defeat.

Looking for scapegoats for the embarrassing defeats at Bull Run and Ball's Bluff, Congress created the Joint Committee on the Conduct of the War. Benjamin Wade, a staunchly abolitionist senator from Massachusetts, chaired the committee, which was dominated by other Radical Republicans, including Zachariah Chandler and Lyman Trumbull. Critics of the committee denounced it as "Jacobin," an attempt to besmirch the reputations of prominent Democratic generals and to hide the effects of cronyism in the army that was Lincoln's responsibility. The committee's supporters, however, championed it as a "foe of inefficiency and corruption in the army," a mechanism that exposed the ineptitude of commanders and the gross corruption that hampered the war effort.

General Charles P. Stone was the committee's first victim. Members produced witnesses who testified to Stone's supposed dealings with Confederate officers and misuse of "contraband" slaves in his regiment. In a testament to the Jacobin nature of the proceedings, Stone was not allowed to speak or to produce a witness on his own behalf. He was arrested and briefly imprisoned. After a short time in jail, Stone was released and given several minor commands, but neither his military career nor his reputation ever fully recovered from the joint committee hearings.

General McClellan, a prominent New York Democrat with many friendships among Confederate officers that predated the war, assumed that he was the next target. With no one able to escape the committee's reach, politics in the Union, already encumbered by the war and the infighting that it caused, suffered considerably. Lincoln and McClellan's relations further deteriorated as a result. The general consistently ignored the president's advice, orders, and dispatches, even going so far as to call Lincoln a "well meaning baboon." The ill will that the committee created had dire consequences for the Union and its army.

Militarily the Battle of Ball's Bluff was another humiliating defeat precipitated by tactical errors and poor planning. Politically it widened the schism between loyal Democrats and radical Republicans, with the creation of the Joint Committee on the Conduct of the War the most partisan abuse of power. The defeat also prompted Lincoln to take an even more active role in the day-to-day operations of McClellan's Army of the Potomac.

See also *Joint Committee on the Conduct of the War*

—PETER SMITH

BIBLIOGRAPHY

Donald, David Herbert. *Lincoln.* New York: Simon and Schuster, 1996.

Foote, Shelby. *The Civil War: A Narrative—Fort Sumter to Perryville.* New York: Random House, 1958.

Foner, Eric. *Politics and Ideology in the Age of the Civil War.* Oxford: Oxford University Press, 1980.

Johnson, Michael, ed. *Abraham Lincoln, Slavery, and the Civil War.* New York: Bedford/St. Martin Press, 2001.

McPherson, James. *Battle Cry of Freedom: The Civil War Era.* Oxford: Oxford University Press, 1988.

Paludan, Phillip Shaw. *A People's Contest: The Union and Civil War 1861–1865.* Lawrence: University of Kansas Press, 1989.

White, G. Edward. *Oliver Wendell Holmes Jr.* Oxford: Oxford University Press, 2006.

Williams, T. Harry. "The Committee on the Conduct of the War: An Experiment in Civilian Control." *Journal of the American Military Institute* 3 (Autumn 1939): 138–156.

Baltimore Convention, 1860

See *Democratic Conventions, 1860*

Baltimore Mob

At the beginning of the Civil War, Baltimore, Maryland, was a city seething with Southern sentiment and one that had such a history of violent politics that it had the nickname "Mobtown." Baltimore was the biggest city on the Chesapeake, and although a Southern city, it had a sufficiently diverse population to have something of a split personality in 1861. The downtown waterfront area was renowned for its street-gang political warfare and was home to "clubs" (or street gangs) such as the Plug Uglies, the Blood Tubs, the Butt Enders, the Red Necks, and many others. Street violence as a form of political expression was a Baltimore tradition. Geographically it lay right along the fault line of a nation divided by sectionalism and slavery. Because Maryland, a slave state, surrounded Washington, D.C., on three sides, the many Marylanders who clamored for secession in spring 1861 constituted a significant threat to the capital and thus to national security.

Baltimore was the largest railway center anywhere near Washington, and it stood between the capital and the rest of the loyal Union, operating very much as a funnel for all rail traffic coming to the capital from the free states. The many railroads that converged just north of Baltimore became a single line that went through town to the waterfront, ending at President's Street Station. Those wishing to proceed on to Washington by train would have to disembark there and walk or otherwise travel the nearly two miles to the Camden Street Station, where they would board another train to complete the trip to the capital. The route between the two stations traversed the heart of the area where the street gangs roamed and was notorious for its late-night rowdiness and drunken revelry.

On the evening of February 22, 1861, the anniversary of the birthday of George Washington, Abraham Lincoln spoke at Independence Hall in Philadelphia. He then traveled on to Harrisburg. Had the schedule proceeded as planned, Lincoln was to travel by train the next day through Baltimore and on to Washington. However when he arrived in Harrisburg, he was informed that an attempt would be made on his life while his entourage passed through Baltimore. Because of the location of the two train stations in Baltimore, and the nearly two miles of cobblestone streets that would have to be traversed from one to the other, there was fear that he would simply be too vulnerable if he made the trip as announced. Detective Allan Pinkerton and Major General Winfield Scott had each, independently of the other, gleaned information about the assassination attempt that was supposed to be made the following day. Therefore late in the evening, and in spite of his reluctance to do so, Lincoln put on a disguise. He pulled a long blanket over his shoulders, removed the characteristic stovepipe hat, and joined only by Ward Hill Lamon boarded a train in Harrisburg that would several hours later deliver the two men to the President's Street Station. There they met Pinkerton, who joined them in the car they occupied at the rear of the train, which was then uncoupled and pulled by a team of mules along the streets of the Baltimore waterfront to Camden Street Station. There they would be coupled to another train that would take them on to Washington. All other trains were "side-tracked" until Lincoln's had passed, and all telegraph lines from Harrisburg had been cut on February 22 until word was received of the president's safe arrival. The party arrived in Washington at six o'clock in the morning.

The media excoriated Lincoln over the incident. A *New York Times* reporter, Joseph J. Howard Jr., wrote a story saying that Lincoln had "sneaked" through Baltimore wearing a "Scotch plaid cap and a very long military cloak." Though it was untrue, the story was picked up by journalists and political cartoonists who had a field day with it. Lincoln was greatly embarrassed and felt that it had undermined all the efforts he had been making to present a dignified front and provide trappings of legitimacy to every act he performed as president-elect. He felt that this single incident had done much to undermine those efforts, and it may have accounted for much of the carelessness about his own personal security that he later demonstrated as president.

The Baltimore mob genuinely threatened national security two months later. It happened soon after the surrender of Fort Sumter. Washington had only a few hundred military personnel in the entire city. There was real concern that one of the Maryland or Virginia militia units training within sight of the capital might attempt to seize the government and all of its officials, and that the city's weak defenses could be overwhelmed. Lincoln and other government officials desperately hoped that troops would begin arriving soon. Because Harpers Ferry, Virginia, had been abandoned to the Confederates, the only way for trains coming from the North to reach Washington was to pass through Baltimore. On April 18 the first Northern militia began to pass through Mobtown. Four companies of unarmed troops made the passage through the waterfront area on foot. As they passed, a crowd gathered and shouted epithets at the soldiers. Even though the soldiers were flanked by the Baltimore police, the mob began throwing bricks and chunks of pavement. Several soldiers were injured, but the troops made it to Camden Street Station and quickly boarded the train for Washington.

The much more serious situation occurred the next day, when the Sixth Massachusetts regiment attempted to pass through the city. Knowing ahead of time the kind of reception that awaited them in Baltimore, the colonel of the regiment ordered that ammunition be distributed and weapons loaded. When they arrived at President's Street Station about 10:30 that morning, the troops were loaded onto horse-drawn train cars that pulled them along Pratt Street toward Camden Street Station. As the cars passed, the mob continued to grow in size and surliness and began throwing bottles and bricks and jeering at the soldiers, daring them to fire. The first seven companies of the regiment made it through, but when a sand cart was dumped out on the track, followed by anchors, chains, and large rocks, it made further passage impossible. The frustrated driver of the car unhitched his team of horses, took them around and hitched then to the opposite end of the car, and started back toward President's Street Station. A major logjam ensued as the remainder of the regiment tried to get back to the station. A captain took charge of the four companies that were now hopelessly separated from the rest of the regiment. He ordered the troops into marching formation, and they started through the crowd again. When they picked up the pace to the double-quick, the crowd seemed to become even more infuriated. As they crossed the Jones Falls Bridge the first shots rang out, and several soldiers fell. The troops now began firing back into the crowd, attempting to move, reload, fire, and avoid the missiles raining down on them. The mob grew bolder and in several instances rioters rushed the soldiers and wrestled their muskets away from them. At least one soldier was killed with his own musket, which was used to bayonet him to death. Rioters cheered for Jefferson Davis and secession. They left no question as to which side they were on in the secession crisis.

Only when a force of Baltimore police, guns drawn, inserted themselves between the rioters and the troops as the procession neared Camden Station was order restored. By one o'clock in the afternoon the troops were boarded and the train was on its way. Four soldiers had been killed and thirty-six wounded in the rioting, and twelve Baltimoreans were dead and an unknown number wounded. That afternoon a giant rally was held in Monument Square, at which both the mayor of the city and the governor of Maryland spoke. Later that day both of them forwarded dispatches to Lincoln urging him not to send any more troops through Baltimore. When no reply came from the president that day, Maryland militiamen and Baltimore policemen burned bridges along the rail lines that led north from the city. Union troops could no longer enter Baltimore from the North. Washington D.C., facing its greatest crisis ever, was cut off.

These were the events that caused Abraham Lincoln, on April 27, 1861, to suspend for the first time the writ of *habeas corpus* "at any point on or in the vicinity of the military line...between the City of Philadelphia and the City of Washington." In the weeks and days that followed some of the most sensational arrests in American history took place, including those of the Baltimore marshal of police, George P. Kane; Baltimore mayor William Brown; and several months later nine members of the Maryland legislature and the chief clerk of the Maryland Senate.

—David E. Long

BIBLIOGRAPHY

McPherson, James M. *Battle Cry of Freedom: The Civil War Era.* New York: Oxford University Press, 1988.

Mills, Eric. *Chesapeake Bay in the Civil War.* Centreville, Md.: Tidewater Publishers, 1996.

Banking and Monetary Policy

The expansion of the federal government's powers was one of the most dramatic changes that the Civil War brought to America. Perhaps nowhere was this change more evident than in banking and monetary policy, where the Union government took unprecedented steps that expanded its involvement in the nation's economy.

Before the Civil War, the United States had no national currency except for gold and silver coins. Money made of such precious metals was called "specie," and many believed that it was the only real money. The disastrous inflation experienced with the Continental dollar during the American Revolution had soured many Americans on paper currency. Both the First Bank of the United States (1791–1811) and the Second Bank of the United States (1816–1836) issued paper money that found widespread acceptance and facilitated transacting business. Despite the benefits, both banks had been killed by political opposition, most notably in President Andrew Jackson's famous "Bank War" against the Second Bank of the United States in the 1830s. Lincoln believed that Jackson's attack on the Second Bank had been a grievous error. In 1840, while campaigning for the Whig presidential candidate, William Henry Harrison, Lincoln made the revival of a national bank a central theme of his speeches.

The Constitution provides that only the federal government can coin money. But paper currency could be issued by private banks (including those chartered by states specifically for the purpose of creating currency) and other businesses. This paper money had no standard valuation, and in a sense was worth whatever the public thought it was worth. All paper money was supposed to be a promise that the bills could be redeemed for specie. On of the eve of the Civil War, thousands of different kinds of paper money were in circulation, some relatively sound and some totally worthless. Many people still distrusted all paper currency.

In December 1861 the demand for gold forced banks and private businesses to suspend the conversion of banknotes into gold. On January 1, 1862, the U.S. Treasury also stopped converting its Treasury notes into gold. Lincoln bemoaned the crisis, saying, "The bottom is out of the tub. What am I to do?" It was becoming evident that the nation needed a reliable circulating medium besides specie. In February 1862 Congress passed the Legal Tender Act, which authorized a national paper currency; the notes came to be called "greenbacks" because of their color. The phrase "legal tender" meant that businesses were required to accept this money in any transaction. Many Congress members from both parties opposed the issuance of the greenbacks, and many who supported it saw it as an unavoidable emergency measure brought on by the war. Although the Union printed $450 million in greenbacks over the course of the war, it paid most of its war expenses by borrowing and with increased taxes. That limited the inflation experienced by Northern consumers. In the North, the cost of living roughly doubled during the Civil War, but wages and business profits also rose, albeit to a lesser extent. The Union never experienced the kind of runaway inflation that the Confederacy did.

Both Lincoln and Salmon P. Chase, his first secretary of the Treasury, were initially "sound money" men who distrusted paper currency, but they eventually came to see its necessity. In his annual message to Congress in 1862, Lincoln voiced approval of Chase's arguments on the legal tender and banking issues. Lincoln believed that the greenbacks had met the need for a uniform currency—which in fact they had. Although their purchasing power rose and fell with the fortunes of the Union's war effort, greenbacks were immediately accepted as the standard circulating medium.

The National Banking Acts passed in 1863, 1864, and 1865 were among the clearest examples of expanding federal power during the Civil War. Under the 1863 law, federally chartered banks could be established if they met certain standards. These banks could issue banknotes if they held a required percentage of their assets in U.S. government bonds, as guarantees that their banknotes could be redeemed.

Because of this provision, not only did these banks supply a sound currency, but they also made an expanded market for the government's bonds. In his annual message to Congress in December 1863, Lincoln strongly supported Chase's banking proposals. In fact, it appears that the first National Banking Act represented one of the few times that Lincoln did much political arm-twisting on legislation. Lincoln apparently intervened with key Republican Congress members who opposed the bill, and they eventually fell into line. The second banking act, passed in June 1864, was an amendment to deal with minor problems in the first bill and made no major changes. The 1865 act imposed a 10 percent tax on transactions using state banknotes. Since anyone using greenbacks or the notes of the federally chartered banks could avoid paying the tax, the state banknotes were quickly driven out of circulation.

Historian Gabor S. Boritt has suggested that Lincoln presided over a revolution that changed the government's role in the American economy. Boritt believed that even though Lincoln did not "organize or direct" that revolution, he "repeatedly applied what appears to have been a crucial touch." Many of the innovations were brought on by the demands of the war, but both Lincoln and the Republicans in Congress knew that some of these fundamental changes would endure after the crisis had passed.

See also *Cooke, Jay; Income Taxes: Legal Tender Act of 1862*

—MARK S. JOY

BIBLIOGRAPHY

Boritt, G. S. *Lincoln and the Economics of the American Dream.* Memphis: Memphis State University Press, 1978.

Curry, Leonard P. *Blueprint for Modern America: Nonmilitary Legislation of the First Civil War Congress.* Nashville: Vanderbilt University Press, 1968.

Gordon, John Steele. *Hamilton's Blessing: The Extraordinary Life and Times of Our National Debt.* New York: Penguin, 1997.

Hammond, Bray. *Sovereignty and an Empty Purse: Banks and Politics in the Civil War.* Princeton: Princeton University Press, 1970.

Banks, Nathaniel

Nathaniel Prentice Banks (1816–1894), politician, member of the Republican Party, Speaker of the U.S. House of Representatives, and American Civil War general, was born in Waltham, Massachusetts. In his early life he worked in his father's cotton mill, which led to his nickname, the "Bobbin Boy of Massachusetts." In 1839 he was admitted to the bar with little formal education. Banks was elected to the Massachusetts legislature ten years later, and in 1852 he became speaker of the Massachusetts House of Representatives. He was elected president of the state's constitutional convention in 1853 and in that same year elected to the U.S. House of Representatives.

Throughout his political career Banks switched party affiliations to suit the political climate at the time. At his first election to the U.S. Congress, he allied himself with Democrats and Free-Soilers. In the 1854 national election, he ran as a Know-Nothing. In 1856 Banks was elected Speaker of the U.S. House of Representatives by the Republican majority. In that influential position he appointed Republicans to a number of important posts. He also presented John C. Frémont as a presidential candidate at the 1856 Republican National Convention. Banks tapped into a vein of Know-Nothing and Republican sentiment in his home state for political support and served as governor of Massachusetts from 1858 to 1860. Banks sought, but was never a serious contender for, the Republican presidential nomination in 1860.

As did many politicians, Banks offered his services to the United States upon the outbreak of the Civil War. President Abraham Lincoln appointed him major general of volunteers based on his political base and his ability to recruit in the New England states. Banks commanded a two-division demi-corps in the

Shenandoah Valley in spring 1862. His forces proved unequal to the task of repulsing Confederate Major General Thomas (Stonewall) Jackson's Valley campaign, though at Cedar Mountain, Virginia, on August 9, 1862, Banks's corps nearly defeated Jackson. In November 1862, Banks recruited men for the Army of the Gulf, which was to help secure the Mississippi River for the Union. He laid siege to Port Hudson, Louisiana, and the Confederate garrison surrendered after the capture of Vicksburg, Mississippi, on July 9, 1863. Banks's last major operation was the Red River campaign of 1864, which was a strategic failure. None of its objectives were reached because of the low waters of the Red River, and the Union river fleet was nearly lost. President Lincoln relieved Banks of command and placed him on administrative leave in Washington, D.C., for the rest of the war.

Upon leaving the army, Banks resumed his political career in Congress. He broke with the Republican presidential administrations and returned to serve in the Massachusetts Senate. He won election to the U.S. Congress as an independent and later as a Republican again from 1875 to 1877. After almost ten years as a U.S. marshal for his state, Banks won another term in Congress from 1889 to 1891, but he was unable to obtain renomination for his congressional seat. Banks passed away in Waltham in 1894.

—WILLIAM H. BROWN

BIBLIOGRAPHY

Eicher, John H., and David J Eicher. *Civil War High Commands.* Stanford: Stanford University Press, 2001.

Harrington, Fred H. *Fighting Politician: Major General N.P. Banks.* Westport, Conn.: Greenwood Press, 1970.

Hollandsworth, James G. *Pretense of Glory: The Life of General Nathaniel P. Banks.* Baton Rouge: Louisiana State University Press, 1998.

Warner, Ezra. *Generals in Blue: Lives of the Union Commanders.* Baton Rouge: Louisiana State University Press, 1964.

Bates, Edward

Edward Bates (1793–1869) served as attorney general in the Lincoln administration from March 1861 to September 1864. After serving in the War of 1812 the Virginia-born Bates had moved to Missouri in 1814. There he dedicated his career to practicing law and to public service, as a Whig politician and later a somewhat reluctant Republican. Bates was a member of the Missouri Constitutional Convention in 1820, when the Missouri Compromise facilitated the territory's admission to the Union as a slave state. Bates served as attorney general for the newly admitted state from 1821 to 1822. He represented Missouri in the U.S. House of Representatives from 1827 to 1829, between stints as a state representative (1822) and state senator (1830–1834). He also chaired the 1847 Rivers and Harbors Convention that Abraham Lincoln attended.

Bates was a candidate for the presidential nomination at the 1860 Republican National Convention held in Chicago in May. Though he initially had the support of the influential Horace Greeley, of the *New York Tribune,* Bates obtained a mere 48 votes on the first ballot, running behind Sen. William H. Seward of New York, with 173.5 votes; Abraham Lincoln with 102; Sen. Simon Cameron of Pennsylvania with 50.5; and Ohio's Salmon P. Chase with 49. Bates again trailed badly on the second ballot, and Lincoln prevailed on the third, having emerged as the anti-Seward candidate. All of Lincoln's closest rivals for the nomination would become members of his sometimes fractious cabinet. In addition to Bates as attorney general, Seward became secretary of state, Cameron became secretary of war, and Chase became secretary of the Treasury.

Though he was loyal to Lincoln, Bates was initially skeptical of his ability to lead a nation at war, an opinion that changed over time. A political conservative, Bates vehemently opposed the Radical Republican agenda. As attorney general, however, he implemented policies that comported with his view of the law even if they flew in the face of his personal opinions. He supported the Emancipation Proclamation, although his attitudes toward African Americans were never more progressive than an advocacy of colonization back to Africa. Bates also suggested to Lincoln that African American soldiers merited pay equal to that of their white comrades, despite his personal dislike of their serving in the military, which he thought implied an unwarranted equality.

As attorney general Bates defended Lincoln's suspension of the writ of *habeas corpus* in the face of Chief Justice Roger Taney's claim in *Ex parte Merryman* that only Congress could suspend the writ. Bates argued that the Constitution created three independent branches of government and that the judiciary could not interfere with the executive's chosen method of putting down insurrections.

On the death of Chief Justice Taney in October 1864 Bates indicated to Lincoln his desire to succeed to the position, which he said he would hold for only a few years before retiring, leaving Lincoln to make another appointment during his second term. Bates resigned from the cabinet when it became apparent that Lincoln would instead appoint Salmon P. Chase. Bates returned to Missouri where he died in 1869.

See also *Cabinet, Lincoln's; Rivers and Harbors Convention*

—David E. Arthur

BIBLIOGRAPHY

Bates, Edward. *The Diary of Edward Bates, 1859–1866.* Edited by Howard Kennedy Beale. Washington: Government Printing Office, 1933. Reprint, New York: Da Capo, 1971.

Cain, Marvin R. *Lincoln's Attorney General: Edward Bates of Missouri.* Columbia: University of Missouri Press, 1965.

Bedell, Grace

Grace Bedell (1848–1936), Abraham Lincoln's eleven-year-old "image consultant," encouraged him to grow a beard in 1860.

Born on November 4, 1848, Grace Bedell was unusually interested in the election of 1860. As occurred in many American families, the election divided the Bedell household. Two of Grace Bedell's brothers considered themselves Democrats, and the rest of the family, including Grace, sided with the Republicans. That October, Grace's father brought home a campaign broadside that featured a portrait of the Republican hopeful. Discouraged by his sunken features, Grace wrote to Lincoln on October 15, 1860, and offered him a bit of advice.

"Let your whiskers grow," she urged. A beard would make Lincoln look more attractive because his face was so thin. "All the ladies like whiskers," she assured him, "and they would tease their husband's to vote for you and then you would be President."

Lincoln sent his precocious correspondent a playful reply on October 19. "As to the whiskers, having never worn any, do you not think people would call it a piece of silly affectation if I were to begin it now?" Lincoln asked. Nonetheless, by the time he left Springfield, Lincoln did indeed have a full beard, making him the first president to make such a fashion statement.

On February 16, 1860, the president-elect's train stopped briefly in Westfield, New York. Instead of giving a political speech at the depot, Lincoln told the well-wishers about his young correspondent. "Some three months ago, I received a letter from a young lady here," he explained. "It was a very pretty letter, and she advised me to let my whiskers grow, as it would improve my personal appearance; acting partly upon her suggestion, I have done so; and now, if she is here, I would like to see her." When Grace came forward, Lincoln kissed her, much to the delight of the crowd.

Grace wrote at least two more letters to the president. In 2007, a researcher in the National Archives uncovered a letter from Grace dated January 10, 1864. Grace told the president that her father had fallen on hard times and had "lost nearly all his property." She complained that she had written previously, but had received no reply. "I feel that I ought and could do something for myself," she told Lincoln. Though she was only fourteen, she wanted Lincoln to give her a job in the Treasury Department. However, there is no evidence that Lincoln ever saw the letter.

After the Civil War, Grace married a former Union soldier named George Billings. The couple eventually settled in Delphos, Kansas, where Billings made a living as a farmer and then as a banker. The couple had a boy named Harlow Drake Billings. Grace died on November 2, 1936, two days shy of her eighty-eighth birthday.

Sometime in the 1930s, Michigan congressman and Lincoln collector George A. Dondero (1883–1968) acquired Grace's celebrated letter to Lincoln. He willed the letter to the Burton Historical Collection of the Detroit Public Library, where it remains today. Grace gave Lincoln's reply to her son. When he died in the 1960s, the letter was sold at auction for $20,000. In 1976, the letter was again offered at auction, this time for $65,000. Today Lincoln's letter belongs to a private collector who wishes to remain anonymous.

—SAMUEL P. WHEELER

BIBLIOGRAPHY

Basler, Roy P., ed. *The Collected Works of Abraham Lincoln.* New Brunswick, N.J.: Rutgers University Press, 1953.

Trump, Frederick L. *Lincoln's Little Girl.* Salina, Kansas: Heritage Books, 1977.

Woodlin, Debbie. "More Letters Found from Lincoln's 'Little Correspondent.'" *Joplin* [Missouri] *Globe,* October 30, 2007.

Bell, John

John Bell (1797–1869) was a senator and representative from Tennessee and secretary of war (1841). Bell is most noted for his unsuccessful bid for the presidency under the banner of the Constitutional Union Party in 1860.

John Bell was born near Nashville, Tennessee, on February 15, 1797, to Samuel (a farmer) and Margaret Bell. After graduating from Cumberland College in 1814, Bell studied law and was admitted to the bar in 1816. The following year, he was elected to the Tennessee state senate to represent the district around his new home of Franklin. After serving only one term in the state senate, Bell relocated to the state capital of Nashville. There he became well connected in local Democratic circles and successfully ran for a seat in the U.S. House of Representatives in 1826, defeating Andrew Jackson's close friend Felix Grundy. Bell served continuously in the House until 1841, including a term as Speaker of the House in 1834–1835.

Finding himself at odds with President Andrew Jackson's attacks on the Bank of the United States, Bell abandoned the Democratic Party and joined the ranks of the newly organized Whig opposition, thus gaining the nickname "the Great Apostate." After the election of Whig William Henry Harrison, the party rewarded Bell by naming him secretary of war. The untimely death of President Harrison, however, and the new president's (John Tyler) repeated vetoes of Whig-sponsored legislation, left Bell little choice but to join his fellow Whigs in resigning his post.

Bell then returned to Tennessee to look after his business interests. In 1847 Nashville Whigs once again sent Bell to the state legislature, this time to the statehouse. There he was selected by the Whig majority to serve Tennessee in the U.S. Senate, a position that he held until 1859. While serving in the Senate, Bell was one of but two Southern senators (Sam Houston of Texas was the other) to vote against the Kansas-Nebraska Act, with its explicit repeal of the Missouri Compromise line, in 1854.

The passage of the Kansas-Nebraska Act dealt a deadly blow to the already debilitated Whig Party. Many partisans joined newly emerging political movements, such as the nativist Know-Nothing Party or the antislavery Republican Party, whereas others, such as John Bell and Abraham Lincoln (until 1856), refused to follow suit and desperately tried to hold their party together.

With sectional tensions mounting and the presidential election of 1860 approaching, Bell, along with other Upper South Whigs, created a moderate coalition with former Know-Nothings and amenable Democrats and Republicans. Taking the name the "Constitutional Union Party," the group pledged to maintain the Union and Constitution as they were and nominated Bell as its candidate for the presidency, with Edward Everett of Massachusetts as his running mate. The party's moderate platform proved appealing to many Upper South voters, and thanks to the Democratic Party's national division, it managed to capture the electoral votes of Kentucky, Virginia, and Tennessee, though it was unsuccessful in its bid for the White House, losing to Abraham Lincoln and the Republicans.

Angered by the secession of the Deep South in response to Lincoln's election, Bell worked tirelessly to keep his home state of Tennessee from following suit. "Secession," Bell wrote in a widely published letter penned in early December 1860, "is but another name for an organized resistance by a State to the laws and constituted authority of the Union, or which is the same thing, for revolution." In spite of such pleas, however, Bell accepted his home state's decision to join the Confederacy after the attack on Fort Sumter and Lincoln's call for volunteers from the loyal states to put down the rebellion. Disgusted with politics, Bell retired to private life and focused on running his many businesses, including the Cumberland Furnace Ironworks. Situated at the heart of a major theater of combat, many of Bell's business ventures were destroyed during the war. John Bell died at his Tennessee home in 1869.

See also *Campaign of 1860, Presidential; Constitutional Union Party*

—MARTIN J. HERSHOCK

BIBLIOGRAPHY

Crofts, Daniel W. *Reluctant Confederates: Upper South Unionists in the Secession Crisis.* Chapel Hill: University of North Carolina Press, 1989.

Holt, Michael. *The Political Crisis of the 1850s.* New York: Norton, 1983.

Knupfer, Peter. "Aging Statesmen and the Statesmanship of an Earlier Age: The Generational Roots of the Constitutional Union Party." In *Union and Emancipation: Essays on Politics and Race in the Civil War Era,* edited by David W. Blight and Brooks D. Simpson. Kent, Ohio: Kent State University Press, 1997.

Mering, John V. "The Slave-State Constitutional Unionists and the Politics of Consensus." *Journal of Southern History* 43, no. 3 (1977): 395–410.

Parks, Joseph Howard. *John Bell of Tennessee.* Baton Rouge: Louisiana State University Press, 1950.

Benton, Thomas Hart

A five-term U.S. senator from Missouri, serving from 1821 to 1851, Thomas Hart Benton was known as one of the West's foremost spokesmen, a staunch Democrat, and a reliable voice for hard money and Union. Though the two were from neighboring states, little directly connected Benton with Abraham Lincoln, largely because Benton's career was ending before Lincoln's had really begun. Yet Benton was an inveterate foe of Henry Clay—the Kentucky Whig who was Lincoln's "beau ideal" of a statesman—and he was also the father-in-law of John

Frémont, the first Republican presidential candidate and a Union general. Political rivalry and familial ties would thus have their impact on Lincoln.

As a young Whig in the late 1830s and early 1840s, Lincoln campaigned against Benton's positions on the independent Treasury and the distribution of surplus federal revenue from public land sales. Numbered among Martin Van Buren's closest supporters, Benton had tirelessly advocated the removal of federal funds from the Second National Bank of the United States. Nor did he esteem the "pet banks" that emerged as holders of federal deposits after Andrew Jackson's Bank War with Henry Clay. Supporting currency of intrinsic value and fearful of the deleterious effects of speculation above all else, Benton preferred to keep the government's funds out of the nation's banking system. Lincoln opposed that policy. He favored depositing federal monies in the nation's banks to promote commerce and increase the money supply.

As a supporter of Clay's American System, moreover, Lincoln favored binding the nation more closely together via federally financed internal improvements. Clay proposed funding projects such as roads and canals with revenues collected from public land sales; a percentage of the surpluses so generated would be distributed back to the states. Benton opposed this program because it was predicated on relatively high land prices. Wishing to promote his section's growth as rapidly as possible, Benton favored "graduation," or cutting the price of public lands that did not sell rapidly, to encourage settlement. Through these proposals he sought to increase the West's population and representation.

Benton and Lincoln were thus on opposite sides of the pivotal economic issues of the Age of Jackson. Inherent in those differences was a fundamental disagreement between Democrats and Whigs on the question of expansion. Democrats tended to urge western development and territorial expansion, while Whigs strove for national consolidation and commercial expansion. Those issues would not come to the forefront of American politics until John Tyler, a Virginia Democrat turned Whig, became president and found himself on the wrong side of his party on economic matters. In trying to improve his election prospects, Tyler promoted the Democratic view of expansion by acquiring Texas. But that did not gain him Benton's support; the senator had long sponsored the Santa Fe trade with Mexico.

During the Mexican-American War, which followed the annexation of Texas, when Benton was in the Senate and Lincoln in the House of Representatives, the two men finally found common ground. Though Benton loyally supported President James Polk and Lincoln was one of the president's sharpest critics on the question of the war's origins, both men had opposed how the country had been brought to that point. Both also correctly feared the consequences of annexation in terms of the expansion of slavery and sectional discord.

As sectionalism heightened in the wake of the Mexican-American War, Benton's view that slavery should be limited and the Union should be privileged rendered his position in Missouri fundamentally insecure. Not unlike

Tyler, Benton had become a man without a party. Benton's position on California—he favored the rapid and unencumbered admission of California as a free state, in accord with President Zachary Taylor—was the last straw. The Missouri legislature's pique with Benton by that time was such that they refused to reelect him to the Senate. Benton's last major political stands came against the Kansas-Nebraska Act and the ruling in the *Dred Scott* case. Opposition to the former rejuvenated Lincoln's political career, and opposition to the latter helped make him president. Though Lincoln criticized the Supreme Court's decision because of its negation of African American citizenship, whereas Benton focused on its limitation of congressional power over the territories, the two were closer politically than ever. The irony in both instances was that Benton was now defending Clay's most significant legislation, the Missouri Compromise of 1819–1821.

Benton's career declined dramatically before his death, but his family's prominence and his influence in American politics remained. Benton's savvy daughter, Jessie Benton Frémont, posed a different challenge to Lincoln: that of working with someone like her father from within the same party. Absorbing her father's insights and keen political skills, Jessie Benton Frémont put them to work on behalf of her husband. When John Frémont went beyond the first Confiscation Act and ordered the slaves of Confederate sympathizers freed in his Department of the West, on August 30, 1861, Lincoln countermanded the order, dreading its effects on Border States such as Kentucky. He would not be dissuaded from this course, even after meeting with Jessie Frémont, whom he ungallantly dismissed as a "female politician." The simmering dispute thus begun would cause Lincoln much grief, as it quickly ruptured the Frémonts from the Blair family, to whom the Frémonts were related through Benton's wife. Though Frank Blair Jr. and Montgomery Blair, Lincoln's first postmaster general, had been protégés of Thomas Hart Benton in Missouri, the rift that opened between the Frémonts and the Blairs in the wake of this quarrel led to political ruin for the Frémonts and Blair's dismissal from the cabinet in 1864. Benton's legacy fortunately proved more durable in federal land policy, where the Homestead Act that Lincoln signed on May 20, 1862, resembled the senator's approach, most notably in its provisions for those of lesser means.

—ROBERT W. BURG

BIBLIOGRAPHY

Chaffin, Tom. *Pathfinder: John Charles Frémont and the Course of American Empire.* New York: Hill and Wang, 2002.

Chambers, William Nisbet. *Old Bullion Benton: Senator from the New West.* Boston: Little, Brown, 1956.

Smith, Elbert B. *Magnificent Missourian: The Life of Thomas Hart Benton.* New York: Lippincott, 1958.

Black Hawk War

The Black Hawk War was fought in Illinois and Wisconsin in 1832, over issues of land. The land in question was near the confluence of the Mississippi and Rock Rivers, where the Sauk had their great tribal community of Saukenuk. The place was home to about 6,000 people each summer, and the Sauk believed it a place of extraordinary spiritual power.

Although they ceded fifteen million acres of their territory in a questionable treaty with William Henry Harrison in 1804, the Sauk assumed that they retained possession of Saukenuk itself and were stunned when the government put it up for sale in the autumn of 1829. Once settlers arrived, there was trouble. The Jackson administration sent in a large military force in June 1831 to evict the Sauk from Saukenuk, and it banished them beyond the Mississippi.

After a hard, hungry winter in Iowa, a large faction of the tribe was determined to return to Saukenuk. They turned to Black Hawk, a staunch traditionalist with a reputation for personal courage, to lead them. The band consisted of about 1,600 people, including as many as 500 mounted warriors. Their crossing into Illinois in early April 1832 panicked the settlers.

General Henry Atkinson steamed upriver from St. Louis with 220 infantry soldiers. Governor John Reynolds of Illinois mobilized 1,700 mounted militia volunteers. The two forces converged at Rock Island and prevented the Sauk from reoccupying their village.

Among the volunteers was twenty-three-year-old Abraham Lincoln, from New Salem. Young Lincoln was elected captain of his militia company, and that, he said years later, was "a success which gave me more pleasure than any I have had since."

The troops pursued the Sauk up the Rock River valley into Wisconsin. Their first battle occurred near Dixon's Ferry. Known as "Stillman's Run," after the incompetent militia commander who initiated the action, it was a humiliating rout for the Americans. Following that the militia lost heart and decided to give up the fight. They disbanded on May 28. Reynolds pleaded with those mustering out to stay temporarily to protect the frontier until new troops arrived. Lincoln was among the few who remained, and he reenlisted as a private on June 16. Since he was "out of work" at the time he "could do nothing better than enlist again," he said.

Lincoln never encountered hostile Indians. But he saved an old Potawatomi man when members of his own company intended to kill and scalp him, and he participated in the burial of the grotesquely mutilated bodies of Illinois volunteers killed by the Sauk at Kellogg's Grove.

The new militia and regulars moved into Wisconsin to hunt down Black Hawk's band among the swamps around Lake Koshkonong. Running low on provisions, Atkinson discharged many of the amateur soldiers. Lincoln mustered out on July 10 and set off with George Harrison. Because their horses were stolen the night before their departure the two walked all the way to Peoria. There they bought a canoe, paddled down the Illinois River to Havana, and then trudged the rest of the way to New Salem. Concerning his somewhat uneventful experience at soldiering Lincoln later remarked self-mockingly, "I had a good many struggles with the mosquitoes; and although I never fainted from loss of blood, I can truly say I was often very hungry." Such as it was, this was the sum total of Lincoln's military experience when he entered the White House.

Meanwhile, Black Hawk's band broke out of the swamps and fled westward, hoping to cross the Mississippi to safety. A hard-riding force led by Henry Dodge and James Henry caught up with them near the Wisconsin River, where the Battle of Wisconsin Heights was fought on July 21. The Sauk retreated, struggling on through the forested hills and reaching the Mississippi on August 1. The next morning the soldiers descended upon them near the Bad Axe River. A terrible massacre occurred. When the slaughter ended, only thirty-nine Indians—all women and children—were taken captive. The night before this battle, Black Hawk and his closest supporters abandoned the people to their own fate to seek refuge among the Ojibwa to the north. But after nearly a month in hiding, the old leader gave up and surrendered to the Indian agent at Prairie du Chien.

Black Hawk was imprisoned for a time. Artists rushed to paint his image, and when his autobiography was published in 1833 he became the most famous Indian in America. But for the Sauk people the war brought on their tragic demise. Banished from their homeland, they were forcibly resettled in Iowa, then Kansas, and finally in Oklahoma, where their numbers dwindled to near-extinction and the few who survived sank into abject destitution.

—KERRY A. TRASK

BIBLIOGRAPHY

Herndon, William H., and Jesse W. Weik. *Abraham Lincoln: The True Story of a Great Life.* Vol. 1. 1889. Reprint, New York: D. Appleton, 1923.

Jackson, Donald, ed. *Black Hawk: An Autobiography.* 1833. Reprint, Urbana: University of Illinois Press, 1955.

Jung, Patrick J. *The Black Hawk War of 1832.* Norman: University of Oklahoma Press, 2007.

Trask, Kerry A. *Black Hawk: The Battle for the Heart of America.* New York: Henry Holt, 2006.

Black Suffrage

Black suffrage was one of the most controversial issues of midcentury America and affected Abraham Lincoln's career in a variety of ways.

At the time of the American Revolution free blacks could vote, on the same basis as whites, in Massachusetts, New Hampshire, New York, New Jersey, Pennsylvania, and North Carolina. In addition, there is evidence that some free blacks may have voted in Maryland in this period. Vermont, the fourteenth state, and Tennessee, the sixteenth, also allowed free blacks to vote. By the end of the War of 1812, New Jersey had taken the vote away from both blacks and women. When Maine entered the Union it continued the policy of universal adult male suffrage that had existed when it was part of Massachusetts. In 1821 New York repealed its property requirement for white voters but maintained it for blacks, thus giving blacks "unequal suffrage." In the 1830s Jacksonian Democracy expanded suffrage for whites but also led to the end of suffrage for blacks in Pennsylvania, North Carolina, and Tennessee. In 1842 Rhode Island expanded its suffrage to include blacks. In the 1850s Michigan allowed blacks to vote in school bond elections but not in regular elections. In 1848 the voters in Wisconsin supported a black suffrage referendum, but the state's supreme court later ruled that the vote was insufficient because it did not carry a majority of those who voted in the overall election, but only a majority of those who cast a ballot on this particular issue.

When Lincoln first entered politics, in the 1830s, there were very few blacks in Illinois. They were hemmed in by black laws and had no access to the ballot. In one of his earliest political statements Lincoln asserted his support for "admitting all whites to the right of suffrage, who pay taxes or bear arms (by no means excluding females)." The legal status of blacks had not changed by the 1850s, when Lincoln helped organize the Republican Party, although there were considerably more blacks in the state. Despite a black code that discouraged black migration into the state, the total black population grew from about 2,400 in 1830, to about 5,400 in 1850, and more than 7,600 in 1860. These census figures probably undercount the black population because many blacks who were fugitive slaves, or in the state in violation of the black codes, probably avoided notice as much as possible.

In his 1858 senatorial race Lincoln faced the questions of racial equality and black suffrage. Despite the small black population and their complete lack of political rights in the state, Sen. Stephen A. Douglas constantly played the race card in his debates with Lincoln, trying to convince the electorate that Lincoln was in favor of racial equality. In their debates Lincoln consistently denied that he supported black suffrage, asserting, for example, in the Charleston debate that he was not "in favor of bringing about in any way the social and political equality of the white and the black races—that I am not nor ever have been in favor of making voters or jurors of Negroes." He did, however, argue that political disabilities for blacks did not justify slavery. Furthermore, he argued that blacks should be entitled to all that they earned through their own labors. This was a position that Lincoln maintained throughout the campaign against Douglas. Supporting black suffrage—in a state where blacks had almost no rights—would have been political suicide.

Whether Lincoln actually believed his own arguments on race and inequality is a subject of much historical controversy. Many Lincoln scholars argue that his own views on equality and fundamental justice pointed toward universal adult suffrage. Other scholars note that Lincoln was a product of a region—the upper South and the lower Midwest—and that he held fairly conventional views on race until late in his life.

Whatever Lincoln truly believed, other Republicans were more openly progressive on black suffrage. In the 1850s New York Republicans put a measure on the ballot to remove the property requirement for black voters. The measure failed to gain a majority of the electorate but did gain significant support. Similarly, an equal suffrage proposal passed one house of the Connecticut legislature. In Ohio blacks could not vote, but the state supreme court ruled that people who were more than half white could vote. The legislature reversed this result just before the Civil War. Although blacks could not vote in Ohio, they could hold office, and in the 1850s white voters in Lorraine County elected the black attorney John Mercer Langston to office as a county prosecutor. Blacks had held office in New Hampshire before and immediately after the Revolution, and they had done so in Vermont in the 1830s. In the 1850s blacks held minor offices in Massachusetts and Rhode Island.

When the Civil War began most blacks in the North were without the ballot. They also were denied the right to serve in the army. Political considerations—most significantly, holding onto the border slave states, Delaware, Kentucky, Maryland, and Missouri—led Lincoln to pursue a cautious policy on slavery, emancipation, and race. With the loyalty of the upper South secured by mid-1862 Lincoln addressed the issues of slavery and black troops. He had issued the Emancipation Proclamation and authorized the enlistment of black troops by January 1, 1863.

The likely end to slavery raised significant issues for Lincoln and others who took Constitutionalism and republican theory of government seriously. If four million slaves became free—which seemed likely—it would be impossible to imagine a just or representative government without their political participation. In the North the black population was tiny; less than 3 percent of all blacks in the nation lived there on the eve of the Civil War. Thus, it was possible to disfranchise this small number of people and still maintain a government that represented the vast majority of the population. But in the South blacks constituted

30 percent to 55 percent of the populations of the states. If free they would have to be able to participate in the government; otherwise, there could not be a representative democracy. Furthermore, Lincoln and other Republicans understood that once blacks served in the military it would be difficult to argue that they could not also vote. Without black suffrage the postwar nation would witness the absurd result that those who fought to preserve the Constitution could not vote, but former Confederates, who fought against the Constitution, would be able to vote.

In 1864 Lincoln suggested to the governor of Louisiana, which was by then under the control of the United States, that blacks be allowed to vote. He congratulated Governor Michael Hahn on being the "first free-state Governor of Louisiana." He noted that the state was about to call a constitutional convention, which would "define the elective franchise." Lincoln cautiously noted, "I barely suggest for your private consideration, whether some of the colored people may not be let in—as, for instance, the very intelligent, and especially those who have fought gallantly in our ranks." He believed that black voters "would probably help, in some trying time to come, to keep the jewel of liberty within the family of freedom." He told Hahn this in confidence and did not state it for public consumption. Nevertheless, this was a remarkable change for Lincoln and the nation. Only six years earlier he had declared his opposition to black suffrage. Now he was urging the governor of a state to move toward enfranchising blacks. This was the first time in the history of the United States that a president—or any important national politician—had taken such a position.

By the end of the war many—perhaps a majority—of the Republicans in Congress were advocating black suffrage. More than 200,000 blacks had served in the army and navy, with more than 30,000 dying for the Union cause. Hundreds of thousands more had served the army and navy in civilian capacities, as cooks, nurses, burial crews, and teamsters. Many Republicans believed that blacks had earned the right to vote. Moreover, Republicans understood that former slaves needed the ballot to protect themselves from their former masters in the postwar South. In addition, black ballots might provide the margin of victory for their party in future elections.

In his last recorded speech, on April 11, 1865, Lincoln publicly declared that the franchise should be given to "the very intelligent" blacks as well as "those who serve our cause as soldiers." He was reluctant to force this on the new governments forming in the South but believed they ought to follow this path. This position was consistent with Lincoln's general approach to race—he moved cautiously, suggesting solutions to the states, but in the end, when necessary, as with emancipation, he could act decisively. There is good reason to believe that had he lived, Lincoln would have moved with more vigor to guarantee black suffrage. Instead, Congress took up this role after the president's death, forcing the former Confederate states to enfranchise blacks before they could be readmitted to the Union, and ultimately sending the Fifteenth Amendment to the states, which prohibited discrimination in voting on the basis of race or previous condition of servitude.

—PAUL FINKELMAN

BIBLIOGRAPHY

Finkelman, Paul. "Prelude to the Fourteenth Amendment: Black Legal Rights in the Antebellum North." *Rutgers Law Journal* 17 (1986): 415–482.

Lewinson, Paul. *Race, Class, and Party: A History of Negro Suffrage and White Politics in the South.* New York: Russell and Russell, 1963.

Nieman, Donald G. *Promises to Keep: African Americans and the Constitutional Order: 1776 to the Present.* New York: Oxford University Press, 1992.

Wang, Xi. *The Trial of Democracy: Black Suffrage and Northern Republicans, 1860–1910.* Athens: University of Georgia Press, 1997.

Blair, Austin

Austin Blair (1818–1894), Republican governor of Michigan from 1861 to 1865, was an important western ally of President Abraham Lincoln. He supplied the Union with thousands of well-equipped troops, voiced early support for emancipation, and kept Michigan's Democrats in check during the most difficult days of the Civil War.

Blair was born on February 8, 1818, to a farming family in Caroline, New York. He graduated from Union College in 1839, apprenticed to become an attorney while working as a clerk at Sweet and Davis, a law firm in Oswego, New York, and joined the bar in 1841. That same year Blair wed Persis Lyman and shortly thereafter left New York, where attorneys were plentiful. He migrated to Jackson, Michigan, setting up practice in 1842 with Reule C. Baker. When the firm struggled, Blair moved from Jackson to Easton Rapids, Michigan. Failing to find much more success in that community, Blair, a Whig, turned to politics.

He lost his bid to enter the lower house of the Michigan legislature in 1843. The following year, however, Blair won a new job—clerk of Eaton County. He quit after his wife and baby daughter died and returned to Jackson to resume his career as an attorney. But Blair could not stay away from politics for long and won election to the Michigan House of Representatives in 1845. As a state legislator, he helped lead the fight to abolish Michigan's death penalty in 1846. The same year he remarried, taking Elizabeth Pratt as his second wife. Blair also fought unsuccessfully to enfranchise blacks by amending Michigan's constitution. Partly in response to this defeat, in 1848 Blair joined the Free Soil Party, which sought to prevent the spread of slavery.

His involvement with the Free Soilers was interrupted by personal tragedy, when he lost his second wife and young son in 1848. Wracked by grief, Blair temporarily abandoned politics for the law. He soon recovered from this second loss, marrying a third wife, Sarah Louis Ford, the following year. With her he had five children, one of whom died in childhood.

Blair was elected as Jackson County's prosecuting attorney in 1852 and two years later became a founding member of the Republican Party. He won election to the Michigan Senate as a Republican in 1854, and there he battled to curb the consumption of alcohol, to create a college for women, and to grant married women property rights. Despite his successes Blair's efforts to win the Republican nomination to the U.S. Senate failed because of intense competition in the party.

Blair instead became the Republican gubernatorial nominee in 1860 and soundly defeated his Democratic opponent, John Barry, in the general election. Fort Sumter fell the following April, and one of Blair's first challenges was to supply President Lincoln with the troops needed to defeat the Confederacy. The state legislature, however, had adjourned earlier that year without appropriating the funds needed for this task. To make up for the shortfall, Blair borrowed from private donors, who were reimbursed after Blair called the state legislature into special session on May 7, 1861.

Overall Blair provided the Union with more than 80,000 troops, and he made sure that those soldiers possessed the equipment needed to fight effectively. His early support for abolishing slavery helped boost support for President Lincoln's Emancipation Proclamation in 1863. Nonetheless, Blair's reelection as governor in 1862 was much closer than had been the contest for that office two years earlier.

Blair served in Congress from 1866 to 1873, but because of his frustration with scandals in the nation's capital, he joined the Liberal Republicans in 1872, becoming their unsuccessful candidate for Michigan governor that year. Blair rejoined the Republican Party in 1880 and also served as a regent of the University of Michigan between 1882 and 1890. He died four years after leaving office.

—JAMES SCHWARTZ

BIBLIOGRAPHY

Messner, Vivian T. "The Public Life of Austin Blair, War Governor of Michigan, 1863–1894." Master's thesis, Wayne State University, 1937.

Smith, Earl O. "The Public Life of Austin Blair, War Governor of Michigan, 1845–1863." Master's. thesis, Wayne State University, 1934.

Blair, Francis

As the patriarch of a prominent family from the Border South and an adviser to presidents from Andrew Jackson to Abraham Lincoln, Francis Preston Blair made an indelible mark on antebellum politics. Blair first achieved renown as a contributor to the *Argus of Western America,* the Frankfort, Kentucky, newspaper published by Amos Kendall. He later edited the *Argus* when Kendall moved to Washington to become an adviser to President Andrew Jackson. In 1830, Blair followed Kendall to Washington to become editor of the *Globe,* the administration's paper of record. Consolidating his influence both within and outside of Jackson's inner circle, Blair made valuable connections within the Democratic Party, particularly with Sen. Thomas Hart Benton. Differences with proslavery Democrats, however, led him to abandon the Democratic Party, first for the Free Soil Party in 1848, and then for the Republican Party in 1856. Blair backed Edward Bates at the Chicago convention in 1860 and worked against William Seward, but strongly supported Lincoln's nomination. Lincoln in turn made use of Blair, as Blair took up his familiar role of adviser once more. Blair helped Lincoln become Jackson's heir as a staunch defender of the Union.

Blair was singularly placed to counsel Lincoln and became one of his foremost advisers. As he had with Jackson, Blair proved congenial, loyal, and consistent. He called on the White House from the neighboring Blair House daily while in residence, and Lincoln visited Blair's Silver Spring home in Maryland on occasion, as well. Blair was given the opportunity to comment upon the president's first inaugural address; he also encouraged Lincoln's decision to take a firm stand against secession, particularly on resupplying Fort Sumter. Blair's course was so steadfastly against secession, in fact, that he opposed the creation of West Virginia in June 1863. His advice throughout was shaped by Jackson's response to the nullification crisis in 1832. But Blair's prominence was not simply a result of vicinity or past associations. It was also due to his knowledge, position, and family ties.

Ex-Whigs in the Republican Party had reached out to Blair in 1856 not only as an organizer but to help win over Democrats. Blair provided insight to Lincoln on how to appeal to and hold the support of Democrats during the war. The relationship between General George McClellan and Lincoln was at first central to such efforts. Blair traveled with Lincoln in July 1862 to meet with McClellan. He defended the general through October 1862 and, like McClellan, advocated "soft war" toward the South. That would open Blair up to censure from Radical Republicans and was the wrong approach to winning the war in the long run, but it was critical to maintaining the Border South's loyalty in the short run. Besides being the foyer through which to invade the Confederate homeland, the Border South contributed 200,000 white troops to the North rather than the South. By keeping the region in the Union, Lincoln denied the slave states half their potential industrial capacity as well. Raised in Kentucky, well connected in Missouri, and residing in Maryland, Blair brought inestimable knowledge of the Border South to Lincoln and reinforced his priorities there.

As a slaveholder, Blair was particularly attuned to the wishes of many in the Border South on the question of colonization. By 1860 the region contained only about 11 percent of the South's slaves. As slavery dwindled, its importance lessened. In Blair's view, if the federal government compensated slaveholders for their slaves and relocated emancipated blacks, slavery's demise could come that much more quickly. Blair's support of emancipation, even with colonization, hastened his departure from the Democratic Party, but it also alienated him from those in the Republican Party who favored emancipation alone. It suited Lincoln, however, given his Border South focus. Blair thus investigated the possibility of colonizing freed slaves to Chiriqui (in modern-day Panama) and wrote a report on the project for Lincoln in November 1861, but the endeavor proved stillborn. Though worried about Republican electoral prospects, Blair would support the Emancipation Proclamation and gradually liberate his remaining slaves.

Perhaps Blair's greatest contribution to the preservation of the Union was his family. His older son, Montgomery, was Lincoln's first postmaster general, and his younger son, Frank Jr., was a Missouri congressman and a major general simultaneously. Moreover, his sons-in-law Gustavus Fox and Samuel Lee served respectively as assistant secretary of the navy and as an acting rear admiral. More distant relations included Sen. Benjamin Gratz Brown of Missouri. Besides adding weight to Blair's counsel—influence his advice would not have had with Jackson—these connections served Lincoln well in keeping Missouri in the Union and in trimming the ambitions of Treasury secretary Salmon Chase. Feuds stemming from these ties, however, would lead to an irreparable break in 1861 with John Frémont and would also force Montgomery Blair's resignation from Lincoln's cabinet in 1864. Through the tumult, however, Blair remained steadfastly behind Lincoln.

It was as a diplomat that Blair had his least success, yet ironically achieved the most recognition, during Lincoln's presidency. Lincoln had Blair approach Robert E. Lee before the war in an effort to secure his services for the Union. Blair also crossed military lines at Horace Greeley's behest, and with the president's blessing, to meet twice with Jefferson Davis near the war's close in January 1865. Under cover of a request to search for papers lost in a Confederate raid on his property, Blair put out peace feelers to Davis, proposed a joint effort against France in Mexico, advised Davis to negotiate so as to get better reconstruction terms, and gathered intelligence on Richmond. Blair's efforts ultimately led to the Hampton Roads conference in February. In this as in other matters, Blair's conservatism ably counterbalanced radical sentiments, serving Lincoln as the president thought best.

See also *Blair, Montgomery*

—ROBERT W. BURG

BIBLIOGRAPHY

Freehling, William W. *The South vs. the South: How Anti-Confederate Southerners Shaped the Course of the Civil War.* New York: Oxford University Press, 2001.

Smith, Elbert B. *Francis Preston Blair.* New York: Free Press, 1980.

Smith, William Ernest. *The Francis Preston Blair Family in Politics.* 2 Vols. New York: Macmillan, 1933.

Blair, Montgomery

Montgomery Blair (1813–1883) was the oldest son of Francis P. Blair Sr., a veteran Maryland Democrat-turned-Republican editor and politician. Montgomery Blair's younger brother, Frank Jr., was also a prominent Republican. Montgomery was a West Point graduate. After his military service he moved to St. Louis, where he was a successful attorney and a close ally of Sen. Thomas Hart Benton. In the mid-1850s Blair was co-counsel on Dred Scott's legal team. Lincoln appointed Montgomery Blair postmaster general in 1861 in deference to his family's political prominence, his strong support among formerly Democratic elements within the Republican coalition, and the widely recognized need to win support from Border State Unionists, particularly in the strategically vital state of Maryland but also in Missouri, where Blair had lived. Although the position of postmaster general was generally viewed as a sinecure, with minimal responsibilities related to routine patronage disbursement, Blair proved an able but remarkably controversial figure in the wartime cabinet.

Blair and Lincoln established a strong relationship, and Blair was one of Lincoln's strongest supporters within the administration. Blair proved his value early on, advising Lincoln during the 1861 Fort Sumter crisis not to surrender to Southern demands and turn over the installation. Drawing on his military background and his lifelong residence in slave states, among the elite of the South, Blair argued that such a move would be interpreted as a sign of weakness and would embolden the rebels. Blair was initially the only cabinet member to directly oppose secretary of state William H. Seward and general in chief Winfield Scott's plan to abandon Fort Sumter, although his colleagues, and Lincoln himself, soon swung over to that position. Although this hard-line stance resulted in the bombardment and surrender of the fort, it succeeded in uniting the North in defense of the flag and cast Jefferson Davis and the Confederacy as the aggressors. Lincoln subsequently expressed his appreciation for Blair's excellent advice in this tense period.

Blair also offered Lincoln much-appreciated advice regarding another crisis in 1861. Captain Charles Wilkes of the USS *San Jacinto* precipitated an international dispute by boarding the British ship *Trent* at sea and removing two Confederate diplomats, John Slidell and James Mason. The House of Representatives passed a resolution praising Wilkes, but Blair quickly informed Lincoln that the Confederates should be freed, as their removal violated international law and would not be tolerated by the British government. When it soon became evident that Britain was contemplating going to war with the United States in response to this provocation, Lincoln grudgingly accepted the wisdom of Blair's position and surrendered the envoys, thus averting British entry into the conflict.

Blair was widely regarded as unduly conservative and reactionary, a view that William Lloyd Garrison, as he wrote in *The Liberator,* considered unjust, as Blair was a long-standing supporter of emancipation. Although Blair was initially against Lincoln's plan to issue the Emancipation Proclamation in fall 1862, fearing that it would result in the Republican Party's defeat in the upcoming elections, he wrote a public letter loyally supporting the president's decision to end slavery in the South as a military necessity. Blair, like Lincoln, hoped to colonize African Americans following emancipation, perhaps to the Caribbean or Latin America. Blair did not believe that African Americans could peacefully coexist on terms of civic and legal equality with whites in the United States, a stance that bitterly antagonized radical Republicans, but which again echoed Lincoln's own views, particularly as represented by his statements on these issues during his 1858 debates with Stephen Douglas.

The postmaster general, a remarkably contentious man, feuded with most of his fellow cabinet members and a number of important Republican leaders. He did not get along with Seward, who had opposed Blair's appointment to the cabinet. Attorney general Edward Bates, a rival Border State leader, felt that Blair denounced anything that he proposed during cabinet meetings out of jealousy. Blair and Chase were on bad terms, particularly after Blair's former friend John C. Frémont published private correspondence in which Blair insulted Chase's competence and good faith. Blair's relations with secretary of war Edwin Stanton were even worse, and the two men generally did not speak or acknowledge one another's presence at cabinet meeting. Though the ever-tolerant Lincoln liked and respected the postmaster general, according to his private secretaries John G. Nicolay and John Hay the president became increasingly annoyed with Blair's relentless infighting and penchant for controversy, realizing that it undermined his usefulness.

Montgomery Blair vigorously supported Lincoln's policy of attempting to restore the occupied Southern states to the Union quickly. Blair and Lincoln both viewed secession as a movement carried out by a small cadre of proslavery leaders, for which the majority of Southern whites should not be blamed or held responsible. Neither Blair nor Lincoln agreed with radical demands for postwar confiscation of rebel property or the execution of Confederate leaders. Both favored generous amnesty terms that they believed would quickly win the renewed loyalty of Southern whites following the end of the war. Both also argued that the president, and not Congress, should supervise the political reorganization of the Southern state governments. Blair's vigorous public support for Lincoln's reconstruction plan and his attacks on radical opponents of that policy, particularly a vituperative speech at Rockville, Maryland, in October 1863, led to intensified demands for Blair's dismissal from the cabinet.

Although Lincoln was reluctant to dismiss the loyal Blair, political reality forced his hand, and he asked for Blair's resignation in September 1864. Blair's ouster was very well received by the Republican press and in fact apparently persuaded radical critic of the administration John C. Frémont, by this time a bitter enemy of the Blairs, to withdraw from the presidential race. Radical Maryland congressman Henry Winter Davis, another fierce critic of Lincoln, pledged his support to the president in the wake of his enemy Blair's dismissal, in another example of the remarkable effect of this seemingly minor personnel change in the cabinet.

Blair remained a loyal supporter of Lincoln for the duration of the war, although he and his family switched allegiance to the Democrats during Reconstruction. Blair died at his estate in Silver Spring, Maryland, which he had rebuilt after it was burned by Confederate troops during the war.

See also *Blair, Francis; Cabinet, Lincoln's*

—MICHAEL T. SMITH

BIBLIOGRAPHY

Maroney, Rita Lloyd. *Montgomery Blair: Lincoln's Postmaster General.* Washington: U.S. Government Printing Office, 1963.

Smith, Michael Thomas. "The Meanest Man in Lincoln's Cabinet: A Reappraisal of Montgomery Blair." *Maryland Historical Magazine* 95 (Summer 2000): 190–209.

Smith, William E. *The Francis Preston Blair Family in Politics.* 2 vols. New York: Macmillan, 1933.

Bleeding Kansas

In the summer of 1856 Republican newspapers decried "Bleeding Kansas," their phrase for the violence and turmoil in Kansas Territory. Tensions had been high in the territory since its founding in 1854, when the Kansas-Nebraska Act opened

The sacking of the Free Soil capital of Lawrence, Kansas, by proslavery men in May 1856. Incensed by the antislavery "Topeka movement," which sought to make Kansas a free state, the proslavery, official territorial government tried to assert its authority using the pretext of carrying out a court injunction.
Source: The Granger Collection, New York

the territory to settlement, with the provision, known as "popular sovereignty," that it would be the settlers themselves who would decide whether to permit slavery. The act politicized migration to the territory, pitting New England, Midwestern, and Missouri settlers against one another. In addition, there was considerable fraud in early elections. Nonresident Missourians crossed the river to vote, intimidated free-state voters into avoiding the polls, and elected proslavery men to the territorial legislature. Indignant free-staters subsequently formed their own government, called the "Topeka movement" after the town where it was established. At Topeka, the free-staters wrote their own constitution and elected a governor and legislature. Although Congress never accepted the legitimacy of the Topeka government, deeming it treasonous, it existed as an extralegal, free-state alternative to the legally sanctioned, proslavery territorial legislature.

Conflict inevitably arose from the existence of two governments in the territory. The territorial government viewed itself as the upholder of law and order against the extralegal free-state government. But the Topeka movement believed it had more legitimacy than the fraudulently elected, "bogus" legislature. The two sides nearly came to blows in the winter of 1855–1856, when the territorial militia surrounded Lawrence in the Wakarusa War. The territorial governor, Wilson Shannon, and leading Missourians intervened to prevent violence, but the contradiction of two governmental authorities was not resolved.

In May 1856 conflict in the territory erupted into a guerrilla war. Determined to assert its authority, the territorial government decided to crack down on the free-state movement. On the pretext of carrying out the injunction of a territorial court, a posse led by the local sheriff ravaged Lawrence. Charles Robinson, governor under the free-state movement, was arrested on his way east. Charged with treason, Robinson and other free-staters were held prisoner at the territorial capital of Lecompton for most of the summer. In 1857 Robinson was tried—and acquitted—for usurping office. A. H. Reeder, the former territorial governor, who had converted to the free-state side, escaped to the east disguised as a common laborer. Tempers were further heated by the attack in the U.S. Senate on Charles Sumner of Massachusetts by South Carolina congressman Preston Brooks. In a speech on Kansas policy, Sumner had insulted Brooks's uncle, a South Carolina senator. It was amid this turmoil that Kansas settler John Brown led a party of men who killed five proslavery settlers near Pottawatomie Creek.

These events broke the precarious quiet. Bands of armed guerrillas roamed the territory during the summer of 1856, warning settlers of opposing political views to leave the territory or be burned out. Under the ineffective Shannon, the territory descended into lawlessness. U.S. troops disbanded armed parties, but they quickly re-formed. Shannon would soon leave the territory. Acting governor Daniel Woodson openly favored the proslavery side. Before departing, Shannon ordered the U.S. army to disperse the Topeka legislature, which was to meet on July 4. The job fell to Colonel Edwin Sumner, whose dispersal of the free-state legislature "at the point of the bayonet" made excellent propaganda for the antislavery cause.

Although migration into the territory was much diminished because of the fighting, one of the army's duties was to intercept heavily armed immigrant bands. Missourians also searched migrant parties passing through their state for weapons. As the river route through Missouri became increasingly difficult for Northern migrants, they turned to alternative routes through Iowa and Nebraska. James H. Lane, a free-state leader, returned to Kansas along such a route with a band—his "Army of the North"—of several hundred men. When Woodson declared the territory in rebellion and called for help from the territorial militia—moving large numbers of Missourians to cross the border and join the melee—the army lost faith in him and refused to carry out his requests.

Although most of the battles of Bleeding Kansas are more properly seen as skirmishes, they nonetheless became legendary in Kansas history. At Black Jack on June 2, John Brown and his men captured Henry Clay Pate of the territorial militia. A ruse in which Frederick Brown rode around Pate's camp shouting that they were outnumbered persuaded Pate to surrender. In early August, Brown and his men attacked a settlement of Georgians at Osawatomie. A few days later, free-state men attacked Franklin, capturing "Old Sacramento," the cannon that Missourians had won in the U.S.-Mexican War. The next day, free-staters attacked Henry Titus's fortified cabin near Lawrence. Two weeks later, proslavery forces burned Osawatomie. John Brown participated in the town's unsuccessful defense, and his son Frederick was killed there.

In September 1856, a new territorial governor arrived in Kansas. He was John W. Geary, a veteran of the Mexican War and former gold rush mayor of San Francisco. A Democrat, Geary understood that his mission was to restore order to the territory before the presidential election. Geary reassured the army of his impartiality in the conflict, secured the help of Missouri governor Sterling Price in dispersing proslavery bands, and informed a proslavery band threatening Lawrence that if they attacked the town, they would be fired on by the U.S. Army. The governor's new measures interrupted fighting between proslavery Kickapoo Rangers and free-state forces under James H. Lane at Hickory Point. The rangers were secure within log walls that free-staters, lacking artillery, could not penetrate. Lane withdrew, learned of the governor's order to disband, and did not return to fight on the next day. Another free-state party, however, renewed the fight and was taken prisoner by federal troops. Under Geary's crackdown, guerrilla bands began to disperse and leave the territory. By mid-November, the army considered the territory quiet enough to go into winter quarters. Estimates are that thirty-eight people were killed in the fighting in Kansas in 1856 and an estimated $2 million worth of property was destroyed.

Bleeding Kansas helped shape the political realignment of the 1850s. Abraham Lincoln, who had reentered political life in 1854 to argue against the Kansas-Nebraska Act, had by 1856 joined the new Republican Party. Not only was Lincoln, like many Northerners, personally outraged by the violence in the territory, but Bleeding Kansas also provided him with a political opportunity. The attack on Lawrence occurred at the same time that anti-Nebraska forces in Illinois were holding a convention at Bloomington. The attack lent credence to Lincoln's call at the Bloomington convention for the antislavery forces to unite in resisting an increasingly aggressive Slave Power.

When the Republicans nominated explorer John C. Frémont for the presidency, they considered Lincoln as a possible vice presidential nominee. Lincoln was passed over for William L. Dayton of New Jersey. The Democrats, much weakened by the turmoil in Kansas, nominated James Buchanan, in part because he had been out of the country as U.S. minister to Great Britain and therefore had not been involved in the Kansas-Nebraska Act. Bleeding Kansas was a staple of Republican propaganda during the 1856 election. Lincoln campaigned actively for the Republicans during that election, but unlike other Republican politicians, he did not use the specific events in Bleeding Kansas to excite his audiences. Instead Lincoln concentrated on the larger issue of slavery's incompatibility with self-government to appeal for resistance to slavery's expansion.

In the short term the Democrats managed to hold onto power by winning the 1856 presidential race. But Bleeding Kansas had done much to persuade

Northerners that the Democratic policy in Kansas was flawed. As the Democratic administrations of Franklin Pierce and James Buchanan struggled with turmoil in Kansas, the Republican Party gained stature. Abraham Lincoln continued his rise to prominence by challenging Illinois senator Stephen A. Douglas, the Democratic architect of the Kansas policy. The continued turmoil in Kansas provided support for Lincoln's argument that popular sovereignty aided slavery's expansion and undermined the republic's commitment to freedom.

See also *Kansas-Nebraska Act; Lawrence, Kansas*

—NICOLE ETCHESON

BIBLIOGRAPHY

Basler, Roy P., ed. *The Collected Works of Abraham Lincoln.* New Brunswick, N.J.: Rutgers University Press, 1953.

Cawardine, Richard J. *Lincoln.* London: Pearson, 2003.

Donald, David Herbert. *Lincoln.* New York: Simon and Schuster, 1995.

Etcheson, Nicole. *Bleeding Kansas: Contested Liberty in the Civil War Era.* Lawrence: University Press of Kansas, 2004.

Fehrenbacher, Don E. *Prelude to Greatness: Lincoln in the 1850s.* Stanford: Stanford University Press, 1962.

Rawley, James A. *Race and Politics: "Bleeding Kansas" and the Coming of the Civil War.* Philadelphia: Lippincott, 1969.

Winkle, Kenneth J. *The Young Eagle: The Rise of Abraham Lincoln.* Dallas: Taylor, 2001.

Blockade, Union Naval

After the formation of the Confederate States of America, President Abraham Lincoln issued the "Proclamation of Blockade against Southern Ports" on April 19, 1861. Initially the Union navy concentrated its effort along the Atlantic coast, but as numbers of ships and sailors expanded and bases were captured along the Southern coast the blockade was expanded into the Gulf of Mexico to the Rio Grande in Texas. The blockade required the patrolling of more than 3,500 miles of coast and the closure of more than ten major ports.

The blockade was one of the main elements of General Winfield Scott's Anaconda Plan to subdue the Confederacy. Its purpose was to strangle the

Southern economy and weaken the Confederate military sufficiently that the South could be divided at the Mississippi River, invaded, and defeated. The blockade attempted to prevent the South from exporting cotton and other agricultural goods and importing military and other supplies.

The blockade is often underestimated as a determinant of the war's outcome. Many observers and scholars consider the blockade a "leaky affair," and rightly so. However, the actual impact on the Southern economy and the Confederate military was enormous, and it ultimately was a primary reason for the Union victory. Yes, cotton was exported, and the majority of blockade-running attempts were successful, but the cost was high and the overall flow of trade greatly reduced. Moreover, the actual volume of blockade running was limited, and the small and fast blockade runners could not carry as much cargo as larger, prewar cargo ships.

Blockade running was considered glamorous, whereas blockade patrolling was considered boring. But both were motivated by profit. Successful blockade running could make a captain and crew wealthy, but those serving in the Union navy could also profit by capturing and auctioning ships and cargoes, with the proceeds divided among the crew by rank. In sharp contrast to land battles, runners would typically offer little resistance once they were cornered. All they could do was return quickly with a new ship. Union naval vessels would do little more than fire a shot across the bow, for fear of damaging or destroying the prize. For the most part, only when the Confederate navy offered resistance were ships destroyed and sailors killed.

Typically blockades are insufficient to win a war, but the Union blockade was more successful than most for two primary reasons. First was the capture of Southern port cities, such as New Orleans, and the operation of bases on land and barrier islands near the ports. Second was the South's own "King Cotton" strategy, which was based on the idea that if Southern cotton was withheld from world markets then European powers would intervene on behalf of the South. Thus, with the exception of military goods, Confederate policy tended to discourage, but not prohibit, trading through the blockade, creating a de facto Confederate blockade of the South.

One paradoxical impact of the blockade was the importation of luxury goods into a country where basic goods were in short supply. Luxury goods tend to be expensive and small, while basic goods tend to be inexpensive and bulky. Blockade runners could import more value in luxury goods in their small, fast ships and thereby economically justify the costs and risks of the venture. The import of luxuries in the face of shortages of basic goods was an important factor in the demoralization of the Southern population.

In addition to the effect on international trade, the blockade also greatly diminished trade along the Southern coast. Products such as beef from Texas could not be shipped easily to New Orleans, Charleston, or Richmond, so that such products, as well as people and soldiers, had to be transported by railroad. That increased pressure on railroads already facing shortages of replacement rails, engines, locomotives, and cars, as the existing stocks depreciated or were destroyed. When Fort Fisher was captured in January 1865, the last major port open to blockade running, Wilmington, North Carolina, was closed. It had been the main source of supplies for the Army of Northern Virginia, which quickly disintegrated in the aftermath. In total the blockade captured more than a thousand blockade runners and destroyed several hundred, helping achieve Scott's plan to strangle the Southern economy.

The blockade was also a central political issue during the Civil War. Lincoln's blockade proclamation was an act of war, and in the absence of a congressional declaration of war it was considered illegal by many, albeit justified by emergency conditions. Although later ratified by Congress, Lincoln's actions are considered a critical precedent in extending the war powers of the executive branch in cases of national emergency.

The blockade also had the effect of de facto recognition of the Confederacy as a foreign belligerent nation because a unified nation would not blockade itself or part of itself. It would instead declare and enforce the closure of its ports. The blockade solved an important political problem for Lincoln in that it justified, under international law, the searching of foreign ships in open waters, providing legal backing for the blockade fleet to stop and search ships from neutral nations, particularly those from Britain.

The de facto recognition of the Confederacy was also a key feature in political and economic interactions with the European powers during the Civil War. If Lincoln had declared the Southern ports closed, the Confederates would have been considered insurrectionists; the blockade made them belligerents who could legally interact with foreign powers. The Confederacy could thus buy military goods and obtain loans from neutral nations. Other nations could choose which side to support, creating the possibility that King Cotton might induce Britain to side with the Confederacy. Instead, Britain declared its neutrality and became the primary source of military goods for the Confederacy without having to go to war.

Lincoln's blockade was a risky but necessary component of Union victory. It was critical to economic and military strategy and was the central issue in international politics. Had the Confederacy committed either to a strong King Cotton strategy or to encouragement of blockade running and coastal defense, the outcome might have been different.

See also *Anaconda Plan; Scott, Winfield*

—Mark Thornton

BIBLIOGRAPHY

Surdam, David G. *Northern Naval Superiority and the Economics of the American Civil War.* Columbia: University of South Carolina Press, 2001.

Thornton, Mark, and Robert B. Ekelund Jr. *Tariffs, Blockades, and Inflation: The Economics of the Civil War.* Wilmington, Del.: Scholarly Resources, 2004.

Wise, Stephen R. *Lifeline of the Confederacy: Blockade Running during the Civil War.* Columbia: University of South Carolina Press, 1988.

Booth, John Wilkes

From the moment that Abraham Lincoln was shot in his private box at Ford's Theatre in Washington, D.C., on April 14, 1865, the identity of his killer was never in doubt. His assailant, the actor John Wilkes Booth (1838–1865), had planned his act to include a dramatic leap to the stage, a pause, and a Latin declamation—"Sic semper tyrannis!"—in full view of the audience. Clearly, Booth wanted the world to know who had killed the president, and why. To Booth, the assassination of the president was an act of heroism.

This misguided view went far beyond a mere sympathy for the South, and the only way to understand it is to look at the peculiar circumstances of Booth's home state and his extraordinary family legacy that seemed to give special meaning to the events of 1861–1865.

The ninth of ten children, John Wilkes Booth was raised on a farm near Bel Air, Maryland, and in Baltimore. Like his two older brothers, he followed his father, British-born actor Junius Booth, to a successful career on the stage. The elder Booth was a colorful man, known for his bizarre offstage antics, his eclectic literary tastes, and an almost fanatical respect for life in all its forms. In his politics, he shared the views of his father, Richard Booth, who insisted that visitors to his London parlor bow to a portrait of George Washington. Richard had named his sons Junius Brutus and Algernon Sydney, after his political heroes. In the same tradition, his grandson was named after their supposed ancestor, the English radical John Wilkes.

Booth's ancestral politics might have gone unnoticed, but as the sectional crisis exploded, the heated rhetoric of the day called up images of ancient history and the fate of liberty in earlier times. More and more, Booth found special relevance in what he called "the teachings of our fathers," and he cited them often in justifying the course he eventually took.

Booth had grown up in Maryland, a slave state with deep divisions and with many citizens who had a serious grudge against the president. The war's earliest fatalities had occurred in Booth's own neighborhood, on April 19, 1861, when the Sixth Massachusetts Infantry was met by an angry mob as they passed through Baltimore in response to President Lincoln's first call for troops. The soldiers fired into the crowd, and when the fracas was over, more than a dozen people lay dead.

For the Lincoln administration, this was both a political and a military crisis. Troops needed to pass unimpeded through Maryland, but that did not sit well with the more ardent Southerners in the state. Virginia was almost certain to secede, and Maryland seemed ready to follow Virginia out of the Union—surrounding Washington with rebellious territory.

Lincoln's response was to declare martial law. He suspended the writ of *habeas corpus,* setting aside the usual protections of the law and suppressing newspapers. Within months, Baltimore was under martial law, and dozens of Maryland legislators had been sent to prison to keep them from leading their state out of the Union. To Abraham Lincoln, these were commonsense measures made necessary by the wartime emergency. To his critics, they were tyranny and oppression. They vilified Lincoln, and more often than not they blamed secretary of state William H. Seward, whom they viewed as the brains of the administration and the instigator of the martial law policy. It was no accident that John Wilkes Booth formed his conspiracy in Maryland and that it targeted both Lincoln and Seward.

Booth enjoyed an extraordinarily successful stage career, but money and popularity did little to dampen his resentment over the course of the war. He had often heard Lincoln's opponents call the president a modern Caesar, and their words rang true to

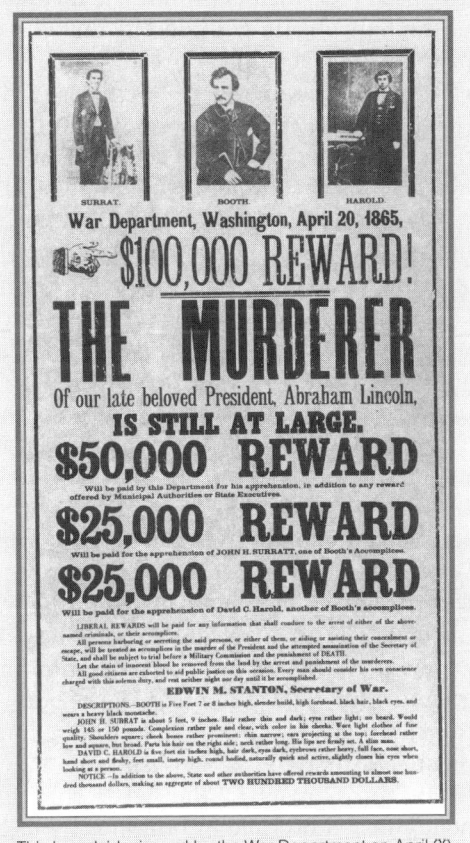

This broadside, issued by the War Department on April 20, 1865, offered rewards for the apprehension of John Wilkes Booth and his fellow conspirators.
Source: The Granger Collection, New York

Booth, who spent his formative years reading tales of the Roman Republic and its martyrs in the cause of liberty. As an actor, Booth had performed in countless plays that glorified the killing of tyrants. Oftentimes the happy ending, so to speak, was the death of the king.

For the sake of family harmony, John Wilkes had promised his mother that he would not join the ranks of the Confederacy. It was a pledge he soon regretted. When the South's fortunes waned, he began telling people that he had contributed to the cause as a smuggler of quinine. This was patently false, but it answered critics who taunted him for doing nothing while so many others had died for their beliefs. In truth, the critics were right, and Booth was tormented by what he called his "idleness."

That changed in the summer of 1864, when Booth ran into two old friends in Baltimore. Fueled by alcohol, and perhaps a sense of helplessness, Booth proposed a daring plan to lift the fortunes of the Confederacy, while saving lives in the bargain. He pointed out that the combatants were no longer exchanging prisoners of war, and, as a result, captive U.S. soldiers were left indefinitely in the care of the starving South. Men were dying by the thousands, but as long as the public blamed the Confederacy, the Lincoln administration had little incentive to do anything about it. If someone were to capture the president and hold him hostage, his government would have little choice but to resume the exchange.

Booth said it would not be difficult to abduct Lincoln on his way to or from his summer residence at the Soldiers' Home, to which he often traveled alone and unguarded. He persuaded his friends Samuel Bland Arnold and Michael O'Laughlen Jr. to join him in the effort. Little transpired until October 1864, when Booth traveled to Montreal, Canada. There he met a blockade runner from Maryland named Patrick C. Martin, who gave Booth a letter of introduction to a network of pro-Confederate smugglers in their home state.

This underground system was well known to David Edgar Herold, a Washington pharmacy clerk who had befriended Booth in the spring of 1863. Herold spent much of his time hunting in Southern Maryland, and he knew John Harrison Surratt Jr., whose mother, Mary, ran a tavern on the main stage line out of Washington. Surratt was a courier for the Confederate State Department and was eager to take a more active role in the war. Booth offered him a chance, and by the end of 1864, both Surratt and Herold had joined the abduction plot.

As a courier, John Surratt would have been very familiar with the underground routes to Richmond that Booth and his cohorts would need to use in transporting a captive Lincoln to the South. Surratt, however, lacked good judgment. His first act as a conspirator was to engage George Andrew Atzerodt to ferry the party across the lower Potomac River to Virginia. Atzerodt, an alcoholic, wasted no time in bragging about his newfound importance. His indiscretions made him more of a threat than an asset, and Booth was compelled to move him to Washington, where he and Herold could watch his every move.

Surratt soon redeemed himself by bringing Lewis Thornton Powell into the plot. A former Confederate soldier and prisoner of war, Powell had an impressive war record that included service with Mosby's Rangers. He was strong, discreet, and would become Booth's right-hand man.

Booth's plot continued to develop slowly, and by some accounts its membership would grow to include Mary Surratt and Dr. Samuel A. Mudd. The evidence for their complicity—especially that of Dr. Mudd—is vigorously disputed.

Nevertheless, the conspirators were idle until the final weeks of the war, when Sam Arnold convinced Booth that their window of opportunity was closing. Booth called a meeting, and only then did the original conspirators learn that others had also been involved in the plot. Their meeting was contentious, and after a round of drunken threats, Sam Arnold issued an ultimatum to do something or he would leave. A day later, on March 17, Booth assembled his men for an abduction attempt. Lincoln failed to appear, and Booth announced that the conspiracy was finished. This, like so many of his claims, was untrue.

A few of Booth's men remained with him, but their goal had changed. The government had resumed its prisoner exchange in mid-January, taking away the motive for which some people had joined the plot. Furthermore, the fall of Richmond on April 3 left Booth with no place to take a captive Lincoln. After Robert E. Lee's surrender on April 9, the possibility of bartering for prisoners seemed even more remote, yet Booth refused to give up.

On Thursday, April 13, Booth and his remaining cohorts got together in Lewis Powell's hotel room, just around the corner from Ford's Theatre. The city was lit up that night in celebration of Lee's surrender, but Booth was in a bitter mood. He ordered Lewis Powell to kill Secretary of State Seward, who was bedridden after a recent carriage accident. George Atzerodt was assigned to kill the vice president, Andrew Johnson; David Herold would assist in their escape from the city. For himself, Booth reserved the greatest glory: he was going to kill the president.

Things did not go as planned. President Lincoln decided to forgo the festivities and remained at home with a headache that night. With their main target out of reach, Booth and his men awaited another opportunity. It came the following night.

The assassination and its aftermath are a familiar story. Booth entered the Lincolns' private box in Ford's Theatre and shot the president. The Lincolns' guest, Major Henry Rathbone, tried to stop the assassin, but Booth drew a dagger and inflicted a serious wound on Rathbone's arm. He then leaped to the stage below and fled the scene. In the meantime, Lewis Powell botched his attack on Secretary Seward, and he fled the secretary's house leaving five men horribly wounded in his wake. All would survive. George Atzerodt made no attempt to kill the vice president or anyone else. He simply walked away and got staggeringly drunk.

Booth eluded capture for more than eleven days before a detachment of the Sixteenth New York Cavalry trapped him in a tobacco barn near Port Royal, Virginia. David Herold, who fled with Booth, gave himself up, but Booth refused to be taken alive. He made a break for the door and was shot in the neck. He died a couple of hours later, on the morning of April 26.

Three weeks later, Herold and seven others stood trial before a military commission on charges of murder and conspiracy. Arnold, O'Laughlen, and Dr. Mudd were convicted and sentenced to life in prison. Edman Spangler, a stagehand at Ford's Theatre, was convicted of a lesser charge and sentenced to six years. Powell, Atzerodt, Herold, and Mary Surratt were sentenced to death and were hanged together on the afternoon of July 7. John Surratt would not be captured until late 1866. He was released in 1868 after his trial ended in a hung jury, but the public seemed satisfied that justice had been done.

The Lincoln conspiracy trial left many questions unanswered, and to this day the full scope of Booth's plan remains the subject of heated debate. In spite of its efforts, the government was never able to prove that the Confederate government was involved in the plot, and recent efforts to revive the theory have left most people unconvinced.

Conspiracy theorists have made much of the fact that John Wilkes Booth was able to develop a plot right under the noses of federal authorities and escape detection for the better part of a year. To his contemporaries, though, this was not such a mystery. As lawyers and detectives unraveled the details of the plot, they found a number of people who had known of Booth's intentions but felt powerless to report him to the authorities.

Ironically, Booth had conspired under the protective shield of the law. Long before the days of plea bargains, a prosecutor was legally bound to file charges against anyone implicated in a crime. This was common knowledge in 1865, and Booth used it to full advantage. In developing his plot, he spoke to many people and pitched many ideas and proposals. But before he did, he always made a point of gathering evidence that could implicate those people in his schemes. Then, if they refused to cooperate, he would tell them about the predicament he had put them in. It worked every time.

See also *Assassination*

—Michael W. Kauffman

BIBLIOGRAPHY

Kauffman, Michael W. *American Brutus: John Wilkes Booth and the Lincoln Conspiracies.* New York: Random House, 2004.

Smith, Gene. *American Gothic: The Story of America's Legendary Theatrical Family—Junius, Edwin, and John Wilkes Booth.* New York: Simon and Schuster, 1992.

Taper, Louise, and John Rhodehamel. *Right or Wrong God Judge Me: The Writings of John Wilkes Booth.* Urbana and Chicago: University of Illinois Press, 1997.

Border States, Lincoln and

Lincoln had a special relationship with the Border States, which included the northernmost of the slave states—Delaware, Kentucky, Maryland, and Missouri—none of which seceded. (West Virginia, formed from a group of breakaway Virginia counties and formally admitted to the Union as a state on June 20, 1863, is often included among the Border States.) Kentucky in particular held personal meaning for Lincoln: Born in that state, he married into a prominent Lexington family, the Todds, and good friends of his, such as Joshua and James Speed, resided there.

The Border States also held strategic importance for Lincoln and for the Union war effort. Had Maryland seceded, Lincoln's capital would have been completely surrounded by Confederate territory. Kentucky contained or bordered strategically important waterways, including the Mississippi, Ohio, Cumberland, and Tennessee Rivers; the latter two would prove especially important as invasion routes into Tennessee in early 1862. Missouri's militarily important geographic features included its sections of the Missouri and Mississippi Rivers, as well as the key commercial center of St. Louis. These states also produced food crops that would have been enormously helpful to the Confederacy.

Moreover, the Border States ultimately provided far more men to the Union army than to the Confederate forces. Delaware supplied perhaps 10,000 white soldiers and 1,000 black soldiers to the Union cause; the Confederates drew perhaps 1,000 men from the state. Maryland's total of 44,000 Union soldiers (35,000 whites and 9,000 blacks) was more than twice the size of its contingent of 20,000 Confederate troops. Similarly, whereas about 35,000 Kentuckians wore Confederate gray, nearly 74,000 men from the state (about one-third of them African American) wore Union blue. Missouri's Union forces consisted of 80,000 whites and 8,000 blacks; about 30,000 Missourians fought in regular Confederate units and another 3,000 as pro-Confederate guerrillas. Finally, Union forces from West Virginia included approximately 25,000 men, while the Confederates mustered around 15,000 there.

Lincoln recognized the political importance of the Border States by including several of their prominent citizens in his cabinet: Edward Bates of Missouri was attorney general from 1861 to 1864; Montgomery Blair of Maryland was postmaster general from 1861 to 1864; and James Speed of Kentucky was attorney general from 1864 to 1866.

Because they contained key resources and potential military recruits—and they were slave states—the Border States presented Lincoln with major challenges. His first problem concerned whether the Border States would secede following the outbreak of fighting at Fort Sumter (April 12, 1861). Delaware offered Lincoln the least trouble. Its close connections to Northern commerce and weak commitment to slavery (slaves were less than 2 percent of its 1860 population) made it unlikely that the state would secede. Indeed, the governor did not even call the legislature into session to consider secession after Fort Sumter.

Maryland's situation was less certain, and nervous presidential advisers urged Lincoln to arrest troublesome legislators to prevent the calling of a secession convention. Lincoln refused, and his gambit worked. On May 14, 1861, Maryland legislators approved resolutions refusing to call a secession convention. But it was not a total victory for Lincoln: the resolutions also supported recognizing the Confederacy and apprising both Lincoln and Confederate president Jefferson Davis of the legislature's actions. Before a planned September legislative session, which some in Washington believed secessionists would dominate, secretary of war Simon Cameron ordered the arrests of more than a dozen legislators. As a result, the legislature lacked a quorum and could take no action. The presence of U.S. troops and the suspension of *habeas corpus* (first proclaimed for part of Maryland on April 27, 1861) made it certain that secessionists would never be successful there.

In Missouri, at the March 1861 convention considering secession, Unionists defeated efforts to take the state out of the Union. Then, in the midst of violent clashes between pro-Union and pro-Confederate forces, the convention took control of the state government. It deposed the pro-Confederate governor, appointed new state leaders, and acted as a legislature during most of the war.

The Kentucky legislature, controlled by Unionists, refused to call a secession convention and declared the state neutral, but Governor Beriah Magoffin secretly allowed the Confederates to muster men on Kentucky soil. Lincoln carefully respected the state's neutrality. The Union army, for instance, received Kentucky recruits across the Ohio River in Cincinnati. Confederate General Leonidas Polk openly violated Kentucky's neutrality by moving troops in to take Columbus, on the Mississippi (September 3, 1861); the legislature then invited Union forces into the state to repel the invasion. Soldiers under General Ulysses S. Grant arrived on September 6, 1861, to secure Kentucky for the Union.

Even with secession defeated in the Border States, Lincoln faced growing problems with the region's slaveholders as emancipation policies evolved during the war. As slaves rushed to Union lines along the Virginia coast, General Benjamin Butler declared them contraband of war that could be legally seized. On August 6, 1861, Lincoln approved the first Confiscation Act, which essentially ratified Butler's policy and allowed the taking of any property—including slaves—used to aid the Confederate military cause. Although the law did not necessarily emancipate slaves, it set an important antislavery precedent upsetting to pro-Union slaveholders in the Border States.

Two weeks later, on August 30, 1861, Union General John C. Frémont went beyond the Confiscation Act by declaring Missouri under martial law and declaring free all slaves of rebels in the state. Border State Unionists panicked. James Speed, writing from Louisville, advised Lincoln that Frémont's proclamation would seriously damage pro-Union sentiment in Kentucky. The president feared that result, too. In September 1861 he wrote U.S. senator Orville Browning of Illinois of his concern about the dangers that Frémont's actions posed: "I think to lose Kentucky is nearly the same as to lose the whole game. Kentucky gone, we can not hold Missouri, nor, as I think, Maryland. These all against us, and the job on our hands is too large for us. We would as well consent to separation at once, including the surrender of this capitol." Lincoln therefore repudiated Frémont's orders and similar ones issued by General David Hunter in the South Carolina Sea Islands. Lincoln continued to tie emancipation to the Border States up until the moment he announced his plans to end slavery. As late as September 13, just days before issuing the Preliminary Emancipation Proclamation, he argued that a premature emancipation would take "fifty thousand bayonets" from Kentucky out of the Union army and give them to the Confederates.

Lincoln recognized that attacking slavery constituted an important means of defeating the Confederacy—and preventing the recognition of the Davis government by foreign powers. But antislavery action, he believed, should occur while taking into consideration views of the Border States.

Lincoln only moved toward emancipation after military victories in Tennessee and Arkansas had ensured that the Confederacy could not invade Kentucky or Missouri and that neither state was likely to secede. By this time Unionist forces in Maryland were strong enough to prevent secession in that state. Even though the Border States were secure for the Union cause, Lincoln wanted their support—especially that of Kentucky—as he moved against slavery. As Lincoln moved toward emancipation, always couching it as a war measure, he sought to enlist the support of Border State officials. In a March 6, 1862, message to Congress, he proposed a plan of gradual, compensated emancipation for any state willing to take part. Meeting with Border State congressmen, he strongly urged them to support his proposal. Should they do so, Lincoln believed, the Confederacy would see the futility of trying to win over the Border States and would be forced to end the war. Compensated emancipation would also be far less expensive, in treasure let alone blood, than continued warfare. He also argued in a July 12, 1862, meeting that "by mere friction and abrasion," the war was ending slavery in their states. So why not take compensation for an inevitable occurrence? The Border State representatives, however, rejected his entreaties.

When Lincoln issued the Preliminary Emancipation Proclamation (September 22, 1862, exactly one year after his letter to Browning), the Border States reacted more negatively than any other Union area. Although the proclamation (issued in its final form January 1, 1863) did not affect slaves in the Border States, many residents of the region feared that it would inspire slaves from farther south to sweep into their own states. But Lincoln held firm. The president told a group of Kentucky Unionists on November 21, 1862, "that he would rather die than take back a word of the Proclamation of Freedom" and he urged them again to accept his plan for gradual emancipation.

None of the Border States took Lincoln up on his offer of compensated emancipation, although two—Maryland in 1864 and Missouri in early 1865—abolished slavery outright before the end of the war, and West Virginia, at the insistence of Congress, included gradual emancipation in its 1863 constitution. But more important, the Border States remained officially loyal to Lincoln's government and contributed vast resources to the Union war effort.

—ROBERT S. TINKLER

BIBLIOGRAPHY

Basler, Roy P., ed. *The Collected Works of Abraham Lincoln. Vols. 4 and 5.* New Brunswick, N.J.: Rutgers University Press, 1953.

Berry, Stephen. *House of Abraham: Lincoln and the Todds, a Family Divided by War.* New York: Houghton Mifflin, 2007.

McPherson, James M. *Ordeal by Fire: The Civil War and Reconstruction*. 3rd ed. Boston: McGraw Hill, 2001.

Neely, Mark E., Jr. *The Fate of Liberty: Abraham Lincoln and Civil Liberties*. New York: Oxford University Press, 1991.

Paludan, Philip Shaw. *The Presidency of Abraham Lincoln*. Lawrence: University Press of Kansas, 1994.

Wooster, Ralph A. *The Secession Conventions of the South*. Princeton: Princeton University Press, 1962.

Wright, William C. *The Secession Movement in the Middle Atlantic States*. Rutherford, N.J.: Fairleigh Dickinson University Press, 1973.

Brady, Mathew

Mathew Brady (c.1823–January 15, 1896) was born in Warren County, New York, to Irish immigrants. He had little formal education, learning artistic techniques from his friend the portraitist William Page. When Brady was about seventeen he moved to New York City, where he was introduced to daguerreotyping by Samuel F. B. Morse.

In 1844 Brady opened his Daguerrean Miniature Gallery on Broadway and began photographing distinguished Americans. He went to Washington in 1849 to photograph Zachary Taylor's inauguration, also making daguerreotypes of Clay, Webster, and Calhoun. In 1851 Brady won first prize at the first world's fair, at London's Crystal Palace.

Brady was at the forefront of technical innovation in photography, switching to wet-plates in 1855, which allowed enlargements and reproductions. His business expanded dramatically in 1859 when he began producing thousands of photo postcards, "cartes de visite." Brady's eyesight had seriously deteriorated, however, so he was seldom behind the camera, leaving that to assistants. In January 1858 Brady opened the National Photographic Art Gallery on Pennsylvania Avenue in Washington, hiring Alexander Gardner as manager.

Brady photographed Abraham Lincoln for the first time in New York on February 27, 1860, before the Cooper Union speech. This Lincoln portrait was made into a carte de visite and widely reproduced. *Harper's Weekly* also published it in May. As Lincoln later said, "Brady and the Cooper Institute made me president." On his first day in Washington as president-elect, February 23, 1861, Lincoln went to Brady's studio for his inaugural portrait.

With the coming of war, soldiers rushed to Brady's studios to have their pictures taken. Brady himself resolved to record history: "I can only describe the destiny that overruled me.... I felt I had to go. A spirit in my feet said, 'Go', and I went." Lincoln granted him permission to photograph military operations but insisted that Brady finance the operation himself.

Brady accompanied the Union army to Bull Run, returning with a few images of the battlefield. In early 1862 he equipped teams to photograph all the theatres of the war, an undertaking that eventually cost over $100,000. Brady and Gardner traveled to Maryland for the Antietam campaign, where Gardner took the haunting images of Confederate dead near the Dunker Church. He also photographed Lincoln, in stovepipe hat, in camp with General John McClernand. In October, *Harper's Weekly* published the Antietam images, the first to show bodies of the fallen. Brady later displayed the pictures in his New York gallery to stunned viewers.

Brady did not take all the pictures credited to him; rather, he was the studio owner, employing around fifteen photographers, including Gardner and Timothy O'Sullivan. In keeping with the portraitist practices of the day, photographers sometimes altered or rearranged objects to create more memorable scenes. The dead sharpshooter at Gettysburg, for example, was actually moved by the photographer to make that famous image of Devil's Den. Brady and his photographers made around 3,500 pictures during the Civil War, the first to be extensively photographed. Brady, however, usually refused to give his individual photographers credit, a practice that led Gardner to leave Brady's employ and set up his own studio in Washington in late 1862.

Throughout his years in Washington, Lincoln frequented both Brady's and Gardner's studios. In February 1863, Lincoln sat for a "full-length landscape," joking that it would take more than one negative. "Just look natural," the photographer said. "That is just what I would like to avoid," replied the president. The famous seated image of Lincoln on the old five-dollar bill was made in Brady's studio, probably by his assistant Andrew Burgess, on February 9, 1864, the same day as the photograph of Lincoln reading to his son Tad. Other famous portraits were taken by Alexander Gardner, including the frontal portrait taken the Sunday before the Gettysburg Address, as well as the haunting image from April 10, 1865.

After Lincoln's assassination, Brady photographed the visitors to Lincoln's deathbed for Alonzo Chappel's painting *The Last Hours of Lincoln*. Gardner photographed the conspirators in their cells and recorded their hangings.

The expenses of his vast photographic operations ruined Brady financially. In 1866 he was unable to sell his collection for $30,000 to the New York Historical Society "as a nucleus of a national historical museum." Instead Brady exhibited his war photographs, but the public was weary of images of the recent conflict.

After the war Brady continued his political portraits but was in and out of court because of bankruptcy. Congress finally purchased his photographs for $25,000 in 1875, but even that was not enough. After closing his New York and

Washington studios, Brady spent his remaining years working for his nephew and passed away in January 1896.

Americans first saw Abraham Lincoln through Mathew Brady's photographs, as candidate and then as president, and they experienced the images of war through his eyes. Summarizing his life's work Brady said, "My greatest aim has been to advance the art [of photography] and to make it what I think I have, a great and truthful medium of history."

—Fred Beuttler

BIBLIOGRAPHY

Horan, James D. *Mathew Brady: Historian with a Camera.* New York: Crown Publishers, 1955.

Panzer, Mary. *Mathew Brady and the Image of History.* Washington, D.C.: Smithsonian Institution Press for the National Portrait Gallery, 1997.

Breckinridge, John Cabell

John Cabell Breckinridge (1821–1875), U.S. representative, vice president of the United States, U.S. senator, Confederate general, was born in Lexington, Kentucky, to a distinguished family from Virginia. He graduated from Centre College in 1839 and completed law studies at Transylvania University. Breckinridge was admitted to the bar in 1840. During the Mexican War he served as major of the Third Kentucky Volunteers.

As a Democrat in a state dominated by the Whig Party, Breckinridge was elected to represent Fayette County in the Kentucky State House of Representatives in 1849. Afterward he was elected to the U.S. House of Representatives from 1851 to1855. In 1856 Breckinridge became the youngest person to serve as vice president of the United States. Breckinridge brought a Southern balance to the Democratic ticket in 1856 and along with the Southerners in his cabinet strengthened President James Buchanan's reputation in the South as a proslavery, Northern doughface.

In the presidential election of 1860, Breckinridge became the choice of the proslavery faction of the Democratic Party. When the Southern delegates walked out of the Democratic National Convention in Charleston, South Carolina, in 1860, Breckinridge became their choice to run for president on the national ticket against Stephen Douglas, the nominee of the Northern wing of the party. Breckinridge's platform affirmed the extreme proslavery stance of the Southern states by calling for a slave code for the federal territories, supporting the annexation of Cuba (with its large slave population), and denouncing Northern opposition to the Fugitive Slave Law of 1850. Breckinridge received seventy-two electoral votes from the states of the Deep South but was unable to carry the border slave states, including his home state of Kentucky.

Despite his loss in the election for president, Kentucky elected Breckinridge to the U.S. Senate in 1860. He served only nine months in office, but long enough to work with several other senators on the Crittenden Compromise to prevent civil war. While still a U.S. senator, Breckinridge accepted the rank of brigadier general in the Confederate army, even though his state voted to remain loyal to the Union. For that action, the U.S. Senate moved, on December 4, 1861, to expel him on a charge of disloyalty to the Union.

Breckinridge was a bright star among the Confederate military leaders in the Western Theater of the Civil War. General Breckinridge led troops superbly at major engagements such as Shiloh, Stones River, and Chickamauga. He was the initial commander of the Confederate Kentucky Brigade, known as the "Orphan Brigade." After a falling-out with General Braxton Bragg, Breckinridge was sent east where he compiled a strong military record with victories at New Market, Virginia, in May 1864 and in the successful raid on Saltville, Virginia. In February 1865 Breckinridge was tapped to be the Confederate secretary of war, in the hope that his military experience could pull victory out of defeat. After the fall of Richmond, Breckinridge fled southward with the Confederate cabinet and was able to escape to Europe.

Breckinridge traveled through Europe, Great Britain, and Canada before returning to the United States in 1869. He stayed away mainly because of the Senate expulsion of 1861, fearing that he might be tried as a traitor. The U.S. government offered him amnesty in 1868. Breckinridge returned to Kentucky and died at home in 1875.

See also *Campaign of 1860, Presidential*

—WILLIAM H. BROWN

BIBLIOGRAPHY

Butler, Anne, and Wendy Wolf. *United States Senate Election, Expulsion, and Censure Cases, 1793–1990.* Washington, D.C.: U.S. Government Printing Office, 1995.

Davis, William C. *Breckinridge: Statesman, Soldier, Symbol.* Baton Rouge: Louisiana State University Press, 1974.

Heck, Frank Hopkins. *Proud Kentuckian: John C. Breckinridge, 1821–1875.* Lexington: University Press of Kentucky, 1976.

Warner, Ezra. *Generals in Grey: Lives of the Confederate Commanders.* Baton Rouge: Louisiana State University Press, 1959.

Brooks, Preston

The 1856 caning of Massachusetts Republican senator Charles Sumner by Preston S. Brooks (1819–1857), representative from South Carolina (1853–1857), on the floor of the U.S. Senate exacerbated sectional tensions and contributed to the growth of the Republican Party throughout the North.

On May 19, 1856, Charles Sumner delivered a speech titled "The Crime against Kansas." His oration attacked the institution of slavery, proslavery factions in Kansas, and his enemies in the Senate—Democrats Stephen Douglas (Illinois) and Andrew Butler (South Carolina). Sumner accused Douglas of crafting the Kansas-Nebraska bill to pander to the interests of slave owners and made shocking sexual innuendoes in reference to Butler and slavery. Butler was rumored to have a slave mistress, and Sumner's speech was considered beyond the pale of acceptable debate. In addition, Sumner did not know that Butler was not on the floor of the Senate at the time, which meant that the Massachusetts senator had verbally attacked Butler without giving him a chance to defend his honor. Sumner also declared South Carolina a stain on the Union. Finding these insults too much to bear, Butler's cousin, Rep. Preston Brooks, decided to take action.

Born in Edgefield, South Carolina, on August 5, 1819, Preston Brooks graduated from South Carolina College in 1839; he then studied law and was admitted to the bar in 1845. In 1856 Brooks had served three years in the House of Representatives and was considered by most of his colleagues to be a politician of average ability and a moderate national Democrat. Brooks, as a member of the House, had not heard Sumner's speech. He read the published version in Washington newspapers the following day. He first thought of challenging Sumner to a duel, but friends reminded him that duels were to be fought among social equals and that Sumner's remarks deprived him of that right. Determined to punish Sumner physically nonetheless, Brooks entered the Senate chambers on May 22 armed with a gutta-percha cane. He strode up to Sumner, who was seated (with his back to Brooks) at his desk autographing copies of his speech. Addressing him by name, Brooks said something to the effect that Sumner had grossly insulted his relative and his state of South Carolina, then immediately began raining blows upon the seated senator's head. Pinned under his desk, which was bolted to the floor, the bloodied Sumner wrenched himself free before collapsing, unconscious, but Brooks continued to flog the senator until his cane shattered to bits and onlookers finally intervened. All the while another Southern congressman brandished a pistol to prevent anyone from coming to Sumner's aid. The attack was so severe that the injuries kept Sumner from his Senate duties for four years. As for

Brooks, congressional measures failed to expel him, and he resigned in July—only to be reelected by his constituents to fill his own vacancy. He served in the House until his sudden death on January 27, 1857.

Public reaction to the caning of Charles Sumner was divided along sectional lines. To many Northerners Brooks's action proved slave owners to be tyrannical bullies who sought to squelch free speech through violence. Conversely, Southerners praised Brooks as a gentleman who acted to protect the honor of the South against the insults of Northern abolitionists. Republican strategists gained new party members, as they took advantage of Northern outrage and connected the attack to the brutality exhibited by the proslavery faction in Kansas.

The Sumner caning may have helped to impel Abraham Lincoln to deliver one of his most passionate speeches against slavery and the Democratic Party. Only days after the attack, on May 29, county delegates met in Bloomington, Illinois, to create a state Republican Party. Comprising conservative Whigs, anti-Nebraska Democrats, and Know-Nothings, the convention agreed that the Illinois Republican Party would continue opposition to the Kansas-Nebraska Act and stand against the spread of slavery into the western territories. Lincoln was the last of the delegates to speak that day, and the speech he delivered marked a public break with the waning Whig Party and emphasized his antislavery convictions. It was considered by many to be the greatest speech of his life. Listeners were so spellbound by Lincoln's impassioned oration that unfortunately no one took notes. Those who attended remembered that in this "Lost Speech" Lincoln argued that slavery could only be maintained by violence, as evinced in Kansas, and that Brooks's beating of Sumner demonstrated the brutal methods employed by slave owners to wield their power in Washington. Given that Lincoln's speech went unrecorded, his exact words are in dispute, but so many people present that day recalled his vehement fury against slave owners and their desire to spread slavery that many historians believe the caning may have served as a catalyst for Lincoln's fiery tone. What is not in dispute is that the "Lost Speech" established Lincoln firmly as one of Illinois's most ardent and outspoken Republicans.

Two years after the Bloomington convention, Lincoln was nominated by the Illinois Republican Party to run for the Senate against the incumbent Democrat, Stephen Douglas. In a July 17, 1858, speech, Lincoln used Brooks to denounce Southern slave owners—charging that they sought to nationalize slavery. Lincoln maintained that the founders of the Constitution intended the slow demise of slavery, and he believed that national politics had followed that course up until the repeal of the Missouri Compromise in 1854. Slave owners, Lincoln argued, thought the opposite. He told his audience that Preston Brooks—who had been showered with gifts by fellow Southerners after his attack on Sumner—had once declared that the Constitutional framers were wrong in their assumptions that slavery would eventually become extinct and that wiser and more experienced men of the present day recognized the necessity of slavery as vital to the Southern economy. Lincoln lost the 1858 election, but his nationally publicized speeches cast him as an enemy of slavery and Southern interests, which prompted the secession of several Southern states after Lincoln won the presidency in 1860.

See also *Sumner, Charles*

—ALISON MANN

BIBLIOGRAPHY

Basler, Roy P., ed. *The Collected Works of Abraham Lincoln. Vol 2, 1848–1858.* New Brunswick, N.J.: Rutgers University Press, 1953.

Crissy, Elwell. *Lincoln's Lost Speech: The Pivot of His Career.* New York: Hawthorne Books, 1967.

Donald, David Herbert. *Lincoln.* New York: Simon and Schuster, 1995.

Mathis, Robert. "Preston Smith Brooks: The Man and His Image." *South Carolina Historical Magazine* 79 (October 1978): 296–310.

Wyatt-Brown, Bertram. *Southern Honor: Ethics and Behavior in the Old South.* New York: Oxford University Press, 1982.

Brown, John

John Brown (1800–1859) was born in Connecticut and raised in Ohio, where he spent much of his life. He was at various times a tanner, land speculator, local postmaster, tradesman, sheep herdsman, wool merchant, and farmer. He had only limited successes in these enterprises, and he spent much of his adult life fending off creditors.

A fierce opponent of slavery, Brown occasionally wrote on the subject, and after the passage of the Fugitive Slave Law of 1850 he helped blacks in Springfield, Massachusetts, into a self-defense organization, prosaically called the League of Gileadites. In 1855 some of Brown's sons moved to Kansas, both to settle on the land in that recently organized territory and to be part of the movement of Northerners determined to prevent slavery from gaining a new western foothold under Stephen A. Douglas's policy of popular sovereignty. Suffering from disease, hunger, and the elements, Brown's sons begged their father to join them later that year, and in Kansas he was quickly drawn into the emerging civil war between proslavery and antislavery settlers.

In the spring of 1856 Brown and his sons killed five proslavery settlers along the Pottawatomie Creek, including at least one man who had threatened to kill the Browns. Brown denied any involvement in the killings. He soon headed east to raise money for Kansas and then returned to the territory. In December 1858 Brown led a raid into Missouri, where he killed a slave owner and helped rescue eleven slaves from bondage. Wanted for murder, he evaded authorities, taking the slaves to Illinois, from which they were later transported to Michigan and then Canada.

In early 1859 Brown began to plan for an invasion of the South in which he hoped to lead a guerrilla war against slavery and help slaves. He toured the North under a variety of *noms de guerre,* raising money for vague plans and only telling a few trusted individuals, including Frederick Douglass, of his true goals.

On October 16, 1859, Brown and eighteen followers seized the U.S. armory at Harpers Ferry, Virginia, with the intention of stealing arms, gathering slaves, and then running into the mountains. But Brown delayed once he had captured the armory and was soon surrounded by the local militia. The next day marines, led by Colonel Robert E. Lee, the future Confederate general, stormed the building where Brown was, capturing him and seven others. By this time ten of Brown's men, including two of his sons and two of his sons-in-law, were dead. Brown was wounded but alive. A few weeks later he was tried and sentenced to death. He was hanged on December 2.

An idealized 1863 lithograph imagined the American abolitionist John Brown meeting a slave mother and her child on the steps of the Charles Town, Virginia, jail on the way to his execution. Images such as this reflected the emerging Northern wartime image of Brown, not as a madman, but as a prophet martyred in the holy crusade against slavery.

Source: The Granger Collection, New York

In the period between his capture and his death Brown wrote scores of letters and gave numerous interviews. In the process he remade himself into a martyr for freedom in the struggle against slavery. Millions of Northerners came to admire the bearded abolitionist, who took on the aura of an Old Testament prophet while in jail and became for many a Christ-like martyr after his execution. On the day of his execution hundreds of thousands in the North demonstrated in his support, ministers gave sermons praising him, and intellectuals wrote essays and poems in his honor. Southerners viewed this outpouring of sympathy with horror. To them Brown was a homicidal madman who had invaded the South, destroyed property, and killed people.

Most Republicans scrambled to distance themselves from what Lincoln's campaign manager, David Davis, called the "mad affair that was Harpers Ferry." William H. Seward, the front-runner for the presidential nomination, moved quickly, "clearing his skirts effectually of John Brown," and Lincoln bragged that no Republicans were implicated in the raid or proved to be any of Brown's backers.

Yet despite their desire to prove that they were not in favor of Brown's violent attacks on slavery, Republicans could not entirely condemn him. Too many rank-and-file Republicans admired him. Speaking in Elwood, Kansas, just before Brown's execution, Lincoln said that "no man, North or South, can approve of violence or crime," but he also said that Brown had shown "great courage, rare unselfishness." The day after Brown's execution Lincoln told an audience in Lawrence, Kansas, that no one could "object" to his execution, "even though" they "agreed with us in thinking slavery wrong." Lincoln also used Brown's execution to warn Southerners that if they "undertake to destroy the Union, it will be our duty to deal with" them "as old John Brown has been dealt with." At Leavenworth, a few days later, a reporter noted that Lincoln "sympathized" with "Brown's hatred of slavery," even as he "emphatically denounced" his "insurrectionary attempt." Lincoln asserted that Brown was "insane" and declared that he "had yet to find the first Republican who endorsed his proposed insurrection," but at the same time he asserted that "slavery was responsible" for such "uprisings."

In his great speech at Cooper Union in New York City, in February 1860, Lincoln emphatically declared, "John Brown was no Republican" and that Southerners had "failed to implicate a single Republican in his Harper's Ferry enterprise." He openly challenged Southern leaders either to show what Republicans were involved or cease their "malicious slander" that Lincoln's party supported Brown. Condemning the raid as "absurd," Lincoln nevertheless warned his political opponents that if they used "John Brown" to "break up the Republican organization" it would not "destroy" the "judgment and feeling against slavery in the nation." Moreover, he rhetorically asked Southerners who were already talking about secession, "Would the number of John Browns be lessened or enlarged?" if they destroyed the nation.

Clearly for Lincoln, Brown was a madman and a threat to the public order. But he was also admirable in his "unselfishness" and his hatred for slavery. Other Republicans were less conflicted than Lincoln about Brown. Horace Greeley, the editor of the *New York Tribune*, correctly predicted that Brown's raid would "drive the slave power to new outrages" and make the "irrepressible conflict... ten years nearer." John Andrew, the popular Republican governor of Massachusetts, perhaps best summed up the conflict within the party, refusing the comment on the wisdom of the raid at Harpers Ferry but declaring that "John Brown himself is right."

Brown's execution took place eleven months before the presidential election of 1860, and the event profoundly affected the campaign. Some Southerners claimed that Brown was an agent of the Republican Party and a potent example of Northern aggression against the South. Many referred to Lincoln and his party as "John Brown Republicans." Democrats increasingly charged that Republicans had been behind Brown and even circulated a rumor that Lincoln had been one of his financial backers.

In Virginia Governor Henry Wise gave speeches while holding a pike that Brown had brought to Virginia to arm slaves. Other Southern governors used Brown to gain support for military appropriations. In the North strongly antislavery Republicans, such as Governor Andrew, Horace Greeley, and Sen. Charles Sumner, gave lip service to condemnations of Brown's violence but could not hide their admiration for the brave martyr to freedom. More moderate Republicans, such as Lincoln, stressed that the Republicans had nothing to do with the raid and denounced Brown's violence, but also used him as an example of what would happen to Southern traitors if they tried to destroy the nation and the Constitution.

When war broke out in April 1861 the Northern image of John Brown was less complex. Brown was not so much a madman as a prophet, who understood that slavery could only be crushed by violence. The most popular marching song for the U.S. Army quickly became "John Brown's Body," which included the following lyrics:

> *John Brown's body lies a-mouldering in the grave;*
> *John Brown's body lies a-mouldering in the grave;*
> *John Brown's body lies a-mouldering in the grave;*
> *His soul's marching on!*
> ....
> *They will hang Jeff. Davis to a sour apple tree!*
> *They will hang Jeff. Davis to a sour apple tree!*
> *They will hang Jeff. Davis to a sour apple tree!*
> *As they march along!*

Later in the war Julia Ward Howe would write new lyrics for this tune, titling her song, "The Battle Hymn of the Republic." But even with the new lyrics the song evoked Brown as the martyred biblical prophet who saw the vision of a holy crusade against slavery. After Lincoln's own martyrdom, popular art, including mass-produced posters, often showed portraits of Brown and Lincoln overlooking photographs of war heroes and later, during Reconstruction, leading black politicians. Indeed, after the war thousands of households had pictures of both Brown and Lincoln on their walls, especially middle-class African American families.

See also *Abolitionism; Antislavery*

—PAUL FINKELMAN

BIBLIOGRAPHY

Abels, Jules. *Man on Fire: John Brown and the Cause of Liberty.* New York: Macmillan, 1971.

Carton, Evan. *Patriotic Treason: John Brown and the Soul of America.* New York: Free Press, 2006.

Finkelman, Paul, ed. *His Soul Goes Marching On: Responses to John Brown and the Harpers Ferry Raid.* Charlottesville: University Press of Virginia, 1995.

Oates, Stephen B. *To Purge This Land with Blood: A Biography of John Brown.* New York: HarperCollins, 1970.

Russo, Peggy, and Paul Finkelman, eds. *Terrible Swift Sword: The Legacy of John Brown.* Athens: Ohio University Press, 2005.

Browning, Orville

Orville Hickman Browning (1806–1881) was a longtime friend of Abraham Lincoln, despite political disagreements and Browning's uncertainty about Lincoln's capacity for the presidency.

Browning and Lincoln had similar backgrounds: Both were Kentucky born, practiced law in Illinois, served in the Black Hawk War (1832), were Whig members of the Illinois legislature in the 1830s and 1840s, harbored antislavery sentiments, and fostered the Republican Party in Illinois. Browning, however, came from a well-to-do family, was college educated, and considered himself more refined and sophisticated than Lincoln. Nevertheless, the two men and their wives were friends.

Their friendship did not always carry over into politics. In 1860 Browning initially supported Edward Bates for the presidency, but he fell into line when the Illinois Republicans pledged their support to Lincoln. Browning later solicited Bates's endorsement of Lincoln. Privately, though, Browning continued to think that nominating Lincoln was a mistake.

Lincoln, although aware of Browning's attitudes, trusted him. Browning was among the few people with whom Lincoln spoke freely about the secession crisis in 1860 and 1861. Lincoln also accepted Browning's advice to delete from his inaugural address a potentially provocative promise to "reclaim" federal property in the seceding states, instead confining his rhetoric to an intention to "hold, occupy, and possess" such property.

In July 1861 the Brownings joined the Lincolns in Washington, after Browning was appointed to the Senate seat left vacant by the death of Stephen

Douglas. For the next year, Browning shared some of Lincoln's most unguarded conversations. Mary Lincoln encouraged Browning's frequent social calls, hoping that they relieved some of the pressure on her husband. When the Lincolns' son Willie died in February 1862, the Brownings stayed at the White House for days.

Still, Browning and Lincoln sometimes diverged politically, most importantly in their attitudes toward slavery's place in wartime policy. In 1861 Browning favored General John C. Frémont's order emancipating slaves in Missouri and objected to Lincoln's insistence that it be modified to comport with the Confiscation Act (1861). Lincoln maintained that Frémont's order was a political decision not properly within a general's purview. A year later, Browning and Lincoln reversed roles when Browning questioned the constitutionality of the Second Confiscation Act (1862) and unsuccessfully urged Lincoln to veto it. Browning also opposed Lincoln's plans for an emancipation proclamation, doubting the efficacy of such a proclamation and predicting damaging effects on public sentiment.

After the elections of 1862, the Illinois legislature chose a Democrat to replace Browning in the Senate, and the Brownings temporarily left Washington early in 1863. Lincoln might have kept Browning on hand by appointing him to a cabinet post or—as Browning desired—to the Supreme Court, but he never did. Although Browning and Lincoln remained friendly, Browning manifested scant willingness to campaign for Lincoln in 1864.

After Lincoln's death, Browning became secretary of the interior (1866–1869), and he joined the Democratic Party in the late 1860s.

—CARA L. SHELLY

BIBLIOGRAPHY

Baxter, Maurice G. *Orville H. Browning: Lincoln's Friend and Critic*. Bloomington: Indiana University Press, 1957.

Browning, Orville Hickman. *The Diary of Orville Hickman Browning*, 2 vols. Ed. Theodore C. Pease and James G. Randall. Springfield: Illinois State Historical Library, 1925–1933.

Donald, David Herbert. *Lincoln*. New York: Simon and Schuster, 1995.

———. *"We Are Lincoln Men": Abraham Lincoln and His Friends*. New York: Simon and Schuster, 2003.

Goodwin, Doris Kearns. *Team of Rivals: The Political Genius of Abraham Lincoln*. New York: Simon and Schuster, 2005.

Guelzo, Allen C. *Abraham Lincoln: Redeemer President*. Grand Rapids, Michigan: William B. Eerdmans, 1999.

———. *Lincoln's Emancipation Proclamation: The End of Slavery in America*. New York: Simon and Schuster, 2004.

Oates, Stephen B. *With Malice toward None: The Life of Abraham Lincoln*. New York: Mentor, 1978.

Buchanan, James

James Buchanan (1791–1868) was born in Mercersburg, Pennsylvania, graduated from Dickinson College, in Carlisle, Pennsylvania, in 1809, and moved to Lancaster, where he began to practice law in 1812. At the age of twenty-three, Buchanan started his political career when he was elected to the Pennsylvania legislature.

Buchanan was a prominent political figure for nearly half a century. After ten years in the House of Representatives, he served as a U.S. diplomat in Russia from 1832 to 1833. On his return he was elected to the U.S. Senate, where he became a leading spokesman for the Democratic Party and supported the policies of both Andrew Jackson and Martin Van Buren. Later he was secretary of state in the administration of President James Knox Polk. Among Buchanan's contributions to U.S. foreign affairs were his work on the Oregon boundary claim and his efforts in the dispute with Mexico over Texas. He sought but failed to secure the Democratic presidential nomination in 1848 and again in 1852. Franklin Pierce, who defeated Buchanan for the nomination in 1852, made him ambassador to Great Britain. In that position he issued the Ostend Manifesto, which justified U.S. seizure of Cuba if Spain would not sell the colony to the United States. The manifesto failed to place Cuba in American hands and also undermined the credibility of the Pierce administration, but it made Buchanan extremely popular with the Southern wing of the Democratic Party.

In 1856, with the aid of Southern backers, Buchanan finally won the Democratic nomination for president. He narrowly beat John C. Frémont, representing the new Republican Party, in the general election. Buchanan carried five Northern states, including his home state of Pennsylvania, but was essentially a sectional candidate who was swept into the White House by the South. He was the first president in more than two decades who had not carried a majority of states in both the North and the South. Buchanan's cabinet included four slaveholding Southerners and also included several Northern "doughfaces" sympathetic to slavery and the South.

The growing division between North and South over slavery in the territories was the most important issue during Buchanan's presidency. During his campaign Buchanan promised to resolve it. In his inaugural address Buchanan declared that the problem of slavery in the territories was a "judicial question" and urged the nation to accept whatever the Supreme Court decided in the *Dred Scott* case, which would be announced two days after his inauguration. Before he gave the address, Chief Justice Roger B. Taney, in full view of the audience, stood up and whispered something to Buchanan. Many Republicans, including Lincoln, later argued that Taney had told Buchanan how *Dred Scott* would be decided, and that that was why Buchanan endorsed the as-yet-unannounced decision. No one knows what Taney said to Buchanan, but historians now know that Justice Robert Grier had in fact told Buchanan what the outcome of the case would be.

The *Dred Scott* decision awarded slavery a privileged status under the Constitution. Taney declared that the federal government had no power to regulate slavery but instead had a duty to protect slave owners and their rights. Northerners, believing that the decision would expand slavery, were in a frenzy, but Buchanan did nothing to subdue their fears.

Buchanan also took steps to settle the ongoing debate over slavery in Kansas spawned by passage of the Kansas-Nebraska Act, which permitted settlers to decide whether Kansas would be a free or a slave territory. Proslavery forces held the Lecompton Convention and created a proslavery state constitution for Kansas. Ignoring the antislavery forces in Kansas—who were in the majority—the president asked Congress to admit Kansas as a slave state. Illinois senator Stephen A. Douglas, breaking with his own Democratic Party, opposed the Lecompton constitution and argued that Buchanan was trying to override the will of the people. Ultimately Congress refused to admit Kansas under Lecompton, and Buchanan retaliated against Douglas by engineering his removal as chair of the Senate Committee on the Territories. At the very end of Buchanan's administration Kansas would enter the Union as a free state.

Abraham Lincoln began his 1858 senatorial campaign against Stephen Douglas with an attack on both Douglas and Buchanan, even though the two were at odds with each other. Lincoln accused them, along with Chief Justice Taney and former president Franklin Pierce, of conspiring to open all of the territories to slavery and hinted that they also wanted to impose slavery on the North. Douglas had to defend against Lincoln while at the same time battling the Buchanan administration, which had not forgiven Douglas for defying them on the Lecompton constitution. The Lincoln–Douglas debates, which occurred throughout the campaign, made Abraham Lincoln a well-known figure for the Republican Party, even as Douglas won the election.

After the 1858 elections Buchanan's administration continued to struggle with the slavery issue, which was intensified when radical abolitionist John Brown and a band of eighteen men seized the town of Harpers Ferry, Virginia, and the U.S. arsenal located there, on October 16, 1859. Brown became a martyr for the abolitionists when he was convicted of criminal conspiracy, murder, and treason. Buchanan not only condemned the attack but tried to blame it on the Republicans, who denied any connection to Brown. Buchanan also placated the South by allowing Virginia to prosecute and ultimately hang Brown, even though he probably should have been tried in federal court. During the election of 1860 the Democratic Party split. Stephen Douglas was nominated at the national convention, but Southern Democrats, demanding a proslavery platform, held a convention of their own and nominated Buchanan's vice president, John C. Breckinridge. The Republicans, whose platform opposed the spread of slavery but did not call for its abolition, nominated Lincoln. The Constitutional Union Party, whose aim was to save the Union, nominated John Bell of Tennessee.

The split gave Lincoln the popular plurality and a large electoral vote majority, and he was elected. With the election of a Republican president, the South considered secession. Buchanan believed that peace could be restored if the abolitionists stopped agitating slave states and let them alone to manage their own affairs. As Southern states moved toward secession he did nothing to stop them, arguing that secession was illegal but that he had no constitutional authority to stop it. Preparing to secede, some Southern states ordered new weapons for their militias, which the Buchanan administration initially allowed. Only in the last few months of his administration were the arms shipments halted.

On December 20, 1860, secession began with South Carolina. Over the next month Mississippi, Florida, Alabama, Georgia, and Louisiana followed, and together these states formed a new nation, the Confederate States of America.

In January 1861 Buchanan sent the merchant vessel *Star of the West* to Charleston, South Carolina, with supplies for Fort Sumter. Confederate guns fired on the ship, forcing it to withdraw. Federal forts, arsenals, and navy yards began to be turned over to Confederate states without additional shots being fired. Believing he had inadequate military forces, Buchanan did nothing but wait for his term to expire.

On inauguration day Buchanan escorted Lincoln to the ceremony and then to the White House. He later told neighbors that his parting words to Lincoln were, "If you are as happy, my dear sir, on entering this house as I am in leaving it and returning home, you are the happiest man in this country."

In March 1861 Buchanan returned to Wheatland, his Pennsylvania home, leaving Lincoln to resolve the crisis. Buchanan later wrote *Mr. Buchanan's Administration on the Eve of the Rebellion,* a book defending his tenure. Throughout the war he opposed almost every one of Lincoln's policies. Until the end, Buchanan blamed the Civil War on the work of a handful of Northern fanatics. He died June 1, 1868, at age seventy-seven.

See also *Campaign of 1856, Presidential*

—Paula Cochran

BIBLIOGRAPHY

Cahalan, Sally Smith. *James Buchanan and His Family at Wheatland.* James Buchanan Foundation, 1988.

Donald, David Herbert. *Lincoln.* New York: Simon and Schuster, 1996.

Goodwin, Doris Kearns. *Team of Rivals: The Political Genius of Abraham Lincoln.* New York: Simon and Schuster, 2006.

Harris, William C. *Lincoln's Rise to the Presidency.* Lawrence: University Press of Kansas, 2007.

Howe, Daniel Walker. *The Political Culture of American Whigs.* Chicago: University of Chicago Press, 1984.

Mearns, David. *The Lincoln Papers.* Vols. 1 and 2. New York: Doubleday, 1948.

Miller, William Lee. *Lincoln's Virtues: An Ethical Biography.* New York: Random House, 2003.

Potter, David M. *The Impending Crisis.* New York: Harper and Row, 1976.

Wilson, Douglas. *Honor's Voice: The Transformation of Abraham Lincoln.* New York: Vintage, 1999.

Bull Run, First Battle of (First Manassas)

The Civil War as a military conflict started slowly in spring 1861. Both sides spent several months mobilizing, concentrating, equipping, and training their respective armies. Although a number of minor clashes occurred, not until summer was either side prepared to undertake a major military operation. In light of the Confederate decision to transfer its national capital from Montgomery, Alabama, to Richmond, Virginia, it seemed logical that both sides would look to north-central Virginia to fight what might be the decisive battle in a short, sharp conflict, in which the opposing capitals were a mere hundred miles apart.

Just north of Manassas Junction, twenty-five miles from Washington, D.C., Pierre G. T. Beauregard, the hero of Fort Sumter, was gathering a command some 22,000 strong. A second force of 12,000, under the command of Joseph E. Johnston, held Winchester, Virginia, in the Shenandoah Valley. Meanwhile in Washington, President Lincoln and General Winfield Scott chose Irwin McDowell to take charge of the Union forces arriving in the nation's capital and transform them into a fighting force poised to advance.

Pressure grew on McDowell to do something. Horace Greeley's *New York Tribune,* observing that the Confederate Congress was to convene for the first time at Richmond on July 20, called on the administration to make sure that that never happened. "On to Richmond!" headlines blared. Observers noticed that the ninety-day enlistment period for the first wave of militia regiments was about to expire. But the Union commander believed that his men were not yet ready to take the field, let alone engage in combat. When he raised that point with Lincoln, the president replied, "You are green, it is true, but they are green also; you are all green alike." That simple truism obscured the fact that offensive operations required a much higher degree of training to coordinate movements and execute tactics effectively.

McDowell commenced his advance on July 16, 1861. Within two days his army had reached Centreville, Virginia. Lead elements probed southward toward two fords across Bull Run, which ran south and west of Centreville. There they encountered Confederate defenders and drew back after a short skirmish. That led McDowell to consider sweeping westward, crossing Bull Run, and driving south against the Confederate left flank.

Unfortunately for McDowell, his plans were already unraveling. All along he had assumed that General Robert Patterson would use his command of 18,000 men to keep an eye on Johnston at Winchester. But Johnston evaded Patterson's scrutiny and began shifting his men by rail toward Manassas Junction, fifty miles to the southeast. Together Johnston and Beauregard would present McDowell with an enemy force of nearly equal strength.

As McDowell made his plans, Johnston's men began detraining at Manassas Junction. Beauregard planned to drive north towards Centreville and what he believed to be the Union left. Thus both armies intended to go on the offensive by crossing Bull Run and driving in their opponent's left. Much would depend on who moved first.

Mere hours after midnight on July 21 three Union divisions commenced the movement against the Confederate left. Two divisions swung north, forded Bull Run, and marched due south, while a third division headed for Stone Bridge, which was defended by a lone Confederate brigade. The flanking march proved difficult and encountered delays; eventually the Union attack drove the badly outnumbered Confederates back onto Henry House Hill. Thwarted in his desire to attack the Union left, Beauregard hurriedly shuttled commands to meet the attackers, and by midday the situation appeared to be stabilized. Union assaults were piecemeal and uncoordinated. By late afternoon the Confederates launched a counterattack and succeeded in cracking the Union line, sending the disorganized and somewhat panicked Yankees scampering back toward Washington. Later much would be made of the stand of one Virginia brigade, under the command of Thomas J. Jackson, who earned the nickname "Stonewall" for holding his ground. But it was the botched Union attacks, the summer heat, and Union artillerists' mistaking blue-clad Confederate attackers for friendly forces that were decisive.

Union losses approached 3,000 total casualties, while the Confederates suffered a loss of 2,000 killed, wounded, and missing. Spectators who had ridden out from Washington to watch what they thought would be the decisive battle of the war fled headlong in chaos.

The Union defeat proved humiliating, but nothing more. Although some Confederates later speculated that Beauregard and Johnston should have pursued the retreating Union forces, in truth they were disorganized by their triumph and unprepared to exploit it. If the battle put an end for the moment to hopes for a quick victory and raised Confederate morale, it caused Lincoln to reassess how he wanted to prosecute military operations. He laid out plans for new offensives, continued recruiting and outfitting his armies, and called for a new general with a record of previous success, George B. McClellan, to replace McDowell as commander of what would soon become known as the Army of the Potomac.

—BROOKS D. SIMPSON

BIBLIOGRAPHY

Davis, William C. *Battle at Bull Run: A History of the First Major Campaign of the Civil War.* 1977. Baton Rouge: Louisiana State University Press, 1981.

Detzer, David. *Donnybrook: The Battle of Bull Run, 1861.* New York: Harcourt, 2004.

Hennessy, John. *The First Battle of Manassas: An End to Innocence, July 18–21, 1861.* Lynchburg, Virginia: H.E. Howard, 1989.

Burial and Tomb, Lincoln's

After his death on Saturday, April 15, 1865, Lincoln lay in state in the East Room of the White House. On the morning of Tuesday, April 18, more than 25,000 mourners waited hours to pay final respects to the fallen president. The funeral, attended by 600 invited guests, was held the next day. After the guests departed, the funeral procession taking the coffin to the Capitol commenced. Mournful crowds lined the streets to pay their last respects.

That Friday, the funeral train left Washington for Springfield, Illinois. Aboard the funeral train were 300 mourners and two caskets. One casket was the president's, and the other was the casket of Willie Lincoln, Lincoln's son who had died at age eleven and who was now to be buried alongside his father. The train followed a 1,654-mile route, stopping along the way so that citizens could mourn their martyred president. The train arrived in Springfield on May 3. A funeral was held the next day at Oak Ridge Cemetery, the burial site that Mrs. Lincoln had requested.

Lincoln's remains were moved to a temporary vault that December, while a memorial tomb was constructed in Springfield by the National Lincoln Monument Association. In 1871 Lincoln and his three sons (Willie, Edward, and Tad, who had died earlier in the year) were moved into the partially built structure. The memorial tomb was completed in 1874, and Lincoln's remains were again buried, this time encased in marble in the center chamber.

In 1876 an attempt was made to steal Lincoln's body and hold it for ransom. The thieves were unsuccessful, but the attempt caused the National Lincoln Monument Association to move the corpse to a hidden, and safer, place within the tomb. At the death of Mrs. Lincoln in 1882, her remains were buried with those of her husband. Both were moved in 1887 to a more secure brick vault under the floor of the burial room.

In 1899 the state of Illinois, which had acquired the vault in 1895, began restoring the tomb. The five caskets of the Lincoln family were moved to a nearby underground vault until the construction was complete, and Lincoln's corpse was returned to the center vault it had formerly occupied.

At the request of Lincoln's only surviving son, Robert Todd Lincoln, the body was moved for the seventeenth time to its final resting place: a cement vault ten feet below the surface of the burial room.

With its marble walls and ceiling of gold leaf, the burial room is dominated by a centrally located, seven-ton block of marble marking the approximate location of the vault. On it are inscribed the dates of Lincoln's birth and death. It also contains the remains of Mrs. Lincoln, three of Lincoln's four sons, and a grandson. Nine flags surround the vault. Seven represent the homes of Lincoln and his family, and the remaining two are U.S. and presidential flags. On the wall above the U.S flag is inscribed, "Now he belongs to the ages."

—PAULA COCHRAN

BIBLIOGRAPHY

Donald, David Herbert. *Lincoln.* New York: Simon and Schuster, 1996.

_____. *Lincoln at Home: Two Glimpses of Abraham Lincoln's Domestic Life.* New York: Simon and Schuster, 1999.

Neely, Mark E., Jr., and Harold Holzer. *The Lincoln Family Album: Photographs from the Personal Collection of a Historic American Family.* New York: Doubleday, 1990.

Butler, Benjamin

Benjamin Franklin Butler (1818–1893) was a controversial politician, lawyer, and general who was both famous and infamous for his conduct during the Civil War, particularly his military governorship of New Orleans. An ambitious, quarrelsome man, Butler spent his life making enemies and generally besting them. A capable, if corrupt, administrator and masterly businessman, Butler was remarkably unsuccessful in all of his tactical field commands. The politically powerful Butler was alternately a valuable ally for President Abraham Lincoln and an unwelcome nuisance, who posed problems until he resigned his commission in 1864.

The son of Captain John Butler and Charlotte Ellison Butler, Benjamin graduated Waterville College (now Colby College) in Maine in 1838 and gained admission to the Massachusetts bar in 1840. Always interested in a good fight and particularly clever, Butler earned a reputation as an impressive courtroom performer and quickly found himself in demand. Butler married Sarah Hildreth in

1842, and the two had four children, three of whom survived. Butler was elected to the Massachusetts House of Representatives in 1853 and to the state senate in 1859; he was a delegate to the 1860 Democratic National Convention, where he cast more than fifty votes for Jefferson Davis during the contested proceedings. Butler opposed Stephen Douglas and supported Democrat John C. Breckinridge in the 1860 election.

When the Civil War began in April 1861 Butler was a brigadier general in the Massachusetts militia. He was assigned to keep the rail lines between Baltimore and Washington open. His performance there, successfully bringing troops to Washington through the hostile city of Baltimore, along with his political influence, led Lincoln to promote him to major general on May 13, 1861. Butler was assigned to Fortress Monroe, Virginia, where he promptly embarked on an unsuccessful assault on the Confederate position at Big Bethel, the first of many failures in the field.

While the Lincoln administration was groping for a position to take with regard to slaves in occupied territory, Butler, relying on his legal training, concluded that under the laws of war slaves who escaped to his lines were "contraband" of war and thus not subject to return to their masters. Republicans and the press immediately embraced the concept, but the Lincoln administration was more cautious and waited until August 6, two weeks after the Battle of Bull Run, to confirm the legality of Butler's order.

Butler later became an autocratic and allegedly corrupt military governor of New Orleans. Butler believed in making examples of lawbreakers to maintain order, but he was instrumental in arranging food and trade to feed the starving city. Believing that festering garbage contributed to rampant disease, he directed work crews to keeping the city clean. Other actions earned Butler greater notoriety, however, particularly the execution of William Mumford, a pro-Confederate New Orleans citizen who tore down an American flag in the occupied city. The action caused Confederate president Jefferson Davis to issue a presidential order authorizing the execution of Butler on sight. Also notorious was Butler's General Order No. 28, issued to stop local women from spitting on or otherwise insulting federal troops. The order declared that any woman doing so would be treated as a prostitute. It outraged the city, leading a resident to name him "Beast Butler." Local hostility contributed to the decision to remove Butler from New Orleans.

Butler's recall was also encouraged by a stream of complaints from abroad that reached the desk of secretary of state William H. Seward, as Butler constantly antagonized foreign consuls in New Orleans. On December 17, General Nathaniel P. Banks replaced Butler in New Orleans. Butler returned to Lowell, Massachusetts, with a great deal of money illicitly earned and several nicknames, including "Spoons," for what was said to be his habit of stealing silverware from local houses, and "Beast," the nickname that remained with him ever after. Many of Butler's policies in New Orleans, such as imposing loyalty oaths on the population or supporting the seating in Congress of representatives elected from federally controlled areas of Louisiana, prefigured Reconstruction; indeed, some historians argue that Reconstruction began with Butler in New Orleans. His decision to arm and organize the city's free black population also anticipated later Union policy.

An idle Butler was a political liability for Lincoln, however, given his penchant for stirring up trouble. In October 1863, Lincoln convinced Butler to return to Fortress Monroe and head the Department of Virginia and North Carolina. In May 1864, Butler proposed landing an army at Bermuda Hundred, on the James River between Richmond and Petersburg. From there, Butler proposed to attack Richmond. At Bermuda Hundred, however, Butler immediately began to dig into a defensive position. He not only failed to attack but was kept in check by a vastly inferior force under the command of Confederate General P.G.T. Beauregard. That debacle reinforced his reputation as a poor field commander and caused Butler irreparable political damage. In 1864 Butler's political star was still ascendant, and Lincoln at one point considered him as his vice presidential running mate. The failure at Bermuda Hundred scuttled any chance of Butler's appearing on Lincoln's ticket, and his subsequent, disastrous attack on Fort Fisher in North Carolina led to his recall. On November 30, 1864, Butler resigned his commission, ending his military career.

Butler joined the Radical Republicans at the end of the war and served in the U.S. House of Representatives from 1867 to 1875 and from 1877 to 1879. He was one of the managers of the impeachment of Andrew Johnson in 1868, sponsored the Civil Rights Act of 1871, and, working with Sen. Charles Sumner, proposed the Civil Rights Act of 1875. At the same time, however, Butler became associated with the corruption that marred Ulysses S. Grant's presidency, and he was frequently blamed for the failures of Reconstruction. Governor of Massachusetts from 1883 to 1884, Butler died in January 1893.

—ANTHONY SANTORO

BIBLIOGRAPHY

Butler, Benjamin F. *Autobiography and Personal Reminiscences of Major-General Benjamin F. Butler: Butler's Book.* 2 vols. Whitefish, Montana: Kessinger Publishing, 2006.

Dawson, Joseph G., III. *Army Generals and Reconstruction: Louisiana, 1862–1877.* Baton Rouge: Louisiana State University Press, 1982.

Hearn, Chester G. *When the Devil Came Down to Dixie: Ben Butler in New Orleans.* Baton Rouge: Louisiana State University Press, 1997.

Trefousse, Hans Louis. *Ben Butler: The South Called Him Beast.* New York: Twayne, 1957.

West, Richard. *Lincoln's Scapegoat General: A Life of Benjamin F. Butler.* Boston: Little, Brown, 1965.

Westwood, Howard C. "Benjamin Butler's Enlistment of Black Troops in New Orleans in 1862." *Journal of Louisiana History* 26 (Winter 1985): 5–22.

Cabinet, Lincoln's

Following his presidential election victory in November 1860, Abraham Lincoln immediately began assembling his cabinet. The nation was fragmenting, and Lincoln needed to construct an administration with the utmost ability, talent, and statesmanship to steer the republic back to unity.

Lincoln's presidential nomination had resulted from a coalition representing discordant political views from across the Northern states. In return for their support, Lincoln sought to award cabinet positions to the most able men from a cross section of those interests. That meant, Lincoln concluded, appointing his political opponents. As many of these men were strong in personality and opinion, Lincoln realized that he would have to sacrifice harmony in favor of the expertise and knowledge that each could bring to the table. Lincoln saw advantages to having those individuals working for him instead of against him. Still, his chosen political advisers would create political challenges for him.

Appointing William Henry Seward to a prestigious position was an obvious choice. Lincoln needed a secretary of state knowledgeable about foreign affairs, and Seward was. A former Whig governor and U.S. senator from New York, Seward gained national fame in the 1850s with his impassioned speeches against the slave power. Seward's presidential aspirations and qualifications were apparent, but he was perceived as too radical. The most promising prospect for president in 1860 had to accept a cabinet position that he did not really want, under a man he thought he should have defeated. His inclusion in the cabinet was significant; Seward's presence in the administration provided crucial respect and credibility both at home and abroad.

Lincoln tapped another 1860 presidential rival for secretary of the Treasury. A U.S. senator, then Ohio governor, Salmon P. Chase was also a famed antislavery champion and a free-soil Democrat before helping create the Ohio Republican Party. Pompous and urbane, Chase considered the victorious frontier rail-splitter beneath him. Chase's attitudes toward Lincoln would prove detrimental at times, but the secretary of the Treasury would be of vital importance to Lincoln. Chase would brilliantly keep the financial ship afloat during four years of war and would introduce to the country the first federal paper currency. He was also unwavering in his opposition to slavery and would provide Lincoln with important support in the cabinet when Lincoln first proposed the Emancipation Proclamation.

War had not yet broken out in early 1861, so the post of war secretary seemed relatively insignificant. In return for the support of the state's delegates at the 1860 Republican convention, Lincoln felt obligated to select a Pennsylvanian. He reluctantly chose Sen. Simon Cameron, but after only a year Cameron resigned under charges of corruption. In his place Lincoln gave the nod to renowned lawyer Edwin Stanton, attorney general briefly under President Buchanan. Not exactly friends, Stanton and Lincoln had been hired as team lawyers in a case in the early 1850s, and Stanton snubbed Lincoln throughout its duration. But Stanton was respected. Now he had an enormous task in helping the president organize and equip thousands of soldiers in the field. With necessary military orders constantly emanating from the secretary of war, Stanton's office would grow to be a major command center.

For attorney general, Lincoln selected another 1860 presidential rival—Missourian Edward Bates. From a loyal Border State, the conservative Bates would be essential to maintaining Union solidarity in the crucial borderland between slavery and freedom. Though their legal and constitutional interpretations sometimes differed, Lincoln occasionally used Bates as a sounding board for guidance in matters of the arrest and imprisonment of possible traitors and on emancipation. Another conservative, Border State addition was postmaster general Montgomery Blair, a politically well connected Marylander who also had political and family ties in Missouri and who had served as a legal counsel in 1857 for Dred Scott. Blair would help engineer a money order system and rapid mail delivery by railway.

For secretary of the navy, Gideon Welles, a former lawyer and journalist with naval experience, fit the role. A Connecticut Democrat before he became a Republican, Welles added a New England presence and helped balance the cabinet between former Whigs and former Democrats. Welles found the navy in shambles but surprisingly rebuilt it into a force that effectively blocked Southern ports and strangled the Southern economy. Rounding out his cabinet, Lincoln chose Caleb Smith as secretary of the interior. A lawyer and Indiana congressman, Smith was rewarded for his work in helping secure Lincoln's nomination for president in 1860. Smith was never very content in his position and passed many of his duties on to assistant interior secretary John Usher. Smith resigned in late 1862, and Usher was appointed to fill the post. The Interior Department in Lincoln's presidency would be important in paving the way for the transcontinental railroad and unveiling the Homestead Act.

Lincoln's first vice president was Hannibal Hamlin, of Maine. The extent of Hamlin's contribution to the administration was as a running mate to give the Republican ticket a New England balance. Hamlin had been a free-soil Democrat and thus also balanced Lincoln's Whig background. Hamlin was largely excluded from major cabinet decisions.

Lincoln's first and perhaps most difficult task would be to gain his cabinet's trust and respect, convincing his team to reconcile their differences and jealousy. It would not be easy. Seward and Chase each believed that he should be the one occupying the executive's chair, and consequently, for the first half of the term each distrusted the ambitions and intentions of the other. General consensus among the cabinet was that Chase consistently sought to upstage and embarrass the president and that Seward actually intended to run the government with Lincoln as a puppet president. Smith felt like an outcast. The more conservative and somewhat stuffy Welles clashed with both Seward and Chase. Stanton was often snobbish, brash, and humorless, which was offensive to many. The Border State cabinet members, Blair and Bates, who seemingly should have had much in common, distrusted each other intensely. The immediate crisis for the administration—the Confederate seizure of Fort Sumter in April 1861—demonstrated cabinet discord and revealed the members' contempt and animosity for the president and for one another. Then in 1862 several cabinet members, in a near-coup, signed a paper demanding that the president remove General McClellan. Lincoln squelched the discontent but shortly thereafter did in fact remove McClellan as head of the army.

Lincoln's qualities enabled him to corral his team. Seward fired off a scathing memo to Lincoln during the Fort Sumter crisis pompously declaring that the president had no policy. Instead of demanding Seward's resignation, Lincoln deftly handled the situation with him personally. Seward concluded that he had underestimated his chief and eventually became one of Lincoln's most intimate friends. Though Stanton was not an affable personality and found Lincoln's humor juvenile, Lincoln began to spend more time in the War Department and slowly penetrated Stanton's prickly exterior. Stanton, too, would grow to be a strong ally and friend to the president. Lincoln would develop a friendship with the socialite Blair clan as well. Though he did not have the social interaction with others in the cabinet that he did with Stanton and Seward, Lincoln showed respect and cordiality to all. Lincoln tried to stay above the feuds in this political family and knew the weaknesses of each of the members, cleverly working that knowledge to his advantage. When Chase and Seward once simultaneously offered to resign, Lincoln played the upper hand and for a while kept the two resignations in each pocket before rejecting both.

Ever cognizant of their strengths and service to the country in the crisis that the Union faced, Lincoln was willing to defend his cabinet against criticism from Congress, the newspapers, and from inside. The president waved off Chase's repeated, brazen efforts to publicly disparage him, even when it was evident that the secretary was undermining the administration. Lincoln defended Seward against claims that the secretary's influence and countenance excessively swayed him. Lincoln upheld Stanton's military decisions, though he was famously more lenient than his war secretary when it came to punishing soldiers who had been court marshaled. And Lincoln repeatedly rebuffed those in Congress who sought to replace Blair, Seward, and Chase. Most telling, when Simon Cameron was under fire early in the term for corruption, Lincoln stepped in and saved Cameron from further public humiliation—an act Cameron never forgot.

Despite deep differences, the cabinet solidified. When in 1862 Chase informed key senators that the cabinet was a dysfunctional mess and that Lincoln had run roughshod over any joint decision making, each cabinet secretary was given the opportunity to speak candidly about the divisiveness among them. One by one, each secretary testified to their general harmony and that together they had built a team. Even Chase reluctantly agreed. Assessing the team and the leader that guided them, Seward wrote in 1862 that executive force and vigor are rare qualities, and that the president was the best of them.

Late in 1864, Lincoln decided that he could no longer weather Chase's incorrigibility and accepted his resignation, only to nominate him as chief justice of the U.S. Supreme Court. Sen. William Fessenden of Maine served the rest of the first term, and then Treasury official Hugh McCulloch served for the one month of Lincoln's second term. Attorney General Bates resigned in 1864, and James Speed, of Kentucky, served for the remainder of Lincoln's presidency. Blair also resigned in late 1864, and Ohio governor William Dennison succeeded him. John Usher resigned after the first term, and Iowa senator James Harlan took over. Both Welles and Seward served the remainder of Lincoln's presidency and into Andrew Johnson's term.

See also *Bates, Edward; Blair, Montgomery; Cameron, Simon; Chase, Salmon Portland; Fessenden, William; Seward, William; Stanton, Edwin; Welles, Gideon*

—RON J. KELLER

BIBLIOGRAPHY

Brownstein, Elizabeth Smith. *Lincoln's Other White House.* Indianapolis: Wiley, 2005.

Carpenter, Francis. *The Inner Life of Abraham Lincoln: Six Months at the White House.* Lincoln: University of Nebraska Press, 1995.

Chase, Salmon P. *Inside Lincoln's Cabinet: The Civil War Diaries of Salmon P. Chase.* New York, London: Longmans, Green, 1954.

Goodwin, Doris Kearns. *Team of Rivals.* New York: Simon and Schuster, 2005.

Hendrick, Burton J. *Lincoln's War Cabinet.* Boston: Little, Brown, 1946.

Rothschild, Alonzo. *Lincoln, Master of Men: A Study in Character.* Boston: Houghton Mifflin, 1906.

Welles, Gideon. *Diary of Gideon Welles: Secretary of the Navy under Lincoln and Johnson.* Boston: Houghton Mifflin, 1911.

Cameron, Simon

Simon Cameron (1799–1889) was the most politically powerful man in mid-nineteenth-century Pennsylvania and set the course for politics in the state for half a century. Cameron was born on March 8, 1799, in Maytown, Lancaster

County, Pennsylvania, and when he was six the family moved to Sunbury. He was orphaned at the age of nine and left to fend for himself. He was apprenticed to the town's physician and later at the *Northumberland Gazette*. Cameron went on to serve as journeyman and editor of several newspapers in Pennsylvania and Washington, D.C., allowing him to mingle with the politicians of the day. These connections led to Cameron's first political appointment in 1822, when he was chosen to serve as Pennsylvania's state printer. Seven years later he was appointed adjutant general of the state militia.

Though known for his political pursuits, Simon Cameron was also a successful businessman. In the post–War of 1812, internal improvement boom, he began his rise to wealth and political power. In 1826, with no experience but sufficient capital, Cameron built a section of the Pennsylvania Canal along the Susquehanna River, and in 1831 he organized the construction of a canal from Lake Pontchartrain to the Mississippi River at New Orleans.

To help finance his endeavors Cameron started the Bank of Middletown and served as its cashier. With his own bank, he undertook railroad building, helping to create a rail system across the state. In 1834 James Buchanan became president of one of Cameron's railroads. Cameron later assisted Buchanan in obtaining a Senate seat. In 1838, at Buchanan's suggestion, President Martin Van Buren gave Cameron the responsibility of reimbursing the Winnebago Indians of the Wisconsin Territory for lands taken by the federal government. Cameron was accused of cheating the Indians, and although the charges were never proved, the scandal persisted throughout his life.

In 1845, having formerly declined to get into politics, Cameron reconsidered and was elected to the U.S. Senate, as a Democrat, to finish out the term of James Buchanan, who had resigned to join James K. Polk's cabinet as secretary of state. Cameron challenged Buchanan and other leading Pennsylvania Democrats when, in seeking the Senate seat, he rejected the party's support of free trade and low tariffs. Instead, Cameron proposed higher import duties to protect Pennsylvania industry against foreign competition. Confidently he challenged his party's choice before the state General Assembly (which elected senators during the nineteenth century). He was elected by a coalition of opposition Whigs and high-tariff Democrats. This stand cost him many of his friends in the Democratic Party, in particular President James K. Polk and future president James Buchanan.

In Congress Cameron supported the Mexican War as well as high tariffs. More famously, when he was interrupted by Sen. Henry Foote while making a speech, Cameron slugged the Mississippi senator, knocking him to the floor. As sectional animosities increased in the 1850s, Cameron had a certain cachet for defending Northern honor against Southern aggression. He was not elected to a full term in 1849 and left public office. In the fluid party system of the 1850s, Cameron was a Democrat in 1852 and a Know-Nothing in 1854. By this time he was openly opposed to the spread of slavery into the territories, which led him to the new Republican Party in 1856 and to a Senate seat in March 1857.

Cameron was now the darling of the iron and coal interests of Pennsylvania and was widely accused of gaining his Senate seat through corruption if not outright bribery. Despite this reputation, he quickly became a leader of the Republicans, vigorously opposing the proslavery Lecompton constitution that would have made Kansas a slave state.

In 1860 Cameron was a presidential candidate. He placed third behind Lincoln and Seward in the Republican convention balloting, and having been promised a post in the presidential cabinet by Lincoln's aides, endorsed Lincoln. After Lincoln was elected, he honored the promise and made Cameron secretary of war.

Lincoln found Cameron ignorant, selfish, obnoxious, and discourteous. He was also probably corrupt, supporting military contracts for substandard weapons and working with dishonest vendors. When a special committee was formed to investigate allegations of fraud in the War Department, Lincoln sought a way to fire Cameron gracefully. Hoping to rally support, Cameron responded by having his staff create a report for Congress in which he included comments showing his support of freeing and arming slaves to save the Union. This he promptly released to the press, without Lincoln's permission. Infuriated, Lincoln demanded recall of the report.

On January 11, 1862, Lincoln relieved Cameron of his current duties by letter and offered him a position as minister to Russia. When he learned that Cameron was devastated by the news, Lincoln allowed him to save face and resign. Cameron went to Russia just long enough to be introduced to the tsar, before returning home to Pennsylvania to run for the Senate. His 1863 bid failed, but he was successful in 1867.

Despite their problematic relationship, Cameron served as an honorary pallbearer at Lincoln's funeral. Cameron resigned his Senate seat in 1877, so that his son could take his place, and he died in 1889.

See also *Cabinet, Lincoln's; Corruption in the Federal Government*

—Paula Cochran

BIBLIOGRAPHY

Donald, David Herbert. *Lincoln.* New York: Simon and Schuster, 1996.

Goodwin, Doris Kearns. *Team of Rivals: The Political Genius of Abraham Lincoln.* New York: Simon and Schuster, 2006.

Harris, William C. *Lincoln's Rise to the Presidency.* Lawrence: University Press of Kansas, 2007.

Howe, Daniel Walker. *The Political Culture of American Whigs.* Chicago: University of Chicago Press, 1984.

Mearns, David. *The Lincoln Papers.* 2 vols. New York: Doubleday, 1948.

Miller, William Lee. *Lincoln's Virtues: An Ethical Biography.* New York: Random House, 2003.

Wilson, Douglas. *Honor's Voice: The Transformation of Abraham Lincoln.* New York: Vintage, 1999.

Campaign of 1856, Presidential

In 1856 the Republican Party fielded a presidential candidate for the first time, marking its meteoric rise in American politics. Although the party had won local and state elections throughout the North, including electing Salmon P. Chase governor of Ohio in 1855, in early 1856 it remained unorganized in many Northern states. In the first half of the year, Republicans worked assiduously at the state and local levels to fuse diverse groups. Former Whigs, anti-Nebraska Democrats, racial conservatives and abolitionists, immigrants, and nativists—all had to unite if the Republicans were to achieve victory in state and presidential elections. On February 22, 1856, Republican leaders met at Pittsburgh to lay plans for a national convention and to prepare to oppose the Democratic and American Parties in the November election.

On the same day, the American Party convened in Philadelphia. Although delegates from some Northern states bolted from the convention, those that remained named former president Millard Fillmore the party's candidate. Democrats, convening in Cincinnati June 2–5, nominated James Buchanan, a former U.S. senator from Pennsylvania, who had most recently served as ambassador to Great Britain. The Republicans would have preferred to face a Democratic candidate with a clear role in the passage of the Kansas-Nebraska Act; Buchanan was out of the country for the controversy. But it was Fillmore's candidacy that posed the greatest challenge for the new party, providing a political home for nativists as well as conservative Whigs uncomfortable with the radical antislavery elements of the new Republican Party.

The Republican Party's national convention met in Philadelphia June 17–19. Its first national platform proclaimed that the nation's founders held constitutional doctrines opposed to the expansion of slavery and that Congress had a duty to prohibit slavery's expansion into the territories. It called for the admission of Kansas under the free-state Topeka constitution, for federal aid for internal improvements, and the construction of a railroad to the Pacific. The platform remained vague on issues relating to immigrants and nativists, seeking to hold both groups within the party. Capping off months of maneuvering among Republican operatives, the convention passed over its known leaders in choosing its nominee. Ohio's Republican governor, Salmon P. Chase, an architect of the party who was associated with both antislavery politics and nativism, was seen as too radical and had little support in the East. New York senator William Seward had both antislavery credentials and nativist opposition that limited his appeal. Moreover, Seward supporters hesitated to run their leader in a three-way race in which he would have scant chance of victory. Many former Whigs, such as Abraham Lincoln, favored Supreme Court justice John McLean. An Ohioan, McLean was conservative, appealing to the voters

Lincoln believed were crucial to Republican Party success in Illinois. McLean, however, alienated Republican antislavery activists by his rulings that upheld the fugitive slave laws of 1793 and 1850. His flirtation with nativism also threatened German support for the party. Party operatives instead put forth John C. Frémont as the nominee. A former Democrat, the western explorer was attractive precisely because he lacked a significant political record and because his candidacy conveyed an image of youthful vigor that was appealing to the new party.

In Illinois, Abraham Lincoln played a central role in the formation of the Republican coalition, known as the Anti-Nebraska Party. In the wake of the Kansas-Nebraska Act of 1854, efforts to unite opposition groups failed in the state, owing to the persistence of the Whig Party, especially in the central and southern regions of the state; the strength of the American Party; issues of temperance; and the influence of Stephen A. Douglas and the Nebraska Democrats. Abolitionist Owen Lovejoy's unsuccessful efforts to unite anti-Nebraska elements underscored the need for more moderate leadership of a fusion movement. Indeed, by 1855 prohibition had been rejected by voters and nativism had devolved into anti-Catholicism, opening the possibility of attracting Protestant immigrants to the anti-Nebraska coalition.

Although Lincoln had been elected a delegate to the Pittsburgh convention, he remained in Illinois, focusing on organizing the state. On February 22, 1856, Lincoln attended a meeting of anti-Nebraska editors in Decatur, Illinois, and was instrumental in drafting a declaration of principles that sought to attract conservative Whigs while alienating neither foreign-born nor nativist voters. Those in attendance pledged their opposition to slavery's expansion into the territories, while maintaining that Congress did not have to admit new territories. The meeting upheld the legality of the Fugitive Slave Law, pledged not to interfere with slavery where it existed, and called for restoration of the Missouri Compromise. The group also organized a state meeting to be held at Bloomington on May 29 to organize Illinois's Anti-Nebraska Party. Sangamon County elected Lincoln a delegate, and although he was not nominated for state office at the convention, he gave the meeting's final speech. The newspaper the *Alton Weekly Courier* reported that in the speech Lincoln assailed the Slave Power and pledged himself to the new fusion party. Lincoln's work at the state level, as well as his growing national reputation, was apparent at the Philadelphia convention in June, where he was the runner-up for the party's vice presidential nomination.

Although Lincoln believed that Buchanan would win the three-way race for president and carry Illinois, he campaigned throughout Illinois and traveled to a rally in Michigan, giving over fifty speeches in support of Republican candidates. In his speeches he spoke against slavery's expansion but did not use the violence in Kansas or the caning of Charles Sumner to assail the Democratic Party. Lincoln was more concerned with appealing to conservative voters in his own state. As Lincoln explained in his correspondence, the election of gubernatorial candidate William Henry Bissell seemed probable because both Republicans and the American Party supported him, but Frémont was unlikely to carry Illinois because Fillmore attracted nativists and conservative Whigs. Lincoln sent out lithographed letters, dated and signed, to Fillmore supporters, calling on them to support Frémont against Buchanan and argued that Fillmore's proclaimed neutrality on slavery's expansion made him unfit to govern.

Lincoln's belief that conservative Whigs in southern Illinois would support Fillmore was borne out on election day, November 4, 1856. Bissell was elected governor, but the Democratic Party carried Illinois in the presidential race, with Buchanan taking just over 44 percent of the votes cast. Frémont polled just over 40 percent, with his greatest strength coming from the northern districts of the state. As Lincoln predicted, Fillmore's candidacy made the difference, as the American Party candidate garnered almost 16 percent of the vote, giving the Democrats a majority in the southern districts. Buchanan carried Illinois by more than nine thousand votes, earning a plurality but not a majority. Lincoln interpreted the results with optimism and continued his efforts to strengthen the Republican Party in Illinois and eventually throughout the North.

See also *Buchanan, James*

—CHRISTINE DEE

BIBLIOGRAPHY

Anbinder, Tyler G. *Nativism and Slavery: The Northern Know-Nothings and the Politics of the 1850s.* New York: Oxford University Press, 1992.

Basler, Roy P., ed. *The Collected Works of Abraham Lincoln.* Vol. 2. New Brunswick, N.J.: Rutgers University Press, 1953.

Donald, David Herbert. *Lincoln.* New York: Simon and Schuster, 1995.

Gienapp, William E. *The Origins of the Republican Party, 1852–1856.* New York: Oxford University Press, 1987.

Holt, Michael F. *The Rise and Fall of the American Whig Party: Jacksonian Politics and the Onset of the Civil War.* New York: Oxford University Press, 1999.

Campaign of 1858, Lincoln's Senatorial

Abraham Lincoln's 1858 campaign for the U.S. Senate is perhaps the most famous senatorial campaign in American history. In 1855 Lincoln ran unsuccessfully for the Senate, ultimately bested by former Democrat Lyman Trumbull, who held the balance of power among the various anti-Nebraska factions in the Illinois General Assembly. In 1858 the Republican Party had become firmly established in the state, and Lincoln was widely regarded by many Republican leaders as a logical choice for the Senate. In a somewhat unorthodox move, the party nominated him at its June 16, 1858, convention in Springfield. Because senators were not popularly elected, but chosen instead by both houses of the state legislatures, the decision to nominate a senatorial candidate was unusual. No Illinois voter would cast a ballot directly for Lincoln or his Democratic opponent, Stephen A. Douglas; however, in voting for state legislators voters knew that they were choosing candidates pledged to support one or the other.

Douglas, Illinois's powerful senior senator, was a two-term veteran and among the most prominent Democrats in the country. He was the author of the Kansas-Nebraska Act of 1854 and a perennial presidential candidate. The election was complicated by the course Douglas had taken in the fight over the Lecompton constitution, the controversial document that proslavery forces in the territory of Kansas hoped to use to bring Kansas into the Union as a slave state. With the full backing of the administration of President James Buchanan, support of the Lecompton constitution was made a test of Democratic Party loyalty in the winter of 1857–1858. Because Douglas believed that supporting Lecompton compromised the principle of popular sovereignty, whereby the residents of a territory decided whether that territory would legalize slavery, he led the fight against it. Douglas's break with the Buchanan administration would have important ramifications for his bid for reelection in 1858. In an effort to defeat Douglas, key administration allies would organize an opposition to him within the Illinois Democratic Party. Known as the "National Democrats" or "Danites," these supporters of Buchanan would nominate their own candidate, Sidney Breese, in an effort to disrupt Douglas's reelection effort. Throughout the fall election campaign there were frequent rumors of cooperation between prominent Republicans and National Democrats.

Douglas's course on the Lecompton constitution also complicated Lincoln's campaign because a number of eastern Republicans, most prominently *New York Tribune* editor Horace Greeley, became enthusiastic about Douglas's defection on the Lecompton issue, believing it might be possible to induce him to defect to the Republican Party. Greeley and other party leaders advised Illinois Republicans to forgo a candidate for the Senate and unite behind Douglas. Lincoln and Illinois party leaders largely ignored such advice. Illinois Republican leaders were wary of the enormously popular "Little Giant," as he was known, and had battled Douglas for nearly two decades. They believed that Douglas was vulnerable.

One issue dominated the entire campaign, namely, the status of slavery in the territories. Beginning with his speech accepting his nomination at Springfield, known as the "House Divided" speech, Lincoln set the tone for his campaign against Douglas. The nation, he said, could not indefinitely exist both slave and free. Lincoln argued that all the prominent members of the Democratic Party (Douglas, Presidents Pierce and Buchanan, and Chief Justice Roger Taney) had acted in concert in recent events—the Kansas-Nebraska Act, the *Dred Scott* decision (1857), the fight over Kansas—with the principal purpose of making slavery a national institution. Responding to Lincoln on July 9, from the balcony of the Tremont House in Chicago, Douglas advanced several arguments that he would use throughout the campaign. Slavery, he maintained, was a local decision that was best left to the residents of a territory through the mechanism of popular sovereignty. Labeling Lincoln a consolidationist who could not allow for diversity of customs at the local level, Douglas maintained that it was perfectly acceptable and possible that the nation could continue half-slave and half-free. Local control, for Douglas, was paramount. Decrying his opponent as a "black Republican," Douglas charged that Lincoln and the Republicans were a party of black equality, whereas the founders had intended a republic that was organized for the benefit of white Europeans only.

As the campaign moved into the fall, both candidates would log nearly 10,000 miles on railroads, conventional roads, and rivers. To maximize exposure, Lincoln followed Douglas from county to county and town to town, listening to the senior senator's speeches and then responding later in the day or the next day at his own campaign rallies. To take advantage of Douglas's immense popularity, Lincoln finally challenged him to a series of debates. Although it was risky for the more popular Douglas, the "Little Giant" finally relented, lest he be accused of cowardice. At the same time, Douglas would set the rules. Eventually the candidates agreed to a series of joint appearances in each congressional district (the candidates' respective speeches in Springfield and Chicago exempted those districts). The format would be an hour opening, followed by an hour and one-half rebuttal, concluding with a thirty-minute rejoinder. Douglas would make four openings and Lincoln three. The sites were Ottawa (August 21), Freeport (August 27), Jonesboro (September 15), Charleston (September 18), Galesburg (October 7), Quincy (October 13), and Alton (October 15). Political oratory was a popular form of entertainment in the nineteenth century, and the debates drew wide attendance in many Illinois towns, attracting numerous residents from surrounding counties. Attendance varied from a scant 2,000 in Jonesboro to an estimated 10,000 to 25,000 at Galesburg.

The debates did not start favorably for Lincoln. At Ottawa, in his booming baritone, Douglas opened aggressively, attacking Lincoln and the Republican Party for its connection to abolitionism. He posed a series of questions to Lincoln: Did Lincoln favor the repeal of the Fugitive Slave Act? Would he allow new slave states into the Union? Would he forbid slavery in all national territories? Although the Republican Party had articulated opinions on many of the issues, Lincoln appeared timid and cautious, failing to answer Douglas's questions directly. At Freeport, in northern Illinois, after Lincoln had been urged by party leaders to become more aggressive, he recovered some momentum. He asked Douglas several pointed questions designed to force him onto the defensive and put him at odds with Southern Democrats. In light of the Supreme Court's recent *Dred Scott* decision, Lincoln asked Douglas whether the people of a territory could prohibit slavery in any legal way prior to statehood. Although Douglas had addressed this issue on several previous occasions, he reaffirmed his position in what became known as the "Freeport doctrine," arguing that the people of a territory could lawfully exclude slavery by failing to adopt positive laws to protect the institution.

A few weeks later, at Jonesboro, Lincoln was again cautious. When Douglas predictably attacked him and the Republican Party as advocates of racial equality, Lincoln avoided the issue, knowing that he was already unpopular in the southern portion of Illinois. At Charleston, in east-central Illinois, Lincoln again downplayed racial radicalism, telling the audience that he had never endorsed the political or social equality of African Americans. Perhaps the lowest point of the debates for Lincoln, the Republican candidate spent the bulk of his time providing a tedious account of behind-the-scenes Senate proceedings that supposedly demonstrated that Douglas, despite his public opposition to the Lecompton constitution, had favored an earlier arrangement that would have denied the free settlers of Kansas a choice on the slavery issue. Arcane and cryptic, Lincoln's speech could not have impressed the residents of Coles County.

At Galesburg, Quincy, and Alton, many historians maintain, Lincoln became more aggressive and articulate, framing the issue of slavery's expansion in moral terms and arguing that slavery was inconsistent with the Declaration of Independence. At Galesburg, Lincoln challenged Douglas's oft-repeated assertion that African Americans were never included under the Declaration of Independence and said that Douglas could not show that the Founding Fathers meant to exclude African Americans. At Alton, Douglas was clearly weary from the long and arduous campaign. Lincoln, however, seemed to be gaining his stride. Making use of the economic argument that the territories needed to remain open for free, white labor, Lincoln contended that slavery's expansion must also be stopped for moral reasons. He denounced Douglas for his moral neutrality on slavery, particularly Douglas's repeated statement that he did not care whether slavery was voted up or down. Lincoln maintained that the real debate on slavery was a matter of right or wrong. The Republican Party, he said, believed that slavery was wrong, whereas the Democrats occupied the morally ambiguous ground that saw nothing inherently wrong with it. While Lincoln would not challenge the institution where it already existed, its fundamental unfairness required that slavery's growth be curtailed.

In 1858 Illinois consisted of two distinct cultural and political regions. Southern Illinois was settled primarily by Border State migrants—conservative, Democratic, and fervently antiblack. Northern Illinois was populated by New England migrants, Protestant in religion, primarily antislavery, and overwhelmingly committed to the Republican Party. The central portion of the state was a mixture of the two groups, and whoever carried the central counties would likely have enough votes in the General Assembly to win the election. When Illinois voters went to the polls on November 2, 1858, they favored Republican candidates by a narrow margin, roughly 50 percent to 48 percent. The defection of the National Democrats peeled off just enough votes to allow the Republicans to win the popular vote. Predictably, Democrats carried the southern counties and Republicans the northern ones. But because the legislative apportionment of Illinois was based on the 1850 Census, which gave more representation to southern Illinois, the Democrats controlled the General Assembly by a 54–46 margin. Douglas would be reelected to a third term in early January 1859.

An important element in Lincoln's defeat was his failure to carry a number of counties in central Illinois. His previous connection to the Whig Party might have been expected to help him there, but the defection of several key former Whigs may have been damaging. One who deserted Lincoln was his former law partner John Todd Stuart. Another was Kentucky senator John J. Crittenden, a prominent national figure whom Lincoln had counted on for support. Yet another was Lincoln's friend Judge T. Lyle Dickey, from Ottawa, who now considered Lincoln and the Republican Party too radical.

Although Lincoln's defeat was a bitter pill, the Illinois Republican rose in prominence through a senatorial campaign that drew national attention. It contributed to Lincoln's reputation and allowed him to gain the stature to become a viable presidential candidate in 1860.

See also *Douglas, Stephen A.; Lincoln-Douglas Debates of 1858*

—BRUCE TAP

BIBLIOGRAPHY

Carwardine, Richard. *Lincoln: A Life of Purpose and Power.* New York: Vintage, 2007.

Donald, David Herbert. *Lincoln.* New York: Simon and Schuster, 1995.

Guelzo, Allen C. *Lincoln and Douglas: The Debates That Defined America.* New York: Simon and Schuster, 2008.

Johannsen, Robert W. *Stephen A. Douglas.* New York: Oxford University Press, 1973.

———, ed. *The Lincoln-Douglas Debates.* New York: Oxford University Press, 2008.

Campaign of 1860, Presidential

The election of 1860 formally began with the Democratic national convention at Charleston, South Carolina, in April and concluded with Abraham Lincoln's victory on November 6, 1860. The campaign was influenced by the tumultuous sectionalism of the preceding decade. Violence stemming from the Kansas-Nebraska Act, the Republicans' strong showing in their first presidential

An 1860 cartoon indicating Republican success shows John Bell warning Stephen Douglas of Abraham Lincoln's approach, while James Buchanan tries unsuccessfully to help John C. Breckinridge into the White House.

Source: The Granger Collection, New York

campaign in 1856, controversy over the *Dred Scott* ruling, public response to John Brown's raid, and the contest for the speakership in the House of Representatives all fueled sectionalism. In the years leading up to the 1860 election, aspiring politicians sought to advance their national profiles and strengthen their support among party operatives and voters. At issue was the status of slavery within the nation—whether it should be allowed in the federal territories and whether the federal government was bound to protect slave owners' property rights. The 1860 campaign encompassed four candidates and employed a vast array of communications that included newspapers, campaign speeches, published biographies, political cartoons, songs, and pageantry. The results were astounding. More than 81 percent of eligible voters cast ballots—a rate of participation surpassed only once in U.S. history, in the election of 1876. Americans correctly understood that the campaign would determine the fate of the nation.

Illinois Democratic senator Stephen A. Douglas was the recognized front-runner for his party's presidential nomination. He was hamstrung, however, by his commitment to the doctrine of popular sovereignty, which was opposed within his party by fire-eating Southern radicals and by supporters of the James Buchanan administration. In an essay published in *Harper's* magazine in September 1859, Douglas attempted to carve out support among moderates in the Democratic and Republican ranks. He presented the doctrine of popular sovereignty as a middle ground between Southerners' demands for a federal slave code and Republicans' opposition to slavery's expansion. Douglas's opponents worked against his nomination. President James Buchanan had asserted, in the wake of the *Dred Scott* ruling, that the federal government was bound to protect slaveholders' property. Buchanan's vice president, John Breckinridge of Kentucky, had stated his support for a federal slave code in 1860, and Sen. Jefferson Davis of Mississippi made a resolution to the same effect in early 1860. A faction of Northern Democrats benefited from political patronage under the Buchanan administration, and they were willing to assent to slavery's expansion. These Democrats resented Douglas's power and blurred sectional divisions by allying themselves with states' rights Southerners.

The Republican nomination was unsettled, as well, in the spring of 1860. The contenders included New York senator William Seward, former Ohio governor Salmon P. Chase, and Missouri politician Edward Bates. A significant conservative movement within the party favored the aged Supreme Court justice John McLean of Ohio. Seward sought to move away from critics' claims that he was radical and favored abolition. In his speech against the Fugitive Slave Law of 1850 he had argued that there was a "higher law than the Constitution." His reputation as a radical was enhanced in his "Irrepressible Conflict" speech of 1858, in which he stated that slavery and free labor were at odds and that the nation would eventually become all one or all the other. In February 1860, in an effort to quell the fears of conservatives in his party, Seward made a speech on the Senate floor in which he softened his earlier rhetoric, emphasizing the ties that bound both sections of the country together and the right of states to control slavery where it already existed. Salmon P. Chase had support within his home state of Ohio but did not have its delegates' unanimous backing. Moreover, he lacked his opponents' deft campaign management and grass-roots support. Bates garnered support from nativists and conservatives in the party, but moderate and radical Republicans questioned his commitment to halting slavery's expansion. When Chase did state his positions more clearly, he managed to alienate his conservative base by disavowing the *Dred Scott* decision.

Abraham Lincoln maneuvered skillfully through Republican Party politics in the months before the Chicago convention. He had raised his national profile following the Lincoln-Douglas debates of 1858 and campaigned for Republican candidates in midwestern state elections in 1859. Lincoln compiled his debates with Douglas along with campaign speeches for publication and aided a Pennsylvania newspaper editor in writing a brief biographical account. In February 1860 Lincoln made perhaps the most important speech of his political career at the Cooper Union in New York City. His speech impressed the New York audience. Before the speech many in the East considered him a hayseed from the far western prairies; after it they realized that he was a serious and significant politician.

The speech was widely circulated in the national press and presented Republicans as a national party of moderation. Lincoln then embarked on a speaking tour of the New England states that further enhanced his national reputation. Returning to Illinois, Lincoln focused his attention on uniting the factions within the state party organization. Lincoln knew his political ambitions required the unified support of the Illinois Republican Party, and he worked to bring together radical Republicans in the northern part of the state and conservatives in the southern part. In early May, a week before the Republican national convention was scheduled to begin, Illinois Republicans voted to cast their convention support in whole for Lincoln.

The Republicans' convention of 1860 stood in stark contrast to the chaos of the Democrats' convention. In April at Charleston, the Democrats had been unable to come together on a party platform. Supporters of Douglas championed popular sovereignty, while Southern radicals demanded a federal slave code protecting slavery in the territories. When eight Southern delegations left the convention, the remaining delegates were unable to nominate Douglas, and the party scheduled another convention for Baltimore on June 18.

In the interim, the Republicans came together in Chicago and rallied around a platform intended to broaden the party's appeal and knit together former Whigs, anti-Nebraska Democrats, Know-Nothings, naturalized immigrants, and political abolitionists. The party opposed slavery's expansion and called for a protective tariff to benefit industry and a homestead act to promote access to western lands. The Republicans also supported federal aid for internal improvements, including a transcontinental railroad, and equal rights for naturalized citizens. When the convention turned to nominating a presidential candidate, the strategic importance of the conservatives became paramount. Republicans recognized from the election of 1856 that they had to carry the lower Northern states and the voters who remained conservative and unwilling to interfere with slavery within the states. Conservatives and moderates grew stronger in their opposition to Seward, and Lincoln became, as he had hoped, the second choice of many. Over the course of two ballots, Lincoln secured delegates from numerous Northern states, including Indiana, Pennsylvania, and Ohio. On the third ballot, he surpassed Seward and became the Republican nominee.

Democrats reconvened in Baltimore in June and were again unable to unite on a candidate. Douglas supporters from the South presented rival delegations. The delegations that had bolted at Charleston planned to unite with Upper South delegates and demand a slave code in the platform. When anti-Douglas delegates again bolted from the convention, they convened separately and nominated Vice President John C. Breckinridge on a platform that supported a federal slave code. The remaining Democratic delegates then nominated Douglas, on a platform that pledged to support the Supreme Court's determination on territories' ability to pass legislation on slavery and that opposed personal liberty laws thwarting the Fugitive Slave Law. Both Douglas and Breckinridge ran for president as Democrats.

Former Whigs and Know-Nothings who were unwilling to join with either the Republicans or Democrats formed a new party, the Constitutional Union Party. They nominated John Bell of Tennessee and Edward Everett of Massachusetts to run on a platform that supported the Union and the Constitution, in an effort to return to a political order uncomplicated by the issue of slavery's expansion. With four candidates, the election of 1860 was impassioned, but most observers believed that the split in Democratic ranks guaranteed Lincoln's election in November.

Republicans took nothing for granted. They organized clubs of young Republicans, known as "Wide-Awakes," which held parades throughout the Northern states. Merchants sold campaign memorabilia that capitalized on Lincoln's reputation as a "rail-splitter." Photographers and painters scrambled to distribute images of Lincoln throughout the North. Campaign biographers rushed accounts of Lincoln's life into print. Lincoln provided his own account to an editor of a Chicago newspaper, and William Dean Howells wrote a biography as well. Although Lincoln did not take a public role in the campaign, he adroitly managed the flow of information from Springfield, assuring Pennsylvanians that he favored the tariff and writing private letters to combat rumors about his views on topics such as religion and immigration. He also benefited from the stump speeches of his supporters, including former rivals William Seward and Salmon Chase. It was a campaign strategy designed to avoid mistakes.

In response, Democrats in the North used the press to caricature Lincoln as illiterate, uneducated, ape-like, and unfit for the presidency. Rumors circulated that he was an atheist, an abolitionist, and a nativist. Douglas broke with tradition and embarked on a cross-country campaign tour that took him from New England to the Southern states. From train platforms and hotel balconies he made speeches that championed popular sovereignty, railed against radicals of both parties, and positioned himself as the Democrat who could lead the party to victory in 1864, if not in 1860. Following state election results in October, in which Republicans carried Pennsylvania, Ohio, and Indiana, Douglas was again campaigning in the South, where he hoped to solidify his position at the head of a national Democratic Party. Ultimately Douglas failed, as the campaign in the Southern states was fought primarily between Breckinridge and Bell, reflecting the depth of sectional feeling and Southerners' distrust of Douglas.

On election day, November 6, Republicans' success in capturing Northern voter support was complete. The careful selection of a candidate with broad appeal to all factions, the adroit management of Lincoln's image in the media, the successful use of campaign proxies to speak on his behalf, the successful grass-roots organizing all came together to secure the majority for Lincoln. It was the electoral votes of the most populous states—New York, Pennsylvania, Ohio, Illinois, and Indiana—that allowed an upstart, sectional political party to elect a president.

See also *Bell, John; Breckinridge, John Cabell; Constitutional Union Party*

—CHRISTINE DEE

BIBLIOGRAPHY

Basler, Roy P., ed. *The Collected Works of Abraham Lincoln.* Vol. 2. New Brunswick, N.J.: Rutgers University Press, 1953.

Carwardine, Richard. *Lincoln: A Life of Purpose.* Harlow, England: Pearson Longman, 2003.

Donald, David Herbert. *Lincoln.* New York: Simon and Schuster, 1995.

Foner, Eric. *Free Soil, Free Labor, Free Men: The Ideology of the Republican Party before the Civil War.* New York: Oxford University Press, 1995.

Gienapp, William E. *Abraham Lincoln and Civil War America.* New York: Oxford, 2002.

Goodwin, Doris Kearns. *Team of Rivals.* New York: Simon and Schuster, 2005.

Hesseltine, William B., ed. *Three against Lincoln: Murat Halstead Reports the Caucuses of 1860.* Baton Rouge: Louisiana State University Press, 1960.

Johannsen, Robert W. *Stephen A. Douglas.* New York: Oxford University Press, 1973.

Nevins, Allan. *The Emergence of Lincoln: Prologue to Civil War, 1859–1861.* New York: Scribner's, 1950.

Campaign of 1864, Presidential

After nearly four years of war and unprecedented carnage, at issue in the election of 1864 was not merely Abraham Lincoln's political career, but the fate of the nation. Lincoln's Democratic opponent, former general George McClellan, had campaigned in favor of a negotiated peace with the South. That would have meant an end to the Union as it existed before the war and an end to the possibility that slavery would be abolished in the South. Perhaps in no other election in American history were the stakes so high. Although Lincoln feared he might lose, he did not. In the process he demonstrated that, contrary to the impressions of his opponents and many in his own party, he was one of the finest politicians of his time. He succeeded in ensuring his own reelection and his party's control over the government and demonstrated that most of his party's differences involved personalities and tactics rather than ideological disputes.

Before Lincoln's reelection, no president since Andrew Jackson had won a second term. By early 1864 Lincoln had taken several steps toward his reelection. Late in 1863, he wrote several speeches and letters—most notably the Gettysburg Address and a letter to a rally in Springfield, Illinois—and an annual message that managed to please radicals and conservatives alike. He and Mary Todd Lincoln expanded the White House social calendar in an effort to woo supporters. Early in 1864, his appointment of Ulysses S. Grant as general in chief won plaudits, inspired confidence, and reduced pressure for immediate victories while Grant mapped out his plans. Meanwhile, Lincoln's most loyal cabinet members—secretary of state William Henry Seward of New York, postmaster general Montgomery Blair of Maryland, and secretary of the navy Gideon Welles of Connecticut—worked in their states and with their friends to build support for him. So did Lincoln's friends elsewhere, including Pennsylvania's Simon Cameron, whose departure from the War Department Lincoln had eased, and the young moderate William Chandler, who engineered an early endorsement in New Hampshire.

An 1864 political cartoon shows President Abraham Lincoln viewing his Democratic Party opponent, General George B. McClellan, as a rival of little stature. It plays on Lincoln's celebrated reputation for joking.
Source: The Granger Collection, New York

Some Republicans, however, wanted to displace Lincoln, for personal advancement, because of the military struggles of the war, or because of what they perceived as Lincoln's slow progress toward emancipation and black equality. These Republican opponents of Lincoln were mystified by his early success in moving toward renomination: he was outmaneuvering them, and the party rank and file seemed devoted to him.

Lincoln overcame challenges that included public displeasure with the war's seemingly slow military progress, as no major victories occurred for much of the summer of 1864, as well as displeasure among some party members with Lincoln's political moderation. Balancing radicals and conservatives, he often vexed both, but more often the radicals, whose strong antislavery beliefs had kept them on the political periphery before the war and who often found it hard to adapt and compromise once they were in power.

Another challenge was that Lincoln led not just Republicans but the Union Party, a hybrid party created to attract Democrats who supported the war. This enterprise was complicated by Democratic hostility to emancipation, the suspension of *habeas corpus* in the Border States, and the draft. It also disaffected some of Lincoln's fellow Republicans. They considered turning from him to one of two generals who had been prewar Democrats: Grant, who seemed apolitical, or Benjamin Butler of Massachusetts, who had shifted from supporting Southern

Democrats to radicalism. Another general, radical Republican John Frémont, had been the first Republican nominee in 1856 and had personal reasons to oppose Lincoln, who had twice removed him from command and then removed him.

The most formidable challenge came from within Lincoln's cabinet: secretary of the Treasury Salmon Chase. A lifelong abolitionist, Chase deemed Lincoln slow and conservative. The humorless Chase was never comfortable with Lincoln's manners, style, lack of piety, and storytelling. Nakedly ambitious and denying it all the while, Chase never appreciated Lincoln's subtle management of people (including himself) and government. He demanded a more activist presidency and curried favor with anyone who might help his presidential prospects, offending almost as many as he attracted. Early in 1864 Chase's friends and allies sent out two circulars, one under the congressional frank of Sen. Samuel Pomeroy of Kansas, the other through Chase's fellow Ohioans Sen. John Sherman and Rep. James Ashley. The pamphlets attacked Lincoln, declaring his reelection impossible. When the embarrassed Treasury secretary offered his resignation, Lincoln declined to accept it. Shortly thereafter, early in March, after the National Union Party committee overwhelmingly endorsed Lincoln's reelection, Chase announced his withdrawal from the race. By then Lincoln seemed to have the nomination in hand. He felt secure enough that when Chase, trying to back him into a corner, offered his resignation over a patronage dispute, Lincoln shocked him by accepting it.

Although some radicals still counseled delaying the convention because five months remained before the election, the National Union meeting that June proved to be a coronation. The party chair, *New York Times* editor Henry Raymond, was a Seward ally, and presiding officer William Dennison soon joined the cabinet. At Lincoln's urging, the convention endorsed a constitutional amendment banning slavery. In keeping with Lincoln's efforts to build Union Party support among Democrats and in border slave states, the convention chose as his running mate Andrew Johnson, the Tennessee Democrat who had refused to secede with his state and served as military governor and U.S. senator. How much of a role Lincoln played in his selection remains uncertain, but this much is obvious: the leaders of what had been the Northern, antislavery Republican Party chose a slave-owning Southern Democrat. The Union Party thought Republican but acted more broadly. Even naming it a "Union" Party was intended to make support for Lincoln less partisan and, in effect, to make the election about preserving the Union rather than supporting Lincoln or the Republican agenda.

Lincoln's reelection was likely only in hindsight. In Virginia, Grant gradually wore down Robert E. Lee's army, but he seemed to be banging his head against a gray wall. Sherman was moving across the South, but his stunning success was not yet clear to most Northerners. The Democrats nominated George McClellan, confronting Lincoln with a handsome young general whose soldiers professed to love him. He offered peace and an end to the carnage. But as the new name for Lincoln's party made clear, McClellan offered it at the cost of preserving the Union. For his part, in August a dejected Lincoln wrote what became known as the "blind memorandum," which he required his cabinet to sign sight unseen.

Lincoln wrote that with his defeat probable, and his opponent having promised peace with the South, the administration would do its best to save the Union before the next president took office.

Lincoln also came under radical fire. Upset with his opposition to their reconstruction plan, Sen. Benjamin Wade of Ohio and Rep. Henry Winter Davis of Maryland issued a manifesto blistering Lincoln; while their intemperate language and timing cost them support, their actions showed that Lincoln could hardly take radical support for granted. Late in the summer, three radical Republican editors—Greeley, Parke Godwin of the *New York Evening Post,* and Theodore Tilton of the *Independent*—asked state party leaders whether Lincoln should be replaced atop the ticket, and while the responses said no one could do better, the affair betrayed the lack of enthusiasm for Lincoln. A fringe group of radicals put forth Frémont as an alternative candidate, and if he had drawn off Republican support, Lincoln could have been in trouble.

Although Lincoln began to think that he might eke out a victory, calculating that he held a razor-thin lead over McClellan in the Electoral College, he actually was better positioned than he realized. Lincoln had told his secretary that the divided Democrats would nominate either a war candidate on a peace platform or a peace candidate on a war platform. McClellan was the former, with peace Democrat George Pendleton of Ohio as his running mate, and their platform declared the war in which McClellan had fought a failure. As September began, Sherman announced the capture of Atlanta and Admiral David Farragut took Mobile, giving Lincoln the major military victories he needed to puncture the opposition's balloon inside and outside of the Union Party.

Managing a great deal of the campaign behind the scenes, Lincoln also demonstrated his political canniness. To counter the Frémont threat, bilious radical Sen. Zachariah Chandler of Michigan brokered a deal: he helped induce Frémont to fold his insurgent challenge, and Montgomery Blair, whom the radicals despised for his blunt conservatism, loyally resigned from the cabinet. Chase had sulked since resigning, but Chief Justice Roger Taney's death in October gave Lincoln an opportunity. Chase wanted Taney's position and Lincoln wanted to give it to him; when the president made clear to the radical's friends that his support would aid his cause, Chase promptly began stumping for the Union Party ticket.

The result was a strong majority for Lincoln that November. He defeated McClellan in the Electoral College, 212 to 21. The Democrat carried only Delaware, his home state of New Jersey, and Kentucky, where Lincoln was born. Lincoln easily won the popular vote, 55 percent (2,218,388) to 45 percent (1,812,807). Lincoln gained strong support from farmers, skilled urban workers, and, to the surprise of those who expected the former general to retain his men's loyalty, soldiers. But Democrats fought a strong campaign and could expect to regain Southern support when the Confederate states returned to the Union.

The election proved several points. Though often criticized within the party, Lincoln's steely determination and homey approach resonated with the public and the soldiers he sent to fight. The Union Party remained a reasonable facsimile of the Republican Party and gained support beyond those who voted Republican in

1860, but the Democratic Party remained viable. The country supported its platform, including abolition of slavery—a major advance from four years before, when Republicans had sought only to stop slavery's spread. Even during civil war, the nation could conduct an election without undue problems—and that war would be fought to the bitter end. Of that, both North and South could be sure.

See also *McClellan, George B.*

—MICHAEL GREEN

BIBLIOGRAPHY

Donald, David Herbert. *Lincoln.* New York: Simon and Schuster, 1995.

Green, Michael S. *Freedom, Union, and Power: Lincoln and His Party during the Civil War.* New York: Fordham University Press, 2004.

Hyman, Harold M. "Election of 1864." In *History of American Presidential Elections, 1789–1868,* edited by Arthur M. Schlesinger Jr. and Fred L. Israel, 1155–1244. New York: Chelsea House, 1971.

Long, David E. *The Jewel of Liberty: Abraham Lincoln's Re-election and the End of Slavery.* Mechanicsburg, Pa.: Stackpole Books, 1994.

Waugh, John C. *Reelecting Lincoln: The Battle for the 1864 Presidency.* New York: Crown, 1997.

Cass, Lewis

Lewis Cass (1782–1866), a prominent Democratic politician from Michigan and the "father of popular sovereignty," lost the presidency to Zachary Taylor in the election of 1848. He was born at Exeter, New Hampshire, to Jonathan and Mary Gilman Cass; educated at Phillips Exeter Academy; and trained as a lawyer. As a young man Cass moved to Ohio, married Elizabeth Spencer, and served in the state legislature. A militia officer during the War of 1812, he was included in General William Hull's ignominious surrender of Detroit. Cass was appointed governor of Michigan Territory in 1813 and held that post for eighteen years. In 1831 he became President Andrew Jackson's secretary of war and five years later, U.S. minister to France. Cass was a U.S. senator from 1845 to 1857 and concluded his long public career as secretary of state under President James Buchanan.

The doctrine of popular sovereignty, which helped secure Cass the Democratic nomination in 1848, was an attempt to defuse the explosive issue of slavery expansion. Repudiating the Wilmot Proviso, Cass rejected the idea that Congress should regulate slavery in the western territories. Instead, he argued that the residents of the territory should decide the question themselves.

Abraham Lincoln was an Illinois Whig serving in the House of Representatives in 1848 and a wholehearted supporter of Zachary Taylor. Lincoln presented a devastatingly humorous attack on the Democratic candidate. Belittling Cass's military contributions as an aide to General William Henry Harrison at the Battle of the Thames, Lincoln sarcastically recounted his own exploits as a "hero" of the Black Hawk War, assaulting not hostile Indians but wild onions. Focusing on the fact that Cass was entitled to ten rations per day while governor of Michigan Territory, Lincoln concluded that the Democratic nominee was "a general of splendidly successful charges—charges...not upon the public enemy, but upon the public treasury." Lincoln subsequently entertained rapt audiences during a campaign swing through New England, a region that generally supported the Whig ticket. Upon returning to Illinois in October, Lincoln campaigned enthusiastically for Taylor in his congressional district. Despite the yeoman's efforts of Lincoln to rally his home state Whigs, however, Illinois voters backed Cass in the election.

Following his defeat by Taylor, Cass supported the Compromise of 1850, which implicitly endorsed popular sovereignty regarding slavery and the western territories. In 1854 Cass only reluctantly backed the Kansas-Nebraska Act as a party measure (even though it incorporated his theory of popular sovereignty) because it reignited the explosive issue of slavery expansion by repealing the Missouri Compromise line.

As secretary of state, Cass backed President Buchanan's support of the proslavery Lecompton constitution for Kansas, believing that further compromise was necessary to save the Union. In the election of 1860, Cass joined Buchanan in supporting the presidential nomination of Southern Democrat, John C. Breckinridge. Cass resigned from Buchanan's cabinet following Lincoln's election, in a dispute over reinforcing the federal troops at Charleston, South Carolina.

The attack on Fort Sumter galvanized Cass, and he enthusiastically addressed several recruitment rallies and subscribed thousands of dollars to help equip volunteer regiments. The former secretary of state also contributed diplomatic advice. In November 1861, a federal cruiser overhauled the British steamer *Trent* and took into custody two Confederate agents, James M. Mason and John Slidell. The British government demanded their immediate release, and war appeared likely. Cass cabled secretary of state William Henry Seward, cautioning the administration to act prudently. Lincoln agreed and defused the crisis by ordering the release of Mason and Slidell.

As the Civil War dragged on, Cass's health deteriorated. He did not play an active role in the presidential campaign of 1864, although he favored George B. McClellan. Lewis Cass died in June 1866, an outdated symbol of antebellum political compromise.

See also *Popular Sovereignty; Taylor, Zachary*

—WILLARD CARL KLUNDER

BIBLIOGRAPHY

Congressional Globe. 30th Cong., 1st sess., app., 1041–1043.

Klunder, Willard Carl. *Lewis Cass and the Politics of Moderation.* Kent, Ohio: Kent State University Press, 1996.

Riddle, Donald W. *Congressman Abraham Lincoln.* Urbana: University of Illinois Press, 1957.

Central Pacific Railroad

On July 1, 1862, President Abraham Lincoln signed the Pacific Railway Act, authorizing the construction of a railroad across the western United States and pledging massive government aid for the project. The bill promised aid to the Central Pacific Railroad and authorized a federal charter for a new corporation, the Union Pacific Railroad. The Union Pacific was to build westward from an unspecified point near the 100th meridian. Under the original legislation, the Central Pacific was authorized to build only from Sacramento, California, to the Nevada border.

The Republican Party platforms in 1856 and 1860 called for a Pacific railroad bill. But before the Civil War, the question of the route for the first transcontinental railroad always became caught up in sectional debate—the North and South each wanted the line to go through their own section. Lincoln had a strong personal interest in the railroad and a long record of supporting internal improvements of various kinds.

The Central Pacific Railroad had been organized in June 1861 by the "big four"—California businessmen Mark Hopkins, Collis P. Huntington, Charles Crocker, and Leland Stanford. Stanford was elected governor of California in 1861. All four were Republicans who had supported Lincoln's candidacy for the presidency. In forming the Central Pacific they were anticipating the imminent fulfillment of the Republican Party's promise to build a Pacific railroad.

Government aid to the two railroads included the right-of-way on which the track was built and additional grants of public land that could be sold to help pay construction costs. The original land grants were ten square miles of land (later increased to twenty square miles) for each mile of track. The government also loaned the railroads $16,000 per mile of track in level country and $48,000 per mile in mountainous territory. Together the two railroads received approximately 45,000,000 acres of government land.

The Pacific Railroad Act left several important decisions to be determined later by the president. One concerned the gauge of the railroad. Huntington convinced Lincoln to choose 5 feet, the gauge already being used by local lines in California. However, most railroads in the East used 4 feet 8½ inches, which would eventually become the standard gauge for U.S. railroads. Congress received so many complaints from railroad officials that it overrode Lincoln and chose the 4 feet 8½ inch gauge. Another decision that fell to Lincoln was determining exactly where the Sierra Nevada Mountains began. This was important because of the higher loan rates for track in mountainous terrain. Supporters of the Central Pacific convinced Lincoln that the mountains begin relatively close to Sacramento, thus qualifying more track for the higher loan rates.

In 1864 Congress passed a second Pacific Railroad Act, which increased the land grants as mentioned previously and also authorized the Central Pacific to build 150 miles beyond the California-Nevada border. The transcontinental railroad was finished with a "golden spike" ceremony at Promontory Summit, Utah Territory, on May 10, 1869. The Central Pacific had built about 690 miles of track, and the Union Pacific approximately 1,084 miles.

In 1885 the Central Pacific merged with the Southern Pacific, which had finished its own transcontinental line from El Paso to Los Angeles in 1883. The Southern Pacific was a dominant force in Pacific Coast railroading for many decades. In 1996 the Union Pacific acquired the Southern Pacific, and the entire route of the first transcontinental railroad came under the control of one company.

See also *Illinois Central Railroad; Railroads; Union Pacific Railroad*

—MARK S. JOY

BIBLIOGRAPHY

Bain, David Haward. *Empire Express: Building the First Transcontinental Railroad.* New York: Penguin, 1999.

Williams, John Hoyt. *A Great and Shining Road: The Epic Story of the Transcontinental Railway.* Lincoln: University of Nebraska Press, 1996.

Chandler, Zachariah

Zachariah Chandler (1813–1879), a U.S. senator from Michigan, is best known as a critic of the Union's early war effort and of President Andrew Johnson's lenient policy toward white Southerners during Reconstruction. Driven by fierce ambition, he also favored aggressive U.S. expansion in North America and protective tariffs to help new American industries prosper.

Chandler's drive probably stemmed from his Yankee upbringing. He was born on December 10, 1813, in Bedford, New Hampshire. Descended from a long line of Puritan ancestors, he grew up in a prosperous New England family. His father, Samuel, was a farmer who served as town clerk, selectman, and justice of the peace in Bedford. Zachariah, one of seven children, was a top student in Bedford schools. After his student days, he tried teaching and worked briefly as a retail clerk. In 1833 he joined the first big surge of migration to Michigan in search of economic opportunity.

It did not take him long to find it. After ending a retail partnership with his brother-in-law, Franklin Moore, in 1836, Chandler survived the Panic of 1837 and prospered in Detroit's burgeoning economy. Working from dawn to dusk to ensure that his dry goods store succeeded, the tall, thin young man even slept on the premises some nights. He shifted from retail to the wholesale trade during the 1840s, becoming one of the richest men in Michigan. By 1857 his business became the first in the state to achieve revenues of $50,000. Despite his busy schedule Chandler found time for romance, marrying Letitia Grace Douglass, a New Yorker, eleven years after he moved to Michigan. Their sole child, Mary Douglass Chandler, was born in 1848.

Chandler also became increasingly active in politics. A staunch abolitionist, he contributed generously to the Underground Railroad and worked for Whig candidates in the 1840s. These activities prompted Chandler to run for political office. He was elected Detroit's mayor in 1851 and lost a hard-fought contest to become governor of Michigan the following year. Despite that defeat Chandler, a founding member of the Republican Party, won election to the U.S. Senate in 1857.

In Washington, Chandler bitterly attacked the Democrats for their role in foisting the proslavery Lecompton Constitution on Kansas. After Abraham Lincoln's election in 1860, Chandler turned his vitriol on secessionists, strongly supporting the war to defeat the Confederacy. But he soon became a thorn in the side of President Lincoln and Union generals. From his perch on Congress's Joint Committee on the Conduct of the War, he criticized General McClellan's timidity and sought a much more vigorous prosecution of the war. One of Congress's Radical Republicans, many of whom hailed from the Old Northwest, Chandler was an early advocate of emancipation, urging Lincoln in 1861 to transform the war into a crusade against slavery. He also favored recruiting African American troops and confiscating Confederate property to punish the rebel elite and discourage others from emulating them. Later Chandler denounced both President Lincoln and President Andrew Johnson's plan to rebuild the war-torn nation. Urging that greater care be taken to protect the rights of former slaves, he favored enfranchising freedmen and imposing harsher penalties on Confederate leaders. He favored convicting Johnson of high crimes and misdemeanors during Congress's failed effort to impeach the seventeenth president in 1868.

Chandler also helped to shape the nation's postwar economy. In 1861 he began a fourteen-year stint as head of the Senate Committee on Commerce, where he battled against easy money and fought for trade barriers to protect fledgling American industries, especially those in Michigan. He also favored acquiring Canada and increasing U.S. dominance of the Americas. After losing his Senate seat in 1874, Chandler served as President Ulysses S. Grant's secretary of the interior, and he is credited with helping to clean up that agency's Land Office, Pension Bureau, and Office of Indian Affairs. After leaving office Chandler continued to fight for African American rights, denouncing President Rutherford B. Hayes's decision to let white supremacists regain control of the South. In early 1879 the Michigan legislature reelected Chandler to the Senate, but he died shortly after taking office.

—JAMES SCHWARTZ

BIBLIOGRAPHY

Detroit Tribune and Post. Zachariah Chandler: An Outline Sketch of his Life and Public Service. Detroit: Post and Tribune Company, 1880.

George, Sister Mary Karl. *Zachariah Chandler: A Political Biography.* East Lansing: Michigan State University Press, 1969.

Charleston Convention, 1860

See *Democratic Conventions, 1860*

Chase, Salmon Portland

Salmon Portland Chase (1808–1873), longtime advocate of abolition, began his antislavery efforts in defense of fugitive slaves and abolitionists as a Cincinnati attorney in the 1830s. A key Liberty Party strategist, Chase sought to move antislavery politics into the two-party system by seeking the support of Northern Democrats and Whigs. In 1848, he was the chief architect of the Free Soil Party (which opposed extending slavery into the territories) and won election by the Ohio legislature to the U.S. Senate the following year. In 1855 he was elected the first Republican governor of Ohio and hoped to use that position as a springboard to the presidency. Denied the nomination in 1856, Chase accelerated his efforts in 1860. With Abraham Lincoln's nomination and election Chase accepted appointment as Treasury secretary, a position he held for three years. Still ambitious for the presidency, he resigned in June 1864, only to be appointed chief justice of the United States in December. Chase had a long and contentious relationship with President Lincoln and clearly influenced him in his decisions regarding emancipation and civil rights.

The two men had little contact through the 1840s, as Lincoln remained a loyal Illinois Whig and Chase was an active third-party organizer with Democratic Party leanings. When Chase entered the Senate in 1849, Lincoln had retired to Springfield after his single term in the U. S. House of Representatives. The first meeting of the two may have come in 1858 when Chase came to Illinois to speak on Lincoln's behalf during his contest for the U.S. Senate seat of Stephen A. Douglas. After Douglas's reelection, Lincoln, always the moderate, urged Chase not to pursue a platform plank condemning the Fugitive Slave Law because it would jeopardize Illinois Republican voter support. Differences in antislavery ideology— or at least tactics and strategy—were thus obvious by the late 1850s.

As the Republicans prepared to choose a presidential nominee in 1860, Lincoln at first expressed interest in Chase, noting the Ohioan's willingness to campaign on his behalf against Douglas. Since Lincoln never openly sought the nomination, Chase enthusiastically congratulated him on his nomination and eventual election. As always, Chase had a political motive, hoping to be part of Lincoln's cabinet.

The president-elect had to satisfy the many factions of his party in choosing his cabinet and waited until the inauguration to nominate Chase for the Treasury post. The two men had always been cordial, and Lincoln assumed that Chase would be a loyal administrator. His appointment would also satisfy the antislavery wing of the party as well as those Republicans who had formerly been Democrats. Yet in making Chase secretary of the Treasury Lincoln angered the new secretary of state, William H. Seward of New York, and his many partisans. The president would need all of his political skill to keep the loyalty of his two leading cabinet members in the tumultuous war years ahead.

Had Chase confined himself to financing the war he would have been considered a highly successful Treasury secretary. Like many in the North, he was slow to recognize that the defeat of the Confederacy would be long and costly. Yet once that reality sank in, and with it the need for massive loans and currency and banking reform, Chase labored valiantly to put in place an economic program unprecedented in the country's history. With the aid of financier Jay Cooke, the government floated loans of millions of dollars to augment the meager revenue it realized through tariffs and land sales. And with the full and active support of the president, Chase engineered legislation to approve the issuance of hundreds of millions of dollars of Treasury notes as legal tender. This, combined with new taxes and a system of banking associations, put the Union on a sounder, if still tenuous, financial basis as war costs accelerated. Chase had firm allies in Congress, led by Sen. John Sherman of Ohio, who steered the necessary bills through the legislature. Never solving the financial crisis completely, Chase nevertheless overcame conservative opponents, and with the president using his influence to persuade the undecided, the war effort moved steadily forward on firmer financial footing.

Perhaps Chase's greatest achievement in his relationship with Lincoln was entirely outside of his Treasury responsibilities, as he helped persuade Lincoln to move more quickly toward emancipation. As one of those Republicans who consistently advocated making the war one to free the slaves as well as save the Union, Chase never fully appreciated the pressures Lincoln felt from all directions, including those in slaveholding Border States that remained in the Union, who sought to prevent federal intervention on the issue, and conservative Republicans who opposed any war goal but preserving the Union. Initially, Chase advised Lincoln to let Union generals pursue emancipation in their respective war theaters, but the president instead revoked emancipation orders by Generals John C. Frémont in Missouri and David Hunter in the Southeast, insisting that such decisions must be reserved to the commander in chief. Similarly, Chase was among those who urged the removal of General George C. McClellan, in part because of his failure to engage the enemy and in part because of his proslavery policies.

In July 1862 the president informed his cabinet of his decision to pursue a preliminary emancipation proclamation. Although unhappy with some of the details, Chase could feel satisfaction that his views were at last being heard. The proclamation, issued on September 17 after the Union victory at Antietam, included Chase's phrase invoking "the considerate judgment of mankind, and the gracious favor of Almighty God." The proclamation also urged the recruitment of freedmen into Union armies, another of Chase's goals. Later in the war Chase combined with others to achieve greater equality of black troops with white. His pressure had helped push the reluctant president toward emancipation, and without him it would have been a slower and more limited policy. Chase also urged that the president back the concept of black suffrage, something that Lincoln was moving toward at the time of his death.

Chase always believed that he was intellectually superior to the president and more deserving of the top office. His efforts to maneuver into position for his party's nomination in 1864 were unrelenting. In late 1862, feeling unappreciated, he sought to force Lincoln's hand to remove his chief rival, the more conservative Secretary Seward, who appeared to have the president's ear on key policy matters. With Radical Republican senators he met with Lincoln in December, only to be outmaneuvered by the politically adroit president, who forced him to acknowledge Seward's loyalty. Chase also attempted to use his patronage power in several Union-occupied Confederate states, including Louisiana and Florida, to create Chase organizations. In early 1864 a committee of backers issued a circular to boost his candidacy. Again such moves backfired and left the president more entrenched in power. In March 1864 Chase was forced to issue a letter disavowing his candidacy, and in late May the party overwhelmingly renominated Lincoln.

It was a patronage struggle that finally led the president to accept Chase's resignation in mid-1864. In a battle with the Seward faction over lucrative

Treasury-related offices in New York City, Chase insisted that his people be allowed to retain the offices. Safely renominated, with key economic policies in place, Lincoln no longer judged Chase's presence in the cabinet critical. Thus, rather than yield, Lincoln surprised Chase by accepting his resignation.

The aging chief justice of the United States, Roger B. Taney of Maryland, died in October 1864. Lincoln waited until he had been reelected and then chose a replacement who he knew would uphold emancipation and other key wartime legislation. Chase had campaigned faithfully for Lincoln against his Democratic rival, George B. McClellan, knowing that loyalty had its rewards. In early December, the president nominated Chase as Taney's successor, hoping that once on the Court he would confine himself to judicial matters, as he had never been able to do in regard to financial issues while in the cabinet. Lincoln would not live long enough to see those hopes frustrated, but the chief justice did move to make permanent the constitutional changes the war had brought. At the same time Chase, although denied his presidential aspirations, could take solace that Lincoln had moved closer to him on racial equality as the nation entered the Reconstruction process.

See also *Cabinet, Lincoln's*

—FREDERICK J. BLUE

BIBLIOGRAPHY

Blue, Frederick J. *Salmon P. Chase: A Life in Politics.* Kent, Ohio: Kent State University Press, 1987.

Donald, David Herbert. *Lincoln.* New York: Touchstone, 1996.

Goodwin, Doris Kearns. *Team of Rivals: The Political Genius of Abraham Lincoln.* New York: Simon and Schuster, 2005.

McPherson, James M. *Ordeal by Fire: The Civil War and Reconstruction.* New York: McGraw-Hill, 1992.

Niven, John. *Salmon P. Chase: A Biography.* New York: Oxford University Press, 1995.

Oates, Stephen B. *With Malice toward None: A Life of Abraham Lincoln.* New York: Harper and Row, 1977.

Van Deusen, Glyndon G. *William H. Seward.* New York: Oxford University Press, 1967.

Chicago Convention, 1860

See *Republican Convention, 1860*

Circuit Courts

Abraham Lincoln practiced law primarily in the circuit courts of Illinois during the twenty-five years he was an attorney. Circuit riding was a very important aspect of his legal career. It gave him the opportunity to make political connections in central Illinois, meeting and working with fellow lawyers who would help him in later elections. Arguing issues of debt, economic development, and personal conflict gave Lincoln a rich exposure to the issues of importance to the general public. Lincoln also was able to hone his oratory and logic, as he had to deal with cases and issues quickly on the circuit.

The circuit court system in antebellum Illinois changed frequently. The federal circuit court system was the model under the first Illinois Constitution, with supreme court justices presiding in the circuit courts so as to remain in contact with the general population. During the antebellum period the Illinois General Assembly changed the system from one of appointing circuit judges—relieving supreme court justices of circuit duty—to again requiring circuit duty for justices, and finally to election of circuit judges by the general population. Lincoln worked under all three of these systems.

During this period of robust growth in Illinois's population, circuits became larger as the legislature carved new counties out of existing ones. Then circuits became smaller as judges complained about the large circuit sizes and excessive travel time. When Lincoln became a lawyer in 1836, there were only five circuits in the state; when he left Illinois in 1861, there were twenty-six circuits. Several contiguous counties made up a circuit. Counties generally had a spring and a fall term, with some larger counties having an additional summer term. After the completion of a two- or three-day term, the judge and lawyers would move to the next county seat, and so on, until the last county in the circuit was completed.

Circuit riding was an integral part of the lawyer's professional life. Many counties only had one or two lawyers, and itinerant lawyers filled the demand for legal representation. Later in the antebellum period, attorneys were able to earn a good livelihood by practicing in their home county and a few neighboring ones. Lincoln was one of only a few attorneys who continued to travel the entire circuit with the judge and the state's attorney. He normally traveled the Eighth Judicial Circuit, but early in his career, he would travel outside of the Eighth Circuit to handle cases.

Although other attorneys complained about difficult roads, less-than-adequate living conditions, poor food, and swollen streams, Lincoln did not complain and appeared to enjoy himself on the circuit. Lincoln typically carried his personal items—a change of clothes, a nightshirt, and other necessities—in his carpetbag.

He also carried a few books to read for pleasure. For outerwear, he generally brought his linen duster and umbrella and in colder weather would wear a shawl or cloak. For entertainment the judge and attorneys would frequently attend parties at a local lawyer's house, go fishing at a nearby pond or stream, or tell stories and jokes.

During the course of his legal career, Lincoln handled at least two thousand cases on the circuit, almost always visiting the core counties of Tazewell, McLean, Logan, and De Witt. During the height of Lincoln's law practice, from 1849 to 1853, Lincoln traveled the fourteen-county circuit every spring and fall term, leaving his Springfield home for two months at a time. Lincoln represented plaintiffs slightly more often than he represented defendants. On the circuit, however, that figure was reversed, reflecting the nature of that type of circuit traveling. Since court cases had to be filed ten days before the term of court began, itinerant lawyers generally were not able to begin lawsuits in other counties. As a result, when traveling lawyers came to town, defendants generally solicited their representation. Lincoln did represent plaintiffs, of course, when asked by a local attorney that the plaintiffs had already retained.

The nature of Lincoln's practice on the circuit was varied. The bulk involved debt collection in some form—unpaid promissory notes, mortgage foreclosures, and partnership settlements. However, Lincoln also handled a number of replevin, slander, divorce, inheritance, and other cases. Lincoln was a general practice attorney, not specializing in any particular area of the law. That was typical of most antebellum Illinois attorneys, but by the mid-to-late 1850s, some attorneys devoted substantial time to particular areas, such as railroad or real estate litigation. While Lincoln handled a number of cases both for and against railroad companies, he never stopped handling other types of litigation.

Even though politics was Lincoln's first love, it did not prevent him from working with attorneys of the opposing party. In fact, politics rarely influenced whom Lincoln practiced with on the circuit. In many counties he acted as a co-counsel to Democratic attorneys as frequently as to Whig and Republican attorneys. The most notable example was *People v. Turner,* a murder case in De Witt County in which Lincoln and Stephen A. Douglas (later U.S. senator, 1847–1861) represented the defendant.

Lincoln's circuit practice was not confined to the county courts of Illinois. Lincoln also fashioned a lucrative business in the federal circuit courts, primarily practicing in Springfield. With the growth of Chicago, Congress added a term of court in Chicago to the district of Illinois. In 1854 Congress divided Illinois into two districts. Lincoln continued his practice in the southern district in Springfield and frequently traveled to Chicago for business in the northern district.

—John A. Lupton

BIBLIOGRAPHY

Benner, Martha L., Cullom Davis, et al., eds. *The Law Practice of Abraham Lincoln: Complete Documentary Edition, DVD-ROM.* Urbana: University of Illinois Press, 2000.

Duff, John J. *A. Lincoln: Prairie Lawyer.* New York: Bramhall House, 1960.

King, Willard L. *Lincoln's Manager: David Davis.* Cambridge, Mass.: Harvard University Press, 1960.

Stowell, Daniel W., et al., eds. *The Papers of Abraham Lincoln: Legal Documents and Cases.* 4 vols. Charlottesville: University of Virginia Press, 2008.

Civil Liberties

Because his presidency coincided with the American Civil War, Abraham Lincoln is often scrutinized more than other chief executives on whether his administration furthered or limited civil liberties of citizens. Though most assessments are critical of President Lincoln's policies on civil liberties, a comprehensive analysis reveals a more balanced record than Lincoln is generally given credit for.

The position of the Lincoln White House on slavery developed as the Civil War progressed. At first Lincoln contemplated retaining slavery if the Union itself could be saved. As the two became inextricably intertwined, the president realized that only freedom for blacks would bring about necessary changes in American society.

Lincoln drafted the Emancipation Proclamation in July 1862 and issued the preliminary Emancipation Proclamation in September. He warned that unless the Confederate states returned to the Union, he would free all of their slaves. When his directive was ignored, Lincoln issued the Emancipation Proclamation, on January 1, 1863. The proclamation freed only the slaves in the rebellious states, while exempting all or parts of seven states from its provisions because those places were either back under U.S. control or had never left the Union. Lincoln understood that the Fifth Amendment to the Constitution prevented the national government from taking private property—including slaves—from people under the jurisdiction of the United States. Even though it did not include all slaves, the Emancipation Proclamation represented an unprecedented use of the executive order or presidential proclamation for implementing policy. Later, in his final annual message as president, Lincoln called on Congress to reconsider passing a constitutional amendment to eradicate slavery. To this end, the Thirteenth Amendment was ratified just a year later in 1865. It was followed by the Fourteenth Amendment in 1868 and the Fifteenth in 1870.

The Lincoln administration was responsible for furthering the civil liberties of blacks in at least two other ways. In July 1862 the Union army formed its first black regiment. Many of the soldiers in this regiment were former slaves. In the same year Congress passed and Lincoln signed the first Morrill Act. This law provided public lands to states to finance agricultural colleges. After the Civil War a second Morrill Act would provide land grant colleges for African Americans in the South. These institutions became the primary vehicle for the education of blacks for a century.

In 1862 Lincoln also signed the Morrill Anti-Polygamy Act, which was the first of a series of nineteenth-century laws designed to marginalize, persecute, and destroy the Mormon Church. The Supreme Court would uphold this law in *Reynolds v. United States* (98 U.S. 145 [1879]). Two states—West Virginia (1863) and Nevada (1864)—entered the Union during the Lincoln presidency, both as free states, with all citizens enjoying rights under the Constitution.

Many actions of the Lincoln administration during the Civil War were challenged as violations of the Constitution or of the rights of citizens. However, Lincoln was careful to explain the rationale for his policies and mindful of the need to have them approved eventually if not immediately.

The opening of the Civil War witnessed the first alleged affronts to civil liberties. Following the battle at Fort Sumter in April 1861, the Lincoln White House placed a blockade on Confederate ports. Although the strategy was successful in impeding importation of war supplies, it was attacked by those on the merchant ships who were captured and detained. Congress eventually granted President Lincoln permission to declare that an insurrection existed and retroactively supported his military moves. In its April 1863 decision in *the Prize Cases,* the U.S. Supreme Court ruled by a vote of five to four that Lincoln's actions at the outset of the War between the States did not violate his constitutional authority. Lincoln had justified his moves by equating the Civil War with an international conflict.

In prosecuting the Civil War, the Lincoln administration found it necessary to implement martial law in parts of the United States. The accompanying policies were diverse and controversial. First, the designation was employed to arrest dissenters and those suspected of being disloyal. Second, it was used to justify censorship of mail and telegraph communications and suppression of unfriendly newspapers. Third, it was the impetus behind the 1862 Confiscation Law, which made it easier to seize rebel property. In the latter instance, the U.S. Supreme Court upheld the government's actions in 1871 in *Miller v. United States.*

Probably the starkest threat to Americans' civil liberties during the Civil War had to do with the judicial rights of those detained, arrested, or caught. According to the Constitution, the right of *habeas corpus*—to be arrested only under charges consistent with the rule of law and to be incarcerated only after a fair trial—may only be suspended in cases of rebellion. The *habeas corpus* clause is in Article I of the Constitution, which deals with Congress, and it does not specify how—or by which branch of the government—*habeas corpus* may be suspended. Lincoln issued orders suspending the writ in April 1861, when Congress was not in session. Four months later, after it returned, Congress acted to legitimate the move. Chief Justice Roger B. Taney attempted to thwart Lincoln's suspension in the case of John Merryman, a Confederate militiaman who had been arrested by the army in Maryland after he had sabotaged bridges and attempted to raise troops for the Confederacy. The commander at Fort McHenry, acting under orders from Lincoln, ignored Taney's writ, and the Lincoln administration ignored Taney's opinion in *Ex parte Merryman* (1861). Taney acted in his role as a circuit judge, and the case never went to the Supreme Court. Later the president expanded the suspension of the writ, and that was followed by the passage of the Habeas Corpus Act by Congress in March 1863. The April 1863 U.S. Supreme Court ruling in the *Prize Cases* upheld the actions of the president in this area.

Once captured, certain rebel leaders and citizens suspected of disloyalty were subject to military tribunals. Such courts operated with rules similar to military courts martial. Though the military tribunals were attacked as violating civilians' rights, the Lincoln administration defended them as the most efficient and fair mechanism for meting out justice during war. Congress acted several times to support Lincoln's policies on military tribunals. For example, an 1862 law authorized the president to appoint a judge advocate general for a military commission; two laws passed in 1863 specified certain punishments for conviction by a military tribunal; and an 1864 law provided for penalties against quartermasters who had been found guilty by such courts. Conversely, the U.S. Supreme Court ruled unanimously in *Ex Parte Milligan* (1866) that the 1864 military trial of an Indiana citizen who was charged with conspiracy was unconstitutional, as the area where he was captured was not in a theater of military operations and civil courts were still functioning.

Another way in which the Lincoln administration was accused of limiting or violating civil liberties was by the imposition of a draft, the first in the nation's history. This policy may have been initiated by the Lincoln White House, but it was approved by Congress in March 1863. The Conscription Act required registration of males between the ages of twenty and forty-five—both citizens and those undergoing naturalization—with exemption if a substitute was designated or on payment of a $300 fee. When protests against conscription turned violent, as they did in New York during the summer of 1863, federal troops were dispatched to restore order.

Given the overwhelming need to defeat the Confederate forces, the Lincoln administration nonetheless demonstrated compassion and concern for civil liberties in selected policies toward rebels. For instance, Lincoln issued a proclamation of amnesty and reconstruction in December 1863, which offered a full pardon to those who voluntarily took a prescribed oath. Further, the U.S. and Confederate governments approved periodic exchanges of prisoners of war. That practice was discontinued by General Ulysses S. Grant a month after his appointment as leader of Union troops in March 1864, in part because the Confederacy refused to treat captured black soldiers under the traditional rules of war, but instead sought to enslave them.

The tragic death of Abraham Lincoln at the hands of an assassin, within days of the end of the Civil War, made it difficult to determine certain elements of his legacy. Having just been reelected, Lincoln was busy planning reconstruction policy. After his death, President Andrew Johnson and the Republican-controlled Congress battled bitterly over the future of the country, particularly over the rights of freedmen and how Confederate states would be permitted to rejoin the Union.

Several consequences of the Lincoln presidency for civil liberties deserve attention. First, Lincoln's reputation as the president who saved the Union is equaled only by his initiative in freeing those who had been enslaved. Black citizens showed their loyalty for Lincoln's action, as a majority voted for Republican candidates for another seventy years.

A second outcome had to do with the actions of a wartime administration. Subsequent administrations that had to govern domestically and fight a war at the same time looked to the precedents established during the Lincoln administration. These guideposts proved particularly valuable to the Woodrow Wilson administration during World War I and the Franklin Roosevelt administration during World War II. Though the courts tended to defer to the executive branch during wartime, outcomes such as the Supreme Court's 1952 decision in the case of *Youngstown Sheet and Tube v. Sawyer* served as a warning to presidents not to overstep their constitutional authority.

See also *Habeas Corpus*

—SAMUEL B. HOFF

BIBLIOGRAPHY

Baker, Thomas E., and John F. Stack Jr., eds. *At War with Civil Rights and Liberties.* Lanham, Md.: Rowman and Littlefield, 2006.

Fisher, Louis. *Military Tribunals and Presidential Power: American Revolution to the War on Terrorism.* Lawrence: University Press of Kansas, 2005.

Irons, Peter. *War Powers: How the Imperial Presidency Hijacked the Constitution.* New York: Henry Holt, 2005.

Javits, Jacob. *Who Makes War: The President versus Congress.* New York: William Morrow, 1973.

Murray, Robert Bruce. *Legal Cases of the Civil War.* Mechanicsburg, Pa.: Stackpole Books, 2003.

Randall, James G. *Constitutional Problems under Lincoln.* Urbana: University of Illinois Press, 1964.

Schlesinger, Arthur M., Jr. *War and the American Presidency.* New York: Norton, 2005.

Tushnet, Mark, ed. *The Constitution in Wartime: Beyond Alarmism and Complacency.* Durham, N.C.: Duke University Press, 2005.

Waldrep, Christopher, and Lynne Curry. *The Constitution and the Nation: The Civil War and American Constitutionalism, 1830–1890.* New York: Peter Lang, 2003.

Clay, Henry

Henry Clay (1777–1852), senator and congressman from Kentucky and U.S. secretary of state, was a renowned antebellum political leader and founder of the Whig Party. Known as "the Great Compromiser" for his role in settling sectional controversies, he sought the presidency in 1824, 1832, and 1844 but was never elected. Always insistent that diverse interests were not dangerous to the nation but combined to improve its welfare, Clay was devoted to ideals of national and personal improvement and coined the term "self-made man." Lincoln greatly admired him and called Clay "my beau ideal of a statesman."

Born in Virginia, Clay studied law there before moving to Kentucky, where he entered the legislature as a Jeffersonian Republican in 1803. Like Lincoln, Clay criticized slavery in his early career and championed the institutions of modern economic development, including banks and internal improvements. A large slaveholder himself, Clay later became a leader of the American Colonization Society.

After two brief stints in the Senate, Clay won election as Speaker when he joined the House of Representatives in 1811. Clay was a leading "War Hawk," who helped incite the War of 1812 but helped negotiate its conclusion in 1814. Following the war, Clay joined the "National" wing of the Republican Party in supporting economic development. He embraced the Second Bank of the United States and proposed an "American system" of protective tariffs to stimulate domestic industry and a national network of roads, canals, and other internal improvements funded by the sale of public lands. Lincoln supported the same objectives in his early career, and they would underpin the platforms of the Whig Party.

Clay launched his reputation as a sectional compromiser in the Missouri crisis of 1819–1820. Although others devised the basic provisions of the famous Missouri Compromise, permitting slavery in Missouri but barring it from the rest of the Louisiana Purchase north of 36° 30', Clay found ambiguous language to defuse a subsequent dispute over the rights of free blacks under the new state's constitution.

In 1824 Clay was among four major candidates to succeed President James Monroe. He finished last in the balloting but helped obtain the victory of John Quincy Adams over Andrew Jackson in the House of Representatives. When Adams then named him secretary of state, Clay drew charges of a "corrupt bargain" and cemented the lifelong enmity of Jackson and his followers.

Returning to private life when Jackson defeated Adams in 1828, Clay reentered the Senate and won the National Republican presidential nomination in 1831. Seeking a campaign issue, Clay persuaded Congress to recharter the Bank of the United States, but the president responded with a popular veto, and Clay lost to Jackson by a wider margin than Adams had in 1828. Lincoln cast his first presidential vote for Clay in this contest.

That election coincided with rising sectional tension. When protests failed against the protective tariff, South Carolina "nullified" the Tariff of 1828 and threatened secession if federal authorities attempted to enforce it. Jackson countered with military preparations and a proclamation of federal supremacy, but Clay and South Carolina's Sen. John C. Calhoun averted possible civil war by agreeing to the Compromise of 1833, mandating a gradual retreat from protectionism over nine years.

Convinced that the Bank of the United States would attempt to manipulate elections in its continued quest for a new charter, Jackson resolved to destroy the bank and ordered withdrawal of the government's deposits in the fall of 1833. Clay marshaled opposition in the Senate, denouncing Jackson's actions as illegal and dictatorial. Within a year, a broad range of Jackson's opponents had coalesced under the name "Whig," and for the next two decades, Whigs and Democrats competed for power in the Second American Party System.

The new party ran three sectional candidates in 1836 but failed to defeat Martin Van Buren, Jackson's chosen successor. Clay and his fellow Whigs blamed Democratic economic policies when depression struck in 1837, and their candidate, General William Henry Harrison, ousted Van Buren in the election of 1840. When Harrison died after a month in office, Clay failed to enact the Whig economic program over opposition from the new president, John Tyler.

Clay successfully claimed the Whig presidential nomination in 1844, and Abraham Lincoln led his campaign in Illinois. He expected to run on familiar economic issues, but Democrat James K. Polk prevailed on a platform of western expansion. Defying the Whigs (including congressman Abraham Lincoln), Polk made war on Mexico in 1846, reaffirming the U.S. annexation of Texas and securing California, the future southwestern, and some mountain states when the war concluded in 1848. Victory touched off bitter debate when Northern efforts to bar slavery from these territories led to Southern threats of secession, and Congress was once more deadlocked by sectional recriminations.

Returning to the Senate, Clay proposed a comprehensive solution to all outstanding issues in early 1850. His plan included strengthening the Fugitive Slave Act, admitting California as a free state, allowing other new territories to decide on slavery for themselves, and compensating Texas for surrendering territory to New Mexico. For most of the spring and summer, Clay struggled to pass these measures as a single omnibus package, with support from all sections, but finally admitted defeat and left Washington to recover his shattered health. After his departure, Sen. Stephen A. Douglas assembled a different sectional coalition to pass each individual feature of the Compromise of 1850.

Clay and his colleagues received widespread acclaim for saving the Union, but the compromise proved very unstable, leading the historian David Potter to call it "the armistice of 1850." The Fugitive Slave Act became deeply unpopular in the

North and split the Whigs into irreconcilable sectional factions before they collapsed after 1852. Seeking Southern support for his presidential ambitions, Stephen A. Douglas reopened sectional divisions with his Kansas-Nebraska Act of 1854, inspiring Lincoln to reenter politics in the newly formed Republican Party. Henry Clay did not witness the nation's final descent into sectional violence but died in Washington in 1852, aged seventy-five. Two weeks afterward, at a ceremony in the Illinois statehouse, Abraham Lincoln delivered a eulogy in Clay's honor. Throughout the rest of his career Lincoln continued to venerate Clay, even as he moved away from the politics of compromise to the politics of emancipation during the Civil War.

See also *American System; Whig Party*

—HARRY L. WATSON

BIBLIOGRAPHY

Hamilton, Holman. *Prologue to Conflict: The Crisis and Compromise of 1850.* Lexington: University Press of Kentucky, 1964.

Holt, Michael. *The Rise and Fall of the American Whig Party: Jacksonian Politics and the Onset of the Civil War.* New York: Oxford University Press, 1999.

Howe, Daniel Walker. *The Political Culture of the American Whigs.* Chicago: University of Chicago Press, 1980.

———. "Why Abraham Lincoln Was a Whig." *Journal of the Abraham Lincoln Association* 16, no. 1 (Winter 1995): 27–38.

Moore, Glover. *The Missouri Controversy, 1819–1821.* Lexington: University of Kentucky Press, 1953.

Peterson, Merrill D. *The Great Triumvirate: Webster, Clay, and Calhoun.* New York: Oxford University Press, 1987.

———. *Olive Branch and Sword: The Compromise of 1833.* Baton Rouge: Louisiana State University Press, 1982.

Potter, David. *The Impending Crisis, 1848–1861.* Edited and completed by Don E. Fehrenbacher. New York: Harper and Row, 1976.

Remini, Robert V. *Henry Clay: Statesman for the Union.* New York: Harper and Row, 1991.

Cleveland Convention, 1864

Some of the most venomous opposition to Abraham's Lincoln's reelection in 1864 came not from the opposing Democratic Party but from radicals in his own Republican Party. The radicals believed he had not vigorously prosecuted the war and that he had not come down hard enough against slavery but had dragged his feet on emancipation. They were ardent abolitionists who believed that freeing the slaves should have equal priority with winning the war and saving the Union. Lincoln put nothing above saving the Union. The radicals feared that when the war was won, Lincoln's reconstruction policies would be far too lenient and liberal toward the South. They wanted control to be in their hands, not Lincoln's, and they wanted hard-hearted vengeance.

In early May of the election year a small core of the radicals in New York issued a national call to a special convention to nominate a man more to their liking to run against Lincoln on a third-party ticket. Some 400 of these alienated radicals met in Cleveland on May 31. In a single day they drafted a platform and nominated John Charles Frémont, a bitter Lincoln foe, for president—the man they had intended to nominate from the beginning.

Frémont had been the first presidential nominee of the Republican Party in 1856. He was a dashing, compelling figure, a former army officer, and a famous western explorer. He was a romantic figure in the American psyche, a dreamer, wanderer, and adventurer who fired the imagination. In the Mexican War Frémont had played a part in wresting California from Mexico and setting it up as a U.S. territory. After it became a state, Frémont had been California's governor for a time and one of its U.S. senators.

In 1841 he married a mate to match his larger-than-life persona—Jessie Benton, the headstrong daughter of Thomas Hart Benton, the powerful Democratic U.S. senator from Missouri, who frowned on the match. The couple had married secretly without Benton's consent; eventually the senator mellowed and came to accept and like his dashing son-in-law, even though he opposed him politically.

In 1856 the newly minted Republican Party picked Frémont to be its first candidate for president, and he ran a strong race before losing to Democrat James Buchanan. Lincoln had campaigned vigorously for Frémont in Illinois and then himself became the Republican nominee in the party's second—and successful—bid for the presidency in 1860.

When the Civil War came Lincoln appointed Frémont a major general in command of the important Western Department in Missouri. There Frémont came crossways with Lincoln when he unilaterally freed the slaves of secessionists in that key Border State. It was an act popular with abolitionists, but it threatened the tenuous bond keeping Missouri in the Union. It was an act too far ahead of its time, and Lincoln could not tolerate it. He ordered Frémont to modify the order. When Frémont refused, Lincoln rescinded it himself and reassigned Frémont to the Mountain Department in Western Virginia. When Frémont performed poorly Lincoln replaced him, causing the disgruntled general to ask to be relieved. After that he was not reassigned. Not only was Frémont bitter, but so were his radical backers, who had admired his unilateral freeing of slaves in Missouri. He was the special darling of the Germans, particularly in St. Louis. Indeed St. Louis and New York were the two centers of his greatest support.

When the irreconcilable Republican Radicals thought of putting up somebody to unseat Lincoln in 1864, Frémont was their first choice. Driven by a hatred of the president, detesting what they called the "imbecile and vacillating policy" of his administration, they called "in thunder tones" for the convention in Cleveland to nominate their man.

The convention that met was single-minded and short. Disgruntled anti-Lincoln radicals came from fifteen Northern and Border States, especially Germans. But there was little concern for credentials. Anybody who wanted to attend could participate. The convention quickly shaped a platform that contained the long-cherished aims of the radical wing of Lincoln's party—swift subjugation of the South, followed by immediate emancipation of all blacks Union-wide, with absolute equality of all men before the law regardless of color, and confiscation of the property of all rebel slaveholders. The platform also called for a one-term policy for the presidency, so that there could never be another second-term anathema such as Lincoln, and for wresting reconstruction policy from the president and lodging it in the far more radical hands of Congress. A plank that was thrown out suggested that members of the convention not accept any offices of trust, honor, or profit from the administration in power during the next presidential term. That was thought to be going too far.

The press covering and commenting on the convention either egged on these dissidents or ridiculed them. Manton Marble, the avidly anti-Lincoln editor of the hotly pro-Democratic *New York World,* praised the convention as "a political flank movement" and predicted that it would draw delegates to Cleveland in "immense numbers," which it didn't. James Gordon Bennett, the maverick editor of the *New York Herald,* who favored Ulysses S. Grant for president, thought it "only another radical abolition fiasco."

The unsympathetic *Cleveland Herald* looked at the convention's 200 to 400 participants (the number seemed to fluctuate) and called it a convention of "sly politicians from New York, impetuous hare-brained Germans from St. Louis, abolitionists, and personal friends and parasites of Frémont." The equally unsympathetic *Cincinnati Commercial* called it a collection of "long-haired radicals."

On the morning of May 31 delegates began drifting into Chapin Hall in Cleveland. The *New York World* reported that the convention was studded with "gentlemen whose hair is brown, and long, and parted in the middle" (i.e., radical theorists), who "are not, never have been, and never will be politicians, nor can they be made such by any sort of process. Not one of them ever had an opinion worth entertaining upon the subject of the government of a nation."

Henry Raymond, the editor of the *New York Times* and also the Republican national chairman, saw the Cleveland affair as a kind of "mental hallucination," a "precious piece of foolery" run by a set of "witless fellows." He dismissed it as "simply a flank movement against the Administration" that had no hold whatever on public confidence or sympathy.

When the time came that evening to nominate the candidate, there was an eleventh-hour effort by a small knot of delegates on behalf of Grant for president instead of Frémont, despite the fact that Grant, the general of the Union armies trying to win the war, was utterly uninterested in running against the president who was his commander in chief. That apostasy quelled, Frémont was nominated by acclamation, and the hall rocked for fifteen minutes in wild celebration. The *Chicago Tribune* correspondent, who drastically reduced the estimated number attendees, admitted that he "never before supposed that one hundred men—not even Missouri border ruffians—could raise such a yell."

After Frémont was nominated the convention picked the presiding officer of the convention, John Cochrane, a former New York congressman and Union general, as his running mate. Having named its ticket, the convention then had to pick a name for the new party. A committee was appointed, and after what the *Chicago Tribune* described as "many sittings and conferences among the wet nurses and old ladies of the Convention," decided to call itself the "Radical Democracy."

Frémont accepted its nomination, with the reservation that the plank on confiscation be dropped as impracticable. He also specified that if the upcoming Union (Republican) Party Convention in Baltimore on June 7 nominated any other man than Lincoln, he would drop his candidacy and support him, whoever he was. However, if Lincoln should be nominated, as expected, he would stay in the race and do whatever possible to prevent his reelection. Lincoln was easily nominated in Baltimore.

From the start there was no thought that the ticket nominated at the so-called "bolter's convention" could be elected. It was generally thought to be but the handiwork of a bunch of "ultra patriots, sore-heads, and cranks." The most prominent and public of the Republican Radicals in the country did not attend. But the ticket could siphon off important votes from Lincoln that could be telling in a close canvass that pitted Lincoln against the Democratic nominee, George B. McClellan, another former general whom he had sacked.

In late September, after the fall of Atlanta made it apparent that Lincoln would likely win the election, Frémont was persuaded by intermediaries to drop his candidacy. Although there was still much radical discontent, there was no longer any organized, effective radical opposition to Lincoln's reelection, and zero prospects for Frémont's maverick candidacy.

Frémont's withdrawal and reluctant falling into line was another tribute to Lincoln's careful and astute political maneuvering. Despite the bitter radical opposition to him, he had been able to blunt and counter it all, and in the end demonstrated once again that he was the master politician of the Civil War era.

See also *Frémont, John C.; Radical Republicans*

—John C. Waugh

BIBLIOGRAPHY

Bartlett, Ruhl J. *John C. Frémont and the Republican Party.* 1930. Reprint, New York: DaCapo, 1970.

Long, David E. *The Jewel of Liberty: Abraham Lincoln's Re-election and the End of Slavery.* Mechanicsburg, Pa.: Stackpole Books, 1994.

Waugh, John C. *Reelecting Lincoln: The Battle for the 1864 Presidency.* New York: Crown, 1997.

Zornow, William Frank. *Lincoln and the Party Divided.* Norman: University of Oklahoma Press, 1954.

———. "The Cleveland Convention, 1864, and Radical Democrats." *Mid-America* 36 (January 1954): 39–53.

Colfax, Schuyler

Schuyler Colfax (1823–1885), an Indiana Republican and Speaker of the House from 1863 to 1869, enjoyed a friendly but wary relationship with Abraham Lincoln. A Radical Republican nicknamed "the Smiler," Colfax later became engulfed in scandal as vice president (1869–1873).

Colfax was born in New York City on March 23, 1823. When he was thirteen, his family moved to New Carlisle, Indiana. At nineteen, he became editor of the Whig *St. Joseph Valley Register.* Reporting on Indiana for the *New York Tribune,* he formed close ties with *Tribune* editor Horace Greeley that affected his relations with Lincoln.

Sharing Lincoln's antislavery whiggery, Colfax lost his first campaign for Congress in 1850 but won in 1854 on an anti-Nebraska platform. Whereas Lincoln remained reluctant to abandon the Whigs after the Kansas-Nebraska Act and detested Know-Nothingism, Colfax dallied with the nativists before joining the Republicans. He soon became chair of the Post Offices and Post Roads Committee. Hoping to build the new party in a neighboring state, he campaigned for Lincoln in the 1858 Senate election, but there were rumors that, like Greeley, he considered supporting Stephen Douglas after the "Little Giant" broke with Democratic president James Buchanan.

At the 1860 Republican Convention, Colfax joined Greeley in backing Missouri's Edward Bates. After Lincoln's nomination, Colfax's congratulation prompted Lincoln to reply, "You distinguish between yourself and my *original* friends—a distinction which, by your leave, I propose to forget." Lincoln appreciated Colfax's campaigning that year and considered him for secretary of the interior before naming Caleb Smith, a conservative former Whig from Indiana. To Colfax's concerns that his rumored support for Douglas influenced the decision, Lincoln offered reassurance: Colfax had been "most honorably and amply recommended," but he thought, "Colfax is a young man—is already in position—is running a brilliant career, and is sure of a bright future in any event. " He said, "With Smith, it is now or never."

Lincoln proved prescient. In 1863 Colfax became Speaker of the House of Representatives—in spite of Lincoln's initial support for others. Lincoln initially supported Frank Blair for Speaker because of his friendship with the Blair family, Blair's moderate tendencies, and perhaps because of concerns about Colfax's ties to Greeley and secretary of the Treasury Salmon Chase. With Blair unable to leave the army to seek the post, Lincoln supported fellow Illinoisan Elihu Washburne. But Colfax's popularity prompted Lincoln to concede the issue, meet with Colfax, and win assurances that as Speaker, he would treat all branches of the Republican Party fairly.

As Speaker for the second half of Lincoln's presidency, Colfax caused no major problems or controversies. He supported Lincoln's efforts to pass the Thirteenth Amendment so strongly that he took the unusual step of leaving the Speaker's chair to address the House on its behalf and to vote for the measure. On April 14, 1865, Colfax stopped by the White House to discuss a pending cross-country trip. He made the trip—telling those who greeted him that on the day Lincoln was shot, the president gave him a message attesting to the West's importance and encouraging its economic and population growth.

Lincoln and Colfax fostered that growth by supporting construction of the transcontinental railroad, but Colfax paid for that support. While in Congress, he accepted stock in the Crédit Mobilier, a construction company that Union Pacific Railroad executives used to enrich themselves and political supporters. In 1868, before his relationship to the Crédit Mobilier became public, he was elected vice president, running with Ulysses S. Grant. Eventually, however, the House investigated Colfax's connection to the Crédit Mobilier, and his denials of corruption were easily disproved. Defeated for renomination as vice president in 1872, Colfax left politics, becoming well paid for speeches recounting his memories of Lincoln. He died en route to one such speech on January 13, 1885.

See also *Thirteenth Amendment*

—MICHAEL GREEN

BIBLIOGRAPHY

Basler, Roy P., et al., eds. *The Collected Works of Abraham Lincoln*. 9 vols. New Brunswick, N.J.: Rutgers University Press, 1953–1955.

Donald, David Herbert. *Lincoln*. New York: Simon and Schuster, 1995.

Smith, Willard H. *Schuyler Colfax: The Changing Fortunes of a Political Idol*. Indianapolis: Indiana Historical Bureau, 1952.

Colonization

Even though slavery had been banned in the Northern states by the early 1800s, the laws brought only a limited freedom for blacks. Theoretically free, they endured blatant discrimination, as most white Americans dismissed them as inferior and incapable of being assimilated into American society or politics, at least for the foreseeable future. Colonization of free blacks to Africa, the West, or some other place seemed an appropriate solution.

After the American Revolution Thomas Jefferson advocated deportation as a way to achieve gradual emancipation without inviting race war and social anarchy in the South. A committee in the Virginia legislature explored the idea, and Jefferson included this proposal in his 1787 *Notes on the State of Virginia*. The Virginia General Assembly took action in 1800, requesting Governor James Monroe to propose to President Jefferson a plan for establishing a penal colony for blacks beyond the limits of Virginia in the western territory of the United States. Jefferson replied that he could not recommend purchasing land in or near the territory of the United States because such an area might eventually become part of the Union. The West Indies, in particular Santo Domingo, he believed, had better possibilities, and Africa might be considered if no other territory could be found. Jefferson also considered the possibility of colonizing freed American slaves in the British-sponsored African settlement of Sierra Leone. The nation's preoccupation with diplomatic troubles growing out of the Napoleonic wars ended that endeavor.

In 1817 a group of concerned citizens formed the American Colonization Society, intending to resettle free blacks to Africa. Its founders and promoters included Robert Finley, Elias Caldwell, Francis Scott Key, Supreme Court justice Bushrod Washington, Henry Clay, and John Randolph. Although the society began as a private endeavor, its founders assumed that once a colony had been established to demonstrate the concept's feasibility, the federal government would accept the cost of maintaining it. As it became apparent that Congress was unwilling to commit to any action, however, the society focused on building local auxiliaries throughout the country to raise funds and build public support for colonization.

The society evolved through several phases over the years. In its formative period during the 1820s, it gained strength and popularity throughout the country. Between 1830 and 1840, however, serious financial difficulties hindered the organization's progress largely as a result of attacks from militant abolitionists such as William Lloyd Garrison, who dismissed colonization as an unwarranted compromise with slavery. But as quarrels over slavery intensified and popular opinion increasingly polarized Americans during the 1850s, interest in the colonization society revived. State legislatures such as those of Virginia, New Jersey, Pennsylvania, Missouri, and Maryland reexamined colonization and appropriated money for the emigration of free blacks. President Millard Fillmore prepared a recommendation that federal funds be appropriated for colonization in his 1852 State of the Union address but later removed the proposal from his message.

Like his hero, Henry Clay, Lincoln had always seen colonization as an answer to slavery, although he never spoke much about the utter impracticality of moving millions of people to another part of the world. Speaking at Peoria, Illinois, in 1854, Lincoln admitted the difficulty of eradicating the institution of slavery in any satisfactory way but suggested as his first impulse that all slaves be freed and dispatched to Liberia. Three years later in his Springfield, Illinois, debate with Stephen A. Douglas, Lincoln maintained that should there be a separation between the white and black races it "must be effected by colonization." He acknowledged the task's difficulty, "but 'when there is a will there is a way'; and what colonization needs most is a hearty will."

As president, Lincoln's first annual message to Congress, in 1861, included the possibility of colonization of free blacks who desired to leave the United States. Concerning the acquisition of new territory, Lincoln argued that acquiring colonization territory through congressional appropriations met the critical need of the country. Key to this proposal and all his others on colonization was the requirement that it be voluntary on the part of those leaving the country. Again addressing colonization in his second annual message to Congress, Lincoln revealed that he was negotiating with countries in the Caribbean basin for suitable sites.

Lincoln also raised the matter of colonization with his cabinet. With secretary of the interior Caleb B. Smith, Lincoln approved a contract for the use of money appropriated by Congress to voluntarily colonize ex-slaves living in the District of Columbia to Central America. Lincoln also believed that that site would benefit the United States because the contract would include coal for the navy. When the Central American countries rejected this prospect, Lincoln and Smith looked to an island under the control of Haiti. This possibility was seriously investigated. Negotiations had brought a preliminary agreement, and there was even a tentative settlement party when Lincoln ordered secretary of state William H. Seward not to countersign or affix the seal of the United States to the new contract. Having discovered massive fraud in the project, Lincoln canceled the contract. In February 1864 he ordered secretary of war Edwin M. Stanton to dispatch a ship to bring back the pioneering colonists who had been transported to the island but now desired repatriation.

In both speeches and policy considerations Lincoln consistently supported colonization but only on the conditions that free blacks give their consent and that the host country guarantee protection of their persons and their rights. Lincoln also expressed concern about whether free blacks would be willing to migrate to these countries. As it became more apparent that free blacks adamantly opposed relocation, Lincoln drew back from colonization. With the Civil War's end and Lincoln's death, colonization as a viable movement came to an end.

See also *American Colonization Society*

—ALLAN YAREMA

BIBLIOGRAPHY

Basler, Roy P., ed. *The Collected Works of Abraham Lincoln.* 7 vols. New Brunswick, N.J.: Rutgers University Press, 1953.

Ford, Paul Leicester, ed. *The Writings of Jefferson.* 10 vols. New York: G.P. Putnam's Sons, 1889.

Fox, Early Lee. *The American Colonization Society, 1817–1840.* Baltimore: John Hopkins University Press, 1919.

Hamilton, Stanislaus Murry, ed. *The Writings of James Monroe.* 6 vols. New York: G.P. Putnam's Sons, 1900.

Litwack, Leon F. *North of Slavery: The Negro in the Free States, 1790–1860.* Chicago: University of Chicago Press, 1961.

Staudenraus, P.J. *The African Colonization Movement, 1816–1865.* New York: Columbia University Press, 1961.

Yarema, Allan. *The American Colonization Society: An Avenue to Freedom?* Lanham, Md.: University Press of America, 2006.

Compensated Emancipation

Compensated emancipation proposals in the United States (1783–1865) sought to end slavery while providing some compensation to slave owners. Before the Civil War no laws were ever passed at the state or federal level to accomplish this. In the revolutionary era Massachusetts and New Hampshire ended slavery outright with no compensation. Pennsylvania, Connecticut, Rhode Island, New

York, and New Jersey adopted gradual emancipation, decreeing that slaves born after passage of the law would have to serve until a certain age. These laws did not "take" slaves from masters but provided that only the children of slaves would become free. The laws also provided for the indenture of these children, which gave masters compensation for their loss in the form of labor. Starting with New York in 1827, all the Northern states eventually passed laws freeing the remaining slaves in their jurisdictions, without any compensation to masters.

From the time of the American Revolution some opponents of slavery suggested that the national government fund a system of compensated emancipation for the slaves in the South. There were economic, political, and constitutional reasons why this could never happen. The cost, as Southerners constantly pointed out, would have been prohibitive. In addition, Southerners in Congress would have done everything in their power to prevent such a law from even being debated. Strict Constitutionalists also argued that the national government had no constitutional power to touch slavery in the states, and thus they maintained that any form of compensated emancipation had to be completely voluntary on the part of the slave owner. Most discussions of compensated emancipation also included the colonization of the former slaves. This too would have been enormously expensive, and Southerners argued that forced colonization would also exceed the powers of Congress.

Congress did have the power to regulate the District of Columbia and the territories, and in those places compensated emancipation was constitutional. From the beginning of his career Abraham Lincoln favored using the powers of Congress to accomplish it. In 1837 he presented a memorial in the Illinois legislature declaring that Congress did have "the power under the constitution, to abolish slavery in the District of Columbia." This memorial did not pass, but it indicates Lincoln's early interest in the subject. A decade later, in his single term in Congress, Lincoln proposed a bill for the gradual abolition of slavery in the District of Columbia. Such an emancipation scheme would avoid the Fifth Amendment problem of taking property without due process or just compensation because gradual emancipation did not free those presently enslaved but only guaranteed that their as-yet-unborn children would be free. Lincoln read the proposed emancipation bill on the floor of Congress but in the end did not introduce it; a powerless freshman congressman, he explained, "I was abandoned by my former backers." In fact, with acrimonious debate over the Wilmot Proviso tearing Congress apart, a serious discussion of a bill to end slavery in the District was not even remotely plausible. Nevertheless this bill, like his state legislature resolution, underscores that Lincoln was always interested in ending slavery where he could but had not adopted a radical abolitionist vision of ending slavery everywhere in the United States through federal action.

When Lincoln was inaugurated as president in March 1861, seven states had seceded; four more followed a month later. Lincoln recognized that the perceived threat to slaveholders was a primary cause of secession, and he feared that the slaveholding Border States, Delaware, Maryland, Missouri, Kentucky, and West Virginia, might follow suit. Part of Lincoln's strategy to prevent the loss of the

Border States to the Confederacy involved a proposal in March 1862 for gradual, federal compensation to slave owners in those states, but delegates rejected the offer. Historians remain divided as to Lincoln's commitment to black equality, but it is clear that his constitutional beliefs and his commitment to the preservation of the Union kept him on a moderate course of emancipation. His support for compensated emancipation in the District of Columbia in 1862 illustrates this point: That act was achieved under the constitutional authority of Congress and provided compensation for masters and immediate freedom for slaves. It appropriated a small amount of money to encourage free blacks voluntarily to leave the United States, but it did not tie emancipation to colonization, and no blacks ever took advantage of the provision.

In July 1862 Lincoln sent a bill to Congress that would have appropriated money to pay masters in the Border States who freed their slaves, but Congress never acted on it. In December of that year, in his annual message to Congress, Lincoln advocated the principles of colonization and gradual, compensated emancipation as a means of ending the war through a constitutional amendment. The federal cost of compensation for slaves in the states that adopted the amendment, he stated, would be far less than war expenditures. But Congress did not pursue Lincoln's proposal. In February 1865 Lincoln made another unsuccessful attempt to use compensation to end the war peacefully, proposing that four hundred million dollars be distributed among the remaining slave states as recompense for the loss of slave property—provided that those states ratified the Thirteenth Amendment and rejoined the Union. Although historians cannot agree on Lincoln's racial thinking with respect to emancipation, his compensation proposals demonstrate an unwavering commitment to restoring the Union while ensuring the eradication of slavery.

See also *Slavery*

—Alison Mann and Paul Finkelman

BIBLIOGRAPHY

Blight, David, and Brooks Simpson, eds. *Union and Emancipation: Essays on Politics and Race in the Civil War Era*. Kent, Ohio: Kent State University Press, 1997.

Cox, LaWanda. *Lincoln and Black Freedom: A Study in Presidential Leadership*. Columbia: University of South Carolina Press, 1981.

Fladeland, Betty L. "Compensated Emancipation: A Rejected Alternative." *Journal of Southern History* 42, no. 2 (May 1976): 169–186.

Frederickson, George. "A Man but Not a Brother: Abraham Lincoln and Racial Equality." *Journal of Southern History* 41, no. 1 (February 1975): 39–58.

Holzer, Harold, and Sara Vaughn Gabbard, eds. *Lincoln and Freedom: Slavery, Emancipation, and the Thirteenth Amendment*. Carbondale: Southern Illinois University Press, 2007.

Lind, Michael. *What Lincoln Believed*. New York: Doubleday, 2004.

Compromise of 1850

Throughout the first half of the nineteenth century the annexation of new land by the United States sparked intense sectional debate over the question of the expansion of slavery into the newly acquired territory. Conflict had arisen in 1819–1820, when Missouri applied for statehood as a slave state, thrusting into the limelight the question of slavery's extension into the Louisiana Purchase. Similar controversy ensued when the U.S. Army wrested California, New Mexico, and Utah from Mexico in the U.S.–Mexican War in 1848, and Congress took up the question of its authority to legislate the issue for the region.

Southern slaveholders demanded the right to take their slave property into the new territories, while Northerners, stirred by growing antislavery sentiment, bitterly opposed it. Driving Southern demands was the fear that if the new territories entered the Union as free states, that would dramatically change the balance of political power in Congress and put the institution of slavery, which they deemed a cornerstone of the American republic, at the mercy of hostile sentiment in the North.

The issue was explosive, and the nation's two main political parties, the Democrats and the Whigs, had done everything in their power to downplay it, compromising where possible, employing partisan restraints when necessary, or simply avoiding the issue altogether. Though certainly not perfect, this strategy had largely succeeded in maintaining the peace. That delicate balance ended, however, when David Wilmot, a relatively obscure Democratic representative from Pennsylvania, attached a rider to a wartime appropriations bill to exclude slavery from any territory gained as a result of the war with Mexico. With the question now in the open, Congress ground to a halt. Hoping to circumvent the troublesome issue, presidential aspirants Lewis Cass, the Democrat, and Zachary Taylor, the Whig, organized campaigns in 1848 to ease tensions. Taylor and the Whigs chose to remain silent on the question, and Cass promoted a policy known as "popular sovereignty," under which the question of allowing slavery or not would be left to the residents of the territories to decide.

The Whig strategy, which lent itself to divergent sectional spins, proved the more appealing, and Zachary Taylor was elected to the White House. Unfortunately for Taylor, however, the discovery of gold in California, and the unorganized region's explosive settlement, necessitated immediate action by federal authorities. Once again Congress found itself confronting the issue of slavery's expansion. Intending to bypass the sticky question of congressional authority over slavery in federal territories, the new president proposed bringing California immediately into the Union as a free state. Taylor's proposal did not sit well with Southerners, and Congress again stood deadlocked.

Compromise of 1850

Eager to settle the dispute and keep the nation whole, Sen. Henry Clay proposed an omnibus compromise bill that focused on five outstanding issues: (1) California's proposed admission as a free state; (2) the organization of the New Mexico and Utah Territories and the question of whether they would be admitted, when ready, as slave or free states; (3) an outstanding boundary dispute between Texas, a slave state, and its territorial neighbor, New Mexico; (4) slavery and the slave trade in the District of Columbia; and (5) the problem of fugitive slaves' fleeing north and not being returned.

Clay's task loomed as even more difficult because of two factors: The House of Representatives was so divided over the issues that it took nearly a month to organize and elect a Speaker; it had been ruled out as a vehicle for compromise. Additionally the president, Zachary Taylor, was stubbornly clinging to his plan and opposing any other, more comprehensive compromise. Accordingly Clay determined to wage his battle in the Senate. In January 1850 he introduced a compromise package addressing all five problems. His plan called for immediate statehood for California as a free state; the other territories when ready would be admitted free or slave, with no restrictions either way; Texas would relinquish its claim to New Mexico territory and in return the federal government would assume the state's debt contracted prior to its annexation in 1845; slavery would not be abolished in the District of Columbia, but the slave trade would be; and finally, the Fugitive Slave Law, to enforce the return of runaway slaves to their masters, would be tightened.

Clay's compromise would not win easy acceptance. The Senate was sharply divided. Two of the nation's other notable statesmen, John C. Calhoun of South Carolina and Daniel Webster of Massachusetts, were at opposite poles—Calhoun speaking against compromise just before he died the first day of April, and Webster speaking eloquently for it in a famed speech on the Senate floor on May 7.

The environment for compromise changed dramatically, however, when President Taylor fell ill in early July and died. Clay's omnibus legislation, in a fast-moving series of motions, collapsed less than a month later. Clay threw up his hands in despair, but the young, first-term senator from Illinois, Stephen A. Douglas, chair of the Committee on the Territories, who had sponsored the various pieces of Clay's compromise, stepped in and guided the package through the Senate and then through the House, not as a package, but measure by individual measure, piece by piece. The new president, Millard Fillmore, who favored the compromise, signed it all, and the nation heaved a huge sigh of relief. It was not perfect and was widely viewed as but a patch over the trouble, but it put down the immediate crisis.

The relief was to last four years, until Stephen Douglas himself unhinged the compromise with the Kansas-Nebraska Act, which abolished the Missouri Compromise line, allowing slavery into any territory that would accept it. This was the "popular sovereignty" solution—leaving it to the individual territories to decide to enter free or slave—vigorously favored by Douglas as the ultimate solution to the slavery problem.

Lincoln, who had been in Illinois practicing law, riding the judicial circuit and virtually out of politics since 1849, played no role in the Compromise of 1850. But like most Americans he thought it a reasonable, if not a permanent, solution. When the Kansas-Nebraska Act was passed, Lincoln, who vigorously opposed the spread of slavery into the territories, charged out of political retirement to oppose it and Douglas. This would lead to the great debates over the issue between Lincoln and Douglas in the Illinois Senate race of 1858, and to their nomination for president by their respective parties and Lincoln's election in 1860.

See also *Fillmore, Millard; Taylor, Zachary*

—JOHN C. WAUGH

BIBLIOGRAPHY

Freehling, William W. *The Road to Disunion: Secessionists at Bay, 1776–1854.* Vol. 1. New York: Oxford University Press, 1990.

Hamilton, Holman. *Prologue to Conflict: The Crisis and Compromise of 1850.* Lexington: University Press of Kentucky, 1964.

———. "Democratic Senate Leadership and the Compromise of 1850." *Mississippi Valley Historical Review* 41 (December 1954): 403–418.

Harmon, George D. "Douglas and the Compromise of 1850." *Journal of the Illinois State Historical Society* 21 (January 1929): 453–499.

Hodder, Frank H. "The Authorship of the Compromise of 1850." *Mississippi Valley Historical Review* 22 (March 1936): 525–536.

Rozwenc, Edwin C., ed. *The Compromise of 1850.* Problems in American Civilization. Boston: D.C. Heath, 1957.

Waugh, John C. *On the Brink of Civil War: The Compromise of 1850 and How It Changed the Course of American History.* The American Crisis Series: Books on the Civil War Era, No. 13. Wilmington, Del.: Scholarly Resources, 2003.

Confederate States of America

The Confederate States of America (1861–1865) was the name adopted by the Southern states that attempted to break away from the federal Union in response to the election of Abraham Lincoln. Shortly after secession the new Confederate vice president, Alexander Stephens, declared that slavery was the "cornerstone" of the new Southern nation. Convinced that the founders, many of whom were slave owners, readily understood the connection between slavery and white liberty, the secessionists believed that the election of Abraham Lincoln—a Republican committed to an antislavery agenda—made it necessary to leave the union and to create a new republic devoted to the intentions of the founders. They sought to create a nation that stood as a conservative bulwark of the deep connections between slavery and liberty.

Between Lincoln's election in November 1860 and March 1861, seven states—South Carolina, Mississippi, Alabama, Florida, Georgia, Louisiana, and Texas—seceded. Prior to Lincoln's inauguration in February 1860, their representatives met at Montgomery, Alabama, to organize as the Confederate States of America. To justify the creation of an independent nation, the seceding states employed a philosophy formulated by South Carolina senator John C. Calhoun (1782–1850). Calhoun believed that secession was a constitutional right, on the theory that the states had voluntarily created the nation and therefore could voluntarily withdraw from it. On February 9, the assembled delegates unanimously elected Jefferson Davis of Mississippi as the nation's new president and Alexander H. Stephens of Georgia as vice president.

Lincoln's policies toward the Confederacy evolved over time. Initially the president reacted with caution. He did not believe that states had the right to secede from the Union, nor was he convinced that the majority of the Southern population, which was overwhelmingly non-slaveholding, supported secession. Thus he urged moderation, hoping that time would enable latent Unionism to coalesce. Lincoln also feared that vigorous action would alienate the slave states that remained loyal to the Union and incite them also to secede

In the aftermath of the Fort Sumter crisis and Lincoln's call for 75,000 volunteers from the loyal states, four more states—Virginia, Tennessee, Arkansas, and North Carolina—seceded. Thereafter, the story of the Confederacy became that of the Civil War.

Lincoln's policies remained consistent with his belief that the seceding states did not have the right to leave and create an independent nation. Publicly he refused to acknowledge the Confederacy and instead referred to the states as "rebellious" entities. Nonetheless, at least one of Lincoln's actions, the imposition of a blockade around the Confederate coastline, raised questions of whether, as the Confederacy insisted, under international law the action validated its claim to be an autonomous state. Lincoln, however, remained firm in his denial of any such claim.

Initially Lincoln's policies toward the Confederacy were designed to effect their return to their former positions within the Union, with slavery intact. He insisted on the protection and efficient enforcement of the Fugitive Slave Law that provided for the rendition of runaway slaves to their owners, and he refused to allow initiatives by Union generals such as John C. Frémont to emancipate slaves in areas under their jurisdiction. As Lincoln consistently made clear, his primary objective was to preserve the Union.

By 1862, however, epic campaigns and battles forced Lincoln to change his belief that Southern Unionists could overthrow the secessionist powers. He concluded that the war could no longer be treated as though it were a limited police action. Ensuring the survival of the republic required the war to be fought all-out—the rebel armies had to be destroyed. To achieve that goal, the federal army began consuming, confiscating, or destroying civilian property that could be used to support or supply the Confederate armies, including slaves.

The Confiscation Acts of 1861 and 1862 allowed confiscation of Confederate slaves—deemed contraband of war—as a means of undermining the Confederacy's ability to wage war. The measures did not, however, lead to the emancipation of most slaves because a judicial proceeding was required to seize a slave. The Second Confiscation Act freed all slaves that fled to the U.S. Army or were seized under the act, but this left most Southern slaves still in bondage. Continued misfortune on the military front and difficulty recruiting soldiers, along with a growing threat of European recognition of the Confederacy, however, forced Lincoln to consider more dramatic action on slavery. Lincoln's Emancipation Proclamation, issued in September 1862 and effective January 1, 1863, declared freedom for slaves in states or portions of states then in rebellion against the United States.

Though the proclamation shifted Union war aims and broadened the war to include a commitment to the destruction of slavery, Lincoln continued to support peaceful reunification. This conciliatory tone was very much in evidence in his 1863 reconstruction policy that offered pardon and amnesty to Southerners who took an oath of allegiance and created the opportunity to establish new, loyal state governments within the Union. The policy also allowed compromise on all wartime policies except slavery and emancipation. Portions of Tennessee, Arkansas, and Louisiana took advantage of this opportunity, abolishing slavery along the way to further demonstrate their loyalty to the Union. Lincoln's vision, however, remained largely unfulfilled because of congressional opposition.

By 1864 hope for peaceful negotiation began to wane on both sides. Confederate president Jefferson Davis rejected any consideration of peace that did not include the independence of the Confederate states. Lincoln continued to insist on the preservation of the Union, and now, bolstered by Union military successes, he also required Southern states to abolish slavery before the war could end. Emancipation had become the North's tool for subduing the rebellion.

The final push for total war and unconditional surrender brought the Confederacy to its knees. With his reelection in 1864, Lincoln's policy of unconditional surrender altered military tactics. Since the Confederacy refused to surrender, federal troops worked to break the South's "unconquerable defiance" by burning and destroying Southern crops, railroads, bridges, factories, and other property, as most famously carried out during General William T. Sherman's devastating march from Atlanta to the sea. The magnitude of wreckage undermined the morale of all Confederates, both civilian and military. The use of unconditional surrender and total warfare proved a winning combination. On April 7, 1865, near the Appomattox Courthouse, General Robert E. Lee found himself surrounded by Ulysses Grant's army. Understanding that a retreat would lead to guerrilla warfare and needless further destruction, Lee surrendered his battered troops to Grant, along with hopes of an independent Confederacy.

See also *Davis, Jefferson; Lee, Robert E.*

—ALYSSA ARNELL

BIBLIOGRAPHY

Coulter, E. Merton. *The Confederate States of America, 1861–1865. A History of the South*. Vol. 7. Baton Rouge: Louisiana State University Press, 1950.

Cowley, Robert, ed. *With My Face to the Enemy: Perspectives on the Civil War.* New York: Putnam's, 2001.

Johannsen, Robert W. *Lincoln, the South, and Slavery: the Political Dimension.* Baton Rouge: Louisiana State University Press, 1991.

McPherson, James M. *Battle Cry of Freedom.* New York: Oxford University Press, 1988.

———. *Abraham Lincoln and the Second American Revolution.* New York: Oxford University Press, 1991.

Oates, Stephen B. *Our Fiery Trial: Abraham Lincoln, John Brown, and the Civil War Era.* Amherst: University of Massachusetts Press, 1979.

Sandburg, Carl. *Abraham Lincoln: The Prairie Years and the War Years.* New York: Harcourt Brace, 1954.

Thomas, Emory. *The Confederate Nation, 1861–1865.* New York: Harper and Row, 1979.

Confiscation Acts

Following the election of Abraham Lincoln as president of the United States, the seven states of the Deep South seceded from the Union, believing that his election threatened slavery. Four Upper South states—Virginia, North Carolina, Tennessee, and Arkansas—joined the Confederacy following the attack on Fort Sumter on April 12, 1861. Almost immediately, enslaved African Americans came to the same conclusion as their white Southern counterparts, that the election of Lincoln and the appearance of Northern armies in the South meant freedom for the slaves. Slaves began to run away from their masters as U.S. armies moved deeper into the South.

For political reasons Lincoln moved slowly to enact emancipation. He faced the problem of losing support from loyal slave owners in seceded Southern states and in the Border States. Even though he opposed slavery, Lincoln did not believe that he had the constitutional authority to free the slaves. He also understood that Northerners—especially Unionist Democrats—would oppose the war effort if he made war on slavery.

Following his appointment as commander of Fort Monroe in Virginia, General Benjamin F. Butler (1818–1893) immediately had to decide how to deal with runaway slaves fleeing to the Union lines. Increasingly Union soldiers came to resent enforcing the Fugitive Slave Act of 1850. Butler also recognized the value of slave labor to the Confederacy. When he received no clear instructions on what to do with the fugitive slaves, Butler, a lawyer before the war, came up with a brilliant legal solution. He declared slaves to be contraband of war because they were being used by the Confederates in the war effort. He welcomed and freed all slaves who fled to his lines, allowing them to work in exchange for shelter, food, and clothing.

Congress followed Butler's action with passage of the first of two Confiscation Acts on August 6, 1861. The act granted the army authority to seize rebel-owned property, including slave property "employed in hostile service against the government."

The first challenge to Lincoln's authority on slavery came on August 30, 1861, after John C. Frémont (1813–1890), military commander of the Department of the West, declared martial law in Missouri. Fearing that the confiscation and liberation of slaves would frighten Unionists in the South, Lincoln asked that the proclamation be rescinded, but Frémont refused, leading to his removal in November 1861. Lincoln's fears proved prescient when the loyal Kentucky legislature demanded nullification of Frémont's proclamation. Lincoln also believed that the proclamation was a violation of the Confiscation Act.

In the following year Lincoln sought an alternative to the Confiscation Act. Even though Lincoln did not veto the act, he nonetheless did not support it. He saw gradual emancipation combined with compensation to slave owners as the preferred government policy. In a special message to Congress on March 6, 1862, Lincoln recommended a joint resolution in support of compensated, gradual emancipation. He saw this as far less expensive than the war, in both money and lives, although he doubtless knew that most of the Southern states would not have returned to the Union under such a program. On April 10, 1862, Congress endorsed compensated, gradual emancipation for only the Border States and followed this with the abolition of slavery in the District of Columbia on April 16, 1862.

Public hostility to the Confederacy increased as battlefield casualties mounted. The anger translated into desire for revenge against what many saw as

Southern aggression. Many saw confiscation and emancipation of the slaves as punishment of the aggressors. On May 9, 1862, General David Hunter issued General Order Number 11, which declared martial law in Georgia, Florida, and South Carolina. He used this declaration to free all slaves in his district. Lincoln immediately responded by denying any foreknowledge of Hunter's order; he proclaimed that the military had no authority to issue such a declaration, saying that this authority was reserved to himself as commander in chief.

On July 17, 1862, Congress passed the Second Confiscation Act, authorizing the freeing, without compensation, of slave property confiscated from those in rebellion against the United States. It also authorized the president to colonize the newly freed people to a "tropical country." By the time Lincoln signed this bill he had already written, but not yet released, the Emancipation Proclamation, and thus the congressional action dovetailed with his plans to end slavery as a war measure.

During the following months Lincoln saw no favorable response to his plan for gradual and compensated emancipation of slaves. He even added the promise of their deportation to either Liberia or Haiti. Still, no one responded to his proposal. Lincoln concluded that he should exercise presidential authority to accomplish emancipation through his war powers. The Emancipation Proclamation (September 22, 1862) was a direct challenge to Congress and the Confiscation Acts.

See also *Confiscation Act, Second*

—Bradley Skelcher

BIBLIOGRAPHY

Belz, Herman. *Emancipation and Equal Rights: Politics and Constitutionalism in the Civil War Era.* New York: Norton, 1978.

Berlin, Ira, et al., ed. *Freedom: A Documentary History of Emancipation, 1861–1867: The Destruction of Slavery.* Series 1. Volume 1. New York: Cambridge University Press, 1985.

Current, Richard. *The Lincoln Nobody Knows.* New York: Hill and Wang, 1958.

Johnson, Michael P., ed. *Abraham Lincoln, Slavery, and the Civil War: Selected Writings and Speeches.* Boston: Bedford/St. Martin's, 2001.

McPherson, James M. *Abraham Lincoln and the Second American Revolution.* New York: Oxford University Press, 1992.

Oates, Stephen B. *With Malice toward None: The Life of Abraham Lincoln.* New York: New American Library, 1977.

Siddali, Silvana R. *From Property to Person: Slavery and the Confiscation Acts, 1861–1862.* Baton Rouge: Louisiana State University Press, 2005.

Syrett, John. *The Civil War Confiscation Acts: Failing to Reconstruct the South.* New York: Fordham University Press, 2005.

Confiscation Act, Second

The Thirty-seventh Congress passed the Second Confiscation Act on July 17, 1862. The act followed the First Confiscation Act, passed on August 6, 1861. In response to the first act, the Confederacy had passed the Sequestration Act on August 30, 1861, allowing the confiscation of property owned by "alien enemies" or pro-Unionists. These seizures were to be permanent. The North responded with the Second Confiscation Act.

The First Confiscation Act only allowed Union forces to confiscate property used for military purposes by the Confederacy. By the second act Congress used confiscation to punish rebels by seizing their property without hope of its return.

In many respects the Second Confiscation Act represented the frustrations and anger of Northerners over the prosecution of the war by Lincoln and his generals at the time. The growing number of casualties prompted many Northerners to clamor for revenge and the punishment of rebels by confiscating and freeing their slaves and taking other property without compensation. To many, secessionists had committed treason and should be punished regardless of due process. Sen. Lyman Trumbull of Illinois, chair of the Judiciary Committee, led the movement to punish disloyal Southerners through permanent confiscation of their property. In the end, Congress considered this a war necessity.

On April 10, 1862, Congress had endorsed Lincoln's proposal for gradual, compensated emancipation of slaves. That proposed legislation included the appropriation of funds to finance compensation and for voluntary resettlement of freedmen in Liberia and Haiti. On April 16, 1862, Congress abolished slavery in the District of Columbia, providing compensation to loyal slave owners. These measures followed on the heels of legislation passed on March 13, 1862, forbidding the return of seized slaves by the army or navy. Lincoln complied and ordered the army and navy not to return seized slaves to their owners. Congress then passed the Territorial Emancipation Act, on June 19, 1862

Confiscation also applied to property other than slaves. Salmon P. Chase, as secretary of the Treasury, had the responsibility of disposing of confiscated property and collecting the revenue from its sale. As the U.S. Army moved south, the largest seizures of property were of cotton and other agricultural products, especially after Congress passed the Internal Revenue Act on July 1, 1862. The Internal Revenue Act allowed for the collection of income taxes by the federal government to finance the war effort. There were numerous accusations of corruption following the seizure of contraband property and its auction.

As Union military forces moved throughout the South, they seized more property, such as plantations, and including the home of General Robert E. Lee in Arlington, Virginia. As General William T. Sherman occupied and seized more Confederate territory, he issued Field Order No. 15 on January 16, 1865, proclaiming the redistribution of abandoned and seized land in allotments of forty acres to former slaves. Sherman based his action on the Confiscation Acts, as he had done earlier while occupying Memphis, Tennessee. Following passage of the Second Confiscation Act in 1862, Sherman proclaimed its sovereignty over any existing slave codes within the municipality. The Freedmen's Bureau used this as precedent in its land redistribution plans.

Still Lincoln, and others such as Sen. Orville Browning of Illinois, saw the Second Confiscation Act as a challenge to the Constitution and to presidential powers. They were concerned about taking private property without trial and conviction. Lincoln objected to Congress's assertion of the power to free slaves within a state. Under the threat of a veto, Congress changed this language. Sen. John Sherman of Ohio believed that confiscation could only come through judicial action.

Congress continued to maintain that the Second Confiscation Act was a wartime measure authorized by the Constitution. The Supreme Court of the United States upheld the Second Confiscation Act following the Civil War in the *Confiscation Cases* (87 U.S. 92 [1873]).

The Second Confiscation Act encouraged more slaves to escape to freedom behind Union lines. Congress took a step toward overturning the Fugitive Slave Act of 1850 in Section 10 of the act, which did not require the return of fugitive slaves escaping from any territory or state or the District of Columbia.

The act's passage also prompted Lincoln to move toward proclaiming emancipation of slaves held within states that were in rebellion against the United States. On July 22, 1862, Lincoln informed his cabinet that he would issue an emancipation proclamation. He delayed issuing the proclamation until Union forces secured a military victory, which came at the Battle of Antietam on September 17, 1862. In all, the Second Confiscation Act was the culmination of a series of steps leading the North toward prosecuting the war not only to preserve the Union, but also to end slavery.

See also *Confiscation Acts*

—BRADLEY SKELCHER

BIBLIOGRAPHY

Davis, David Brion. *Inhuman Bondage: The Rise and Fall of Slavery in the New World.* New York: Oxford University Press, 2006.

Green, Michael S. *Freedom, Union, and Power: Lincoln and His Party during the Civil War.* New York: Fordham University Press, 2004.

Hamilton, Daniel W. *The Limits of Sovereignty: Property Confiscation in the Union and the Confederacy during the Civil War.* Chicago: University of Chicago Press, 2007.

Johnson, Michael P., ed. *Abraham Lincoln, Slavery, and the Civil War: Selected Writings and Speeches.* Boston: Bedford/St. Martin's, 2001.

Litwack, Leon F. *Been in the Storm So Long: The Aftermath of Slavery.* New York: Vintage, 1979.

McPherson, James M. *For Cause and Comrades: Why Men Fought in the Civil War.* New York: Oxford University Press, 1998.

Siddali, Silvana R. *From Property to Person: Slavery and the Confiscation Acts, 1861–1862.* Baton Rouge: Louisiana State University Press, 2005.

Syrett, John. *The Civil War Confiscation Acts: Failing to Reconstruct the South.* New York: Fordham University Press, 2005.

Congress, Lincoln's Relations with

Abraham Lincoln's presidency spanned the Thirty-seventh and Thirty-eighth Congresses. During that period Republicans controlled both the House and the Senate, and Lincoln ostensibly enjoyed good relations with a Congress that, with few exceptions, approved his wartime measures and his appointments to both military and patronage positions. In reality, conflict and tension often entered into relations between the president and Congress, particularly in light of the incessant pressures and criticisms emanating from both the Democratic minority and the radical wing of the Republican Party. Though not a majority, even within the ranks of congressional Republicans, the most committed opponents of slavery (who would eventually be called Radical Republicans) were numerous enough to dictate, or at least influence, policy regarding the confiscation of property, the emancipation of the slaves, and the reconstruction of the seceded states. Other than the war itself, these were arguably the most important policy questions facing the federal government during the war. In all of these areas the clashes between Lincoln and leading radicals sometimes threatened the harmony that the majority coalition required to prosecute the war vigorously, and, in 1864 they threatened to undermine Lincoln's reelection.

The representatives and senators elected in November 1860 would not meet as a new Congress until December 1861. On April 15, 1861, however, in response to the crisis at Fort Sumter, Lincoln called for Congress to meet in special session on July 4. When they convened, the clerk read Lincoln's message in which he defended his recent suspension of the writ of *habeas corpus*, first in areas of Maryland and later in Missouri, and the subsequent arrests of hundreds of citizens without formal charges being lodged against them. Lincoln justified his emergency exercise of powers that were constitutionally within the purview of the legislature, such as, the expansion of the size of the regular army and navy. He also explained his proclamation of a blockade of the Southern coast, initially from Texas to South Carolina and later expanded to include North Carolina and Virginia. He expressed confidence that nothing beyond the constitutional competency of Congress had been done and then urged the legislature to "ratify" his use of extraordinary measures. Congress did in fact approve his actions.

The leadership of the Thirty-seventh Congress reflected what would be the prevailing spirit of that legislative body. Galusha A. Grow, of Pennsylvania, who is most remembered as the father of the Homestead Act, was chosen Speaker of the House, and he promptly chose the deeply antislavery Thaddeus Stevens to chair the powerful Ways and Means Committee. Grow, Stevens, and the entire Republican leadership were all strong unionists who would accept no compromise over secession. Five days after his appointment Stevens reported out a bill authorizing secretary of the Treasury Salmon P. Chase to borrow $250 million over the next twelve months. Then Stevens pushed through a suspension of the rules to permit the bill to be considered immediately and obtained approval to limit debate to one hour. Before its adjournment on August 6, this special session passed a remarkable sixty-six bills, all but four of them relating to the war.

The first rumblings of disharmony between this Congress and Lincoln followed the Battle of Bull Run on July 21. Many members of Congress had accompanied the army into the field and witnessed the battle at first hand. What they saw was an unmitigated disaster, as the Union army fled from the battle in disarray. Moreover, many of the witnesses reported seeing slaves performing duties for the Confederate army that would normally have been performed by soldiers. Then on October 21, at the Battle of Ball's Bluff, outside Leesburg, Virginia, west of Washington, an even worse defeat befell the Union army. Union casualty rates were a staggering 50 percent, and many of the dead were carried downstream by the Potomac River, ending up along the Washington waterfront, a grisly reminder of another military disaster.

The defeats led some of the most radical antislavery members of the party, including senators Benjamin Wade of Ohio and Zachariah Chandler of Michigan, to demand that the war be prosecuted to the fullest by officers whose loyalty to the country was above suspicion. Less than a week after convening for their December session, Congress approved the creation of the Joint Committee on the Conduct of the War, with broad investigatory powers and virtually unlimited subpoena power. Its membership was decidedly antislavery and uncompromising over secession, and many of the members harbored deep distrust of the military. During its existence the committee investigated allegations of fraud and incompetence in the War Department (leading to the resignation of secretary of war Simon Cameron and his replacement by Edwin Stanton), questioned officers about both their competence and their loyalty, and even investigated rumors that Mary Todd Lincoln was a Confederate spy. The committee became a source of continuous criticism of Lincoln for his hesitation to implement immediate emancipation in early 1862, for his toleration of General George B. McClellan's lack of aggression, and particularly for his reappointment of McClellan to command of the Army of the Potomac following the Second Battle of Bull Run. Ultimately the committee produced eight volumes of testimony and findings, but

Lincoln largely ignored its recommendations. The committee was reconstituted during the Thirty-eighth Congress, in 1863, but despite much posturing, its influence over the president was never very strong.

The record of the Thirty-seventh Congress was impressive. In February 1862 Congress passed the legal tender bill authorizing the first paper currency for the United States. In April 1862 it abolished slavery in the District of Columbia, through compensated emancipation, something Lincoln had sought as a congressman during his only term in the House (1847–1849). In May the Homestead Act passed, awarding 160 acres of public land to any citizen who would reside on the land and farm it for five years. Twenty-five thousand settlers staked claims to more than three million acres of land before the war's end. In June the Morrill Land Grant College Act was passed, providing land to the states if they would agree to finance the creation of public agricultural and mining colleges. On July 1 Congress passed the U.S. Internal Revenue Act of 1862, creating the first income tax in American history, and on the same day Lincoln signed the Pacific Railroad Act into law, providing land and financial grants to corporations to build the first transcontinental railroad, from Omaha, Nebraska, to Sacramento, California.

A critically important issue during the Thirty-seventh Congress was confiscation. The First Confiscation Act, passed in the aftermath of the First Battle of Bull Run, was essentially a restatement of internationally recognized confiscatory policy recognizing the right of nations at war to seize the property of enemies, including slaves, that was being used by the enemy in its war effort. The Second Confiscation Act, introduced on December 2, differed from the first in that it was intended to be punitive. This measure targeted individuals who supported the rebellion and proposed to punish them by taking their property. There was much precedent for this type of action during the American Revolution. Judicial philosophy, however, had changed during the subsequent three-quarters of a century, as the idea of unfettered and inalienable property rights took hold in the nation. The debate on the Second Confiscation Act consumed most of the session and divided Republicans. Extended debates focused on whether the confiscatory provisions, specifically the liberation of the offenders' slaves, would be more likely to bring the rebels back to their former loyalties or drive them further into rebellion.

In the end, the important thing about the legislation, at least from Abraham Lincoln's perspective, was that it would require *in rem* proceedings in which jurisdiction was not based on the presence of the person but rather on the location of the property. Lincoln did not care for *in rem* jurisdiction, and he objected to the legislation constitutionally because he believed that it violated the constitution's proscription against bills of attainder, or laws that worked a corruption of blood by punishing an offender beyond his lifetime. Since the permanent forfeiture of property would dispossess the heirs of the property owner from any future rights, Lincoln let it be known that he would veto the legislation. This compelled Congress to enact a joint explanatory resolution saying that the forfeiture would not extend beyond the lifetime of the offender. Lincoln then signed the legislation while simultaneously forwarding his proposed veto message to Congress to be made part of the record.

As the president later pointed out, the Second Confiscation Act never freed a slave because it neither inspired nor influenced Lincoln's course with regard to the Emancipation Proclamation. And that presidential decree subsumed any effect that might have been rendered by the confiscation legislation. In the end it was simply a showy display by Congress of its zeal to free those enslaved in the South. But emancipation would come by means of executive actions and the presence of the military.

Congress passed the Thirteenth Amendment as Lincoln's first term came to a close. The amendment finished the process of ending slavery in the loyal slave states and in those regions of the former Confederacy that had been under the control of the United States in 1863 and thus were exempt from the Emancipation Proclamation. More important, the new amendment, which was ratified by the end of 1865, constitutionalized the Emancipation Proclamation, thus preventing any subsequent suits or actions by disgruntled slave owners trying to gain compensation for the loss of their slaves or arguing that the emancipation itself was illegal. The short session of the Thirty-seventh Congress, convening in December 1862 following the midterm elections, had some stirring and controversial moments. Democrats, bolstered by a gain of twenty-eight seats (but not close to a majority) in the House of Representatives, began a systematic attack on the administration and its policies, particularly the suspension of the writ of *habeas corpus* and the jailing of dissenters. Peace Democrats, or "copperheads" as they were widely known, engaged in antiadministration activities that sometimes seemed to border on outright support of Southern independence. And immediately after the signing of the Emancipation Proclamation on January 1, 1863, radical House leader Thaddeus Stevens successfully sponsored a bill calling for the recruitment of 150,000 black soldiers. In addition, on the last day of the session, March 3, 1863, Congress passed the Conscription Act, by which all men between the ages of twenty and thirty-five were subject to the draft. It was the first military draft in U.S. history. In a gesture that further aroused copperhead antagonism, Stevens also introduced and gained passage of a measure giving the president the authority, at his discretion, to suspend the writ of *habeas corpus* and extended that authority until the end of the war.

The Thirty-eighth Congress was contentious throughout its life. Democrats were badly split between supporters and opponents of the war (many Democrats who genuinely supported the war joined with the Republicans in a "Union Party" coalition for the remainder of the conflict). Border State Unionists were divided between those who supported Lincoln and those who condemned him, and Republicans divided between the radicals and moderates. In the House of Representatives there was an early attempt at a coup when Democrats and Border State Unionists tried to form a coalition that would deny the credentials of some Republicans and permit the coalition to organize and control the House. Republicans were alerted to the danger and met in special caucus on December 6, the day before the opening of Congress. The principal author of the coup attempt, Tennessee Unionist Emerson Etheridge, who had been chosen clerk of the Thirty-seventh Congress to reward his loyalty in remaining in Congress when his state seceded, ended by losing his clerkship as a result of his efforts. The debate on the issue had been particularly confrontational and would set the tone for the rest of the session.

In spite of the turmoil, however, the Thirty-eighth Congress also produced a raft of important legislation, particularly Stevens's Ways and Means Committee, which reported out bills to raise the tariff by an average of 47 percent and to impose the first income tax in American history. The tax ranged from a low of 5 percent on annual incomes starting at $600 to a high of 10 percent on incomes over $5,000. Excise taxes were also enacted for the first time since the Jefferson administration on a long list of items. Additionally, Congress approved the National Banking Act, thus ensuring that the funds to finance the war would come primarily from American lending institutions. The Freedmen's Bureau, in spite of sharply racist Democratic opposition, was also created by this Congress; it was the first social welfare agency established by the United States. Congress also banned segregation when chartering new street car companies in the District of Columbia, the first time the national government had passed a law to guarantee racial equality. As Northern victories placed large sections of the former Confederacy under Union control in 1863, Lincoln and congressional Republicans addressed how best to reconstruct the shattered nation; that debate amplified the rift between Lincoln and congressional radicals.

Lincoln pursued a lenient plan of reconstruction, often referred to as the "10 percent plan," designed as a temporary expedient for undermining immediate support for the Confederacy and rallying pro-Union dissent in a time of ongoing conflict. Dissatisfied with the low threshold for readmission established by Lincoln, and believing that the Southern states had abrogated their rights as states, congressional radicals, led by Ohio senator Benjamin Wade and Maryland representative Henry Winter Davis, rejected the credentials of those elected by the reconstructed Southern states and passed, on July 4, 1864 (the last day of the spring session), a more stringent plan of reconstruction that mandated the immediate abolition of slavery and would ensure congressional authority over the defeated states into the future. Intent on avoiding being "committed to any single plan of restoration" and uncomfortable with the measure's abolition provision, which suggested that the seceded states had actually been out of the Union (Lincoln believed that the pending Thirteenth Amendment was the only constitutional way to abolish slavery), Lincoln pocket-vetoed the bill, refusing to sign it within the time constitutionally allowed. The issue of reconstruction would remain in controversy between Lincoln and congressional radicals and would not be resolved until after Lincoln's death and the war's end in 1865.

The most important matter that the Thirty-eighth Congress considered was the enabling legislation for the Thirteenth Amendment to the Constitution, the first amendment in over a half-century, which would permanently end slavery in the United States. When it came before the House during the long session in spring 1864, it fell fifteen votes short of the two-thirds vote necessary. However, in the lame duck session following Lincoln's reelection in 1864, the president played a larger role in influencing Congress than he had at any other time in his presidency. His Annual Message in December 1864 made very clear that he wanted a constitutional amendment that would make the end of slavery permanent and universal throughout the United States. He referred to it as a "King's remedy for a monstrous wrong," and he and other members of his administration, particularly secretary of state William Seward, used every skill of influence, pressure, moral suasion, and power of patronage available to them to change as many Democratic votes as possible. The fifteen-vote loss of the previous April had been a virtual party line vote. Now, following Lincoln's reelection and the Republican successes in the congressional elections, about half that number of Democrats changed their votes, and the other half absented themselves the day of the vote. On January 31, 1865, in a roll call vote before packed galleries in the House of Representatives, the measure passed 119 to 58, winning three votes more than the necessary two-thirds. The House chamber erupted in a celebration such as had never before been seen there. People hollered and danced and cheered and climbed on tables. It was pandemonium, and when order was finally restored, the House adjourned for the rest of the day. It was one of the greatest days in the history of the U.S. Congress. Abraham Lincoln's journey to emancipation had been completed.

—David E. Long

BIBLIOGRAPHY

Donald, David Herbert. *Lincoln.* New York: Simon and Schuster, 1995.

Long, David E. *The Jewel of Liberty: Abraham Lincoln's Reelection and the End of Slavery.* Mechanicsburg, Pa.: Stackpole, 1994.

McPherson, James M. *Battle Cry of Freedom: The Civil War Era.* New York: Ballantine, 1988.

Conscription Act

Abraham Lincoln signed the first U.S. military draft on March 3, 1863.

After the fall of Fort Sumter in April 1861, Lincoln issued a call for 75,000 volunteers to serve ninety days to put down the rebellion. The president, as did most people both North and South, believed that the conflict would end quickly. Loyal states were given a quota of troops to raise, but the massive number of eager volunteers prompted some governors to ask the Lincoln administration to accept more regiments.

Conscription Act

The Union defeat at the battle of Bull Run in July 1861 partially dispelled the image of a quick victory. The day after the battle, Lincoln signed a bill authorizing the recruitment of 500,000 volunteers. Only three days later, the president approved another 500,000 recruits. Rather than ninety-day terms, these new enlistments were for three years. Again volunteers swamped recruiting offices across the North, and by the end of 1861 the U.S. war effort seemed to have sufficient troops to defeat the Confederacy.

By mid-1862, however, battlefield defeats had frustrated the Union war effort and damaged Northern morale. High casualties wore down the Union and Confederate armies, and both governments struggled to raise and equip replacements. In April 1862 the Confederacy took the monumental step of authorizing the first military draft in American history with the passage of a conscription act. The United States also moved in that direction. On July 2, 1862, after conferring with Northern governors, Lincoln called for another 300,000 volunteers. Unlike previous calls for enlistment, though, this time volunteers were slow in coming. To help entice recruits, the federal government offered $100 enlistment bounties. The government also took its first step toward coercing military service. On July 17, 1862, Congress passed a militia act. This measure placed all able-bodied men between eighteen and forty-five in the militia and empowered the president to call the state militias into federal service for nine months.

On August 4, 1862, Lincoln's War Department placed a new quota of 300,000 for the nine-month militia on top of the previous call for 300,000 men. If any state was unable to raise its quota, the federal government threatened to draft men from within that state. To fill their quotas, some states did implement a draft. Resistance to these enlistment efforts prompted the War Department to send soldiers to some Northern towns. Nonetheless, by the end of 1862 the Union recruiting drive netted 421,000 three-year enlistees and nearly 88,000 militiamen.

In early 1863, the United States again faced a manpower crisis. Casualties from battle and disease continued to drain the army. The excitement of war had long passed, and most men drawn to the conflict for patriotic reasons were already in the ranks. More than three dozen Union regiments and almost one hundred nine-month militia regiments were about to complete their terms of service and go home. Replacements were badly needed. Congress reacted with the Enrollment Act, or Conscription Act, which Lincoln approved on March 3, 1863.

The Conscription Act was primarily, but not only, designed to entice men to enlist. Provost marshals in congressional districts enrolled male citizens between twenty and forty-five years of age. When a draft was announced, a predetermined percentage of names were drawn from among the enrolled. The selection of one's name did not automatically mean military service. In fact, most men drafted did not serve. Many were rejected because of health or mental problems. Furthermore, the act offered means for draftees to avoid service. They could hire a substitute to take their place or were allowed to pay a fee of $300. Bribery, feigning illness, or other kinds of fraud helped keep many others out of the army. As a result, of the nearly 207,000 men drafted, only 46,000 actually entered the army.

Critics of the Republican administration lambasted the draft. Some Democrats criticized the $300 commutation fee, declaring that it favored the wealthy. Opposition to that exemption policy grew so strong that Congress repealed the commutation option in July 1864.

The depth of the draft's unpopularity in the North was tragically realized in New York City in July 1863. New York had a large immigrant Irish population, whose living and working conditions were appalling. Fear of having to compete with freed blacks for jobs had created strong resentment toward the Lincoln administration's emancipation policies. New York City's powerful Democratic presence also fueled the opposition to the draft. In this atmosphere, on Saturday, July 11, draft officers began the first conscription lottery in the city. On Monday morning, July 13, disgruntled New Yorkers attacked the draft offices and incited the worst riot in American history. For four days, rioters attacked Republican and abolitionist property, burned police stations, and took their frustration out on numerous African Americans. Finally, federal soldiers were called in to suppress the uprising. When it ended, more than one hundred people were dead.

New York's Democratic governor, Horatio Seymour, requested a suspension of the draft. Lincoln replied that the military situation made the draft a necessity, since the Confederacy placed every able-bodied man into its ranks. The Union, the president argued, could not afford to hesitate strengthening its own armies. On August 19 the draft resumed in New York. By that time the New York City Council had raised enough funds to pay the commutation fees of its draftees.

The draft continued to be controversial. Many complained of the expansion of federal power, and some state officials impeded the draft by refusing to enforce draft laws and even releasing drafted men from service. Lincoln responded by suspending the writ of *habeas corpus* in draft cases. Democrats focused on its unpopularity to hurt Republican candidates in wartime elections. Yet the Lincoln administration continued to use the draft well into 1864, as a threat to bolster recruiting and as a real means of obtaining soldiers to keep Union ranks battle worthy.

See also *Draft, Military; Draft Riots, New York City; Volunteers, Ninety-Day*

—IAN MICHAEL SPURGEON

BIBLIOGRAPHY

Bernstein, Iver. *The New York City Draft Riots: Their Significance for American Society and Politics in the Age of the Civil War.* New York: Oxford University Press, 1990.

Donald, David Herbert. *Lincoln.* New York: Simon and Schuster, 1995.

McPherson, James. *Battle Cry of Freedom: The Civil War Era.* Oxford: Oxford University Press, 1988.

Neely, Mark E., Jr. *The Fate of Liberty: Abraham Lincoln and Civil Liberties.* Oxford: Oxford University Press, 1991.

Nevins, Allan. *The War for the Union. Vol. 3: The Organized War, 1863–1864.* New York: Scribner's, 1971.

Constitution and Slavery, The

The Constitution of 1787 protected slavery in a variety of ways. Article I, Section 2 counted slaves for purposes of representation on a three-fifths basis. This clause gave the South added seats in the House of Representatives that enabled Southerners to protect slavery in Congress. Without the representatives created by counting slaves, the South would have been outvoted, and it is unlikely that such proslavery acts as the admission of Missouri as a slave state, Texas annexation, and the Fugitive Slave Law of 1850 could have been passed. The three-fifths clause also gave the South a bonus in the Electoral College. In 1800 Thomas Jefferson's slim margin of victory over the non-slaveholding John Adams was based on the electors created by counting slaves for purposes of representation.

Article I, Section 9 protected the African slave trade from congressional interference for at least twenty years and led to the importation of as many as 70,000 new slaves. Article I, Sections 9 and 10 banned export taxes, which protected the economic interests of the commodity-producing slave states. Two clauses—one in Article I and another in Article IV—guaranteed that the federal government would help suppress slave rebellions, as it did in the case of the Nat Turner rebellion (1831) and John Brown's raid (1859). The Fugitive Slave Clause of Article IV guaranteed that masters could recover runaway slaves who escaped to the North. Article V required three-quarters of the states to ratify a constitutional amendment, giving the slave states an absolute veto over all constitutional amendments. Finally, the structure of the Constitution created a government of limited powers, which made it impossible for the national government to touch slavery where it existed. As General Charles Cotesworth Pinckney told the South Carolina House of Representatives after the Constitutional Convention, "We have a security that the general government can never emancipate them, for no such authority is granted and it is admitted, on all hands, that the general government has no powers but what are expressly granted by the Constitution, and that all rights not expressed were reserved by the several states."

The Constitution did give Congress plenary power to regulate federal territories and the District of Columbia, which meant that at least in theory Congress could end slavery in both those places. However, the Fifth Amendment prohibited the taking of property without due process of law or just compensation, and thus emancipation in federal territory would have required compensation to the master and perhaps a judicial hearing.

As a competent and successful lawyer and a student of the U.S. Constitution, Abraham Lincoln began his presidency with a strong sense of the limitations that the Constitution placed on any emancipation scheme. In his first inaugural he urged the seven states that claimed to have left the Union to cease their efforts to secede and return to their proper political relationship within the United States. In making this case Lincoln reminded these Deep South states that slavery was safe within the Union. Quoting from one of the speeches that he made leading up to his election, Lincoln declared: "I have no purpose, directly or indirectly, to interfere with the institution of slavery in the States where it exists. I believe I have no lawful right to do so, and I have no inclination to do so." He then reiterated the point by quoting the Republican Party platform:

> Resolved, *That the maintenance inviolate of the rights of the States, and especially the right of each State to order and control its own domestic institutions according to its own judgment exclusively, is essential to that balance of power on which the perfection and endurance of our political fabric depend; and we denounce the lawless invasion by armed force of the soil of any State or Territory, no matter what pretext, as among the gravest of crimes.*

He added that his administration would stand for the principle "that all the protection which, consistently with the Constitution and the laws, can be given, will be cheerfully given to all the States when lawfully demanded, for whatever cause—as cheerfully to one section as to another."

This position was based on an orthodox and well-understood interpretation of the U.S. Constitution. This understanding dated from the drafting of the Constitution and had never been successfully challenged in law or politics. In 1787 the understanding of the Constitution by all parties was quite clear: the national government had no power to interfere with the "domestic institutions" of the states. Therefore the states, and not the national government, had sole power to regulate all laws concerning personal status. That included the regulation of marriage, divorce, child custody, inheritance, voting, and freedom—whether one was a slave or a free person.

The Republican platform of 1860 opposed the spread of slavery into the federal territories, but only the most radical antislavery theorists ever imagined a federal law banning the movement or sale of slaves in interstate commerce. Moreover, such a law would not have ended slavery where it already existed.

Thus when Lincoln entered office he understood that he had "no lawful right" to "interfere with the institution of slavery in the States where it exists." In his attempt to bring the seceding states back into the Union he also declared, "I have no inclination to do so." This statement in his inaugural address could be interpreted to mean that Lincoln had no personal interest or desire to end slavery, but Lincoln chose his words carefully. His personal views on slavery were clear: he hated slavery and had always believed that "if slavery is not wrong, nothing is wrong." But his personal desires could not overcome the constitutional realities of his age. Thus, because he had no power to touch slavery where it existed, he could honestly say he had no inclination to attempt to do what was not constitutionally possible. Reflecting his long-standing Whig ideology, Lincoln surely rejected the idea of acting outside the Constitution. Reflecting his sense of the politically possible, Lincoln was willing to reassure the seceding states that he had no "inclination" to do what he could not constitutionally, legally, or politically accomplish. When circumstances changed, so would Lincoln's "inclination," but in early March 1861 Lincoln had no reason to think circumstances would change as they did.

During the Civil War Lincoln concluded that he could attack slavery as a war measure but only in those places that claimed to be out of the Union. Thus the Emancipation Proclamation was limited to the slaves living in the Confederacy. Lincoln did not attempt to end slavery in the border slave states because he had no constitutional authority to do so. He did sign a law to end slavery in the District of Columbia, but that law provided for compensated emancipation, thus avoiding a challenge under the Fifth Amendment.

The irony of the Civil War is that slavery was fully protected by the Constitution as long as the slave states remained in the United States. Once they made war against the United States, Lincoln found constitutional authority, in his role as commander in chief of the army, to free slaves. In the end, however, a constitutional amendment was necessary to end slavery everywhere in the United States. Lincoln urged Congress to pass such an amendment in the summer of 1864, and shortly before the new year Congress did so. Within a year it was ratified, thus forever ending slavery in the United States.

See also *Slavery*

—Paul Finkelman

BIBLIOGRAPHY

Finkelman, Paul. Dred Scott v. Sandford: *A Brief History.* Boston: Bedford Books, 1995.

Finkelman, Paul. *Slavery and the Founders: Race and Liberty in the Age of Jefferson.* 2nd ed. Armonk, N.Y.: M.E. Sharpe, 2001.

Foner, Eric. *Free Soil, Free Labor, Free Men: The Ideology of the Republican Party before the Civil War.* New York: Oxford University Press, 1970.

Robinson, Donald L. *Slavery in the Structure of American Politics, 1765 to 1820.* New York: Harcourt Brace Jovanovich, 1971.

Vorenberg, Michael. *Final Freedom: The Civil War, the Abolition of Slavery, and the Thirteenth Amendment.* New York: Cambridge University Press, 2001.

Wiecek, William M. *The Sources of Antislavery Constitutionalism in America, 1760–1848.* Ithaca, N.Y.: Cornell University Press, 1978.

Constitutional Law, Lincoln and

Throughout his career Abraham Lincoln's views of the Constitution shaped his political behavior and his public policy initiatives. Lincoln saw the Constitution as an almost sacred text and believed fidelity to the Constitution and the preservation of the Union to be his most important obligation as a public servant and as a citizen. Constitutional law for him included not only decisions of the U.S. Supreme Court, but also commonly understood views of constitutional interpretation and implementation. Most of all, he believed that the Union and the Constitution were the paramount "law" in the United States. In a famous speech concerning slavery, Sen. William H. Seward had said that there was a "higher law than the Constitution." But Lincoln would never have agreed. His First Inaugural Address was almost entirely devoted to explaining why the Constitution was paramount, why Southerners had not been denied their constitutional rights, and why, most of all, the Union had to be preserved so the Constitution could be preserved. Thus, he closed his inaugural by reminding Southerners, "*You* have no oath registered in Heaven to destroy the government, while *I* shall have the most solemn one to 'preserve, protect and defend' it." For Lincoln the "government" and the Constitution were one and the same. This was the keystone of his constitutional law.

Preserving the Union, and thus ultimately sustaining the Constitution, was Lincoln's paramount goal throughout his presidency. This led him to make hard choices about the meaning of Constitutionalism. The United States had never fought a long, sustained war since the Constitution had been written. Nor had the United States ever witnessed sustained, protracted, and horribly bloody rebellion. The Constitution provided few guidelines for the operation of the rule of law under such circumstances. Not only were there no Supreme Court precedents for these circumstances, but there were in fact very few Supreme Court precedents on many of the issues Lincoln faced, including free speech in wartime, treasonous activities in wartime, the suspension of *habeas corpus*, military conscription, and the disposition of the property of citizens who are in rebellion against the government.

Most of all, Lincoln believed that secession violated the Constitution and constituted rebellion and treason. There was no case law on this issue. Lincoln operated from the text of the Constitution itself, arguing that the document contemplated a perpetual Union that could not be dissolved without the consent of all the parties. It was on this basis that he would prosecute the war against secession.

While campaigning for the Senate in 1858 and the presidency in 1860, Lincoln rejected the arguments of Chief Justice Roger Taney in the *Dred Scott* case. There Taney had argued that Congress did not have the power to prohibit slavery in the territories. Lincoln flatly disagreed with this interpretation of the text of the Constitution. He argued that all of Taney's claims on this issue were mere *dicta* because earlier in the case, Taney had asserted that the federal courts had no power to hear the case because no black could be a citizen of the United States, and thus Dred Scott, whether free or slave, could never sue in federal court. Thus, in attacking Taney's *Dred Scott* opinion Lincoln never attacked the legitimacy of the Supreme Court ruling on constitutional issues, but rather he narrowly attacked part of the decision as not being legitimately before the Court.

Once in office Lincoln faced a similar problem. In Maryland pro-Confederate saboteurs and organizers were aggressively attempting to disrupt the movement of troops to protect the national capital and to get Maryland to secede. The army, on Lincoln's orders, arrested a small number of activists, including John Merryman. The army held Merryman in the brig at Fort McHenry without any formal charge. Lincoln acted under the clause in Article I, Section 9 of the Constitution that allowed for the suspension of *habeas corpus* during a "rebellion." The clause did not say which branch of the government had the power to suspend. With Congress not in session, Lincoln acted on his own. Although held by the military, Merryman was allowed access to an attorney, who quickly went to Chief Justice Taney, who issued a writ of *habeas corpus* directed at the commander of Fort McHenry. Since the president had suspended the writ, the military might have simply ignored Taney. Instead, an army officer appeared before Taney to explain why his writ would be ignored. Taney then issued an opinion chastising the administration, but he issued no order. Lincoln ignored the writ and the opinion, and the full Court never responded to the issue. Taney had argued that under the Constitution the president had no power to unilaterally suspend the writ. Lincoln and the lawyers in his administration disagreed, but when Congress came into session it passed legislation authorizing the suspension of the writ.

Lincoln faced a complicated constitutional issue when military authorities arrested, tried, and convicted Clement Vallandigham, a pro-Confederate politician from Ohio for his speech on the war. Lincoln argued that Vallandigham was not tried for criticizing the government—which Lincoln argued was protected even in wartime—but rather for attempting to obstruct the draft. The U.S. Supreme Court rejected Vallandigham's petition in 1864, saying that it had no power to interfere with a military trial. This result in effect confirmed the constitutionality of Lincoln's actions. Commenting on the case and its implications for free speech, a frustrated Lincoln asked, "Must I shoot a simpleminded soldier boy who deserts, while I must not touch a hair of a wiley agitator who induces him to desert?" Lincoln then solved the problem by ordering Vallandigham released but banished to the Confederacy. Vallandigham later sneaked back into Ohio, in June 1864, and began his agitations all over again, without any interference from the army or the administration.

The issue of slavery and constitutional law bedeviled Lincoln not only as president but throughout his life. In 1837, as a twenty-eight-year-old legislator, Lincoln was one of six members of the Illinois state assembly to vote against a proslavery resolution supported by eighty-three members of that body. He voted against the resolution condemning abolitionists not only because he was personally opposed to slavery, but also because his understanding of constitutional liberty included a right to free speech. He then joined one other representative in framing his own resolution, declaring that slavery was "founded on both injustice and bad policy" but that the national government had "no power, under the constitution, to interfere with the institution of slavery in the different States." However Lincoln also asserted, again consistent with traditional constitutional understandings, that Congress did have "the power under the constitution, to abolish slavery in the District of Columbia." This early foray into the constitutional issues of slavery suggests that Lincoln, even as a young man, understood the constitutional limitations as well as the constitutional possibilities of fighting slavery.

Four years after he voted against slavery in the legislature he argued *Bailey v. Cromwell* (1841) before the Illinois Supreme Court, winning a decision in which the Illinois court held that the "presumption of law" in Illinois was "that every person was free, without regard to color." This result was consistent with Lincoln's view that the states were free to regulate slavery and that under both the Northwest Ordinance and the Illinois constitution slavery could not exist in the Prairie State.

Lincoln, however, also understood that the Constitution protected the right of Southern masters to recover their fugitive slaves. Thus he once argued in favor of a Kentucky man who claimed a black woman as a fugitive slave. He lost the case and never again served a slave owner in this manner. But he understood the constitutionality of the fugitive slave laws. He wrote his Kentucky friend Joshua Speed, "I also acknowledge *your* rights and *my* obligations, under the constitution, in regard to your slaves. I confess I hate to see the poor creatures hunted down, and caught, and carried back to their stripes, and unrewarded toils; but I bite my lip and keep quiet." Similarly, in his First Inaugural Address he noted that when members of Congress or the president "swear their support to the whole Constitution" it included the fugitive slave clause, and he pledged "to conform to and abide by all those acts which stand unrepealed," including the fugitive slave laws, as long as they were held to be constitutional.

When he entered the White House Lincoln agreed with the generally accepted understanding of the Constitution and slavery, that the national government had no power to interfere with slavery in the states but could regulate slavery in the District of Columbia. Lincoln also accepted the argument—which had been a fixture of American politics from 1787 to 1857—that the national government had a right to regulate slavery in the territories. In *Dred Scott v. Sandford* (1857) the Supreme Court had held that the national government could not ban slavery in the territories, but Lincoln considered this to be illegitimate *dicta* since the Court also said it had no jurisdiction to hear the case at all.

As he entered the presidency, Lincoln thus understood the Constitution to allow Congress to interfere with slavery only in federal jurisdictions. He also understood the Fifth Amendment to the Constitution to bar freeing slaves without some compensation. But the Constitution gave him few guidelines on how to deal with slaves in the Confederacy. During the war Lincoln developed different policies for slaves in different places. He never proposed any law to end slavery in the Border States, but did urge the state governments there to end slavery, and he offered federal assistance, including compensation for masters, if the loyal slave states ended slavery. Eventually he also allowed for the conscription of slaves in the Border States, which dramatically undermined slavery, especially in Kentucky. Lincoln encouraged Congress to pass a compensated emancipation bill for the District of Columbia, which quickly ended slavery there when Lincoln signed it. He later signed bills that simply ended slavery in all the federal territories, on the theory that despite *Dred Scott*, Congress still retained plenary power to govern the territories. In 1864 Lincoln also happily signed legislation repealing the federal fugitive slave laws, effectively ending the return of runaway slaves.

Slavery in the Confederacy was more complicated. Lincoln ultimately concluded that in his role as commander in chief—a constitutionally recognized role—he had the power to take slaves from all people in rebellion against the national government. There was no constitutional precedent for this; but then again, there was no constitutional precedent for secession or civil war. Lincoln issued the Emancipation Proclamation as a war measure, directed only at the slaves in the rebellious states, because that was the only place where he, as commander in chief of the army, had the constitutional power to act.

In his first message to Congress, on July 4, 1861, Lincoln acknowledged that some people questioned the constitutionality of some of his actions, such as suspending *habeas corpus* on his own or calling out troops without an authorization from Congress. But he argued that at the time, the laws of the nation "were being resisted, and failing of execution in nearly one-third of the States," and that as someone who had just taken an oath to "take care that the laws be faithfully executed," he necessarily had to act. He asked Congress, "Are all the laws, *but one,* to go unexecuted, and the government to go to pieces, lest that one be violated?" This part of the speech was in response to criticism of his suspension of *habeas corpus,* but it truly served as a metaphor for Lincoln's understanding of the Constitution and the need to preserve it under unique circumstances.

Nearly three years later, on April 4, 1864, Lincoln summarized his constitutional theory—and his implementation of constitutional law—in a letter to Albert G. Hodges, a newspaper editor from Kentucky:

> *I did understand however, that my oath to preserve the constitution to the best of my ability, imposed upon me the duty of preserving, by every indispensable means, that government—that nation—of which that constitution was the organic law. Was it possible to lose the nation, and yet preserve the constitution? By general law life and limb must be protected; yet often a limb must be amputated to save a life; but a life is never wisely given to save a limb. I felt that measures, otherwise unconstitutional, might become lawful, by becoming indispensable to the*

preservation of the constitution, through the preservation of the nation. Right or wrong, I assumed this ground, and now avow it. I could not feel that, to the best of my ability, I had even tried to preserve the constitution, if, to save slavery, or any minor matter, I should permit the wreck of government, country, and Constitution all together.

—Paul Finkelman

BIBLIOGRAPHY

Farber, Daniel A. *Lincoln's Constitution.* Chicago: University of Chicago Press, 2003.

Finkelman, Paul. *An Imperfect Union: Slavery, Federalism, and Comity.* Chapel Hill: University of North Carolina Press, 1981.

Neely, Mark E., Jr. *The Fate of Liberty: Abraham Lincoln and Civil Liberties.* New York: Oxford University Press, 1991.

Striner, Richard. *Father Abraham: Lincoln's Relentless Struggle to End Slavery.* New York: Oxford University Press, 2006.

Constitutional Union Party

The Constitutional Union Party was a short-lived third party created in December 1859 to prevent secession by defeating Republican Party candidate Abraham Lincoln. Meeting in Baltimore on May 9, 1860, the party's national convention eschewed any stance on the slavery-related issues that dominated the politics of the day, instead highlighting the danger of disunion and rallying behind the Constitution and the Union.

Led by its presidential candidate, John Bell of Tennessee (former Speaker of the House, secretary of war, and senator), and vice presidential candidate, Edward Everett of Massachusetts (former governor, secretary of state, and senator), the Constitutional Unionists hoped to attract conservative former Whigs, particularly those who in 1856 had voted with the nativist American Party. Those voters, accounting for about 22 percent of the electorate (14 percent of crucial Northern voters), had been the balance of power that had permitted Democrat James Buchanan to defeat Republican John C. Frémont.

The new party had no illusions of winning an electoral majority but instead sought to ally with Democrats in what were called "fusion" tickets. The group's efforts gained urgency after October 9 state elections in Indiana and Pennsylvania—states that had voted Democratic in 1856—produced significant Republican majorities. Constitutional Unionists now pinned their hopes on capturing New York, thereby preventing a Republican majority in the Electoral College and forcing the election into the House of Representatives, where the Republicans did not control a majority of the state delegations. If no candidate had an Electoral College majority each state delegation in the House would have one vote, and thus even though the Republican candidate might have a plurality in popular and electoral votes, he would not become president. However, mutual antipathy between rival Democratic factions and between Democrats and the former Whigs of the Constitutional Union Party frequently prevented fusion. In New York an alliance was delayed until late October, just before the election, and even then was rejected by Illinois senator Stephen A. Douglas, the presidential candidate of the Northern wing of the Democrats.

Officially the Bell-Everett ticket won just 3 percent of the Northern vote and 13 percent overall. Although these totals underestimate the party's support, as they do not reflect fusion votes in several Northern states, the Constitutional Union movement had failed signally: On election day, November 6, Republicans captured not only New York but almost every electoral vote from the free states. As in most third-party campaigns, the Constitutional Unionists suffered from a widespread perception that they could not win, which seems to have persuaded many of the conservative Whigs whom they hoped to attract either to support the Republicans or to abstain. The party ran fourth in the popular vote, with just over 590,000 votes. Most of the votes that the party attracted were in the Upper South, where it captured Virginia, Kentucky, and Tennessee. In the Electoral College, however, the party ran third, with thirty-nine electors, easily defeating Stephen A. Douglas, who won just twelve. The party's support in the Upper South formed the nucleus of what would become, during the secession crisis, a new Union Party built around containing secession to the Deep South and forging a Union-saving sectional compromise.

See also *Bell, John; Campaign of 1860, Presidential*

—RUSSELL MCCLINTOCK

BIBLIOGRAPHY

Crofts, Daniel W. *Reluctant Confederates: Upper South Unionists in the Secession Crisis.* Chapel Hill: University of North Carolina Press, 1989.

Gienapp, William E. "Who Voted for Lincoln?" In *Abraham Lincoln and the American Political Tradition,* edited by John L. Thomas. Amherst: University of Massachusetts Press, 1986.

Kirwan, Albert D. *John J. Crittenden: The Struggle for the Union.* Lexington: University of Kentucky Press, 1962.

Knupfer, Peter. "Aging Statesmen and the Statesmanship of an Earlier Age: The Generational Roots of the Constitutional Union Party." In *Union and Emancipation: Essays on Politics and Race in the Civil War Era,* edited by David W. Blight and Brooks D. Simpson. Kent, Ohio: Kent State University Press, 1997.

Mering, John V. "The Slave-State Constitutional Unionists and the Politics of Consensus." *Journal of Southern History* 43, no. 3 (1977): 395–410.

Parks, Joseph Howard. *John Bell of Tennessee.* Baton Rouge: Louisiana State University Press, 1950.

Stabler, John Burgess. "A History of the Constitutional Union Party, a Tragic Failure." PhD diss., Columbia University, 1954.

Contrabands

At the beginning of the Civil War, Abraham Lincoln pledged not to interfere with slavery where it already existed, and Congress passed the Crittenden-Johnson Resolution in summer 1861, which directed that the war effort sought only to maintain the Union, without disturbing the domestic institutions of the states. Despite these early efforts to leave slavery out of the conflict, fugitive slaves fled into Union lines as federal armies marched South. Frustrated slave owners often followed, determined to retrieve their property.

Lincoln was placed in a tricky political situation. The slaveholding Border States of Missouri, Kentucky, Maryland, and Delaware remained loyal to the Union but had sizable secessionist populations. Lincoln feared that those states might join the Confederacy if U.S. armies harbored runaway slaves or threatened the institution of slavery. Yet many antislavery Northerners sympathized with the fugitive slaves and wanted no part in protecting slavery. Lincoln needed their political support for the war effort.

Caught between two important but opposing interests, Lincoln remained silent on the matter of fugitive slaves. He allowed army commanders to establish their own policies in the field. Many officers willingly returned runaways to their masters. George B. McClellan, for example, assured citizens in Virginia that his troops would put down any attempt by the local slave population to revolt and would respect Southern domestic rights and interests.

Not all Union officers were eager to preserve secessionist slaveholding interests. In late May 1861, General Benjamin F. Butler took command of federal forces at Fortress Monroe in Virginia. Shortly after his arrival, three slaves came into Union lines and explained that their master planned to send them South to work on Confederate defenses. This information, and the knowledge that slaves were already being used to construct artillery positions against his fort, prompted Butler to declare the fugitive slaves "contraband of war." The general term "contraband" referred to any property subject to confiscation on the ground that it aided the

Former slaves arrive at an unidentified Union camp in the South. The Second Confiscation Act declared that all slaves who reached U.S. Army lines were free. Later, the Emancipation Proclamation would free all slaves in rebellious states.
Source: The Granger Collection, New York

enemy's war effort. The slaves' master, Confederate Colonel Charles K. Mallory, sent another officer, Major M. B. Carey, to demand the return of his slave property. When Carey approached under a flag of truce Butler met with him outside the fort and rejected the demand. Butler argued that since Virginia claimed to be out of the Union, he was not bound to enforce the Fugitive Slave Law. Furthermore, because slaves were considered property and were used by the Confederate war effort, Butler concluded, he was justified in retaining the runaways.

Butler's classification of fugitive slaves as "contrabands" quickly caught on as Northern newspapers popularized the term. Many Northerners who opposed abolishing slavery nonetheless accepted the technical confiscation of slaves as property from Confederate masters. The Confederacy used slaves in its war effort, for constructing defenses, driving wagons, and producing supplies and tools for war. Most Northerners understood that returning slaves would help the enemy.

Lincoln did not oppose Butler's policy. In contrast, the president did intervene when Generals John C. Frémont and David Hunter tried to emancipate slaves in their respective military districts. Lincoln declared that they had overstepped their authority by overturning domestic laws without his consent. He also feared that the generals' actions would jeopardize the status of the loyal slave states, especially Kentucky. Yet Butler's contraband policy did not abolish slavery or emancipate slaves. The "contraband" classification dealt with slaves as property and technically only applied to slaves used by the Confederacy who escaped to the lines of the Union army. The Lincoln administration accepted Butler's policy but took no steps to expand it. Nonetheless, the image of freedom behind Union lines spread among the slave population, and soon hundreds of "contrabands" fled to Fortress Monroe and other Union camps in the South.

Lincoln's tacit acceptance of Butler's contraband policy helped open a new set of problems. First, how were officers to distinguish between slaves used by the Confederacy and those of Unionists? Some owners provided proof of their loyalty to the United States in order to regain their runaway slaves; others were given vouchers by the government for compensation. The federal government also had to deal physically with tens of thousands of refugees. Contraband camps sprang up along Union army lines across the nation. Many of the former slaves served as laborers, teamsters, or cooks, or filled other positions in the Union army. An increasing number of people called upon Lincoln to arm these former slaves to bolster the war effort further. He resisted the calls for months, but pressure to use black soldiers mounted.

The rising numbers of refugees soon taxed the military's resources. By the end of 1862, some Union military districts had over 10,000 refugees within their lines. Relief organizations helped provide medicine, food, and education to the former slaves, but many of the camps were badly managed and in poor shape. Refugees continued to pour in.

The legal status of the contrabands proved a particularly important problem. Were they people or property? Their status as "contraband of war" meant that they were no longer secessionist property. But the "contraband" classification did not establish a new legal status. Butler wrote to the War Department in July 1861 asking whether the contrabands were slaves or free. The administration gave no direct answer. Congress partly responded to the contraband issue with the First Confiscation Act, in August 1861, which authorized federal authorities to retain only slaves who had worked for the Confederacy. However, the bill did not declare them free. The status and fate of thousands of runaway slaves remained in limbo. In July 1862 Congress passed a second, more sweeping confiscation act that authorized the army to free the slaves of all secessionists through a judicial proceeding and also declared that slaves who escaped to U.S. Army lines were free. The act also authorized the president to use black soldiers. These confiscation acts paved the way for Lincoln's own Emancipation Proclamation and his approval of using black soldiers.

The contraband policy blurred the line between freedom and slavery early in the war, drew thousands of slaves to federal lines, and ultimately helped make slavery a central element of the Civil War.

—Ian Michael Spurgeon

BIBLIOGRAPHY

Guelzo, Allen C. *Lincoln's Emancipation Proclamation: The End of Slavery in America.* New York: Simon and Schuster, 2005.

Klingaman, William K. *Abraham Lincoln and the Road to Emancipation, 1861–1865.* New York: Viking, 2001.

McPherson, James. *Battle Cry of Freedom: The Civil War Era.* Oxford: Oxford University Press, 1988.

Trudeau, Noah Andre. *Like Men of War: Black Troops in the Civil War, 1862–1865.* Boston: Little, Brown, 1998.

Cooke, Jay

Jay Cooke (1821–1905) was an American investment banker active in financing the U.S. government during the Civil War. Cooke was from a prominent Ohio family. His father, Eleutheros Cooke, was a lawyer, businessman, and U.S. congressman. In 1861 Jay Cooke formed his investment banking firm, Jay Cooke and Company. Through family connections he was acquainted with Salmon P. Chase, the former Ohio governor who became Abraham Lincoln's first secretary of the Treasury. Although Jay Cooke and Chase never became close, Cooke was offered the position of assistant treasurer, which he declined. Chase eventually commissioned Cooke to sell war bonds. In March 1862 Lincoln suggested that Cooke be appointed supervisor of all government bond sales. By the war's end Cooke had raised more than $3 billion through bond sales and bank loans that he negotiated.

Cooke went directly to the people and sold bonds in denominations as small as $50, on installment payments. He believed that many people who had never made investments of any kind would buy war bonds out of patriotism. Cooke employed a sales staff of over 2,500, paid for out of his own commissions. He made widespread use of advertising and well-placed patriotic stories and is often credited with inventing the modern bond drive.

Although Cooke was a wealthy man before the war, he had a tremendous fortune by its end. His commission for selling government bonds was relatively modest—one-fourth of one percent. But his access to the government's financial plans and purchasing needs gave him inside information that he used to make wise investments. Criticism eventually arose over Cooke's virtual monopoly on the government's bond issues, and Chase stopped using Cooke as the government's agent.

Cooke's relationship with Lincoln is a matter of debate, though Cooke himself did not like to admit that he never developed an intimate relationship with the president. The suspicion with which Lincoln regarded Salmon Chase's political ambitions may have colored his relationship with Cooke. After General

George B. McClellan's failure to move on Richmond in the Peninsula Campaign in the fall of 1862, Cooke met with Lincoln and asked him to replace McClellan; in his personal memoir he recorded imploring Lincoln for almost two hours, "earnestly and almost pleadingly." Although Lincoln and Cooke were not close, after William Fessenden replaced Chase as secretary of the Treasury, Lincoln encouraged Fessenden to again engage Cooke for selling war bonds, ignoring the criticisms of Cooke's earlier domination of the process.

After Lincoln's assassination Cooke realized that the tragic news might set off a run to sell government bonds. He ordered his agents to buy all the government bonds they could, to stem any sell-off. Cooke told the secretary of the Treasury "that I would thus fully maintain the credit of the nation in this crisis."

After the Civil War, Cooke became involved in financing the Northern Pacific Railroad. When the Northern Pacific declared bankruptcy in 1873, Cooke's banking firm also failed, and he lost much of his personal fortune. He rebuilt his fortune in later years through various business endeavors, including a brokerage house, Charles D. Barney and Company, which was enormously profitable and eventually merged to become the modern giant Smith-Barney. Cooke retired, living out his last years with his daughter until his death in 1905.

See also *Banking and Monetary Policy*

—Mark S. Joy

BIBLIOGRAPHY

Lubetkin, John M. *Jay Cooke's Gamble: The Northern Pacific Railroad, the Sioux, and the Panic of 1873*. Norman: University of Oklahoma Press, 2006.

Oberholtzer, Ellis Paxson. *Jay Cooke: Financier of the Civil War*. 2 vols. Philadelphia: George W. Jacobs, 1907.

Sandburg, Carl. *Abraham Lincoln: The War Years. Vol. 2*. New York: Harcourt, Brace, 1939.

Cooper Union Address

Abraham Lincoln's Cooper Union address, of February 27, 1860, his oratorical debut in New York City, was one of the most influential and successful speeches of his pre-presidential career and probably did more than any other to propel him into contention for the presidency.

Cooper Union Address

In December 1859, a group of anti-Seward Republicans in New York invited Lincoln—and other western political orators—to come east to participate in a lecture series. Their speeches were meant to show voters there that there were electable alternatives to Seward for the 1860 Republican presidential nomination. These Republicans believed that Seward, an easterner, could not win western support, whereas a viable western candidate could succeed in both regions. They offered Lincoln $200 plus expenses. Lincoln accepted but delayed his trip for so long that the original lecture series, planned for the Plymouth Church in Brooklyn, had ended by the time he arrived in New York. Instead he became part of a second lecture series staged at the Cooper Institute (now Cooper Union), a new, tuition-free college for men and women, on the Bowery in Manhattan.

Lincoln prepared meticulously for his appearance, doing all his own research and writing his complex, 7,500-word text by hand. As his theme, he planned to attack a recent magazine article by his longtime political rival, Democratic senator Stephen A. Douglas, which argued that the nation's founders did not believe the federal government had the power to restrict the spread of slavery or to interfere with states that exercised local control over the institution. Lincoln's own investigations gave him the confidence to reply that most of the signers of the Constitution had, in fact, voted in subsequent years for legislation that gave the federal government precisely that power. If he was correct, then the current Republican argument for halting the spread of slavery had the backing of history.

The fifteen-hundred-mile train journey from Springfield to New York took several exhausting days, and Lincoln did not discover that his speech had been rescheduled for Cooper Union until he arrived. He had to revise his manuscript for a secular audience in just a day and a half. Meanwhile he toured the city, met influential Republicans, and had an iconic photograph taken at Mathew Brady's studio on Broadway. The distinguished pose, quickly reproduced in countless engravings and lithographs, helped introduce Lincoln to the national electorate and allay fears that he was too homely to stand successfully for the presidency.

About twelve hundred people paid twenty-five cents to attend Lincoln's speech—three hundred fewer than could be accommodated in the college's vast Great Hall. But Lincoln made a highly favorable impression on his audience, many of whom expected the speaker to be a slam-bang, frontier style stump speaker. Instead, the Illinoisan began his two-hour address with a sophisticated legal and historical argument to support his claim that the founders had intended to place slavery "on the course of ultimate extinction." The first and longest section of the speech provided a lawyerly argument for his case, spiced with brilliant use of humor.

In the second part of his long address, Lincoln offered a riveting direct appeal to Southerners, contending that Republicans meant the region no harm and would not interfere with slavery where it already existed. Adopting a conservative posture, he assured slave owners that Republicans had not supported abolitionist John Brown and had no desire to foment slave insurrections.

But in the third and final section of his speech, Lincoln changed course yet again and turned his attention back to Republicans, shifting gears unexpectedly to remind them that they indeed had a moral obligation to continue their fight to rid the country of slavery.

Lincoln ended his long, carefully reasoned address with a direct appeal to emotion, arguing in an impassioned peroration that justice always prevailed in long struggles for freedom, and that in this case Republicans were clearly on the side of justice:

> Neither let us be slandered from our duty by false accusations against us, nor frightened from it by menaces of destruction to the Government nor of dungeons to ourselves. Let us have faith that right makes might, and in that faith, let us, to the end, dare to do our duty as we understand it.

Lincoln's ringing conclusion brought the elite crowd to its feet. Horace Greeley, editor of the influential *New York Tribune*, declared, "No man ever before made such an impression on his first appeal to a New-York audience."

Lincoln, Greeley, and others made sure that the speech was not forgotten. The *Tribune* and several other newspapers printed it in full the next day, but not before Lincoln himself visited the typesetting rooms and proofread the drafts to make sure they were accurate. Heading north to visit his son at prep school, he went on to deliver versions of the same speech to appreciative audiences in New Hampshire, Connecticut, and Rhode Island. Pamphlet reprints quickly appeared in several languages, and again contributing his own time and effort, Lincoln personally supervised the publication of a handsome, footnoted reprint that became the standard source of his approved text. By the end of the political campaign, the speech had reached hundreds of thousands of American voters.

Although the Cooper Union address never earned Lincoln massive support in New York City, which remained overwhelmingly Democratic, his triumphant appearance convinced many skeptical eastern Republicans that he could be a successful presidential standard-bearer in their region. The reputation he earned at Cooper Union helped him win the nomination when Seward faltered at the May 1860 convention and helped him sweep the North and the East in the November elections.

Nearly a year after his New York debut, Lincoln reached Washington for his presidential inauguration, where he paused to visit Mathew Brady's new capital gallery for another photographic sitting. Offered an introduction to the famous artist, Lincoln explained that he needed no such introduction. As he put it—a view most historians have since come to share—"Brady and the Cooper Institute speech made me President."

See also *Gettysburg Address; House Divided Speech; Rhetoric in Lincoln's Public Speeches*

—HAROLD HOLZER

BIBLIOGRAPHY

Barondess, Benjamin. *Three Lincoln Masterpieces.* Charleston: Education Foundation of West Virginia, 1954.

Freeman, Andrew. *Abraham Lincoln in New York.* New York: Coward McCann, 1960.

Holzer, Harold. *Lincoln at Cooper Union: The Speech that Made Abraham Lincoln President.* New York: Simon and Schuster, 2004.

Copperheads

Abraham Lincoln never had the full support of the Northern people in fighting the Civil War. On the contrary, conservative Democrats, popularly known as "Copperheads" (a Republican appellation that alluded to the highly poisonous snake), opposed many of the steps Lincoln took to wage war, especially emancipation and conscription. Although quite visible at the local level in the first year of the war, these conservatives did not have a national profile until the summer of 1862, when the Union armies were faring poorly on the battlefield. In a pattern that would hold for the rest of the war, the influence and power of the Peace Democrats operated inversely to how well the armies were doing in the field. Thus the Copperheads were most potent in the summer of 1864. When the Democrats held their nominating convention in late August, the Copperheads nearly took over the party and forced the War Democrats—those who supported Lincoln's policies—to make concessions that would taint the party for years to come.

Peace Democrats generally emerged from one of three positions. First were those who had Southern roots. Although some of these were outright sympathizers, many in this category thought the South was within its rights to secede. There was nothing in the Constitution, after all, that stated the terms of admission or of secession. The second group comprised immigrants, particularly Irish and German Catholics. Long targeted for either abuse or reform by Protestants who wound up in Lincoln's Republican Party, some immigrants wanted nothing to do with a Republican war. The third group consisted of native-born conservatives who embraced a strict-constructionist approach to the Constitution. These people considered themselves the heirs of Thomas Jefferson and Andrew Jackson, who were suspicious of a large, centralized federal government and of industrialization. Their rhetoric, which framed most issues in constitutional terms, became the dominant voice of the antiwar movement. All three segments of Copperheadism were also

THE COPPERHEAD PARTY.—IN FAVOR OF *A VIGOROUS PROSECUTION OF PEACE!*

This Northern newspaper cartoon of 1863 shows the Union threatened by political serpents wearing the hats of Midwest Democratic congressmen, such as Clement Vallandigham of Ohio.
Source: The Granger Collection, New York City

virulently racist, even by the standards of their own time, and routinely used race-baiting sentiments to persuade others to their side. Although Republicans regarded them as traitors, most Peace Democrats were not Southern sympathizers. They genuinely wanted reunion and were deeply concerned about where Lincoln was taking the country. However, they never seemed to realize that secession and the war threatened the very existence of the nation, they never acknowledged the Confederates' desire for independence, and they never came to terms with a modernizing, industrializing nation.

From the beginning of the war, Peace Democrats worried about the actions Lincoln and the Republican Congress took to fight the war: raising troops without congressional approval, declaring martial law in Maryland, suspending *habeas corpus,* creating paper currency and an income tax. From early on, these conservatives viewed Lincoln as a tyrant—a word they used very specifically to hark back to the American Revolution and George III. The greatest concern of the Copperheads was that Lincoln would emancipate the slaves. They had long suspected that the Civil War was really a fight to free bondsmen, not, as Lincoln claimed, to restore the Union. When Lincoln issued the Preliminary Emancipation Proclamation in September 1862, it was a peculiar victory of sorts for the Copperheads. Although their greatest fear had come to pass, the proclamation pushed many who had been willing to give Lincoln the benefit of the doubt into the camp of the Peace Democrats. The feelings against the president and his party spilled over into the elections of that year, as Democrats scored significant gains in Congress and Copperheads took the governorships of New York and New Jersey and majorities in the Illinois and Indiana state legislatures.

The success of antiwar Democrats attracted the attention of soldiers, who saw the Copperheads as dismissive of their sacrifices in the field. The increasing sense of alienation moved many soldiers to support emancipation (the army was deeply divided about this initially) and prompted many Democrats in the army ranks to join the Republican Party. These soldiers became an important source of support for Lincoln, regularly including their endorsement of him in their letters home.

Despite increasing favor in the army, Lincoln saw his support among civilians drop considerably in the first half of 1863, partly because of continued embarrassments on the battlefield and partly because Congress had passed a conscription law in March. The draft, with its power to pull the unwilling into the military, deeply alienated many in the North. Nevertheless, support for the war substantially recovered in July with the victories at Gettysburg and Vicksburg. Although a number of draft riots broke out that summer—most notably in New York City—civilian support for the war generally remained strong until the middle of 1864.

Public enthusiasm for Lincoln and his policies rose even higher in March 1864, when Lincoln appointed Ulysses S. Grant as head of all the Union armies. Many in the North believed that this tenacious general would smash the Confederacy in a few months. But his Overland Campaign seemed to yield nothing good. For its thousands of casualties and wrenching scenes of battle, the campaign ended only in a stalemate outside of Petersburg, Virginia. A Union effort to move into Texas was stymied at Shreveport, Louisiana, and General William Tecumseh Sherman's advance into Georgia ended in a siege at Atlanta. Copperheads attacked Lincoln for his policies and cried for an immediate end to the war. One Wisconsin newspaper refused even to mention the president's name, referring to him instead as either "the widow-maker" or "the orphan-maker."

Support for the Union cause and for Lincoln plummeted as war-weary Northerners lost hope. Even the North's most prominent Republican editor, Horace Greeley, begged Lincoln to reach a compromise peace with the Confederates. Many in the North blamed Lincoln and his position on emancipation for the South's refusal to rejoin the Union—despite Jefferson Davis's repeated statements that the Confederates wanted independence, not reunion. By the middle of August, it appeared that Lincoln would lose his reelection bid. Leading party figures thought so, and so did Lincoln, who drafted a document laying out the terms of transition to the next administration. Under pressure from the chairman of the Republican Party, Lincoln considered abandoning his insistence on emancipation as one of his prerequisites for a peace accord (the other being reunion) but then thought better of it. He remained committed to the African Americans whom the war had liberated and who were fighting for the Union.

In this environment the Democrats held their nominating convention. The power of the Copperheads was at its zenith. War Democrats succeeded in placing one of their own, the former head of the Army of the Potomac, George B. McClellan, at the top of the ticket. To placate the restless peace wing, Democrats named Copperhead congressman George Pendleton of Ohio as their vice presidential candidate and put the most notorious Copperhead in the country, former Ohio congressman Clement Vallandigham, in charge of the party platform. This was a mistake. Vallandigham and the other peace men on the committee inserted language that deemed the war a "failure" and called for an immediate cessation of hostilities.

The party's timing was terrible, for less than two days after the convention broke up, Sherman took Atlanta. Literally overnight, Northern sentiment turned 180 degrees. Now civilians in the North believed the war was won; what was left was a mop-up job. Events such as Philip Sheridan's destructive romp through the Shenandoah Valley only confirmed this point of view. Democrats were tarred by their own platform as traitors to the Union, and McClellan went down to an ignominious defeat. The former general did not muster even 20 percent of the soldier vote.

In the wake of the election, most Peace Democrats went silent, but many Unionists in the North—especially former soldiers—did not forget or forgive. The Democrats remained largely out of power for the rest of the nineteenth century, until the Civil War generation died and their memories of defeatism in the midst of travail went with them.

See also *Vallandigham, Clement Laird*

—Jennifer L. Weber

BIBLIOGRAPHY

Gray, Wood. *The Hidden Civil War: The Story of the Copperheads.* New York: Viking, 1942.

Klement, Frank L. *Copperheads in the Middle West.* Chicago: University of Chicago Press, 1960.

Milton, George Fort. *Abraham Lincoln and the Fifth Column.* Washington, D.C.: Infantry Journal, 1942.

Weber, Jennifer L. *Copperheads: The Rise and Fall of Lincoln's Opponents in the North.* New York: Oxford University Press, 2006.

Corruption in the Federal Government

The issue of corruption in government was a major factor in American politics during the Civil War era. It was commonplace during the war for both Republican and Democratic newspapers to cite corruption as the underlying cause of the conflict. The widespread, intense suspicion of corruption, exacerbated by the vast growth of government bureaucracy and spending during the war, reflected the persistent political ideology of republicanism. This influential concept focused on the need to check government power and warned of social and political decline if citizens did not guard vigilantly against corruption.

The apparently fairly substantial increase in legislative corruption in the decades preceding the Civil War fueled public interest in the issue. The development of corporate lobbying, along with the competition attending the return to prosperity and economic growth during the 1840s and most of the 1850s, helped earn state as well as national government a not undeserved reputation for dishonesty. Historian Michael F. Holt observed that public interest in the corruption issue in Northern states during the early 1850s was sufficiently powerful to ensure the electoral defeat of whichever party proved most vulnerable to such charges.

Lincoln's nomination in 1860 partly stemmed from his reputation for unimpeachable integrity—his image as "Honest Abe"—which contrasted sharply with those of other possible nominees, including William H. Seward, Simon Cameron, and John C. Frémont, whose candidacy might have enabled the opposition once again to make much of the immensely useful corruption issue. The Republicans in 1860 intended to, and did, capitalize on the Buchanan administration's many corruption scandals, reprinting thousands of copies of a congressional committee report on the scandals as a campaign document. It would not have done for their nominee to be less than solid on this issue; hence Lincoln's superior "availability."

Despite Lincoln's sterling reputation for personal honesty, scandals dogged his administration and provided fuel for vocal critics in both the Democratic and Republican ranks. Widespread corruption in government contracting contributed to the ouster of the notorious Pennsylvania political boss Simon Cameron from his post as head of the War Department in early 1862. But the ouster of Cameron hardly ended accusations of corruption, and the Navy, Interior, and Treasury Departments all suffered through major scandals of their own. Much of the alleged corruption centered on the practice of trading between the lines in cotton. Although trade beyond Union lines was illegal, and even within occupied regions technically subject to Treasury Department supervision, it persisted throughout the conflict along the vast, indistinct, ever-shifting, and difficult-to-police boundary between the two "nations" at war. With the war playing havoc with the supply of cotton, prices soared by 1864 and 1865 to the highest rates of the entire nineteenth century, making these ventures (often carried out by investors with presidential permits) even more than usually profitable.

Efforts to dramatize links between the hated corruptionists and the Lincoln administration peaked in the critical election year of 1864. Few Democratic editors or orators overlooked an opportunity to portray Lincoln as the tool of selfish private interests. Radical supporters of John C. Frémont and other Republican rivals of Lincoln similarly portrayed their preferred candidates as the best alternative to the continuation of rule by the reputedly contractor-enriching, "shoddy" dynasty. Lincoln's well-known personal incorruptibility likely shielded him to some extent from the full impact of these allegations, but their persistence reflects the centrality of the corruption issue to the era's political culture.

See also *Cameron, Simon*

—MICHAEL T. SMITH

BIBLIOGRAPHY

Holt, Michael F. *The Political Crisis of the 1850s*. New York: Norton, 1978.

Meerse, David E. "Buchanan, Corruption, and the Election of 1860." *Civil War History*, 1966, 116–131.

Nicklason, Fred. "The Civil War Contracts Committee." *Civil War History*, 1971, 232–244.

Smith, Michael Thomas. "The Enemy Within: Corruption and Political Culture in the Civil War North." PhD diss., Pennsylvania State University, 2005.

Summers, Mark W. *The Era of Good Stealings*. New York: Oxford University Press, 1993.

Crittenden Compromise

The Crittenden Compromise (1860–1861)—though it was ultimately rejected—received more attention than any other attempt to resolve the secession crisis peacefully. The compromise originated with Sen. John J. Crittenden (1786–1863), a Kentuckian who had served in the U.S. Senate intermittently since 1817—first as a Democratic Republican, then as a Whig, and as an American or "Know-Nothing" from 1855 until 1861. Crittenden held other state and national posts along the way, ending his career as a Unionist in the U.S. House of Representatives (1861–1863).

Crittenden first proposed the compromise on December 18, 1860, before any states declared their withdrawal from the Union but with threats of secession rampant. Having struggled for years to dampen sectional antagonisms, Crittenden now hoped to avert a cataclysm for the nation and for his state. The Crittenden Compromise envisioned a series of constitutional amendments, including amendments to (1) restore the Missouri Compromise boundary of 36° 30', extend it to the Pacific so that it would divide all territory currently part of the United States "or hereafter acquired," and allow slavery south of that parallel while prohibiting it to the north; (2) prohibit Congress from abolishing slavery in areas under its jurisdiction within slave states; (3) limit congressional ability to abolish slavery in the District of Columbia; (4) bar Congress from interfering with the interstate slave trade; (5) provide for federal reimbursement of slaveholders who were prevented by local resistance from recovering fugitive slaves; and (6) prohibit any future amendments altering or repealing the above provisions or enabling Congress to abolish or interfere with slavery in slave states. Additional resolutions attached to the Crittenden Compromise emphasized enforcement of fugitive slave laws, eradication of state personal liberty laws that interfered with fugitive slave legislation, modification of the Fugitive Slave Act of 1850, and enforcement of the law banning the importation of slaves. Among various compromise efforts Crittenden's proposals, because they seemed to be the most comprehensive and the most likely to mollify the Deep South, generated the most support from Northern businessmen, some legislators, and pro-Union citizens' meetings.

With the Union facing uncertain prospects, each chamber of Congress formed a special committee to weigh possible options. The Senate's Committee of Thirteen included Crittenden, William Henry Seward (a New York Republican whose Senate service spanned 1849 to 1861 and who became Lincoln's secretary of state), Benjamin Wade (an Ohio Republican who served in the Senate from 1851 until 1869), Stephen Douglas (Lincoln's Democratic rival from Illinois, a senator from 1847 until 1861), Robert Toombs (a Democratic senator from Georgia from 1853 to 1861, later secretary of state for the Confederacy and a brigadier general in the Confederate military), and Jefferson Davis (a Democratic senator from Mississippi from 1847 to 1861, later the president of the Confederacy). In late December 1860 the committee declined to recommend the Crittenden Compromise. All five Republicans on the committee opposed the plan, joined by Southerners Toombs and Davis, who claimed that a lack of Republican support would doom any compromise. (Because of the committee's rule requiring a concurrent majority of both Republicans and non-Republicans, the minority Republican members alone could prevent the committee from endorsing any deal.)

Crittenden believed that his compromise could attract popular, peace-seeking majorities in both the North and South. Republicans, however, could not stomach the territorial provisions of the deal, and the Deep South was indifferent, at best, to political compromise. When Crittenden tried to introduce his proposals on the floor of the Senate in January 1861, Republicans stymied his efforts, and they continued to stifle later attempts in both the Senate and the House to enact the

Crittenden Compromise or modified versions of it, including a variation proposed by a Peace Convention in February 1861, which would have allowed the expansion of slavery into Southern territories already held by the United States but eliminated the "or hereafter acquired" phrase. The application of Crittenden's proposals to territories "hereafter acquired" seemed especially troublesome to some Republicans, including Abraham Lincoln, who predicted that such a provision would produce endless Southern demands for more Central American and Caribbean territory. But many opponents of the Crittenden Compromise could not accept it even if it were limited to territory already held by the United States.

Although supporters of the Crittenden Compromise saw it as a means to avoid war, Lincoln doubted that the plan would ensure peace. At most, he thought, it might postpone a more severe crisis. As president-elect, Lincoln reinforced Republican opposition to Crittenden's territorial provisions, writing to Republicans in both houses of Congress to insist that they hold firm against any potential expansion of slavery. He would promise to enforce fugitive slave laws, urge Northern states to repeal personal liberty laws, avoid interference with the interstate slave trade or slavery in the District of Columbia, and support a proposed constitutional amendment protecting slavery in states where it already existed, but he would concede no more. Lincoln and other Republicans rejected the Crittenden Compromise because they would not cast aside their party's central tenets against the extension of slavery.

Many historians think that no compromise would have stopped the Deep South from seceding because none could erase the trigger for secession—Lincoln's election.

—CARA L. SHELLY

BIBLIOGRAPHY

Kirwan, Albert D. *John J. Crittenden: The Struggle for the Union.* Lexington: University Press of Kentucky, 1962.

Knupfer, Peter B. *The Union as It Is: Constitutional Unionism and Sectional Compromise, 1787–1861.* Chapel Hill: University of North Carolina Press, 1991.

McPherson, James M. *Battle Cry of Freedom: The Civil War Era.* New York: Oxford University Press, 1988.

_____. *Ordeal by Fire: The Civil War and Reconstruction.* New York: Knopf, 1982.

Nichols, Roy Franklin. *The Disruption of Democracy.* New York: Macmillan, 1948.

Oates, Stephen B. *With Malice toward None: The Life of Abraham Lincoln.* New York: Mentor, 1978.

Potter, David M. *The Impending Crisis, 1848–1861.* Completed and edited by Don E. Fehrenbacher. New York: Harper and Row, 1976.

_____. *Lincoln and His Party in the Secession Crisis.* New Haven: Yale University Press, 1942.

Stampp, Kenneth M. *And the War Came: The North and the Secession Crisis, 1860–1861.* Baton Rouge: Louisiana State University Press, 1950.

Curtin, Andrew Gregg

Born in Centre County, Pennsylvania, Andrew G. Curtin (1817–1894) began practicing law in 1837 and spent the next fifty years at the forefront of Pennsylvania and national political life. He canvassed for Whig presidential candidate Henry Clay in 1844 and became the party's state chairman. In 1854 Curtin established his antislavery stance and opposition to the Kansas-Nebraska bill, but with Whig support diminishing and candidates dividing votes among Know-Nothing legislators, he lost a U.S. Senate race to Democrat Simon Cameron. As consolation, he entered the administration of Governor James Pollock in 1855 as secretary of the commonwealth and superintendent of public schools, initiating a system of normal schools to train teachers. That same year, Curtin joined Cameron in the state's Republican Party, called the People's Party, but in 1860, after receiving the party's nomination for governor, he challenged Cameron for control.

The division in the People's Party carried over into the presidential race. At the Republican National Convention, Curtin rejected Cameron's candidacy and balked at supporting William Seward. He doubted the New Yorker's electability and worried that lukewarm support for Seward would harm his own chance to be governor. In positioning himself for the nomination, Abraham Lincoln counted on the rejection of such better-known candidates, and Curtin's influence turned an important delegation his way. During the campaign Lincoln recognized the importance of Pennsylvania's electorate, and he carefully muted disharmony within the state's fractious party. Curtin's victory in October ensured Lincoln's victory in Pennsylvania, and despite continued discord caused by Cameron's selection as secretary of war, the new governor became a valued ally during the secession crisis and the fighting that followed.

Responding to Lincoln's call for troops in April 1861, Curtin sent five companies to defend Washington, D.C. His recruitment efforts exceeded the requested quotas, and he created a facility, Camp Curtin, outside Harrisburg, to train more than 300,000 Union soldiers. The governor worked closely with federal authorities in organizing for the war, but he fretted over Pennsylvania's security. When the Confederate army advanced into Maryland in late summer 1862, Curtin telegraphed the president and the War Department asking for information, ammunition, reinforcements, and permission to raise additional state militia. Officials mocked the anxious governor, particularly his reports overstating rebel movements and inflating troop counts, but Lincoln endorsed Curtin's requests and welcomed whatever intelligence the governor could offer. In the days before the battle of Antietam, Curtin became Lincoln's principal source for determining the whereabouts of the opposing armies, and throughout September he demonstrated his loyalty to the president and the Union cause.

On September 6, Curtin invited Northern governors to meet in his state for a discussion of the war and its outlook. The Loyal War Governors' Conference convened in Altoona on September 24 and 25, with Curtin in a leading role; its topics included George B. McClellan's generalship and the merits of the Emancipation Proclamation. Critics then and historians since have argued about the purpose and consequences of the conference, but the gathering reinforced Curtin's loyalty to Lincoln and his policies. Curtin tirelessly supported the war effort, and Pennsylvania soldiers appreciated his concern for their well-being. He visited camps and hospitals, created a state agency to assist the men and their families, and arranged for the wounded and dead to be returned home. Throughout May 1863, Lincoln reassured Curtin that the Confederates posed no threat, but when they moved into Pennsylvania in late June, the president backed Curtin's plea for 60,000 citizens to defend the state.

When the fighting ended at Gettysburg, Curtin was mortified that unburied corpses lay on the battlefield and body parts protruded from hurriedly dug graves. He authorized David Wills, a local banker who had studied law with Thaddeus Stevens, to purchase seventeen acres to establish a cemetery. He then commissioned a landscape architect to design the space and invited other states to share the cost of interring their dead from the battle. Wills arranged to dedicate the site on November 19, inviting Edward Everett to be the principal orator and asking Lincoln to offer some remarks. Lincoln used the opportunity to celebrate a rare Union victory, explain his expanding war aims, and encourage unity among the Curtin and Cameron factions. Curtin arrived late on the eve of the dedication but, along with several governors and federal officials, joined in the next day's pageantry.

These year-long achievements overshadowed the exhaustion that nearly drove Curtin from office. In the spring, with his health declining, the governor contemplated retirement, and Lincoln considered him for a diplomatic post. Instead Curtin ran for reelection, defeating a peace Democrat endorsed by McClellan. The victory continued the strong relationship between Lincoln and Curtin, and it encouraged the president's bid for a second term.

Curtin remained as governor until 1867, then lost another Senate race to his rival, Cameron. President Ulysses S. Grant appointed him minister to Russia in 1869, but returning home in 1872, Curtin opposed Grant's reelection. He finished his political career representing Pennsylvania as a Democrat in Congress from 1881 to 1887.

—J. Thomas Murphy

BIBLIOGRAPHY

Albright, Rebecca G. "The Civil War Career of Andrew Gregg Curtin." *Western Pennsylvania Historical Magazine* 47 (October 1964): 323–341 and 48 (January 1965): 51–73.

Beers, Paul B. "Andrew Gregg Curtin." *Civil War Times Illustrated* 6 (1967): 12–20.

Bradley, Erwin Stanley. *The Triumph of Militant Republicanism: A Study of Pennsylvania and Presidential Politics, 1860–1872*. Philadelphia: University of Pennsylvania Press, 1964.

D

Davis, Jefferson

Jefferson Davis (1808–1889) was a leading Mississippi politician who became the president of Confederate States of America. First elected to the U.S. House of Representatives from Mississippi in 1845, Davis resigned in 1846 to fight in the Mexican War, where he won recognition for heroism in the battles of Monterrey and Buena Vista. He was elected to the U.S. Senate in 1847 and served until 1853, when he became secretary of war under President Franklin Pierce. In 1857 he returned to the Senate and served until his resignation on January 21, 1861, twelve days after Mississippi seceded from the Union. Although both Abraham Lincoln and Davis served in the Thirtieth Congress (1847–1849), there is no evidence of any direct contact between the two men.

A lifelong Democrat, Davis was not a fomenter of secession as the conflict between the North and the South grew in the latter part of the 1850s. He was never identified with the Southern "fire eaters," though he was a slaveholder with strong proslavery attitudes. Davis's advocacy of states' rights earned him the name "Calhoun of the South." Throughout his life Davis defended slavery and never gave up his belief in the superiority of the white race. A leading candidate for the presidency of the Confederacy from its inception, Davis was elected on February 8, 1861. Supporters looked to his military background, political and administrative experience, and basic conservatism.

A native of Kentucky, Davis was born on June 3, 1808, in Fairview (now Todd County), about 125 miles from the birthplace of Abraham Lincoln. Two years after his birth his parents moved west, eventually settling in southwestern Mississippi, where they became prominent members of the slaveholding planter class. Although Davis started his education in a log cabin school in Mississippi, he obtained his formal education in his native Kentucky before entering the U.S. Military Academy at West Point, graduating in 1828 ranked twenty-third in a class of thirty-four. After a somewhat tumultuous career in the military, during which he served in various posts in the western territories, Davis resigned from the army in 1835. The same year, he married Sara Knox Taylor, the daughter of Zachary Taylor, who would later be the twelfth president of the United States.

Within months of his marriage both Davis and his wife contracted malaria, which took Sara's life. As Lincoln suffered from depression after the death of Ann Rutledge, Davis suffered similarly after his wife's death. He spent the next ten

Jefferson Davis
Source: Library of Congress

years secluded at his Mississippi plantation, Brierfield, where he read extensively and enhanced his education before reentering public life.

Recurring bouts of malaria plagued Davis for most of his life, along with virtual blindness in his right eye. These and other health problems caused Davis to be absent from the presidency of the Confederacy for considerable periods. Historians speculate that poor health contributed to his difficulty dealing with people and helped shape his personality, which was described as aloof, stubborn, inflexible, and lacking in humor.

In 1843 Davis married Varina Howell (1826–1905), a woman eighteen years his junior. Like many Confederate wives, Varina would do much in the years after her husband's death to mold his legacy. Of the six children born to them, only two daughters reached adulthood. Five-year-old Joseph Evan Davis died as a result of a fall from the balcony of the Confederate White House in 1864, two years after the Lincolns suffered the loss of twelve-year-old Willie.

Unlike Lincoln, who sought the office of president, Davis was a reluctant candidate, having originally been named major general of the Mississippi militia, a post he seemingly preferred. As president he faced the daunting task of forming a central government while at the same time financing and fighting a war. Portrayed as an ideologue, Davis has been criticized for his poor political skills, micromanagement of his generals, and inability to deal with his cabinet members. Whereas Lincoln struggled to find the right general to fight the war and dealt primarily with the long-range goals of the conflict, Davis essentially was his own secretary of war. Throughout the war he was strongly criticized by North Carolina governor Zebulon Vance and Georgia governor Joseph Brown. Both during and after the war, critics placed much of the blame for the Southern defeat on Davis. The eminent historian David M. Potter, writing in the 1960s, argued in an oft-cited essay that if Lincoln and Davis had exchanged positions, the Confederacy would have prevailed.

Historian Paul Escott argues that Davis failed to gain the support of the nonslaveholding, yeoman farmer segments of the Confederacy, a failure that prevented the development of Confederate nationalism, which Escott alleges was needed to hold the fledgling government together. Escott further contends that Davis's strong identification with the planter/aristocratic class caused him to make too many wartime concessions to slave owners, which further angered yeoman farmers. More sympathetic historians such as Frank E. Vandiver present Davis as a modernizer who improved the administration and business management of the South and did much to equip the South for modern times.

Asked late in the war about the fate of Davis at the conclusion of the conflict, Lincoln told an anecdote that revealed his hope that Davis would escape "unbeknown" to him. There is every indication that Lincoln would have shown compassion to Davis and had no desire to impose severe sanctions against his Confederate counterpart.

With the evacuation of Richmond on April 2, 1865, Davis and his cabinet retreated south. Hoping to join with Edmund Kirby Smith in the Trans-Mississippi region, Davis and his entourage engaged in a futile attempt to keep the Confederate government together. On May 10, 1865, Davis was arrested in Georgia for participation in an alleged Confederate conspiracy that resulted in the assassination of Lincoln. Though the charges of treason were ultimately dropped, Davis was incarcerated for 720 days before his release on bond on May 14, 1867.

Staunchly defending his position that secession was not treason, Davis pushed for a trial. After numerous delays by the prosecution, the case was dismissed by Chief Justice Salmon P. Chase, who was assigned to hear the case in Richmond, Virginia, as a circuit court judge. Chase ruled that since Davis suffered punishment by virtue of his inability to hold public office, which was imposed by Section 3 of the Fourteenth Amendment, any further punishment would be double jeopardy. Before the appeal of that decision could be heard by the U.S. Supreme Court, President Andrew Johnson issued a final amnesty on December 28, 1868, that terminated any further proceedings against Davis.

Upon the conclusion of the legal proceedings, Davis lived briefly in Canada and traveled in Europe before returning to the United States to assume the role of the consummate unreconstructed Confederate. For the rest of his life he only wore grey suits and maintained that the Confederate cause was correct and noble. His two-volume work *The Rise and Fall of the Confederate Government,* first published in 1881, was a lengthy defense of his position that he was not a rebel but a constitutional patriot. Davis opposed any new rights for blacks, rejoiced in the failure of Reconstruction, and praised the reassertion of white supremacy. In an 1873 speech he asserted that because the Union had turned the war into an antislavery crusade, the South had been cheated, not conquered. In his role as an unreconstructed Confederate, Davis never asked for a pardon or for the removal of the political disabilities imposed by the Fourteenth Amendment.

From the mid-1870s Davis lived on the Mississippi Gulf Coast at Beauvoir, where he wrote his memoirs, as the guest of a wealthy Confederate widow, Sarah Dorsey, who ultimately sold him the property. Davis died in New Orleans on December 6, 1889. He was temporarily interred in New Orleans while several cities vied to be his final resting place. On May 31, 1893, he was buried in Hollywood Cemetery, in Richmond, Virginia, in an elaborate funeral that drew thousands of mourners. Although numerous highways, buildings, and monuments throughout the former Confederacy bear the name of Jefferson Davis, the epitaph on his memorial in the City of Richmond, dedicated on June 3, 1907, represents the legacy that Davis would most likely have preferred: "Exponent of Constitutional Principles and Defender of States Rights." In 1978 Mississippi senator Trent Lott obtained passage of a bill that restored the citizenship of Jefferson Davis. In 1998 the state of Mississippi dedicated a state-financed Jefferson Davis Presidential Library, located in Biloxi.

See also *Confederate States of America*

—C. ELLEN CONNALLY

BIBLIOGRAPHY

Cooper, William J. *Jefferson Davis, American.* New York: Knopf, 2000.

Escott, Paul D. *After Secession—Jefferson Davis and the Failure of Confederate Nationalism.* Baton Rouge: Louisiana State University Press, 1978.

Potter, David M. "Jefferson Davis and the Political Factors in Confederate Defeat." In *Why the North Won the Civil War,* edited by David Herbert Donald. Baton Rouge: Louisiana State University Press, 1960.

Vandiver, Frank E. *Jefferson Davis and the Confederate State.* Oxford: Clarendon Press, 1964.

Declaration of Independence, Lincoln's View of

Shortly before his first inauguration, Abraham Lincoln claimed that he "never had a feeling politically that did not spring from…the Declaration" of Independence, which he regarded as the nation's founding document and statement of purpose. Sixteen years old when the United States celebrated the fiftieth anniversary of the declaration, Lincoln grew up in a culture that revered that document but disagreed about its meaning. Today Americans most readily remember the phrase, "We hold these truths to be self-evident, that all men are created equal" and assume that the central principle expounded by the declaration is equality. Yet the declaration's meaning was once ambiguous: Did it mean equality for all or the right of revolution for some? Lincoln believed that the main ideal espoused by the declaration was a specific definition of equality. As president during the Civil War, he enshrined that interpretation even as the war replaced his belief that halting slavery's extension was the best way to achieve equality with the conviction that realizing the declaration's promise required emancipation.

Whereas the Declaration of Independence pays tribute to many (sometimes contradictory) ideals, Lincoln insisted that the central principle on which its signers intended to base the United States was an affirmation of every person's fundamental humanity and equal right to rise in the world. Many Americans held the contrasting view that the declaration's chief tenet was the right of some people to replace a government that did not promote their interests with one that did. Southern secessionists and many white Northerners, including Lincoln's rival, Illinois senator Stephen A. Douglas, maintained that the declaration meant the equality of whites only and was fully reconcilable with black slavery. Lincoln answered such claims by countering, as he did in the 1858 debates with Douglas, that "the negro is included in the word 'men,'" and where "the right to life, liberty, and the pursuit of happiness" were concerned, black men were "as much entitled to these as the white man." For Lincoln, therefore, the animating principle of the Declaration of Independence and founding tenet of the nation was incompatible with slavery because if all people were equal, none could be property.

At first Lincoln believed that the most politically feasible way to achieve the equality that the declaration promised was to stop the extension of slavery. He articulated this position in a speech in Peoria, Illinois, delivered in response to passage of the Kansas-Nebraska Act (1854), which replaced a ban on the spread of slavery into the Kansas Territory with popular sovereignty, or the right of white males in the territory to vote on slavery. Senator Douglas, the bill's author, portrayed popular sovereignty as successor to the guarantee of self-government in the Declaration of Independence. Lincoln countered that popular sovereignty was a perversion of the declaration because what the declaration really said was, "Allow *all* the governed an equal voice in the government, and that, and that only is self-government." Because popular sovereignty would determine the fate of slaves without permitting them a say in that fate, and might result in the expansion of slavery, which denied the equality of some people by making property of them, it contradicted the declaration. The genuine way to "re-adopt the Declaration of Independence," and thus make the nation "forever worthy of the saving," was to stop slavery from spreading, Lincoln argued, at Peoria and repeatedly through the election of 1860.

Secession, the formation of the Confederacy, and the outbreak of Civil War affirmed Lincoln's belief that the heirs of the declaration must preserve its legacy of equality, but the progress of the war forced him to reconsider how best to do so. Once the Southern states established a Confederacy, founded, as Confederate vice president Alexander Stephens said, not on equality but on the opposite principle, that blacks were inferior to whites, preserving equality would take more than stopping slavery's spread; it would require the defeat of the Confederacy. The duration and intensity of the military conflict and the actions of slaves convinced Lincoln that defeat of the Confederacy and vindication of the principles of the declaration required destruction of slavery, as an institution wholly incompatible with the tenets of the declaration and responsible for bringing on the war that threatened those tenets.

The events of July 1863 created opportunities for Lincoln to embed his vision of the declaration's meaning within the national consciousness. On July 4, Union armies celebrated key victories at Gettysburg and Vicksburg. In remarks delivered on July 7, Lincoln noted three times that Gettysburg and Vicksburg vindicated the declaration signed eighty-seven years earlier because armies fighting for the "self-evident truth that all men were created equal" defeated troops trying to "overthrow that principle." At a November ceremony dedicating the national cemetery at Gettysburg, Lincoln delivered the address that historians have since credited with definitively shaping Americans' understanding of the Declaration of Independence as the articulation of the nation's founding ideals. The Gettysburg Address achieved this feat in three steps. First, the matter-of-fact tone in which the opening sentence identified "the proposition that all men are created equal" as the heart of the declaration settled the question of the declaration's core meaning. Second, by portraying the Civil War as a test of "whether that nation or any nation so conceived and so dedicated" could survive, the address located the founding of the nation squarely within the declaration and its ideals. Finally, the Gettysburg Address concluded with the conviction that the only way to save that nation and vindicate its founding principles was to bring about a "new birth of freedom" without the equality-denying institution of slavery. In short, today's widely shared assumptions that the Declaration of Independence marked the founding of the nation and that its main principle is a definition of human equality antithetical to slavery come from the way in which Lincoln explained the document's meaning to a nation in the midst of a war that had changed his own understanding of how best to achieve what the declaration promised.

—Chandra Manning

BIBLIOGRAPHY

Basler, Roy P., ed. *The Collected Works of Abraham Lincoln.* New Brunswick, N.J.: Rutgers University Press, 1953–1955.

Burton, Orville Vernon. *The Age of Lincoln.* New York: Hill and Wang, 2007.

Cuomo, Mario M., and Harold Holzer, editors. *Lincoln on Democracy.* New York: HarperCollins, 1990.

Jayne, Allen. *Lincoln and the American Manifesto.* Amherst, New York: Prometheus Books, 2007.

Wills, Garry. *Lincoln at Gettysburg: The Words That Remade America.* New York: Simon and Schuster, 1992.

Wilson, Douglas L. *Lincoln's Sword: The Presidency and the Power of Words.* New York: Knopf, 2006.

Democratic Conventions, 1860

In the summer of 1860 Abraham Lincoln's political prospects were closely tied to the Democratic Party's selection of a presidential candidate. If the Democrats nominated Sen. Stephen A. Douglas of Illinois, whom Lincoln ran against for the Senate in 1858, some Republicans believed, the party would need to nominate a westerner to gain support in Douglas's region. Divisions within the Democratic Party complicated Douglas's nomination prospects. Democrats scheduled their convention for Charleston, South Carolina, April 23–May 3, but the convention divided and failed to make a nomination. In the period between the Charleston convention and the Baltimore convention that was held June 18–23, Republicans held their national convention in Chicago, May 16–18. The prospect of Douglas's nomination was beneficial to Lincoln because it weakened the position of Sen. William H. Seward of New York, the front-runner for the Republican nomination. Lincoln supporters capitalized on their advantage, and Lincoln was nominated on the third ballot. The Democrats' final split, at the Baltimore convention, resulted in two different candidates, increasing the likelihood of Lincoln's election in November.

As the Democratic convention approached, Stephen A. Douglas worked to unite the Democratic Party behind his nomination. He struggled to generate Southern support during a Senate session dominated by the issue of slavery's status in the federal territories. Although the Illinois senator supported legislation mandating the federal suppression of conspiracies such as John Brown's raid and avowed his opposition to racial equality, numbers of "ultra" or "fire-eating" Southern Democrats refused to support Douglas because of his support for popular sovereignty. They believed that popular sovereignty—letting territorial settlers determine slave or free status—was inadequate protection for slavery. Douglas attempted to gain support for the idea that the Supreme Court was the final arbiter of whether a territorial government could pass legislation regarding slavery, as the Democratic platform drafted at Cincinnati for the 1856 election had affirmed, but sectional tensions continued to increase. In January a proposal to remove Congress's right to veto territorial legislation resulted in a Senate debate in which radical Southern Democrats tried to undermine Douglas's support. The next month, Mississippi senator Jefferson Davis presented resolutions stating that neither Congress nor territorial legislatures could prevent people from bringing slaves into the territories and that the federal government had to safeguard slave owners' property through a national slave code. The debate framed the sectional animosities in politics and set the stage for the selection of delegates to the Charleston convention.

In the North some rival groups nominated anti-Douglas delegates, but most delegates from the middle western and New England states favored the Illinois senator as the party's nominee. In the South, Democrats were sharply divided over a number of possible nominees. Although Douglas enjoyed support among individuals in the Southern states, Southern convention delegates favored a federal slave code, opposed the Cincinnati 1856 platform, and generally opposed Douglas's nomination. Alabama took the lead in the opposition when Sen. William Lowndes Yancey pledged that if a federal slave code was not part of the party platform, the state's delegation would withdraw from the Charleston convention. Midwestern delegations proved equally intransigent, declaring that they would do the same if popular sovereignty were not upheld.

When the convention began on April 23, many believed that the party was hopelessly divided. The Deep South states were united in their support of the Alabama plan, even as they could not agree on an acceptable alternative to Douglas. A group of pro-Buchanan delegates were arrayed against Douglas on personal grounds, and Illinois and New York had each sent two slates of delegates to the convention. Douglas supporters prevented the rival delegations from being seated and also secured a rule change that allowed delegates who were not bound to support a candidate as a bloc to vote individually. Many of these unbound delegations included Southern supporters of Douglas, and he secured a majority of the individual delegates. Douglas opponents succeeded in electing Caleb Cushing, a pro-Buchanan Massachusetts delegate, as president of the convention. Murat Halstead, a reporter for the *Cincinnati Commercial,* believed that after the second day of the convention the tide of opinion favored Douglas, but that there were "inextinguishable feuds" in the party that would emerge in the battle over the platform.

Although Northern states held the advantage in number of delegates at the convention, the decision to draft a platform before nominating a candidate neutralized Northern influence. Each state had a single vote on the party platform, and California and Oregon voted with the Southern states in favor of a slave code. Douglas supporters pressed for a platform that affirmed the party's Cincinnati platform of 1856 and upheld the Supreme Court's ruling in *Dred Scott,* a position that was compatible with popular sovereignty. The Southern group insisted on a federal slave code. After three days, the committee on the platform reported out three separate platforms. The majority report rejected the power of territorial legislatures to make decisions regarding slavery, rejecting Douglas's Freeport doctrine, and called for a federal slave code. It was supported by a bare majority of the committee. The Douglas minority reaffirmed their position on the Cincinnati platform and the power of the Supreme Court. The final minority report, presented by Benjamin Butler of Massachusetts, supported the Cincinnati platform only. All the reports favored the acquisition of Cuba and the construction of a transcontinental railroad, disavowed personal liberty laws passed by states as a violation of the Fugitive Slave Laws, and pledged to uphold the rights of naturalized citizens.

Following the presentation of the reports, Senator Yancey of Alabama rose to speak and was greeted by an ovation. In a speech that lasted an hour and a half, Yancey called for Southerners to unite in defense of their rights and honor and said that defeat on principle was preferable to victory by ambiguous platforms and misleading the people. Ohioan George Pugh answered Yancey's speech. He argued against the constitutionality of protecting slavery in the territories and claimed that Northern Democrats had long sacrificed their political lives to uphold the doctrines of Southerners. He promised that the Northern Democrats would no longer do the bidding of the South and that the Democracy of the Northwest would be heard. When a Connecticut delegate moved to vote on the platform, the convention broke into chaos.

Days of maneuvering followed, but the division between Southern and midwestern delegations proved insurmountable. On April 30, Douglas supporters made a motion to substitute the minority Douglas platform and to vote on each resolution separately. The Southern delegates refused to vote, and seven Southern state delegations left the convention—Alabama, Mississippi, Louisiana, South Carolina, Florida, Texas, and Arkansas. Georgia followed the next day. Those that remained required that a two-thirds vote of all delegates to the convention would be necessary to nominate a candidate. The decision made Douglas's nomination at Charleston impossible, and on May 3 the delegates determined to recess and reconvene in Baltimore on June 18. Some observers predicted that the Republicans, meeting in Chicago weeks later, would nominate the next president.

The division of the Democrats influenced Lincoln's actions. While he doubted that Douglas would be nominated in Charleston, he had waited to reveal his political plans in case a nominee was chosen. After the failed convention, Lincoln admitted to Illinois senator Lyman Trumbull, in a letter of April 29, 1860, that he desired the Republican nomination. He also measured Republicans' prospects in Illinois. With Douglas on a Democratic ticket, Lincoln believed that neither Seward nor Missourian Edward Bates could carry the state and surmised that the more moderate associate justice John McLean of Ohio could do so. Lincoln noted that Illinois Republicans needed to control the state legislature, and that would be jeopardized by the nomination of Seward. Lincoln believed the bolt of the Southern convention delegates would facilitate Douglas's nomination, but other Republicans were less certain. Seward remained the front-runner, even as he was perceived as too radical on the issue of slavery to carry the critical states of Pennsylvania, Ohio, Indiana, and Illinois in the election. Lincoln, perceived as a moderate, worked to shore up his support among the Illinois delegation and those of other middle western states. His supporters presented him as the candidate most able to unite diverse factions within the Republican ranks and counter Douglas's western influence.

Between the Charleston and Baltimore conventions, Douglas supporters in the Southern states succeeded in presenting new delegations to compete with those that had walked out at Charleston. The delegates who had bolted planned to unite with Upper South delegates in Baltimore to push for a slave code platform or bolt again in larger numbers. In Baltimore the Democrats battled over credentials and anti-Douglas Southerners bolted again. They were joined by some delegates from the Upper South and the North. The bolters convened separately in Baltimore and nominated Vice President John C. Breckinridge of Kentucky on a platform that supported a federal slave code. Those who remained nominated Douglas on the second ballot on a platform that opposed state laws thwarting the Fugitive Slave Law and affirmed the Supreme Court's right to determine if territorial governments could pass legislation pertaining to slavery. Split in two, the Democrats ran both Douglas and Breckinridge in the 1860 election. Lincoln associates, including Illinois representative Elihu B. Washburn and senator Lyman Trumbull, believed that the Democrats' split secured Lincoln's election and wrote him to that effect on June 24 and 28. Lincoln himself was optimistic after Baltimore, writing to friend Anson G. Henry on July 4, 1860, that even with the financial resources of the Democratic Party, the results of the Baltimore convention made a Republican victory likely.

See also *Republican Nominating Convention of 1860*

—CHRISTINE DEE

BIBLIOGRAPHY

Basler, Roy P., ed. *The Collected Works of Abraham Lincoln. Vol. 2.* New Brunswick, N.J.: Rutgers University Press, 1953.

Hesseltine, William B., ed. *Three against Lincoln: Murat Halstead Reports the Caucuses of 1860.* Baton Rouge: Louisiana State University Press, 1960.

Johannsen, Robert W. *Stephen A. Douglas.* New York: Oxford University Press, 1973.

Mitchell, Charles W. "The Madness of Disunion: The Baltimore Conventions of 1860." *Maryland Historical Magazine* 100, no. 3 (2005): 326–349.

Parkhurst, John G., ed. *Official Proceedings of the Democratic National Convention Held in 1860 at Charleston and Baltimore.* Cleveland, Ohio: Plain Dealer Job Office, 1860.

Democratic Party

The Democratic Party was deeply entwined in the political career of Abraham Lincoln. As a Whig Party activist in Illinois in the 1830s, Lincoln battled against the local Democrats and their ideas, which he opposed with great vigor, first as a state legislator and later during his single term in Congress in the late forties. There he won fame among his partisan colleagues for his savage assaults on the administration of the Democratic president, James K. Polk. Lincoln always considered himself a "Henry Clay Whig" devoted to the commercial and nationalizing policies of the Whig leader, in particular a national bank, a protective tariff, federal aid for the building of roads and the improvement of harbors, and the primary role of Congress in determining the government's direction.

The Democrats, in contrast, since their original coming together in the 1820s had carved out a distinct ideological focus that stressed strict Constitutionalism—that is, limited federal government intervention in economic affairs and in the lives of American citizens. The Democrats' laissez-faire approach included opposition to all of the Whigs', and Lincoln's, favorites: a national bank, a protective tariff, and federal spending for internal improvement projects, as well as to any attempts to regulate people's personal behavior. In foreign policy, the Democrats under Jackson and his successors took an aggressive stance that culminated in Polk's leading the country into war with Mexico and annexing large portions of its territory in the peace treaty.

The Whigs were appalled. Congressman Lincoln drew applause from friends and ridicule from enemies, as he unhesitatingly went after the president during the war with Mexico for what he deemed Polk's provocations and his excessive and dangerous course of conquest. His opposition to the war, though supported by his party colleagues, cost the Whigs Lincoln's congressional seat in the next election.

During the 1850s, as resistance to the further expansion of slavery came to the center of political affairs, Lincoln took a strong stance against the Democrats' policy of popular sovereignty—that is, allowing the people of a territory to decide whether to permit slavery there or not. Such a policy, the new Republican Party argued, could lead to additional slave states in the Union. When Lincoln debated the Democratic leader Stephen A. Douglas, in the 1858 race for senator from Illinois, both candidates drew a sharp line on the matter. Lincoln articulated the "free soil" demand that there be no additional slave territory, a position he carried with him into the presidential campaign of 1860.

The Democrats had a very difficult time during the Civil War. When Lincoln became president, he faced a badly weakened political enemy. Once the nation's usual majority party, the Democratic Party had lost many of its supporters and split wide open over the territorial issue in 1860. Then when the Southern states seceded, they took many party supporters with them. The Democrats had to find new leaders as well, since prominent Southerners such as former House Speaker Howell Cobb and Sen. Jefferson Davis, among many others, were gone; Douglas died in 1861. The party's Northern remnant was badly divided over whether to support the war that was now upon them and to what extent to contest Lincoln's policies for carrying it out. A small group of "War Democrats" argued that they should rise above normal partisanship in this unprecedented emergency; they actively supported the Lincoln administration and its policies as necessary to win the war and save the Union. Some would eventually join the Republicans permanently. "Peace Democrats" ("copperheads" to their enemies) just as vigorously challenged the war, its costs, and its unacceptable disruption of American society. They would accept no compromise with the enemy—that is, the Lincoln administration. The largest group of Democrats, led by new leaders such as Governor Horatio Seymour of New York and Rep. Samuel S. Cox of Ohio, rejected both extremes and tried to mark out a middle-of-the-road position. They wished to legitimate themselves as a loyal opposition to the Lincoln administration, dedicated to the Union and restoring it by military action. But at the same time, following their party's traditional outlook, they were determined to defend the constitutional proprieties and social commitments that they defined as important even during wartime.

After a brief period of peace between the parties at the outset of the war, partisan conflict emerged once again as the middle Democratic bloc went along with the notion of "constitutional purity." They articulated their support for the war effort but refused to accept that wartime exigencies should permit the federal government to go as far as Lincoln was moving, as he aggressively assumed additional power, increased regulation over the economy and American citizens, and began to undermine accepted social realities as part of the administration's war aims. What these Democrats saw as the Lincoln administration's aggressive centralization policies, social experimentation, and puritanical regulative outlook about people's behavior by 1862 provoked them against a government that they argued "is in rebellion against the Constitution." They were determined to oppose the administration's overreaching. "The Constitution as it is, the Union as it was," became their rallying cry.

In particular, Democrats argued that in the name of national security and prosecuting the war the Lincoln administration was seriously overstepping constitutional limits on interference with freedoms of speech and of the press. Some of the administration's more enthusiastic officials, usually military officers, closed down several Democratic newspapers, including the most important one, the *New York World,* and arrested party officeholders and candidates, such as Rep. Clement Vallandigham, running for governor of Ohio, because of their outspokenness—and alleged treason. These actions were few and temporary, but Democrats from the majority and the peace wing saw them as devastating attacks on civil liberties. Both blocs also adopted a virulent racist, antiblack, stance, arguing that the United States was a white man's country and that government authority should not be used to uplift blacks, as the Lincoln administration was engaged in doing. They decried in the bitterest terms the Emancipation Proclamation and the enlistment of African Americans into the army and opposed conscription.

Democratic leaders hoped to build a conservative coalition against Republican despotism, attracting former Whigs from the Border States and uncomfortable, less-radical members of Lincoln's party to their side. But this strategy never got far. The Republicans took advantage of their opponents' divisions and often unpopular complaints, labeling all Democrats (except the War Democrats) treasonous cowards—that is, Copperheads, indifferent to the nation's survival. Their angry assaults worked well in a series of wartime elections, particularly when the Democrats ran candidates such as Vallandigham, from their peace wing, or when in the interest of party unity they allowed the peace bloc leeway in platform matters.

The Lincoln administration suffered a setback in congressional and state elections in 1862, when the Democrats won governorships in such key states as New York and New Jersey. But the Republicans successfully held onto their power in 1863 and, most critically, in Lincoln's reelection in 1864 against a hybrid Democratic ticket of General George McClellan, who supported the war, for president, and Ohio's George Pendleton, a prominent member of the peace bloc, for vice president, The Democrats' platform was portrayed as copperhead influenced—which it was, in part. In these elections the party retained the loyalty of many of its traditional supporters in urban Catholic centers in eastern cities and in other ethnic enclaves in upstate New York and in Pennsylvania, and that of farmers and small town entrepreneurs in the lower Mississippi Valley, in particular. But in their difficult position, and demonized by the Republicans, the Democrats' support had grown very little since the war began. Lincoln and his party retained the support of most of those who formed the Republican Party in the 1850s.

The aftermath of the 1864 presidential election found the Democratic Party in a deep valley. They had hectored and bothered the administration during wartime but never could block its pursuit of, as the Democrats saw it, a social and governmental revolution in the nation. And the Democrats were up against as wily a politician as they had ever faced. They were not traitors, but they were outargued and outmaneuvered, the charges of treason sticking to them even after the war's end. They would be unable to regain the presidency for two decades.

—Joel H. Silbey

BIBLIOGRAPHY

Katz, Irving. *August Belmont: A Political Biography.* New York: Columbia University Press, 1968.

McJimsey, George. *Genteel Partisan: Manton Marble, 1834–1917.* Ames: Iowa State University Press, 1971.

Silbey, Joel H. *A Respectable Minority: The Democratic Party in the Civil War Era, 1860–1868.* New York: Norton, 1977.

Smith, Adam I. *No Party Now: Politics in the Civil War North.* New York: Oxford University Press, 2006.

Democrats, Peace

The Peace Democrats, contemptuously labeled "copperheads" by their Republican adversaries, shared with their party's mainstream bitter hostility to the Lincoln administration's wartime policies. Like their Democratic colleagues, they challenged the president's war against the South and sought to derail the administration's plans to transform America's racial situation. But the Peace Democrats went much farther than most of their party peers in their opposition to the war and their demands that it be ended before it further damaged the Union. To them, what Lincoln and his associates were doing was not only wrongheaded but both unconstitutional and futile. They believed that abolitionists controlled the Republican Party and that these hectoring puritans were determined to use coercive government power to reshape the Union in their image. Splitting from other Democrats, therefore, the Peace Democrats refused to support the administration's military efforts and advanced an extremely chaste constitutional outlook on all other matters. Arguing that trying to bring the South back into the Union by force would not succeed, they demanded negotiations as the only effective means of settling the differences ripping the nation apart and returning it to its normal and preferred situation.

Particularly strong in the lower Middle West, among a population largely descended from original settlers from the Southern states, the Peace Democrats fought to control the Democratic Party, advance their variation of its advocacy both locally and nationally, and remove the "Black Republicans" from power. Their militantly antiblack, anticoercion, anti-Lincoln stance won them much support in the early years of the war. They were able to dominate Democratic Party affairs in Ohio and to a lesser extent in Indiana and Illinois. In New York City, Mayor Fernando Wood represented the same attitudes among restive Democrats there. Several Peace Democrats were elected to Congress from Ohio, and one of the most dogged of them, Clement Vallandigham, was the party's candidate for governor in 1863.

The copperheads became the focus of much partisan opprobrium for their advocacy of what Republican propaganda asserted was treason. But their strict, unbending constitutional and social conservatism was not necessarily treasonous (although some of them were prepared not only to oppose the war effort but to disrupt it). They resisted the draft law when it was enacted, never let up in their loud calls to end the conflict, and called for a halt to the coercive powers that the Lincoln administration had taken up. The issuance of the Emancipation Proclamation in late 1862 drove them to despair. It summed up all that had gone wrong under Lincoln. A government-imposed social revolution was now far advanced. As the Peace Democrats grew more desperate, they encouraged men to resist the draft by refusing to report when called up, and some of them participated in destructive riots against enforcing the law, incidents that took particular aim at African Americans, scapegoating them for all that had gone wrong.

The copperheads' stance, Vallandigham's fiery oratory, local military officials' claim that Democratic-led secret societies were engaging in subversion, and the outbreak of riots led outraged federal officials to arrest the bloc's leaders and suppress their meetings and newspapers, including some that did not represent the Peace Democrats' viewpoint. But because all Democrats were being labeled treasonous copperheads in Republican propaganda, distinctions among them were readily ignored. In Ohio, the longtime Democratic leader and editor of the party's major newspaper there, Samuel Medary, was among those seized. The most prominent of them, Vallandigham, was imprisoned in a military jail for a time and then, at Lincoln's order, deported to the Confederacy. He made his way north and continued his campaign for governor from Canada, but was badly beaten that autumn.

The copperheads' strength in some areas made the leaders of the national Democratic Party tread carefully around them. Their votes were needed on election day in the areas where they had strength, as well as in Congress, even as party leaders realized that their reputation, as painted by their opponents and by government actions against them, could significantly harm the party at the polls in many places. Both elements were present in the presidential election of 1864 when a Peace Democrat leader, Ohio congressman George Pendleton, was selected as the party's vice presidential nominee. He and his colleagues strongly influenced the Democrats' national platform which, among other things, declared the war a "failure." The Republicans effectively countered the Democrats by continuing to characterize them as hostile to the Union and as friends of slavery and traitors to the war effort. With the war going better in the fall of 1864, Lincoln won reelection against his partisan enemies, most of whom, to repeat, were not copperheads, no matter what the Republicans claimed.

The copperheads were never really the danger that the Republicans claimed they were. Despite the provocative actions of some of them, they did not have the strength, the organization, or the intent to accomplish what was charged against them. They were important for two reasons: for the resistance that they offered to the demands imposed on Americans by the wartime emergency and as an effective and convenient target for the Lincoln administration as it attempted to undercut resistance to its policies.

—Joel H. Silbey

BIBLIOGRAPHY

Cowden, Joanna. *Heaven Will Frown on Such a Cause as This: Six Democrats Who Opposed Lincoln's War.* Lanham, Md.: University Press of America, 2001.

Klement, Frank L. *Lincoln's Critics: The Copperheads of the North.* Shippensburg, Pa.: White Mane Publishing, 1999.

———. *The Limits of Dissent: Clement L. Vallandigham and the Civil War.* New York: Fordham University Press, 1998.

Mushkat, Jerome. *Fernando Wood: A Political Biography.* Kent, Ohio: Kent State University Press, 1990.

Desertions/Presidential Pardons

Despite the fragmentary nature of existing records, the handful of scholars who have studied desertion agree that well over two hundred thousand Union soldiers were absent without leave at some point during the Civil War. In many instances, homesickness or feelings of loyalty and obligation to family motivated even patriotic enlisted men to leave the service permanently or temporarily. As the war progressed, the institution of the draft and the temptation of the bounty system filled the ranks with less-principled men, who oftentimes fully intended to desert at the first opening. After returning home, many deserters received help from civilians in evading arrest by provost marshals, who captured and returned to the ranks only about eighty thousand deserters. The significant loss of manpower prompted several Union generals to urge Lincoln to take stronger measures to help enforce military discipline.

However, as commander in chief Lincoln favored leniency and forgiveness in the cases of most deserters. In a presidential proclamation of March 10, 1863, he offered amnesty to all soldiers absent without leave who returned to their regiments by April 1. Over the course of the war Lincoln received almost one hundred fifty petitions from apprehensive family and friends or accommodating politicians regarding reprieves for soldiers condemned to be executed for desertion. Despite his busy schedule and the numerous cares of office, he always devoted time to review the known details of each case, for he sincerely hoped to find any pretense to save a man's life. Taking into account the age and previous service record of each soldier, Lincoln typically suspended the death sentence, preferring to place the impenitent deserter in prison and offering full pardon to the repentant soldier who agreed to serve out the remainder of his enlistment term. On February 26, 1864, Lincoln's growing concern that too many deserters faced the firing squad before their cases came to his attention prompted him to commute all executions for desertion to imprisonment.

Lincoln's penchant for pardoning Union deserters demonstrated his compassion for the common Union soldier and his keen understanding of human frailty. Recognizing that the heat of battle could cause a man's instinctive desire for self-preservation to overcome his best intentions to obey orders, Lincoln generally gave each man the benefit of the doubt when considering such "leg cases." Realistic enough to know that a few unscrupulous men may have been the recipients of his mercy, the president preferred to err on the side of caution, since taking a man's life afforded him no opportunity to redeem his character. Above all, Lincoln took great satisfaction in knowing that his pardoning a deserter would bring immeasurable happiness to the soldier and his family. Numerous letters from forgiven soldiers convey their sincere gratitude and attest to their high regard for the beneficent man who allowed them a second chance in life. Far from undermining discipline in the army, Lincoln's presidential pardons for deserters clearly revealed the magnanimity of his nature and his genuine love for his fellow man.

—Sean A. Scott

BIBLIOGRAPHY

Cashin, Joan E. "Deserters, Civilians, and Draft Resistance in the North." In *The War Was You and Me: Civilians in the American Civil War,* edited by Joan E. Cashin, 262–285. Princeton: Princeton University Press, 2002.

Davis, William C. "The Quality of Mercy." In *Lincoln's Men: How President Lincoln Became Father to an Army and a Nation.* New York: Free Press, 1999.

Weitz, Mark A. "Preparing for the Prodigal Sons: The Development of the Union Desertion Policy during the Civil War." *Civil War History* 45 (1999): 99–125.

Doughface

The term "doughface," part of a substantial lexicon of colorful labels in nineteenth-century American politics, appears to trace its political roots to the debate over the Missouri Compromise (1820), when John Randolph, of Roanoke, an eccentric, erratic member of the Virginia delegation in the House of Representatives, deplored the pliability of Northerners who had voted with the South to allow Missouri to enter the Union as a slave state. Randolph railed, "They were scared at their own dough faces—yes, *they were scared at their own dough faces!*" (quoted in Leonard Richards, *The Slave Power,* 85). Some thought that Randolph meant that "doe"-faced men were as timid as skittish deer, but others perceived his odd term as a reference to "dough"-like malleability. The latter interpretation prevailed.

In the late 1840s *Webster's* dictionary defined "doughfacism" as "willingness to be led about by one of stronger will." By then, "doughface" applied not only to Northern politicians who voted with the South (or absented themselves from important votes on sectional issues in Congress) but also to Northern newspapers, clergy, or others who seemed to truckle to the South. The term connoted subservience, weakness, cowardice, insincerity, unreliability, and corruption.

Historians frequently define "doughfaces" as "Northern men with Southern principles," but in many instances, critics in the antebellum period considered doughfaces to be men with no principles whatsoever. Devoid of firm convictions, the logic ran, doughfaces were easily swayed, molded, or bought. Southerners, too, despised doughfaces, as the initial attack by Virginia's John Randolph suggests. Although the South benefited from doughface support, some Southerners resented dependence on such men and shared the opinion that doughfaces were weak, corrupt, and inherently untrustworthy.

Because of the mathematics of representation in each house of Congress, doughfaces often provided the margin of victory for the Southern or proslavery side in sectional disputes. Of those in politics who were stigmatized as doughfaces, most were Democrats. The Democratic Party's opponents accused doughface Democrats of abetting the corrupting influences of the so-called Slave Power—a theme that the Republicans, free of any need to cater to a Southern wing of their own, exploited even more heavily than could the Whigs. Republicans portrayed the Democratic Party as so internally debased by Southern proslavery interests and Northern doughfacism that the Democrats could no longer be trusted.

Abraham Lincoln shared Republicans' contempt for doughfaces and their role in bolstering the Slave Power. In the 1850s Lincoln made strong statements linking Democratic politicians such as Sen. Stephen Douglas and Presidents Franklin Pierce and James Buchanan—all of whom were viewed as doughfaces—with the alleged Slave Power conspiracy to dominate the nation. Lincoln considered Douglas the worst and most dangerous doughface because of Douglas's powerful influence in politics and public opinion.

In the secession winter of 1860–1861 some Republicans, including Lincoln, discounted the seriousness of secession, suspecting that it was a Southern ploy to stampede doughfaces and other spineless Northerners into supporting unconscionable concessions to the South. By then, however, many Southerners loathed doughfaces, especially Stephen Douglas, and neither sought nor expected anything from them.

See also *Missouri Compromise*

—CARA L. SHELLY

BIBLIOGRAPHY

Carwardine, Richard. *Lincoln: A Life of Purpose and Power.* New York: Vintage, 2006.

Donald, David Herbert. *Lincoln.* New York: Simon and Schuster, 1995.

Goodwin, Doris Kearns. *Team of Rivals: The Political Genius of Abraham Lincoln.* New York: Simon and Schuster, 2005.

Johannsen, Robert W. *Stephen A. Douglas.* New York: Oxford University Press, 1973.

Richards, Leonard L. *The Slave Power: The Free North and Southern Domination, 1780–1860.* Baton Rouge: Louisiana State University Press, 2000.

Summers, Mark W. *The Plundering Generation: Corruption and the Crisis of the Union, 1849–1861.* New York: Oxford University Press, 1987.

Douglas, Stephen A.

Until his death in 1861, Stephen A. Douglas (1813–1861) was Abraham Lincoln's great Illinois political opponent. Douglas had a meteoric career in American politics. He was born April 23, 1813, in Brandon, Vermont, and later resided for a few years in upstate New York. He moved to Illinois at age twenty to seek his fortune, and he quickly earned admittance to the legal profession and entered politics. A founder of the Illinois Democratic Party, Douglas rapidly rose in politics. His fierce debating skills combined with his small stature led to his nickname, "the Little Giant." In 1843 Douglas was elected to Congress, just when the nation commenced a vast western movement; Douglas became one of the North's most prominent advocates of this territorial expansion, known as Manifest Destiny.

But Manifest Destiny led to a destructive quarrel: whether slavery could move into newly acquired territories. David Wilmot raised the issue in 1846 when he presented a proviso that banned slavery from all the territories acquired from Mexico. For four years Congress fought over the proviso, several Southern states threatening secession if such a prohibition ever became law. Lewis Cass found a way out of the dilemma by formulating the doctrine of "popular sovereignty"—that Congress should not pass any law about slavery in the territories but rather permit settlers to decide the question for themselves. Becoming a U.S. senator in 1847, Douglas earned national fame by bringing about a resolution of the quarrel. An attempt by Henry Clay to compromise all sectional disputes, a piece of legislation called the "Omnibus," failed to pass Congress because it united Northern and Southern radicals against it. Douglas stepped in and broke the Omnibus into separate bills, which passed Congress in late 1850, becoming the "Compromise of 1850." Everyone recognized that Douglas deserved the credit for its passage, and for his role he became a serious presidential contender in 1852.

Douglas's political fortunes soon were reversed because of the slavery extension issue, which consumed the nation after 1854. Douglas rekindled the debate by a gross miscalculation of Northern popular attitudes when he sponsored the Kansas-Nebraska Act. To mollify Southerners, Douglas's measure divided Nebraska Territory into two parts, Kansas and Nebraska, repealing the Missouri Compromise's prohibition against slavery's expansion into the area and establishing popular sovereignty to handle the question of slavery. Douglas believed that if the issue was taken out of the halls of Congress, sectional passions would disappear. He was in error.

The immediate impact of the Kansas-Nebraska Act was to dethrone the Northern Democratic Party. The Northern Democrats were slaughtered in the congressional elections of 1854, and the Republican Party came into being. The act energized Abraham Lincoln and brought him back into the political arena.

In the 1830s Lincoln and Douglas had encountered each other in Springfield, Illinois. Lincoln had chosen the Whig Party—popular in Sangamon County but not the rest of the state—whereas Douglas became a Democrat. So their rivalry began early in their lives; they had served concurrently in the state legislature, debated each other in the presidential election of 1840, and for a while rode legal circuit together. But Lincoln's activism faded after his congressional term (1847–1849), and he remained in Springfield tending his law practice while Douglas went on to claim national glory. The Kansas-Nebraska Act changed the direction of the two men's lives. Lincoln was outraged that slavery was being allowed to expand. He held that slavery undermined freedom and believed that

Douglas was acting in the interest of slavery instead of freedom—antislavery partisans called such an individual a "doughface." Lincoln and Douglas met face to face in October 1854 and argued about the effects of the Kansas-Nebraska Act, with Lincoln denouncing the doctrine of popular sovereignty as a fraud that betrayed the hopes of the founding generation and Douglas justifying it as pure democratic practice.

Affairs connected with Kansas continued to damage the Democratic Party and Douglas's reputation. Sensational event followed sensational event: attacks by Missourians on antislavery Kansas settlers, the "sack of Lawrence," the John Brown murders at Pottawatomie Creek, and the caning of Charles Sumner. Even though the Democrats narrowly elected James Buchanan president in 1856, events in Kansas continued to intrude on national politics. In March 1857 the Supreme Court ruled in the *Dred Scott* decision that Congress could not exclude slavery from the territories. Shortly thereafter came the Lecompton Constitution controversy, in which the proslavery faction in Kansas wrote a state constitution (the Lecompton Constitution) and sent it to Congress in a move to gain admittance to the Union as a slave state. In the congressional battle over the legislation in 1858, Douglas opposed the Lecompton Constitution as a perversion of popular sovereignty that was based on fraudulent voting; for his opposition he earned the enmity of President James Buchanan and Southern leaders.

Douglas faced a difficult year in 1858 when he sought reelection against a formidable Republican opponent, Abraham Lincoln. Out of this situation came the famous Lincoln-Douglas debates. During the fall of 1858, the two men faced each other in seven Illinois towns. In these matches Douglas stressed the vitality of popular sovereignty, insisted that the nation need not worry about slavery, and argued for white supremacy. Lincoln warned that popular sovereignty was dead because of the *Dred Scott* decision, that slavery was morally wrong, and that the nation had to return to the policy of no expansion of slavery. Against tremendous odds, Douglas won reelection. At the time senators were actually elected by the state legislature, and Douglas's victory partially resulted from the weighting of the electoral districts after the Census of 1850, an apportionment that favored the Democratic southern part of the state but that by 1858 underrepresented the rapidly growing northern, and Republican, part.

Douglas believed that the Democratic Party in the North was in danger of being destroyed by Southern demands that slavery always be protected in the territories, and thus he was determined to get the Democratic Party's nomination at the 1860 national convention in Charleston. But the Charleston convention divided between Gulf State Southerners, who wanted federal protection of slavery in the territories, and Northerners who demanded a platform based on popular sovereignty. This breach was then widened at a subsequent convention in Baltimore, where Border State Southerners left the party and joined Gulf State Southerners to offer a distinctly Southern presidential candidate. The Baltimore nomination went to Douglas.

Republicans understood that they could win the election of 1860 because the Democratic Party vote would be split between the Northern and Southern candidates (Douglas and John C. Breckinridge). To play it safe, the Republicans chose Abraham Lincoln as their nominee. But there would be no Lincoln-Douglas debates in 1860 because Lincoln followed the custom of staying home and letting others campaign for him. Douglas broke tradition altogether and decided to take his message directly to the nation's voters. The Little Giant traveled throughout the country denouncing sectional extremism on the slavery issue and arguing for popular sovereignty. By late September, realizing that he was not going to win, he toured the Southern states and, facing hostile crowds, told Southern audiences that secession would not be tolerated.

In November 1860 Abraham Lincoln won the presidential contest, and as many had feared, the Gulf States reacted by producing secession ordinances in December and January. By March 1 a new nation, the Confederate States of America, had been formed. Douglas strove to find a compromise that would bring these states back into the Union but failed. As time went on, he was beginning to accept a division of the Union because he feared the use of military force. When Lincoln became president, he and Douglas had in common many viewpoints about secession, but they differed on whether force should be used to stop it and whether Fort Sumter should be resupplied or evacuated. Whatever disputes may have existed between them were rendered moot when the Confederates fired on Fort Sumter on April 12. Lincoln responded with a proclamation calling for a volunteer army to put down the rebellion. In response four more slave states—North Carolina, Virginia, Tennessee, and Arkansas—joined the Confederacy.

Douglas reacted to the firing on Fort Sumter the way most Northerners did: it was an act of war that required retaliation. In late April, Douglas went back to Illinois to urge support for Lincoln's war against the Confederacy, but he did not live to see the actual fighting. He had been in ill health for several years, and his exertions in 1858 and 1860 proved too much for his weakened constitution. He fell into a deep illness and died on June 4.

The most important issue Douglas faced during his life was the question of slavery's expansion, and he wanted to manage the problem so that it would not divide the country into warring parts. He differed from Lincoln in believing that slavery was not a danger to free society. Indeed Douglas declared in his 1858 debates with Lincoln that he did not care if slavery was "voted up or down." His struggles during the 1850s reveal the erosion of moderates on the issue of slavery during the antebellum decade and the failure of political leaders to find a compromise solution. In the larger processes of U.S. history, Douglas's political career showed the power of racist sentiment in the Anglo-American population during the nineteenth century, a racism that not only got in the way of moral judgments on the institution of slavery but also foiled attempts to end it short of war.

See also *Campaign of 1858, Lincoln's Senatorial; Lincoln-Douglas Debates*

—JAMES L. HUSTON

BIBLIOGRAPHY

Huston, James L. *Stephen A. Douglas and the Dilemmas of Democratic Equality.* Lanham, Md.: Rowman and Littlefield, 2006.

Johannsen, Robert W. *Stephen A. Douglas.* 1973. Reprint, Urbana: University of Illinois Press, 1997.

Douglass, Frederick

Born enslaved in Talbot County, Maryland, Frederick Washington Augustus Bailey, later known as Frederick Douglass (1818–1895), was the son of Harriet Bailey, a field hand, and a white man. His father was most likely his first master, Aaron Anthony. During his twenty years in bondage, Douglass experienced both plantation and urban slavery, living on various plantations in Maryland and in Baltimore. He also learned to read during this period and surreptitiously read the *Columbian Orator.* When he was about eighteen years old Douglass was allowed to live outside the confines of his master's home, arranging his own boarding and enjoying considerable freedom so long as the bulk of his weekly wages were turned over to his owner. During this time Douglass came to believe that he deserved more than the quasi freedom available to him in Baltimore. In September 1838, he borrowed the papers of a free black sailor and boarded a train for the North. Douglass joined his soon-to-be wife, Anna Murray, in New York City, and the pair eventually settled in New Bedford, Massachusetts.

In New Bedford, Douglass became acquainted with the movement to abolish slavery, and in 1841 he was hired as a lecturing agent for the Massachusetts Anti-Slavery Society. He soon gained a reputation as a powerful orator with the ability to testify personally to the evils of slavery. He became a close associate of prominent antislavery activists and the protégé of William Lloyd Garrison. In 1845 Douglass published the first of three autobiographies, *Narrative of the Life of Frederick Douglass,* which was read widely in the United States and Great Britain. While he was touring Great Britain and Ireland in 1845 to mid-1847, British abolitionists raised funds and purchased Douglass's freedom, and he returned to the United States a free man in April 1847. Moving his family to Rochester, New York, Douglass began to edit and publish his own antislavery weekly newspaper, the *North Star.*

During the decade of the 1850s, Douglass toured the country and became America's most famous former slave. He worked tirelessly for the causes of abolition, black civil rights, and the rights of the women with whom he often shared a speaking platform. Although he initially supported Garrison, who rejected politics and considered the U.S. Constitution a proslavery document, Douglass came to believe that political means were necessary to bring an end to slavery. By June 1851 he had broken with Garrison and converted his newspaper to a Liberty Party vehicle, renamed *Frederick Douglass' Paper*. In the 1850s he campaigned for politicians who supported abolition but eventually came to believe that the more moderate Republican Party was the best hope for freeing those still in bondage.

Douglass voted for Abraham Lincoln in the presidential election of 1860. Like most African Americans who enjoyed the right of suffrage, he believed that the man from Illinois was the nation's best hope for bringing an end to slavery. In Douglass's

The noted African American abolitionist Frederick Douglass photographed circa 1885. Lincoln encouraged Douglass to share his opinions on slavery, emancipation, and the direction of the war on a number of occasions, and invited Douglass to social events; inviting an African American to such events was unprecedented for an American president.

Source: The Granger Collection, New York

view Lincoln was not a perfect candidate. In the month between Lincoln's inauguration and the beginning of the Civil War in April 1861, Douglass became highly critical of the president's actions. The conciliatory tone of Lincoln's First Inaugural Address brought Douglass's worst fears to life. Although he supported the new president's desire to preserve the Union, he detested Lincoln's vow to leave slavery in place in the Southern states. In an editorial blasting Lincoln's inaugural address, Douglass proclaimed him "the most dangerous advocate of slave-hunting and slave-catching in the land."

In early spring 1861, while Lincoln was preparing to lead the nation, Douglass was preparing to leave on a trip to Haiti to investigate it as a potential site for black emigration. When the opening shots of the Civil War were fired on April 12, he canceled his trip, becoming hopeful that the Union was about to engage in a righteous war against slavery. Douglass became a vocal advocate of the use of force to end both the war and slavery. He used his newspaper to launch vicious attacks against the South, blaming slaveholding planters for the current conflict and decrying poor Southern whites as "ignorant, besotted, and servile," men who were tools of the slaveholders and caught up in a great and horrible Slave Power. For the first two years of the war Douglass's main message pushed

Northerners toward hatred of the slaveholders. He also advocated a more active role for African Americans in the conflict, especially the recruitment of black troops, but placing such troops in direct conflict with Southerners was in opposition to Lincoln's conciliatory plans in the war's early days. Finally, in fall 1862, following Lincoln's preliminary Emancipation Proclamation, official policy moved to allow the participation of African American troops.

In 1863 Douglass devoted much of his time to the recruitment of black troops for the famed 54th Massachusetts regiment. Two of his sons, Charles and Lewis, were among his first recruits, and by late spring he had sent over one hundred young black men to the unit. Once ending slavery became an important war aim, Douglass's criticism of Lincoln tempered, but he was deeply disturbed about the inequality of pay and the unchallenging assignments designated to black soldiers, as well as the horrendous treatment of blacks captured by the Confederacy. On August 10, 1863, Douglass met Lincoln for the first time. He came to Washington to personally bring the grievances of black soldiers to the president's attention. Lincoln listened politely to Douglass's complaints about unequal pay; he maintained that popular prejudice precluded offering equal pay immediately but promised future parity. Douglass came away from this first meeting with a new respect for the man in the White House, believing him to be sincere and honest. In a December 1863 address, Douglass told the American Anti-Slavery Society that Lincoln was a sincere man and that he would be remembered as "Honest Abraham."

Although he sometimes disagreed with Lincoln's policies, Douglass campaigned for the president in 1864. When it seemed that his reelection prospects were questionable, in summer 1864, Lincoln drafted a letter in which he denied that he was standing in the way of peace and proclaiming that he could not sustain a war against slavery if Congress and the nation did not support it. He called Douglass to the White House and shared the letter and his potential plans to abandon abolition as a war goal. Douglass urged Lincoln to keep to the current course, and while the weight of his influence cannot be ascertained, the president did not publish the letter. Douglass was also active in a presidential plan to encourage active resistance among the enslaved population of the Confederate states, but it was abandoned once prospects for Lincoln's reelection brightened.

The last months of the war found Douglass offering a number of orations predicting a bright future for African Americans. In an address delivered before a black convention in October 1864, he remarked, "The change is great, and increasing, and is viewed with astonishment and dread by all those who had hoped to stand forever with their heels upon our necks." He came to believe that Lincoln's presidency was the major turning point toward full acceptance and citizenship for his race. Douglass and Lincoln met for the last time at the president's second inaugural reception, held at the White House. The unprecedented appearance of an African American at the event led door guards to try to turn Douglass away, but he persisted in his desire to see the president. Douglass later recalled sending someone he knew to tell the president he was detained, and within minutes he was invited into the reception, with Lincoln himself calling out, "Here comes my friend Douglass."

Douglass's celebration of the end of slavery and the Civil War was tempered by the assassination of the man he now called friend and leader in April 1865. At home in Rochester when he learned of the president's death, Douglass was called on to deliver an impromptu eulogy. "A dreadful disaster has befallen the nation," he told those assembled at Rochester's City Hall, "it is a day for silence and meditation; for grief and tears." But Douglass mourned his friend as well as his president, calling his death a "personal as well as a national calamity." He remembered the words of Lincoln's Second Inaugural Address, quoting a lengthy passage from memory and concluding that Lincoln was an honest and good man. If "an honest man is the noblest work of God, we need have no fear for the soul of Abraham Lincoln."

A few months after the president's death, Douglass received a parcel and a note from Mary Todd Lincoln. Some time before his death, she noted, her husband had desired to do something to show his regard for Douglass. To honor his wish, she sent Douglass Lincoln's walking stick as a memento. He accepted it with graciousness and in recognition of Lincoln's "humane interest in the welfare of [his] whole race."

See also *Abolitionism; Garrison, William Lloyd*

—L. Diane Barnes

BIBLIOGRAPHY

Blight, David W. *Frederick Douglass' Civil War: Keeping Faith in Jubilee*. Baton Rouge: Louisiana State University Press, 1989.

Oakes, James. *The Radical and the Republican: Frederick Douglass, Abraham Lincoln, and the Triumph of Antislavery Politics*. New York: Norton, 2007.

Draft, Military

The Civil War draft was one of the most controversial issues that the administration of President Abraham Lincoln faced. When the war began, the Union army had no need for a draft because hundreds of thousands of men volunteered. Repeated Union defeats in 1861 and early 1862, however, combined with the expiration of short-term enlistments, made clear that more men were needed but also quenched enthusiasm for volunteering. Accordingly Lincoln and the

Republican Congress turned to conscription, passing the Militia Act of July 17, 1862. The act obligated every male citizen between the ages of eighteen and forty-five to nine months of potential service in a state militia, and it authorized the president to call the state militias into federal service. To head off legal challenges to the measure, Congress justified its actions by citing the Constitution's provision on federal authority to establish a "well-regulated militia." The act, however, raised very few troops directly.

More effective was the Enrollment Act of March 3, 1863. That act declared that the U.S. armed forces comprised all male citizens between the ages of twenty and forty-five, each of whom might be obligated to serve for three years. The Enrollment Act, unlike the Militia Act, obligated citizens directly to the federal government and was predicated on Congress's authority to raise armies rather than on the militia clause. Congress, knowing that draftees were often stigmatized for a lack of patriotism, designed the act primarily as a means of producing volunteers.

Enforcement of the act was entrusted to provost marshal general James Barnett Fry, a capable executive. In each congressional district, draft officials enrolled potential draftees, who often resisted. Following presidential calls for troops in summer 1863, spring 1864, fall 1864, and spring 1865, the provost marshal general assigned a quota to each district, to be met with either volunteers or draftees. Communities generally thought it shameful to meet their quotas through the draft, so they offered substantial bounties to raise volunteers. If volunteer enlistments did not meet the quota, draft officials chose soldiers publicly by lottery. Once selected, a draftee had three choices: he could enlist, he could commute his service by paying $300, or he could furnish a substitute at his own expense.

Many profiteers abused the draft. High bounties that ranged from several hundred dollars at the war's beginning to over a thousand dollars at war's end enticed the unscrupulous. Many "bounty jumpers" enlisted, collected their money, and then deserted. Though President Lincoln declared draft resisters subject to martial law, jumpers were rarely punished severely. Draft brokers tried to profit from the naïveté of draftees and potential volunteers. The best of the brokers only interjected themselves as third parties in enlistment or furnished substitutes to draftees, keeping most of the bounties or payment for themselves. The worst offered for enlistment men whom they drugged or got drunk, blacks whom they threatened, criminals they had bailed out, old or infirm men whom they made appear healthy, or even boys they persuaded or kidnapped.

Resistance to the draft was fierce. Many Northerners resented being drafted for a war they opposed. This was especially true in the aftermath of the Emancipation Proclamation. With the abolition of slavery now an explicit war aim, many Northern men, mired in the region's pervasive racism, balked at fighting a war to emancipate slaves. Others objected to the Enlistment Act's commutation clause, viewing it as setting "the rich man's money against the poor man's blood." Political resistance took the form of repeated petitions to repeal the law, to lower quotas, or to dismiss Provost Marshal General Fry. Democratic politicians also used the act's unpopularity (along with its perceived connection to emancipation) to good effect to challenge Republican control at the state and national levels, diminishing Republican hegemony in Congress after the fall elections of 1862 and taking control of several key Northern states. Some citizens obstructed the draft by fleeing, feigning disability, or refusing to be enrolled. Other resistance turned violent, as gangs murdered some draft officials, stole the enrollment lists, and terrorized draft supporters. The worst outbreak of violence was the New York City draft riot in July 1863, which resulted in several hundred deaths and several million dollars in property damage.

To alleviate public discontent and curb abuses, Congress amended the Enrollment Act in February 1864, repealing the commutation clause because of its negative impact on actual enrollments. Congress added a section permitting conscientious objectors either to commute their obligation for $300 or to serve as noncombatants. Some conscientious objectors, such as Quakers, were a harder case because they refused both alternatives, but the War Department treated them leniently by drafting but then paroling them.

President Lincoln strongly supported the draft. He wrote a forceful address in which he refuted charges that the draft was unconstitutional and decried opponents of the draft as unpatriotic. Lincoln had the tact, though, not to deliver the address. Some of Lincoln's measures were stern—for example, he permitted the prosecution of newspaper editors opposed to the draft, suspended *habeas corpus* for draft resisters, and subjected draft dodgers to martial law—but those measures were rarely enforced. Lincoln also proved himself just to both draft officials and draft objectors. Despite resistance, abuse, and overwhelming unpopularity, the Civil War draft succeeded in raising troops for the Union army. In the end very few men were actually drafted, and of those only about 46,000 served. Another 87,000 commuted, and nearly 74,000 furnished substitutes. The draft law was intended, however, to raise volunteers, and that it did: After the law was passed nearly 835,000 Northern men volunteered for service. In total the draft raised, directly or indirectly, about one million men. The Civil War draft also gave the nation experience with conscription, and lessons learned during the Civil War led to fairer drafts for later wars.

See also *Conscription Act; Draft Riots, New York City*

—LINCOLN AUSTIN MULLEN

BIBLIOGRAPHY

Leach, Jack Franklin. *Conscription in the United States: Historical Background.* Rutland, Vt.: C. E. Tuttle, 1952.

Murdock, Eugene Converse. *One Million Men: The Civil War Draft in the North.* Madison: State Historical Society of Wisconsin, 1971.

———. *Patriotism Limited, 1862–1865: The Civil War Draft and the Bounty System.* Kent, Ohio: Kent State University Press, 1967.

Draft Riots, New York City

As a result of the massive losses that the Union sustained during the first two years of the Civil War and decreased enlistments due to low morale, on March 3, 1863, President Abraham Lincoln signed the Enrollment Act into law. The act required all able-bodied men between the ages of twenty and forty-five to register for possible military service. A lottery determined the order in which men were called up. The names of conscripts would subsequently be printed by the draft office and in newspapers. The act contained a loophole, however. Men who could afford to pay a commutation fee of $300, or who could arrange for a substitute, could buy their way out of service.

Opposition to the order was quick and widespread. Throughout the spring and early summer protests occurred throughout the Northeast. But the upheaval that occurred in New York City between July 13 and 17, 1863, was by far the longest and most violent.

Several circumstances created tinder for the riots that raged in New York. To begin with, the city had a long history of control by corrupt Democratic political bosses, who were vocal in their opposition to conscription. The Democratic governor of New York, Horatio Seymour, in particular was a longtime critic of Lincoln and his policies. Although New York City had a Republican mayor at the time of the riots, George Opdyke, he was exceptionally unpopular among common people, particularly because he vetoed a three-million-dollar draft exemption fund passed by the Democrat-dominated City Council.

Additionally the city was home to a large population of Irish immigrants who opposed the draft for a number of reasons. Irish immigrants and their descendants had increased in New York City from the 1840s to the 1860s. At the time of the Civil War one out of every four people living in New York City was of Irish descent. They were often stigmatized because they practiced Catholicism, and many considered them racially distinct from, and inferior to, people of Anglo stock. Irish immigrants lived in the worst parts of the city and were forced to toil in jobs that few others would take. Usually poor and marginalized, few in New York's Irish community felt allegiance to the Union, and fewer still wished to risk their lives defending it. They particularly resented the commutation fee, viewing it as proof that they were being exploited because of their economic status while wealthy Anglo-Americans could avoid service and death.

Finally, partially as a result of the propaganda of Democrats and newspapers allied with the Democratic bosses, the Irish believed that the sole cause of the war was wealthy Northerners' desire to liberate African Americans in the South

A mob lynches a black man on Clarkson Street during the New York City draft riots of July 13–16, 1863. Angered by the perceived unfairness of the military draft, a working-class mob burned buildings and attacked innocent African Americans. Lincoln called troops fresh from combat at Gettysburg to quell the violence.

Source: The Granger Collection, New York

(who they believed would immediately migrate north), a claim that gained additional credence after the Emancipation Proclamation of January 1, 1863. Because Irish immigrants frequently competed with African Americans for jobs, the two groups had a rocky relationship. Tensions had already flared between the two communities during the war years. Earlier in 1863, for example, the Union army was summoned to defend African Americans who crossed picket lines to work jobs vacated by striking Irish longshoremen. Convinced that they were being sent to their deaths in a war being fought to defend and to liberate their economic competitors, the Irish immigrants expressed their frustration through the only means they saw available: violence and vigilantism.

The rioting began after the names of draftees were published in the New York City newspapers on July 12. Groups of working-class people—many but not all of whom came from the downtown Irish immigrant communities—began gathering in the streets. Other working-class whites, including German immigrants and native-born Protestants, joined their ranks. On the morning of July 13, an angry mob marched to the draft office and set it on fire. After destroying the clearest symbol of their oppression the rioters turned their ire on less-obvious targets. Some gathered in large numbers and worked out concerted plans to attack other symbols of their subjugation—the uptown mansions of the rich, banks, and shops that sold goods to New York's wealthy residents. Others engaged in unplanned attacks on their perceived enemies—most frequently African Americans.

As the riots spread in the days following July 13, African Americans increasingly became the targets of violence. No African American could expect safe passage on the streets of New York City. In many instances angry mobs chased down, beat, and sometimes killed individual African Americans who made the mistake of leaving their homes. Rioters also committed lynchings, hanging African American men from trees, burning them, and dismembering them in several cases. Rioters' ire was not restricted to individual African Americans. They also attacked African American institutions, burning both an African American church and an orphanage and looting establishments that were owned or patronized by African Americans.

Eventually Lincoln ordered troops from the Army of the Potomac, still recovering from the bloodying it took at Gettysburg, to march to New York City and restore order. In spite of the chaos, however, martial law was not enacted in New York. Lincoln left the restoration of order in the hands of local politicians.

Although more than one hundred people died during the four days of rioting, the New York City draft riots did not cause Lincoln to change the Enrollment Act. Through various means, most of the men opposed to fighting in the Union army were exempted—the New York Board of Supervisors funded the replacement of many drafted working-class men, and New York's governor successfully lobbied for a decrease in the number of troops that the state of New York was required to provide. Lincoln, therefore, was not particularly pressured by the events in New York to alter his policy. In the summer of 1863 the New York City draft riots were merely one of the many ways that Northerners expressed their dissatisfaction with the war and Lincoln's governance.

See also *Conscription Act; Draft, Military*

—G. MEHERA GERARDO

BIBLIOGRAPHY

Bernstein, Iver. *The New York City Draft Riots: Their Significance for American Society and Politics in the Age of the Civil War.* New York: Oxford University Press, 1990.

Donald, David Herbert. *Lincoln.* New York: Simon and Schuster, 1995.

McPherson, James. *Battle Cry of Freedom: The Civil War Era.* Oxford: Oxford University Press, 1988.

Neely, Mark E., Jr. *The Fate of Liberty: Abraham Lincoln and Civil Liberties.* Oxford: Oxford University Press, 1991.

Dred Scott v. Sandford (1857)

Between 1854 and 1860 Abraham Lincoln rose from successful lawyer and midlevel state politician, who was barely known outside Illinois, to the Republican presidential nominee, taking a huge victory in the Electoral College, with a substantial plurality of the popular vote in a four-way contest. A key factor in Lincoln's rise was his brilliant critique of the Supreme Court's decision in *Dred Scott v. Sandford* (1857). That case dominated the senatorial race of 1858 and to a great extent the presidential race of 1860.

Dred Scott was born a slave in Virginia around 1800, taken by his master to Missouri in 1830, and then sold to an army surgeon, Dr. John Emerson. Scott accompanied Emerson to Fort Armstrong, in Illinois, and to Fort Snelling, in what is today Minnesota but at the time was part of the Wisconsin Territory. The Illinois Constitution prohibited slavery in that state, and the Missouri Compromise of 1820 banned slavery in the Wisconsin Territory. Under well-accepted legal doctrine, Dred Scott became free when his master voluntarily took him to those free jurisdictions.

When his master died, Scott sued his master's widow, Irene Emerson, to gain his freedom, and in 1850 a jury of twelve white men in St. Louis, following nearly thirty years of Missouri precedents, found in his favor. However, the newly reorganized and popularly elected Missouri Supreme Court ruled against Scott, rejecting the older precedents and declaring, "Times are not now as they were when the former decisions on this subject were made. Since then, not only individuals but States have been possessed with a dark and fell spirit in relation to slavery, whose gratification is sought in the pursuit of measures, whose inevitable consequence must be the overthrow and destruction of our Government." Thus, Missouri would no longer recognize freedom obtained in non-slave states.

By this time Mrs. Emerson had remarried, moved to Springfield, Massachusetts, and transferred ownership of Scott to her brother, John F. A. Sanford, who lived in New York City. This allowed Scott to begin a new suit, in federal court, because the U.S. Constitution allowed citizens of one state to sue citizens of another state in federal court. This was known as "diversity jurisdiction" because there was "diversity" of citizenship between the two parties. Claiming to be a free citizen of Missouri, Scott asserted in his lawsuit that he was a "citizen" of Missouri who had been wronged by Sanford, a "citizen" of New York. Sanford responded that no black, even a free black, could ever be a citizen of the United States. The federal judge in St. Louis, Robert Wells, rejected this argument, asserting that *if* Scott were free he could be considered a "citizen" for purposes of diversity jurisdiction. After a trial, however, Wells ruled that he had to apply Missouri law to the case, and thus Scott would remain a slave.

The case was then appealed to the U.S. Supreme Court, with Montgomery Blair arguing the case for Scott. The Court heard arguments on the case in early 1856, but refused to decide the case at that time, and instead ordered re-argument for the December 1856 term. The Court thus avoided rendering a decision on the eve of the 1856 presidential election, in which the new Republican Party ran on a platform of banning slavery in the federal territories. Lincoln and other Republicans would later claim that the Court deliberately delayed issuing an opinion in the case to avoid giving the Republicans a campaign issue they might have ridden to victory. Lincoln argued that this was part of a larger conspiracy to nationalize slavery, just one of the ways that Lincoln would capitalize on *Dred Scott*.

After the election and inauguration of James Buchanan, Supreme Court Chief Justice Roger B. Taney issued a massive opinion—almost sixty pages long—in which he held three things: First, he held that blacks, whether slave or free, could never be citizens of the United States, and thus Dred Scott, even if free, was not entitled to sue in "diversity" in federal court. Elaborating on this theme Taney declared that when the Constitution was adopted blacks were "regarded as beings of an inferior order, and altogether unfit to associate with the white race, either in social or political relations; and so far inferior, that they had no rights which the white man was bound to respect; and that the negro might justly and lawfully be reduced to slavery for his benefit." Second, Taney held that the Constitution did not allow Congress to pass laws to regulate the territories. He reached this conclusion through a tortured reading of the Constitution's provisions for governing the territories. Third, Taney argued that the Constitution protected slaves as property, and that therefore American citizens must have a right to carry their constitutionally protected property into the federal territories. He asserted that "an act of Congress which deprives a citizen of the United States of his liberty or property, merely because he came himself or brought his property into a particular Territory of the United States, and who had committed no offence against the laws, could hardly be dignified with the name of due process of law."

Most Southerners applauded the decision. The *New Orleans Picayune* asserted that it gave "the sanction of established law, and the guarantees of the constitution, for all that the South has insisted upon." The paper also gloated that the decision was "a heavy blow to Black Republicanism and its allies." Northern Democrats saw the decision as a key to undermining, even destroying, the new Republican Party. The main plank of that party was to prohibit slavery in the territories, but under *Dred Scott* that was impossible. Republicans would be forced either to abandon the principles on which their party was based, or to advocate a position of semianarchy by which Congress could ignore a Supreme Court decision.

Republicans considered the opinion to be the worst in the history of the Court. Horace Greeley's *New York Tribune,* the most important Republican paper in the country, declared that the decision was "entitled to just so much moral weight as would be the judgment of a majority of those congregated in any Washington bar-room. It is a *dictum* prescribed by the stump to the bench—the Bowie-knife sticking in the stump ready for instant use if needed."

Lincoln responded to *Dred Scott* in a speech in Springfield on June 26, 1857. The speech offered a critique of the decision, asserting that it was based on bad history and wrong facts, and that the territorial issues were not legitimately before the Court because early in the decision Chief Justice Taney had held that blacks cannot sue in federal courts. At this point Lincoln did not attack the Court itself. Rather, Lincoln argued that the decision was wrong in so many ways that it could not be good law. He also argued that the Court was not the only branch of the government that could interpret the Constitution. These were the arguments of a good lawyer trying to undermine a bad decision.

The speech was in response to one given by Sen. Stephen A. Douglas two weeks earlier. Lincoln noted Douglas's claim that "all who question the correctness of the decision" were "offering violent resistance to it." But, Lincoln asked, "who resists it?" No one, he asserted, "resisted the authority of his master over him," which of course was the narrow holding in the case. Lincoln not only denied that Republicans offered resistance to the decision, but emphatically asserted that Republicans "believe…in obedience to, and respect for the judicial department of government" and that the courts' "decision on Constitutional questions, when fully settled, should control…subject to be disturbed only by amendments to the Constitution." This set of arguments was carefully designed to head off Douglas's arguments that Lincoln was attacking a venerable institution—the Supreme Court. Lincoln boldly argued that the decision was "erroneous" and made by a Court that had "often over-ruled its own decisions." Lincoln claimed the only goal of the Republicans was to "do what we can to have" the Court "over-rule this" one.

He then proceeded to undermine the decision by chipping away at it. He noted that the decision was not unanimous, that it had been made with "apparent partisan bias," and that it was based "on assumed historical facts which are not really true."

In his famous "House Divided" speech, in June 1858, Lincoln offered a more mature, sophisticated, and politically savvy attack on the *Dred Scott* decision. Lincoln now personalized the attack, focusing on Chief Justice Roger B. Taney, Sen. Stephen A. Douglas, President James Buchanan, and the previous president, Franklin Pierce. He alleged a conspiracy among these men not only to open up the territories to slavery but in the end to nationalize slavery. There were three steps in the conspiracy, and the first two were in place. First, there was the Kansas-Nebraska Act, which repealed most of the Missouri Compromise and opened most of the existing federal territories to slavery. That law was the brainchild of Douglas. Next was the *Dred Scott* decision, which not only allowed slavery in all the remaining federal territories, but furthermore prohibited Congress or the territorial governments from banning slavery in the territories. The third piece would be a nationalization of slavery by the Supreme Court.

Lincoln began this speech by setting out the nature of the conspiracy. He noted, "We are now far into the fifth year since a policy was initiated with the avowed object, and confident promise, of putting an end to slavery agitation." But rather then ending the agitation, the crisis over slavery in the territories had worsened. Lincoln was convinced that the problem would not be solved—the agitation would not cease—"until a crisis shall have been reached and passed." He then set out the nature of the crisis in a series of short statements:

> "A house divided against itself cannot stand."
>
> *I believe this government cannot endure permanently half slave and half free.*
>
> *I do not expect the Union to be dissolved—I do not expect the house to fall—but I do expect it will cease to be divided.*
>
> *It will become all one thing, or all the other.*
>
> *Either the opponents of slavery will arrest the further spread of it, and place it where the public mind shall rest in the belief that it is in the course of ultimate extinction; or its advocates will push it forward, till it shall become alike lawful in all the States, old as well as new—North as well as South.*

Lincoln ominously asked: "Have we no tendency to the latter condition?"

Lincoln then set out the conspiracy that was leading to that tendency. *Dred Scott* was the most recent and most important part of the conspiracy, which had begun when Senator Douglas proposed the Kansas-Nebraska Act. It included all of the politics leading to *Dred Scott,* in which Taney had declared that the national government could not limit slavery in the territories. How could such a monstrous conspiracy actually play out in the end? How could people go to bed thinking Missouri would become a free state and "awake to the reality instead, that the Supreme Court has made Illinois a slave State"? Lincoln noted that Dred Scott had in fact lived in the free state of Illinois, and yet both the federal court in Missouri and the U.S. Supreme Court held that he was a slave. Thus, there was a "logical conclusion that what Dred Scott's master might lawfully do with Dred Scott, in the free State of Illinois, every other master may lawfully do with any other one, or one thousand slaves, in Illinois, or in any other free State." He warned, "Such a decision is all that slavery now lacks of being alike lawful in all the States." The threat was real, and Lincoln warned, "Welcome, or unwelcome, such decision is probably coming, and will soon be upon us." If Lincoln and his party were not victorious, and the "present political dynasty shall be met and overthrown," then freedom would be in danger throughout the nation. Thus he believed, "We shall lie down pleasantly dreaming that the people of Missouri are on the verge of making their State free, and we shall awake to the reality instead, that the Supreme Court has made Illinois a slave State."

Central to this conspiracy was the *Dred Scott* decision. Lincoln offered a devastating analysis of the history of the case from 1857 until he entered the White House in 1861. His election as president, he might have said, prevented the nationalization of slavery, just as it ultimately led to the nationalization of freedom.

—PAUL FINKELMAN

BIBLIOGRAPHY

Fehrenbacher, Don E. *The Dred Scott Case.* New York: Oxford University Press, 1978.

Finkelman, Paul. Dred Scott v. Sandford: *A Brief History.* New York: Bedford Books, 1997.

E

Ellsworth, Elmer Ephraim

Elmer Ephraim Ellsworth (1837–1861), a friend of the Lincolns and one of the first casualties of the Civil War, had aspired to attend West Point, but his modest education thwarted his hopes for admission. After moving from his native New York to Rockford, Illinois, in the mid-1850s, he became involved with local militia units.

Fascinated by accounts of the Zouave regiments organized by the French in Algeria, Ellsworth copied the drill and clothing styles of the Zouaves, transforming the National Guard Cadets of Chicago into the United States Zouave Cadets. Garbed in brightly colored uniforms, featuring baggy pants, short jackets, fezzes, and gaiters, Ellsworth's Zouaves mastered maneuvers impressive enough to enthrall audiences for hours. The prize-winning, sixty-man unit toured the East in the summer of 1860, creating a sensation with its performances and making the handsome, charismatic Ellsworth something of a celebrity. Early in 1861, he published a manual about training militia units, trying not only to delineate drills, commands, and maneuvers but also to enhance the appeal of militia service.

In 1859, pressed by his fiancée's father to choose a reliable profession, Ellsworth had begun reading law. He went to Springfield in 1860 to clerk in Abraham Lincoln's law office. Intelligent, charming, and boyishly exuberant, Ellsworth quickly became a favorite of the Lincoln family.

Ellsworth helped Lincoln's campaign in 1860 and traveled to Washington, D.C., with the Lincolns in 1861. Lincoln tried to have a Bureau of Militia created within the War Department, planning to appoint Ellsworth to head it. When that effort failed, Ellsworth formed an eleven-hundred-man Zouave unit in New York. Composed largely of volunteer firefighters, Colonel Ellsworth's colorfully clad regiment, officially the 11th New York, was nicknamed "the Fire Zouaves." Responding to Lincoln's call for troops after the attack on Fort Sumter (April 1861), the regiment arrived in Washington in early May 1861. Ellsworth drilled them on the South Lawn of the White House, sometimes with the Lincolns as an appreciative audience.

Ellsworth's men and other Union forces crossed into Virginia on May 24, 1861, virtually as soon as Virginia formally ratified its ordinances of secession. Ellsworth's mission to take Alexandria met little resistance. At the Marshall House, a hotel near the telegraph office that Ellsworth had successfully secured, a Confederate flag flew. Ellsworth climbed the hotel stairs and seized the banner. As he descended with the flag, the hotel proprietor shot and killed him.

One of the earliest Union casualties of the Civil War, Ellsworth was cast as a martyr in many Northern communities. Northerners named towns, streets, and children in his honor. The 44th New York Volunteer Infantry Regiment called itself "the Ellsworth Avengers," and the patriotic rallying cry "Remember Ellsworth" reverberated throughout the North in the early phases of the Civil War.

News of Ellsworth's death shocked Lincoln, who called the slightly built Ellsworth "the greatest little man I ever met." He wrote to Ellsworth's parents, praising their son's character, and Ellsworth's body lay in state in the East Room of the White House before its return to New York for burial. The confiscated Confederate flag stained with Ellsworth's blood was presented to the Lincolns, who accepted it graciously but quietly packed it away, horrified by its association.

See also *Zouaves*

—CARA L. SHELLY

BIBLIOGRAPHY

Donald, David Herbert. *Lincoln.* New York: Simon and Schuster, 1995.

Goodwin, Doris Kearns. *Team of Rivals: The Political Genius of Abraham Lincoln.* New York: Simon and Schuster, 2005.

Perrett, Geoffrey. *Lincoln's War: The Untold Story of America's Greatest President as Commander in Chief.* New York: Random House, 2004.

Randall, Ruth Painter. *Colonel Elmer Ellsworth: A Biography of Lincoln's Friend and First Hero of the Civil War.* Boston: Little, Brown, 1960.

Emancipation Monument (Freedmen's Memorial to Abraham Lincoln)

On April 14, 1876, the eleventh anniversary of the slain president's assassination, the Freedmen's Memorial to Abraham Lincoln (Emancipation Monument) enjoyed a well-attended dedication in Washington, D.C. The statue, created by Thomas Ball and funded entirely by black people (primarily Civil War military veterans), was intended to pay tribute to the fallen leader for issuing the Emancipation Proclamation in 1863, as well as to depict the significance of freedom to African Americans. Instead, however, the monument enshrines the quintessential portrait of Lincoln as noble liberator, generously bestowing freedom upon a grateful and submissive slave. Featuring a nearly naked black man, with broken shackles on his wrists, crouched at the feet of a fully clothed, erect President Lincoln, whose outstretched arm beckons the ex-slave to arise, the Emancipation Monument immortalizes an image of white paternalistic authority over black people.

Shortly after Lincoln's assassination in 1865, Charlotte Scott, a woman emancipated as a result of the proclamation, entrusted her former master with a five-dollar contribution toward the construction of a monument in the assassinated president's memory. This much-publicized event precipitated a vigorous fund-raising campaign by James Yeatman and William Greenleaf Eliot, leaders of the Western Sanitary Commission, who became the custodians of Scott's initial donation and of subsequent offerings. Prominently highlighting the efforts of the humble former slave to honor "Massa Lincoln," Yeatman and Eliot institutionalized their own conception of black deference into the process by which the monument came into being. They called on the nation's black population to demonstrate appropriate gratitude for the sacrifices that others had made on their behalf. Consistent with their understanding of a racial hierarchy, Yeatman and Eliot never considered allowing those who funded the project to have an actual say in its content.

The decade-long debate over the form of the sculpture paralleled the nation's broader struggle to come to grips with the meaning of freedom for black Americans. Many of the early proposals for a monument revealed the postwar expectation that black people would become full-fledged citizens of an interracial nation. The artist originally chosen, Harriet Hosmer, crafted an elaborate sculpture that included four standing black men who represented important moments along the time line of African American history. The figures range from a downtrodden and manacled slave to a uniformed black Union soldier, rifle at the ready. However, this and other sculptors' early conceptions of black men's newfound empowerment were ultimately cast aside in favor of the more palatable image constructed by Ball.

Thomas Ball (1819–1911) had actually conceived his design for a sculpture long before he was contacted by the committee to construct a freedmen's memorial. In 1874, Eliot and Yeatman offered the artist a $17,000 commission for his rendition of emancipation. Ball enthusiastically agreed, although he made one change from the original proposal: Where the form of the slave had initially been modeled after Ball's own body, in the final product the kneeling slave was crafted from a photograph of William Eliot's former slave Archer Alexander. Congress appropriated $3,000 to build a pedestal for the statue and declared the dedication day a holiday. Thousands attended the unveiling in the nation's capital.

Ball's monument became the most frequently photographed nineteenth-century sculpture of Lincoln. The work helped to forge the image of the former president as the Great Emancipator, and its popularity entrenched that perception up through contemporary times. Three years after the original memorial was dedicated in Washington's Lincoln Park, its duplicate was unveiled in Boston, Massachusetts.

Yet not everyone felt comfortable with the symbolism captured by the Freedmen's Memorial. Frederick Douglass, invited to address the audience at the unveiling in 1876, reminded his listeners that Lincoln was, ultimately, "the white man's president," who would have sacrificed black freedom to save the Union. Douglass and others complained that the kneeling slave implied black inferiority. Nevertheless, the monument emerged as the prevailing image of Lincoln, and it inspired the production of posters, medallions, and postcards that were marketed to a mass audience. The widespread consumption of these icons normalized the view of Lincoln as a benevolent liberator. It simultaneously suggested that black people passively awaited their salvation from white people, Lincoln specifically, who beneficently bestowed it upon them. Only in recent times has that story come to be challenged and the role of African Americans in their own emancipation begun to emerge.

—MARCY S. SACKS

BIBLIOGRAPHY

Brown, Thomas J. *The Public Art of Civil War Commemoration: A Brief History with Documents.* Boston: Bedford/St. Martin's, 2004.

Hatt, Michael. "'Making a Man of Him': Masculinity and the Black Body in Mid-Nineteenth-Century American Sculpture." *Oxford Art Journal* 15, no. 1 (1992): 21–35.

Holzer, Harold. "Picturing Freedom: The Emancipation Proclamation in Art, Iconography, and Memory." In *The Emancipation Proclamation: Three Views [Social, Political, Iconographic],* by Harold Holzer, Edna Greene Medford, and Frank J. Williams, 83–156. Baton Rouge: Louisiana State University Press, 2006.

Sandage, Scott. "A Marble House Divided: The Lincoln Memorial, the Civil Rights Movement, and the Politics of Memory, 1939–1963." *Journal of American History* 80, no. 1 (June 1993): 135–167.

Savage, Kirk. "The Politics of Memory: Black Emancipation and the Civil War Monument." In *Commemorations: The Politics of National Identity,* edited by John R. Gillis, 127–149. Princeton: Princeton University Press, 1994.

———. *Standing Soldiers, Kneeling Slaves: Race, War, and Monument in Nineteenth-Century America.* Princeton: Princeton University Press, 1997.

Emancipation Proclamation

The Emancipation Proclamation is probably the best known, and least read, document written by Abraham Lincoln. In the proclamation Lincoln declared that most of the slaves in the Confederate states were to be immediately freed. Lincoln signed the proclamation on January 1, 1863, exactly one hundred days after he had issued the Preliminary Emancipation Proclamation. Although he de-

The first reading of the Emancipation Proclamation before President Abraham Lincoln's cabinet in 1862. Standing left to right: Treasury secretary Salmon P. Chase, secretary of the interior Caleb B. Smith, postmaster general Montgomery Blair; seated left to right: secretary of war Edwin M. Stanton, President Lincoln, secretary of the navy Gideon Welles, secretary of state William H. Seward, and attorney general Edward Bates.

Source: The Granger Collection, New York City

clared millions of slaves to be free, Lincoln had to await military victories across the South to enforce his proclamation.

Critics point out that Lincoln did not emancipate any slaves in the United States, but that the proclamation only applied to those areas of the United States—the Confederate States—where he had no political power to actually end slavery. Critics also note that the proclamation contains none of the rhetorical flourishes normally associated with Lincoln's writing and speeches. Writing in 1948 the historian Richard Hofstadter caustically noted that it had all the "moral grandeur of a bill of lading." Even admirers of Lincoln describe it as "boring" and "pedestrian."

The proclamation is in fact a narrowly written, tightly focused, and highly legalistic document. Lincoln intended this because he feared that the Supreme Court (still presided over by the proslavery Confederate sympathizer Chief Justice Roger B. Taney) would overturn the proclamation. While some modern scholars bemoan the lack of flowery rhetoric and sweeping assertions of liberty, keen observers at the time understood Lincoln's strategy. Karl Marx, writing for a London newspaper during the war, had a clear fix on what Lincoln had done and his strategy: the "most formidable decrees which he hurls at the enemy and which will never lose their historic significance, resemble—as the author intends them to—ordinary summons, sent by one lawyer to another."

From the beginning of the war, Lincoln faced pressure to end slavery from Republican activists, abolitionists, and army generals. Meanwhile, slaves on their own abandoned their masters and fled to the lines of the U.S. Army. Lincoln opposed slavery as deeply as any abolitionist, believing as he wrote in his famous letter to Albert G. Hodges in 1864, "If slavery is not wrong, nothing is wrong." But in 1861 he believed that he was in no position to move against slavery. In his inaugural he had implored the Confederate states to return to the Union. So initially all of his policies were directed at convincing the first seven states that left the Union to return. When this policy failed and war broke out, he focused on keeping the four border slave states—Delaware, Maryland, Kentucky, and Missouri—in the Union. Clearly any move against slavery early in the war would have pushed Kentucky, with its 200,000 slaves, into the Confederacy. This shift would have put a Confederate army on the Ohio River, threatened America's heartland, and enormously increased Confederate military resources. Early in the war a group of ministers urged Lincoln to free the slaves because God would be on his side. He allegedly responded, "I hope to have God on my side, but I must have Kentucky." Just weeks before he announced his emancipation plans, he worried that a precipitous move against slavery would take "fifty thousand bayonets" from Kentucky out of the Union army and give them to the Confederates. Thus Lincoln could make no move against slavery until the spring of 1862. By then General Ulysses Grant had won major victories at Forts Donelson and Henry, pushing Confederate forces out of Tennessee and thus securing Kentucky from Confederate invasion. Confederates were defeated in Arkansas, at Pea Ridge, thus preventing a Confederate invasion of Missouri.

Securing Kentucky and Missouri was only a first step toward emancipation. Without some likelihood of actually winning the war, a declaration of emancipation would be useless, even counterproductive. As he explained to a group of Chicago ministers, emancipation was useless without a military victory and would be "like the Pope's bull against the comet." He asked how he "could free the slaves" when he could not "enforce the Constitution in the rebel States." Not until significant victories in late 1861 and the first half of 1862 did Lincoln feel his position was militarily strong enough to move against slavery. Even then, he waited to announce his preliminary proclamation until he could report a major victory at Antietam.

Finally, Lincoln still needed a legal or constitutional basis for the proclamation. Lincoln had long believed, as almost all constitutional scholars did at the time, that the national government had no power to touch slavery in the states. While he urged Kentucky and the other loyal slave states to begin a process of emancipation, and even offered to help secure federal funds to do so, he did not see any legally permissible method of forcing emancipation on those states, short of a constitutional amendment. Similarly, he initially doubted that he had the power to interfere with slavery in the Confederate states, which in theory were still part of the

Union. Gradually, however, Lincoln concluded that he could emancipate slaves in those states that were in rebellion under his powers as commander in chief.

Having concluded he had the constitutional authority to issue the proclamation, Lincoln bided his time throughout the summer of 1862. Calls for emancipation increased and Lincoln coyly deflected them. By this time he had personally decided to move against slavery and had told his Cabinet so, but he refused to tip his hand to anyone. When Horace Greeley published an editorial urging Lincoln to free the slaves, the president took the time to answer with an unprecedented letter to the editor. He told the American people that his goal was to "save the Union" and that he would accomplish that in any way he could. He would free some slaves, all slaves, or no slaves to save the Union. He also noted that this position was a description of his "*official* duty" and not a change in his "oft-expressed *personal* wish that all men every where could be free." In fact he had already resolved to free as many slaves as he constitutionally could.

On September 22, shortly after the battle of Antietam, Lincoln issued the Preliminary Emancipation Proclamation, essentially warning the South that in one hundred days he would declare all the slaves in the rebellious states free, unless those states returned to the Union. Lincoln doubtless had no expectation that this would happen. The purpose of the proclamation was "restoring the constitutional relations" between the nation and all the states. The preliminary proclamation authorized the enlistment of black troops immediately, even before the hundred days were up.

The hundred days ended on January 1, 1863, and Lincoln signed the Emancipation Proclamation. He framed the proclamation as within his right "by virtue of the power in me vested as Commander-in-Chief, of the Army and Navy of the United States in time of actual armed rebellion." This was, constitutionally, a war measure designed to cripple the ability of those in rebellion to resist the lawful authority of the United States. It applied only to those states and parts of states that were still in rebellion. This was constitutionally essential. Where the Constitution was in force, federalism and the Fifth Amendment prevented presidential emancipation. The proclamation was narrowly written, carefully designed to withstand the scrutiny of the Supreme Court. It narrowly applied only to the states in rebellion. It would not threaten Kentucky or Missouri or those parts of the South that were firmly under the authority of the United States. Thus the proclamation did not threaten the constitutional relationship between the states and the federal government. Ironically, it only had force where Lincoln had no power to enforce it—in the Confederacy. But the proclamation served as a carefully crafted, narrow document: a bill of lading, to use Professor Hofstadter's phrase, for the delivery of freedom to some three million Southern slaves. The vehicle for delivery would be the army and navy—of which he was commander in chief. As the armies of the United States moved deeper into the Confederacy they would bring the power of the proclamation with them, freeing slaves every day as more and more of the Confederacy was redeemed by military success. This carefully constructed plan, and not any towering rhetoric, was the moral grandeur of the proclamation and of Lincoln's careful and complicated strategy to achieve his personal goal that "all men every where could be free."

See also *Antietam Campaign; Slavery*

—PAUL FINKELMAN

BIBLIOGRAPHY

Blight, David W., and Brooks D. Simpson. *Union and Emancipation: Essays on Politics and Race in the Civil War Era.* Kent, Ohio: Kent State University Press, 1997.

Franklin, John Hope. *The Emancipation Proclamation.* Garden City, N.Y.: Doubleday, 1963.

Holzer, Harold, and Sara Vaughn Gabbard, eds. *Lincoln and Freedom: Slavery, Emancipation, and the Thirteenth Amendment.* Carbondale: Southern Illinois University Press, 2007.

Quarles, Benjamin. *Lincoln and the Negro.* New York: Oxford University Press, 1962.

Everett, Edward

Edward Everett (1794–1865), was a professor, orator, and politician. Many accounts of Lincoln's Gettysburg Address include the vignette that Lincoln's two-minute speech followed a two-hour-long oration by some rarely mentioned speaker. Edward Everett was that speaker, the author of the *other* Gettysburg address.

Before Everett spoke at the Gettysburg cemetery dedication on November 19, 1863, he had developed a reputation as one of the leading orators of his time. He was born in 1794 in Dorchester, Massachusetts, and educated at Boston Latin School and Harvard University, from which he graduated in 1811. Everett then studied for the ministry and was ordained a Unitarian minister in 1814. He subsequently studied for the Ph.D. at the University of Göttingen, in Germany, from 1815 to 1819, afterward returning to teach at Harvard from 1820 to 1826.

When Ralph Waldo Emerson spoke in 1880 on the early days of Transcendentalism, he credited Everett with bringing German ideas about literary criticism to Boston. As Emerson wrote, "The novelty of the learning lost nothing in the skill and genius of his relation, and the rudest undergraduate found a new morning opened to him in the lecture-room of Harvard Hall." Emerson thought Everett's contribution was in his oratory, for Everett's "power lay in the magic of form; it was in the graces of manner; in a new perception of Grecian beauty, to which he had opened our eyes." One of Everett's most famous orations is "The Circumstances Favorable to Literary Improvement in America," which was given to Harvard's Phi Beta Kappa Society in 1824. Everett identified circumstances that assisted literary development, including democracy, such common bonds as geography, language, and culture, and America's progress.

Everett was a Whig politician as well as an educator. He served in the U.S. House of Representatives from 1825 to 1835 and as governor of Massachusetts from 1836 to 1840. He served as envoy to Great Britain from 1841 to 1845. In 1846 he returned to Harvard as president. In 1852, following Daniel Webster's death, Everett was appointed to Webster's seat in the Senate, and he was subsequently elected to the seat. He resigned in 1854. Everett was a candidate for vice president of the United States on the Constitutional Union ticket in 1860, along with Sen. John Bell of Tennessee. After the beginning of civil war, Everett experienced a conversion to the antislavery cause, traveling the Union in support of the war effort.

Everett's Gettysburg address began with an appeal to God and to nature: "Standing beneath this serene sky, overlooking these broad fields now reposing from the labors of the waning year, the mighty Alleghenies dimly towering before us, the graves of our brethren beneath our feet, it is with hesitation that I raise my poor voice to break the eloquent silence of God and Nature." He then spoke at length about the battle and the Union cause and concluded with an appeal for reconciliation. Following their addresses, Everett and Lincoln corresponded. Everett remarked, "I should be glad, if I could flatter myself that I came as near to the central idea of the occasion, in two hours, as you did in two minutes." President Lincoln returned the compliment. He told Everett that his "point made against the theory of the General Government being only an agency whose principals are the States, was new to me, and, as I think, is one of the best arguments for the national supremacy. The tribute to our noble women for their angel ministering to the suffering soldiers surpasses in its way, as do the subjects of it, whatever has gone before."

Everett died in Boston on January 15, 1865, without seeing his beloved Union restored.

—ALFRED L. BROPHY

BIBLIOGRAPHY

Emerson, Ralph Waldo. "Life and Letters in New England." In *Lectures and Biographical Sketches*. Boston: Houghton Mifflin, 1911.

Miller, Perry *The Transcendentalists*. Cambridge: Harvard University Press, 1954.

Reid Ronald F. *Edward Everett: Unionist Orator*. Westport, Conn.: Greenwood Press, 1990.

Varg, Paul. *Edward Everett: The Intellectual in the Turmoil of Politics*. Selinsgrove: Susquehanna University Press, 1992.

Ex parte Merryman

On April 15, 1861, in response to the attack on Fort Sumter, President Lincoln called for 75,000 volunteers to suppress the rebellion. Two days later, on April 17, Virginia called for a secession convention. If Virginia left the Union—which it formally did on May 23—the nation's capital would come under immediate threat of attack. Lincoln was particularly anxious that Northern troops reach Washington before Virginia's troops could attack the city. To reach Washington, Northern soldiers had to cross Maryland, a slave state that had not left the Union but was threatening to do so. Troops from the North could reach Baltimore by train, but they had to march across the city to a second train station to continue on to Washington. This peculiarity of the railroad lines leading in and out of Baltimore set the stage for mob violence. On April 19 a Pennsylvania regiment, rushing to protect the nation's capital, needed a police escort to march between Baltimore's two train stations. A day later a Massachusetts regiment was attacked by a pro-Confederate mob, leading to a riot and the deaths of four soldiers and twelve civilians. Maryland authorities and pro-Confederate citizens began to destroy bridges connecting the state to the North.

On April 27 Lincoln authorized General Winfield Scott to suspend the writ of *habeas corpus* in Maryland and to arrest anyone the army believed was a threat to the security of the nation or was likely to commit sabotage. Many state officials were unwilling to keep the peace in Maryland and were in fact complicit in sabotaging vital rail networks. Lincoln lacked a national police force to stop the destruction of bridges and the organizing of militias planning to join the Confederacy. Nor did Lincoln have at his disposal a body of law that allowed the national government to arrest and prosecute civilians for what would have been, in normal times, a criminal trespass or arson. Such legal regulations were traditionally the responsibility of the states. Yet to do nothing at all would have imperiled the nation. Though the constitution provided for the suspension of *habeas corpus* "when in cases of rebellion or invasion the public safety may require it," it was silent on whether the president or Congress had the power to do it. Congress was not in session at the time, and indeed, if the rail lines into Maryland were severed, Congress might never be able to meet. Thus Lincoln instructed General Scott to use the army to arrest saboteurs and those organizing military opposition to the United States. Significantly, he refused to authorize the arrest of pro-Confederate politicians in Maryland, who were agitating for secession.

On Saturday, May 25, soldiers under the command of General William H. Keim arrested John Merryman, a local planter and secessionist, and confined him to Fort McHenry in Baltimore. Merryman was arrested for his role in the destruction of bridges and other transportation infrastructure, hindering the U.S. mail, and organizing troops to join the Confederacy. He was arrested without any formal charge because with *habeas corpus* suspended the army did not need any particular charge to hold him. Keim's men delivered Merryman to Fort McHenry, under the command of General George Cadwalader, a veteran of the Mexican War and the highest ranking officer in the Pennsylvania militia.

Although in the custody of the military, with the normal rule of law suspended, Merryman was allowed to see his attorney. That he was allowed to do so illustrates military officers' uncertainty about the nature of suspension. It may also reflect that Cadwalader was well educated, a successful attorney before the war; his brother was the U.S. district judge in Philadelphia. As both a lawyer and a longtime officer in the militia, who had been a minor hero in the Mexican War, Cadwalader obeyed his commander, General Scott, and his commander in chief, while retaining respect for some sense of due process. Cadwalader may also have understood that allowing Merryman access to counsel would defuse some of the local hostility over the suspension.

Merryman's lawyers met with him at Fort McHenry and then asked General Cadwalader for a copy of the process under which Merryman was held. The general refused to provide any information other than to say that Merryman was in custody of the army under orders that emanated from the president of the United States and the general in chief of the army, Winfield Scott. Merryman's attorneys immediately went to Washington, where they applied for a writ of *habeas corpus* from Supreme Court chief justice Roger B. Taney, whose duties also included serving as the circuit justice for Maryland. On Sunday, May 26, Taney issued the writ, commanding Cadwalader to personally bring Merryman to his court in Baltimore the next day and explain under what authority he held him.

Instead of complying, on Monday the 27th Cadwalader sent a subordinate officer, who explained to Taney that Merryman was in custody under the suspension of *habeas corpus* authorized by the president and requested a delay in the proceeding so that the general could confer with the president. Taney refused this seemingly reasonable request and ordered General Cadwalader to appear on Tuesday to respond to a contempt citation. On Tuesday a marshal reported to Taney that he had been unable to serve General Cadwalader with the contempt process because he was denied access to Fort McHenry. Taney noted that he might order the marshal to organize a *posse comitatus* to arrest Cadwalader, but he admitted that it would be a futile gesture, given the stronger force of the army. Instead he limited himself to writing a scathing, twenty-page opinion castigating Lincoln for suspending the writ of *habeas corpus* and for delegating the power to arrest under the suspension to subordinates, such as General Cadwalader.

Using a narrow structural analysis of the Constitution, Taney asserted that because the suspension clause is found in Article I of the Constitution, only Congress could suspend the writ. He ignored the facts that Congress was not in session at the time and that Merryman's acts were designed in part to prevent members of Congress from even getting to Washington to hold a session. Relying on the text of the Constitution, Anglo-American legal history, and the few existing treatises that discussed the issue, such as Story's *Commentaries on the Constitution,* Taney asserted that the president had no power to suspend the writ, that the military was obligated to obey the courts, and that even if Congress did suspend the writ, the military had no power to hold civilians in custody because all Americans were entitled to a "speedy" and "public" trial. Taney's anger bristled throughout the opinion and in many ways undermined his argument. Taney's claim that the military could not hold civilians if Congress suspended the writ seemed to make no sense because the whole purpose of suspension was to allow for the incarceration of dangerous people without charges. And if not charged with any crime, then they could not be tried.

Taney's opinion quickly appeared in newspapers and pamphlets. Secessionists, Confederate sympathizers in the North, and anti-Lincoln politicians and editors used the opinion to label Lincoln a tyrant and a despot. Supporters of Lincoln and the Union cause dismissed the opinion as the ravings of the same justice who had written the overwhelmingly proslavery opinion of the Court in *Dred Scott.* For Republicans, the opinion confirmed their suspicion that Taney was a Confederate sympathizer who was more interested in undermining the war effort and protecting slavery than in upholding the Constitution.

Lincoln ignored Taney's opinion, and Merryman remained in military custody until July, when the situation in Maryland had stabilized and the state was firmly on the side of the Union. At that point he was turned over to state authorities, who charged him with treason but never put him on trial. Meanwhile, in July Lincoln addressed Congress, noting that the suspension of *habeas corpus* "has purposely been exercised but very sparingly." He noted that some believed he had violated the law by the suspension, and to this he responded that the laws of the United States were being violated throughout the Confederacy, and he had sworn to uphold those laws. He then asked, "Are all the laws but one to go unexecuted, and government itself go to pieces, lest that one be violated?" This was as close as Lincoln came to acknowledging Taney's argument. But he then denied that he had violated any law. He argued that as president and commander in chief he had the power to suspend *habeas corpus* in response to a "rebellion." Responding to Taney's one-sided originalism, Lincoln noted, "It cannot be believed the framers of the instrument [the Constitution] intended that, in every case, the danger should run its course, until Congress could be called together; the very assembling of which might be prevented, as was intended in this case by the rebellion."

On August 6, Congress passed legislation ratifying the legality of all actions taken by the president, and by the military on behalf of the president, to preserve the Union. Taney's opinion was mostly a dead letter. However, after the war, in *Ex parte Milligan* (1866), the Supreme Court accepted the claim articulated by Taney that even if *habeas corpus* is suspended the military cannot try civilians if the regular civilian courts are operating.

—Paul Finkelman

BIBLIOGRAPHY

Farber, Daniel. *Lincoln's Constitution*. Chicago: University of Chicago Press, 2003.

Finkelman, Paul. "Civil Liberties and the Civil War: The Great Emancipator as Civil Libertarian." *Michigan Law Review* 91 (1993): 1352–1381.

Freedman, Eric. *Habeas Corpus: Rethinking the Great Writ of Liberty*. New York: New York University Press, 2001.

Hyman, Harold M., and William M. Wiecek. *Equal Justice Under Law: Constitutional Development, 1835–1875*. New York: Harper and Row, 1982.

Jackson, Jeffrey D. "The Power to Suspend Habeas Corpus: An Answer from the Arguments Surrounding *Ex parte Merryman*." *University of Baltimore Law Review* 34 (2004): 11–54.

Neely, Mark E., Jr. *The Fate of Liberty: Abraham Lincoln and Civil Liberties*. New York: Oxford University Press, 1991.

Vladeck, Stephen I. "The Field Theory: Martial Law, the Suspension Power, and the Insurrection Act." *Temple Law Review* 80 (2007): 391–438.

F

Fessenden, William Pitt

William Pitt Fessenden (1806–1869), a member of a prominent political family, completed a degree at Bowdoin College (1823), was admitted to the bar in Maine (1827), and entered politics as a Whig. He served several nonconsecutive terms in Maine's House of Representatives between 1832 and 1854 and one term in the U.S. House of Representatives (1841–1843). Elevated to the U.S. Senate in 1854, Fessenden joined the fray over the Kansas-Nebraska bill (1854) and aided in organizing the Republican Party. He remained in the Senate until 1869, except for an eight-month tenure as secretary of the Treasury (July 1864–March 3, 1865).

A powerful senator widely respected for integrity and political acumen, Fessenden stumped diligently for Republicans in 1860, despite his fragile health and his skepticism about Abraham Lincoln's capacities. When several Southern states reacted to Lincoln's election by seceding, Fessenden opposed compromise, insisting that there could be no lasting accord until the recurrent threat of disunion had been resolved. Named as a delegate to an unofficial peace conference (February 1861), he refused to attend.

Early in the Civil War, Fessenden doubted Lincoln's mettle, judgment, and willingness to move against slavery. Nevertheless, he cooperated with the administration in meeting the exigencies of war. As chairman of the Senate Finance Committee (1861–1864), Fessenden influenced taxation, tariffs, debt management, and other financial measures. Although appalled by some policies, including the issuance of paper money (greenbacks), he pragmatically acknowledged their necessity.

Fessenden's role entailed consistent contact with secretary of the Treasury Salmon P. Chase (1861–1864). They worked well together, but the conniving Chase fed the concerns that Fessenden had about Lincoln and secretary of state William Henry Seward (1861–1869). Chase drew Fessenden into an attempt to force Seward from the cabinet (December 1862), but Lincoln adroitly foiled the scheme and exposed Chase's duplicity.

After repeated difficulties with Chase, in July 1864 Lincoln replaced him with Fessenden, who did not want the post but agreed to serve. He was among the stronger members of Lincoln's evolving cabinet, and his interactions with Lincoln transformed him into an admirer of the president.

Satisfied that the Union's finances were sound by early 1865, Fessenden returned to the Senate at the beginning of Lincoln's second term. Chosen to lead the congressional Joint Committee on Reconstruction (1865–1867), Fessenden tried to ensure protection of freedmen's rights and safe restoration of former Confederate states. Congressional factionalism and the attitudes of President Andrew Johnson (1865–1869) frustrated many efforts. Despite his disillusionment with Johnson, Fessenden was one of seven Republican senators who voted for acquittal when Johnson was impeached in 1868.

Fessenden remained in the Senate until his death in 1869.

See also *Cabinet, Lincoln's*

—CARA L. SHELLY

BIBLIOGRAPHY

Benedict, Michael Les. *The Impeachment and Trial of Andrew Johnson.* New York: Norton, 1973.

Bogue, Allan G. *The Earnest Men: Republicans of the Civil War Senate.* Ithaca, New York: Cornell University Press, 1981.

Cook, Robert. "'The Grave of All My Comforts': William Pitt Fessenden as Secretary of the Treasury, 1864–1865." *Civil War History* 41 (September 1995): 208–226.

Donald, David Herbert. *Lincoln.* New York: Simon and Schuster, 1995.

Foner, Eric. *Reconstruction: America's Unfinished Revolution, 1863–1877.* New York: Harper and Row, 1988.

Goodwin, Doris Kearns. *Team of Rivals: The Political Genius of Abraham Lincoln.* New York: Simon and Schuster, 2005.

Hendrick, Burton J. *Lincoln's War Cabinet.* Boston: Little, Brown, 1946.

Jellison, Charles A. *Fessenden of Maine: Civil War Senator.* Syracuse: Syracuse University Press, 1962.

McPherson, James M. *Battle Cry of Freedom: The Civil War Era.* New York: Oxford University Press, 1988.

———. *Ordeal by Fire: The Civil War and Reconstruction.* New York: Knopf, 1982.

Oates, Stephen B. *With Malice toward None: The Life of Abraham Lincoln.* New York: Mentor, 1978.

Fillmore, Millard

Millard Fillmore (1800–1874) was the thirteenth president of the United States and the second "accidental president," taking office when President Zachary Taylor died in July 1850. Fillmore and Abraham Lincoln had much in common.

They were both Whigs. Both grew up poor, were largely self-educated, became lawyers, and served in their state legislatures. Fillmore was from rural upstate New York and ultimately settled in Buffalo. He served three terms in Congress (1837–1843) and also served as state comptroller. In New York he was considered a conservative, unsympathetic to the antislavery politics of the party's most important figure, William Henry Seward. He was chosen as Taylor's running mate in 1848 in part because Seward wanted to remove him as a force in state politics.

Like most vice presidents of the time, Fillmore was on the road to obscurity when Taylor's death catapulted him to the White House. At the time of Taylor's death Congress was debating what became the Compromise of 1850. Taylor opposed some of the compromise, and Seward, still the leader of the New York Whigs, was a vocal opponent of the proposed fugitive slave law. Fillmore was a supporter of the compromise, which had first been proposed by Lincoln's idol, Henry Clay. When compromise failed as a single omnibus bill, President Fillmore assiduously worked with Sen. Stephen A. Douglas to get it through Congress as a series of separate measures. He happily signed each component bill, including the Fugitive Slave Law of 1850, which was the most controversial piece of the package because it failed to provide due process protections for alleged fugitive slaves.

Fillmore appointed the conservative Whig Daniel Webster as secretary of state, and Webster and Fillmore both pledged to vigorously enforce the new Fugitive Slave Law. In 1851 Fillmore's administration arranged the arrest of a fugitive known as Jerry (with various last names including "Henry" and "McHenry") in Syracuse, New York, a hotbed of abolition not far from where the president had grown up. The arrest led to a huge embarrassment for the administration when an estimated 5,000 people rushed the jail and freed the fugitive in what became known as the Jerry Rescue. Indictments led to only one conviction, which was on appeal when the defendant died. Meanwhile, Senator Seward provided money to post bond for those indicted.

While the Jerry trials were taking place the administration also pushed for the largest treason trial in American history, in which more than fifty Pennsylvanians were placed on trial for refusing to help return a fugitive slave in what became known as the Christiana Slave Riot. In that case the owner of a fugitive was killed by his own slave, who then successfully made his way to Canada. The trials ended in another disaster for the administration, as even the doughface Justice Robert Grier, who heard the case while riding circuit, concluded that refusal to help enforce the 1850 law was not treason.

The Whigs did not nominate Fillmore in 1852, and he left office as a politician without a party. In 1856 he tried to resurrect his political career as a Know-Nothing, while most of his former party members were moving into the new Republican Party. He carried only Maryland and won a mere 22 percent of the popular vote, which mostly came from Southerners who could not stand the Democratic nominee, James Buchanan. Fillmore angered most Northerners—even those who might have been Know-Nothings—by asserting, very early in his campaign, that the South would have the right to secede if the antislavery

Republican, John C. Frémont, won the election. This set the stage for Fillmore's further alienation from his earlier political roots. Most New York Whigs had become Republicans in 1860, but Fillmore had not. He opposed secession in theory but also opposed the war effort and publicly denounced Lincoln as a tyrant. His status as a former president protected him from mobs or even arrest, but by the end of the war he was thoroughly marginalized and irrelevant.

See also *Taylor, Zachary*

—PAUL FINKELMAN

BIBLIOGRAPHY

Anbinder, Tyler. *Nativism and Slavery: The Northern Know Nothings and the Politics of the 1850s.* New York: Oxford University Press, 1992.

Hamilton, Holman. *Prologue to Conflict: The Crisis and Compromise of 1850.* Lexington: University Press of Kentucky, 1964.

Potter, David M. *The Impending Crisis, 1848–1861.* New York: Harper and Row, 1976.

Rayback, Robert J. *Millard Fillmore: Biography of a President.* Published for the Buffalo Historical Society by H. Stewart, 1959.

Smith, Elbert B. *The Presidencies of Zachary Taylor and Millard Fillmore.* Lawrence: University Press of Kansas, 1988.

Florville, William

William Florville, or William de Fleurville (1807–1868), nicknamed "Billy the Barber," was a Haitian-born, Catholic, black resident of Springfield, Illinois, in the mid-1800s. Having made Abraham Lincoln's acquaintance in the early 1830s, Florville sustained one of the most lasting relationships with Lincoln of any of the people of color Lincoln knew in Springfield.

Florville came to the United States in his midteens and eventually made his way to Illinois, where he married and fathered five children in the 1830s. In 1832 he opened a barbershop in Springfield. Lincoln, who had met and befriended Florville earlier in New Salem, Illinois, was among the first customers. Florville's shop became a popular gathering place frequented by Lincoln and other men who enjoyed swapping stories and news. At some point Florville adopted a French spelling of his name, "de Fleurville," but Lincoln continued to refer to him as "Florville" or simply "Billy."

As his business thrived, Florville accumulated land and invested in other ventures. A shrewd businessman, Florville ran an array of notices in local newspapers, announcing new features of his shop, gently nudging delinquent customers to pay their bills, and cleverly advertising the advantages of his services. When Florville's substantial property holdings required legal defense or services, Lincoln handled various proceedings for him, including several lawsuits and routine matters such as tax payments, or recruited others to help if Lincoln himself could not be present.

During Lincoln's presidency, Florville wrote to Lincoln about matters great and small. Always friendly and supportive, Florville penned letters heralding Lincoln's Emancipation Proclamation, hoping for Lincoln's reelection in 1864, expressing shock and sympathy over the death of Lincoln's son Willie, and assuring Lincoln that both the Lincolns' Springfield residence and the dog that the Lincoln children had left in Springfield were fine.

Florville does not appear prominently in most biographies of Lincoln, and fleeting glimpses of the relationship between the two reflect varying emphases in historians' interpretations. Most of Lincoln's biographers agree, however, that mutual esteem and friendship characterized the tie and that Lincoln welcomed warm letters from familiar friends like Florville during trying times in the White House. Perhaps most importantly, Lincoln's relationship to Florville may have helped him change his views on race and made him more comfortable in the presence of successful blacks—such as Frederick Douglass—than any other president in the nineteenth century.

Florville shared the stunned horror of most Americans when Lincoln was assassinated and was an honorary pallbearer in Lincoln's Springfield funeral procession. When Florville died in 1868, his own well-attended funeral illustrated the breadth of his circle of acquaintances. He is buried in Springfield's Calvary Cemetery, the Roman Catholic cemetery adjacent to Oak Ridge Cemetery, the site of Lincoln's tomb.

—CARA L. SHELLY

BIBLIOGRAPHY

Donald, David Herbert. *Lincoln.* New York: Simon and Schuster, 1995.

Guelzo, Allen C. *Abraham Lincoln: Redeemer President.* Grand Rapids: Eerdmans, 1999.

Finkelman, Paul. "Abraham Lincoln: Prairie Lawyer." In *America's Lawyer Presidents: From Law Office to the Oval Office,* edited by Norman Gross, 128–137. Evanston: Northwestern University Press, 2004.

Hudson, Gossie Harold. "William Florville, Lincoln's Barber and Friend." *Negro History Bulletin* 37, no. 5 (August–September 1974): 279–281.

McDermott, Stacy Pratt. "Lincoln and Race: The Great Emancipator didn't advocate racial equality. But was he a racist?" *Illinois Issues Online,* February 2004, http://illinoisissues.uis.edu/features/2004Feb/lincoln.html.

Washington, John E. *They Knew Lincoln.* New York: Dutton, 1942.

Foreign Relations and Diplomacy, Lincoln's

The most crucial foreign policy achievement of Abraham Lincoln and his diplomatic team during the Civil War was preventing recognition of the Confederacy by any foreign nation. Although the president was frequently preoccupied with domestic and military issues he nevertheless kept close watch on events in Europe and was in daily communication with secretary of state William H. Seward. The president and the secretary, along with minister to Great Britain Charles Francis Adams and the chairman of the Senate Committee on Foreign Relations, Charles Sumner, were the chief architects of the successful policy.

At the beginning of the war Lincoln had to restrain Seward's efforts to assume authority with his proposal to demand explanations from Great Britain, France, Spain, and Russia for their allegedly pro-Confederate actions. If the responses were not satisfactory Seward proposed that the United States should declare war; he believed that a foreign war would bring Americans together. In rejecting Seward's proposals Lincoln firmly established control over his own administration, ending Seward's efforts to become a kind of premier. From this point in early April 1861, the president and the secretary of state acted effectively as a team, with Seward accepting his role as adviser rather than policy maker.

The administration maintained throughout the long struggle that the war was a domestic insurrection, requiring foreign nations to avoid any involvement, especially diplomatic recognition of the Confederacy. Yet in proclaiming a blockade of Confederate ports in April 1861 Lincoln opened the door to other interpretations. The European powers, led by Great Britain and secondarily France, would gladly have seen their upstart rival, the United States, divided in two. Moreover, Britain's market for Southern cotton implied a need to break the blockade. Britain's response was to proclaim neutrality, thus granting the Confederacy the right to seek foreign loans and purchase supplies abroad. At the same time, as long as Union warships could effectively patrol Southern ports, Britain gave tacit recognition to the Lincoln blockade.

A crisis in Anglo-American relations developed on November 8, 1861, when an American naval vessel captained by Charles Wilkes stopped the British mail packet *Trent* en route from Havana to St. Thomas. Wilkes ordered two Confederates onboard, James M. Mason and John Slidell, seized and imprisoned. They were traveling to Europe to seek English and French aid. Although Wilkes was initially hailed in Congress and throughout the North as a hero, cooler heads prevailed after prime minister Lord Henry Palmerston threatened war. With advice from Senator Sumner, Lincoln calmed the angry passions and advised "one war at a time." Sumner convinced the president that the United States had violated international law in seizing Mason and Slidell. Secretary Seward found a face-saving way out of the crisis in releasing the two, suggesting that Wilkes had acted in error and on his own authority. Mason and Slidell then sailed unmolested to Europe and spent the next three years seeking English and French recognition in vain.

British intervention remained a real possibility through much of 1862, as Union defeats on the battlefield continued, British demand for cotton increased, and the purpose of the war remained simply to save the Union without challenging slavery. But in September, a Union victory at Antietam was followed by the preliminary Emancipation Proclamation, which promised an attack on slavery to begin the next year. Palmerston now faced rising pro-Union sentiment among British voters and assumed a more cautious policy. Earlier that year, Britain and the United States had accepted a minor treaty pledging the two nations to more effective suppression of the African slave trade. The Senate, with Senator Sumner's urging, ratified the treaty unanimously.

A new crisis developed in 1863 when Napoleon III proposed joint French-British recognition, a step that was abandoned following Union victories at Vicksburg and Gettysburg in early July. But when Confederate representative James D. Bulloch arranged with Liverpool shipyards to build blockade-running vessels and ships with ironclad prows to be used as rams against the wooden ships of the U.S. Navy, tensions accelerated. Seward authorized Minister Adams to say that Lincoln would regard the Confederate use of the vessels as an act of war by England. The two raiders, the *Florida* and the *Alabama,* did sail and before the war's end captured or sank more than a hundred U.S. merchant ships. During the crisis, U.S. consul in Liverpool Thomas H. Dudley had secured evidence that the construction of the ships violated British law, and on September 6, 1863, the British government detained the rams. The Confederates were now forced to concentrate on France, as Britain declined to take any further provocative steps.

Napoleon III had made no effort to hide his pro-Confederate sympathies and had used the American preoccupation with the war to intervene in Mexico. His pretext was Mexico's financial instability and inability to pay its European debts. In June 1863 French troops seized Mexico City and overthrew the government of Benito Juarez, making the Austrian Archduke Ferdinand Maximilian Napoleon's puppet emperor. Seward, with Lincoln's full support, skillfully played a waiting game, applying pressure and offering incentives to France, and with the fall of the Confederacy in April 1865 sent 50,000 troops to the border. Within two years France withdrew its troops and the Maximilian government fell. The defeat of the Confederacy was at least in part due to the successful diplomacy of President Lincoln and his skilled team of advisers.

See also *Adams, Charles Francis;* Alabama *Claims; Great Britain, Relations with;* Trent *Affair*

—Frederick J. Blue

BIBLIOGRAPHY

Crook, David P. *Diplomacy during the American Civil War.* Indianapolis: Wiley, 1975.

Donald, David Herbert. *Lincoln.* New York: Touchstone, 1996.

Jones, Howard. *Union in Peril: The Crisis over British Intervention and the Civil War.* Chapel Hill: University of North Carolina Press, 1992.

McPherson, James M. *Ordeal by Fire: The Civil War and Reconstruction.* 2nd ed. New York: McGraw Hill, 1992.

Oates, Stephen B. *With Malice toward None: A Life of Abraham Lincoln.* New York: Harper and Row, 1977.

Van Deusen, Glyndon F. *William H. Seward.* New York: Oxford University Press, 1967.

Fort Pickens

Fort Pickens was a pentagon-shaped stronghold situated on Santa Rosa Island, in Pensacola Harbor, off Florida's northwestern Gulf coast. Although surrounded by hostile forces, the fort remained in the Union's possession throughout the Civil War. The decision to reinforce Fort Pickens illustrated a divided presidential cabinet and brought to light the competing ideologies that offered Lincoln vastly different solutions for, and compromises with, secession.

In response to the often uncontested British landings on American soil during the War of 1812, the United States had embarked upon a twenty-year project to strengthen port and naval fortifications. The government hired French architect Simon Bernard to update Fort Pickens. Reconstruction of the fort began in 1829 and ended in 1834. Slaves were the primary source of labor for the fort's modifications, unintentionally foreshadowing the nation's impending crisis.

After the 1860 presidential election, President Buchanan sent two hundred federal troops to Fort Pickens to quell secessionist unrest. Local Confederate forces were lying in wait outside the fort and did not permit the men to land. Under an "informal truce," the Confederates promised not to attack the fort if it was not reinforced. Southern sympathizers, however, broke the truce in January 1861, when an unorganized band of rebels attacked Union positions in Florida, making these engagements, not the attack on Fort Sumter on April 12, the first clashes between the United States and armed Southerners.

The Confederacy's future president, Jefferson Davis, sent three emissaries to Washington to "negotiate for the transfer of Forts Sumter and Pickens." This diplomatic proposal did not seem feasible since many in the South wanted to provoke the Union into responding with force, and the Union could not risk giving up fortifications and dividing its territory. A heavy-handed military response by the United States would galvanize Southern opposition and push the uncommitted Border States to the Confederacy's cause. Secessionists in Florida, however, made the difficult decision that had confounded Lincoln when they attacked Fort Pickens.

On January 8, 1861, a band of secessionist sympathizers launched an attack on U.S. fortifications including Fort McRee, the Pensacola Naval Yard, and Fort Pickens. Lieutenant Adam J. Slemmer, the commanding officer, determined that of the three forts, Fort Pickens was the most defensible. Slemmer and his troops abandoned Fort Barrancas, spiked its guns, destroyed its powder supply, and took refuge in Fort Pickens. The rebels made several frontal assaults but were easily repelled. Over the course of the Civil War, subsequent attempts by Confederates to take the fort failed. It remained in Union control, providing a physical and psychological rallying point for the Union.

President Lincoln could not afford to lose the Union fortifications in the South. Doing so would, in the words of historian James McPherson, "divide the North, demoralize the Republican Party, and fatally wreck his administration." Lincoln vacillated between using the might of the military and preserving peace at all costs, often going to bed at night with a "sick headache." Competing ideologies in his cabinet urged the president either to make war or allow secession. He sent emissaries to the South to avoid war. When he heard General Winfield Scott's report from Virginia that "there is no attachment to the Union," Lincoln grew despondent as members of his cabinet expressed the opinion that reinforcing Fort Pickens and Fort Sumter would lead to open war.

Having made the decision to hold Fort Pickens "at all costs," Lincoln ultimately decided that there was no other alternative than war. He reminded his cabinet that since his election Fort Pickens had been under "constant siege" and that the duty fell to him, as commander in chief, to "hold, occupy, and protect the places belonging to this government." Lincoln, resigned to the inevitability of war, gave the orders to reinforce Fort Pickens and Fort Sumter.

The two expeditions to Forts Pickens and Sumter were emblematic of the confusion in Lincoln's administration. Secretary of state William Seward, wanting to demonstrate that reinforcing a fort in Confederate territory would not lead to conflict, began a tacit campaign to weaken the larger, naval expedition to Fort Sumter. He issued orders reassigning the warship *Powhattan,* under the command of Lieutenant David Porter, from the naval force designated to supply Sumter to the smaller, army-led effort to reinforce Pickens. On April 6, 1861, Lincoln learned that his order to reinforce Fort Pickens had been ignored by Captain Montgomery Meigs, the "leader" of the expedition, thus illustrating the deep divide within his cabinet and the inefficiency that Lincoln faced throughout the Civil War.

See also *Fort Sumter*

—PETER SMITH

BIBLIOGRAPHY

Amedeo, Michael. *Armchair Reader Civil War: Untold Stories of the Blue and Gray.* New York: West Side Books, 2007.

Donald, David Herbert. *Lincoln.* New York: Simon and Schuster, 1996.

Foner, Eric. *Politics and Ideology in the Age of the Civil War.* Oxford: Oxford University Press, 1980.

Foote, Shelby. *The Civil War: A Narrative—Fort Sumter to Perryville.* New York: Random House, 1958.

Johnson, Michael, ed. *Abraham Lincoln, Slavery, and the Civil War.* New York: Bedford/St. Martin's, 2001.

Lanning, Michael. *The Civil War 100: The 100 Most Significant Leaders, Battles and Events.* New York: Sourcebooks, 2008.

McPherson, James. *Battle Cry of Freedom: The Civil War Era.* Oxford: Oxford University Press, 1988.

Fort Sumter

Although the elements of sectional conflict had been in place since the inception of the United States, intensifying over time with events such as "Bleeding Kansas" and John Brown's raid, Abraham Lincoln's victory in the presidential election of 1860 brought the situation to its final, critical juncture.

During the two administrations preceding Lincoln's, those of Franklin Pierce and James Buchanan, the nation had slid steadily toward violence and disunion. Historians continue to debate whether his predecessors' inaction was detrimental to the Union or merely delayed the advent of civil war by a few years, but it is certain that when Lincoln came into office in March 1861 immediate action was necessary to ensure the continued safety of Fort Sumter, a besieged fortification at the mouth of Charleston Harbor in South Carolina.

As a member of the fledgling Republican Party, Lincoln had run on a platform that called for halting the spread of slavery into new territories, protective tariffs for American industry, and granting free land to homesteaders in the West. All of these policies created hostility to Lincoln and his party throughout the South, where residents viewed him as a direct threat to their livelihood and way of life. A Republican in office, they reasoned, would not be content to stop slavery from entering new areas but would naturally be driven to end the institution in states where it had been well established for centuries.

Interior of Fort Sumter during the bombardment, April 12, 1861. The reaction in the upper South was exactly what Lincoln had feared. Virginia again voted on secession and decided to join the Confederacy.

Source: Library of Congress

In the months before the presidential election of 1860, public opinion in the South, particularly in the city of Charleston, South Carolina, long a hotbed of proslavery activism, reached a fevered, almost paranoid pitch. Many citizens sincerely believed that Republican and abolitionist agents at large in the region were inciting slaves to rebellion, setting fires, and in the words of the *Charleston Courier* and the *Montgomery Mail,* preparing "our people for the rule of Lincoln."

In October the Palmetto State's governor, William Henry Gist, wrote to fellow state executives declaring that his state was likely to secede from the Union should Lincoln win the election and urging them to join with her. A week later Gist issued a call for the state legislature to convene in Columbia on November 5, the day before the presidential election, ready to act if word reached them that Lincoln had won. The closer the election drew, the more tense the situation became. Just days before the vote, a crowd gathered outside a Columbia hotel to hear U.S. senator James Chestnut proclaim that "a line of enemies is closing around us," before demanding to know whether Northerners should be allowed to govern the affairs of the South.

When news reached Charleston that Lincoln had been elected, a federal grand jury "respectfully decline[d] to proceed with their presentments," as Lincoln's election had "swept away the last hope for the permanence, for the stability, of these sovereign states." Following that proclamation, the presiding judge resigned his office. In an instant, the first official links between South Carolina and the United States government had been severed. The process would be made official on December 20, 1860, when South Carolina became the first state to secede from the Union.

The newly independent republic of South Carolina faced an unusual problem. Within its borders were several U.S. military fortifications occupied by what it now considered a foreign power, most prominently a series of emplacements around Charleston Harbor designed to protect the city from naval assault. Almost immediately, South Carolina dispatched emissaries to Washington, hoping to arrange the peaceful transfer of these properties from one government to another. President Buchanan, however, had failed to address the issue of slavery for the majority of his presidency; they did not expect him to change drastically now that he was a lame duck.

President-elect Lincoln's carefully chosen public remarks suggest a man who sincerely hoped and believed that the situation, though dire, would not result in civil war. Yet Lincoln rejected either appeasement or compromise in dealing with any Southern state seeking to sever ties with the United States. To him, none of the three scenarios widely acknowledged as potential outcomes—disunion, acceptance of slavery, or civil war—was palatable. Yet it is also clear which of his principles Lincoln held most dear: the perpetuity of the Union.

Lincoln's public remarks and private letters make clear that he would not shy away from military action if it proved necessary. In his famous 1858 "House Divided" speech, he stated emphatically that he did not expect the Union to be dissolved, a topic he had touched on more deeply in an 1856 speech at Galena, Illinois. There Lincoln stated, "The Union...won't be dissolved. We don't want to dissolve it, and if you attempt it, *we won't let you*. With the purse and sword, the army and the navy and the treasury in our hands and at our command you *couldn't do it.*" Yet despite this ultimate resolve, Lincoln retained a deep-seated hope that war could be avoided by the Southern states' choosing to desist from their secessionist course, a belief he reiterated at many of his stops en route to Washington in preparation for his inauguration.

Meanwhile, Major Robert Anderson, a career soldier and a native of the slaveholding Border State of Kentucky, commanded the U.S. forces in Charleston Harbor. Since South Carolina's secession ordinance he had received no instructions from his superiors in Washington, and he grew increasingly concerned that his troops were vulnerable to attack by the state militia. For six days after the ordinance of secession was passed, the situation remained tense but static. Realizing how exposed his situation was, Anderson determined to move his troops from Fort Moultrie, an aging fortification easily assaulted by land, to the greater safety of Fort Sumter, located on an isolated, man-made island at the mouth of the harbor. The evacuation of Fort Moultrie and the spiking of her guns were conducted so efficiently that citizens of the city didn't realize what had happened until the following morning. Many prominent Carolinians considered

Anderson's course tantamount to an act of war, believing that an informal agreement to maintain the status quo until word arrived from Washington had been violated.

At Fort Sumter, Anderson and his troops were considerably safer from attack, but they had only a limited supply of provisions. Anderson was convinced that a concerted attack against his small garrison would be successful. The odds would become all the greater when South Carolina was joined by other seceding states in the Deep South. By February, Mississippi, Florida, Alabama, Georgia, Louisiana, and Texas had also withdrawn from the Union, forming the Confederate States of America on February 4, 1861.

During this time there came from Washington a single, largely symbolic attempt to support Anderson. Uncharacteristically, President Buchanan dispatched an unarmed merchant vessel, *Star of the West*, to resupply the fort and land an additional two hundred soldiers. Almost as soon as the ship entered Charleston Harbor, on January 9, 1861, it was fired upon by cannon. Once the ship turned about, the Buchanan administration made no further attempt to send aid.

Lincoln's private letters during this time express a steely resolve to retain Fort Sumter. A message Lincoln sent to General Winfield Scott, federal general in chief, directed the soldier "to be as well prepared as he can to either hold or retake the forts, as the case may require, at, and after the inauguration." To others he wrote that if the forts fell (and in another letter, "if Mr. Buchanan surrenders the forts"), they must be retaken. In fact, so keenly aware was Lincoln of the potential for military intervention that his first order of business on February 23, 1861, the day he arrived in Washington, was to call on President Buchanan and immediately thereafter on General Scott. Later that day, Lincoln met with representatives of the Confederacy dispatched to Washington as a peace convention, who stressed to him that it was his decision as the incoming president whether there would be peace or war. Lincoln replied carefully, reiterating that the Constitution must be upheld, whatever the potential consequences might be. He was about to take an oath, he said, to ensure that that document was "respected, obeyed, enforced, and defended."

With secession now a reality, Lincoln was intensely concerned with strategies that might keep the eight slave states that had not yet seceded in the Union. The states of the upper South, including Virginia, North Carolina, Kentucky, and Tennessee, had cultures far less dependent on slave-supported agriculture and even had pockets of strong pro-Union sentiment. At this stage it was unlikely that the status quo, despite its volatility, would inspire them to secede. If the federal government should fire on fellow Southerners, however, the situation was likely to change dramatically.

On February 26, Lincoln met with representatives of Virginia. The state's proximity to Washington, its position as the most populous and industrialized state in the South, and its historical status as a political leader in the nation made Virginia's position of paramount importance to Lincoln. Several weeks earlier a vote on secession in Virginia had failed to pass. However the delegation's elderly leader, William C. Rives, said that if violence were used against any Southern state, Virginia would surely secede, and he himself would fight if necessary. Lincoln replied that if it would keep Virginia in the Union, he would withdraw federal troops from Fort Sumter. When asked by a European diplomat if the reported exchange was true, Lincoln replied, "A state for a fort is no bad business." Despite that quip, Lincoln remained unwilling to negotiate seriously regarding the status of Fort Sumter.

On March 4, a letter arrived at the White House from Fort Sumter, which Buchanan, on his last day in office, pointedly ignored. In it Major Anderson predicted that to hold Fort Sumter permanently he would need 20,000 troops, and he would need them soon; his supplies were dwindling and would last only another month to forty days. The new president would not see the letter until the following day.

Abraham Lincoln's inaugural address was eagerly anticipated by both North and South. The speech, though it vowed to avoid war, made clear that Lincoln remained firm in his belief that it was unlawful for any state to withdraw from the Union. At no point did he mention Fort Sumter by name, but when he declared that "the power confided in me will be used to hold, occupy and possess the property and places belonging to the government," there was little doubt what he was referring to. In his closing paragraphs, Lincoln also pledged that he would not order the first blow of any war:

> *In your hands, my dissatisfied fellow-countrymen, and not in mine, is the momentous issue of civil war. The government will not assail you. You can have no conflict without being yourselves the aggressors. You have no oath registered in heaven to destroy the government; while I have the most solemn one to "preserve, protect, and defend" it.*

The next day Lincoln was presented with Anderson's report by Joseph Holt, who had agreed to continue acting as secretary of war until Lincoln's choice, Simon Cameron, was confirmed by the Senate. For the first time, Lincoln faced the full, grim reality of the situation in Charleston Harbor. When Lincoln shared Anderson's bleak outlook with General Scott, the old soldier responded that there was no alternative but surrender—an option that would humiliate the new president and his party. Still, Lincoln was somewhat hesitant to take Anderson's dire warnings at face value, knowing that he was a Southerner by birth and might be sympathetic to the Confederate cause. Lincoln ordered Scott to carefully examine the situation at other forts throughout the South, lest they devolve as well.

On March 9 Lincoln's cabinet met for the first time, and many were shocked to hear that Fort Sumter was near to being starved into submission, with a nonexistent army and fleet the only way to resupply it. It was reported in Charleston that the general opinion of the cabinet and General Scott was that the fort would be evacuated and surrendered, perhaps in the next two weeks. But no official announcement came as Lincoln himself remained uncertain. On March 15 Lincoln posed a question to his advisers: "Assuming it is possible to now provision Fort Sumter, under all the circumstances is it wise to attempt it?"

The answers were not heartening. Even if it were theoretically possible to get supplies to the fort, when weighed against the possibility of civil war it seemed unwise, reasoned most of the cabinet. Secretary of War Cameron was firmly opposed, responding that a failed attempt would embarrass them, and even a successful one would only last so long before it had to be repeated. Only the secretary of the Treasury and the postmaster general supported an attempt to resupply. Lincoln was still not ready to give up the fort and sent trusted friends to Charleston to gather more information. It seemed likely that any ship entering the harbor, even if it contained only food, would be stopped.

Ward Hill Lamon, one of Lincoln's law partners, who participated in the fact-finding mission, caused quite a stir in Charleston. So curious was his trip that some historians theorize that Lincoln or his secretary of state, William Seward, was purposely using Lamon to mislead Southerners, knowing that his actions and comments would be widely distributed. Lamon met with Anderson at the fort—the only official visitor from Washington the major had received—and told him he was soon to be evacuated. He also met with South Carolina governor Charles Pickens, with whom he began—without authorization—to negotiate the possibility of sending a civilian vessel into the harbor to facilitate the evacuation. Based on a passing remark made by Fort Sumter's commander, Lamon began spreading the rumor that Anderson intended to blow up his post as he left. In denying this rumor, Anderson wrote to Washington that he thought his government had "left me too much to myself, has not given me instructions, even when I have asked for them, and that responsibilities of a higher and more delicate character have been devolved upon me than was proper."

As Lincoln contemplated taking action, he received a memo from General Scott on March 28. In it, Scott urged Lincoln to abandon not only Fort Sumter but also Fort Pickens in Pensacola, Florida, to appease Border State sentiments. This came after Lincoln had previously ordered the Florida fort to be reinforced—an order that, unknown to Lincoln, was seriously delayed by issues of bureaucracy between the army and the navy.

At a cabinet meeting the following day, Lincoln again polled his advisers and found their opinion shifting toward resupplying Sumter. Immediately he began to plan an expedition to relieve Anderson, though he did not make a full commitment. Perhaps, Lincoln thought, when word arrived that Pensacola had been reinforced, he would be able to withdraw from Charleston without its appearing that his administration lacked backbone. Thus preparations to resupply Fort Sumter continued with the understanding that if the situation changed, they could be reversed.

The resupply plan hatched by Gustavus Vasa Fox, a fifteen-year navy veteran, called for several smaller boats to sneak into Charleston Harbor under cover of night. In late March, Fox visited Charleston to reconnoiter, and Major Anderson attempted to convince him of the futility of his plan. The shallow landing area meant that only rowboats or similar vessels could reach the docks, and they would be within range of Confederate-occupied Fort Moultrie. Fox did not trust Anderson's Southern sympathies—as others in the Lincoln administration also did not—and therefore did not tell him that the visit had confirmed his belief that a relief mission could be successful. He also did not relay Lincoln's recommendation that the fort be reduced to half rations to buy him more time. Instead Fox returned to Washington with a list of items he would need to accomplish his mission, and Lincoln directed that they should all be collected by April 6. However, one key element of the plan was denied to Fox when Secretary Seward unilaterally ordered the *Powhatan,* the most powerful vessel in the Atlantic fleet, to Pensacola instead.

On April 4, Lincoln ordered Fox to deliver subsistence—and two hundred additional troops—to Fort Sumter. Fox protested that he was not ready, that he had to go to New York to retrieve several specialized tugboats and then travel more than six hundred miles to Charleston. Lincoln replied, "You will best fulfill your duty to your country by making the attempt."

Meanwhile, on April 3 Anderson had urgently wired Washington for instructions, telling them his food could last only four or five days. His pleas were met with silence. He had no way of knowing that while he waited, Fox was in New York preparing to sail south. During this period of inaction, a schooner entered the harbor unwisely flying the Stars and Stripes, causing the batteries on Morris Island to open up. Seeing their national flag under enemy fire, the men of Fort Sumter were eager to return fire, but Anderson demurred—only patience would keep them out of civil war at this stage.

Anderson had begun to suspect that the government was allowing him to run out of food without orders so he would be forced to surrender and then be pilloried for it, perhaps even court-martialed. "After thirty-odd years of service," he wrote to Washington, "I do not wish it to be said that I have treasonably abandoned a post and turned over to unauthorized persons public property entrusted to my charge. I am entitled to this act of justice at the hands of my Government, and I feel confident that I shall not be disappointed."

Washington's silence ended on April 4. Major Anderson's messages had finally informed Lincoln that his instructions to cut to half rations had not been delivered and that estimates of how long the fort could last were drastically off. Lincoln wrote that he was ordering the immediate launch of a resupply effort and that he hoped that the fort would still stand on April 12. If, when the fleet arrived, South Carolina's coastal batteries made any attempt to stop it, the fleet would try to land reinforcements as well. "You will therefore hold out, if possible, till the arrival of the expedition," the orders ran, going on to say that if "in your judgment, to save yourself and your command, [you feel that] capitulation becomes a necessity, you are authorized to make it." To Anderson the message was a stinging blow, raising questions about his honor and commitment to the Union. In despair, Anderson wrote a heartfelt note to a personal friend in the Adjutant General's Office and sent it with his next official dispatch reporting more activity on the shore batteries. This fateful note fell into the lap of Governor Pickens, alerting the Confederacy to the relief expedition.

On April 6 Lincoln issued the final orders for the relief expedition, after learning that his numerous efforts to reinforce Fort Pickens in Pensacola were still delayed. He dispatched a messenger to Governor Pickens with the following message, in accordance with an agreement put in place by Buchanan whereby he had to notify the South Carolina government prior to any attempt to resupply Fort Sumter: "An attempt will be made to supply Fort Sumter with provisions only, and that if such attempt be not resisted, no effort to throw in men, arms, or ammunition will be made without further notice, [except] in case of an attack on the fort."

With Lincoln's message and Anderson's letter in hand, the Confederate government met in Montgomery, Alabama, on April 9 and determined to begin a bombardment of Fort Sumter before a resupply fleet arrived. Only secretary of state Robert Toombs dissented, saying, "You will wantonly strike a hornet's nest.... Legions now quiet will swarm out and sting us to death. It is unnecessary. It puts us in the wrong. It is fatal." On April 11 General Pierre G. T. Beauregard dispatched emissaries to Fort Sumter with an ultimatum: If Anderson did not surrender, he would compel him to do so. Anderson replied that if Beauregard did not batter his command into surrender, he would soon be starved out. Reporting this to his superiors, Beauregard was directed to approach Anderson again, asking him to name the date and time he would surrender the fort. The response came that Fort Sumter would capitulate by noon on the fifteenth, unless Anderson received other orders or additional supplies. At approximately 3:20 a.m. on April 12, Beauregard informed Anderson that his specified date was unacceptable and that Beauregard's batteries would begin bombardment of the fort in one hour.

In the predawn darkness, at 4:30 a.m., the Confederate guns opened up, beginning with a single shot from Fort Johnson. Anderson withheld fire until 7:00 a.m. and only continued firing until sundown. Confederate shore batteries did noticeable damage to Fort Sumter; Union counterfire was less effective, the fort being designed to defend against a naval assault. Repeated hits splintered and broke the central flagpole, but the defenders were able to quickly rig another way to fly the Stars and Stripes. Several incoming shots started fires that Union soldiers struggled to contain, lest they ignite their powder stores.

After thirty-four hours of intense bombardment, Fort Sumter raised a white flag of surrender, signaling the end of the first battle of the Civil War. Despite the intense fire, remarkably few casualties occurred, and no combat deaths. Confederate officials arranged generous terms for the departing Union soldiers, including the promise of a one-hundred-gun salute to the U.S. flag. Anderson and his command were transported back to Union territory by the Northern fleet that had been dispatched to resupply them and that had prompted the bombardment. Anderson smuggled out the battered American flag that had flown over the fort. It would return to Charleston in 1865, when he would again raise it over the fort after years of Confederate occupation.

Public opinion in the North was suddenly galvanized against any who would presume to fire on the American flag. President Lincoln called for 75,000 volunteers to combat the insurrection and many states responded enthusiastically. The reaction in the upper South, however, was exactly what Lincoln had feared. While the Union soldiers were steaming north to New York harbor, Virginia again voted on secession and decided to join the Confederacy. In the next two months Arkansas, North Carolina, and Tennessee followed.

Though Lincoln never publicly stated that he sent the fleet to Charleston to force the issue to a head, he certainly recognized that hostilities were the most likely outcome. Lincoln did not choose his course because he found war acceptable. To his mind, he chose the option to, as he phrased it in his inaugural address, "hold, occupy and possess the property and places belonging to the government and to collect the duties and imposts." This option, particularly when compared with the alternatives of accepting disunion or allowing the steady spread of slavery throughout that union, was the best path available to him. Should war come from his decision to uphold the Constitution, he had at least served his highest duty. Four years later, in his second inaugural address, Lincoln eloquently expressed his philosophy: "Both parties deprecated war, but one of them would make war rather than let the nation survive, and the other would accept war rather than let it perish, and the war came."

See also *Fort Pickens*

—Jim Campi

BIBLIOGRAPHY

Detzer, David. *Allegiance: Fort Sumter, Charleston, and the Beginning of the Civil War.* New York: Harcourt, 2001.

Klein, Maury. *Days of Defiance: Sumter, Secession, and the Coming of the Civil War.* New York: Knopf, 1997.

Forts Henry and Donelson

As the Confederacy prepared to defend its borders in 1861, military planners decided to build a series of forts to contest a Union advance into western Tennessee along the Mississippi, Tennessee, and Cumberland Rivers. Just south of the Kentucky/Tennessee border the Confederates began construction on a brace of forts, named Henry and Heiman, to protect the Tennessee River, as well as Fort Donelson, which was located along the south bank at a bend of the Cumberland. Along with Columbus, Kentucky, on the east bank of the Mississippi, which the Confederates occupied in September 1861, these forts were deemed essential to securing the Confederate perimeter.

No sooner had Confederate forces invaded Kentucky, in September 1861, than Brigadier General Ulysses S. Grant countered by occupying Paducah, Kentucky, located where the Tennessee and Cumberland Rivers empty into the Ohio. For the next several months, Grant wrestled with the idea of ousting the Confederates from Columbus. This activity, including a sharp clash on November 7, at Belmont, Missouri, just across the river from Columbus, led the Confederates to pay more attention to a possible Union advance down the Mississippi. In contrast, Fort Heiman remained unfinished, and low-lying Fort Henry could mount only seventeen cannon. There was more satisfactory progress at Fort Donelson but no effort to establish additional fortifications farther north in Kentucky.

At the end of January 1862 Grant traveled to St. Louis to present a plan for advancing against Fort Henry in conjunction with a naval flotilla under the command of flag officer Andrew H. Foote. Grant later recalled that General Halleck rather briskly dismissed the idea, but within days he changed his mind. Perhaps the reason was that Halleck had learned that Foote supported the operation, or it may have been a report that the area was being reinforced. As Lincoln had grown impatient with the failure of Union forces to advance and was especially frustrated with the inertia of his western commands—part of the reason why he issued General War Order No. 1 on January 27, 1862, calling for a general offensive to begin by February 22, 1862—Halleck's reversal was timely.

Grant and Foote commenced their advance on February 3. Grant estimated his command at 15,000 men; Foote's seven vessels included four ironclad gunboats. As the Union advance approached the forts, the Confederate commander, judging the area indefensible because of high waters that had flooded Fort Henry, had withdrawn the majority of his command to Fort Donelson, leaving a token force to inflict what damage it could before surrendering Fort Henry to Foote's flotilla. When Grant arrived, he decided to follow up on the victory, wiring Halleck that he would "take and destroy" Donelson in the next few days before returning to Henry. As Foote's gunboats sailed back to the Ohio River to make their way to the Cumberland River and to Fort Donelson (after undergoing some repairs), Grant took stock of the situation, waited for the roads to dry, and finally set out for Donelson on February 12.

Upon learning of the fall of Fort Henry, Confederate commander Albert Sidney Johnston decided to withdraw his forces from Kentucky to south of the Cumberland River. To facilitate that move he decided to hold Fort Donelson, and he quickly reinforced it to the point that the Confederate troops could now meet Grant on equal terms. By February 13 Foote's fleet, shy one gunboat put out of commission at Fort Henry, arrived. The following day Confederate cannon severely punished the gunboats, wounding Foote—there would be no repeat of the quick victory at Henry. That evening, Confederate commander John B. Floyd, working with subordinates Gideon Pillow and Simon B. Buckner, devised a plan whereby the Confederates would drive back the Union right flank south of the fort and escape through the opening.

Attacking before dawn on February 15, the Confederates succeeded in prying back the Union line. Grant was returning from a visit to the wounded Foote when he learned of the Confederate success. With a cigar in hand (a gift from the flag officer), he discerned that the Confederates were making a break for it. He immediately rallied his forces and counterattacked. Losing sight of the original plan, Floyd inexplicably passed up the opportunity to escape and ordered his subordinates to return to the fort after Pillow had fallen back to his initial position to refit. That night, Floyd convened a second meeting of his generals. Concluding that the garrison was doomed, Floyd, afraid of being prosecuted for treason (he had served in James Buchanan's cabinet as secretary of war before resigning in the winter of 1860–1861), turned over command to Pillow, who immediately passed it on to Buckner. Floyd, Pillow, and a small number of Confederates, including Nathan Bedford Forrest, escaped: Buckner contacted Grant (an old friend from the prewar army) to ascertain the conditions of capitulation. Grant's reply was short and to the point: "No terms except unconditional and immediate surrender can be accepted. I propose to move immediately upon your works." The following morning Buckner surrendered what remained of the garrison, some 13,000 men. Grant, who had been reinforced to some 25,000 men by the close of the siege, had suffered some 2,800 casualties, while Confederate losses (aside from the captured) approached 2,000, with perhaps 2,500 men having escaped.

The Union victory made Ulysses S. Grant a hero. Wags argued that his initials stood for "unconditional surrender"; admirers showered the pipe smoker with cigars. Lincoln sent his name to the Senate for promotion to major general. Forgotten in the wake of the triumph was that Halleck, who had succumbed to fears of disaster as Grant approached Donelson, had unsuccessfully sought to replace him with another general. Just as important, the loss of the fort and its garrison forced Johnston to abandon western Tennessee, including Nashville, presenting Lincoln with an opportunity to appoint a military governor, Andrew Johnson, to undertake the construction of a new, loyal state government. At a time when Lincoln was frustrated with George B. McClellan's seeming inaction, Grant's victory offered cause for optimism.

See also *Grant, Ulysses S.*

—BROOKS D. SIMPSON

BIBLIOGRAPHY

Cooling, Benjamin F. *Forts Henry and Donelson: The Key to the Confederate Heartland.* Knoxville: University of Tennessee Press, 1987.

Engle, Stephen D. *Struggle for the Heartland: The Campaigns from Fort Henry to Corinth.* Lincoln: University of Nebraska Press, 2001.

Gott, Kendall D. *Where the South Lost the War: An Analysis of the Fort Henry–Fort Donelson Campaign, February 1862.* Mechanicsburg, Pa.: Stackpole Books, 2003.

Simpson, Brooks D. *Ulysses S. Grant: Triumph over Adversity, 1822–1865.* New York: Houghton Mifflin, 2000.

Founding Fathers, Lincoln's View of

Abraham Lincoln viewed the United States as an experiment to demonstrate that self-government based on the ideals of the Founding Fathers could work. Yet even as many Americans shared Lincoln's devotion to the founders, the content of the founders' ideas remained ambiguous and contested. For Lincoln, the founders' legacy consisted of specific definitions of equality, freedom, liberty, and self-government, which shaped his views on economics and slavery, his perception of the secession crisis, and his conduct of the Civil War.

The most important principle that Lincoln attributed to the founders was equality, by which, Lincoln said, the founders meant a basic human dignity and right to opportunity that neither governments nor individuals could impugn. Lincoln's definition of "equality" influenced his interpretation of the other ideals. "Freedom" referred to every person's right to be free from the command of other people and to be rewarded for his or her labor. "Liberty" involved every human being's right to rise in the world. "Self-government" meant that no human being could be governed by another without consent. The mission bequeathed to subsequent generations by the founders, as Lincoln saw it, was to show that government founded on these principles could succeed.

Lincoln's political views grew directly from his interpretation of the founding principles of equality, freedom, liberty, and self-government. Initially a Whig, the young Lincoln first applied founding ideals to economic matters. He endorsed an active role for government in stimulating the economy through measures such as internal improvements (government subsidized transportation projects), tariffs, and a national bank to promote opportunity and upward mobility. Lincoln's lifelong antipathy toward slavery was at root a moral objection, but his opposition was enhanced by his economic ideals because slavery limited opportunity and upward mobility for non-slaveholders and denied them to slaves. Yet Lincoln's respect for the founders moderated his antislavery position; because the founders' Constitution protected slavery, Lincoln respected the property rights of slave owners in existing slave states, while hoping that slavery would eventually die.

As the United States gained territory in the 1840s, Lincoln focused on slavery's extension. The Kansas-Nebraska Act of 1854 crystallized Lincoln's thinking because it invoked a contradictory view of founding principles. Designed by Illinois senator Stephen A. Douglas, the Kansas-Nebraska Act replaced the prohibition of slavery in Kansas with popular sovereignty, meaning that white men in the territory voted on slavery. Supporters of popular sovereignty cited principles of equality and self-government: white men in Kansas should have the same right to choose their form of government that residents of states did. Lincoln explained his contrasting view in a speech in 1854, in Peoria, and in a series of debates when he ran against Douglas for the Senate in 1858. The humanity and therefore equality of black Americans meant that no other human beings could justly vote to rob them of the fruits of their labors, the right to rise in the world, or the right to govern themselves, and therefore founding principles argued for no extension of slavery. Douglas won, but the debates heightened Lincoln's profile within the Republican Party.

As the election of 1860 approached, Lincoln deepened his analysis of the founders' opposition to slavery's expansion. In the 1860 Cooper Union (New York) Address, a speech that introduced him to a national audience, Lincoln invoked the revolutionary generation by repeating the phrase, "our fathers, who framed the government" fifteen times, citing George Washington eight times, Thomas Jefferson twice, Alexander Hamilton once, and Benjamin Franklin once, and systematically analyzing the writings and voting records of the thirty-nine signers of the Constitution to argue that the founders opposed the spread of slavery. Of the twenty-three who had voted on the Northwest Ordinance, the organization of Mississippi Territory, or the Missouri Compromise, all twenty-three had voted that Congress *could* regulate slavery in the territories, and twenty-one voted that Congress *should* restrict slavery. Of the remaining sixteen signers, fifteen privately supported restriction, while only one wrote that the federal government could not limit slavery. After rendering the 36–3 decision, Lincoln ended his speech with an exhortation to uphold the founders' moral legacy by opposing slavery's expansion.

Lincoln viewed the secession of the Southern states in response to his election to the presidency in 1860 as a threat to the survival of the founders' experiment in republican government for three main reasons: First, secession destroyed the Union that Lincoln regarded as the concrete legacy of the founders, as he indicated when he explained to well-wishers in Springfield, Illinois, that his task was to save the government that George Washington's generation created. Second, by leaving the Union because of dissatisfaction with election results, Southern states rejected the only workable basis for self-government. As Lincoln observed in July 1861, secession and war presented "the question, whether a constitutional republic, or a democracy—a government of the people, by the same people—can, or cannot maintain its territorial integrity, against its own domestic foes." Third, by founding itself on the cornerstone of slavery and inequality, as Confederate vice president Alexander Stephens stated, the Confederacy debased the ideals of equality, freedom, and liberty by replacing them with their opposites.

Lincoln's prosecution of the Civil War, especially his decision to turn a war for the Union into a war against slavery, grew from his sense of obligation to the founders' legacy. As he said in the Gettysburg Address, the war tested whether a nation "conceived in Liberty, and dedicated to the proposition that all men are created equal" could "long endure." Because dedication to slavery had led Southern states to jettison the nation, secession and war demonstrated to Lincoln that slavery was incompatible with equality, freedom, liberty, and self-government and that only a "new birth of freedom" without slavery could save the nation. Lincoln issued the Emancipation Proclamation of January 1, 1863, and supported a constitutional amendment eradicating slavery nationwide to make the Union worthy of saving by realizing the ideals that he attributed to the founders. In so doing, Lincoln altered the United States from the slaveholding republic the founders had known to a free nation that he believed they had envisioned. Guided by his own sense of what the Founders intended, Lincoln led the nation through what some historians have called a Second American Revolution, which answered questions left unanswered by the founders' Revolution.

—Chandra Manning

BIBLIOGRAPHY

Basler, Roy P., ed. *The Collected Works of Abraham Lincoln.* New Brunswick, N.J.: Rutgers University Press, 1953–1955.

Boritt, Gabor S. *Lincoln and the Economics of the American Dream.* Memphis: Memphis State University Press, 1978.

Burton, Orville Vernon. *The Age of Lincoln.* New York: Hill and Wang, 2007.

Holzer, Harold *Lincoln at Cooper Union: The Speech That Made Abraham Lincoln President.* New York: Simon and Schuster, 2004.

McPherson, James M. *Abraham Lincoln and the Second American Revolution.* New York: Oxford University Press, 1990.

Simon, John Y., Harold Holzer, and Dawn Vogel, eds. *Lincoln Revisited: New Insights from the Lincoln Forum.* New York: Fordham University Press, 2007.

Fredericksburg and Chancellorsville, Battles of

Fredericksburg (December 13, 1862) and Chancellorsville (April 30–May 6, 1863) marked the climax of two Union efforts to breach the Confederate defense line in central Virginia between late autumn 1862 and spring 1863. In each case, the Army of Northern Virginia defeated the Army of the Potomac in a costly battle; each Confederate victory led to despondency in the North and raised Confederate morale to the point that Robert E. Lee and many of his fellow Confederates were convinced that they were invincible on the battlefield, an attitude they would take with them as they invaded the North in June 1863.

In November 1862, just as the midterm elections passed, Abraham Lincoln decided to replace George B. McClellan as commander of the Army of the Potomac with Ambrose Burnside. Lincoln had considered replacing McClellan before, but Burnside had previously declined the president's offer and expressed concern that he might not be up to the task. Within weeks of taking charge of the Army of the Potomac, Burnside had devised a plan whereby his army would march around Lee's right, cross the Rappahannock River at Fredericksburg, located midway between the rival capitals at Washington and Richmond, and force Lee to engage him or risk losing his capital. Essential to the plan were speed and the arrival of bridging equipment in timely fashion at Fredericksburg. Unfortunately, as a result of bureaucratic confusion, when Burnside's lead elements arrived opposite Fredericksburg, the pontoon bridges were nowhere to be found. Instead of forcing a crossing, Burnside decided to wait for the pontoons to arrive: In the interim Lee moved his army to Fredericksburg and began forming a defensive position west and south of the town.

When Union engineers began attempting to assemble the bridges on December 11, they came under fire. Burnside shelled Fredericksburg and crossed infantry to stifle the resistance. By December 12 much of the Army of the Potomac had deployed on the west bank of the river, and Burnside prepared to attack the next day. The major blow would be delivered against the Confederate right, held by Stonewall Jackson's corps. A more limited demonstration would take place against James Longstreet's corps, which was deployed on the heights west of town, including a stone wall beside a sunken road that served as an ideal fortified position with excellent fields of fire. After initial success in the morning, the Union attackers south of the town fell back in the face of a Confederate counterattack. From late morning through the afternoon wave after wave of Union infantry assaulted Longstreet's position along Marye's Heights. Time and again they were cut down before they could even approach the Confederate position. Watching, Lee observed, "It is well that war is so terrible, else we should grow too fond of it." It was one of the most disastrous frontal assaults of the war.

Deterred from personally leading an assault on December 14, Burnside withdrew the next day. His losses totaled 12,653 men out of a force of some 110,000 effectives, while Confederate casualties reached 5,377 out of some 70,000 engaged. It was left to Lincoln to point out that over time, a Fredericksburg a week would eventually destroy Lee's army, a calculation of the terrible impact of attrition. But this Union defeat, coming on the eve of the Emancipation Proclamation, triggered a cabinet crisis provoked by secretary of the Treasury Salmon P. Chase, who urged congressional Republicans to call for the resignation of secretary of state William H. Seward. Lincoln so shrewdly thwarted the effort that Chase offered his own resignation, whereupon the president rejected both cabinet members' efforts to leave.

Burnside proved less able in stifling dissent among some of his officers, who went to Washington to complain about him to Lincoln. When Burnside sought to fire these officers, Lincoln decided to transfer them and replace Burnside with Joseph Hooker. Ambitious and loud, Hooker had declared that the nation needed a dictator and that he would not be averse to playing that role. Lincoln reminded him that only generals who won battles became dictators. Thus admonished, Hooker did what he could to revive army morale, and by spring 1863 the Army of the Potomac approached 134,000 men, its top strength during the war. At the same time, Lee had dispatched Longstreet with two divisions to secure forage and to protect southeast Virginia, with the result that Hooker outnumbered Lee by the largest margin there would ever be between the two armies at the beginning of a campaign. Hooker devised a plan whereby his cavalry would sweep around and threaten the Confederate rear, while four infantry corps would swing west, cross the Rapidan and Rappahannock Rivers, and come up on Lee's rear at Fredericksburg. The rest of the army would keep Lee in check.

With just over 60,000 men Lee moved quickly to stave off disaster. Leaving an augmented division behind at Fredericksburg, he moved 46,000 men west to check Hooker's advance just east of Chancellor's Tavern. Hooker did not press his advantage, whereupon Lee divided his army yet again, sending some 26,000 men under Stonewall Jackson to march concealed through the thick woods to a position where they could smash the unguarded Union right flank. Lee would keep the rest of Hooker's army occupied, accepting the chance that the Yankees might overwhelm them. The plan worked perfectly, as Jackson's attack on May 2 rolled up the Union right: Only darkness, followed by Jackson's being hit by friendly fire, halted the charge. Over the next several days Lee pushed Hooker back and successfully countered a Union effort that overran Fredericksburg but failed to advance past Salem Church. On the evening of May 5, Hooker decided to pull back north of the rivers.

Hooker's losses exceeded 17,000 men, and the Confederates suffered more than 13,000 casualties, the most important of which was Jackson, who died on May 10. The news of the defeat shocked Lincoln, who moaned, "My God! My God! What will the country say?" Nevertheless, the Army of the Potomac had fought better than had its generals. Lee realized that simply maintaining his defensive line at such a high cost would not be enough. With that in mind, he planned to invade the North once more.

—Brooks D. Simpson

BIBLIOGRAPHY

Furgurson, Ernest B. *Chancellorsville 1863: The Souls of the Brave.* New York: Knopf, 1992.

O'Reilly, Francis A. *The Fredericksburg Campaign: Winter War on the Rappahannock.* Baton Rouge: Louisiana State University Press, 2003.

Rable, George C. *Fredericksburg! Fredericksburg!* Chapel Hill: University of North Carolina Press, 2001.

Sears, Stephen W. *Chancellorsville.* New York, Houghton Mifflin, 1996.

Free Soil Party

The Free Soil Party was an antislavery third party formed in 1848 to oppose the expansion of slavery into territories acquired in the Mexican War. On the grounds that slavery was a state institution, not a federal one, it endorsed the Wilmot Proviso, then under debate in Congress, to prohibit the spread of slavery into the newly acquired territories. The party attempted to continue the efforts of the Liberty Party to force Democrats and Whigs to stop catering to the interests of what it called the Slave Power and to the Southern demand that slavery be legal in all territories.

Abraham Lincoln was a young Whig member of the House of Representatives in 1848. He endorsed the Wilmot Proviso but refused to jeopardize his position in the Whig Party to join an untried and inexperienced third party that had little chance of national or even regional success.

Even before the Mexican War the issue of slavery in the territories had come to dominate American politics with the controversy over annexation of Texas. With annexation complete in March 1845 and statehood secured by the end of the year, the issue shifted to war with Mexico over the Texas boundary and territories farther west. After four terms in the Illinois legislature Lincoln was elected to the House of Representatives in 1846, a few months after the war began. Like numerous other northern Whigs in Congress he became an active opponent of the war and a proponent of the Wilmot Proviso. Most important was Lincoln's introduction, in December 1847, of his "Spot Resolutions," to embarrass Democratic President James K. Polk by challenging his contention that Mexico had invaded American soil and claiming that the spot where the war had started was in territory to which Mexico had a stronger claim. The war, Lincoln argued, was a Slave Power conspiracy to expand slavery. Lincoln believed that if confined to the South slavery would gradually die out.

Although a firm opponent of the expansion of slaveholding, Lincoln was not as sensitive to the danger as he would be a decade later, and he rarely spoke of it during his one term in the House. Like most antislavery advocates, he thought that Congress had no power over slavery in the South but could constitutionally legislate on it for the territories, where Congress had full jurisdiction. Similarly, Congress controlled the District of Columbia, and Lincoln proposed an abolition bill for that jurisdiction. But when it came to joining the Free Soil party, which endorsed his stance, his beliefs were not strong enough to make him willing to risk Whig unity and jeopardize his future as a Whig.

Thus when many northern Whigs bolted from their party after it nominated Louisiana slaveholder and Mexican War general Zachary Taylor, the young Illinois representative remained loyal. Lincoln would have preferred the nomination of his political idol, Henry Clay of Kentucky, but he enthusiastically supported Taylor after attending the nominating convention. The threat of Whig defections to the third party was strongest in Massachusetts, where young Whigs Charles Francis Adams and Charles Sumner led the walkout, and Lincoln delivered several campaign addresses there to counter their appeal. His key argument was his belief that General Taylor would not veto the Wilmot Proviso because its constitutionality was not in dispute. He rationalized that the Free Soil endorsement was no stronger than that of the Whigs and that the third party, by drawing away Whig votes, would actually aid the Democrats and their candidate, Michigan senator Lewis Cass who, he said, was less likely than Taylor to promote freedom in the territories.

Lincoln's decision to remain a loyal Whig was made easier by the Free Soil nomination of former Democrat Martin Van Buren, a longtime opponent of the Whig economic program. But his own partisan appeals indicate that Lincoln was a party man first and an advocate of containing slavery second. Because both parties were silent on the issue of racial equality, Lincoln's racial beliefs were as secure as a Whig as they would have been as a Free-Soiler. Most adherents of both parties thought that the territories should be kept free of slavery to protect the interests of small, white farmers of the North, the Illinois constituents whom Lincoln sought most to champion. Thus his decision to remain aloof from the Free Soil movement could be made on grounds other than the issue of slavery.

Following Taylor's election, the Free Soil party continued for six years but in 1852 attained only half of its 1848 vote. In the election of 1852 Lincoln, having returned to private law practice, campaigned for the Whig Party and its presidential candidate, Mexican War hero General Winfield Scott. After Scott's defeat the party rapidly declined. Its decline was accelerated by the party's ineffectiveness in resisting Illinois senator Stephen A. Douglas's Kansas-Nebraska bill of 1854, which repealed the Missouri Compromise ban on slavery in the territories north of 36° 30'. By the next year, 1855, a new political party, which soon came to be called the Republican Party, had gained unprecedented power throughout most of the North. The new party combined Whigs, antislavery Democrats, and Free-Soilers on a platform pledged to keep slavery out of the western territories. It was a position similar to that of the Free-Soilers of 1848. With the Whig organization on the verge of collapse, Lincoln, like most northern Whigs, joined the new party. The primary difference was that the Republicans emerged as part of the two-party system, with a real chance of victory, whereas the Free-Soilers were destined to remain on the fringe of political power as a third party.

See also *Liberty Party*

—Frederick J. Blue

BIBLIOGRAPHY

Blue, Frederick J. *The Free Soilers: Third Party Politics, 1848–54.* Urbana: University of Illinois Press, 1973.

Fehrenbacher, Don. *Prelude to Greatness: Lincoln in the 1850s*. Stanford: Stanford University Press, 1962.

Foner, Eric. *Free Soil, Free Labor, Free Men: The Ideology of the Republican Party before the Civil War*. New York: Oxford University Press, 1970.

Morrison, Michael A. *Slavery and the American West: The Eclipse of Manifest Destiny and the Coming of the Civil War*. Chapel Hill: University of North Carolina Press, 1997.

Oates, Stephen B. *With Malice toward None: The Life of Abraham Lincoln*. New York: Harper and Row, 1977.

Sewell, Richard H. *Ballots for Freedom: Antislavery Politics in the United States, 1837–1860*. New York: Oxford University Press, 1976.

"Free Soil, Free Labor, Free Men"

The Northern veneration of "free labor" as the cornerstone of a good society undergirded the profound ideological rift that eventually precipitated the American Civil War in 1861. Free labor ideology honored the dignity of paid work and stressed its efficacy in providing opportunities for upward mobility and personal autonomy. In the 1850s, the nascent Republican Party embraced the philosophy of "Free Soil, Free Labor, Free Men." In the campaign of 1856 the party's slogan also included "free speech." The party and its slogan gave political voice to the growing conviction that North and South had become competing, antagonistic societies that could not successfully coexist under a single political system.

The belief in the nobility of labor predated American independence. It derived in large part from the Calvinist theological doctrine that every person had a divinely appointed "calling," which God required the individual to pursue to his fullest capacity. In an overwhelmingly Protestant society, most Americans accepted the strong work ethic as an article of faith and associated the ascetic characteristics generally required for financial success with moral righteousness. Conversely, idleness and excessive luxury implied moral decay and seemed incompatible with this version of Christian values.

The embrace of "free labor" also drew on American republican traditions that emerged in the revolutionary era. Republican government, America's founders asserted, demanded the existence of a virtuous and economically independent citizenry and of relatively egalitarian economic circumstances across society. Wide disparities of wealth or opportunity threatened to breed alienation and resentment, potentially wreaking havoc on a system in which ultimate authority is vested in the electorate. Consequently, the "middling sort" of economic entrepreneur represented the ideal republican citizen, and in a country with an abundance of available land, the yeoman farmer became its most glorified embodiment.

In the antebellum era, Northerners increasingly adapted the principles of the Protestant work ethic and their understanding of republicanism to a broader vision of a good society. While the notion of a calling might imply that people must necessarily remain permanently in their particular profession, thereby cementing social stratification, an emergent capitalist philosophy emanating from Northern industrial centers asserted that hard work promised the reward of upward mobility. Individual effort would combine with the virtually limitless opportunity offered by a dynamic economy and an expanding geography to preclude the entrenchment of rigid class structures.

This dignified view of labor applied to all types of producers—wage workers, artisans, farmers, and entrepreneurs. According to its precepts, a man might begin life as a wage laborer, but through self-discipline, sobriety, and effort he could seize the possibilities available and eventually buy a farm or open his own shop. Furthermore, the free labor ideology posited harmony of interests among all producers and both the promise of upward mobility and the irrelevance of class identity. The prospect of improving one's economic status undermined the fundamental causes of social strife. The individual, then, rather than the collective, was the building block of a good society. Through personal effort, ambition, and intelligence one could dictate one's own economic and social success. Within this social and economic model, disparities in wealth resulted from differences in personal characteristics rather than systemic problems.

Because proponents of free labor asserted that every man held his individual fate in his own hands, they disdained those who worked for wages their entire life. A wage earner only remained so because he lacked the personal characteristics that would elevate his status and allow him to secure economic independence. Poverty or persistent dependence derived from individual deficiencies; adherents to the frugal, industrious ways of the Protestant work ethic would surely rise. "Free labor," then, meant labor with economic choices and the eventual opportunity to escape the wage-earning class.

The conviction that in America workers could legitimately aspire to improvement in their status rested fundamentally on the ample availability of cheap land to the West. Free land offered a safety valve against frustration and antagonism in eastern urban centers. The westward migration of urban laborers to the territories would limit the excessive concentration of workers, thereby preserving a constant, and high, wage rate. Furthermore, the accessibility of land guaranteed the option of leaving the wage labor system altogether in favor of becoming a prosperous farmer. In the absence of land, growth of the labor supply would exert downward pressure on wages and the avenues for advancement would diminish. It was precisely that belief in the possibility of escaping economic dependency that served to inhibit the formation of class identities and maintain the harmony of interests between capital and labor. Geographical mobility ensured the expectation of social mobility.

This credo led to the promotion by the 1850s of a specific homestead plan among Northern political adherents of the free labor ideology. Offering inexpensive—or even free—land in the territories to settlers seeking to flee urban poverty would assist them in achieving middle-class respectability and independence. They would raise families who would similarly value hard work. The evils of a permanent class of urban poor and a sharply demarcated class structure, as evident in Europe, could be avoided in the United States because free land gave everyone the chance for an economic alternative.

The Republican Party, founded in 1854, embraced the free labor ideology as its organizing principle. Republicans, including Abraham Lincoln, insisted that the North best exemplified a good society because of its adherence to the values promoted by the Founding Fathers. Lincoln often spoke publicly about the strength of the North's middle class, its economic egalitarianism, and the plentiful opportunities for achieving financial independence. Republican champions pointed to the rural landscape, dotted with small farms, as proof of the success of the free labor ideology.

Most importantly, proponents of free labor found it fundamentally incompatible with the Southern slave institution. Slavery appeared to deny every core belief inherent in the free labor ideology. Southern society, free labor adherents argued, denigrated work rather than honoring it. As a result, slaves lacked any incentive to work and were forcibly held in ignorance. Furthermore, poor whites, ensnared in a system that viewed labor with contempt, had no hope of raising their social status. The moral values of hard work, sobriety, and republican virtue were absent in the South; in a complete negation of Northern values, Southern whites glorified idleness, not labor. Where the North served as a beacon of progress, the South represented decadence and seemed to impede national advancement. With both sections stubbornly claiming their own moral superiority over the other and simultaneously requiring geographic expansion to ensure their own survival, ideological conflict over the proper use of available land became increasingly contentious.

Once the free labor ideology gained widespread credence in the North, permitting the creation of a political party premised on its tenets, the viability of the two-party system that had sustained compromise over slavery since the nation's founding finally collapsed. A fundamental prerequisite of democratic politics—that competing parties view one another as offering a legitimate political alternative—no longer held true within the United States. Republican politicians warned the public about the spreading influence of the South's "slavocracy" and that left unchecked, it would destroy republican values, which included free labor and free speech. The South was notorious for stifling freedom of speech and the press by preventing discussion of slavery. The continued political ascendancy of slaveholders, the Republicans argued, would be fatal to the economic, political, and civil liberties of Northern white workers, forcing them into a life of servile dependence such as Southern white workers endured. Republicans successfully mobilized Northern voters with these claims, and their rally behind the free labor ideology led to Lincoln's election in 1860.

Meanwhile Southern slaveholders alleged that a Northern abolitionist menace had emerged with the object of destroying the South's way of life. By making fundamental ideological claims in this way, the two sections found themselves unable to diffuse their competing beliefs through the democratic process. The two systems simply could not coexist under a single political umbrella, and the momentum of conflict could no longer be arrested.

Although Northern proponents of the free labor ideology denounced slavery and the slave institution, their antislavery stance rarely corresponded with sympathy for slaves or black people. Some advocates of free labor were also staunch abolitionists, but the widespread acceptance of the free labor creed among Northern whites went hand in hand with racist beliefs that America belonged only to white people. Nevertheless, the notion of "Free Soil, Free Labor, Free Men" pushed slavery into the forefront of the competing—and ultimately irreconcilable—visions of a good society that eventually rent North and South in the 1860s.

—MARCY S. SACKS

BIBLIOGRAPHY

Engs, Robert F., and Randall M. Miller, eds. *The Birth of the Grand Old Party: The Republicans' First Generation.* Philadelphia: University of Pennsylvania Press, 2002.

Foner, Eric. *Free Soil, Free Labor, Free Men: The Ideology of the Republican Party before the Civil War.* New York: Oxford University Press, 1970.

———. *Politics and Ideology in the Age of the Civil War.* New York: Oxford University Press, 1980.

Gienapp, William E. *The Origins of the Republican Party, 1852–1856.* New York: Oxford University Press, 1987.

Holt, Michael F. *The Political Crisis of the 1850s.* New York, Norton, 1978.

Messner, William F. *Freedmen and the Ideology of Free Labor: Louisiana, 1862–1865.* Lafayette: Center for Louisiana Studies, 1978.

Richardson, Heather Cox. *The Death of Reconstruction: Race, Labor, and Politics in the Post–Civil War North, 1865–1901.* Cambridge, Mass.: Harvard University Press, 2001.

———. *The Greatest Nation of the Earth: Republican Economic Policies during the Civil War.* Cambridge, Mass.: Harvard University Press, 1997.

Freeport Doctrine

During the Lincoln-Douglas debates of 1858, Abraham Lincoln posed a question to Stephen A. Douglas about the validity of the doctrine of popular sovereignty in light of the Supreme Court's decision in the case of *Dred Scott v. Sandford*. Douglas reaffirmed the legitimacy of popular sovereignty and his belief that the

Supreme Court ruling had little bearing on the issue, noting that slavery could not survive without a slave code, and under popular sovereignty the settlers could kill slavery simply by not protecting it. News of Douglas's pronouncement spread and angered Southerners. The Freeport Doctrine thus played a part in dividing Northern and Southern Democrats over slavery in the territories, generating animosities that would divide the party into sectional halves at the 1860 Charleston convention.

Two factors were important in Douglas's quest for reelection to the U.S. Senate in 1858. First, he had defied President Buchanan and important Southern leaders when he argued against congressional acceptance of the Lecompton Constitution; approval of that constitution would have made Kansas a slave state. Douglas had to defend his actions to the Illinois public while trying to soothe Southern anger at his rebellion. Second, the *Dred Scott* decision in March 1857 undermined Douglas's pet doctrine of popular sovereignty. The Supreme Court had declared that a territorial legislature could not ban slavery because slaves, as a form of property, were protected by the U. S. Constitution; only when a territory wrote its state constitution could residents decide for or against the peculiar institution. Douglas's version of popular sovereignty stated that territorial legislatures could pass laws for or against slavery at any time and that Congress should not interfere. The dilemma he faced was how to make his version of popular sovereignty compatible with the Court's ruling.

Lincoln faced different challenges in his quest to defeat Douglas's bid for reelection. Because Douglas had voted with Republicans to defeat the Lecompton Constitution, some easterners courted him and hoped he would join the party. Lincoln wanted to thwart that attempt by showing that Douglas had no antislavery inclinations at all. Second, Lincoln intended to prove that Douglas was actually proslavery, virtually an active conspirator in bringing about the nationalization of slavery. Lincoln saw the practice of slavery as a threat to individual freedom and representative government. His solution to the problem of slavery was a policy of no expansion; he thought—and believed the founders of the country thought—that restricting slavery to its current boundaries would eventually produce the institution's death. Lincoln feared that Douglas's popular sovereignty would keep slavery alive and enable it to move north. Therefore Lincoln had to prove in the debates that Douglas's doctrine was a means to transform the nation into a slaveholders' republic.

Lincoln's tactics were actually more convoluted. In two major speeches prior to the debate at Freeport, Douglas had already indicated that he had a response to the difficulties produced by the *Dred Scott* decision—and Lincoln was probably aware of them. Moreover, Lincoln had to be wary about his argument because Douglas had just split from President Buchanan over the Lecompton Constitution; if Lincoln pressed too strongly on these matters, he would make Douglas out to be freedom's champion, not its enemy.

At the first debate, at Ottawa, Douglas asked Lincoln a series of questions, trying to show that Lincoln had abolitionist leanings running counter to the

Republican Party platform. Lincoln seized this opening to ask Douglas questions at the second debate at Freeport, held on August 27, 1858. The second question Lincoln asked—he had four—was how the people of a territory could legally exclude slavery—in short, how Douglas could trumpet the doctrine of popular sovereignty as a means to deny slavery's expansion into a territory when the Supreme Court had determined that a territorial legislature could not do so. Douglas responded with what became known as the Freeport Doctrine: The Supreme Court makes no difference, for "the people have the lawful means to introduce it or exclude it as they please, for the reason that slavery cannot exist a day or an hour anywhere, unless it is supported by local police regulations" (Johannsen 1965, 88). In other words, if the territorial legislature did not pass laws that protected slaveholders in their property, then slavery could not exist.

Lincoln knew what Douglas's answer would be and did not return to it in subsequent debates. He probably asked it to remind people of the role of the Supreme Court in the slavery controversy. A legend grew up, started by Chicago newspaper editor Joseph Medill, that Lincoln purposely sought to eliminate Douglas as a presidential candidate by ruining him with the South and opening his own path to the Republican nomination. The story was made up. Lincoln was more interested in winning the Senate seat, and to do so he pressed Douglas on the morality of slavery and the possibility of a second *Dred Scott* decision that would nationalize slavery.

The Freeport Doctrine undoubtedly did Douglas no favors in his standing with Southern Democrats, but animosity toward him already had boiled over as a result of the Lecompton fight. Southerners, however, wanted to repudiate Douglas's version of popular sovereignty, and so by February 1859, Sen. Albert Gallatin Brown of Mississippi declared that to make the verdict of the Supreme Court in the *Dred Scott* case mean something, Congress needed to pass a federal slave code for the territories in which the federal government took up the duty of ensuring the sanctity of slave property in the territories; Congress should not leave it to territorial legislatures. In April 1860, both Jefferson Davis and Brown pressed resolutions containing a territorial slave code in the Senate. Southern radicals adopted the idea and pressed for adoption of the code in the platform at the Charleston Democratic National Convention. Northerners refused to accept the slave code provision and instead adopted a (pro-Douglas) popular sovereignty platform; that action drove Gulf state Southerners out of the party. This was the train of events involving the Freeport Doctrine that over time produced a divided Democratic Party in the election of 1860, enabling Abraham Lincoln to win the presidency.

—James L. Huston

BIBLIOGRAPHY

Cooper, William J., Jr. *Jefferson Davis, American.* New York: Vintage, 2000.

Fehrenbacher, Don E. *Prelude to Greatness: Lincoln in the 1850s.* Stanford: Stanford University Press, 1962.

_____. *The Dred Scott Case: Its Significance in American Law and Politics.* New York: Oxford University Press, 1978.

Freehling, William W. *The Road to Disunion, Vol. 2: Secessionists Triumphant, 1854–1861.* New York and Oxford: Oxford University Press, 2007.

Jaffa, Harry V. *Crisis of the House Divided: An Interpretation of the Issues in the Lincoln-Douglas Debates.* Garden City: Doubleday, 1959.

Johannsen, Robert W., ed. *The Lincoln-Douglas Debates.* Oxford and New York: Oxford University Press, 1965.

Zarefsky, David. *Lincoln, Douglas, and Slavery in the Crucible of Public Debate.* Chicago: University of Chicago Press, 1990.

Frémont, John C.

John Charles Frémont (1813–1890) was the illegitimate son of a French émigré, Jean Charles Fremon, and Anne Beverley Whiting Pryor, a Virginian who abandoned her aging husband to live with Fremon. Frémont (he changed his name after his father died) was raised in Charleston, South Carolina, and attended the College of Charleston from 1829 to 1831. He then worked as a mathematics teacher and a surveyor until 1838, when his South Carolina patron, Joel R. Poinsett, became secretary of war and commissioned Frémont as a second lieutenant in the U.S. Army Corps of Engineers. He was sent to help map and explore the West. While assigned to Washington, Frémont met seventeen-year-old Jessie Benton and over the objection of her father, Sen. Thomas Hart Benton, married her in 1841.

In the 1840s Frémont traveled in the West, mapped routes to the Pacific Coast, and published two books about his explorations. In February 1846 Frémont arrived in California with sixty armed men, but then left for Oregon. In May he returned and helped ignite the Bear Flag Revolt, which led to California's breaking away from Mexico, just as the Mexican War broke out. Conflicts with his military superiors led to Frémont's court martial and dismissal from the army. President Polk reinstated him, but then Frémont resigned. By 1849 Frémont was back in California, where he invested in land that would eventually make him wealthy and served a short time as one of California's first U.S. senators. In the Senate he emerged as a moderate opponent of slavery, but he left politics for more explorations of the Rockies. In 1856, as a charismatic and famous hero, he was the first presidential candidate of the Republican Party. The party did well, capturing eleven states and over 1.3 million votes, but James Buchanan, the Democrat, captured 1.8 million votes and won more states and thus the election. Frémont then went back to California and his gold and land interests until the Civil War began.

When the war began, Lincoln immediately appointed Frémont a major general, headquartered in St. Louis and in command of all troops in the West. The appointment was a disaster. Frémont was poorly organized and knew little about actual military command. His army was defeated at Wilson's Creek, Missouri, in August 1861, and as a result the Confederates seized control of most of southwest Missouri. On August 30, without consulting Lincoln or anyone else, Frémont declared martial law in Missouri and announced that all slaves owned by Confederate activists in that state were free. This order went well beyond the recently passed Confiscation Act and threatened Lincoln's policy of keeping the four loyal slave states in the Union. Lincoln immediately and unambiguously urged Frémont to withdraw his proclamation, pointing out that it undermined efforts to keep Kentucky in the Union: "I think there is great danger," he told Frémont, that "the confiscation of property, and liberating slaves of traitorous owners, will alarm our Southern Union friends, and turn them against us—perhaps ruin our rather fair prospect for Kentucky." Lincoln tactfully asked the headstrong general to "modify" his proclamation "on his own motion." Aware of the exaggerated egos of his generals, Lincoln noted, "This letter is written in a spirit of caution and not of censure."

While Lincoln waited for Frémont to act, letters poured in from Border State Unionists urging the president to directly countermand Frémont's order. One Kentucky Unionist told Lincoln, "There is not a day to lose in disavowing emancipation or Kentucky is gone over the mill dam." Lincoln told Sen. Orville Browning of Illinois that "to lose Kentucky is nearly...to lose the whole game." Lincoln incorrectly thought that Frémont would be politically savvy enough to withdraw the order. Instead, Frémont, who hoped to score points with the abolitionist wing of the Republican Party, embarrass Lincoln, and set himself up to be the Republican candidate in 1864, refused to comply with the request of his commander in chief. Frémont asked Lincoln to formally countermand the proclamation. This would allow Frémont later, in effect, to accuse the president of undermining emancipation. Lincoln "cheerfully" did so, ordering Frémont to modify the proclamation. Still playing politics, Frémont claimed that he never received the order but only read about it in the newspapers, and even after Lincoln issued it, Frémont continued to distribute his original order. Frémont's stubbornness and lack of political sense led to his dismissal by Lincoln on November 2, 1861. In Missouri Frémont showed valor, personally leading troops into battle and eventually chasing most of the Confederate forces out of the state, but this was not enough to save his command.

Popular with radicals and abolitionists, Frémont gained another command, in western Virginia, where he proved unable to cope with Stonewall Jackson's forces and tactics, even though he had numerical superiority. He subsequently lost command permanently. In the summer of 1864 a small group of radicals and disgruntled Republicans nominated Frémont for the presidency on an independent ticket, but he wisely withdrew in September. He was as incompetent as a politician as he had been as a general, and there were too many rumors that hinted at a financial scandal. After the war he was involved in various railroad ventures that failed. He served three years as the governor of the Arizona Territory but resigned under a taint of corruption. Frémont died nearly penniless, in New York City in 1890.

See also *Cleveland Convention, 1864*

—PAUL FINKELMAN

BIBLIOGRAPHY

Gienapp, William E. *Abraham Lincoln and Civil War America: A Biography.* New York: Oxford University Press, 2002.

Jackson, Donald, and Mary Lee Spence, eds. *The Expeditions of John Charles Frémont.* Champaign: University of Illinois Press, 1970–1984.

Nevins, Allan. *Frémont: Pathmarker of the West.* New York: Longmans, Green,1955.

Garrison, William Lloyd

William Lloyd Garrison (1805–1879) was the best known and most important white abolitionist in the antebellum United States. He was the editor of the *Liberator* and one of the founders of the American Anti-Slavery Society, the most radical abolitionist organization in the nation. In addition to his lifelong commitment to ending slavery, he advocated numerous other reforms, including women's rights, abolition of the death penalty, complete racial equality, and pacifism. He took extreme positions and advocated radical, but peaceful, apolitical tactics to reach his goals. He considered the Constitution a "covenant with death" and an "agreement in Hell" because of its many proslavery provisions. When the Fugitive Slave Law passed, he publicly burned a copy of it, which brought cheers from a large crowd, and followed that by burning of a copy of the Constitution, which offended many in his audience. But Garrison was undaunted by lack of popular support. For most of his public career, he refused to vote or participate in politics and urged his followers to do likewise. He infuriated many Northerners when he persistently argued that the North should secede from the nation, adopting the slogan "No Union with Slaveholders." He only abandoned that position after 1861, when the South left the Union and it became obvious that civil war would doubtless destroy slavery.

Garrison was raised in poverty in Newburyport, Massachusetts, in a precarious household. His father, Abijah, was a seaman, but his alcoholism often left the family teetering on the edge of destitution. Abijah abandoned the family when Garrison was thirteen. That year William Lloyd, who had become a devout Baptist like his mother, Frances "Fanny" Lloyd Garrison, was apprenticed to the owner of the *Newburyport Herald*. He would spend the rest of his working days in the printing and newspaper business. After numerous failed attempts to start his own paper, Garrison joined Benjamin Lundy, the publisher of the nation's only significant antislavery paper, which had the unwieldy name *The Genius of Universal Emancipation* and was published in Baltimore. Garrison's vitriolic moralism led him to condemn a shipowner as a "murderer" for participating in the interstate slave trade. The merchant had Garrison prosecuted for libel, and the young editor spent seven weeks in a Baltimore jail. He then headed for Massachusetts where, in January 1831, he began publishing the *Liberator,* the most influential abolitionist paper in the nation. Although its circulation was

William Lloyd Garrison circa 1860. Garrison, editor of the *Liberator* and one of the founders of the American Anti-Slavery Society, was the best-known white abolitionist in antebellum America and an early patron of Frederick Douglass. A critic of Lincoln's measured actions to end slavery, Garrison became a supporter of the president after the Preliminary Emancipation Proclamation.

Source: The Granger Collection, New York City

small, the paper's uncompromising hostility to slavery and persistent call for immediate abolition gave it a prominent presence among American reformers. For Southerners and their Northern allies, Garrison became the living embodiment of opposition to slavery. During his debates with Lincoln, Sen. Stephen A. Douglas accused Lincoln of being an advocate of as "bold and radical abolitionism as ever...Garrison enunciated," although that did not in fact represent Lincoln's views. For Douglas it made good political sense, in conservative Illinois, to accuse Lincoln of being aligned with Garrison.

Garrison and his followers were uncompromising opponents of slavery and racism. Most practiced what they preached. Garrison hired blacks to work on the *Liberator*. His chief typesetter—a skilled and important profession—was William C. Nell, one of the nation's first blacks to publish work on African American history. When traveling with blacks on segregated trains, Garrison insisted on sitting in the cars reserved for blacks, while he publicly denounced segregation and agitated to end it. Garrison was the first activist to hire blacks and women as speakers. He was an early patron of Frederick Douglass and helped to launch his career as a speaker and writer.

Garrison advocated "moral suasion" as a way to end slavery. The refusal of Garrison and his follower to engage in politics infuriated more political abolitionists, such as Salmon P. Chase, who worked with the Liberty Party and the Free Soil Party before becoming a Republican and ultimately serving in Lincoln's cabinet and then as Chief Justice of the United States. Although not participating in politics, Garrisonians always commented on politics, attacking politicians and parties whenever they supported slavery in any way. After his decision in *Prigg v. Pennsylvania* (1842) upholding the constitutionality of the Fugitive Slave Law of 1793, the *Liberator* referred to Justice Joseph Story as the "slave-catcher-in-chief" for New England.

Garrison's attitude to politics is illustrated by the response of his followers to Lincoln's presidential candidacy. In 1847 Lincoln had represented a slave owner in his attempt to recover a slave. Lincoln was unsuccessful in the litigation, known as the Matson fugitive slave case. When Lincoln ran for president, Garrison's most brilliant ally, Wendell Phillips, called Lincoln "that slave hound from Illinois." Garrisonians mistrusted Lincoln, in part because he was not as morally pure as they were and in part because he was an unpolished, self-educated hick from the frontier, whereas many of Garrison's followers were college-educated intellectuals. Wendell Phillips, for example, was a Boston Brahmin with a Harvard degree. Thus Phillips, speaking for the Garrisonians, condemned Lincoln as "a first-rate second-rate man....A mere convenience waiting like any other broomstick to be used."

When the slave states began to secede Garrison at first responded with a diffident attitude. He had long called for the North to leave the Union, so having the South do so would accomplish the same thing. Also, as a pacifist and a nonresistant, Garrison did not want to support a war, especially since it did not appear to be a war against slavery. Shortly after the war began, however, Garrisonians moved to support the effort, while advocating for emancipation and the use of black troops. By the end of April 1861 Garrison was arguing that it was not really a war "to defend the 'stars and stripes,'" but was "really a struggle between freedom and slavery." But he was frustrated by Lincoln's refusal to move quickly against slavery. He claimed that Lincoln was "unwittingly helping to prolong the war" by not moving against slavery, and wrote, "If he *is* 6 feet 4 inches high, he is only a dwarf in mind." In 1862 he denounced Lincoln in the *Liberator* for failing to "put an end to slavery."

The Preliminary Emancipation Proclamation moved Garrison into Lincoln's camp—it was "certainly matter for great rejoicing," but it was clearly not strong enough for Garrison because it left slavery alone in the Border States. Still, despite his carping Garrison understood that after thirty years of fighting slavery and the national government, he now had the national government on his side. Garrison no longer advocated disunion and he publicly defended Lincoln and his policies even when some of his colleagues, including Wendell Phillips, were more critical of Lincoln for his slow pace toward emancipation.

As Lincoln moved to end slavery, Phillips claimed that if the president had grown it was "because we have watered him." This seems unlikely. But the three decades that Garrison and his followers spent agitating for an end to slavery did have an impact on the changes that the war brought. Northerners were clearly more prepared for an end to slavery because they had heard for years how deeply immoral the system was. By the end of the war the once-radical Garrison had been transformed into a respected "prophet" who had advocated emancipation long before it was politically acceptable. In June 1864 Garrison had a private meeting with Lincoln in the White House, and it thrilled him. In January 1865 Garrison sent Lincoln a painting titled *Watch Night—or, Waiting for the Hour,* portraying blacks on the evening of December 31, 1862, waiting for the next day when Lincoln would sign the final Emancipation Proclamation. By this time Garrison, like Frederick Douglass and many other abolitionists, had come to respect and admire Lincoln, even if they did not always agree with his actions. With the adoption of the Thirteenth Amendment, Garrison retired from public life.

See also *Abolitionism; Douglass, Frederick; Whittier, John Greenleaf*

—PAUL FINKELMAN

BIBLIOGRAPHY

Mayer, Henry. *All on Fire: William Lloyd Garrison and the Abolition of Slavery.* New York: St. Martin's, 1998.

Merrill, Walter. *Against Wind and Tide: A Biography of William Lloyd Garrison.* Cambridge, Mass.: Harvard University Press, 1963.

Stewart, James Brewer. *William Lloyd Garrison and the Challenge of Emancipation.* Arlington Heights, Ill.: Harlan Davidson, 1992.

Thomas, John L. *The Liberator, William Lloyd Garrison: A Biography.* Boston: Little, Brown, 1963.

General War Order Number One

Issued January 27, 1862, President Abraham Lincoln's General War Order Number One set February 22, George Washington's birthday, as the date for a general movement of land and naval forces under his command. The order is important for what it reveals about Lincoln as commander in chief and how he wished to fight the Civil War.

When war broke out in 1861, Lincoln realized that he needed to learn a great deal about combat quickly. His only military experience came during the Black Hawk War of 1832 and was so scant that he mocked it himself on the campaign trail. In summer 1861 he set about learning as much as he could about conducting a war. Following the Union defeat at Bull Run in July, Lincoln called for 500,000 volunteers and brought General George B. McClellan to Washington to take command of and train the eastern armies. On November 1, Lincoln relieved General Winfield Scott of command and named McClellan general in chief of all Union forces.

Lincoln was one of the few politicians to recognize that patience was required, that McClellan needed time to train and equip his army before moving south into battle. At the same time, however, Lincoln was impatient that the war be concluded as swiftly and decisively as possible. As fall 1861 wore on with no sign of movement from McClellan, Lincoln became less patient and queried frequently when McClellan would be ready to commence offensive operations. The president's relationship with his general was souring because of Lincoln's impatience and McClellan's characteristic caution. On January 15, 1862, McClellan was summoned to explain his inactivity before the congressional Joint Committee on the Conduct of the War, but McClellan, suspicious of politicians generally and Republicans specifically, withheld the details of the plan he was working on, the Peninsula Campaign.

McClellan was only the most visibly inert of the Union generals; Lincoln was also perplexed by the failure of units in the Gulf of Mexico to advance on and seize the mouth of the Mississippi River. By late January, his patience exhausted, Lincoln issued General War Order Number One, directing that the Union forces in Virginia, the Army of the Potomac, the Army of Western Virginia, and the units stationed near Fortress Monroe, in Hampton, were to begin a general movement against rebel forces by February 22. Also included in the order were the units then in Kentucky, the army and riparian forces stationed at Cairo, Illinois, and naval forces in the Gulf of Mexico. The order was Lincoln's first direct attempt to order his general in chief into action.

In contrast to McClellan, Lincoln's tendency was to be highly aggressive in conducting the war. This was partially a product of his temperament and characteristic disdain for procrastination; when faced with an obstacle, Lincoln preferred to meet it head-on, rather than try to avoid it or deal with it at a later time. Lincoln had understood the need to train and prepare for battle at the beginning of the war, but by this time he was ready for action. This tendency expressed itself in early 1862 in his repeated suggestions that McClellan march directly against the Southern forces concentrated around Manassas Junction.

The order also shows Lincoln starting to combine his natural inclination toward conducting the war aggressively with the military theory he was learning. Lincoln recognized that each side possessed a distinct advantage that the opponent would need to overcome: The North had an overwhelming advantage in manpower and armament, and the South fought along interior lines. Southern forces thus could be moved from place to place rapidly to meet consecutive threats from Union armies. To capitalize on the Union's numerical advantage, therefore, Northern armies would have to attack multiple points simultaneously, forcing the Confederates to react to the threats in one region by transferring units from another. A succession of coordinated efforts would, Lincoln believed, overcome the Confederates' interior lines and weaken their armies sufficiently that Union armies could begin to overwhelm them, beginning at their weakest points.

Critics note that General War Order Number One ignored factors beyond the control of the field commanders, such as weather, roads, readiness, logistics, and the disposition and strength of Confederate forces, but such criticisms fail to take account of two elements of Lincoln's thought process. First, as he wrote to McClellan later in 1862, factors inhibiting Union army movement, such as weather and road condition, worked equally to the disadvantage of Confederate forces and thus should be overcome rather than used as an excuse for inactivity. Second, Lincoln's order did not put forward a specific plan of battle but simply ordered his commanders into action; it would be up to them to devise the plans of attack.

The order did achieve one immediate result, once it was supplemented with Lincoln's Special Order Number One, issued January 31, which specifically directed McClellan to move against the Confederate army at Manassas. McClellan responded to the order with a twenty-two-page letter to secretary of war Edwin M. Stanton and, when questioned by Lincoln, finally divulged the details of his Peninsula Campaign. Lincoln was skeptical of the plan's success but relented, and preparations for the attack went forward.

General War Order Number One did not prompt a major, coordinated Union offensive, but it did set several attacks in motion. More importantly, the order reveals how Lincoln approached the Civil War as commander in chief. Recognizing the Union's principal advantage, Lincoln sought ways to capitalize on his armies' overwhelming numerical superiority by bringing superior numbers to bear on several fronts simultaneously. Lincoln believed that his armies should focus primarily on destroying the rebel armies rather than on what the enemy could do to him.

—Anthony Santoro

BIBLIOGRAPHY

Adams, Michael C. *Fighting for Defeat: Union Military Failures in the East, 1861–1865.* Lincoln: University of Nebraska Press, 1992.

Donald, David Herbert. *Lincoln.* London: Jonathan Cape, 1995.

Hattaway, Herman, and Archer Jones. *How the North Won: A Military History of the Civil War.* Urbana: University of Illinois Press, 1983.

Lincoln, Abraham. "General War Order No. 1." In *The Collected Works of Abraham Lincoln.* 8 vols. Edited by Roy P. Basler. Vol. 5, 111–112. New Brunswick, N.J.: Rutgers University Press, 1953.

———. "Letter to George B. McClellan," October 13, 1862. In *The Collected Works of Abraham Lincoln.* Edited by Basler. Vol. 5, 460–462.

Neely, Mark J., Jr. *The Last Best Hope of Earth: Abraham Lincoln and the Promise of America.* Cambridge, Mass.: Harvard University Press, 1993.

German Americans, Lincoln and

The 1850s in the United States are commonly remembered as a time of heated controversy over the future of Southern slavery and its westward expansion. But they were also a period of mass immigration. Parallel to the escalating sectional conflict, immigration from Europe between 1840 and 1860 soared to record numbers, with more than four million people entering the country, aggravating the debates over race, nationality, and citizenship in the young republic. About one-third of the newcomers came from the German states. German-speaking people made up the second-largest immigrant group of the time, outnumbered only by the Irish. German immigrants spread out more evenly across the continent than the Irish and were particularly attracted to the extensive farmlands and burgeoning communities of the Midwest. New England and the plantation South were largely avoided.

Highly diverse along regional, occupational, generational, and religious lines, German Americans never constituted a monolithic bloc in antebellum society. Many disagreed strongly over a range of social and political issues, among them the question of how to retain ethnic identities in a country demanding nothing less than total assimilation. The arrival of the "Forty-Eighters," refugees from the failed European revolutions of 1848–1849, augmented intraethnic divisions. Their espousal of radical causes such as socialism, opposition to established religion, and the abolition of slavery not only set them apart from their conservative countrymen but also made them unruly elements in the eyes of nativist Americans.

Abraham Lincoln, forthright in his denunciation of the antiforeign Know-Nothings, had no such misgivings. His image of Germans as a law-abiding, industrious people dovetailed neatly with his ideal of a free-labor republic where every individual could escape permanent dependency and climb up the social ladder through hard work. Lincoln was also quick to realize that many German Americans, the recent Forty-Eighter arrivals in particular, shared his displeasure with the Kansas-Nebraska Act of 1854. Because the act theoretically opened the two territories to the introduction of slave labor, they believed that it seriously undermined the promise of free homesteads for white settlers in the West. Eager to mobilize this ethnic group for the nascent Republican Party, Lincoln established close ties to Illinois's liberal German American leadership. He won the advice and trust of the Belleville lawyer and immigrant politician Gustav Körner and benefited from the support of two illustrious Forty-Eighter exiles, Friedrich Hecker and Dr. Ernst Schmidt. During the presidential campaign of 1860, Lincoln secretly purchased the *Illinois Staats-Anzeiger,* Springfield's German-language newspaper, in the hope of swaying German American public opinion in his home state. Contrary to the "myth of 1860," however, which claims that securing the German vote was central to Lincoln's triumph at the polls, the Republicans never enjoyed the backing of the entire German American constituency. Although the number of Germans voting Republican increased among Northern urban workingmen, political and religious conservatism stayed a powerful force in rural areas, where German immigrants, Catholics for the most part, continued to go with the Democratic Party.

Lincoln's tenuous relationship with the German Americans persisted throughout the Civil War, although German immigrants from the Northern states initially flocked en masse to the Union colors. Slavery and secession were generally denounced, but the far greater motivation for these men to enlist was to refute nativist accusations and prove themselves worthy citizens of the republic. To ensure German American support for the Northern war effort, the Lincoln administration early on endorsed the formation of ethnic regiments. Over time, twelve German immigrants were promoted to the rank of general officers, among them the Forty-Eighters Franz Sigel, August Willich, Ludwig Blenker, and Carl Schurz, whom Lincoln in 1861 also sent as U.S. minister to Spain.

Such politically motivated commissions notwithstanding, German American support for the president remained volatile and was put to the test on several occasions. Lincoln's removal of General John C. Frémont, an outspoken friend of the immigrant and an enemy of slavery, in November 1861 angered liberal and radical German immigrant factions across the North. Cries of indignation grew even louder after Franz Sigel, the popular German American war hero, was relieved from command of the Army of the Potomac's XI Corps under mysterious circumstances. Lincoln, partly responding to public pressure from immigrant politicians and journalists, had Sigel reinstated as head of the new Department of West Virginia. Radical German American spokesmen, however, were unimpressed and became increasingly critical of the president's moderate antislavery policies, as well as his allegedly soft handling of Confederate "rebels and traitors." Some ultimately broke with the party in power and participated in the 1864 Cleveland Convention organized by Radical Republicans, abolitionists, and War Democrats, where Frémont was nominated for the presidency on a third-party ticket. That Schurz and other German American leaders loyal to the president stumped tirelessly for his reelection helped Lincoln survive this crisis.

The military victories of the last war months reconciled most German American dissenters with the president but without bridging all the differences. Nor did the news of Lincoln's assassination in April 1865 and his subsequent apotheosis transform him into a statesman unanimously revered in the German immigrant community. Because there was no single German America, German American opinions about Lincoln's presidency differed widely. Unlike his liberal followers, conservatives dreaded black emancipation and the wartime expansion of federal authority. Radicals, on the other hand, saw their hopes betrayed that Lincoln would set out forcefully to remodel the country in accordance with their democratic ideals. Political disagreements, ethnic prejudices, and fears of nativism erected high barriers, which not only impinged on Lincoln's relationship with a heterogeneous German American populace but complicated interactions between native-born and ethnic citizens in Civil War America at large.

—Mischa Honeck

BIBLIOGRAPHY

Bergquist, James M. "The Forty-Eighters: Catalysts of German-American Politics." In *The German-American Encounter: Conflict and Cooperation between Two Cultures, 1800–2000,* edited by Frank Trommler and Elliott Shore, 22–36. New York: Berghahn, 2001.

Donald, David Herbert. *Lincoln.* New York: Simon and Schuster, 1995.

Levine, Bruce. *The Spirit of 1848: German Immigrants, Labor Conflict, and the Coming of the Civil War.* Urbana: University of Illinois Press, 1992.

Öfele, Martin W. *True Sons of the Republic: European Immigrants in the Union Army.* Westport, Conn.: Praeger, 2008.

Gettysburg, Battle of

The Battle of Gettysburg, fought July 1–3, 1863, pitted General Robert E. Lee's Confederate Army of Northern Virginia against Major General George G. Meade's Union Army of the Potomac in the Civil War's most costly clash of arms on free soil.

In late June, with his forces spread through south-central Pennsylvania from the Maryland border to the Susquehanna River near Harrisburg, Lee ordered his forces to concentrate near Gettysburg. On July 1 the Confederate army clashed with Union troops north and west of Gettysburg, finally forcing them to retreat to the defensible hills and ridges south of the town. On July 2, the bloodiest of the battle's three days, Lee believed he had achieved a partial victory after assaults against both flanks of Meade's fishhook-shaped line. Intending to exploit the previous day's success, Lee initially planned on July 3 to continue his attacks against the Union flanks. A sustained firefight, starting at first light, on Meade's right flank, however, caused Lee to reconsider, and he determined instead to assault the Union center. The resulting Confederate attack—best known as "Pickett's charge"—ended in bloody repulse. On July 4, Lee began his withdrawal to Virginia. Confederate casualties topped 30,000. Even in victory, Meade's army suffered at least 23,000 casualties, including the loss of several senior generals.

In Washington, President Lincoln watched for news of the military events in Pennsylvania with unease. While news from far-off Vicksburg seemed to presage a decisive Union victory in the western theater, the advance of Lee's army onto free soil created a significant political crisis in the East. Since the Union army's crushing defeat at Chancellorsville in May, Republican leaders increasingly worried that continued military failure in the eastern theater might bode ill for the party's candidates in upcoming state elections. In Pennsylvania, in particular, Governor Andrew Gregg Curtin faced a tough contest for reelection. In the 1862 midterm elections, a Democratic resurgence had ousted significant numbers of the Keystone State's Republican officeholders. Worse, Curtin faced increasingly uncertain health, and he could not mend a rift in a splintered Pennsylvania

Republican party, in which one faction backed him but the other allied with his political nemesis, former secretary of war Simon Cameron. But Curtin ranked near the top of Lincoln's most devoted and energetic allies, and he had hosted the Loyal Governors Conference in Altoona in the fall of 1862 to offer tangible political support for the Emancipation Proclamation. Lincoln simply could not lose Curtin. Thus, even beyond the military necessity of repulsing the Confederate army, Lincoln approved several specific War Department initiatives designed both to defend Pennsylvania and to enhance Curtin's political profile.

On June 9, 1863, Lincoln approved the creation of two new military districts. As commander of the Department of the Monongahela, Brigadier General William H. T. Brooks prepared to defend western Pennsylvania. Major General Darius N. Couch took command of the Department of the Susquehanna to establish the state's first line of defense in central and eastern Pennsylvania. Lincoln also approved the deployment of the New York and New Jersey militias to serve alongside Pennsylvania's own state troops. In managing the deployment and logistical needs of these forces, Curtin held the political spotlight, often communicating directly with his fellow governors. He also forwarded a steady stream of requisitions and information directly to Lincoln, often ignoring secretary of war Edwin M. Stanton, with whom he often clashed. Indeed, much of the governor's correspondence to Lincoln appeared in newspapers throughout the North, spotlighting Curtin's active role defending his home state. In the end, Curtin's outstanding service in a time of severe crisis—and Lincoln's unobtrusive assistance—helped to secure his reelection. In November, Curtin personally hosted Lincoln in Gettysburg for the dedication of the new national cemetery.

For Lincoln, the Battle of Gettysburg also exacerbated an especially nagging military concern. By mid-1863, Lincoln's strategic vision differed significantly from that of many of his senior generals. Whereas military men continued to embrace Jominian concepts of military strategy taught at West Point, Lincoln viewed the path to victory differently. After two years of failed efforts to capture Richmond—Jomini had stressed the importance of capturing or controlling such geographical "strategic points"—Lincoln made clear to Major General Joseph Hooker as early as January 1863 that the Army of the Potomac's primary objective was destroying Lee's army, not capturing Richmond. Six weeks after Lee smashed the Army of the Potomac at Chancellorsville in May, Lincoln replaced Hooker—just three days before the opening shots at Gettysburg—with General Meade. Lincoln knew little of General Meade's capacity, and the worried president haunted the telegraph office for news from Pennsylvania.

By sundown on July 3, Lincoln's confidence in Meade and his elation at Lee's repulse seemed unbounded. On July 4 the president congratulated the Army of the Potomac for covering itself with "the highest honor" and offered "profoundest gratitude" to God for the victory. He also saluted Meade's generalship, quickly approving his promotion to brigadier general in the regular U.S. Army, effective July 3.

Lincoln's joy quickly evaporated, however. In his own congratulatory message, General Meade had saluted his soldiers' hard work and encouraged them to "drive from our soil every vestige of the presence of the invader." Lincoln immediately took sharp exception to Meade's phraseology, noting to General in Chief Henry W. Halleck on July 6 that the use of the words "the invader" essentially acknowledged Confederate independence.

Worse, a cautious pursuit of Lee left the president feeling "a good deal dissatisfied." On July 6 Lincoln fumed at a message from a Union general that reported the passage of Confederate wounded across the Potomac "without saying why he does not stop it, or even intimating a thought that it should be stopped." On July 7 Meade had halted his own pursuit, unclear about Lee's intentions. That same day, a frustrated Lincoln wrote Halleck that if Meade moved quickly to destroy Lee in Maryland, "the rebellion will be over." Halleck sent the president's message to Meade, who bristled at the implied rebuke but replied on July 8, "Be assured I most earnestly desire to try the fortunes of war with the enemy on this side of the river, hoping, through Providence and the bravery of the men to settle the question." Nonetheless, he wanted Halleck—and Lincoln—to appreciate his army's exhausted condition and the likelihood of a stout defense by Lee. Meade possessed no "desire to imitate [Lee's] example at Gettysburg and assault a position when the chances are so greatly against success," and wished "to moderate in advance the expectations of those who, in ignorance of the difficulties to be encountered, may expect too much."

When Lee completed his withdrawal across the Potomac on July 14, without significant opposition, Lincoln was distraught. Lee's escape "created great dissatisfaction" in Lincoln's mind, Halleck advised Meade and encouraged him to launch "an active and energetic pursuit" immediately to "remove the impression that it has not been sufficiently active heretofore." Stung by presidential censure he deemed wholly unfair, Meade asked to be relieved of command. Halleck convinced him to withdraw his request, however, and within the month Lincoln acknowledged that Meade had done his full duty. In a letter to Major General Oliver O. Howard on July 23, Lincoln admitted he had felt deep frustration that "General Meade and his noble army had expended all the skill and toil and blood up to the ripe harvest, and then let the crop go to waste." He acknowledged further, "I had always believed—making my belief a hobby possibly—that the main rebel army going north of the Potomac could never return, if well attended to." Now, however, he felt "profoundly grateful for what was done, without criticism for what was not done," and declared Meade "a brave and skillful officer and a true man."

In March 1864, however, the Joint Committee on the Conduct of the War opened hearings on military decision making in the Pennsylvania campaign, essentially a referendum on Meade's leadership. Most who testified were friends of deposed General Hooker or senior officers who held grudges against Meade. The most damning allegations accused Meade of planning to retreat back into Maryland on July 2, rather than standing and fighting at Gettysburg. Meade refuted all charges, and the committee saw no need for further action. Still, Meade wanted those who testified against him to answer for what he considered their libelous claims, and he stepped outside the formal chain of command to ask Lincoln to approve the calling of a military Court of Inquiry to clear his name and, perhaps, to prefer charges against some of his accusers. Lincoln, however, denied Meade's request, thanking him for his "good services" and advising him "that it is much better that you be engaged in trying to do more" in 1864 than become diverted by proceedings concerning 1863. With the Overland Campaign about to begin, Lincoln understood when and how to make his most necessary senior officers—even the victor of Gettysburg—understand their duty.

See also *Gettysburg Address*

—CAROL REARDON

BIBLIOGRAPHY

Coddington, Edwin B. *The Gettysburg Campaign: A Study in Command.* New York: Scribner's, 1968.

Hyde, Bill, ed. *The Union Generals Speak: The Meade Hearings on the Battle of Gettysburg.* Baton Rouge: Louisiana State University Press, 2003.

Meade, George Gordon, Jr., ed. *The Life and Letters of George Gordon Meade, Major-General United States Army.* 2 vols. New York: Scribner's, 1913.

Sears, Stephen. *Gettysburg.* New York: Houghton Mifflin, 2003.

Gettysburg Address

Lincoln delivered what would become his most famous speech on November 19, 1863, at the dedication of a cemetery in Gettysburg, Pennsylvania, for thousands of soldiers who had been killed in battle there four months earlier. Today the address ranks among the most hallowed texts in the political culture of the United States, regarded as an indispensable expression of a national creed. Countless Americans memorized it as schoolchildren. Twenty-five million annual visitors to the Lincoln Memorial in Washington, D.C., see the speech etched into a high marble wall. Citizens of nations from Hungary to China have invoked Lincoln's words in protest against dictatorship.

The Gettysburg Address has become the subject of considerable lore: that Lincoln was not even the featured speaker at the ceremony (true), that he hastily composed the speech on the back of an envelope (false), that the speech's brevity left photographers no time to capture an image of the president as he spoke (true), that Lincoln disparaged his own remarks as soon as he left the stage (uncertain). A century and a half of extensive scholarly attention—by historians, rhetoricians, and political theorists, among others—has resolved many questions about the speech, but its sparing text continues to generate discussion about critical issues in American history and politics.

The battle fought at Gettysburg between July 1 and July 3, 1863, represented a military turning point in the Civil War, as U.S. forces repelled the Confederate army's deepest advance into Northern territory. On July 4, the strategically crucial port of Vicksburg, Mississippi, fell to General Ulysses S. Grant after a weeks-long siege, shifting control of the Mississippi River to the United States and severing Confederate territory in two. This fortuitous sequence of military successes portended a quick end to the war, but within two weeks the outlook had dimmed. To Lincoln's frustration, General George G. Meade neglected to reengage General Robert E. Lee's weakened army as it retreated from Gettysburg. The politics of war had become more complicated, too. Opposition to Lincoln's Emancipation Proclamation and the Conscription Act of March 1863 erupted in the New York draft riots of July 13 to July 16, in which eleven black men were lynched on the streets of Manhattan. By autumn, victory no longer seemed imminent, nor was popular support for the war as fervent as in early July. In the ceremony at Gettysburg, Lincoln detected an opportunity to fortify political will behind the war effort and to articulate the war's purpose.

So massive was the carnage at Gettysburg that many soldiers had been buried hastily in poorly marked graves; under the authority of the Commonwealth of Pennsylvania, a Gettysburg Cemetery Commission undertook to re-inter fallen soldiers and plan a ceremony of dedication. As their keynote speaker, the organizers invited Edward Everett, formerly a U.S. senator, secretary of state, and president of Harvard University, and one of the country's most respected orators. They later invited Lincoln to offer "a few appropriate remarks." Though his son Tad lay sick on the morning of November 18, Lincoln embarked by train for Pennsylvania, carrying a draft of his remarks written on White House stationery.

The next day, following Everett's two-hour speech, Lincoln took about three minutes to deliver his address of fewer than three hundred words. In keeping with a classical tradition exemplified by the funeral oration of Pericles, the speech honors the dead, interprets their deaths as a noble sacrifice to a just cause, and enlists the survivors' continued commitment to that cause. Like a gentle jeremiad (the Puritan sermon that is English-speaking North America's first indigenous rhetorical form), the Gettysburg Address deprecates its listeners and then charts for them a path to greater worthiness. In a rhythmic string of negative statements Lincoln avers, "In a larger sense, we can not dedicate—we can not consecrate—we can not hallow—this ground. The brave men, living and dead, who struggled here, have consecrated it, far above our poor power to add or detract." No sooner does Lincoln so belittle himself and his audience—his listeners on the field at Gettysburg and the tens of thousands of readers he would reach in newspapers the next day—than he calls on them to fulfill a grand purpose: "It is rather for us to be here dedicated to the great task remaining before us—that from these honored dead we take increased devotion to that cause for which they gave the last full measure of devotion." The same political community that has only a "poor power" to honor Gettysburg's heroes possesses in Lincoln's final sentence the awesome capacity to "resolve" that "this nation, under God, shall have a new birth of freedom." From weakness comes strength, and from death on the battlefield a national rebirth.

Within a form that he derives from ancient Greek and colonial American traditions, Lincoln asserts a distinctly untraditional, even controversial account of American history and politics. Today's readers of the speech easily can neglect to recognize its almost revolutionary content, for many of Lincoln's key phrases have become axiomatic, the raw material of American political discourse. But not all of Lincoln's contemporaries agreed with his characterization of the cause for which he sought the nation's "increased devotion." In the speech, Lincoln notably forbears from any direct reference to the Confederacy, slavery, or political conflicts in the North. Nevertheless, the Gettysburg Address interprets the Civil War as a struggle for equality—not, as many at the time would have insisted, for the restoration of the Union alone.

Lincoln had begun to formulate the content of the address—his first prepared speech since his inauguration in 1861—as early as July 7, 1863, when he offered an extemporaneous response to a crowd outside the White House celebrating the Gettysburg and Vicksburg victories: "How long ago is it?—eighty odd years—since on the Fourth of July for the first time in the history of the world a nation by its representatives, assembled and declared as a self-evident truth that 'all men are created equal.'" At Gettysburg in November, Lincoln rendered "eighty odd years" more precisely as "four score and seven years," but his thesis remained the same: the United States traces its origin to the signing of the Declaration of Independence on July 4, 1776—not, as his Democratic opponents frequently argued, to the crafting of the Constitution in 1787—and the declaration's assertion of human equality forms the nation's guiding principle. Amid fractious debates over slavery, many Americans regarded the Declaration of Independence more dubiously than they do today; in 1854, one Democratic senator called the proposition that all men are created equal a "self-evident lie." Lincoln's controversial focus on equality as a war goal did not escape notice; opposition newspapers complained that he dishonored the buried soldiers by misstating the cause for which they died.

By placing language from the Declaration of Independence at the head of the Gettysburg Address, Lincoln crowned a political campaign that he had waged throughout the late 1850s. In speeches against the Kansas-Nebraska Act of 1854 and in his 1858 debates with Stephen Douglas, Lincoln opposed the extension of slavery into western territories with repeated appeals to Thomas Jefferson's assertion of universal equality. In 1863 the same appeal tacitly sought to expand support for the Emancipation Proclamation—a limited measure framed as a matter of military necessity—into a broader commitment to the abolition of slavery, which would begin to take shape a month later when the Thirteenth Amendment to the Constitution first was introduced in Congress. By characterizing equality not as a "self-evident truth" but rather as a "proposition" whose validity the war was "testing," Lincoln turned human equality from a supposed *fait accompli* into the moral purpose of the war—and of the nation. The Declaration of Independence arguably holds its sanctified place in American consciousness today because of the Gettysburg Address, and perhaps because of the Gettysburg Address, "All men are created equal" is the best-known line in that document.

See also *Cooper Union Address; Gettysburg, Battle of; House Divided Speech; Rhetoric in Lincoln's Public Speeches*

—CHRISTOPHER HAGER

BIBLIOGRAPHY

Blight, David. *Race and Reunion: The Civil War in American Memory.* Cambridge, Mass.: Harvard University Press, 2001. See esp. pages 12–15.

Boritt, Gabor. *The Gettysburg Gospel: The Lincoln Speech That Nobody Knows.* New York: Simon and Schuster, 2006.

Holzer, Harold. "Lincoln's 'Flat Failure': The Gettysburg Myth Revisited." Chap. 10 in *Lincoln Seen and Heard.* Lawrence: University Press of Kansas, 2000.

Jaffa, Harry V. "The Declaration of Independence, the Gettysburg Address, and the Historians." Chap. 2 in *A New Birth of Freedom: Abraham Lincoln and the Coming of the Civil War.* Lanham, Md.: Rowman and Littlefield, 2000.

McPherson, James. *Abraham Lincoln and the Second American Revolution.* New York: Oxford University Press, 1990. See esp. pages 110–112.

Mearns, David C., and Lloyd A. Dunlap, eds. *Long Remembered: Facsimiles of the Five Versions of the Gettysburg Address in the Handwriting of Abraham Lincoln.* Washington, D.C.: Library of Congress, 1963. See also www.loc.gov/exhibits/gadd/.

Nevins, Allan. *Lincoln and the Gettysburg Address: Commemorative Papers.* Urbana: University of Illinois Press, 1964.

Schmitz, Neil. "Doing the Gettysburg Address: Jefferson/Calhoun/Lincoln/King." *Arizona Quarterly* 62, no. 2 (Summer 2006): 145–152.

Wills, Garry. *Lincoln at Gettysburg: The Words That Remade America.* New York: Simon and Schuster, 1992.

Grant, Ulysses S.

Ulysses S. Grant (1822–1885) emerged from obscurity in 1861 to become Abraham Lincoln's choice as general in chief in 1864. Under his direction Union armies won victories that contributed to Lincoln's reelection and crushed the Confederacy in 1865. The Ohio-born Grant graduated from West Point in

General Ulysses S. Grant at his headquarters in Cold Harbor, Virginia, 1864. The Lincoln-Grant partnership was essential to achieving a Union victory.

Source: Library of Congress

1843 in the middle of his class; after seeing distinguished service in the Mexican-American War, he spent time at several posts before resigning his captain's commission in 1854 amid rumors that he had become a drunkard. He struggled to succeed in civilian life, first in St. Louis, then in Galena, Illinois, where he moved in 1860 to work in his father's general store.

At the outbreak of the Civil War, Grant battled to gain a colonel's commission. It was not until June that Illinois governor Richard Yates appointed him to command the Twenty-first Illinois, to replace an inept colonel. Grant whipped the regiment into shape and took it to Missouri. There he learned that he had been promoted to brigadier general of volunteers, courtesy of Rep. Elihu B. Washburne, who had sought the commission for his Galena townsman from Lincoln. In September Grant gained national notice for occupying Paducah, Kentucky, in the wake of the Confederate decision to violate that state's neutrality. Two months later Grant's men clashed with Confederate forces at Belmont, Missouri, withdrawing after achieving initial success. In the aftermath of that battle Lincoln for the first time heard rumors about Grant's drinking, but Washburne denounced the rumors.

Grant became a national hero in February 1862 when he won victories at Forts Henry and Donelson, opening up Tennessee. At Donelson some 13,000 Confederates surrendered, earning Grant the nickname of "Unconditional Surrender" and a promotion to major general of volunteers, courtesy of Lincoln. Weeks later Grant's superior officer, Henry W. Halleck, accused Grant of neglecting his duties, adding that rumor had it that he was drinking again. General in chief George B. McClellan authorized Grant's arrest, although Halleck preferred to order him to remain behind while his men advanced. Grant challenged the accusations, and after Lincoln intervened, Halleck backed down rather than press charges and restored Grant to field command.

Grant rejoined his command, which was encamped at Pittsburgh Landing, on the west bank of the Tennessee River just north of the Tennessee-Mississippi border. There he awaited the arrival of Don Carlos Buell's army. Confederate General Albert Sidney Johnston decided to attack Grant before Buell arrived. In the ensuing battle of Shiloh (April 6–7, 1862), Grant's command was driven back to the landing after a day of fierce combat. Buell's men and other reinforcements began arriving as the first day of battle drew to a close, and on the following day a Union counterattack drove the Confederates away. Two days of combat had cost the Union forces 13,000 casualties, and Grant came under heavy criticism for being unprepared for a Confederate attack. When Lincoln inquired whether Grant was to blame for what had happened, Halleck, who had arrived at Pittsburgh Landing days after the battle, fended off the inquiry, although he decided to name Grant his second-in-command, effectively removing him from field command. Later narratives would cite Alexander McClure's claim that Lincoln responded to a request to remove Grant by declaring, "I can't spare this man; he fights," but that tale is of dubious validity. A disheartened Grant sought a transfer and contemplated taking an extended leave, but he regained a field command in July 1862 when Halleck left for Washington to assume the post of general in chief.

Through the summer of 1862 Grant wrestled with the responsibilities of occupation duty in West Tennessee: In September and October he fended off Confederate offensives at Iuka and Corinth. Before long he began to contemplate the capture of Vicksburg, Mississippi, to solidify Union control of the Mississippi River and drive a wedge through the Confederacy. Unknown to him, one of his subordinates, John A. McClernand, was lobbying Lincoln for command of an independent force to take Vicksburg. Lincoln's orders authorizing the idea contained a critical loophole, for they provided that Grant would determine whether he could spare men for McClernand's mission. Learning of McClernand's imminent return, Grant prematurely launched a two-pronged offensive in December, but the Confederates thwarted both drives. Over McClernand's protests, Grant decided at the end of January 1863 to take control of operations against Vicksburg.

For the next ten weeks Grant tried a number of schemes to take Vicksburg, only to encounter failure each time. Reports filtered north that his men were dying in the Louisiana swamps. McClernand sought to undermine Grant with Lincoln, once more raising the issue of Grant's drinking. By March Lincoln was curious enough to send two envoys west to report back on what was going on. By the time they arrived, Grant was ready to implement his preferred plan, whereby a naval flotilla would run the Vicksburg batteries and then ferry Grant's command across the Mississippi south of the city. Once back on dry land, Grant swung east, captured the state capital at Jackson, Mississippi, and turned to drive the Confederates back into Vicksburg in mid-May. After a siege of forty-seven days, Grant entered the city on July 4, 1863. Lincoln, ecstatic, secured Grant's promotion to major general in the regular army. In a letter to Grant he shared his earlier doubts about Grant's plans but admitted that the results indicated that Grant was correct. He also shared with others Grant's letter endorsing the enlistment of black soldiers as a way to strengthen the Union while simultaneously weakening the Confederacy. At last Grant had secured Lincoln's unwavering support. Lincoln did not protest when Grant removed McClernand from command during the siege.

Although Lincoln did not give Grant the go-ahead to advance on Mobile in the immediate aftermath of Vicksburg, he did not hesitate to elevate Grant to overall command in the western theater (between the Appalachian Mountains and the Mississippi River) in October 1863. Grant delivered on that trust by forcing the Confederate Army to abandon its siege of Chattanooga, Tennessee, in November 1863. The next month Washburne introduced a bill reviving the rank of lieutenant general. Although this measure is usually identified with Lincoln, the president did not initiate it. House Republicans, fearing that Lincoln might promote Halleck instead, attempted to specify Grant by name in the bill. The president first wanted to learn whether Grant harbored any presidential ambitions for 1864. When Grant signaled through intermediaries that he did not, Lincoln made it known that he would submit Grant's name for the new rank and would elevate him to the position of general in chief. The two men met for the first time at a White House reception on the evening of March 8. The following day Grant accepted his new commission and within days he assumed command of the armies of the United States.

In 1864 Grant mapped out a campaign featuring simultaneous advances against the major Confederate field armies in Virginia and Georgia, with the hope that other offensives would threaten Confederate logistics. In Georgia his chief subordinate, William T. Sherman, advanced against Atlanta. Grant accompanied the Army of the Potomac as it moved against Robert E. Lee's Army of Northern Virginia, while other Union advances threatened Richmond and the Shenandoah Valley. For forty days Grant and Lee marched and fought in central Virginia, with Grant driving Lee to the outskirts of Richmond while his other Virginia offensives failed. Then Grant crossed the James River, laid siege to Petersburg and Richmond, and kept Lee from regaining the strategic initiative. However, the long casualty lists and the resulting siege disappointed Northern expectations for a decisive victory that spring, and with Sherman also laying siege to Atlanta it looked as if Grant's strategy would not produce results in time to secure Lincoln's reelection. However, the fall of Atlanta in September and dramatic victories by Philip Sheridan in Virginia's Shenandoah Valley clinched the election for the president, and Grant celebrated the victory at the polls as essential to victory on the battlefield.

In the winter of 1864–1865 Grant urged Lincoln to meet Confederate representatives at Hampton Roads, Virginia. The president journeyed south to Grant's headquarters at City Point and was present when Grant captured Petersburg and Richmond. Meeting with Grant and Sherman aboard the presidential steamer *River Queen,* he outlined his hopes for a lenient peace. Grant implemented those wishes with the terms he offered Lee at Appomattox. Delighted, Lincoln welcomed Grant when the general returned to Washington, but Grant declined to accompany the president to Ford's Theatre on the night of April 14.

As general in chief under Lincoln's successor, Andrew Johnson, Grant became a supporter of congressional Republican efforts to reconstruct state governments and protect black civil rights and eventually political rights. Elected president in 1868, Grant served two terms, during which time he reluctantly conceded defeat on Reconstruction. His *Personal Memoirs* (1885–1886) portray a much more harmonious relationship between Lincoln and Grant than was the case, but there is little doubt that their partnership was essential to achieving Union victory.

See also *Forts Henry and Donelson; Overland Campaign; Vicksburg Campaign*
—BROOKS D. SIMPSON

BIBLIOGRAPHY

Bunting, Josiah, III. *Ulysses S. Grant.* New York: Times Books, 2004.

Catton, Bruce. *Grant Moves South.* New York: Little, Brown, 1960.

———. *Grant Takes Command.* New York: Little, Brown, 1969.

Simpson, Brooks D. *Let Us Have Peace: Ulysses S. Grant and the Politics of War and Reconstruction, 1861–1868.* Chapel Hill: University of North Carolina Press, 1991.

———. *Ulysses S. Grant: Triumph over Adversity, 1822–1865.* New York: Houghton Mifflin, 2000.

Smith, Jean E. *Grant.* New York: Simon and Schuster, 2001.

Williams, T. Harry. *Lincoln and His Generals.* New York: Knopf, 1952.

Great Britain, Relations with

The early American pattern wherein a seasoned diplomat later became a president (Jefferson, J. Adams, Monroe, and J. Q. Adams) gradually broke down and ended entirely with Abraham Lincoln. Yet despite his initial heavy reliance on secretary of state William Seward for policy toward the European powers, most of all Great Britain, Lincoln soon constructed his own foreign policy. Lincoln's native caution and conservatism gradually impressed the parties involved.

Among the key issues between the United States and Britain was the matter of the rights of neutrals on the high seas. Lincoln ordered the blockade of Southern ports two weeks after Fort Sumter, and because British ships carried most cotton and other goods eastward, the move seriously threatened their maritime dominance. Meanwhile, the Union sought to protect its own goods, ships, and expanding markets. Quickly the British shipbuilding industry became the source of many Confederate warships. Through intense pressure from minister Charles Francis Adams in London and consul Thomas Dudley in Liverpool this source was partly closed off, but British-made commerce raiders continued to bolster Confederate forces throughout the war. On technicalities, Britain was free to build, but not arm, those ships.

Separately the *Trent* affair was the nadir of Anglo-American relations and led to Lincoln's best moment in his relations with Britain. On November 8, 1861, a U.S. frigate intercepted the British mail steamer *Trent,* near Cuba. Aboard the *Trent* were two Confederate diplomats, James Mason and John Slidell, whom the Americans seized. Britain protested vehemently, while the English and American publics clamored for redress, even war. Because there was no transatlantic cable at this time—it had broken in 1858 and would not to be restored until 1866—the hottest words took several days to reach either shore by ship. Lincoln toned down a key dispatch that Seward had written before its courier sailed for London, and Prince Albert, just before he died on December 14, did the same with a testy missive by Lord Russell, the British foreign minister. At a four-hour cabinet meeting on Christmas Day, Lincoln acceded to the point made by Seward and attorney general Edward Bates that Mason and Slidell had been wrongly taken; they were released, with minimal apology.

The economics of the cotton trade and the ever-present threat of British recognition of an independent Confederacy were the proximate causes of Anglo-American tensions. British textile manufacturers relied extensively on Southern-grown American cotton to produce their goods and thus, Lincoln and many others feared, they would pressure the British government into formal recognition of the Confederate States. This fear, in fact, gave Lincoln pause when he considered establishing a blockade of the Southern states, inasmuch as doing so, according to international law, conferred belligerent status on the Confederacy and thus opened the door for easier British recognition. In the end, however, British hostility toward slavery, that nation's dependence on Northern wheat, the increasing availability of cotton grown elsewhere, and the South's inability to demonstrate convincingly that it had the power to win and hold its independence ensured that no formal recognition would be forthcoming.

Perhaps the chief factor keeping Anglo-American relations from flaming into open warfare was that neither country had anything to gain by war against the other. Seward early on threatened a foreign war to reunite the United States, but Lincoln immediately rejected this absurd suggestion. The president had rare contact with the British ambassador in Washington, Lord Lyons, but he left him with one memorable notion: "Tell the English people I mean them no harm," he said as Lyons departed for home. Lincoln's Emancipation Proclamation of January 1, 1863, ended any moral case British leaders could make for coming into the war against the Union, and the victories of July 1863 ended the military possibility. Thereafter Britain's affairs in Europe—particularly the Dano-

Prussian war of 1864 and French intervention in Mexico—seriously distracted British officials.

In one popular print of Lincoln sold after his death, Liberty's right foot rests on the British lion. This is not how Lincoln viewed the denouement of the Civil War, nor did the average Briton. Lincoln had sent friendly missives to British workingmen. Hand-drawn condolences poured into Washington when he died, from scores of civic, political, and religious groups in England and Canada. The widows Victoria and Mary exchanged notes. By his death as by his policy, Lincoln stabilized, then improved, relations with Britain.

See also *Adams, Charles Francis;* Alabama *Claims; Foreign Relations and Diplomacy, Lincoln's;* Trent *Affair*

—James M. Cornelius

BIBLIOGRAPHY

Jenkins, Brian A. *Britain and the War for the Union.* 2 vols. Montreal: McGill-Queens University Press, 1974–1980.

Mahin, Dean B. *One War at a Time: The International Dimensions of the American Civil War.* Washington, D.C.: Brassey's, 1999.

Monaghan, Jay. *Diplomat in Carpet Slippers: Abraham Lincoln Deals with Foreign Affairs.* Indianapolis and New York: Bobbs-Merrill, 1945.

Great Emancipator

In 1866 Joshua F. Speed, Lincoln's close friend during his early years in Springfield, recalled a conversation of 1841 in which the dejected lawyer lamented that he had accomplished nothing that would cause people to remember his life as having benefited humanity. More than two decades later, Lincoln had not forgotten the incident, and he identified the Emancipation Proclamation as the act that would fulfill his youthful aspiration. Indeed Lincoln did not miss the mark when emphasizing the magnitude of that measure, for his own contemporaries hailed him as the Great Emancipator, as would future generations. Although some recent scholars have attempted to downplay and even discredit this image, the prevalence of the Great Emancipator icon in material culture has enabled the depiction of Lincoln as the liberator of slaves to become a primary and indelible facet of his legacy.

After the Emancipation Proclamation took effect on January 1, 1863, African Americans embraced the image of Lincoln as the Great Emancipator. For example, the spontaneous outpouring of gratitude that occurred on the streets of Richmond when Lincoln unexpectedly visited the fallen rebel capital on April 4, 1865, demonstrated the depth of many freedmen's admiration for the man whom they regarded as their deliverer. Lincoln's assassination ten days later and subsequent apotheosis as a martyred saint secured his status as the Great Emancipator, the American Moses who delivered his countrymen from bondage without living to enter the Promised Land.

Because of racial conservatism, many white Americans were reluctant at first to envision Lincoln as Great Emancipator. Thus artistic renderings of Lincoln emancipating slaves did not appear until the presidential campaign of 1864, and several of the early depictions thoroughly condemned his action. In 1864, however, two best-selling prints based on recent paintings helped popularize the image of Lincoln as Great Emancipator. John Sartain's engraving of Edward Dalton Marchant's painting *Abraham Lincoln, 16th President of the United States* portrayed Lincoln with quill in hand, having just signed the Emancipation Proclamation. In the background, a broken chain crushed by the foot of Liberty underscores the document's monumental import. The print adapted from Francis Bicknell Carpenter's painting *The First Reading of the Emancipation Proclamation before the Cabinet* enjoyed even greater popular success, selling tens of thousands of copies and going through several reissues over the next four decades. Carpenter's zeal in promoting the Emancipation Proclamation as the crowning achievement of Lincoln's administration earned him the designation as the man most responsible for establishing Lincoln's image as Great Emancipator.

After the assassination, artists and printers rushed to depict the slain president as the Great Emancipator. Fanciful renderings of a mythic "emancipation moment," which portrayed Lincoln breaking the shackles of a kneeling slave, typified the growing emphasis on viewing him as the moving force behind the eradication of slavery. Even the statue erected by the Freedmen's Memorial Society in Washington, D.C., on April 14, 1876, presented Lincoln towering over a genuflecting African American. Although generally complimentary in his speech at the unveiling ceremony, Frederick Douglass, Lincoln's friend and admirer, who had become the acknowledged spokesperson for black Americans, nonetheless foreshadowed future controversy by calling Lincoln "the white man's president" and labeling blacks as "only his step-children."

In the early twentieth century, a generation of blacks who had not known slavery had to square the popular image of Lincoln as Great Emancipator with the realities of segregation and racism that dominated the nation. Although most African Americans still held Lincoln in high esteem, black leaders differed over how to make him relevant. The educator Booker T. Washington held up Lincoln as a model of hard work whom blacks could emulate and urged them to interpret their freedom as the ability to become self-supportive within a society rank with inequality. In contrast, activist W. E. B. DuBois asserted that African Americans needed to replace the figure of the submissive slave kneeling at the feet of Lincoln with one symbolizing strength and independence.

By the heyday of the Civil Rights Movement, in the late 1960s, some black activists sought to eradicate completely the Great Emancipator image, asserting that slaves had secured their own freedom through their actions and personal resistance. In its most bitter form, this revisionist position claimed that whites created and promoted the myth of Lincoln freeing the slaves with the Emancipation Proclamation to keep blacks in a subservient and inferior position. Professional historians have attempted to strike a balance between a top-down perspective that emphasizes Lincoln's decisive hand in the destruction of slavery and a bottom-up approach that stresses the slaves' role in obtaining their freedom. However, proponents of both views still debate whether to regard Lincoln as merely another factor among slaves, Union soldiers, Northern civilians, and congressmen who together achieved the abolition of slavery, or as the primary, indispensable agent without whom neither the Civil War nor the swift destruction of slavery would have occurred. Nevertheless, the abundance of Great Emancipator images in print and art attests to the historic affection of the American people for Lincoln and their need for a hero of mythic proportions.

See also *African Americans and Lincoln*

—SEAN A. SCOTT

BIBLIOGRAPHY

Berlin, Ira. "Who Freed the Slaves? Emancipation and Its Meaning." In *Union and Emancipation: Essays on Politics and Race in the Civil War Era,* ed. David W. Blight and Brooks D. Simpson, 105–121. Kent, Ohio: Kent State University Press, 1997.

Holzer, Harold. "'Prized in Every Liberty-Loving Household': The Image of the Great Emancipator in the Graphic Arts." In *Lincoln Seen and Heard.* Lawrence: University Press of Kansas, 2000.

Holzer, Harold, Edna Greene Medford, and Frank J. Williams. *The Emancipation Proclamation: Three Views (Social, Political, Iconographic).* Baton Rouge: Louisiana State University Press, 2006.

McPherson, James M. "Who Freed the Slaves?" In *Drawn with the Sword: Reflections on the American Civil War.* New York: Oxford University Press, 1996.

Peterson, Merrill D. *Lincoln in American Memory.* New York: Oxford University Press, 1994.

Schwartz, Barry. *Abraham Lincoln and the Forge of National Memory.* Chicago: University of Chicago Press, 2000.

Greeley, Horace

One of the most important newspaper editors of his time, Horace Greeley (1811–1872) was both a political ally and a constant critic of Abraham Lincoln. Born in New Hampshire and raised in Vermont, Greeley came to New York City in 1831 as an apprentice printer, created an arts and news journal called the *New Yorker* and the *New York Tribune* (1841), and by the 1850s was the most recognizable and widely read newspaper editor of his day. With his acerbic tongue, encyclopedic political knowledge, and slangy prose, "Uncle Horace" suffered no fools and criticized virtually everyone.

The colorful New York editor and the lanky Illinois attorney shared a common enthusiasm for republican virtue, the "right to rise," and the Whig Party. In the 1850s Greeley joined Albany, New York, editor Thurlow Weed and politician William Henry Seward Jr., later secretary of state (1861–1869), in the triumvirate behind the formation of a Republican Party in New York. In 1860 Greeley helped nominate Lincoln and defeat Seward, who by then was a political enemy.

Greeley and Lincoln first met at the Northwest River and Harbor Convention in Chicago, in July 1848, where Greeley was a featured speaker. During the winter of 1848–1849, the two served together in the U.S. Congress. Greeley took a more radical stance than Lincoln against slavery and made himself unpopular by publishing statistics demonstrating that most members of Congress, including Lincoln, had overcharged the public for their mileage to and from Washington, D.C.

Greeley went on to build a great newspaper, become an innovative pioneer in journalism, and establish a worldwide reputation for candor, honesty, and hard truths. As a capitalist utopian, he dabbled in literary and philosophical fads, publishing the work of many with whom he disagreed, including the little-known London scribbler Karl Marx.

In 1858 Greeley supported Stephen A. Douglas against Lincoln in the Illinois U.S. Senate race, arguing that Douglas in Washington would be a divisive force within the Democratic Party and would help elect a Republican president in 1860. Lincoln was understandably annoyed at Greeley's apparent sellout of a fellow Republican and would never quite trust Greeley again, much as he feared and respected the editor's power and influence.

Nevertheless Greeley attended the Republican Convention of 1860 in Chicago and, by throwing his voting bloc behind Lincoln, helped defeat Seward (the favorite) and nominate Lincoln. Greeley became an ardent supporter of the president-elect and visited him in Springfield and on the train headed for his Washington, D.C., inauguration.

Whereas Lincoln came to support a Union with or without slavery, Greeley argued for an end to slavery, with or without Union. In December 1860 Greeley wrote that the "errant sisters" of the Confederacy should "depart in peace." Within a month, he shifted his ground and urged Lincoln to stand firm against the rebel cause. In June 1861 the *Tribune* ran a series of banner headlines urging federal troops "On to Richmond!" and was widely blamed for the premature Union campaign and defeat in July at Bull Run. (Greeley took responsibility for the headlines but did not write them himself.)

Crushed by the news of Bull Run, Greeley had a nervous breakdown ("brain fever") and wrote Lincoln that he was "hopelessly broken" by the "awful disaster." Lincoln put the letter in his desk drawer for future use.

In 1862 Greeley's campaign against Southern "slavocracy" made him a staunch ally of the president in the moves toward emancipation. On August 19 Greeley published his "Prayer of 20 Millions," favoring immediate liberation of the slaves. Lincoln's famous response, urging Union with or without slavery, is the more famous, and briefer, document. Lincoln's public response to Greeley illustrates Lincoln's savvy use of the press. While claiming his only goal was to preserve the Union, Lincoln in fact was laying the groundwork for the Emancipation Proclamation, which he had already written and was simply waiting for the right time to announce. For Greeley, the Emancipation Proclamation was a "Proclamation of Freedom," signaling that America would lead the world from liberty for some to freedom for all. Both Greeley and Lincoln now embraced Union and emancipation as the same cause, as they did the Homestead Act for settling the American West.

Greeley and Lincoln were wary allies on press freedom during the Civil War. Greeley relentlessly criticized Union generals for their incompetence and the president for his inaction on various matters. But he also published stories desired by the White House in return for advance notice of important policy changes. Lincoln absorbed the criticism from the press and rarely shut down any newspapers.

On personal liberties, Greeley defended the Ohio Peace Democrat, Clement Vallandigham, arrested for his antiwar rhetoric, but respected Lincoln's right to restrict personal liberties in time of war. Greeley shared, and even anticipated, Lincoln's call in the Gettysburg Address (November 19, 1863) for a transformation of liberty into freedom, borrowing the republican rhetoric of the day from Europe.

In 1864 Greeley deeply annoyed Lincoln by his abortive attempt to help negotiate peace with self-proclaimed Confederate representatives at Niagara Falls, in Canada. Lincoln regaled his cabinet with the story, adding that Greeley was like "an old shoe, good for nothing new, whatever he has been."

Greeley also opposed Lincoln's nomination for a second term, although he campaigned for the president after his nomination and the Union victory at Atlanta. The editor remained a critic of Lincoln, even writing a sharply worded editorial the night Lincoln was shot, April 14, 1865. (The *Tribune* staff refused to run it.) Greeley then joined in the eulogies for a great president.

Greeley and Lincoln were, for almost two decades, respectful allies in the campaign against slavery and for a new Republican Party. They shared a philosophy of universal freedom and human rights, but they also respected each other's right to disagree, as they often did. Each at times disdained and feared the other. Greeley's dedication to freedom and Lincoln's dedication to Union finally fused only during a bloody Civil War.

Greeley and the Republican Party parted ways after 1865. But Greeley was still a formidable voice in the public arena. In 1872 Ulysses S. Grant defeated Greeley when he ran for president on both the Liberal Republican and Democratic tickets. A few months later Grant and other dignitaries attended Greeley's funeral in New York. Greeley would be enshrined in American history as a pioneering journalist, if not as a great politician or national leader.

See also *New York Tribune*

—ROBERT C. WILLIAMS

BIBLIOGRAPHY

Horner, Harland Hoyt. *Lincoln and Greeley.* Urbana: University of Illinois Press, 1953.

Howe, Daniel. *The Political Culture of the American Whigs.* Chicago: University of Chicago Press, 1979.

Williams, Robert C. *Horace Greeley, Champion of American Freedom.* New York: New York University Press, 2006.

Greenbacks

Paper currency issued by the Union government under the Legal Tender Act of 1862 came to be called "greenbacks" because of its color. Prior to the Civil War, the federal government had not issued paper money since the disastrous experience with the Continental currency during the American Revolution. The only money that the federal government produced was gold and silver coin, which was called "specie." Many people believed that specie money was the only real money.

The Constitution specified that only the federal government could produce gold and silver coins. But before the Civil War, state governments, private banks, and other businesses issued paper money or "bank notes." This money had no set, standard value, but all paper currency was supposed to be a pledge that the holder could take it to the issuer and convert it into specie.

In December 1861 the high demand for gold forced U.S. banks to suspend the conversion of bank notes into specie. On January 1, 1862, the federal

Treasury also suspended the conversion of its Treasury notes into gold. Despite the traditional distrust of paper money, many business and government leaders reluctantly concluded that some kind of national currency was needed besides specie. In February 1862, Congress passed the Legal Tender Act, which authorized the printing of the greenbacks. By declaring this money "legal tender," Congress was requiring that all businesses accept it in transactions. The federal government also accepted the money for all payments due to the U.S. Treasury, except for import taxes, which still had to be paid in gold. The first issue of greenbacks was $150,000,000. By the war's end, $450,000,000 had been issued.

Both Lincoln and Salmon P. Chase, his first secretary of the Treasury, were initially "sound money" men who distrusted paper currency but eventually came to see its necessity. Lincoln did not much involve himself in the push for the Legal Tender Act. In his annual message to Congress in 1862, Lincoln voiced approval of Chase's arguments on the legal tender issue. Lincoln believed the greenbacks had met the need for a uniform currency—which in fact they had. Although the purchasing power of the greenback rose and fell with the fortunes of the Union war effort, they were immediately accepted as the standard circulating medium.

Although the Union printed a massive amount of currency, it met most of its war expenses through taxation and borrowing. This limited the inflation experienced by Northern consumers. In the North, the cost of living roughly doubled during the Civil War, but wages and business profits also rose, albeit to a lesser extent. But the Union never experienced the kind of runaway inflation that the Confederacy did.

Many in Congress believed that the greenbacks were a temporary expedient and should be retired after the war. In the late 1800s, the monetary system became a major political issue, as groups such as the Greenback Party wanted the paper money to stay in circulation, in part because a larger money supply helped debtors pay off their debts. In one of history's fine ironies, Chase, appointed chief justice of the United States by Lincoln in December 1864, would later rule that issuing the greenbacks had been unconstitutional.

—MARK S. JOY

BIBLIOGRAPHY

Curry, Leonard P. *Blueprint for Modern America: Nonmilitary Legislation of the First Civil War Congress.* Nashville: Vanderbilt University Press, 1968.

Gordon, John Steele. *Hamilton's Blessing: The Extraordinary Life and Times of Our National Debt.* New York: Penguin, 1997.

Hammond, Bray. *Sovereignty and an Empty Purse: Banks and Politics in the Civil War.* Princeton: Princeton University Press, 1970.

Habeas Corpus

The suspension of *habeas corpus* during the Civil War was a significant element in the war on the home front in both the United States and the Confederacy. The Confederacy used suspension more often and on a much higher percentage of its citizens than did the United States. Even before the war began military authorities in the South began to arrest civilians, and throughout the war, as historian Mark E. Neely has demonstrated, there were always political prisoners held in the South. Far fewer people were arrested in the United States, but most historical scholarship has focused on the suspensions by Lincoln during the war.

The writ of *habeas corpus* allows a prisoner to be brought before a judge to determine if there is proper cause to hold the person in custody. Often called "the great writ," it has historically been considered central to the fair administration of justice. Without the writ government officials—the police, the army, or some other agency—could hold people in custody or jail for any reason, or no reason at all. The Framers of the Constitution understood the importance of the writ but also understood that in times of emergency it is sometimes necessary to suspend it. The Constitution thus provides that "the privilege of the writ of *habeas corpus* shall not be suspended, unless when in cases of rebellion or invasion the public safety may require it." Once *habeas* was suspended other rights—such as freedom of speech, press, and assembly, or the guarantee of a fair trial—could no longer be enforced because people could be arrested for any reason the government saw fit and not brought to trial. The clause provided specific circumstances for suspension: rebellion or invasion had to have taken place and the public safety had to "require" a suspension.

The Constitution did not explicitly say how the writ could be suspended or indeed what branch of the government could suspend it. The clause appears in Article I, Section 9 of the U.S. Constitution, which is generally, although not wholly, devoted to limitations on the powers of Congress. But structurally and linguistically there were arguments for assuming that the president, in response to an invasion or rebellion, might suspend the writ on his own. Some of the clauses in Article I, Section 9 of the Constitution specifically referred to Congress or to the passage of laws, which clearly were direct limitations on Congress. Some of the clauses, however, could also apply to other branches as well, such as the statement that "the United States" could not bestow upon anyone a title of nobility. Thus the suspension clause might be seen as applying to the executive as well as the legislative branch. There was also a logical reason to believe that the president could act on his own. An invasion or rebellion might easily prevent Congress from meeting—the British, after all, had seized Philadelphia during the Revolution and Washington, D.C., during the War of 1812. Under such circumstances Congress would be unable to meet at all, and thus if the president could not suspend the law to repel the invasion, the nation might fall.

At the beginning of the Civil War Lincoln ordered the suspension of *habeas corpus* in response to chaos and sabotage in Maryland. The crisis began when Northern militias trying to reach Washington, D.C., were attacked by pro-Confederate mobs in Baltimore. On April 20, 1861, Lincoln sent a letter to the governor of Maryland and the mayor of Baltimore, declaring that "troops *must* be brought here [Washington, D.C.] but I make no point in bringing them *through* Baltimore." Lincoln informed them that General Winfield Scott had already agreed to "march them *around* Baltimore, and not through it."

On April 25 Lincoln ordered General Scott not to interfere with the forthcoming meeting of the Maryland legislature, even though he feared the legislature would "take action...against the United States." Lincoln noted that the legislature had a "clearly legal right to assemble" and until the legislature acted against the government, the army should do nothing. In the event of a vote to secede Lincoln was prepared to act and "in the extremest necessity" order "the suspension of the writ of *habeas corpus*." In the next two days, however, Confederate sympathizers, with the support of local officials in Baltimore, began to burn the railroad bridges connecting Baltimore to the North. If these bridges were destroyed it would be extremely difficult to bring troops to the national capital to protect it from a Confederate attack.

On April 27 Lincoln authorized General Scott to suspend the writ of *habeas corpus* along every "military line" between Washington, D.C., and Philadelphia to protect roads, bridges, and railroads from sabotage. This order allowed the military to arrest anyone the army believed was a threat to the security of the nation or was likely to commit sabotage. Among those arrested at this time was John Merryman, a local planter and secessionist who was organizing troops to join the Confederacy and who had also participated in the burning of bridges. The April 27 order was the beginning of expansive use of the suspension of *habeas corpus* during the war. On July 2 Lincoln would expand the order to include the rail line from New York City to Washington.

Lincoln's critics immediately denounced the act as tyranny, asserting that only Congress could suspend *habeas corpus.* Supreme Court Chief Justice Roger Taney took this position in issuing a writ of *habeas corpus* in *Ex parte Merryman* (1861); the full Court never heard the case or took a position on suspension. Lincoln argued that because Congress was not in session, he had the authority and the obligation to suspend the writ to maintain the Union and the

Habeas Corpus

Constitution. As he told General Scott, "You are engaged in repressing an insurrection against the laws of the United States," which was precisely the condition the Constitution required for suspension.

On July 4 Congress came back into session, and in a long message to Congress Lincoln discussed the suspension of *habeas corpus*. He noted that this authority had "purposely been exercised but very sparingly," but nevertheless its "legality and propriety" had been questioned. Lincoln noted that the argument against his suspension was "that one who is sworn to 'take care that the laws be faithfully executed' should not himself violate them." Lincoln famously responded to this argument:

> *The whole of the laws which were required to be faithfully executed were being resisted and failing of execution in nearly one-third of the States. Must they be allowed to finally fail of execution, even had it been perfectly clear that by the use of the means necessary to their execution some single law, made in such extreme tenderness of the citizen's liberty that practically it relieves more of the guilty than of the innocent, should to a very limited extent be violated? To state the question more directly, are all the laws but one to go unexecuted and the Government itself go to pieces lest that one be violated? Even in such a case would not the official oath be broken if the Government should be overthrown, when it was believed that disregarding the single law would tend to preserve it?*

Lincoln, having made this point, then denied that in fact he had violated the law. He noted that the Constitution was silent on which branch was allowed to suspend the writ, but not silent on the concept that it could be suspended in case of rebellion. He emphasized that the suspension clause "was plainly made for a dangerous emergency" and, Lincoln thought, "it cannot be believed the framers" of the Constitution "intended" that "the danger should run its course, until Congress could be called together; the very assembling of which might be prevented, as was intended in this case, by the rebellions." Lincoln could have pointed out, but did not, that many, perhaps most, members of Congress might not have been able to attend the session in Washington if Confederate sympathizers had destroyed the railroad lines and bridges going through Maryland.

On July 12 attorney general Edward Bates sent Congress a detailed legal analysis of Lincoln's actions and a defense of their constitutionality. Congress debated the issue of *habeas corpus* in the emergency session that began on July 4, but the members apparently accepted the arguments of Lincoln and Bates because they took no action on the matter in that session. Instead, on August 6 Congress passed the First Confiscation Act, which allowed for confiscation of all private property used for "insurrectionary purposes." This law in effect suspended the Fifth Amendment's prohibition against taking private property without due process of law or compensation. The same day Congress passed legislation obscurely titled "An Act to Increase the pay of Privates…and for other purposes." This law, sometimes called the "Ratification Act," provided that "all the acts, proclamations and orders of the President of the United States after the fourth of March, eighteen hundred and sixty-one, respecting the army and navy...are hereby approved and in all respects legalized and made valid." In this act Congress approved Lincoln's suspensions of *habeas corpus*.

On September 24, 1862, Lincoln extended his suspension of *habeas corpus* to the entire United States. This suspension applied to "all Rebels and Insurgents, their aiders and abettors within the United States, and all persons discouraging volunteer enlistments, resisting militia drafts, or guilty of any disloyal practice, affording aid and comfort to Rebels...." The proclamation authorized trial by court martial or military commission. The proclamation would be implemented by the military and was necessary because "disloyal persons are not adequately restrained by the ordinary process of law" from aiding the insurrection. This sweeping assertion of power might easily have been used against anyone dissenting from government policy. In fact, despite the complaints of "lost cause" partisans, modern scholarship shows that there were relatively few arrests for mere words, and many of those were countermanded by Lincoln himself. When generals arrested opposition editors, Lincoln famously urged them to spare him the "embarrassment" of such attempts to stifle the opposition. Most of those arrested and held under the *habeas* suspension had in fact been involved in aiding the Confederate cause. In March 1863 Congress finally passed a *habeas corpus* act. This act legitimated all of the arrests under Lincoln's proclamations and authorized the president to suspend the writ as he believed necessary during the rest of the war.

The use of the military to arrest civilians and the incarceration of civilians by the military strike modern Americans as tyrannical. But for Lincoln there were probably no other options. There were a few federal marshals in every state, but there was no national police force like the modern FBI and thus no way to enforce federal law at the local level on a large scale. Most law in the antebellum period was enforced at the local level under the authority of the states. Under normal circumstances the state of Maryland, for example, would have arrested John Merryman for attempting to destroy railroad bridges and prosecuted him under state law. But Maryland not only refused to restrain Confederate operatives like Merryman, but state officials actually encouraged such actions. There were, however, few if any federal laws that could have been used to arrest Merryman, even if there had been a federal marshal available to arrest him. Thus Lincoln could either suspend *habeas corpus* and prevent the destruction of vital communication and transportation networks, or he could stand by and watch them destroyed as he waited for Congress to assemble and suspend *habeas*. For Lincoln there was no alternative to using the military for this job. Merryman was held at Fort McHenry until the crisis in Maryland had passed, and then he was quietly released, as were hundreds of others in the North who were arrested by the military.

After the war the Supreme Court ruled, in *Ex parte Milligan* (1866), that it was unconstitutional to try civilians in military courts if the civil courts were open and operating. Milligan was charged with organizing a conspiracy in Indiana to raise troops to aid the Confederacy. By the time of his trial, late in the war, there were statutes available to prosecute him in civilian court and the courts were open and operating in Indiana. Thus the Court overturned Milligan's conviction. By then the emergency was over, and the normal rule of law was in place. Milligan might have been indicted at that point and brought to trial, but no one had an interest in such a step.

See also *Civil Liberties*

—PAUL FINKELMAN

BIBLIOGRAPHY

Duker, William F. *A Constitutional History of Habeas Corpus.* Westport, Conn.: Greenwood, 1980.

Finkelman, Paul. "Civil Liberties and the Civil War: The Great Emancipator as Civil Libertarian." *Michigan Law Review* 91 (1993): 1352–1381.

Freedman, Eric M. *Habeas Corpus: Rethinking the Great Writ of Liberty.* New York: New York University Press, 2001.

Hyman, Harold M., and William M. Wiecek. *Equal Justice under Law: Constitutional Development, 1835–1875.* New York: Harper and Row, 1982.

Jackson, Jeffrey D. "The Power to Suspend Habeas Corpus: An Answer from the Arguments Surrounding *Ex parte Merryman*." *University of Baltimore Law Review* 34 (2004):11–54.

Neely, Mark E., Jr. *The Fate of Liberty: Abraham Lincoln and Civil Liberties.* New York: Oxford University Press, 1991.

———. *Southern Rights: Political Prisoners and the Myth of Confederate Constitutionalism.* Charlottesville: University Press of Virginia, 1999.

Hamlin, Hannibal

Hannibal Hamlin served as vice president under Abraham Lincoln from 1860 to 1864. Dropped from the ticket for the 1864 presidential race, he missed the presidency by five weeks. One can only wonder what the nation's history would have been had Hamlin, who favored a radical reconstruction of the South, become our seventeenth president.

Hamlin was born in Paris Hill, Maine, on August 27, 1809. His father, Cyrus Hamlin, was a Harvard graduate and a physician. Hannibal grew up in a prosperous family and was an athletic young man and an avid reader. He got a good education, first in public schools and then at Hebron Academy.

Hamlin's ambition to become a lawyer was delayed several times because of a sick brother and his father's death. At twenty-one he was finally able to go to work at the law offices of Fessenden and Deblois. There Hamlin worked for Samuel C. Fessenden, a staunch abolitionist who influenced his views. He was thereafter an antislavery man himself.

His home state was solidly Democratic, and Hamlin joined the party. In 1835 he was elected to the state house of representatives. Hamlin had a good reputation, got along with other members, and earned respect as a man who could get things done.

In 1856 Republicans were anxious for the popular Hamlin to join their party to help balance their radical membership. Hamlin left the Democratic Party to run as the Republican candidate for governor of Maine. Though he did not formally break with the Democrats until 1856, he was credited with broadening the Republican base.

The Republican Party that nominated Hamlin for vice president had not completely coalesced. Hamlin's selection was based more on his position as a senior senator from the East and his Democratic Party roots than on his ability to perform in office. He brought balance to the Republican ticket.

With the 1860 election won, Lincoln and Hamlin, who had never met, convened in Chicago for a three-day meeting to discuss the process of selecting Lincoln's first cabinet. Hamlin, experienced in Washington politics, functioned as an intermediary for Lincoln and his new cabinet members. William H. Seward needed placating after his disappointing failure to be nominated for the presidency. Hamlin worked to recruit Seward, Lincoln's former rival, into the cabinet as secretary of state. Hamlin was also successful in naming Gideon Welles, also a former Democrat, as New England's cabinet representative. Once the cabinet was selected, Hamlin found himself disappointed, realizing that his office was something of a nonentity.

As vice president Hamlin's main responsibility was to preside over the Senate, a duty he found so boring that he rarely attended. Hamlin's chronic absence from Senate proceedings caused embarrassment when William Salisbury, a Democrat from Delaware, called the president a weak and imbecilic man. Republicans objected that the remarks were not in order. Hamlin, who paid little attention to the proceedings, had not even heard the remarks. Hamlin ordered Salisbury to sit for questions from the objecting Republicans. When the senator refused, Hamlin ordered the sergeant-at-arms to place him in custody. A staunch temperance man, Hamlin blamed Salisbury's hostile outburst on his drinking. He sobered the institution by banning liquor from the Senate chamber and committee rooms and outlawing the sale of liquor in the Senate restaurant.

Hamlin's relationship with Lincoln was more courteous than inclusive. As vice president he felt like a fifth wheel. He did not intrude upon Lincoln but gave his views and advice when asked. Lincoln did not call on him as one of his chief advisers. A strong supporter of black rights, Hamlin pressed Lincoln to issue the Emancipation Proclamation and to enlist and arm African Americans. Lincoln knew that such policies would give the war a greater moral purpose but feared that they would divide the North, and thus he did not move in that direction until he judged that the actions were politically feasible.

Hamlin thought that the president was too passive and generally found himself more comfortable with congressional radicals than with Lincoln. However, it was Hamlin who Lincoln invited to dinner to see the first draft of the Emancipation Proclamation and offer suggestions, the first person to do so. Moved by the gesture, the vice president encouraged the proclamation's immediate release.

Despite the fact that Hamlin felt like an inactive observer and the least important man in Washington, he was willing to stand for reelection in 1864. Hamlin had been a loyal supporter and said that Lincoln, though exclusionary in most respects, had always treated him with kindness and consideration. He assumed that Lincoln supported his renomination as vice president.

The Republican Party wanted Lincoln to replace Hamlin. To win the election Lincoln believed that he needed the support of Northern Democrats and the War Democrats. Hamlin was a Radical Republican, and that faction initially tried to supplant Lincoln with Salmon Chase or some other staunch abolitionist. But after the failed Cleveland Convention the radicals were no longer a threat to Lincoln's renomination, and Lincoln understood that they would ultimately support him. Thus Hamlin was not necessary to the ticket in 1864. Although Lincoln saw no need for a change, he agreed to replace Hamlin with the Tennessee governor, Andrew Johnson. Years later Hamlin would admit that although he never complained to anyone, he was hurt and believed he had been treated unfairly by Lincoln and his party.

His successor took office in March 4, 1865. Vice President Andrew Johnson made his first appearance before the Senate after drinking an overabundance of whisky and gave a long-winded, incoherent speech, infuriating Republicans. Ironically, it was the temperate Hamlin who had served him the whisky. On the same occasion Hamlin gave a short but eloquent speech of his own and then promptly left Washington to return to Maine.

On April 14, 1865, President Lincoln was assassinated at Ford's Theatre. Hamlin and Johnson stood side by side at Lincoln's casket. Five weeks into his term Johnson would become president.

President Johnson nominated Hamlin as collector of the port of Boston. After a short time in the post, horrified by Johnson's policies, Hamlin resigned. In 1869 he returned to the Senate and served two terms. By 1877 Hamlin had fallen ill with the first signs of heart disease. His last public engagement was a celebration of Lincoln's birthday. In 1882 he retired from public office. Hamlin died on July 4, 1891. He was eighty-one.

See also *Johnson, Andrew*

—Paula Cochran

BIBLIOGRAPHY

Donald, David Herbert. *Lincoln.* New York: Simon and Schuster, 1996.

Goodwin, Doris Kearns. *Team of Rivals: The Political Genius of Abraham Lincoln.* New York: Simon and Schuster, 2006.

Miller, William Lee. *Lincoln's Virtues: An Ethical Biography.* New York: Random House, 2003.

Hampton Roads Conference

The Hampton Roads Conference (February 3, 1865) was the most conspicuous of several unsuccessful peace initiatives in 1864–1865.

The conference stemmed from overtures by Francis P. Blair Sr. (1791–1876), the founder and former editor of the influential *Washington Globe,* who was well connected to both Union and Confederate leaders. In January 1865, Abraham Lincoln, having rebuffed Blair's earlier efforts to open discussions with the Confederacy, allowed him to approach Confederate president Jefferson Davis unofficially. Blair thought that Lincoln's reelection and recent Union military successes had piqued Confederate interest in peace talks. Lincoln was less optimistic but willing to see what developed.

Blair, searching for ways to unite North and South, sketched a plan for suspending hostilities between the Union and the Confederacy so that they might join forces against a French puppet regime in Mexico. Lincoln rejected this absurd scheme, but both he and Davis, confronting vocal antiwar factions at home, perceived advantages in demonstrating willingness to explore peace prospects at this juncture.

Davis agreed to send Confederate commissioners to meet Union counterparts "with a view to secure peace to the two countries." Lincoln's reply emphasized "securing peace to the people of our one common country." The clash between "two countries" and "one common country" nearly scuttled the meeting before the participants even convened, but when General Ulysses S. Grant welcomed the Confederate delegation to his headquarters on January 29, 1865, he believed them to be sincere and advised against peremptorily dismissing them. Lincoln thereupon decided to join secretary of state William Henry Seward to confer with the Confederates, including vice president Alexander H. Stephens, senator and former Confederate secretary of state Robert M. T. Hunter, and assistant secretary of war John A. Campbell.

On February 3, 1865, aboard the Union steamer *River Queen,* at Hampton Roads, Virginia, the men conducted four hours of informal talks, keeping no official minutes. Old friends Lincoln and Stephens greeted each other warmly, and the conference remained generally cordial, despite immutable disagreements. Lincoln was adamant that the Union must be restored, that measures already taken against slavery must be sustained, and that there could be no armistice short of the end of the war. On other matters, however, he indicated flexibility, hinting at leniency in restoring Southern political participation, consideration of how emancipation would actually be implemented, and possible compensation for slave owners.

Despite such conciliatory signals, the Confederate delegates were disappointed in Lincoln's rigid commitment to his fundamental terms for ending the war, and they were appalled by Seward's announcement that Congress had approved the Thirteenth Amendment, which would abolish slavery, furthering its progress toward adoption. (Stephens later claimed that Lincoln helpfully suggested that states might ratify the Thirteenth Amendment "prospectively," allowing themselves several years before considering it binding, but historians disagree over the plausibility of Stephens's account on that point.) The Confederate commissioners attempted to circumvent differences by reviving Blair's Mexico plan or advocating a cease-fire as a precursor to a convention of all of the states, but Lincoln relentlessly maintained that only the Confederacy's surrender could end the war.

The Hampton Roads Conference concluded without substantive achievements, as expected by both Davis and Lincoln. The conference did, however, underscore the irreconcilability of Confederate and Union goals. Davis used reports of the talks to reinvigorate Confederate determination, deliberately casting the Union's terms and actions as insulting. Meanwhile, Northern critics who had feared that Lincoln would concede too much applauded his firmness on key principles.

—Cara L. Shelly

BIBLIOGRAPHY

Davis, William C. *Jefferson Davis: The Man and His Hour.* Baton Rouge: Louisiana State University Press, 1991.

Donald, David Herbert. *Lincoln.* New York: Simon and Schuster, 1995.

Gienapp, William E. *Abraham Lincoln and the Civil War.* New York: Oxford University Press, 1992.

Goodwin, Doris Kearns. *Team of Rivals: The Political Genius of Abraham Lincoln.* New York: Simon and Schuster, 2005.

Johnson, Ludwell H. "Lincoln's Solution to the Problem of Peace Terms, 1864–1865." *Journal of Southern History* 34, no. 4 (November 1968): 576–586.

McPherson, James M. *Battle Cry of Freedom: The Civil War Era.* New York: Oxford University Press, 1988.

———. *Ordeal by Fire: The Civil War and Reconstruction.* New York: Knopf, 1982.

Sanders, Charles W., Jr. "Jefferson Davis and the Hampton Roads Peace Conference: 'To Secure Peace to the Two Countries.'" *Journal of Southern History* 63, no. 4 (November 1997): 803–826.

Schott, Thomas E. *Alexander H. Stephens of Georgia.* Baton Rouge: Louisiana State University Press, 1988.

Hay, John

John Milton Hay (1838–1905), Lincoln's highly capable assistant personal secretary, was a surrogate son to the president, far more like Lincoln in temperament and interests than his own son Robert Todd Lincoln. Hay's humor, intelligence, love of wordplay, fondness for literature, and devotion to his boss made him a source of comfort to the beleaguered president in the loneliness of the White House. Though twenty-nine years younger than Lincoln, Hay became as much a friend and confidant to the president as their age difference would allow.

Hay was born in Indiana, raised in a small town in western Illinois, and educated at Brown University. In 1860, while apprenticing in the Springfield law office of his uncle, Milton Hay, young John was recruited to assist Lincoln's private secretary, John G. Nicolay, a school chum from Pittsfield, Illinois. Attorney Hay said that his nephew had "great literary talent and great tact," and that he "will never make a lawyer," but that he "may be a poet some day, and he can at least write good English." Indeed he could. In the White House, Hay frequently composed letters for Lincoln's signature. Most of them were routine, but one—the famous 1864 letter of condolence to the widow Bixby—achieved world renown. In addition, he contributed dozens of anonymous and pseudonymous articles to newspapers during the Civil War, giving the administration's interpretation of events. In those pieces, he in effect served the function that would later be handled by a presidential press secretary.

Hay also acted as one of Lincoln's troubleshooters, helping to solve difficult problems. In early 1864 Hay spent weeks in Florida promoting that state's return to the Union in accordance with the president's so-called Ten Percent Plan for reconstruction. After that effort fizzled, he was dispatched to Niagara Falls a few months later to investigate Confederate peace feelers that the influential newspaper editor Horace Greeley had urged the administration to heed. Hay helped expose the Confederate effort as nothing more than a ruse to bolster the Peace

President Abraham Lincoln photographed with his secretaries, John M. Hay (standing) and John G. Nicolay, in November 1863.
Source: The Granger Collection, New York City

Democrats, who were insisting that the war be abandoned. That same year Lincoln also sent Hay to St. Louis to investigate rumors of a potential uprising.

Hay greatly admired his boss. In summer 1863 he wrote Nicolay that the president

> *is in fine whack. I have rarely seen him more serene & busy. He is managing this war, the draft, foreign relations, and planning a reconstruction of the Union, all at once. I never knew with what tyrannous authority he rules the Cabinet, till now. The most important things he decides & there is no cavil. I am growing more and more firmly convinced that the good of the country absolutely demands that he should be kept where he is till this thing is over. There is no man in the country, so wise, so gentle and so firm. I believe the hand of God placed him where he is.*

Hay scouted rumors that radicals dominated administration policy:

> *You may talk as you please of the Abolition Cabal directing affairs from Washington: some well meaning newspapers advise the President to keep his fingers out of the military pie: and all that sort of thing. The truth is, if he did, the pie would be a sorry mess. The old man sits here and wields like a backwoods Jupiter the bolts of war and the machinery of government with a hand equally steady & equally firm.*

Three years later he told a biographer, "Lincoln with all his foibles, is the greatest character since Christ."

Hay did not like Mary Todd Lincoln, referring to her in an 1862 letter as devilish and a "Hell-Cat." The First Lady resented Hay's unwillingness to engage in various unethical schemes to defraud the government, including misuse of the presidential stationery fund and misappropriation of a White House servant's salary.

The relations between Hay and Lincoln resembled those between Alexander Hamilton and George Washington when Hamilton served as Washington's principal aide. The journalist John Russell Young recalled that Hay

> *knew the social graces and amenities, and did much to make the atmosphere of the war[-]environed White House grateful, tempering unreasonable aspirations, giving to disappointed ambitions the soft answer which turneth away wrath, showing, as Hamilton did in similar offices, the tact and common sense which were to serve him as they served Hamilton in wider spheres of public duty.*

Young, who often visited the White House during the Civil War, called Hay "brilliant" and "chivalrous," quite "independent, with opinions on most questions," which he expressed freely. At times sociable, Hay could also be "reserved" and aloof, "with just a shade of pride that did not make acquaintanceship spontaneous." Hay, Young said, combined "the genius for romance and politics as no one…since Disraeli"; he judged that Hay was well "suited for his place in the President's family." Young depicted Hay as "a comely young man with [a] peach-blossom face," "exceedingly handsome—a slight, graceful, boyish figure—'girl in boy's clothes,' as I heard in a sniff from some angry politician." This "young, almost beardless, and almost boyish countenance did not seem to match with official responsibilities and the tumult of action in time of pressure, but he did what he had to do, was always graceful, composed, polite, and equal to the complexities of any situation which might arise." Hay's "old-fashioned speech" was "smooth, low-toned, quick in comprehension, sententious, reserved." People were "not quite sure whether it was the reserve of diffidence or aristocracy," Young remembered. The "high-bred, courteous" Hay was "not one with whom the breezy overflowing politician would be apt to take liberties." Young noticed "a touch of sadness in his temperament" and concluded that Hay "had the personal attractiveness as well as the youth of Byron" and "was what Byron might have been if grounded on good principles and with the wholesome discipline of home."

In 1863 an Ohio journalist described Hay as "that fellow five feet tall, that walks like lightning down the street," wearing "a turtle-backed hat, just the shape of his cranium, with well oiled locks, and handsome kid gloves." A "stranger might mistake him for a stray Englishman," and a "close observer will notice at once the air of weighty secrets by which he is surrounded." Hay expressed himself "in the choice and expressive language which prevails at the 'Chebang,' as he pleasantly terms the White House. Inquire affectionately after the health of the President of the mightiest nation on the earth, and John will inform you that the 'old Tycoon is in high feather.'"

A newspaperman who saw Hay in 1861 recalled that he was

> *a young, good-looking fellow, well, almost foppishly dressed, with by no means a low down opinion of himself, either physically or mentally, with plenty of self-confidence for anybody's use, a brain active and intellectual, with a full budget of small talk for the ladies or anybody else, and both eyes keeping a steady lookout for the interests of "number one."*

When a classmate from Brown congratulated him on winning the post of assistant presidential secretary, Hay replied: "Yes. I'm Keeper of the President's Conscience."

During his service in the White House, Hay kept an invaluable diary. When he and Nicolay wrote a ten-volume biography of Lincoln (published in 1890), they relied heavily on that document, as subsequent biographers have also done. With Nicolay, he also edited an edition of Lincoln's speeches and letters. Hay achieved eminence as a diplomat, serving as assistant secretary of state (1879–1881), ambassador to Great Britain (1897–1898), and secretary of state (1898–1905). He originated the "Open Door Policy" (1899, 1900) to protect equal commercial privileges for all countries dealing with China and protect that nation's territorial integrity. He also kept up his writing, composing editorials for the *New York Tribune,* publishing poetry, travel literature, and regional stories that anticipated the works of Bret Harte. His anonymous 1883 novel, *The Breadwinners: A Social Study,* was widely read.

See also *Nicolay, John G.*

—MICHAEL BURLINGAME

BIBLIOGRAPHY

Burlingame, Michael. "The Authorship of the Bixby Letter." In *At Lincoln's Side: John Hay's Civil War Correspondence and Selected Writings,* edited by Michael Burlingame. Carbondale: Southern Illinois University Press, 2000.

———. *The Inner World of Abraham Lincoln.* Urbana: University of Illinois Press, 1994.

Burlingame, Michael, and John R. Turner Ettlinger, eds. *Inside Lincoln's White House: The Complete Civil War Diary of John Hay.* Carbondale: Southern Illinois University Press, 1997.

Henry and Donelson, Forts

See *Forts Henry and Donelson*

Herndon, William H.

William Henry Herndon (1818–1891), Abraham Lincoln's third and last law partner, remains Lincoln's most controversial biographer.

Born on Christmas Day 1818, in Greensburg, Kentucky, Herndon was living in Sangamon County, Illinois, by the age of five. In 1836 Herndon entered Illinois College at Jacksonville, where he reportedly addressed a group of students who had gathered to protest the murder of abolitionist Elijah Lovejoy (1802–1837). Not only did Herndon condemn the murder, but he denounced the institution of slavery. When Herndon's father, Archer G. Herndon (1795–1867), a local Democratic politician, heard about the episode, he withdrew his son from the school, saying he would not tolerate "a damned abolitionist pup." Though Herndon's biographer doubts the story, there is no question that Herndon withdrew from the college after only one year and returned to Springfield with a political outlook clearly different than his father's.

In Springfield Herndon found employment as a clerk in Bell and Co., Joshua F. Speed's (1814–1882) general store. Speed offered Herndon $700 per year, plus board. Along with Speed, Lincoln, and another clerk, Herndon boarded at the store until he married Mary J. Maxey on March 26, 1840. The couple had six children during their marriage.

At Lincoln's suggestion, Herndon began reading law in the office of Logan and Lincoln. He studied in the firm for three years and was admitted to the bar on December 9, 1844. Shortly thereafter, Logan and Lincoln dissolved their partnership, and Lincoln asked Herndon to become his law partner. Years later, when asked why Lincoln had chosen him, Herndon admitted, "I don't know and no one else does."

The Lincoln and Herndon law firm was remarkably successful. They handled nearly 3,400 cases, including an average of fifteen cases per year on appeal to the

Illinois Supreme Court. They also had an extensive federal practice. While Lincoln spent much of his time traveling the law circuit, Herndon typically remained in Springfield in the office.

Herndon was deeply interested in politics. But he never craved elective office, although he served a single term as mayor of Springfield and helped establish the Republican Party in Illinois. Unlike his law partner's, Herndon's antislavery views grew increasingly radical. He carried on a lively correspondence with such prominent eastern abolitionists as Theodore Parker (1810–1860), Wendell Phillips (1811–1884), and Horace Greeley (1811–1872).

By 1858 Lincoln and other key Republicans began to distance themselves from Herndon's radicalism. In December 1860, as South Carolina threatened secession and Congress searched for a compromise, Herndon wrote a characteristically fiery letter to Charles Sumner: "Compromise—Compromise! Why I am sick at the very idea. Fools may compromise," Herndon exclaimed. "I am thoroughly convinced that two such civilizations as the North and the South cannot co-exist on the same soil and be co-equal in the Federal brotherhood. Let this natural war—let this inevitable struggle proceed—go on, till slavery is *dead—dead—dead."*

Nonetheless, before Lincoln left for Washington in 1861 he met with Herndon a final time and told him to keep the law firm open. "If I live I'm coming back some time," Lincoln said, "and then we'll go right on practicing law as if nothing ever happened."

Herndon continued his radical course throughout Lincoln's presidency. When the Confederacy fired on Fort Sumter, he hoped his law partner would immediately abolish slavery and execute the leaders of the rebellion. "He ought to hang somebody and get up a name for will or decision—for character," Herndon wrote a fellow Illinois radical. "Let him hang some Child or woman, if he has not Courage to hang a *man."* Though he was clearly frustrated with Lincoln's moderate course, Herndon remained loyal to Lincoln. He campaigned for the Republican ticket in 1862 and had plans to do so again in 1864, before an illness slowed his efforts.

Herndon visited Lincoln in the White House in January 1862. Shortly after Herndon's wife died the previous year, he had begun courting Anna Miles. By most accounts, she was a beautiful young woman, some eighteen years Herndon's junior and not terribly interested in the fiery Springfield lawyer. Nonetheless, Herndon was persistent. He promised her sister's husband that he would secure a federal appointment for him if he and his wife could convince Anna that he would make a suitable husband. When they agreed to the proposition, Herndon went to Washington to see the president. He told Lincoln about his whirlwind courtship, as well as the promise he had made. Lincoln thought it all was "wonderfully funny" and agreed to help his law partner. Not only did the president appoint Herndon's future brother-in-law an agent for the Cherokee Indians, but that July, Herndon and Anna were indeed married.

Within weeks of the assassination Herndon decided to "write & publish the *subjective* Mr Lincoln—'the inner life' of Mr L." He wanted to show the nation that Lincoln "was not God—was man: he was not perfect—had some defects & a few positive faults."

Herndon sent hundreds of letters to people who knew Lincoln during his time in Kentucky, Indiana, and Illinois. He traveled to interview old acquaintances and gathered letters and documents. Using his collection of primary source material, Herndon delivered a series of disastrous lectures in 1865 and 1866. He revealed, among other things, that Lincoln's one true love was not his wife of more than twenty years, but a girl from New Salem named Ann Rutledge (1813–1835). "Mr. Wm H Herndon is making an ass of himself," wrote Lincoln's oldest son a short time later. Neither he nor his mother forgave Herndon.

By 1869, Herndon was no closer to finishing his long-awaited Lincoln biography. Money problems forced him to sell his collection of primary source material for $4,000 to Ward Hill Lamon (1828–1893), who produced a poorly received, ghostwritten biography in 1872.

After a decade of financial troubles, alcoholism, and declining health, Herndon went into partnership with a young writer named Jesse W. Weik (1857–1930). By 1889 *Herndon's Lincoln: The True Story of a Great Life* finally hit bookstores. As promised, the book was indeed controversial. After questioning whether Lincoln was truly Thomas Lincoln's son, Herndon described his childhood in particularly pitiful terms. He expanded on the Rutledge romance and even claimed that Lincoln never became a Christian and died an infidel. "It is one of the most infamous books ever written," wrote a particularly harsh reviewer. "The book is the shame and disgrace of American literature. The obscenity of the work is surprising and shocking.... [W]e declare that this book is so bad it could hardly have been worse."

"Though poor, I am a happy man," Herndon wrote near the end of his life. "My life has been a happy one—saw much—learned some things of life; and now I enjoy myself as much as any person on the globe." On March 18, 1891, Herndon died, leaving an estate valued at $107.85, with debts greatly exceeding that amount. He is buried in Oak Ridge Cemetery in Springfield.

Herndon's reputation has steadily improved among Lincoln scholars. His collection of primary source material, published for the first time in 1998 by the Lincoln Studies Center at Knox College, remains the most important resource for information regarding Lincoln's pre-presidential life. Though he remains controversial, Herndon is also Lincoln's most important biographer.

—SAMUEL P. WHEELER

BIBLIOGRAPHY

Basler, Roy P., ed. *The Collected Works of Abraham Lincoln.* New Brunswick, N.J.: Rutgers University Press, 1953.

Donald, David. *Lincoln's Herndon.* New York: Knopf, 1948.

Donald, David Herbert. *"We Are Lincoln Men:" Abraham Lincoln and His Friends.* New York: Simon and Schuster, 2003.

Herndon, William H., and Jesse W. Weik. *Herndon's Lincoln.* Publication of the Knox College Lincoln Studies Center Series. Ed. Douglas L. Wilson and Rodney O. Davis. Urbana: University of Illinois Press, 2006.

Lupton, John A. "A. Lincoln, Esquire: The Evolution of a Lawyer." In *A. Lincoln, Esquire: A Shrewd, Sophisticated Lawyer in His Time,* by Allen D. Spiegel. Macon, Ga.: Mercer University Press, 2002.

Wilson, Douglas L., and Rodney O. Davis, eds. *Herndon's Informants: Letters, Interviews, and Statements about Abraham Lincoln.* Urbana: University of Illinois Press, 1998.

Hicks, Thomas Holliday

Thomas Holliday Hicks (1798–1865), a native of Maryland's Eastern Shore, held various local and state offices before narrowly winning the governorship of Maryland in 1857; he remained in that post until 1862. An erstwhile Whig, Hicks joined the American (or "Know-Nothing") Party in the mid-1850s and was the only non-Democratic governor of a slave state during the secession crisis of 1860–1861.

Although he was a slaveholder with proslavery attitudes, Hicks did not think that Maryland should automatically align with the lower South. Urging Marylanders to disregard both the secession threats from the Deep South and the antislavery rhetoric from the North, Hicks attempted to minimize divisiveness in the election of 1860. Hicks was unhappy with Abraham Lincoln's victory, but he conceded the constitutionality of the election and did not condone drastic reactions to it. When states of the Deep South seceded, Hicks counseled moderation and resisted pressures to call Maryland's Democratic-dominated legislature into session lest it act on pro-secession sentiment.

Believing that Maryland might suffer some of the worst harm in a war between North and South and unconvinced that Maryland's interests coincided with those of either faction, Hicks hoped for an amicable solution. When a multistate peace conference was slated for early 1861, Hicks appointed Maryland's representatives. All of them voted for compromise, although none unequivocally renounced secession. Hicks also urged Lincoln to name prominent Border State moderates to cabinet and Supreme Court positions, in the belief that such appointments would mitigate slave state suspicions of Lincoln.

Hicks's steadfast refusal to summon Maryland's legislature during the secession winter and his interest in compromise efforts often blur into assumptions that he was pro-Union and anti-secession in those perilous months. He was neither. Hicks reserved the option of secession if circumstances deteriorated, but he favored a central confederacy of Border States, rather than affiliation with the Deep South. He contacted other Border State governors, pressing the idea that a Border State confederacy would best serve those states' interests and could help maintain peace by buffering the extremes of North and South.

The Confederacy's firing on Fort Sumter (April 12–14, 1861) and Lincoln's request for troops (April 15, 1861) from the remaining Union states set in motion events fatal to Hicks's vision of Border State solidarity, as more states joined the Confederacy and others, including Maryland, endured internal strife. On April 19, the Sixth Massachusetts, on its way to Washington, D.C., clashed with a pro-secession mob in Baltimore. Hicks, struggling to prevent more incidents, assured an angry Baltimore crowd that Maryland would not fight the Southern states. He also allegedly approved efforts to destroy bridges and rail lines to block the flow of Northern troops through Maryland, although he later denied supporting such tactics. Lincoln, willing to take reasonable steps to avoid trouble, allowed that Northern troops might temporarily bypass Baltimore, but the point became moot when Union forces entered Maryland and seized key routes to Washington.

With Union control a reality and his own idea of a central confederacy evaporating, Hicks converted to Unionism. By late summer 1861, he was helping to stifle pro-Southern elements in Maryland, and he cooperated with the Lincoln administration's arrests of pro-secession state legislators. Sent to the U.S. Senate in 1862, he continued to offer advice on how to stymie Confederate sympathizers in Maryland. Hicks died in February 1865.

—Cara L. Shelly

BIBLIOGRAPHY

Hesseltine, William B. *Lincoln and the War Governors*. New York: Knopf, 1948.

Nichols, Roy Franklin. *The Disruption of Democracy*. New York: Macmillan, 1948.

Radcliffe, George L. P. *Governor Thomas H. Hicks of Maryland and the Civil War*. Baltimore: Johns Hopkins University Press, 1901.

Wright, William C. *The Secession Movement in the Middle Atlantic States*. Cranbury, N.J.: Associated University Presses, 1973.

Homestead Act

The Homestead Act, passed in 1862, allowed settlers to claim 160 acres of government land, free except for a small filing fee, provided that they resided on the land and made certain improvements. The act was part of the Republican agenda, dating from 1856, to encourage the settlement of the West by non-slaveholders. The term "free soil," in the Republican slogan, "Free Soil, Free Speech, Free Labor, Free Men" had the double meaning of wanting no slavery in the West but also endorsing allowing land to be sold cheaply, or just given, to settlers. The Homestead Act accomplished this.

Sentiment for homestead legislation mounted for two decades before the law was enacted. The House of Representatives passed several homestead bills in the 1850s, but the Senate never concurred. An 1860 bill passed both houses, but President James Buchanan vetoed it. The Republican platform in 1860 called for a homestead law.

Although many Republican positions on internal improvements and economic issues were similar to the earlier Whig agenda, homesteading was something of an exception. The Whigs had favored an activist government that would intervene to help the nation's economy, but on land issues they often favored policies tailored more to investors and speculators than to settlers. Abraham Lincoln followed this Whig philosophy in some cases but departed from it in others. During his term in the U.S. House, Lincoln opposed Illinois Democrat John McClernand's proposal that the government should get land into the hands of producers as cheaply as possible, as long as the costs of administering the land policy were met. McClernand's resolution was tabled and never acted on by Congress. On the other hand, Lincoln supported a homesteading proposal advocated by *New York Tribune* editor Horace Greeley in 1847. In the midst of the 1860 campaign, Greeley recalled that support after Buchanan's homestead veto, asking, "Does anyone suppose Abraham Lincoln would ever veto such a bill?"

The issue of free land for settlers was very much tied to the Republican Party's "free soil" ideology that opposed the expansion of slave territory. Republicans believed that the potential mobility of eastern workers, who might go west and become farmers under favorable government policies, helped to maintain social stability in the eastern cities. Workers who went west lessened the competition for jobs, allowing better wages for those who remained. Allowing slavery in the western lands might block this potential migration of free settlers. Moreover, and just as favorable to the Republicans, land filled with many small farms would effectively block plantation slavery from being introduced.

Lincoln supported the homestead plank in the 1860 Republican platform but never pushed it strongly. On the way to Washington for his inauguration, Lincoln spoke to German immigrants in Cincinnati, assuring them of his support for the homestead proposal. In his 1863 message to Congress Lincoln noted that the early settlement and cultivation of the public lands had long been advocated by some of America's wisest statesmen, and he suggested that that policy was now implemented in the Homestead Act.

Rep. Cyrus Aldrich of Minnesota introduced a homestead bill during the special session of Congress that Lincoln called in spring 1861. Nothing was done on the measure because of the press of war business. In December 1861, as the Thirty-Seventh Congress began its second regular session, Elijah Lovejoy of Illinois called for consideration of Aldrich's earlier bill. Some members of

Congress opposed homesteading because they believed that veterans of the Civil War would eventually be offered land bounties, and there were concerns about how that might conflict with a homestead law. Others argued that the government needed the revenue from land sales. Despite debates and opposition the Homestead Act passed by overwhelming majorities in the House in late February 1862 and in the Senate in May. Lincoln signed the bill on May 20, 1862.

Under the terms of the Homestead Act, any head of a household could claim 160 acres of surveyed public domain land by paying a $10 filing fee. Homesteaders had to reside on their claim for five years and make specified improvements on it, a process often called "proving up." This was an important provision, as fully two-thirds of the homesteaders failed to "prove up" in the first thirty years the law was in effect. After six months of residency, a homesteader could purchase their claim at the standard government price of $1.25 per acre. This provision was called "commutation." If settlers had the funds to do so, they might choose to commute their homestead because the land could then be sold, if values were rising, or it could be mortgaged to buy supplies, equipment, or more land.

The intent of the Homestead Act was to establish family farms, but it did not work as intended. There were many problems that the law's supporters never foresaw. Many of the landless poor were simply too poor to move west and support themselves while they brought a farm into production. Speculators and other business interests acquired large tracts of public land through fraud. Another problem was that whereas 160 acres was a good-sized farm in the East, it was simply not enough land for wheat farming or cattle ranching in the semi-arid West.

The Homestead Act found its greatest success in the first tier of Plains States—Kansas, Nebraska, and the Dakotas. In Nebraska and the Dakotas, 56.5 percent of the federal land was distributed under the Homestead Act. There were many later amendments to the homesteading law and many separate bills for homesteading in particular areas. Most homesteading activity was curtailed by an executive order issued by President Franklin Delano Roosevelt in the 1930s. By that time, more than 400,000 settlers had received about 285 million acres of land via homesteading.

—Mark S. Joy

BIBLIOGRAPHY

Boritt, G.S. *Lincoln and the Economics of the American Dream.* Memphis, Tenn.: Memphis State University Press, 1978.

Cardwardine, Richard. *Lincoln: A Life of Purpose and Power.* New York: Vintage, 2006.

Curry, Leonard P. *Blueprint for Modern America: Nonmilitary Legislation of the First Civil War Congress.* Nashville: Vanderbilt University Press, 1968.

Foner, Eric. *Free Soil, Free Labor, Free Men: The Ideology of the Republican Party before the Civil War.* New York: Oxford University Press, 1970.

Gates, Paul. *History of Public Land Law Development.* Washington, D.C.: Zenger, 1968.

Hine, Robert V., and John Mack Faragher. *The American West: A New Interpretive History.* New Haven: Yale University Press, 2000.

White, Richard. *"It's Your Misfortune and None of My Own": A New History of the American West.* Norman: University of Oklahoma Press, 1993.

Honest Abe

Abraham Lincoln's political supporters used the designation "Honest Abe" in various electoral campaigns to build up public trust and to elicit votes. The moniker's origins are somewhat unclear, but the image that it conveys has become for many a core element in the public memory of the man.

Nineteen-year-old Abraham Lincoln left his father's home and settled in New Salem, Illinois, in 1828. He tried many professions including grocer, postmaster, surveyor, and rail-splitter. Although he failed in some ventures, each allowed him to make personal connections in the surrounding area. It was his business venture with partner William Berry that earned him the nickname "Honest Abe." When their store went out of business, Lincoln repaid his own share of the debt and, after Berry's death, assumed his former partner's share as well.

Lincoln began his political career in 1832, unsuccessfully campaigning for the Illinois legislature as a member of the Whig Party. Despite that initial setback, he would gain victory two years later and go on to serve four two-year terms in the Illinois House of Representatives (1834–1842). Lincoln's rise to become chairman of the Whig Party made him a household name in Illinois.

John T. Stewart, a fellow Whig politician, encouraged Lincoln to study law. Lincoln joined Stewart's law firm in Springfield as a junior partner and became certified by the Sangamon County bar in 1837. There Lincoln handled hundreds of cases, furthering his reputation for fairness and honesty. In 1841 he joined the law firm of Stephen T. Logan. Lincoln had a knack for winning the respect of jurors, many of whom knew him as "Honest Old Abe." He made it a point to treat his clients honorably, and his opponents viewed him as fair and honest in the courtroom. Logan and Lincoln ended their successful partnership when Logan opted to go into business with his son, David. Lincoln started his own law firm with William H. Herndon in 1844.

In 1846 Lincoln ran for the U.S. Congress. His opponent, Peter Cartwright, was a frontier preacher. Cartwright tried to woo voters by claiming that Lincoln was an atheist, which Lincoln denied. Lincoln's reputation as an honest lawyer and politician, now firmly established across the state, held firm, and he won the election, serving in the U.S. House of Representatives from 1847 to 1849.

Over the years Lincoln traveled widely, visiting circuit and county courts. For many years Lincoln traveled with David Davis. When Davis was elected judge of the Eighth Circuit Court in 1848 he already knew Lincoln well and regarded the self-taught lawyer as fair and honest in his dealings. When Davis was absent, it was "Honest Abe" he trusted to preside as judge in his place.

Around 1850 Lincoln encapsulated his views of honesty in notes he wrote for a lecture, stating that any man choosing to be a lawyer should not yield to the public opinion that all lawyers are dishonest. Instead, he urged those choosing the profession to be honest in all associations. He then advised that if one could not be an honest lawyer, one should at least be honest in another profession. It was following his own advice that earned him the nickname "Honest Abe."

Lincoln was again elected to the Illinois legislature in 1854. In 1855 he was in the running for election to the U.S. Senate by the Illinois legislature before Lyman Trumbull prevailed. In 1856 Lincoln joined the Republican Party. In 1858, as the slavery issue boiled, Lincoln ran for the Senate against Democrat Stephen Douglas. Although he did not win the Senate seat, reports about Lincoln's debates with Douglas appeared in major newspapers, making Lincoln known outside of Illinois. The national recognition facilitated Lincoln's nomination for president in 1860. While the Whigs and Democrats lost power in the conflict over slavery, Lincoln was the perfect man to gain ground for the Republicans, relying in part on his solid reputation for honesty to win the election.

—Paula Cochran

BIBLIOGRAPHY

Donald, David Herbert. *Lincoln.* New York: Simon and Schuster, 1996.

Goodwin, Doris Kearns. *Team of Rivals: The Political Genius of Abraham Lincoln.* New York: Simon and Schuster, 2006.

Miller, William Lee. *Lincoln's Virtues: An Ethical Biography.* New York: Random House, 2003.

House Divided Speech

On June 16, 1858, at a convention in Springfield, the Illinois Republican Party named Abraham Lincoln its "first and only choice" for the U.S. Senate seat held by Stephen A. Douglas. Lincoln's speech on that occasion has come to be known by the scriptural quotation from which it draws its central idea: "A house divided against itself cannot stand." The address initiated the campaign that featured the Lincoln-Douglas debates, laid out key positions on which Lincoln would elaborate in those debates, and articulated in strident terms the views on slavery and union—the national "house" and ways to resolve its division—that would animate Lincoln's politics in the years leading up to his presidency.

As dozens of book titles attest, "the house divided" has become a favorite phrase of scholars and one of American cultural memory's most resonant descriptions of the Civil War era. Lincoln's use of the image was not entirely original, but it foreshadowed the audacity of his subsequent political career. Because of this speech, Lincoln's opponents imputed to him a belligerent intention to eradicate slavery from the United States. As was Lincoln's political position in 1858, the speech is more moderate than that, but it does describe in harrowing tones the threat of slaveholding interests and enjoins Republicans to resist them. At the risk of appearing radical, Lincoln crystallized in this speech his vision of the Republican Party's antislavery purpose, while also articulating the Republican fear that the "slavocracy" was poised to spread slavery across the nation.

The Republicans' meeting at Springfield was not formally a nominating convention; in the nineteenth century, U.S. senators still were elected indirectly, by state legislatures. The Republican Party took the unusual step of formalizing its support for a single candidate largely to quell speculation that Illinois Republicans would make common cause with their longtime nemesis, Stephen Douglas. In late 1857, Douglas broke with President James Buchanan, a fellow Democrat, over the legitimacy of the Kansas Territory's proposed Lecompton Constitution. Some Republicans outside of Illinois perceived that Douglas now could be a powerful ally in the fight to prevent slavery's extension into Kansas and that an alliance with him could fracture and weaken the Democrats.

The Springfield convention's nomination of Lincoln was a rebuke to that strategic plan, and Lincoln's speech served in part to explain why Republican voters should not be enticed to support Douglas. Notwithstanding Douglas's opposition to Lecompton and his cooperation with Republicans on the issue, Lincoln argued, the Democratic senator stood opposed to fundamental Republican principles. As he would do numerous times in the coming years, Lincoln attacked Douglas's remark that he didn't care how Kansas voted on slavery. Republicans' political work, he said, "must be intrusted to, and conducted by its own undoubted friends.... who *do care* for the result." Lincoln cited another biblical proverb, "A *living* dog is better than a *dead* lion," and cast himself as the living dog: If not as fearsome a political force as Stephen Douglas, he still was a fitter champion in the political struggle ahead.

Lincoln's view of that struggle constitutes the main subject of the speech. It was not—as were many of his most famous speeches—an address directly to the public. It was delivered at a party convention, to a partisan audience, in an effort to promote party unity. Lincoln begins with a prosaic introduction (echoing Daniel Webster's famous reply to Robert Hayne) that signals his practical interest in charting a course of political action: "If we could first know *where* we are, and *whither* we are tending, we could then better judge *what* to do, and *how* to do it." As to "where we are," Lincoln observes that the nation is in a state of increasing agitation over slavery, which *"will* not cease, until a *crisis* shall have been reached, and passed." This speech was not the first time Lincoln expressed the idea that the United States "cannot endure, permanently half slave and half free," nor was he the first to express it, but his description of the path forward—"whither we are tending"—is more striking. He says, "I do not expect the Union to be *dissolved*—I do not expect the house to *fall*—but I *do* expect it will cease to be divided. It will become *all* one thing, or *all* the other." This unambiguous account of the possibilities raises the stakes of slavery politics: the Republican policy of opposing slavery's extension into the western territories, though more moderate than abolitionism, now becomes a means to the same eventual end of eradicating slavery. Like most people at the time, Lincoln believed that the Constitution forbade interference with slavery in the Southern states, but he insists that "to arrest the further spread" of slavery will be to "place it where the public mind shall rest in belief that it is in course of ultimate extinction."

In Lincoln's view, "ultimate extinction" follows logically from a policy of slavery restriction. If no new slaves are imported from Africa and the institution is contained in the states where it already exists, eventually it will die out. The "founding fathers" themselves, Lincoln believed, harbored the same expectation; slavery always had been "in course of ultimate extinction," from the framing of the Constitution until 1854. Then, the Kansas-Nebraska Act gave slavery a new life in the western territories, conjuring up the other possibility in Lincoln's all-or-nothing vision of the house divided: If slavery's foes do not fight to restrict it, then its *"advocates* will push it forward, till it shall become alike lawful in *all* the States, *old* as well as *new—North* as well as *South."*

The House Divided speech may be most notable historically for its broad appraisal of the politics of slavery, but most of its text is devoted to the details of a precise political moment. Lincoln's original audience heard not only a statement of principles but also an intricate allegation that the Democratic Party was then engaged in a conspiracy to nationalize the institution of slavery. Lincoln charged that Douglas was a key player in this conspiracy, along with Franklin Pierce, the Democratic former president; Buchanan, his successor; and chief justice of the United States Roger B. Taney, who wrote the Supreme Court's infamous *Dred Scott* decision. Step by step, Lincoln explained, these men were paving the way for a full-scale reversal of slavery's course toward extinction. With the Kansas-Nebraska Act of 1854, they had repealed the Missouri Compromise and empowered all federal territories to legalize slavery; the 1857 *Dred Scott* decision deemed it unconstitutional to exclude slavery from those territories. The next logical step, Lincoln claims, is a second Supreme Court decision—the next *Dred Scott* decision—that would declare it unconstitutional for even existing states to disallow slavery. Historians disagree about the likelihood of such a decision, but even if Lincoln exaggerated the possibility, his warning about that prospect galvanized an audience of Republicans who greatly feared it. "Welcome or unwelcome," Lincoln says, "such decision is probably coming, and will soon be upon us, unless the power of the present political dynasty shall be met and overthrown. We shall *lie down* pleasantly dreaming that the people of *Missouri* are on the verge of making their State *free;* and we shall *awake* to the *reality,* instead, that the *Supreme* Court has made *Illinois* a *slave* State."

Lincoln acknowledged he could not prove that Douglas, Pierce, Taney, and Buchanan colluded, but the cumulative effects of their actions were the same as if they had. If "different workmen—Stephen, Franklin, Roger and James, for instance" separately crafted timbers that, when "joined together...exactly make the frame of a house or mill," it is impossible not to believe, Lincoln argues, that they worked from the same plan. By redeploying the speech's central image of a national "house," which must become all one thing or all the other, Lincoln warns that a new house, entirely open to slavery, already is being constructed by Democratic carpenters. Republicans must preserve the house as it had stood before, with slavery destined for extinction.

To many of his opponents, Lincoln's call to resist the conspiracy sounded like a counterplot to make the national house entirely free, and Lincoln sounded like an abolitionist; confidants who read Lincoln's draft urged him to exclude the house divided passage. He afterwards explained that the speech had not expressed his "wish" to end slavery throughout the country but rather his "expectation" that it eventually would end, as long as it was not allowed to expand. If conservative in its refusal expressly to wish slavery away, the House Divided speech nevertheless is uncompromising about which of two possible courses the nation ought to follow. Its "careful aggressiveness," to borrow one scholar's phrase, demonstrates the coexistence in Lincoln of a cautious politician and an adamant opponent of slavery.

See also *Cooper Union Address; Gettysburg Address; Rhetoric in Lincoln's Public Speeches*

—Christopher Hager

BIBLIOGRAPHY

Briggs, John Channing. "The 'House Divided' Speech: The Logic of Hopeful Resolve." In *Lincoln's Speeches Reconsidered.* Baltimore: Johns Hopkins University Press, 2005.

Donald, David Herbert. *Lincoln.* New York: Simon and Schuster, 1995. 206–209.

Fehrenbacher, Don E. "The Origins and Purpose of the House Divided Speech." In *Prelude to Greatness: Lincoln in the 1850s.* Stanford: Stanford University Press, 1962.

Finkelman, Paul. *An Imperfect Union: Slavery, Federalism, and Comity.* Chapel Hill: University of North Carolina Press, 1981.

Forgie, George. *Patricide in the House Divided: A Psychological Interpretation of Lincoln and His Age.* New York: Norton, 1979. 265–277.

Jaffa, Harry V. *Crisis of the House Divided: An Interpretation of the Issues in the Lincoln-Douglas Debates.* 1959. Reprint, Chicago: University of Chicago Press, 1982.

Pfau, Michael William. "The House That Abe Built: The 'House Divided' Speech and Republican Party Politics." *Rhetoric and Public Affairs* 2, no. 4 (Winter 1999): 625–651.

Zarefsky, David. *Lincoln, Douglas, and Slavery: In the Crucible of Public Debate.* Chicago: University of Chicago Press, 1990. Esp. 43–47 and 83–87.

Hunter, David

David Hunter (1802–1886) was a U.S. Army general and political ally of President Abraham Lincoln. David Hunter graduated twenty-fourth in his class from the United States Military Academy in 1822, served at various western posts, and at the time of Lincoln's election was a major stationed at Fort Leavenworth, Kansas.

While at Fort Leavenworth, Hunter began a correspondence with Abraham Lincoln through which he expressed his support for Lincoln and the abolitionist movement. Hunter's views won him a place with Lincoln and his supporters, and on Lincoln's election as president, Hunter was invited to accompany him on his inaugural train from Springfield, Illinois, to Washington, D.C. In Buffalo, New York, Hunter suffered a dislocated collarbone from the crowds pressing in to see Lincoln.

From April to May 1861 Hunter rose from colonel of the Third U.S. Cavalry to brigadier general of volunteers, commanding a brigade in the Washington, D.C., defenses. By June 1861, he commanded a division. A month later, Hunter was wounded at the Battle of First Manassas, Virginia, on July 21. In August 1861, after he recovered, he was promoted to the rank of major general and transferred to the Department of the West. After Major General John C. Frémont was relieved of command, Hunter served as temporary commander of the department.

In March 1862, Hunter was appointed commander of the Department of the South, which was deployed in the low country of South Carolina and Georgia. As departmental commander, he issued General Order No. 11, which emancipated the slaves in Florida, Georgia, and South Carolina. President Lincoln quickly rescinded the order before it could have any long-term political effect. Hunter raised the First South Carolina Volunteers (African Descent), one of the first African American units of the war. For his actions, Hunter was branded a felon by the Confederate government.

David Hunter, seated, center, with other members of the military commission that tried and convicted the Lincoln conspirators, sentencing half of them to hang. Hunter, a political ally of Lincoln, also served as president of the court martial proceedings against Major General FitzJohn Porter and conducted the investigation into the surrender of Harpers Ferry in September 1862.

Source: Library of Congress

As a political ally of the presidential administration, Hunter served as president of the court martial proceedings against Major General FitzJohn Porter after the Second Manassas campaign of August 1862. He also helped to investigate the surrender of Harpers Ferry, Virginia, during the Antietam campaign of September 1862.

In May 1864, General Hunter relieved Major General Franz Sigel as commander of the Army of the Shenandoah, after Sigel's defeat at New Market, Virginia. Hunter advanced southward through the Shenandoah Valley with orders to destroy the Virginia Central Railroad and defeated the main Confederate force at the Battle of Piedmont on June 5, 1864. He captured and burned the Virginia Military Institute, and sacked Lexington, Virginia. Hunter was defeated by Confederate reinforcements before he could attack Lynchburg. He was removed from command and did not serve again in a field command during the remainder of the war.

After Lincoln's assassination Hunter accompanied the president's body back to Springfield, Illinois. Hunter then returned to Washington, where he presided over the military trial of those accused of conspiring to kill Lincoln. He conducted the trial with dignity, but it was criticized at the time and later as being unfair. All the defendants were found guilty, and the court, led by Hunter, sentenced half of them to hang. Hunter retired from the army in 1866 and died in Washington in 1886.

—WILLIAM H. BROWN

BIBLIOGRAPHY

Eicher, John H., and David J. Eicher. *Civil War High Commands.* Stanford: Stanford University Press, 2001.

Gallagher, Gary W., ed. *Struggle for the Shenandoah: Essays on the 1864 Valley Campaign.* Kent, Ohio: Kent State University Press, 1991.

Warner, Ezra. *Generals in Blue: Lives of the Union Commanders.* Baton Rouge: Louisiana State University Press, 1964.

Iconography

The field of iconography—technically speaking, "the collected representations illustrating a subject" along with "a set of traditional or specified symbolic forms associated with that subject or theme"—was completely unknown to Lincoln himself, who once admitted that he knew nothing about artistic matters and was an entirely "indifferent judge" of his own portraits. Yet consciously or otherwise, Abraham Lincoln also made sure that the field of Lincoln iconography thrived. During the last five years of his life, he kept himself consistently, and surprisingly, available to photographers, painters, and sculptors, who in turn helped establish his image in the public mind, subsequently refining it several times over, until Lincoln evolved into the quintessential American icon.

When he was first nominated for the presidency in 1860, few people outside of Illinois knew what Lincoln looked like—and to make matters worse, rumors abounded that the newly anointed candidate was too homely to hold high office. Turning to the few existing photographic models then in existence, engravers and lithographers managed to generate a significant outpouring of imagery— both flattering portraits and wicked caricature—that helped cement Lincoln's early image with the voting public. Featuring props like log rails, axes, mauls, surveyors' tools, and flatboat oars, the pro-Lincoln pictures emphasized the self-made man who had risen from poverty through education and hard labor. Such pictures served usefully to focus on Lincoln as a personality, deflecting criticism of his progressive anti-slavery-expansion views by ignoring contentious campaign issues. Anti-Lincoln cartoons, on the other hand, assailed him as a crude and rustic country bumpkin who intended to impose a culture of racial equality on the bitterly divided nation. Such caricatures often featured Lincoln as a grotesquely tall scarecrow with disheveled hair, wearing an open-necked linsey-woolsey shirt, and in the company of supposedly dangerously radical politicians and cruelly lampooned African Americans.

While still a presidential candidate, though he did no campaigning of his own, Lincoln used iconography to make sure he "appeared" almost everywhere. The nominee wisely found time to obligingly pose for photographers, painters, and sculptors in his Springfield hometown, cooperating with several ventures specifically designed to yield original new portraits that might romanticize his homely features. These works, too, often inspired popular prints, which in turn became treasured keepsakes for the American parlor. One such example, commissioned by one of Lincoln's worried supporters in decisive Pennsylvania, was designed to generate a good-looking picture "whether the original would justify it or not." Rushed into production in October, the engraved adaptation was widely circulated in that crucial state in the weeks before election day. Ever modest, Lincoln typically joked with visiting image makers that he was too homely to sit for pictures. One painting he declared had a "somewhat pleasanter expression" than the original, hastily adding, "But that perhaps is not an objection." Despite such quaint comments, Lincoln undoubtedly appreciated the potential impact of the results and, no matter how busy he was with visitors and correspondence, made ample time for sittings.

All of these early images, careful and crude alike, became suddenly outdated when Lincoln abruptly modified his image after his election in 1860, growing a beard that buried his rugged, log cabin–to–White House frontiersman image under an avuncular new visage as a bearded statesman. Publishers had no choice but to issue a whole new body of Lincoln portraiture. The resulting, dignified-looking new pictures, many of them little more than hastily revised versions of clean-shaven, campaign-era poses, nevertheless may have helped to cool fears that the inexperienced Lincoln was not up to the sectional crisis.

The major image transformation of Lincoln's lifetime was propelled by the Emancipation Proclamation in 1863. Overnight Lincoln's reputation changed dramatically. He was often portrayed thereafter as a liberator and a modern Moses. However few such images were issued that year—as nervous picture publishers evidently hesitated before testing the market for scenes that featured black people. The first real flurry of "Great Emancipator" imagery appeared in time for Lincoln's 1864 reelection campaign, a hotly contested race that also reinvigorated the market for anti-Lincoln cartoons. Even as some printmakers showed Lincoln literally lifting enslaved people to freedom, others assailed him as a secret integrationist, bloodthirsty dictator, and hapless military failure.

Lincoln was far more than a silent witness to this image transfiguration. He welcomed two artists-in-residence to the White House—Edward Marchant in 1863 and Francis Carpenter in 1864—to facilitate the creation of heroic paintings celebrating emancipation, sensing its importance to the country's history—and his own. For Carpenter he posed for three separate sets of photographs, as well, and also gave him open access to his office to make sketches and observe him carefully for six months. The New York artist's final work inspired one of the best-selling engravings of the century, and the original canvas was later obtained by the U.S. Capitol, where it remains on display to this day.

The image makers barely had time to take stock of the newly reelected president when assassin John Wilkes Booth killed him in April 1865. But nothing Lincoln had done in life inspired the engravers and lithographers as much as did his death. Within months the market was flooded with vivid (often inaccurate) interpretations of his murder, mournful depictions of his final moments, panoramic scenes of his funerals, unlikely scenes of family gatherings in the White

House, and wildly imagined portrayals of his ascent to heaven. Old photographs were richly tinted and romanticized to create handsome memorial portraits, and when the printmakers' creative imagination lagged, some produced composites that showed Lincoln's head on the squat bodies of celebrities of the previous generation. In the mad scramble to own a Lincoln icon, almost any picture proved marketable. Paintings were adapted into prints, and marble busts were photographed as keepsakes for family albums. By the end of the 1860s Lincoln's was the most familiar face in American history, eclipsing even the ubiquitous George Washington. In iconography as in public memory, Lincoln became a national saint.

It is important to remember, however, that neither Lincoln nor other contemporary politicians directly controlled their image the way modern politicians do today. Artists, printmakers, and publishers devised their own approaches to the Lincoln theme, usually motivated by profits, not admiration or enmity. In fact, many picture publishers, including the famous New York lithographers Currier and Ives, initially produced both pro- and anti-Lincoln prints, concurrently supplying images for admirers and enemies alike. Only when his assassination rescued him from the realm of pictorial criticism did American iconography fully accept—and reflect—Lincoln's new status as a peerless hero. American iconography not only illustrated this transfiguration, it influenced it.

—HAROLD HOLZER

BIBLIOGRAPHY

Bunker, Gary L. *From Rail-Splitter to Icon: Lincoln's Image in Illustrated Periodicals, 1860–1865.* Kent, Ohio: Kent State University Press, 2004.

Holzer, Harold, Mark E. Neely, and Gabor S. Boritt. *The Lincoln Image: Abraham Lincoln and the Popular Print.* New York: Scribner's, 1984.

Illinois

Illinois, once part of the Northwest Territory, achieved statehood on December 3, 1818. Early Illinois pioneers recognized the rich soil and the advantages offered by the navigable Illinois, Mississippi, and Ohio Rivers. A generation after statehood, Chicago was already rising steadily as a new urban commercial center of the western frontier. In the territorial and early statehood years many settlers moved in from the Southern states, locating mainly in the southern part of Illinois.

Illinois entered the Union with a free-state constitution and a ban on slavery, but a clause in the constitution allowed seasonal slavery and indentured servitude for the next thirty years. A heated movement in 1822 to overturn Illinois's constitution was stymied by the voters, but it demonstrated the intense division within the state over slavery. The outcome of the vote secured Illinois as a free state and made it more attractive to settlers who were hostile to slavery, such as Thomas Lincoln, who had left Kentucky because of his distaste for slavery and moved to Illinois in 1830.

While the Lincolns had settled south of Decatur, the enterprising young Abraham Lincoln moved on to New Salem, near Springfield, eagerly seeking new opportunities. He became engaged as a storekeeper, a surveyor, and the captain of a Black Hawk War regiment and entered politics and law. With each successive venture, Lincoln built central Illinois connections and foundations vital to his later rise to national prominence. Lincoln and fellow assemblymen in the state legislature noted the state's northerly population trend and successfully relocated the state capital from Vandalia to Springfield, where Lincoln also moved.

The new home of the Lincolns was a small state. In 1830 the entire population was about 157,000, of whom only 2,400 were black, including about 750 who were still held in bondage. By the time Lincoln ran for the presidency, Illinois had grown to more than 1.7 million people, with 7,600 blacks. The black population would nearly quadruple in the next decade, reaching about 29,000 in 1870, when the total population would be just over 2.5 million. During Lincoln's three decades in Illinois, Chicago would grow from an insignificant hamlet of about one hundred people to a city of over 100,000. The city would grow rapidly between 1860 and 1865 and attain a population of just under 300,000 by 1870. Lincoln's success as an attorney and his rise to fame would mirror the growth of his adopted state.

With the growing population came the need to expand transportation. As a state legislator, Lincoln in 1837 helped lead the fight for a system of internal improvements. This program would improve navigation among Illinois waterways and, more important, approve the construction of railroads to traverse the state. Though the law saddled Illinois with a debt, it brought the beginnings of an expansive network of railroads tying the state to other markets across the country. Northern Illinois had used the Michigan and Erie Canal for transport of goods and produce eastward, but for lower Illinois the Mississippi River served as the main artery for transport to New Orleans. Had it not been for the railroads, the state would have naturally looked economically and culturally more toward the South and may have found it difficult to retain its pro-Union stance in the days before and during the Civil War. In that case, Illinois might not have produced the great president Abraham Lincoln.

In 1837 Lincoln first dealt with the politics of slavery in Illinois. In that year a mob in Alton destroyed the abolitionist newspaper of Elijah Lovejoy, killing the unrelenting Lovejoy as he tried to defend his press. Lincoln opposed a resolution in the state legislature attacking abolitionists and instead proposed a resolution, which failed, condemning slavery.

Until the 1850s Illinois was a relatively minor frontier state. In 1850 Sen. Stephen A. Douglas guided the Compromise of 1850 through Congress, becoming a politician of national significance and raising the political profile of Illinois. The importance of the state, and Douglas, grew the moment Douglas introduced the Kansas-Nebraska Act in Congress in 1854. This law also reignited the issue of slavery in the territories and made Illinois the focus of national politics. In response to Douglas's Kansas-Nebraska Act Lincoln helped organize the Republican Party in Illinois just as other opponents of the expansion of slavery did elsewhere. Fearing the danger to the country if slavery were allowed to spread, Abraham Lincoln and others took to the stump across the state speaking in opposition to Senator Douglas and the new law. Lincoln amassed a following, and the Republican Party drafted him to run against Douglas in his reelection bid in 1858.

From the state capitol building Lincoln that year delivered his eloquent admonition that "a house divided against itself cannot stand." The two politicians canvassed the Prairie State, and the national spotlight focused on Illinois as the stage for the great debates over slavery between one of the nation's most prominent men and one of its most promising. The state legislatures elected U.S. senators at that time, and the 1850 apportionment favored the Democrats, which tipped the victory to Douglas.

Though he lost the 1858 race, the political base that Lincoln had built in Illinois stood ready to nominate him for president in 1860, and that the Republican Party convention was held in Chicago boded well for Illinois's favorite son. Among the candidates in the 1860 election, Illinois forwarded two. Stephen Douglas opposed Lincoln again, and this time Lincoln prevailed. On February 11, 1861, Lincoln departed Illinois, never again to return except aboard his own funeral train in 1865.

After the first shots at Fort Sumter in 1861, Lincoln called on the states for volunteers. Illinois more than fulfilled the request. The Wigwam in Chicago, where Lincoln was nominated for president in 1860, housed soldiers. Troops were also mustered at Camp Douglas in Chicago and Camp Butler in Springfield. Cairo became a gathering point for troops from several Northern states to receive their training and final orders before departing south. Politicians including John Logan, John McClernand, and future governor Richard Oglesby came forward to offer their services for the Union cause. General Ulysses S. Grant, from Galena, led several units from Cairo into Confederate territory. Most Illinois soldiers were sent south, participating in such fierce battles as Fort Donelson and Shiloh in Tennessee, and Vicksburg, Mississippi. General George B. McClellan, former chief engineer of the Illinois Central Railroad, served as chief commander of Union forces.

Illinois proffered nearly 260,000 men for the Union cause, very few being drafted. The willingness could be attributed partly to the fact that *their* Abraham Lincoln was commander in chief. But not all of Illinois was united. Strong pro-Confederate sympathies infiltrated southern Illinois counties particularly. Democratic opposition and copperhead influence rose in Illinois after Union progress stalled in 1862 and early 1863. Particularly vociferous was an antiwar riot between soldiers and copperheads in Charleston, Illinois, in 1864. Racial prejudice in the state hindered some residents' full appreciation and approval of the Emancipation Proclamation in 1863, though others acclaimed its long-awaited release. Illinois collectively celebrated the end of Civil War and mourned the assassination of Lincoln in April 1865. His body was interred in Springfield on May 4, 1865.

See also *Yates, Richard; Vandalia, Illinois*

—Ron J. Keller

BIBLIOGRAPHY

Cole, Arthur. *The Centennial History of Illinois, Volume 3: The Era of the Civil War, 1848–1870.* Springfield: Illinois Centennial Commission, 1919.

Davidson, Alexander, and Bernard Stuve. *A Complete History of Illinois from 1673 to 1873.* Springfield: Illinois Journal Company, 1876.

Ford, Governor Thomas. *A History of Illinois.* Chicago: S.C. Griggs, 1854.

Howard, Robert. *Illinois: History of the Prairie State.* Grand Rapids: Eerdmans, 1972.

Mather, Irwin F. *The Making of Illinois: A History of the State from the Earliest Records to the Present Time.* Chicago: Flanagan, 1937.

Page, Roy, et al. *Illinois at War: 1861–1865.* Springfield: Office of the Superintendent of Public Instruction, 1968.

Illinois Central Railroad

The Illinois Central Railroad (IC) was chartered by the state of Illinois in 1851. As early as the 1830s there was interest in Illinois in a "central" railroad that would connect the Illinois-Michigan canal in the northern part of the state with the mouth of the Ohio River in the south. The IC was the first railroad to receive a federal land grant; Illinois senator Stephen A. Douglas was instrumental in obtaining congressional approval for it. In 1850 Congress granted federal lands to Illinois and other states along a route from northern Illinois to Mobile, Alabama, with the understanding that the states would then grant the lands to a railroad company. The state of Illinois chartered the Illinois Central and selected a group of eastern investors and industrialists to build and operate the line. By 1856 the

IC had 700 miles of track in Illinois. At that point it was probably the longest railroad in the world.

Abraham Lincoln, as a lawyer in Springfield, Illinois, did considerable legal work for the IC. In the Illinois legislature and during his one term in the U.S. House, Lincoln was an avid supporter of internal improvements projects. In the Illinois legislature in 1837 Lincoln supported a huge internal improvements program that proposed to spend $10 million on various projects, 90 percent of it going to railroad schemes.

In his history of the Illinois Central, John Stover suggests that in the mid- and late 1850s, Lincoln and his law partner, William Herndon, probably received more fees and retainers from the IC than from any other single client. Lincoln represented the IC in more than fifty cases, including eleven before the Illinois Supreme Court. The most important of these was the McLean County tax case, *Illinois Central Railroad v. the County of McLean.* When the state chartered the IC, it exempted the corporation from all state and local taxes except for an annual "charter fee" paid to the state. McLean County officials argued that the state had no right to do this and billed the railroad for property taxes on its lands within the county. Lincoln was hired to help present the railroad's case, along with the IC's staff attorney James F. Joy. A lower court found in the railroad's favor, and the county appealed to the Illinois Supreme Court. Herndon did most of the research for the appeal and provided several precedents from other states where similar exemptions had been upheld. After two hearings, the Supreme Court found in the railroad's favor in a decision handed down in January 1856.

Lincoln submitted a bill to the IC for $2,000. Railroad officials considered the amount exorbitant and refused to pay. Lincoln then decided his services were worth even more. When he billed the railroad $5,000 and still received no payment, he sued the Illinois Central. The case, ironically, was heard in McLean County by the same judge who had heard the original tax case, and the court found in Lincoln's favor. Even after Lincoln sued for his fee, the railroad continued to retain him in later cases. While Lincoln was often on retainer for the IC, he was never a permanent staff lawyer for the railroad. He also represented other railroads and transportation interests.

See also *Central Pacific Railroad; Railroads; Union Pacific Railroad*

—Mark S. Joy

BIBLIOGRAPHY

Finkelman, Paul. "Abraham Lincoln: Prairie Lawyer." In *America's Lawyer Presidents: From Law Office to the Oval Office,* edited by Norman Gross. Evanston: Northwestern University Press, 2004.

Starr, John W., Jr. *Lincoln and the Railroads: A Biographical Study.* New York: Dodd, Mead, 1927.

Stover, John F. *History of the Illinois Central Railroad.* New York: Macmillan, 1975.

Inaugural Address, First

The First Inaugural Address, delivered March 4, 1861, signaled Abraham Lincoln's early desire to maintain federal authority in the Deep South without endangering the fragile peace that had prevailed during the four months since secession had commenced. At the moment of its delivery, seven Deep South states had declared their independence and formed a government. The eight remaining slave states had rejected secession, yet might still leave the United States should the federal government exert authority in the seceded states. Thus Lincoln occupied a delicate position.

Lincoln opened his address by insisting that Southerners had no cause for apprehension at his election; he and his party had pledged many times to uphold all facets of the Constitution in every state, Southern as well as Northern. In particular, he promised to enforce one of the most controversial rights claimed by Southerners, the heavy-handed 1850 Fugitive Slave Law, adding, however, that he believed it should be amended to protect free people from false arrest.

Secessionists now threatened the Union, Lincoln continued. Despite their claims, he argued, the Union was not a legal contract created by the Constitution but a nation whose existence preceded that document, and for a nation to provide the means for its own destruction was absurd. Therefore, secession ordinances were invalid and violence against federal authority would be revolution. Lincoln swore to maintain all federal property remaining in the government's hands, collect import duties in Southern ports, and if possible deliver the mails.

The new president quickly tempered this expression of forcefulness, avowing that he wanted peace and would act only in defense. There would be no bloodshed, he declared, unless it was forced upon the government. He asked loyal Southerners to take time to view all aspects of the situation. After all, the Constitution had not been violated, and the Republicans had pledged repeatedly to uphold it, so disunionists could not claim even the natural right of revolution. More immediately, popular government would collapse if the minority would not abide by a legitimate election; the precedent would simply be repeated endlessly. Similarly, demanding concessions under the threat of secession also undermined electoral government, forcing Lincoln and his party to betray those who had elected them. Secession, then, meant anarchy.

Lincoln appealed to Southerners to have faith in the ultimate justice of the constitutional system, the proper means of ensuring which was not secession but future elections and possibly amendment of the Constitution itself—in fact, he

Abraham Lincoln's first inaugural was held on the steps of the unfinished Capitol building on March 4, 1861. Seven Deep South states had already seceded, and with others threatening to follow, Lincoln tried to balance firmness with magnanimity. His address pleased Republicans, Upper South Unionists, and even many Northern Democrats. Predictably, secessionists insisted that the address had been bellicose.

Source: The Granger Collection, New York

endorsed a constitutional amendment that Congress had just approved protecting slavery in the Southern states. Again he urged Southerners to act with calmness and forbearance, to take their time. And again Lincoln reminded them that while his administration would not act aggressively against disunionists, neither would it back down from its obligation to maintain federal authority. But he emphasized his desire to avoid conflict, concluding with a heartfelt appeal to Americans' shared history and mutual devotion to the Union: "I am loth to close. We are not enemies, but friends. We must not be enemies. Though passion may have strained, it must not break our bonds of affection. The mystic chords of memory, stretching from every battle-field, and patriot grave, to every living heart and hearthstone, all over this broad land, will yet swell the chorus of the Union, when again touched, as surely they will be, by the better angels of our nature."

The address Lincoln delivered on March 4 differed significantly from his original draft of just over a month earlier. In both speeches his tone was mild, exuding fair-mindedness and reason, but the earlier draft had been far more forceful in its opposition to secession. For example, Lincoln's opening assurance that he had neither ill will toward Southerners nor malign intentions toward slavery had been preceded by a firm assertion that he had been elected on the Republican Party platform and was bound to follow it. As the centerpiece of that platform was the exclusion of slavery from the western territories, placing it counter to every significant compromise proposal before Congress that winter, this established his firm opposition to compromise. More menacingly, the earlier draft had also vowed not just to maintain federal property in the Deep South but to recapture that already seized by secessionists, a profoundly more assertive policy. And the speech had closed not with an eloquent plea for harmony and peace but abruptly with the implied threat, "With *you*, and not with *me*, is the solemn question of 'Shall it be peace, or a sword?'"

Historians continue to debate the specific influences behind Lincoln's changes. What seems clear, however, is that the environment of Washington itself played no small part: Like many Republican leaders, once he was in the capital Lincoln found himself swayed by the immediacy of responsibility and the desperate pleas of Southern Unionists. Also plain is the key role played by Lincoln's secretary of state–designate, former New York governor and senator William Henry Seward, who throughout the crisis had led a minority faction of procompromise Republicans in Congress.

Seward not only surrounded Lincoln with Southern Unionists from the moment the president-elect arrived in the capital, but also responded to Lincoln's request for an opinion on his inaugural draft with a six-page letter. Appearing bellicose and inflexible, Seward wrote, would utterly alienate Northern conservatives and Upper South Unionists; in particular, the opening paragraphs pledging the administration's loyalty to the Republican platform would drive Virginia and Maryland to secede, forcing a battle for the capital itself. He advised Lincoln to follow the example of Thomas Jefferson's 1800 inaugural address, which had asserted Jefferson's intention to govern for the good of all, not just his own party. Seward suggested about fifty specific revisions, most of which involved subtle changes in phrasing—for example, replacing "on our side, or on yours" with "on the side of the North, or of the South," or describing the secession movement as "revolutionary" rather than "treasonable." He advocated more substantive alterations as well, eliminating Lincoln's blunt rejection of compromise and, not surprisingly, his pledge to recapture the Southern forts. Finally, Seward drafted a peroration that stressed Americans' shared heritage and need for unity.

Seward's suggestions found a ready ear; already Lincoln had proved open to the idea that the administration should appear flexible. A week earlier, his old Illinois friend and fellow lawyer Orville Hickman Browning had advised Lincoln to eliminate the vow to retake seized federal property in the South—not because he disagreed with the idea but because there was no need to announce it. If the administration maintained an overtly defensive posture, Browning explained, the secessionists would inevitably hand it an opportunity to recapture the seized forts without ever appearing to be aggressive. This was in line with Lincoln's desire to uphold the laws without provoking Southerners and probably reflected the spirit in which the president-elect took Seward's later, more extensive suggestions.

Lincoln adopted over thirty of Seward's revisions, but perhaps the most significant was one that he rejected. With reference to the Southern forts and collection of import duties, rather than adopt Seward's long, deliberately ambiguous passage supporting peace, Lincoln instead followed Browning's counsel and simply dropped the word "reclaim," while still pledging to "hold, occupy, and possess" government property and collect the tariff. Despite the new, gentler tone, Lincoln had conceded little of substance.

Predictably, response to Lincoln's inaugural address broke primarily along party lines. Republicans supported its masterful balance of firmness and magnanimity, while secessionists condemned its bellicosity. Yet the revisions did have a positive effect among Upper South Unionists, many of whom seemed relieved at its peaceful tone, and even among Northern Democrats, many of whom followed the lead of Illinois senator (and recent presidential hopeful) Stephen A. Douglas in praising the speech's conciliatory tone.

See also *Inaugural Address, Second*

—RUSSELL MCCLINTOCK

BIBLIOGRAPHY

Basler, Roy P., ed. *The Collected Works of Abraham Lincoln.* New Brunswick, N.J.: Rutgers University Press, 1955.

Crofts, Daniel W. *Reluctant Confederates: Upper South Unionists in the Secession Crisis.* Chapel Hill: University of North Carolina Press, 1989.

Einhorn, Lois J. *Abraham Lincoln, the Orator: Penetrating the Lincoln Legend.* New York: Greenwood Press, 1992.

McClintock, Russell. *Lincoln and the Decision for War: The Northern Response to Secession.* Chapel Hill: University of North Carolina Press, 2008.

Nichols, Marie Hochmuth. "Lincoln's First Inaugural." In *American Speeches,* edited by Wayland Maxfield Parrish and Marie Hochmuth Nichols, 60–100. New York: Longmans, Green, 1954.

Potter, David M. *Lincoln and His Party in the Secession Crisis.* 1942. Reprint, Baton Rouge: Louisiana State University Press, 1995.

White, Ronald C. *The Eloquent President: A Portrait of Lincoln through His Words.* New York: Random House, 2005.

Wilson, Douglas L. *Lincoln's Sword: The Presidency and the Power of Words.* New York: Vintage, 2006.

Inaugural Address, Second

Delivered March 4, 1865, Abraham Lincoln's Second Inaugural Address ranks among his greatest speeches and is also, at 703 words, among the shortest presidential inaugural addresses in American history. The address succinctly conveys how Lincoln viewed the war and the suffering that it brought to both sides and indicates the vision that Lincoln had in mind for postwar reconstruction. A jeremiad in the American tradition, the Second Inaugural remains debated by historians, who disagree as to what the speech says about, among other things, the evolution of Lincoln's thoughts on civil rights for African Americans. Less contested is what the address reveals about the evolution of Lincoln's thoughts on race, the role of God in history, and culpability for the Civil War.

Lincoln's first inaugural address was a mixture of a lawyer's brief and a public policy statement. Amid the 1861 secession crisis, Lincoln's speech laid out specific policy positions that he intended for his administration and also laid out his argument that the Constitution supported maintenance of the Union against those Southerners who would seek to dissolve it. In this sense, the speech was a lawyer's brief arguing that the North was correct in its position, while the South was incorrect. In the second inaugural, by contrast, Lincoln dismissed policy concerns, focusing instead on the meaning and the significance of the war. If the first inaugural address was delivered by Lincoln the lawyer, then the second was delivered by Lincoln the president, looking over his war-ravaged nation in the closing days of its Civil War.

The term "jeremiad" refers to a particular type of sermonic text in which the community is assumed to exist in a covenantal relationship with God. The sermon argues that the community has failed to live up to its covenantal obligations, usually in specific detail, and urges a return to true Christian beliefs and practices. The community in the jeremiad has suffered the judgment of God, but this judgment is corrective and restorative, rather than merely punitive. Lincoln's address, particularly its emphasis on shared culpability and the restorative feature of divine justice, marks the second inaugural as a jeremiad and lends credence to assessments that the address was more sermon than speech.

Lincoln's faith deepened during his years in the White House; he began to refer to God and God's will more and more often and began to state more frequently that he believed himself an agent in a Divine plan. Somewhat paradoxically, however, the more Lincoln saw God's hand at work in the Civil War, the less clearly he felt he could understand God's will. This ambiguity is reflected in the second inaugural; both sides read the same Bible and invoke the same God, but God's will may be opposed to both sides, and must be opposed to one. The invocation of God's will is ambiguous in the second inaugural, particularly as Lincoln declares that the North needs to remain steadfast in the pursuit of what is right, insofar as God allows them to see what is right; here Lincoln states his belief that the will of God is hidden from men. In this way, the second inaugural shows Lincoln expressing his desire to be on God's side, rather than an expectation that God was on his.

Though he came to believe that the war was God's punishment for slavery, Lincoln held both North and South culpable for the national sin. Referring to the expulsion from Eden, when Adam and Eve were commanded to seek their daily bread by the sweat of their own brows, Lincoln reminds his audience that the Southern slave society earned its bread by the sweat of others and thus disobeyed God's command to humanity. Immediately thereafter, however, Lincoln reminds his audience of Jesus' command to "judge not, that ye be not judged" (Matthew 7:1). The reason Lincoln would not blame the South was the continuation of the war and the damage that was being done to South and North alike. In Lincoln's view, God's judgment fell on both sides because both sides were complicit in the sin of slavery, one by seeking to expand and perpetuate it, the other by tolerating it and not confronting it sooner. For Lincoln, both sides had sinned together and had been judged together; both, therefore, must suffer together. Lincoln's biblical allusions, and the idea of togetherness that they conveyed, are strong signs that Lincoln was thinking deeply and beginning to speak about his plans for postwar reconstruction.

The idea of redemptive justice emerges clearly in the last paragraph of the address. Lincoln declares the need to remain steadfast and complete the task before the nation, to bring the Civil War to a successful conclusion, but declares also the need to forge a redemptive, restorative peace. Arguing for a just peace, Lincoln commits to binding the nation's wounds; to caring for veterans, widows, and orphans; and to creating a just peace, not only between North and South but between the reunited United States and the nations of the world. Lincoln's comment about caring for widows and orphans should not be understood to speak only to the practical realities of a postwar population, however; widows and orphans are frequently used in the Bible as metaphors for social justice. In speaking to the concerns of widows and orphans alongside the need for a just peace, Lincoln is reinforcing the redemptive message of his jeremiad.

The second inaugural reveals two primary evolutions in Lincoln's thought. The first, on the cause of the Civil War, is much more clearly stated in this second address than in Lincoln's first inaugural address. The cause of the war, Lincoln states, was slavery. The entire nation was thus to blame for the war in Lincoln's mind: The South bore blame for maintaining and seeking to expand slavery, while the North bore blame for tolerating slavery. This is a strong departure from the first inaugural address, in which Lincoln stated bluntly that he did not believe that his office possessed the authority to act against slavery where it stood but that he would work to prevent its expansion into new states or new territories.

More importantly, the second inaugural reveals the change in Lincoln's attitudes toward race. Early in his political career, he espoused the belief that whites were naturally superior to blacks and that African Americans did not deserve rights of citizenship equivalent to those enjoyed by whites. For nearly two full years during the Civil War Lincoln argued strongly in favor of colonization, by which all African Americans would be removed from the United States, which would become, as Lincoln then believed it properly was, a white man's country. However, as the necessities of war dictated changes in policy, primarily arming and organizing African Americans into combat regiments, Lincoln's views on race began slowly to change. As these units demonstrated bravery and capability on the battlefield, Lincoln slowly began to see African Americans less as an inferior race and more as his countrymen, fighting to preserve their nation. It would be an overstatement to say that Lincoln completely shed his racist views or that he came to support full, unequivocal rights for blacks and whites alike, but it is clear in the second inaugural that he was at least moving in that direction. The change in his assessment of blame, from placing it on the South to placing it on the nation wholesale, is one indication of this change. A second indication is Lincoln's statement that the nation's wounds needed to be bound. In the address, Lincoln spoke of the wounds brought both by the sword and by the lash—the wounds caused both by the war and by slavery. Stating that both sets of wounds needed to be bound, Lincoln hinted that he was thinking about how the nation could treat all of its inhabitants more equitably.

The extent of Lincoln's movement toward an endorsement of African American civil rights remains debated among historians. Though his assassination prevented him from pursuing his plans further, the second inaugural address makes clear that Lincoln did not view African Americans the same way at the end of the Civil War as he did at the beginning. The address reveals the extent to which Lincoln's views on religion, the cause of the Civil War, and the role of African Americans in American society had been changed during the four years of combat and shows Lincoln looking toward a just peace.

See also *Inaugural Address, First*

—ANTHONY SANTORO

BIBLIOGRAPHY

Berkovitch, Sacvan. *The American Jeremiad.* Madison: University of Wisconsin Press, 1978.

Guelzo, Allen C. *Abraham Lincoln: Redeemer President.* Grand Rapids, Mich.: Eerdmans, 1999.

McPherson, James M. *Abraham Lincoln and the Second American Revolution.* New York: Oxford University Press, 1990.

Paludan, Phillip Shaw. *The Presidency of Abraham Lincoln.* Lawrence: University Press of Kansas, 1994.

Takach, James. *Lincoln's Moral Vision: The Second Inaugural Address.* Jackson: University Press of Mississippi, 2002.

White, Ronald C., Jr. *Lincoln's Greatest Speech: The Second Inaugural.* New York: Simon and Schuster, 2002.

White, Ronald C., Jr. "Lincoln's Sermon on the Mount: The Second Inaugural." In *Religion and the American Civil War*, edited by Randall M. Miller, Henry S. Stout, and Charles Reagan Wilson, 208–228. New York: Oxford University Press, 1998.

Wills, Garry. "Lincoln's Greatest Speech." *Atlantic Monthly* 284, no. 3 (September 1999): 60–70.

Wilson, Edmund. *Patriotic Gore: Studies in the Literature of the American Civil War.* New York: Oxford University Press, 1962.

Wolf, William J. *Lincoln's Religion.* Philadelphia: Pilgrim Press, 1970.

Income Taxes

The outbreak of Civil War meant that the U.S. government needed not only immediate revenue to fight the war, but also revenue streams that could be used to provide guarantees to lenders. To obtain such increases in revenue was challenging for a government that had been small. It was difficult to sell war bonds. Foreigners and Southerners had flooded the market with older bonds. There was also real fear that the United States could not raise enough revenue to repay bonds. Secretary of the Treasury Salmon P. Chase was forced to travel to New York to persuade bankers to purchase or underwrite federal bonds.

An income tax was not immediately suggested as a means of raising revenue. Instead, taxes on manufactures and property were recommended. A property tax could piggyback onto existing state and local taxes and could be easily administered. However, because it was considered a direct tax, the Constitution required that it would have to be allocated among the states based on population size, not wealth or property values. Landowners in states where land was less valuable could face higher property tax rates than landowners in states with higher land values. It seemed unfair that a wealthy state would be able to tax property at a lower rate than a poor state. Furthermore, there was fear that financial property would be exempt while real property would be taxed.

Historian James McPherson called the tax fairness issue the second-most-divisive issue of the Civil War. The Republican Congress would need to carefully construct a set of policies to keep disparate groups content. Manufacturers, farmers, financiers, and the Border States would have to form some sort of coalition to fight and pay for the war. The new taxes must have the appearance of fairness; farmers could not be expected to fight the war and pick up the lion's share of the cost. Failure to settle on an equitable system of taxation would aid not only the South, but also copperhead Democrats in the next election. While they explored the options, lawmakers noted that the British had instituted a successful income tax that raised revenue and appealed to poor farmers' sense of fairness. Hence, an income tax was included in the Civil War tax measures, despite its omission in Salmon Chase's original report to Congress.

In August 1861 a multifaceted compromise bill that raised excise taxes, raised tariffs, and taxed income above $800 was introduced and eventually passed both houses of Congress. Most families did not earn over $800 annually. Profits from federal bonds were tax exempt. In the rush and confusion of that first year, no income tax forms were printed and no income tax was collected. Despite its first U.S. appearance, the income tax received little attention. The tariff gained most of the attention because members of Congress from manufacturing districts were eager to impose protective tariffs such as had been thwarted in the past by members from the South.

Although tariffs received the most attention, the strong Democratic showing in the midterm elections convinced Republican leaders that they would have to proceed cautiously on the tax issue. Hence, the 1862 bill taxed income above $600 at 3 percent and income above $10,000 at 5 percent. The House proposed a rate of 7.5 percent on income above $50,000, but the conservative Senate killed that in conference.

As the war dragged on into its third year and the nation's debt and deficit mounted, Secretary Chase argued for a progressive income tax, which he felt would raise more money than a flatter tax. Northeastern Congress members, however, opposed the plan because their constituents would pay the greatest share. More than 10 percent of Northern households paid the income tax. In the Northeast, 15 percent of households paid the income tax. By 1865 the income tax raised $32,050,000, or 37 percent of the amount that the tariff raised.

Although Reconstruction was very costly, the Republican leaders preferred to raise revenue through protective tariffs. Tariffs helped manufacturing areas and hurt agricultural areas, but farmers were bought off with protective tariffs on wool to compensate for higher manufacturing prices. Financiers had supported the income tax in the interest of winning the war and returning the country to the gold standard, but they withdrew their support once the return of the gold standard was within easy reach. The income tax ended in 1872.

See also *Banking and Monetary Policy; Legal Tender Act of 1862*

—David T. Mitchell

BIBLIOGRAPHY

Bolles, Albert S. *The Financial History of the United States from 1774–1885. Vol. 1–3.* New York: Appleton and Co. 1886 [1969 reprint].

Hill, Joseph A. "The Civil War Income Tax," *Quarterly Journal of Economics* 8, no.4 (1894): 416–452.

McPherson, James. *Battle Cry Freedom: The Civil War Era.* New York: Oxford University Press. 1988.

U.S. Printing. *Congressional Globe.* Sess. 1 and 2. 37th, 38th, 39th, 40th, and 41st Congresses. Washington, D.C.

Indiana

Shortly after Indiana entered the Union on December 11, 1816, Lincoln's father, Thomas, moved his family out of slaveholding Kentucky into the state carved from the former Northwest Territory. Thomas purchased land from the federal government and put seven-year-old Abraham to work clearing timber. Over the next fourteen years—one-quarter of his lifetime—Lincoln matured on Indiana soil before moving to Illinois in 1830. He worked at farming, carpentry, and manual labor in an era when four out of five men moved during their lifetimes and one out of four children lost a parent before age fifteen. While living in Indiana, the youth conscientiously rejected local values—hunting, fishing, and farming, as well as drinking, smoking, and gambling. Most strikingly, he matured among Kentucky transplants, in a state with black laws that was named for its displaced indigenous inhabitants, yet he felt neither sympathy for slavery nor hatred of Indians. Among Lincoln's Indiana neighbors were both Democrats and future Whigs. Lincoln's personal rejection of frontier life later aligned with the Whigs' ideological program of nationalism and economic development.

Lincoln attended three brief school sessions between 1818 and 1824, and he repeatedly read a few dozen identifiable books, including the Bible, Aesop's *Fables,* and biographies of Benjamin Franklin and George Washington. Though he did not join the local Little Pigeon Creek Baptist Church with his family, he did acquire a distrust of professional clergy, a dislike of sectarian bickering, a Calvinistic sense of providential predestination that he would describe as a "doctrine of necessity," and a religious fluency that later permeated his public speeches in the form of biblical phraseology and metaphors, most evidently in his House Divided speech, Gettysburg Address, and second inaugural.

Other experiences in Indiana offer tantalizing but ambiguous clues about Lincoln's psychological development. On October 5, 1818, his mother, Nancy Hanks Lincoln, died suddenly of milk sickness—tremetol poisoning acquired by drinking the milk of cows that had digested the white snakeroot plant. The following year Lincoln was kicked in the head by a horse and remained unconscious overnight. On January 28, 1828, his sister Sarah Lincoln Grigsby died in childbirth. The following year Abraham hired out to carry surplus farm produce by flatboat to New Orleans. Lincoln's alienation from his father had its roots in Indiana, where the father hired out the son for pay and whipped him for reading. In October 1844 Lincoln returned to Indiana to campaign for Whig presidential candidate Henry Clay. The reunion with childhood acquaintances stirred mixed memories that found expression in a series of mostly melancholy poems drafted during 1846. Many of the jokes Lincoln later told were set on the Indiana frontier.

Every assessment of Lincoln's adult political life turns in some measure to his adolescent experience in Indiana. During the campaign of 1860, Lincoln presented himself as a self-made man who overcame the inadequacies of a frontier boyhood. Early biographers contrasted Lincoln's greatness with an exaggerated portrait of the frontier family's poverty and vagrancy. In the early twentieth century, defenders rightly demonstrated the family's industry while romanticizing the frontier into a pastoral scene of husking bees and honorable books. Over the past thirty years historians have reexamined the reminiscences of Lincoln's Indiana neighbors and worked to contextualize Lincoln's political, religious, moral, and psychological development within the broad social history of American frontier life. Since 1963 the family homestead and Nancy's gravesite have been maintained by the National Park Service.

—Keith A. Erekson

BIBLIOGRAPHY

Miller, William Lee. *Lincoln's Virtues: An Ethical Biography.* New York: Knopf, 2002.

Winkle, Kenneth J. *The Young Eagle: The Rise of Abraham Lincoln.* Dallas: Taylor Trade, 2001.

Indian Relations, Lincoln and

Relations with American Indians during the Civil War have not gained a great amount of attention because the country and Abraham Lincoln dedicated their time and resources to fighting the rebellion. Even though an American Indian killed Lincoln's grandfather, and the future president served, however inconsequentially, in the Black Hawk War, Lincoln's record with respect to American Indian relations was consistent with historical governmental policy. The president wanted to limit white-Indian interaction to "protect" both groups while promoting Manifest Destiny.

The 1862 Dakota uprising in Minnesota led to Lincoln's legacy as the American president to have ordered the execution of, and clemency toward, more people than any other. The violence arose partially from the Dakotas' desperation because of their poor treatment by the federal government, but it came primarily from the push of white settlers onto Dakota lands. Once the outbreak began Lincoln responded forcefully on the side of the white settlers. Moderately, his support came out of the often indiscriminate violence the Dakota perpetrated on white civilians. However, the main reason for the president's backing settlers involved the fact that the Civil War was not going well for the Union, and Minnesota was a key state for Republican support. Lincoln sent John Pope, the failed general at Second Bull Run, to crush the Dakota uprising. Pope succeeded this time but at the expense of Dakota lives and legacy.

Dakota rebels were tried and over three hundred convicted and sentenced to execution in farcical trials. The possibility of injustice and the idea of hanging so many people caused Lincoln to act. The president pored over the trial transcripts and made the decision to spare all but thirty-eight of the perpetrators.

In the Indian Territory (present-day Oklahoma) a mini–Civil War occurred during the Lincoln administration. At the outset many Indians sided with the Confederacy as a result of its government's early pleas and $500 enlistment bounties paid to members of the "five civilized" tribes who joined the Southern cause. These tribes had little affection for the U.S. government, especially after the Union abandoned its forts and supplies at the war's outbreak. These tribes also had slaves and thus had an affinity toward the Confederacy, which was founded, according to Confederate vice president Alexander Stephens, on the "cornerstone" of slavery. Throughout the war, the nations proved largely divided, battling fiercely, at least partly over the issue of slavery. This division caused turmoil that Lincoln had little knowledge of and little real desire to solve. Union troops eventually occupied Indian Territory leading to postwar white encroachment.

One other famed incident that occurred during the Civil War involved Lincoln indirectly—the 1864 Sand Creek Massacre of the Cheyenne in Colorado by the state's militiamen. In March 1863, the Cheyenne leader Black Kettle had met with Lincoln in Washington. The president assured him the United States wanted peace, but the militia ignored the chief executive's wishes, as well as the white flag flown in the Cheyenne camp, and indiscriminately killed Indian men, women, and children.

Finally, the Navajos' (Dine) "Long Walk" took place during the Lincoln presidency, but without much influence or input from the president. Union General James H. Carleton defeated the Navajo, who had long raided in the northern Arizona and New Mexico Territories. In the winter of 1863, Carleton, with the help of Kit Carson, commenced a four-hundred-mile march from the nation's home territory to Bosque Redondo in far eastern New Mexico, a site not compatible with healthy living. Nearly two hundred Navajos died along the way from exposure and starvation. Carleton had misled federal officials about the quality of land and trading contracts. With the help of secretary of war Edwin Stanton, the government called for an investigation of the general, which led to his reassignment in 1867. After the war the federal government returned the Navajo to their homeland.

One notable American Indian served prominently in the Union army during the war and met and liked Lincoln. Ely Samuel Parker, or Do-He-No-Geh-Weh (meaning "keeper of the western door"), was a full-blooded Seneca who would become the first American Indian to head the Office of Indian Affairs, today's Bureau of Indian Affairs. Parker grew up in upstate New York on a reservation, where he attended the missionary school. He obtained law and engineering degrees before serving as an officer on General Ulysses S. Grant's staff during the Civil War. Parker was the only nonwhite at Robert E. Lee's surrender, for which Parker wrote out the terms.

As a midwesterner who had represented railroads as a lawyer, Lincoln was not one to try to stop Euro-American westward expansion. His meetings with Black Kettle and several other American Indian leaders promoted peace through assimilation. Then, as a result of the Dakota uprising and a visit to the Executive Mansion by the famed reformer Episcopal Bishop Henry Whipple, Lincoln announced that he wanted to improve the corrupt Indian system. But the president was unable to secure passage of the legislation because Minnesota congressmen who opposed Indian Office reform held key congressional positions.

Like most of his predecessors, Lincoln tried reform but failed. Unsurprisingly and through no real fault of his own, Abraham Lincoln left Indian relations little better than he found them.

See also *Sioux Uprising; Long Walk, The*

—Scott L. Stabler

BIBLIOGRAPHY

Danziger, Edmund. *Indians and Bureaucrats.* Urbana: University of Illinois Press, 1974.

Nichols, David A. *Lincoln and the Indians: Civil War Policy and Politics.* Columbia: University of Missouri Press, 1978.

Inflation

As the Civil War began, the United States had no uniform paper currency. The only money created by the federal government was gold and silver coins. Paper money was printed by state-chartered banks. This currency circulated

Inflation

widely, but since its reliability and actual value were often questionable, businesses often discounted it in transactions. All paper money was supposedly redeemable at the issuing bank for gold or silver coin, which was called "specie," but lax state banking regulations meant that many banks lacked sufficient specie to support their banknotes.

In December 1861 the high demand for gold forced U.S. banks and private businesses to suspend the conversion of paper currency into specie. On January 1, 1862, the federal government also suspended the conversion of its Treasury notes into specie. Many in Congress and in Lincoln's administration were driven to the conclusion that the nation needed a paper currency, despite their misgivings about the inflationary dangers inherent in such money. In February 1862 Congress authorized the issuance of the first "greenbacks." By the end of the war, over $450 million of this paper currency had been issued. This money was made "legal tender," which meant that businesses were required to accept it in transactions. There were no provisions for the ultimate conversion of the greenbacks into specie.

In his annual message to Congress in 1862, Lincoln noted the success of the greenbacks and suggested that the notes had met the nation's need for a uniform currency. While the value of the greenback against gold fluctuated widely during the war, the paper money was immediately accepted by businesses and the public without great outcry.

The value of the greenbacks depreciated when the war seemed to be going badly for the Union, but the North never experienced the kind of runaway inflation that the nation had seen with the Continental paper dollar during the Revolution, nor what the Confederacy was experiencing during the Civil War. In part the reason was that the Union did not resort to the printing press to pay for most of its war costs. The Union raised about 13 percent of its expenditures through printing money, 20 percent through increased taxation, and the balance through the sale of bonds.

In January 1863, when Congress authorized issuing an additional $100 million in greenbacks, Lincoln signed the legislation but expressed "sincere regrets" at its necessity. He recommended that Congress proceed with the national banking legislation proposed by secretary of the Treasury Salmon P. Chase. Lincoln also urged Congress to start taxing the use of paper currency from state-chartered banks. Such a tax would drive those banknotes out of circulation, and that would reduce the money supply. Chase had advocated such a tax in his annual Treasury reports of both 1861 and 1862.

Estimates of the rate of inflation for both the Union and the Confederacy are imprecise. It is often suggested that the cost of living roughly doubled in the North. But it did not approach the hyperinflation that the Confederacy experienced, in which the inflation rate may have reached 9,000 percent. Although the discussion of wartime inflation is often tied to the fluctuation of the greenback against gold, it is important to note that the massive outlays of the government for war supplies would have caused significant inflation even if all purchases had been made with gold. Lincoln expressed anxiety over inflation and publicly spoke out against those who speculated in gold while disregarding the best interests of their nation. But he believed that the resort to paper currency with its attendant inflationary dangers was a risk the nation had to take to win the war and preserve constitutional government.

—MARK S. JOY

BIBLIOGRAPHY

Curry, Leonard P. *Blueprint for Modern America: Nonmilitary Legislation of the First Civil War Congress.* Nashville, Tenn.: Vanderbilt University Press, 1968.

Hammond, Bray. *Sovereignty and an Empty Purse: Banks and Politics in the Civil War.* Princeton: Princeton University Press, 1970.

Richardson, Heather Cox. *The Greatest Nation of the Earth: Republican Economic Policies during the Civil War.* Cambridge, Mass.: Harvard University Press, 1997.

Internal Improvements

In the nineteenth century, projects that today are labeled "public works" or "infrastructure" were called "internal improvements." The question of whether or not the federal government should fund internal improvements of less than national scope was hotly debated. The Whigs favored federal funding for projects such as canals; turnpikes; railroads; and river, harbor, and port improvements. The Democrats generally argued that these were state or local issues and should be funded at those levels.

There were also regional differences on the subject. Southern plantations were often located on rivers that provided easy movement of their crops to markets, so Southerners generally opposed federal spending on internal improvements. They also saw federal funding as a broadening of constitutionally defined powers and thus feared that such actions could be a precedent for federal action against slavery. Long settled areas such as the Eastern Seaboard had already developed much of their own infrastructure and did not want to be taxed at the federal level to pay for such projects in other regions. The newer parts of the nation, of course, took precisely the opposite view, and the new states of the trans-Appalachian West were among the strongest supporters of federal expenditures for internal improvements. However, there were numerous exceptions to these party and sectional patterns, as many politicians supported any project that might benefit their particular constituents.

Lincoln greatly admired the Kentucky statesman Henry Clay and strongly supported Clay's "American System," which called for internal improvements, a protective tariff, and a national bank. When he entered Illinois politics in 1832, Lincoln wholeheartedly embraced internal improvements. He pointed to his own experience freighting goods on the Sangamon River and suggested he knew the types of projects that could benefit his district. In 1837 the Illinois legislature passed an ambitious program of internal improvements that Lincoln strongly supported. However, when the Panic of 1837 hit later that year, the projects came to a halt and the state's economy was crippled. The legislature would pass no more improvement bills for some time, but Lincoln continued to advocate such projects.

During Lincoln's one term in the U.S. House of Representatives (1847–1849), his attention was focused primarily on the war with Mexico and the resultant question of the extension of slavery into newly acquired territory. Nevertheless he regularly presented petitions from his district, many of which were requests for land grants for railroads. In June 1848, Lincoln addressed Congress, setting out the Whig doctrine on internal improvements and criticizing President James K. Polk's position that many such projects were of local benefit only. Lincoln argued that there was nothing so local as not to be of some general advantage to the nation.

As president, Lincoln was naturally occupied primarily with the crisis of the Civil War. But Lincoln did not have to lobby for internal improvements because his party, which favored them, controlled the White House and both houses of Congress. In 1862 Lincoln signed the Pacific Railroad Act—the largest internal improvement project undertaken by the federal government to that time. During the same session, Congress passed the Homestead Act and the Morrill Land Grant Act, both of which significantly influenced the nation's future economic development. These laws did not exactly constitute internal improvements, but they reflected Whig/Republican support for federal stimulus to economic and geographic development. Throughout his administration Lincoln often praised internal improvement projects in his annual messages to Congress. He consistently maintained that America could pursue such development programs even in the midst of a tragic and costly war.

—MARK S. JOY

BIBLIOGRAPHY

Boritt, G. S. *Lincoln and the Economics of the American Dream.* Memphis, Tenn.: Memphis State University Press, 1978.

Larson, John Lauritz. *Internal Improvements: National Public Works and the Promise of Popular Government in the Early United States.* Chapel Hill: University of North Carolina Press, 2001.

Neely, Mark E., Jr. *The Last Best Hope of Earth: Abraham Lincoln and the Promise of America.* Cambridge, Mass.: Harvard University Press, 1993.

J

Jackson, Andrew, As a Model for Lincoln

Both Abraham Lincoln (1809–1865), the sixteenth president of the United States, and Andrew Jackson (1767–1845), the seventh president, who served from 1829 to 1837, grew up on the frontier. Uneducated and poor, both prospered in frontier law and rode their hardscrabble backgrounds to the presidency. Both had nicknames—Jackson's "Old Hickory" and Lincoln's "the Rail-Splitter"—that reflected their frontier background. Raised among supporters of Andrew Jackson, Lincoln was initially a Jacksonian Democrat. Frontiersmen readily identified with Jackson, the hero of the Battle of New Orleans in 1814, and his personification of nineteenth-century manliness. Lincoln never achieved Jackson's martial success (he served in the Black Hawk War of 1832 but saw no action). Rather, Lincoln's physical manliness was expressed in typical boyhood contests—wrestling, foot races, and feats of strength. Although Jackson's toughness and tenacious personality were evident in his many duels and gunfights, Lincoln, who didn't even use guns to hunt, preferred unassuming persuasion to a physical altercation. He showed courage instead in his remarkable work in the political arena, where he would, perhaps surprisingly, find a role model in the presidency of the man whose politics he subsequently rejected.

William Jones, an anti-Jackson shopkeeper from Indiana, convinced Lincoln to embrace the growing anti-Jackson coalition and join the Whigs. Lincoln's rejection of Jacksonian politics was also influenced by his personal views about the importance of policies that promoted sustained commercial development. Thus Lincoln was drawn to the Whig Party's support for the Second Bank of the United States, government-sponsored internal improvements, and protective tariffs to encourage economic development. For the rest of his life Lincoln followed Whig doctrine and almost worshiped its standard-bearer, Henry Clay.

Jackson's veto of the recharter of the Second Bank of the United States led to its demise in 1836. Jackson believed the national bank threatened the economy and served to expand government powers. He began banking reform, including the promotion of hard money, silver and gold, rather than the use of unregulated paper money. Whigs used Jackson's overthrow of the bank as a means of increasing membership in their party.

Jackson, although supportive of internal improvements, believed that federally sponsored improvements would endanger republican government. He believed that internal improvements were constitutionally acceptable for national defense and if they provided national benefit, but he rejected support for local projects that benefited a state, a segment of a state, or a corporation. Jackson's opposition to social and economic modernization was counter to Whig dogma. Jackson supported an agricultural society of commoners. Lincoln favored the Whig view of government supporting an industrial economy in which the federal government would subsidize banks, factories, and railroads.

Jackson, unlike previous presidents, did not yield to Congress. He sought to fully exercise his presidential power. Whigs proclaimed themselves defenders of liberty against the tyrannical Jackson. Hostile cartoons portrayed Jackson as "King Andrew I." While "King Andrew" cleared out opponents, vetoed internal improvements, and killed the Bank of the United States, Whigs argued that Congress, not the president, reflected the will of the people.

Though Jackson favored a federal government of limited powers, his views changed somewhat with the Nullification Crisis. In 1832, displeased by a federal tariff, South Carolina declared that it had the right to nullify the tariff and would do so by force if necessary. Jackson believed that this nullification of federal law was tantamount to treason, and he threatened to send federal troops to enforce the law. In the Nullification Crisis Jackson headed off any thoughts some South Carolinians might have had of leaving the Union. He went on to redefine constitutional law by stating that the people forged the union and therefore the people alone could dissolve it. States surrendered essential parts of their independent power in becoming part of the nation, including the right to declare war, make treaties, or exercise exclusive judicial and legislative powers. American citizens owed obedience to the nation's Constitution and its laws. The crisis was averted when Congress passed a compromise in 1833, reducing the tariff. Jackson had clearly placed the power of the federal government over that of a state. But although a crisis had been avoided, the question of nullification had not been resolved.

When Lincoln became president in 1860, he adhered to Whig (now Republican) views in ordinary matters of government. He rarely interfered with the work of Congress and gave freedom to members of his cabinet. He tripled the average tariff, subsidized the construction of a transcontinental railroad, created a national banking structure, signed the Homestead Act with its offer of free land to actual settlers, and supported the Legal Tender Act, which provided for the issue of paper money. Lincoln believed that the purpose of government was to do for the people whatever they needed to have done but could not do for themselves.

But in spite of Lincoln's solid support for Whig and Republican policies, during the crisis of the Union, facing the threat of secession over slavery from the time he took office, Lincoln sought guidance in the actions and words of Andrew Jackson, who had confronted similar threats during the Nullification Crisis. Lincoln used a Jacksonian response to defend the nation's sovereignty. Indeed, Lincoln's first inaugural address is often compared to Jackson's nationalistic writings. It contained language similar to that used by Jackson to make legal and constitutional arguments against secession. Lincoln reiterated Jackson's beliefs that "no state, upon its own mere motion, can lawfully get out of the Union"; that "resolves and ordinances to that effect are legally void: and that acts of violence, within any State or States, against the authority of the United States, are insurrectionary or revolutionary." Lincoln reiterated that the people are sovereign, that the Union was perpetual, that disunion by armed force is treason and secession is the very essence of anarchy. Like Jackson, he was willing to preserve the Union at any price.

In 1861, Lincoln suspended civil law in territories where resistance to federal authority threatened to lead to the withdrawal of additional states from the Union.

Like Jackson, Lincoln began to rely more on his own judgment than on the counsel of his advisers. Exercising the strength of the presidency, Lincoln doubled the size of the army and navy, instituted a naval blockade of the Confederacy, spent Treasury funds, and in 1862, with Congress out of session, suspended *habeas corpus* throughout the nation. When Lincoln was criticized, he again turned to the example of Andrew Jackson. In 1815, Jackson had established martial law in New Orleans. The military acted as the police, the courts, and the legislature. Jackson had several citizens arrested under martial law, including a judge who later fined Jackson $1,000. Jackson paid the fine but was later reimbursed by Congress. Jackson, as a military general, had proved that he could declare martial law in time of war. Lincoln, as president, assumed the right as well.

After Lincoln suspended the writ of *habeas corpus* thousands of people were arrested. Among them was a Maryland secessionist named John Merryman. Supreme Court Chief Justice Roger B. Taney issued a writ of *habeas corpus*. Justice Taney ruled that the suspension was unconstitutional because Lincoln had suspended the writ without an act of Congress. Lincoln ignored the decision (much as Jackson had ignored Justice John Marshall's decision in *Cherokee Nation v Georgia*) and Congress subsequently validated his decision.

Lincoln tried to find a balance between liberty and order during wartime but was criticized nonetheless. It was now Lincoln who was portrayed as the hostile "king." Lincoln defended his stance on civil liberties and their relation to the Constitution: "Often one limb must be amputated to save a life; but life is never given to save a limb." Like Jackson, he exercised his presidential power to preserve peace and enforce the nation's laws to save the Union and the principles he believed it stood for. And like Jackson, he was willing to preserve the United States at any price.

—Paula Cochran

BIBLIOGRAPHY

Donald, David Herbert. *Lincoln.* New York: Simon and Schuster, 1996.

Goodwin, Doris Kearns. *Team of Rivals: The Political Genius of Abraham Lincoln.* New York: Simon and Schuster, 2006.

Harris, William C. *Lincoln's Rise to the Presidency.* Lawrence: University Press of Kansas, 2007.

Howe, Daniel Walker. *The Political Culture of American Whigs.* Chicago: University of Chicago Press, 1984.

Mearns, David. *The Lincoln Papers: Vols. 1 and 2.* New York: Doubleday, 1948.

Miller, William Lee. *Lincoln's Virtues: An Ethical Biography.* New York: Random House, 2003.

Wilson, Douglas. *Honor's Voice: The Transformation of Abraham Lincoln.* New York: Vintage, 1999.

Jackson, Claiborne Fox

Born in Kentucky in 1806, Claiborne Fox Jackson (1806–1862) moved to Missouri in 1827, where he eventually served five terms in the state legislature and became an outspoken champion of Southern slaveholding interests. Personal and political problems—including a rivalry with Missouri senator Thomas Hart Benton—during the 1840s pushed Jackson out of public office for a time. However, the struggle over the slaveholding future of Kansas Territory in the 1850s drew him back to action, and he joined other Missourians in resisting antislavery efforts there, even crossing into Kansas and voting illegally.

Jackson's reputation as an extreme defender of Southern rights aided his political reemergence in the latter part of the 1850s, as many Missourians grew frustrated with the success of antislavery efforts in Kansas and across the North. By 1860 Jackson was the state's Democratic candidate for governor. But Democrats in Missouri and across the nation were strongly divided. The national Democratic Party split into Northern and Southern factions, each nominating its own candidate for president—Stephen A. Douglas in the North and John C. Breckinridge in the South. Jackson backed Douglas, a controversial choice that lost him some support among the Southern-rights Democrats but drew in moderates. He narrowly won the election.

Jackson took the governor's seat just as the nation was thrust into the secession crisis following Abraham Lincoln's election. He openly identified with the slaveholding South but officially took a neutral stance on secession. Nonetheless, when the Missouri legislature scheduled a convention to determine the state's future, Jackson worked behind the scenes preparing for the state's secession. He corresponded with secession commissioners and even made plans to secure 60,000 muskets from the federal arsenal in St. Louis if Missouri seceded.

The Missouri convention overwhelmingly voted against secession, but affirmed its state's sovereignty and denounced attempts by the U.S. government to coerce the Deep South back into the Union. Jackson sought to use the conditional Unionism of many Missourians against the federal government. Since Northern troops would invariably go through Missouri, by land or river, if the government attempted to forcefully end secession, Jackson planned to portray those efforts as an assault on the sovereignty of Missouri. His plan was aided when Francis P. Blair Jr., a strong Missouri Unionist—and the brother of Montgomery Blair, who served in Lincoln's cabinet—recruited a large number of German immigrants in St. Louis to prevent secession or a Confederate invasion. When the War Department transferred the rabidly anti-secessionist army captain Nathaniel Lyon and a contingent of regular soldiers to St. Louis, many conditional Unionists in Missouri turned against the federal government.

Following the attack on Fort Sumter in South Carolina, Lincoln issued his call for volunteers to put down the rebellion. Missouri was asked to provide roughly 3,000 men. Jackson responded that Lincoln's act was unconstitutional and illegal. He denounced the effort to coerce the Deep South back into the Union as an unholy crusade. Secessionists in Missouri celebrated their governor's rejection of Lincoln's request. Jackson then ordered militia commanders to assemble their men at key locations for "training." Behind the scenes, Jackson communicated with Confederate officials about Missouri's chances for secession. But he still acted carefully, as much of the state remained loyal to the Union.

Jackson's hopes for secession received an unexpected boost when Blair and Lyon led a force of 6,500 troops in a surprise assault against one of the militia training camps on May 10. Around 670 secessionists were captured, and 200 more escaped. When the Union troops paraded their captives downtown, a small fight led to a large riot in St. Louis. Allegations of federal soldiers shooting women and children turned even more Missourians against the Lincoln administration. Jackson quickly took advantage of the situation and ordered the Missouri militia to defend the state. The excitement abated, however, when officials in St. Louis restored order and established an uneasy peace.

In June, Jackson and Confederate General Sterling Price met with Lyon and Blair to discuss Missouri's neutrality. Lyon rejected the idea of taking a middle ground and stormed out of the meeting, threatening to go to war to prevent the state from joining the Confederacy. Jackson seized on this as a hostile act by the U.S. government and encouraged Missourians to resist. Lyon, in turn, sent federal troops to capture the governor in Jefferson City. Jackson hastily evacuated the town and gathered up nearly 4,000 volunteers to combat U.S. forces. In early July, he successfully led his force against a smaller contingent of federal soldiers under Franz Sigel at Carthage, Missouri. Despite this military victory, Jackson relinquished command of the soldiers and headed into Arkansas to use his diplomatic skills to aid Missouri's Confederate cause.

While Jackson was out of the state, the Missouri state convention met again and, despite opposition from a small group of pro-Confederate delegates, declared the governor's seat vacant. Hamilton Gamble was chosen to replace Jackson. A staunch Unionist, Gamble supported the Lincoln administration for the rest of the war.

Jackson still considered himself governor of Missouri and met with Confederate president Jefferson Davis. With a promise from Davis of Confederate support once Missouri seceded, Jackson returned to southern Missouri and issued a "proclamation of independence," declaring the state independent from the United States. The proclamation had no legal authority, but he hoped it would influence Missourians to secede. In October 1861, the exiled governor formed a group of pro-Confederate legislators into a convention (guarded by Price's Confederate army) and had them pass an ordinance of secession. He signed the act and sent it to Richmond, where the Confederate government admitted Missouri as the twelfth Confederate state on November 28, 1861.

Jackson's secessionist state government, though, was on the run and received little aid from the Confederacy. He spent most of 1862 unsuccessfully pressing Confederate authorities to regain Missouri from Union forces. That year his health broke down. Stomach cancer and tuberculosis weakened his body. On December 7, 1862, Jackson died in Arkansas.

—IAN MICHAEL SPURGEON

BIBLIOGRAPHY

Hesseltine, William B. *Lincoln and the War Governors.* New York: Knopf, 1948.

Monaghan, Jay. *Civil War on the Western Border: 1854–1865.* Lincoln: University of Nebraska Press, 1984.

Phillips, Christopher. *Missouri's Confederate: Claiborne Fox Jackson and the Creation of Southern Identity in the Border West.* Columbia: University of Missouri Press, 2000.

Johnson, Andrew

Andrew Johnson (1808–1875) proved to be of great help to Abraham Lincoln as military governor of Tennessee and a loyal War Democrat, service for which he was rewarded by being named as Lincoln's running mate in 1864. That proved a momentous decision, for as his successor after Lincoln's death, always claiming that he was following in Lincoln's footsteps, Johnson pursued a policy of reconstruction that sought to restore white supremacy and the subjugation of African Americans in the postwar South. Ultimately, his willingness to obstruct Congress's plan of reconstruction led to his impeachment and near-conviction in 1868.

Born in North Carolina, Johnson migrated to Tennessee, where he set up shop as a tailor in Greenville. Before long he became engaged in politics, protesting local land policy as unfair. That pattern—of battling aristocrats and interests—was evident throughout his climb up the political ladder, from alderman and mayor of Greenville, through service in both houses of the Tennessee legislature, to five terms in the U.S. House of Representatives (1843–1853), two terms as governor (1853–1857), and finally election to the U.S. Senate in 1857. Johnson was a passionate Jacksonian Democrat; he was also a defender of slavery. He railed against the planter aristocracy but did not question the institution upon which its power rested. Once in the Senate, Johnson pressed for the adoption of a homestead bill that he had first advocated as a congressman but coupled that with speeches that reaffirmed his proslavery credentials. By 1860 Johnson entertained thoughts of running for president; when he failed to gain the nomination, he decided to support the candidacy of John C. Breckinridge, in part because he distrusted the Democratic nominee, Stephen A. Douglas, and in part because he despised Constitutional Unionist candidate (and Tennessee political rival) John Bell.

In the secession crisis Johnson proclaimed both at local meetings and on the floor of the U.S. Senate that secession was unconstitutional. He returned to Tennessee to battle secession advocates, only to find himself on the losing end of that argument when in June Tennessee formally voted to secede. Buoyed by pro-Union support in East Tennessee, Johnson returned to Washington, where he gained renown as the only U.S. senator from a state that had joined the Confederacy. Although he endorsed Lincoln's strong use of executive power, he also cosponsored what became known as the Crittenden-Johnson resolutions, which declared that the purpose of the war was reunion alone and not the destruction or impairment of slavery or states' rights. Johnson secured an appointment to the Joint Committee on the Conduct of the War, although his service on that committee proved short-lived. Despite the conservatism on slavery inherent in the Crittenden-Johnson resolutions, he supported the passage of the First Confiscation Act, which targeted slaves being used to support the Confederate war effort.

Frustrated by the failure of Union armies to liberate East Tennessee, Johnson took some satisfaction when Union advances in February 1862 opened up portions of Middle and West Tennessee. On March 4, 1862, Lincoln named Johnson military governor of Tennessee. Johnson would have to oversee the restoration of civil rule where possible and would otherwise manage the occupation of the state. It proved difficult to restore civil government in the midst of military operations, and Johnson often clashed with military commanders over spheres of authority and his concern that Union generals were not doing enough to drive the Confederates from the state. Moreover, Johnson's reputation as a vindictive and bitter foe raised questions about whether his tough approach would foster reconciliation. The new military governor dealt harshly with secessionists and other dissenters at first, although over time he showed some ability to woo back opponents. He initially remained a steadfast supporter of slavery, persuading Lincoln to exempt the state (including the portions still under Confederate control) from the final Emancipation Proclamation.

Circumstances began to change for Johnson in 1863. In February he journeyed to Washington, making speeches along the way in which he conceded for the first time that slavery might have to be destroyed to save the Union. Lincoln began to press him on the prospect of raising black regiments. By the end of August, Johnson declared himself in favor of emancipation; Union military successes over the next three months placed most of Tennessee under his control. The military governor resisted Lincoln's calls for a quick statewide election, for he was unsure about the strength of Unionism in Tennessee, especially in the wake of emancipation. It would not be until January 1864 that Johnson would initiate a process looking toward the restoration of civil government and a final decision on emancipation in Tennessee. That process proved controversial, in part because Johnson wanted voters to take an oath that made explicit their support for the Union and the war effort. Initial efforts proved futile, in part because of low turnout in a March 1864 election, and the process languished for months.

In the presidential election year of 1864 Lincoln, anxious to attract support from War Democrats, showed no interest in keeping his vice president, Maine's Hannibal Hamlin, on the Republican ticket. The president supposedly considered a number of running mates, including Benjamin F. Butler of Massachusetts, New York's Daniel S. Dickinson, and Johnson. The degree to which Lincoln desired Johnson's nomination remains a matter of much discussion. Pennsylvania newspaperman and politico Alexander K. McClure first advanced the argument that Lincoln had secured Johnson as his running mate, but Lincoln's secretary, John J. Nicolay, believed otherwise. What is clear is that Lincoln expressed no objection to the Tennessean's presence on the ticket. It did not hurt that secretary of state William H. Seward feared that if fellow New Yorker Dickinson secured the nomination, he might lose his cabinet post in a reorganization of a second Lincoln administration (for it would be difficult to have two high-ranking officials hail from the same state). When Republicans, meeting under the name of the National Union Party, met in Baltimore in June, they made quick work of nominating Johnson.

In fall 1864 Johnson kept one eye on his national political prospects and the other on the progress of reconstruction in Tennessee. He campaigned for the ticket in Indiana, a state where the Republicans needed to woo Democratic support; he went so far as to tell a gathering of Tennessee blacks that he would be their "Moses," leading the way from slavery to freedom. Although Congress eventually decided not to take into account Tennessee's vote in the fall contest, the Lincoln-Johnson ticket prevailed, making Johnson vice president–elect.

Before he left Tennessee to take the oath of office, Johnson pressed to restore civil government to the state. Measures abolishing slavery and nullifying secession were rammed through a makeshift constitutional convention, and Johnson proclaimed the result on February 25, just before he departed for Washington. The Tennessean was in poor health, and when he arrived in Washington he decided to do a little celebrating on inauguration eve, which did not help matters. On the morning of March 4, Johnson arose, still unsteady and ailing. He downed three glasses of whiskey in an effort to fortify himself, but the alcohol had the opposite effect. At noon he addressed a packed Senate chamber in a rambling manner that offered all-too-clear evidence of his condition before taking the oath of office.

In the aftermath of this public humiliation Johnson escaped public scrutiny by staying at the Blair family residence in Silver Spring, Maryland, for several weeks. Although Lincoln did not believe that Johnson was a drunkard, he maintained his distance from his new vice president. When, in the aftermath of the fall of Richmond, Lincoln learned that Johnson had come down to City Point from Washington, he did his best to avoid him. It does not appear that the two men met until April 14, when the vice president questioned whether Grant's surrender terms at Appomattox treated the former Confederates too leniently. Less than twenty-four hours later Andrew Johnson was the seventeenth president of the United States.

In years to come many people would claim that as president, Johnson sought to put into place the reconstruction policy that Lincoln had advocated. Johnson himself did what he could to encourage that impression. Indeed, there are remarkable similarities between Johnson's postwar proclamations and his predecessor's wartime pronouncements. However, with war's end Lincoln prepared to reconsider his previous policies; it is evident that the two men held different views on emancipation and what freedom might mean for African Americans. In retrospect, Lincoln's greatest mistake as president might have been his failure to ensure that his possible successor shared his own outlook on reconstruction and emancipation, a very real consideration given Lincoln's own awareness that he was the target of a possible assassination plot.

See also *Hamlin, Hannibal; Reconstruction*

—BROOKS D. SIMPSON

BIBLIOGRAPHY

Bowen, David W. *Andrew Johnson and the Negro.* Knoxville: University of Tennessee Press, 1989.

McKitrick, Eric L. *Andrew Johnson and Reconstruction.* Chicago: University of Chicago Press, 1960.

Sefton, James E. *Andrew Johnson and the Uses of Constitutional Power.* Glenview, Ill.: Scott Foresman, 1980.

Trefousse, Hans L. *Andrew Johnson: A Biography.* New York: Norton, 1989.

Joint Committee on the Conduct of the War

After the firing on Fort Sumter, on April 12, 1861, many Northerners expected a brief and relatively painless conflict to put down secession and reunite the nation. Battlefield defeats at Big Bethel (June 10, 1861), the First Bull Run (July 21, 1861), Wilson's Creek (August 10, 1861), and Ball's Bluff (October 21, 1861) quickly altered those unrealistic expectations. For many congressmen, these early setbacks created doubts about the competency of the nation's commander in chief, Abraham Lincoln. Lincoln, some argued, had also failed to advance the Union war effort by failing to attack the institution of slavery. When Major General John C. Frémont, commander of the Department of the West, issued a proclamation that liberated slaves in his department (August 30, 1861), Lincoln quickly overruled him. A few months later, Frémont was removed from command. As a result of dissatisfaction with Lincoln, when it met in early December 1861, one of the first acts of the Thirty-seventh Congress was to create the Joint Committee on the Conduct of the War.

The Joint Committee on the Conduct of the War had three Senate members and four members from the House of Representatives. The senators were Republicans Benjamin F. Wade of Ohio and Zachariah Chandler of Michigan; Andrew Johnson, the only senator from a seceded Southern state to remain in the Senate, represented Senate Democrats. After he was appointed military governor of Tennessee, Johnson left the Senate and the joint committee. He was replaced by Joseph Wright, the former governor of Indiana. House members were Republicans Daniel W. Gooch of Massachusetts, George W. Julian of Indiana, and John Covode of Pennsylvania. The lone house Democrat was Moses Fowler Odell, who represented Brooklyn, New York. Because of his legal experience, Benjamin Wade was chosen to chair the committee.

The committee was reappointed in the Thirty-eighth Congress, and Wade stayed on as chair. The membership stayed the same with a couple of exceptions. Pennsylvania representative John Covode retired from Congress and was replaced by Republican Benjamin F. Loan from St. Joseph, Missouri. In the Senate, Joseph Wright, who failed to win reelection, was replaced by Oregon Democrat Benjamin F. Harding. Early in 1865 Harding resigned from the committee and was replaced by Pennsylvania Democrat Charles R. Buckalew.

Congress gave the joint committee wide discretion to investigate all aspects of the conduct of the war, past and present. Armed with subpoena power, the committee investigated many facets of the Northern war effort. During the Thirty-seventh and Thirty-eighth Congresses, it looked into military supply contracts, the negotiation of ice contracts, the manufacture of heavy ordnance, and the construction of light draught monitors. It investigated Confederate mistreat-

Soldiers stand at a gravesite following the Battle of Antietam. The Joint Committee on the Conduct of the War spent a great deal of time investigating the causes of Union military defeats and the operations of the Army of the Potomac, including the Antietam Campaign.

Source: Library of Congress

ment of Union army prisoners and inquired into the massacre of black U.S. soldiers captured by Confederates under the command of General Nathan Bedford Forrest at Fort Pillow, Tennessee, on April 12, 1864. The committee also examined the massacre of Indians—mostly women and children—by territorial militia at Sand Creek, in the Colorado Territory, on November 29, 1864.

Despite these wide-ranging investigative interests the joint committee spent the bulk of its efforts examining the causes of Union military defeats, particularly in the Eastern Theater. During the Thirty-seventh Congress the committee spent a great deal of time examining and exonerating the operations of John C. Frémont in the Department of the West. It spent most of its time, however, investigating the operations of the Army of the Potomac, particularly the battles of Bull Run and Ball's Bluff, the Peninsular Campaign (March–July 1862), Antietam (September 17, 1862), and Fredericksburg (December 13, 1862). During the Thirty-eighth Congress the committee focused mainly on the Army of the Potomac, particularly the battles of Chancellorsville (May 2–3, 1863) and Gettysburg (July 1–3, 1863), and the pursuit of Lee's army after Gettysburg.

The Joint Committee on the Conduct of the War attempted to influence military policy in a variety of ways. Committee members sometimes delivered impassioned speeches to Congress to support and bolster the committee's point of view. Zachariah Chandler, for instance, delivered a brutal attack on Major General George McClellan and the strategy of the Peninsula Campaign on the floor of the Senate in July 1862. In some cases committee testimony, supposedly confidential, was leaked to newspapers and released to the public. When the committee investigated Frémont's operations in the Department of the West, for instance, favorable testimony on Frémont's behalf was leaked to the *New York Tribune.* No doubt this played a role in obtaining for Frémont the command of the Mountain Department on March 29, 1862. Probably the most forthright committee method of communication was its formal reports, published periodically and released to the public. In April 1863 the committee published its first major findings on the Army of the Potomac, roundly criticizing McClellan for his management and for not bringing the war to a successful conclusion. At the same time, the committee criticized the Lincoln administration for unfairly removing Frémont from command in the Department of the West. Probably the most sensational committee publication was its report on the treatment of Union prisoners in Confederate prisons and the Fort Pillow massacre, which was released to the public in May 1864. This report painted the Confederacy as a benighted, brutal society that starved Union prisoners and massacred Union soldiers, particularly African Americans after they tried to surrender.

Throughout the Civil War, the committee's relationship with Abraham Lincoln was sporadic and uneven. Convinced that Lincoln was not up to the task of organizing the Union war effort, the committee members believed it was their task to force the president to prod the generals into action. Early in the conflict, committee members were outraged when they discovered that Lincoln knew little or nothing about McClellan's plans for the Army of the Potomac. Indeed the committee members, particularly its Republican majority, were skeptical about the quality of the army's West Point–educated officers from the war's beginning. Because West Point was regarded as Democratic and conservative, many members regarded top Democratic generals such as McClellan, Major General Fitz-John Porter, Major General William B. Franklin, and others as proslavery and Southern sympathizers. As a result the committee was constantly maneuvering to replace the army's top leadership with officers it believed embodied Republican values, particularly a commitment to attacking and eradicating the institution of slavery. Since the committee had a rather naïve concept of military strategy, its recommendations were not always the most appropriate and wise. Lincoln, also a military amateur, did not always accept the committee's recommendations. In many cases Lincoln's decisions on key military appointments were undoubtedly the wiser. Had he listened to the committee, such generals as Major General Benjamin F. Butler and Frémont, both inept in terms of tactical skill, would have been accorded major field commands. Moreover, generals such as Major General Joseph Hooker and Major General Ambrose Burnside, both of whom had disastrous results while commanding the Army of the Potomac, would have been kept in these important positions of leadership.

Committee members seemed to live by the formula that sound ideology trumped military experience. Lincoln was not averse to having generals in command who supported the policies of the Republican Party, and he was often suspicious of military professionals, but he did not discount all professional soldiers on account of the poor performance of some. The congressional joint committee met frequently with the president and attempted to influence his decisions, particularly when it came to the top position in the Army of the Potomac. During the Thirty-seventh Congress the committee worked steadfastly to prod the Army of the Potomac into action and to force Lincoln to remove McClellan from command. During the Thirty-eighth Congress it targeted Major General George Meade, seeking to remove him from command and replace him with Joseph Hooker, who had presided over the disastrous Union defeat at Chancellorsville and was removed from command just prior to the battle of Gettysburg.

The committee's investigations were often a forum where disgruntled army officers were at liberty to criticize superiors and try to advance their fortunes. Moreover, committee members were all too willing to smear unsuccessful Democratic generals with the brush of disloyalty. One consequence of the committee's work was to foster a spirit of distrust among the army's officer corps. Lincoln's relationship with the army officer corps was markedly different and was characterized by a willingness to listen and learn. When necessary, Lincoln could be firm, especially when he decided to remove McClellan from command. At the same time, when the congressional committee was lobbying for Meade's removal on grounds of incompetence and questionable loyalty, Lincoln would not give in, recognizing that lack of military success was not necessarily a sign of disloyalty. Because of his flexibility, Lincoln eventually developed successful relationships with Lieutenant General Ulysses Grant and Major General William Sherman based on mutual respect and trust. Fortunately for the country, Lincoln's approach, based on fostering unity and cooperation, prevailed over the divisive tactics of the Joint Committee on the Conduct of the War.

See also *Ball's Bluff, Battle of*

—BRUCE TAP

BIBLIOGRAPHY

Tap, Bruce. *Over Lincoln's Shoulder: The Committee on the Conduct of the War.* Lawrence: University Press of Kansas, 1998.

———. "Amateurs at War: Abraham Lincoln and the Committee on the Conduct of the War." *Journal of the Abraham Lincoln Association* 23 (Summer 2002): 1–18.

Trefousse, Hans L. *The Radical Republicans: Lincoln's Vanguard for Racial Justice.* New York: Knopf, 1969.

Williams, T. Harry. *Lincoln and the Radicals.* Madison: University of Wisconsin Press, 1941.

K

Kansas-Nebraska Act

The legislation known as the Kansas-Nebraska Act opened the Kansas and Nebraska Territories to settlement. More importantly, it reopened the slavery issue that had been settled by the Compromise of 1850, and it provoked the birth of a new political party, the Republicans. In so doing, the Kansas-Nebraska Act created the opportunity for Abraham Lincoln to return to politics.

Home to a number of Native American tribes, the region west of Iowa and Missouri was unorganized territory in 1854. There was neither territorial government nor legal white settlement. Stephen A. Douglas, the U.S. senator from Illinois who chaired the Committee on Territories, had long hoped to provide a territorial government for the region and to open it to white settlement. He believed that would facilitate the construction of a transcontinental railroad (with a proposed eastern terminus in Chicago, in Douglas's home state) linking the eastern states and the Pacific Coast. A believer in Manifest Destiny, Douglas thought the greatness of the United States lay in continued westward expansion. But several bills to organize the region had failed in Congress for lack of Southern support. Because the region lay in the northern part of the Louisiana Purchase, the 1820 Missouri Compromise prohibited slavery in any territories formed there.

In late 1853, Iowa senator Augustus C. Dodge introduced yet another bill to organize the region west of the Missouri River. Sen. David Atchison of Missouri made it clear to Douglas that the bill would fail unless it contained provisions to gain Southern support. Douglas revised the bill. In addition to creating the territories of Kansas and Nebraska, the legislation now removed the Missouri Compromise's prohibition of slavery in the territory and replaced it with "popular sovereignty." Douglas would proclaim that popular sovereignty was nothing other than "the great principle of self-government," namely, letting the people decide.

First introduced by Democratic presidential candidate Lewis Cass in 1848 as a policy for handling slavery in the territories, popular sovereignty was now adopted by Douglas, who insisted that provisions in the Compromise of 1850 concerning New Mexico and Utah Territories had been based on popular sovereignty. The New Mexico and Utah Territories had been opened to settlement with no restrictions on slavery. Douglas further insisted that the Compromise of 1850 had superseded the Missouri Compromise. Accordingly, the new Kansas-Nebraska

VOTING IN KICKAPOO.

"Border ruffians" from Missouri at the polls in 1855 in Kickapoo, Kansas Territory, voting for a proslavery legislature.
Source: The Granger Collection, New York

proposal would not repeal the Missouri Compromise prohibition of slavery, as that prohibition had already been rendered invalid by the Compromise of 1850.

Douglas's reasoning did little to convince the bill's foes. Although Southerners were delighted at the removal of the prohibition, many Northerners—even Democrats—were outraged. White Southerners felt that a stigma, the prohibition of slavery, had been removed, and that an equal right to go into the territories with all their property was now acknowledged. Northerners, however, called the bill a violation of a sacred compact between North and South. "The Appeal of the Independent Democrats" voiced the unhappiness of Northern Democrats. Its authors, antislavery Democrats including Salmon P. Chase of Ohio and Charles Sumner of Massachusetts, insisted that Douglas's bill violated a "sacred compact," the Missouri Compromise, by which that region had been "consecrated to freedom." The Kansas-Nebraska Act was part of "an atrocious plot" to exclude free labor from these territories and turn them into "a dreary region of despotism, inhabited by masters and slaves."

Despite a storm of opposition, the bill passed Congress in May 1854. Securing its passage required all of Douglas and his allies' tactical skill to move Kansas-Nebraska to the top of the legislative calendar and rally wavering Democrats. Almost all Southern Democrats supported the legislation, but Northern Democrats were badly divided. In the House of Representatives, forty-four Northern Democrats supported Kansas-Nebraska, but an equal number opposed it.

The Kansas-Nebraska bill shaped the political realignment of the 1850s. The Whig Party had been foundering. Its last presidential candidate, Winfield Scott, had been solidly defeated in the 1852 election. In response to the Kansas-Nebraska Act, a new fusion movement of old Whigs, anti-Nebraska Democrats, antislavery men, and anti-immigrant or "Know-Nothing" voters came together in 1854 to form the Republican Party. The new party opposed extending slavery into the territories. Although Abraham Lincoln was reluctant to leave the Whig Party and its program for government-sponsored economic development, by 1856 he had become a Republican. In that national election Lincoln was considered as a possible vice presidential candidate. Despite being passed over, he actively campaigned for the ticket of John C. Frémont and William L. Dayton. Although the Democrat, James Buchanan, won the presidency, the Republicans performed well in the election, winning almost two-thirds of the Northern states and a third of the popular vote. The Republicans might have done even better if not for the third-party candidacy of Millard Fillmore, who ran for the anti-immigrant Know-Nothings.

Turmoil in the new Kansas Territory would undermine Buchanan's presidency and the Democratic Party. Popular sovereignty did not provide Kansas a stable foundation: it did not specify when settlers decided about slavery—during the territorial stage or in a state constitution. The lax residency requirements of the period encouraged nonresident Missourians to vote in the first territorial elections. Kansas Territory became notorious for election fraud and for polarization between proslavery and free-state settlers, which would lead to violence and national political controversy.

Before 1854, Abraham Lincoln's political career was largely moribund. A Whig in a heavily Democratic state, he was unable to win significant office and concentrated instead on his successful legal career. The Kansas-Nebraska Act provided Lincoln with both a political cause and a political opportunity. He viewed popular sovereignty as wrong because it ignored the immorality of slavery. Although Douglas championed popular sovereignty as basic to democracy, Lincoln insisted that it was subversive of republican principles to accept the subordination of any group of people. Although Lincoln accepted slavery as guaranteed by the Constitution, he argued that as a moral evil and a violation of republicanism it should not be extended to the territories. Lincoln set out his position on these issues at Springfield and Peoria. By 1858 he was arguing that the Kansas-Nebraska Act had been merely the latest step in a larger Slave Power conspiracy to expand slavery into even the free states. Lincoln based this contention on the 1857 *Dred Scott* decision, in which the Supreme Court denied the constitutionality of prohibiting slavery in the territories. Lincoln, in the 1858 House Divided speech, predicted that there might soon be another Supreme Court decision legalizing slavery in the free states.

Not only did Kansas-Nebraska provide Lincoln with a political cause, but by undermining Democratic power it gave Lincoln a renewed chance at political office. Of the forty-four Northern Democrats who voted for Kansas-Nebraska, only seven were reelected in 1854. The new Republican Party elected Lyman Trumbull, an anti-Nebraska Democrat, as U.S. senator in 1855. Lincoln was a close contender for that seat but finally directed that his supporters give their votes to Trumbull to avoid a Democratic victory in the state assembly.

In 1858 Lincoln challenged Stephen A. Douglas for Douglas's Senate seat. That campaign and the Lincoln-Douglas debates provided a forum for both men to articulate their views of popular sovereignty and to debate the effects of the Kansas-Nebraska Act on both territory and nation. Although Douglas won the election, Lincoln nearly triumphed. Republicans won the state's popular vote, but Democrats controlled the state's general assembly, which would elect the U.S. senator. This campaign brought Lincoln national attention as the near-victor over the powerful Douglas. The 1858 senatorial election set the stage for Lincoln to become a contender for the presidency.

See also *Bleeding Kansas; Lawrence, Kansas*

—Nicole Etcheson

BIBLIOGRAPHY

Basler, Roy P., ed. *The Collected Works of Abraham Lincoln.* 8 vols. New Brunswick, N.J.: Rutgers University Press, 1953.

Cawardine, Richard J. *Lincoln.* London: Pearson, 2003.

Donald, David Herbert. *Lincoln.* New York: Simon and Schuster, 1995.

Etcheson, Nicole. *Bleeding Kansas: Contested Liberty in the Civil War Era.* Lawrence: University Press of Kansas, 2004.

Fehrenbacher, Don E. *Prelude to Greatness: Lincoln in the 1850s.* Stanford: Stanford University Press, 1962.

Rawley, James A. *Race and Politics: "Bleeding Kansas" and the Coming of the Civil War.* Philadelphia: Lippincott, 1969.

Wolff, Gerald W. *The Kansas-Nebraska Bill: Party, Section, and the Coming of the Civil War.* New York: Revisionist Press, 1977.

Kentucky (as Lincoln's Birthplace and in the Civil War)

Abraham Lincoln was born on February 12, 1809, near Hodgenville, Kentucky. The son of Thomas and Nancy Hanks Lincoln, Abraham spent his first seven years in present-day Larue County, first at his birthplace and then several miles away on Knob Creek. In 1816 the Lincoln family moved to Indiana. They would later move again, to Illinois, where Lincoln rose to prominence as a lawyer in the 1830s and 1840s.

Although Lincoln left Kentucky as a child, his connections to the state extended into his adult life. Many of the people he met and worked with in Indiana and Illinois were Kentuckians. Both his wife, Mary Todd, and his best friend, Joshua Fry Speed, came from Kentucky. Kentucky also played a prominent role in the development of Lincoln's political ideology. A staunch Whig, Lincoln idolized Henry Clay, who served Kentucky in both houses of the U.S. Congress and was a perennial presidential candidate. Lincoln followed Clay's political lead and adopted much of his ideology.

In the 1850s the Whig Party dissolved, and like many Northern Whigs, Lincoln joined the antislavery Republican Party, which mustered little support in Lincoln's native Kentucky. Although a small, indigenous antislavery movement existed in Kentucky during the 1830s and 1840s, few Kentuckians actively opposed slavery after 1850. In general, Kentuckians viewed Republicans as radical abolitionists obsessed with the immediate end of slavery. As the candidate of the antislavery party in the 1860 presidential election, Lincoln received little support from Kentucky. Most Kentuckians backed either John Bell of the Constitutional Union Party or John C. Breckinridge, a native son who was the candidate of the Southern wing of the Democratic Party. Although he achieved victory nationally, Lincoln received less than 1 percent of the votes cast in Kentucky.

Following his inauguration, Lincoln worked to prevent the Border States from seceding. Of particular concern to him was Kentucky, which he saw as the keystone of the Border States. Even though Kentucky did not leave the Union at the beginning of the war, secession remained a possibility for the state until September 1861. Lincoln knew that Kentucky remained undecided in its allegiance and that its governor, Beriah Magoffin, favored secession. Lincoln thus proceeded cautiously in all matters that might aggravate the situation in Kentucky. In May, when the state adopted a policy of armed neutrality, Lincoln announced that he would respect the position rather than attempt coercion. Covertly, however, Lincoln supported the state's Unionists and worked to arm loyal militia regiments. With the help of Joshua Speed and other allies in the state, Lincoln prevented secession long enough that when the Confederate army invaded Kentucky in September, the recently elected Unionist legislature ended the state's neutrality and sided with the North.

After the threat of secession passed, Lincoln continued to work to appease Kentuckians, who resisted both military policy in the state and federal efforts at emancipation. Throughout the war, Lincoln paid close attention to affairs in Kentucky and often interceded when civilians requested his help. Many Kentuckians thought the federal army treated them as though they were disloyal, despite their professed Unionism. Much of the dissatisfaction stemmed from military interference in elections. Kentuckians charged that federal troops prevented dissenters from voting in both the 1863 gubernatorial election and the 1864 presidential election.

Kentuckians also complained about the policies of General Jeremiah T. Boyle and his successor, General Stephen G. Burbridge, who between them commanded the Department of Kentucky for most of the war. Beginning in 1862, the Union military had to suppress a guerrilla war in Kentucky. Boyle arrested many civilians suspected of disloyalty and of supporting the guerrillas. As the war intensified, Lincoln suspended the writ of *habeas corpus* in the state. Boyle and Lincoln were harshly criticized for their antiguerrilla tactics. Lincoln, however, tried to appease the state's Unionists, and in January 1864 he replaced Boyle with Burbridge. Yet Burbridge continued Boyle's method of arresting suspected guerrillas and began executing them. In February 1865 Lincoln acquiesced to the Kentuckians' demands and relieved Burbridge of duty as well.

Kentuckians also resisted federal emancipation policy. During the secession crisis, many Kentucky Unionists believed that remaining in the United States would allow them to preserve slavery in the state. Lincoln, however, knew that slavery would be a casualty of the war, and in March 1862 he offered the Border States a proposal for gradual, compensated emancipation. Kentucky's congressional delegation, along with those of the other Border States, overwhelmingly rejected the offer. By the end of 1862, Lincoln's preliminary Emancipation Proclamation had added black freedom to federal war goals. Many Kentuckians believed that they had been misled by the Lincoln administration. Kentucky politicians, journalists, soldiers, and civilians all disapproved of Lincoln's efforts at emancipation, but they especially resisted the use of black soldiers. Although Lincoln at first exempted Kentucky from black enlistment, by March 1864 recruiting offices opened across the state. The combination of emancipation and black enlistment eroded slavery in Kentucky, but it was not until 1865 that most Kentuckians realized that they could not maintain slavery in the state.

As president, Lincoln had few supporters in Kentucky. Although Lincoln won the 1864 presidential election, Kentuckians once again voted against him, and the state was one of three that supported the Democrat, General George B. McClellan.

Lincoln's assassination in April 1865 softened much of Kentucky's disdain for him. Many who had opposed his policies publicly praised him and lamented his death. By the late nineteenth century, most Kentuckians were proud of Lincoln's Kentucky heritage, and they made efforts to preserve both of his childhood homes in the state.

—JACOB F. LEE

BIBLIOGRAPHY

Coulter, E. Merton. *The Civil War and Readjustment in Kentucky.* Chapel Hill: University of North Carolina Press, 1926.

Harrison, Lowell H. *The Civil War in Kentucky.* Lexington: University Press of Kentucky, 1975.

———. *Lincoln of Kentucky.* Lexington: University Press of Kentucky, 2000.

Townsend, William H. *Lincoln and the Bluegrass: Slavery and Civil War in Kentucky.* Lexington: University Press of Kentucky, 1955.

King Cotton

The South's fortunes were inextricably linked to cotton, the region's principal cash crop and the mainstay of its economy. In 1855 David Christy postulated as much in his book *Cotton Is King*. Christy's work would come to encapsulate the thinking of a cadre of Southern nationalists and secessionists, who argued that cotton was so important to the world economy that it would be the utmost folly for the North or the industrial powers of Europe to challenge the system that produced it. Doing so, they said, would lead to massive unemployment and class revolution in mill towns or districts across the world, whether Lowell, Lancashire, or Lyons. To avoid such a fate, sectional tensions had to be moderated, or the South had to be allowed to secede peacefully. Failing those possibilities, as others, such as New Orleans editor J. D. B. De Bow and South Carolina planter James Henry Hammond came to believe, Great Britain and France would have to intervene on the South's behalf if a civil war ensued. In a famous speech before the war, Senator Hammond declared, "No, you dare not make war on Cotton. No power on earth dares make war upon it. Cotton is King." A great part of Abraham Lincoln's challenge, as he led the North during the Civil War, involved how best to dethrone the economic and diplomatic power of King Cotton.

Although not absolute, King Cotton's power was nearly as strong as it appeared in theory. By 1860 the South supplied Great Britain with three-quarters or more of its cotton. With the eventual disruptions of supply brought on by a Confederate embargo and a Union blockade, more than a million mill workers would be displaced or forced onto the dole in France and Great Britain combined. The wealth generated by the millions of bales of cotton (a bale weighed 400–500 pounds) sold every year (4.6 million were produced in 1860) could raise the foreign currency the South needed to supply its deficiencies in armaments and foodstuffs. Taxes on cotton could even fund the war directly. In short, King Cotton had the potential to strengthen the Confederacy at the same time as its loss weakened the Union. Yet this did not prove to be the reality.

Economically, King Cotton's power was not as complete as was assumed. The Confederate embargo on cotton in 1861–1862 combined later with an effective, seven-hundred-ship Union blockade to prevent the South from gaining foreign currency. At most, only an estimated 1.5 million bales were smuggled out of the South after April 1862. Demand did not slacken, however, and the price of cotton increased exponentially, such that it could have more than offset the revenue lost in decreased sales. But increases in the cost of transportation within the South and across the Atlantic wiped out much of the potential profit. Because of costs, blockade runners sought to transport luxury items from Europe, which tended to be less bulky and more lucrative, instead of needed armaments and foodstuffs.

In these circumstances it made sense for the Union to allow some cotton through the blockade or between lines. Unionists in the South were encouraged to sell cotton to agents of the federal government in selected ports. Bales captured as spoils of war could also be used in Northern industry or exported overseas, mitigating the effects of the war at home and abroad. Lincoln's policy in this regard was so flexible as to suggest that he did not have one; instead he seemed to respond in ad hoc fashion, often deferring to army commanders and Treasury Department bureaucrats. The president was admittedly concerned about the blockade's effect on prices and sought to bring some cotton to market to drive them down. Though correct in theory, the trade conducted probably benefited the South's war effort more than it hurt cotton's profitability in Norfolk toward the war's close; the trade contributed earlier to the demoralization of the Confederacy in the Mississippi Valley.

Diplomatically King Cotton's power was not employed as well as it might have been. With demand remaining high, Europeans cultivated other suppliers in Egypt and India. Market forces also compelled substitution, particularly of wool and linen, for cotton. However, the impact of these outlets and replacements was limited. Given the universal expectation that the war would end quickly—the work necessary to exploit new sources or substitute different fibers was frequently delayed—it proved fortunate that demand for wartime goods created enough opportunities and jobs in other areas to offset the losses in textiles.

Union diplomacy only added to Confederate miscalculations. In his first annual address to Congress, Lincoln appealed to the morality of the Europeans.

Disputing the Southern estimation that their motivation was principally economic, Lincoln argued that even if it were, the proper course would be not to intervene but to aid the Union in bringing the war to a close as speedily as possible. The threat of a Union wheat embargo likely also had some impact, causing the British to fear the prospect of a famine in wheat as well as cotton. Without British cooperation, the French proved unwilling to intervene and chose to be content with posing a challenge to the Monroe Doctrine in Mexico.

Lincoln thus effectively took advantage of the havoc wreaked by the Union blockade, purchasing cotton in such a way as to foster Unionist sentiment in the South while sowing despair among those forced to burn their harvests. By appealing to the humanitarianism of the Europeans, particularly via the Emancipation Proclamation, he also limited the leverage of King Cotton's diplomacy. But these victories were not without cost. Rampant illicit cotton trading contributed to a corrupt postwar culture, and the blockade's damage to international law forced significant diplomatic adjustments during Ulysses Grant's presidency.

—ROBERT W. BURG

BIBLIOGRAPHY

Basler, Roy P., ed. *The Collected Works of Abraham Lincoln.* New Brunswick, N.J.: Rutgers University Press, 1955.

Finkelman, Paul. *Defending Slavery: Proslavery Thought in the Old South.* Boston: Bedford/St. Martin's, 2003.

O'Connor, Thomas H. "Lincoln and the Cotton Trade." *Civil War History* 7 (1961): 20–35.

Owsley, Frank Lawrence. *King Cotton Diplomacy: Foreign Relations of the Confederate States of America.* Chicago: University of Chicago Press, 1931.

Surdam, David G. *Northern Naval Superiority and the Economics of the American Civil War.* Columbia: University of South Carolina Press, 2001.

Knights of the Golden Circle

The Knights of the Golden Circle began as the particular brainchild of George W. L. Bickley, a resident of Cincinnati with a reputation for engaging in shady financial schemes. The principal idea of the organization, which Bickley created in the 1850s, was to colonize portions of Central America, establishing slavery and minimizing the influence of the Catholic Church. Bickley published rules, invented rituals and titles, and traveled around the country trying to raise support for this endeavor. By selling memberships for five dollars, he hoped to profit financially. Bickley had little intention of following through on the colonizing schemes. He was eventually exposed as a fraud and was denounced in various Southern newspapers as nothing more than a confidence man. As a result, the actual number of members was inconsequential.

On the eve of the Civil War, the Knights of the Golden Circle gained new notoriety when rumors circulated that members of President James Buchanan's cabinet were members of the society and that the society was prominently involved in creating support for secession and for the South. Once civil war erupted, some Republican editors and party officials seized on the Golden Circle rumors as a way to discredit Democratic opponents and gain advantage in elections. Bickley facilitated many of the rumors by his own propaganda, especially after he wrote an "open letter" in which he claimed to have 8,000 Golden Circle members in the state of Kentucky. Published in numerous Kentucky papers, the letter was seized on as proof of the influence of the secret society. Particularly in states that bordered Kentucky—Ohio, Indiana, and Illinois—a flurry of exposés appeared in summer and fall 1861 that exaggerated the membership and influence of the knights. Indianapolis journalist James Hiatt, for instance, published an exposé in fall 1861 that attributed the annexation of Texas, the war against Mexico, the sectional turmoil in territorial Kansas in the 1850s, and the growth of secession sentiment to the knights.

As early as fall 1861 Republican journalists and political leaders claimed that the knights were in league with prominent members of the Democratic Party. As the war became less popular in parts of southern Indiana, Illinois, and Ohio, the Knights of the Golden Circle began to play a more prominent role in Republican electoral strategy. In Illinois, Chicago *Tribune* correspondent and friend of Governor Yates, Joseph K. C. Forrest, used Knights of the Golden Circle rumors to discredit Democratic opponents of the war. Forrest published a dubious exposé in the August 26, 1862, issue of the *Tribune* that claimed an increase in Knights of the Golden Circle activities and linked them to members of the Democratic Party. After Democrats captured the state legislature in the fall election, Forrest and Yates continued the smear campaign against the Democratic legislature, claiming that it was dominated by disloyal men who wanted to end the war against the South.

In Indiana, Governor Oliver Morton, aided by Colonel Henry B. Carrington, adopted a parallel style to discredit Democrats who captured control of the state legislature in the fall 1862 election. Carrington wrote two reports in early 1863, which he forwarded to the War Department, that "documented" the activities of the Knights of the Golden Circle. The threat of actions by the Golden Circle could be used to suppress newspapers, search the mails, and even, in the case of Governor Morton, prorogue the Democratic-controlled state legislature.

Bickley, meanwhile, spent time in the South during the war and served as a surgeon in the Confederate Army of the Tennessee, commanded by Braxton

Bragg. He eventually deserted Confederate service and was captured by Union forces in July 1863. He was sent north with instructions to report to Department of Ohio commander Ambrose Burnside. Instead Bickley headed for central Indiana, where he was arrested at Albany, Indiana, by a government detective. Although Bickley's arrest was a propaganda coup for the Republican Party, no evidence was found on him that linked Northern Democratic leaders with the knights. Imprisoned until October 1865, Bickley wrote to President Lincoln on two occasions. In each case, the president did not respond to the leader of the Knights of the Golden Circle.

By 1864 Golden Circle rumors decreased. Instead of the Knights of the Golden Circle, other secret societies—in particular, the Order of American Knights and the Sons of Liberty—began to attract attention. Although historians are divided as to the threat that such secret societies posed, some prominent Democrats, Clement Vallandigham for instance, did affiliate with the Sons of Liberty. Moreover, there was some evidence of plots and conspiracies, but not by the Knights of the Golden Circle, whose existence, although real, was widely exaggerated.

How much credence did Abraham Lincoln accord shadowy groups such as the Knights of the Golden Circle? Lincoln biographers note that the sixteenth president was concerned about the potential threat they posed. As a political ally of Republican governor Richard Yates, Lincoln undoubtedly put stock in Yates's reports regarding the Knights of the Golden Circle. At the same time, Lincoln was skeptical about the linkage that some Republicans made between the knights and leading members of the Democratic Party. Realizing that the opposition could make political hay on the issues of false arrests and suppression of free speech, Lincoln was also careful to avoid measures that would unnecessarily inflame the political opposition. As a result, when Major General Ambrose Burnside arrested Vallandigham for violating General Order No. 38, which prohibited speech that expressed treasonable sentiments, Lincoln decided to banish the recalcitrant former Ohio congressman to the Confederacy, instead of keeping him imprisoned in the North where he would be a lightning rod for the political opposition. When Burnside suppressed the Chicago *Times*, edited by Lincoln critic Wilbur F. Storey, on June 1, 1863, Lincoln overruled his decision on the grounds that suppression would do more harm than good. As with many controversial issues in the Civil War, Lincoln approached the handling of the Knights of the Golden Circle and secret societies with balance, common sense, and restraint.

—Bruce Tap

BIBLIOGRAPHY

Donald, David Herbert. *Lincoln*. New York: Simon and Schuster, 1995.

Klement, Frank L. *Dark Lanterns: Secret Political Societies, Conspiracies and Treason Trials during the Civil War*. Baton Rouge: Louisiana State University Press, 1984.

Know-Nothing (American) Party

The Know-Nothings were an anti-immigrant, anti-Catholic political movement that arose in the early 1850s. Upset by the influx of Irish and Germans, the Know-Nothings began as a secret organization before going public in 1854. Their popularity persisted until the late 1850s. Know-Nothing candidates often ran under the American Party label.

With the disintegration of the Whig Party in the early 1850s, the controversy over the Kansas-Nebraska Act of 1854, and high immigration rates, many discontented Whigs and Democrats sought new political homes. The Know-Nothings argued that the three million immigrants who came between 1845 and 1854, many of whom were Catholic, threatened the republic. From 1854 to 1856 the American Party seemed destined to become the major opponent of the Democrats.

The success of the anti–slavery-expansion Republican Party ultimately depended on the incorporation of the Northern Know-Nothings. When his attempts to revive the Whig Party in Illinois failed, Abraham Lincoln looked to the Republicans. Despondently Lincoln wrote Owen Lovejoy, an Illinois abolitionist, on August 11, 1855, that the prospects of the nascent Republican Party were grim until the Know-Nothing fervor somehow dissipated. But the practical Lincoln added that he was willing to "fuse" with "any body who stands right" in opposition to extending slavery.

Lincoln's relationship with the Know-Nothings was complicated. Clearly the nativist beliefs of the Know-Nothings repulsed him. In a now-famous letter of August 24, 1855, to his old friend Joshua F. Speed, Lincoln confided, "I am not a Know-Nothing. That is certain. How could I be? How can any one who abhors the oppression of negroes, be in favor of degrading classes of white people?" His disgust for the Know-Nothings led Lincoln to underestimate them; he was frequently surprised by their persistence. With ambitions for the U.S. Senate, and later the presidency, Lincoln had to keep his feelings private.

Lincoln's activities in the political campaigns of the mid- and late 1850s indicate that he encouraged Know-Nothings to make common cause against the Democrats. He often helped negotiate fusion tickets in Illinois. Across the North, Republicans in state and local elections adopted issues that Know-Nothings favored, such as temperance and protecting public schools from Catholic influence. In 1855 when a small movement of Protestant immigrants, the "Know-Somethings," tried to combine anti–slavery extension with anti-Catholicism, they were swallowed up by the more aggressive Republican Party. Most effectively, Republicans castigated wealthy slaveholders and Democratic Party leaders (backed by immigrant votes) for creating a Slave Power conspiracy to spread slavery. In his final debate with Stephen A. Douglas, at Alton, Illinois, on October 15, 1858, for example, Lincoln decried the "combination and conspiracy to make the institution of slavery national." Nowhere did Lincoln attack immigrants; he merely let former Know-Nothings in the audience make their own conclusions.

In 1860 Lincoln's nomination for the presidency over William H. Seward was helped by Seward's earlier attacks on the Know-Nothings. In the presidential campaign Republicans created "Wide Awake" political clubs, with elaborate initiations reminiscent of the rituals of the secret Know-Nothing lodges earlier in the decade.

By 1860 the American Party had largely disappeared. It could not expand beyond its one-issue platform, nor could the Know-Nothings dodge the issue of slavery expansion. The success in 1860 of Lincoln and the Republicans was only possible with the absorption of the Know-Nothings into their ranks.

—M. PHILIP LUCAS

BIBLIOGRAPHY

Anbinder, Tyler. *Nativism and Slavery: The Northern Know-Nothings and the Politics of the 1850s.* New York: Oxford University Press, 1992.

Fehrenbacher, Don E. *Prelude to Greatness: Lincoln in the 1850s.* Stanford: Stanford University Press, 1962.

Gienapp, William E. *The Origins of the Republican Party, 1852–1856.* New York: Oxford University Press, 1987.

Holt, Michael F. *The Political Crisis of the 1850s.* New York: John Wiley, 1978.

Lawrence, Kansas

Home to the antislavery newspaper the *Herald of Freedom* and the Free-State Hotel, a fortress-like structure, Lawrence became the most notorious free-state settlement in the Kansas Territory. In fall 1854, migrants from both Missouri and the North camped on the site of Lawrence. New England settlers, who were sponsored by the New England Emigrant Aid Company, platted the town—prompting some claim disputes with Missourians—and made Massachusetts Street the main avenue. They named the town after the principal financial backer of NEEAC, Massachusetts industrialist Amos Lawrence.

Armed forces threatened Lawrence several times during the 1850s conflict between proslavery and free-state settlers. In the winter of 1855–1856, the territorial militia surrounded the town in the Wakarusa War. This "war" originated when Franklin M. Coleman murdered Charles W. Dow in a land dispute. When Dow's friends retaliated against Coleman, who was a Missourian, Sheriff Samuel Jones, who was also a Missourian, arrested one of them—Jacob Branson, a member of a free-state militia—for disturbing the peace. Free-state men soon rescued Branson from the sheriff and his posse and took him into Lawrence. Sheriff Jones then called for help in recovering his prisoner from the territorial militia. Volunteers from Missouri supplemented the militia and threatened a general attack on the town. Aided by bitterly cold weather, which sapped the resolve of the Missourians camped around the town, territorial governor Wilson Shannon and leading Missourians such as David Atchison brokered a peace agreement. The crisis passed when Governor Shannon ordered the forces surrounding Lawrence to disband.

The legal dispute over resisting the sheriff, however, remained unresolved. In April 1856, Sheriff Jones returned to Lawrence, where he intended to arrest the men who had taken Branson from his custody. Several attempts and the help of U.S. troops were required to make any arrests. As Jones camped outside the town, someone shot him. Although initially reported dead, Jones soon recovered, and in May he returned armed with legal processes against the hotel and the newspaper. The posse set fire to the hotel and destroyed the newspaper office. Jones's men then looted houses. One proslavery man was killed by masonry falling from the hotel and no one else was hurt; however, property damage was substantial. Republican newspapers exploited the incident as the "sack of Lawrence."

The sack of Lawrence began the summer of fighting known as "Bleeding Kansas." Clashes between free-state and proslavery guerrillas occurred at a number of Kansas settlements. In September 1856 a proslavery guerrilla force again threatened Lawrence but was turned back by territorial governor John W. Geary's threat to use the U.S. army against the Missourians.

The problems of Bleeding Kansas were a staple of Republican propaganda during the election campaign of 1856. Abraham Lincoln, who campaigned actively for the party that fall, vigorously opposed repealing the Missouri Compromise prohibition of slavery in Kansas (1854). His rhetoric, however, focused less on the details of proslavery transgressions in Kansas than on the moral and ideological dilemma posed by the territory's plight. Lincoln was concerned with whether the republic could encourage the expansion of a moral evil such as slavery and still retain its free and egalitarian nature. Unlike other Republicans, Lincoln did not reiterate specifics about Bleeding Kansas in his speeches. Nonetheless, the sack of Lawrence, in furthering the ascendance of the Republican Party, furthered Lincoln's career. As an aspiring presidential candidate in 1859 Lincoln made a brief tour of Kansas and spoke in several places—but Lawrence was not one of them.

Because many New England settlers in Kansas were abolitionist, Lawrence became a haven for runaway slaves. This trend accelerated as African Americans seized the opportunities presented by the Civil War to flee bondage. Many slaves from Missouri and Arkansas fled into Kansas Territory, and many found their way to Lawrence.

In part because Lawrence was known as a destination for runaway slaves, as well as for property that Kansas troops looted from Missourians, Missouri bushwhacker William Clarke Quantrill targeted the town. On August 21, 1863, Quantrill attacked Lawrence at daybreak with several hundred men. In a couple of hours' time, the raiders slaughtered 150 men and boys. Among the first victims were the black and white army recruits camped on southern Massachusetts Street. But almost all the victims were civilians, many still in bed when the raiders struck. When Lawrence residents realized that women were being spared, many men fled to the cornfields or hid. Wives tried to protect their husbands. The raiders looted and set fire to houses. Because of the fire, some bodies were never recovered or were unrecognizable. The raid panicked the entire Kansas border region for months afterward.

In the aftermath of the raid, many Kansans called for the removal of General John Schofield, who refused to allow a retaliatory raid into Missouri. President Lincoln sided with Schofield, agreeing that such a raid might lead to "indiscriminate" killings of Missourians. Although Quantrill's raid was deeply felt in Kansas, Lincoln placed it in the context of raids by other Confederates, such as John Hunt Morgan, which exemplified the bloody nature of civil war. The internecine conflict in Missouri, which threatened to take Missouri into the Confederacy, concerned Lincoln as president far more than events in Kansas. Although Quantrill's raid was murderous, it did not threaten to remove Kansas from the Union.

See also *Bleeding Kansas; Kansas-Nebraska Act*

—Nicole Etcheson

BIBLIOGRAPHY

Abraham Lincoln to Charles D. Drake, et al., October 5, 1863. Abraham Lincoln Papers at the Library of Congress, http://memory.loc.gov.

Castel, Albert E. *A Frontier State at War: Kansas, 1861–1865.* Ithaca, N.Y.: Cornell University Press, 1958.

Etcheson, Nicole. *Bleeding Kansas: Contested Liberty in the Civil War Era.* Lawrence: University Press of Kansas, 2004.

Leslie, Edward E. *The Devil Knows How to Ride: The True Story of William Clarke Quantrill and His Confederate Raiders.* New York: Random House, 1996.

Territorial Kansas Online, www.territorialkansasonline.org.

Lee, Robert E.

Robert E. Lee (1807–1870) was the Confederacy's most dominant military leader. As commander of the Army of Northern Virginia (1862–1865) he thwarted Union offensives during 1862 and 1863, only to fail to carry out successful invasions northward across the Potomac. In 1864–1865 he battled Ulysses S. Grant; if he inflicted heavy damage on Grant's forces, he failed to regain the initiative. Lee's battlefield successes in 1862 forced Lincoln to embrace measures to escalate the conflict. Lee's successes in Virginia overshadowed Union triumphs elsewhere, until Grant effectively neutralized him in 1864.

Born in Virginia, the son of Revolutionary War hero "Light Horse" Harry Lee, Lee entered West Point in 1825. Four years later he graduated second in his class, with a sterling reputation and a commission as a brevet second lieutenant of engineers. For the next seventeen years he served in a number of army assignments, most notably on the Mississippi River at St. Louis. In 1846 he was ordered to report to Texas as part of the army's mobilization to wage war against Mexico. In the following year he distinguished himself as a member of General Winfield Scott's staff during Scott's campaign that resulted in the capture of Mexico City. In the 1850s Lee served as superintendent of West Point. He gained public attention in 1859 when he led a detachment of marines to Harpers Ferry and captured John Brown.

Although Lee had reservations about slavery, they were rooted in the burdens he believed the peculiar institution placed on white men; he thought it the best way to manage race relations and had no qualms about disciplining the slaves he owned. Lee blamed abolitionists for sectional strife; although he believed that secession was nothing but revolution, he added that he had no use for a Union held together by force. During the secession crisis Lee stated that he would not lead United States soldiers into war against fellow Americans; however he might remain in military service to defend his native state of Virginia.

On April 18, 1861, six days after Confederate forces fired on Fort Sumter, Lee met separately with general in chief Winfield Scott and Francis P. Blair Sr., long a Washington political elder, whose son was Lincoln's postmaster general. Blair sounded Lee out on the prospect of taking command of a newly raised army; Scott advised Lee to resign if he was not going to put down the rebellion. Upon learning that the Virginia convention meeting in Richmond had voted to secede, Lee tendered his resignation on April 20. He left Arlington for Richmond, where he accepted command of Virginia's forces. The following month he was commissioned a brigadier general in the Confederate army, and at the end of August he was elevated to the rank of general.

During the first year of the war Lee's assignments included preparing Virginia's defenses, overseeing its mobilization, attempting (and failing) to check Union advances in western Virginia, overseeing the establishment of defensive positions along the South Atlantic coast, and serving as Confederate president Jefferson Davis's military adviser. Perhaps his most important service was in assisting Confederate general Thomas J. Jackson's operations in the Shenandoah Valley, which did so much to distract Lincoln in spring 1862 and helped facilitate a rift between Lincoln and Union general George B. McClellan over withholding reinforcements in favor of protecting Washington and pursuing Jackson. When Confederate general Joseph E. Johnston was wounded at the battle of Fair Oaks, Lee took command of the Army of Northern Virginia, on June 1, 1862. He brought Jackson's force east and attacked McClellan's army on the outskirts of Richmond. In a series of battles known as the Seven Days (June 25–July 2, 1862), Lee drove McClellan away from Richmond, ending any hope of a quick Union victory by the middle of 1862 and reviving Confederate morale.

In August 1862 Lee moved northward to engage Union general John Pope's Army of Virginia, defeating it at Second Bull Run (August 27–30). As Union forces regrouped around Washington under McClellan's command, Lee invaded Maryland in hopes that pro-Confederate Marylanders would rally and foreign powers might consider intervening to mediate a peace settlement. He also targeted the Union supply base at Harpers Ferry, which he captured on September 15. By that time, however, McClellan was advancing, and he attacked Lee at Antietam (September 17). Lee barely held his position in the bloodiest single day of combat in the war; after remaining in place the following day he retreated across the Potomac.

Lincoln, unhappy with McClellan's lethargic pursuit of Lee, turned to new generals. On December 13, 1862, Lee repulsed a series of attacks by Ambrose Burnside at Fredericksburg; nearly five months later his brilliant generalship at Chancellorsville thwarted Joseph Hooker's offensive. Once more he decided to cross the Potomac and take the war to the North, after warding off suggestions that he detach portions of his army to assist in the relief of Vicksburg. As the Army of Northern Virginia advanced in June, entering Maryland and then Pennsylvania, Lincoln urged Hooker to cut off the Confederates and bring Lee to decisive battle far from his own Virginia. When Hooker offered his resignation due to a dispute over the control of Union detachments, Lincoln hurriedly replaced him with George G. Meade. In three days of battle at Gettysburg (July 1–3, 1863) Meade checked a series of attacks launched by Lee, with both sides suffering heavy losses. Lee then managed to make his way south across the Potomac once more, leaving Lincoln again frustrated that Meade could not deal a crippling blow to the Confederates. For the remainder of 1863 Lee and Meade maneuvered back and forth across northern Virginia, with each army detaching forces to participate in the Chickamauga and Chattanooga campaign.

Through the end of 1863, Lee had successfully checked every Union offensive in Virginia and protected the Confederate capital at Richmond. He had done so in a series of brilliant campaigns capped by skillfully fought battles against numerically superior Union forces. However, he had not enjoyed similar success north of the Potomac, and his preference for offensive operations had come at a high cost in casualties. His Army of Northern Virginia had become the symbol of continued Confederate resistance: so long as Lee was in the field, it looked as if the Confederacy had a chance to win. With these considerations in mind Lincoln brought Ulysses S. Grant east in march 1864 to assume overall command of the armies of the United States. Grant soon realized that he would have to remain in the East and supervise operations against Lee while directing the rest of the war effort by telegraph and courier. In a series of bloody battles stretching out over six weeks, Grant drove Lee back from the Rapidan River to Richmond and Petersburg. Grant's losses were high (nearly 60,000 men), and so were Lee's (about 35,000 men). Moreover, as Lee himself recognized, Grant now had Lee pinned against the Confederate capital, and unless the Confederate commander found a way to wriggle free, he would have to abandon Richmond. With Lincoln running for reelection, Lee was under pressure to do something on the battlefield that might persuade war-weary Northern voters that the end of the war was as far off as ever.

Lee attempted to retake the initiative when he sent Jubal Early into Maryland in July, but Grant sent reinforcements in time to defend Washington. That fall, Phillip Sheridan defeated Early in a series of battles and devastated the Shenandoah Valley. Lee proved unable to force Grant to abandon his siege operations. With Lincoln's reelection the Confederate commander struggled to keep his army together as desertion and demoralization ate away at his ranks.

Elevated to command of all the Confederate armies in February 1865, Lee decided to risk everything by evacuating Richmond and Petersburg to join forces with Joseph E. Johnston's army in North Carolina and attack William T. Sherman's army before Grant could arrive on the scene. But Grant thwarted Lee's effort to set up the breakout at Fort Steadman (March 25, 1865); a week later Sheridan's victory at Five Forks rendered Lee's position untenable. Evacuating Petersburg and Richmond on the night of April 2, Lee tried to join Johnston. When Grant's pursuit blocked those routes, Lee marched westward, only to be headed off by Union forces near Appomattox Court House, where he surrendered his army to Grant on April 9, 1865.

In surrendering as he did Lee set aside talk of continuing the war as a guerrilla struggle. Grant's generous terms were in line with Lincoln's expressed wishes about how to secure Confederate surrender and provide a basis for postwar reconciliation. But although Lee accepted defeat and subsequently served as president of Washington College in Lexington, Virginia, he questioned Reconstruction policy and asserted that during the war he had been overwhelmed, not beaten.

—Brooks D. Simpson

BIBLIOGRAPHY

Connelly, Thomas L. *The Marble Man: Robert E. Lee and His Image in American Society.* New York: Knopf, 1977.

Fellman, Michael. *The Making of Robert E. Lee.* New York: Random House, 2000.

Freeman, Douglas Southall. *R. E. Lee.* New York: Scribner's, 1934.

Nolan, Alan T. *Lee Considered: General Robert E. Lee and Civil War History.* Chapel Hill: University of North Carolina Press, 1991.

Pryor, Elizabeth B. *Reading the Man: A Portrait of Robert E. Lee through his Private Letters.* New York: Viking, 2007.

Thomas, Emory M. *Robert E. Lee: A Biography.* New York: Norton, 1995.

Legal Tender Act of 1862

The Legal Tender Act was passed in February 1862 in the midst of a funding crisis for the United States during the Civil War. The chief architect of the law was secretary of the Treasury Salmon P. Chase. The act was the first sustained effort at moving the United States toward a national currency. It also created the country's first form of fiat money at a national level.

The act passed after intense debate and scrutiny by Congress and in the face of intense opposition by the banking lobby. It was assumed that it would be a temporary expedient for funding the Civil War. The act formally allowed the U.S. government to print and issue up to $150 million in notes, in denominations of $5 or more. Unlike previous Treasury issues, these new notes did not pay interest and were declared legal tender for the payment of all public and private debts. The new notes were not redeemable for specie, a critical characteristic of previous Treasury notes. By the end of 1863 the Treasury had issued nearly $450 million in notes, which eventually became known as "greenbacks" because the back of the note was printed in green ink.

Permitting the issue of greenbacks to help fund the Civil War was the main reason for the Legal Tender Act. Lincoln and Congress faced the daunting prospect of increased expenditures at a time when taxation was new and the bond market was undeveloped. The economy of the United States had not improved from the depression that followed the banking panic of 1857. With production not yet fully recovered, the Union entered the Civil War running a large deficit. Tax revenues were not likely to increase in the near future, as the trade embargoes would most likely reduce revenue from import duties. At the same time, the instability of war led to a flight of specie from the United States to banks and institutions abroad. Eventually the drain of specie, combined with the large expenses of the war, led the U.S. government to suspend all specie payments. If specie payment had not been suspended, the government would not have had the gold to honor all specie conversions, and a financial crisis would have ensued.

The departure from specie redemption meant that the Union had to issue fiat money and require that it be deemed legal currency. However, distrust of paper currency that was not backed by precious metal was high. Opponents' arguments ranged from the unconstitutionality of fiat money to fears that paper money would bring inflation that would ruin the living standards of all Americans. Eventually a Republican-dominated Congress passed the authorizing bill, however, and Lincoln signed it into law on February 26, 1862.

The inflation fears of opponents of the Legal Tender Act were somewhat justified; greenbacks' value against gold fell steadily over the course of the war. But the fear that greenbacks would suffer the same inflationary levels that Continentals did during the Revolutionary War was not. The cost of living in the North at the end of the Civil War was 75 percent higher than when the war began, a rise much less than the hyperinflation seen during the Revolutionary War.

The lasting effects of the Legal Tender Act were the movement toward a national currency and the introduction of a permanent fiat method of payment in the United States. Abraham Lincoln would continue the movement toward formalizing a unified currency with the National Banking Act of 1863. Lincoln was concerned that the Supreme Court would strike down that law, and when he appointed Chase to be chief justice he did so in part because he believed Chase supported it. However, in *Hepburn v. Griswold,* 75 U.S. 603 (1870), Chase wrote the majority opinion striking the law down. A year later, in *Knox v. Lee,* 79 U.S. 457 (1871), also known as the Second Legal Tender Case, the Court reversed that decision in a five-to-four vote, with Chase writing a dissent.

—Patrick Van Horn

BIBLIOGRAPHY

Atack, Jeremy, and Peter Passell. *A New Economic View of American History: From Colonial Times to 1940.* New York: Norton, 1994.

Brands, H. W. *The Money Men: Capitalism, Democracy, and the Hundred Years' War over the American Dollar.* New York: Norton, 2008.

Knox, John J. *A History of Banking in the United States.* New York: Bradford Rhodes and Co., 1900.

Liberty Party

The Liberty Party was organized in 1839 by abolitionists who believed that political activity would be an effective tool in fighting slavery. Early Liberty Party organizers broke off from William Lloyd Garrison's American Anti-Slavery Society because Garrison rejected electoral politics. The key organizer was James G. Birney, a former slaveholder with roots in Kentucky and Alabama. In April 1840 a national Liberty Party Convention, with delegates from six states, nominated Birney for the presidency. Most Northern opponents of slavery were either followers of Garrison, and thus utterly alienated from electoral politics, or were unwilling to waste their ballot on a third party with dim political prospects. Birney received only 6,797 votes (0.3 percent of the popular vote) in the 1840 election, one of the few antebellum elections that pitted two Northerners—Martin Van Buren and William Henry Harrison—against each other.

By 1844 the Liberty Party had greater traction. The controversy over the annexation of Texas made slavery a more significant political issue. In 1844 both parties nominated Southern slaveholders—Henry Clay of Kentucky on the Whig ticket and James K. Polk of Tennessee on the Democratic ticket. Their nominations left opponents of slavery with no national ticket that they could support. Birney, again the Liberty Party presidential nominee, received 62,103 votes (2.3 percent of the popular vote) but again, as in 1840, carried no states. The party did demonstrate the power of antislavery voters, however. Polk won only 39,000 more popular votes than Clay, which meant that if the Liberty voters had supported the Whig Party, Clay would have outpolled Polk. More significant, Clay lost New York State by 5,100 votes while Birney won more than 15,000 votes in the state. Had Clay won New York he would have won the election. Whigs later blamed the Liberty Party for taking votes away from Clay, but there is no reason to believe that any of the antislavery Liberty voters would have voted for Clay. In Illinois Abraham Lincoln tried to persuade Liberty voters to support Clay with the argument that Clay was personally opposed to slavery because he was active in the colonization movement. This argument did not impress Liberty voters, who hated colonization as well as slavery.

Although Lincoln rejected the Liberty Party, other future Republicans began their careers with the party or worked with it. In New York the Liberty Party questioned candidates on various issues in 1840 and 1844, and that may have helped the rising antislavery Whig William H. Seward, who responded positively to Liberty Party queries about his willingness to provide greater protections for free blacks and fugitive slaves and repeal the New York law that allowed visiting masters to keep their slaves in the state for up to nine months. With Seward's support that law was repealed in 1841. Seward never joined the Liberty Party but worked with it. In Ohio Salmon P. Chase joined the Liberty Party in 1841 and worked for seven years to build it into a viable political force, developing a platform that was constitutionally possible by agitating for an end to slavery in the territories and in the District of Columbia.

In 1846 Liberty Party candidates received 74,017 votes in various state elections. In October 1847 the party nominated Sen. John P. Hale of New Hampshire for the presidency, but his candidacy was withdrawn the following year when the Liberty Party joined the broader-based Free Soil Party. The 1848 election was crucial for tying opposition to slavery with electoral politics. In Ohio, for example, Chase won a seat in the U.S. Senate, when Free-Soilers who had once been Liberty Party men held the balance of power in the state legislature. Gamaliel Bailey, one of the party's organizers in Ohio, became the publisher of the *National Era*, the Washington, D.C., based antislavery paper that first published Harriet Beecher Stowe's *Uncle Tom's Cabin* in serial form. The Liberty Party continued into the 1850s but was never again a factor in national politics. It was significant, however, as a harbinger of the antislavery wing of the Republican Party.

See also *Free Soil Party*

—Paul Finkelman

BIBLIOGRAPHY

Harrold, Stanley. *Gamaliel Bailey and Antislavery Union*. Kent, Ohio: Kent State University Press, 1986.

Sewell, Richard H. *Ballots for Freedom: Antislavery Politics in the United States, 1837–1860*. New York: Oxford University Press, 1976.

The Life of Washington, by Parson Weems

Abraham Lincoln read *The Life of Washington,* by Mason Locke Weems (1756–1825), while still a youth in southern Indiana. The book apparently made an impression on his young mind. Nearly forty years later, as president-elect, Lincoln made a reference to the book in a speech before the New Jersey Senate.

By most accounts, Weems was born in Maryland, educated in London, and ordained in the Protestant Episcopal Church; however, he did not gain fame as a minister. Weems instead embarked on a colorful career as an itinerant bookseller and popular author. Without a doubt, *The Life of Washington* remains his most well-known book.

Originally published in 1800, the book was a standard biography of the nation's first president. But Weems was dissatisfied with it because it simply detailed Washington's public life. In 1806 Weems revised the book, adding a number of anecdotes designed to highlight Washington's many private virtues. Most notably Weems added the story of the cherry tree, which featured a young Washington famously confessing to his father, "I can't tell a lie, Pa; you know I can't tell a lie. I did cut it with my hatchet." Like many of the most popular stories in Weems's books, the scene was certainly a work of fiction.

Lincoln read one of the later editions of *The Life of Washington,* which featured the many dubious anecdotes and woodcut illustrations. He borrowed a copy from an Indiana neighbor, Josiah Crawford. While the book was in Lincoln's possession, however, it became damaged. Though young Lincoln was friendly with Crawford, he knew his reputation: A neighbor called him a "close penurious man," and another claimed he was "noted for his littleness in all his dealings with his neighbors." Instead of shirking responsibility, Lincoln confessed that the book was damaged while in his possession. To pay for the damage, Crawford required two days of labor from Lincoln. According to a neighbor, Lincoln resented Crawford's terms.

Nonetheless, more than forty years later, Lincoln fondly recalled reading the book. On February 21, 1861, the president-elect spoke to the New Jersey Senate in Trenton. He recalled reading *The Life of Washington* "away back in my childhood" during "the earliest days of my being able to read." Of all the memorable scenes in the book, "none fixed themselves upon my imagination so deeply as the struggle here at Trenton, New Jersey."

Lincoln remembered thinking "that there must have been something more than common that those men struggled for; that something even more than National Independence; that something that held out a great promise to all the people of the world for all time to come."

The president-elect wanted to assure the nation that his administration would be consistent with the promise of the founders. "I am exceedingly anxious that this Union, the Constitution, and the liberties of the people shall be perpetuated in accordance with the original idea for which that struggle was made," Lincoln concluded, "and I shall be most happy indeed if I shall be an humble instrument in the hands of the Almighty, and of this, his almost chosen people, for perpetuating the object of that great struggle."

—SAMUEL P. WHEELER

BIBLIOGRAPHY

Houser, M.L. "Some Books That Lincoln Read." In *Lincoln's Education and Other Essays.* New York: Bookman Associates, 1957.

Warren, Louis A. *Lincoln's Youth: Indiana Years, 1816–1830.* Indianapolis: Indiana Historical Society, 1959.

Weems, Mason Locke. *The Life of George Washington; with Curious Anecdotes, Equally Honourable to Himself, and Exemplary To His Young Countrymen.* Philadelphia: Joseph Allen, 1809.

Wilson, Douglas L., and Rodney O. Davis, eds. *Herndon's Informants: Letters, Interviews, and Statements about Abraham Lincoln.* Urbana: University of Illinois Press, 1998.

Lincoln, Childhood and Youth

Abraham "Abe" Lincoln was born to Thomas and Nancy Lincoln in a log cabin near Hodgenville, Kentucky, on February 12, 1809. He was named in honor of his father's father, Abraham, who was killed by Indians in 1786.

In 1811 Lincoln's father, in search of more fertile land, moved the family to a farm on Knobs Creek. Lincoln's earliest memories were of following his father through the field; as his father planted corn, young Abe followed planting pumpkin seeds. He remembered vividly the year that a heavy storm washed their work away. Abe would also remember the birth at Knobs Creek of the third Lincoln child, Thomas, who only lived a short time.

Abe Lincoln's parents were illiterate, but education was very important to his mother, Nancy. She would often recite to the children Bible passages that she had memorized. On occasion young Abe and his sister, Sarah, attended ABC school to learn basic skills from teachers Zachariah Riney and later Caleb Hazel. Abe was a bright child and a quick learner. He was known to review material over and over until he had it memorized.

In 1816, when Abe was seven, the family moved across the Ohio River to Indiana. Thomas Lincoln had had problems with land claims in Kentucky, as well as a religious disagreement over slavery. Indiana was a free, but also a wild and untamed, state. The family lived in a rough shelter until a cabin could be built. The land needed to be cleared for planting, so the Lincolns depended on deer and bear to survive the winter. Young Abe, only eight years old, shot a turkey through the cabin chinking. That was the first time, and the last, that he would ever use a gun to obtain food.

Despite his tender age, Lincoln assisted his father in clearing the land. Ax in hand, he cut down trees and underbrush, learned the land, made rails, and tended the crops. Lincoln later wrote of the years in the region:

> *When first my father settled here,*
>
> *'Twas then the frontier line;*
>
> *The panther's scream, filled night with fear*
>
> *And bears preyed on the swine.*

Lincoln's mother was thrilled to have the company of her aunt and uncle, Elizabeth and Thomas Sparrow, when they moved to the area with eighteen-year-old Dennis Hanks, an illegitimate nephew of Elizabeth's. But the excitement was short-lived. When milk fever swept the area, Elizabeth and Thomas were afflicted and died. Then Abe's mother, Nancy, died of the illness on October 5, 1818.

His mother's death left Abe in bitter agony. Dennis provided a much-needed extra hand to Thomas and Abe's sister. Sarah, only twelve, tried to take on her mother's duties, but it was too much for her to handle. Thomas returned to Kentucky and sought a bride in Sarah Bush Johnston, a widow with three children. The arrangement had little to do with romance; he needed a wife and she a husband. Thomas paid her deceased husband's debt, married her on December 2, 1819, and returned home with a wife.

Besides her three children—Elizabeth, twelve; John, nine; and Matilda, eight—Sarah Bush Johnston brought with her possessions the Lincoln children had never known, such as silverware, furniture, and books. Sarah provided much-needed emotional support and enthusiasm and helped the two families blend without incident. Abe would refer to his biological mother as his "angel mother," but always loved and revered Sarah, whom he fully accepted as a mother.

Abe and his stepmother became very close. Sarah, though illiterate, appreciated education and encouraged the children to learn to read and write. Abe, though erratically schooled, learned by reading. When he was able to attend school he showed up in his coonskin hat and pants that were many inches too short for his long legs and lanky frame. Despite his awkward appearance, Abe, who had learned the skill of storytelling from his father, made friends easily.

As Abe grew he was depended upon to handle more of the chores on the farm. Abe loved to learn and was known to walk miles to borrow books from neighbors. To his father's dismay, Abe could often be found sitting under a tree reading one of his favorite books—*Pilgrim's Progress, Arabian Nights, Robinson Crusoe,* or Aesop's *Fables.* Abe preferred reading and learning to manual labor. Dennis Hanks would later describe Abe as lazy. He spent more time reading, scribbling, and writing than working. The father and son were never close, and their relationship grew more distant as Abe reached adolescence.

Another source of tension between father and son was on the topic of religion. Thomas and Sarah belonged to the Little Pigeon Baptist Church, but Abe, though he attended services, never felt inclined to join. He preferred to mock the sermons for the neighbor children until his father, unhappy with the jesting, would stop the activity and put Abe to work.

In 1826 Abe Lincoln's only surviving sibling, Sarah, married Aaron Grigsby and moved several miles away. His stepsister, Matilda, also wed and moved away. On January 28, 1826, a year and a half after marrying, Sarah died in childbirth; she was buried with her stillborn child. Abe, angry that no one had called a doctor for Sarah and her child, quarreled with the Grisby family.

When not working for his father, Abe did side jobs. After trying unsuccessfully to sell firewood to steamships on the Ohio River, Abe and his two partners traded nine cords of wood for a bolt of white fabric. Abe had his share made into a shirt, the first white shirt he had ever owned. He was more successful as a ferryman, taking passengers from shore to steamers on the Ohio.

In 1828, James Gentry hired Abe to deliver a load of meat, corn, and flour to New Orleans with Gentry's son Allen. The adventure took a turn for the worse when seven black men attacked the boat, hoping to steal the goods onboard. The two young men held the assailants off and continued on their way to New Orleans. There Abe witnessed slavery for the first time in his life. Abe enjoyed his travel away from home and longed to escape Little Pigeon Creek and his father, but legally he was obligated to stay with and work for his father until the age of twenty-one.

In 1830 the Lincoln family, fearing an outbreak of milk fever in Indiana, moved to Illinois. Abe drove the oxen there, and he helped his father build a cabin on the bank of the Sangamon River. It was there that Abe would give his first political speech, calling for internal improvements, a protective tariff, and a national bank.

In 1831 Abe, finally of age, was able to leave home for good. He leapt at the opportunity to visit New Orleans for the second time when Denton Offett hired him to deliver a flatboat of goods to the city. Offett had promised him a job in his store upon his return. Though Offett didn't come through, Abe found himself a home in New Salem, Illinois, where he boarded at Rutledge's Tavern, worked odd jobs, and began his long journey to adulthood and a new life. The friends and business associates he made in New Salem would be instrumental in his political career and his eventual rise to the presidency.

See also *Lincoln, Young Manhood to Eve of Political Career; Lincoln, Legal and Early Political Career; Lincoln, As a National Figure, 1854–1865*

—PAULA COCHRAN

BIBLIOGRAPHY

Davis, Herbert, and David Donald. *Lincoln.* New York: Simon and Schuster, 1996.

Donald, David Herbert. *Lincoln at Home: Two Glimpses of Abraham Lincoln's Domestic Life.* New York: Simon and Schuster, 1999.

Harris, William C. *Lincoln's Rise to the Presidency.* Lawrence: University Press of Kansas, 2007.

Neely, Mark E., Jr., and Harold Holzer. *The Lincoln Family Album: Photographs from the Personal Collection of a Historic American Family.* New York: Doubleday, 1990.

Lincoln, Young Manhood to Eve of Political Career

Abraham Lincoln was born and spent the first seven years of his life in Kentucky. In 1816 Thomas Lincoln moved his family north across the Ohio River from Kentucky and settled on a wooded, 160-acre claim in Spencer County, Indiana. Lincoln later attributed his father's move north to his dislike of slavery and his efforts to establish an uncontested claim to property—a problem that plagued Thomas in Kentucky. In migrating north of the Ohio River, the Lincolns joined thousands of other Southerners seeking cheap federal land on which to practice subsistence agriculture. Soon relatives from Kentucky joined the Lincolns in Indiana, settling on nearby claims and establishing a small community of security and exchange.

As a young boy, Lincoln assisted his father in the grinding labor of clearing woods, splitting rails for fencing, and planting and harvesting corn. Opportunities for education were few and inconsistent, and much of what Lincoln learned during his years in Indiana he learned from reading whatever he could find. His infrequent attendance at nearby schools ended altogether when he reached adolescence and became old enough to find work in the community. Lincoln hired himself out as a farm laborer, ferryman, store clerk, and flatboat operator. Working in the context of subsistence agriculture and a nascent market economy, his pay often came in the form of produce or the promise of reciprocal labor and always went to supplement his family's needs.

Lincoln likely inherited his political loyalties from his father. Thomas Lincoln was a follower of fellow Kentuckian and Speaker of the U. S. House of Representatives Henry Clay and later supported the Whig Party. As a teen working in nearby towns, Lincoln may have followed Clay's 1824 presidential bid through the newspapers or may have witnessed local political campaign activities. Lincoln may also have inherited his father's negative views on slavery. While in Kentucky, the Lincolns attended churches with known antislavery stances, and after they left slavery behind in favor of the free soil of Indiana, they joined a Baptist church with similar antislavery leanings. During a flatboat trip to New Orleans in 1828, Lincoln was said to have expressed disgust after witnessing the city's slave markets.

In early 1830 Thomas Lincoln sold his farm and moved his family, including twenty-one-year-old Abraham, to Illinois to establish a farm in Macon County. By the 1830s central Illinois contained a mix of settlers from the North and South. Settlers from the upland South (Kentucky, Virginia, and Maryland), such as the Lincolns, represented the largest group of migrants. The Lincolns settled land in a part of Macon County on the north side of the Sangamon River, alongside a "Yankee" settlement. While there Lincoln worked as a farm laborer in much the same way he had in Indiana. He is said to have made his first political speech while working for a family near the county seat of Decatur. During the winter Lincoln made plans with his cousin John Hanks and his stepbrother John D. Johnston to ship a cargo of produce by flatboat to New Orleans in the spring for Denton Offutt, a merchant in nearby Springfield.

During their journey down the Sangamon River, Lincoln, Hanks, Johnston, and Offutt came upon the village of New Salem. In an event memorable to many witnesses in the village, Lincoln displayed his ingenuity by directing the difficult task of floating the flatboat over a milldam. Offutt was also impressed with Lincoln and offered him a job as clerk in a store he wished to open in New Salem. Lincoln accepted, and after he returned from New Orleans he set off for New Salem.

Though it had been established only two years prior, in 1831 New Salem was a central market for the surrounding countryside, a place where farmers could trade for goods and obtain the services of skilled craftsmen and professionals. A group of young men from the nearby settlement of Clary's Grove used the village as a meeting place during times of leisure. The so-called Clary's Grove boys immediately took an interest in Lincoln, who earned their admiration and support by proving his worth in a wrestling match with their leader, Jack Armstrong. Lincoln also gained acceptance among the village's professionals and artisans. He attended meetings of the debating society, studied grammar under the tutelage of a local schoolmaster, studied law, and befriended the village's justice of the peace.

Confident of the backing of his new community, Lincoln announced his candidacy for the state legislature in a local newspaper on the platform of improving the navigability of the Sangamon River, improving educational resources, and limiting usurious lending. By promoting the Sangamon River as a mode of getting agricultural produce to market, Lincoln's platform exhibited his interest in supporting internal improvements to facilitate economic growth.

Offutt's store never flourished, and Lincoln found himself facing unemployment in 1832. When Illinois governor John Reynolds mobilized the state militia in April, at the outset of the Black Hawk War, Lincoln promptly volunteered. In northern Illinois, Native American followers of Chief Black Hawk had reentered traditional Sac and Fox tribal lands east of the Mississippi River. Fearing an uprising, the federal government called on the Illinois militia to supplement the regular army units in the area. Lincoln joined one of ten companies raised in Sangamon County, a company formed mostly of volunteers from the New Salem area. The company elected him captain, indicating Lincoln's rise to leadership in his community after only a brief residence.

After an uneventful march to northern Illinois, Lincoln's company disbanded at the end of its thirty-day service. Thereafter Lincoln reenlisted several times and served for another two months. During this time he encountered men who would influence his political career, including future Whig congressmen John T. Stuart, John J. Hardin, and Edward D. Baker. These men, themselves rising political stars in Illinois, encouraged Lincoln to pursue his candidacy for the state legislature. Stuart, Lincoln's future law partner, also encouraged him to study law.

After returning to New Salem in July, Lincoln resumed his campaign for the state legislature. With only a few weeks until the election, he had little time to campaign and placed eighth among thirteen candidates vying for the county's four seats. He managed to earn nearly all of the votes from his largely pro–Andrew Jackson precinct, despite being an avowed supporter of Henry Clay.

Lincoln subsequently entered into a partnership with New Salem merchant William F. Berry. Their general store, one of three in the village, was not successful despite their having obtained a license to dispense liquor. In April 1833, after a few months of fitful business, the store folded, leaving Lincoln deeply in debt. In May Lincoln received a presidential appointment as postmaster of New Salem. This was a surprise given his declared anti-Jackson leanings. Although it is unlikely he would have been appointed without some support from local Democrats, Lincoln later mused that this oversight was due to New Salem's unimportance in the spoils scheme that characterized patronage during President Jackson's administration. As postmaster, Lincoln had free access to newspapers, and the political news therein, and he had even greater contact with residents of the surrounding countryside.

In the fall of 1833 the county surveyor, a Democrat, hired Lincoln as deputy county surveyor. He quickly learned his new profession and continued in the job until he began the practice of law full-time in 1837. Despite this success, Lincoln could not pay his lingering debts, and after being sued, he had to sell most of his personal belongings to satisfy a debt from his partnership with Berry. It would be years before Lincoln fully paid off the accumulated debt from his early forays into the developing market economy.

Undeterred, Lincoln gathered his resources, continued to foster his reputation in Sangamon County, and in spring 1834 made another bid for the state legislature. His reputation had grown since his first candidacy in 1832; his roles in the community as militia captain, postmaster, and surveyor made him more widely known. In the developing two-party system of the 1830s, Lincoln ran a campaign in which he garnered support both from the Jacksonian Democrats of the countryside and from his fellow Clay supporters, including the growing Whig stronghold of nearby Springfield. This coalition of support gave Lincoln enough votes to win a seat in the state legislature, launching his political career.

See also *Lincoln, Childhood and Youth; Lincoln, Legal and Early Political Career; Lincoln, As a National Figure, 1854– 1865;*

—CHRISTOPHER SCHNELL

BIBLIOGRAPHY

Miller, Richard L. *Lincoln and His World: The Early Years, Birth to Illinois Legislature.* Mechanicsburg, Pa.: Stackpole Books, 2006.

Thomas, Benjamin P. *Lincoln's New Salem.* Springfield, Ill.: Abraham Lincoln Association, 1934.

Warren, Louis A. *Lincoln's Youth: Indiana Years, 1816–1830.* Indianapolis: Indiana Historical Society, 1959.

Wilson, Douglas L. *Honor's Voice: The Transformation of Abraham Lincoln.* New York: Knopf, 1998.

Winkle, Kenneth J. *The Young Eagle: The Rise of Abraham Lincoln.* Dallas: Taylor Trade Publishing, 2001.

Lincoln, Legal and Early Political Career

In 1830 Thomas Lincoln moved with his family, including his son, Abraham, from Indiana to Macon County, Illinois. During the year that Abraham Lincoln lived there he gave his first political speech in the county seat of Decatur. Striking out on his own in the nearby community of New Salem, Lincoln decided to run for the Illinois General Assembly after living in the state for only two years. He lost that first election, running eighth in a field of thirteen, with the top four winning election. At this point Lincoln considered a career in the law, but he believed that his lack of education would prevent him from succeeding.

Lincoln ran for the Illinois legislature again in 1834. With support from local Democrats, the Whig Lincoln took second in the field of thirteen. During his first session in the General Assembly, at the state capital of Vandalia, Lincoln observed and learned the art of lawmaking. As his first term progressed, he became more comfortable and began making speeches and helping to draft bills. He and fellow Whig John T. Stuart became quick friends, and Stuart encouraged Lincoln to study the law, loaning him law books from his Springfield law office.

Lincoln won a second term in the Illinois legislature in 1836. The members of the Sangamon County delegation became known as the "Long Nine" because the seven representatives and two senators were all over six feet tall. Lincoln helped pass a massive internal improvements act to build canals and railroads across Illinois, but the Panic of 1837 thwarted the grandiose plan and nearly bankrupted the state. The other major law passed in that session was a measure to move the capital of Illinois to Springfield, which was more centrally located in the state. Finally, Lincoln made his first antislavery statement by adding a protest to a resolution that condemned abolitionism. Lincoln and another Long Nine member believed that "the institution of slavery is founded on both injustice and bad policy."

In 1836 Lincoln became licensed to practice law in Illinois when the justices of the Illinois Supreme Court examined him and found him competent in his knowledge of the law. Although he handled a couple of cases, Lincoln did not begin his practice until spring 1837. John T. Stuart had invited Lincoln to become his junior partner, and the two began practicing law in Springfield. The partnership generally handled debt-related litigation but also had cases involving divorce, replevin, and criminal actions. Stuart and Lincoln rode the circuit together, traveling to counties in the First Judicial Circuit, which included their home county of Sangamon. In 1838 Stuart won election to the U.S. House of Representatives and left the young Lincoln to manage a prominent law firm on his own.

Lincoln won a third term in the Illinois legislature in 1838 and began to be a leader in the Illinois General Assembly. He ran for speaker but lost in a legislature with a slight Democratic majority. Lincoln helped to deal with banking issues in the state and continued to support expensive internal improvements legislation despite the public outcry against it. Lincoln also worked on many other bills as Whigs in the state looked to him for legislative guidance. During the presidential campaign of 1840, Lincoln campaigned actively for the Whig nominee, William Henry Harrison, against incumbent Democrat Martin Van Buren. Lincoln traveled all over Illinois—concentrating in heavily Democratic southern Illinois—making stump speeches on behalf of Harrison and debating Democratic politicians. Van Buren won Illinois, but Harrison won the election. Lincoln also won his fourth and last term in the Illinois legislature.

In the first assembly in the new state capital of Springfield, the two legislative bodies met in local churches while construction continued on the new capitol building. Lincoln's most notable act was not legislative but rather an attempt to prevent legislation. Lincoln and two other Whig representatives jumped out of a window to prevent a quorum on a banking bill. Unfortunately for Lincoln, the leap did not stop the vote, and the local Democratic press excoriated Lincoln. Also during the session Lincoln experienced his "fatal first" of January 1841, an episode in which he plunged into a deep depression over his broken engagement with Mary Todd. Lincoln had served eight productive years—his longest elected service—in the Illinois General Assembly, learning the political lawmaking process and discovering that he had the ability to debate issues with prominent Illinoisans.

After a couple years of practicing law without his law partner and mentor, Stuart, Lincoln thought that he needed more guidance in the legal profession. Stephen T. Logan invited Lincoln to join him as a law partner, and the two began practicing law together in spring 1841. Both the federal court and the Illinois Supreme Court moved to Springfield when the city became the state capital. Logan sensed the possibility that a federal bankruptcy act would generate a large amount of business, and he wanted help in that area of law. Logan introduced Lincoln to a substantial federal practice beyond bankruptcy. Even though Lincoln handled a small number of cases on appeal to the Illinois Supreme Court, Logan also introduced him to a large appellate practice. During their partnership they became lawyer's lawyers—handling in Springfield appeal cases that originated across the state. Lincoln also continued his practice of riding the circuit, typically carving his own circuit out of two or three jurisdictional circuits, most notably the Eighth Judicial Circuit. Logan provided Lincoln important legal guidance, teaching him the importance of fees, introducing him to other areas of the law, and stressing the importance of preparation.

In 1844 Logan wanted to take his son David into the practice, and Lincoln, after seven years of being junior partner, was ready to form his own firm. Lincoln asked the young William Henry Herndon, a law clerk in the Logan and Lincoln law office, to become his partner. Lincoln continued his practice of riding the circuit, handling cases at the Illinois Supreme Court, and arguing cases at the federal court in Springfield. By the sheer volume of his cases, Lincoln became one of the more prominent attorneys in the state and evolved into a consummate general practice attorney.

Not long after his service in the Illinois legislature ended, Lincoln set his eyes on the U.S. Congress. Stuart decided not to run again in 1842, and three Whigs—Lincoln, Edward Dickinson Baker, and John J. Hardin—all vied for the newly created seventh congressional district of eleven counties hugging the Illinois River. The district nominating convention chose Hardin as its candidate but with an implicit agreement that Baker would run in 1844 and Lincoln in 1846. Accordingly Lincoln began preparing for his run for Congress in 1845. Hardin, however, announced his desire to return to Congress, and he and Lincoln mobilized their forces against each other. Hardin finally withdrew when newspapers and party leaders agreed that it was Lincoln's turn. Lincoln secured the Whig nomination and opposed Democrat Peter Cartwright, an itinerant Methodist preacher. Lincoln easily won the election in August 1846.

The Thirtieth Congress did not meet until December 1847, and Lincoln devoted himself to the practice of law during the time between his election and his move to Washington. Most notably, one week before packing up his family to move east Lincoln participated in the Matson slave case. Kentuckian Robert Matson had brought slaves to his farm in Coles County, Illinois. With the help of some local abolitionists, the slaves—a mother and her four children—sued for their freedom. Lincoln represented Matson in the case but lost when the judges hearing the case ruled that since slavery was illegal in Illinois, the slaves were free upon entering the state.

See also *Lincoln, Childhood and Youth; Lincoln, Young Manhood to Eve of Political Career; Lincoln, As a National Figure, 1854–1865*

—John A. Lupton

BIBLIOGRAPHY

Benner, Martha L., Cullom Davis, et al., eds. *The Law Practice of Abraham Lincoln: Complete Documentary Edition, DVD-ROM.* Urbana: University of Illinois Press, 2000.

Donald, David. *Lincoln.* New York: Simon and Schuster. 1995.

Riddle, Donald W. *Lincoln Runs for Congress.* New Brunswick, N.J.: Rutgers University Press, 1948.

Simon, Paul. *Lincoln's Preparation for Greatness: The Illinois Legislative Years.* Norman: University of Oklahoma Press, 1965. Reprint, Urbana: University of Illinois Press, 1971; paperback ed., 1989.

Steiner, Mark E. *An Honest Calling: The Law Practice of Abraham Lincoln.* DeKalb: Northern Illinois University Press, 2006.

Stowell, Daniel W., et al., eds. *The Papers of Abraham Lincoln: Legal Documents and Cases.* 4 vols. Charlottesville: University of Virginia Press, 2008.

Stowell, Daniel W., ed. *In Tender Consideration: Women, Families, and the Law in Abraham Lincoln's Illinois.* Urbana: University of Illinois Press, 2002.

Winkle, Kenneth J. *The Young Eagle: The Rise of Abraham Lincoln.* Dallas: Taylor Trade Publishing, 2001.

Lincoln, As a National Figure, 1854–1865

Born in obscurity in Kentucky, Abraham Lincoln trod a slow and arduous path to national recognition. By 1854 the resident of Springfield, Illinois, had accomplished more than most people achieve in a lifetime. A successful lawyer, Lincoln had served several terms in the Illinois General Assembly, and in 1846 he was elected to a term in the U.S. House of Representatives. After his term in Congress ended, Lincoln had few political prospects, particularly as a member of the Whig Party in a state controlled by Democrats. Although Lincoln was well known in Illinois by the early 1850s, he was virtually unknown outside his native state and the familiar eighth judicial circuit, where he plied his legal practice. Although Lincoln craved high office and political distinction, his prospects early in the decade appeared bleak. The situation would begin to change in 1854 as a result of the Kansas-Nebraska Act, introduced in Congress by Lincoln's political rival, Sen. Stephen Douglas. Some would argue that Lincoln's opposition to the Kansas-Nebraska Act ultimately put him on a path to the presidency.

Beginning in fall 1854 Lincoln delivered a series of speeches that criticized the Kansas-Nebraska Act, saying that the policy set forth in it directly contradicted the wishes of the Founders, who Lincoln claimed wished to see the growth of slavery limited so that it would eventually perish. In fall 1854, ostensibly campaigning on behalf of congressional candidate Richard Yates, an anti-Nebraska Whig, Lincoln had his sights on the U.S. Senate. A Senate seat would confer national stature on Lincoln, as it had on his political idol, the Whig senator from Kentucky Henry Clay. Also running as an anti-Nebraska Whig, Lincoln initially received the most votes in the Illinois General Assembly when it began balloting to choose a senator in early February 1855. He would not receive the required majority, however, because of the opposition of a group of anti-Nebraska Democrats who distrusted Lincoln's Whig affiliations. Led by Norman B. Judd, these Democrats supported the anti-Nebraska Democratic candidate, Lyman Trumbull. Rather than risk the election of the regular Democratic candidate, Governor Joel Matteson, Lincoln threw his support to Trumbull.

By 1856 Lincoln was prominently identified with the new Republican Party, having played an important part in a Decatur, Illinois, meeting of newspaper editors that worked to organize the party in Illinois. At the 1856 Republican national convention in Philadelphia, members of the Illinois delegation nominated Lincoln as a favorite son candidate for the vice presidency. Not well known outside of his native state, Lincoln finished second to the eventual nominee, William Dayton. With the Senate term of Stephen Douglas soon expiring, Lincoln once again focused on a U.S. Senate seat and the 1858 elections.

It was during the 1858 senatorial campaign that Lincoln began to attract national attention. Ironically, a large part of this attention was due to Lincoln's opponent, Stephen Arnold Douglas. It was Douglas who was the larger-than-life figure in 1858. Running for his third term in the Senate, Douglas was one of the most prominent Democratic leaders in the antebellum United States. He had worked behind the scenes to bring about the Compromise of 1850. It was his controversial Kansas-Nebraska bill that brought Lincoln back to the Illinois political scene and eventually into the Republican Party. Finally it was the determined opposition of Douglas to approval of the proslavery Lecompton Constitution for the state of Kansas that made his reelection campaign so widely followed. Because of his national stature, Douglas had nothing to gain by accepting the challenge to a series of debates with the lesser-known Republican candidate. A perennial risk taker, however, Douglas did not like to back down from challenges.

Given the opportunity to share the spotlight with Douglas, Lincoln took a major step toward becoming a national figure. Since Douglas was known throughout the country, his presence in the debates was responsible for large audiences and national press reporting. As the debates were covered across the nation, Americans became familiar with Lincoln's "House Divided" speech; his challenge to Douglas at Freeport, and his soaring moral rhetoric at the final three debates at Galesburg, Quincy, and Alton. Lincoln made the moral case for blocking the spread of slavery in the western territories as effectively as any Republican leader. Although Lincoln lost the senatorial contest, he became a speaker who was frequently sought by Republican candidates throughout the North.

As a result of the stature he gained during the 1858 elections, Lincoln was invited by the Ohio state Republican committee to speak at Columbus, Dayton, Hamilton, and Cincinnati on behalf of Republican candidates in the 1859 state elections. During the same year, Lincoln also spoke in Indiana, Iowa, Wisconsin, and Kansas. Perhaps the culmination of Lincoln's rise to become a pre-presidential national figure occurred when he accepted an invitation to speak at the famous Cooper Union in New York City, in February 1860. Speaking on February 27, Lincoln made a favorable impression on the eastern Republican audience despite his ungainly appearance and Kentucky accent. Lincoln followed up this successful speech with a speaking tour in New England. Despite two unsuccessful tries for the Senate, on the eve of the 1860 Republican convention Abraham Lincoln was an emerging national figure.

Ultimately Lincoln's popularity resulting from his senatorial campaign against Douglas made him a viable candidate for the Republican nomination in 1860. In the first place, Lincoln was now widely recognized as a significant Republican politician. Second, many of the more prominent Republicans, such as William Henry Seward, Salmon Chase, Simon Cameron, and Edward Bates, had baggage that did not encumber Lincoln. Seward was widely known as too radical on the slavery issue—as was Chase. A former Democrat, Cameron had a reputation for shady financial dealings, while Bates was too closely affiliated with the anti-immigrant Know-Nothing Party of the mid-1850s. Lincoln had none of these problems; hence his managers set about a strategy to make him the second choice of those supporting the more favored candidates. When front-runner Seward was not able to secure a majority, Lincoln's stock began to rise, and he was universally nominated on third ballot at the Republican Party convention in Chicago on May 18, 1860.

Lincoln was elected president by a plurality of popular votes but a majority of electoral votes. Southern states greeted his election with secession that eventually erupted into civil war, and the majority of Lincoln's presidency was devoted to putting down rebellion and restoring the Union. Abraham Lincoln's skill in handling critical war issues, such as slavery, as well as his use of speeches and letters to articulate and justify his course as president during the Civil War would add to his prominence as a national leader. Despite the unpopularity of the war in many areas of the North and despite the many low points for Union military fortunes, Lincoln was nevertheless overwhelmingly reelected in November 1864, proof that his stature as a national figure was augmented, not diminished, by his presidency.

Lincoln's course on the slavery issue helped build his national prominence. Recognizing that moving too quickly against the "peculiar institution" would jeopardize the support of Border State conservatives as well as members of the Democratic Party, Lincoln bided his time, waiting for the correct opportunity to move against slavery. He tried to shape popular opinion through skillful public letters, such as his August 22, 1862, response to *New York Tribune* editor Horace Greeley's editorial, "The Prayer of Twenty Million." In his response to Greeley's appeal for the abolition of slavery, Lincoln made the case that preserving the Union was paramount. Slavery might have to perish but only if it helped restore the Union. When Lincoln issued the preliminary Emancipation Proclamation after the battle of Antietam on September 22, 1862, he could justify his action as necessary to restore the Union. Similarly, Lincoln skillfully defended his administration's policies on civil liberties, as in his June 12, 1863, letter to New York Democrat Erastus Corning, which also appeared in the *New York Tribune*. Defending the arrest and imprisonment of Clement Vallandigham, Lincoln argued that restrictions of civil liberties were necessary to fight the rebellion. Finally Lincoln's public speeches were also critical in creating a context for the significance and meaning of the American Civil War. At Gettysburg, on November 19, 1863, Lincoln's short address was pivotal in equating sacrifices on the battlefield with the Declaration of Independence and the promise of equality set forth by the nation's Founders.

Probably the greatest single factor in augmenting Lincoln's stature was his role as commander in chief. Lacking military experience, Lincoln nevertheless became a competent commander in chief who, particularly through the cooperation and participation of Ulysses Grant and William Sherman, developed a successful strategy to subdue the Confederacy. The recognition of Lincoln's ability to develop this strategy was an important factor in his reelection in 1864. By the time of his assassination at the hand of John Wilkes Booth, Lincoln had emerged as the most significant political figure of the era.

—Bruce Tap

BIBLIOGRAPHY

Carwardine, Richard. *Lincoln: A Life of Purpose and Power.* New York: Vintage, 2007.

Donald, David Herbert. *Lincoln.* New York: Simon and Schuster, 1995.

Gienapp, William E. *Abraham Lincoln and Civil War America: A Biography.* New York: Oxford University Press, 2002.

Guelzo, Allen C. *Lincoln and Douglas: The Debates that Defined America.* New York: Simon and Schuster, 2008.

Thomas, Benjamin P. *Abraham Lincoln: A Biography.* New York: Knopf, 1952.

Lincoln, Memory of

Since the moment he died, Abraham Lincoln has held endless fascination for Americans. He is the subject of more than 15,000 books, as well as hundreds of songs, films, and statues and thousands of artworks and advertisements. The meaning of his life and legacy has been analyzed and debated, as various individuals and groups have tried to lay claim to some small piece of the sixteenth president.

When it came to securing his place in American memory, Lincoln died under nearly ideal circumstances. On that Saturday in 1865, he was only six days removed from Robert E. Lee's surrender at Appomattox and so was at the height of his popularity. He escaped the difficult challenge of reconstructing the shattered nation. He was even shot on Good Friday, the same day that Jesus was martyred, a fact not lost on the deeply religious Americans of the nineteenth century.

Lincoln's death caused an overwhelming outpouring of grief. For two days his body lay in state in the White House and then in the Capitol. More than 50,000 mourners waited as much as six hours to view the president's body. After a funeral service, Lincoln's coffin traveled by train to the major population centers of the North, stopping for spectators and services in New York, Philadelphia, Buffalo, and a dozen other cities before reaching the president's final resting place in Springfield, Illinois.

During this time, songs celebrating Lincoln's life poured from the pens of composers—"A Nation Mourns Her Chief," by H.S. Thompson; "Our Martyr President," by W. Dexter Smith Jr.; and "President Lincoln's Funeral March," by Karl Metz, to name only three. The nation's poets joined in the mourning as well. Most notable was Walt Whitman, whose melancholy Lincoln tribute "O Captain! My Captain!" famously concludes:

> *My Captain does not answer, his lips are pale and still;*
>
> *My father does not feel my arm, he has no pulse nor will;*
>
> *The ship is anchor'd safe and sound, its voyage closed and done;*
>
> *From fearful trip, the victor ship, comes in with object won;*
>
> > *Exult, O shores, and ring, O bells!*
> >
> > > *But I, with mournful tread,*
> > >
> > > > *Walk the deck my Captain lies,*
> > > >
> > > > > *Fallen cold and dead.*

Individuals are often lionized in the days and weeks after their deaths. In Lincoln's case, however, the frenzy did not abate once he had been buried. Millions of Americans purchased photographs and works of art portraying the president for display in their houses. The most popular, an 1865 print entitled "Apotheosis," shows Lincoln being welcomed into heaven by George Washington. Some Americans decided to go even farther in commemorating the president, naming their hometowns or local landmarks after him. More than twenty cities bear Lincoln's name, as do six mountains, several lakes, and countless roads.

Americans of the late nineteenth and early twentieth centuries were deeply enamored of statues and other monuments, and in the decades after his death Lincoln was regularly honored with memorials. A magnificent tomb was built on his gravesite in 1871, and between 1887 and 1889 the famed sculptor Augustus Saint-Gaudens created a pair of statues for the city of Chicago. In 1917 the famous Lincoln Memorial in Washington, D.C., was dedicated, and eight years later Lincoln was immortalized on Mount Rushmore in South Dakota. In addition to these famous works were hundreds of other memorials to the president erected throughout the United States. Almost without exception, these works portray Lincoln in the same way—larger than life, heroic, stately, bearded, and dressed in the garb of his presidential years.

Lincoln's status as an American icon, then, was secure by the start of the twentieth century. The U.S. government has freely traded on that status, using him as a symbol of strength, civic virtue, and national unity. In addition to funding construction of the Lincoln Memorial, government officials have placed Lincoln on currency—the penny beginning in 1909, and the five dollar bill beginning in 1914—and have applied his name to warships, schools, government buildings, and even the 3,000-mile Lincoln Highway. Politicians, both Democrats and Republicans, are eager to lay claim to Lincoln's legacy. Ronald Reagan, for example, regularly quoted Lincoln in his speeches, attributing to him such conservative wisdom as, "You cannot help the poor man by destroying the rich" and "You cannot help men permanently by doing for them what they could and should do for themselves." Reagan continued to use these quotations even after learning that, as is the case with many Lincoln "quotes," he never said or wrote any such things.

Undoubtedly the twentieth-century politician with whom Lincoln is most closely connected is John F. Kennedy. As have all occupants of the Oval Office, Kennedy liked to link himself to Lincoln. The connection was strengthened by the commonalities between the two men: their charisma, their talent as speakers, their commitment to social justice, and perhaps most significantly, the fact that both died at the hands of an assassin. On the day after Kennedy died, an editorial cartoon in the *New York Times* showed Lincoln weeping. The two presidents continue to be associated with one another, most notably in the hit 1968 song "Abraham, Martin, and John" and in lists of assassination "coincidences" that are reproduced endlessly in books and on the Internet.

The linking of Lincoln with Martin Luther King Jr.—the Martin of "Abraham, Martin, and John"—illustrates another significant dimension to Lincoln's memory, the "Great Emancipator" as an important symbol for civil rights activists. He was often a subject of the Harlem Renaissance poets; "Let's Go See Old Abe," the 1920 composition by Langston Hughes, is a notable example. In 1936, after black athletes dominated the Berlin Olympics, the *Los Angeles Times* headline read, "Abraham Lincoln Won 1936 Olympic Games." In 1939 African American singer Marian Anderson was, because of her race, denied permission to give a concert at the Daughters of the American Revolution's Constitution Hall, in Washington, D.C. The performance was quickly moved to the Lincoln Memorial, where Anderson delighted the crowd with a rendition of "My Country, 'Tis of Thee." Martin Luther King Jr.'s "I Have a Dream" speech was also delivered on the steps of the Lincoln Memorial, in 1964.

Abraham Lincoln was a politician and a crusader for civil rights, so it is understandable that civil rights groups would seize upon his memory. Other claims, however, are more tenuous. For example, in 1918 the Red Square Toy Company introduced Lincoln logs and began to cash in on the president's name. In subsequent decades, it became fairly common to treat Lincoln's memory as a commodity—the Ford Motor Company's Lincoln Continental was introduced in 1939, Lincoln Financial Group incorporated in 1968, and Honest Abe Log Homes opened for business in 1979, to choose but three examples from among many. Of course, businesses are not the only ones to have traded on Lincoln's memory; it has also become customary for various social groups to try to co-opt Lincoln as one of their own. In the 1980s, for example, depression advocacy groups laid claim to Lincoln as a role model for coping with clinical depression. In 1999 author and gay activist Larry Kramer announced that he had proof that Lincoln was gay, though he refused to release the alleged proof for scrutiny.

The desire of so many Americans to lay claim to Lincoln speaks to his enduring place in American memory. There are exceptions to the rule, however. Naturally, hatred of Lincoln persisted in much of the South throughout the nineteenth century and into the twentieth. During this time, anti-Lincoln Southerners published several widely read books condemning the president, notably Charles Minor's *The Real Lincoln* (1901) and Edgar Lee Masters's *Lincoln the Man* (1931). In the 1960s these Southern critics were joined by a handful of African American activists, notably Lerone Bennett, who made a career of arguing that Lincoln should be remembered as a white supremacist and not as a hero. Bennett's writings are collected in *Forced into Glory: Abraham Lincoln's White Dream* (2000). The anti-Lincoln crusade has also been joined by a handful of neoconservatives, most prominently Thomas DiLorenzo, whose *Lincoln Unmasked: What You're Not Supposed to Know about Dishonest Abe* (2006) blames Lincoln for many modern ills, particularly the large size of the federal government. These books are not the only evidence that Lincoln remains unpopular with some Americans. In 2003, for example, there was much controversy when a statue to Lincoln was unveiled in Richmond, Virginia, the onetime capital of the Confederacy. Though welcomed by most residents, some protestors made clear that the memorial was not welcome in their city,

As vocal as they may be, the opponents of Lincoln are in the clear minority. For the vast majority of Americans, affection for Abraham Lincoln remains strong. The still brisk trade in books about Lincoln and writings by him is evidence of that fact, as are the many Lincoln museums scattered across the nation, the dozens of men who make a living traveling the country as Lincoln impersonators, and the existence of the 5,000-member Abraham Lincoln Association. Undoubtedly the celebration of Lincoln's two hundredth birthday in 2009 and the release of the Steven Spielberg–directed *Lincoln* in 2010 will serve to affirm his central place in American historical memory.

—CHRISTOPHER BATES

BIBLIOGRAPHY

Ferguson, Andrew. *Land of Lincoln: Adventures in Abe's America.* New York: Grove Press, 2004.

Peterson, Merrill D. *Lincoln in American Memory.* New York: Oxford University Press, 1995.

Prokopowicz, Gerald J. *Did Lincoln Own Slaves? And Other Frequently Asked Questions about Abraham Lincoln.* New York: Pantheon, 2008.

Sandage, Scott A. "A Marble House Divided: The Lincoln Memorial, the Civil Rights Movement, and the Politics of Memory, 1939–1963." *Journal of American History* 80, no. 1 (June 1993): 135–167.

Steers, Edward, Jr. *Lincoln Legends: Myths, Hoaxes, and Confabulations Associated with Our Greatest President.* Lexington: University Press of Kentucky, 2007.

Lincoln, Edward Baker

Edward Baker Lincoln (1846–1850), the second son of Abraham and Mary Todd Lincoln, was named after Lincoln's friend Edward Dickinson Baker (1811–1861), who later died in the battle of Ball's Bluff (October 21, 1861).

Indulgent parents, the Lincolns left their sons, only Robert Todd and Eddie at the time, free of most rules and restraints, sometimes to the dismay of other people who considered the boys too rambunctious. Lincoln, although often busy and preoccupied with his law practice and politics, enjoyed playing with his sons and sometimes brought them to his Springfield office while he was working, allowing them to do as they pleased amid the books, papers, desks, and files.

While Lincoln served his single term in Congress, Eddie and the rest of the family came to Washington, D.C., for several months in late 1847 through early 1848. Although the few surviving stories about Eddie usually depict him as a sweet-natured, gentle boy, the Lincoln children were sometimes noisy and boisterous enough to irritate other residents of the boardinghouse where the Lincolns stayed. Lincoln knew of some of the difficulties their presence created, but he missed them when Mary Lincoln took the boys home in the spring of 1848.

Eddie, a somewhat frail child, had been unwell in Washington, and he was still sickly later in 1848 when Mary Lincoln took the children east again to join their father on a campaign tour of New England. The continued uncertainty of Eddie's health figured into Lincoln's decision to decline the governorship of the Oregon Territory when it was offered to him in 1849. In December 1849, Eddie fell seriously ill with pulmonary tuberculosis, and despite attentive care from both parents, he died on February 1, 1850, at the age of three.

The Reverend James Smith, a Presbyterian minister recently arrived in Springfield, conducted Eddie's funeral and subsequently comforted Mary Lincoln in her grief. Lincoln, grateful for the relief she seemed to find in religion, rented a pew at Smith's First Presbyterian Church, but he remained unable fully to share his wife's faith and tended instead to take refuge in work.

Eleven years after Eddie's death, when the Lincolns again left Springfield for Washington, D.C., Lincoln's farewell remarks highlighted his ties to Springfield, including a reminder that his children had been born there and that one was buried there.

—Cara L. Shelly

BIBLIOGRAPHY

Donald, David Herbert. *Lincoln.* New York: Simon and Schuster, 1995.

Goodwin, Doris Kearns. *Team of Rivals: The Political Genius of Abraham Lincoln.* New York: Simon and Schuster, 2005.

Oates, Stephen B. *With Malice toward None: The Life of Abraham Lincoln.* New York: Mentor, 1978.

Lincoln, Mary Todd

Mary Ann Todd (December 13, 1818–July 16, 1882) was born in Lexington, Kentucky. The daughter of Robert Smith and Eliza Todd, she was the fourth of seven children and was only six years old when her mother died, in 1825, from childbirth complications. In 1827 Robert Todd married his second wife, Elizabeth Humphreys, who eventually bore him nine children. Robert Smith Todd was a wealthy and influential banker and politician and counted among his friends such men as Henry Clay. Mary was reared in a typically Southern, aristocratic style by a family that owned slaves. Mary was unusual for a girl of that time and place in that she completed twelve years of schooling; she loved politics and was outspoken in her opinions. A physician-historian, W.A. Evans, in a clinical analysis of Mary Lincoln, said that one key to understanding her personality was that as a child she was indulged, but then, after the death of her mother, she was lost in the chaos of a large family and failed to acquire virtues such as patience and self-control.

Mrs. Abraham Lincoln photographed by the studio of Mathew Brady in 1861. During her years in the White House, Mary Todd Lincoln endured the death of her son Willie and the assassination of her husband.
Source: The Granger Collection, New York

In 1839, at the age of twenty-one, Mary moved to Springfield, Illinois, to live with her sister Elizabeth Edwards. Elizabeth and her husband, Ninian Edwards, were the leaders of the young and fashionable socialites of the town, and upon her arrival Mary immediately became one of the belles of Springfield. She charmed everyone with her culture and grace, high intelligence, quick wit, and noticeable beauty. She intoxicated the eligible bachelors and counted among her suitors a grandson of Patrick Henry; future U.S. senators Stephen A. Douglas, Edward D. Baker, James Shields, and Lyman Trumbull; and the future president, Abraham Lincoln.

She met Lincoln at a ball in 1839, when he was a member of the state legislature and a junior partner in the law firm of Stuart and Lincoln. Mary is said to have declared as a girl that she would one day marry a man who would be president of the United States, and according to tradition, she believed that she had found that man in Abraham Lincoln. After twelve months of courting they were engaged in 1840, but on January 1, 1841, Lincoln broke off the engagement because of his own fears of being a good husband and father. After an eighteen-month hiatus, they reconciled and were wed in November 1842.

The Lincolns spent the next eighteen years in Springfield. They had four sons: Robert Todd (Bob), born in 1842; Edward (Eddie), born in 1846; William (Willie), born in 1850; and Thomas (Tad), born in 1853. Only Robert Todd would survive to adulthood. During their years in Springfield, Abraham

Lincoln rose from a junior to a senior partner in his own law firm; he served one term in the U.S. House of Representatives (1847–1849); ran for the U.S. Senate twice (1854 and 1858) but lost both times; and finally ran for president and was elected in 1860. During those years Lincoln, as an attorney, rode the Eighth Judicial Circuit, traveling the state of Illinois for six to eight months of the year. Mary stayed home with her children while her husband was away and was the primary caregiver. One historian has even labeled her a "single mother," given the frequency of her husband's absences. In 1850 Mary and Abraham suffered the loss of their four-year-old son Eddie, who died of tuberculosis.

William Herndon, Abraham Lincoln's junior law partner, said that Lincoln's ambition was "a little engine that knew no rest." Mary Lincoln's ambition for her husband, and her encouragement of his goals, was certainly as relentless. There is no evidence of a political partnership between Mary and Abraham, in the sense that she "advised" him on politics or strategy, but Lincoln certainly respected his wife's opinions and discussed political items with her.

As first lady, Mary Lincoln both helped and hindered her husband. The White House that she inherited from outgoing President James Buchanan was a dilapidated shack, and Mary transformed it into a grand house worthy of the president. She filled her role as hostess with grace and culture, dressing well, throwing elegant parties, dances, and receptions; she also visited the military hospitals to give gifts and solace to wounded soldiers. As a wife and mother she was a great comfort and support to her husband as he endured the trials of leading the nation through the Civil War. But Mary Lincoln also did many things that embarrassed her husband and caused him headaches and worry. She overspent her decorating budget by $20,000; she falsified and padded White House accounts and took the money herself; she befriended individuals who had shady reputations; and she accepted gifts and bribes in exchange for influence with her husband and on government appointments.

Mary Lincoln was not only cheerful, graceful, and loving, but also vain, arrogant, and jealous. This dichotomy brought her many enemies. She also suffered what is now believed to have been bipolar disorder, the symptoms of which were evident in her early life and worsened over time. During the White House years she suffered mainly from anxiety, paranoia, narcissism, mood swings, and depression, but in later years she suffered hallucinations and delusions. Mary's mood swings and depression intensified in 1862, after the death of the Lincolns' eleven-year-old son Willie. Her grief was so pronounced that her husband actually warned her that if she did not overcome it, it would drive her mad and he would be forced to commit her to an asylum. Mary also became interested in spiritualism, the solace of contacting the spirits of the dead to talk with them. The deaths of Eddie and Willie and the constant threats of assassination against her husband terrified Mary. Her fear of death, especially after 1862, also caused her to refuse the request of her oldest son, Robert, to join the Union army. President Lincoln acquiesced to his wife's refusal, causing himself great embarrassment. Newspapers criticized him as a hypocrite, willing to let other men's sons die but not his own.

On the night of April 14, 1865, Mary accompanied her husband to Ford's Theatre to watch the play *Our American Cousin*. She was holding his hand when he was shot by John Wilkes Booth and accompanied the body across the street from the theater to the Petersen House. While doctors attended to the dying president and government officials came and went, Mary spent the night either at her husband's side or crying in the front parlor, often lamenting, "Why didn't he shoot me?" When Abraham Lincoln died on the morning of April 15, Mary was inconsolable.

After her husband's assassination, Mary Lincoln moved with her two sons, Robert and Tad, to Chicago, where she spent most of her time writing letters to various government officials seeking a government pension. In 1868, after the marriage of oldest son Robert, Mary and Tad went to Europe, where Tad attended school and Mary traveled. They returned to America in 1871, but Tad, who caught pneumonia on the trip, died of pleurisy in July. Mary was distraught and spent the next four years alone, traveling America visiting health spas. In May 1875, after she had behaved erratically for years, Robert Lincoln believed his mother to be mentally ill and, after consulting with medical experts and old friends of Abraham Lincoln, had her declared insane by a jury trial and committed to Bellevue Place Sanitarium in Batavia, Illinois. In June 1876 Mary was declared sane by another Chicago jury, after which she immediately estranged herself from her son, who she thought had her locked up in order to steal her money.

She went into a self-imposed exile in Europe from 1876 to 1880, living mostly in Pau, France, and traveling extensively across the Continent visiting health spas and popular tourist sites. In December 1879, while hanging a painting, Mary fell and severely injured her spine, causing her intense pain on her left side and difficulty walking. Six months later, because of the pain and weakness in her left side, Mary fell down a flight of stairs, further injuring her back. Because of her injuries and generally declining physical health, she decided in late 1880 to return to America. She went to live with her sister Elizabeth Edwards at the Edwards home in Springfield. Mary reconciled with her son, Robert, in 1881. Mary Lincoln died of a stroke, most likely a complication of untreated diabetes, on July 16, 1882, at age sixty-four. Despite the fact that she was constantly criticized after her husband's death as an embarrassment to his memory, Mary was typically eulogized at her death as a great support and comfort to Lincoln as he endured the trials of his office.

See also *Todd Family*

—Jason Emerson

BIBLIOGRAPHY

Baker, Jean. *Mary Todd Lincoln: A Biography*. New York: Norton, 1987.

Burlingame, Michael. *The Inner World of Abraham Lincoln*. Urbana and Chicago: University of Illinois Press, 1994.

Emerson, Jason. *The Madness of Mary Lincoln.* Carbondale: Southern Illinois University Press, 2007.

Evans, W. A. *Mrs. Abraham Lincoln: A Study of Her Personality and Her Influence on Abraham Lincoln.* New York: Knopf, 1932.

Randall, Ruth Painter. *Mary Lincoln: Biography of a Marriage.* Boston: Little, Brown, 1953.

Turner, Justin G., and Linda Levitt Turner. *Mary Todd Lincoln: Her Life and Letters.* New York: Knopf, 1972.

Lincoln, Nancy Hanks

Nancy Hanks Lincoln (1784–1818), Abraham Lincoln's mother, remains a somewhat shadowy figure about whom biographical information is sketchy and sometimes uncertain.

Nancy Hanks was born in 1784 in Virginia, to a woman named Lucy Hanks, but her father's identity has never been clear. She moved to Kentucky while still a child and grew up largely in the care of relatives. In 1806 she married Thomas Lincoln, with whom she had three children, Sarah (1807–1828), Abraham (1809–1865), and Thomas (b. 1812; died in infancy).

Physical descriptions of Nancy Lincoln vary, and no likeness of her is known to exist. Of her character and personality, people who knew her commonly recalled kindness, religiosity, strong-mindedness, and intelligence as her defining traits and believed her to be superior to her husband in intellect. Many, including her son, also remembered her as prone to sadness. Although she signed documents with an *X* and probably could not write, sources disagree on whether she could read. Most, however, hold that she tried to instill her values and religious beliefs in her children and taught them her favorite biblical passages, which she either read or had memorized.

The Lincolns moved to Indiana in 1816, where they continued to eke out a living as subsistence farmers, as they had been doing in Kentucky. In the fall of 1818 Nancy Lincoln contracted a dreaded illness then known as "milk sickness" because people suspected that it resulted from the consumption of tainted milk. "Milk sickness," or brucellosis, is now known to stem from drinking the milk of animals that have eaten plants poisonous to humans. In Indiana, cows routinely left to roam free and to forage for themselves might easily have fed on such plants, particularly snakeroot foliage. Victims of milk sickness usually suffered dizziness, nausea, and an irregular heartbeat, leading to coma and death within a week. Nancy Lincoln was no exception. She died in 1818. Abraham Lincoln was nine years old.

With no clergy readily available in the sparsely populated Indiana frontier, no formal service or funeral attended Nancy Lincoln's burial. The gravesite, neglected in subsequent years, became too overgrown to be clearly identifiable. A family friend, however, eventually erected a marker in the approximate location, and the Lincoln Boyhood National Memorial in Lincoln City, Indiana, later incorporated the site.

All historians and biographers agree that Nancy Lincoln's death was a severe blow to her children. Some believe that the early loss deepened Abraham Lincoln's lifelong tendency toward melancholy. In 1844, when Abraham Lincoln returned to Indiana after a long absence to campaign for the Whigs, he visited old friends and some of his boyhood haunts. For several months thereafter, he wrote poetry about the memories stirred by the visit. Some of his verses evoked pleasant images and ideas, but reflections on death often tinged his musings. By then he had lost several other loved ones in his life in addition to his mother.

Lincoln rarely spoke or wrote specifically about his mother, but when he did, he expressed fondness and admiration. He considered her intelligent, gentle, and loving and referred to her as his "angel mother," which reflected his memory of her nature and which served, as well, to differentiate her from his stepmother, of whom he also thought highly. His stepmother was still living at the time of some of the "angel mother" references to Nancy Lincoln.

Lincoln's law partner William Herndon remembered a conversation in which Lincoln credited his own superior talents and ambition to his mother's background. Rumors and lore within the Hanks family hinted that Nancy was the illegitimate daughter of a distinguished Virginia gentleman. Herndon claimed that Lincoln thought that his own abilities might have sprung from those roots. Some historians question the accuracy of Herndon's recollection of Lincoln's remarks on this subject, but others conclude that Herndon's account is not inherently incredible, incompatible with other evidence, or undeserving of serious consideration.

—CARA L. SHELLY

BIBLIOGRAPHY

Donald, David Herbert. *Lincoln.* New York: Simon and Schuster, 1995.

Goodwin, Doris Kearns. *Team of Rivals: The Political Genius of Abraham Lincoln.* New York: Simon and Schuster, 2005.

Thomas, Benjamin P. *Abraham Lincoln: A Biography.* 1952. Reprint, New York: Modern Library, 1958.

Lincoln, Robert Todd

On August 1, 1843, Mary and Abraham Lincoln welcomed the birth of their first son, Robert Todd Lincoln (1843–1926). He was named after Mary's father, Robert Smith Todd.

In contrast to his father, Robert was short and stocky, and he had a personality that did not match either parent's. During his childhood he spent little time with his father, who was frequently away for long periods riding the judicial circuit. Shy and reticent, Robert was never as close to his father as his younger siblings. With Abraham Lincoln's work, political life, and then the presidency, Lincoln and Robert just didn't have time to develop a relationship.

At seven Robert lost his younger brother Edward to diphtheria. The two had been close and the death had a profound effect on him. Another brother, Willie, was born in 1850, but their age difference prevented them from being close. When the youngest Lincoln, Tad, was born, Robert was already a teenager.

Robert was the only one of the Lincoln sons who lived into adulthood. The best educated of the Lincoln boys, he began school at an early age in Springfield. Abraham Lincoln, who had little formal education, desired that his eldest son be well educated and encouraged him to attend Harvard. When Robert failed the entrance exam he spent a year at Phillips Exeter Academy, a college prep school. He subsequently passed the exam in 1860 and spent the majority of the war years at college, graduating from Harvard in 1864.

In February 1865, Robert joined general in chief Ulysses S. Grant's staff as a captain and worked with Grant until the end of the war. He returned to Washington with Grant on April 13, 1865, and spent some time with his father discussing his war experiences, including witnessing the surrender of Robert E. Lee at Appomattox Court House. The visit with his father would be his last. That evening Lincoln would be shot and killed by John Wilkes Booth at a performance at Ford's Theatre.

When the news reached Robert he rushed to the Peterson House (where the dying president had been taken), and he remained at his father's bedside until his death the next morning. Robert then spent several weeks at the White House caring for his grieving mother and brother and making preparations for his father's funeral. After the funeral, Robert, Mary, and Tad left Washington for Chicago.

Ironically, John Wilkes Booth's brother, Edwin Booth, had once saved Robert Lincoln's life after a fall on a train. In 1865 Edwin Booth was commended for his act by Colonel Adam Badeau, then serving as an officer on Grant's staff.

After the death of his father, Robert graduated from the Chicago Law School and was admitted to the Illinois bar in 1867. The following year he married Mary

Eunice Harlan, the daughter of Sen. James Harlan of Iowa. The couple had two daughters, Mary and Jesse, and one son, Abraham "Jack" Lincoln II. Jack, who would die at seventeen, had the honor of unveiling the statue of his grandfather in Lincoln Park, Chicago, in 1887.

Robert would be called on again to comfort his mother and make funeral arrangements when his brother Tad died in 1871. Funeral services were held for Tad in Robert Lincoln's Chicago home the next day, with a more formal service following later in Springfield. Robert Lincoln, his mother too distraught to travel, accompanied Tad's body to Springfield and later to its final resting place with his father and two brothers, Eddie and Willie, in the Lincoln Tomb in Springfield.

The sole surviving Lincoln son was a successful corporate attorney. He returned to Washington in 1881 to serve as secretary of war for President James Garfield. President Benjamin Harrison appointed him U.S. Minister to England, a post he held from 1889 to 1893.

Robert never sought nomination for office but seemed to find himself in his father's political shadow. He was frequently mentioned as a candidate for president or vice president at various Republican National Conventions but was never elected. Robert was very private and, as a man who preferred a business over a political life, did not appear offended by not being nominated.

Having served as counsel to the Pullman Palace Car Company, Robert became acting president of the company in 1897, when George Pullman died, and president in 1901. He retired from the Pullman Company in 1911 at age sixty-nine but remained as chairman of the board until 1922. He also was a director for the Commonwealth Edison Company and the Chicago Telephone Company.

A wealthy man, Robert built a summer home on several hundred acres in Vermont. The estate, named Hildene, included gardens, lawns, and woodlands. In 1911 Robert sold his home in Chicago and bought a mansion in Washington, D.C. He spent his summers at Hildene, enjoying golf and astronomy, and his winters in Washington, traveling between the two in his private Pullman car, called the *Advance.*

Robert made his last public appearance on May 30, 1922, at the dedication of the Lincoln Memorial. He died from a cerebral hemorrhage, at his summer home, on July 26, 1926. He was eighty-three. His wife, Mary Harlan Lincoln, chose to have Robert buried at Arlington Cemetery, rather than in the Lincoln Tomb in Springfield because, she wrote, Robert "was a personage, who made his own history, independently of his great father, and should have his own place 'in the sun'!" Mary Harlan Lincoln died in 1937.

Robert was successful but also very private, keeping the family photo album and Lincoln's papers well guarded. The Lincoln papers were deeded to the Library of Congress by Robert Todd Lincoln with the requirement that they remain sealed until twenty-one years after his own death. On July 26, 1947, the Lincoln papers were officially opened to the public.

—Paula Cochran

BIBLIOGRAPHY

Goff, John S. *Robert Todd Lincoln: A Man in His Own Right.* Norman: University of Oklahoma Press, 1969.

Lincoln, Sarah Bush Johnston

Sarah Bush Johnston Lincoln, Abraham Lincoln's stepmother, was born in 1788 to a prosperous family in Elizabethtown, Kentucky. In 1806 she married her first husband, Daniel Johnston. A struggling farmer, Johnston was in debt and listed as a delinquent taxpayer in Hardin County in 1806. In 1816 he died, leaving Sarah with the outstanding debts. For the next three years she supported herself and her three children.

Thomas Lincoln, whose first wife, Nancy Hanks Lincoln, had died of milk sickness, needed a wife and a mother for his children. Acquainted with Sarah from his days in Kentucky, Thomas returned to the state in 1819 to visit her and asked her to marry him. Sarah was unable to accept the proposal before her debts were paid off, so Thomas agreed to pay them himself. They were married on December 2.

They brought to the Lincoln farm in Indiana Sarah's walnut dresser, table and chairs, spinning wheel, and knives, forks, and spoons. These luxuries impressed the Lincoln children, who appeared dirty, raggedly dressed, and hungry. Although Sarah found the area desolate and wild, she set about reorganizing the little cabin to make it a comfortable home. The men took time off from hunting to install a wood floor, complete the unfinished roof, replace the door, and add a window. Sarah also had the men build a loft so the boys would have a proper place to sleep.

Thomas and Sarah and their five children—Sarah and Abraham Lincoln, and Elizabeth, John, and Matilda Johnston—along with Dennis Hanks, Abraham Lincoln's cousin, lived together in the eighteen-by-twenty log cabin. Sarah treated the children fairly but later admitted that Abraham was her favorite, even over her own children.

She found her stepson a diligent reader and a student who would study continuously until he got it right. Although Sarah was illiterate, as was Lincoln's father, Sarah encouraged Abraham's interest, though his father seemed to find it an annoyance.

Sarah's small collection of books was a great resource for the curious young man. Their limited number meant that Abraham reread the same books many times, perfecting his reading and writing skills and writing favorite passages repeatedly until he had memorized them. The collection included a family Bible, which Sarah later claimed that he didn't read much, and *Pilgrim's Progress,* a work that Abe Lincoln would later quote in his speeches. The morals in Aesop's *Fables* also became deeply ingrained. Lincoln would later make famous a line from the four bulls' fable, "A kingdom divided against itself cannot stand."

Abraham Lincoln was a gawky young man, prone to sensitivity, and honest to the point that his presidential election would be based on that reputation. He was often ridiculed and teased for his unusually large stature and his homely looks, which would one day gain him the nickname "Gorilla." Sarah's acceptance and emotional support must have brought him great comfort. The two shared an abiding trust and a common way of thinking, whereas he and his father were always estranged. Yet it was his father's humor and storytelling skills that Lincoln used to overcome awkward moments and to find acceptance during his lifetime.

Throughout Lincoln's life he described his stepmother as good and kind, fondly referring to her as "Mother." In all the vast literature recounting Lincoln's early years, there is hardly an unkind word about Sarah Bush Johnston Lincoln, and she always spoke fondly of him.

As an adult Abraham remained close to his stepmother. He visited her every year or two and attended to her welfare after his father's death in 1851, providing her a forty-acre plot of land to live on until her death. On January 31, 1861, Abraham visited his stepmother for the last time before going to Washington for his inauguration.

In April 1865 Sarah grieved deeply when she learned of Lincoln's assassination and fondly remembered his final visit. She had been neither proud nor glory bent when Abraham was elected president, as she sensed some harm would come to him because of it. In a September 8, 1865, interview with William Herndon, Lincoln's former law partner, she depicted her stepson as a model child who was honest and witty, and she said that she had never known him to drink, bet, use profane language or tobacco, or utter a cross word.

Sarah Bush Johnston Lincoln died in 1869. She is buried next to her husband Thomas Lincoln in the Shiloh Cemetery, in Coles County, Illinois.

—Paula Cochran

BIBLIOGRAPHY

Donald, David Herbert. *Lincoln.* New York: Simon and Schuster, 1996.

Goodwin, Doris Kearns. *Team of Rivals: The Political Genius of Abraham Lincoln.* New York: Simon and Schuster, 2006.

Miller, William Lee. *Lincoln's Virtues: An Ethical Biography.* New York: Random House, 2003.

Lincoln, Thomas

Thomas Lincoln was born to a prosperous family in Virginia on January 6, 1778. Although he grew up on more than five thousand Kentucky acres, he had a difficult time making ends meet after his father, Abraham, was killed by local Indians while clearing his land in 1786. Under the law of primogeniture, all the family's land and holdings went to the eldest son, Mordecai, leaving the younger brothers, Thomas and Josiah, to fend for themselves. Thomas was left penniless and struggled economically, relying on low-paid wage labor.

Thomas, a man with black hair, an average build, and a large nose, worked hard. When he accumulated enough savings he purchased a 238-acre farm on Mill Creek, in Harden County, Kentucky. He was respected in the community and was known as an honest man. In 1806 he married Nancy Hanks, and the two had their first child, Sarah. In 1809 Thomas purchased a new farm, known as the Sinking Spring Farm, where he built his family a one-room log cabin. It was there that the future president, Abraham Lincoln, was born on February 12, 1809.

The soil proved to be of poor quality, so the family moved ten miles north to a more fertile farm on Knobs Creek. There Nancy had a third child, Thomas, who died in infancy. That was also the locale of Abraham Lincoln's earliest memories. Abraham and his father worked side by side in the fields, Thomas planting corn while Abraham dropped a pumpkin seed in every other hill.

In 1816, because of some difficulty with land claims in Kentucky and because of Thomas's opposition to slavery, the Lincoln family relocated to Indiana. The Lincolns were members of an antislavery Baptist church, and when they moved to Indiana Thomas Lincoln was an active member of the Pigeon Creek Baptist Church, serving as a trustee and attending church conferences. The family lived in the wilderness on Little Pigeon Creek, in a three-sided, rough shelter with no floor, until a cabin could be built. Not long after the move, Thomas's wife, Nancy, died of milk fever.

The next year Thomas married Sarah Bush Johnston, a widow with three small children. Sarah was a godsend for the family, bringing with her worldly goods, love, and an appreciation for reading, writing, and knowledge. Sarah also became a member of the Pigeon Creek Baptist Church, but Abraham did not, and as a young boy often entertained his friends by mimicking the preacher's sermons. This caused tension between the father and son, as did Abraham's interest in reading, which Thomas considered a sign of laziness.

In 1830 Thomas moved the family to Macon County, Illinois, and a year later to Coles County, Illinois, where he remained for the rest of his life. By this time

Abraham was almost grown, and the relationship between father and son became strained. Thomas saw little need for education, while his son desired knowledge and soon departed to seek it.

In 1841 Abraham, by then a successful lawyer, purchased a third of his father's land when his father fell into financial difficulty. Seven years later he purchased the rest of the property to save it from a forced sale. Even after his father's death Abraham kept the land for his stepmother, whom he adored, providing her a place to live until her death.

Thomas Lincoln died January 17, 1851, at age seventy-three. Abraham, long estranged from his father, did not attend the funeral.

—Paula Cochran

BIBLIOGRAPHY

Donald, David Herbert. *Lincoln.* New York: Simon and Schuster, 1996.

_____. *Lincoln at Home: Two Glimpses of Abraham Lincoln's Domestic Life.* New York: Simon and Schuster, 1999.

Harris, William C. *Lincoln's Rise to the Presidency.* Lawrence: University Press of Kansas, 2007.

Neely, Mark E., Jr., and Harold Holzer. *The Lincoln Family Album: Photographs from the Personal Collection of a Historic American Family.* New York: Doubleday, 1990.

Lincoln, Thomas "Tad"

Thomas Lincoln (1853–1871), the youngest child of Mary and Abraham Lincoln, was born on April 4, 1853. Though he was named after Lincoln's father, it would not be until 1867 that Mary Lincoln would mention to the president's mother that Thomas "Tad" Lincoln was indeed named for her husband, who had died in 1851. After noting the child's unusually large head, Lincoln nicknamed Thomas "Tadpole." Shortened to Tad, the nickname would stick for the rest of the boy's life.

A doting father, Lincoln cared for and frolicked with his boys in such a way that it spawned gossip and disparaging comments. Indeed Lincoln was often seen around Springfield with the boys in tow or riding on their father's shoulders. The boys frequently went to Lincoln's law office with him where, to the dismay of his partner William Herndon, the boys would tear the office apart and dance on the clutter they created. Later, in the White House, it was not uncommon to find Lincoln wrestling on the floor with the boys.

Tad was just eight years old when the Lincolns moved into the White House. A handsome young man with dark hair like his father's, Tad talked rapidly and with a lisp, probably caused by a slight cleft palate. His speech impediment endeared him to his father all the more. An exasperating and difficult young man, Tad was also loving and emotional, and the Lincolns, never disciplinarians, allowed his wild spirit to roam where it might.

Tad was full of mischief and pranks. To him the White House was a huge playground. Despite the serious state of the nation, Tad and his brother Willie enjoyed having the "Bucktail" Pennsylvania regiment on the grounds and used them as playmates. With friends Buddy and Holly Taft, children of a federal judge who lived nearby, the boys commanded a military post from the White House roof, complete with painted log cannon, and drilled neighborhood children on the White House lawn.

The Lincoln boys also had many pets, including a pony and two goats, Nanko and Nannie who, like the boys, often had the run of the house. On one occasion Tad harnessed Nanko to a chair and rode the goat-driven device through a formal reception in the East Room.

In February 1862 the White House was filled with visitors celebrating the expected victory over the Confederacy. The president and his wife, however, were distracted by the suffering of their young boys in their rooms upstairs, and both repeatedly slipped away from guests to check on their condition. Both Tad and Willie were suffering from "bilious fever," likely typhoid fever. Over the next few weeks Willie became worse, and he died on Thursday, February 20. Both Lincolns were devastated, but Mary was inconsolable and was unable even to care for Tad who, although weak, recovered from his brush with death.

After Abraham Lincoln's death in April 1865, Tad Lincoln returned to Chicago with the rest of his family. In Chicago Tad went to school for the first time. Though the boys had tutors at the White House, Tad had never taken learning seriously and, being more indulged than ever after Willie's death, was not required to do so. The eldest Lincoln son, Robert, had attended school from the age of seven, and Willie wrote poetry at eleven. Tad, at the age of twelve, was just learning to read and write. Tad would return to Washington with his older brother, Robert, in 1867 to testify in the trial of John Surratt, who was accused of conspiring with John Wilkes Booth to assassinate his father.

In 1868 Mary and Tad left for Europe for three years, where Tad attended boarding school. Tad fell ill on the journey home and was not well when he arrived in Chicago. Suffering from what was likely tuberculosis, he was unable to breathe lying down and had to sleep upright in a chair. As the illness progressed he was in severe pain and lost a great deal of weight. Tad died on Saturday, July 15, 1871, at the age of eighteen.

Funeral services were held for Tad in Robert Lincoln's Chicago home. Mary Lincoln, again distraught with grief, did not accompany his body to Springfield.

Robert Lincoln laid Tad to rest with his father, Abraham, and his two brothers, Eddie and Willie, in the Lincoln Tomb in Springfield.

—Paula Cochran

BIBLIOGRAPHY

Donald, David Herbert. *Lincoln.* New York: Simon and Schuster, 1996.

———. *Lincoln at Home: Two Glimpses of Abraham Lincoln's Domestic Life.* New York: Simon and Schuster, 1999.

Harris, William C. *Lincoln's Rise to the Presidency.* Lawrence: University Press of Kansas, 2007.

Neely, Mark E., Jr., and Harold Holzer. *The Lincoln Family Album: Photographs from the Personal Collection of a Historic American Family.* New York: Doubleday, 1990.

Lincoln, William "Willie" Wallace

William "Willie" Wallace Lincoln (1850–1862) was the third child born to Mary Todd and Abraham Lincoln. He was named for his uncle William Wallace, a physician in Springfield, who was married to Mary Todd Lincoln's sister Frances.

Willie was described as a lovable boy who was bright, sensible, sweet tempered, and gentle mannered. At the same time, he and his younger brother, Tad, were also prone to mischievous and prankish behavior. Abraham Lincoln had been away for much of the childhood of his eldest son, Robert, but he devoted a great deal of time to Willie and Tad, so much so that the gossips of Springfield called him "henpecked."

The Lincolns were never good disciplinarians, and after the death of their son Edward in 1850 they indulged their boys all the more. Lincoln would pull the boys in a wagon or carry them on his shoulders through Springfield, even bringing them to his office, where his partner found them a great nuisance.

Lincoln's election to the presidency in 1860 thrust his sons into the national spotlight. The family's move into the White House in 1860 annoyed Willie, who found the constant stares and public attention bothersome. The public not only stared, but they also showered the boys with presents. The boys had a menagerie of pets, including a pony and two goats which, despite Mrs. Lincoln's wishes, ran about the White House lawn and sometimes the White House itself.

When the undisciplined duo were not disrupting formal proceedings at the White House they could be found playing with the soldiers posted to protect the Lincolns or drilling the neighborhood children on the South Lawn of the White House. They often accompanied their father when he visited troops in their camps.

Both Willie and Tad were educated by tutors at the White House, but Willie was more academically disciplined than his younger brother. Among his most noted achievements was a poem that he wrote in honor of Colonel Edward Baker, a senator for whom the Lincolns' second son was named, who died in the Battle of Ball's Bluff. The poem was printed by the *National Republic,* and Lincoln openly wept when he read it. Willie's poem ran,

> *There was no Patriot like Baker*
> *So noble and so true;*
> *He fell as a soldier in the field,*
> *His face to the sky of blue.*
>
> *His voice is silent in the hall,*
> *Which oft his presence grac'd.*
> *No more he'll hear the loud acclaim*
> *Which rang from place to place.*
>
> *No squeamish notions filled his breast,*
> *The Union was his theme;*
> *'No surrender and no compromise,'*
> *His day-thought and night's dream.*
>
> *His Country has her part to play,*
> *To'rd those he has left behind;*
> *His widow and his children all,*
> *She must always keep in mind.*

Mrs. Lincoln had planned a grand ball and dinner for representatives of Washington society for February 5, 1862. Excited to show off the redecorated White House, her new gown, and "The Mary Lincoln Polka," she invited a crowd of five hundred. Upstairs the boys suffered with fevers. Lincoln told General John C. Frémont that his sons were very ill and that he feared the worst. Both Lincolns excused themselves from the party several times to be with the boys.

Tad recovered, but Willie became worse and died in the White House on February 20, 1862. The typhoid (or bilious) fever that took his life was probably caused by the polluted water in the White House.

Willie's death cast a dark shadow over the remaining years of Lincoln's presidency. Lincoln described Willie's death as his greatest personal tragedy. Willie, he said, was too good for this earth. Mrs. Lincoln, crushed with grief, sought relief through mediums and spiritualists.

On February 24 Willie's funeral took place in the East Room of the White House. He was buried in Oak Hill Cemetery in Georgetown. Abraham, Eddie, and Willie were later interred in the Lincoln Tomb in Springfield, Illinois.

—PAULA COCHRAN

BIBLIOGRAPHY

Donald, David Herbert. *Lincoln.* New York: Simon and Schuster, 1996.

_____. *Lincoln at Home: Two Glimpses of Abraham Lincoln's Domestic Life.* New York: Simon and Schuster, 1999.

Harris, William C. *Lincoln's Rise to the Presidency.* Lawrence: University Press of Kansas, 2007.

Neely, Mark E., Jr., and Harold Holzer. *The Lincoln Family Album: Photographs from the Personal Collection of a Historic American Family.* New York: Doubleday, 1990.

Lincoln–Douglas Debates

Although the Lincoln-Douglas debates were the most notable event of the 1858 senatorial contest between Abraham Lincoln and the Democratic incumbent, Stephen Arnold Douglas, it is important to note that the debates were only a small fraction of numerous speeches that both candidates gave throughout the state of Illinois. After his nomination by the Republican state convention at Springfield on June 16, 1858, Lincoln began to follow the more popular Douglas around the state, responding to the senator's speeches later in the day. Hoping to capitalize on Douglas's popularity and reputation for not backing down from challenges, the Republican state committee, led by Norman B. Judd, convinced Lincoln in late July to challenge Douglas to a series of joint appearances before the electorate.

Although he had much to lose by sharing the political platform with a much less popular opponent, Douglas finally agreed to debates in seven of Illinois's congressional districts. Because both candidates had already given major speeches in Chicago and Springfield, they omitted the congressional districts in those cities. The format called for one candidate to deliver a one-hour opening address. This would be followed by a ninety-minute rebuttal. The debate would then conclude with a thirty-minute rejoinder by the opening candidate. It was agreed that Douglas would have four openings and Lincoln three. Because of the importance of the campaign, both Republican and Democratic newspapers hired stenographers to cover and carefully record the speeches.

On August 21 the candidates squared off at Ottawa, located some eighty miles southwest of Chicago in the third congressional district, represented by abolitionist Owen Lovejoy. Facing a largely Republican audience gathered in the town's Washington Square, Douglas began aggressively, accusing Lincoln of entering into

An artist's reconstruction of one of the Lincoln-Douglas debates of 1858. Although Stephen Douglas won the election, the debates helped Abraham Lincoln gain prominence on the national political stage and propelled him toward the Republican presidential nomination in 1860.

Source: The Granger Collection, New York

a conspiracy with Sen. Lyman Trumbull to undermine and "abolitionize" the great Whig and Democratic Parties. Although they differed on many issues, these parties, Douglas contended, had always compromised on slavery and so prevented it from dividing the nation. Douglas then read a portion of resolutions, quite radical in temperament, supposedly adopted at an October 1854 state Republican convention in Springfield. With these resolutions in mind, he then aimed seven interrogatories at Lincoln: Did Lincoln support the repeal of the Fugitive Slave Law? Would Lincoln vote to allow new territories into the Union if they would result in additional slave states? Would Lincoln vote to allow the admission of additional slave states into the Union even if the residents of said states desired slavery? Did Lincoln favor the abolition of slavery in the District of Columbia? Did Lincoln favor abolishing the interstate slave trade? Would Lincoln vote to prohibit slavery in any of the territories of the United States? Would Lincoln oppose the acquisition of additional territories if those territories allowed slavery? Blasting Lincoln's "House Divided" speech as the call to a war between sections, Douglas criticized Lincoln as promoting black equality while denying the people of both states and territories the right to decide on the status of slavery at the ballot box.

Lincoln's response to Douglas's charges was evasive. Although he forthrightly denied that he and Trumbull had conspired to break up the major parties to form the Republican Party, he then spent a great deal of time reading from an 1854 speech at Peoria to rebut Douglas. Lincoln argued that he had answered Douglas's interrogatories in previous speeches and refused to do so here. While refusing to answer Douglas's questions, Lincoln did address other Douglas accusations. Denying that he favored "perfect equality" between whites and African Americans, Lincoln maintained that the Declaration of Independence did apply to blacks in its guarantee of the right to life, liberty, and the pursuit of happiness. Returning to a theme raised in the "House Divided" speech of June 16, 1858, Lincoln reiterated his contention that Douglas was part of a gigantic proslavery conspiracy that would make slavery national, a conspiracy that might be consummated when the Supreme Court handed down another *Dred Scott* decision declaring that a state, in addition to territories, could not exclude slavery from its constitution.

Illinois Republican leaders advised Lincoln that his performance had been too passive at Ottawa, and he became more aggressive at the next debate, on August 27 at Freeport, in solidly Republican Stephenson County, the northernmost of the debate sites. Addressing a sympathetic audience, Lincoln answered each of Douglas's questions at Ottawa: Lincoln did not favor repeal of the Fugitive Slave Act, nor would he oppose the admission of slave states. Neither did Lincoln support the cessation of the domestic slave trade or the abolition of slavery in the District of Columbia. Although Lincoln was not generally opposed to the acquisition of more territories, he was unalterably opposed to the extension of slavery in any U. S. territory and believed it was the right of Congress to legislate against the expansion of slavery.

Having answered Douglas, Lincoln now flung a series of interrogatories at the incumbent senator. In light of the recent *Dred Scott* decision, Lincoln's point was to expose popular sovereignty, the crux of Douglas's philosophy on solving the slavery issue, as ineffective. Could the people of the Kansas Territory exclude slavery in any legal sense prior to statehood? How would Douglas respond if the

Supreme Court ruled that a state, not merely a territory as in the *Dred Scott* decision, could not exclude slavery? Did Douglas favor the acquisition of new territory regardless of how it touched on the slavery question? Then Lincoln delivered his knockout punch, revealing that Douglas's charge at Ottawa, that Lincoln was party to a radical platform on slavery that had been adopted at Springfield, had not been adopted at Springfield at all, but at a convention in Aurora, Illinois. In other words, Douglas had deliberately deceived the audience at Ottawa.

A skilled debater, Douglas, who was frequently interrupted by a hostile audience, quickly responded to the Lincoln interrogatories. Knowing full well that they were designed to embarrass him with Southern Democrats, Douglas pointed out that regardless of the *Dred Scott* decision, the people of a territory could exclude slavery by failing to enact positive legislation to protect slave property. Indeed he chided Lincoln for asking the question because he, Douglas, had answered this same inquiry on numerous occasions. Although the position was not original to this debate, it became known as the Freeport doctrine. The question about forcing states to adopt slavery in their constitutions was greeted with scorn by Douglas. Even Southerners, he remarked, regarded this as an absurdity. As to the charge that Douglas had misled the audience at Ottawa by claiming to have read the platform from a state Republican convention at Springfield, Douglas now skillfully turned this on Lincoln, arguing that his opponent was preoccupied with the "spot" where the resolutions were adopted instead of their radical content. In such fashion, Douglas turned the discussion back to Lincoln and his unpopular opposition to the Mexican War when he served in Congress and had demanded to know the exact "spot" on American soil where American blood had been shed. Although Lincoln had not delivered a decisive blow to the "Little Giant," his performance at Freeport encouraged his supporters.

The joint debates now moved south into hard-core Douglas territory. Jonesboro was a small town of less than a thousand inhabitants, located midway between Carbondale and Cairo in sparsely populated Union County, in the ninth congressional district. It drew the smallest audience of all the debates, less than two thousand people. Opening the debate, Douglas repeated his accusation that Lincoln and Trumbull had conspired to break up and "abolitionize" the old Whig and Democratic Parties. He then attacked Lincoln, as he would in each and every debate, for inciting sectional war with his "House Divided" speech, for undermining the Supreme Court by questioning the *Dred Scott* decision, and for advocating equality for African Americans. Lincoln's response to Douglas also covered familiar ground. Although Lincoln agreed with Douglas that states and territories should be free to decide many issues, slavery was different. Denying that he intended to wage war on the South, Lincoln argued that his policy simply returned the nation to the course set by the Founders. If anyone had stirred up controversy on the slavery issue, it was Douglas with his infamous Kansas-Nebraska bill. As Douglas had tried to discredit Lincoln with Republican resolutions passes at Aurora, Illinois, Lincoln pointed out that there were currently two Democratic factions in Illinois: those who supported Douglas and the so-called

National Democrats, who opposed Douglas's position on the Lecompton Constitution and supported fellow Democrat Sidney Breese for the U.S. Senate. Was Douglas responsible for all the platforms and resolutions adopted by all these Democratic factions throughout the state?

After the less-than-vigorous debate at Jonesboro, the scene shifted to east-central Illinois. Here in the so-called Whig belt of central Illinois, the fourth debate took place in the town of Charleston, in Coles County, on September 18. As Democratic southern Illinois was considered safe for Douglas, and northern Illinois solidly Republican, the campaign in the central counties might tip the election to either Lincoln or Douglas. Hence the performance of each candidate was crucial. Coles County was familiar territory for Lincoln, as his father and stepmother resided at Goosenest Prairie to the east of Charleston. When Charleston was part of the eighth judicial circuit, Lincoln had tried many cases in the town. Attended by an audience estimated at 15,000 to 20,000, the debate at Charleston was unique. Beginning by denying that he advocated social and political equality for African Americans, Lincoln then launched into a tedious and detailed review of behind-the-scenes Senate maneuvering on an Enabling Act that would allow the residents of Kansas to form a constitution. Repeating charges that had been raised by Lyman Trumbull, Lincoln asserted that Douglas had personally tried to remove an amendment, submitted by Sen. Robert Toombs of Georgia, that specifically called for the constitution to be submitted to the residents of Kansas for ratification. Lincoln's intent was to show that Douglas's commitment to popular sovereignty and the voice of the people was a sham. Before delivering his standard critique of Lincoln and the Republican Party, a somewhat puzzled Douglas wondered why Lincoln had wasted time defending Trumbull's actions in the Senate and neglected to make a speech of his own. Although the issue Lincoln raised seemed arcane, the Charleston debate suggested that Lincoln could hold his own against his more popular and experienced rival.

After a three-week hiatus the debates shifted north to Galesburg, about fifty miles northwest of Peoria, on October 7. Galesburg had been founded by antislavery evangelicals, and the crowd that gathered at Knox College to witness the debate, estimated from 10,000 to 25,000, was solidly behind Lincoln. As he had in previous debates, Douglas punched away at Lincoln, using familiar themes. Defending his course on Kansas as a defense of popular sovereignty, Douglas blasted the Republican Party for making common cause with the National Democrats, those Democrats who opposed Douglas's course on the Lecompton Constitution and were working against Douglas's reelection with the full support of President James Buchanan. Criticizing the Republicans as a sectional party, Douglas charged that Lincoln could not remain consistent on his positions even in different regions of Illinois, arguing that African Americans were the equals of whites in Freeport and Chicago but denying equality in places like Jonesboro and Charleston. In replying to Douglas at Galesburg, Lincoln seemed to acquire new eloquence, which would characterize his performances at the final debates at

Quincy and Alton. Taking issue with Douglas's contention that the Founders did not include African Americans in the Declaration of Independence, Lincoln also claimed there was nothing inconsistent in maintaining that African Americans were included in the promises of the declaration but were not the social and political equals of whites. According to Lincoln, Douglas's reading of history on the slavery issue was a distortion that required "blowing out the moral lights around us."

Located on the Mississippi River across from Hannibal, Missouri, Quincy, like Charleston, was in the pivotal Whig belt of central Illinois, important in determining the outcome of the election. Beginning at 1:30 on October 13 in the city's Washington Square, Douglas and Lincoln for the most part repeated the same arguments and counterarguments that they had used throughout the campaign. Again, however, it was Lincoln who, as he had at Galesburg, took the moral high ground, arguing that the Republican Party took the position that slavery was wrong and therefore sought to prevent its expansion. Douglas and the Democrats, noted Lincoln, were animated by a policy that regarded the issue of slavery through the lens of moral neutrality. For Douglas, slaves were property to be considered in the same way as other forms of property.

Two days later the final debate took place at Alton, south of Quincy on the Mississippi River, a little northeast of St. Louis. Most historians agree that Douglas was suffering from fatigue and the effects of excessive drinking. In a voice that was hoarse, Douglas opened the debate, briefly repeating many of the same charges against Lincoln but then providing an extensive defense of his actions on the Lecompton Constitution. His central point was that his entire course on the Lecompton Constitution was motivated by his desire to ensure that the residents of Kansas freely chose to accept or reject the constitution. While he did not care whether Kansas came into the Union with or without slavery, Douglas would do all in his power to make sure that the people's right to choose was not violated. Lincoln responded to many of Douglas's charges with the same arguments that he had used throughout the debates, but he again captured the high moral ground when he discussed slavery. Using the familiar argument of many Republican and Free Soil Party advocates, who believed it was necessary to keep the western territories free from slavery, Lincoln argued that opportunities for white laborers would be preserved by this policy. But Lincoln did not end on this pragmatic note, arguing in addition that slavery was a moral wrong that needed to be curtailed. Douglas and the Democratic Party, Lincoln contended, ignored the moral dimensions of the slavery issue, and that was not in the best interest of the nation.

When the November elections came, Republican candidates won the majority of votes; however, the Illinois General Assembly was controlled by Democrats. The legislative districts were based on the state's 1854 reapportionment plan, which overrepresented Democratic southern Illinois. Douglas, consequently, would be reelected to his third term, as the state legislatures, not the populace, actually elected U.S. senators at the time. Douglas won in the legislature 54–46. Lincoln, although disappointed and defeated, would become a prominent Republican figure and presidential candidate as a result of his performance in the debates. Although their actual impact on Illinois voters of the time is not entirely clear, the debates have rightly acquired legendary status in American political history.

—BRUCE TAP

BIBLIOGRAPHY

Donald, David Herbert. *Lincoln.* New York: Simon and Schuster, 1995.

Guelzo. Allen C. *Lincoln and Douglas: The Debates That Defined America.* New York: Simon and Schuster, 2008.

Johannsen, Robert W., ed. *The Lincoln-Douglas Debates.* New York: Oxford University Press, 2008.

———. *Stephen A. Douglas.* New York: Oxford University Press, 1973.

See also: *Douglas, Stephen; Campaign of 1858, Lincoln's Senatorial*

Lincoln Historic Sites, Preservation of

From a Kentucky log cabin meant to symbolize his humble beginnings, to the Washington, D.C., boardinghouse where he succumbed to an assassin's bullet, to the ornate Illinois tomb where is interred, an enormous variety of sites associated with the life, career, and even death of Abraham Lincoln have been maintained to commemorate our sixteenth president. In the nearly 150 years since his death, such spots have become akin to shrines celebrating the legacy of the Great Emancipator, allowing a curious posterity to explore virtually every phase of his journey from splitting fence rails to delivering the Gettysburg Address. Not only has the immense public fascination with Lincoln led to an impressive number and variety of public sites interpreting his life and legacy, but it has also ensured that many such locations are preserved and meticulously cared for.

Through the efforts of federal and state agencies, as well as local historical societies and private groups, it is possible to follow the course of Lincoln's life through various restored buildings, museums, and other historic sites and monuments. For example, the National Park Service maintains three different homes connected to Lincoln, as well as several locations connected to his trip to Pennsylvania to dedicate Gettysburg National Cemetery; Fort Stevens, where he

The log cabin said to be the birthplace of Abraham Lincoln in Hodgenville, Kentucky, was shortened and narrowed in the early twentieth century to fit inside a memorial building. Tests in 2004 confirmed that the cabin was built no earlier than 1848, requiring the National Park Service to call it a "symbolic cabin."
Source: The Granger Collection, New York

became the only sitting American president to come under enemy fire; Ford's Theatre, where he was shot by John Wilkes Booth; and the Peterson House, where he died the next morning.

One of the National Park Service–maintained spots is also one of the most curious. Abraham Lincoln Boyhood National Historic Site in Hodgenville, Kentucky, encompasses 146 acres of farmland where Lincoln spent his earliest years. For many years legend had it that the one-room log cabin where Lincoln was born still stood, leading to the erection of a massive marble memorial hall around it during the first years of the twentieth century. Unfortunately, during construction it was determined that the cabin was slightly too large to fit in the designated space in the memorial, and so it was shortened by four feet in width and one foot in length. In the 1940s rumors began to circulate that the enshrined cabin was not the actual structure in which Lincoln was born, and in 2004 it was established that the earliest possible date of construction for the cabin inside the memorial was 1848, when Abraham Lincoln would have been forty years old. Today, despite the Park Service's reference to the memorialized structure as a "symbolic cabin," the site draws more than 200,000 visitors annually.

Several other sites whose connections to Lincoln's youth are also somewhat spurious have also been preserved for visitors, who may be disappointed if they do not read the fine print. In Decatur, Illinois, guests can visit the Lincoln Trail Homestead State Historic Site, where a stone monument commemorates the spot where the Lincoln family crossed from Indiana into Illinois. A plaque elsewhere on the grounds marks the location of the first family homestead in the Prairie State, the original structure and a replica built to attract tourists having been destroyed. Two other state historic sites with reproduction structures are meant to evoke the time during which Abraham Lincoln was associated with the area. Visitors to Lincoln's New Salem can visit an "imagined recreation" of the village where he spent his young adult years. More than a dozen buildings have been constructed and furnished to echo the small town where Lincoln lived from 1831 to 1837, a period that included his days as a rail-splitter, postmaster, and deputy surveyor, his service in the Black Hawk War, and his election to the Illinois General Assembly. Meanwhile, at the Lincoln Log Cabin State Historic Site in Lerna, visitors can see a reconstructed cabin on the site of Lincoln's parents' final home, where he said farewell before traveling to Washington, D.C., for his presidential inauguration.

Scattered across Illinois are a vast array of sites associated with Lincoln's legal and early political career, including at least six courthouses where he tried cases as a prairie lawyer. Several, including the Macon County Historic Complex and Metamora Courthouse State Historic Site, feature restored courthouses open to visitors, while the Pottsville Courthouse State Historic Site features a re-created building, the original having been moved to the Henry Ford Museum in Michigan in the 1920s. Only the Beardstown Courthouse, where Lincoln famously tried the "almanac case"—in which he discredited a witness who claimed the scene was illuminated by moonlight, by using a *Farmer's Almanac* to show that the night in question had been dark, and thereby secured his client's acquittal of a murder charge—remains active. Also scattered across the state are the seven sites of the famed 1858 Lincoln-Douglas debates, a plaque or monument marking each location. The Old Main Building at Knox College in Galesburg is the only building associated with the debates still standing; it has just undergone a comprehensive renovation.

In Springfield curious tourists can visit the law offices that Lincoln shared with junior partner William Herndon, at the intersection of Sixth and Adams

Streets, overlooking the Old State Capitol, where he served in the Illinois legislature and in 1858 delivered his famous "House Divided" speech. Nearby is the Lincoln Home National Historic Site, a four-square-block district of preserved buildings that includes the only home that Lincoln ever owned, where the Lincoln family resided for seventeen years before they departed for the White House. True Lincoln devotees can travel to the lobby of the Marine and Fire Insurance Company at Bank One, near the intersection of Sixth and Washington Streets, to view his financial accounts. Lincoln opened his account with a deposit of $310 on March 1, 1853, and it continued until the settlement of his estate in 1867. Also open to visitors during the summer months is the Lincoln Depot, the station from which Lincoln departed for his inauguration. Though heavily damaged by fire in the 1960s, today the site is interpreted through a cooperative agreement of the National Park Service and the *State-Journal* newspaper.

Published itineraries for the president-elect's whistle-stop tour en route to Washington called for him to ride in an open carriage, but rumors of an assassination plot caused the route to be secretly altered. Originally, Lincoln's train was scheduled to arrive at Baltimore's Calvert Street Station from Harrisburg, Pennsylvania, around noon on February 23, 1861. Lincoln would then have to transfer trains, traveling by coach across the city; it was during this journey that a group of conspirators planned to ambush him. Once the plot came to light, Lincoln's advisers prevailed on him to alter his plans, taking a private train from Harrisburg to Philadelphia and from there to Baltimore, arriving in the city from a different direction and several hours ahead of schedule. As an added precaution telegraph service between Baltimore and Pennsylvania was impeded to prevent the conspirators from communicating if they noticed anything was amiss. Lincoln arrived in Washington without fanfare at about 6:00 a.m. on February 23 and took up residence in the Willard Hotel, which is still operating, though in a new building, on Pennsylvania Avenue.

Although named in his honor, the White House Lincoln Bedroom served a very different purpose during the Lincoln administration than its name would suggest. It and the adjoining Lincoln Sitting Room were used primarily as a private office and cabinet meeting room during the nineteenth century, well before construction of the West Wing. Thus, contrary to popular modern stories, Lincoln would only have slept here if he fell asleep working at his desk. Today the room contains one of five copies of the Gettysburg Address in Lincoln's own hand, the only one signed, dated, and titled.

During the Civil War, Lincoln took an extremely active role as commander in chief of the nation's armed forces. In May 1862 he visited Fort Monroe, in Hampton, Virginia, and helped plan a Union assault against the nearby city of Norfolk. Tours of the fort's many historic features are available, even while it remains an active military base. On his return journey to Washington, Lincoln met with Major General Irvin McDowell at Chatham—now a part of Fredericksburg and Spotsylvania National Military Park—in Stafford County, Virginia, to discuss plans for the army's movement south toward Richmond. All told, Lincoln would visit the area, which served as a Union base of operations, six times in 1862 and

1863. In November 1863 he famously traveled to Gettysburg, Pennsylvania, to help dedicate the Soldier's National Cemetery. The next summer, Lincoln became the only sitting president to come under enemy fire during the Battle of Fort Stevens, when Confederate raiders were rebuffed in an attempt to breach the defenses of the capital city. Throughout the war Lincoln was a frequent visitor to the War Department offices, particularly the telegraph offices, located in what is now the Eisenhower Executive Office Building, adjacent to the White House.

Many of the buildings familiar to Lincoln during his time in Washington are still there and in active use, though occasionally by other entities. For example, the Patent Office of Lincoln's day, which was the scene of a tremendous ball following his second inauguration, today houses the Smithsonian American Art Museum and National Portrait Gallery. The original building of the Smithsonian Institution, sometimes called "the Castle," once hosted popular lectures that Lincoln would occasionally attend and today continues to hold special exhibitions. Standing immediately east of the White House, the Treasury Building continues in the same use today as during the 1860s, although troops are no longer bivouacked on the lawn. The buildings where the eminent portraitist and pioneer of photojournalism Mathew Brady, who photographed Lincoln many times, kept his studio and offices on Pennsylvania Avenue have been renovated and combined with adjoining structures to house international offices for the Sears department stores. Mary Surratt's boardinghouse, where conspirators plotted the Lincoln assassination, still stands in the city's Chinatown area, a plaque on the exterior of the restaurant commemorating the building's former use.

Lincolniana—the study and collection of Lincoln-related objects—has advanced greatly in recent years, as many sites anticipated the two-hundredth anniversary of his birth in February 2009. Although nearly every site even tangentially related to Lincoln has planned some sort of special event to capitalize on the upsurge in popularity, several particularly prominent sites have received major facelifts, renovations, and upgrades for the observance.

In August 2007 one of the most famous sites, and certainly the most tragic one, associated with Abraham Lincoln, Ford's Theatre National Historic Site, closed to the public for an eighteen-month, $40 million renovation and expansion. The site is part of a "campus" along Tenth Street, N.W., featuring a fully upgraded working theater, a reimagined and interactive museum, and the new Center for Education and Leadership, as well as the Peterson House, where Lincoln died. Although best remembered as the place where actor and southern sympathizer John Wilkes Booth shot Lincoln during a performance of *Our American Cousin* on April 14, 1865, Ford's Theatre has been an active performance space since 1968. Following Lincoln's assassination, public outcry forced the curtains shut on the Ford's Theatre stage, and the site languished for ninety years, intermittently serving as federal government offices or a storage facility. The current renovation, the first since President Dwight Eisenhower authorized the site's reconversion to a theater in the 1950s, features new seating, heating and air conditioning, and restrooms, as well as providing the handicap accessibility necessary in a modern theater.

Elsewhere in Washington, a far less known Lincoln landmark has recently opened to visitors for the first time. President Lincoln's Cottage on the grounds of the Armed Forces Retirement Home served as the family's residence from June to November 1862, 1863, and 1864, when the heat and humidity in the city originally built on swampland became too oppressive. The president would commute approximately three miles to the White House daily, although he would often conduct important business or meet with his generals at the cottage, making it the Camp David of its day. Much of the planning, drafting, and revision of the Emancipation Proclamation was done at the cottage. Living at the cottage also allowed the Lincoln family a degree of privacy not available to them when they were staying at the White House. Their stays were welcome respites from the constant demands of government, despite the emergency conferences that could call Lincoln away in the middle of the night.

Four Civil War–era buildings at the Soldier's Home, as the Armed Forces Retirement Home is often colloquially called, were designated a National Historic Landmark by the secretary of the interior in 1974. In 2000 President Bill Clinton made the cottage and 2.3 acres surrounding it a National Monument, although ownership is maintained by the nonprofit National Trust for Historic Preservation. Shortly thereafter, a seven-year, $15 million renovation began on the cottage's interior, exterior, and grounds. Archaeological excavations were also undertaken and a visitor center was built to help interpret the site. With the extensive project complete, President Lincoln's Cottage opened to the public for the first time in February 2008.

—Jim Campi

See also *Soldiers' Home*

Lincoln in Film

The emergence of the film industry in the early 1900s coincided with the 1909 centennial of Abraham Lincoln's birth and the resulting surge of interest in the sixteenth president. Lincoln was a popular subject for early moviemakers, though interest in him waned over time.

The first known film to feature Lincoln is *The Reprieve: An Episode in the Life of Abraham Lincoln* (1908). Only a few minutes in length, the movie shows Lincoln pardoning a sleeping sentry. This basic story line, apparently easy to communicate via silent film, was the foundation for many early Lincoln shorts, including *Abraham Lincoln's Clemency* (1910), *The Sleeping Sentinel* (1914), *The Heart of Lincoln*

(1915), and *The Dramatic Life of Abraham Lincoln* (1924). The Gettysburg Address was another popular subject, serving as the basis for at least two different films titled *Lincoln's Gettysburg Address* (1912, 1922) and for *The Battle of Gettysburg* (1913). A few early directors attempted more ambitious projects. Francis Ford, for example, undertook a multipart biography in 1913 that included *When Lincoln Was President, The Battle of Bull Run, The Toll of War, When Lincoln Paid,* and *From Rail Splitter to President.* The foremost visionary among the first generation of filmmakers was D.W. Griffith, who twice turned his attention to Lincoln. Griffith's three-hour epic, *Birth of a Nation* (1915), which presents American history from the Civil War through Reconstruction, has Lincoln as a central character for its first half. Fifteen years later, near the end of his career, Griffith produced a highly regarded biography of the president titled *Abraham Lincoln* (1930). It was the first Lincoln movie—and the first Griffith movie—to feature sound.

The early film portrayals of Lincoln were, almost without exception, fawning. Lincoln is presented as a great hero and a symbol of whatever virtue the filmmaker wanted to emphasize—compassion, industry, honesty, and so forth. Even *Birth of a Nation,* which is highly critical of Northern actions during and after the Civil War, portrays Lincoln in a sympathetic fashion. These early Lincoln films also share another common feature—they are exceedingly ahistorical. Many, particularly the sleeping sentry films, are based on events that never actually happened. Others, particularly *Birth of a Nation,* so badly distort history as to render it unrecognizable. Some make laughable errors. *The Battle of Gettysburg* shows Lincoln delivering the Gettysburg Address against a backdrop that is clearly the Malibu Hills in California. Griffith's *Abraham Lincoln* has him delivering the Second Inaugural Address at Ford's Theatre moments before his assassination.

In 1926 and 1939, Carl Sandburg published a two-volume biography of Lincoln. The second book, *Abraham Lincoln: The War Years,* was a runaway best seller and Pulitzer Prize winner stimulating renewed interest in Lincoln among filmmakers. The result was a pair of movies generally regarded as the finest ever made about Abraham Lincoln—*Young Mr. Lincoln* (1939) and *Abe Lincoln in Illinois* (1940), starring Henry Fonda and Raymond Massey, respectively. The former was chosen for inclusion in the National Film Registry in 2003, and the latter was nominated for multiple Academy Awards. Though the two movies are not as problematic as the films of D.W. Griffith from a historical standpoint, they are nonetheless highly flattering to Lincoln and frequently fudge events and details so as to enhance their stories.

In 1939, only a few months before the release of *Abe Lincoln in Illinois, Gone With the Wind* arrived in theaters. The character of Lincoln, however, does not appear in the three-hour-long film, whose backdrop is the Civil War. This proved to be the beginning of a trend. Perhaps because Lincoln's story had already been told, or because the burgeoning civil rights movement made Lincoln controversial, the sixteenth president all but disappeared from the silver screen after this. He is entirely absent from all the important Civil War films made in the last sixty years, including *The Red Badge of Courage* (1951), *Shenandoah* (1965), *Glory* (1989), *Gettysburg* (1993), *Gangs of New York* (2002), *Gods and Generals* (2003), and *Cold Mountain* (2003).

Though he was all but gone from theaters, the emergence of television allowed Lincoln to be portrayed on the small screen. Lincoln was a popular subject in the television of the 1950s and 1960s, appearing in episodes of *The Philco Television Playhouse* ("Ann Rutledge," 1950); *Omnibus* ("Mr. Lincoln," with five parts, 1952–1953); *General Electric Theater* ("Love Is Eternal," 1955); *Ford Star Jubilee* ("The Day Lincoln Was Shot," 1956); *The Twilight Zone* ("The Passersby" and "Back There," 1961); *Doctor Who* ("The Chase," 1964); and *Star Trek* ("The Savage Curtain," 1969), among others. As with earlier filmic representations, the portrayals of Lincoln were very positive. In "The Passersby," for example, Lincoln is presented as the tragic final victim of the Civil War. In "The Savage Curtain," Captain James Kirk summons his hero, Lincoln, to help defeat a quartet of enemies in hand-to-hand combat.

After 1970, Lincoln faded from television, just as he had from movies, appearing only in documentaries and the occasional made-for-TV movie. Since 2000, however, there has been a resurgence of interest. Portrayals of Lincoln are again appearing on television, as in the 1950s and 1960s, sometimes as comic relief, sometimes as part of a dramatic story line. He is even being portrayed again, as for example, *National Treasure: Book of Secrets* (2007). It remains to be seen if the bicentennial of Lincoln's birth in 2009 and the release of a Steven Spielberg–directed biopic in 2010 will accelerate the trend.

—CHRISTOPHER BATES

BIBLIOGRAPHY

Chadwick, Bruce. *The Reel Civil War: Mythmaking in American Film.* New York: Vintage, 2002.

Gallagher, Gary W. *Causes Won, Lost, and Forgotten: How Hollywood and Popular Art Shape What We Know about the Civil War.* Chapel Hill: University of North Carolina Press, 2008.

Thompson, Frank. *Abraham Lincoln: Twentieth Century Popular Portrayals.* Dallas: Taylor, 1999.

Lincoln in Music

For the five years that he was at the center of national politics, Abraham Lincoln was the subject of all manner of songs. After his death, songwriters' interest in him slowly waned, such that by the 1960s he was virtually absent from popular music.

Lincoln first found himself the subject of songs during the presidential campaign of 1860. At that time it was considered unseemly for presidential candidates to campaign for the job. Instead, candidates' followers were expected to communicate their message, and one of the best ways to do so was through song. The Lincoln songs of 1860 emphasized his humble roots ("Rail Splitter's Polka"), his integrity ("Old Honest Abe for Me"), his willingness to stand up to the South ("Lincoln and Liberty, Too"), and his excellent chances for victory ("The Wigwam Grand March").

Once Lincoln was in the White House, the number of Lincoln songs only increased. Singing was a popular activity on both the home and war fronts, and songwriters were happy to supply the demand for music. There were recruitment songs such as "The Union Volunteers" (1861) and "We Are Coming Father Abraham, Three Hundred Thousand More" (1862). There were patriotic songs such as "Uncle Abe and the Rebellious Boys" (1863) and "Old Abe the Battle Eagle" (1865). Lincoln's signing of the Emancipation Proclamation unleashed a storm of songs in favor—"We'll Fight for Uncle Abe" (1863), "Old Abe Has Gone and Did It, Boys" (1862)—and against—"Oh! Massa's Gwine to Washington" (1863) and "The Unhappy Contraband." Naturally the election of 1864 produced even more campaign songs, most notably "Our Nation's Captain" (1864), "Vote for Abraham" (1864), and "Three Cheers for Abe and Andy" (1864).

The president's assassination brought yet another wave of Lincoln songs—"A Nation in Tears" (1865), "A Nation Weeps" (1865), "Our Martyr President" (1865), "Our Noble Chief Has Passed Away" (1865), "President Lincoln's Funeral March" (1865), "Rest, Noble Chieftain" (1865), and "Toll the Bell Mournfully" (1865), along with dozens of others. Once the president was buried, however, the flood of songs slowed to a trickle. For the rest of the nineteenth century, songwriters would only occasionally compose a song about Lincoln, such as "Will You Ever Give the Colored Race a Show" (1868) and "Washington and Lincoln" (1890).

In the first decades of the twentieth century, songwriters' attention returned to Lincoln, in part because of the celebrations of Lincoln's one hundredth birthday in 1909. "Lincoln Centennial Grand March" (1909), for example, was popular. In 1942, Aaron Copland was asked to compose a work in honor of an "eminent American" to help drum up support for World War II. Copland responded with "Lincoln Portrait," a composition that blends orchestral instruments and passages from Lincoln's speeches. The work is generally considered the most important and the best of all Lincoln-inspired compositions.

After World War II, Lincoln all but disappeared from the world of music. The dominant musical styles of the postwar era—rock and roll and hip-hop—have little room for a white man who symbolizes the authority of the government. Lincoln did merit mention in a few of the protest songs of the 1960s, notably Bob Dylan's "Talking World War III Blues" (1963) and Dion's "Abraham, Martin, and John" (1968). He has since been used for ironic or surrealistic effect, as in Holopaw's "Abraham Lincoln" (2003) or Five Iron Frenzy's "Abraham Lincoln

Beard" (2003). However, Abraham Lincoln's days at the center of the popular music world are clearly long past.

—CHRISTOPHER BATES

BIBLIOGRAPHY

Bernard, Kenneth A. *Lincoln and the Music of the Civil War.* Caldwell, Idaho: Caxton Printers, 1966.

Brands, Pearl Brown. *Music Written about Abraham Lincoln.* Bryn Mawr, Pa.: T. Presser Co., 1938.

Cornelius, Stephen. *Music of the Civil War Era.* Westport, Conn.: Greenwood Press, 2004.

Lincoln Memorial

The Lincoln Memorial in Washington, D.C., has become deeply embedded in American iconography. Yet every aspect of the memorial was still being hotly debated in the first decades of the twentieth century. The first effort to erect a national monument enshrining President Lincoln's memory got under way in 1867 with congressional authorization, but the initiative withered for lack of interest and money. Thirty-five years later, in 1902, Congress created the Lincoln Memorial Commission, which authorized Rep. James McCleary of Minnesota to travel through Europe, gather information on monuments, and report back with a recommendation. McCleary's proposal was an arresting one. He envisioned a monumental highway 72 miles long and 200 feet wide, running between the nation's capital and Gettysburg. Down the middle would run a 50-foot-wide greensward with gardens, fountains, and statues. Hundreds of thousands of Americans would visit the Gettysburg battlefield and the national cemetery there via this splendid highway, McCleary argued, and return to Washington ennobled in spirit.

Road-building interests, tire companies, automobile manufacturers, and property owners along the route enthusiastically supported the plan, but as time passed with no action, their hopes dimmed. In 1911 the memorial commission finally won an appropriation of $2,000,000 but decided to defer to the Fine Arts Commission on the form the memorial should take. The Fine Arts Commission was made up of artists and architects who envisioned a traditional memorial of marble or bronze rather than an asphalt roadbed. From that point on, the questions were where the memorial would be located, who would design it, and what it would look like.

Fort Stevens, where President Lincoln had watched Union forces repulse Confederate troops in July 1864, Capitol Hill, and Union Station all had their supporters, but the Fine Arts Commission strongly favored the current site on the Potomac River, where the Lincoln Memorial would provide a strong anchor for the west end of the National Mall. The Lincoln Memorial Commission asked architects Henry Bacon, well known for his work on the Chicago World's Fair in 1893, and John Russell Pope, a rising star in American architecture, to submit designs. Pope submitted ten drawings, including one for a massive funeral pyre from which a thin stream of smoke would perpetually waft. Bacon submitted only one, the winning one, of a dignified Doric temple.

Ground for the Lincoln Memorial was broken on February 12, 1914, the one-hundred-fifth anniversary of Lincoln's birth. That same year the commission chose the preeminent American sculptor, Daniel Chester French, to execute the statue of Abraham Lincoln that would stand at the heart of memorial. French chose to concentrate on the dignity and force of character of Lincoln the statesman. He submitted a full-scale, twelve-foot-tall model of his seated Lincoln in 1916, but he and Bacon immediately realized that it was far too small. Lincoln would look insignificant, dwarfed by the enormous columns. To decide just how much larger the statue should be, French and Bacon made progressively larger solar prints and mounted them on wooden frames. Not until they reached nearly twenty feet did the statue seem properly proportioned. Although the cost of the memorial was already inching toward $2,500,000, and would eventually exceed $3,000,000, the commission approved the larger, more expensive statue.

French turned the actual carving over to Piccirilli Brothers, noted marble carvers in New York City, who fashioned the twenty-eight blocks of white Georgia marble so perfectly that when assembled, the 175-ton statue seemed carved from a single huge block. French, however, was horrified when he first saw it. Lincoln's face looked out not with quiet dignity but with a blank stare. His head rose up into darkness. His knees were far too prominent. Lighting was the problem. French had carefully modeled Lincoln's features on the assumption that the memorial would have a large glass skylight. But the plans had changed, and translucent marble covered the ceiling. What light there was came through the doorway, flattening Lincoln's face and highlighting his shins. The problem of proper illumination plagued French and Bacon for years.

The Lincoln Memorial was completed in 1921. Inside, the memorial is divided into three sections by fifty-foot-high Ionic columns. The two side chambers contain murals by Jules Guerin and the words of Lincoln's most famous speeches: on the left, the mural *Emancipation* and the Gettysburg Address; on the right, a mural with allegorical figures portraying Unity flanked by Fraternity and Charity and Lincoln's Second Inaugural Address. French's statue of Lincoln dominates the central chamber. Lincoln sits gracefully in a flag-draped chair, whose posts are formed by fasces. His coat unbuttoned; his powerful hands resting on the arms of the chair; his face, properly lit, is strong but benign. On the wall behind Lincoln is the following inscription: IN THIS TEMPLE AS IN THE HEARTS OF THE PEOPLE FOR WHOM HE SAVED THE UNION THE MEMORY OF ABRAHAM LINCOLN IS ENSHRINED FOREVER.

More than 50,000 people, including a complement of elderly Civil War veterans and Lincoln's only surviving son, Robert Todd Lincoln, attended the dedication of the Lincoln Memorial on May 30, 1922, Decoration Day, later Memorial Day. Former president and current chief justice William Howard Taft officiated. He spoke of Lincoln's qualities—patience, mercy, love, courage, sacrifice, honesty, and imagination—and told the audience, "Here is a shrine at which all can worship." In his dedication speech President Warren G. Harding spoke of Lincoln's trials, concluding, "Today, American gratitude, love and appreciation, give to Abraham Lincoln this lone white temple, a parthenon for him alone." Dr. Robert Moton, the president of Tuskegee Institute, gave the main speech at the dedication. The presence of a black leader on the podium, in what was by this time a thoroughly segregated national capital, suggests the importance of Lincoln to the enduring issue of race in America. Since the dedication the memorial has been a significant icon for civil rights, most notably as the background for Dr. Martin Luther King Jr.'s "I Have a Dream" speech, at the famous March on Washington in 1963.

—Kathryn Allamong Jacob

BIBLIOGRAPHY

Concklin, Edward F. *The Lincoln Memorial.* Washington, D.C.: U.S. Government Printing Office, 1927.

McCreary, James T. "What Shall the Lincoln Memorial Be?" *American Review of Reviews* 38 (September 1908): 340–344.

National Archives. Record Group 42, Records of the Office of Public Buildings, Entry 195, Lincoln Memorial Commission Papers. Washington, D.C.: National Archives.

Peterson, Merrill D. *Lincoln in American Memory.* New York: Oxford University Press, 1994.

Richman, Michael. *Daniel Chester French, An American Sculptor.* New York: Metropolitan Museum of Art, 1976.

Sandage, Scott A. "A Marble House Divided: The Lincoln Memorial, the Civil Rights Movement, and the Politics of Memory, 1939–1963." *Journal of American History* 80 (June 1993): 135–167.

Steers, Edward, Jr., and Joan Chaconas. *Everlasting in the Hearts of His Countrymen: A Guide to the Memorials to Abraham Lincoln in the District of Columbia.* Washington, D.C., 1984.

Lincoln on Currency

Several American presidents and other notable figures in the nation's history have been pictured on U.S. currency. Abraham Lincoln's image first appeared on U.S. currency in 1869, on a one-hundred-dollar "large note," so called because the dimensions of this currency were slightly larger than those of today's paper money. The engraving on this bill was based on the photograph of Lincoln taken by Andrew Berger in Mathew Brady's photography studio in February 1864. Robert Lincoln, the president's son, believed that this was the best photograph ever taken of his father. This same picture was also later used on the Lincoln five dollar notes.

The first of the five dollar notes with Lincoln's image appeared in 1914; they were printed until 1923. These were also "large notes." In 1923 the design of the bill was changed, and the portrait's format became more circular, rather than oval. Collectors came to call this the "porthole portrait." In 1928 the "small note" series was begun, with the dimensions of the bills similar to those in use today. On the five dollar bill, the portrait returned to the oval format.

In 1996, as part of a continuing program to redesign U.S. currency to make counterfeiting more difficult, a new design for the Lincoln five dollar note was introduced. It featured a larger portrait, printed off-center on the face of the note. In 2008, the bicentennial of Lincoln's birth, another new design was introduced, but the larger, off-center portrait remained.

By far the most-reproduced image of Abraham Lincoln is his portrait on the U.S. penny. Production of this coin began in 1908 to mark the centennial of Lincoln's birth in 1909. The portrait on the face of the penny was based on a sculpture by Victor Brenner. When the Lincoln penny was first introduced demand for it was so great that traders sold it for more than the face value. To mark the 150th anniversary of Lincoln's birth in 1959, the back of the penny was redesigned, with a depiction of the Lincoln Memorial replacing the stalks of wheat that had previously been used. By the 1990s, over 250 billion Lincoln pennies had been minted.

Another member of Lincoln's administration also appeared on U.S. paper money, Salmon P. Chase, Lincoln's first secretary of the Treasury. Like Lincoln, Chase was originally a "sound money" man who distrusted paper currency and had to be convinced of the necessity of using the greenbacks that were adopted during the Civil War. Despite his misgivings, Chase had his own portrait printed on the first issue of greenbacks, perhaps thinking that the publicity might help him in future political endeavors. Chase resigned from the Treasury in 1864, and

Lincoln appointed him Chief Justice of the Supreme Court. In a case during the Reconstruction era, Chase ruled that issuing the greenbacks had been unconstitutional. Chase was also featured on a ten-thousand-dollar bill that was first produced in 1928. These large-denomination bills never circulated in large numbers and were used primarily for transfers of funds between banks. The Treasury stopped producing these bills during World War II and withdrew them from circulation in 1969.

The secretary of the Treasury has the final decision on the design of U.S. paper money and coins, including the selection of the portraits. At present, federal law prohibits the image of any living person being used on U.S. currency.

—Mark S. Joy

BIBLIOGRAPHY

Lange, David W. *The Complete Guide to Lincoln Cents.* Irvine, Calif.: Zyrus Press, 2005.

Peterson, Merrill D. *Lincoln in American Memory.* New York: Oxford University Press, 1994.

Sullivan, George. *Picturing Lincoln: Famous Photographs That Popularized the President.* New York: Clarion, 2000.

Lincoln Penny

The Lincoln penny, introduced in 1909 to commemorate the centennial of Abraham Lincoln's birth, replaced the Indian-head penny, long a popular American icon. The decision to depict a specific person on a circulating U.S. coin, which had never been done before, generated controversy at the time. Some Americans thought that placing the image of an actual person on currency was redolent of Old World monarchy and should not happen in America. Some who had despised Lincoln during the Civil War objected to the use of his likeness, in particular. Others revered Lincoln and insisted that he belonged on a higher denomination than the lowly penny. Defenders of the choice, though, believed that placing him on the face of the most common American coin was the most appropriate honor for Lincoln.

Several years before the coin's introduction, President Theodore Roosevelt, perceiving American coins as staid and dull, became interested in having

American currency redesigned, hoping to imbue it with a more energetic, fresh image. Roosevelt influenced the selection of sculptor Victor David Brenner for the project. Brenner based the penny's portrait of Lincoln on a 1907 plaque that he had carved, which he had modeled on a photograph of Lincoln taken in February 1864 in Mathew Brady's studio. Lincoln faces to the right on the penny because that is the direction of the original photograph—not for any of the reasons suggested by some legends.

Early controversy notwithstanding, the Lincoln cent proved popular when it was introduced and sold for more than face value in its early days of circulation. Originally 95 percent copper and 5 percent zinc, the coin underwent significant changes in its alloys and composition in ensuing decades, especially during World War II, when pennies were made of zinc-coated steel until copper no longer needed to be conserved for wartime purposes. In the 1980s pennies shifted to a copper-plated zinc composition, resulting in a content of more than 97 percent zinc and less than 3 percent copper, but preserving the copper appearance of the coins.

The reverse of the Lincoln penny featured a wheat-head until 1959, the Lincoln sesquicentennial, when the Lincoln Memorial replaced the wheat motif. "FG," the initials of Frank Gasparro, the engraver responsible for the new image, appeared near the right-hand side of the depiction of the memorial for the duration of this design, and the initials "VDB" remained in tiny letters on the obverse of the coin, located above the bevel at the base of Lincoln's portrait. Brenner's initials had been made much smaller, but not removed, after protests against their original prominence.

In 2005, Title III of the Presidential $1 Coin Act declared that the reverse of the Lincoln penny would be refreshed again in 2009 in observance of the bicentennial of Lincoln's birth. Four designs, each emphasizing a different phase of Lincoln's life, would be used on the reverse, while Brenner's likeness of Lincoln remained on the obverse. The law further stipulated that in 2010, after the bicentennial series had run its course, another image emblematic of Lincoln's importance would be chosen for the reverse of the coin.

Hundreds of billions of Lincoln pennies have been produced since the coin's inception, and they account for a majority of all U.S. coins struck.

—Cara L. Shelly

BIBLIOGRAPHY

Presidential $1 Coin Act of 2005. Public Law 109-145, 119 Stat. 2664.

U.S. Department of the Treasury. "History of the Lincoln Cent." www.ustreas.gov/education/fact-sheets/currency/lincoln-cent.shtml.

U.S. Mint. "Nuggets from the Vault: The History of Presidents on Our Coins." Washington, D.C.: U.S. Department of the Treasury. www.usmint.gov/historianscorner/index.cfm?action=DocDL&doc=nugget07-12-06.doc.

Logan, Stephen T.

Stephen Trigg Logan (1800–1880) was Abraham Lincoln's second law partner, from 1841 to 1844. An "exceptionally acute and technically skilled lawyer and former judge," Logan is often credited for much of Lincoln's legal training.

Logan was born on February 24, 1800, in Franklin County, Kentucky, and moved to Springfield, Illinois, in 1832. Shortly after his arrival, he saw Lincoln make a speech at the courthouse. Though he thought the speech was "very sensible," he walked away thinking Lincoln was "sort of a loafer."

Logan went on to establish one of the most successful law practices in Illinois, but by 1841 he had had a falling-out with his law partner, Edward D. Baker (1811–1861), over money. At about the same time, Lincoln split with his first law partner, John Todd Stuart (1807–1885). In 1841 Logan invited Lincoln to form a law partnership.

According to Logan, Lincoln was not a good lawyer at that time. He had little legal knowledge, never studied enough, and lacked confidence in his ability. But Logan was impressed by Lincoln's ability "in getting the good will of juries." During their partnership Lincoln did not hold or run for political office; instead, he spent his time absorbing Logan's legal knowledge. On at least one occasion, for example, Logan read and corrected one of Lincoln's complaints for a slander case. "By close study of each case as it came up," remembered Logan, "he got to be quite a formidable lawyer."

During their four years together, Logan and Lincoln handled about 850 cases. They specialized in bankruptcy law and enjoyed a robust appellate practice, averaging an astonishing twenty-five cases before the supreme court of Illinois each term. Logan was crucial to Lincoln's legal career. He emphasized the importance of preparation and collecting fees in a timely manner and helped establish Lincoln as a formidable lawyer, not simply on the circuit but also in the appellate and federal courts in Springfield. Logan and Lincoln dissolved their partnership in fall 1844. Logan wanted to work with his son, and Lincoln was ready to become the senior partner in a firm of his own. Lincoln emerged from the partnership with Logan as a more prepared, experienced, and confident lawyer.

Logan's political career was never as distinguished as his legal reputation, though he was a member of the Illinois legislature in 1842, 1844, and 1846. He ran for Lincoln's vacated congressional seat in 1848 but lost. In 1854 Logan again won a seat in the state legislature, but in 1855 he set his sights on the supreme court of Illinois. Not only did he lose the election, but Lincoln later commented that Logan was "worse beaten than any other man ever was since elections were invented."

Logan was a delegate to the Chicago Republican National Convention in 1860, where he helped Lincoln secure the nomination for president. When the war started, Lincoln appointed him as a commissioner to investigate procurement claims against the government in Cairo, Illinois. Logan died at his home in Springfield on July 17, 1880. He is buried in Oak Ridge Cemetery in Springfield.

—SAMUEL P. WHEELER

BIBLIOGRAPHY

Burlingame, Michael. *An Oral History of Abraham Lincoln: John G. Nicolay's Interviews and Essays.* Carbondale: Southern Illinois University Press, 1996.

Lupton, John A. "A. Lincoln, Esquire: The Evolution of a Lawyer." In *A. Lincoln, Esquire: A Shrewd, Sophisticated Lawyer in His Time,* by Allen D. Spiegel. Macon, Georgia: Mercer University Press, 2002.

Memorials of the Life and Character of Stephen T. Logan. Springfield: H.W. Rokker, 1882.

Long Walk, The

The Navajo Removal occurred in 1864. The forced march of 9,000 Indians from their homeland to a reservation three hundred miles away became a footnote in a year filled with the huge battles in which the United States defeated the Confederacy. A tragedy for the Native Americans, it marked only one more event in the western expansion of the United States.

With their hogans, flocks of sheep, finely woven blankets, and peach trees on the one hand and their fighting ability on the other, the Navajo balanced a warrior culture with a pastoral subsistence in the arid lands of the desert Southwest. Although leaders on both sides promised peace, conflict continued as Americans moved into Navajo land in search of gold and Navajo warriors raided towns and ranches.

When the Civil War distracted U.S. military power, the Navajo stepped up their attacks. In response, General James Carleton, commander of New Mexico, turned to Colonel Kit Carson for help. By the 1860s Kit Carson enjoyed a national reputation, thanks in large part to John C. Frémont, who made the mountain man a hero in his published accounts of his expeditions. Uncomfortable with his fame and disillusioned when he was sometimes unable to live up to his reputation in real situations, Carson had settled into a quiet life with his family. But when duty called again at the outbreak of the Civil War, he answered. A dedicated Unionist and longtime opponent of slavery, the old scout defended New Mexico against Confederate invaders.

Carleton ordered Carson to defeat the Navajo and move them to a reservation. Pursuing the Navajo into their strongholds in Canyon de Shelle, he burned their crops, destroyed their peach orchards, and shot their livestock. Eventually the Navajo surrendered. Within a few weeks, the Long Walk began, as the military forced the Indians to move to the Bosque Redondo Reservation in southern New Mexico. About five hundred died during the walk, and things only got worse after their arrival.

Poorly planned and even more poorly located, the reservation was ill-suited to sustain the Navajo. Crops would not grow, the wood supply quickly gave out, and their old Indian enemies attacked them. Moreover, it turned out that the Navajo homeland did not contain rich gold and silver mines. Despite Carleton's fervent dedication to keeping the reservation, William Tecumseh Sherman, now serving as a peace commissioner, listened to the eloquent plea of Barboncito, and in June 1868 he allowed the Navajo to return home.

Nationally the Long Walk represented the ways in which the United States continued to expand westward even during the Civil War. It also was an example of how the Lincoln administration implemented the Republican ideology of freedom, union, and power during the war. Long justified as a means of securing liberty, territorial expansion fit nicely with Republican support for free soil. And now it was needed to preserve the Union. To achieve both freedom and union, Lincoln and the Republicans extended the power of the national government. Earlier Indian removals cost more lives than the Long Walk, and unlike other Native Americans, the Navajo returned to their homeland. But the West now coincided with a crisis and became part of broader plans to fulfill an ideology that would change the nation.

See also *Indian Relations, Lincoln and*

—A. James Fuller

BIBLIOGRAPHY

Dunlay, Thomas. *Kit Carson and the Indians.* Lincoln: University of Nebraska Press, 2000.

Green, Michael S. *Freedom, Union, and Power: Lincoln and His Party during the Civil War.* New York: Fordham University Press, 2004.

Sides, Hampton. *Blood and Thunder: An Epic of the American West.* New York: Doubleday, 2006.

Magoffin, Beriah

Beriah Magoffin (1815–1885), governor of Kentucky during the secession crisis, presided over the state's adoption of armed neutrality and later resigned after a Unionist majority in the legislature rendered him ineffective. Born in Harrodsburg, on April 18, 1815, Magoffin was educated at Centre College and Transylvania University, where he earned a law degree in 1838. Magoffin then worked as an attorney and entered politics. A staunch Democrat, Magoffin was a frequent delegate at the party's national conventions. In 1859 Magoffin defeated Joshua F. Bell in Kentucky's gubernatorial election.

As governor, Magoffin guided Kentucky through secession and the beginning of the Civil War. Under his administration the state chose to pursue a course of armed neutrality. Magoffin personally supported slavery and states' rights, and historians have argued over whether he actually believed in neutrality or was secretly a secessionist. Most recent scholarship has contended that he was a neutral and believed that states had the right to secede but should not. On April 15, following Fort Sumter and President Lincoln's call for volunteers, Magoffin famously replied that Kentucky would supply no troops to the federal government for the purpose of coercion. The following week, he also rejected a Confederate request for soldiers. Regardless of his personal beliefs, Magoffin stated that it was his duty to follow the will of the people, and on May 20 he announced the state's neutrality. Kentucky would support neither side. Unionists, however, continued to suspect that Magoffin was a secessionist.

In September, Confederate troops under the command of General Leonidas Polk invaded western Kentucky, violating the state's neutrality. In response, Union forces under General Ulysses S. Grant also moved into the state. Magoffin wanted both armies to leave. However, state elections the previous month had placed an overwhelming Unionist majority in the state legislature, and they only ordered the withdrawal of the Confederates. The governor vetoed the bill, but he was soon overruled by the Unionist majority in the legislature. Having lost his veto power, Magoffin was rendered powerless. The legislature proceeded as it wished without worrying about the views of Magoffin, whom they considered disloyal.

As early as September 1861, members of the legislature called for Magoffin's resignation. He remained governor until August 1862, but for the final year of his administration he was frustrated by his own ineffectiveness. On August 10, 1862, Magoffin stated the conditions for his resignation. Particularly, he desired that his replacement be a conservative. Magoffin's lieutenant governor, Linn Boyd, had died shortly after the 1859 election and had not been replaced. As a result, Magoffin and members of the state legislature carried out a series of maneuvers that resulted in state senator James F. Robinson's ascension to the governorship. On August 18, the legislature accepted Magoffin's resignation.

Magoffin's political career effectively ended with his resignation as governor. From 1867 to 1869 he served one term in the Kentucky House of Representatives, but he remained out of step with most Kentuckians. By and large, Kentuckians resisted emancipation until the Thirteenth Amendment passed in December 1865 and then worked to curb civil and political rights for blacks. Despite his earlier proslavery stance, Magoffin encouraged Kentuckians to accept both emancipation and black civil rights. Magoffin retired to his hometown of Harrodsburg, where he died on February 28, 1885.

—Jacob F. Lee

BIBLIOGRAPHY

Coulter, E. Merton. *The Civil War and Readjustment in Kentucky.* Chapel Hill: University of North Carolina Press, 1926.

Harrison, Lowell H. "Governor Magoffin and the Secession Crisis." *Register of the Kentucky Historical Society* 72 (April 1974): 91–110.

Harrison, Lowell H., ed. *Kentucky's Governors, 1792–1985.* Lexington: University Press of Kentucky, 1985.

Mason, James

James Murray Mason (November 3, 1798–April 28, 1871) was a senator from Virginia before serving as Confederate envoy to Great Britain. A grandson of George Mason, he was the son of farmer and businessman John Mason and Anna Maria Murray. Mason was born in Georgetown, District of Columbia. Graduating from the University of Pennsylvania in 1818, Mason earned his law degree from the College of William and Mary in 1820 and moved to Winchester, Virginia, to establish his law practice. In 1822 he married Eliza Chew, with whom he had eight children.

Mason served in the Virginia House of Delegates from 1826 to 1831, served in the 1829 Virginia constitutional convention, and was a member of the U.S. House of Representatives from 1837 to 1838. Upon the death of Isaac S. Pennybacker, Mason was elected to the Senate in 1847. He won reelection in 1850 and 1856 and remained in the Senate until March 28, 1861. From 1851 to 1861, Mason headed the Senate Foreign Relations Committee; he chaired the congressional committee that investigated John Brown's 1859 raid at Harpers Ferry.

A member of John C. Calhoun's Southern "mess," Mason was a strident advocate of Southern rights and a passionate defender of slavery. Mason was a dedicated secessionist and delivered the seriously ill Calhoun's final speech in the Senate during the 1850 compromise debates, warning of disunion unless the South was guaranteed perpetual equal representation in Congress. He was a strict constructionist and drafted the Fugitive Slave Law of 1850; he argued that slavery should be introduced into the territories without limitation. Mason also strongly opposed the Homestead Act, fearing that it was a means to create more free states and tilt the congressional balance permanently toward Northern interests.

When Virginia seceded, Mason joined the Confederate government. On August 24, 1861, Confederate president Jefferson Davis appointed Mason special envoy to Great Britain, where he sought formal diplomatic recognition of Confederate independence. Before he reached London, however, Mason was part of a major diplomatic crisis, the *Trent* affair. On November 8, 1861, en route from Cuba to Britain, Mason and James Slidell, Confederate envoy to France, were seized and removed from the British mail steamer *Trent*. They were imprisoned in Boston until January, when the diplomatic crisis was resolved and they were permitted to sail to Europe.

Mason's diplomacy was generally passive and reactive. Taking his lead from Davis, Mason preferred to allow events to run their course rather than press his British contacts on issues of importance to the Confederacy. Mason's passivity reflected both his own belief that the British were bound to recognize Confederate independence and the passive approach that Richmond took to diplomacy with Britain. Believing that cotton was king, and that Britain would soon support the Confederate cause, Mason and the Confederate government in Richmond believed that time was on their side. Though he achieved some diplomatic successes, such as the $3 million Erlanger bond issue and the legal maneuverings that permitted the commerce raiders *Florida* and *Alabama* to escape, Mason failed to persuade the European powers to recognize Confederate independence or to help lift the Union blockade. Mason also failed to have the Laird rams delivered to the Confederate navy for use against the blockade.

Mason lived in Canada until 1868, when he returned to Virginia. He died April 24, 1871, and was buried in Alexandria, Virginia.

See also *Slidell, John; Trent Affair*

—ANTHONY SANTORO

BIBLIOGRAPHY

Baylen, Joseph O., and William W. White. "James M. Mason and the Failure of the Confederate Naval Effort in Europe, 1863–1864." *Louisiana Studies* 2, no. 2 (1963): 98–108.

Ferris, Norman B. *The Trent Affair: A Diplomatic Crisis.* Knoxville: University of Tennessee Press, 1977.

Warren, Gordon H. *Fountain of Discontent: The Trent Affair and Freedom of the Seas.* Boston: Northeastern University Press, 1981.

Young, Robert W. *Senator James Murray Mason: Defender of the Old South.* Knoxville: University of Tennessee Press, 1998.

McClellan, George B.

George B. McClellan (1826–1885), Union general and 1864 Democratic presidential candidate was, in the words of Ulysses S. Grant, "one of the mysteries of the war." Rising to prominence during the first months of the conflict, he won Abraham Lincoln's trust, only to lose it as general in chief and commander of the Army of the Potomac. Opposed to the administration's escalation of the war in 1862, McClellan became more clearly identified with the Democratic Party, eventually securing that party's presidential nomination in August 1864, days before Union forces occupied Atlanta.

The son of a prominent Philadelphia physician, McClellan was something of a prodigy as a youth, quickly advancing through a series of private schools. Admitted to West Point while he was still fifteen, McClellan proved a model cadet, graduating second in the class of 1846. During the Mexican-American War he served as an engineering officer under Winfield Scott, winning promotion to brevet captain. He returned to West Point and commanded the engineering company based there before taking on a series of assignments, the most important of which was that of a military observer during the Crimean War. He gained some renown for inventing the McClellan saddle, which became standard issue for United States cavalry units. In 1857 he resigned his commission to join the management of the Illinois Central Railroad, although he retained an interest in military matters and contemplated a return to service. It was during these years that he first encountered Abraham Lincoln, who represented the railroad in several cases. It was a sign of McClellan's politics that he preferred Stephen A. Douglas. In 1860 he accepted the presidency of the Ohio and Mississippi Railroad.

President Abraham Lincoln and General George B. McClellan on the battlefield in Antietam, Maryland, in October 1862. Lincoln twice appointed and twice removed McClellan as commander of the Army of the Potomac. McClellan would run against Lincoln as the Democratic nominee for president in 1864 on a platform advocating peace with the Confederacy.
Source: The Granger Collection, New York

With the advent of hostilities in April 1861 McClellan accepted a commission as major general in charge of Ohio's volunteers. A commission as a major general in the regular army followed in May. In June and July he directed a successful Union advance into western Virginia. Called to Washington in the aftermath of the Union defeat at First Manassas to replace Irvin McDowell, McClellan threw himself into organizing and training what he would soon christen the Army of the Potomac. Lincoln, still smarting from charges that he had rushed unprepared Union forces into combat, was willing to bide his time, but as summer turned to fall people began wondering if the army would ever actually move. During these months McClellan's chief objective appeared to be to supplant Winfield Scott as general in chief, and that he achieved on November 1, 1861. He declared, "I can do it all."

As general in chief, McClellan proved unable to push Union forces forward. He had virtually nothing to do with the Union success at Mill Spring, Kentucky, and the capture of Forts Henry and Donelson by forces under Ulysses Grant. Nor did he show any signs of moving against Confederate forces in Virginia, making the report, "All quiet along the Potomac" into a derisive remark. When McClellan finally moved forward to Manassas, he discovered only abandoned Confederate works and logs painted black to resemble cannon—which soon became known as "Quaker guns." Lincoln began to prod him to take the offensive, whereupon McClellan proposed a waterborne campaign against Richmond. After much discussion, especially concerning the number of men McClellan would have to leave behind to defend Washington, Lincoln sanctioned the plan but in the process stripped McClellan of his position as general in chief, ostensibly so that he could concentrate on his advance along the James River.

McClellan advanced deliberately on Richmond from the east. He called for more men and was especially unhappy when Lincoln refused to release soldiers from the defense of Washington and the Shenandoah Valley. Before long the president and the general fell into the practice of trading hostile dispatches, with McClellan declaring that he was greatly outnumbered. In the months that followed both men were guilty of undermining faith in the other and engaging in disparaging remarks, resulting in a less-than-ideal command relationship. At the end of May Confederate commander Joseph E. Johnston fell wounded while directing an attack against McClellan's forces. McClellan welcomed the news that he would now face Robert E. Lee, whom he believed was "too cautious & weak under grave responsibility—personally brave & energetic to a fault, he yet is & is likely to be timid & irresolute in action." With McClellan's men within sight of Richmond's church spires, Lee decided to attack. In the multiple battles that followed, collectively known as the Seven Days (June 25–July 2, 1862), Lee drove McClellan away from the Confederate capital. As McClellan managed a fairly able fighting withdrawal, he launched message after message calling for reinforcements and seeking to shift blame elsewhere. "If I save this Army now I tell you plainly that I owe no thanks to you or any other persons in Washington," he wired secretary of war Edwin Stanton in a dispatch that was edited by a supervisor; "you have done your best to sacrifice this Army."

Meeting with Lincoln at Harrison's Landing less than a week after the campaign's conclusion, McClellan handed the president a letter in which he deplored measures that would escalate the war and strike at slavery. Lincoln's response was to elevate another general, Henry W. Halleck, to the post of general in chief. In what proved to be a controversial decision, Halleck ordered McClellan to abandon his position along the James and join forces with John Pope's Army of Virginia in preparation for an overland advance against Richmond. Although lead units of the Army of the Potomac did reach Manassas in time to be part of the Union defeat at Second Bull Run (August 28–30), Lincoln wondered whether McClellan had given Pope his full support. Nevertheless he decided to place McClellan in command of the Union forces regrouping around Washington. On September 4 Lee crossed the Potomac into Maryland, and several days later McClellan moved out to find and fight Lee. Aided by the capture of a copy of Lee's plan of campaign, McClellan pressed westward, overcoming Confederate resistance at several passes along South Mountain, and prepared to engage Lee in battle.

On September 17, McClellan engaged in what was the bloodiest single day of combat in the Civil War, along Antietam Creek just east of Sharpsburg, Maryland. Time and again Union assaults made initial headway, only to be checked by a skillfully managed Confederate defense. That night Lee decided not to retreat: McClellan declined to send freshly arrived reinforcements into action and chose instead to lick his wounds. When Lee finally withdrew, McClellan followed at a distance, and the Confederates recrossed the Potomac after a sharp rearguard action at Shepherdstown.

Although frustrated that McClellan could not achieve more, Lincoln rested content with declaring Antietam enough of a victory to allow him to issue the Preliminary Emancipation Proclamation on September 22. Although McClellan questioned the wisdom of the measure, as well as Lincoln's decision two days later to suspend the writ of *habeas corpus,* he reminded his men that the remedy to any complaint lay at the polls. When McClellan showed no signs of pursuing Lee preparatory to another battle, Lincoln decided to replace him, and he did so just after the November 1862 midterm elections. Never again would McClellan exercise command in the field.

At first McClellan receded into retirement, content to prepare a report of his military operations. In 1863, however, he became involved in politics when he endorsed George W. Woodward, the Democratic candidate for governor of Pennsylvania. Many observers saw this act as McClellan's first step toward seeking the Democratic nomination for president in 1864. He failed to support efforts to pressure Lincoln to restore him to a command, perhaps to take charge of the forces around Washington after a Confederate thrust in July 1864 came close to entering the capital itself. On August 31, Democratic delegates meeting at Chicago selected McClellan as their candidate for president on the first ballot. But they coupled the choice with a platform that declared the war a failure and called for a negotiated peace, in addition to saddling McClellan with a peace advocate, George H. Pendleton of Ohio, as his running mate.

Union victories on the battlefield doomed McClellan's chances. Ironically, it was William T. Sherman's capture of Atlanta on September 2, 1864, which looked much like the sort of victory McClellan had sought in 1862, that proved most damaging to his presidential candidacy. By the beginning of November additional Union triumphs had secured Lincoln's reelection. McClellan still polled 45 percent of the popular vote, although he proved far less popular with soldiers who cast ballots in the field and claimed only twenty-one electoral votes. Accepting defeat, he resigned his commission in the army.

After the war, McClellan remained interested in business and politics. He once more headed a railroad, served a term as governor of New Jersey, and campaigned for Grover Cleveland in 1884. The following year he unexpectedly passed away. McClellan's posthumous "memoir," *McClellan's Own Story,* in fact cobbled together by William C. Prime, proved most damaging to McClellan's reputation, in part by displaying his harshness toward Lincoln.

See also *Antietam Campaign; Campaign of 1864, Presidential*

—BROOKS D. SIMPSON

BIBLIOGRAPHY

Hassler, Warren W. *General George B. McClellan: Shield of the Union.* Baton Rouge: Louisiana State University Press, 1957.

Rafuse, Ethan S. *McClellan's War: The Failure of Moderation in the Struggle for the Union.* Bloomington: Indiana University Press, 2005.

Rowland, Thomas J. *George B. McClellan and Civil War History: In the Shadow of Grant and Sherman.* Kent, Ohio: Kent State University Press, 1998.

Sears, Stephen W. *George B. McClellan: The Young Napoleon.* New York: Ticknor and Fields, 1988.

McLean, John

Born in New Jersey, John McLean (1785–1861) grew up a farmer's son. His family moved to Virginia and Kentucky before finally settling in Ohio in 1796. He had only two years of formal education, from ages sixteen to eighteen, and at nineteen he was apprenticed to the Hamilton County Court of Common Pleas while he studied law under Arthur St. Clair Jr., the son of the former territorial governor. McLean edited a newspaper, practiced law, worked for the federal land office, and served in Congress (1813–1816) and on the Ohio Supreme Court (1816–1822). President James Monroe made him commissioner of the General Land Office in 1822 and in 1823 brought him into his cabinet as postmaster general. McLean held that position until 1829, serving three successive presidents—Monroe, John Quincy Adams, and Andrew Jackson. He then went to the Supreme Court where he served from 1829 to 1861. When McLean died in 1861 he was the last surviving member of the administrations of Monroe and Adams, a living link between the nation's founding and the secession crisis.

McLean was universally acknowledged as the most competent and honest postmaster general to have held the position up to that time. During the 1828 campaign he did not support Andrew Jackson, but he also refused to use the Post Office, with its national presence and veritable army of patronage appointees, to help reelect John Quincy Adams. Because of his neutrality in the campaign and his popularity and competence, McLean was the only Adams official whom Jackson kept in his cabinet. However, McLean was no Jacksonian, and he refused to remove local postmasters so that Jackson could replace them with loyal party men. Jackson did not want to fire McLean, and McLean had no interest in leaving government service. The solution, which satisfied both men, was his nomination to an open seat on the Supreme Court.

Although nominated by Jackson, McLean was not a Jacksonian on a Court dominated by Jacksonians. He was also a Northerner who hated slavery on a Court dominated by proslavery Southerners and a string of Northern doughfaces who almost always voted to support slavery. McLean was never an abolitionist, but on the antebellum Court he stood out for his relatively strong commitment to freedom and his hostility to slavery.

In addition to his ambivalent political position on the Court, McLean was also clearly interested in higher office. Whig Party historian Michael Holt argued that his "passion for the presidency...burned almost as long and torridly" as Daniel Webster's. John Quincy Adams noted in his diary that Justice McLean "thinks of nothing but the Presidency by day and dreams of nothing else by night." It is hard to gauge how much McLean's quadrennial quest for the White House affected his position on the Court, but it surely must have. As Chief Justice Roger Taney handed out assignments for important majority opinions he must have understood that allowing McLean to write an important opinion would only serve to heighten his political profile. Since McLean and Taney were not political allies, the chief justice had little reason to support McLean's aspirations.

McLean's pursuit of the presidency began less than two years after he went on the bench. In 1830 the Anti-Masonic Party emerged out of fear that Masons were a threat to the nation. The party was a strange coalition built mostly around hatred of Andrew Jackson (who was a Mason). Among its members were a number of men who would eventually become prominent political leaders as Lincoln rose to national office, including James Buchanan, William H. Seward, Thaddeus Stevens, William Sprague, and Thurlow Weed. Almost immediately the party began to woo McLean, who initially indicated that he would accept its nomination. But shortly before the party's convention—the first national political convention in American history—McLean withdrew from consideration. McLean had his eye on the White House, but knew he could never get there through an obscure third party. Four years later he actively sought the nomination of the Whig Party, and as early as 1835 the Whig Party in Ohio officially endorsed his candidacy. But he proved unacceptable to a majority of Whigs, who believed he was a closet Jacksonian. Others mistrusted him because he appeared to have no real political principles. In the end the Whigs nominated no one that year and instead ran four regional candidates, in the hope that with so many candidates the election would go to the House of Representatives, where one of the Whigs could emerge victorious. This strategy failed miserably, as Martin Van Buren carried fifteen states and 170 electoral votes, while the four regional candidates together carried eleven states and 124 electoral votes.

In 1840 McLean stood on the sidelines as the popular war hero William Henry Harrison, who was also from Ohio, won the Whig nomination and the election. Harrison died in office only a month after his inauguration and was succeeded by John Tyler, a former Democrat who alienated almost every member of the Whig Party. Tyler offered McLean the cabinet post of secretary of war, but McLean decided not to leave the Supreme Court. He understood that being a one-term cabinet member in the administration of an unpopular, unelected president would not help him to the presidential nomination, which was all he really wanted. He remained on the bench, waiting for the election of 1844 and another shot at the White House. By 1844 McLean had long shed any taint of Jacksonianism and was acceptable to mainstream Northern Whigs. But now Southern Whigs distrusted him on slavery. Given his recent dissent in *Prigg v. Pennsylvania* (1842) that was totally sensible. McLean's name was put forward as a vice presidential candidate, but he withdrew himself from consideration. The Whig ticket of Clay and Frelinghuysen lost in a close election.

Starting in 1846 Justice McLean actively sought the Whig nomination for 1848. He wrote letters, dined with important politicians, and had his supporters reach out to Whigs across the nation. He tried to sell himself as the last remnant of the founding era—a veteran of James Monroe's administration who could rise above party politics and partisanship. In March 1846 he seemed to be the candidate to beat. But the Mexican War changed everything, as General Zachary Taylor's victory at Buena Vista in February 1847 made him the most logical Whig candidate. McLean was also hampered by his position on the Court, which made it impossible for him to campaign actively, give speeches, or take positions on a number of issues. At the Whig convention, which met from June 7 to June 9, McLean's name was put forward, but he received only two votes on the first ballot and none after that.

Having lost the Whig nomination, McLean still had a chance to be nominated as the candidate of the newly created Free Soil Party, which emphatically opposed the spread of slavery into the territories but avoided an extreme antislavery position that would alienate most Northern voters. In October 1847, before the Free Soil Party was created, Charles Sumner of Massachusetts asked Salmon P. Chase "how much Anti-Slavery there is in Judge McLean." Sumner, a dedicated foe of slavery, declared, "I have strong personal predilections in his favor. I honor his character." Sumner believed that "if Judge McLean could be induced to take any practical ground against the extension of Slavery, he would be a popular candidate," and running for president with John Hale of New Hampshire it would be a "strong ticket." Chase agreed, declaring that McLean was "the most reliable man, on the slavery questions, now prominent in either party." The Free-Soilers met in Buffalo, New York, on August 9 and 10. McLean might have had a shot at a place on the ticket, but having just openly sought the Whig nomination he would not allow his name to be put forward at the convention of another party. Furthermore, McLean was ambivalent about third parties. His lifetime seat on the Supreme Court was better than a quixotic run for the White House or vice presidency on a third-party ticket that was bound to lose.

In 1852 McLean was no longer unwilling to consider a third-party candidacy. Most likely he understood that at his age he had to run soon, or he would never realize his dream of becoming president. Thus he allowed his name to be put forward to the Free Soil Democratic Party. His was one of seven names offered at the party convention, but he won few votes. The convention chose John P. Hale, who polled slightly more than 150,000 votes out of the more than three million cast.

By 1856 McLean, at age seventy-one, seemed desperate to get a nomination. He had tentatively offered himself to the Know-Nothings and received eleven votes at that party's convention in February 1856. McLean then made himself available to the North American Party, which had split off from the American (Know-Nothing) Party. The North Americans nominated Nathaniel Banks of Massachusetts, who eventually withdrew from the campaign to support the Republican Party.

Party membership was fluid and affiliations changed quickly. By this time McLean was unalterably hostile to the Democratic Party, which had become a proslavery bastion. He seemed to be willing to run on any party ticket that opposed the Democrats. Thus, having failed to win the nomination of either of the nativist parties, McLean became an active candidate at the Republican convention. He was the senior statesman of the new party, considered an attractive candidate who could appeal to Know-Nothings, former Whigs, "westerners" (today's Midwest), and moderate opponents of slavery. Unlike his leading opponent, John C. Frémont, McLean was an experienced politician, who had been in Washington for three decades. Despite his strengths, McLean lacked the charisma of Frémont, the heroic western explorer and soldier. On an informal first ballot McLean ran second, with 196 votes to Frémont's 359. Frémont was then nominated by acclamation. The 1856 Republican convention was the closest McLean would ever come to winning a presidential nomination.

The 1856 election sent the doughface Democrat James Buchanan to the White House. Two days after Buchanan's inauguration the Supreme Court announced its decision in *Dred Scott v. Sandford* (1857). It held 7–2 that the Missouri Compromise was unconstitutional, that Congress had no power to prohibit slavery in the territories, and that free blacks could never be citizens of the United States, even if they were able to vote and hold office in the states where they lived. McLean's lengthy dissent castigated Chief Justice Taney's opinion and provided ammunition for Republicans, such as Abraham Lincoln, who denounced the decision. Had the Court decided the case in the spring of 1856, it is possible that McLean's dissent would have bolstered his presidential candidacy enough to overcome Frémont's appeal. His dissent made it clear that McLean was solidly antislavery. But it came too late in his career to gain him a presidential nomination.

But in 1860, at age seventy-five, he made one more run. With the party system and the nation collapsing, a motley collection of former Whigs, Know-Nothings, and moderate Democrats organized the Constitutional Union Party which, like the Know-Nothings in 1856, also called itself the American Party. The party met in Baltimore on May 9–10, and on the first ballot McLean ran sixth among ten candidates, with nineteen votes. On the second ballot the party nominated John Bell, a former senator from Tennessee. Not quite finished as a presidential candidate, Justice McLean was proposed at the Republican convention in Chicago a week later. On the first ballot McLean ran seventh among thirteen candidates, with twelve votes. On the third ballot Abraham Lincoln won the nomination, but McLean was one of seven candidates still in contention, running fifth with a few convention votes.

In less than year McLean would be dead, opening a seat on the Supreme Court for Lincoln to fill just as he entered the White House. McLean had been on the Court for thirty-two years, and for almost all that time he had been running for president or vice president. McLean remained in national politics while on the bench and at various times in his career was considered to be a National Republican, Jacksonian Democrat, Anti-Masonic, Free Democrat, Whig, Free-Soiler, Know-Nothing, North American, and Republican before finally seeking the presidential nomination of the Constitutional Union Party in 1860. He had been considered a viable candidate by at least eight different parties, and at least three times his name had been put forward at more than one political convention in the same year. This is a record of sorts, unmatched by any political figure in the history of the nation. From 1848 until 1860 McLean stood for moderate antislavery politics and helped lay the groundwork for another former Whig who was moderately antislavery to be elected president in 1860.

—PAUL FINKELMAN

BIBLIOGRAPHY

Carney, Thomas E. "The Political Judge: Justice John McLean's Pursuit of the Presidency." *Ohio History* 111 (2002): 121–144.

Finkelman, Paul. "Story Telling on the Supreme Court: *Prigg v. Pennsylvania* and Justice Joseph Story's Judicial Nationalism." In *Supreme Court Review, 1993*, edited by Dennis J. Hutchinson, David A. Strauss, and Geoffrey R. Stone. Chicago: University of Chicago Press, 1994.

Holt, Michael F. *The Rise and Fall of the American Whig Party*. New York: Oxford University Press, 1999.

Kahn, Michael A. "The Appointment of John McLean to the Supreme Court: Practical Presidential Politics in the Jacksonian Era." *Journal of Supreme Court History*, 1993, 70.

Weisenburger, Francis P. *The Life of John McLean: A Politician on the United States Supreme Court*. Columbus: Ohio State University Press, 1937.

Merryman, Ex parte

See *Ex parte Merryman*

Mexican War

The Mexican War resulted from a complex mix of American designs on Mexican territory, especially California, the Texas Revolution and the subsequent annexation of Texas, internal Mexican politics, and the American ideology of Manifest Destiny. In the short run it led to the acquisition of a huge amount of land, including all of the present-day states of California, Utah, and Nevada, and portions of present-day Arizona, New Mexico, Colorado, and Wyoming. However, the acquisition of this land destabilized political accommodations over slavery in the territories, creating a huge political crisis that led to the Compromise of 1850 and the Kansas-Nebraska Act. This in turn led to Abraham Lincoln's reentry into politics in 1854 and the creation of the Republican Party.

Abraham Lincoln was a first-term congressman during the Mexican War, and his opposition to it is credited with derailing his political career from 1849 until he returned to politics in the mid-1850s. Lincoln may have learned a valuable political lesson through this experience: that a successful politician cannot be too far out in front of his constituents. The Mexican War also was a training ground for many of the men who would later be key officers and politicians in the Civil War, including generals Ulysses S. Grant, Robert E. Lee, and George B. McClellan, as well as Confederate president Jefferson Davis. But the lessons they took from their experience may not have been helpful for some of them. Many of the officers—such as Lee, McClellan, and Davis—left the Mexican War believing that wars were easily and quickly won and that frontal charges at a fortified enemy could be successful. These ideas would lead to disastrous results for both armies in the Civil War.

The immediate cause of the war was American annexation of Texas in 1845 and American designs on California. Mexico had never recognized Texas independence, and the Mexican government warned the United States that it would consider

View of the camp of the army commanded by General Zachary Taylor near Corpus Christi, Texas, in October 1845. Lincoln was a congressman during the Mexican war, and his opposition to it was unpopular.

Source: Library of Congress

Texas annexation tantamount to an act of war. However compromise might have averted war. Mexico claimed that the boundary of Texas had always been the Nueces River. Texas, however, claimed that its boundary extended another 150 miles south, to the Rio Grande. After annexation President James K. Polk sent American troops into the disputed area, which seemed a direct provocation of Mexico. At the same time, Polk attempted to buy California from Mexico, which from the Mexican perspective was deeply insulting. By early May 1846 Polk had decided to ask for a declaration of war against Mexico, although he had no strong reason to do so. Over the weekend between his decision to go to war and the time when he could bring his request to Congress, Polk got welcome news: Troops under General Zachary Taylor had engaged in a battle with Mexican soldiers. He asked for a declaration of war, declaring that Mexico had "invaded our territory and shed American blood upon the American soil."

In December 1847 Lincoln, in his famous "spot resolutions," demanded that the administration show the "spot" on American soil where American blood had been shed; Lincoln suspected that the blood had been shed on disputed soil. Lincoln's opposition to the war was unpopular, and later politicians would call him "spotty Lincoln." In January he voted for the Ashmun Resolution, which demanded that the administration show evidence that "Mexico herself became the aggressor by invading our soil in hostile array." Lincoln argued that the war was "unnecessarily and unconstitutionally commenced by the President." Opponents of the war argued that it was part of a conspiracy to spread slavery into new territories. Northern Democrats, who supported the war but not slavery, thus supported the Wilmot Proviso, sponsored by Rep. David Wilmot of Pennsylvania, which would have banned slavery in any territory acquired during the war against Mexico. The House passed the proviso a number of times, but it died in the Senate. The proviso led to a stalemate in politics that was finally broken by the Compromise of 1850.

Meanwhile American military success was swift and relatively painless, with only about 1,700 combat deaths—although another 11,000 men or more died from disease. In the Treaty of Guadalupe Hidalgo, in 1848, Mexico ceded about 500,000 square miles—some 40 percent of its territory—to the United States in return for $15 million. The political cost of the war was much greater because it led to more than a decade of debate over the status of slavery in the new territories. In 1848 many disaffected Northern Democrats joined with committed opponents of slavery to form the Free Soil Party, which failed to win the election but took enough votes from Lewis Cass to put General Zachary Taylor in the White House. John C. Frémont, who had helped capture California, emerged as a national hero and would become the Republicans' first presidential candidate in 1856. Although Lincoln suffered politically for his opposition to the war, he would later become politically successful when the territorial acquisitions from the war led to the creation of the new Republican Party. Some Southerners, including John C. Calhoun and the future Confederate vice president, Alexander Stephens, also opposed the war as an unnecessary war of aggression, and they understood that it would dangerously upset the delicate political compromises over slavery in the territories. On that point they were correct.

See also *Polk, James K.; Spot Resolutions; Wilmot Proviso*

—PAUL FINKELMAN

BIBLIOGRAPHY

Frazier, Donald S., ed. *The United States and Mexico at War: Nineteenth Century Expansion and Conflict.* New York: Macmillan, 1998.

Johannsen, Robert W. *To the Halls of Montezuma: The Mexican War in the American Imagination.* New York: Oxford University Press, 1995.

Schroeder, John H. *Mr. Polk's War: American Opposition and Dissent, 1846–1848.* Madison: University of Wisconsin Press, 1973.

Missouri Compromise, The

Though it was an entire generation distant from his presidency, the Missouri Compromise of 1820 was perhaps the most important piece of congressional legislation influencing Abraham Lincoln's political career. Both its repeal in the Kansas-Nebraska Act of 1854 and its judicial defeat in the *Dred Scott* decision of 1857 helped catapult Lincoln onto the national political stage, positioning him against Sen. Stephen Douglas. It was at the very center of the Lincoln-Douglas debates in the 1858 Illinois campaign for the U.S. Senate. Those debates were picked up and printed by major newspapers around the country, making Lincoln a well-known name and a national political figure. Though Lincoln lost the election, the debates showcased his political acumen and eloquence and marked his initial step toward election as president two years later.

The Missouri Compromise of 1820 was a political watershed in its own right, for it set the tone and defined the terms by which the nation would address the issues of territorial expansion, the extension of slavery, statehood, secession, and sectional agreement for the remainder of the antebellum period. Anchored chronologically between the "Great Compromise" during ratification of the Constitution and the Compromise of 1850, the Missouri Compromise of 1820 cemented a pattern of political compromises between North and South, kept the weight of their power in the federal government balanced, and sounded a chord for national harmony and sectional unity. Before the Missouri Compromise, slavery was not a dramatically divisive political issue in the newly formed United States, although the debates over ratification of the Constitution and over regulating and then closing the African slave trade illustrated its potential to create sectional conflict. Mentally tying it to the colonial industry that produced it, many Northerners naïvely believed, or at least hoped, that the institution of slavery would either wither away along with the declining tobacco economy in the South or remain only in the states that had not yet abolished it. But a thriving cotton market emerged by the end of the 1790s and then exploded after the War of 1812. Even before the invention of the cotton gin, however, slavery was profitable, prices for slaves were high, and Southerners insisted on the right to reopen the African slave trade that they had voluntarily closed during the Revolution. In 1803 South Carolina did reopen the trade, bringing in more than 50,000 new slaves in the next five years. By 1819 slavery was a booming institution, and many in the North feared that the increased weight of a slaveholding South would tip the scales and upset the sectional balance of representational power in the federal government that had thus far existed.

When Missouri applied for statehood in 1819, James Tallmadge, a congressman from New York, introduced what would be called the Tallmadge amendment, requiring a ban on future slave importation and a program of gradual emancipation as prerequisites for the admission of Missouri as a state. With the ensuing debates turning hostile and heated, Southerners threatening secession, and the House of Representatives evenly divided between North and South, Speaker of the House Henry Clay engineered a compromise that put an end to the stalemate. Under it Missouri entered the Union as a slave state and Maine entered as a free state, thus retaining the balance of slave and free states. The compromise also banned slavery north and west of Missouri, thus guaranteeing that most of the federal territories existing at the time would be free soil. At one level the compromise followed the legislative precedents of both the Northwest Ordinance of 1787, which prohibited slavery north of the Ohio River, and the

Southwest Ordinance of 1790, which permitted slavery south of it. However Northerners objected to the compromise because Missouri was in fact north of the southern terminus of the Ohio River. The compromise reaffirmed congressional authority to prohibit the institution and established a new geographical boundary for slavery in the federal territories of the Louisiana Purchase. Although the congressional debates surrounding the 1820 legislation unleashed mounting sectional resentment, the end product remained in place for over thirty years and represented the inherent optimism of the "Era of Good Feelings." It stood as yet another legislative precedent for North-South accord.

But when westward migration into the territories acquired from the Mexican War began in earnest at midcentury, it renewed questions of whether slavery should expand there and whether Congress, resident citizens ("popular sovereignty"), or states had the authority to ban it altogether in those areas. As the threads of unity began to unravel in the 1850s, politicians were forced to revisit the merit, legitimacy, and constitutionality of the Missouri Compromise.

As growth continued, some Americans believed that the country needed a transcontinental railroad in the territories, but they bitterly disagreed over whether it should go above or below the 36° 30' parallel. In 1854 Sen. Stephen Douglas of Illinois introduced legislation for the railroad that would split the Nebraska Territory in two, with the implicit understanding that Kansas, to the south, would become a slave state and Nebraska, to the north, a free one. Pitching the idea of "popular sovereignty," Douglas believed that the residents of the territories should decide the slavery issue and not Congress. The Kansas-Nebraska Act passed in August, and Southerners were allowed to bring slaves into areas of the territory where they had previously been prohibited, effectively repealing the Missouri Compromise of 1820 and replacing it with sectional fear, animosity, and discord.

Northerners believed that Southerners were conspiring to restrict their political and economic liberties in the federal territories, while Southerners believed that the North was conspiring to reduce the South's political and economic influence there. Soon a groundswell of outrage against the Kansas-Nebraska Act prompted various camps in the North to unite to form the first truly sectional political organization in the United States, the Republican Party. The act also stoked the ire, and resuscitated the political career, of a former, one-term congressman, Abraham Lincoln. With the backing of the Illinois Republican Party, Lincoln ran against the Democratic incumbent, Douglas, for the Senate in 1858.

The *Dred Scott* decision of 1857 and its ruling on the Missouri Compromise set the stage for the Lincoln-Douglas debates and the Senate campaign. In his decision, chief justice Roger B. Taney ruled that the Missouri Compromise was unconstitutional because it deprived citizens of their property (slaves) without due process of law as guaranteed by the Fifth Amendment. In effect, the Supreme Court determined that Congress did not have the authority to ban slavery in federal territories.

Lincoln and the Republican Party disagreed. Both believed that Congress did have the authority to ban slavery, but only in the territories, not in the states where the institution already existed. Although Lincoln believed that slavery was morally wrong and privately hoped for its demise, he separated himself politically from both Douglas and the abolitionists, arguing against "popular sovereignty" and pushing only for Congress's right to ban the institution in the federal territories, not its complete and immediate abolition. Although Lincoln was not a proponent of racial equality, he believed that preventing the spread of slavery was his moral obligation.

The debates were instrumental in elevating Lincoln's political stature and putting Lincoln and Douglas on the Republican and (Northern) Democratic presidential tickets two years later. The presence of the Constitutional Union Party alongside their names on the ballots reminded voters of the historical importance of compromise.

See also *Doughface*

—John Macaulay

BIBLIOGRAPHY

Forbes, Robert Pierce. *The Missouri Compromise and Its Aftermath: Slavery and the Meaning of America.* Chapel Hill: University of North Carolina Press, 2007.

Moore, Glover. *The Missouri Compromise, 1819–1821.* Gloucester: P. Smith, 1967.

Morgan's Raid

From June 11 to July 26, 1863, Brigadier General John Hunt Morgan led approximately 2,500 Confederate soldiers on a raid through Kentucky, Indiana, and Ohio. A veteran of the Mexican War and a Lexington businessman, Morgan had conducted successful raids on U.S. Army posts and communication lines in Kentucky in July, October, and December 1862. In the summer of 1863 General Braxton Bragg authorized Morgan to create a diversion in Kentucky, but on July 8 the "Thunderbolt of the Confederacy" disobeyed his commanding officer and crossed the Ohio River. When Major General Ambrose Burnside cut off his retreat routes to the South, Morgan fled northward. Over the course of six weeks, the raiders engaged in passing skirmishes and direct battles, captured federal soldiers and local militiamen, burned bridges and rail lines, seized horses and supplies, and ransacked private homes and stores. Lincoln grew impatient with the raid's duration and asked Burnside to report Morgan's whereabouts to him personally. Most of Morgan's men were injured or captured, others drowned while attempting to cross the Ohio River, and the remaining 400 finally surrendered with Morgan near Lisbon, Ohio.

From a tactical standpoint, Morgan's raid accomplished very little: he liberated no prisoners, aroused no Confederate sympathies, and was captured before creating a diversion significant enough to relieve Union pressure on Bragg's army in Tennessee. Seen in the long view of 1863, the raid represented yet another Confederate defeat contemporary with the campaigns at Vicksburg (May 18–July 4) and Gettysburg (July 1–3). But in the moment Southerners hailed the "Great Raid" and Northerners recoiled in fear as terror spread throughout the midwestern home front. Previous Confederate attempts to cross the Ohio River had been deflected by Union troops or aborted in mid-execution. Morgan's Raid made a reality of the fears held by wary residents of the Old Northwest.

Five months after the raid Lincoln remained nervous about the potential danger of Confederate raiding. In Indiana such fears had been stirred into political frenzy by Governor Oliver P. Morton, whose labeling of all political opponents as Copperheads created a bitter partisan climate in the state. Many midwesterners believed that the southern counties along the Ohio River in Ohio, Indiana, and Illinois harbored untold numbers of Southern sympathizers just waiting for a chance to join the rebellion. That Morgan also believed the rumors is evident from his secret dispatch of spy Thomas Hines in June to curry advance support from Indiana Copperheads for the impending raid. Hines and his men were chased out of Indiana before securing any assistance, and Morgan's Raid ultimately galvanized Union support along the north side of the Ohio River because the raiders stole from all residents, independent of their political leanings. When their homes and property were on the line, residents stood with the Union and supported the war as necessary to its preservation.

Local historians in search of notable accomplishments celebrate the raid as the "longest" of the Civil War and "the northernmost penetration of the Confederacy" (Vermont residents cite a Confederate-led raid on a Burlington bank as their claim to the same honor). Claims of exceptionalism aside, the raid briefly brought the war to the midwestern home front and strengthened support for Lincoln and the war. On November 27, 1863, Morgan escaped from the Ohio Penitentiary in Columbus with six of his men by crawling through an underground passageway to the courtyard and then scaling the prison wall. He commanded troops in southwest Virginia in 1864, and on September 3, 1864, he was surprised and killed by U.S. Army troops in Tennessee. Upon hearing the news Lincoln reportedly said, "Well, I wouldn't crow over anybody's death; but I can take this as resignedly as any dispensation of Providence."

—Keith A. Erekson

BIBLIOGRAPHY

Duke, Basil Wilson. *A History of Morgan's Cavalry.* Cincinnati: Miami Printing and Publishing Company, 1867.

Horwitz, Lester V. *The Longest Raid of the Civil War: Little-Known and Untold Stories of Morgan's Raid into Kentucky, Indiana and Ohio.* Cincinnati: Farmcourt Publishing, 2001.

Mormons, Attacks on

There is no evidence that Abraham Lincoln was ever directly involved in matters related to attacks on Mormons in Illinois during 1844–1845 or at the time of their ultimate expulsion from Illinois in 1846. As a politician during the 1850s, he chose not to exploit negative public feelings toward the Mormons for political expediency beyond citing them to illustrate inconsistencies in how Stephen A. Douglas applied his "popular sovereignty" doctrine. As a Republican, however, Lincoln endorsed his party's 1856 platform, which declared it the imperative duty of Congress "to prohibit in the Territories those twin relics of barbarism—Polygamy, and Slavery." As president, Lincoln's Mormon policy was to keep a wary eye but basically to leave them alone.

During the winter of 1838–1839 Mormons fleeing a Missouri extermination order arrived in western Illinois in large numbers. Their prophet, Joseph Smith, founded a new gathering place, the city of Nauvoo, on a picturesque bend of the Mississippi River. Lincoln was a member of the state house of representatives in December 1840 when the Illinois legislature granted Nauvoo a charter. Lincoln joined the majority in approving the charter, even though Mormon voters had scratched his name from the list of Whig electors in the recent presidential election.

Lincoln never visited Nauvoo. Records show, however, that he was at home in Springfield on two occasions when Joseph Smith visited the city—once in November 1839 and again in January 1843. It is possible that Lincoln met Joseph Smith on one or both of these occasions, but there is no conclusive evidence. That Lincoln was keenly aware of the local political importance of the Mormons is shown in a letter he wrote to his law partner, Whig congressman John Todd Stuart: "Joshua Speed says he wrote you what Jo Smith said about you as he passed here. We will procure the names of some of his people here and send them to you before long."

There are no known writings or statements by Lincoln regarding the conflict between Mormons and anti-Mormon extremists in western Illinois from 1844 through 1846. Lincoln was in Springfield at the time of Joseph Smith's murder at Carthage, Illinois, in June 1844. He was attending court at Tremont when the last Nauvoo Mormons were expelled from the city by an unauthorized militia in September 1846. Several of his Whig associates played roles in events. That Lincoln may not have viewed the Mormons in as menacing a light as some of his associates is suggested in a letter he wrote in July 1842, shortly after Mormon apostate John C. Bennett published an exposé: "There is nothing new here. Bennett's Mormon disclosures are making some little stir here, but not very great."

Lincoln refused to attack his rival Stephen A. Douglas on the "Mormon question" (though colleagues encouraged him to do so) beyond publicly noting an inconsistency in Douglas's "popular sovereignty" position—if Douglas would permit people to vote their moral conscience to allow slavery in the territories, why shouldn't he allow the Mormons to vote their moral conscience to allow polygamy in the Utah Territory?

The Mormon question complicated Utah territorial patronage matters for President Lincoln. He listened politely to Mormon emissaries pleading for appointees sympathetic to them. He made several unsuccessful appointments before finally settling on federal officials tolerable to both eastern Republicans and Utah Mormons. Brigham Young and other Mormon officials were generally ambivalent about Lincoln. They were disappointed when he did not back Utah statehood petitions and when he signed the Morrill Anti-Bigamy Act of 1862, attacking polygamy (though Lincoln did not enforce it). But the Mormons appreciated his ultimate policy: "Tell Brigham Young that if he will let me alone, I will let him alone."

—BRYON C. ANDREASEN

BIBLIOGRAPHY

Andreasen, Bryon C. *Mormon Connections to Lincoln-Era Springfield*. On file, Abraham Lincoln Presidential Library, Springfield, Ill.

Hubbard, George U. "Abraham Lincoln as Seen by the Mormons." *Utah Historical Quarterly* 31 (Spring 1963): 91–108.

Long, E.B. *The Saints and the Union: Utah Territory during the Civil War*. Urbana: University of Illinois Press, 1981.

Simon, John Y. "Lincoln, Douglas, and Popular Sovereignty: The Mormon Dimension." In *Lincoln Revisited: New Insights from the Lincoln Forum*, ed. John Y. Simon, Harold Holzer, and Dawn Vogel. New York: Fordham University Press, 2007.

Morrill, Justin Smith

Born in Strafford, Vermont, Justin Smith Morrill (1810–1898) was the precocious son of a blacksmith, who left school at age sixteen to apprentice in retail merchandising. By 1848 he retired from business a wealthy man and thereafter devoted his time to horticulture, landscape design, and Whig Party politics. Morrill, who married Ruth Barrell Swan, a Massachusetts teacher, in 1851, was known as a Free Soil or Webster Whig when he won election to Congress in 1854. Before assuming his seat Morrill helped organize the Republican Party that controlled Vermont government from 1855 to 1962. After serving in the House of Representatives (1855–1867) he moved to the Senate (1868–1898).

In Congress Morrill was first known as an opponent of slavery in the western territories, a fierce foe of Mormon polygamy, and an advocate of the protective tariff. The Morrill tariff of 1860 first made him a national figure. Most Southern Congress members favored free trade, and this tariff was one factor leading to secession. But Morrill, who was vilified in Virginia newspapers as a Yankee protectionist, was also interested in the distribution of western lands to farm families. Since his visit to relatives farming on the Illinois prairie in 1841 he had favored plans to sell farm land to settlers. The Morrill Act was introduced in 1857 and vetoed by President Buchanan in 1860, passing only after its Southern opponents left Congress. This homestead bill derived from Morrill's antislavery views and coincided with Republican free-soil ideology. When President Lincoln signed the landmark law in 1862, it began a tradition of federal support for higher education and vocational education and made Morrill the father of the land-grant colleges.

The law granted public lands for the establishment of institutions known as land-grant colleges. For each congressional district, 30,000 acres of federal land was designated as an endowment for a college. Sale of the land provided funds to establish or expand the state college or university, and by 1865 more than 15,000 claims were filed. It expanded public higher education to include practical training in engineering, science, agriculture, and military science, as well as the traditional classics curriculum. Eventually the Homestead Act of 1862, as it was known, fostered more than one hundred colleges and universities, despite some early scandals when states hard-pressed to cover wartime expenses sold their land grants quickly and cheaply to wealthy speculators. The New York telegraph tycoon Ezra Cornell, for example, purchased 500,000 acres in the Middle West to benefit Cornell University.

Large state universities in Wisconsin (1848), Michigan (1855), and Minnesota (1869) soon developed; some, such as Texas A&M (1871), were known as agricultural and mechanical schools. This law, in conjunction with the transcontinental acts passed in 1862 and 1864, promoted settlement in the western territories. It derived from the Jeffersonian idea of an educated electorate of yeoman farmers and transformed education in the United States by opening higher education to women, immigrants, and working-class Americans. New, scientific agricultural methods originated or were popularized in the new land-grant colleges and their agricultural experiment stations and cooperative services. Especially in dry farming, hard wheat, alfalfa, peanuts, and soybeans, their work helped to feed expanding populations in the United States and abroad. Morrill, who served continuously in Congress for forty-three years, was known as the father of the Senate when he died in Washington, D.C., on December 28, 1898.

—PETER C. HOLLORAN

BIBLIOGRAPHY

Cross, Coy F. *Justin Smith Morrill: Father of the Land-Grant Colleges.* East Lansing: Michigan State University Press, 1999.

Parker, William B. *The Life and Public Services of Justin Smith Morrill.* New York: Da Capo, 1971.

Williams, Roger L. *The Origins of Federal Support for Higher Education.* University Park: Pennsylvania State University Press, 1991.

Morrill Land Grant Act

On July 2, 1862, Abraham Lincoln signed the Morrill Land Grant Act, sponsored by Republican representative Justin Smith Morrill, of Vermont. This act granted public lands to any state that would use the funds from their sale to endow a school for teaching agricultural and mechanical arts. Morrill and others had been urging passage of such a bill for several years. Morrill was born in Strafford, Vermont, in 1810. First elected in 1854, he served in Congress for more than forty years, first in the House and from 1867 to 1898 in the Senate.

Morrill first attempted to develop national support for agricultural education in 1856, when he asked the House Committee on Agriculture to establish a national board of agriculture and one or more national agricultural schools modeled after the naval and military academies. That proposal was never acted on. In 1857 Morrill introduced a bill similar to the one that passed in

1862; Congress approved this measure, but President James Buchanan vetoed it in 1860.

Many western congressmen opposed the Morrill Act initially. Because the measure was passed at virtually the same time as the Homestead Act and the Pacific Railroad Act (with its large land grants to the railroads), some believed the bills would be at cross purposes. Others feared that the sale of these "endowment lands" would lead to large-scale purchases by absentee speculators, so that the lands would remain unsettled while the owners waited for the value to rise. Some members of Congress opposed the bill because they believed the government itself needed the revenue from land sales.

Under the Morrill Act, each state could claim 30,000 acres of public land for each member of its congressional delegation. States that did not have public lands within their own borders would receive scrip that could be sold to people who could use it to acquire public lands. States had to establish a school within five years. The money from the sale of the public lands or the land scrip had to be invested in government bonds or some other safe investment that would yield 5 percent or more per year. The funds from the endowment lands could not be used to erect buildings for the schools; they had to be paid for by the states themselves.

Besides his interest in schools for teaching the agricultural and mechanical arts, other factors influenced Morrill's support of this legislation. He believed that the older, eastern states received little benefit from the large land grants that had been made for various development purposes. He also believed that the low prices of federal land led to poor land use, since an owner could ruin land through poor farming and then move on to purchase cheap land elsewhere.

Lincoln and the Republican Party supported Morrill's bill, but support was not universal. In the Senate, the seven "no" votes included five Republicans, all from western states that had extensive public lands. Generally, however, the bill was strongly supported in many parts of the Northeast and the Old Northwest, where the Republicans found their greatest strength. Although Lincoln signed the act, he apparently took no major role in encouraging its passage. Most studies of Lincoln's life and presidency give more attention to Morrill's contributions on the tariff and other economic issues than to the land-grant college act.

—MARK S. JOY

BIBLIOGRAPHY

Cross, Coy F., Jr. *Justin Smith Morrill: Father of the Land-Grant Colleges.* East Lansing: Michigan State University Press, 1999.

Nevins, Allan. *The Origins of the Land-Grant Colleges and State Universities.* Washington, D.C.: Civil War Centennial Commission, 1962.

Morrill Tariff

In 1857 Congress eliminated the tariff (import tax) on a number of items. This was done partly out of concern over large federal Treasury surpluses. Justin Smith Morrill, a Republican congressman from Vermont, was a strong believer in a protective tariff that would shield American industry from cheap foreign competition. He voted against the tariff reductions.

Within only a few months after the new tariff took effect, the government was facing its more common problem of falling revenues. Morrill proposed reinstituting the earlier tariffs but the proposal went nowhere.

In 1858 Morrill easily won reelection. When Congress convened for its first session in December 1859, Republicans controlled the House. Ohio Republican John Sherman became chairman of the Ways and Means Committee, and he urged Morrill to write a new tariff measure. Morrill wrote a bill that the House approved on May 10, 1860. Morrill believed his bill would increase federal revenue by $60 million per year. Trying to allay Southern fears about a protective tariff, he described his measure as a revenue-producing tariff. In the Senate, Virginia Democrat Robert M. T. Hunter, an advocate of lower tariffs, used parliamentary maneuvers to hold up consideration of the Morrill bill until the second session of Congress, which would begin in December 1860. This meant that the Senate would not consider the bill until after the November 1860 presidential election, and it made the tariff an issue in the presidential campaign.

The Republican platform called for a higher tariff, which Abraham Lincoln firmly supported. Both Lincoln and Morrill had been Whigs before the Republican Party was born, and the protective tariff was a principal part of the Whig agenda. Pennsylvania, with a significant iron industry, wanted the high tariff, as did several western states where wool production was important. The tariff issue may have been significant in bringing the votes of Pennsylvania and several western states to Lincoln in the election. William McKinley, the future president, who was in Congress at the time, believed that without the tariff issue the Republicans would not have carried Pennsylvania, and that would have dramatically reduced Lincoln's electoral majority to a mere three votes.

By the time the Senate returned to consideration of the tariff after the second session of the 36th Congress began, many anti-tariff Southern senators were leaving the Senate as their states seceded. When the Senate continued to delay action on the tariff, Lincoln announced in February 1861 that if the Morrill tariff was not in place by the time he was inaugurated, he would make its passage an immediate priority. The Senate finally approved the Morrill tariff in late February 1861. President James Buchanan signed the bill two days before Lincoln's inauguration, and the law took effect on April 1, 1861.

Great Britain opposed a high tariff because of its heavy export trade with the United States. Some scholars have suggested that the Morrill tariff may have been part of the reason for the strong sympathy of some British leaders for the South during the early stages of the Civil War. The Republican-dominated Congress raised the tariff more significantly during the Civil War. Rates were revised downward somewhat during the Reconstruction period, but in general a high, protective tariff remained U.S. policy until President Woodrow Wilson's administration.

—Mark S. Joy

BIBLIOGRAPHY

Cross, Coy F., Jr. *Justin Smith Morrill: Father of the Land-Grant Colleges.* East Lansing: Michigan State University Press, 1999.

Richardson, Heather Cox. *The Greatest Nation of the Earth: Republican Economic Policies during the Civil War.* Cambridge, Mass.: Harvard University Press, 1997.

Morton, Oliver P.

Governor Oliver P. Morton (1823–1877) of Indiana was one of the most important governors during the Civil War. He remains a controversial figure among historians. Some nineteenth-century authors saw him as a heroic genius, while others denounced him as a manipulator and opportunist who ignored constitutional limits and broke the law to increase his own power. In the twentieth century, Progressive historians saw him as an able administrator whose emotional instability hampered his efforts and made him paranoid. Thus, they argued, he became a nuisance to Lincoln, who outsmarted Morton while using him in his own heroic work to save the Union. Later historians continued to see Morton as an efficient leader but still argued that his prickly personality and arrogance caused problems and deepened divisions in Indiana politics. Examining Morton's career in the context of the Lincoln administration begins to shed light on Indiana's war governor.

Born in 1823 in eastern Indiana, Oliver Morton became an attorney and worked mostly for the railroads before entering politics. First elected as a circuit court judge, he made a name for himself as an antislavery Democrat before the party expelled him in 1854 for his strident opposition to the Kansas-Nebraska Act. Quick to act, Morton joined the loosely organized People's Party in time to run for governor in 1856. He lost the race, but the campaign made him a rising star in the new Republican Party. In 1860 the Republicans devised a scheme in which Henry S. Lane would be the candidate for governor, while Morton ran for lieutenant governor. If the Republicans won a majority in the legislature, Lane would resign and be elected to the U.S. Senate and Morton would become governor. The plan worked. Lane resigned after two days in office and Morton took the governor's chair on January 16, 1861.

The national crisis set the context for his governorship, and Morton responded with great energy and confidence. He became one of Lincoln's strongest allies at the state level, constantly defending the president against criticism from Democrats. A dedicated supporter of the war effort, Morton remained zealous for the cause during the darkest days of the conflict. His support for the Union and Lincoln became the stuff of legend. Morton was an aggressive recruiter of soldiers, and his efforts resulted in Indiana ranking second in the number of troops contributed to the Northern armies. Often using creative accounting and ingenuity in procurement, Morton became the "Soldiers' Friend" by working with the Indiana Sanitary Commission, churches, and women's groups to keep the troops supplied.

Indiana Democrats took advantage of battlefield losses and war weariness to win control of the state legislature in the elections of 1862. Peace Democrats critiqued Republican policies by pointing to the loss of constitutional rights, denouncing emancipation, and attacking the growing power of the national government. They tried to appoint a military board to control the state militia and finances, which would effectively take away the governor's executive power. To prevent that, the Republicans bolted the session, and without a quorum the Democrats could not pass the bill. The legislative session ended without an appropriations bill, and many expected Morton to call a special session.

Instead Morton turned to one-man rule. For almost two years he did not call the legislature into session and ran the state himself. To pay expenses, he employed all of his administrative skills. He got some money from the War Department, borrowed on his own credit, raised funds from the county governments, and asked wealthy friends for help. He used technicalities in the law to shift funds around and found ways to get around the constitutional and legal obstacles to what he needed to do. His enemies denounced him as a dictator, but Morton plowed forward, centralizing power in Indiana in the state government and in the executive branch.

When criticism mounted Morton accused the Democrats who opposed him of treason, arguing that they were members of secret organizations that sympathized with the Confederacy and plotted to overthrow the government. Later historians doubted the existence of such groups (or at least thought that Morton exaggerated their size and influence), but the accusations resonated in a state where many citizens had Southern roots. Treason trials before a military tribunal confirmed Morton's fears and bolstered his reputation. More important,

Morgan's Raid raised the specter of a Confederate invasion of Indiana and rallied flagging support for the war.

After the war Morton spent time in Europe, where he went to recover from a stroke in the fall of 1865. In 1867 he was elected to the U.S. Senate, and he was reelected in 1873. Morton became a staunch supporter of the Radical Republicans, promoting rights for African Americans with his work on behalf of the Reconstruction Amendments to the Constitution. A contender for the party's nomination for the presidency in 1876, Morton eventually helped decide the election in favor of Rutherford B. Hayes, serving on the Electoral Commission that settled the disputed contest by giving the Republican the victory over Democrat Samuel J. Tilden, who had won the popular vote. Morton died after suffering another stroke in 1877.

—A. James Fuller

BIBLIOGRAPHY

Foulke, William Dudley. *Life of Oliver P. Morton, Including His Important Speeches.* Indianapolis: Bowen-Merrill Company, 1898.

French, William M. *Life, Speeches, State Papers and Public Services of Gov. Oliver P. Morton.* Cincinnati: Moore, Wilstach, and Baldwin, 1866.

Green, Michael S. *Freedom, Union, and Power: Lincoln and His Party during the Civil War.* New York: Fordham University Press, 2004.

Runden, Ed. "Oliver P. Morton." In *The Governors of Indiana,* edited by Linda C. Gugin and James E. St. Clair. Indianapolis: Indiana Historical Society, 2006.

Towne, Steven E. "Scorched Earth or Fertile Ground: Indiana in the Civil War, 1861–1865." In *The State of Indiana History 2000: Papers Presented at the Indiana Historical Society's Grand Opening,* edited by Robert M. Taylor Jr. Indianapolis: Indiana Historical Society, 2001.

N

National Banking Act of 1863

Originally titled the National Currency Act, the National Banking Act of 1863 was designed to transform the banking sector in the United States into a more secure and centralized system that could facilitate a market for government bonds. The banking system in the United States prior to the act was one in which counterfeit banknotes circulated and charter applications were determined by the state legislatures, which led to rampant bribery and inefficiency. The National Banking Act was an attempt to remove these characteristics and promote commerce through a sound financial system. The act also continued Lincoln's movement toward establishment of a national currency for the United States.

The act formally established a Comptroller of the Currency, which would oversee and audit all national banks. National banks were required to maintain a level of paid-in capital, a feature not standard among the state banking systems. The capital requirements were tied to the population of the town where the bank was located: $50,000 if less than 6,000 people, $100,000 if between 6,000 and 50,000 people, and $200,000 for towns with a population over 50,000. At least one-third of this capital had to be held in U.S. Treasury bonds. National banks could issue their own banknotes at 90 percent of the total face value of the Treasury bonds).

The act was passed in February 1863, and conversion of existing state banks to national banks was voluntary. However, many state banks were reluctant to trade their state charters for a new system of regulations that were much more stringent. Initially the act was unsuccessful in generating the desired large number of national banks. To encourage more state banks to apply for national bank charters, Lincoln signed a revision of the act into law in June 1864. The revision imposed a 2 percent tax on all banknotes issued by state banks. When this did not encourage the creation of more national banks, the tax was raised to 10 percent in March 1865.

The National Banking Act produced three main outcomes: the establishment of a national currency, a federal chartering system for banks, and the financing of the Civil War for the Union. The main goal was a national currency, which Lincoln had begun working toward with the Legal Tender Act of 1862. Prior to the National Banking Act, circulating currency in the United States consisted mainly of notes issued by state banks. By 1860 there were more than 10,000 types of these notes in circulation. Although many were issued by banks that were financially sound, many were also issued by banks of questionable soundness. If a bank failed after it issued notes, then those notes became worthless, as there was no institution that would convert them to specie. Additionally there were continual efforts to counterfeit banknotes. As a result, the notes often traded at a discount.

To create a more stable national currency the acts, as previously mentioned, instituted a tax on all state bank–issued notes. The impact of the tax was large, and by 1870 there were virtually no state banknotes in circulation. After the act, only national banks could issue banknotes. Besides being backed by U.S. Treasury securities they had a uniform format, which made it easier to judge authenticity. These national banknotes solved the major problems that plagued the fractured state banknote market: the difficulty of identifying counterfeit notes and the questionable soundness of their financial backing.

A second effect of the National Banking Act was the creation of a national chartering system for banks. Each state had control over issuance of its own state bank charters, and therefore the conditions for entry into the banking industry varied from state to state. Many states required approval by the state legislature. This format created the incentive for bribery, either to restrict entrance of new banks or to promote a new bank in the interest of someone willing to pay for the charter. The problem led to the adoption of "free banking" laws, starting in Michigan in 1830. Under this system, banking applications were developed that contained standard requirements to be met to obtain a charter. This removed the incentives for bribery and resulted in a sounder method for introducing banks. In effect, the National Banking Acts formed a federal policy for free banking extending to all the states. By 1868, a mere four years after Lincoln's revisions to the original act, the number of state banks had plunged to 16 percent of the number in 1864, and these banks held only 9 percent of all bank-held assets in the United States. The audits performed by the Comptroller of the Currency placed national banks under greater oversight than many of the state banking systems had. In the event of failure of a national bank, the paid-in capital was sold off, and those who held the bank's notes were reimbursed for their value.

The third effect of the National Banking Acts was the funding of the Civil War for the Union. Every bank with a national charter had to hold one-third of its paid-up capital in U.S. Treasury bonds. This solved the problem of an underdeveloped bond market that had hobbled the financing of the war effort. In essence, the National Banking Act required national banks to help fund the Union's costs. When national banks bought the Treasury bonds, they were deposited with the Comptroller of the Currency. In return the bank was issued national banknotes, which were then lent to borrowers and entered circulation. By the war's end in April 1865 more than $123 million in national banknotes was in circulation, all backed by U.S. Treasury bonds.

Overall, the National Banking Act of 1863 continued Abraham Lincoln's movement toward a unified banking system and a national currency. The problems of corrupt state chartering systems, unstable state banking systems, and discounted state banknotes were no longer impediments to national commerce. Furthermore, the capital and banknote structure of the new national banks provided the necessary funding for the Civil War, which allowed the Union to avoid relying on heavy taxation or inflation, as occurred in the Confederacy.

—PATRICK VAN HORN

BIBLIOGRAPHY

Atack, Jeremy, and Peter Passell. *A New Economic View of American History: From Colonial Times to 1940.* New York: Norton, 1994.

Hughes, Jonathan, and Louis P. Cain. *American Economic History.* New York: Pearson, 2007.

Knox, John J. *A History of Banking in the United States.* New York: Bradford Rhodes and Co., 1900.

National Union Party

When the Confederates fired on Fort Sumter on April 12, 1861, it led to a surge of patriotism in the North, but the defeat at the First Battle of Bull Run, on July 21, 1861, dampened political unity, as it became apparent that the war would not end quickly. In fall 1861 several state Republican Party organizations, responding to the nation's long-standing hostility toward political parties, particularly during time of war, worked with Democrats to create "fusion" tickets of pro-war candidates running as the Union Party. Union Party platforms stressed patriotism and ignored most of the economic and social issues that divided the two regular parties. President Abraham Lincoln used military commissions and patronage to promote fusionism and collaboration with pro-war Democrats. In fall 1861 Union Party tickets won critical races in Ohio, Rhode Island, and New York. Throughout the war, the Union Party ran strongly in the slaveholding Border States of Kentucky, Maryland, and Missouri.

Fusion appealed less to Democrats in 1862 because war weariness, emancipation, the tariff, and civil liberties provided them with strong antiadministration issues. In addition, Democrats disliked Republican domination of the fusion movement. Fusion revived in 1863 because of the increasing power of the peace

A campaign banner for Republican presidential candidate Abraham Lincoln and his running mate, Andrew Johnson. The National Union Party won the election of 1864 in a landslide, and Lincoln received 55 percent of the popular vote.

Source: Library of Congress

Democrats, who opposed not only Lincoln but also the pro-war faction within their own party.

President Lincoln was alarmed by the 1862 electoral successes of the Democrats. The fusion rebound of 1863 showed that the he would have a better chance of winning re-election by running on the broadest theme possible, patriotism, on a National Union Party ticket. By focusing on the war, the National Union Party donned a moderate mantle and reached beyond the strictly ideological and sectional basis of the Republican Party of 1860 to appeal to pro-war Democrats and Border State voters. The regular Republican Party provided almost all of the state-level apparatus of the National Union Party. Few regular party leaders objected to assuming the new name, as they understood it was a good electoral strategy.

Lincoln's biggest headache in forming a National Union Party came from Radical Republicans who thought the president was an incompetent war leader and weak on securing rights for freedmen. At the end of May 1864 a band of Radicals gathered in Cleveland, Ohio, and nominated General John C. Frémont for the presidency.

In the first week of June 1864 the National Union Party held its convention. In keeping with the Unionist message, they gathered in Baltimore, Maryland, a Border State. Robert Breckenridge, a Presbyterian minister from Kentucky who had sons serving on both sides of the conflict, acted as the temporary chairman. The delegates nominated Lincoln for president without opposition. When attention turned to selecting a vice president, several candidates received consideration. President Lincoln did not express a preference for a particular individual, but it was assumed that the incumbent, Hannibal Hamlin of Maine, would be replaced by a pro-war Democrat. After some deliberation, the convention nominated Andrew Johnson of Tennessee for the second position on the ticket. As a Democrat, governor, and the only senator from a seceding state to remain loyal, Johnson poignantly personified the message of the National Union Party. Lincoln was happy with the choice of his running mate.

The National Union Party platform called for solidifying the freedom of the slaves with a constitutional amendment and continued prosecution of the war without compromise. It expressed approval of the Lincoln administration and the armed forces and also contained a strong statement asserting the Monroe Doctrine. It expressed support for the new national banking system, wounded veterans, immigration, and the transcontinental railroad. Trusting in the wisdom of the party leaders to craft the best platform to win the election, Lincoln made only a single demand, a plank calling for a constitutional amendment guaranteeing the freedom of the slaves.

This platform made peace with the Radicals by calling for the Thirteenth Amendment and appealed to the normally Democratic-leaning immigrant population of the urban North. Overall the platform was solidly nationalistic. There was no mention of the controversial topics of tariffs or reconstruction, although the latter would become a hotly debated issue during the summer of 1864.

The National Union Party gained greater appeal when the Democratic Party nominated General George McClellan on a platform that called for ending the war. Three weeks after the Democratic convention, Frémont ended his candidacy, and the remaining Radicals rallied to the National Union Party.

The National Union Party won the election of 1864 in a landslide, carrying all the states except for New Jersey, Delaware, and Kentucky. Abraham Lincoln received 55 percent of the popular vote. He did especially well with soldiers, gaining nearly 80 percent of their vote.

After Lincoln's assassination, President Andrew Johnson continued to claim affiliation with the National Union Party. Although the political situation had changed, Johnson continued to use the 1864 National Union Party platform as his guide and argued that he could go no further than what he had been elected to do. Johnson tried to reshape the National Union Party into a conservative, Democratic-leaning organization to promote his failed plan of reconstruction, but this proved impossible. Northern Democrats and Southerners of all persuasions refused to join what once had been the party of Lincoln. After Johnson's rebuke in the midterm elections of 1866 the National Union Party faded into history.

See also *Campaign of 1864, Presidential; Republican Party*

—Gregory J. Dehler

BIBLIOGRAPHY

Green, Michael S. *Freedom, Union, and Power: Lincoln and His Party during the Civil War.* New York: Fordham University Press, 2004.

Hyman, Harold M. "The Election of 1864." In *History of American Presidential Elections, 1789–1968,* vol 2., edited by Arthur Schlesinger Jr., 1155–1244. New York: McGraw-Hill, 1971.

Long, David E. *The Jewel of Liberty: Abraham Lincoln's Re-Election and the End of Slavery.* Mechanicsburg, Pa.: Stackpole, 1994.

Neely, Mark E., Jr. *The Union Divided: Party Conflict in the Civil War North.* Cambridge: Harvard University Press, 2002.

Paludan, Phillip S. *A People's Contest: The United States Civil War, 1861–1865.* 2nd ed. Lawrence: University Press of Kansas, 1996.

Rawley, James A. *The Politics of Union: Northern Politics during the Civil War.* Lincoln: University of Nebraska Press, 1980.

Smith, I.P. *No Party Now: Politics in the Civil War North.* New York: Oxford University Press, 2007.

Zornow, William F. *Lincoln and the Party Divided.* Norman: University of Oklahoma Press, 1954.

New Salem, Illinois

New Salem, Abraham Lincoln's home in Illinois from 1831 to 1837, was a small village located on the Sangamon River. It was founded in 1829, and about twenty-five families lived there at its peak.

Denton Offutt (ca. 1803–ca. 1860), a young entrepreneur from Kentucky, saw potential in New Salem. Like its founders, he believed that riverboats were destined to navigate the Sangamon River. In 1831 he made arrangements to rent the local sawmill and gristmill; he also opened a general store in the village. Offutt recruited Lincoln, then just a twenty-two-year-old laborer, who had recently taken a flatboat down the Mississippi River to New Orleans for him, to run the mill and serve as the "chief and head clerk" in the store. Within a year the store closed and Offutt fled town, but Lincoln remained in the village.

The people of New Salem embraced Lincoln. He earned the respect of the roughest frontiersmen when he wrestled local strongman Jack Armstrong (ca. 1803–ca. 1857), but the intellectuals were also impressed with him. Schoolteacher Mentor Graham (1800–1886) began teaching Lincoln the finer points of "English grammar," and village philosopher Jack Kelso introduced him to the works of William Shakespeare and Robert Burns. Others encouraged him to join the local debating club, and when Lincoln showed an interest in studying law, the local justice of the peace invited him to attend court sessions.

By 1832 the villagers encouraged Lincoln to run for a seat in the Illinois state legislature. In addition to being charismatic, he had experience as a flatboatman and understood the importance of river trade. The villagers hoped he might be able to persuade the legislature to help improve the Sangamon River. On March 15, 1832, Lincoln officially announced his candidacy for the legislature and declared his platform in an article published by the *Sangamon Journal.* Though he was in favor of limiting usury and promoting education, Lincoln devoted the majority of his address to the improvement of the Sangamon River. Unfortunately Lincoln's service in the Black Hawk War prevented him from mounting an effective campaign. Even though he was not elected, however, he proudly recalled that he carried his local precinct 277 to 7.

When Lincoln returned to the village, he partnered with William F. Berry and opened a general store of his own, but the store soon "winked out," leaving him out of work and heavily in debt. Shortly thereafter, Lincoln was appointed postmaster of New Salem and deputy surveyor of Sangamon County.

Lincoln again ran for the legislature in 1834, and this time he succeeded. He was reelected in 1836, 1838, and 1840. Lincoln's election signaled the beginning of the end of his time in New Salem, however. Encouraged by his colleagues in the legislature, Lincoln earned his law license in 1837 and entered into a law partnership with fellow Whig John Todd Stuart (1807–1885). On April 15, 1837, Lincoln officially left New Salem and settled in Springfield.

The Sangamon River never proved navigable, and New Salem died shortly after Lincoln left. Nonetheless, interest in the village grew after William H. Herndon (1818–1891) published his long-awaited Lincoln biography, which featured interviews with several old residents, as well as the Ann Rutledge (1813–1835) love story.

By the turn of the century, a new generation of boosters sought to unlock New Salem's rich potential. In 1902 T.G. Onstott predicted that New Salem was destined to become the "Mount Vernon of the West." Four years later, William Randolph Hearst (1863–1951) delivered a lecture before the Old Salem Chautauqua and toured the deserted village. He ended up purchasing sixty-two acres that encompassed the village, for $11,000, and conveyed it to the Chautauqua Association in trust. By 1919 the Illinois legislature not only agreed to take over the site but promised to restore all of the buildings that were there in Lincoln's time. Restoration work began in earnest in 1932. Lincoln's New Salem was added to the National Register of Historic Places in 1972. In 2006 approximately 600,000 people visited the park, which consists of the reconstructed village and two hundred campsites.

—Samuel P. Wheeler

BIBLIOGRAPHY

Thomas, Benjamin P. *Lincoln's New Salem.* Springfield, Illinois: Abraham Lincoln Association, 1934.

Winkle, Kenneth J. *The Young Eagle: The Rise of Abraham Lincoln.* Dallas: Taylor Trade Publishing, 2001.

New York Tribune

Founded by Horace Greeley in 1841, the *New York Tribune* became one of the most important Republican Party newspapers in the 1850s and 1860s. Greeley was a committed abolitionist and a significant player in Republican politics, both for his relations with party leaders and for his ability to shape public opinion within the party and outside it.

Greeley was the quintessential nineteenth-century reformer. In addition to abolition, Greeley advocated women's rights, an end to capital punishment, prison reform, vegetarianism, and world peace while opposing liquor, tobacco, and all sorts of personal immorality. By 1860 his paper, which came out as a daily, weekly, and semiweekly, had a combined circulation of nearly 300,000 and was the leading Republican paper. In addition to the newspaper, the *Tribune* published political pamphlets, especially during elections. In 1860, for example, the *Tribune* published a 104-page pamphlet containing Supreme Court chief justice Roger Taney's opinion in the *Dred Scott* case and justice Benjamin R. Curtis's stinging dissent. That year the *Tribune* also published a pamphlet version of the *Lemmon Slave Case,* in which the New York Court of Appeals held that a slave voluntarily brought to the state became instantly free, even if the master was merely changing ships in New York harbor. Many Republicans feared that the U.S. Supreme Court would reverse that decision, thus allowing slavery in the North.

The *Tribune* was well known for excellent reporting, often sending its own reporters to the scene of an event rather than relying on stories by people working for local papers. It was also famous for Greeley's biting editorials. The paper declared on March 7, 1857, for instance, that Chief Justice's Taney's opinion in *Dred Scott v. Sandford* was "entitled to just so much moral weight as would be the judgment of a majority of those congregated in any Washington bar-room. It is a dictum prescribed by the stump to the bench—the Bowie-knife sticking in the stump ready for instant use. If needed."

The *Tribune* shaped itself as the national voice of the Republican Party, but it was not always sensitive to local issues. In December 1857, for example, Abraham Lincoln complained of the *Tribune*'s "constant eulogizing, and admiring, and magnifying" editorials about Sen. Stephen A. Douglas, whom Lincoln was about to challenge in the Senate race. Lincoln wondered if the *Tribune* "concluded that the republican cause, generally can be promoted by sacraficing [sic] us here in Illinois?" He noted that at the moment all Republicans in the state were opposed to Douglas, but recognizing the strength of the New York paper, he

The field of presidential candidates and their supporters is parodied in this editorial cartoon from the 1860 campaign. Lincoln has mounted a balance beam constructed of wooden rails, whose crossbar represents the Republican nomination, which Lincoln won in large part due to the support of Horace Greeley, founder of the *New York Tribune*.

Source: Library of Congress

feared "if the Tribune continues to din his praises into the ears of its five or ten thousand republican readers in Illinois, it is more than can be hoped that all will stand firm." Eventually the paper supported Lincoln in his losing effort against Douglas. The *Tribune* also published an early version of Lincoln's Cooper Union speech as "Tribune Tracts No. 4." When correspondents asked for copies of the speech, Lincoln directed them to the *Tribune* offices.

Despite Greeley's constant support for reform, the *Tribune* initially supported Edward Bates for the 1860 Republican presidential nomination and opposed New York's favorite son, William H. Seward, as too radical. When Lincoln won the nomination the *Tribune* campaigned heavily for him.

When the war began the *Tribune* firmly supported the administration yet at the same time criticized it for not moving faster on slavery or against the Confederacy. The *Tribune* supported conscription and kept its offices open during the draft riots in 1863.

The most important interaction between Lincoln and the *Tribune* came in August 1862. On August 20 the *Tribune* printed an editorial titled "A Prayer for Twenty Millions," urging Lincoln to end slavery. The editorial complained that Lincoln was overly influenced by "certain fossil politicians hailing from the Border Slave States" and urged him to rigidly enforce "the emancipating provisions of the new [Second] Confiscation Act." The editorial declared "that what an immense majority of the Loyal Millions of your countrymen require of you is a frank, declared, unqualified, ungrudging execution of the laws of the land."

Lincoln responded with a letter to the editor, something that was unprecedented in the history of the presidency. By this time Lincoln had already drafted the Preliminary Emancipation Proclamation and was waiting for the appropriate time— a military victory in a major battle—to announce his intention to end slavery. He took advantage of the *Tribune* editorial to help prepare the American people for what was coming. His letter was written on August 22, exactly a month before he would issue the Preliminary Emancipation Proclamation, although he could not know that at the time. Lincoln had in fact decided that he no longer needed to placate the "fossil politicians" from Kentucky and Missouri, but he did need to prepare them, and the rest of the American people, for his monumental plan, which was far greater than merely implanting the confiscation act. Thus, he wrote in the *Tribune*:

> *I would save the Union. I would save it the shortest way under the Constitution. The sooner the national authority can be restored; the nearer the Union will be "the Union as it was." If there be those who would not save the Union, unless they could at the same time save slavery, I do not agree with them. If there be those who would not save the Union unless they could at the same time destroy slavery, I do not agree with them. My paramount object in this struggle is to save the Union, and is not either to save or to destroy slavery. If I could save the Union without freeing any slave I would do it, and if I could save it by freeing all the slaves I would do it; and if I could save it by freeing some and leaving others alone I would also do that. What I do about slavery, and the colored race, I do because I believe it helps to save the Union; and what I forbear, I forbear because I do not believe it would help to save the Union. I shall do less whenever I shall believe what I am doing hurts the cause, and I shall do more whenever I shall believe doing more will help the cause. I shall try to correct errors when shown to be errors; and I shall adopt new views so fast as they shall appear to be true views.*
>
> *I have here stated my purpose according to my view of official duty; and I intend no modification of my oft-expressed personal wish that all men everywhere could be free.*

Critics of Lincoln often use this letter to argue that he had little interest in emancipation, but others feel that that analysis does not hold up when the letter is read in the context of the Greeley editorial and the decision, already made, to issue the Emancipation Proclamation.

For the rest of the war the *Tribune* continued to support Lincoln, even though Greeley was personally unhappy with his pace toward emancipation and briefly considered supporting an opposition candidate within the party in 1864. At the same time the paper pushed for victory, emancipation, and blacks rights— issues on which Lincoln agreed with it, even when they required more deft political responses than the paper and its editor wanted.

See also *Greeley, Horace*

—PAUL FINKELMAN

BIBLIOGRAPHY

Basler, Roy P., ed. *Collected Works of Abraham Lincoln.* 7 vols. New Brunswick, N.J.: Rutgers University Press, 1953.

Greeley, Horace. *Recollections of a Busy Life.* New York: J.B. Ford and Company, 1868.

Schulze, Suzanne. *Horace Greeley: A Bio-Bibliography.* Westport, Conn.: Greenwood Press, 1992.

Van Deusen, Glyndon G. *Horace Greeley: Nineteenth-Century Crusader.* Philadelphia: University of Pennsylvania Press, 1953.

Nicolay, John G.

Born in Germany, John G. Nicolay (1832–1901) came to the United States with his family at the age of six. They settled first in Cincinnati, then moved to Indiana, then to Missouri, and finally to Illinois. His mother died around 1842, shortly after the family had settled in Pike County, Illinois. His father passed away in 1846. Two years later John Nicolay obtained a job in the office of the *Pittsfield Pike County Free Press,* soon rising to the editorship. He became active in the Illinois Republican Party and in 1856 befriended its rising star, Abraham Lincoln.

He soon moved to Springfield, where he clerked for Ozias M. Hatch, secretary of state for Illinois and a friend of Lincoln's. At Hatch's office, which served as a kind of Republican Party headquarters, young Nicolay often saw Lincoln, who came to regard the young man highly. In 1858 he recommended Nicolay to Horace Greeley as a correspondent, calling him "entirely trust-worthy." A year later, Lincoln had Nicolay deliver to a publisher in Ohio his carefully prepared scrapbook of the 1858 debates with Stephen A. Douglas. When Lincoln won the presidential nomination in May 1860, he hired Nicolay as his personal secretary and after the election kept him on as his principal White House secretary.

Not everyone approved of the choice. Some thought Nicolay lacked sufficient polish and savoir faire. In fact, at the White House Nicolay became known as "the bulldog in the anteroom," with a disposition "sour and crusty." A New Yorker complained to the president early in his first term, "If the stories I hear about Nicolay...are true, you ought to dismiss him. If he is sick, he has a right to be cross and ungentlemanly in his deportment, but not otherwise. People say he is very disagreeable and uncivil." Alexander K. McClure described Lincoln's principal secretary as "a good mechanical, routine clerk" but whose "removal was earnestly pressed upon Lincoln on more than one occasion because of his want of tact and fitness for his trust." McClure claimed that "only the proverbial kindness of Lincoln saved him from dismissal."

Noah Brooks, a California journalist, deemed Nicolay a "grim Cerberus of Teutonic descent who guards the last door which opens into the awful presence." Nicolay, in Brooks's view, "has a very unhappy time of it answering the impatient demands of the gathering, growing crowd of applicants which obstructs passage, hall and ante-room." Brooks recommended that "an inside guardian of affable address, as well as flintiness of face," be "placed on duty…where the people come almost in actual contact with the great man within, whom they learn to love or dislike, according to their treatment by his underlings." Lincoln, Brooks noted, "is affable and kind, but his immediate subordinates are snobby and unpopular."

Other observers were more charitable. According to John Russell Young, a journalist who frequently observed Nicolay during the Civil War, the young man from Pike County "had the close, methodical, silent German way about him. Scrupulous, polite, calm, obliging, with the gift of hearing other people talk; coming and going about the Capitol like a shadow; with the soft, sad smile that seemed to come only from the eyes; prompt as lightning to take a hint or an idea; one upon whom a suggestion was never lost, and if it meant a personal service, sure of the prompt, spontaneous return." Young thought Nicolay had "great powers of application" and "endurance." Withal, he was a "man without excitements or emotions, never saying anything worth quoting, and in that regard invaluable as a private secretary; absorbed in the President, and seeing that the Executive business was well done."

William O. Stoddard, who served as an assistant personal secretary during the Civil War, gave a balanced assessment of Nicolay in the White House: "A fair French and German scholar, with some ability as a writer and much natural acuteness, he nevertheless—thanks to a dyspeptic tendency—had developed an artificial manner the reverse of 'popular,' and could say 'no' about as disagreeably as any man I ever knew." But, Stoddard added, Nicolay served Lincoln well: "That…for which we all respected him, which was his chief qualification for the very important post he occupied, was his devotion to the President and his incorruptible honesty Lincoln-ward." Nicolay "measured all things and all men by their relations to the President, and was of incalculable service in fending off much that would have been unnecessary labor and exhaustion to his overworked patron." Stoddard believed that Nicolay "deserves the thanks of all who loved Mr. Lincoln" and observed that "people who do not like him—because they cannot use him, perhaps—say he is sour and crusty, and it is a grand good thing, then, that he is. If you will sit in that chair [Nicolay's] a month or so, you will see what has become of any easy good-nature you sat down with."

Stoddard concluded that Lincoln "showed his good judgment of men when he put Mr. Nicolay just where he is, with a kind and amount of authority which it is not easy to describe." Stoddard acknowledged that Nicolay "was much better qualified" for the secretary's job than he himself was: Nicolay "was older, more experienced, harder, had a worse temper, and was decidedly German in his manner of telling men what he thought of them. I was more reticent."

On occasion Nicolay went on troubleshooting and fact-finding missions for the president, which he handled with characteristic efficiency.

Nicolay did not get along with the First Lady, who resented the young secretary for resisting her schemes to defraud the government. For the same reason, she disliked John Hay, a young man who served as Nicolay's principal assistant.

After the war, Nicolay and Hay wrote a ten-volume biography of Lincoln, which appeared in 1890, and edited two volumes of the president's letters, speeches, and other papers.

See also *Hay, John*

—MICHAEL BURLINGAME

BIBLIOGRAPHY

Burlingame, Michael. *Abraham Lincoln: The Observations of John G. Nicolay and John Hay.* Carbondale: Southern Illinois University Press, 2007.

_____. *An Oral History of Abraham Lincoln: John G. Nicolay's Interviews and Essays.* Carbondale: Southern Illinois University Press, 1996.

_____. *With Lincoln in the White House: Letters, Memoranda, and Other Writings of John G. Nicolay, 1860–1865.* Carbondale: Southern Illinois University Press, 2006.

Ninety-Day Volunteers

See *Volunteers, Ninety-Day*

Northwest Ordinance

On July 13, 1787, the Continental Congress enacted "An Ordinance for the Government of the Territory of the United States, North-West of the River Ohio," which provided for the orderly settlement of the territory to the north and west of the Ohio River (the present-day states of Ohio, Indiana, Illinois, Michigan, and Wisconsin, and a portion of Minnesota). The Northwest Ordinance, as it has come to be called, fundamentally altered the fledgling government's path and eventually became the template for turning most federal territories into states. The document included references to providing for freedom of religion, educational opportunities, and friendly relations with the Native Americans already occupying the newly opened territories. It also has received high praise for its provisional language regarding the prohibition of slavery. This latter point became a political tool for Abraham Lincoln in his struggle against division and slavery.

Ideas asserted in the Northwest Ordinance are believed to have been drafted by Thomas Jefferson, Manasseh Cutler, Rufus King, and Nathan Dane. The act included the outline for three phases of government. The first phase included provisions for the appointing of governors, judges, militia, and law enforcement officers. It also outlined the setting up of the legal codes and lower courts. The territory had to have more than five thousand free men living there before the second phase could begin. Once all of these stipulations were met, the second phase started.

The second phase provided for the arrangement of the legislature (two houses—a legislative council and a house of representatives) as well as the requirements for voting privileges in the territory. The ordinance declared a voter as an adult male who owned at least fifty acres of land. Once the second phase of conditions was met, the territory moved to the statehood process.

According to the ordinance a territory could apply for statehood after it contained more than sixty thousand residents. The residents then had to create a state constitution, to be submitted to the United States Congress. The ordinance outlined the requirements for the newly created state to include freedom of religion, trial by jury, educational opportunity, and the abolition of slavery.

The Northwest Ordinance figured greatly in Lincoln's political agenda. On October 16, 1854, Lincoln delivered a speech at Peoria that rebutted Sen. Stephen A. Douglas's stand on the Kansas-Nebraska Act. In the speech Lincoln objected strongly to the act and its repeal of the Missouri Compromise line delineating the geographical boundary for slavery. Lincoln referred to the nation's Founders and their interpretation of slavery via the Northwest Ordinance. In a country bitterly divided over slavery, Lincoln's reliance on the ordinance as a political authority firmly established his political agenda.

—Dawn P. Hutchins

BIBLIOGRAPHY

Duffey, Denis P. "The Northwest Ordinance as a Constitutional Document." In *Columbia Law Review* 95, no. 4 (May 1995): 929–968.

Finkelman, Paul. "Slavery and the Northwest Ordinance: A Study in Ambiguity." In *Journal of the Early Republic,* Winter 1986, 343–370.

———. "Evading the Ordinance: The Persistence of Bondage in Indiana and Illinois." In *Journal of the Early Republic* 9, no. 1 (Spring 1989): 21–51.

———. *Slavery and the Founders: Race and Liberty in the Age of Jefferson.* Armonk, N.Y.: M.E. Sharpe, 1996.

Hurt, R. Douglas. "Historians and the Northwest Ordinance." In *Western Historical Quarterly* 20, no. 3 (August 1989): 261–280.

Williams, Frederick D., ed. *The Northwest Ordinance: Essays on Its Formulation, Provisions, and Legacy.* East Lansing: Michigan State University Press, 1989.

Zarefsky, David. *Lincoln, Douglas, and Slavery: In the Crucible of Public Debate.* Chicago: University of Chicago Press, 1990.

O

Old Northwest

Lincoln was a product of the Old Northwest in his personal, professional, and political life. The region was derived from the Northwest Ordinance of 1787, and its territories would give rise to the states of Ohio, Indiana, Illinois, Michigan, Wisconsin, and Minnesota. The 1787 ordinance prohibited slavery in the territory, and the southernmost of the states that emerged—Ohio, Indiana, and Illinois—would be shaped by their status as free states that bordered the slave states of Virginia, Kentucky, and Missouri.

Lincoln was born in the slave state of Kentucky. His family moved to Indiana and then Illinois, leaving behind both irregular land titles and competition with slave labor. In his youth Lincoln lived the hard, rural agricultural life that characterized the states carved from the Old Northwest in the early decades of the nineteenth century. It was this life that he desired to leave behind when he embraced the economy of the greater Mississippi River Valley, piloting a flatboat down the river to New Orleans. When he moved to New Salem, Illinois, in 1831, he hoped to prosper in the new market town located on the Sangamon River. He worked in stores, ran for the state legislature on a platform of improving navigation of the river and local roads, and surveyed land to supplement his meager wages as postmaster. He was elected to the state legislature in 1834 as a Whig, and promoted economic development at the state capital, in Vandalia. Yet the market economy had left New Salem behind and so did Lincoln. In the 1836–1837 legislative term, Lincoln helped draft legislation that relocated the state capital to Springfield. Lincoln, attuned to the promise of economic development and party politics, gained admission to the bar and moved to the Illinois state capital.

The states of the Old Northwest were crucial to Lincoln's political career and eventual election in 1860. As a Whig, Lincoln operated in a Democratic state throughout the 1840s and the early 1850s, winning a single term in the U.S. House of Representatives. Following passage of the Kansas-Nebraska Act, Lincoln became a prime architect of the Republican Party in Illinois. He succeeded in holding together radicals in the rapidly growing lake city of Chicago and the state's more conservative members in the southern counties. At the same time, his leadership kept nativists and naturalized German immigrants within party ranks. When he challenged Stephen A. Douglas for the Senate in 1858, the candidates' debates garnered national attention. In 1859 Lincoln toured the North giving campaign speeches for Republicans. In Ohio, Wisconsin, and Kansas, he highlighted the differences between the slave South and the free labor of the North, identifying the Old Northwest with the virtues of free labor and seeing the region as rife with opportunity. He cited his own history as an example of this opportunity and argued that it was the responsibility of the federal government to protect the interests of free labor in the territories.

When he returned to Illinois, Lincoln continued to build his political network and increase Republican support throughout the middle western states. At the same time, he positioned himself for a possible presidential nomination. That the presidency was even a possibility for Lincoln was the result of his careful political maneuverings and the solid base of support he enjoyed in Illinois. In preparation, Lincoln's loyal supporters secured Chicago as the site of the Republican National Convention of 1860. Lincoln managed the state's delegates and gained their unanimous support. From this foundation, Lincoln was able to garner the unanimous support of Indiana's delegation and gathered the support of Ohio's splintered delegation as well. From the solid political foundation laid in the Middle West, Lincoln was able to defeat front-runner William Seward on the third ballot.

In his presidential leadership Lincoln drew on practical political experience and life in the diverse region of the Middle West. His experience balancing diverse factions within his own state and party contributed to Lincoln's image as a moderate Republican, neither a radical desiring to abolish slavery nor a conservative willing to accede to a compromise on slavery's expansion. As a lawyer and a solid member of the middle class Lincoln embodied the upward mobility that appealed to Republicans and residents of the growing and expanding urban West. He also possessed an unremarkable, hardscrabble and rural background that gave him an affinity with small farmers and rural Northerners. In the election of 1860 Lincoln swept all of the Old Northwest states, as well as Pennsylvania and New England. He garnered support in upstate New York as well, enabling Republicans to overcome Democratic strength in New York City. Indeed, during the Civil War, as dissent and disaffection festered in the middle western states, Lincoln's solid base of political support and adroit use of politicians and governors in the Old Northwest states allowed the president and his party to withstand considerable Democratic assaults in 1862 and 1863 and to execute federal mobilization and conscription, providing the manpower necessary to achieve military victory.

See also *Northwest Ordinance*

—CHRISTINE DEE

BIBLIOGRAPHY

Carwardine, Richard. *Lincoln: A Life of Purpose and Power.* Harlow, UK: Pearson Longman, 2003.

Donald. David Herbert. *Lincoln.* New York: Simon and Schuster, 1995.

Wilson, Douglas L. *Honor's Voice: The Transformation of Abraham Lincoln.* New York: Knopf, 1998.

Wilson, Douglas L., and Rodney O. Davis, eds. *Herndon's Informants: Letters, Interviews, and Statements about Abraham Lincoln.* Urbana: University of Illinois Press, 1998.

Winkle, Kenneth. "'The Great Body of the Republic': Abraham Lincoln and the Idea of a Middle West." In *The Identity of the American Midwest: Essays in Regional History,* edited by Andrew R.L. Cayton and Susan E. Gray. Bloomington: Indiana University Press, 2001.

Order of Retaliation

On July 30, 1863, President Abraham Lincoln issued the Order of Retaliation in response to Confederate executions of African American soldiers and threats against their white officers who were captured while serving in the United States Army.

As early as August 1862, before the enlistment of black soldiers had even been officially sanctioned by the U.S. government, the Confederate army issued a peremptory general order encouraging the "execution as a felon" of any white officer commanding black troops. In November 1862 Confederate president Jefferson Davis and secretary of war James A. Seddon approved the execution of four black soldiers whom Confederate troops had taken prisoner in South Carolina. They hoped to set an example.

In his Christmas Eve Declaration issued one month later, President Davis announced that any African American soldiers subsequently taken prisoner would be sold into slavery and that their white commanding officers would face execution. Davis went further in his January 12, 1863, message to the Confederate Congress, declaring the Emancipation Proclamation (issued by Lincoln on January 1, 1863) "the most execrable measure in the history of guilty man." He said that all captured Union officers would be executed as "criminals engaged in inciting servile insurrection."

In formulating a response to Davis, Abraham Lincoln was politically constrained in part by the potential reaction of non-abolitionist Northerners to retaliation against white soldiers, over and above their ongoing reluctance about the enlistment of black soldiers. Nevertheless, on July 30, 1863, Lincoln declared in his Order of Retaliation that Davis's edicts were "a relapse into barbarism and a crime against the civilization of the age." He went on to order that "for every soldier of the United States killed in violation of the laws of war, a rebel soldier shall be executed; and for every one enslaved by the enemy or sold into slavery, a rebel soldier shall be placed at hard labor on the public works and continued at such labor until the other shall be released and receive the treatment due to a prisoner of war."

The Order of Retaliation did little to halt sporadic atrocities. Ample evidence shows that black soldiers and their white officers were informally executed by their Confederate captors on numerous occasions. But the order would finally be put to the test after the most notorious controversy of the war involving black soldiers. In April 1864 Confederate forces under General Nathan Bedford Forrest, at the Battle of Fort Pillow in Tennessee, were reported to have massacred as many as 200 African American soldiers—along with some of their white comrades—who had attempted to surrender.

The Confederates, after first celebrating the lopsided victory—the Confederate Congress voted thanks to Forrest for the campaign—soon denied that a massacre had taken place. Lincoln's cabinet pondered a response, ultimately deciding to punish only those members of Forrest's command who might be captured and warn the Confederacy that imprisoned Southern officers would be set aside as hostages to ensure against another such incident—measures they apparently never carried out. Meanwhile the U.S. Congress launched an investigation by a subcommittee of the Joint Committee on the Conduct of the War, which was dominated by Radical Republicans. They wasted little time in denouncing Lincoln, who they felt was soft on slavery and abolition, for hesitancy in seeking revenge.

Lincoln apparently outlined a possible stance toward the rebels in a letter to secretary of war Edwin Stanton that he never sent. He also ordered Forrest to appear in federal court, an action he surely knew to be futile. Insight into Lincoln's personal struggle with this issue is revealed by a meeting he had with the black abolitionist Frederick Douglass, who pushed for a reprisal to the Fort Pillow killings. Lincoln said of retaliation, "It's a terrible remedy. Once begun, I don't know where it would end. If I could punish the soldiers who actually committed atrocities, I would do it. But hanging innocent men for the crimes of others is a revolting idea. I think—I hope—the threat of retaliation will convince the rebels to stop waging barbaric warfare." The question of retaliation was eventually overcome by events, as the public and Lincoln were increasingly distracted by General Ulysses S. Grant's highly successful Wilderness Campaign that put Confederate forces on the defensive in Virginia.

Practically speaking, the Fort Pillow incident caused a permanent end to prisoner exchanges, which had occurred sporadically throughout the war, but little more. Lincoln, caught in a political tempest with angry radicals on the one side and skeptical Northern whites on the other, took the moral high ground by not enforcing the Order of Retaliation. As he had said during the post–Fort Pillow cabinet meetings, "Blood cannot restore blood, and government should not act for revenge."

—David E. Arthur

BIBLIOGRAPHY

McPherson, James M. *Battle Cry of Freedom: The Civil War Era*. New York: Ballantine, 1988.

Oates, Stephen. *The Whirlwind of War: Voices of the Storm, 1861–1865*. New York: HarperCollins, 1999.

Ward, Andrew. *River Run Red: The Fort Pillow Massacre in the American Civil War*. New York: Viking, 2005.

Overland Campaign

The Overland Campaign (May 4–June 18, 1864) saw Ulysses S. Grant take on Robert E. Lee and the Army of Northern Virginia in the spring of 1864. At the end of seven weeks of marching and fighting, Grant managed to pin Lee against Richmond and Petersburg, Virginia, and inflict a high number of casualties but at great cost to his own army. For Northerners hoping for a quick knockout blow, the campaign proved a disappointment: its high cost fed war weariness in the North. However, Grant had wrested the initiative from Lee, retained it, inflicted great damage on his foe, and maneuvered him into a position where even Lee believed that the loss of Richmond was inevitable. Although Lincoln publicly claimed he was satisfied with the result, privately he wondered about the battlefield cost.

When Grant took over as general in chief in March 1864, he set aside an earlier plan that would have taken the war into North Carolina in favor of a multipronged approach against Lee, Richmond, and Confederate logistical infrastructure. One offensive would clear out southwestern Virginia and strike at Confederate resources there; a second drive would cut south through the Shenandoah Valley, depriving the Confederacy of a favored invasion route as well

Gen. Ulysses S. Grant examines a map held by Gen. George G. Meade in Massaponax Church, Va., in May 1864. Union and Confederate armies suffered terrible losses in the Overland Campaign, and Northern public opinion viewed it as a costly stalemate with no end in sight, an impression that might have proved fatal to Lincoln's chances for reelection.

Source: Library of Congress

as a supply source. The newly formed Army of the James would move along its namesake river, land between Richmond and Petersburg, and threaten Richmond while cutting it off from the Confederate heartland. Finally, the main Union field army, the Army of the Potomac, augmented by another infantry corps, would advance against Lee in central Virginia. If Lee turned south to save Richmond, the Army of the Potomac would fall upon his rear; if Lee decided to stand and fight, the Army of the James would compromise Richmond's defense and threaten to take the Confederate capital.

On May 4, Grant, Meade, and the augmented Army of the Potomac moved out, crossing the Rapidan and Rappahannock Rivers. Lee chose to engage Grant in the heavily wooded area known as the Wilderness. In two days of fighting (May 5–6) each army punished the other in a series of hard-fought clashes. Union losses totaled 17,666, and Confederate casualties exceeded 11,000—approximately the same number of losses each side had suffered a year earlier at Chancellorsville. Grant pressed southward once more, and Lee barely beat him to the critical crossroads at Spotsylvania Court House, where for the next two weeks (May 8–21) Grant sought weaknesses in Lee's fortified lines. Twice he came close to achieving a breakthrough.

At the beginning of the campaign Grant had sought to soothe Lincoln's anxieties, telling a newspaper correspondent bound for Washington to assure the president that there would be "no turning back." On May 11, as he prepared to assault Lee's center at Spotsylvania (which resulted in what would become known later as the Bloody Angle), Grant reassured his civil superiors that he would "fight it out on this line if it takes all summer." Within days of that declaration, however, he learned that two of his supporting offensives, in the Shenandoah Valley and on the James River, had been thwarted and that it would be left to the Army of the Potomac to shoulder the main burden. Thus Grant decided to slide once more around Lee's right toward Richmond. The two armies confronted each other along the North Anna River (May 23–26), where Lee failed to spring what looked to be a trap. Extricating his forces from their precarious situation Grant slid around the Confederate right once more, and the two armies clashed at Cold Harbor, due east of Richmond. Grant, believing that Lee's army was on the point of collapse, ordered a frontal assault for June 2, but delays caused him to postpone the assault until the early morning of June 3. He left the details of planning the assault to the commander of the Army of the Potomac, George G. Meade. The June 3 assault was a bloody disaster, and although later accounts exaggerated the extent and cost of that setback, Grant concluded that it was time to turn to an alternative he had long contemplated. He decided to cross the James River to strike at Petersburg, south of Richmond. At best, by severing the supply links connecting Richmond to the rest of the Confederacy, Grant would isolate the city; at worst he would pin Lee down in a siege. The Confederate commander dreaded that prospect, observing that if Grant crossed the James, the resulting siege would make the evacuation of Richmond "a matter of time."

Union forces crossed the James and attacked Petersburg (June 15–18) but failed to crack the Confederate defenses, whereupon Grant settled down to lay siege to the city. The campaign had been a costly one for both sides, with Union forces suffering some 60,000 in total losses and the Confederates at least 33,000. The relentless combat had taken a toll on both armies. What Grant had been able to achieve militarily—the pinning of Lee—was somewhat nullified by the fact that Northern public opinion, which had entertained hopes of a quick and decisive battlefield triumph by the North's newest hero, saw the resulting siege as a costly stalemate with no end in sight. That impression might have proved fatal to Lincoln's chances for reelection.

Lincoln himself was unsure as to what to make of the campaign. Unlike other observers, he labored under no illusions about overwhelming the Confederates at a single stroke. As Grant commenced crossing the James, Lincoln informed him, "I begin to see it. You will succeed." The next week, however, when he visited Grant's headquarters at City Point, Virginia, he expressed the hope "that all may be accomplished with as little bloodshed as possible." It would not be until September and October that Grant's strategic plan—of placing pressure on the Confederacy from several points at the same time—would bear fruit with the capture of Atlanta and Philip H. Sheridan's victories in the Shenandoah Valley.

See also *Grant, Ulysses S.*

—Brooks D. Simpson

BIBLIOGRAPHY

Grimsley, Mark. *And Keep Moving On: The Virginia Campaign, May–June 1864*. Lincoln: University of Nebraska Press, 2002.

Rhea, Gordon C. *The Battle of the Wilderness, May 5–6, 1864*. Baton Rouge: Louisiana State University Press, 1994.

———.*The Battles for Spotsylvania Court House and the Road to Yellow Tavern, May 7–12, 1864*. Baton Rouge: Louisiana State University Press, 1997.

———. *Cold Harbor: Grant and Lee, May 26–June 3, 1864*. Baton Rouge: Louisiana State University Press, 2002.

———. *To the North Anna River: Grant and Lee, May 13–24, 1864*. Baton Rouge: Louisiana State University Press, 2000.

Rhea, Gordon C., and Chris E. Heisey. *In the Footsteps of Grant and Lee: The Wilderness through Cold Harbor*. Baton Rouge: Louisiana State University Press, 2007.

Simpson, Brooks D. *Ulysses S. Grant: Triumph over Adversity, 1822–1865*. New York: Houghton Mifflin, 2000.

P

Patronage, Lincoln and

With the formation of the second party system, patronage became critical to prominent politicians. Passing legislation or winning reelection depended on the ability to distribute government offices to friends while denying foes comparable opportunities. The skillful kept party discord low and personal popularity high. To master the art required time, skill, and effort; Lincoln noted in June 1862 that patronage had been more "troublesome" to him to that point than even slavery. Yet in spite of his difficulties and the tensions inherent in the practice, Lincoln managed matters like a virtuoso in comparison with his immediate predecessor and successors.

Democrats had pioneered the concept of rotation in office; Whigs and then Republicans preferred maintaining civil servants in office. Though Lincoln philosophically disliked the need for patronage, he pragmatically accepted its necessity. He thus took Democrats to task over the issue as early as 1844, though by 1849 he was requesting inclusion in President Zachary Taylor's patronage counsels. When the Republicans ran Lincoln in 1860, they built their campaign in part on investigations of President James Buchanan's appointments, on the issue of undue Southern influence in national politics, and on Lincoln's reputation as "Honest Abe." Once elected, Lincoln faced considerable challenges and special opportunities in patronage matters because his party was new and because of the sectional crisis facing the country.

Lincoln would replace almost all of Buchanan's lower-ranking appointees (1,195 out of 1,520) with Republican loyalists for reasons of policy and partisanship. At the cabinet level he would spread appointments among friends and rivals, seeking to ensure representativeness but also party cohesion. Historians have noted Lincoln's willingness to take prominent leaders into subordinate positions, even though such men had presidential aspirations of their own and thus might privilege their careers over Lincoln's. Because his was the first Republican administration elected, ensuring the party's continued existence required some consideration. Lincoln's personal skills, however, made the arrangements more than functional. Only secretary of war Simon Cameron failed Lincoln notably in his service.

Southerners feared in 1860 that Lincoln might use federal patronage to appoint abolitionists intent on subverting the institution of slavery. To alleviate such fears, Lincoln explored the possibility of selecting Rep. John A. Gilmer of North Carolina for his cabinet. In corresponding with Gilmer, Lincoln pledged not to investigate whether prospective appointees were slave owners and also said that he would take local views into consideration. These assurances were not enough to lure Gilmer into Lincoln's cabinet, though Lincoln would more effectively use patronage in Border States and those undergoing Reconstruction in the future.

Because the federal government expanded exponentially during Lincoln's tenure, he had added appointment opportunities and thus could please many Republicans. The war's bipartisan support allowed Lincoln to make use of prominent War Democrats as well, and he gave preference to competency and efficiency wherever he found them. What emerges through analysis of Lincoln's correspondence is how little debate exists in his letters on questions of patronage, given the disappointments that inevitably occurred. Lincoln handled a successful reelection campaign that might have caused greater tumult in 1864, successfully building a coalition ticket while dropping both vice president Hannibal Hamlin and postmaster general Montgomery Blair to fend off an internal challenge. Presidents Andrew Johnson and Ulysses S. Grant would fail similar tests. Lincoln did so while espousing rules of conduct that encouraged supporters of individual candidates not to fear retaliation as long as they remained party loyalists. Hence his reputation.

—Robert W. Burg

BIBLIOGRAPHY

Basler, Roy P., ed. *The Collected Works of Abraham Lincoln.* New Brunswick, N.J.: Rutgers University Press, 1955.

Carman, Harry J., and Reinhard H. Luthin. *Lincoln and the Patronage.* New York: Columbia University Press, 1943.

Peoria Speech, Lincoln's

Lincoln delivered a speech in Peoria, Illinois, on October 16, 1854, that detailed his objections to the Kansas-Nebraska Act. That measure had been signed into law the previous May, and though Lincoln had primarily been concentrating on his legal career since leaving Congress in 1849, he claimed that the act "aroused" him "as he had never been before." Accordingly Lincoln took an

In a three-hour campaign speech in Peoria, Illinois, on October 16, 1854, for Richard Yates, a Whig candidate for the House, Abraham Lincoln delineated arguments against the extension of slavery to the territories. He opposed the Kansas-Nebraska Act of 1854, which allowed settlers in the territories—including Kansas and Nebraska, shown here on a map from 1854—to decide for themselves whether to allow slavery within their boundaries.

Source: The Granger Collection, New York

active part in the 1854 election campaign and thereby established himself as a central figure in the opposition to the Kansas-Nebraska Act in Illinois.

The Kansas-Nebraska Act created intense political turmoil, and the figure at the center of the controversy was Democratic senator Stephen A. Douglas, Lincoln's longtime political rival. Douglas was the person most responsible for the legislation's passage. Lincoln and many others were alarmed by the Kansas-Nebraska Act because it repealed the Missouri Compromise prohibition of the extension of slavery into the remaining territory of the Louisiana Purchase lying above 36° 30' north latitude. Rather than maintain the federal ban on slavery, the Kansas-Nebraska Act allowed settlers in those territories to decide the issue for themselves. Douglas touted this principle of popular sovereignty as the ideal solution to the slavery controversy because it enabled the people in the territories to exercise their right of self-government, which in Douglas's view was the primary achievement of the American Revolution.

Not only did Whigs such as Lincoln oppose repeal of the Missouri Compromise Line, but the prospect of slavery expanding into territory where it had previously been prohibited also upset some Democrats. When Douglas returned to Illinois after Congress adjourned, he attempted to defend his course of action in a speech in Chicago, but an angry crowd shouted him down and prevented him from speaking. Douglas then proceeded to travel the state to explain his position and campaign for support.

With the ostensible purpose of assisting Richard Yates, the Whig candidate for the U.S. House of Representatives from the congressional district that included Springfield, Lincoln began to speak out publicly against the Kansas-Nebraska Act in the late summer and agreed to be a candidate for the Illinois General Assembly. Inasmuch as the Peoria speech and several other speeches during the campaign were delivered in locales that were not part of either Lincoln's legislative district or Yates's congressional district, it is apparent that Lincoln had a larger purpose in mind. The political situation presented Lincoln with an opportunity to drive a wedge into the Democratic Party that could deal a crippling blow to Douglas and perhaps also aid his own prospects.

An examination of the Peoria speech, however, reveals that more than mere partisanship and political opportunism motivated Lincoln's opposition to the Kansas-Nebraska Act. Lincoln and Douglas had shared the same platform in Bloomington and Springfield prior to October 16 when they met in Peoria, but the three-hour address Lincoln delivered that evening is his best-known speech from the 1854 campaign because it is the one for which the most complete text is available. The Peoria speech is also significant because it contains the primary arguments and core principles that Lincoln would employ against Douglas's doctrine of popular sovereignty for the remainder of the decade.

Lincoln made it clear in his speech that he was opposed to the extension of slavery into the territories, rather than advocating the abolition of slavery in the states where it already existed. In fact Lincoln claimed that Southerners were no more responsible for slavery than Northerners, and if the roles were reversed, he suspected that Northerners would not behave any differently. Lincoln also assured his audience that he was not in favor of repeal of the controversial Fugitive Slave Act of 1850 and that he was not seeking the abolition of slavery in Washington, D.C., even though Congress had the authority to end slavery in the nation's capital. Despite these moderate positions on many of the key issues of the slavery controversy, Lincoln did not mince words when he denounced slavery as a "monstrous injustice" that contradicted the "fundamental principles of civil liberty" and deprived the American experiment in republican government of its influence on the world.

While Douglas asserted that self-government was the leading principle of the founders of the republic, Lincoln argued that his "ancient faith" taught him that it was the idea that all men are created equal. Lincoln worried that the repeal of the Missouri Compromise was an insidious effort to replace the democratic principles embodied in the Declaration of Independence with a new faith in despotism that enabled some men to rule over others without their consent. Though

Lincoln argued that African Americans were human beings and therefore entitled to natural rights, such as life and liberty, it did not necessarily follow that they should be elevated to a position of social and political equality. Lincoln further claimed that the founders agreed with his position, as evidenced by their restricting the spread of slavery into the Northwest Territory and by using the word "person" rather than "slave" in the Constitution.

Lincoln saw a clear distinction between an African American slave and other kinds of property, and he believed that Douglas's failure to acknowledge the distinction made it impossible for him to maintain that popular sovereignty was somehow neutral on the slavery issue. Supporters of popular sovereignty claimed not to care about the fate of slavery in the territories, yet Lincoln dismissed this alleged indifference as "covert *real* zeal" for the spread of slavery. For Lincoln, the logic that justified repeal of the Missouri Compromise would make possible the resumption of the African slave trade and also enable slavery to spread "wherever in the wide world, local and unorganized opposition can not prevent it."

For Lincoln, nothing less than the future of the republic was at stake in the contest. Douglas was a major figure on the national political stage, yet Lincoln proved himself a worthy adversary during the 1854 campaign. Lincoln's opposition to the Kansas-Nebraska Act was based on the firm conviction that slavery was a moral injustice that violated the principles upon which the republic had been founded. The Peoria speech offered no easy solution to the slavery issue, but Lincoln hoped that restoration of the Missouri Compromise would be an important step in reviving both the spirit of sectional compromise and the "spirit of seventy-six." Lincoln believed it was time to "repurify" the republic by returning to the principles of the Declaration of Independence, and the themes he raised in the Peoria speech would be further developed throughout the rest of the decade. Yates failed to win the congressional election against a Democratic supporter of Douglas, but Lincoln won election to the state legislature, an office he declined to accept so that he could be a candidate for the U.S. Senate when the legislature convened in 1855.

—Matthew Norman

BIBLIOGRAPHY

Donald, David Herbert. *Lincoln.* New York: Simon and Schuster, 1995.

Fehrenbacher, Don E. *Prelude to Greatness: Lincoln in the 1850s.* Stanford: Stanford University Press, 1962.

Fornieri, Joseph R. *Abraham Lincoln's Political Faith.* DeKalb: Northern Illinois University Press, 2003.

Johannsen, Robert W. *Stephen A. Douglas.* New York: Oxford University Press, 1973.

———. *Lincoln, the South and Slavery: The Political Dimension.* Baton Rouge: Louisiana State University Press, 1991.

Lincoln, Abraham. "Speech at Peoria, Illinois, October 16, 1854." In *The Collected Works of Abraham Lincoln,* edited by Roy P. Basler et al., 2: 247–283. New Brunswick, N.J.: Rutgers University Press, 1953.

Personal Liberty Laws

Personal liberty laws, adopted in fourteen free states before the Civil War, countered efforts by Southern slaveholders to recapture fugitive slaves in the North. During the winter of 1860–1861 Abraham Lincoln sought to accommodate the demands of slave state politicians for the repeal of these laws, while maintaining a commitment to legal protections for accused fugitive slaves. That proved impossible.

The fugitive slave clause of the Constitution (Article IV, section 2, paragraph 3) states that any "person held to service or labor in one State under the laws thereof" (a euphemism to describe a slave) who escaped to another state "shall be delivered up" when claimed by "the party to whom such service or labor may be due" (i.e., a slave owner). No law or regulation of the state to which the slave fled would free him, the clause declared. To enforce this constitutional clause, Congress passed the Fugitive Slave Acts of 1793 and 1850.

Personal liberty laws presumed the freedom of a state's residents and provided protections to accused fugitives. Provisions varied from state to state, but often the laws granted alleged runaway slaves the privilege of the writ of *habeas corpus* and the right to a jury trial. Some states barred state officials from assisting in the capture of fugitive slaves or their return to any slave state. These legal measures made more difficult the rendition of fugitive slaves.

Passage of the laws occurred in response to federal legislative or judicial action. Some states protected persons of color before 1793, but most enacted personal liberty laws in response to the 1793 law, the U.S. Supreme Court's 1842 *Prigg v. Pennsylvania* decision (which implied that enforcement was a purely federal matter), or the 1850 law. Lincoln's Illinois adopted its only personal liberty measure, an anti-kidnapping provision, in 1833, the year before he took his seat in the legislature. Apparently Illinois lawmakers did not consider other protections during Lincoln's state legislative career.

During the secession crisis, questions related to enforcement of the Fugitive Slave Act assumed special importance. Southern Unionists sought evidence of Northern moderation on slavery to help them counteract secessionist appeals. Consequently, efforts to repeal personal liberty laws, long a Southern demand, increased in intensity. The situation forced Lincoln, who had never spoken publicly or apparently written privately on the constitutionality or desirability of the laws, to take a stand.

In a December 15, 1860, letter to John Gilmer, a North Carolina Unionist congressman, Lincoln claimed to "really know very little of" personal liberty laws. "I have never read one," he wrote. "If any of them are in conflict with the fugitive slave clause, or any other part of the constitution, I certainly should be glad of their repeal." He went on to note, however, that he "could hardly be justified, as a citizen of Illinois, or as President of the United States, to recommend the repeal of a statute of Vermont, or South Carolina."

Despite claiming a lack of justification to call for change in the laws, the president-elect did press members of Congress to compromise on fugitive slave issues. Five days after his letter to Gilmer, Lincoln dispatched a set of three resolutions to U.S. senator William Seward of New York for consideration by the Senate's Committee of Thirteen, tasked with developing sectional compromise measures. Lincoln urged enforcement of the Constitution's fugitive slave clause and recommended the modification or repeal of state laws that conflicted with the Fugitive Slave Act. Still, his language showed that he approved of some sort of personal liberty law. State law, he wrote, should include "the usual safeguards to liberty, securing free men against being surrendered as slaves." Presumably those safeguards might include *habeas corpus* rights and jury trials in free states, precisely the provisions about which slaveholders and their allies had long complained.

A version of Lincoln's resolution, reworded by Seward, fell short of approval in committee. The committee chair, Sen. John J. Crittenden of Kentucky, as part of his compromise efforts, offered a resolution labeling personal liberty laws unconstitutional and calling for their repeal. Crittenden's set of proposed constitutional amendments and congressional resolutions failed in the committee (December 28, 1860) and later on the Senate floor (January 16, 1861) thanks to a combination of Republican opposition and Southern Democratic abstentions.

Even without direct congressional prodding, several Northern state legislatures debated modification or repeal of their personal liberty laws during the secession winter. In Massachusetts, for example, a group of conservative citizens, including former state chief justice Lemuel Shaw and Governor Nathaniel Banks, urged legislators to repeal the state's personal liberty provisions. They hoped such action would strengthen Upper South Unionists in their struggles against secessionists. But supporters of the personal liberty law fought back. Governor John Andrew, who succeeded Banks in January 1861, strongly backed rights for accused fugitive slaves. In early March the legislature approved a bill modifying, but not repealing, protections for persons of color. The law stated its intention not to interfere with federal statutes, but it also provided for trials for the accused. Such a measure, although not acceptable to most Southern officials, accorded with Lincoln's ideas.

In his inaugural address, on March 4, 1861, Lincoln publicly stated his views on personal liberty laws for the first time, in essentially the same language as his draft resolutions of December 1860. He paired support for the Fugitive Slave Act with a call to employ "all the safeguards of liberty known in civilized and humane jurisprudence...so that a free man may not, in any case, be surrendered as a slave." That formulation proved unsatisfactory to slaveholders, who demanded unrestricted freedom of action in recovering runaway slaves.

—ROBERT S. TINKLER

BIBLIOGRAPHY

Basler, Roy P. *The Collected Works of Abraham Lincoln.* Vol. 4. New Brunswick, N.J.: Rutgers University Press, 1953.

Campbell, Stanley W. *The Slave Catchers: Enforcement of the Fugitive Slave Law, 1850–1860.* Chapel Hill: University of North Carolina Press, 1968.

Finkelman, Paul. *An Imperfect Union: Slavery, Federalism, and Comity.* Chapel Hill: University of North Carolina Press, 1981.

Morris, Thomas D. *Free Men All: The Personal Liberty Laws of the North, 1780–1861.* Baltimore: Johns Hopkins University Press, 1974.

Phillips, Wendell

Wendell Phillips (November 29, 1811–February 2, 1884), orator, abolitionist, and civil rights activist, was one of the nineteenth century's most outspoken critics of slavery. Born in Boston to John Phillips and Sally Whalley, Phillips enjoyed a life of privilege among the elite Boston Brahmins. After graduating from Harvard College, Phillips earned a Harvard law degree in 1833 and was admitted to the bar the following year. In 1835 he was introduced to Boston abolitionist circles and to his future wife, Ann Terry Greene, who is largely credited with inspiring Phillips to dedicate his life to the antislavery cause.

With his first major antislavery speech in December 1837, in which he expressed his outrage at the recent murder of abolitionist editor Elijah Lovejoy, Phillips gained a reputation for his powerful oratorical style. He was widely regarded as the most forceful and talented speaker on the abolitionist lecture circuit. He also became the closest associate of William Lloyd Garrison and modeled his brand of activism after Garrison's, rejecting political activism, opposing denominational religion, and championing women's rights. However, Phillips did not share Garrison's pacifism, holding that coercive force might be necessary to bring an end to the evil institution of slavery.

During the 1850s Phillips managed the executive committee of the American Anti-Slavery Society and fought against the Fugitive Slave Act of 1850. As a leader of the Boston Vigilance Committee, Phillips worked with other abolitionists to protect fugitive slaves from being captured and returned south. While carefully observing the political changes of the 1840s and 1850s, Phillips held to the Garrisonian premise that the U.S. Constitution was a proslavery document, as he expressed in his two pamphlets *The Constitution—A Proslavery Document*

(1842) and *Can an Abolitionist Vote or Hold Office under the United States Constitution?* (1843). Arguing that the political system implicated all Americans in the crime of slavery, he recommended that abolitionists agitate for disunion, espousing Garrison's famous mantra, "No Union with Slaveholders."

As the nation approached the end of the 1850s, Phillips used his oratory to dramatize his position: it was the responsibility of the people of the North to destroy slavery. In a series of speeches reprinted in newspapers and books, Phillips urged defiance of the Fugitive Slave Act, supported free-soil activism in Kansas, praised John Brown's raid on the federal arsenal at Harpers Ferry, and predicted a war that would end slavery. As the election of 1860 loomed, Phillips steadfastly condemned the Republican Party for what he saw as its antislavery pretensions. Although other abolitionists, including Garrison, came to support the Republican platform and its candidate, Phillips did not. He tagged Abraham Lincoln "The Slavehound of Illinois," in reference to a bill sanctioning the Fugitive Slave Law of 1793, which Lincoln supported while in Congress in 1849. Upon hearing of Lincoln's election, however, Phillips was more hopeful, calling it a victory for the American Anti-Slavery Society. Although Lincoln was not an abolitionist in Phillips's eyes, he "consents to represent the antislavery idea."

Once the Civil War was under way, Phillips rejected disunionism, calling secession treason. He argued that abolitionists must convince Lincoln to make emancipation a war aim but soon lost patience with the president's unwillingness to act on behalf of the slave. He took to the lecture circuit, condemning Lincoln and the moderate Republicans, and formed an alliance with such Radical Republicans as Henry Wilson, Charles Sumner, and Thaddeus Stevens. In the spring of 1862 the radicals arranged for Phillips to deliver an antislavery address in the U.S. Capitol, before an audience of hundreds of representatives and senators. On this March 1862 visit to Washington, Phillips finally found himself face to face with President Lincoln in an interview that lasted more than an hour. Phillips left the meeting feeling "rather encouraged" that Lincoln was inclined toward emancipation. From then until Lincoln acted to emancipate slaves in the South, Phillips continued to use his power as a public speaker to pressure the president to act on slavery. By the end of the war Phillips was again disappointed with Lincoln and his lack of support for black civil and voting rights. In his eulogy for the martyred president in 1865, Phillips conveyed his mixed feelings about the leader's passing: "God has graciously withheld him from any fatal misstep and has withdrawn him at the moment when…the nation needed a sterner hand for the work God has given to do."

—L. Diane Barnes

BIBLIOGRAPHY

Finkelman, Paul, et al., eds. *The Encyclopedia of African American History, 1619–1895*. 3 vols. New York: Oxford University Press, 2006.

Stewart, James Brewer. *Wendell Phillips: Liberty's Hero*. Baton Rouge: Louisiana State University Press, 1976.

Pickens, Fort

See *Fort Pickens*

Pierce, Franklin

Franklin Pierce (1804–1869) was elected the fourteenth president of the United States in 1852. Pierce had served loyally and without distinction in the U.S. House of Representatives from 1833 to 1836 and in the Senate from 1837 to 1842. At the outbreak of the Mexican War, Pierce volunteered as a private but was quickly promoted to colonel and then brigadier general. Again he served without distinction. Yet Pierce was handsome, always affable, and made few enemies in public life. When the Democratic Party found itself deadlocked at its presidential nominating convention in 1852, Pierce emerged as a dark horse candidate. He was nominated on the forty-ninth ballot.

The Whigs ran Mexican War hero Winfield Scott. Party members ridiculed Pierce's service during the war (he fainted twice from injuries sustained in battle). Lincoln told the Springfield Scott Club in August 1852 that the Democratic attempt "to set him up as a great General, is simply ludicrous and laughable." But it was Pierce who had the last laugh. In November he and his running mate William R. King annihilated the Whig ticket, taking 254 electoral votes to the opposition's 42.

Franklin Pierce proved as inept a president as he was a congressman, senator, and brigadier general. His party continued to divide over economic issues and the extension of slavery into the West. Pierce's ineffectiveness led Sen. Stephen A. Douglas to attempt to reinvigorate the party through western expansion and the construction of a transcontinental railroad. The Kansas-Nebraska Act (1854) organized those territories and embraced the principle of popular sovereignty, allowing the settlers there to decide for themselves the status of slavery. The bill also repealed the Missouri Compromise (1820) ban on slavery north of the line 36° 30'.

The effect of the Kansas-Nebraska Act was to destroy Lincoln's Whig Party, which had already divided along sectional lines over slavery extension. In its stead the Republican Party emerged throughout the North. Throughout 1854 Lincoln repeatedly denounced the act as unnecessary and a repudiation of the accord reached in the Compromise of 1850 that had appeared to settle sectional differences.

The act did not specify when citizens could decide the status of slavery in Kansas, which lay west of slaveholding Missouri. There was a sense of urgency in the free and slave states to settle the territory with "right-minded settlers." In the election of the territorial legislature in 1855, thousands of Missourians crossed into Kansas to cast fraudulent ballots. The proslavery legislature then passed a harsh slave code for the territory. Free-state settlers refused to accept the legitimacy of the territorial legislature and its laws. They established a shadow government in Topeka.

Political conflict in Kansas soon gave way to armed combat. In 1856 the territorial governor, Wilson Shannon, called upon President Pierce to allow him to use federal troops stationed in Kansas to restore order. Pierce refused. He pledged to support the laws of Kansas and to uphold the proslavery government against the rebellious free-soil movement. Pierce's reputation as a "doughface"—a Northern man with Southern sympathies—had already been established through his cabinet appointments. His support of the Kansas territorial legislature confirmed it.

As Republicans began to advance a conspiracy thesis to explain the onset and continued agitation of the territorial issue in Kansas, the ineffective Pierce began to assume a more prominent role in its development. In his House Divided speech at Springfield, in June 1856, Lincoln charged that "Stephen, Franklin, Roger, and James" had "all understood one another from the beginning, and all worked upon a common *plan* or *draft* drawn up before the first lick was struck." Although his metaphor drew on the construction of a house, Lincoln's audience knew full well that Douglas, Pierce, Taney, and Buchanan were doing the bidding of the Slave Power to divide the Union.

By the end of his presidency Pierce was scorned by Northern Republicans and distrusted by free-state Democrats. He did not enjoy enough Southern support to obtain renomination and was the first elected president to suffer that humiliation. He retired to Concord where a lifelong problem with alcohol adversely affected his health. When Pierce died in October 1869 the *New York Times* noted simply that his record as a statesman did not "command the approbation of the nation" and that "his place will not be missed by those actively engaged in public affairs." Once the conspirator, Pierce was now a nonentity.

—MICHAEL A. MORRISON

BIBLIOGRAPHY

Basler, Roy P., ed. *The Collected Works of Abraham Lincoln.* New Brunswick, N.J.: Rutgers University Press, 1953–1955.

Gara, Larry. *The Presidency of Franklin Pierce.* Lawrence: University Press of Kansas, 1991.

Holt, Michael F. *The Fate of Their Country: Politicians, Slavery Extension and the Coming of the Civil War.* New York: Hill and Wang, 2005.

Nichols, Roy Franklin. *Franklin Pierce: Young Hickory of the Granite Hills.* 1931. 2nd ed. Philadelphia: University of Pennsylvania Press, 1958.

Political Culture, Lincoln and

The political culture of any time and place consists of the essential values within which the political system operates. They not only help define the legitimacy of political words and actions but also often give form and substance to the everyday workings of the political process. The political culture of Lincoln's America was primarily defined by four core values: equality, democracy, individualism, and capitalism. Lincoln's success in reaching the heights of this political culture and his enduring legacy in American history are largely the result of his remarkable ability to both advocate for and embody all of these central values.

Nineteenth-century Americans were egalitarians. In their recent Revolution they had thrown off not merely a monarchy but monarchical society itself, with all its trappings of hierarchy and rank. They rejected the age-old notion of privilege and sought to fashion a new society in which individual merit could hold its own against the advantages of birth and wealth. Most of all, men were to be accorded equal dignity. The inherent equality of all men that Jefferson's Declaration found self-evident meant that no man should look down upon another. The plowman and the professor, the laborer and the lawyer were all entitled to the same respect.

It was Lincoln's fate and good fortune to be associated with the greatest egalitarian achievement of the century: the elimination of slavery. But long before he accomplished that task he had spoken out for the possibilities of humble farmers and laborers, the acceptance of the immigrant, and even the equal dignity of the sober and the inebriate. Later, as president, Lincoln regularly took time out from his lofty responsibilities to mitigate the severity of military justice meted out to common soldiers. In these acts he demonstrated that all were equally deserving of his esteem and compassion. The example of his own life helped justify the merits of this outlook. Who could have foreseen the benefits that came to society from allowing such a common-looking, humbly born individual the opportunity to show what he could accomplish?

Democracy was a natural consequence of these egalitarian notions. If all were inherently equal in society, why should not all be equally entitled to determine its future? By the time Lincoln had come of age most property and religious requirements for voting and office holding by white men had fallen away. Though people of the time thought of it as "universal suffrage," our age must note that women and African Americans were not yet considered part of the political universe. But fairness to Lincoln's age requires us to recognize that no country on Earth had such an expansive electorate. Politicians no longer "stood" for election but had to "run" for office. They had to seek the support of masses of ordinary people to attain power, and they had to publicly justify their actions to the people at regular intervals to hold onto it. Lincoln was well suited to such a democratic milieu. He was a dedicated party worker as well as campaigner and officeholder. His ability to speak and interact with common people—after all, he was one of them—helped his early successes in the local politics of Illinois. After he stepped onto the national stage in the 1850s, his superb mastery of the written word carried his message and his popularity to masses of people he could never personally encounter.

Individualism was also a consequence of equality. If no man was better than another, no one must bend a knee and accept another's control over his life. This left each individual cut off from the hierarchical bonds that had held society together for centuries. Each man was to be free to pursue his own interests in his own way. This conception called into question the very notion of society and put increased importance on the remaining ties among individuals and the sources of order within these independent men. Lincoln's passion for the law, his reverence for the Constitution, his devotion to Henry Clay ("the Great Compromiser"), and his dedication to the Union were all evidence of his recognition that, now that necessary bonds had disappeared, the consensual rules and order of American society must be preserved. At the same time, his advocacy of economic opportunity, education, and self-control revealed his understanding that for an individualistic society to last, individuals must be able to support themselves and be responsibly independent.

Lincoln's America was also a capitalistic world. The rights of private property were firmly established in the laws, and few questioned that an open, competitive economic order was central to the success of their society. Most of the legislation in Lincoln's time was economic in nature, and contests between the parties reflected only differing notions of how best to regulate and maintain such an order. The one glaring exception to this core American value was the institution of chattel slavery. The challenge this institution posed to the American belief in free labor and, as Lincoln often said, the right of each man to the product of his own toil would ultimately result in its demise in 1865. Much of Lincoln's hatred of the institution (and that of the Republican Party he ultimately led), was due to its violation of this basic capitalistic value. Lincoln's longtime support of the Whig Party was based largely on its willingness to use the engine of government to help propel America's capitalistic economy forward, to make it sufficiently productive to open abundant opportunities for America's individualistic population to sustain and even better themselves. Economic opportunity, in Lincoln's eyes, laid the foundation for equality, individualism, and democracy itself. He saw the meaning of the Civil War in extending such opportunity to all. His own life, from his youth as a rail-splitter to an inhabitant of the White House, embodied it.

—Lawrence Frederick Kohl

BIBLIOGRAPHY

Ellis, Richard J. *American Political Cultures.* New York: Oxford University Press, 1993.
de Tocqueville, Alexis. *Democracy in America.* New York: Library of America, 2004.

Political Philosophy, Lincoln's

Lincoln's political philosophy is found in his articulation and defense of the core ideals, principles, and ends that guided his statesmanship. Though primarily a man of action, Lincoln reflected about the nature of politics in a way that was highly philosophical. When deliberating on a particular policy, such as slavery, he probed its underlying moral foundations and its inherent goodness or evil in the abstract. The related crises of slavery and disunion impelled him to provide an ultimate justification of democratic government that was informed by an overarching vision of God, man, society, and history. Lincoln's political philosophy thus developed as an urgent response to rival visions of American public life, both Northern and Southern, that competed for public authoritativeness during the Civil War era. Lincoln's proslavery opponents of the South included theologians such as Frederick Ross, who argued that servitude was ordained by God; apologists such as George Fitzhugh, who defended the superiority of slave society over free society; and the adherents of John C. Calhoun's states' rights philosophy. The latter interpreted the Constitution as a compact of free and independent states, affirmed slavery as a "positive good," and claimed a national duty to protect, perpetuate, and extend it. Before the war, Lincoln directed much of his intellectual firepower against the Northern doctrine of popular sovereignty as propounded by his nemesis from Illinois, Stephen A. Douglas. Popular sovereignty defended the right of territorial settlers to decide for themselves whether or not to have slavery. Lincoln condemned the moral relativism of this doctrine because it denied the inherent evil of slavery, thereby trivializing a great moral wrong, dulling the nation's moral conscience, and preparing the public mind for its indefinite perpetuation.

The Whig ideology of the antebellum period exerted an early and enduring influence on Lincoln's political philosophy. Lincoln esteemed Henry Clay as his "beau ideal of a statesman." In regard to slavery, the young Lincoln shared Clay's policies of gradualism and colonization. As a Whig politician, Lincoln shared his party's commitment to economic nationalism, internal improvements, the national bank, moral restraint, and the rule of law against the populist impulses of Jacksonian Democracy. Indeed, his Lyceum Address of 1838 constitutes a Whig manifesto in its repudiation of mob violence and its call for a "political religion" based on reverence for the laws as the best means to perpetuate the nation's political institutions. Daniel Webster's view of the inseparability of liberty and Union was yet another important Whig doctrine that influenced Lincoln's mature view of the moral character and destiny of the American regime.

Lincoln's experience as a lawyer also influenced his political philosophy. His command of the English language, his attention to legal detail, his ability to communicate complex ideas in layman's terms, and the logical precision and clarity that are hallmarks of his writing may be attributed, in part, to the habits of thought and mind that he cultivated in the legal profession. His legal training prepared Lincoln for the greatest constitutional crisis the nation has faced, that over secession and slavery. It equipped him to do legal battle with chief justice Roger B. Taney, in *Dred Scott,* over the moral foundations of the Constitution. And as president, Lincoln's legal abilities were brought to bear in his defense of the Union, his critique of secession, and his justification of the broad exercise of executive power during the war in suspending the writ of *habeas corpus* and in emancipating the slaves as a war measure. In view of the underlying legal justifications of these policies, Lincoln has been called the "attorney general in chief."

The core principles of Lincoln's political philosophy are to be found in the natural law and rights teaching of the Declaration of Independence. Lincoln interpreted the Declaration as a moral covenant that served as a rule and measure to judge the moral progress of the nation. He viewed the self-evident truth of human equality as preeminent among the Declaration's principles: it constituted the "the central idea" of the American regime and "the father of all moral principle." Indeed Lincoln regarded the fundamental principles of equality, consent, and liberty in the Declaration as a "political faith" or a "political religion." Fidelity to this political creed was the very basis of a shared public life. Unlike his proslavery opponents of both the North and South, Lincoln understood equality as a universal and inclusive principle that applied in the abstract to all people at all times. It was an affirmation of our common humanity and moral worth. The founding principle of equality was therefore irreconcilable with slavery. The Civil War was a test of the nation's fidelity to its political faith.

Lincoln's reliance on the natural law teaching of the Declaration as the basis of his moral opposition to slavery appears prominently for the first time in his Peoria address of 1854, in which he defends the "ancient faith" of the Founders against the heretical "new faith" of popular sovereignty. The doctrine of popular sovereignty in the North and the defense of slavery in the South violated the principle of equality and consent by debasing an entire class of human beings to the level of a beast and by exalting the "allegedly" superior to a higher plane of authority, in which they wielded absolute power over their fellow human beings. According to Lincoln, the underlying principle justifying slavery and denying consent was identical to the Divine Right of Kings, which had been overthrown by the American Revolution but was now being revived in defense of slavery. Moreover, Lincoln's view of equality appreciated both the equal dignity and the depravity of human nature: Given that we are all equally imperfect, "no man is good enough to govern another man, without that other's consent. I say this is the leading principle—the sheet anchor of American republicanism."

The intellectual sources that inform Lincoln's mature political philosophy can be described in terms of the three Rs of his political faith: Reason, Revelation, and Republicanism. Lincoln combined and integrated the complementary truths from each of these traditions to provide an ultimate moral justification of American public life. Lincoln trusted in reason's ability to discern self-evident truths about politics and universal laws of nature. He thus considered the principles of Jefferson to be "the axioms and definitions" of free society. His appeal to natural theology against slavery was influenced by the Enlightenment thinker William Paley; and his view on political economy and self-improvement borrows from the Enlightenment rationalism of Francis Wayland.

The teachings of Revelation, as conveyed by the King James Bible, were also a crucial ingredient of Lincoln's political thought. The moral precepts of the Bible confirmed and complemented the teachings of unaided reason. Lincoln's case against slavery drew upon the following biblical precepts: man created in the image of God, in Genesis 1: 27; the Golden Rule to "do unto others," in Matthew 7: 12; the Great Commandment, to "love one's neighbor as oneself," in Matthew 22: 37–40; and the injunction to "earn bread by the sweat of thy brow," in Genesis 3: 19. As manifested in his Second Inaugural, a speech that has been aptly described as an expression of his living faith, Lincoln humbly bore witness to the role of Divine Providence in human affairs, without self-righteously confounding his will—and that of the victorious North—with the will of God.

Finally, Lincoln's political philosophy relied on his interpretation of the Founders' republicanism. He maintained that the Founders intended to restrict the spread of slavery in the territories and looked forward to its ultimate extinction through a natural death. He provided compelling evidence of this intent in his celebrated Cooper Union address of 1860, in which he distinguished between those parts of the Constitution based on principle and those based on compromise. In sum, Lincoln saw himself as affirming, conserving, and defending the Founders' legacy of republican government.

More specifically, Lincoln viewed the republicanism of the Founders as consistent with Webster's interpretation of the inseparability of liberty and Union. This meant the preservation of a national Union pledged to the principles of the Declaration of Independence and the rule of law under the Constitution of 1787. According to Lincoln, the loftier aspirations of freedom and equality for all were to be realized within the legal framework and safeguards of the Constitution. Lincoln's political philosophy was governed by the practical virtue of prudence, the ability to apply moral principle under myriad legal and sociopolitical circumstances. Lincoln used the biblical metaphor of the apple of gold and picture of silver to convey the complementary roles of the Declaration and the Constitution in maintaining an ordered liberty under the auspices of a national union:

> *The assertion of that* principle, *at* that time, *was* the *word,* "fitly spoken" *which has proved an "apple of gold" to us. The* Union, *and* the Constitution, *are* the picture *of* silver, *subsequently framed around it. The picture was made, not to* conceal, *or destroy* the apple; *but to* adorn, *and* preserve it. *The picture was made for the apple*—not *the apple for the picture. So let us act, that neither* picture, *or* apple *shall ever be blurred, or bruised or broken.*

Preserving the Union for Lincoln thus meant preserving the principles for which it stood. He defined the Civil War as a war over the American dream and its promise of equal opportunity for all. According to Lincoln, the success or failure of the American democratic experiment during the Civil War was tied to the fate of democracy throughout the world. He saw America as an exemplar of democracy that provided inspiration and hope to all those laboring under oppression. En route to his inauguration and under the cloud of assassination, Lincoln clearly proclaimed the core beliefs that animated his statesmanship:

> *I have often inquired of myself, what great principle or idea it was that kept this Confederacy so long together. It was not the mere matter of the separation of the colonies from the mother land; but something in that Declaration giving liberty, not alone to the people of this country, but hope to the world for all future time. It was that which gave promise that in due time the weights should be lifted from the shoulders of* all *men, and that all should have an equal chance. This is the sentiment embodied in that Declaration of Independence.*

Indeed, such clear and compelling articulations of the ultimate meaning, purpose, and promise of self-government make Lincoln one of the greatest teachers of democracy the world has ever known.

—Joseph R. Fornieri

BIBLIOGRAPHY

Anastaplo, George. *Abraham Lincoln: A Constitutional Biography.* Lanham: Md.: Rowman and Littlefield, 1999.

Belz, Herman. *Abraham Lincoln, Constitutionalism, and Equal Rights in the Civil War Era.* New York: Fordham University Press, 1998.

Boritt, G.S. *Abraham Lincoln and the Economics of the American Dream.* Urbana: University of Illinois Press, 1988.

Carwardine, Richard J. *Lincoln: Profiles in Power.* London: Pearson, 2003.

Diggins, John Patrick. *On Hallowed Ground: Abraham Lincoln and the Foundations of American History.* New Haven: Yale University Press, 2000.

Fehrenbacher, Don E. *Prelude to Greatness: Lincoln in the 1850s.* Stanford: Stanford University Press, 1962.

Foner, Eric. *Free Soil, Free Labor, Free Men: The Ideology of the Republican Party before the Civil War.* New York: Oxford University Press, 1970.

Fornieri, Joseph R. *Abraham Lincoln's Political Faith.* DeKalb: Northern Illinois University Press, 2003.

Greenstone, J. David. *The Lincoln Persuasion: Remaking American Liberalism.* Princeton: Princeton University Press, 1993.

Guelzo, Allen C. *Abraham Lincoln: Redeemer President.* Grand Rapids, Mich.: Eerdmans, 1999.

Hein, David. "Lincoln's Theology and Political Ethics." In *Essays on Lincoln's Faith and Politics,* ed. Kenneth W. Thomson. 105–179. Lanham, Md.: University Press of America, 1983.

Jaffa, Harry V. *Crisis of the House Divided: An Interpretation of the Issues in the Lincoln-Douglas Debates.* Chicago: University of Chicago Press, 1982.

_____. *A New Birth of Freedom.* Lanham, Md.: Rowman and Littlefield, 2000.

Miller, William Lee. *Lincoln's Virtues: An Ethical Biography.* New York: Knopf, 2002.

Morel, Lucas. *Lincoln's Sacred Effort.* Lanham, Md.: Lexington Books, 2000.

Thurow, Glen E. *Abraham Lincoln and American Political Religion.* Albany: State University of New York Press, 1976.

White, Ronald C., Jr. *Lincoln's Greatest Speech: The Second Inaugural.* New York: Simon and Schuster, 2002.

Williams, Frank J. *Judging Lincoln.* Carbondale: Southern Illinois University Press, 2002.

Winger, Stewart L. *Lincoln, Religion, and Romantic Cultural Politics.* DeKalb: Northern Illinois University Press, 2002.

Polk, James K.

The eleventh president of the United States, James Knox Polk, was born on November 2, 1795, near Charlotte, North Carolina. The son of a prosperous planter, he moved in 1803 with his family to Columbia, Tennessee. After graduating from the University of North Carolina, Polk returned to Columbia, where he took up a career in law. In 1825 he was elected to the first of seven terms in the U.S. Congress.

Polk, James K.

A protégé of Andrew Jackson, Polk rose quickly up the ranks of the Democratic Party. As a member of the Ways and Means Committee he played a key role in Jackson's successful campaign to remove federal deposits from the Second Bank of the United States. In 1835 he was elected Speaker of the House, a position he would hold for four years. Polk resigned the speakership in 1839 to run for governor of Tennessee but served only one two-year term. After twice being defeated in subsequent gubernatorial campaigns, Polk's political future appeared dim. His fortunes changed dramatically, however, at the Democratic convention in Baltimore in 1844. Former president Martin Van Buren, the likely nominee, had angered expansionists in his party by opposing annexation of the Texas Republic, a policy much favored by Southern planters. On the ninth ballot the convention delegates turned to Polk, who had hitherto been regarded only as a potential vice presidential candidate. Polk defeated Henry Clay in the fall election, becoming at age forty-nine the youngest president in U.S. history to that time.

James K. Polk, who served as the eleventh president from 1845 to 1849, oversaw the annexation of Texas, resolution of the Oregon boundary dispute, and the Mexican Cession. Polk's expansionism increased the territory of the United States by 1.2 million square miles and fueled the sectional debate about slavery. These tensions would eventually lead to the Civil War.

Source: Library of Congress

In domestic affairs Polk hewed faithfully to the laissez-faire policies of his Democratic predecessors. Believing that a government that promoted economic development would only invite a "disreputable scramble for the public money," Polk successfully vetoed internal improvements bills and pushed through a tariff schedule that eliminated protection of textiles and iron (the 1846 Walker tariff). In addition, he restored the Independent Treasury system, which removed federal funds from general circulation.

In his single term as president Polk would make his biggest mark in the area of foreign affairs. An avowed expansionist, Polk shared with many Americans the belief that the nation had a "Manifest Destiny" to extend its territorial limits. Congress had narrowly approved the annexation of Texas shortly before Polk took office, a move that was angrily denounced by Mexico, which still claimed the land it had lost as a result of the Texas Revolution in 1836. Even before Texas formally approved the offer, Polk dispatched fifteen hundred U.S. troops into the trans-Nueces, the land between the Nueces River and the Rio Grande, in what Mexico regarded as a hostile act.

Meanwhile, the administration found itself embroiled in an escalating crisis with Great Britain over control of the Pacific Northwest. Although Polk had campaigned on a promise to acquire the entire Oregon Territory, which the United States had occupied jointly with Britain since 1818, once in office he offered to divide the territory roughly in half, at the 49th parallel. The proposal was initially rejected by the British minister in Washington, prompting the president to abruptly cease negotiations. Both sides, however, were anxious to avoid a confrontation over the issue. When the British Foreign Office overruled its diplomatic representative and agreed to accept the 49th parallel compromise line with modifications, Polk referred the matter to the Senate, which ratified the agreement. But the Oregon treaty angered many in the North, who believed the president had reneged on his "All of Oregon" pledge.

Polk took a far more confrontational course toward Mexico. Convinced that Mexican leaders would submit to U.S. pressure, the president dispatched John Mason Slidell to Mexico City in November 1845 with instructions to settle the Texas boundary issue. The Mexican government refused to negotiate with Slidell, a rebuff that Polk believed gave the United States "ample cause of war." Having already resolved to ask Congress for a declaration of war against Mexico, the president learned on May 9, 1846, that U.S. troops had been attacked on the eastern bank of the Rio Grande. Congress passed the president's war bill two days later.

Popular support for the war initially appeared strong (by some estimates, more than 200,000 men responded to the War Department's call for 50,000 volunteers). But the surge of patriotic feeling was short-lived. Whig leaders were disturbed by the sweeping new opportunities for executive power and patronage that the war had created. More ominously, many Northern politicians of both parties were troubled by the fact that the expansionist president appeared determined to acquire vast new territories for the benefit of the slaveholding South. Opposition to the war grew steadily, even as U.S. armies racked up a string of victories in the field. Critics of the administration included Abraham Lincoln, a freshman Whig representative from Illinois. In late 1847 Lincoln presented to Congress a set of resolutions condemning the war as unnecessary and unconstitutional. These became known as the "spot" resolutions because Lincoln demanded to know the exact spot where American blood had been spilled. Soon afterward U.S. and Mexican negotiators signed the Treaty of Guadalupe Hidalgo, by which Mexico ceded its northern territories, an area that included California and much of the American Southwest, to the United States for an indemnity of $15 million.

With the annexation of Texas, the settlement of the Oregon boundary dispute, and the Mexican Cession, the national domain had grown by 1.2 million square miles during Polk's four years in office, an increase of 64 percent. No other nineteenth-century chief executive would do more to establish the United States as a world power. But Polk's expansionist agenda sparked a furious sectional debate over the expansion of slavery, aggravating the tensions that would lead to the Civil War.

After leaving office, Polk embarked on a speaking tour of the Southern states before returning home to Tennessee. The grueling itinerary took a severe toll on the former president's fragile health, and he died of cholera in Nashville on June 15, 1849.

See also *Mexican War; Spot Resolutions; Wilmot Proviso*

—SAM W. HAYNES

BIBLIOGRAPHY

Haynes, Sam W. *James Polk and the Expansionist Impulse.* 3rd ed. New York: Longman, 2005.

Seigenthaler, John. *James K. Polk.* New York: Times Books, 2004.

Pomeroy Circular

In February 1864 dissatisfied Radical Republicans sought to prevent Abraham Lincoln's renomination for president by declaring their support for secretary of the Treasury Salmon P. Chase. Chase, a U.S. senator, former Ohio governor, and ardent abolitionist, had been a leading contender for the Republican nomination in 1860 and subsequently joined Lincoln's cabinet.

During his four years as head of the Treasury, Chase continually plotted to replace Lincoln on the 1864 Republican ticket. Chase used his patronage powers to win supporters and earn favors from numerous powerful politicians. He continually sought to undermine Lincoln, his most famous attempt being the manipulation of several Republican senators who called for the removal of secretary of state William Seward—Chase's political enemy—from the cabinet. During this "cabinet crisis" in 1862, both Seward and Chase tendered their resignations, but Lincoln's political adroitness placated the senators, embarrassed Chase, and kept both secretaries in office. Lincoln always knew of Chase's ambitions. Lincoln kept him in his cabinet not only because he was an effective Treasury secretary, but also because he knew that Chase would cause him less trouble in the government than outside it.

Chase and his supporters saw an opportunity to advance his presidential candidacy for 1864 after Lincoln announced his Proclamation of Amnesty and Reconstruction on December 8, 1863, the leniency of which angered many radicals. A group calling itself the "Organization to Make S.P. Chase President" issued, on February 9, 1864, a document titled "The Next Presidential Election," which decried the ineptitude of the Lincoln administration and called for a new candidate. On February 20, 1864, Kansas senator Samuel C. Pomeroy issued a circular—labeled "strictly private" but leaked to the press—that repeated the arguments against Lincoln and advocated the nomination of Chase in his stead.

The movement to replace Abraham Lincoln as the 1864 Republican nominee was not a surprising development. Lincoln's renomination and reelection were in no way certain. No president had been renominated by his party since 1840, and none had been reelected since 1832. Republican Party radicals resented Lincoln's slow road to emancipation and thought him a weak and vacillating leader. The country showed signs of disenchantment with a four-year war with few major victories, continual shifting of commanding generals, high casualty rates, and suspension of some civil liberties. Chase and his radical supporters saw an opportunity, but they underestimated Lincoln's popularity as a leader.

After the circular's release, Republican representatives in numerous state legislatures immediately caucused and supported Lincoln's renomination. The embarrassed Chase disingenuously denied any knowledge of, or involvement in, Pomeroy's statements. The resounding indignation at the Pomeroy circular effectively destroyed Chase's presidential candidacy and ensured Lincoln's renomination. But Lincoln's patience with Chase's political plotting was at an end, and Chase's removal from the cabinet soon followed. In June 1864, in a dispute over a political appointment, Chase again tendered his resignation, and Lincoln accepted.

The backlash from the Pomeroy circular not only doomed Chase but also hobbled the Radical Republicans in Congress. They had believed that the American people supported their harsh and punitive reconstruction policies and would therefore reject Lincoln. Instead, the circular boosted the president's approval and sanctioned his more lenient reconstruction policy. Lincoln's assassination changed the political dynamic, however, and the resentful radicals reasserted themselves and their policies against the weaker and less politically skilled new president, Andrew Johnson. Their ascension ultimately led to Johnson's impeachment and the unforgiving reconstruction policies that helped create great sectional dissatisfaction in the aftermath of the war.

—Jason Emerson

BIBLIOGRAPHY

Donald, David, ed. *Inside Lincoln's Cabinet: The Civil War Diaries of Salmon P. Chase*. New York: Longman's, Green, 1954. 211–223.

Nicolay, John G., and John Hay. *Abraham Lincoln: A History*. 10 vols. New York: Century Company, 1890. 8: 309–325.

———. "Abraham Lincoln: A History—The Pomeroy Circular—The Cleveland Convention—The Resignation of Chase." *The Century Magazine* 38, no. 2 (June 1889): 278–298.

Waugh, John C. *Reelecting Lincoln: The Battle for the 1864 Presidency*. New York: Crown, 1997. 110–120.

Wilson, Charles R. "The Original Chase Organization Meeting and the Next Presidential Election." *Mississippi Valley Historical Review* 23, no. 1 (June 1936): 61–79.

Winchell, J.M. "The Pomeroy Circular." *New York Times.* September 15, 1875, 1.

Popular Sovereignty

Popular sovereignty was proposed in 1847 to solve the problem of the legality of slavery in territories that the United States might acquire as a consequence of the Mexican-American War. The issue first arose in August 1846, when Democratic representative David Wilmot of Pennsylvania proposed an amendment to a $2 million appropriation bill to purchase a peace with Mexico. Wilmot's proviso stipulated that slavery would be prohibited in any territory acquired as a result of the war. It passed along sectional lines in the House, but the Senate failed to act on it before the congressional session ended. In February 1847, Sen. John C. Calhoun of South Carolina offered a series of four resolutions that denied that Congress had the power to restrict slavery on the ground that it was the exclusive creature of the states. Calhoun and other Southerners used a narrow construction of the Constitution to disclaim the right of Congress to appropriate territory to the exclusion of any state or citizen.

Congress and the nation now found themselves caught between two extreme solutions to the territorial issue. Wilmot's rested on the fundamental principle of liberty and the broader goal to extend American free institutions into the West. Calhoun's emphasized the equality of slaveholders under the Constitution and of the South within the Union. When the Senate ratified the Treaty of Guadalupe Hidalgo in March 1848 the United States acquired 525,000 square miles of Mexican territory, including California and New Mexico. The hypothetical and principled conflict over slavery extension now became real. Some moderates proposed extending the Missouri Compromise, which banned slavery north of a line at 36° 30' latitude, through the new territories to the Pacific Ocean. Although territorial division was proposed in the House in 1848, it failed to pass.

Moderates then turned to the idea of local self-determination, or as it would become known, "popular sovereignty." First articulated by Daniel S. Dickinson of New York and hinted at by members of Congress North and South in 1846 and 1847, popular sovereignty was put squarely before the public in the 1848 campaign. Lewis Cass, a Democratic presidential hopeful, outlined the doctrine in a public letter in December 1847. He refused to take a clear stand on Congress's power over slavery in the commonly owned territories. Instead Cass maintained that the people of the territories, acting through their legislatures, should determine the status of slavery for themselves. Cass's argument resonated with Democrats who had long supported a strict construction of the Constitution, a limited national government, and local self-determination. Cass and other supporters of popular sovereignty maintained that the meaning of the American Revolution lay in the determination of the colonists to manage their own affairs.

The Democrats nominated Cass for president in 1848 and placed him on a platform that simply endorsed the principles and compromises of the Constitution. Cass's letter, however, clearly put him and his party on the side of local self-determination. Having once won with a military hero, the Whigs followed the same formula and nominated Zachary Taylor, a general with no established party identification and no clear political views. But Taylor was popular and eminently electable. Abraham Lincoln excoriated Cass for his waffling position on Wilmot's Proviso. Lincoln also maintained that he preferred "a candidate who, like General Taylor, will allow the people to have their own way regardless of his private opinion." He shrewdly concluded that the Whigs could elect no other candidate and that with Taylor, "we can...make great inroads among the rank and file of the democrats." Lincoln was right. Taylor bested Cass in 1848, 163 electoral votes to 127.

From 1848 to 1850 Congress deadlocked over the status of slavery in the territories. Following Taylor's death in the summer of 1850, it passed a series of measures known as the Compromise of 1850 that seemed to resolve all of the outstanding and hotly debated issues regarding slavery. California was admitted as a free state, and the remaining territories were organized without any restrictions on slavery. Thus the central problem of territorial organization had been resolved on the basis of nonintervention. The Compromise of 1850 seemed to leave extremists North and South little on which to focus anti- and proslavery agitation.

Although the Democrats won a convincing victory in 1852, essentially ending the political viability of the Whig Party, Franklin Pierce's advantage in the popular count was only 1.6 percent of three million votes cast. Pierce quickly proved to be an inept president. In the absence of effective political leadership, Stephen Douglas took it upon himself to reassert his party's basic political tenets and in the bargain reinvigorate the democracy. To that end he would combine western expansion, internal improvements (a transcontinental railroad), and popular sovereignty into a program that was embodied in the Kansas-Nebraska bill. It organized the lands west of Iowa and Missouri. Needing the support of Southerners and believing that the Compromise of 1850 established nonintervention with slavery in the territories, Douglas wrote the principle of popular sovereignty into the bill and repealed the Missouri Compromise (1820) ban on slavery north of 36° 30'.

Douglas was excoriated then and thereafter for repealing this "sacred" ban on slavery extension, and no one was harsher than Abraham Lincoln. In the fall of 1854 Lincoln told an audience in Bloomington, Illinois, that slavery would only expand if it was able to gain a foothold in a territory before a government could be organized to ban it. Asserting that the right of self-government "rightly understood" was sacred, Lincoln charged that the Nebraska Act was a gross violation of that principle. Here his indictment of popular sovereignty took a significant turn. If blacks were not humans, he claimed, "then it is right to allow the South to take their peculiar institution with them and plant it on the virgin soil of Kansas and Nebraska." If they were human, "then there is not even the shadow of popular sovereignty in allowing the first settlers upon such soil to decide whether it shall be right in all future time to hold men in bondage there."

By 1856 any semblance of constitutional government, law, and order had wilted on the dusty plains of Kansas. Vote fraud led to the election of a proslavery legislature, which proceeded to enact a series of laws (some draconian) that legalized slavery. Enraged free-soil settlers adopted their own constitution establishing a shadow government that excluded slavery. Political turmoil in the territory divided the settlers into warring camps. The middle ground of popular sovereignty provided the context for a battleground.

Faring poorly in Kansas, popular sovereignty was dealt a severe blow by the Supreme Court in 1857. In *Scott v. Sandford* the Court ruled that Congress could not ban slavery in the territories, as it had in 1820. Lincoln maintained that by extension the Court had also barred the people of a territory from excluding slavery. Douglas would counter that slavery could not exist without local regulations that legalized and supported it. Thus local legislatures could prevent slavery from taking root in the territory by simply not protecting the institution.

Douglas first made this argument in 1857, but it became the centerpiece of his debate with Lincoln in Freeport in August 1858. And the dispute over the meaning and future of "squatter sovereignty" became an important theme in their exchanges thereafter. Lincoln's scorn for Douglas's dodge, a "sort of *do nothing Sovereignty,*" dripped with sarcasm. At their debate in Quincy in October, he declared that despite Douglas's continuing adherence to the doctrine, the Supreme Court had "*squatted* his Squatter Sovereignty out." The Freeport doctrine, he hooted, had rendered popular sovereignty "as thin as the homeopathic soup that was made by boiling the shadow of a pigeon that had starved to death.... The Dred Scott decision covers the whole ground, and while it occupies it, there is no room even for the shadow of a starved pigeon to occupy the same ground."

For all of the humor and invective, Lincoln's attack on popular sovereignty illustrated larger, more principled differences between himself and Douglas. The senator insisted that the Founders had recognized the diversity of interests and institutions in the nation and founded the Union on the basis of self-governance and states' rights. The nation was born half-free and half-slave, and it should remain on the basis upon which the Founders placed it. Lincoln maintained that the Founders had intended to restrict the scope, the evils, and the lifespan of slavery. The effect, if not intent, of popular sovereignty was to make slavery permanent and national. Therefore the differences over popular sovereignty were eclipsed and transcended by the larger imperative of the survival of republican institutions.

Although Douglas would continue to advocate for popular sovereignty, making it his platform in the 1860 campaign, Lincoln's view of the Founders' intent and the moral imperative to restrict the expansion of slavery into the West prevailed in that election. The House would cease to be divided.

See also *Cass, Lewis*

—MICHAEL A. MORRISON

BIBLIOGRAPHY

Basler, Roy P., ed. *The Collected Works of Abraham Lincoln.* 8 vols. New Brunswick, N.J.: Rutgers University Press, 1953–1955.

Etcheson, Nicole. "The Great Principle of Self-Government: Popular Sovereignty and Bleeding Kansas." *Kansas History* 27 (2004): 14–29.

Huston, James L. "Democracy by Scripture versus Democracy by Process: A Reflection on Stephen A. Douglas and Popular Sovereignty." *Civil War History* 43 (1997): 189–200.

———. "Putting African Americans in the Center of National Political Discourse: The Strange Fate of Popular Sovereignty." In *Politics and Culture of the Civil War Era: Essays in Honor of Robert W. Johannsen,* edited by Daniel McDonough and Kenneth W. Noe. Selinsgrove: Susquehanna University Press, 2006.

Johannsen, Robert W. *Stephen A. Douglas.* New York: Oxford University Press, 1973.

Klunder, Willard Carl. *Lewis Cass and the Politics of Moderation.* Kent, Ohio: Kent State University Press, 1996.

Postage Stamps

See *Stamps, Postage*

Pottawatomie Creek Massacre

On the night of May 24–25, 1856, the abolitionist John Brown and his followers murdered five proslavery settlers near Pottawatomie Creek in Kansas Territory. The Pottawatomie massacre helped to ignite guerrilla fighting that became known as "Bleeding Kansas."

Brown, a lifelong opponent of slavery, was a migrant from Ohio with a checkered economic past. He came to Kansas to aid his adult sons who had migrated to the territory, where he intended to help make Kansas a free state. Having become frustrated with the ineffectiveness of nonviolent abolitionism, Brown brought guns with him when he came west. After he arrived Brown became increasingly disenchanted with the cautious leadership of the free-state movement in Kansas.

In late May, Brown was on his way to Lawrence, Kansas, with other free-state men from the southeastern part of the territory to defend the town from proslavery forces gathered there. While camped en route, they learned that the town had already been attacked in the "sack of Lawrence." They may also have learned of the caning in the U.S. Senate chamber of Sen. Charles Sumner of Massachusetts, who was attacked by Rep. Preston Brooks of South Carolina. Brooks defended the honor of his uncle, South Carolina senator Andrew P. Butler, whom Sumner had insulted in a speech on Kansas policy. Brown decided to retaliate against proslavery men.

A guide led Brown and a small party to the cabins of James Doyle, Allen Wilkinson, and James Harris. Pretending to be travelers in need of directions, they entered the Doyle cabin, where they seized James Doyle and his eldest sons, William and Drury. They left the younger children and Doyle's wife, Mahala, in the cabin. In the morning, Mahala Doyle found the bodies of her husband and sons, hacked by broadswords, near the creek. The next victim was Allen Wilkinson, who, like the Doyles, had migrated from Tennessee. When Wilkinson surrendered, Brown told Louisa Wilkinson that they were taking her husband prisoner. Neighbors found Wilkinson's body with his throat slashed. Finally, Brown's party went to James Harris's cabin. One by one they took men outside for questioning. They returned the others who had been interrogated, but not William Sherman. Harris found Sherman's corpse the next day.

Kansas historian James Malin called these murders political assassinations. All the victims were associated with the proslavery party. James Doyle and his sons had worked for the court run by the proslavery territorial justice and had participated in intimidating free-state settlers into leaving the territory. Wilkinson was a member of the proslavery territorial legislature. William Sherman's brother, "Dutch" Henry, ran a store that was a rendezvous point for Southern migrants.

The Pottawatomie massacre sparked guerrilla war in Kansas Territory. Because the Democratic Party was in power, Northerners blamed it for the fighting in the territory. Bleeding Kansas became a staple of Republican Party propaganda and contributed to the rise of the party and its candidates, including Abraham Lincoln. It was not well known outside the territory, however, that John Brown had led what Missourians called "midnight assassinations." Lincoln did not comment directly on the Pottawatomie massacre, but he would later condemn Brown for "violence, bloodshed, and treason" in the attack on Harpers Ferry.

See also *Bleeding Kansas*

—NICOLE ETCHESON

BIBLIOGRAPHY

Etcheson, Nicole. *Bleeding Kansas: Contested Liberty in the Civil War Era.* Lawrence: University Press of Kansas, 2004.

Oates, Stephen B. *To Purge This Land with Blood: A Biography of John Brown.* New York: Harper and Row, 1970.

Reynolds, David S. *John Brown, Abolitionist.* New York: Knopf, 2005.

U.S. House of Representatives, 34th Cong., 1st sess., *Report 200 (Howard Report)*, serial 869.

Prayer of Twenty Millions, The

"The Prayer of Twenty Millions," by Horace Greeley (1811–1872), ranks among the most famous and significant editorials in American history. Dated August 19, 1862, and written as an open letter to Abraham Lincoln, the "Prayer" appeared in Greeley's *New York Tribune* on August 20, 1862. It voiced Greeley's frustration with Lincoln's handling of slavery in the context of the Civil War.

Unknown to Greeley until it was too late to hold publication of the "Prayer," Lincoln was already formulating an emancipation proclamation and simply awaiting an auspicious time to announce it. Lincoln privately shared a draft of his proclamation with writer James R. Gilmore (1822–1903), who often functioned as an intermediary in behind-the-scenes communications between Lincoln and Greeley. Initially reluctant to inform Greeley of his intentions for fear that Greeley might reveal the plan prematurely or try to force him to issue the proclamation immediately, Lincoln eventually agreed to allow Gilmore to tell Greeley, knowing that such leaks sometimes softened the often-irascible editor. Gilmore, however, delivered the news on the same day that the *Tribune* trumpeted Greeley's "Prayer."

In "The Prayer of Twenty Millions" Greeley claimed that many who had supported Lincoln's election and wanted the Confederacy crushed were "sorely disappointed" with Lincoln's cautious policy toward slavery. Greeley castigated the president for being "unduly influenced by…fossil politicians" from the Border States and by warnings that bold measures against slavery would damage public support for the war. Greeley maintained that reasonable people at home and abroad recognized that slavery lay at the heart of "the Rebellion" and that to try to eradicate the insurrection without destroying its cause would be "preposterous and futile." The Union government, Greeley warned, "cannot afford to temporize with traitors." Blasting Lincoln for undermining earlier emancipation orders from Generals John C. Frémont and David Hunter, Greeley claimed that Lincoln's actions manifested too much "tenderness" toward slaveholding rebels. "We have fought wolves with the devices of sheep," Greeley complained.

Adamant that Lincoln had been "strangely and dangerously remiss" in enforcing "the emancipating provisions of the new Confiscation Act," Greeley demanded that Lincoln fulfill his duty to "EXECUTE THE LAWS." The recently adopted Confiscation Act (1862) went beyond its predecessor, adopted a year earlier, and provided for confiscating the property and freeing the slaves of people in rebellion against the Union. Greeley—slighting constitutional qualms that many, including some Republicans, expressed about the act—accused Lincoln of allowing legal provisions "designed to fight Slavery with Liberty" to languish.

Accounts of Lincoln's personal reaction to Greeley's "Prayer" vary. Some indicate that its tone and allegations irritated the president, whereas others observe that when the editorial appeared in the *Tribune* Lincoln welcomed it as an opportunity to mold public attitudes. Lincoln chose the unusual course of responding in a public letter of his own, dated August 22, 1862, published first in a Washington, D.C., newspaper and then in Greeley's *Tribune* and other papers.

Lincoln's letter, briefer than Greeley's, is one of his most quoted statements on emancipation and the Union. Declining to refute Greeley's specific assertions but implying that some of them were erroneous, Lincoln focused instead on framing his own position for the public. He wrote, "My paramount object in this struggle is to save the Union, and is not either to save or to destroy slavery. If I could save the Union without freeing any slave I would do it, and if I could save it by freeing all slaves I would do it; and if I could save it by freeing some and leaving others alone I would also do that." Lincoln closed with his "oft-expressed personal wish that all men everywhere could be free."

Lincoln's statement attempted both to avoid alienating people who objected to transforming the war into an abolitionist crusade and to signal that he was contemplating action against slavery. In his formulation, with saving the Union as the "paramount" (but not necessarily "sole") object, Lincoln believed that both goals—maintaining the Union and ensuring the ultimate demise of slavery—could coincide. Many historians see Lincoln's statement as a masterly stroke both for its content and for the way in which such an open letter allowed Lincoln to articulate his views publicly but unofficially.

Other editors, some of whom considered Greeley's "Prayer" presumptuous, quickly spread this unusual public exchange, often seeming pleased with the perception that Lincoln had bested the cantankerous Greeley. Greeley, undaunted, published his own replies to Lincoln, continuing to complain that Lincoln's current course was foolish and fatally flawed. Privately Greeley grumbled that Lincoln had not truly responded to the "Prayer" but had treated it unfairly as a meddling demand for abolition. Greeley insisted that all he demanded was that Lincoln enforce existing laws. Greeley soon suspected, probably accurately, that Lincoln had already drafted his letter and had been waiting for a chance to publish it. Still, Greeley congratulated himself on eliciting a statement from Lincoln. Now aware of Lincoln's as-yet-unannounced plans for an emancipation proclamation,

Greeley waited to see if the president would act. When Lincoln finally revealed his intentions on September 22, 1862, and then issued his Emancipation Proclamation on January 1, 1863, Greeley heralded the development.

—Cara L. Shelly

BIBLIOGRAPHY

Franklin, John Hope. *The Emancipation Proclamation.* Garden City, N.Y.: Doubleday, 1963.

Guelzo, Allen C. *Abraham Lincoln: Redeemer President.* Grand Rapids, Mich.: Eerdmans, 1999.

———. *Lincoln's Emancipation Proclamation: The End of Slavery in America.* New York: Simon and Schuster, 2004.

Hale, William Harlan. *Horace Greeley: Voice of the People.* New York: Harper, 1950.

Horner, Harlan Hoyt. *Lincoln and Greeley.* Urbana: University of Illinois Press, 1953.

Stoddard, Henry Luther. *Horace Greeley: Printer, Editor, Crusader.* New York: G. P. Putnam's Sons, 1946.

Striner, Richard. *Father Abraham: Lincoln's Relentless Struggle to End Slavery.* New York: Oxford University Press, 2006.

Williams, Robert C. *Horace Greeley: Champion of American Freedom.* New York: New York University Press, 2006.

Prize Cases, The (1863)

In the *Prize Cases* the Supreme Court upheld the constitutionality of the Lincoln administration's blockade of the Confederacy. The Court heard oral arguments in December 1862 and issued its opinion on March 10, 1863. In a five-to-four vote, the Court decided that Lincoln had the authority to establish the blockade without congressional support under his powers as commander in chief.

The case essentially combined four different cases that arose out of Lincoln's blockade orders of April 19 and April 27, 1861, before Congress's approval of his military actions on July 13, 1861. In that time, the U.S. Navy captured the *Amy Warwick,* the *Crenshaw,* the *Hiawatha,* and the *Brilliante* as prizes of war for their violation of the blockade.

The nature of a blockade in a civil war and its relation to international law created serious questions concerning the president's powers and the legal status of the Confederacy. Prior to the *Prize Cases,* the war powers of the president were largely unclear. Contemporary international law stated that a blockade could only exist between two sovereign states. Thus it appeared to some foreign nations that Lincoln had indirectly recognized the sovereignty of the Confederacy. Lincoln also created the blockade without a declaration of war from Congress, raising the question of the president's power to use military force without legislation.

The blockade was a vital part of Lincoln's strategy to defeat the Confederacy. Several European states, especially Great Britain, depended on Southern cotton to fuel their economies. In turn, the Confederacy could not manufacture all the goods it needed to carry on the war. Confederate officials saw the trade of cotton and other crops for food and military equipment as vital to their war effort. Lincoln's blockade sought to cordon off the South and cut its supply line as a way to shorten the war. Great Britain responded by declaring its neutrality but granted the Confederacy full belligerent rights on the open sea and the power to contract loans and purchase goods abroad. Secretary of state William H. Seward sent a diplomatic message to Great Britain that emphatically stated that the blockade in no way imparted sovereignty to the rebel states; rather the United States had a right to put down insurrections with force, secure its borders, and deprive its rebels of valuable supplies. Seward's arguments did not clearly correspond with international law, and several shipowners brought the United States to court to question the validity of the blockade and the president's powers to use military force without congressional approval.

The Court accepted Lincoln's power to create the blockade without a declaration from Congress and rejected the notion that a blockade was only possible between two sovereign states. Associate justice Robert C. Grier wrote the opinion of the majority, holding that civil war was not a legal condition between two independent states but a fact that the Court was bound to recognize. A state had the right to use all the military might it needed to defend itself, including blockades, which other neutral states had to respect. Grier noted that the president had a duty to react swiftly to an insurgency without waiting for Congress's assent. The president could not start a war "but is bound to accept the challenge without waiting for any special legislative authority."

The *Prize Cases* represented an important victory for the Lincoln administration and expanded the powers of the executive. Lincoln's initial use of military force had aroused claims of unconstitutionality by many critics in the Union. The Supreme Court's imprimatur helped put to rest many questions about Lincoln's legal basis for action. It also helped maintain the government's denial of the Confederacy's sovereignty, thus making sure that no European powers recognized the Confederacy as an independent state. Constitutionally it vindicated Lincoln's actions of 1861, including the suspension of *habeas corpus,* and empowered the executive branch to take decisive military action in the face of insurrection.

To Lincoln, the *Prize Cases* underlined the potential danger of the Supreme Court to his war strategy. The narrow vote in favor of the government's position reflected a closely divided Court. In the 1861 circuit case *Ex parte Merryman,* Chief Justice Taney had condemned Lincoln's suspension of *habeas corpus* without congressional approval. Taney almost carried a majority in the *Prize*

Cases. Justice Samuel Nelson's dissent echoed Taney's *Merryman* opinion in arguing that the Constitution vested the authority to make war in Congress. There were also political considerations at play. The majority of the sitting justices belonged to the Democratic Party, and all four dissenters were Democrats. Of the five positive votes, three were Republicans appointed by Lincoln. Without the votes of two Democrats, Grier and James Moore Wayne, the minority could have turned into a majority against Lincoln.

A decision against the government would not have meant an end to the blockade, but it could have had serious political ramifications. All the dissenters agreed that Lincoln had the power to enact the blockade after Congress's declaration in July 1861. What concerned the minority was the execution of vast powers by the president without regard to the legislature. Even so, a defeat in the *Prize Cases* could have had a detrimental effect on the political situation in the North. Lincoln faced an election in 1864, and a Supreme Court decision that declared that Lincoln had acted unconstitutionally in 1861 would have been a valuable tool for the Democratic campaign. Seeing this danger, Lincoln ushered a bill through Congress to add a tenth justice to the Supreme Court bench, thus heading off any potential future hindrances from the Court. In the end the *Prize Cases* represented the precarious and complex problems that faced Lincoln's presidency and the administration's strategy in the war.

—MICHAEL T. CAIRES

BIBLIOGRAPHY

Bernath, Stuart L. *Squall across the Atlantic: American Civil War Prize Cases and Diplomacy.* Berkeley: University of California Press, 1970.

Hyman, Harold M., and William Wiecek. *Equal Justice under Law: Constitutional Development, 1835–1875.* New York: Harper and Row, 1982.

Randall, J. G. *Constitutional Problems under Lincoln.* Urbana: University of Illinois Press, 1964.

Swisher, Carl Brent. *The Taney Period, 1836–64.* New York: Macmillan, 1974.

Proclamation Calling Militia and Convening Congress

In the six weeks between Abraham Lincoln's inauguration as president and the outbreak of hostilities at Fort Sumter, South Carolina, there was much uncertainty as to how the administration would respond to the crisis. Despite assurances to the South in his inaugural address that he had "no purpose, directly or indirectly, to interfere with the institution of slavery" where it already existed, Lincoln had also pledged to possess and defend all federal property in the seven seceded states. The two major points of concern here were Fort Sumter, in Charleston Harbor, and Fort Pickens, off Pensacola, Florida. Of the two, Fort Sumter was by far the more visible and volatile situation. Lincoln faced tremendous pressure to achieve a compromise that would help defuse the crisis at Charleston and stave off imminent military and political crisis.

Acting on the advice of assistant secretary of the navy Gustavus Fox, Lincoln decided on a middle course that might allow him to achieve his goal of holding onto the fort without provoking a military confrontation. He had a naval force outfitted to transport provisions to the starving men at Fort Sumter. When it set sail from New York, Lincoln notified South Carolina governor Francis W. Pickens that the ships were carrying provisions only, and that no attempt would be made to supply either troops or munitions to the fort without prior notice to South Carolina officials. Pickens, a fire-eating secessionist during the summer of 1860, when the presidential election campaign had heated up, had earlier in the 1850s been a moderate cooperationist. Cooperationists were those Southerners who had opposed secession if there was some compromise solution that could avoid the breakup of the country. In April 1861 Pickens appeared to change hats again, as he refused to take action regarding Fort Sumter until the Confederate government acted. The new government, attempting to establish itself in Richmond, did not yet have the standing to order action by Pickens, but when they learned that Lincoln intended to resupply the troops defending Fort Sumter, they urged him to act to prevent it. Pickens ordered the South Carolina militia surrounding Fort Sumter to commence an attack on the fort. In the early morning hours of Friday, April 12, 1861, they opened fire on the incomplete structure located at the entrance to the harbor. South Carolina and Confederate authorities realized that federal ships carrying supplies were just beyond the harbor, and if they were permitted to provision the fort, then the small garrison there could potentially remain indefinitely. Shelling began around 4:30 a.m. and continued for more than thirty hours before Major Robert Anderson, commander of the garrison of U.S. troops inside, surrendered the facility. The war had begun.

Everything that was happening during this secession spring was without precedent in American history. Thus Lincoln found little in the historical record to guide his response to the unprovoked attack on a federal installation, and he had to rely on his political skill and instincts. The firing on Fort Sumter galvanized the Northern public. On April 15 Lincoln responded to the initiation of hostilities by issuing the Proclamation of Insurrection, stating that "combinations of individuals too powerful to be suppressed by the ordinary means" had taken control of Southern governments and that therefore he was declaring martial law. To suppress the rebellion he called for 75,000 volunteers for military service of ninety days duration. He also called for a special session of Congress, to convene on July 4.

The attack on Fort Sumter presented Lincoln with an enormous problem of great constitutional significance. When he called on the states to provide volunteers to suppress the rebellion and assigned each state a quota, a firestorm of indignation issued from border and upper South states. On the same day the call was issued, both North Carolina and Kentucky refused, making it clear they would supply no troops to suppress their sister states. Governor Isham Harris of Tennessee, who had already been organizing the state militia, declared, "Tennessee will furnish not a single man for coercion, but fifty thousand if necessary for the defense of our rights and those of our Southern brothers." Harris asked the Confederacy for "protection" and thereby took the state into the secessionist camp, in spite of an earlier plebiscite in which voters had rejected that action by 10,000 votes. On April 17 Kentucky refused to send troops in response to Lincoln's call, and the governor of Missouri called the requisition "illegal, unconstitutional, revolutionary, inhuman, diabolical" and said it "cannot be complied with." Virginia's response the same day claimed that since Lincoln had chosen to "inaugurate the war" Virginia would send no troops. The governor proclaimed that "the people of this Commonwealth are free men, not slaves." That day, in a secret ballot, a Secession Convention voted 88–55 for Virginia to join the Confederacy. On this very eventful day, Jefferson Davis, who had been elected the provisional president of the Confederate States of America, issued a proclamation inviting all interested in "service in private armed vessels on the high seas" to apply for letters of marque and reprisal. This was the international practice among maritime nations at the time for setting up legalized piracy and encouraging attacks at sea on ships of nations with which they were at war.

Though it was strenuously opposed in the South, Lincoln's proclamation met with enthusiastic approval in much of the North. Tens of thousands of Northern men rushed to volunteer, eager to play a hand in chastising their treasonous Southern brethren. Among the volunteers could be counted a number of African American men, who saw the war as an opportunity both to strike a deadly blow against slavery and also to show their worth to their white counterparts. Unfortunately for these prospective soldiers, as well as for some white volunteers, they were not able to enlist under the Proclamation Act—African Americans because they were not allowed to enlist and whites because the quota of 75,000 had been filled.

Lincoln declared a blockade of Southern ports in spite of an evenly divided cabinet. Welles, Chase, Bates, and Blair took the position that the government should simply close the ports of the insurrection based on the policing powers of municipal law to seize entering or departing ships. Seward, Cameron, and Smith argued for a declared blockade in accordance with the law of nations. This declaration was perhaps the greatest constitutional inconsistency of Lincoln's early presidency because history and the law of nations do not anticipate nations imposing blockades of their own shores. This act gave Confederate officials their strongest argument for recognition as an independent country, since only nation-states were subject to naval blockade under international law.

On Friday, May 3, Lincoln expanded on his first call for troops, calling for 42,000 volunteers to serve for three years. He also expanded the size of the regular army to 23,000 and authorized enlistment of naval personnel to 18,000. Lincoln's actions were unprecedented in that all of these things were done without congressional approval. On May 6 Tennessee and Arkansas became the ninth and tenth Confederate states, as secession ordinances were passed. On May 20 North Carolina became the eleventh and last state to secede.

When it convened on July 4, Congress retroactively endorsed all of Lincoln's actions that could have been interpreted as in excess of his constitutional powers.

—David E. Long

BIBLIOGRAPHY

Denney, Robert E. *The Civil War Years: A Day-by-Day Chronicle of the Life of a Nation.* New York: Sterling Publishing, 1992.

Goodwin, Doris Kearns. *Team of Rivals: The Political Genius of Abraham Lincoln.* New York: Simon and Schuster, 2005.

McPherson, James M. *Battle Cry of Freedom: The Civil War Era.* New York: Oxford University Press, 1988.

Proclamation of Amnesty and Reconstruction

See *Ten Percent Plan*

Racism and Racial Thought, Lincoln and

Racism and racial thought are among the most controversial subjects in recent Lincoln studies. This was not always so. Until the 1960s few scholars considered such topics, and Lincoln's relationship with black Americans was dominated by his image as the Great Emancipator. The civil rights movement sparked a wide-ranging reconsideration of U.S. history as a whole, and it cast a new light on Abraham Lincoln.

Among other effects, the civil rights movement rescued the long-suffering reputation of the radical abolitionists and in so doing called into question the image of Republican moderates, as well as Lincoln's complicated relationship to both factions of his party. Beginning in the 1960s, critics pointed out that while most radicals urged Americans to grant blacks full civil and political rights, and many went further and embraced the vision of a truly color-blind society, Lincoln repeatedly asserted his opposition to racial equality. During the 1858 senatorial campaign he declared,

> *I am not nor ever have been in favor of making voters or jurors of negroes, nor of qualifying them to hold office, nor to intermarry with white people; and I will say in addition to this that there is a physical difference between the white and black races which I believe will for ever forbid the two races living together on terms of social and political equality. And inasmuch as they cannot so live, while they do remain together there must be the position of superior and inferior, and I as much as any other man am in favor of having the superior position assigned to the white race.*

Such utterances reflected Lincoln's understanding of the complexity of antebellum racism and the deeply held view among most whites that blacks could never be fully integrated into American society. Thus Lincoln pondered the response to the question that had long vexed antislavery activists: What to do with the freed slaves? In an 1854 speech in Peoria, Illinois, Lincoln confessed to having no good answer to this problem:

> *If all earthly power were given me, I should not know what to do, as to the existing institution. My first impulse would be to free all the slaves, and send them to Liberia,—to their own native land. But a moment's reflection would convince me, that whatever of high hope, (as I think there*

is) there may be in this, in the long run, its sudden execution is impossible.... What then? Free them all, and keep them among us as underlings? Is it quite certain that this betters their condition?... What next? Free them, and make them politically and socially, our equals? My own feelings will not admit of this; and if mine would, we well know that those of the great mass of white people will not.

As this passage suggests, Lincoln endorsed colonization—the voluntary movement of African Americans outside the country—as the only possible solution, a position that has further riled modern sensibilities. Critics have charged that Lincoln's inability to envision a racially integrated society weakened his stance against slavery itself, pointing to his consistently putting opposition to slavery after his commitment to the Union. For example, not only did his prewar political efforts against slavery focus merely on trying to prevent the institution from spreading, but in an effort to halt secession in 1861 he actually endorsed a constitutional amendment that would permanently protect slavery in the Southern states. Moreover, as president Lincoln lagged conspicuously behind his party's radical wing in pushing for emancipation. While the radicals fought for a policy of confiscating and freeing slaves, he repeatedly offered federal compensation to loyal slave states if they would institute gradual emancipation. When Lincoln finally did announce his intention to act against slavery in the fall of 1862, he gave three months' notice, during which time rebellious states could keep their slaves if they returned to the Union. The Emancipation Proclamation that Lincoln finally signed on January 1, 1863, freed no slaves in the loyal states or in the recaptured regions of the Confederacy.

Lincoln's defenders point out that, as all people are, he was a product of his age. Despite the radical views of a small abolitionist minority, a virulent, deep-rooted racism prevailed throughout the antebellum North, particularly in the Indiana of Lincoln's formative years and among the Illinoisans whose votes he courted later. Both states were among those that passed "black laws," which attempted to prevent free blacks from entering and restricted the civil and political rights of those who did live there. As late as 1848 almost three-fourths of Illinois voters supported a clause in the state constitution banning African Americans; five years later the legislature instituted a law that punished anyone convicted of bringing blacks into the state with severe fines and prison terms. Defenders note that it was virtually inevitable

Artist Thomas Nast's illustration celebrates the emancipation of Southern slaves with the end of the Civil War. A picture of Lincoln hangs near a family's mantel in one scene, and an oval portrait of Lincoln is set at the bottom of the drawing. Many historians contend that Lincoln's racial views evolved over time.

Source: Library of Congress

that such prejudice would influence Lincoln's own thinking, especially given his upbringing and residence in the central and southern parts of the Northwest, where racism was fiercest. Moreover, in such a political climate no politician could have achieved political success by advocating equality.

In this context, what seems striking is not the depth of Lincoln's racism but its mildness. Although he clearly embraced white supremacy, his language in doing so was far more temperate and qualified than the virulent race-baiting of political opponents such as Democrat Stephen A. Douglas, so much so that Douglas regularly accused him of favoring racial amalgamation. Moreover, Lincoln consistently spoke against slavery not so much as an inefficient, uncompetitive labor system that victimized whites, as many of his Republican colleagues did, but as a moral wrong. At the center of his antislavery argument was an insistence that as fellow human beings, blacks possess full natural rights; thus what modern readers perceive as Lincoln's racism was accompanied by his insistence that

> *there is no reason in the world why the negro is not entitled to all the natural rights enumerated in the Declaration of Independence, the right to life, liberty and the pursuit of happiness.... I agree with Judge Douglas he is not my equal in many respects—certainly not in color, perhaps not in moral or intellectual endowment. But in the right to eat the bread, without leave of anybody else, which his own hand earns, he is my equal and the equal of Judge Douglas, and the equal of every living man.*

Thus Lincoln placed equality of opportunity, regardless of race, at the heart of his conception of the American Union he so dearly prized.

With regard to Lincoln's war record, defenders acknowledge that Lincoln did indeed place saving the Constitution and the Union above ending slavery, which led him to seek first a quick end to the war without touching slavery, then a state-driven policy of gradual emancipation. Yet they also note that Lincoln faced political realities that Radical Republicans could afford the luxury of ignoring: The president could not prosecute the war effectively if he alienated either the pro-administration "war Democrats" or the loyal border slave states, which any appearance of antislavery radicalism would have done. Some conclude that both Lincoln's push for colonization in 1862, which took its most public form after he had privately decided on emancipation, and the hundred-day delay after the preliminary announcement of emancipation stemmed less from racism than from Lincoln's concerns with maintaining a conservative image and preparing the public mind in the North and Border South for the shock of abolition. It is also important to understand that the colonization schemes he proposed were entirely voluntary and that no blacks ever accepted the government aid offered for voluntary colonization. Many scholars conclude the colonization proposals were window dressing that Lincoln knew would never be implemented. In addition, they point out that once Lincoln had committed to emancipation he refused to back away from it, despite severe pressure, and played a critical role in Congress's 1865 adoption of the Thirteenth Amendment, permanently abolishing slavery.

Finally, defenders argue that Lincoln's racial views evolved over time. Although he would never endorse the color-blind, racially integrated vision of the abolitionists, over the course of the war he moved from insisting that the Constitution protected slavery in the Southern states to using his own constitutional powers as president to ban slavery in the rebellious states, even as he used the political influence of his office to fight for a change in the Constitution itself. With regard to the social and political status of free African Americans, once Lincoln had committed himself to emancipation he quietly dropped the colonization schemes that had long lain at the core of his antislavery ideas, urged popular respect for the contributions and sacrifices of black soldiers and sailors, and as early as spring 1864 even suggested extending the vote to "the very intelligent, and especially those who have fought gallantly in our ranks," a stance he endorsed publicly just before his assassination. He also publicly invited Frederick Douglass to join him for tea at his summer residence—an act of social integration that shocked most white Americans. In addition, Lincoln sought the advice of blacks, such as Douglass, and met with them at the White House. No other American president had ever publicly and officially met with blacks or treated them with such respect and dignity.

There is no definitive answer to the question of Lincoln's views on race and how they influenced his attitude and policies toward slavery. As Lincoln was notoriously reticent with regard to his private thoughts, virtually all of his statements on the subject were the public pronouncements of a politician seeking office or trying to influence legislation and/or public opinion. Moreover, as historian Don E. Fehrenbacher has argued, Lincoln's views on race were vague and undeveloped; he seems to have thought about race, per se, very little, if at all, prior to the 1854 furor over the Kansas-Nebraska Act. His racial thought, such as it was, was always secondary to his antislavery ideals; until emancipation became a reality in the last years of Lincoln's life, there was little incentive for his ideas on race to move beyond a core belief that African Americans had certain basic natural rights possessed by all human beings.

Clearly, then, Lincoln was a product of his time; just as clearly, he was not among that handful of individuals able to transcend the harsh racial prejudices of that time. As critics charge, the president was well behind the abolitionists in overcoming the racism of his age, and he never did catch up to them. As defenders point out, racism did not prevent him from playing a central role in shaping the Republican antislavery message that sparked the war or from being the pivotal figure in bringing the weight of the federal government to bear against the institution of slavery.

See also *African Americans and Lincoln*

—RUSSELL MCCLINTOCK

BIBLIOGRAPHY

Basler, Roy P., ed. *The Collected Works of Abraham Lincoln.* New Brunswick, N.J.: Rutgers University Press, 1953–1955.

Bennett, Lerone, Jr. *Forced into Glory: Abraham Lincoln's White Dream.* Chicago: Johnson Publishing Co., 2000.

Duberman, Martin, ed. *The Antislavery Vanguard: New Essays on the Abolitionists.* Princeton: Princeton University Press, 1965.

Fehrenbacher, Don E. "Only His Stepchildren: Lincoln and the Negro." In *Lincoln in Text and Context: Collected Essays.* 95–112. Stanford: Stanford University Press, 1987.

Fredrickson, George M. *Big Enough to Be Inconsistent: Abraham Lincoln Confronts Slavery and Race.* Cambridge, Mass.: Harvard University Press, 2008.

Guelzo, Allen. *Lincoln's Emancipation Proclamation: The End of Slavery in America.* New York: Simon and Schuster, 2004.

Litwack, Leon. *North of Slavery: The Negro in the Free States, 1790–1860.* Chicago: University of Chicago Press, 1961.

Radical Republicans

Radical Republicans saw the Civil War as an instrument to level the old slaveholding society of the South and replace it with an egalitarian system in which blacks would enjoy the full rights of citizenship. Radicals included members of Congress, the cabinet, press, and intelligentsia. Senators Charles Sumner of Massachusetts and Benjamin Wade of Ohio and representatives Thaddeus Stevens of Pennsylvania and Owen Lovejoy of Illinois led the Radicals in Congress. Governor John Andrew of Massachusetts was a leading Radical, as was secretary of Treasury Salmon Chase. Activists Frederick Douglass, Wendell Phillips, and William Lloyd Garrison advocated the Radical position from outside government. To their supporters, Radicals were fighting nobly to extend human rights and the ideals of the Declaration of Independence and Constitution to a group for whom it was long overdue. To their enemies, Radicals were dangerous idealists reminiscent of the bloodthirsty Jacobins of the French Revolution. Although they were members of the same party, the Radicals were a constant thorn in President Lincoln's side.

The Radical Republicans formed in the prewar sectional confrontations. They had roots among abolitionists, the Liberty Party, conscience Whigs, and free-soil Democrats. These diverse groups were united by a fear that the Southern slaveholders were subverting the Constitution through the Fugitive Slave Act, denial of the free-soil majority in Kansas, and the Supreme Court's decision in the *Dred Scott* case. By 1860 the Radical antislavery group had coalesced into a powerful faction within the Republican Party. The members tended to support

Salmon P. Chase of Ohio for president but could not overcome the moderates and conservatives, who succeeded in obtaining the nomination for Abraham Lincoln.

When forming his cabinet, President Lincoln appointed the Radical Salmon Chase as secretary of Treasury. However, Lincoln checked Radical influence in the executive departments by also including William Henry Seward as secretary of state and Montgomery Blair as postmaster general.

When the war began in 1861 Radicals urged a swift and vigorous military campaign and brooked no compromise with the rebels. Although Lincoln responded to their demands and ordered his raw recruits forward (which resulted in the defeat at First Bull Run on July 21, 1861), the Radicals were never satisfied with how his administration prosecuted the war. They despised Lincoln's appointment of Democrats General George B. McClellan and General Henry W. Halleck, among others, to significant commands. To pressure Lincoln, the Radicals got Congress to create the Joint Committee on the Conduct of the War. This committee launched investigations, extracted testimony, and generally pressured Lincoln without unduly embarrassing their party leader.

Radicals saw the war as an opportunity to rid the nation once and for all of the original sin of slavery. Lincoln, however, considered slavery within the larger objective of winning the war. When General John C. Frémont, a Radical Republican, attempted to free the slaves in his district of command in Missouri, in July 1861, Lincoln forced him to rescind the order. The same thing happened to General David Hunter, another Radical, on the coast of South Carolina the following year. Lincoln and the Radicals made common cause by banning slavery in the territories and the District of Columbia. And Lincoln also signed the Confiscation Acts that the Radicals favored. Radicals were pleased with the Emancipation Proclamation, but they worried (as Lincoln did) about its constitutionality and were unhappy that it did not reach all the slaves in the nation. They supported a constitutional amendment to end slavery everywhere in the United States. The Radicals fought hard to get Congress to propose what became the Thirteenth Amendment, which Lincoln also favored.

Radicals openly and seriously criticized Lincoln's reconstruction policy. Lincoln proposed lenient terms to readmit states into the Union. The Radicals, however, were determined to reshape Southern society to prevent the emergence of any form of pseudo-slavery. In the Wade-Davis bill of 1864 Radicals set much stricter standards for readmission than Lincoln had in his own proposal, including requiring ratification of the Thirteenth Amendment. For most Radicals the Wade-Davis bill was still too easy on the rebels, but they wanted a bill that could pass in Congress. An impasse developed when Lincoln pocket-vetoed the Wade-Davis bill and Congress responded by refusing to seat the delegations of the three states that met readmission requirements under the president's plan. Voicing the frustrations of the Radicals, Sen. Benjamin Wade and Rep. Henry Winter Davis of Maryland published a surprisingly stern rebuke of the president's reconstruction policy in several newspapers on August 5, 1864.

Despite the growing animosity between the president and the Radicals over reconstruction, Lincoln tried to maintain cordial personal relations as best he could. He often invited Sen. Charles Sumner to the White House for social occasions and conversation. Sumner even accompanied Mrs. Lincoln to the theater when the president was unavailable.

As the presidential election of 1864 approached, many Radicals hoped to replace Lincoln as the Republican candidate. They feared he might respond to peace overtures and remained concerned over the direction of the war after Grant's Overland Campaign stalled around Petersburg, Virginia, after sustaining 50,000 casualties. Following Secretary of the Treasury Chase's flubbed candidacy, some Radicals gathered at the end of May in Cleveland, Ohio, to nominate John C. Frémont for president. Not all Radicals supported Frémont. Although some important Radicals, such as Frederick Douglass and Wendell Phillips, backed him, most Radicals in government lined up behind Lincoln after the Democrats nominated General George McClellan for president on a peace platform. Frémont withdrew from the race in September, and his supporters generally joined Lincoln. To appease the Radicals, Lincoln got a plank added to the National Union Party platform of 1864 calling for an amendment guaranteeing the end of slavery.

Radicals reached the zenith of their power in 1866–1869 when they passed their reconstruction program over the serial vetoes of President Andrew Johnson and then impeached him (although they failed by one vote to remove him from office).

The Radicals failed in their quest to completely remake the social and political landscape of the South. The weakness of their policy was that once states were readmitted, the federal government lost any ability to shape state politics. Efforts in 1870 and 1871 to curb acts of violence against the freedmen largely failed. Radical efforts were undone by more than violent acts of political intimidation in the South. Northern apathy in the wake of the new, emerging economic order, Supreme Court decisions that undercut the protections of the Fourteenth and Fifteenth Amendments, and a new generation of political leaders who placed national restoration over the rights of the freedmen took their toll as well. The Civil Rights Act of 1875 was the last gasp of Radicalism. Passed as a posthumous tribute to Sen. Charles Sumner, it was very much watered down from its original scope and then was further vitiated by the Supreme Court.

In the final analysis it is difficult to judge exactly the relationship between Lincoln and the Radicals. Since 1865 historians have been debating this topic. Some argue that Lincoln was a pragmatist who placed his larger objective of winning the war over any other social goal, but that he still agreed in principle with the central aim of the Radicals, granting full citizenship rights to the newly freed slaves. There are several variations of this theory. Lincoln is either leading the Radicals or evolving toward them. Others argue that Lincoln and the Radicals did, in fact, have serious policy disagreements. Lincoln may have absorbed some of their ideas, but he was still essentially a moderate, or even a conservative, who disagreed with fundamental elements of the Radical program.

Abraham Lincoln's last public speech, on April 11, 1865, is a good example of how hard it is to gauge Lincoln's relationship with Radical goals. On one hand he made several concessions to Radical positions, including a statement accepting that the freedmen should have the right to suffrage—something that he had never before championed. On the other hand, Lincoln's speech was still a defense of his own reconstruction policies and a plea to seat the delegations of the states that were established under his own lenient, non-Radical policy.

See also *Cleveland Convention, 1864*

—GREGORY J. DEHLER

BIBLIOGRAPHY

Bogue, Allan G. *The Earnest Men: Republicans of the Civil War Senate.* Ithaca, N.Y.: Cornell University Press, 1981.

Donald, David. *Charles Sumner and the Rights of Man.* New York: Knopf, 1970.

Foner, Eric. *Reconstruction: America's Unfinished Revolution, 1863–1877.* New York: Harper and Row, 1988.

Green, Michael S. *Freedom, Union, and Power: Lincoln and His Party during the Civil War.* New York: Fordham University Press, 2004.

Harris, William C. *With Charity for All: Lincoln and the Restoration of the Union.* Lexington: University Press of Kentucky, 1997.

Paludan, Phillip S. *The Presidency of Abraham Lincoln.* Lawrence: University Press of Kansas, 1994.

———. *A People's Contest: The United States Civil War, 1861–1865.* 2nd ed. Lawrence: University Press of Kansas, 1996.

Trefouse, Hans L. *The Radical Republicans: Lincoln's Vanguard for Radical Justice.* New York: Knopf, 1969.

Williams, T. Harry. *Lincoln and the Radicals.* Madison: University of Wisconsin Press, 1941.

Railroads

The transportation revolution that followed the War of 1812 integrated the isolated towns and regions of the United States into a new market economy. Canals led the way in developing this new social and economic order, but by the 1830s they were being replaced by railroads. Railroads conquered natural limitations, created new markets, fostered the growth of corporations, and dramatically decreased costs while increasing the speed at which goods, individuals, and services traveled. By 1860 there were over 30,000 miles of railroad track across the United States. The Northern regions possessed approximately two-thirds of the total mileage.

Throughout his political and legal careers Abraham Lincoln was intimately involved with the expansion of railroads. As an adherent of Whig founder Sen. Henry Clay's American System, Lincoln believed strongly that the government should promote economic growth through internal improvements. During his tenure in the Illinois state legislature during the 1830s Lincoln advocated and voted for granting charters to railroads, but many of the new corporations could not raise money from the eastern banking system. As a remedy Lincoln and his fellow Whigs chartered a state bank to provide needed capital. After he left office, Lincoln lobbied the legislature to charter the Illinois Central Railroad, which became the first railroad in the United States to receive land grants.

During the 1850s cases involving railroads were an important part of Lincoln's legal practice. He represented the Illinois Central Railroad in more than fifty cases, as well as several other lines. Although Lincoln supported railroads and worked for them, he also represented passengers, landowners, and small businesses filing suit against them in about as many instances. Lincoln's railroad cases were a part of the emerging corpus of railroad and investor liability law.

Throughout the 1850s a transcontinental railroad connecting California to the East was a topic of political interest. Like many of his contemporaries Lincoln believed such a national undertaking should receive assistance from the federal government. In 1853 Congress requested the War Department to survey the most practicable route a transcontinental railroad could take, but sectional animosities and rivalries precluded any agreement on a route to California. The Republican Party platform of 1860 included a plank calling for federal aid in the construction of a transcontinental railroad.

On July 1, 1862, President Lincoln signed the Pacific Railroad Act. The act created both the Union Pacific and Central Pacific railroads and provided them with monetary subsidies and land grants in a pattern similar to the Illinois Central charter. In 1864 Lincoln persuaded Congress to increase the subsidies because the companies had difficulty raising money through private means. The act also obligated the president to name the eastern terminus of the transcontinental railroad. After consulting engineer Richard Dodge, Lincoln selected Omaha, Nebraska.

Railroads played a critical role in the Union war effort. The Lincoln administration worked with railroads to establish reasonable rate formulas for government traffic of men and supplies but exercised little oversight as the companies profited immensely from the war. Congress granted Lincoln the right to take over the operation of railroads during the war, but Lincoln only wielded that power in several temporary and minor instances.

See also *Central Pacific Railroad; Illinois Central Railroad; Union Pacific Railroad*

—GREGORY J. DEHLER

BIBLIOGRAPHY

Ambrose, Stephen. *Nothing Like it in the World: The Men Who Built the Transcontinental Railroad, 1863–1869.* New York: Simon and Schuster, 2000.

Dirck, Brian. *Lincoln the Lawyer.* Urbana: University of Illinois Press, 2007.

Thomas, Benjamin P. *Abraham Lincoln: A Biography.* New York: Knopf, 1994.

Paludan, Phillip S. *A People's Contest: The United States Civil War, 1861–1865.* 2nd ed. Lawrence: University Press of Kansas, 1996.

Rail-Splitter Image, Lincoln's

The political application of the "rail-splitter" image to Abraham Lincoln began on May 9, 1860, at the Illinois state Republican convention in Decatur, when Lincoln's cousin John Hanks entered the hall carrying a pair of split rails inscribed, "ABRAHAM LINCOLN. The Rail Candidate FOR PRESIDENT IN 1860. Two rails from a lot of 3,000 made in 1830 by John Hanks and Abe Lincoln—whose father was the first pioneer of Macon County." The presentation sparked an enthusiastic demonstration for Lincoln, who responded by acknowledging that he didn't know if he had made these particular thirty-year-old rails, but that "he had mauled many and many better ones since he had grown to manhood." With the strong support of the Illinois delegation Lincoln went on to win the Republican presidential nomination in Chicago later that month.

Throughout the presidential election campaign that followed, Lincoln was widely portrayed in speeches and political cartoons as a "rail-splitter." Since the rise of Andrew Jackson in the 1820s, and especially since the 1840 "Log Cabin and Hard Cider" electoral campaign of William Henry Harrison, presidential candidates had recognized the value of presenting themselves to the public as sharing the experiences of the common man. For Lincoln, a successful, solidly middle class lawyer, there was great advantage in being portrayed as a manual laborer, splitting logs into rails to be used for fences on frontier farms. Democratic opponents and foreign observers mocked Lincoln for lacking formal education and social sophistication, which only cemented the rail-splitter image further in the public mind. Currier and Ives published a cartoon of the four 1860 candidates as baseball players, with Lincoln using a rail for a bat, and after the election reporters nicknamed Lincoln's eldest son, Robert, the "Prince of Rails."

Lincoln himself did not come up with the idea for the image. Credit for that belongs to Richard J. Oglesby, Republican politician and later governor of Illinois, who brought John Hanks and his rails to the Decatur convention. But Lincoln understood the image's power and did nothing to discourage it, even though he had spent most of his life trying to rise above his frontier origins. In a campaign autobiography written for John L. Scripps in June 1860, Lincoln wrote that in 1830 he "made sufficient of rails to fence ten acres of ground" and that these rails "are, or are supposed to be, the rails about which so much is being said just now, though they are far from being the first, or only rails ever made by A." The rail image was ubiquitous in the 1860 campaign, appearing, for example, as a rail fence border on the campaign photograph that inspired Grace Bedell to write to Lincoln and urge him to grow a beard. It is impossible to determine the precise effect that the rail-splitter image had on the outcome of the election, but given the narrowness of Lincoln's victory in some key Northern states, it is safe to say that its contribution was significant.

A cartoon from the presidential campaign of 1864 or shortly thereafter, showing the "Rail Splitter," Abraham Lincoln, and his running mate, Andrew Johnson, the Tennessee tailor, and pointing to the task of reconstruction that lay ahead.

Source: The Granger Collection, New York

—GERALD J. PROKOPOWICZ

BIBLIOGRAPHY

Basler, Roy P., ed. *Collected Works of Abraham Lincoln.* New Brunswick, N.J.: Rutgers University Press, 1953.

Plummer, Mark A. *Lincoln's Rail-Splitter: Governor Richard J. Oglesby.* Champaign: University of Illinois Press, 2001.

Reconstruction

Lincoln's reconstruction efforts actually began with his inauguration in March 1861. In his inaugural address Lincoln announced his intention to maintain the federal laws and possessions in the South and restore the seceded states to the Union. He reasoned that individuals, not states, had rebelled and had overturned legitimate governments in the states that had seceded. Lincoln believed that it was his responsibility under the Constitution, as president and commander in chief, to suppress the insurrection and restore republican (and loyal) forms of government in each state. In his mind the states were indestructible, and except for acts supporting secession, their laws should remain intact unless amended or repealed by the regular constitutional processes. Lincoln assured Southerners in his first inaugural address that they would be protected in all of their rights under the Constitution, including their property rights in slavery. As Lincoln knew, slavery was the fundamental reason for the sectional division. Although emancipation would later become a war aim, Lincoln continued to insist that his purpose was to return the seceded states to their "proper practical relation with the Union." He preferred to call his policy one of restoration, not reconstruction, a word that suggested a desire for significant or even radical changes in Southern institutions and society.

Lincoln favored a large measure of self-reconstruction that would be led by a nucleus of Southern Unionists as federal armies penetrated the rebel states. He had faith in the "good sense" of the Southern people to want reunion once they understood that his government was no threat to their rights. Lincoln often overestimated the strength of Southern Unionism and underestimated the support of the Southern people for independence.

When Congress met in July 1861, it gave Lincoln good reason to believe that it would cooperate with his plan to suppress the rebellion and restore loyal governments in the South. Congress overwhelmingly passed the Crittenden-Johnson resolutions affirming Lincoln's purpose that the war was fought not to interfere with the institutions of the South but "to defend and maintain the supremacy of the Constitution and to preserve the Union, with all the dignity, equality, and rights of the several States unimpaired."

Lincoln's first attempt to implement his restoration policy occurred in western Virginia soon after that state seceded. At the time, Lincoln opposed the separation of the western counties from Virginia, believing that such action would contradict his purpose of preserving the sanctity of the states. Encouraged by the president, western Virginia Unionists met in Wheeling in June 1861 and formed the Restored Government of Virginia. The Wheeling convention selected Francis H. Pierpont governor and elected members of Congress under the laws of Virginia. Lincoln gave his consent to the work, and Congress seated the representatives of the Restored Government. In 1862, the Pierpont government approved the formation of the state of West Virginia. Lincoln reluctantly agreed, and Congress admitted the new state after its founders provided for the abolition of slavery in its constitution. The Restored Government of Virginia moved to Alexandria, where it functioned as a rump regime until Pierpont assumed control in Richmond after the war.

Lincoln had high hopes in 1862 that states where federal forces had penetrated could be quickly restored to the Union. When Nashville, Tennessee, fell to federal forces on February 25, Lincoln appointed Union senator Andrew Johnson as military governor of Tennessee and dispatched him to Nashville to begin the work of restoring civil government. Despite the existence of a strong Union base in East Tennessee, Johnson resisted pressure from Lincoln to hold elections until the area could be liberated from Confederate control and the Unionists could prevent rebels from overwhelming the new government. Although Johnson initially opposed the Emancipation Proclamation, by 1864 he had announced his support for Lincoln's antislavery policy. After the federal army had redeemed East Tennessee, a state convention of Unionists in early 1865 abolished slavery and made provisions for the restoration of the state to the Union.

A positive reaction in the North and the Border States to Johnson's appointment in 1862 encouraged Lincoln to dispatch military governors to other Southern states where federal enclaves had been established. After General Ambrose E. Burnside seized areas in eastern North Carolina in early 1862, the president appointed Edward Stanly military governor of the state. Federal armies, however, failed to extend their control much beyond New Bern, and Stanly found himself stymied in his efforts to restore loyalty and civil government in the occupied area. When Lincoln issued the Emancipation Proclamation, Stanly, who had attempted to maintain the state's slave code, resigned in January 1863, and the president did not appoint a replacement.

A more hopeful situation for Lincoln occurred in Louisiana. After New Orleans fell to federal forces in May 1862, Lincoln appointed Colonel George F. Shepley military governor, instructing him to seek the restoration of civil government and the election of congressmen in the two occupied districts. After much prodding by Lincoln, two Union representatives were elected and seated in early 1863 to serve out the congressional term. Efforts to restore civil government in the New Orleans area floundered until early 1864. The president's appointment of military governors for Texas and Arkansas proved fruitless, mainly because the Union controlled only a sliver of territory in each state.

Disappointed by the meager success of his military governors, Lincoln changed course on December 8, 1863, issuing a Proclamation of Amnesty and Reconstruction designed to encourage Southerners to resume their allegiance to the Union and, with the support of the federal military, to initiate civil governments in their states. The time appeared ripe for such an initiative. Federal successes at Gettysburg, Vicksburg, Chattanooga, and elsewhere during summer and fall 1863 caused Lincoln to conclude, as he said in his annual message to Congress on the same day as the proclamation, that "in some States the elements for resumption" of Union governments "seem ready for action, but remain inactive, apparently for want of a rallying point—a plan of action." Lincoln's plan granted amnesty to the great majority of rebels who would take a simple oath of future loyalty to the Union, the Constitution, and the laws and proclamations regarding slavery. Certain classes of Confederate officials and those who had abused prisoners of war would be excluded from amnesty. The proclamation offered no process by which the banned classes could be pardoned, though the assumption existed that those individuals could apply directly to the president. A year later

Lincoln informed Congress that all applications of persons in the excepted classes had been approved and that he had no intention of withholding pardons.

The second part of the December 8 proclamation provided a method to restore loyal state governments. Lincoln indicated that whenever one-tenth of the voters in any rebel state in the 1860 presidential election had taken the oath of allegiance and had not subsequently violated it, they could "re-establish a State government which shall be republican" in character. The 10 percent would be a "tangible nucleus" to launch Union state governments. Lincoln did not explain what he meant by "republican," though he cited the guaranty clause of Article IV of the Constitution. He required that the restored governments agree to the abolition of slavery, though as a "temporary arrangement" they could adopt measures that recognized the freedmen and freedwomen's "present condition as a laboring, landless, and homeless class." However, they must acknowledge the former slaves' permanent freedom and provide for the education of black youth. Lincoln also reaffirmed that Congress was the sole judge for the admission of Southern members to seats in that body. He further said that his plan of restoration was the best that he could suggest, but "it must not be understood that no other possible mode would be acceptable."

A flurry of reconstruction activity in the federally occupied areas followed Lincoln's proclamation, though the process was not completed in any state until after the war. Louisiana became the model. There in early 1864, with General Nathaniel P. Banks's encouragement and despite the fact that most of Louisiana had not been pacified, a Union government and a constitutional convention were elected. Before the convention assembled, a delegation of prominent New Orleans blacks visited Lincoln and presented him with a petition asking for black suffrage. Though the president informed the delegation that he could not impose a suffrage requirement on the state, he wrote the new governor, Michael Hahn, "barely suggest[ing] for your private consideration, whether some of the colored people may not be let in—as, for instance, the very intelligent, and especially those who have fought gallantly in our ranks." When the convention met in April, the governor showed Lincoln's letter to the leading delegates, but they ignored the president's suggestion. Still, as required by Lincoln, they abolished slavery in the new constitution. Congress, however, postponed action on seating Louisiana's representatives until after the war.

When the war became stalemated during the summer of 1864, and Lincoln's reelection was in doubt, Radical Republicans in Congress secured the passage of the stringent Wade-Davis reconstruction bill to replace the president's lenient plan. Lincoln pocket-vetoed the bill.

After his reelection Lincoln moved unsuccessfully to secure an early restoration of the Union on the basis of the surrender of the Confederate armies, emancipation, and, as he affirmed in his second inaugural address, "with charity for all." Two days after Lee's surrender in April, but not before the end of hostilities, Lincoln made his last statement on reconstruction; it was also his last speech. In this address he declared that differences among "the loyal people" regarding "the mode, manner, and means of reconstruction" had caused "embarrassment," but he stood by his 1863 plan. Lincoln admitted, however, that "no exclusive, and inflexible plan can safely be prescribed as to details and colatterals [sic]." The president specifically defended the reconstruction efforts in Louisiana against the Radicals who wanted to disfranchise rebel leaders and provide federal protection for black freedom, including political rights. He announced—for the first time in public—that he preferred that the elective franchise "were now conferred on the very intelligent" blacks in Louisiana "and on those who serve our cause as soldiers." But he would not impose it upon the leaders of the new state government who, he contended, were "fully committed to the Union, and to perpetual freedom." Lincoln also put pressure on Congress, scheduled to meet in December, to seat the senators and representatives from Louisiana and his other loyal Southern governments. Lincoln indicated that "it may be my duty to make some new announcement to the people of the South." With the war ending, Lincoln was probably thinking about a declaration extending temporary military control to states, such as North Carolina, where no loyal government existed. This purpose became clearer when Lincoln met with his cabinet three days later and asked secretary of war Edwin M. Stanton to develop a plan for North Carolina that the cabinet could discuss on April 18. The meeting was never held.

See also *Johnson, Andrew; Ten Percent Plan; Wade-Davis Bill*

—WILLIAM C. HARRIS

BIBLIOGRAPHY

Belz, Herman. *Reconstructing the Union: Theory and Policy during the Civil War.* Ithaca, N.Y.: Cornell University Press, 1969.

Cox, LaWanda. *Lincoln and Black Freedom: A Study in Presidential Leadership.* Columbia: University of South Carolina Press, 1981.

Foner, Eric. *Reconstruction: America's Unfinished Revolution, 1863–1877.* New York: Harper and Row, 1988.

Harris, William C. *With Charity for All: Lincoln and the Restoration of the Union.* Lexington: University Press of Kentucky, 1997.

Republican Nominating Convention of 1860

On May 16, 1860, at high noon, Governor Edwin D. Morgan of New York called to order an estimated 12,000 Republican delegates gathered in the Chicago "Wigwam" to nominate a presidential candidate. The Wigwam was a two-story, wooden meeting hall that had been built by city leaders for the express purpose of attracting the Republican convention to Chicago. Located at the corner of Lake Street and Market (today's Wacker Drive), it was intended to be temporary but survived until at least 1867.

The Democratic Party had split over the issue of extending slavery into the territories at its Charleston, South Carolina, convention of April 23–May 3, 1860, and a second convention had been scheduled for June 18–23, in Baltimore, to try to agree on a nominee. With schism in the Democratic Party, Republicans knew that they had an excellent chance of winning the White House and perhaps even guiding the eventual demise of slavery, the peculiar institution that had vexed the nation since its birth. It was apparent that the nation was beginning to crumble along sectional lines. Indeed, there were no delegations in Chicago to represent Tennessee, Arkansas, Mississippi, Louisiana, Alabama, Georgia, South Carolina, or North Carolina, slaveholding Southern states where the Democratic Party dominated.

At the outset the heavy favorite for the Republican nomination was Sen. William H. Seward of New York. In the months leading to the convention Seward had worked to broaden his appeal by distancing himself from the radical stances that undercut his support among conservative members of the party. He sought to increase his chances of winning Pennsylvania and Indiana or Illinois—states viewed as key to winning the nomination and the general election. Seward went so far as to disavow John Brown and his ideals. Nevertheless, as the convention began, a substantial anti-Seward movement was evident.

Who among the other candidates would step into the vacuum created if Seward faltered remained a question. The other serious contenders were Sen. Simon Cameron of Pennsylvania, Sen. Salmon P. Chase of Ohio, the conservative Edward Bates of Missouri, Justice John McLean of the U.S. Supreme Court, and Abraham Lincoln, a former U.S. representative from Illinois.

Lincoln was a successful lawyer who had served several terms in the Illinois state legislature and one term in the U.S. House of Representatives (1847–1849). Lincoln had committed to serve only one term in Congress to begin with, but his ill-received criticism of President Polk and the Mexican War meant that he left office under a cloud. His efforts to secure a position in the administration of President Zachary Taylor came to naught and he returned to Illinois. Lincoln redeemed himself politically and achieved national fame during his failed 1858 campaign against Stephen Douglas for a seat in the U.S. Senate and his selfless campaigning for other Republicans throughout the North in the 1859 elections. Lincoln hoped to be the presidential nominee in 1860, but as a dark horse he certainly didn't expect it. At a minimum he hoped to boost his chances of securing a Senate seat in 1864.

As was the custom of the time, none of the candidates attended the convention in person; they were represented by influential backers, including journalists, who advocated, brokered deals, and otherwise did the bidding of the nominees. Seward was backed by Thurlow Weed of the *Albany Evening Journal*. Edward Bates of Missouri was initially supported by Horace Greeley of the *New York Tribune*, who bitterly opposed a Seward nomination as a result of a personal split he'd had with Seward and Weed years before. Lincoln very much wanted to attend the convention, but he knew that doing so would make him appear too eager and ambitious. His fate rested in the hands of a relatively unknown but talented team of Illinois political allies led by Judge David Davis, whom Lincoln would eventually nominate to the U.S. Supreme Court, and including Joseph Medill of the *Chicago Tribune*.

The convention first agreed on a platform less strident than the one that had failed to win them the 1856 election. It acknowledged that John Brown's actions in Harpers Ferry had been a crime. It supported a homestead act, as well as internal improvements, including work on rivers and harbors and the creation of a transcontinental railroad. It also, however, issued a pointed warning to Southern states that "contemplated treason."

With the platform settled, balloting for the presidential nomination commenced on the convention's third day. The first ballot ended with Seward garnering 173.5 votes, Abraham Lincoln 102, Simon Cameron 50.5, Salmon P. Chase 49, and Edward Bates 48. Seven other men, including Supreme Court justice John McLean, received 14 or fewer votes apiece. John C. Frémont, who had been the party's nominee in 1856, received only one vote on the first ballot and none after that. Though Seward led, there were already cracks in what should have been his solid New England base. New Hampshire had gone for Lincoln, and he had also received votes from Maine, Massachusetts, and Connecticut. Most important, "Honest Abe" had taken both Illinois and Indiana, which allowed him to double the vote total of the other contenders. With no candidate having obtained a majority, a second ballot was ordered.

On the second ballot Vermont went for Lincoln, and, even more significant, Pennsylvania withdrew its support for Simon Cameron, throwing most of its votes behind Lincoln. Lincoln had nearly pulled even with Seward. The vote totals were Seward with 184.5 votes, Lincoln with 181, Chase with 42.5, Bates with 35, Cameron with only 2. William Dayton of New Jersey had 10 votes, Justice McLean had 8 votes, and a new candidate, Cassius Marcellus Clay of Kentucky, now had two votes.

The Chicago convention provided many advantages to Lincoln, not least of which was the ease with which his supporters could travel to it. Lincoln's team executed a well-conceived strategy stressing a positive message about their candidate who, in spite of his modest political résumé, had earned a growing national reputation from his debates with Stephen Douglas. Lincoln brought few weaknesses to the table and many strengths. As was often the case during the era, Lincoln's advisers were rumored to have suggested the availability of plum appointments in his administration to those who could deliver delegates. Pennsylvania's Cameron would become Lincoln's first secretary of war, and Bates, Seward, and Chase would also join the presidential cabinet. If any such promises were actually made they were no doubt implied in a manner that preserved flexibility for the candidate. Indeed, Lincoln had instructed his representatives to "[m]ake no contracts that will bind me."

With Lincoln's momentum apparent, the anti-Seward forces began swarming to Lincoln on the third ballot. On the third roll call he received 231.5 votes, to Seward's 180, with 54.5 votes scattered among Chase, Bates, Dayton, McLean, and Clay. Before the roll call was over, however, delegates began spontaneously to change their votes to Lincoln. When the dust of the third ballot had cleared, Lincoln had 364 votes and the nomination. Amid a frenzy of celebration Lincoln officially became the 1860 Republican candidate for president. Sen. Hannibal Hamlin of Maine was then nominated for vice president. As a New Englander and former Democrat, he was chosen to balance Lincoln's western, Whig roots. That evening Lincoln greeted and spoke to revelers who gathered outside his Springfield home, while celebrations occurred throughout the North as news of the nomination spread.

Not all were happy, however. Remaining conservative elements of the Whig Party and some elements of the Know-Nothing Party who did not ally with the Republicans assembled as the Constitutional Union Party, nominating slaveholding Tennessean John Bell for president and Massachusetts "Cotton" Whig Edward Everett for vice president. In the meantime, the Democrats had finally nominated Stephen Douglas for president, and the disaffected Southern Democrats put up Kentuckian John Breckinridge. The presidential campaign would be a four-way race pitting Lincoln against Douglas in the North and Breckinridge against Bell in the South.

When Lincoln emerged the victor in the general election, without carrying a single Southern state, proslavery firebrands in the Deep South began agitating for secession, as they had promised to do if Lincoln was elected. Compromise proposals to avert war came to nothing, in part because Lincoln refused to abandon his position that slavery should not be allowed to expand beyond the existing slave states. When South Carolinians fired on Fort Sumter in April 1861, Civil War became certain.

See also *Democratic Conventions, 1860*

—David E. Arthur

BIBLIOGRAPHY

Carwardine, Richard. *Lincoln: A Life of Purpose and Power*. New York: Vintage, 2006.

Havel, James T. *U.S. Presidential Candidates and Elections: A Biographical and Historical Guide*. New York: Macmillan, 1996.

Maihafer, Harry J. *War of Words: Abraham Lincoln and the Civil War Press*. Washington, D.C.: Brassey's, 2001.

McPherson, James. *Battle Cry of Freedom: The Civil War Era*. New York: Ballantine, 1988.

Proceedings of the Republican National Convention held at Chicago, May 16, 17 and 18, 1860. Albany: Weed, Parsons, and Co., printers, 1860.

Republican Party, The

The Republican Party and the Democratic Party composed what has become known as the Third American Party System (1856–1896). Established in the mid-1850s as an antislavery political organization, the Republican Party quickly eclipsed other, contemporary third-party political movements that arose in the midst of the Whig Party's collapse to become the primary opposition to the national Democratic Party by 1856. Four years later the party, with Abraham Lincoln as its presidential nominee, captured the White House, precipitating Southern secession and civil war. In spite of ongoing Democratic competition and internal party differences, the party retained control of the federal government throughout the Civil War, which greatly enhanced Lincoln's ability to lead and conduct the war. Republican hegemony in the federal government would outlive the twin crises of war and Reconstruction and would continue virtually unabated into the late 1920s.

The party's origins can be traced most immediately to the disintegration of the national Whig Party in the early to mid-1850s. Many disillusioned Whigs and some disgruntled Democrats sought new political movements organized around issues such as nativism, temperance, banking, railroad expansion, and increasingly, in the aftermath of the controversial Kansas-Nebraska Act of 1854, antislavery or anti-Southernism.

Although long a political minefield, debate over slavery, and most especially its expansion into the western territories of the United States, had been largely mitigated by the early 1850s through hard-fought compromise measures constructed in 1820 and 1850 and through intense party management. The Kansas-Nebraska Act's overt repeal of the 1820 Missouri Compromise ban on slavery in the Louisiana Purchase territory north of 36° 30′, however, wounded Northern sensibilities and thrust the issue of slavery's extension back into the national spotlight. In the days immediately following passage of the act, protest meetings erupted across the North. Animated by their desire to preserve the western territories for free white settlers and to reverse the national political fortunes of the imagined Slave Power, a number of Northern politicians of diverse political lineage called for the creation of a new, antislavery political movement to protect the republic and American liberty from destruction and ruin. The new party that emerged in the Northern states after May 1854 organized under various names (anti-Nebraska, the People's Party, the Fusion Party, etc.) but eventually assumed the moniker "Republican Party." Though most famously known for its hostility to slavery, the party also embraced a host of other, often local, ethno-cultural and economic issues that were important to contemporary voters and linked in the minds of many to the ongoing battle to control the fate of the territories.

The new party quickly gained momentum and won a number of important races, particularly in the Midwest, in the fall campaigns of 1854. Building on these victories and on intensifying sectional tensions in Kansas, Republican influence spread eastward in 1855 and then surged after the sack of Lawrence and the caning of Republican senator Charles Sumner in the spring of 1856. After these shocking events, Republicans gathered for their first national convention in Philadelphia, Pennsylvania, on June 17, 1856. There the party adopted a platform strongly worded against slavery's extension and nominated outspoken abolitionist and military hero John C. Frémont for president. Campaigning under the slogan "Free Speech, Free Press, Free Soil, Free Men," Frémont made a remarkable showing against his victorious Democratic rival James Buchanan and the American (or Know-Nothing) Party candidate, former president Millard Fillmore, capturing nearly one-third of the total votes cast and 114 electoral votes (all from free states).

Over the next few years, the Republican Party played upon growing Northern fear and resentment spawned by the Supreme Court's *Dred Scott* decision (1857); ongoing violence and fraud surrounding the proposed proslavery Lecompton Constitution (1858) in Kansas; and Southern reaction to John Brown's failed attempt to foment slave rebellion at Harpers Ferry (1859) to broaden its support among Northern voters, who increasingly gave credence to the party's allegations of an organized Slave Power conspiracy. Confident in the appeal of their platform, yet eager to avoid the taint of radical abolitionism, Republicans turned to a moderate westerner, Abraham Lincoln, as their standard-bearer for the 1860 presidential campaign.

Lincoln's personal path to Republicanism was gradual and measured. Deeply devoted to the Whig Party and its principles, Lincoln, after a term in the U.S. House of Representatives (1847–1849), returned to practicing law in Illinois. The passage of the Kansas-Nebraska Act, however, stunned Lincoln and drew him back into political activity in opposition to it. Determined to oppose the act without doing direct harm to his own political fortunes, Lincoln initially avoided the nascent Illinois Republican Party, formed in 1854, because of its abolitionist bent. He also shunned the thriving but controversial Know-Nothing movement, remaining committed instead to the Whig Party as the best vehicle for espousing his moderate anti-Nebraska and antislavery extension views. The Whigs' collapsing fortunes and escalating tensions in the new Kansas Territory led Lincoln finally to abandon his old party in early 1856 and take the lead in fusing disparate anti-Nebraska forces into a new, moderate, antislavery extension political movement under the banner of the Republican Party.

At the heart of the new party's antislavery extension platform lay a set of ideas collectively known as "free-soil" ideology. According to proponents of free-soilism, it had been the intention of the Founders to frame the American republic on an antislavery basis, as demonstrated by their omission of explicit, positive support of slavery from the founding documents and their exclusion of the institution from the Northwest Territory. While acknowledging that slavery was protected constitutionally in the states where it already existed, Republicans were determined to prevent its further spread, viewing it as an affront to the Founders and as a direct threat to the freedoms of nonslaveholding whites.

In recognition of his leadership and effectiveness as a spokesperson for the new party's platform, Republicans chose Lincoln to challenge Democrat Stephen Douglas, the architect of the Kansas-Nebraska Act, for the U.S. Senate in 1858. Though not able to unseat the powerful incumbent, Lincoln garnered much attention in Illinois and the Midwest and a modicum of recognition elsewhere in the North for his rhetorical prowess and forceful articulation of antislavery thought.

With tensions mounting between North and South, the 1860 presidential election loomed large. Convinced that the fate of the republic hung in the balance and that Southern aggression had gained the upper hand, Republican leaders plotted to maximize the party's electoral appeal. Many believed that the Republican front-runner, William Seward, darling of the party's radical wing, would alienate a large portion of the Northern electorate because of his ties to abolitionism. Lincoln's eloquent and widely publicized Cooper Union Address (February 27, 1860), as well as his astute bridge building and extensive contact base, quickly established him as a viable moderate alternative to Seward. At the party's May 18 nominating convention in Chicago, Lincoln emerged as the moderate and conservative Republicans' choice, capturing the party's presidential nomination and, in short order, on the strength of free-state votes, the White House.

Republican ascendancy prompted the secession of the Deep South, and after Lincoln's post–Fort Sumter request for troops, four additional slave states followed. Resignations by Southern congressmen and senators gave Republicans a tremendous legislative advantage, which the party was able to preserve for the duration of the war.

His party's dominance proved both a help and a hindrance to Lincoln. On the one hand, internal party divisions, particularly strong pressure from the radical wing for emancipation, became a constant source of difficulty and a potential stumbling block for the president and party leaders and regularly threatened to undermine the Republicans' ability to rule. On the other hand, partisan loyalty and formal party structures enabled Lincoln to rein in potential trouble through threats of political retribution and/or the withholding of patronage and to rally the party faithful behind even the most controversial of actions. In this way, partisans fell in line behind the president's decisions to suspend the writ of *habeas corpus,* to institute conscription, and most notably to destroy slavery in the Confederacy. Additionally the party took advantage of its position to pass a series of economic measures (the Homestead Act, the Morrill Land Grant Act, a tariff, a National Banking Act, the Pacific Railroad Act, etc.)—traditionally blocked by Southern representatives but highly prized by the erstwhile Whigs who had joined the Republicans—that set the stage for the nation's postwar industrialization.

Legislative unity and success, however, were harder to accomplish in Reconstruction policy. Here, perhaps more than in any other area, internal division vexed Lincoln and party leadership. Lincoln's April 1865 assassination destroyed any opportunity for Lincoln and congressional Republicans to work through their differences on this issue. That task fell to Andrew Johnson and the postwar Congress. The long, strenuous battle between Johnson and congressional Republicans over Reconstruction and the associated question of African American rights resulted in a mixed legacy that the nation has not yet fully resolved.

The modern Republican Party, though in many respects philosophically distant from its Civil War predecessor, continues to benefit from its connections to Abraham Lincoln. Lincoln's skillful and bold wartime leadership, his historical reputation, the party's ability to preserve the republic during its darkest hour, its advocacy of emancipation, and Lincoln's martyrdom persist as symbols of the party and have ensured that it will forever be known as the "party of Lincoln."

See also *Campaign of 1860, Presidential; Campaign of 1864, Presidential; National Union Party*

—Martin J. Hershock

BIBLIOGRAPHY

Donald, David Herbert. *Lincoln.* New York: Simon and Schuster, 1995.

Foner, Eric. *Free Soil, Free Labor, Free Men: The Ideology of the Republican Party before the Civil War.* New York: Oxford University Press, 1995.

Gienapp, William E. *The Origins of the Republican Party.* New York: Oxford University Press, 1987.

Goodwin, Doris Kearns. *Team of Rivals: The Political Genius of Abraham Lincoln.* New York: Simon and Schuster, 2005.

Holt, Michael. *The Political Crisis of the 1850s.* New York: Norton, 1983.

Neely, Mark. *The Union Divided: Party Conflict during the Civil War.* Cambridge, Mass.: Harvard University Press, 2002.

Rhetoric in Lincoln's Public Speeches

The political culture of Abraham Lincoln's time prized rhetoric. Americans listened attentively to political speeches of great length. Becoming increasingly literate, they pored over politicians' words in newspapers. Intellectual elites studied classical Roman and Greek oratory, and even a child of the frontier who received little formal education might still grow up, as Lincoln did, saturated in the language of Shakespeare and the King James Bible. Accordingly, antebellum Americans recognized that rhetoric could have profound consequences. As the politics of slavery grew fractious and intense, many worried that rhetoric was powerful enough to unsettle the nation's tenuous sectional balance; Congress even imposed a "gag rule" to prohibit debate over slavery. Lincoln evoked widespread anxiety about rhetoric's power to manipulate public opinion when he accused Stephen Douglas of basing an argument on "a specious and fantastic arrangement of words, by which a man can prove a horse chestnut to be a chestnut horse."

Such aphoristic humor glimmered in many of Lincoln's speeches, and his contemporaries recalled him as a gifted teller of folksy stories and occasionally ribald jokes—in private conversation. In public, the hallmark of Lincoln's rhetoric was a logical seriousness befitting a high-stakes endeavor. His legal practice afforded him extensive training in persuasive speaking. He argued thousands of cases during his twenty-five-year career, and in his speeches he often assumed the bearing of a lawyer methodically presenting a case. For his 1860 Cooper Union Address, he researched, compiled, and systematically presented the nation's Founders' voting records regarding slavery in the territories. In many speeches he relied on a tactic, honed in the courtroom, of paring away counterarguments to focus on the essential core of his position.

In their first debate, Sen. Stephen Douglas denied the equality of the races, and Lincoln replied: "I agree with Judge Douglas [that the black man] is not my equal in many respects—certainly not in color, perhaps not in moral or intellectual endowment. But in the right to eat the bread, without leave of anybody else, which his own hand earns, he is my equal and the equal of Judge Douglas, and the equal of every living man." The qualifying first sentence betokens political pragmatism (and has raised questions ever since about Lincoln's beliefs about race), but it also typifies one of Lincoln's chief rhetorical modes: By conceding peripheral and more controversial points, he focuses attention on his most indisputable claim, the logical bedrock of his argument.

Famously plainspoken, Lincoln generally avoided ornate or excessively metaphorical language, but his rhetoric rarely was simplistic. Even as famously succinct a speech as the Gettysburg Address makes use of rhetorical figures such as parallelism—"government of the people, by the people, for the people shall not perish from the earth"—and anaphora—"in a larger sense, we cannot dedicate, we cannot consecrate, we cannot hallow this ground." Such repetition served not only for oratorical effect but also to bolster Lincoln's logic of persuasion, as in his 1862 letter to newspaper editor Horace Greeley, written to allay Northern concerns that Lincoln was on a crusade to end slavery: "If I could save the Union without freeing any slave I would do it, and if I could save it by freeing all the slaves I would do it; and if I could save it by freeing some and leaving others alone I would also do that."

Nineteenth-century culture valued speakers who both engaged the mind and excited listeners' "passions," and Lincoln expressed his eminently logical arguments not only in careful rhetorical forms but also in affecting language. Over the course of his career, Lincoln's speeches exhibited an abiding interest in the ways that citizens come to feel connected as a political community and the ways that rhetoric itself forges such connections. In his address to the Springfield Young Men's Lyceum in 1838, Lincoln lamented the "fading" memories of the Revolutionary War, and he wondered what, in place of those memories, would unite Americans. By 1858, speaking in Chicago, he described the Fourth of July as an occasion for all Americans, both native born and immigrant, to "trace their connection" to the nation's founding; the Declaration of Independence acts as an "electric cord," Lincoln said, "that links the hearts of patriotic and liberty-loving men together." Both ideas converge in the First Inaugural Address, in the final paragraph of which Lincoln envisioned the restoration of the political community that had been rent by secession: "The mystic chords of memory, stretching from every battle-field, and patriot grave, to every living heart and hearthstone, all over this broad land, will yet swell the chorus of the Union, when again touched, as surely they will be, by the better angels of our nature."

As Lincoln's rhetoric of national identity evolved from analytical scrutiny of fading memories to a stirring appeal to "the mystic chords of memory," it bridged distinct moods in American cultural history. Though still deeply influenced by the secular, Enlightenment thinking of the colonial and early national eras, Lincoln's language began to convey the sentimentalism of mid-nineteenth-century American culture. Under the strains of the Civil War, his speeches became both more religious and more disconsolate, as the Second Inaugural Address exemplifies. They remained, as that last major speech also shows, committed to a belief in rhetoric's power to create political unity: Speaking to "both parties," who "read the same Bible, and pray to the same God," Lincoln enjoined both "to bind up the nation's wounds."

See also *Cooper Union Address; Gettysburg Address; House Divided Speech*

—Christopher Hager

BIBLIOGRAPHY

Black, Edwin. "The Ultimate Voice of Lincoln." *Rhetoric and Public Affairs* 3 (2000): 49–57.

Briggs, John Channing. *Lincoln's Speeches Reconsidered*. Baltimore: Johns Hopkins University Press, 2005.

Wills, Garry. *Lincoln at Gettysburg: The Words That Remade America*. New York: Simon and Schuster, 1992.

Wilson, Edmund. *Patriotic Gore: Studies in the Literature of the American Civil War*. 1962. Reprint, New York: Norton, 1994. 99–130.

Zarefsky, David. *Lincoln, Douglas, and Slavery: In the Crucible of Public Debate*. Chicago: University of Chicago Press, 1990.

Richmond, Lincoln's Arrival in

On April 4, 1865, Abraham Lincoln began one of the most memorable trips of his life. He was aboard the *Malvern*, the flagship of Admiral David Dixon Porter's fleet, and he was traveling up the James River to Richmond, Virginia, which had fallen to Union troops less than twenty-four hours earlier. When he heard the news of the city's fall on April 3, Lincoln had told Admiral Porter, "Thank God I have lived to see this. It seems to me that I have been dreaming a horrid dream for four years, and now the nightmare is over." The *Malvern* started upriver the following day at 8:00 a.m. but was soon thwarted by wreckage of all sorts as it entered the channel that approached the city. Carcasses of dead horses, artillery caissons, wrecked boats, and even floating torpedoes, some of which had not yet been defused, littered the river. The party was forced to leave the admiral's ship and board a smaller, captain's barge that was towed by a tug manned by a small contingent of marines. When even that went aground, they had to resort to a rowboat powered by a dozen sailors. When the boat finally made it to Rockett's Landing, the presidential party debarked, only to be quickly surrounded by a group of black workers who immediately recognized Lincoln.

Hundreds of African Americans began pressing in, shouting and invoking the heavens as they witnessed the unbelievable scene taking place in their midst. Several began falling to their knees, praising God and speaking of Lincoln as though he were a messiah in their midst. The president, in an emotion-filled voice, told them, "Don't kneel to me. That is not right. You must kneel to God only, and thank Him for the liberty you will hereafter enjoy." As Lincoln and his small entourage continued up Main Street toward the Confederate White House, the streets, which had been nearly empty, came alive with crowds of former slaves "tumbling and shouting, from over the hills and from the waterside." The crowd that followed him as he proceeded on foot, protected only by a half-dozen marines, grew larger and larger. From windows above the street, hundreds of whites peered out at him, while Lincoln, scarcely noticing the potentially dangerous situation he was in, continuously looked around, taking in everything, seemingly fascinated to be walking the streets of the capital of the rebellion.

At the end of the two-mile walk, Lincoln and the crowd arrived at the residence that had been abandoned by Jefferson Davis only two days earlier. General Godfrey Weitzel had made it his headquarters when he occupied Richmond, and he and his staff breathed a sigh of relief as Lincoln entered the mansion and went into Davis's office, where he sat in the chair that had been used by the Confederate president. To all present it seemed "a supreme moment," but Lincoln's first words, softly spoken, were to ask for a glass of water. The old black servant,

An artist's depiction of Lincoln being greeted by Union soldiers and freedmen in City Point, Virginia, in late March 1865. Lincoln's bodyguard thought it a miracle that Lincoln completed his tour of the fallen Confederate capital without an attempt on his life.

Source: The Granger Collection, New York

still at his post, supplied the water along with a bottle of whiskey and informed those present that "Mrs. Davis had ordered him to have the house in good condition for the Yankees." After touring the mansion and meeting with members of General Weitzel's staff, Lincoln met with Confederate assistant secretary of war John Campbell. The president was acquainted with Campbell from their meeting two months earlier at the Hampton Roads Conference. Though there is some dispute as to what Lincoln and Campbell discussed, it seems apparent that the president agreed to allow the Virginia legislature to convene, but with the condition that it repeal the state's order of secession and remove the Virginia troops from the war.

That afternoon Lincoln went for a carriage ride through the city and visited the Confederate statehouse, which was in total disorder—evidence of the sudden flight of the Confederate government—with desks turned over, large quantities of Confederate scrip lying everywhere in the chamber, and many seemingly significant documents scattered about. After seeing a number of the sights of Richmond, Lincoln returned to the *Malvern*, much to the relief of both Admiral Porter and William Crook, the president's bodyguard. Crook wrote that night that it was nothing short of a miracle that no attempt on Lincoln's life occurred that day. It had been a very long day for Crook, with the president for hours totally exposed in the midst of a city whose residents had come to hate him for everything that he represented, at the very moment of their humiliation and defeat. Many Southerners would later characterize Lincoln's visit to Richmond as something of a "victory lap," a showy display of bravado intended to make them feel worse than they already did.

Lincoln remained at City Point for several more days, receiving his wife, Mary, and a delegation of officials who were arriving to celebrate the capture of Richmond and Petersburg and who wished to see the capital city. He did not return to Richmond when his guests visited, but he did join them for a visit to Petersburg during which he had the carriage stopped so he could get out and explore more closely a "very tall and beautiful" oak tree, admiring the strength of its trunk and intricate development of its branches. He had the carriage stopped a second time when it passed an old country graveyard. Lincoln turned to his wife and said, "Mary, you are younger than I. You will survive me. When I am gone, lay my remains in some quiet place like this." And on the train back to City Point later in the day, he observed a turtle basking in the sun along the wayside. He had the train stopped so the animal could be brought on board, and for the remainder of the ride he and Tad laughed together as they enjoyed the ungainly movements of the turtle.

Lincoln ended the day by spending five hours in an army hospital at City Point. He held the hand of each man he visited, including one twenty-four-year-old captain who had been cited for bravery. As Lincoln took his hand, the horribly wounded captain opened his eyes, smiled, and died.

The following morning, Sunday, April 9, Lincoln returned to Washington aboard the *River Queen*. During the trip the president talked with the Marquis de Chambrun about literary subjects. At one point Lincoln was quoting from a passage in *Macbeth* when the king is delivering his pained eulogy to the murdered Duncan:

> *Duncan is in his grave;*
> *After life's fitful fever he sleeps well;*
> *Treason has done his worst; nor steel, nor poison,*
> *Malice domestic, foreign levy, nothing,*
> *Can touch him further.*

Lincoln was taken by "how true a description of the murderer that one was, when the dark deed achieved, its tortured perpetrator came to envy the sleep of his victim." Lincoln seemed so fascinated with the passage that he read it again, causing his friend James Speed to remind him about the increased threat to his own life. "He stopped me at once," Speed recalled later, "saying he would rather be dead than to live in continued dread." Plus he regarded it essential "that the people know I come among them without fear."

—David E. Long

BIBLIOGRAPHY

Goodwin, Doris Kearns. *Team of Rivals: The Political Genius of Abraham Lincoln.* New York: Simon and Schuster, 2005.

Thomas, Benjamin P. *Abraham Lincoln: A Biography.* New York: Random House, 1952.

Winik, Jay. *April 1865: The Month That Saved America.* New York: HarperCollins, 2001.

Rivers and Harbors Convention

In 1846 President James K. Polk vetoed a bill that designated federal funds for construction projects to improve western harbors and waterways. Polk based his veto on a strict reading of the Constitution and asserted that the government could not support such regional improvements because they did not benefit the nation as a whole. Northerners, residents of the old Northwest specifically, including many Democrats, saw the veto as a slight to their interests in opening the West to trade.

In response to the veto, an organizing committee met in New York City to plan a nonpartisan convention to promote the improvement of inland waterways: the rivers of the West and harbors of the Great Lakes. The committee chose Chicago for the convention, and a crowd estimated in excess of 10,000 delegates and visitors arrived in the city in early July. The convention opened on July 5, 1847, and it quickly elected officers, including a president, Missouri delegate Edward Bates (later U.S. attorney general from 1861 to 1864).

Abraham Lincoln was the lone Whig congressman from Illinois in 1847, and his presence as one of three delegates from Sangamon County was due largely to his strong reputation for supporting internal improvements in the Illinois General Assembly. The convention was a first for Lincoln in two respects: It marked his first visit to Chicago, and it afforded him his first opportunity to speak before a national audience.

Despite the best efforts of its organizers, the convention took on a partisan (anti–Polk administration) and sectional tone. During the convention's second day, New York Democrat David Dudley Field spoke before the delegates and defended President Polk's veto. He asserted that any federal projects should have a national character that would return benefits to all citizens equally. Appropriations for the improvement of the Chicago harbor, for instance, were too local in nature and could not benefit all citizens, especially those in the Southern states.

After Field finished to a chorus of boos and hisses, Lincoln took the podium. He called for a more unified convention, but in refuting Field, he insisted that no internal improvement project could satisfy President Polk's strict construction of the Constitution and benefit all citizens equally. Regional improvements, such as those proposed for western waterways, would benefit the nation as a whole. In his speech, reported in the July 12, 1847, *Missouri Daily Republican* (St. Louis), Lincoln traced his differences with Field to their opposing views of the Constitution: "He [Field] loves the Constitution. I hope I may love it as well as he does, but in a different way. He looks upon it as a net work, through which may be sifted the seeds of discord and dissension. I look upon it as a complete protection of the Union."

The convention passed resolutions calling for federal support to improve navigation on western waterways, and it authorized a memorial containing the resolutions to be presented to Congress. During the following year Congress was the scene of much wrangling over the appropriation of funds for internal improvements. On June 20, 1848, Congressman Lincoln spoke on internal improvements before the House of Representatives, supporting the memorial. Not until 1852, however, would President Millard Fillmore approve internal improvements legislation.

See also *Bates, Edward*

—Christopher Schnell

BIBLIOGRAPHY

Fergus, Robert, comp. "Chicago River and Harbor Convention: An Account of Its Origin and Proceedings." *Fergus Historical Series* 18, Chicago, 1882.

Shaw, James. "A Neglected Episode in the Life of Abraham Lincoln." *Transactions of the Illinois State Historical Society* 29 (1922): 51–58.

Williams, Mentor L. "The Chicago River and Harbor Convention, 1847." *Mississippi Valley Historical Review* 35 (1948–1949): 607–626.

Ruffin, Edmund

Edmund Ruffin (January 5, 1794–June 17, 1865), Southern nationalist and agricultural reformer, was born in Prince George County, Virginia, to the wealthy planter George Ruffin and Jane Lucas. Just before his father's death in 1810, Edmund Ruffin enrolled at the College of William and Mary. Although he withdrew after a year of study, while in college Ruffin met Susan Hutchings Travis, whom he married in 1813. Following brief militia service during the War of 1812, Ruffin settled into a gentleman's life as master of his Coggin's Point plantation, which he later named Beechwood.

Intent on keeping his plantation lands fertile, Ruffin explored various fertilization techniques and in 1818 began experimenting with marl, a shell-like mineral deposit rich in calcium carbonate. This pioneering agricultural reform reduced excess soil acidity and helped to rejuvenate his exhausted lands. Ruffin published the results of his experiments in the journal *American Farmer* in 1821 and then in a 242-page book titled *An Essay on Calcareous Manures,* in 1832. Ruffin's theory that soil fertility could be altered as a result of organic action was a major contribution to soil chemistry and earned him a national reputation as an agricultural reformer. In 1832 Ruffin abandoned active farming to publish the *Farmers' Register,* and in 1835 he moved from his plantation to Petersburg, Virginia, where he became temporarily active in the Petersburg Benevolent Mechanic Association. The *Farmers' Register* gained a reputation as a leading vehicle for the exchange of agricultural skill and knowledge, but it lost readership after Ruffin began attacking the banking establishment. It ceased publication in December 1842.

Ruffin returned to farming on a new plantation some fifteen miles northeast of Richmond, aptly named Marlbourne, in the late 1840s. There Ruffin continued his agricultural studies, proving again that his progressive theories provided a solid

Southern firebrand Edmund Ruffin committed suicide when the Confederacy fell.

Source: The Granger Collection, New York

program for soil enhancement. In the mid-1850s Ruffin turned his zeal to politics. Taken aback by the vocal attacks on slavery by Northern abolitionists and Free-Soilers, Ruffin vigorously defended the institution using historical, racial, and economic arguments. The master of nearly 200 slaves, Ruffin argued that disunion was the only path to preserving the institution he viewed as the cornerstone of Southern society. In the last years of the 1850s, Ruffin traveled widely preaching disunion and published a series of works that earned him a reputation as one of the nation's leading "fire-eaters." Among them were two lengthy pamphlets, "The Political Economy of Slavery" and "African Colonization Unveiled," both of which appeared in 1858, and a novel, *Anticipations of the Future, to Serve as Lessons for the Present Time* (1860), which was inspired by John Brown's raid on the federal arsenal at Harpers Ferry, Virginia. Although far too old for military service, Ruffin had joined a militia company in 1859 so that he could witness Brown's execution. In the novel Ruffin predicted the election of Abraham Lincoln in 1860 and the election of William Seward in 1864. In Ruffin's fictional America, it was the prospect of the election of Seward in 1868 that sparked a civil war, which was fought in Virginia alone. In hopes of preventing his fiction from turning into reality, Ruffin delivered a series of pro-secession speeches in October 1860.

Despite his efforts, Ruffin had little influence on the events leading to secession, and he was especially disgusted by the Virginia Convention, which initially rejected secession. As the presidential election approached in 1860, Ruffin traveled south and was on hand to witness the secession of both South Carolina and Florida. He was at Fort Sumter, serving as part of South Carolina's Palmetto Guard, when the first shots of the Civil War were fired on April 12, 1861. Many contemporary observers credited him with firing the first shot. Gaining the status of popular hero, Ruffin returned to Virginia and remained devoted to the cause of Southern independence even as his plantations were overrun and pillaged by federal troops. When the Confederacy fell, Ruffin's carefully constructed ideological world collapsed. Ruffin committed suicide on June 17, 1865.

—L. DIANE BARNES

BIBLIOGRAPHY

Mitchell, Betty L. *Edmund Ruffin: A Biography.* Bloomington: Indiana University Press, 1981.

Ruffin, Edmund. *Diary of Edmund Ruffin.* Edited by William Scarborough. Baton Rouge: Louisiana State University Press, 1972.

Rutledge, Ann

Ann Rutledge (1813–1835), Abraham Lincoln's first romantic interest, whose sudden death in 1835 plunged him into a profound depression, has also been the subject of intense historiographical debate.

Born in Kentucky on January 7, 1813, Ann Mayes Rutledge was the third of ten children born to James and Mary Rutledge. In 1816 James Rutledge moved his young family to Illinois, and in 1829 he founded the village of New Salem, on the Sangamon River. In addition to building a sawmill and a gristmill, Rutledge converted his home into a tavern to accommodate travelers.

When Lincoln arrived in New Salem, Ann Rutledge was the most desirable girl in the village, but she was already engaged to be married. She had accepted the marriage proposal of John McNeil (1801–1879), a smooth-talking young businessman from New York. McNeil, however, was keeping a secret.

McNeil surprised villagers when he revealed that his real name was John McNamar. He claimed that his father had run up crippling debts in the East and that he had left home and traveled west in hopes of earning enough money to help his father pay his creditors. McNamar told his fiancée that his recent business dealings had been so lucrative that he was going back east to bring his parents to central Illinois. When he returned, he promised Ann, he would marry her.

When McNamar arrived at his parents' home in 1832, he found his father in poor health. His condition steadily worsened, and he died on April 10, 1833. For the next two years McNamar attended to the details of his father's muddled estate. Though it would seem likely, historians simply do not know if he wrote to Ann Rutledge during this time.

With McNamar out of the picture, Lincoln began spending more time with Ann. He boarded at the Rutledge Tavern and attended classes with her at Mentor Graham's (1800–1886) school. The friendship soon blossomed into something more. According to Ann's brother, Lincoln proposed marriage, and Ann accepted on the condition that she could speak with McNamar and obtain release from their engagement. "There is no kind of doubt as to the existence of this engagement," her brother emphasized. Ann's cousin claimed that she sought his advice during that time and echoed much of her brother's account. More than thirty years later, more than a dozen of New Salem's former residents corroborated the Lincoln-Rutledge engagement.

Of course, the marriage never happened. In August 1835, Ann became sick with what contemporaries called "brain fever," which was probably typhoid. She was confined to bed, her condition rapidly deteriorated, and on August 25, 1835, she died.

Lincoln was inconsolable. He told neighbors that he could not "bare the idea of it raining on her grave." A villager referred to him as "temporarily deranged," and another said simply, "The community said he was crazy." Neighbors feared that he was suicidal.

Eventually Lincoln recovered, and a little more than a year later he was courting another woman. However, the Lincoln-Rutledge romance resurfaced more than twenty-five years later. On February 15, 1862, an article appeared in the *Menard Axis,* in Petersburg, Illinois, that detailed the entire episode. The editor had heard the story from his father, who had been not only a villager but also one of Ann's failed suitors.

The story made an impression on Lincoln's law partner William H. Herndon (1818–1891). Shortly after Lincoln's assassination, Herndon began interviewing New Salem residents, several of whom quickly convinced him that the story was genuine. On November 16, 1866, Herndon outlined his findings in a lecture in Springfield. Herndon claimed that Ann suffered from a "conflict of duties, love's promises, and womanly engagements." She was engaged to two men at the same time and died, as it were, from a broken heart. Moreover, Herndon claimed that the story of lost love explained Lincoln's lifelong melancholy, as well as his aversion to organized religion. With Lincoln's widow still very much alive, Herndon callously told his audience that his law partner never again loved another woman after Ann Rutledge died.

Lincoln's family was understandably outraged. His oldest son, Robert Todd Lincoln (1843–1926), wrote that Herndon was "making an ass of himself" and traveled to Springfield to confront him. Similarly Lincoln's widow, Mary Todd Lincoln (1818–1882), dismissed the story outright. *"Ann Rutledge* is a myth," she wrote.

For the next fifty years, Herndon's interpretation of the Rutledge romance dominated the historiography. The height of sentimentality came in 1915 when Edgar Lee Masters (1868–1950) penned a poem for Ann Rutledge, which was later engraved on a bronze tablet and placed beside her grave.

However, a 1928 article in the *Atlantic Monthly,* which featured an astonishing collection of Lincoln and Ann's purported love letters, was simply too much. When the collection was ultimately deemed fraudulent, historians became hostile to the Rutledge romance.

James G. Randall's (1881–1953) multivolume *Lincoln the President* (1945–1955) featured a curious appendix titled, "Sifting the Ann Rutledge Evidence." Randall attacked Herndon's credibility, the memories of New Salem residents, and the veracity of oral history testimony. Though the existence of a relationship, much less an engagement, was not "*dis*proved," he reminded his audience that it was also "*un*proved." The episode was little more than "a famous subject of conjecture."

Randall's wife, Ruth Painter Randall, and graduate student, David Donald, both adopted the Randall thesis. Benjamin P. Thomas's much-heralded Lincoln biography followed suit, as did the major reference work of the period, *The Collected Works of Abraham Lincoln,* edited by Roy P. Basler.

In 1990, John Y. Simon boldly challenged the prevailing historiography. Simon conceded that Herndon had "grossly mishandled a major incident in the Lincoln story." Herndon had never liked Lincoln's widow, and now he used "Ann as a weapon" to injure her. "Neither Herndon's reputation nor that of Ann Rutledge ever recovered from this series of blunders," Simon concluded. He called on scholars to reevaluate the Ann Rutledge evidence.

Historians answered the call. In 1982 Charles Strozier wrote that there was "no single thread of good evidence on the subject"; almost twenty years later, however, Strozier changed his interpretation. By 2001 he had concluded that the "oral history evidence of Lincoln's old friends and neighbors should be taken seriously indeed." Similarly, David Herbert Donald revised his initial skepticism. Nearly half a century after he endorsed the Randall interpretation, Donald argued that Lincoln and Ann were engaged to be married at the time of her death. Just eight years later, however, Donald backed away from that conclusion, though he acknowledged that it was indeed "hard to reach a reasoned judgment."

—Samuel P. Wheeler

BIBLIOGRAPHY

Donald, David. *Lincoln's Herndon.* New York: Knopf, 1948.

———. *Lincoln.* New York: Simon and Schuster, 1995.

———. *"We are Lincoln Men": Abraham Lincoln and His Friends.* New York: Simon and Schuster, 2003.

Fehrenbacher, Don E. "The Minor Affair: An Adventure in Forgery and Detection." In *Lincoln in Text and Context: Collected Essays.* Stanford: Stanford University Press, 1987.

Randall, James G. "Sifting the Ann Rutledge Evidence." Appendix in *Lincoln the President: Springfield to Gettysburg.* 2 vols. New York: Dodd, Mead, 1945.

Simon, John Y. "Abraham Lincoln and Ann Rutledge." *Journal of the Abraham Lincoln Association* 11 (1990).

Walsh, John Evangelist. *The Shadows Rise: Abraham Lincoln and the Ann Rutledge Legend.* Champaign: University of Illinois Press, 1993.

Wilson, Douglas L., and Rodney O. Davis, eds. *Herndon's Informants: Letters, Interviews, and Statements about Abraham Lincoln.* Urbana: University of Illinois Press, 1998.

Scott, Winfield

Winfield Scott (1786–1866), commanding general of the U.S. Army at the outbreak of the Civil War, had been a general since 1813, when Abraham Lincoln was a four-year-old boy. He had been commanding general since 1841, when Lincoln was still a fledgling lawyer in Springfield, Illinois. While Lincoln was serving his single term in Congress, notable primarily for his opposition to the Mexican War, Scott was off in Mexico leading the brilliant campaign that won that war. When Scott ran for president in 1852 on the Whig ticket, he scarcely noticed the campaign support he received from this still-obscure Illinois Whig. Eight years later, when Lincoln ran for president as a Republican, Scott did not return the favor, supporting the Constitutional Union ticket instead.

Lincoln's victory and the secession crisis it precipitated gave Scott concern that this Illinois politician, whom he had never met, might not be up to the challenges he would face. Having chafed under the vacillations of Franklin Pierce and the dithering James Buchanan, Scott needed assurances. "Is Lincoln a *firm* man?" he asked Illinois congressman Elihu Washburne, who replied that the incoming president would do his duty "in the sight of the furnace seven times heated." "All is not lost," the gratified general replied. For his part, the president-elect had reason to be apprehensive about his commanding general. Scott's advanced age—he would soon be seventy-five and was too feeble to mount a horse without the aid of a stepladder—and Virginia upbringing; his alleged preference for Southern officers; and his contentious history of quarrelling with virtually every president he had served under all gave rise to reasonable grounds for suspicion. In fact, rumors swirled throughout the South that Scott was ready to throw in his lot with the Confederacy. To ease his mind, Lincoln sent an emissary to sound out Scott's dependability. Scott was ill, but the old man lifted himself from his sickbed and guaranteed that Lincoln would have a secure inauguration. "If necessary," he vowed, "I shall plant cannon at the ends of Pennsylvania Avenue," and if any secessionists dared to make trouble, "I shall blow them to Hell!" The promise was kept. Thanks to Scott's elaborate security precautions, the inauguration proceeded smoothly and safely.

There were, however, greater challenges to be met, the most pressing of which was the disposition of federal forts in Confederate territory, particularly Fort Sumter in Charleston Harbor. Even before his inauguration Lincoln had assured Scott of his determination to hold or retake these forts—a policy that Scott had been urging on the indecisive Buchanan administration for months. Yet a week after Lincoln's inauguration Scott advised that Fort Sumter should be abandoned, in view of the greatly strengthened Confederate forces in Charleston. This advice was consistent with Scott's hope that the sectional crisis could be resolved short of war if only the South was not provoked into premature violence. If that should happen, he predicted a three-year war requiring 300,000 soldiers and a quarter-billion dollars. The president and his cabinet overrode Scott's cautious advice, only to see the relief expedition turned back, just as Scott had warned, setting off the costly civil war he had feared.

In the early stages of that war Lincoln, the untutored militia captain of the Black Hawk War, necessarily leaned on the experienced commanding general for advice. In his daily reports Scott, in effect, gave the president a crash course in military science. His influence at that point was so great that it seemed to Edwin Stanton as if Scott was, "in fact, the Government." Under his direction the capital city became an armed camp, as tens of thousands of soldiers poured in to defend it against the rebels just beyond the Potomac. These troops were mostly half-trained volunteers, since the 16,000 regulars of the prewar army, and even the 75,000 volunteers Lincoln initially called for, would be grossly insufficient to fight the vast war that would follow. Scott had fought the Mexican War with an army of 10,000; this war would ultimately require numbers a hundred times greater.

What should be done with this immense army once it was assembled? The press and the cabinet expected an immediate advance on the rebel capital of Richmond, Virginia, but Scott was more cautious. Still hoping to resolve the crisis with a minimum of bloodshed, he advocated slow economic strangulation of the Confederacy through what critics labeled his "Anaconda plan." The impatient civilian voices prevailed, and Scott reluctantly approved an invasion of Virginia which, as he had warned, resulted in a Union defeat at the Battle of Bull Run on July 21, 1861.

That battle signaled the beginning a new kind of war, one that Scott was ill-equipped to manage. He was soon eased out of command in favor of George B. McClellan, forty years his junior, and the following November he retired from the army he had served for more than half a century.

Scott and Lincoln parted on amicable terms which, considering that the contentious general had quarreled with virtually everyone he had ever served under, was a tribute to both men. "I have never served under a president who has been kinder to me than you have been," he told Lincoln. Lincoln, in turn, paid Scott a handsome tribute in his annual message to Congress, "calling to mind how fruitfully, ably and brilliantly he has served his country...when few of those now living had been born, and thenceforth continually—I can not but think we are still his debtors."

After that the old general faded into retirement. In one of his last public appearances he was seen "pale, feeble but resolute," as he paid his respects to

Lincoln's coffin where it lay in state. A little over a year later, May 29, 1866, Scott himself was dead.

See also *Anaconda Plan*

—ALLAN PESKIN

BIBLIOGRAPHY

Elliott, Charles Winslow. *Winfield Scott: The Soldier and the Man.* New York: Macmillan, 1937.

Keyes, E.D. *Fifty Years Observation of Men and Events.* New York: Charles Scribner's Sons, 1889.

Nicolay, John G., and John Hay. *Abraham Lincoln: A History.* New York: Century Co., 1890.

Peskin, Allan. *Winfield Scott and the Profession of Arms.* Kent, Ohio: Kent State University Press, 2003.

Secession

Secession was the 1860–1861 movement of several Southern states to withdraw from the United States and form a new republic. Abraham Lincoln's effort to prevent secession while also avoiding war dominated his months as president-elect and the first weeks of his presidency. It finally failed with the April 12, 1861, attack on Fort Sumter, South Carolina.

Southern talk of secession dated from the Continental Congress, when Southerners threatened to leave the emerging confederation if they did not get their way on slavery issues. Deep South delegates used similar warnings to influence the Constitutional Convention of 1787. In response to the Sedition Act of 1798, the Kentucky Resolutions, written by Thomas Jefferson, presented a radical states' rights protest against abuse of federal power. In 1831 South Carolina flirted with secessionist arguments in asserting the right to nullify a federal law.

Such threats were not the exclusive domain of Southerners: At the Hartford Convention some New England Federalists had discussed seceding during the War of 1812. As late as 1857, radical abolitionists led by William Lloyd Garrison held an abortive secession convention in Worcester, Massachusetts. But Garrison had few followers, and his demands that the North secede from the South never gained serious traction, even among abolitionists. The first serious movement to secede occurred in 1850, when the protracted crisis over whether newly acquired Mexican territories would be slave or free sparked the "Nashville Movement," a plan for Southern radicals to meet in Nashville, Tennessee, to coordinate secession among their various states. Although the movement was defused by a timely congressional compromise, from that point forward secession threats became a staple of national politics, recurring with each new sectional crisis.

A rare illustrated sheet music cover issued under the Confederacy. By the time Lincoln was inaugurated on March 4, 1861, six states—Mississippi, Florida, Alabama, Georgia, Louisiana, and Texas—joined South Carolina to create the Confederate States of America.

Source: Library of Congress

Threats of disunion became especially common with the Republicans' first national campaign in 1856. By 1860 most Republicans had become inured to secession talk, dismissing abundant warnings that if their party should capture the White House secession would follow. To them dealings with the South had developed into a tiresome routine: Southerners demanded political advantages, Northerners balked, Southerners threatened to secede, and Northern Democrats gave in and voted with the South. It took Republicans a while to realize that this time was different. South Carolina disunionists ensured that their efforts would not be bogged down by interstate cooperation or a congressional compromise: Immediately upon Lincoln's election on November 6, 1860, the state legislature called a secession convention, which resolved South Carolina out of the Union on December 20, three days after convening. By the time Lincoln was inaugurated on March 4, 1861, six more Deep South states—Mississippi, Florida, Alabama, Georgia, Louisiana, and Texas—had followed suit and joined South Carolina to create the Confederate States of America.

Lame duck president James Buchanan struggled to maintain federal authority in the Deep South, but he was hampered by a deep sympathy with Southern grievances and a desperate desire to prevent violence from undermining congressional negotiations. In Congress, meanwhile, the efforts of Upper South Unionists and Northern Democrats to forge a compromise were impeded by Deep South secessionists and skeptical Republicans. By mid-December 1860, however, conciliationists were joined by a growing number of Republican representatives, and compromise briefly seemed a legitimate possibility. This movement was killed by the combined efforts of outraged Republican constituents and

President-elect Lincoln, who together pressured conciliatory Republicans into adopting a harder line.

Far from the center of events in Washington, neither Lincoln nor his party's rank and file grasped either the depth of secessionism in the Deep South or the fragility of the Upper South's continued loyalty. They believed falsely that disunion sentiment was not widespread even in the Deep South and that, given time and the absence of direct provocation, the secession fever would break and a latent Unionism come to the fore. Had he had a fuller comprehension of the crisis, though, Lincoln is unlikely to have adopted a more conciliatory stance, for in addition to his faith in Southern Unionism, his secession policy was based on two further assumptions (also shared by most Republicans in the winter of 1860–1861). The first was that secession was impossible under the Constitution and would mark the effective end of the American republic. The second was that giving in to Southern ultimatums would not only embolden secessionists by confirming their belief that Northerners were weak and easily intimidated, but would also subvert the very idea of popular government. These assumptions dictated a policy that balanced firmness with magnanimity. On one hand, Republicans must steadfastly resist both disunion and Southern demands for proslavery concessions. On the other, they must reassure concerned Southerners that they would not violate the South's constitutional rights, particularly with regard to slave property.

Reluctant to give secessionists the opportunity to twist his words to their advantage, Lincoln adhered fairly strictly to a policy of public silence from his election until his departure from Springfield for Washington on February 11, 1861. Privately, however, he extended what he intended to be an encouraging hand, assuring Southern Unionist leaders of the Republicans' commitment to respecting Southern constitutional rights, urging his party's congressional leaders to do the same, and seeking Southerners for cabinet posts. At the same time, he made plain to party leaders his firm opposition both to secession and to the movement to fashion a compromise in Congress. Indeed, he continued to maintain a careful watch over Congress, repeatedly quashing renewed efforts to recruit Republicans to the cause of compromise. His efforts succeeded: Congress adjourned on March 4, 1861, having passed just one compromise measure: a constitutional amendment prohibiting federal interference with slavery in the states, something Republicans believed the Constitution did already.

The two-edged sword of firmness and magnanimity informed Lincoln's March 4 inaugural address. In this long-awaited pronouncement of his secession policy, he denounced secession as anarchy, argued that it was unconstitutional and therefore legally void, and pledged to collect import duties at Southern ports and defend all federal property in the Deep South still in government hands. Yet he also continued to insist that his administration had neither the power nor the desire to interfere with slavery in the Southern states and appealed eloquently to Americans' common history and faith in constitutional government to carry them through the crisis.

On the day after his inauguration Lincoln received word that the federal garrison at Fort Sumter, in Charleston Harbor, South Carolina, would soon run out of supplies and that a successful rescue mission could not be arranged in the limited time available. As Fort Sumter was one of just two significant military posts remaining in the Deep South and was located in the very heart of secessionist sentiment and action, Lincoln believed that its evacuation would mark a de facto acknowledgment of disunion. He postponed a decision as long as possible and then, against the counsel of his chief military and political advisers, decided to resupply the fort. In one of the most controversial moves of his presidency, Lincoln abandoned a plan to force in supplies and reinforcements suddenly and forcefully, which was widely considered to be the most realistic plan for successfully resupplying the fort. Instead, on April 6 he requested that the governor of South Carolina (not the Confederate general commanding the defenses, whose authority Lincoln did not recognize) permit the relief mission through. As he almost certainly knew it would, his message triggered a demand for Sumter's surrender, followed by an assault that, some thirty-three hours later, produced the fort's capitulation on April 13.

In the North the seemingly unprovoked Confederate attack broke down political and ideological lines and instantly united public opinion behind the administration. Two days later Lincoln, still refusing to acknowledge secession, issued a proclamation calling for the suppression not of rebellious states, but of powerful combinations who were preventing the enforcement of federal law in the Deep South. The response to his call for volunteers was overwhelming. In the Upper South, however, Lincoln's proclamation represented naked coercion and drove four more states—Virginia, Tennessee, Arkansas, and North Carolina—into the Confederacy. Of the four remaining slave states, Delaware was too conservative to foster a serious secession movement, and a wide range of sometimes-desperate maneuvers by the administration prevented secession in Kentucky, Maryland, and Missouri until military victories in Kentucky, Missouri, Tennessee, and Arkansas made secession by the loyal slave states all but impossible.

—RUSSELL MCCLINTOCK

BIBLIOGRAPHY

Crofts, Daniel W. *Reluctant Confederates: Upper South Unionists in the Secession Crisis.* Chapel Hill: University of North Carolina Press, 1989.

Dew, Charles B. *Apostles of Disunion: Southern Secession Commissioners and the Causes of the Civil War.* Charlottesville: University Press of Virginia, 2001.

Dumond, Dwight Lowell. *The Secession Movement, 1860–1861.* New York: Macmillan, 1931.

Freehling, William W. *The Road to Disunion.* 2 vols. New York: Oxford University Press, 1990–2007.

Klein, Maury. *Days of Defiance: Sumter, Secession, and the Coming of the Civil War.* New York: Knopf, 1997.

McClintock, Russell. *Lincoln and the Decision for War: The Northern Response to Secession.* Chapel Hill: University of North Carolina Press, 2008.

Potter, David M. *Lincoln and His Party in the Secession Crisis.* 1942. Reprint, Baton Rouge: Louisiana State University Press, 1995.

Stampp, Kenneth M. *And the War Came: The North and the Secession Crisis, 1860–1861.* 1950. Reprint, Baton Rouge: Louisiana State University Press, 1970.

Walther, Eric H. *The Fire-Eaters.* Baton Rouge: Louisiana State University Press, 1992.

Seward, William

William Seward was born in the small, rural town of Florida, New York, on May 16, 1801. As he reached adolescence it became clear that he was the most academically gifted of the Seward children. Though Seward generally subordinated himself to authority throughout his life, at key moments he rebelled. During his time at Union College, such a rebellion occurred when Seward, upset with his father's meager allowance, fled to Georgia where he found a job as a schoolteacher. This experience gave him a close look at slavery in the South that would have a profound effect on his later career. Eventually, at the pleading of his mother, Seward dutifully returned to Union College and finished at the top of his class.

After graduation Seward studied the law and was admitted to the bar in 1822. He involved himself in the anti-masonry movement and was elected to the New York Senate in 1830. In 1838, at the age of thirty-seven, Seward was elected the youngest governor to serve the state. As governor Seward gained a reputation as a radical on the issue of slavery and rights for black Americans. He provoked outrage from Virginia state officials when he refused to turn over three black sailors from New York who had helped a slave escape from Virginia, pointing out that there were no laws in New York forbidding the escape of slaves. Seward also advocated for the rights of black Americans to serve on juries and vote.

In 1846 Seward furthered his reputation as a radical when he used the insanity defense in two separate cases involving black men accused of murder. At the time Seward's involvement was immensely unpopular among his fellow New Yorkers. However, with the rise of the free-soil movement, Seward's political fortunes also rose, and he was elected as a Whig to the U.S. Senate in 1848. In the Senate, Seward emerged in the forefront of the antislavery movement. During the debate over the Compromise of 1850, Seward argued that the Constitution was fundamentally antislavery. Even if it condoned slavery there was a "higher law" that ruled over men, and the expansion of slavery was contrary to that law. In 1858 Seward declared that there was an "irrepressible conflict" between freedom and slavery.

By 1860 Seward was the assumed favorite to win the Republican nomination for president. It was only last-minute fears of Seward's perceived radicalism that allowed the dark horse candidate from Illinois to win the nomination and the presidency. Lincoln chose Seward, his chief Republican rival, to be his secretary of state.

Abraham Lincoln and William Seward had only one previous encounter before 1860. During the 1848 election, Seward and Lincoln stayed at the same hotel in Massachusetts. Lincoln had earlier heard a speech by Seward dealing with slavery and remarked to him, "Governor Seward, I have been thinking about what you said in your speech. I reckon you are right. We have got to deal with this slavery question, and got to give much more attention to it hereafter than we have been doing." Twelve years later the president-elect remarked that their chance encounter "had probably made a stronger impression on" his memory than it had on Governor Seward's.

In the early months of the Lincoln administration Seward assumed that the plainspoken prairie lawyer would be the figurehead for the government, while he would control the real power in the administration. On April 1, 1861, as the crisis over an impending civil war loomed, Seward wrote "Some Thoughts for the President's Consideration." In it he wrote Lincoln, "We are at the end of a month's administration and yet without a policy, either domestic or foreign." The strongly worded opening also contained curious policy recommendations, including the possibility of provoking a war with France or Spain as a means of reuniting the sections of the nation against a common enemy. He closed his letter by asserting that there must be a single figure to execute the administration's policies, and "Either the President must do it himself...or devolve it on some member of his Cabinet." Seward left little doubt who he meant when he finished: "It is not my especial province; but I neither seek to evade, nor assume, responsibility."

A lesser president might have viewed the insubordinate tone of the letter as reason to fire Seward. Instead Lincoln composed a reply in which he refuted Seward's assertions that the administration was without a policy. Referring to Seward's suggestion that there must be one commanding voice in the administration, Lincoln remarked, "If this must be done, *I* must do it." Yet as often happened when Lincoln wrote such letters, he chose not to send it. Presumably he shared many of the ideas in the letter with Seward in person, so as to provide a gentler tone. The episode is another example of the strange quirkiness of Seward's personality, in that his brief outburst of insubordination and rebelliousness quickly turned into unflinching loyalty to his superior.

Throughout most of the war Seward's main foreign policy objective was to prevent European powers from intervening on behalf of the Confederacy. At times this proved difficult. On November 8, 1861, a U.S. warship halted the *Trent*, a British vessel carrying two Confederate agents to England. U.S. authorities removed and arrested the two. The British government threatened war against the United States unless the Confederate agents were released. In spite of pressure in the United States to keep the men detained, Seward was able to convince Lincoln that releasing them was the best way to avoid war with Great Britain.

The personalities of Lincoln and Seward displayed sharp contrasts and perfect similarities. Seward was formally educated and raised in New York, whereas Lincoln grew up on the western frontier and engaged in rough labor early in life. His formal education was rough and sparse. Seward associated with the wealthy and educated, while Lincoln interacted with a cross-section of people along the frontier. Seward was vibrant with optimism and had a spring in his step, whereas Lincoln was often melancholy and walked flat-footed. Yet they shared a keen sense of humor. Seward was fond of retelling the story of coming across Lincoln polishing his shoes. When Seward remarked that no one in Washington "blacken[s their] own boots," Lincoln responded, "Indeed, then whose boots *do* you blacken?"

In spite of Seward's earlier radical positions on slavery, his temperament as secretary of state was remarkably conservative. When Lincoln shared his draft of the Emancipation Proclamation with the cabinet for their comments, Seward expressed support for the idea but persuaded Lincoln to wait until the United States won a major military victory. He was concerned that foreign powers would view the timing of the document as the "last shriek of the retreat." Seward also expressed fear that the European powers might construe the document as a call for a slave insurrection. Such an antagonistic move, coupled with the image that the Union was on the verge of defeat, might induce European nations to recognize the Confederacy. Ultimately Lincoln was sufficiently impressed by Seward's reasoning to delay the Emancipation Proclamation until the Union could claim a military victory.

Though Seward and Lincoln occasionally disagreed on policy, their mutual loyalty was strong. In 1863 Seward wrote privately of Lincoln that he was "the best and wisest man he [had] ever known." Indeed, Seward became the one member of the cabinet who developed a truly warm friendship with Lincoln. The often vain Seward was won over to admiration, as he wrote to his wife upon Lincoln's reelection:

> *The election has placed our President beyond the pale of human envy or human harm, as he is above the pale of ambition. Henceforth all men will come to see him as you and I have seen him—a true, loyal, patient, patriotic, and benevolent man.... Abraham Lincoln will take his place... among the benefactors of the country and of the human race.*

On April 5, 1865, a freak carriage accident left Seward severely injured and bedridden. It was during his recuperation that John Wilkes Booth conspired with several other men to have the top officials in the administration assassinated. On the same night that Lincoln was murdered, fellow Wilkes conspirator Lewis Powell barged into the Seward home. When his revolver would not function, Powell attempted to stab Seward with a dagger. The resulting chaotic struggle left several people, including William Seward and his son, severely wounded.

Though Powell failed to kill Seward, the stress of the events led Seward's wife to die of a heart attack shortly afterward. Within a year, Seward's youngest daughter, Fanny, also died as a result of illness. In spite of these personal tragedies, Seward remained as secretary of state in the Andrew Johnson administration. Seward further cemented his reputation as a conservative by supporting Johnson in many of his Reconstruction policies. During this time Seward completed one of his most famous achievements when he secured the purchase of Alaska from Russia. At the end of the Johnson administration, Seward retired from public life. In his remaining years Seward toured the world, publishing an account of his travels. In October 1872 Seward died of what was likely a mild form of Lou Gehrig's disease. He was seventy-one.

See also *Adams, Charles Francis; Cabinet, Lincoln's; Weed, Thurlow*

—JOHN WICKRE

BIBLIOGRAPHY

Donald, David. *'We Are Lincoln Men': Abraham Lincoln and His Friends.* New York: Simon and Schuster, 2003.

Finkelman, Paul, "The Protection of Black Rights in Seward's New York." *Civil War History* 34 (1988): 211–234.

Goodwin, Doris Kearns. *Team of Rivals.* New York: Simon and Schuster, 2005.

Seward, Frederick William. *Autobiography of William H. Seward from 1801 to 1834: With a Memoir of His Life, and Selections from his Letters from 1831 to 1840.* 1877.

Taylor, John M. *William Henry Seward: Lincoln's Right-hand Man.* New York: HarperCollins, 1991.

Van Deusen, Glyndon. *William Henry Seward.* New York: Oxford University Press, 1967.

Wilson, Douglas, and Rodney Davis, eds. *Herndon's Informants: Letters, Interviews, and Statements about Abraham Lincoln.* Urbana: University of Illinois Press, 1998.

Shenandoah Valley Campaigns of 1862 and 1864

Throughout the Civil War the Shenandoah Valley, located along the western edge of north-central Virginia (as of 1861), offered the Confederacy several important military advantages. Its fertile farms were an important source of foodstuffs and livestock. The Blue Ridge Mountains, which bound the eastern edge of the valley, provided a shield for Confederate advances northward, as well as a base of operations from which to threaten Union forces stationed around Washington. Harpers Ferry, a key strategic point, was located at the northern entrance to the valley. From there the valley runs southwest through Staunton and Harrisonburg. Confederate forces advancing northward would find themselves moving closer to Washington, while Union forces moving south would be drawn away from Richmond.

Although the Confederate redeployment from the valley to Manassas Junction via railroad played a role in determining the outcome of the First Battle of Bull Run, it was not until 1862 that the Confederate high command realized the Shenandoah Valley's full strategic value. That March, as George B. McClellan commenced his waterborne campaign against Richmond, Confederate commander Thomas J. "Stonewall" Jackson was busy responding to a Union advance, with orders to detain as many Union soldiers as possible from joining McClellan. On March 23, Jackson attacked Union forces at Kernstown, just south of Winchester, Virginia. Although the Union forces prevailed, news of the battle caused Abraham Lincoln to pay attention to the defense of Washington in the wake of McClellan's movement. The president had long disagreed with his general about whether McClellan had left enough men behind to secure Washington's safety. After Kernstown, Lincoln decided to retain control of Irvin McDowell's corps, stationed near Fredericksburg. The president preferred that McDowell, along with Union generals John C. Frémont (based in the Allegheny Mountains) and Nathaniel Banks (located in the northern valley), converge upon Jackson's men. However, he failed to appoint an overall commander for the operation.

Encouraged by Robert E. Lee, who was then serving as Jefferson Davis's military adviser, Jackson did what he could to fend off the enemy, which outnumbered him approximately three to one. Jackson marched south through the valley and attacked a portion of Frémont's command at McDowell (May 8–9), driving the Yankees away. Then Jackson dashed northward, first hitting a Union detachment at Front Royal (May 23) and then driving Banks back at Winchester (May 25). Banks pulled back to the Potomac River, and Jackson occupied Harpers Ferry.

Lincoln and secretary of war Edwin Stanton decided to concentrate their attention on crushing Jackson. They ignored McClellan's demand for reinforcements, infuriating that commander, who was nearing Richmond. Jackson evaded the trap, marching southward once more. He hit the heads of two of the converging columns when he pushed back Frémont at Cross Keys (June 8) and then a portion of McDowell's force at Port Republic (June 9). Union forces fell back to lick their wounds, while Jackson and his men joined Lee, now in command of the forces around Richmond, in time to launch an offensive against McClellan at the end of June.

For several months Jackson had detained upwards of 60,000 Union soldiers with his force of 17,000 men, marching approximately 650 miles in the course of seven weeks. His men became known as "Jackson's foot cavalry" because of the speed with which they moved. As brilliant as Jackson's generalship may have been, however, it was because of Lincoln that he was able to occupy the attention of so many Union soldiers. The president's failure to appoint someone to coordinate operations allowed Jackson to hit in turn the spearheads of various Union advances.

The Shenandoah Valley played a far lesser role throughout the rest of 1862, with the exception of Lee's decision to capture Harpers Ferry during his September invasion of Maryland. Still, the surrender of the Union garrison, some 12,500 strong, on September 15 should be included in the calculations of losses incurred during the Maryland campaign. In June 1863 Lee would employ the valley once more as he crossed the Potomac and invaded Maryland and Pennsylvania, and he sought shelter there following his defeat in July 1863. By spring 1864 Union forces again occupied Harpers Ferry, while the Confederates remained in position to the south.

In 1864 Ulysses S. Grant planned to have Union forces advance south through the valley to deprive the Confederates of both a supply source and an avenue to advance. However, a Confederate triumph at New Market (May 15) brought a quick end to the initial campaign. Grant ordered General David Hunter to renew the effort, and by early June, Hunter was moving southward through the valley and beyond, with Lynchburg as his target. Lee responded by detaching Jubal Early from the Army of Northern Virginia to confront Hunter. Early's victory at Lynchburg (June 17–18) opened the way for the Confederates to advance across the Potomac in July, where they threatened Washington (July 11–12) and set fire to Chambersburg, Pennsylvania, in retaliation for Hunter's burning of the Virginia Military Institute and several homes. Lee hoped that Early's campaign would repeat Jackson's earlier successes and force Grant to abandon his siege of Richmond and Petersburg, but Lincoln endorsed Grant's decision to remain where he was: "Hold on with a bulldog grip, and chew and choke as much as possible." Nevertheless, units earmarked for the Richmond-Petersburg front had been diverted to Washington in response to Early's operations, and during July they were not brought under unified command, an echo of what had happened in 1862.

Aware of the possible political impact of the presence of a Confederate army near Washington and the North during a presidential election year, Grant finally decided to place Philip H. Sheridan in charge of the newly formed Army of the Shenandoah with orders to smash Early and devastate the valley. Sheridan's victories at Winchester (September 19), Fisher's Hill (September 22), and Cedar Creek (October 19) removed Early as a military threat, while he implemented Grant's directive to devastate the valley such that "a crow flying across the Valley would have to carry its own rations."

Sheridan's victories were critical in large part because they raised Northern morale. Especially important in this regard were the dramatic circumstances under which he rode to the field at Cedar Creek and found his men re-forming after a Confederate attack early that morning had caught them unawares. Waving his hat and riding forward, Sheridan helped rally his men and mounted a counterattack in the afternoon that drove Early from the field. Occurring a week after several October elections had suggested that the Republicans had an edge in some closely contested states, Sheridan's victory gave the president some breathing room as the November presidential election approached. Sheridan completed driving Early out of the valley in 1865, removing it once and for all as a source of support to Confederate military operations.

—BROOKS D. SIMPSON

BIBLIOGRAPHY

Patchan, Scott C. *Shenandoah Summer: The 1864 Valley Campaign.* Lincoln: University of Nebraska Press, 2007.

Stackpole, Edward J. *Sheridan in the Shenandoah: Jubal Early's Nemesis.* Mechanicsburg, Pa.: Stackpole, 1961.

Tanner, Robert G. *Stonewall in the Valley: Thomas J. "Stonewall" Jackson's Shenandoah Valley Campaign, Spring 1862.* New York: Doubleday, 1976.

Wert, Jeffry D. *From Winchester to Cedar Creek: The Shenandoah Campaign of 1864.* 1987. Reprint, New York: Touchstone/Simon and Schuster, 1989.

Williams, T. Harry. *Lincoln and His Generals.* New York: Knopf, 1952.

Sherman, John

John Sherman (1823–1900), U.S. representative, U.S. senator, secretary of the Treasury, and secretary of state, was born in Lancaster, Ohio. Sherman was the younger brother of Civil War major general William T. Sherman and Charles Taylor Sherman, a federal judge. John Sherman received his early education in public schools. He later read law and was admitted to the bar in 1844.

Sherman began his political career as a Whig and served as a delegate to the Whig national conventions in 1848 and 1852. He supported the Compromise of 1850 but opposed the Kansas-Nebraska Act (1854), since the act repudiated the Missouri Compromise of 1820. His political beliefs led him to the Fusion Party and later to the Republican Party. He was elected a U.S. representative from 1854 to 1861. Sherman opposed the presidential administration of James Buchanan and the entry of Kansas as a slave state; he developed expertise on national financial policy and became a strong supporter of national tariffs. When Ohio's Sen. Salmon P. Chase resigned his seat to become the secretary of the Treasury in the cabinet of President Abraham Lincoln in 1861, Rep. Sherman was selected to fill out Chase's term of office. Sherman was later elected to the seat in his own right and continued to serve as U.S. senator until 1877.

With the onset of the American Civil War, Sherman was a strong supporter of President Lincoln and the policies of his administration. Initially Sherman planned to resign his office and offer his services to his state, helping to raise the "Sherman brigade" in and around Mansfield, Ohio. He subsequently decided to retain his seat in the U.S. Senate. He was a supporter of the Legal Tender Act of 1862, which allowed the printing of paper currency to finance the Union war effort. In 1863 Sherman introduced the National Bank Act, which allowed the federal government the same powers as public and private banks.

As U.S. senator, Sherman was in a position to assist and support the military career of his older brother, General William T. Sherman, throughout the Civil War. Senator Sherman supported his brother and advocated in his favor to other senators and President Lincoln. This was especially important with General Sherman's supposed mental breakdown as commander in Kentucky in 1861. Senator Sherman and General Sherman's wife used their influence to have the general placed back in an active field command. Sherman was among the senators who participated in a Radical Republican movement to replace Lincoln with secretary of the Treasury Salmon P. Chase—also an Ohioan—as the 1864 Republican presidential nominee. Their efforts backfired and Sherman soon sought reconciliation with the president.

At the end of the Civil War, Senator Sherman was a supporter of the Fifteenth Amendment, which guaranteed the right to vote regardless of race, but he opposed efforts to disfranchise former Confederates. However, he did not agree with President Andrew Johnson's policies toward the states of the former Confederacy. At President Johnson's impeachment trial, Sherman voted to impeach the president.

Sherman went on to serve in the cabinet of President Rutherford B. Hayes, especially because of his knowledge of national fiscal policies. Upon the election of President James A. Garfield, Sherman was again elected to the U.S. Senate. Sherman sought the Republican presidential nomination for the 1880, 1884, and 1888 elections, but each of these bids failed. He remained in the Senate from 1888 to 1897 and served as chairman of the Republican conference and chairman of the Committee on Foreign Relations. In 1890, Sherman drafted the Sherman Anti-Trust Act, one of the earliest attempts to control the growth of business monopolies. He also drafted legislation dealing with silver purchase acts.

With the election of his fellow Ohioan in 1897, Sherman served briefly as secretary of state in the cabinet of President William McKinley, before resigning in protest against the war with Spain and expansionism in general. At the age of seventy-four, Sherman retired from public life. He became ill and died two years later, in Washington, D.C.

—WILLIAM H. BROWN

BIBLIOGRAPHY

Boque, Allan G. *The Earnest Men: Republicans of the Civil War Senate*. Ithaca, N.Y.: Cornell University Press, 1981.

Burton, Theodore E. *John Sherman.* Boston: Houghton Mifflin, 1906.

Eng, Robert F., and Randall Miller, eds. *The Birth of the Grand Old Party: The Republicans' First Generation.* Philadelphia: University of Pennsylvania Press, 2002.

Gould, Lewis L. *The Presidency of William McKinley.* Lawrence: Regents Press of Kansas, 1980.

Hoogenboom, Ari Arthur. *The Presidency of Rutherford B. Hayes.* Lawrence: University Press of Kansas, 1988.

Sherman, John. *Recollections of Forty Years in the House, Senate, and Cabinet; An Autobiography.* 1895. New York: Greenwood Press, 1968.

Simpson, Brooks D. *The Reconstruction Presidents.* Lawrence: University Press of Kansas, 1998.

Socolofsky, Homer E., and Allan B. Setter. *The Presidency of Benjamin Harrison.* Norwalk, Conn.: Easton Press, 1987.

Walters, Everett. *Joseph Benson Foraker: An Uncompromising Republican.* Columbus: Ohio History Press, 1948.

Sherman, William T.

William T. Sherman (1820–1891), although initially skeptical about Abraham Lincoln's abilities as commander in chief, was an important contributor to the ultimate triumph of the Union war effort. In time he would come to appreciate Lincoln; after the president's death he would attempt to negotiate a peace settlement in line with what he believed to be Lincoln's wishes. In the process he would rank behind his close friend Ulysses S. Grant as the general most responsible for the Union's victory.

Born in Ohio in 1820, Sherman was taken in by Whig politician Thomas Ewing Sr. after the death of his father in 1829. He entered West Point in 1836 and graduated near the head of his class four years later, with a commission as a brevet second lieutenant of artillery. After seeing service in the South, where he gained an appreciation for the terrain in Georgia, he was transferred west to California; from there he watched the Mexican-American War and helped transmit the news of the discovery of gold at Sutter's Mill. Resigning from the army in 1853, Sherman became in turn a banker, a lawyer, and superintendent of a military academy in Alexandria, Louisiana (eventually this institution would evolve into Louisiana State University). He had been there just over a year when

General William T. Sherman at Atlanta, Georgia, in 1864. Sherman's capture of the Southern city has often been cited as a factor in securing Lincoln's reelection to the presidency.

Source: The Granger Collection, New York

Louisiana seceded. Refusing to accept delivery of arms taken by Louisiana from the United States arsenal in Baton Rouge, he resigned his position and moved to St. Louis, where he was heading a streetcar company at the outbreak of the war.

Sherman had excellent political connections—his brother John was a U.S. senator, his foster father/father-in-law was a leading Ohio Republican, and family friend Montgomery Blair was the postmaster general—and it was little surprise that in short order he was made a colonel and then a brigadier general. Sherman did not distinguish himself in his first combat action at First Manassas, and in private correspondence and conversation he questioned whether Lincoln and the Republicans were equal to the challenge before them.

That Sherman tended to see conquering the Confederacy as an overwhelming task became evident when he assumed command of the Department of the Cumberland, headquartered in Louisville, Kentucky, in fall 1861. Believing that the Confederates outnumbered him and that he lacked the manpower to accomplish the task at hand, Sherman expressed his opinions so freely and so vehemently that some observers decided that he was crazy. Doubtless he was feeling the pressure of high command, and he had no problem surrendering his position to rest and recover. Fortunately for him, Union general Henry W. Halleck thought highly of Sherman, protected him, and returned him to field command in 1862 as one of Ulysses S. Grant's division commanders. At Shiloh, Sherman's underestimation of the threat posed by nearby Confederates contributed to the unpreparedness of the Union defenders, but he proved far more able under fire, and in the aftermath of the battle he grew closer to Grant, who came to depend on Sherman for his loyalty and his abilities.

During the next several years Grant and Sherman forged a friendship that proved critical in securing Union success. However, Sherman was far more skeptical about how the Lincoln administration chose to wage war. He advocated taking the war to the Southern people, cared little about abolition, and passionately despised politicians and newspaper reporters. In 1862 he participated in Grant's initial failed effort to take Vicksburg, and he shared his superior's suspicion of fellow general John A. McClernand, who boasted of his influence with Lincoln.

When Grant devised his plan to take Vicksburg in spring 1863, Sherman expressed serious reservations about its feasibility, sharing those concerns in correspondence with family members. However, he loyally complied with Grant's directives, which included acting as a decoy to distract the Confederates. When the campaign turned out to be a smashing success, Sherman could but admire Grant, not least because of the neat way in which he dispatched McClernand while dealing with Lincoln's other concerns. Three months later, when Grant took over the Military Division of the Mississippi, Sherman replaced him as commander of the Army of the Tennessee; in November his subpar performance during the Union victory at Chattanooga did not damage his standing with Grant.

In 1864 the new general in chief, Grant, named Sherman to take over his command in the West, with orders to strike into the Confederate interior, target the Confederate Army of Tennessee, and prevent any troop transfers from that army to Virginia. In the campaign that followed, Sherman outmaneuvered his opponents, pushing the Confederates back through northwest Georgia to the outskirts of Atlanta by July. At that point, newly appointed Confederate commander John Bell Hood launched a series of attacks designed to push Sherman back, but he met with little success. In August Sherman methodically chopped away at Atlanta's connections to the outside world and stretched Hood's lines to the breaking point. Finally, on September 1, Hood evacuated Atlanta, and the following day Sherman entered the city.

The capture of Atlanta, coming as it did on the heels of the Democratic convention that had nominated George B. McClellan for president on a platform that declared the war a failure, ignited Northern morale. At the same time, it was a typical Sherman victory, achieved far more by maneuver than by combat. Throughout the war Sherman proved to be a better marcher than he was a fighter: The previous February he had demonstrated this when he marched through Mississippi in what became known as the Meridian Campaign, with the aim of disrupting Confederate logistics. At the same time, Sherman remained skeptical about politics and politicians, wondered whether Northerners were up to waging the all-out war he wanted to fight, argued that the key to defeating the Confederacy was shredding its material and psychological ability to fight, and expressed doubt about emancipation and disdain for the use of blacks as soldiers. It would not be until war's end that he would revise his earlier negative assessment of Lincoln, lending rich irony to the notion that it was his triumph at Atlanta that went far toward securing the president's reelection.

After taking Atlanta, Sherman discovered in Hood an elusive adversary who could threaten his tenuous supply line from Atlanta to Chattanooga. He thus proposed abandoning Atlanta and marching through Georgia, finally settling on Savannah as his ultimate target. Along the way his men would live off the land, destroy Confederate foodstuffs and livestock, and dismantle the Confederate rail system. Lincoln worried that the plan risked a great deal, but Grant approved of it, although Sherman would not commence his march until after the fall presidential contest. It took Sherman a month to make his way from Atlanta to the outskirts of Savannah, which he presented to Lincoln as a Christmas present. Two months later, Sherman resumed marching, this time making his way through the Carolinas toward Richmond. For years afterward the destructiveness of these marches remained a point of controversy, but they appeared to have achieved their objective of physical destruction and psychological demoralization, and Lincoln expressed no complaint about Sherman's way of waging war. Modern scholarship suggests that the March to the Sea was far less destructive of private property than lost cause mythology has led many Americans to believe.

In March 1865 Sherman made his way up to Grant's headquarters at City Point, Virginia, where he conferred with Lincoln and Grant aboard the president's steamer, the *River Queen.* There Sherman learned of the president's desire for a lenient peace settlement and generous treatment of the defeated. Those thoughts remained in his mind when Confederate commander Joseph E. Johnston decided to open surrender negotiations with him, and they became even more important when he learned of Lincoln's assassination. In what Sherman thought to be the spirit of the moment, the terms that he and Johnston worked out at James Bennett's farmhouse at Durham Station, North Carolina, were extremely lenient, to the point that some critics questioned whether they protected slavery. When news of the terms reached Washington, D.C., Grant defended his comrade against criticism before heading to North Carolina to oversee a new agreement based on the blueprint established at Appomattox Court House.

After the war Sherman remained in the army, rising to lieutenant general (1866) and general (1869). He took little interest in Reconstruction, once minimizing the threat posed by the Ku Klux Klan, an attitude that led Grant to rely as president on others to implement Reconstruction policy. A rift developed between the two men over the organization of the chain of command, and for several years Sherman based his army headquarters in St. Louis before returning to Washington in 1876. Retiring from the army in 1883, Sherman moved to New York City, where he died in 1891.

See also *Atlanta Campaign; Sherman's March to the Sea*

—Brooks D. Simpson

BIBLIOGRAPHY

Fellman, Michael. *Citizen Sherman: A Life of William Tecumseh Sherman.* New York: Random House, 1995.

Lewis, Lloyd. *Sherman: Fighting Prophet.* New York: Harcourt, Brace, 1932.

Marszalek, John F. *Sherman: A Soldier's Passion for Order.* New York: Free Press, 1992.

Sherman, William T. *Memoirs of W. T. Sherman.* 1875. Reprint, New York: Library of America, 1990.

Simpson, Brooks D., and Jean V. Berlin. *Sherman's Civil War: Selected Correspondence of William T. Sherman, 1860–1865.* Chapel Hill: University of North Carolina Press, 1999.

Sherman's March to the Sea

William T. Sherman's occupation of Atlanta on September 2, 1864, did not bring military operations in Georgia to an end. John Bell Hood's Army of Tennessee remained a potent fighting force, and before long Hood began exploring ways to sever Sherman's supply lines, which stretched from Atlanta to Chattanooga. Sherman discovered that it would be a hard task to bring Hood to bay, and so he began contemplating an entirely different sort of response—a march through the interior of Georgia, culminating at the Atlantic coast. During the next several months he discussed the plan with general in chief Ulysses S. Grant, who expressed concern about the need to eradicate Hood's army. In October 1864 Sherman assured his superior that he would leave behind enough force to contain Hood, adding, "I can make this march and make Georgia howl." In a more dispassionate vein, he explained that "if we can march a well appointed Army right through his territory, it is a demonstration to the World, foreign and domestic, that we have a power which Davis cannot resist. This may not be war, but rather statesmanship." Grant decided to let Sherman proceed and later reassured Lincoln and Stanton that Sherman knew what he was doing. That Lincoln had been reelected on November 8, 1864, helped to minimize the possible consequences of disaster.

On November 15, 1864, Sherman commenced his march. As his men left Atlanta, they burned places of military value. Over the next month 60,000 men moved through central Georgia, living off the land, destroying railroads and livestock, and bringing fear to Confederate citizens. Aside from harassment by Confederate cavalry commanded by Joseph Wheeler, Sherman encountered little opposition, and that his soldiers handled easily. He made sure that his line of march was spread out enough to conceal his true objective, Savannah. On November 23 Union troops occupied the state capital at Milledgeville, where they sacked the capitol.

As Sherman had cut his line of communications, most Northerners had to trust to Confederate news reports to keep track of the march's progress. One of those who betrayed nervousness was Abraham Lincoln. In his annual message, delivered on December 6, 1864, Lincoln observed that Sherman's march was "the most remarkable feature in the military operations of the year"; he reflected that it was a sign of the Union's military strength that Grant could approve such an operation. Struck from the final draft was an additional comment that Grant must have believed that the nation could risk the loss of the entire army, "while, by the risk, he takes a chance for the great advantages which would follow success." Then he sat back and waited for news of Sherman's appearance. "We all know where he went in at," he told a crowd, "but I can't tell where he will come out at."

Often overlooked in accounts of the march is the essential role played by the man Sherman left behind to keep an eye on Hood and the Army of Tennessee. Headquartered at Nashville, George H. Thomas cobbled together a defense force in the Tennessee capital, while other units delayed Hood's thrust into the Volunteer State. Hood failed to trap retreating Union columns at Spring Hill, Tennessee, on November 29. The following day Hood repeatedly assaulted Union defenses at Franklin, Tennessee, only to suffer tremendous losses. By early December, Hood had limped to the outskirts of Nashville, where Thomas continued to gather and outfit the city's defenders. After several delays, on December 15 Thomas attacked Hood south of Nashville and on the following day completed a decisive victory over the Confederates, as Hood abandoned his campaign and retreated to Alabama.

By December 10 Sherman reached the outskirts of Savannah. Three days later he assaulted Fort McAllister, and on December 17 he called on Confederate commander William J. Hardee to surrender. The city's Confederate defenders managed to escape, and Union forces occupied Savannah on December 21. On December 22 Sherman informed Lincoln, "I beg to present you as a Christmas gift the city of Savannah with 150 heavy guns & plenty of ammunition & also about 25000 bales of cotton." In his reply the president admitted that he had been anxious about the idea but had decided to leave it in the hands of his generals. Now, between the success of the march and Thomas's victory at Nashville, he concluded that the operation as a whole "brings those who sat in darkness, to see a great light."

Much has been made of the destructiveness of Sherman's march. To be sure, Sherman's men stripped farms and plantations bare of whatever foodstuffs and livestock they could find and liberated slaves as they went, but the physical destructiveness of the march has long been exaggerated. What destruction occurred was compounded by the chaos sparked by straggling Union soldiers (sometimes called "Sherman's bummers"), ill-disciplined Confederate cavalry, and the movement of former slaves in the wake of the Union advance. Reports of violence against white civilians were rare; less is known about the violence some Union soldiers committed against black women. Later studies of the physical destructiveness of the march have shown that the notion that Sherman burned his way from Atlanta to Savannah is greatly exaggerated, a point reinforced by the persistence of tours of antebellum homes along the line of the march.

Sherman's objective was not so much physical destruction as intimidation, and here the march proved quite successful. It was a masterly act of psychological warfare. Intimidated white women, fearful of what might happen, called on their husbands to return home, and desertion became a more serious problem for Confederate armies already lacking sufficient manpower.

As Sherman put it in reporting on the conclusion of the march,

> We are not only fighting armies, but a hostile people, and must make old and young, rich and poor, feel the hard hand of war, as well as their organized armies. I know that this recent movement of mine through Georgia has had a wonderful effect in this respect. Thousands who had been deceived by their lying papers into the belief that we were being whipped all the time, realized the truth, and have no appetite for a repetition of the same experience.

With that in mind Sherman made plans for a second march northward through the Carolinas that would close in on what remained of the Confederacy's main field armies.

—BROOKS D. SIMPSON

BIBLIOGRAPHY

Bailey, Anne J. *The Chessboard of War: Sherman and Hood in the Autumn Campaigns of 1864.* Lincoln: University of Nebraska Press, 2000.

Glatthaar, Joseph T. *The March to the Sea and Beyond: Sherman's Troops in the Savannah and Carolinas Campaigns.* New York: New York University Press, 1985.

Grimsley, Mark. *The Hard Hand of War: Union Military Policy towards Southern Civilians, 1861–1865.* New York: Cambridge University Press, 1995.

Kennett, Lee. *Marching through Georgia: The Story of Soldiers and Civilians during Sherman's Campaign.* New York: HarperCollins, 1995.

Shields, James

James Shields (1810–1879) was an Irish born (County Tyrone) Democratic politician with whom Abraham Lincoln literally almost crossed swords. Shields came to America sometime in the 1820s and arrived in Illinois in 1829. There he took up school teaching before turning to the law and politics. He was elected to the state legislature in 1836.

At the time of his September 1842 dispute with Lincoln, Shields was the state auditor of Illinois, and Lincoln was the law partner of Stephen T. Logan in Springfield. Shields had recently prohibited the state from accepting the notes of the State Bank of Illinois because of the weak financial condition of the bank and his party's general opposition to the government's connection with banks. Lincoln, as a Whig partisan, attacked Shields both professionally and personally in letters to the *Sangamon Journal* written over the pseudonym "Rebecca" from the "Lost Townships." The offended Shields, when he could not get Lincoln to retract his statements, challenged him to a duel. Since dueling was illegal in Illinois, the affair was to take place in Missouri, across the Mississippi River from Alton, Illinois. The lanky, long-armed Lincoln, taking advantage of his choice of weapons, offered to fight the much smaller Shields with heavy cavalry broadswords. Luckily for both, their seconds managed to arrange a reconciliation before blood was shed, on September 22, 1842.

Lincoln's willingness to confront Shields may have helped precipitate his marriage to Mary Todd, which occurred only about six weeks later. During the controversy he took responsibility for all the "Rebecca" letters and gallantly hid the fact that Mary and her friend Julia Jayne had actually contributed some of the sharpest personal attacks on Shields using the same pseudonym.

Shields went on to become a close associate and supporter of Stephen Douglas in the Illinois Democratic Party. He served as a United States senator from Illinois (1849–1855) and later represented both Minnesota (1858–1859) and Missouri (1879) in the Senate. He is the only person to represent three different states in this body. Shields also had a distinguished military career in the Mexican War as a brigadier general of Illinois volunteers. During the Civil War Lincoln appointed his old Democratic rival a brigadier general of U.S. volunteers. He commanded a division in the Shenandoah Valley Campaign of 1862 but resigned from the army in 1863, after criticism of his poor performance led to the rejection of his promotion to major general.

—Lawrence Frederick Kohl

BIBLIOGRAPHY

Callan, J. Sean. *Courage and Country: James Shields: More Than Irish Luck.* Bloomington, Ind.: First Books Library, 2004.

Condon, William H. *Life of Major-General James Shields: Hero of Three Wars and Senator from Three States.* Chicago: Blakely Printing, 1900.

Shiloh, Battle of

The Battle of Shiloh, April 6–7, 1862, sometimes also known as Pittsburg Landing, proved to be a bloody Union victory that frustrated Confederate efforts to check Union triumphs in West Tennessee. However the outcome was very much in doubt during the first day of the battle, for the Confederate attack on April 6 came as a surprise to the Union commander, Ulysses S. Grant, and came close to pushing the Army of the Tennessee into its namesake river.

In the aftermath of the Union victories at Forts Henry and Donelson and the occupation of Nashville in February 1862, Grant came under criticism from his immediate superior, Henry W. Halleck, who seized upon supposed irregularities in his subordinate's administration to detain Grant at Fort Henry, while his army, under the command of Charles F. Smith, made its way southward to Pittsburg Landing, located on the west bank of the Tennessee River a few miles north of the Mississippi border. Grant protested his treatment, and President Lincoln called on Halleck to make his case. Halleck relented, directing Grant to take the field once more. Grant hurried south to join his men, though wondering why he had found himself in virtual arrest, as he put it later, less than a month after winning a major battle.

Halleck's plan was a simple one. He would wait until General Don Carlos Buell and his Army of the Ohio linked up with Grant at Pittsburg Landing and then take command of the whole and advance southward against the critical Confederate rail junction and supply depot at Corinth, Mississippi. Worried that Grant might strike out on his own, he cautioned Grant against bringing on a general engagement: Division commander William T. Sherman, seeing his first action in the field in several months after suffering what amounted to a psychological breakdown, was determined to counter rumors that he was petrified of the enemy. He thus discounted reports of enemy activity in his front as the exaggerated concerns of inexperienced subordinates. Grant believed that it was more important to drill his raw soldiers than to fortify his position, especially as he did not expect to be attacked.

These circumstances proved most advantageous to Confederate commander Albert Sydney Johnston, who was determined to regain what the Confederates had lost in February. Determined to attack Grant before Buell joined him, Johnston gathered a considerable force at Corinth. At the beginning of April he ordered his men to advance against Grant's encamped forces. It proved an awkward, noisy movement, but Grant relied on Sherman's reports, which played down news of enemy activity. To press forward to assess the situation would violate Halleck's warnings to await Buell's arrival. Thus Johnston was able to deploy for a massive assault relatively unimpeded.

Johnston ordered his men forward in the early hours of April 6. They soon made contact with Union pickets, and before long the noise of combat and the cries of couriers alerted the encamped Yankees that they were coming under attack. The momentum of the Confederate assault rolled over portions of what passed for the Union front line, hastily assembled and unfortified, and by midmorning the battle was under way in earnest. Grant, who had established his headquarters north of the landing at Savannah, hurried down to coordinate defensive operations. He believed that before long Buell's advance elements would arrive, as well as one of his own divisions, and he determined to fight it out as he awaited their appearance. Many Union soldiers panicked and fled during the morning, but others held their ground.

By early afternoon the Confederates had pushed forward, eventually isolating portions of two Union divisions at a place thereafter called the Hornet's Nest. The Union stand there helped to buy Grant time; so did the loss of Confederate momentum as units became intermixed, soldiers grew exhausted, and the command reorganized as Pierre G.T. Beauregard took over for the mortally wounded Johnston. However, Grant had assembled a compact line of final defense near the landing, and Buell's lead elements began crossing the Tennessee. Beauregard, unaware of the impending appearance of Union reinforcements, decided to regroup, with the expectation of finishing things up the next morning. That night several of Buell's divisions took up positions near the landing, and Grant's other division also arrived. When hostilities resumed in the morning, it was the Confederates' turn to wage a fighting withdrawal before finally retreating on the afternoon of April 7. Grant failed to order an effective pursuit, and the battle was over.

Early reports of a Union victory in Northern newspapers soon gave way to the sobering realization that the losses at Shiloh dwarfed those in previous American wars. Reporters offered sensational accounts of Union soldiers bayoneted in their tents and wildly exaggerated the degree to which Grant had been surprised (although there is no doubt that the Confederates achieved a striking strategic surprise, catching Grant unprepared). Hurrying down to Pittsburg Landing, Halleck was harshly critical of Grant. But when Lincoln inquired whether the losses at Shiloh were due to Grant's negligence, Halleck pointed instead to the bloody nature of battle and dismissed critical newspaper accounts. In later years historians would claim that Lincoln fended off calls for Grant's removal, declaring, "I can't spare this man; he fights," but in truth the president displayed no such confidence. It was Halleck who protected Grant from others even as he was unsparing in his own criticism.

The victory at Shiloh opened the door to additional Union advances southward, including the taking of Corinth in May. It also proved critical in forging a friendship between Grant and Sherman. In retaining control of West Tennessee, the Union victory allowed wartime reconstruction to proceed in Tennessee under military governor Andrew Johnson. Yet it offered a disturbing glimpse into just how bloody the war would become.

—BROOKS D. SIMPSON

BIBLIOGRAPHY

Cunningham, Edward, Gary D. Joiner, and Timothy B. Smith. *Shiloh and the Western Campaign of 1862.* El Dorado Hills, Calif.: Savas Beatie, 2007.

Daniel, Larry J. *Shiloh: The Battle That Changed the Civil War.* New York: Simon and Schuster, 1997.

McDonough, James Lee. *Shiloh—In Hell before Midnight.* Knoxville: University of Tennessee Press, 1977.

Sword, Wiley. *Shiloh: Bloody April.* New York :William Morrow, 1974.

Sioux Uprising

Lasting barely six weeks during the late summer and fall of 1862, the Sioux uprising—or Dakota War—marked the last violent resistance by the Minnesota Dakota to the loss of their territories. Four hundred and thirteen civilians died as a result of the attacks, as did 77 soldiers and 71 Dakota. President Abraham Lincoln intervened to offer clemency to 264 Dakota convicted in the aftermath. Nonetheless it culminated in the largest mass execution in U.S. history.

On August 17, 1862, five young Dakota men argued with a farmer over stolen eggs, ending in the murder of several settlers. Seeking sanctuary, the young Dakota ran to Little Crow (1810–1863), the chief of the Mdewakaton Dakota. In previous years Little Crow might have handed the guilty parties over to the state authorities. By the late summer of 1862, however, the Minnesota Dakota were facing a serious food shortage as result of a poor harvest in 1861 combined with steady waves of farmers settling into their hunting territories and the thinning of the buffalo herds. The shortages were exacerbated by the government's failure to release annuity payments, leaving food locked in agency storehouses while the Dakota people went hungry.

Little Crow allowed himself to be convinced by the Mdewakaton Soldier's Lodge that now was the time to push back against white incursions into Dakota lands. Over the next week Little Crow's forces attacked the Lower Sioux Agency, Fort Ridgely, and New Ulm, Minnesota. The Lower Sioux Agency was destroyed, but both New Ulm and Fort Ridgely survived, though at heavy cost. Bands of Dakota also fanned out and attacked fleeing settlers, killing and capturing hundreds as they went.

In response to the attacks, Minnesota governor Alexander Ramsey (1815–1903), a Republican, appointed his predecessor, Henry Sibley (1811–1891), military commander of a hastily raised regiment. Sibley's troops defeated the outnumbered forces of Little Crow at the Battle of Wood Lake on September 23, and soon after Dakota men began surrendering, even as Little Crow and others retreated north and west. At the same time, a peace party, led by elders of the Sisseton, Wahpeton, and Anglo and Franco Dakota communities, was able to secure the safety and then release of between 100 and 300 civilian hostages.

In October and November, Sibley summarily tried more than 400 full and mixed Dakota for various crimes related to the uprising. In hastily convened military trials, sometimes trying forty or more men in a single day, Sibley's court sentenced 303 Dakota to death. Henry Whipple (1822–1901), Episcopal bishop of Minnesota, appealed to President Abraham Lincoln on behalf of the condemned

Sioux, charging that their cases had been tried unfairly and in haste. President Lincoln had his staff review the cases, and eventually he commuted most of the death sentences to lesser terms. Lincoln's decision was unpopular in a population howling for Indian blood, but he defended it, declaring, "I could not hang men for votes." Governor Ramsey countered that the Republican's slim margin of victory in Minnesota in 1864 was a direct result of Lincoln's clemency.

On December 26, 1862, thirty-eight men were hanged in Mankato, the largest mass execution in U.S. history. Though the death toll was ultimately far lower than the 800 to 1,000 deaths first reported, the Dakota War nonetheless permanently changed the face of Minnesota. The Sioux lost the last of their reservation lands in the state, and settlers came hard on their heels to grow the wheat for which Minnesota would be famous.

See also *Indian Relations, Lincoln and*

—Eleanor L. Hannah

BIBLIOGRAPHY

Carley, Kenneth. *The Dakota War of 1862*. 2nd ed. St. Paul: Minnesota Historical Society Press, 2001.

Schultz, Duane. *Over the Earth I Come: The Great Sioux Uprising of 1862*. New York: St. Martin's, 1992.

Slave Power/Slavocracy

Northern antislavery leaders portrayed the Slave Power/Slavocracy as a conspiracy to control the federal government in behalf of Southern proslavery interests. It consisted of Southern members of Congress and their Northern allies, who were usually members of the Democratic Party. Through it the proslavery interests in the South controlled state and national government and dominated the presidency, Congress and its committees, and the Supreme Court.

The concept of a Slave Power began as early as the Constitutional Convention of 1787, when New York delegate Gouverneur Morris led opposition to the document's indirect endorsement of slavery. Morris and other Northerners were especially upset by the three-fifths clause, which gave the slave states added seats in the House of Representatives by adding three-fifths of their nonvoting slave populations to the state's nonslave numbers. By adding slave state seats in Congress, proslavery elements also augmented their votes in the

Electoral College and thus helped to maintain their control of the presidency and indirectly the Supreme Court. With the passage of the Missouri Compromise in 1820–1821, admitting the slave state of Missouri, Northern opponents intensified their resistance. The Missouri Compromise also included the creation of a dividing line in the Louisiana Territory between slave and free territory at 36° 30'. It was on this line that Abraham Lincoln and other Northern Whigs, and then Republicans, focused their attention in the intense sectional debates over slave territory in the 1840s and 1850s.

Other issues in the 1830s preceded the debates over extending slave territory. The administration of Andrew Jackson pushed through Indian removal, primarily of Southern tribes, with the South's extra seats in Congress and the support of numerous Northern Democrats. Debates in the House over the Gag Rule tabling antislavery petitions resulted in a House rule with the same alliance between 1836 and 1844. Because of the three-fifths clause, by 1833 the South had ninety-eight representatives instead of seventy-three, a margin that ensured the passage of both Indian removal and the Gag Rule and gave the South added power in future contested votes. In addition to Southern votes, the South could count on the votes of numerous Northern Democrats in the House and at least six in the Senate. It was the new territories acquired after the Mexican War in 1848 that brought the issue of a Slave Power conspiracy to a head and enlisted Abraham Lincoln in the ranks of those determined to thwart the efforts of the Slavocracy to expand slavery.

The Mexican War added vast new territories to the United States and expanded its borders from Texas and the Louisiana Territory to the Pacific Ocean. Northerners of both major parties supported the Wilmot Proviso banning slavery in all Mexican War territories. Lincoln had been elected to the House in 1846 and eagerly joined the House majority that approved the proviso, only to see it die in the Senate, where Slave Power interests were more powerful. In the presidential election of 1848, Democrats nominated an ally of the Slave Power, Sen. Lewis Cass of Michigan, one of the so-called doughfaces—meaning Northern men with Southern principles—on a platform endorsing "popular sovereignty," or the right of the territorial residents to decide on slavery. Lincoln campaigned for Cass's Whig opponent, Mexican War general Zachary Taylor, believing that even though Taylor was a slaveholder he would not veto the Wilmot Proviso if Congress passed it. Lincoln strongly opposed any challenge to the 36° 30' line as a permanent barrier protecting free territory and argued that popular sovereignty was a mere pretense for slavery.

This position became central in Illinois politics when Democratic senator Stephen A. Douglas emerged as the leading advocate of popular sovereignty by 1850. Douglas helped push the Compromise of 1850 through Congress; it was a collection of slave-related bills that included the organization of Utah and New Mexico Territories on a popular sovereignty basis. It also included a fugitive slave act that greatly strengthened Slave Power efforts to force Northern and federal government assistance in the return of escaped slaves. To Lincoln and his fellow

Northern Whigs these parts of the compromise represented the ultimate control of government by the Slave Power.

In 1850 Lincoln had returned to private life as an attorney not actively involved in public life. But three years later, when Douglas began his efforts to organize the Nebraska Territory, Lincoln was ready to reenter Whig politics. The Kansas-Nebraska Act that emerged in 1854 repealed the Missouri Compromise line and, in Lincoln's eyes, dramatically changed the issue of the expansion of slavery. Rather than banning slavery, the measure, which Franklin Pierce signed into law in May, left the decision to territorial voters. Large numbers of Northern Democrats supported Douglas's bill. To Lincoln, the senator's efforts reflected Douglas's moral indifference toward slavery and his desire to secure Southern support to achieve the presidential nomination. It was another example of the power of the Slavocracy and the willingness of Northern politicians to do the bidding of their Southern colleagues. As the Whig Party declined it was replaced by a purely Northern party, the Republicans, dedicated to stopping the spread of slavery and thwarting the efforts of the Slave Power. In Illinois, Lincoln emerged as the primary leader of the new party.

In 1857 James Buchanan, Democrat from Pennsylvania, succeeded Pierce in the presidency. To critics such as Lincoln and his fellow Illinois Republicans, Buchanan was even more a tool of the Slavocracy than Pierce had been. The *Dred Scott* decision of March 1857, with chief justice Roger B. Taney of Maryland leading the way, confirmed the role of the Supreme Court in giving the Slave Power all it demanded. The decision denied Congress the right to legislate on slavery in the territories, thus ensuring that slavery would be legal in all territories. Chosen by Illinois Republicans to deliver his party's keynote address in June 1858, Lincoln in his "House Divided" speech charged that the Slave Power conspiracy had taken over government and had destroyed the noble dream of the Founders to restrict slavery. He portrayed Douglas, along with Pierce, Buchanan, and Taney, as dedicated to protecting slavery everywhere. Illinois voters must stop Douglas and his fellow conspirators, for the government could not endure permanently half-slave and half-free. The next step, Lincoln suggested, would be a Supreme Court decision denying even the states the right to exclude slavery.

The convention nominated Lincoln to run for the U.S. Senate against incumbent Douglas that fall. In the famous Lincoln-Douglas debates that followed, the challenger pictured Douglas as an agent of the Slave Power attempting to persuade Northerners to accept slavery with moral indifference. Lincoln saw Douglas as the ringleader of Northern conspirators determined to satisfy the South and enjoy the political benefits of the immoral coalition. Lincoln forced Douglas onto the defensive, costing him much of his Southern support, when he suggested that a territory could still deny slavery despite the *Dred Scott* decision. But Douglas's answer satisfied Illinois voters, and the legislature reelected him to the Senate.

In 1860 Lincoln opposed Douglas again, this time in a four-way contest for the presidency. With Northern Democratic power in Congress already reduced dramatically following the 1858 elections, Republican advocates described the sinister designs of the Slave Power and this time had the votes to back up their charges. Lincoln's election as president ended the more-than-seventy-year Slave Power domination of the federal government. With their power gone Southern states began the secession process, with a bloody civil war and the elimination of slavery to follow.

See also *Antislavery; Brown, John; Compensated Emancipation; Constitution and Slavery, The; Emancipation Proclamation; Garrison, William Lloyd*

—FREDERICK J. BLUE

BIBLIOGRAPHY

Etcheson, Nicole. *Bleeding Kansas: Contested Liberty in the Civil War Era.* Lawrence: University of Kansas Press, 2004.

Fehrenbacher, Don E. *The* Dred Scott *Case: Its Significance in American Law and Politics.* New York: Oxford University Press, 1978.

Finkelman, Paul. Dred Scott v. Sandford: *A Brief History with Documents.* Boston: Bedford, 1995.

Foner, Eric. *Free Soil, Free Labor, Free Men: The Ideology of the Republican Party before the Civil War.* New York: Oxford University Press, 1970.

Forbes, Robert P. *The Missouri Compromise and Its Aftermath: Slavery and the Meaning of America.* Chapel Hill: University of North Carolina Press, 2007.

Johanssen, Robert W. *Stephen A. Douglas.* New York: Oxford University Press, 1973.

Oates, Stephen B. *With Malice toward None: The Life of Abraham Lincoln.* New York: Harper and Row, 1977.

Richards, Leonard L. *The Slave Power: The Free North and Southern Domination, 1780–1860.* Baton Rouge: Louisiana State University Press, 2000.

Stampp, Kenneth M. *America in 1857: A Nation on the Brink.* New York: Oxford University Press, 1990.

Zarefsky, David. *Lincoln, Douglas, and Slavery: In the Crucible of Public Debate.* Chicago: University of Chicago Press, 1990.

Slavery

Slavery was legal in all the colonies on the eve of the American Revolution, but by 1804 there was a distinct "North" where slavery had either been abolished or was in the process of being abolished, and a distinct "South" where slavery was legally, politically, and economically secure. By the mid-nineteenth century, the slave issue threatened to divide the United States along sectional lines.

Slaves were held as legal property in Southern states, and the institution was an essential aspect of Southern economics and culture. North of the Mason-Dixon line, Free Soil advocates and abolitionists called for an end to slavery's expansion, and some for its ultimate extinction. Throughout the 1850s, events such as the Kansas-Nebraska Act of 1854 and the Supreme Court's 1857 decision in the *Dred Scott* case convinced Republicans (who embraced Free Soil ideals) and abolitionists that an organized Slave Power was asserting control over national politics. Similarly, Southern defenders of slavery bristled at Northern criticism of their peculiar institution, especially in the aftermath of abolitionist John Brown's failed attempt to foment armed slave insurrection at Harpers Ferry in 1859, and they aggressively worked to protect slavery. It was in this tumultuous environment that Abraham Lincoln's moderate politics gave rise to his Republican nomination for president in 1860.

Abraham Lincoln was personally opposed to slavery. He believed it to be a moral wrong that threatened the stability of the nation. He always believed that "If slavery is not wrong, nothing is wrong." Yet prior to 1862, he acknowledged the legal right of slave owners to retain slaves and to have fugitive slaves caught and returned. During the presidential campaign of 1860, the position of Lincoln and his party was that slavery should be protected where it existed but restricted from expanding into new territories. Lincoln believed that restricting slavery in this manner would lead to its eventual decline. Southerners also believed that restricting slavery would lead to its demise and threatened disunion if Lincoln won the presidency. Thus the Republican commitment to limiting slavery became the primary cause for Southern secession.

Once elected president, Lincoln repeated his commitment not to interfere with slavery where it existed so as to obtain the support of the Border States and Northern Democrats. In his inaugural address Lincoln reiterated that he understood he had "no lawful right" to "interfere with the institution of slavery in the States where it exists." Nevertheless, the Confederate attack on Fort Sumter (April 12, 1861) sparked the Civil War and eventually altered Lincoln's political conceptions on slavery.

Although he initially resisted his generals' efforts to free slaves in occupied regions, the slave issue ultimately became a political and military tactic that Lincoln used to protect his primary goal of preserving the Union. On August 30, 1861, Major General John C. Frémont, commander of the Union army in St. Louis, declared slaves owned by Missouri Confederates to be free. Fearing the Border States' reactions, Lincoln directed Frémont to limit his directive to include only slaves actively engaged in supporting the Confederacy. This directive reflected the restraints of the 1861 Confiscation Act.

Lincoln also found himself pressed by Republican senators who insisted that he use the president's war powers to emancipate the slaves. From the war's beginning, abolitionists and some Republicans pressured the Lincoln administration to transform the war into a moral crusade to eradicate slavery. Yet Lincoln felt bound by the Constitution to protect slavery in the Southern states. He understood that early emancipation might push Kentucky and Missouri into the Confederacy and cause the United States to lose the war. His stated intention was to limit the effects of war in the rebellious states so as to minimize disruption of Southern institutions and to promote a smooth and quick return of Union control in those territories.

By 1862 it was apparent that the war was not a limited, short engagement. Lincoln hoped to solidify Union loyalty in the Border States by encouraging those states to abolish slavery. Lincoln submitted gradual, compensated emancipation plans to Maryland, Delaware, Kentucky, and Missouri that he hoped would be implemented. The representatives from those states rejected the plans. Although Lincoln's appeal did not lead the Border States to adopt resolutions initiating emancipation, it did prepare the way for a federal sanction on slavery.

The 1862 Confiscation Act gave the president power to employ ex-slaves in the Union army. Just days later, on August 22, 1862, Lincoln submitted a draft of the Emancipation Proclamation to his cabinet. Timing was important to the success of the proclamation, and because of military reverses Lincoln refrained for a time from implementing his new plan. Antislavery advocates attempted to pressure Lincoln into initiating abolition, to which Lincoln responded, "My paramount object is to save the Union, and not either to save or destroy slavery. If I could save the Union without freeing any slave, I would do it; if I could save it by freeing all the slaves, I would do it; and, if I could do it by freeing some and leaving others alone, I would also do that." However, at the time he published those words he had already written the Emancipation Proclamation and was simply waiting for the appropriate moment—a major battlefield victory—to issue it.

The technical language of the Emancipation Proclamation never actually freed slaves in the Border States or in areas of the Confederacy under Union control. Instead the proclamation was directed toward freeing slaves in Confederate territories where the protections of the Constitution did not limit Lincoln's actions. Lincoln was hesitant to push for emancipation in the Border States while the Confederate army had the military advantage. He did not want to provoke sedition in the Union and add strength to the Confederacy. He also did not believe that under the Constitution the U.S. government could interfere with slavery in the loyal Border States.

In September 1862 the tide of war turned, as Confederate general Robert E. Lee suffered losses at South Mountain and Antietam in Maryland. In response, public opinion ripened and on September 22, 1862, President Lincoln issued his preliminary proclamation of emancipation. He gave notice that on January 1, 1863, "all persons held as slaves within any State or designated part of a State the people whereof shall then be in rebellion against the United States shall be then, thenceforward, and for ever free." Again Lincoln stressed that emancipation was a tactic for preserving the Union. On December 1, in his message to Congress, he urged implementation of his plan of gradual, compensated emancipation in Union-occupied territories "as a means, not in exclusion of, but additional to, all others for restoring and preserving the national authority throughout the Union."

In 1863 Lincoln presented his reconstruction policy to loyalists in rebellious states to encourage emancipation in those areas not affected by the Emancipation Proclamation. The reconstruction policy presented pardon and amnesty to Southerners who took an oath of allegiance to the Union. The policy also allowed compromise on all wartime policies concerning slavery and emancipation. Portions of Tennessee, Arkansas, and Louisiana took advantage of the opportunity and abolished slavery to show their loyalty to the Union.

Buoyed by a sweeping change in popular sentiment, Lincoln increased enlistment of African Americans into army regiments. Their gallantry on the battlefield aided the Union cause and solidified emancipation as a war goal. When slavery was abolished in the loyalist regions of the Confederacy, these areas contributed more than 180,000 African American recruits to the Union army and navy. Lincoln credited these soldiers and sailors with turning the tide of the war and argued that their sacrifices earned both freedom and the right to vote. Still, slavery remained a debatable issue. During the winter session of 1863–1864, Lincoln encouraged Congress to abolish slavery by constitutional amendment, but the necessary two-thirds vote of the House of Representatives was not obtained.

The president worried that after the war the courts might nullify his wartime proclamation on grounds that confiscation of "property" required due process of the law. Thus, Lincoln used his reelection victory in 1864 to promote a constitutional amendment that would end slavery throughout the nation. The Republican Party supported Lincoln's platform and endorsed the Thirteenth Amendment (1864). In April, the Senate passed the resolution, and on January 31, 1865, the House did so. Lincoln did not live to see the amendment become part of the Constitution after its ratification. The Thirteenth Amendment provides that "neither slavery nor involuntary servitude, except as a punishment for crime, whereof the party shall have been duly convicted, shall exist within the United States or any place subject to their jurisdiction." Before the end of 1865, twenty-seven of the thirty-six states in the Union gained the three-fourths votes required to ratify the amendment. Slavery formally ended on December 18, 1865, with President Andrew Johnson's official proclamation.

—ALYSSA ARNELL

BIBLIOGRAPHY

Cowley, Robert, ed. *With My Face to the Enemy: Perspectives on the Civil War.* New York: Putnam's, 2001.

Johannsen, Robert W. *Lincoln, the South, and Slavery: The Political Dimension.* Baton Rouge: Louisiana State University Press, 1991.

Jones, Howard. *Abraham Lincoln and a New Birth of Freedom: The Union and Slavery in the Diplomacy of the Civil War.* Lincoln: University of Nebraska Press, 1999.

Klingaman, William K. *Abraham Lincoln and the Road to Emancipation.* New York: Viking, 2001.

McPherson, James M. *Battle Cry of Freedom.* New York: Oxford University Press, 1988.

Sandburg, Carl. *Abraham Lincoln: The Prairie Years and the War Years.* New York: Harcourt, Brace, 1954.

Vorenberg, Michael. *Final Freedom: The Civil War, the Abolition of Slavery, and the Thirteenth Amendment.* New York: Cambridge University Press, 2001.

Slavery in the Thirtieth Congress

Abraham Lincoln was largely a spectator in the frequent and often heated debates over slavery that took place during the Thirtieth Congress (1847–1849), in which he served as a Whig representative from Illinois. The slave trade was a prominent feature of everyday life in Washington and a source of shame for many, including Lincoln, who was appalled that a large slave pen could be seen from the windows of the Capitol. Because the Constitution granted Congress authority over the territories and the District of Columbia, much of the debate in the Thirtieth Congress focused on the Wilmot Proviso and various proposals to abolish the slave trade in Washington. While abolitionists favored an immediate, unconditional end to both the slave trade and slavery in the District, Lincoln conceived of a plan, never formally presented on the House floor, for gradual, compensated emancipation that offered a moderate solution to a problem that was becoming increasingly acrimonious.

Lincoln's actions in Congress indicate that his views had not changed much since 1837 when, as a member of the Illinois state legislature, he submitted a protest that claimed slavery was founded on "injustice and bad policy." Lincoln also asserted in the protest that the federal government had no authority to interfere with slavery in the states where it already existed, yet he believed Congress could abolish slavery in Washington, D.C., provided it was done at the request of citizens. Though Congressman Lincoln stayed at the same boardinghouse as Joshua Giddings, an abolitionist member of the House, Giddings was unable to alter Lincoln's moderate approach to the issue. Lincoln supported the right of citizens to submit antislavery petitions to Congress, and he voted for the Wilmot Proviso and other measures that sought to prevent the extension of slavery into the territories, but he often opposed Giddings and the handful of other abolitionists who sought to inject their agenda into the proceedings.

In April 1848 in Washington, two abolitionists loaded more than seventy slaves onto a ship called the *Pearl* and attempted to take them to freedom. Poor winds foiled the escape, but the incident became the subject of an intense debate after Rep. John G. Palfrey, a Massachusetts abolitionist, introduced a resolution related to the episode. Lincoln did not participate in the debate, but he was part of the majority vote that ended discussion of Palfrey's resolution. Congress also engaged in an acrimonious debate over a resolution that congratulated France on its recent revolution. Abolitionists made much of the fact that one of the first acts of the new French republic was to abolish slavery in its colonial possessions, and though Lincoln voted in favor of the congratulatory resolution, he opposed Palfrey's motion to amend the resolution by including a thinly veiled condemnation of slavery. Lincoln also opposed Palfrey's attempt to introduce a bill that would have repealed all laws relating to slavery in the District. The horror of slavery was brought home to both Lincoln and Giddings when a group of armed men burst into their boardinghouse and seized an African American man who had been working there as a waiter. Following this incident Giddings introduced a resolution to appoint a committee to investigate this outrage and explore the possibility of either abolishing the slave trade in Washington or moving the capital to a free state. Lincoln was part of the minority that voted against tabling Giddings's resolution.

Even though Lincoln believed Congress should not take action regarding slavery in Washington without the approval of the District's citizens, he voted with the majority to table a resolution introduced by Giddings to give Washington residents the opportunity to express their preference for either slavery or freedom. Much of the opposition to the Giddings resolution stemmed from a provision that allowed all men over the age of twenty-one to participate in the referendum. Approval of the resolution would have meant that both free and enslaved African Americans could vote in the election. Giddings argued that there should be no distinctions between men, all of whom came from the same Creator, but for most of his colleagues, including Lincoln, extending the franchise to African Americans was too radical a prospect.

Lincoln's opportunity to present his plan for ending slavery in Washington occurred during debate over a resolution that had been introduced by Daniel Gott of New York. Gott's resolution included a strong condemnation of the slave trade and instructed the House Committee for the District of Columbia to draft a bill to prohibit it in the District. The House approved Gott's resolution on December 21, 1848, with Lincoln voting against it. On January 10, 1849, the House devoted much of the day's session to reconsidering Gott's resolution. Lincoln obtained the floor and stated that if members voted to reconsider Gott's resolution, he would present an alternative plan that would abolish slavery in the District. He then proceeded to detail the particulars of his proposal.

Lincoln's plan would have abolished slavery in Washington through a gradual process that included compensation to slaveholders. All children born to enslaved mothers after January 1, 1850, would be free after a period of apprenticeship. Those slaves born in the District prior to January 1, 1850, would remain enslaved unless slaveholders applied to the federal government for compensation. A board composed of the president, secretary of state, and secretary of the Treasury would be responsible for determining the full cash value of a slave, paying the owner and providing the slave with a certificate of freedom. Lincoln's plan allowed federal employees from slaveholding states to bring personal servants into the District and also required municipal authorities to apprehend fugitive slaves in an "active and efficient" manner. The plan would not go into effect unless a majority of the District's free white male residents voted in favor of it.

Lincoln claimed that he had presented his plan to "about fifteen of the leading citizens" of Washington and it had met with their approval, yet when called upon to provide the names of these supporters, Lincoln did not respond. The effort to reconsider Gott's resolution was successful, and a few days later, Lincoln indicated that he would soon formally introduce his bill for compensated emancipation. Despite his stated intentions, Lincoln never presented the bill.

After Lincoln was nominated for president in 1860, there was interest in this aborted attempt at emancipation. Lincoln agreed to discuss the subject in an interview and explained why he decided not to introduce his bill. He revealed that the mayor of Washington was among the leading citizens who had initially expressed approval of his plan for compensated emancipation. As he prepared to introduce it as a bill, however, Lincoln learned that some of his Southern colleagues had visited the mayor and other local supporters of his measure and were able to change their minds. After Lincoln discovered that his support had melted away, he "dropped the matter knowing that it was useless to prosecute the business at that time."

Lincoln revived his plan for compensated emancipation early in his presidency. In April 1862 Congress acted on his recommendation by passing a bill that abolished slavery in Washington and offered compensation to the District's loyal slaveholders. This act was not contingent upon the approval of any of Washington's residents.

See also *Congress, Lincoln's Relations with*

—MATTHEW NORMAN

BIBLIOGRAPHY

Basler, Roy P., ed. *The Collected Works of Abraham Lincoln.* Vol. 1, 74–75. New Brunswick, N.J.: Rutgers University Press, 1953.

Donald, David Herbert. *Lincoln.* New York: Simon and Schuster, 1995.

Findley, Paul. *A. Lincoln: The Crucible of Congress.* New York: Crown, 1979.

Riddle, Donald W. *Congressman Abraham Lincoln.* Urbana: University of Illinois Press, 1957.

Lincoln's 1849 draft of his bill for compensated emancipation in Washington, D.C., and the notes of his 1860 interview with James Q. Howard are in the Abraham Lincoln Papers at the Library of Congress, available online at http://memory.loc.gov/ammem/ alhtml/ malhome.html.

The debates in Congress can be followed in the *Congressional Globe,* 30th Cong., 1st Sess. and 30th Cong., 2nd Sess. Available online at the Library of Congress's "A Century of Lawmaking" Web site, http://memory.loc.gov/ammem/amlaw/.

Slidell, John

Born in New York City, John Slidell (1793–1871) attended Columbia College (1810), joined his father's chandler business, and moved to New Orleans in 1819. There he studied law and began a practice with Judah P. Benjamin until he became a U.S. district attorney (1829–1833) and was elected as a Democrat to the House of Representatives (1843–1845).

At the suggestion of secretary of state James Buchanan, Slidell resigned from Congress in 1845 to serve as minister to Mexico for President James K. Polk. Slidell was to negotiate the Texas boundary and purchase California and New Mexico, but the Mexican government refused to receive him. He declined other diplomatic appointments and was elected to the Senate (1853–1861). He played a major role in the election of President James Buchanan in 1856. Slidell joined the Southern "fire-eaters" at the 1860 Democratic convention in Charleston, South Carolina, to oppose the presidential nomination of Stephen A. Douglas.

Resigning from the Senate when Louisiana seceded, Slidell was appointed by President Jefferson Davis as the Confederate commissioner to France in August 1861. Traveling with James Murray Mason, the commissioner to Great Britain, he ran the blockade on the *Theodora* to reach Havana for a ship to Europe. While sailing from Cuba to England on their diplomatic mission, aboard the British mail steamer *Trent,* Slidell and Mason were arrested by Captain Charles D. Wilkes of the frigate USS *San Jacinto* on November 8, 1861. Wilkes had deliberately planned the arrest, despite orders to sail to Philadelphia for ship repairs and against the advice of his executive officer. News of the arrest caused public rejoicing in the North, and the House of Representatives unanimously approved a resolution of thanks.

In Britain, however, anger mounted as news spread of the "outrage" by the "piratical" Wilkes, and Henry Adams reported from London that Britain was preparing for war. The Foreign Office sent an ultimatum to Washington, moderated at the urging of Prince Albert, demanding release of the prisoners and an apology. But the note took more than a month to reach the United States, by which time the initial joy in Lincoln's cabinet had cooled. Determined to avoid war or diplomatic conflict with Britain, secretary of state William H. Seward sent an official explanation on December 26, 1861, conceding that Wilkes erred in not bringing any enemy papers carried by Slidell or Mason or the neutral merchant vessel *Trent* to an American prize court for adjudication. The diplomats and their two secretaries, George Eustis and James E. Macfarland, confined at Fort Warren in Boston, were released in six weeks when Britain and France protested this violation of international law. The *Trent* affair, which could have led to war with Britain and recognition of the Confederacy, was a notable diplomatic imbroglio.

In January 1862 Slidell and Mason sailed for France, and Slidell's home in New Orleans was confiscated by the Union army. In Paris, Slidell was received cordially, but his efforts to win official recognition or material aid for the Confederacy from Emperor Napoleon III failed. The French minister in Washington, Mercier, was definitely pro-South, and France suffered from the cotton famine, but this did little to advance Slidell's appeals. Although France's unofficial reception of Slidell offended the United States, it did not violate international law. As did most European governments, the French, the press and the public, disapproved of the seizure of the Confederate agents. But the U.S. minister in Paris, William L. Dayton, and Archbishop John Hughes of New York reported that their discussions with officials in Paris indicated France would not cooperate with Britain in any action hostile to Washington.

After the war John Slidell requested a pardon from President Andrew Johnson but was denied. He died in England on July 29, 1871.

See also *Mason, James;* Trent *Affair*

—PETER C. HOLLORAN

BIBLIOGRAPHY

Diket, Albert L. *Senator John Slidell and the Community He Represented in Washington, 1853–1861.* Washington, D.C.: University Press of America, 1982.

Ferris, Norman B. *The* Trent *Affair: A Diplomatic Crisis.* Knoxville: University of Tennessee Press, 1977.

Fuller, Howard J. *Clad in Iron: The American Civil War and the Challenge of British Naval Power.* Westport, Conn.: Praeger, 2008.

Mordell, Albert. ed. *Civil War and Reconstruction: Selected Essays by Gideon Welles.* New York: Twayne, 1959.

Warren, Gordon H. *Fountain of Discontent: The* Trent *Affair and Freedom of the Seas.* Boston: Northeastern University Press, 1981.

Wilson, Beckles. *John Slidell and the Confederates in Paris, 1862–65.* New York: Minton, Balch and Co., 1932.

Smith, Caleb

See *Cabinet, Lincoln's*

Soldiers' Home

President Abraham Lincoln, his wife, Mary, and son Tad spent a quarter of the Lincoln presidency—roughly June to November in 1862, 1863, and 1864—living in a thirty-four-room, brick-and-stucco country house on the grounds of the Soldiers' Home, situated on the outskirts of the capital about three miles from the White House. The house was built in 1842 by a Washington banker, George Washington Riggs Jr. Riggs soon tired of country life, and in 1851 he sold his house and 200-acre farm to the federal government for use as a home for veterans. Ironically it was secretary of war Jefferson Davis, who was later the Confederate president, who provided the impetus for the purchase. The earliest residents were known as "inmates," until 1859, when the "asylum" officially became the Soldiers' Home.

Abraham Lincoln first rode out to see the Soldiers' Home a few days after his March 4, 1861, inauguration. Soon a local newspaper reported that he and his family planned to summer there. But demands on the incoming president, most importantly the need to respond to the confiscation of federal property in the Southern states, kept the commander in chief preoccupied in the White House. During the summer and autumn months of the next three years, however, Lincoln commuted daily between this country retreat and his White House office. "The President and his family have removed for the summer to the charming country seat known as the 'Soldiers Home,' about three miles from the city," wrote the president's White House secretary William Stoddard on June 23, 1862. "Mr. Lincoln usually rides in on horseback, about nine o'clock in the morning, accompanied by 'little Fred' [Tad] on his pony. His health is better this season than last, and he manages to keep up his spirits in spite of the burdens of anxiety." The president's health was no doubt aided by the Soldiers' Home breezes that offered a respite from the sweltering humidity of the low-lying city.

Soldiers' Home

When the Lincolns first came to stay at their country home in June 1862, they were mourning the sudden death of their son Willie. Mary Todd Lincoln was despondent and, in her own words, "in need of quiet." The president was almost certainly in search of relief from his grief and the stress of pressing the Union's war effort. As it turned out, the Soldiers' Home was not as far removed from the war, or the White House hubbub, as either had hoped. By the autumn of 1862 they shared the grounds with three hundred veterans and soldiers of his military guard. Protection was deemed essential after a number of security breaches. In addition, reminders of the war's horror crowded in on the president from another corner of the Soldiers' Home, as burial details quickly filled a national cemetery hastily established adjacent to the facility. During his time in residence an average of thirty to forty burials a week were conducted in plain view of the Lincoln home.

Soon favor seekers and casual visitors learned the route to the Lincolns' door, just as they did in much greater numbers at the White House. Nonetheless, the president found time here to concentrate on the war and meet with many political friends and foes as he relentlessly pursued his goal of implementing a constitutionally conforming emancipation policy. While living at the cottage from mid-June to mid-November 1862, Lincoln was consumed with finalizing a gradual and compensated emancipation plan that would be acceptable to the Border States. When that initiative fizzled, Lincoln turned to preparing an alternative plan. His Emancipation Proclamation took effect January 1, 1863.

In the summer of 1864, as prospects for Lincoln's reelection dimmed, a number of Republicans and war Democrats found their way to the cottage to discuss policy options that would improve the chances for victory in the coming campaign. For three years Lincoln used his cottage for these types of politically discreet consultations away from White House scrutiny, but this accessibility also left him vulnerable to persistent office seekers, who pursued him even to the Soldiers' Home.

The president found time for relaxation by indulging his love of storytelling and reading Shakespeare, the Bible, poetry, or the light works of contemporary humorists. Here he chatted with the soldiers of his presidential guard, took leisurely carriage rides and walks with his wife, and played games with his youngest son. Mrs. Lincoln encouraged friends and acquaintances to visit and dine.

That any president, but especially a wartime president, would choose to commute to work on a daily basis is startling by today's standards. But the routine provided Lincoln with opportunities to interact with soldiers in transit to or from the fronts, injured soldiers housed in nearby military hospitals, freed African Americans living in "contraband" settlement camps, and ordinary people who traveled to the Soldiers' Home to enjoy its tranquil setting and treed carriage paths. These encounters gave the president firsthand news from those outside of the capital and nearer the battle lines. With those opinions and views Lincoln could better determine the course of the war and the popularity of his political initiatives. The family surely would have returned for the season in 1865.

Mary Lincoln's fondness for the location was reflected in a letter written August 25, 1865: "How dearly I loved the 'Soldiers' Home' and I little supposed one year since, that I should be so far removed from it." Lincoln made the Soldiers' Home his home and was seen riding the grounds in the afternoon of April 13, 1865, just one day before he was assassinated.

Lincoln was not the last president to live there, as Presidents Hayes and Arthur summered at the cottage, as well, and Arthur also stayed there during the winter of 1882–1883 while the White House underwent repairs. In 1889 the cottage was officially named Anderson Cottage after Robert Anderson of Fort Sumter fame, who was one of the founders. In 1973 the cottage, along with three other pre–Civil War structures and six acres of land, was designated a National Historic Landmark. On July 7, 2000, President Bill Clinton declared the Lincoln Cottage and 2.3 acres of surrounding land the President Lincoln and Soldier Home National Monument. Between 2000 and 2008 President Lincoln's Cottage was restored under the auspices of the National Trust for Historic Preservation, and it and a new visitor education center opened to the public February 19, 2008.

See also *Lincoln Historic Sites, Preservation of*

—FRANK D. MILLIGAN

BIBLIOGRAPHY

Brownstein, Elizabeth. *Lincoln's Other White House: The Untold Story of the Man and His Presidency*. Hoboken, N.J.: Wiley, 2005.

Pinsker, Matthew. *Lincoln's Sanctuary: Abraham Lincoln and the Soldiers' Home*. New York: Oxford University Press, 2003.

Soldiers' Vote

Although few Americans today would question the right of a soldier in the field to have a voice in determining the leaders of the government, this issue first received serious consideration during the Civil War. Lincoln viewed the war as the great test of democratic government, and as hundreds of thousands of citizens entered the ranks of the Union army and were sent to places far from their homes, the right of the citizen-soldier to exercise the franchise became a prominent issue. Though the Constitution granted individual states the authority to determine the qualifications for voting and the manner in which elections were conducted, the war witnessed a dramatic increase in the power of the federal government that sometimes blurred the distinction between state and national authority.

Many believed that soldiers' votes would be decisive in elections. One of the first states to test this theory was Lincoln's own state of Illinois. A Democratic-controlled convention produced a controversial new constitution in early 1862. It provided soldiers the opportunity to participate in the referendum on the proposed constitution, appointing commissioners to collect the votes of soldiers outside the state. The commissioners were able to canvass only a fraction of the thousands of soldiers in the field, and despite the hopes of Democrats, Illinois soldiers voted to reject the constitution in a higher proportion than their fellow citizens at home. The 1862 constitution plebiscite would be the only opportunity for Illinois soldiers away from home to vote during the war.

As the 1862 midterm elections approached, the governor of Minnesota wrote to Lincoln requesting federal cooperation with state commissioners appointed to visit regiments and collect the votes of soldiers. Minnesota was one of the first states to allow soldiers to cast absentee ballots, and Lincoln believed that the subsequent midterm losses that the Republicans suffered in the key states of Ohio, Pennsylvania, New York, Illinois, and Indiana could in large part be attributed to the fact that those states had not made provisions for soldiers to vote in the field. Following these setbacks, several states revised their constitutions and passed laws making it possible for soldiers to vote if absent from their home precincts on election day. The two notable exceptions were Illinois and Indiana; both states elected Democratic majorities to their state legislatures in 1862 that refused to approve absentee voting laws proposed by the states' Republican governors.

It was widely believed that the votes of soldiers would determine the outcome in closely contested state and national elections in 1864. The votes of Maryland soldiers had been indispensable in a referendum on a new state constitution that provided for the abolition of slavery, and as one Maryland politician wrote to Lincoln, the "soldiers are quite as dangerous to Rebels in the rear as in front." During the 1864 campaign, Republicans made an issue of the fact that Democrats had generally opposed measures to allow soldiers to cast absentee ballots. In addition to publishing pamphlets that highlighted this difference, such as *The Soldier's Right to Vote, Who Opposes It? Who Favors It?* Republicans also urged Lincoln to ensure that military officials cooperated with state commissioners sent to collect the votes of soldiers. The War Department therefore issued general orders stipulating procedures for granting state election officials access to soldiers. The orders sought to make sure that ballots were distributed and collected in a fair manner, and any attempt to undermine the integrity of the process would be punishable by a court-martial.

Lincoln was also urged to use his powers as commander in chief to assist soldiers from states that had not enacted absentee voting laws. The presidential election would occur on November 8, but Pennsylvania, Ohio, and Indiana were scheduled to hold important state elections on October 11. Many thought that the results in these so-called October states would be a key predictor of the outcome of the November election. Soldiers from both Ohio and Pennsylvania would be able to cast absentee ballots, but the only way for soldiers from Indiana to participate in the election was to obtain leave to return home before October 11. Indiana Republicans appealed to Lincoln to grant furloughs to soldiers and also to suspend the draft that was to take place following his July proclamation calling for an additional 500,000 troops. Even though proceeding with the draft could jeopardize Republican prospects, Lincoln refused to comply with this request. However, the president did write to General William T. Sherman and ask the general to allow as many Indiana soldiers as he could spare to go home and vote in the October election. Lincoln's letter made it clear that this was not an order and that the soldiers did not need to remain in Indiana for the presidential election. Sherman allowed several thousand soldiers to return to Indiana and vote, but it is not known exactly how many furloughed soldiers contributed to Republican victories there.

Favorable results in all three of the October states gave the Republicans great confidence, yet as the November elections drew near, the administration made arrangements to furlough as many Illinois troops as possible so that they could return home in time to vote. Efforts were also made to obtain leave for thousands of civilian employees in Washington, who were not included in absentee voting laws that applied specifically to soldiers. As state and party officials arrived at military camps to collect the soldiers' votes, Republicans and Democrats accused one another of engaging in fraudulent tactics to tamper with ballots. In one high-profile incident, military authorities arrested the New York Democratic commissioners at Baltimore and Washington and tried them on charges of fraud and corruption.

Though the Democrats nominated a popular former general, George B. McClellan, as their candidate for president and adopted a platform that deemed the war a "failure" and resolved to end it as soon as possible, Lincoln's determination to bring the war to a successful conclusion won him overwhelming support from the men who were faced with that grim task. In the states for which the soldiers' vote was tabulated separately, Lincoln garnered over 77 percent of the vote (he won 54 percent of the civilian vote). Lincoln's total would have been even higher if he had taken the advice of a correspondent who suggested that African American soldiers be allowed to cast ballots in the presidential election. The effort to ensure that soldiers in the field would be able to participate in elections was without precedent and also entailed an unprecedented level of federal involvement in an area that had largely been a state responsibility.

See also *Campaign of 1864, Presidential*

—MATTHEW NORMAN

BIBLIOGRAPHY

Benton, Josiah. *Voting in the Field: A Forgotten Chapter of the Civil War.* Boston: Privately printed, 1915.

Chandler, William E. *The Soldier's Right to Vote, Who Opposes It? Who Favors It?* Washington, D.C.: L. Towers, 1864.

Long, David E. *The Jewel of Liberty: Abraham Lincoln's Re-Election and the End of Slavery.* Mechanicsburg, Pa.: Stackpole Books, 1994.

McSeveney, Samuel T. "Re-electing Lincoln: The Union Party Campaign and the Military Vote in Connecticut." *Civil War History* 32, no. 2 (1986): 139–158.

White, Jonathan W. "Canvassing the Troops: The Federal Government and the Soldier's Right to Vote." *Civil War History* 50, no. 3 (2004): 291–317.

Numerous items relating to the soldiers' vote are in the Abraham Lincoln Papers at the Library of Congress, available online at http://memory.loc.gov/ammem/alhtml/malhome.html.

Speed, Joshua F.

Joshua Fry Speed (1814–1882), Abraham Lincoln's closest friend, was born on November 14, 1814, just outside of Louisville, Kentucky. He grew up on a large plantation known as Farmington and attended St. Joseph's College, in Bardstown, but left shortly before earning a degree. Speed secured a clerkship in the largest wholesale store in Louisville. In 1835 he moved to Springfield, Illinois, and bought a part interest in a general store, Bell and Co.

When Lincoln moved to Springfield on April 15, 1837, he stopped at Speed's store on the corner of Fifth and Washington Streets to buy a bed and a few supplies. When Speed told him that the price came to seventeen dollars, Lincoln expressed concern that he could not afford the items. Speed replied that he could put the items on credit, but Lincoln admitted that his ability to pay depended on his success as a lawyer. "If I fail in that I will probably never be able to pay you at all," Lincoln said.

"The tone of his voice was so melancholy that I felt for him," Speed remembered. He generously offered Lincoln an alternative. He told Lincoln that he had "a very large room, and a very large double-bed in it; which you are perfectly welcome to share with me if you choose." Lincoln accepted the offer, and for the next four years, the pair were roommates.

Speed's store soon became a popular meeting spot for other ambitious young men in Springfield. They swapped stories, talked politics, and even formed a "society for the encouragement of debate and literary efforts."

Lincoln's emotional state was shattered in early 1841. Speed, along with a number of others, genuinely feared that he was suicidal. Though the exact nature of Lincoln's depression is not known, it appears to have been connected to his troubled courtship of Mary Todd (1818–1882).

Around the same time as Lincoln's emotional crisis, Speed moved back to Kentucky. At Speed's urging, Lincoln visited Farmington from August to September 1841. Though he seemed "moody & hypochondriac" during his stay, Lincoln was surrounded by people who were sympathetic to his condition. Speed told Lincoln that his brother William had suffered a crippling episode of depression shortly after his wife died; he also confessed that his mother was "naturally of a nervous temperament." During his visit, Speed's mother also spoke with Lincoln. She told him that reading the Bible was the "best cure for the 'Blues'," and the next morning she gave him one of her own. Twenty years later, as the Civil War tested Lincoln's strength, he sent Mrs. Speed a photograph with the inscription, "For Mrs. Lucy G. Speed, from whose pious hand I accepted the present of an Oxford Bible twenty years ago."

Joshua Speed married Fanny Henning (1820–1902) on February 15, 1842. The couple made their home thirteen miles outside of Louisville. Speed was elected to the state legislature in 1848 but never sought political office thereafter. In 1851 he formed a partnership in a real estate business with his wife's brother. The firm flourished, and Speed soon built a large fortune buying and selling property in the Louisville area.

Eventually Lincoln and Speed drifted apart. Now married and living in different states, they differed politically. In 1855 Lincoln wrote Speed a remarkable letter in which he discussed their growing political disagreements. "You know I dislike slavery," Lincoln wrote, "and you fully admit the abstract wrong of it." Yet they were on opposite sides of the slavery question.

Five years later, when Lincoln was elected president, Speed congratulated him. "As a friend, I am rejoiced at your success," Speed wrote, but "as a political opponent I am not disappointed." He had expected the Republicans to win in 1860, but in view of the rise of secessionist sentiment, Speed told his friend, "I can not but tremble for you."

When Lincoln issued the Emancipation Proclamation, Speed complained that he was "so much distressed" that he was "unable to eat or sleep," yet he remained loyal to the Union throughout the war. In 1864 Lincoln appointed his brother, James Speed (1812–1887), attorney general of the United States.

Joshua Speed devoted the rest of his life to various business enterprises in Louisville. By January 1881, his health was failing. He traveled to a healthier climate but returned to Louisville and died on May 29, 1882. He had no children but left an estate worth more than $600,000 to his widow, brothers, and sisters.

In 1999, gay rights activist Larry Kramer made national headlines when he claimed to possess a copy of a previously undiscovered diary written by Joshua Speed. Though he has yet to produce the diary for critical evaluation, Kramer claims that the diary details a homosexual love affair between Lincoln and

Speed. In 2005 sex researcher C. A. Tripp's *The Intimate World of Abraham Lincoln* doubted the existence of a tell-all diary, but he, too, claimed that Lincoln and Speed were lovers. It is important to note that none of Lincoln's contemporaries ever raised the possibility of such a relationship, nor does Tripp provide any concrete evidence. Though intriguing, the Tripp thesis has not found widespread acceptance among Lincoln scholars.

—SAMUEL P. WHEELER

BIBLIOGRAPHY

Basler, Roy P., ed. *The Collected Works of Abraham Lincoln.* New Brunswick, N.J.: Rutgers University Press, 1953.

C. A. Tripp. *The Intimate World of Abraham Lincoln.* New York: Free Press, 2005.

Donald, David Herbert. *"We Are Lincoln Men": Abraham Lincoln and His Friends.* New York: Simon and Schuster, 2003.

Kincaid, Robert L. "Joshua Fry Speed, 1814–1882: Abraham Lincoln's Most Intimate Friend." *Filson Club History Quarterly* 17 (April 1943).

Krause, Susan. "Abraham Lincoln and Joshua Speed, Attorney and Client." *Illinois Historical Journal* 89 (Spring 1996).

Speed, Joshua F. *Reminiscences of Abraham Lincoln and Notes of a Visit to California.* Louisville: Bradley and Gilbert Company, 1896.

Wilson, Douglas L., and Rodney O. Davis, eds. *Herndon's Informants: Letters, Interviews, and Statements about Abraham Lincoln.* Urbana: University of Illinois Press, 1998.

Spot Resolutions

The "spot resolutions" were the antiwar resolutions that Abraham Lincoln presented to the U.S. Congress in 1847. Then a freshman Whig representative from Illinois, Lincoln gained national attention by challenging the Polk administration's justification for the U.S.-Mexican War.

The conflict with Mexico had begun a year earlier, before Lincoln entered Congress. On April 25, 1846, a squadron of U.S. dragoons commanded by Captain Seth Thornton was attacked by Mexican troops near Fort Texas (later renamed Fort Brown, the site of modern-day Brownsville). The engagement left sixteen U.S. troops killed or wounded, and the remaining fifty-two were captured. News of the incident reached Washington, D.C., two weeks later. On May 11 President James Polk asked Congress for a declaration of war, maintaining that a state of war between the two nations already existed. "Mexico has passed the boundary of the United States, has invaded our territory and shed American blood upon the American soil." Two days later, by overwhelming margins and with little debate, both houses voted to declare war.

Despite initial bipartisan support, Polk's war message soon became the subject of considerable controversy, with a growing number of Whigs challenging the president's claim that the attack on Thornton's dragoons had occurred on American soil. Administration critics pointed out that the trans-Nueces, the broad swath of land between the Nueces River and the Rio Grande, was claimed by the United States and Mexico.

The territorial dispute over the trans-Nueces had its roots in the Texas Revolution ten years earlier. The Nueces River had been the southern boundary of Texas under Mexican rule, but Texas claimed the Rio Grande after winning its independence in 1836. Sparsely populated, the trans-Nueces had been a virtual no-man's-land in the years that followed, with neither country able to extend jurisdiction over the area.

The conflicting claims became a problem for Washington when American expansionists began to push for the annexation of Texas in the mid-1840s. Antislavery Northerners managed to block the proposal when it came before the Senate as a treaty in 1844. Presented as a joint resolution in spring of 1845, annexation passed both houses by slender margins. Known as the Brown resolution, the measure left the boundary dispute unresolved, although it was generally accepted among members of Congress who supported annexation that Mexico could be induced to surrender its claim for some form of compensation. Instead, the Brown resolution prompted the Mexican government to break off diplomatic relations with Washington. Insisting that Texas was still a province in revolt, Mexico's leaders maintained that annexation would be grounds for war. Polk, who had favored compensation for Mexico during the presidential campaign, now took the position that vigorous defense of American claims was the best way to deal with the threat of Mexican aggression. Accordingly, he dispatched U.S. troops to the trans-Nueces in summer 1845, stating that he was obligated to protect an area that would soon become part of the United States.

The president's claim that the war had begun as a result of Mexico's violation of U.S. territorial sovereignty was still being hotly debated when Lincoln was elected to Congress in fall 1847. Thirty-eight years old, Lincoln quickly emerged as a prominent administration critic. On December 22 the lone Whig congressman from Illinois introduced the "spot resolutions," a set of eight questions disputing Polk's rationale for war. Arguing that the war had been unnecessary and unconstitutional, Lincoln demanded to know "whether the particular spot on which the blood of our citizens was so shed was or was not at that time our own soil...." Like many Whigs, Lincoln was sensitive to the charge of disloyalty in time of war, and he tempered his remarks by praising the bravery of American soldiers in the field, as well as the conduct of General Zachary Taylor (soon to be the Whig nominee for president). Furthermore, he supported funding for U.S.

troops and favored acquiring some territory from Mexico. Lincoln repeated his argument that the war had been an unprovoked act of aggression by the United States in his first speech to the House of Representatives on January 12, 1848.

Lincoln's antiwar efforts attracted considerable notice in his home state, earning him praise from Whig newspapers and ridicule from Democrats, who nicknamed him "spotty Lincoln." The resolutions did little to enhance his political reputation, for the end of the war was already in sight. U.S. forces had seized Mexico City the previous September, and on February 2, 1848, U.S. and Mexican negotiators would sign the Treaty of Guadalupe-Hidalgo. The Whig representative chose not to run for reelection, making the "spot resolutions" Lincoln's signal accomplishment as a national politician prior to his election in 1860.

See also *Mexican War; Polk, James, K.*

—SAM W. HAYNES

BIBLIOGRAPHY

Donald, David Herbert. *Lincoln.* New York: Simon and Schuster, 1995.

Haynes, Sam W. *James Polk and the Expansionist Impulse.* 3rd ed. New York: Longman, 2005.

Stamps, Postage

The outbreak of the Civil War left various federal facilities in the hands of the Confederacy, including thousands of U.S. post offices with vast quantities of U.S. stamps. At the time, postage stamps functioned like money and were often used when there was a shortage of small coins. To prevent the Confederacy from using the stamps, the United States demonetized all existing postage stamps, and in June 1861 the Post Office contracted with the National Bank Note Company to print all new stamps for the nation. The new stamps would all have arabic numerals on them indicating the denomination. Of the fifteen U.S. Postage stamp designs printed before 1861, all but two either had a roman numeral or spelled out the denomination. Putting the value on the new stamps with a number was a way of distinguishing them from the older, demonetized stamps and making it more difficult for Confederates to use the stamps to enhance their economy and undermine the U.S. economy.

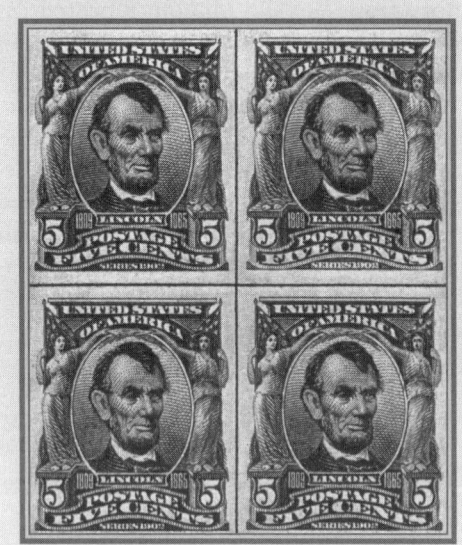

U.S. postage stamps were issued in 1909 to commemorate the 100th anniversary of Lincoln's birth.

Source: The Granger Collection, New York

In March 1863 the Lincoln administration began to use postage as a form of war propaganda with the release of a two-cent stamp bearing the portrait of a grim and determined Andrew Jackson on a black background. Lincoln admired Jackson because he had stood up to the South Carolina extremists in the Nullification Crisis. Like Lincoln, Jackson would not tolerate defiance of the Constitution or deal lightly with those who threatened the integrity of the nation. Jackson was also a Southerner and slaveholder, who symbolized the unity of the nation. The stamp, known as the "Black Jack," was the standard postage for all local mail in the nation, thus reminding everyone who sent a local letter of the president who stood up to the nullificationists. Jackson was also the first person to appear on a stamp who was not one of the Founders. The only other portraits on stamps up to this time were those of George Washington, Benjamin Franklin, and Thomas Jefferson.

The Confederacy also used stamps for political messages, printing them with the Southern nationalist John C. Calhoun, as well as Jefferson, Jackson, and Washington, to underscore the Confederate claim that secession was patriotic. More problematic, of the fourteen postage stamps that the Confederacy issued, eight bore the likeness of the Confederate president, Jefferson Davis. No U.S. stamp had—or has since—showed the likeness of a living person. The Confederate use of Davis's portrait suggests a semi-regal or authoritarian notion of what modern political theorists might call a cult of personality.

Within a year of his death the United States put Lincoln on a stamp, and after that he regularly appeared on everyday postage, along with Washington and Franklin. By 1909 the Post Office was regularly printing stamps to commemorate modern or historical events, and it commemorated Lincoln's birth with a special series of stamps.

—Paul Finkelman

BIBLIOGRAPHY

Brookman, Lester G. *The United States Postage Stamps of the Nineteenth Century.* 3 vols. New York: H.L. Linquist, 1966.

Stanton, Edwin M.

Edwin M. Stanton (1814–1869) served as secretary of war for most of Abraham Lincoln's presidency. Stanton was born in Ohio, where he attended Kenyon College. He began practicing law in 1835 in Steubenville, Ohio, and became active in both Democratic Party politics and antislavery activities, sometimes working with the better-known Salmon P. Chase. Moving to Pittsburgh, Pennsylvania, in 1847, he had an extensive law practice.

In 1854 Stanton encountered Lincoln when the two men were on the same legal team for a case involving the McCormick reaper patent. The legal team defending the patent infringement suit had retained Lincoln because they believed the case would be tried in Chicago. When it was moved to Cincinnati no more thought was given to Lincoln, and Stanton and his colleagues were stunned when Lincoln showed up to join them in Cincinnati. Stanton and all the other lawyers rudely snubbed Lincoln, and Stanton and Lincoln did not part on friendly terms.

In 1856 Stanton remarried, following the death of his first wife. With his new wife, Ellen Hutchinson, Stanton relocated his law practice to Washington, D.C. Although he had a large practice, especially representing railroads, and excellent political connections through Chase, Stanton gained great notoriety in 1859 when he defended Daniel E. Sickles, a man charged with the murder of his wife's lover, Philip Barton Key. To this day people credit Stanton with the first use of the "temporary insanity" defense.

In December 1860, just as South Carolina seceded, James Buchanan named Stanton attorney general in place of Jeremiah Black. During the ensuing secession crisis, Stanton opposed secession and argued against its constitutionality: he shared information about cabinet deliberations and administration decisions with Republican congressional leaders. With Lincoln installed in office, Stanton returned to private life. He expressed intense unhappiness with the new administration in personal correspondence, deploring "the painful imbecility of Lincoln." Before long he assisted the new secretary of war, Simon Cameron, in several legal matters and also became a close confidant of the new general in chief, George B. McClellan. Cameron, always surrounded by rumors of corruption, appears to have been overwhelmed by the responsibilities of his position, and as the war continued it became obvious that he would not do as head of the War Department. In January 1862, Lincoln accepted Cameron's resignation and named Stanton to replace him, a selection endorsed by William H. Seward and Salmon P. Chase, each of whom saw him as a potential ally.

Stanton was a great improvement on his predecessor when it came to administering the War Department, although he erred early on when he called for an end to recruiting, an act that proved both temporary and ill-timed. Nevertheless, he gained a reputation as a hard-working and effective administrator who was devoted to the cause of saving the Union. Although he sometimes found himself at odds with Lincoln on various political and military matters, the two men usually worked well together, and Lincoln valued Stanton's firmness when it came to cracking down on the opposition. At times Stanton defied Lincoln; at times Lincoln circumvented Stanton. But the two men eventually found common ground in their dissatisfaction with the performance of several Union generals, notably McClellan. In the wake of the Union defeat at Second Manassas in August 1862, the secretary strongly remonstrated against the president's decision to place McClellan in charge of the Union forces around Washington, although in the end the president prevailed. Over time Stanton became more active in the prosecution of the war, most notably when he pushed hard to shift reinforcements from Virginia to the relief of Chattanooga less than a week after the Union defeat at Chickamauga.

During the war Stanton became an advocate of emancipation and the enlistment of black soldiers; he also became a passionate advocate of a harsh peace. Lincoln placed a great deal of reliance on Stanton's support of the erection of wartime governments in the occupied South; in turn Stanton supported the president's initiatives on Reconstruction. In 1864 Stanton pushed for a new draft call and did what he could to ensure Lincoln's reelection, including taking steps to make sure that soldiers could vote in the field. By war's end, Stanton the war Democrat had turned de facto Republican. Lincoln rewarded such loyalty by standing by his secretary when he came under criticism, especially from those people who were put off by Stanton's gruff manner, blunt language, and explosive temper. For years people told tales of how the secretary would explode at some of the president's directives, while Lincoln responded to these stories with humor, sometimes even conceding the wisdom of Stanton's objection but never letting anyone forget who was the boss when it mattered.

Throughout the war Stanton displayed concern about Lincoln's personal safety and was frustrated when the president did not heed his warnings. On April 14 he declined Lincoln's invitation to attend the theater that evening and hoped that the president would not go at all. That evening John Wilkes Booth shot Lincoln at Ford's Theatre; there was also an attempt on the life of the bedridden William H. Seward, and it was left to Stanton to take charge in this moment of chaos and tragedy. Although in weeks to come Stanton would build on his determination to capture and prosecute Booth and his associates, he is perhaps best remembered for remarking upon Lincoln's passing, "Now he belongs to the ages."

After Lincoln died Stanton remained in the cabinet. At the end of April he exploded when he heard of the generous terms that General William T. Sherman had given Confederate commander Joseph E. Johnston; it was with some difficulty that the resulting conflict was settled by General Ulysses Grant. Over the next two years Stanton's support of congressional Reconstruction and black rights legislation brought him into conflict with President Andrew Johnson. In August 1867 Johnson, acting under the provisions of the recently passed Tenure of Office Act, suspended him from office, but the Senate failed to concur in January 1868. The following month Johnson's attempt to remove Stanton outright sparked the impeachment crisis of 1868. Stanton resigned his cabinet post at the conclusion of the impeachment trial. In 1869 Grant nominated him to a seat on the Supreme Court, but the ailing Stanton died a day after being confirmed and sworn in.

See also *Cabinet, Lincoln's*

—BROOKS D. SIMPSON

BIBLIOGRAPHY

Flower, Frank A. *Edwin McMasters Stanton: The Autocrat of Rebellion, Emancipation and Reconstruction.* Akron, Ohio: Saalfield Publishing Company, 1905.

Goodwin, Doris Kearns. *Team of Rivals: The Political Genius of Abraham Lincoln.* New York: Simon and Schuster, 2005.

Platt, Fletcher. *Stanton: Lincoln's Secretary of War.* New York: Norton, 1953.

Thomas, Benjamin P., and Harold M. Hyman. *Stanton: The Life and Times of Lincoln's Secretary of War.* New York: Knopf, 1962.

Stephens, Alexander Hamilton

Alexander Hamilton Stephens (1812–1883), born into a modest farm family near Crawfordville, Georgia, was orphaned at fourteen and faced uncertain prospects. Always slight and frail, he was ill-suited to physical labor but lacked the resources to pursue a profession. Benefactors aided his education, enabling him to graduate from Franklin College (later the University of Georgia) in 1832. He then taught school, studied law, passed the bar in 1834, and established a successful practice in Crawfordville. His ambition, interests, and talent for public speaking soon drew him into politics.

After stints in Georgia's House of Representatives (1836–1841) and Senate (1842), Stephens served in the U.S. House of Representatives (1843–1859). Stephens's eloquence transfixed fellow Whig representative Abraham Lincoln (1847–1849). Stephens and Lincoln were among the "Young Indians," Whig congressmen striving to invigorate their party and backing Zachary Taylor for the presidency in 1848, although Taylor later disappointed Stephens during the Crisis of 1850. Stephens supported the Compromise of 1850 but formulated the Georgia Platform (1850), attaching conditions to states' adherence to the compromise. As the Whig Party disintegrated, Stephens joined a Unionist coalition before becoming a Democrat. He pushed the Kansas-Nebraska Bill (1854) through the House but was jarred by the ensuing strife.

Although Stephens and Lincoln did not see each other for sixteen years after Lincoln's departure from Congress, they remained friends. Stephens supported Stephen Douglas's presidential bid in 1860 but regarded many attacks against Lincoln as baseless slander. As some states careened toward secession in response to Lincoln's victory, Stephens delivered a powerful address to the Georgia legislature (November 14, 1860). Calling for calm, he maintained that Lincoln's election was constitutional, that Georgia benefited from the Union, and that there was, as yet, no reason to consider Lincoln or the Union a threat.

Impressed by the speech, Lincoln wrote to Stephens in mid-December, opening a brief, hopeful exchange. Lincoln assured Stephens that a Republican administration would not menace Southerners. Stephens reaffirmed his friendship for Lincoln but warned that Southerners naturally feared and despised Lincoln's party. He urged Lincoln to issue a public statement to alleviate dangerous tensions, but the suggestion was unavailing.

Stephens believed in states' right to secede but opposed precipitous action. In Georgia's secession convention (January 1861), he continued to advocate a conditional Unionist stance and voted against secession. Outvoted, he abided by the majority's choice and participated in the formation of the Confederacy.

Stephens was highly regarded, and he became the Confederate vice president (February 11, 1861–May 11, 1865). In early 1861, although privately worried that war could easily erupt, Stephens was publicly resolute in defining and defending Confederate principles. States' rights were central, and throughout the Civil War Stephens staunchly opposed any encroachment on states' or people's rights and any centralization of power. Unambiguous recognition of slavery was also important to Stephens's view of the Confederacy, as his famous "Cornerstone Speech" (March 21, 1861) demonstrated. Denying that "all men are created equal," he asserted, "Our new government is founded upon exactly the opposite idea; its foundations are laid, its cornerstone rests, upon the great truth that the negro is not equal to the white man; that slavery—subordination to the superior race—is his natural and normal condition."

Having cast his lot with the Confederacy, Stephens committed to Confederate independence, supported the war as long as it seemed necessary to the achievement of that goal, but welcomed opportunities for an honorable peace. In early July 1863, Stephens attempted to meet with Lincoln, purportedly to discuss prisoner exchanges but intending to discuss peace prospects as well. With Union military fortunes languishing, Stephens thought the moment auspicious for peace initiatives. Such expectations shattered when news of Union victories at Gettysburg and Vicksburg (July 1863) arrived almost simultaneously with Stephens's request to pass through Union lines. Lincoln refused to allow Stephens to proceed to Washington.

As Confederate problems mounted later, Stephens and two other prominent Confederates, responding to unofficial Union peace overtures, met Lincoln and secretary of state William Henry Seward (1861–1869) at Hampton Roads, Virginia, and conferred for several hours (February 3, 1865) aboard Lincoln's steamer, the *River Queen*. Although Lincoln indicated flexibility on issues such as compensation for slave owners and the possibility of delayed implementation of the Thirteenth Amendment, the conference foundered because of both sides' unyielding positions on whether an armistice would be predicated on the existence of one nation or two. After failing to reach any general agreements, Lincoln asked if he could do anything personal for Stephens; Stephens requested the release of his nephew, a prisoner of war. Lincoln obliged.

Stephens was arrested on May 11, 1865, and imprisoned for five months. After his parole in October 1865, the Georgia legislature elected him to the U.S. Senate in 1866, but he did not serve because Georgia had not regained its political rights. Stephens instead wrote *A Constitutional View of the War Between the States* (1868–1870), a turgid defense of state sovereignty. Throughout Reconstruction he clung to his convictions regarding states' rights and opposed federal actions that infringed on states' prerogatives.

Although often ailing, Stevens served in the U.S. House of Representatives from 1873 until November 1882, when he resigned to become governor of Georgia. He died on March 4, 1883.

—Cara L. Shelly

BIBLIOGRAPHY

Davis, William C. *"A Government of Our Own": The Making of the Confederacy*. New York: Free Press, 1994.

Donald, David Herbert. *Lincoln*. New York: Simon and Schuster, 1995.

Goodwin, Doris Kearns. *Team of Rivals: The Political Genius of Abraham Lincoln*. New York: Simon and Schuster, 2005.

McPherson, James M. *Ordeal by Fire: The Civil War and Reconstruction*. New York: Knopf, 1982.

Oates, Stephen B. *With Malice toward None: The Life of Abraham Lincoln*. New York: Mentor, 1978.

Perman, Michael. *Reunion without Compromise: The South and Reconstruction, 1865–1868*. London: Cambridge University Press, 1973.

Schott, Thomas E. *Alexander H. Stephens of Georgia*. Baton Rouge: Louisiana State University Press, 1988.

Stephens, Alexander H. *Recollections of Alexander H. Stephens*. New York: Doubleday, Page, 1910.

Von Abele, Rudolph. *Alexander H. Stephens*. New York: Knopf, 1946.

Stowe, Harriet Beecher

Harriet Beecher Stowe (1811–1896), the author of *Uncle Tom's Cabin* (1852) and other novels, was born in Litchfield, Connecticut, the seventh of the nine children of Lyman Beecher and Roxanna Foote. As the daughter of one of the most famous Presbyterian ministers of the nineteenth century, Stowe's early life was shaped by her father and her sister, Catharine Beecher, a pioneer of women's education. Another sibling, Henry Ward Beecher, was also a nationally renowned minister and abolitionist.

As a youth she studied at the Litchfield Female Academy and then entered Catharine Beecher's Hartford Female Seminary, where she undertook a rigorous curriculum that included Latin and moral philosophy. Upon completion of her studies, she taught at the school from 1829 to 1832. That year, along with her family, she relocated to Cincinnati, Ohio, where her father became president of Lane Theological Seminary. It was in Cincinnati, just across the Ohio River from the slave South, that young Harriet came into direct contact with activists engaged in antislavery reform. She also began her literary career there, publishing a geography text, *Primary Geography,* in 1833, and resumed teaching at her sister Catharine's newly formed Western Female Academy. In 1836 she married biblical scholar and Lane professor Calvin E. Stowe, who encouraged her literary career. Together they had seven children, two of whom died in childhood.

Aiming to supplement her growing family's income, Harriet Beecher Stowe wrote vigorously, publishing essays, sermons, and short stories for contemporary publications including the *New York Evangelist* and *Godey's Lady's Book.* In her early writings Stowe took a moderate position on slavery, indicating that both gradual manumission and colonization were acceptable means to end the institution. Her views on slavery were radically altered by the passage of the Fugitive Slave Law of 1850. Strengthening the ability of Southerners to recapture fugitive slaves from Northern states, such as Ohio, and also requiring Northerners to aid in their return, the law turned Stowe into an advocate of immediate abolition.

She began penning *Uncle Tom's Cabin,* which quickly became the most famous and influential novel of the mid-nineteenth century. It appeared as a weekly serial in the Washington, D.C., antislavery *National Era* between June 5, 1851, and April 1, 1852. After it appeared in book form in 1852, the novel sold more than 300,000 copies in the United States during its first year of publication. Telling the tale of faithful slave Tom, who is sold to the Deep South, and of the enslaved family of Eliza and George Harris, who escape to the North, the novel brought slavery home for many American readers. Stowe followed with *A Key to Uncle Tom's Cabin* (1853), which provided factual support for the incidents in her book that she hoped would quell critics who claimed that the novel exaggerated the horrors of slavery.

In the decade leading to the Civil War, Stowe used her newfound political activism to lash out against slavery. As the U.S. Congress debated the Kansas-Nebraska Act, in 1854, she circulated petitions and published essays and pamphlets condemning the bill. Her second antislavery novel, *Dred: A Tale of the Great Dismal Swamp* (1856), reflected her militancy. Unlike the docile Tom, the hero of this novel was depicted as the rebellious and angry son of failed insurrectionist Denmark Vesey. The popularity of *Uncle Tom's Cabin* swelled as the nation teetered on the brink of civil war, and Stowe deserves credit as one of the powerful forces influencing late antebellum politics. Once the war began in April 1861, Stowe insisted that emancipation was an important and necessary outcome.

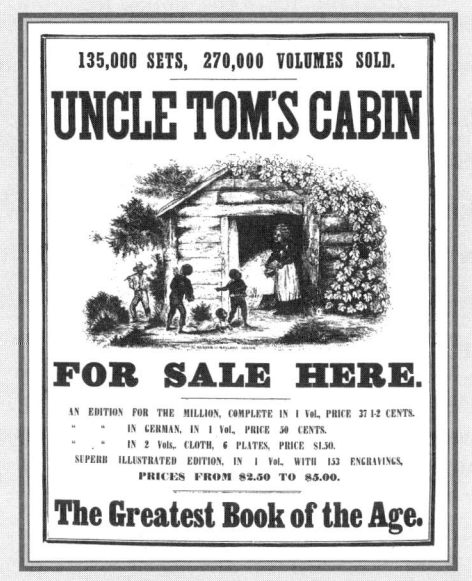

An American booksellers' announcement, c.1860, for Harriet Beecher Stowe's *Uncle Tom's Cabin*, which revealed the horrors of slavery to a widespread audience.

Source: The Granger Collection, New York

In 1862, following Lincoln's announcement of the Preliminary Emancipation Proclamation, Stowe was ecstatic at the possible end of slavery but remained cautious about offering her public support to the measure. Stowe determined to travel to Washington, D.C., where she could personally ascertain the president's commitment to carry out emancipation. While awaiting the invitation she sought, Stowe and her companions visited her son Fred, whose regiment was stationed in the capital, and toured a camp of "contrabands," former slaves who had sought refuge behind Union lines. Stowe was invited to the White House on December 2, along with Massachusetts senator Henry Wilson. The legendary account of this meeting has it that upon meeting Stowe, Abraham Lincoln remarked, "So you're the little woman who wrote the book that started this great war!" (quoted in Hedrick's biography of Stowe). In reality, very little record remains of the exchange between Lincoln and the abolitionist author. Stowe wrote home that her encounter with the president was a humorous one, noting, "It was a very droll time that we had at the White House I assure you." On January 1, 1863, she joined an abolitionist crowd at the Boston Music Hall to celebrate the Emancipation Proclamation.

Stowe continued to publish frequently in periodicals and to write new works of fiction. The sole support of her family after Calvin Stowe retired in 1863, she used her literary skills to create works for a variety of venues. In 1864 she began a monthly column in the *Atlantic* that offered domestic advice. Returning to more conventional topics, her works of the 1860s and 1870s continued to enjoy wide readership. Among her later publications are the novel *The Pearl of Orr's Island* (1862), the collection *Religious Poems* (1867), and a biographic volume, *Men of Our Times* (1868). Her last novel, *Poganuc People,* a fictionalized version of her childhood in Litchfield, appeared in 1878. Stowe died in Hartford in 1896.

—L. Diane Barnes

BIBLIOGRAPHY

Donald, David Herbert. *Lincoln.* New York: Simon and Schuster, 1995.

Hedrick, Joan D. *Harriet Beecher Stowe: A Life.* New York: Oxford University Press, 1994.

Wagenknecht, Edward. *Harriet Beecher Stowe: The Known and the Unknown.* New York: Oxford University Press, 1965.

Strong, George Templeton

George Templeton Strong (1820–1875), a wealthy New York lawyer, helped to establish and run the United States Sanitary Commission during the Civil War. He kept a remarkable diary for nearly forty years. Commencing his diary as a teenager in October 1835, Strong continued to write almost every day for the rest of his life.

Strong was perpetually busy in his law practice, as a vestryman at Trinity Episcopal Church, and as a trustee of his alma mater, Columbia College. His diary details his myriad activities, his happy home life, and his interest in books, music, and public affairs. Keenly observant, Strong monitored the divisive developments of the late 1850s and the onset and progress of the Civil War, recording his own experiences and opinions, his impressions of the public mood, the effects of shifting circumstances on financial markets, and the attitudes expressed by people he knew.

Politically homeless for a time after the collapse of the Whig Party, Strong eventually settled—albeit unenthusiastically—on Abraham Lincoln in 1860.

Once decided, Strong never wavered in his choice, even as his diary filled with dire rumors in the weeks before the election. After Lincoln's victory, Strong decried secession, fretted over bleak news in the winter of 1860–1861, and watched for evidence that Lincoln would be equal to the challenge.

When war erupted, Strong, at forty-one, considered himself too old for military service, but he helped to organize and fund a New York regiment, participated in the Union League Club in New York both during and after the war, and perhaps most important, served as treasurer and a member of the executive board of the United States Sanitary Commission almost from its inception in spring 1861. The Sanitary Commission was a civilian organization that tried to improve military medical care, hygiene, and diet, although the army's Medical Bureau initially resisted civilian "meddling." Lincoln, too, at first saw little need for a civilian adjunct to the military's medical establishment, but the commission proved so effective that it converted Lincoln and many others into supporters.

Strong facilitated many of the commission's projects, raised money, kept meticulous accounts, and conferred with Lincoln and other leaders about the commission's work, finding some receptive but others (including secretary of war Edwin Stanton) hostile. The highly principled Strong sometimes suspected base motives in various officials. He judged Lincoln, however, to be a man of genuine integrity, although he still occasionally worried that the president was too uneducated and unsophisticated. Upon Lincoln's assassination, Strong mourned the loss of a truly good, honest man.

After the Civil War, Strong struggled to rebuild his finances. His law practice had suffered while he focused on the Sanitary Commission, and inflation damaged his investments. Although in declining health, Strong continued to serve Columbia, wrote a financial history of the Sanitary Commission, and became the comptroller of Trinity Church in 1872, retiring from his law firm to take this new job. By June 1875, he was no longer able to work but continued to write in his diary. He died in July 1875.

—Cara L. Shelly

BIBLIOGRAPHY

Maxwell, William Quentin. *Lincoln's Fifth Wheel: The Political History of the United States Sanitary Commission.* New York: Longmans, Green, 1956.

McPherson, James M. *Battle Cry of Freedom: The Civil War Era.* New York: Oxford University Press, 1988.

Olmsted, Frederick Law. *The Papers of Frederick Law Olmsted. Vol. 4: Defending the Union: The Civil War and the U.S. Sanitary Commission, 1861–1863.* Edited by Jane Turner Censer. Baltimore: Johns Hopkins University Press, 1986.

Strong, George Templeton. *The Diary of George Templeton Strong.* 4 vols. Edited by Allan Nevins and Milton Halsey Thomas. New York: Macmillan, 1952.

Stuart, John Todd

John Todd Stuart (1807–1885) was Lincoln's political mentor, his first law partner, and a cousin of Mary Todd Lincoln. Born near Lexington, Kentucky, and educated at Centre College, Stuart opened a law office in Springfield, Illinois, in 1828. After serving in the Black Hawk War with Lincoln in 1832, Stuart encouraged Lincoln to study law and enter politics. In 1834 both men won seats in the state General Assembly where, under Stuart's tutelage, Lincoln emerged as a Whig leader. After his admission to the bar in 1837 Lincoln joined Stuart's law practice at Springfield. The next year Stuart defeated Stephen A. Douglas for Congress and virtually turned over his practice to Lincoln. Desiring a freer hand to engage in politics, Lincoln left the firm in 1841 and joined in a partnership with Stephen T. Logan.

The rise of the antislavery movement during the 1850s distressed Stuart. His ultraconservatism on slavery and his support of the Know-Nothings (nativists) caused him to oppose Lincoln and the Republicans in 1856. When Stuart and other old Whigs established the *Springfield Conservative* to promote the presidential candidacy of Millard Fillmore, Lincoln angrily denounced them as "stool pigeons for the Democracy—brought up like cattle and hogs." But in 1858 Stuart favored Lincoln in his senatorial campaign against his old political foe, Douglas.

In 1860 Stuart, fearful of the sectional implications of a Lincoln victory, again opposed the Republicans and supported John Bell for president. A group of Bell supporters formed the Illinois National Union Party and nominated Stuart for governor. The new, conservative party, however, probably at Stuart's urging, rejected fusion with Douglas in the election. Stuart and his party, which was primarily a shadow of the old Know-Nothing party, lost to Lincoln and the Republicans by a large margin.

Though Stuart supported the Union during the war, he became increasingly disenchanted with what he perceived as the radical policies of Lincoln and Congress. In 1862, with emancipation looming, Stuart ran, with Democratic support, against Lincoln associate Leonard Swett for Congress. Stuart refused to criticize Lincoln, however; he expressed confidence in the president and urged him to "repulse any resort to revolutionary means" in the conduct of the war. Stuart defeated Swett in an election that also saw the Democrats gain control of the state legislature, causing Lincoln great concern.

Stuart's support of Lincoln's congressional opponents did not damage their personal relationship. Occasionally while in Congress (1863–1865) Stuart visited the White House and chatted with Lincoln. However, he continued to fear that Lincoln's war policies, particularly the Emancipation Proclamation, had seriously undermined the Constitution and had made reunion with the South improbable. In 1864 Stuart joined with other disaffected former Whigs to form the Conservative Union Party on a platform pledged to the suppression of the rebellion and the rejection of emancipation as a war aim. Stuart unsuccessfully tried to persuade Millard Fillmore to run for president on a fusion ticket with the Democrats. The effort by the Conservative Unionists to fuse with the Democrats failed when the national Democratic convention adopted a peace or "copperhead" platform at Chicago. The small Conservative Union Party disintegrated, with most of its supporters reluctantly voting for Lincoln.

Defeated in his try for reelection in 1864, Stuart continued to serve in Congress until March 1865. In January he voted against the Thirteenth Amendment, despite a personal appeal by Lincoln. After Lincoln's death, Stuart became a principal director of the National Lincoln Monument Association; he also continued his lucrative law practice and involvement in civic matters in Springfield.

—WILLIAM C. HARRIS

BIBLIOGRAPHY

Cox, Samuel S. *Three Decades of Federal Legislation, 1855 to 1885.* Providence: J. A. and R. A. Reid, 1885.

Donald, David Herbert. *"We Are Lincoln Men": Abraham Lincoln and His Friends.* New York: Simon and Schuster, 2003.

Fillmore, Millard. *Papers.* Buffalo and Erie County Historical Society, Buffalo, N.Y.

Harris, William C. *Lincoln's Rise to the Presidency.* Lawrence: University Press of Kansas, 2007.

McPherson, Edward. *The Political History of the United States of America, during the Great Rebellion.* Washington, D.C.: Philip and Solomons, 1865.

Sumner, Charles

Charles Sumner (1811–1874) and Abraham Lincoln were contemporaries with similar political leanings but totally different backgrounds. Lincoln, the Kentucky-born, Indiana-raised farm boy, who studied law in a frontier setting, differed strikingly from Sumner, the Boston-bred and Harvard-educated scholar, who earned his law degree under the guidance of Supreme Court justice Joseph Story.

Both men entered Whig politics and showed similar interest in resisting the expansion of slavery. While Lincoln was elected to the Illinois legislature, Sumner shocked the establishment in Boston by attacking the immorality of war in general and the aggressive policies of the administration of Democrat James K. Polk in particular. He soon joined other young Whigs in Massachusetts in opposition to the war against Mexico, which they regarded as part of a Slave Power conspiracy to annex additional territories into which to expand slavery. Joining antislavery Whigs and Democrats who supported the Wilmot Proviso banning slavery in such territories, Sumner bolted from the Whigs to join the new Free Soil Party in 1848. In contrast Lincoln, a Whig member of Congress, supported the Wilmot Proviso but remained a loyal Whig in 1848. A future in the two-party system was more important to the moderate Lincoln than chancing his political future with an untried third party, even one dedicated to containing slavery within its existing boundaries.

Despite the divergence in their careers the two men seemed destined eventually to join forces in the effort to contain and eventually destroy slavery. Sumner used a Democratic–Free Soil coalition to win election to the U.S. Senate in 1851; he would remain a part of that body until his death in 1874. Lincoln returned to his Springfield law practice in 1849 but campaigned for Whig candidates and twice was denied election to the U.S. Senate by the Illinois legislature. Sumner joined Salmon P. Chase of Ohio and others in helping to form the Republican Party and spoke out passionately against slavery and the Slave Power that he and others believed controlled the federal government. Lincoln finally abandoned the dying Whig Party and joined the Republicans in early 1856, the same year that Sumner gave his impassioned "Crime against Kansas" speech and was beaten into bloody unconsiousness by Rep. Preston Brooks of South Carolina in May. That event and the escalating violence in Kansas led Lincoln to join Republican efforts locally and nationally in that fall's presidential election. With Sumner too ill to return to the Senate until 1859, Lincoln acquired a national reputation, climaxing with his election as president in 1860. Sumner's health restored, he prepared to work with the president in both foreign policy and domestic, hoping above all to move Lincoln toward emancipation.

Although Sumner wished to see the emancipation process accelerated, he quickly developed a warm and supportive relationship with the president. This was especially true in foreign policy matters, in which Sumner, as chairman of the Senate Committee on Foreign Relations, used his expertise and influence to restrain the aggressiveness of secretary of state William H. Seward and the more militant Republicans in the Senate. His extensive study of European history and his travels there as a young man made Sumner a natural to chair the Senate committee, and the position gave him additional impetus to persuade Lincoln to his thinking on slavery. For it was soon clear that should the war's purpose evolve from merely saving the Union to include ending slavery, Great Britain and France would have to restrain their inclination to aid the Confederacy and thus weaken the Union.

The major crises in foreign relations began in November 1861 when a U.S. naval vessel stopped a British mail packet, the *Trent,* and forced the removal of Confederate commissioners James Mason and John Slidell, who were bound for England to seek assistance. Sumner knew that the prisoners must be released and convinced Lincoln that the United States had violated international law in seizing them. His Senate speech in January 1862 helped tone down Republican militancy. A similarly difficult situation developed when the British agreed to build two Confederate ships, which then preyed on U.S. shipping. In this instance Sumner, Seward, and Charles Francis Adams, the American minister to Great Britain, worked together to force the British to temper their policies. The three also delivered the appropriate strong protest that helped to foil the British plan to release two ironclad warships, the Laird Rams. Sumner convinced the president to restrain Seward in his plans to commission American privateers. He also succeeded in restraining the Senate response to French meddling in Mexico. Sumner knew international law and understood the necessity that the Union not provoke European intervention on the Confederate side at a time when the United States had its hands full. Over the course of the war Lincoln came to depend on Sumner and his expertise in each foreign policy crisis.

As successful as he was in restraining Secretary Seward, Sumner joined other Republicans in backing the efforts of secretary of the Treasury Salmon P. Chase to force Lincoln to remove Seward from the cabinet in late 1862. But Lincoln skillfully outmaneuvered Chase and his Senate allies and forced the protesters to admit Seward's loyalty and indispensability. Though Seward indeed needed to be restrained, Lincoln had grown to depend on him and could not afford to lose him.

Lincoln's defense of Secretary Seward could not, however, soften the resistance of Seward and other conservative party leaders to the efforts of Sumner and others to force the president's hand on emancipation. Here again, despite their differences, Sumner and Lincoln came to appreciate each other's position and developed a close working relationship. Like other radicals, Sumner protested the president's revoking the military orders of Generals John C. Frémont and David Hunter freeing the slaves in their commands. Sumner urged the president to move on emancipation as a military necessity, laying down a stance that Lincoln would eventually adopt. The president respected Sumner, knowing that unlike the ambitious Chase, who constantly maneuvered to be president, he had no other office in mind.

Sumner was instrumental in several steps in the mounting attack on slavery. He pushed for recognition of the black republics of Haiti and Liberia, and he supported the bills to end territorial slavery, as well as the eventual repeal of the Fugitive Slave Act of 1850. As did Chase, he contributed to the final wording of the Emancipation Proclamation of January 1, 1863, and urged that black troops be recruited for Union armies. Sumner led the efforts in each hesitant step toward full equality, including the outlawing of the slave trade and the desegregation of streetcars in the District of Columbia, the same kind of legislation he had helped secure in Massachusetts before the war. He was instrumental in the establishment of the Freedmen's Bureau and urged Lincoln to consider black suffrage. At the same time he showed his genuine humanitarianism by endorsing Lincoln's determination against harsh treatment of Confederate prisoners of war. Although the president always felt more pressure from other factions in his party and usually lagged behind Sumner on issues related to emancipation and equal rights, he could not have found a stauncher ally on such issues.

Yet in early 1865, Lincoln and Sumner realized that reconstruction would severely test their alliance as Congress, with Sumner's urging, attempted to control the terms under which Confederate states would be readmitted to the Union. Still the two were on friendly and supportive terms at the time of the second inaugural on March 6, 1865. Sumner fully endorsed Lincoln's goal of malice toward none. On April 10, he accompanied the president on his tour of recently captured Richmond. Thus it was with shock and disbelief that he heard that Lincoln had been shot. Rushing to the scene, Sumner remained at Lincoln's bedside until he died. He then helped plan Lincoln's funeral. Sumner had lost a close friend in the continuing struggle for equality—as he expressed in the eulogy he delivered in Boston.

See also *Brooks, Preston*

—FREDERICK J. BLUE

BIBLIOGRAPHY

Blue, Frederick J. *Charles Sumner and the Conscience of the North.* Arlington Heights, Ill.: Harlan Davidson, 1994.

Crook David P. *Diplomacy during the American Civil War.* Indianapolis: Wiley, 1975.

Donald, David. *Charles Sumner and the Coming of the Civil War.* New York: Knopf, 1960.

_____. *Charles Sumner and the Rights of Man.* New York: Knopf, 1970.

_____. *Lincoln.* New York: Touchstone, 1996.

McPherson, James M. *Ordeal by Fire: The Civil War and Reconstruction.* New York: McGraw-Hill, 1992.

Oates, Stephen B. *With Malice toward None: A Life of Abraham Lincoln.* New York: Harper and Row, 1977.

Van Deusen, Glyndon G. *William H. Seward.* New York: Oxford University Press, 1967.

Sumter, Fort

See *Fort Sumter*

Supreme Court Appointments

See *U.S. Supreme Court, Lincoln's Appointments to*

Supreme Court, Lincoln's Views of

See *U.S. Supreme Court, Lincoln's View of*

Taney, Roger B.

Roger Brooke Taney (1777–1864) served as chief justice of the United States from 1836 until 1864. Although he headed the Supreme Court during most of Abraham Lincoln's presidency, Taney disagreed strongly with administration policies, using his office to challenge almost every aspect of Lincoln's war policy. Even before Lincoln took office, Taney's most famous ruling—in the *Dred Scott* case (1857)—put him directly at odds with Lincoln and the Republican Party.

The son of Michael Taney V and Monica Brooke Taney (the family name is pronounced as though spelled "Tawney"), he was born March 17, 1777, at the family plantation in Calvert County, Maryland. After graduating from Dickinson College in 1795, he pursued private legal studies in Annapolis and was admitted to the Maryland bar in 1799. In 1806 Roger Taney married Anne Key, the sister of his friend Francis Scott Key. The Taneys had six daughters; their only son died in infancy. Taney, a Roman Catholic, raised his children in the Episcopal church of their mother.

Taney's political career began when he succeeded his father as a member of the Maryland House of Delegates (1799–1800). A Federalist, he lost reelection and failed in another bid for the legislature before winning a state senate seat in 1816. Taney established a successful legal practice in Baltimore and then became Maryland's attorney general in 1827. With the death of the Federalist Party, Taney gravitated to the Jacksonian Democrats by the mid-1820s.

President Andrew Jackson appointed Taney U.S. attorney general in 1831 as part of a major cabinet reorganization, and Taney became a close presidential adviser. He helped shape Jackson's message accompanying his veto of the bill to recharter the Second Bank of the United States. Then, when two successive Treasury secretaries refused to remove federal deposits from the bank as Jackson wished, the president appointed Taney to the post. As secretary of the Treasury, Taney transferred federal funds to Jackson-friendly, state-chartered banks ("pet banks"). The Senate later refused to confirm Taney's recess appointment, as it also did when Jackson sought to name him an associate justice of the U.S. Supreme Court in 1835.

Following chief justice John Marshall's death in July 1835, Jackson submitted Taney's name as his replacement. The Senate, augmented with Democrats in the recent election, approved Taney's nomination 29–15, on March 15, 1836.

In *Dred Scott v. Sandford* (1857) Chief Justice Roger Taney ruled that persons of African descent were not protected by the Constitution, and they could not sue in a federal court. During the Civil War, Taney opposed Lincoln's policies, including suspension of the writ of *habeas corpus* and the naval blockade of Southern ports.

Source: Library of Congress

In one of his earliest opinions, Taney demonstrated his difference from his immediate predecessor by undercutting previous Marshall Court protections for corporate charters. In the *Charles River Bridge* case (1837), he ruled against a corporation's claim that its state-issued charter gave it an exclusive right to operate a toll bridge connecting Boston and Charlestown, Massachusetts. The public's need for an additional (and free) bridge, said Taney, superseded the corporation's rights.

But Taney's rulings on slavery issues most concerned Lincoln in the 1850s. The chief justice's personal relationship to the peculiar institution was complex. Before the mid-1820s, like many Upper South slaveholders, he harbored reservations about holding persons in bondage. He freed seven inherited slaves in 1818 and an eighth in 1821. He retained only two elderly individuals whom he feared would not be able to survive on their own. A supporter of the colonization of freed blacks outside the United States, Taney also worked with an organization seeking to prevent the kidnapping of free blacks into slavery. In 1819 Taney successfully defended Jacob Gruber, a white Methodist minister whose verbal attacks on slavery had led to his indictment on charges of inciting a slave insurrection. As slavery and its white Southern supporters came under increasing attack in the 1820s, however, Taney became more defensive about the institution. Slavery, after all, undergirded the Southern way of life he cherished.

On the Supreme Court Taney ruled in several slavery-related cases, and not always in a decidedly proslavery way. In the *Amistad* case (1841), Taney joined the majority opinion of justice Joseph Story. The case involved determining whether a treaty between Spain and the United States obligated American authorities to turn over to Spanish merchants a group of Africans who had taken over a slave ship off Cuba and ended up in U.S. waters. Story held that the Africans should be considered free because they had been captured by the merchants contrary to Spanish as well as international law.

Taney's opinion in *Prigg v. Pennsylvania* (1842), concerning the Fugitive Slave Act of 1793, showed his heightened concern for protecting the institution of slavery. In another Story majority opinion, the Court upheld the constitutionality of the 1793 law and struck down free-state laws that interfered with the return of runaway slaves to slave states. Story suggested, however, that enforcement was a federal responsibility and that state officials could refuse to aid in the rendition of fugitives. Largely agreeing with Story, Taney emphasized the obligation of free-state officials to enforce the Constitution's fugitive slave clause and related legislation. Taney expressed concern that Story's language might imply that state authorities could not assist in the recapture of a fugitive slave under any circumstances. In fact, Story did not say that, but Taney's reaction made clear his heightened sensitivity about protecting slavery.

Taney's most famous slavery case, *Dred Scott v. Sandford,* began in a Missouri courtroom in 1846, but the underlying events took place in the previous decade. In the 1830s John Emerson, an army doctor, had taken Scott to live in the free state of Illinois for more than a year and then to Fort Snelling in Wisconsin Territory (today part of Minnesota). Because Fort Snelling lay within the old Louisiana Purchase territory, well north of the 36° 30' line established by the Missouri Compromise, slavery was forbidden there. Based on his residence in a free state and a free territory, Scott sued Emerson's widow for his freedom. Precedent lay on his side: In 1836 Missouri's high court freed an enslaved woman taken by her master to Fort Snelling and later returned to Missouri. In Dred Scott's case, however, the Missouri Supreme Court overturned precedent and declared him, his wife, and their daughters still slaves. The Scotts ultimately appealed to the U.S. Supreme Court.

In his majority opinion Taney considered two major questions: First, could Scott sue in a federal court? Second, could Congress ban slavery in a federal territory? To the first question, Taney answered a firm no. Persons of African descent, he claimed, were not meant to be included in the promises of the Declaration of Independence, nor did the Constitution protect them. Simply put, no black person could be a U.S. citizen, and only citizens enjoyed access to federal courts.

Taney's answer to the second query also went against the Scotts. The Fifth Amendment property rights of slaveholders, he declared, trumped any congressional authority over territories. Scott, then, could not claim freedom based on living in Wisconsin because Congress never had the power to make it a free territory. Relying on *Strader v. Graham* (1851), which held that slave-state law governed the status of enslaved persons during sojourns in free states, Taney also ruled that Scott's residence in Illinois had failed to emancipate him.

Lincoln, leader of a party dedicated to preventing the extension of slavery into federal territories, strongly disagreed with Taney's opinion, as he repeatedly made clear in his 1858 debates with Stephen Douglas. Later as president, Lincoln signed legislation abolishing slavery in the territories—a law directly conflicting with Taney's *Dred Scott* decision.

During the Civil War, Lincoln and Taney sparred over most policies, beginning with civil liberties. On April 27, 1861, Lincoln ordered the suspension of the writ of *habeas corpus* in the militarily sensitive corridor between Philadelphia and Washington. Military authorities arrested John Merryman, a Maryland Democratic legislator and Confederate sympathizer, for alleged sabotage against rail and telegraph lines in that region. Taney, sitting on the federal circuit for Maryland, issued a writ of *habeas corpus* at the request of Merryman's attorneys, but army officials refused to honor it, as per Lincoln's orders. Taney responded with his opinion in *Ex parte Merryman,* which declared that only Congress, and not the president acting alone, could suspend *habeas corpus.* Lincoln disregarded Taney's views and, with congressional support, expanded the area in which civilians could be arrested without recourse to the legal system.

Taney also opposed Lincoln's war powers in the *Prize Cases* (decided March 10, 1863). The *Prize Cases* centered on whether the president could, without congressional authorization, order a blockade of Southern ports, as Lincoln had done in April 1861, when he declared a state of insurrection following the firing on Fort Sumter. The cases raised questions not only of presidential power, but also of the Confederacy's status; under international law, a nation blockades an independent or at least a belligerent state. Congress, which was not in session in April, ratified Lincoln's military actions against the rebellious states, including the blockade, after convening in July 1861. Taney joined a minority opinion by Samuel Nelson, which held that ships taken by U.S. authorities for blockade violations before Congress took action had not been legitimately seized. The minority also asserted that once Congress approved the blockade, it accorded belligerent status to the Confederate States. By a 5–4 majority, however, the Court upheld Lincoln's actions, as well as his understanding of the special circumstances of civil war that allowed for blockading Southern ports without granting belligerent status to the Confederacy.

The *Prize Cases* decision was a major victory for Lincoln, but the thinness of the majority cast doubt on whether other Lincoln policies, including those involving emancipation, might be overturned by an unfriendly Court. (Not until after Taney's death and his replacement by Salmon P. Chase did the Court contain a majority of Lincoln-appointed justices.) The fear of a Court challenge to emancipation contributed to Lincoln's support for a constitutional amendment abolishing slavery. Taney continued to oppose Lincoln and his policies until his death on October 12, 1864.

See also *U.S. Supreme Court, Lincoln's Appointments to; U.S. Supreme Court, Lincoln's View of*

—ROBERT S. TINKLER

BIBLIOGRAPHY

Fehrenbacher, Don E. *The Dred Scott Case: Its Significance in American Law and Politics.* New York: Oxford University Press, 1978.

Finkelman, Paul. "'Hooted Down the Page of History': Reconsidering the Greatness of Chief Justice Taney." *Journal of Supreme Court History* 1994 (1995): 83–102.

———. "Story Telling on the Supreme Court: *Prigg v. Pennsylvania* and Justice Joseph Story's Judicial Nationalism." *Supreme Court Review* 1994 (1995): 247–294.

Huebner, Timothy S. *The Taney Court: Justices, Rulings, and Legacy.* Santa Barbara, Calif.: ABC-CLIO, 2003.

Lewis, Walker. *Without Fear or Favor: A Biography of Chief Justice Roger Brooke Taney.* Boston: Houghton Mifflin, 1965.

Ross, Michael A. *Justice of Shattered Dreams: Samuel Freeman Miller and the Supreme Court in the Civil War Era.* Baton Rouge: Louisiana State University Press, 2003.

Simon, James F. *Lincoln and Chief Justice Taney: Slavery, Secession, and the President's War Powers.* New York: Simon and Schuster, 2006.

Steiner, Bernard C. *Life of Roger Brooke Taney: Chief Justice of the United States Supreme Court.* Westport, Conn.: Greenwood, 1970.

Vorenberg, Michael. *Final Freedom: The Civil War, the Abolition of Slavery, and the Thirteenth Amendment.* New York: Cambridge University Press, 2001.

Taylor, Zachary

Zachary Taylor (1784–1850) was a successful U.S. general during the Mexican War and the twelfth president of the United States. Born to Richard and Sarah Taylor near Louisville, Kentucky, Zachary Taylor received a typical frontier education that consisted primarily of tutoring by his parents, who were well-educated members of Virginia's planter class.

In 1808 Taylor was commissioned as a lieutenant in the U.S. Army, at the age of twenty-three. He served during William Henry Harrison's Indian campaigns in the Indiana Territory and saw action in the Ohio Valley during the War of 1812. After briefly leaving the military over a promotion dispute he rejoined as a major and served in various frontier posts. He served in the Black Hawk War and attended Chief Black Hawk's surrender. Promoted to colonel, he was transferred to Florida, where he led troops in the Battle of Lake Okeechobee during the Second Seminole War. Earning the nickname "Old Rough and Ready," Taylor was promoted to brigadier general. By 1841 he was assigned command of the southern division of the army and assigned to Baton Rouge, Louisiana, where he bought a plantation.

Following the U.S. annexation of Texas in 1845, Taylor was ordered by President James K. Polk to enter land between the Nueces River and the Rio Grande that both the United States and Mexico claimed. President Polk sent Taylor to this area knowing that it might very well provoke a war with Mexico. When Mexico declared war, as Polk had hoped, Taylor fought and won a series of battles at Palo Alto, Resaca de la Palma, and Monterrey.

President Polk, a Democrat, began to fear that Taylor's success was making him so well-known among the American public that he could become a presidential candidate for the rival Whig Party. Polk sidelined Taylor, giving command of most of his troops to General Winfield Scott. Taylor was left in command of only 5,000 troops, one of whom was Colonel Jefferson Davis, future president of the Confederacy and Taylor's son-in-law. Taylor's small force fended off an attack by 20,000 Mexicans under General Antonio Lopez de Santa Anna, at the Battle of Buena Vista in February 1847, and Taylor became a national hero despite Polk's best efforts.

On December 22, 1847, Rep. Abraham Lincoln, in what became known as the "spot speech," asked on the floor of Congress "whether the particular spot of soil on which the blood of our *citizens* was so shed, was, or was not, *our own soil,* at that time." He took Polk to task for goading Mexico into a war with the aim of territorial expansion, which would most likely include the expansion of slavery as well. The war having been popular and relatively easily won, Lincoln's speech was poorly received, and his patriotism was even questioned.

In 1848 President Polk honored a pledge not to run for reelection and stepped aside for Democratic presidential nominee Lewis Cass. Zachary Taylor had indeed become the Whig nominee as Polk had feared. Cass lost the electoral vote to Taylor, 163–127, thanks largely to the Free Soil Party candidacy of Martin Van Buren, who split New York's Democratic vote, giving the state to Taylor.

Abraham Lincoln hoped for a position in the Taylor administration but it was not to be. He probably could have been appointed commissioner of the General Land Office when the candidate he was supporting failed to get the appointment, but he refused to be considered for a position for which he had nominated someone else. He was also offered his choice of two positions in the Oregon Territory—as governor or secretary of the territory—but he had no interest in moving west. Thus he returned to Illinois, having previously agreed to serve only one term in the House of Representatives. However Taylor's presidency would have a tremendous impact on Lincoln.

Lacking any political experience, Zachary Taylor took office in 1849, facing the question of whether slavery should be allowed in the western territories that would soon apply for statehood (a question forced into the political spotlight by the explosive growth of California in the aftermath of the discovery of gold there). Southerners worried that the new western states, if allowed to decide the question for themselves as Taylor advocated, would outlaw slavery, thereby making slaveholding states a minority in Congress. Taylor, despite being a slaveholding Southerner himself, opposed a compromise plan being developed by Southern congressmen and declared that if necessary he would use military force to preserve the Union and prevent rebellion against federal authority.

On July 4, 1850, Taylor fell ill during Independence Day celebrations in Washington, D.C., and he died five days later. He was succeeded by Vice President Millard Fillmore who, unlike Taylor, supported what became the Compromise of 1850. Thus, the looming collision over slavery was averted for another ten years, until Lincoln himself was elected president and found himself in a position similar to Taylor's a decade before. When Civil War erupted in 1861, Zachary Taylor's son Richard would become a Confederate general.

See also *Cass, Lewis; Fillmore, Millard*

—DAVID E. ARTHUR

BIBLIOGRAPHY

Bauer, K. Jack. *Zachary Taylor: Soldier, Planter, Statesman of the Old Southwest.* Baton Rouge: Louisiana State University Press, 1985.

Eisenhower, John S. D. *Zachary Taylor: The Twelfth President, 1849–1850.* New York: Times Books, 2008.

Smith, Elbert B. *The Presidencies of Zachary Taylor and Millard Fillmore.* Lawrence: University Press of Kansas, 1988.

Temperance

Early-nineteenth-century Americans drank heavily. Modern scholarship indicates that the country's consumption peaked in 1830, when the average adult imbibed 7.1 gallons of alcohol. The Temperance Movement emerged in response to this high alcohol consumption and from the moralism unleashed by revivalism. Prohibitionism soon arose as well, likewise aiming to create a culture of sobriety.

During this elusive effort, the meaning of "temperance" underwent numerous changes. Initially elites, who tolerated the use of wine but fervently condemned hard liquor, dominated the movement. By the mid-1830s activists shifted from moderation and persuasion toward total abstinence and prohibition, initially through ending liquor licensing. In the early 1840s, temperance activists retreated to moral suasion but soon pursued another prohibitionist method, "local option." Agitation peaked during the 1850s, as enthusiasts throughout the country sought prohibitory legislation for their states patterned after the so-called Maine Law, which briefly outlawed the manufacture and use of alcohol, except for personal medicinal purposes.

An international movement, temperance enlisted thousands of men and women in both the North and South. It was especially popular among evangelical Protestants, and Catholics often despised temperance as a Protestant tool to impose morality. The widespread embrace of temperance led to a three-fourths reduction in alcohol consumption between 1830 and 1845. Prohibitionists' greatest triumph came in the twentieth century, when the federal government outlawed alcohol from 1920 to 1933. During prohibition, and the campaigns preceding it, both "wets" and "drys" invoked Abraham Lincoln's name to support their positions.

Like his contemporaries, Lincoln could escape neither alcohol nor the Temperance Movement. Raised among heavy consumers of liquor, Lincoln drank only moderately as a young man in Indiana. Afterward he imbibed so infrequently that some of his friends thought that he abstained completely. Until he lived in the White House, Lincoln did not serve alcohol in his home and often professed a dislike of it.

Yet Lincoln's public life fell short of the prohibitionist's ideal. In the early 1830s, Lincoln was a partner in a store in New Salem, Illinois, that sold liquor, although the evidence is contradictory as to whether Lincoln sold liquor by the drink. Despite presenting a petition to the Illinois legislature calling for an end to liquor licensing, Lincoln voted against local option and other prohibitionist measures. As an attorney, Lincoln represented saloon keepers as well as temperance enthusiasts who illegally destroyed liquor.

Lincoln endorsed the Temperance Movement's moral suasionist wing. In 1842 Lincoln criticized those activists who condemned liquor drinkers and sellers with "thundering tones of anathema and denunciation" and who never sought to reform drunkards. He also rejected prohibitionist means to limit liquor consumption: "When the conduct of men is designed to be influenced, persuasion, kind, unassuming persuasion, should ever be adopted." Lincoln subsequently spoke to other temperance organizations, but no surviving records indicate that he ever joined a temperance society.

Nor did Lincoln take a position on prohibition during the 1850s, as he then focused on the slavery issue. As an aspirant to the Senate he avoided offending potential supporters, such as German immigrants who opposed both slavery extension and prohibition. Historians reject the claims of James B. Merwin, a lifetime prohibitionist, who in 1904 began asserting that Lincoln was the author of Illinois's proposed prohibition law in 1854 and afterward stumped Illinois with Merwin in support of it.

As president, Lincoln drank wine at state dinners but otherwise abstained. In September 1863, when Lincoln received a Sons of Temperance delegation, he recalled the temperance speeches he gave as a young man and professed to have lived in accord with them, but he did not act on the delegation's request that he combat intemperance in the army more vigorously.

—JOHN W. QUIST

BIBLIOGRAPHY

Basler, Roy P., ed. *Collected Works of Abraham Lincoln.* New Brunswick, N.J.: Rutgers University Press, 1953.

Blocker, Jack S., Jr. *American Temperance Movements: Cycles of Reform.* Boston: Twayne, 1989.

Peterson, Merrill D. *Lincoln in American Memory.* New York: Oxford University Press, 1994.

Rorabaugh, W. J. *The Alcoholic Republic: An American Tradition.* New York: Oxford University Press, 1979.

Townsend, William H. *Lincoln and Liquor.* New York: Press of the Pioneers, 1934.

Tyrrell, Ian R. *Sobering Up: From Temperance to Prohibition in Antebellum America, 1800–1860.* Westport, Conn.: Greenwood Press, 1979.

Ten Percent Plan

Even though it was premature, from nearly the beginning of the American Civil War the question of political reconstruction was prominent in the minds of Abraham Lincoln and other Northern political leaders. Echoing the views of many Border State residents and conservative Republicans who had been members of the Whig Party, Lincoln subscribed to the theory that the Union was not dissolvable; consequently, secession was a legal impossibility. States were not out of the Union but were temporarily under the control of rebellious individuals. If states were not really "out" of the Union, then the process of restoring them—reestablishing civil authority and repairing the relationship with the federal government—should be a painless and straightforward process. Believing that the majority of Southerners were Unionists who had been temporarily seduced into secession by rebel leaders, Lincoln was also convinced that reconstruction ought to be primarily the work of Southerners, with minimal interference on the part of the federal government. For Lincoln, reconstruction would primarily be self-reconstruction by loyal Southern Unionists.

Although Lincoln had broad support for elements of his reconstruction views, there was wide diversity of opinion in Congress. For instance, the Radical Republican senator from Massachusetts, Charles Sumner, believed that states went out of the Union when they seceded; they had committed suicide and reverted into a territorial condition that allowed them to be reconstructed on the terms and conditions applied by the Congress of the United States. Even more rigid was the viewpoint of radical Pennsylvania representative Thaddeus Stevens. Stevens also thought that secession meant that states were out of the Union. As Union armies conquered such states, they could be treated as conquered provinces and reconstructed as the victorious party deemed appropriate. If Congress dictated the abolition of slavery and black suffrage, it was totally within its authority to specify such conditions. To Stevens the argument that states could not legally secede from the Union was absurd. They had seceded de facto and should be dealt with accordingly. Although Lincoln believed that Southern states ought to abolish slavery, he would favor a policy that would allow Southern Unionists to take the initiative. Lincoln's "ten percent plan" and the debate it caused over reconstruction illustrate the differences between the president and congressional Republicans on the issue.

On December 8, 1863, Abraham Lincoln released his Proclamation on Amnesty and Reconstruction, which became popularly known as the "ten percent plan." Impatient that the reconstruction of Southern states had not moved along more promptly under military governors such as Andrew Johnson of Tennessee, Lincoln hoped that the proclamation would expedite the process. Only a paragraph long, the proclamation was nevertheless significant. In rebellious states, whenever 10 percent of the 1860 presidential voting population swore an oath of future loyalty to the Union, that state could begin the process of reestablishing its relationship with the federal government. The amnesty portion of the proclamation specified that Southerners who took the oath would have their property protected, with the exception of slaves, and their political rights restored. High-ranking military officers and political leaders of the Confederacy were excepted from the provision, but on application to the president, the rights of these individuals could be restored. Why did Lincoln specify 10 percent of the 1860 electorate as the significant number? Most likely he realized that wartime conditions would inhibit broad participation. Ten percent seemed like a reasonable number to get the process of reconstruction started.

The reconstruction component of the proclamation was somewhat ambiguous. Once the requisite 10 percent was achieved, a state could form a government, hold elections, and send elected officials to Washington to represent the state in the national government. However Lincoln knew that once representatives were sent to Washington, Congress had the sole authority to recognize them. Since emancipation had been proclaimed by presidential fiat on January 1, 1863, Lincoln's obvious expectation would be that states would abolish the institution of slavery when they formed new state constitutions; however, the proclamation did not state such a requirement. Although states were required to recognize and abide by all congressional acts and presidential proclamations that touched on slavery, no formal act of the central government specifically required reconstructed states to provide for emancipation. Lincoln demonstrated additional flexibility on the slavery issue by allowing such Southern states as Louisiana to implement apprentice-type labor arrangements for slaves in a transitional phase between slavery and freedom. Lincoln wanted and fully expected Southern states to abolish slavery; however, Southern Unionists had to be agents of action, not the federal government.

Lincoln's plan initially drew favorable comment and even enthusiastic praise from some quarters. Conservative Republicans were impressed by the plan's assumption that seceded states had never left the Union and that therefore, restoring the relationship with the central government would be painless. Republicans of a more radical inclination liked the plan because it was founded on antislavery principles. A small minority of radicals, the abolitionist Wendell Phillips for instance, complained that the proclamation did not provide for black suffrage. Finally, there were a few more critics, mainly from the Democratic side, whose principal complaint was that the 10 percent provision was patently undemocratic since it was not rooted in majority rule.

By the middle of 1864, congressional Republicans had soured on the ten percent plan. Congress passed the Wade-Davis reconstruction bill and refused to seat representatives from Louisiana and Arkansas who had been elected under the plan. What went wrong? First, events in Louisiana worked against a favorable perception of the ten percent plan. Under the direction of Major General Nathaniel Banks, commander of the Department of the Gulf, Louisiana held elections for a new state government before it organized a convention to adopt a new constitution. During this interim period, Louisiana's 1860 constitution operated, and it was a constitution that recognized slavery. Critics charged that Banks, proceeding under the ten percent plan, had not done enough to safeguard the rights of newly emancipated slaves. Congressional Republicans cited the clause in the Constitution that requires Congress to provide each state a republican form of government and contended that it provided ample justification for requiring reconstructed states to abolish slavery in their constitutions.

Second, the way Banks had conducted elections to choose some members of the state constitutional convention alienated some Republican congressman. During Banks's Red River campaign (March 10–April 7, 1864), elections were held in various Louisiana parishes that the Union army occupied. For many in Congress, this suggested that the electoral process was compromised by being too closely linked with the presence of Union military forces. Moreover, since the executive branch controlled the military, the whole process smacked of executive corruption, with states such as Louisiana and Arkansas little more than pocket boroughs of the executive. If any branch of government should control reconstruction, most members of Congress believed, it should be the legislative. Finally, partisan politics infected the debate over the ten percent plan. The chair of the House Select Committee on the Rebellious States (the principal House committee charged with following the executive's reconstruction plans) was Maryland representative Henry Winter Davis, a bitter rival of the Blair family in Maryland politics. Because Lincoln was closely allied with the Blairs, and Montgomery Blair was Lincoln's postmaster general, Davis was prevented from controlling his state's patronage.

Passed on July 2, 1864, just before the end of the legislative session, the Wade-Davis bill differed from the ten percent plan in two important respects. First, it required that states explicitly abolish slavery in their state constitutions prior to rejoining the Union. Second, instead of 10 percent of the number that had voted in the presidential election of 1860, this bill required 50 percent participation. Participants were required to swear an ironclad oath that they had never willingly given aid to the Confederacy. When Lincoln killed the bill with the little-used tool of the pocket veto (simply refusing to sign the bill as the legislative session came to an end), he angered Davis and cosponsor Sen. Benjamin F. Wade of Ohio, prompting the two to attack him in the columns of the *New York Tribune,* in what became known as the Wade-Davis manifesto, and seriously dividing the Republican Party on the eve of Lincoln's reelection campaign.

Although the Republican Party would rally around Lincoln, ensuring his reelection in November, the two sides continued to squabble over reconstruction. At the time of Lincoln's death, Congress had refused to recognize the reconstruction governments of Louisiana and Arkansas. Many of the Southern states would eventually come back into the Union only when Congress, after a vigorous and protracted debate with President Andrew Johnson, took nearly complete control of the process. By then the terms for readmission were considerably harsher than the mild and conciliatory policy set forth in the ten percent plan.

See also *Reconstruction*

—BRUCE TAP

BIBLIOGRAPHY

Donald, David Herbert. *Lincoln.* New York: Simon and Schuster, 1995.

Foner, Eric. *Reconstruction: America's Unfinished Revolution, 1863–1877.* New York: Harper and Row, 1988.

Harris, William C. *With Charity for All: Lincoln and the Restoration of the Union.* Lexington: University Press of Kentucky, 1997.

Henig, Gerald S. *Henry Winter Davis: Antebellum Congressman from Maryland.* New York: Twayne, 1973.

Thanksgiving

Days of thanksgiving are deeply rooted in American culture. During the American Revolution, the Continental Congress proclaimed more than a dozen such days. In the two decades before the Civil War, Sarah Josepha Hale persistently urged American presidents to create a national thanksgiving holiday. Born in Newport, New Hampshire, in 1788, Hale was the moderately successful author of *The Genius of Oblivion and Other Original Poems* (1823) and *Northwood: A Tale of New England* (1827), a novel questioning the morality of slavery. She would eventually write more than fifteen books and edit more than twenty. In 1827 she became the editor of *Ladies Magazine and Literary Gazette,* and in 1836 she took over *Godey's Lady's Book,* which she edited until 1877.

In addition to her writing and editing, Hale was involved in social causes, including the formation of the Seaman's Aid Society, fund-raising for the Bunker Hill Monument, and the preservation of George Washington's home, Mount Vernon. She also spent seventeen years trying to convince presidents to make Thanksgiving Day a national holiday. Her sentiments were noted in her book *Northwood,* where she wrote: "We have too few holidays. Thanksgiving, like the fourth of July, should be considered a national festival and observed by all our people."

This became an especially important cause to Hale when the nation faced the Civil War. She sent President Abraham Lincoln a written request explaining that in the midst of a civil war, a national feeling of thanksgiving, a spiritual festival, would be beneficial to the country. She wrote, "The influence of these state seasons of sacred remembrances, high aspirations, and tender rejoicing would not only be salutary on the character of our citizens, but the world would be made better if the germ of good feeling be ever so deeply buried under the cares and riches and pleasures of this life."

Her perseverance paid off in 1863, when Abraham Lincoln issued his Thanksgiving Proclamation, which began, "The year that is drawing to a close has been filled with the blessings of fruitful fields and healthful skies. To these bounties, which are so constantly enjoyed that we are prone to forget the source from which they came, others have been added, which are of so extraordinary a nature, that they cannot fail to penetrate and soften even the heart which is habitually insensible to the ever watchful providence of the Almighty God."

Lincoln's proclamation declared the last Thursday in November to be a day of thanksgiving. Presidents honored the tradition until 1939, when President Franklin Roosevelt changed Thanksgiving to Thursday, November 23, the second-to-last Thursday of the month. In the midst of the Great Depression, the change would allow for an extra week of Christmas shopping, helping businesses and the economy. Although many businesses supported the extra week, the public was outraged. Thanksgiving returned to its former date, and to ensure its permanence, Congress in 1941 declared the fourth Thursday in November to be the legal holiday known as Thanksgiving Day. Though Hale's part in the creation of the holiday is often forgotten, her name lives on as the author of the well-know nursery rhyme, "Mary Had a Little Lamb." Hale died in 1879 at the age of ninety-one.

—Paula Cochran

BIBLIOGRAPHY

Barth, Edna, and Ursula Arndt. *Turkeys, Pilgrims, and Indian Corn: The Story of the Thanksgiving Symbols.* New York: Clarion, 2000.

Fryatt, Norma R. *Sarah Josepha Hale: The Life and Times of a Nineteenth-Century Career Woman.* New York: Hawthorn Books, 1975.

Hodgson, Godfrey. "A Great and Godly Adventure: The Pilgrims and the Myth of the First Thanksgiving." *Public Affairs,* 1943.

Rogers, Sherbrooke. *Sarah Josepha Hale: A New England Pioneer: 1788–1879.* North Haven, Conn.: Shoe String Press, 1985.

Thirteenth Amendment

The states completed ratification of the Thirteenth Amendment to the U.S. Constitution, with Georgia providing the three-quarters-majority vote, on December 6, 1865. Secretary of state William H. Seward (1801–1872) officially declared the amendment adopted on December 18, 1865. Section 1 of the Thirteenth Amendment declared: "Neither slavery nor involuntary servitude, except as a punishment for crime whereof the party shall have been duly convicted, shall exist within the United States, or any place subject to their jurisdiction." All slavery in the United States was abolished.

The election of Abraham Lincoln as president of the United States in 1860 meant the end of slavery to many, even though he was not in favor of its abolition and believed that neither the president nor Congress had the power to end slavery in the states. Lincoln followed the Republican Party platform, which favored containment of slavery—not allowing its extension into the territories—rather than attacking it where it existed. Nonetheless, to contemporaries such as Frederick Douglass (1817–1895) the election of Lincoln "was a judgment against Slavery, and its representatives were aroused." The Southern slaveholding states were so aroused that they began to secede from the Union following Lincoln's election. Thus the issue of slavery led to secession and the Civil War that followed.

At the beginning of the Civil War, Lincoln saw the conflagration as a war to preserve the Union and not one against slavery. Over the course of the Civil War, Lincoln slowly changed his mind. He moved from an antislavery position to advocating abolition. The change began during the war, in 1862. Lincoln slowly came to the conclusion that transforming the war from one to preserve the Union to a war against slavery might conclude it sooner. Following the Union victory at the Battle of Antietam, in Maryland (September 17, 1862), Lincoln issued his Preliminary Emancipation Proclamation on September 22, 1862. The proclamation gave the Confederates one hundred days to end hostilities. If not, the president would proclaim all slaves in states still at war to be free. That Lincoln did on January 1, 1863.

To go further, Lincoln thought, might challenge the U.S. Constitution by endorsing what would amount to a bill of attainder, violating the Fifth Amendment. By focusing the Emancipation Proclamation on those in rebellion, Lincoln believed he could act within his powers as president during crisis to "insure domestic tranquility." Additionally, Lincoln did not want to anger War Democrats. In particular, he did not want to risk alienating the Border States that remained loyal to the Union. During 1862 Lincoln proposed gradual emancipation with compensation to slave owners in the Border States, in a plan that included de-

The Thirteenth Amendment to the Constitution was ratified on December 6, 1865. When elected president, Lincoln favored containment of slavery rather than attacking it where it existed; over the course of the war, however, he concluded that transforming the war from one to preserve the Union to one against slavery might resolve the conflict sooner. Lincoln slowly moved to a position supporting a constitutional amendment abolishing slavery.

Source: Library of Congress

portation or colonization of freed slaves to Liberia or Haiti. Border States regularly rejected this scheme, especially Kentucky and Delaware.

Increasingly Lincoln moved closer to endorsing a constitutional amendment abolishing slavery. In his annual address to Congress on December 8, 1863, Lincoln presented his reconstruction plan, called "Proclamation of Amnesty and Reconstruction." In it he did not endorse an amendment to abolish slavery but suggested that a future Congress or Supreme Court decision could overturn the Emancipation Proclamation. This seemed to open the door to Congress proposing an abolition amendment to the Constitution without threat of opposition from Lincoln.

On January 11, 1864, Sen. John Henderson of Missouri introduced in the Senate Judiciary Committee, chaired by Sen. Lyman Trumbull (1813–1896) of Illinois, the first joint resolution to amend the Constitution to abolish slavery. In the House of Representatives James M. Ashley (1824–1896) of Ohio submitted a bill to protect the freedom of African Americans. James F. Wilson (1828–1895) of Iowa, chairman of the House Judiciary Committee, submitted a proposed amendment allowing for the enforcement of emancipation. Trumbull reported an amendment out of the Judiciary Committee on February 10, 1864, even though he had reservations about amending the Constitution during a time of war. Following a lengthy debate, the Senate voted for the amendment on April 8, 1864.

A faction of Republicans that were dissatisfied with Lincoln met in Cleveland on May 31, 1864, to endorse the third-party candidacy of John C. Frémont for president in the upcoming elections. The group also endorsed an abolition amendment. The Republican Party met in Baltimore on June 7, 1864, and also endorsed an abolition amendment. The delegates renamed their party the National Union Party, thereby demonstrating unity with War Democrats. In the next few months, Union forces won victories throughout the South, which helped lead to Lincoln's overwhelming reelection. The elections also brought Republican control of the House, which had rejected the abolition amendment during summer 1864.

Lincoln appointed Salmon P. Chase (1808–1873), a lifelong abolitionist, chief justice of the United States to replace the deceased Roger B. Taney (1777–1864). All these events together signaled that it was time to endorse the abolition amendment and move for its passage in the House of Representatives. That occurred during the lame duck session, on January 31, 1865. The ratification process concluded after the end of the Civil War, with the Thirteenth Amendment abolishing slavery adopted on December 18, 1865, after it was ratified, ironically, by the former slave state of Georgia.

See also *Colfax, Schuyler*

—Bradley Skelcher

BIBLIOGRAPHY

Belz, Herman. *Abraham Lincoln, Constitutionalism, and Equal Rights in the Civil War Era.* New York: Fordham University Press, 1998.

Blight, David. *Frederick Douglass' Civil War.* Baton Rouge: Louisiana State University Press, 1989.

Holzer, Harold, and Sara Vaughn Gabbard, eds. *Lincoln and Freedom: Slavery, Emancipation, and the Thirteenth Amendment.* Carbondale: Southern Illinois University Press, 2007.

Johnson, Michael P. *Abraham Lincoln, Slavery, and the Civil War: Selected Writings and Speeches.* Boston: Bedford/St. Martin's, 2001.

Kyvig, David E. *Explicit and Authentic Acts: Amending the U.S. Constitution, 1776–1995.* Lawrence: University Press of Kansas, 1996.

McPherson, James. *Abraham Lincoln and the Second American Revolution.* New York: Oxford University Press, 1991.

Vorenberg, Michael. *Final Freedom: The Civil War, the Abolition of Slavery, and the Thirteenth Amendment.* New York: Cambridge University Press, 2001.

Todd Family

The Todd family, prominent in Kentucky and Illinois, helped facilitate Abraham Lincoln's rise to social, political, and professional success. Members of the family played various roles in Lincoln's life as mentor, partner, partisan ally, spouse, and in-law.

The Todds descended from Levi Todd, a soldier in the Revolutionary War, who with his brothers founded Lexington, Kentucky. After the war Todd was awarded the influential post of Fayette County clerk and eventually amassed a sizable fortune through land speculation. He fathered thirteen children, among them Robert Smith Todd. Like his father, Robert was a public official, and like his father, he had numerous progeny. Robert's first wife, Eliza Parker Todd, bore him six children—Elizabeth, Frances, Levi, Mary, Ann, and George—before dying at the age of thirty-one of childbed fever. Todd and his second wife, Elizabeth Humphreys Todd, had eight children—Margaret, Samuel, David, Martha, Emilie, Alexander, Elodie, and Catherine.

Robert's four eldest daughters removed to Springfield, Illinois, in a process of chain migration that began when Elizabeth married Ninian Wirt Edwards (Illinois state representative, 1836–1840), the son of the first territorial governor of Illinois, Ninian Edwards. After his father's death Edwards served briefly as Illinois attorney general before moving his bride to Springfield, where he became a socially prominent merchant. Their house on "aristocracy hill" was widely considered the center of Springfield's social and cultural life. It was also the destination of Frances, Mary, and Ann, in succession, who were sent to Springfield from Lexington to escape the crowded Todd home and to find suitable husbands: Frances married physician William Wallace in 1839, and Ann married dry goods merchant Clark M. Smith in 1846.

The first Todd that Lincoln encountered was not Mary, his future wife, but her cousin John Todd Stuart (U.S. congressman, 1839–1842 and 1863–1864), the son of Robert Todd's sister Hannah. Stuart met Lincoln when both served in the 1832 Black Hawk War in Illinois. Stuart had moved to Springfield from Lexington. He was a rising lawyer and politician who found himself impressed with Lincoln's character and abilities. Both men represented Sangamon County in the Illinois legislature in the 1834 term, and Stuart, a one-term veteran and leading Whig, adopted the role of Lincoln's political mentor. Stuart's departure from the state legislature after an unsuccessful bid for Congress in 1836 left Lincoln the acknowledged Whig Party leader in the chamber, a position he maintained until his final term in 1842.

Stuart was also instrumental in Lincoln's legal training. Lincoln credited Stuart with encouraging his study of the law and loaning him legal texts. In 1837

Lincoln moved to Springfield from New Salem and formally began practice as Stuart's junior law partner. It proved an auspicious beginning for young lawyer Lincoln, who benefited from Stuart's enviable professional reputation and extensive client list. Through his connection to Stuart, Lincoln became a regular guest at the home of Ninian W. Edwards and thus gained entrée into Springfield's elite social circle. As a frequent visitor there, Lincoln developed relationships with a number of prominent citizens, possibly including Stephen T. Logan (delegate to the 1860 Republican convention), who took Lincoln on as a junior partner when Lincoln's partnership with Stuart dissolved in 1841.

Undoubtedly the most important relationship Lincoln formed at the Edwards house was with Mary Todd, who had arrived from Lexington in 1839 for an extended visit with her sister. Like Lincoln, Mary had a sharp mind and loved Whig politics. Their initial courtship, which began against the backdrop of the boisterous 1840 election season, was punctuated by a period of estrangement about which there is great historical speculation but little surviving fact. The pair reconciled late in 1842 and were married on November 4 of that year; Mary was twenty-three, Lincoln ten years her senior.

By marrying a Todd, Lincoln moved up in the world, receiving the benefit of his well-bred wife's supervision regarding clothing and etiquette and acquiring a vast network of well-connected in-laws. It went a long way toward cementing his place among Springfield's social elite and boosted his professional and political careers.

As president of the United States, Lincoln was often vexed by the Todds. John Todd Stuart did not support Lincoln's presidential campaign, and in 1862 he won a seat in Congress as a Democrat. To Lincoln's dismay and the Union's scorn, Mary's brothers George, Samuel, David, and Alexander all joined the Confederate Army, as did her sister Emilie's husband, Benjamin Hardin Helm. Their military exploits were tracked by the newspapers, which frequently speculated that Mary herself might be a Southern sympathizer. Mary's sisters also proved embarrassing to the Lincoln administration. There was a public outcry when Emilie, now the widow of a Confederate officer, spent a week at the White House in 1863, and in 1864 Lincoln's prospects for reelection were jeopardized by a rumor that Martha had carried contraband through the Union lines. Even Edwards proved troublesome. Lincoln had named him Springfield's commissary commissioner in 1861, and by 1863 the president's longtime Republican friends were loudly complaining of graft and mismanagement, forcing Lincoln to transfer Edwards to Chicago. Elizabeth, however, provided much-needed comfort to Mary after the Lincolns' son Willie died of typhoid fever in 1862, and both the Edwardses cared for Mary during the final years of her life.

See also *Lincoln, Mary Todd*

—Erika Nunamaker

BIBLIOGRAPHY

Baker, Jean H. *Mary Todd Lincoln: A Biography.* New York: Norton, 1987.

Berry, Stephen. *House of Abraham: Lincoln and the Todds, a Family Divided by War.* Boston: Houghton Mifflin, 2007.

Wilson, Douglas L. *Honor's Voice: The Transformation of Abraham Lincoln.* New York: Knopf, 1998.

Winkle, Kenneth J. *The Young Eagle: The Rise of Abraham Lincoln.* Dallas: Taylor, 2001.

Trent Affair

The most severe diplomatic crisis of the Civil War, the *Trent* affair brought the United States and Great Britain to the brink of war and nearly helped the Confederacy win diplomatic recognition. On November 8, 1861, the USS *San Jacinto,* commanded by Captain Charles Wilkes, stopped and boarded the RMS *Trent,* a British mail steamer carrying Confederate diplomats James M. Mason and John Slidell, who had been dispatched as envoys to Britain and France, respectively. The Northern press and public were enthusiastic in their praise for Wilkes's action, but London was incensed at the perceived insult to Britain's national honor. Britain demanded a formal apology and immediate release of the prisoners and began strengthening its military forces in Canada and in the Atlantic. After several tense weeks, when war seemed a genuine possibility, the Lincoln administration disavowed Wilkes's action, though it did not apologize, and released Mason and Slidell, who continued their voyage to Europe in January 1862.

Confederate president Jefferson Davis had dispatched Mason and Slidell to Europe on August 24, 1861. The diplomats ran the Union blockade at Charleston aboard the *Theodora* on October 12 and reached Nassau, Bahamas, two days later, before heading to Cuba. On November 7 they left Havana aboard the *Trent,* bound for St. Thomas, there to catch a ship to Southampton, England. Intercepting the *Trent* on November 8, Wilkes sent Lieutenant Donald Fairfax to board the ship and arrest Mason and Slidell. Once the diplomats were aboard, Wilkes turned north and sailed to Boston, where the Confederates were imprisoned at Fort Warren.

An echo of previous Anglo-American naval disputes, the *Trent* affair occurred at a perilous time for the Lincoln administration. During the 1850s, Anglo-American relations had steadily improved, as agreements were reached regarding the Oregon Territory, the Canadian border, and the question of British involvement in Texas. Now, however, the president faced related domestic and international crises at a time of worsening relations with Great Britain. When the British recognized the Confederacy as a belligerent, secretary of state William Henry Seward issued an angry memorandum on April 1, 1861, which declared that British intervention on behalf of the Confederacy would mean war with the United States. In response to the capture of Mason and Slidell, the House of

"You do what's right, my son, or I'll blow you out of the water." A cartoon depicts Great Britain's anger over the removal of Confederate commissioners James M. Mason and John Slidell from the British mail steamer *Trent* on November 8, 1861. Lincoln's decision to release the captives averted British recognition of the Confederacy and possibly an outright war with England.

Source: The Granger Collection, New York

Representatives voted to award Wilkes a gold medal, and Northern newspapers enthusiastically praised Wilkes, opining that the insult done the British was less than similar insults offered the United States by Britain in previous high-seas incidents. The joyous reaction on the part of the Northern press, which lionized Wilkes in part to make up for a lack of battlefield victories, made the situation more difficult for Lincoln to resolve. Initially he could neither condemn the incident nor boast of it; the former would potentially damage the war effort, while the latter would antagonize Britain and push the world's preeminent maritime power closer to the Confederacy, as well as perhaps into a war with the Union.

The *Trent* affair also threatened to impede the Union's ability to make war on the rebellious states. When war broke out in 1861, the Union had only a six-month supply of saltpeter, a component of gunpowder. Some saltpeter could be obtained within the United States, but most had to be purchased from Britain's India colony. The navy authorized Lammot Du Pont to purchase all of the saltpeter available in Britain, approximately 2,300 tons, and to contract for 1,000 tons to be purchased from India. British officials learned of the saltpeter purchases one day before they learned of the *Trent* affair and, fearful that the United States was preparing for war with Britain, moved to stop the shipments.

In December, Lord John Russell, the British foreign secretary, directed the crown's envoy in Washington, Richard Bicketron Pemell, Lord Lyons, to inform Seward that London demanded an apology and the freeing of the prisoners. Russell's memorandum, softened by Prince Albert and delivered December 23, was an ultimatum to the Lincoln administration, in that it instructed Lyons to close down the British legation if Lincoln did not deliver a satisfactory response to the British demand. The modified version, however, hinted that the crisis could be resolved without an apology if it were admitted that Wilkes had acted without orders. Lincoln favored submitting the case to an impartial international arbiter, but during a crucial, Christmas Day cabinet meeting, Seward prevailed upon the president to accept the compromise hinted at in Russell's ultimatum. Arbitration, Seward pointed out, would drag the case out longer, when both sides desired and needed a swift resolution. It was becoming clear that France would side with Britain, thus compounding the problem internationally. The cabinet reconvened on December 26, and Lincoln announced that he would accept Seward's proposal, having been unable to devise a different solution himself. Lyons accepted the message, and Mason and Slidell were released January 1, 1862.

The *Trent* affair brought the United States and Great Britain closer to war than at any other point during the Civil War and marked a low in Anglo-American relations. The resolution of the crisis, however, markedly improved relations between the two nations. Officials in both the North and the South recognized that the rapprochement effectively prevented further British involvement in the Civil War for the time being, while Seward and Lincoln's handling of the crisis improved British opinion of both men.

See also *Adams, Charles Francis; Mason, James; Slidell, John*

—Anthony Santoro

BIBLIOGRAPHY

Adams, Charles Francis, Jr. "The *Trent* Affair." *American Historical Review* 17, no. 3 (April 1912): 540–562.

Adams, Ephraim D. *Great Britain and the American Civil War.* 2 vols. New York: Longmans Green, 1925.

Ferris, Norman B. *The 'Trent' Affair: A Diplomatic Crisis.* Knoxville: University of Tennessee Press, 1997.

Hubbard, Charles M. *The Burden of Confederate Diplomacy.* Knoxville: University of Tennessee Press, 1998.

Jones, Howard. *Union in Peril: The Crisis over British Intervention in the Civil War.* Lincoln: University of Nebraska Press, 1992.

Paludan, Phillip Shaw. *The Presidency of Abraham Lincoln.* Lawrence: University Press of Kansas, 1994.

Warren, Gordon H. *Fountain of Discontent: The* Trent *Affair and Freedom of the Seas.* Boston: Northeastern University Press, 1981.

Trumbull, Lyman

Lyman Trumbull (1813–1896) was a longtime Illinois politician and sometime rival and ally of Abraham Lincoln. Born in Connecticut, Trumbull practiced law in Georgia before moving to Illinois in 1837 and becoming active in Democratic politics. He served in the state senate, as Illinois secretary of state, and on the Illinois Supreme Court before being elected to the U.S. House of Representatives in 1854. The following year, when the Illinois legislature deadlocked over the selection of a U.S. senator between the Republican Lincoln and a Democratic candidate, the antislavery Democrat Trumbull was selected as a compromise choice, with the somewhat grudging support of Lincoln. This coalition helped forge a permanent Republican Party in Illinois out of former Whig and Democratic elements, aided greatly by Lincoln's characteristic magnanimity and political adroitness in dealing with the setback. Lincoln even attended a celebration party for the senator-elect and congratulated Trumbull in person. The defeat of his cherished ambition for a seat in the U.S. Senate was nevertheless a bitter disappointment to Lincoln in the short term, and even more so to Mary Todd Lincoln, who refused afterward to speak to Trumbull's wife, Julia Jayne, previously one of her closest friends.

Relations between Trumbull and Lincoln would at times be strained as well, though Trumbull and his allies supported Lincoln in the 1860 election, repaying the favor from 1854. Lincoln and Trumbull also cooperated in opposing concessions to the South on territorial issues during the secession winter of 1861–1862. They clashed over patronage matters following Lincoln's ascension to the White House, however, with Trumbull believing that his former Democratic allies, particularly Norman B. Judd, the chairman of the Illinois State Republican Party, who aspired to a position in the cabinet, had been slighted in the distribution of offices. The angry Trumbull reputedly vowed never to set foot in the White

House during his former friend's administration because of this perceived snub. Judd's appointment as U.S. minister in Berlin helped repair Lincoln's somewhat testy relations with Trumbull. Owing to both lingering hard feelings and his own undoubted independence and iconoclasm, Trumbull would at times ally himself with radical critics of the administration during the Civil War, and in fact for a time, with other Republican leaders in Congress, he opposed Lincoln's renomination in 1864.

The feisty, bespectacled Trumbull emerged as one of the ablest and most vigorous congressional Republicans of the Civil War era, particularly on issues within the purview of his powerful position as chairman of the Senate Judiciary Committee from 1861 to 1872. Having personally witnessed the Union army's rout at Bull Run in 1861, Trumbull throughout the war feared that the army's leadership lacked competence as well as appropriate aggressiveness, and he participated in the abortive attempt by Republican senators in 1862 to force a reorganization of the cabinet. Trumbull played a vital role in drafting and winning support for much important legislation both during the war and during Reconstruction, such as the Confiscation Acts, the act providing for the suspension of *habeas corpus,* the Freedmen's Bureau legislation, and the Civil Rights Acts. He is perhaps best known, however, for his central role in drafting the Thirteenth Amendment abolishing slavery.

Following the Emancipation Proclamation in 1862, many antislavery leaders, including Trumbull and Lincoln, realized that additional legislation in the form of a constitutional amendment was necessary to ensure the permanent eradication of slavery in the United States. As a temporary war measure that only affected territory in rebellion, the proclamation fell short of being a permanent solution to the problem that Republican leaders of the time (as well as subsequent historians) generally perceived as the cause of the war. As chairman of the Judiciary Committee, Trumbull took charge of the drafting of what would become the Thirteenth Amendment in 1864. He clashed during the process with the more radical Massachusetts senator Charles Sumner, who wanted an abolition amendment that would explicitly grant citizenship rights to freed people. Trumbull instead wrote a more vaguely worded, and he hoped more generally politically acceptable, amendment that did not explicitly define the post-emancipation legal status of African Americans, somewhat disingenuously arguing that it was not necessary, although as the results demonstrated, that was far from the case. With Lincoln's strong support, Trumbull's Thirteenth Amendment passed the Senate in April 1864 and the House of Representatives in February 1865, setting off one of the most joyous celebrations and most remarkable scenes in the history of the U.S. Congress. The Thirteenth Amendment was ratified by the required three-fourth of the states later that year and went into effect.

Following the Civil War, Trumbull broke with most of his fellow Republicans and voted against the impeachment of Andrew Johnson in 1868, doubting the legality and political wisdom of the charges against him. In 1872 he joined the short-lived Liberal Republican insurgency, denouncing the corruption of the Grant administration. During the disputed presidential election controversy of 1876, he served as a counsel for the Democratic candidate, Samuel J. Tilden of New York. Trumbull unsuccessfully ran for governor of Illinois as a Democrat, in 1880. A true political maverick, the former antislavery leader and Lincoln confidant also joined the Populist movement in the 1890s and defended socialist leader Eugene V. Debs and other Chicago railway strikers in 1894.

—MICHAEL T. SMITH

BIBLIOGRAPHY

Donald, David Herbert. *Lincoln.* New York: Touchstone, 1995.

Krug, Mark M. *Lyman Trumbull: Conservative Radical.* New York: A. S. Barnes, 1965.

White, Horace. *The Life of Lyman Trumbull.* Boston: Houghton Mifflin, 1913.

Union Pacific Railroad

On July 1, 1862, President Abraham Lincoln signed the Pacific Railway Act, authorizing the construction of a railroad across the western United States and pledging massive government aid for the project. The bill authorized a federal charter for a new corporation, the Union Pacific Railroad (UP), and promised aid to the existing Central Pacific Railroad (CP). The UP was to build westward from an unspecified point near the 100th meridian, while the CP built eastward from Sacramento, California.

The Republican Party's platforms in 1856 and 1860 called for a Pacific railroad bill. But before the Civil War, the question of the route for the first transcontinental railroad always became caught up in the sectional debate—the North and South each wanted the line to go through its section. Lincoln had a strong personal interest in the railroad and a long record of supporting internal improvements of various kinds. In 1859 Lincoln had visited Council Bluffs, Iowa, and met with Grenville Dodge, who would later become of one of the major figures in the construction of the Union Pacific. Lincoln asked Dodge about a potential route for a western railroad, and Dodge told him about the suitability of the Platte River valley, running westward from the Omaha area into Wyoming.

Government aid to the two railroads included the right-of-way on which the track was built and additional grants of public land that could be sold to help pay construction costs. These land grants were originally ten square miles of land (later increased to twenty square miles) for each mile of track. The government also loaned the railroads $16,000 per mile of track in level country and $48,000 per mile in mountainous territory. Together the two railroads received approximately 45 million acres of government land. Progress on both roads was very slow at first, but the railroad was finished with a "golden spike" ceremony at Promontory Summit, Utah Territory, on May 10, 1869. The Central Pacific had built about 690 miles of track, and the Union Pacific approximately 1,084 miles through Nebraska, Wyoming, and Utah.

The Pacific Railroad Act left several important decisions to be determined later by the president. One was the decision on what would be considered the eastern terminus of the Union Pacific. Lincoln again sought the advice of Grenville Dodge, who was at this time a general serving in the United States Army. Dodge recommended Council Bluffs as the specified starting point, and Lincoln agreed, although

UP officials interpreted Lincoln's directive to specify Omaha, on the west side of the Missouri River.

There were tremendous obstacles to the completion of the first transcontinental railroad, and the problems were exacerbated by numerous frauds and questionable business practices. In some cases track was built quickly, rather than well, to get more of the per-mile subsidies. In the 1870s, several prominent politicians were tainted by the Crédit Mobilier scandal. Many members of Congress and government employees had received corporate stock liberally handed out by the UP and its subsidiary, the Crédit Mobilier, which had been contracted to build the railroad. Because many of the directors of the UP also owned Crédit Mobilier, they were essentially paying themselves to build their railroad.

Undertaking such a massive project during wartime prompted questions about the expense and the diversion of attention from the war effort. However, most of the expenses involved would be paid out as construction went forward, and no significant progress was made until long after the war ended. Lincoln's administration recognized that the completion of the railroad was too far in the future to have much impact on the war, but the idea of tying the Pacific Coast region more firmly to the rest of the nation was seen as an antidote to sectionalism. Despite troubled beginnings, the transcontinental railroad had a tremendous impact on the United States. The UP in particular was instrumental in the settlement and development of the region along its lines through the Great Plains and Rocky Mountain states.

See also *Central Pacific Railroad; Illinois Central Railroad; Railroads*

—MARK S. JOY

BIBLIOGRAPHY

Ambrose, Stephen E. *Nothing Like It in the World: The Men Who Built the Transcontinental Railroad, 1863–1869.* New York: Simon and Schuster, 2000.

Bain, David Hayward. *Empire Express: Building the First Transcontinental Railroad.* New York: Penguin, 1999.

Usher, John

See *Cabinet, Lincoln's*

U.S. Colored Troops (USCT)

President Abraham Lincoln inserted a paragraph in his final Emancipation Proclamation of January 1, 1863, authorizing that suitable emancipated slaves "will be received into the armed service of the United States to garrison forts, positions, stations, and other places, and to man vessels of all sorts in said service." This passage seemingly signaled a major reversal in Lincoln's official policy. Since the start of the war the U.S. Army had turned away free black volunteers.

Soon after the war commenced, however, Lincoln had in fact begun to move cautiously but consistently toward emancipation and the enlistment of African American soldiers. The politics of emancipation and the politics of black enlistment always were closely entwined, and Lincoln's final Emancipation Proclamation underscored the vital nexus in the president's thinking. Lincoln thus charted a more linear course toward the freeing and arming of blacks than his nineteenth-century critics and some modern historians have recognized.

To be sure, from the war's outbreak in April 1861 Lincoln had insisted that the conflict was a constitutional struggle to keep the Union intact, not a war to destroy slavery or to arm blacks. He recognized the political and social implications of emancipation and the use of blacks as armed soldiers. Placing blacks on a political and social par with whites would challenge the nation's racial status quo—white supremacy. It would fuel the racial phobias of conservative Republicans and Democrats and would discourage white enlistments into the Union army. Lincoln also worried that emancipation would alienate non-slaveholders, as well as slaveholders in the loyal Border States, and might further work to unify opposition to the Union cause in the Confederate states.

Despite these concerns, circumstances during the first two years of the war ultimately convinced Lincoln to move slowly but systematically toward freeing the slaves and mobilizing free blacks and liberated slaves as soldiers. Lincoln's failure to suppress the rebellion kept morale low in the North, discouraged Northern whites from filling depleted Union regiments, provided ammunition for his political opponents, and encouraged England to threaten diplomatic recognition of the Confederacy. Significantly, too, the Confederacy's military successes depended heavily on slaves whose labor freed white men to serve in the Southern ranks. Needing to change the direction of the war, in 1862 Lincoln concluded that emancipation and the arming of the blacks were military necessities. "What I do about slavery, and the colored race," Lincoln explained in a public letter to editor Horace Greeley, "I do because it helps to save the Union."

Specifically, in the First Confiscation Act (August 1861) Lincoln's government seized slaves employed by the Confederates and put them to work in auxiliary

U.S. Colored Troops (USCT)

Dress parade of the 1st South Carolina Colored Troops (Union Army), at Beaufort, South Carolina. In August 1863 Lincoln informed General Ulysses S. Grant that he believed the black regiments would become an invaluable "resource which, if vigorously applied now, will soon close the contest."
Source: The Granger Collection, New York

military roles. In March 1862 Congress enacted an additional Article of War that prohibited military and naval personnel from returning to their masters the thousands of fugitive slaves who entered Union lines. The Second Confiscation Act (July 1862) freed slaves of individual rebels and permitted the president "to employ as many persons of African descent as he may deem necessary and proper for the suppression of this rebellion, and for this purpose he may organize and use them in such manner as he may judge best for the public welfare." The Militia Act (July 1862) emancipated family members of bondsmen employed by the Union army and authorized that men so employed be paid "ten dollars per month and one ration, three dollars of which monthly pay may be in clothing." Outraged that Lincoln seemingly was willing only to free slaves to work, not fight, in September 1862 the black abolitionist Frederick Douglass charged that Lincoln had "evaded his obvious duty, and instead of calling the blacks to arms and to liberty he merely authorized the military commanders to use them as laborers, without even promising them their freedom at the end of their term of service."

Though Douglass chafed at Lincoln's apparent lethargy in arming African Americans, Lincoln waited to see how Confederates responded to his Preliminary Emancipation Proclamation, issued on September 22, 1862. If, the president warned, the rebels did not cease their resistance to federal authority, on January 1,

1863, he would emancipate all slaves then residing in a state of rebellion. Hopeful that the Confederates might surrender, and setting the political stage in the North for emancipation and the recruitment of blacks, Lincoln purposely gave the impression that he opposed arming African Americans. For example, nine days before issuing his preliminary proclamation the president informed a delegation of Chicago Christians, "I am not so sure we could do much with the blacks. If we were to arm them, I fear that in a few weeks the arms would be in the hands of the rebels; and indeed thus far we have not had arms enough to equip our white troops."

Behind the scenes, however, Lincoln allowed black troops to be organized on a piecemeal basis in South Carolina (the First South Carolina Colored Volunteers), Louisiana (three regiments of Louisiana Native Guards [Union]), and Kansas (the First Kansas Colored Volunteers). By the time Lincoln issued his final Emancipation Proclamation on January 1, five regiments of blacks, between 3,000 and 4,000 men, already were in service. According to historian Dudley T. Cornish, they were "raised on a catch-as-catch-can basis with little or no control from Washington."

In early 1863 the War Department standardized the recruitment process by establishing the Bureau for Colored Troops, a separate office in the adjutant general's office, to coordinate the organization of black troops. Led by assistant adjutant general Charles W. Foster, this bureau supervised the recruitment of blacks North and South and examined officer candidates for regiments that, by summer 1863, were assigned numbered units in the new U.S. Colored Troops (USCT).

With the exception of a few black regiments formed in Connecticut, Louisiana, and Massachusetts (including the Fifty-fourth and Fifty-fifth Massachusetts Volunteers and the Fifth Massachusetts Cavalry), all other African American units, including those previously mustered on the state level, entered federal service and eventually received USCT regimental designations. In August 1863 Lincoln informed General Ulysses S. Grant that he believed that black regiments would become an invaluable "resource which, if vigorously applied now, will soon close the contest. It works doubly, weakening the enemy and strengthening us. We were not fully ripe for it until the [Mississippi] river was opened. Now, I think at least a hundred thousand can, and ought to be rapidly organized along it's [sic] shores, relieving all the white troops to serve elsewhere."

By war's end, the army had raised 178,975 African American soldiers, organized in 133 infantry regiments, 4 independent companies, 7 cavalry regiments, 12 regiments of heavy artillery, and 10 companies of light artillery. Approximately 19 percent of the men came from the eighteen Northern states, 24 percent from the four loyal slave or Border States, and 57 percent from the eleven Confederate states. Though most of the USCT were ex-slaves, more than 15 percent of the 1860 Northern free black population joined the Union army. All in all, African Americans accounted for between 9 percent and 10 percent of all Union troops who served in the war. Sixteen blacks received the Medal of Honor, awarded to U.S. soldiers for the first time in 1863.

The USCT fought in every military theater, in the East, the West, in the Mississippi Valley, and in the Trans-Mississippi. They entered combat as early as October 29, 1862 (a skirmish at Island Mound, Missouri, by the First Kansas Colored Volunteers), and continued fighting until May 11–12, 1865 (skirmishes at Palmito Ranch, Texas, involving the Sixty-second USCT), a month after General Robert E. Lee surrendered at Appomattox.

To be sure, most of the black troops' fighting was limited to minor engagements, removed from the major campaigns, and under the command of relatively obscure officers. And when the black soldiers finally entered combat, historian Noah Andre Trudeau explains, "they too often entered the fight saddled with the burden of having to prove themselves worthy to their Caucasian comrades. Any misstep during an engagement, or a slip of discipline that would be forgiven a raw white unit, would be held as proof of a black unit's unreliability, a stain that no amount of blood could wash away." Throughout their service black soldiers suffered all manner of discrimination, receiving inferior assignments, inadequate medical care, insufficient training, and insults from white soldiers. Conditions for the USCT generally were separate from and unequal to those of white troops—a condition indicative of their second-class status in the War Department's bureaucracy and in American society at large.

Lincoln, however, appreciated the part that the men of the USCT played in helping to suppress the rebellion. In August 1863, soon after black troops had first distinguished themselves in combat, he predicted that future blacks would "remember that, with silent tongue, and clenched teeth, and steady eye, and well-poised bayonet, they have helped mankind" in saving the Union. The following year Lincoln explained to General James S. Wadsworth that African American troops had "heroically vindicated their manhood on the battle-field, where, in assisting to save the life of the Republic, they have demonstrated in blood their right to the ballot." And in what became his final speech, on April 11, 1865, the president proposed that the franchise in the newly reconstructed Southern states be "conferred on the very intelligent [African American men], and on those who serve our cause as soldiers." An assassin's bullet postponed Lincoln's plan for USCT veterans to receive the right to vote.

—JOHN DAVID SMITH

BIBLIOGRAPHY

Basler, Roy P., ed. *The Collected Works of Abraham Lincoln*. New Brunswick, N.J.: Rutgers University Press, 1955.

Cornish, Dudley T. "African American Troops in the Union Army." In *Encyclopedia of the Confederacy*, ed. Richard N. Current, 1: 9–13. 4 vols. New York: Simon and Schuster, 1993.

———. *The Sable Arm: Negro Troops in the Union Army, 1861–1865*. New York: Longmans, Green, 1956.

Foner, Philip S., ed. *The Life and Writings of Frederick Douglass*. 5 vols. New York: International, 1975.

Guelzo, Allen C. *Lincoln's Emancipation Proclamation: The End of Slavery in America.* New York: Simon and Schuster, 2004.

Hollandsworth, James G., Jr. *The Louisiana Native Guards: The Black Military Experience during the Civil War.* Baton Rouge: Louisiana State University Press, 1995.

Manning, Chandra. *What This Cruel War Was Over: Soldiers, Slavery, and the Civil War.* New York: Knopf, 2007.

Miller, Edward A., Jr. *Lincoln's Abolitionist General: The Biography of David Hunter.* Columbia: University of South Carolina Press, 1997.

Siddali, Silvana R. *From Property to Person: Slavery and the Confiscation Acts, 1861–1862.* Baton Rouge: Louisiana State University Press, 2005.

Smith, John David, ed. *Black Soldiers in Blue: African American Troops in the Civil War Era.* Chapel Hill: University of North Carolina Press, 2002.

Trudeau, Noah Andre. *Like Men of War: Black Troops in the Civil War, 1862–1865.* Boston: Little, Brown, 1998.

U.S. Supreme Court, Lincoln's Appointments to

U.S. Supreme Court appointments by President Abraham Lincoln significantly altered the character and destiny of the bench. In the years between 1862 and 1864, Lincoln appointed five justices to the Court, including the first four Republicans ever seated. These men steered the Supreme Court through the most tumultuous time in American history and in the process elevated the stature of the nation's highest tribunal.

During the Civil War and Reconstruction, the Supreme Court shifted from all Democrats to fully Republican, and it so remained for more than a generation (until 1883). Lincoln selected his nominees on the contradictory expectations that they would demonstrate judicial restraint in chief justice Roger Taney's *Dred Scott* Court, yet also support his war measures in a dependably partisan manner. Lincoln's justices—Noah Swayne, Samuel Miller, David Davis, Stephen Field, and Salmon Chase—were an especially interesting lot. Far too ambitious to leave their politics behind, they were the most politically active group to ever serve on the Court. They schemed with members of Congress, they manipulated the press, and they ran for office. In fact, four of Lincoln's justices ran for president of the United States from the bench. That these justices often sided with the Democrats contributed to the failure of Reconstruction; that they were astute and ambitious politicians added to the development and success of the Supreme Court.

The five justices Lincoln appointed were exceptional in several respects. Noah Swayne, Lincoln's first appointee, was a Quaker who moved from Virginia to Ohio because of opposition to slavery. Dr. Samuel Miller practiced medicine in his home state of Kentucky before becoming Iowa's most successful advocate for small farmers. David Davis served as Lincoln's campaign manager in the presidential election of 1860 and left the Supreme Court when—exhausted by Reconstruction not even a decade after becoming the third Republican justice—he was elected to the same U.S. Senate seat that his dear friend Lincoln failed to secure in 1858. Stephen Field, the only Democrat among this group, is regarded as Lincoln's finest addition to the Court; he buoyed business in most of the 620 opinions he wrote in his thirty-four years of service. Salmon Chase, the former U.S. senator and governor from Ohio who coined the slogan of the Republican Party ("Free Soil, Free Labor, Free Men"), became Lincoln's final appointee and the sixth chief justice of the United States. These five men served as the thirty-fifth through thirty-ninth justices of the U.S. Supreme Court.

Lincoln nominated Noah Swayne to be the thirty-fifth Supreme Court justice. Born in Virginia in 1804, Swayne attended a Quaker academy and after taking up the law moved to Ohio. Swayne was a friend of the recently deceased Justice McLean, also of Ohio, and his selection enabled Lincoln to satisfy residents of an electorally important state. Furthermore, Lincoln liked Swayne because he was prominent as a corporation lawyer and no one believed the war could be won without the support of business. That the new justice's son, Wager, was a general in Lincoln's army also helped his appointment. For Lincoln, everything came back to winning the war. The Senate confirmed Swayne on January 24, three days after his nomination. National press reacted favorably. The *National Intelligencer* praised him for having freed the twenty-five slaves he inherited twenty years earlier. But Swayne's judicial career could be termed a monument to mediocrity. While his unswerving support of Lincoln's war measures was important, as was his emphatic support for black freedom, Swayne's twenty-year career was devoid of meaningful contributions to constitutional law.

Samuel Miller was born in a part of Kentucky where few people owned slaves, yet the Miller family was among those who did. As had his rival, Noah Swayne, Miller studied medicine before entering the legal profession, though Miller actually got a degree and practiced for several years. A large man at over six feet and 200 pounds, he loved to have the fun that went along with telling stories and singing songs. Frustrated by his inability to stem the physical suffering endemic in the hills of Kentucky, Miller started reading law and was admitted to the bar in 1847. He ran for a seat in the Kentucky Convention in 1849 as an advocate for emancipation. Miller's disgust for slavery factored prominently in his decision to leave Kentucky for Keokuk, Iowa. A leader of the new Republican Party in his new state, he lost a race for the state senate and failed to secure nomination in the 1861 Iowa gubernatorial election. Despite his long-standing hatred of slavery, Miller condemned abolitionists as extremist. He wrote the majority opinion in 616 Supreme Court cases—the *Slaughterhouse Cases* most notably—more than any previous justice. Of those decisions, ninety-five dealt with constitutional matters. Justice Miller sat on the fifteen-member commission that resolved the disputed presidential election of 1876.

Born in Maryland eight months after this father's death, David Davis was nursed by a family slave. At thirteen, he entered Kenyon College in Ohio. He studied law at the office of Henry Bishop, in Massachusetts, before entering the New Haven Law School (associated with Yale University) for one of the two years required. Davis campaigned unsuccessfully as a Whig for the Illinois senate in 1840 but won his race for a seat in the state assembly in 1844.

Riding circuit in his very large district, Davis traveled often with his dear friend Abraham Lincoln. Indeed, Lincoln frequently argued before Davis as judge, though one would never have guessed that they were best friends (in fact, Davis served as administrator of the assassinated president's estate). Lincoln lost forty-seven of the eighty-seven cases he argued before Davis. That Davis campaigned feverishly for Lincoln, in two unsuccessful runs for the Senate and as chief strategist for the presidential run in 1860, was but part of their long-standing friendship. Davis not only assisted the new president in the selection of a cabinet, but he also edited various drafts of the inaugural address. When John Campbell resigned his seat on the Supreme Court to join the Confederacy, Lincoln asked Davis to step in. We can only speculate what Lincoln would have thought about his best friend's opinion in *Ex parte Milligan,* yet another example of the idealistic judge overruling the pragmatic politician, to say nothing of the irony that forever laced their relationship. Davis argued the Milligan's rights had been infringed upon when tried by a military court not "ordained and established by Congress." Here was Davis insisting that his best friend, the man who appointed him to the bench fully expecting support for executive war measures, had no power to mandate military tribunals, even at a time of national emergency. Equally ironic perhaps, Davis resigned his place on the Court when the Illinois legislature elected him in 1877 to the U.S. Senate seat that Lincoln could not win.

Many Republicans were shocked when Lincoln selected Stephen Johnson Field, a Democrat, as his fourth nominee to the Court. The pro-Union Field—chief justice of the Supreme Court of California—appealed to Lincoln because he hailed from the isolated, potentially Southern-leaning tenth circuit that Congress had just created on March 3, 1863. His association with business, that essential wartime ally constantly on Lincoln's mind, also recommended him. The sixth of the nine children of Reverend David Dudley Field and his wife, Submit, Field eventually sat on the Supreme Court bench for over thirty-four years and wrote 620 opinions. Stephen Field's siblings had spectacularly successful careers that greatly affected his own. David Dudley Field (1805–1894), named after their father, figured prominently in American political history and was responsible for legal reforms in both the United States (he drove the separation between law and equity proceedings) and Britain (he influenced the English Judicature Acts of 1873 and 1875). David, a bitter opponent of slavery, helped organize the Republican Party and nominate Lincoln for president. Brother Cyrus West Field (1819–1892) led the Atlantic Telegraph Company, the entity that successfully laid the first telegraph cable to span the Atlantic Ocean in 1858. Reverend Henry Martyn Field (1822–1907) wrote a series of world travel books that were very popular and are still classics, with over twenty editions. It is a peculiarity of the times that few were troubled that David Field, a prominent Supreme Court lawyer, later successfully argued cases before his brother, as in *Ex parte Milligan*; in *Cummings v. Missouri* (in which Stephen wrote the majority opinion); in *Ex parte McCardle* (in which David argued for the government); and in the *Legal Tender Cases* (in which David appeared for the U.S. Treasury). All of those were among the most spectacular cases of the era.

Stephen Field's feisty personality contributed mightily to the unfriendly tenor of the Supreme Court, where Justice Miller never trusted Justice Swayne, and David Davis forever harbored hostility toward Field.

After the death of Roger B. Taney, Lincoln appointed Salmon P. Chase chief justice. Chase was certainly the most fascinating character among the justices Lincoln appointed. Of Lincoln's five Supreme Court appointees, none was harder to arrive at than his last. Lincoln was fully aware of the importance of his choice. With the associate justices he had already appointed, the next chief justice would form a majority on the Court that would decide pivotal constitutional issues and the fate of Reconstruction.

Quite a few names were considered, including Edwin Stanton (subsequently appointed by President Grant, only to die four days after confirmation), Montgomery Blair (never a real prospect for lack of support by the Radicals), and Illinois senator Orville H. Browning (whose main goal was to block the appointment of Salmon Chase). The four senior associate justices on the Court—all Democrats—supported Justice Swayne over a Radical like Chase. The letters advocating Swayne were strong, though dull, whereas the support for Chase was vigorous, even zealous. Curiously, Lincoln had promised the job to Swayne, but fearing for his reelection, and because prominent men in the Republican Party were proposing Chase, Lincoln was forced to wiggle free of the pledge he had given Swayne. The quantity and prominence of Chase supporters were too much for Lincoln to ignore, despite his serious reservations. Lincoln worried about Chase's unbridled ambition, a well-known and often-commented-upon aspect of Chase's character.

Chase was born in Cornish, New Hampshire, the eighth child of a father who died when Salmon was only nine years old. Supported by his widowed mother of little means, Salmon attended Dartmouth College, where the eight faculty members elected him to Phi Beta Kappa upon his graduation in 1826. Largely because of his ambition, Chase was the most politically accomplished of Lincoln's justices. Elected first to the Cincinnati City Council in 1840, he became the leader of the Liberty Party in Ohio, U.S. senator from Ohio and the Free Soil Party in 1849, governor of Ohio in 1855, and again U. S. senator (as a Republican) in 1860. At the same time that he ran for the Senate, in 1860, Chase also ran for president of the United States. He served only a few days in the Senate, leaving to become secretary of the Treasury in Lincoln's cabinet (a position from which he rather notoriously, and impishly, offered to resign four times—the fourth having been, to his great surprise, accepted).

Of the five men Lincoln appointed to the Supreme Court, only two had previous judicial experience (Davis and Field, in the state courts of Illinois and California), whereas all of them had been candidates for, or served in, public office (all but Chase at the state level). Three were raised in slave states (Swayne, Miller, and Davis), but all opposed slavery (though one, Miller, had owned slaves, Field was a Democrat, and none was an abolitionist). All were religious (two, Chase and Davis, were raised by ministers); all were extremely well educated; and all continued to be politicians *while on the bench*. Their politics tended to be surprisingly moderate at best or disappointingly unprincipled at worst.

See also *Taney, Roger B.*

—R. Owen Williams

BIBLIOGRAPHY

Basler, Roy P., ed. *The Collected Works of Abraham Lincoln.* New Brunswick, N.J.: Rutgers University Press, 1953.

Fairman, Charles. *History of the Supreme Court of the United States. Vol. 5: "Reconstruction and Reunion, 1864–1888."* In *The Oliver Wendell Holmes Devise.* New York: Macmillan, 1971.

———. *Mr. Justice Miller and the Supreme Court, 1862–1890.* Cambridge, Mass.: Harvard University Press, 1939.

King, Willard L. *David Davis, Lincoln's Manager.* Cambridge, Mass.: Harvard University Press, 1960.

Niven, John. *Salmon P. Chase: A Biography.* New York: Oxford University Press, 1995.

Ross, Michael A. *Justice of Shattered Dreams: Samuel Freeman Miller and the Supreme Court during the Civil War Era.* Baton Rouge: Louisiana State University Press, 2003.

Swisher, Carl Brent. *Stephen J. Field: Craftsman of the Law.* Chicago: University of Chicago Press, 1930.

U.S. Supreme Court, Lincoln's View of

For President Abraham Lincoln, the United States Supreme Court presented both an opportunity and a challenge. The Court could be a powerful ally to the Union during the Civil War, assuming the right justices occupied the bench.

Over the course of his presidency Lincoln had the opportunity to appoint five justices. Unfortunately the Supreme Court was already populated by Democrats and slaveholders who posed a major threat to Lincoln's wartime measures, including the Emancipation Proclamation, the suspension of *habeas corpus,* and the blockade of Southern ports. Chief justice Roger B. Taney—author of the 1857 majority opinion in *Dred Scott v. Sandford* that served as a catalyst for war—represented just the sort of states' rights, proslavery jurisprudence that Lincoln had to avoid.

Lincoln made his living as a lawyer, an especially effective advocate with a reputation as "a lawyer's lawyer," who won most of his 243 cases before the Illinois Supreme Court. He was also admitted to practice law before the U.S. Supreme Court in 1849, and he argued a few cases before the Court while in Washington following his single term in Congress. He argued effectively, yet lost, in *Longworth v. Lewis,* 48 U.S. 776 (1849). Although Lincoln's primary interest in the law was as a means of making a living, he also saw the law as vehicle for effective political engagement. Although he made his living as a lawyer, he nevertheless defined himself as a political man, one very much invested in the political transformation and civic virtue of the Founders.

Early in his career Lincoln had enormous respect for the law and the judicial process; he was reluctant to question the authority of courts or their decisions. Because he distrusted the unreasoned populism of the Democratic Party every bit as much as the moral absolutism of the abolitionists, Lincoln looked to the Supreme Court to resolve tensions over slavery. Delivering one of his many speeches in support of Republican presidential hopeful John Frémont in July 1856, Lincoln professed confidence in the Supreme Court as "the tribunal to decide such questions," while asserting that he and his fellow Republicans "will submit to its decisions."

But Lincoln could not tolerate decisions predicated on "apparent partisan bias," as he made clear in his speech responding to the *Dred Scott* decision, in Springfield, Illinois, on June 26, 1857. To Lincoln, Chief Justice Taney's majority opinion did "obvious violence to the plain unmistakable language of the Declaration." So clearly erroneous a reading of history and the judicial record had Taney offered that Lincoln's trust in judicial precedent was thereafter forever shaken.

At his first inaugural address, March 4, 1861, the new president insisted that decisions of the Supreme Court were "entitled to very high respect and consideration," but he warned that "if the policy of the government, upon vital questions affecting the whole people, is to be irrevocably fixed by decisions of the Supreme Court, the instant they are made … *the people will have ceased to be their own rulers.*" These were the sentiments of a very disappointed post–*Dred Scott* president looking down the barrel of Civil War.

As with so much else in the life and maneuverings of Lincoln, a certain amount of intelligent speculation is required to know just what the clever sixteenth president of the United States really thought. One thing we know is that he had a golden opportunity in the form of three openings on the Supreme Court almost immediately after taking office. Between the years of 1862 and 1864, Lincoln was able to nominate five justices to the Supreme Court, including Taney's replacement as chief justice.

When choosing justices, President Lincoln's first concern was the war; he needed to nominate men he believed would support the Union cause. He needed to appoint men to the bench who could be counted on to support his war measures, including those he made in absence of congressional authority. Lincoln selected his nominees on the contradictory expectations that they would demonstrate judicial restraint on Chief Justice Taney's *Dred Scott* Court (Lincoln did not gain a Republican majority on the bench until mid-1864, when Roger Taney passed away) yet also support his war measures in a dependably partisan manner. Lincoln's justices—Noah Swayne, Samuel Miller, David Davis, Stephen Field, and Salmon Chase—proved loyal to both the president's objectives (until after the war, at least) and the Union.

Few constitutional issues brought greater scorn upon President Lincoln than his suspension of *habeas corpus*. Early in the war he suspended *habeas corpus* in Maryland and then ordered his subordinates to ignore Chief Justice Taney's attempt, in *Ex parte Merryman*, to overrule him. In September 1862, Lincoln issued a proclamation that suspended *habeas corpus* for civilian prisoners held by Union military. Lincoln claimed executive war authority and declared that any and all persons engaged in disloyal acts (for example, discouraging volunteers, resisting the draft, or public speech against the war) could be held by military authorities and tried by military commissions. Although the Supreme Court did not consider the constitutionality of this matter until late in the war (in *Ex parte Vallandigham*), pubic criticism of the perceived assault on civil liberty never abated. At the same time, Lincoln had to defend other war initiatives, such as the issuance of paper money and emancipation (part war aim and part war tactic).

Just as Lincoln needed justices who tended to be inactive yet in step with (Northern) public opinion, thus setting aside *Dred Scott* and supporting the Union, he also wanted justices who would facilitate rapid economic expansion. The 1860s were years of dizzying growth and development. Furthermore, the era put law and lawyers front and center. Constitutional issues had long been hotly contested, but the previous decade's conquests and expansion produced an entrepreneurial spirit best seen in the establishment of the legal profession. Railroads crisscrossed the sprawling nation and touched off myriad property issues, all involving land law. Oil—first discovered in western Pennsylvania in 1859—required huge capital investment that was facilitated through nascent trusts and corporations, yielding corporation law. The host of machines and inventions needed to exploit the burgeoning economy resulted in a never-ending drama of patent law. Lincoln first made his name as a railroad lawyer, and his commitment to America's burgeoning economy never flagged. He certainly expected a similar commitment from the Supreme Court.

See also *Taney, Roger B.*

—R. Owen Williams

BIBLIOGRAPHY

Carwardine, Richard. *Lincoln: A Life of Purpose and Power.* New York: Knopf, 2006.

Donald, David Herbert. *Lincoln.* New York: Simon and Schuster, 1995.

McAfee, Ward M. *Citizen Lincoln.* New York: Nova History Publications, 2004.

Oates, Stephen B. *Abraham Lincoln: The Man behind the Myths.* New York: Meridian, 1984.

Vallandigham, Clement Laird

Ohio congressman Clement Laird Vallandigham was the most visible leader of the antiwar movement during the American Civil War. Born on July 29, 1820, in New Lisbon, Ohio, Vallandigham attended a local academy and Jefferson College. As for many of his generation, law practice provided a starting point for his political career. After a course of private study, Vallandigham began to practice law in New Lisbon in 1842 and three years later was elected to the Ohio House of Representatives as a Democrat.

Relocating to Dayton, Vallandigham was part owner and editor of the *Dayton Empire*. Through this Democratic organ, Vallandigham expressed his belief in states' rights and limited central government. In 1852 and 1854 Vallandigham ran for Congress in Ohio's third congressional district and was narrowly defeated. Two years later, he suffered defeat by a larger margin when his opponents united in opposition to the Kansas-Nebraska Act. In an effort to undercut immigrant support for the Democratic candidate, the Republicans in the district charged that Vallandigham belonged to a Know-Nothing lodge—a charge he denied. In an 1855 speech in Dayton, Vallandigham criticized political extremism and the abolition movement for promoting sectional division. He consistently opposed what he viewed as radicalism. In 1857 he supported the federal government and the Fugitive Slave Law in a fugitive slave case in Ohio.

When Vallandigham ran for Congress in 1856, he challenged the close election that narrowly gave his opponent the seat in the House of Representatives and spent six months in Washington, D.C., pressing his case. In a partisan vote, the House accepted election results that gave Vallandigham a majority of twenty-two votes and seated the Ohio Democrat. He was reelected in 1858 and 1860. Returning from Washington, D.C., in October 1859, Vallandigham had the opportunity to meet with John Brown. Vallandigham inquired about support for Brown's raid in Ohio and sought information that would link Ohio Republicans to Brown. Republicans criticized Vallandigham for his interview, to which Vallandigham responded by laying blame for the raid only in part with Brown. It was instead, he argued, abolitionist agitation that gave rise to Brown's raid.

In the 1860 election, Vallandigham supported Stephen A. Douglas. The Ohio congressman supported numerous compromise measures during the secession crisis of 1860–1861, including the Crittenden Compromise. When war broke out,

A newspaper illustration of antiwar movement leader and congressman Clement Laird Vallandigham as he is turned over to picket guards after President Lincoln banished him to the Confederate lines. Lincoln regarded Vallandigham's arrest and sentencing as warranted in a time of rebellion because Vallandigham's May 1863 speech in Ohio against conscription interfered with the raising of troops and encouraged desertion.

Source: Library of Congress

Vallandigham publicly proclaimed his opposition to both the war and the expansion of executive power in wartime. Believing that Lincoln's call for troops while Congress was in recess was unconstitutional, Vallandigham called for a meeting of Democrats in Chillicothe, Ohio; only three people responded, and the meeting was not held. In the Thirty-seventh Congress, Vallandigham was a vocal critic of mobilization, Lincoln's suspension of the writ of *habeas corpus,* and conscription. When Vallandigham visited the First and Second Ohio Volunteer Infantries outside of Washington, a conflict emerged between companies who demanded that he leave the camp and companies that supported him. An account of the incident was carried in papers throughout the North. During the same session, constituencies in Ohio sent petitions to the House of Representatives protesting Vallandigham's opposition to the war effort. When the Republican-controlled Ohio General Assembly redistricted the state, Vallandigham's support in the third district was undercut. He lost his bid for reelection in 1862.

Vallandigham maintained a high public profile when he left Congress. He spoke and wrote freely in opposition to conscription, military law, and what he saw as the Lincoln administration's violations of civil liberties. With an eye toward the gubernatorial election of 1863, he relished his status as a leader of the Peace Democrats. The War Department had authorized the arrest of civilians interfering with the draft and guilty of "disloyal practices" in August of 1862. A month later, Lincoln suspended the writ of *habeas corpus* throughout the North with the intent of limiting opposition to the draft. In March 1863 Congress passed the *Habeas Corpus* Act affirming the legality of Lincoln's suspension of the writ. In April of the following year, General Ambrose Burnside, commanding the Department of the Ohio, issued General Order No. 38, declaring that anyone who interfered with conscription or expressed sympathies with the enemy would be subject to military arrest.

On May 1, 1863, Vallandigham gave a speech at Mount Vernon, Ohio, in which he stated that the war was being fought for abolition and that conscription and the federal provost marshals that enforced it violated the rights of the people. He also rejected the authority of military officials over civilians. Burnside ordered his arrest, and Vallandigham was tried by military tribunal and sentenced to imprisonment for the duration of the war. Vallandigham promptly applied to the Ohio federal district court for a writ of *habeas corpus*.

Lincoln and his cabinet learned of Vallandigham's arrest after the fact. Lincoln relayed to Burnside that he supported his action, but the incident caused Lincoln to closely analyze the matter of military law and civil liberties in wartime. Within his cabinet, secretary of war Edwin M. Stanton recommended a special suspension of the writ in Vallandigham's case. Ohioan and secretary of the Treasury Salmon P. Chase believed the justice hearing the case, Humphrey Leavitt, would not issue the writ and opposed a directed suspension. Secretary of state William H. Seward also opposed interfering with the court. From the judiciary, Supreme Court justice David Davis offered that military tribunals were unconstitutional in cases like Vallandigham's. The circuit court in Ohio, however, upheld Vallandigham's arrest. It was justified, Burnside stated, because in times of emergency, military law was more efficient than civil law in preventing public dissent, which aided the enemy. Vallandigham's attorney responded with an argument based on freedom of speech, the right to assemble, and the fact that Ohio was not in a state of rebellion and therefore not subject to military law. Democrats throughout the North echoed these arguments, as they rallied to Vallandigham's cause. Indeed, the incident prompted War Democrats to move toward the peace branch of their party, undermining Republican efforts to attract War Democrats to their ranks. Lincoln responded by commuting Vallandigham's sentence, and banishing him to Confederate lines.

The Vallandigham incident provided a rallying point for Lincoln's critics, and the president responded with a letter to a New York Democrat, Erastus Corning. In the letter Lincoln defended the actions taken as appropriate remedies in a time of rebellion and stated that Vallandigham was guilty of interfering with the raising of troops and encouraging desertion, thereby damaging the army. If deserters were liable to be shot, Lincoln argued, then those who encouraged them should be punished as well. Lincoln also recognized the political usefulness of Vallandigham's case for his Democratic opponents. When Burnside suppressed the antiwar Chicago newspaper the *Chicago Times,* Lincoln countermanded his order.

From exile, Vallandigham would continue to plague the Lincoln administration and the Republican Party. The former congressman made his way to Canada and was in Ontario when Ohio Democrats nominated him as their gubernatorial candidate in 1863. Lincoln used the full strength of party patronage to support the Republican campaign in Ohio. His efforts were rewarded when Vallandigham earned less than 40 percent of the votes and Republican John Brough was elected governor. Vallandigham continued to lead the Peace Democrats and attended the Democratic National Convention in Chicago in 1864, where the party nominated General George B. McClellan. Vallandigham was instrumental in drafting a platform that called for immediate peace negotiations. When McClellan maintained his support for the war, Vallandigham refused to campaign for him.

By 1865 Vallandigham recognized that the war had altered the political landscape, and he accepted the passage of the Thirteenth Amendment. He hoped to move the party beyond wartime issues and wanted to counter Republican charges that the Democratic Party was proslavery. In the years following the war, Vallandigham practiced law and supported the Democrats' "New Departure," which accepted the Thirteenth, Fourteenth, and Fifteenth Amendments and Reconstruction; addressed needed reforms in civil service and tax collection; supported hard specie; and opposed the centralization of federal power at the expense of state and local government. Although he remained influential in national and state politics, Vallandigham was never again elected to political office. Clement Vallandigham died on June 17, 1871, in a gun accident while preparing a case for trial.

See also *Copperheads*

—Christine Dee

BIBLIOGRAPHY

Klement, Frank. *The Limits of Dissent.* New York: Fordham University Press, 1998.

Neely, Mark E., Jr. *The Fate of Liberty: Abraham Lincoln and Civil Liberties.* New York: Oxford University Press, 1991.

Vallandigham, James Laird. *A Life of Clement L. Vallandigham.* Baltimore: Turnball Brothers, 1872.

Webber, Jennifer. *The Copperheads: The Rise and Fall of Lincoln's Opponents in the North.* New York: Oxford University Press, 2006.

Vandalia, Illinois (Second State Capital, 1820–1839)

When it became a state in 1818, Illinois established its first capital in Kaskaskia. Because of its location on the Mississippi River, the site was prone to flooding. That led to the capital's relocation in 1820 to Vandalia, located on the Kaskaskia River and the National Road running from Baltimore, Maryland. Abraham Lincoln served three terms in the Illinois legislature while Vandalia was the state capital, from 1834 through 1839.

During his first term in the legislature (1834–1835) Lincoln spent much of his time on two pressing issues: He supported internal improvements legislation that was of utmost importance to Northern frontier states and to the Whig Party. In particular, he backed bills for the construction of canals and railroads.

The other important issue of the day was banking. In 1831 President Andrew Jackson (1829–1837) vetoed legislation to recharter the Second Bank of the United States. Jackson strongly opposed a national bank, but he favored "pet" banks on the state level. Led by Stephen A. Douglas (1813–1861), Democrats in the Illinois legislature also favored state banks. This aligned them with the Whigs, who supported state banks especially after Jackson's successful attack against the national bank. Following his party, Lincoln backed legislation in support of state banks.

During his first term at Vandalia, Lincoln faced two personal challenges. First, William F. Berry, his business partner in New Salem, died leaving him with a debt. Lincoln paid off the debt, earning the nickname "Honest Abe," according to his biographer Benjamin P. Thomas.

Second was the tragic death of Ann Rutledge in 1835. Her father owned a tavern where Lincoln boarded when he first arrived in New Salem. While surveying, he would often visit her. Her death devastated Lincoln, and it showed when he returned to Vandalia. Friends reported that he suffered from severe "melancholy." Some argue that Lincoln's depression was the result of the death of Ann Rutledge, others that he suffered from chronic mental illness. Some say he suffered from the depressing living conditions of the ramshackle town of Vandalia.

Lincoln returned to Vandalia for a second term in the state legislature along with eight other Whigs from the Springfield area. Collectively they were known as the Long Nine because of their height—they were all over six feet tall. The main item on their political agenda was the relocation of the capital to

Springfield. Most people at the time were moving into the northern part of state, and Springfield was close to the center of that growth. The nine also knew what relocation would mean to land values and to their political supporters who had interests in land around Springfield. In 1837, largely through Lincoln's political acumen, the Long Nine secured enough votes to pass legislation making Springfield the capital.

In his second term Lincoln spoke out against slavery. Following the murder of newspaper editor Elijah Lovejoy (1802–1837) in 1837, some southern legislators argued for the suppression of what they deemed incendiary literature that attacked slavery. Lincoln responded in the ensuing debates by proclaiming his antislavery sentiments and opposing the resolution condemning abolitionist speech.

In 1838, Lincoln won a third term in the state legislature. It would be his last legislative session in Vandalia. The following year, the capital officially moved to Springfield. The state transferred the capitol building to Fayette County, where it served as the county courthouse until 1932.

See also *Illinois; Yates, Richard*

—BRADLEY SKELCHER

BIBLIOGRAPHY

Donald, David Herbert. *Lincoln.* New York: Touchstone, 1995.

Jensen, Richard J. *Illinois: A History.* Urbana: University of Illinois Press, 2001.

Oates, Stephen. *With Malice toward None: The Life of Abraham Lincoln.* New York: New American Library, 1977.

Thomas, Benjamin P. *Abraham Lincoln: A Biography.* New York: Modern Library, 1968.

Vicksburg Campaign

Union and Confederate strategists were slow at first to realize the importance of Vicksburg, Mississippi. Located on a bluff on the east bank of the Mississippi River, Vicksburg was ideally located to serve as a fortified point as well as a link to the trans-Mississippi West. In May 1862, in the aftermath of the Union occupation of New Orleans, David G. Farragut's fleet approached the city from the south but did not have the ground forces to occupy the city. A second northward thrust the following month led to the bombardment of the city but not much else, and a third attempt in July also fell short. By summer the Confederates decided to de-

The siege of Vicksburg, illustrated in this lithograph, secured Ulysses S. Grant's reputation as a fighter, earning him a promotion and Lincoln's personal thanks. The victory ensured Union control of the Mississippi and demoralized the Confederates.

Source: Library of Congress

fend Vicksburg vigorously, and as other points along the Mississippi fell under Union control, the city assumed a new importance in everyone's eyes.

One Union general who appreciated Vicksburg's importance was John A. McClernand. Restless with his position as a subordinate in Ulysses S. Grant's command, McClernand visited Lincoln in October 1862, determined to place before the president his own plan for capturing the river citadel. He proposed to raise his own army to take Vicksburg. He believed he had secured Lincoln's consent, but his orders included a rather significant condition: he would be free to command his own expedition only when Grant judged that he had enough troops to spare.

At the same time, Grant commenced planning to take Vicksburg. Initially he contemplated moving due south through northern Mississippi. Getting wind of McClernand's mission, he decided to take the reinforcements that were gathering at Memphis (presumably to form McClernand's strike force), placed them under William T. Sherman's command, and directed Sherman to ferry down the Mississippi, debark north of Vicksburg, and advance toward the city while Grant resumed his push southward. Confederate cavalry raids broke up Grant's advance by striking at his lines of supply and communication. Unaware that he was on his own, Sherman on December 29 unsuccessfully assaulted the Confederates at Chickasaw Bayou. Adding insult to injury, McClernand arrived in the wake of Sherman's repulse, assumed command, and after consulting with Sherman decided to head up the

Arkansas River and capture Fort Hindman, also known as Arkansas Post, on January 12, 1863.

Reassessing the situation, Grant crossed the Mississippi and began to gather his command along the Louisiana/Arkansas border. McClernand protested being superseded, but Grant prevailed when Lincoln declined to sustain McClernand's claim to independent command. However, the president did not deter McClernand from corresponding with him. Thus, McClernand sent the president letters that proclaimed Grant's unfitness (and McClernand's fitness) for directing operations against Vicksburg. What gave such claims credence was that for the next several months, each of Grant's attempts to take Vicksburg proved a miserable failure. Among those attempts was a decision to renew work on a canal that would divert the Mississippi from Vicksburg: Grant understood that Lincoln took a particular interest in such projects. The area north and west of Vicksburg was cold, wet, swampy, and difficult to traverse. Although Grant believed that waiting for spring and dry ground was the best plan to follow, he dared not pass up any opportunity to try some scheme, if for no other reason than to keep his men busy. It would not do to try Lincoln's patience by doing nothing.

That proved a wise idea, for Lincoln entertained doubts about Grant. Reports describing Grant's army as a group of sickly soldiers led by a bumbling, drunken incompetent arrived in Washington, some courtesy of McClernand. Other critics claimed that Grant's generals were not enthusiastic supporters of administration policy regarding emancipation and enlisting blacks. By March 1863 Lincoln had heard enough. Two representatives made their way west to Grant's command with instructions to relay back what they found. Grant's job was in jeopardy.

Grant responded skillfully to the challenges before him. He befriended the representatives from Washington, who were soon singing his praises to their superiors. He ensured that his generals adhered to administration policy on black enlistment and explicitly endorsed it. He also devised a plan whereby a naval flotilla under the command of David D. Porter would run past the Vicksburg batteries, meet the lead columns of his command south of the city, and ferry them across the Mississippi. Sherman would be left to dupe the Confederate commander, John C. Pemberton, as to Grant's intentions. At the same time, a cavalry raid across central Mississippi provided further distraction. Porter's vessels ran the batteries during the night of April 16; at month's end lead elements of Grant's army landed in Mississippi. On May 1, Grant beat back the Confederates at Port Gibson, and two days later he entered Grand Gulf.

Grant discovered that his original plan, which involved cooperating with his fellow army commander Nathaniel Banks, would not come off in timely fashion. He then decided to strike into the interior, driving a wedge between superior enemy forces before turning west to take Vicksburg. Although supply wagons would carry ammunition and supplies, he intended his army to forage off the land. In a series of battles Grant drove away Confederates gathering at Jackson, turned west to defeat Pemberton at Champion Hill, and pursued him back into

Vicksburg. Failing to overwhelm the defenders in two assaults, Grant settled for a siege, with reinforcements allowing him to fend off Confederate efforts to mount a relief operation. He also took advantage of an administrative slip by McClernand to secure the removal of his troublesome rival. On July 3, Grant met Pemberton to discuss terms of surrender. The following day Union forces took possession of the city, paroling approximately 30,000 Confederates.

Coming as it did simultaneously with the Union victory at Gettysburg, Vicksburg proved a decisive blow. Grant's spectacular triumph helped solidify Union control of the Mississippi River, demoralized the Confederates, and boosted Northern morale. Most important, it secured Grant's reputation, earning him both a promotion to major general in the regular army and Lincoln's personal thanks. At long last the president began to suspect that he had found his general.

See also *Grant, Ulysses S.*

—BROOKS D. SIMPSON

BIBLIOGRAPHY

Ballard, Michael B. *Vicksburg: The Campaign that Opened the Mississippi.* Chapel Hill: University of North Carolina Press, 2004.

Bearss, Edwin C. *The Vicksburg Campaign.* 3 vols. Dayton, Ohio: Morningside, 1985–1986.

Grabau, Warren E. *Ninety-Eight Days: A Geographer's View of the Vicksburg Campaign.* Knoxville: University of Tennessee Press, 2000.

Simpson, Brooks D. *Ulysses S. Grant: Triumph over Adversity, 1822–1865.* New York: Houghton Mifflin, 2000.

Winschel, Terrence J., and William Shea. *Vicksburg Is the Key: The Struggle for the Mississippi River.* Lincoln: University of Nebraska Press, 2003.

Virginia Plan

When Andrew Johnson took over the presidency after Abraham Lincoln's assassination, many Republicans in Congress believed that Johnson was better suited to direct reconstruction than was Lincoln. Not only had Lincoln and the Republican Congress been at odds over reconstruction since the summer of 1864 and the president's pocket veto of the Wade-Davis bill, but more recent events reminded Republicans in Congress of the continuing divide. Perhaps no event illustrated congressional mistrust of Lincoln as vividly as the so-called Virginia Plan, which the president formulated in early April 1865.

The context for the Virginia Plan was the rapid dissolution of Confederate military fortunes in April 1865. The precise occasion was Lincoln's visit to Richmond on April 4–5, just after the Confederate capital had fallen into the hands of Union forces. Before visiting Richmond, Lincoln had met with his top military advisers, Ulysses Grant, William Sherman, and David Dixon Porter, at City Point, Virginia. There, in the context of a war that was rapidly coming to an end, Lincoln expressed his desire for a liberal peace that would encourage Southern soldiers to lay down their weapons and return home. Lincoln hoped to take a concrete step in this direction when he met with the Union commander of the occupation of Richmond, Major General Godfrey Weitzel; Gustavus Meyer, a prominent Richmond lawyer; and John A. Campbell, the assistant war secretary of the Confederacy and an important Virginia politician who had occupied a seat on the U.S. Supreme Court. At that meeting, Lincoln informed Campbell that three things were necessary to end the war: national authority had to be reestablished, emancipation recognized, and hostilities totally ceased. Campbell believed that most Virginians recognized that slavery was finished; moreover, a general amnesty would most likely convince them to lay down their arms and come back into the Union.

Hoping to obtain an agreement formally ending military operations from a recognized Confederate authority, Lincoln suggested that Campbell relay to members of the Virginia legislature that they would be given safe conduct passes if they assembled in Richmond for the purpose of formally withdrawing Virginia from the Confederacy. According to Campbell, if the legislature were to meet, it would repeal Virginia's ordinance of secession, and that would prompt Lee and other Virginians to put down their arms and return to their homes.

Although Lincoln would later tell Grant that he expected little to come from this gesture, the president's actions would quickly attract negative publicity. Although Lincoln had wanted Godfrey Weitzel not to publicize the offer, Weitzel felt compelled to publish it in the local Richmond papers so that the members of the Virginia legislature would be aware of the invitation. When Lincoln returned to Washington, D.C., from Richmond on April 9, he would find the entire city buzzing as a result of the publication of his offer. Critics of Lincoln's invitation pointed out that it contradicted the oft-stated position that Confederate institutions and authorities had no real legal standing. Additionally, the plan completely undercut the legitimacy of the loyal Restored Government of Virginia, which had acted as the de facto government of Virginia shortly after the state seceded in April 1861. Among the biggest critics of the Virginia Plan were members of Lincoln's cabinet, and among his most vociferous congressional detractors were the members of the Joint Committee on the Conduct of the War. Several of its members had also recently visited Richmond, and they were appalled and angry when they read about Lincoln's invitation in the local papers.

Embarrassed and surprised, Lincoln met with Francis Pierpont, governor in the Restored Government of Virginia, on April 10 to explain his intentions in calling the rebel legislature together. At Lincoln's prompting and with his support, Pierpont had been a significant force in the organization of the Restored Government of Virginia early in 1861. This government had helped carve out West Virginia as an independent state and drafted a new state constitution for Virginia in 1864 that abolished slavery. Initially the Restored Government primarily represented Unionist western Virginia. With the eventual statehood of West Virginia, the Restored Government consisted of Virginia's eastern shore and areas surrounding Norfolk and Alexandria. Lincoln had sincerely hoped that it would form the core of a reconstructed state of Virginia once the war ended. Indeed, throughout the war both Lincoln and Congress had recognized the legitimacy of Pierpont's government. In his lengthy conference with Pierpont, Lincoln told the governor that his intention was never to replace Pierpont's government; he had extended the offer to the rebel legislature for it to do one thing—namely, end the war by withdrawing the Army of Northern Virginia from the field. Had he known that Lee's surrender was only a few days away, Lincoln claimed, he would never have extended the invitation.

Despite his reassurances to Pierpont, Lincoln did not immediately instruct Weitzel to withdraw the invitation for the Virginia legislature to meet. On the contrary, Lincoln asked Weitzel whether the offer was generating positive responses on the part of rebel legislators. Then on April 12, Lincoln instructed Weitzel to cancel the order. What prompted Lincoln's action was the receipt of a letter that John Campbell had submitted to Weitzel. In it Campbell claimed that Lincoln's intent in calling the legislature together was to negotiate the resumption of relations between the federal government and the state of Virginia. Campbell also inferred that emancipation was still negotiable and not carved in stone. Campbell's letter prompted Lincoln to direct Weitzel to withdraw the invitation.

Although Lincoln claimed that he never recognized the legitimacy of the rebel legislature of Virginia, his actions in the Virginia plan confirmed the worst fears of his critics. Many Republicans in Congress were convinced that Lincoln's approach to reconstruction was too soft and conciliatory, and they considered the Virginia plan a prime example of Lincoln's shortcomings when it came to postwar planning. To them it demonstrated that Lincoln and the executive branch could not be trusted to carry out reconstruction properly. Lincoln's explanation that he imagined only a limited role for the "rebel" legislature was probably accurate, but given the divisive and rancorous debates that had already broken out over the reconstruction issue, it is hard to explain how Lincoln did not foresee that his Virginia plan would upset his fellow Republicans.

—Bruce Tap

BIBLIOGRAPHY

Donald, David. *Lincoln.* New York: Simon and Schuster, 1995.

Harris, William C. *With Charity for All: Lincoln and the Restoration of the Union.* Lexington: University Press of Kentucky, 1997.

Thomas, Benjamin P. *Abraham Lincoln: A Biography.* New York: Knopf, 1952.

Volunteers, Ninety-Day

On April 15, 1861, the day after Fort Sumter fell to the Confederacy, Abraham Lincoln used his authority under a 1795 militia act to call for 75,000 state militiamen to muster into national service for a period of ninety days. The U.S. Army numbered slightly over 16,000 soldiers, and the Union needed more men to suppress the Confederate insurrection. Some historians suggest that Lincoln's call for ninety-day enlistments reflected a common assumption that any conflict would be brief and easily won. Others maintain that Lincoln never expected 75,000 three-month men to suffice. The ninety-day period stemmed from statutory time limits governing the president's ability to bring militias into national service without first securing congressional consent. As soon as possible, Lincoln would seek larger numbers of longer-term volunteers.

Reactions to Lincoln's initial levy of militia varied. Four of the eight slave states that were still in the Union—Virginia, North Carolina, Tennessee, and Arkansas—seceded and joined the Confederacy. Missouri and Kentucky declared that they would not send troops. The governor of Delaware tepidly said that he would not officially commit Delaware units but would not stop volunteers from acting on their own. Maryland's governor tried to limit where and how Maryland units could be used.

Casualties occurred in Maryland on April 19, 1861, when the Sixth Massachusetts, rushing to Washington in response to Lincoln's call for volunteers, clashed with a pro-secession mob in Baltimore. In an effort to avert similar incidents Lincoln acceded to the governor's request that Northern troops bypass Baltimore, but he rejected demands to prevent them from passing through Maryland at all, insisting that the volunteers had to have access to the capital. Because of turmoil in Maryland and elsewhere, Lincoln suspended the writ of *habeas corpus* along the route from Philadelphia to Washington, a controversial decision but one that Lincoln believed necessary to enable militias to reach Washington.

Anxieties escalated in the capital as rumors of imminent Confederate attack swirled, while nervous residents waited for the militiamen to arrive. By late April, however, the early trickle of troops built to a flood, and Lincoln had all the ninety-day men he wanted. The tide of forces rose because of the response to Lincoln's request in the Northern states. Tens of thousands of men volunteered, many motivated by patriotic outrage over the attack on Fort Sumter and many simply seeking adventure. Several Northern governors sought increases in their states' quotas, unwilling to be outdone by other states.

Lincoln had, in fact, earlier received advice to call for larger numbers but settled on 75,000 for both political and practical reasons. Politically he worried that immediately raising a massive army would exacerbate negative reactions in the Border States. In practical terms, he knew that the federal government could not yet feed, arm, organize, or transport vast numbers. Even 75,000 strained existing capacity.

The ninety-day volunteers constituted a hodgepodge of forces, differing in training, discipline, equipment, and dress. Neither Lincoln nor Congress expected these three-month men to subdue the Confederacy. When Congress convened in July 1861, it endorsed most of Lincoln's earlier actions and exceeded his request for 400,000 three-year volunteers. Congress authorized 500,000 three-year enlistments before the first Battle of Bull Run (July 21, 1861) and 500,000 more shortly thereafter.

Meanwhile pressures mounted to use the volunteers already assembled. Some newspapers, politicians, and others impatiently demanded action. Lincoln, alert to the importance of public morale and worried that hastily assembled forces might dissolve when ninety-day enlistments expired, agreed that Union commanders should engage the enemy. Warned that Union armies were not ready for combat, Lincoln reasoned that with troops on both sides similarly green, neither would have an advantage. Some historians accept Lincoln's logic, but others point out that Lincoln overlooked both the greater complexities that Union forces would face in taking the offensive and the psychological effects of short-term enlistments on the ninety-day volunteers, in contrast to the longer commitments characteristic of Confederate units.

Although regular army officers disdained short-term enlistees, three-month men provided the majority of United States forces in the early summer of 1861. Union general Irvin McDowell hoped to exploit his numeric superiority over opposing forces in the vicinity of Bull Run, but delays in setting his plans in motion allowed more Confederates to arrive in time to participate in the engagement. Both sides fought tenaciously on July 21, but Union troops ultimately withdrew. Some (usually alleged to be ninety-day men) fled in panic. Reports also circulated of ninety-day volunteers who departed on the very morning of the battle at Bull Run, when their enlistments expired, bearing out the suspicion that some three-month volunteers had no compunctions about leaving as soon as they discharged their initial commitment, regardless of the circumstances.

The debacle at Bull Run, often exaggerated by Confederate propagandists and Union finger-pointers, failed to shatter Union morale. Instead, Northern will and commitment hardened. With enrollment of a million three-year men sanctioned by Congress, Union armies rapidly eliminated three-month units. Many of the approximately 90,000 ninety-day volunteers reenlisted for three years, and some ninety-day regiments converted themselves into three-year units. Organization, training, and discipline received more rigorous emphasis as true armies took shape with these deeper commitments in mind.

See also *Conscription Act; Draft, Military*

—CARA L. SHELLY

BIBLIOGRAPHY

Detzer, David. *Donnybrook: The Battle of Bull Run, 1861.* Orlando, Fla.: Harcourt, 2004.

Donald, David Herbert. *Lincoln.* New York: Simon and Schuster, 1995.

Goodwin, Doris Kearns. *Team of Rivals: The Political Genius of Abraham Lincoln.* New York: Simon and Schuster, 2005.

Marvel, William. *Mr. Lincoln Goes to War.* Boston: Houghton, Mifflin, 2006.

McPherson, James M. *Battle Cry of Freedom: The Civil War Era.* New York: Oxford University Press, 1988.

Oates, Stephen B. *With Malice toward None: The Life of Abraham Lincoln.* New York: Mentor, 1978.

Paludan, Phillip Shaw. *"A People's Contest": The Union and the Civil War, 1861–1865.* New York: Harper and Row, 1988.

Perrett, Geoffrey. *Lincoln's War: The Untold Story of America's Greatest President as Commander in Chief.* New York: Random House, 2004.

Rawley, James A. *Turning Points of the Civil War.* Lincoln: University of Nebraska Press, 1966.

Wade, Benjamin Franklin

Born on October 27, 1800, in Feeding Hills, Massachusetts, Benjamin Franklin Wade became one of the most prominent Republican senators in the mid-nineteenth century. Following his elder brothers to the Western Reserve area of northern Ohio, Wade was trained as a lawyer and began practicing in Jefferson, Ohio. Wade entered politics as a Whig in 1837 when he was elected to the Ohio state senate. Although he identified with such traditional Whig causes as federally financed internal improvements and protective tariffs, Wade also shared the reformist zeal, working to repeal Ohio's black codes and supporting the antislavery movement. In 1851 he was elected to the United States Senate.

After passage of the Kansas-Nebraska Act of 1854, Wade began distancing himself from the Whig Party and cooperating with so-called fusionist elements that eventually became the Republican Party. During the remainder of the 1850s Wade worked for the restriction of slavery in the federal territories, particularly after he was appointed chair of the Senate Committee on Territories in 1857. During the secession crisis Wade advocated no compromise with the seceded states. Once war broke out, he was an adamant advocate of vigorous war against the South. As chair of the controversial Joint Committee on the Conduct of the War, he had a firsthand view of Union military policy. During the Reconstruction era, Wade quickly became identified with radical Reconstruction and favored such measures as black civil rights and suffrage as embodied in the Fourteenth and Fifteenth amendments. A vociferous critic of President Andrew Johnson, Wade strongly advocated impeachment of the seventeenth president. Because Wade was president pro tempore of the Senate, had Johnson been removed from office, he would have become president. After being defeated for a fourth Senate term in 1869, Wade never again ran for public office. Afflicted with typhoid fever, Wade died on March 2, 1878.

Wade did not have warm relations with Abraham Lincoln. Early in Lincoln's administration, Wade and other Republicans worried that Lincoln was dominated by secretary of state William H. Seward, who was quickly becoming the bête noire of party radicals. As chairman of the Joint Committee on the Conduct of the War, Wade frequently clashed with Lincoln on matters pertaining to army leadership and strategy. As the war progressed, their relations seemed to deteriorate. Wade was part of a group of Senate Republicans who tried to force Lincoln to remove Seward from his cabinet after the Battle of Fredericksburg (December 13, 1862). The most serious rift occurred after Lincoln pocket-vetoed the Wade-Davis reconstruction bill,

Benjamin Franklin Wade, a prominent Republican senator in the mid-1800s, was a reformer and advocated no compromise with the seceded states after the war. Wade clashed with Lincoln over military matters and the Wade-Davis bill, which differed from Lincoln's plan for Reconstruction.
Source: The Granger Collection, New York

which the Senate passed on July 2, 1864. Named after its sponsors, Wade and Maryland Republican congressman Henry Winter Davis, the bill was decidedly different from Lincoln's reconstruction plan, which required only 10 percent of the voters in seceded states to take an oath of allegiance to the Union. The Wade-Davis bill required 50 percent of voters to swear an oath that they had never voluntarily given aid to the Confederacy. The bill also required each state to abolish slavery in its constitution before being readmitted to the Union. Lincoln disagreed with the measure and employed the rarely used pocket veto—allowing the bill to go unsigned while the congressional session expired. Lincoln's action prompted a split with party radicals that threatened to divide the Republican Party and nearly jeopardized the president's chances for reelection in November 1864. After Lincoln was assassinated by John Wilkes Booth, Wade was one of several Republicans who believed that Vice President Andrew Johnson would provide bolder and more aggressive leadership. The Ohio radical was quickly and tragically shown to be mistaken.

—BRUCE TAP

BIBLIOGRAPHY

Trefousse, Hans L. *Benjamin Franklin Wade: Radical Republican from Ohio.* New York: Twayne, 1963.

Wade-Davis Bill

The Wade-Davis bill was the most visible and visceral manifestation of the friction that existed throughout Abraham Lincoln's presidency between the president and Congress. It brought on a battle that threatened Lincoln's reelection prospects in 1864 and challenged the Union coalition that had successfully held together while prosecuting the war. Because it occurred at the moment in Lincoln's presidency when his popularity had reached its ebb, and when members of his own party were holding meetings for the purpose of nominating a different candidate for president, its potential impact on the history of the war and the future of the nation was enormous.

The president and the Radical Republicans in Congress had jockeyed for political advantage and control of wartime policies almost from the moment Congress gathered in special session in 1861. Issues then concerned government policy toward slaves belonging to Southerners, government policy regarding emancipation, whether war policy should be "hard" or "soft" toward the Southern population, and who ultimately controlled the leadership of the military. Lincoln's issuance of the Emancipation Proclamation on January 1, 1863, had doused much of the radical fire of the Thirty-seventh Congress.

That left Lincoln one large and significant hurdle to surmount: With military victory in sight, Lincoln addressed the political issue of how to restore the states of the Confederacy to the United States without planting the seeds for a future war. What would be the minimum adherence to the Constitution required before home rule could safely be returned to the South? And what assurances would have to be enacted to be certain that slavery would not return? Looming even larger was the question of who would have control of the process—the president or Congress.

The president officially had control of the areas that were in rebellion but were currently under the control of U.S. military forces because he was the commander in chief, and martial law was in effect in those places. However there would come a time when there was not a state of war or rebellion, and yet normal relations between the seceded states and the country had not been resolved. Some in Congress, such as the radicals Charles Sumner in the Senate and Thaddeus Stevens in the House, argued that these states had effectively committed "state suicide" by seceding and thereby lost any status they had formerly had as states. Sumner claimed that they had reverted to territorial status, and Congress had the authority to make rules for and regulate the territories. Stevens took the interpretation even further: By waging war against the United States and having unconditionally surrendered, those states were nothing more than "conquered provinces" and had no rights whatsoever under either the Constitution or any international treaty.

Lincoln first broached the subject in his December 1863 annual message to Congress. In it he proposed a Proclamation of Amnesty and Reconstruction. Proceeding under his presidential powers, including the pardon power, he proposed that when 10 percent of the voters who had voted in the 1860 presidential election signed loyalty oaths affirming their allegiance to the Constitution of the United States, they could then hold a state constitutional convention that would renounce the secession decree that the state had adopted and draft a new constitution that did not permit slavery. If the constitution defined a republican form of government, then the state should be qualified at that point to elect representatives to Congress and resume normal relations within the United States.

Lincoln's proposal also called for amnesty and restoration of the right to own property for nearly all Confederates who had supported the rebellion, except those who had been serving in Congress or the federal judiciary when they left to serve the Confederacy; Confederate military officers above the rank of colonel or naval officers above the rank of lieutenant; Confederate civil and diplomatic officials; commissioned officers in the United States Army or Navy who had left their posts to serve the rebellion; and those who had treated prisoners, black or white, "otherwise than lawfully as prisoners of war." The proclamation was a very generous plan that contained no acrimonious or punitive features, and it was highly praised upon its release. However with the passage of time, the radicals in Congress began to snipe at it for being too lenient and making it too easy for traitors to escape the consequences of their disloyalty. At least two things are clear about Lincoln's policy. First, he had changed his thinking since his first inaugural address, when he had doubted that a majority of the legal voters of any Southern state except South Carolina favored disunion. His 10 percent figure would seem to be a concession to the fact that the rebellion had more popular support in the South than he had imagined. Second, it revealed that he was not going to back off on emancipation.

The Wade-Davis bill, Congress's alternative to Lincoln's plan, was first introduced in the House of Representatives in February 1864 by the radical representative Henry Winter Davis. Davis did not care for the manner in which the Louisiana reconstruction government had been set up, and he was angry at Lincoln for not having supported him in a struggle against fellow Marylander Montgomery Blair for control of the Maryland Republican Party. Sen. Benjamin Franklin Wade, who was always ready to take the other side in a squabble with Abraham Lincoln, sponsored the Senate version of the bill. After many amendments and much debate, the bill that finally emerged in July, just before the adjournment of Congress, required much more of Southerners than Lincoln proposed if they were to win back their vacated seats in Congress. It required the president to appoint a military governor to govern the state, in what would be a continuation of martial law, until such time as "half" of the antebellum voting population had signed a loyalty oath and further agree to support all laws and proclamations relating to slavery enacted during the war. At that point, those voters who had signed an "iron-clad" oath claiming that they had never supported the rebellion would be able to draft a constitution that would first have to abolish slavery and repudiate all Confederate debt undertaken by that state.

The Wade-Davis bill was, of course, intended to keep the Confederate states from making any quick return to normal relations within the United States and to make them beholden to Congress to ever be able to return. It was a far cry from Lincoln's forgiving method for restoration. Among many Republicans' points of disagreement with Lincoln's plan was the very notion that the executive branch of government, rather than the legislative branch, would control the process. Wade, Davis, and many other members of the Republican Party in Congress were determined to challenge the idea that a non-vengeful president should have control over such an important process. After long and contentious debates over the legislation, it finally passed on the last day of the session. But when Lincoln came to the Capitol to sign the usual stack of legislation just before adjournment, he set the Wade-Davis bill aside and would not sign it. The action, or inaction, constituted a "pocket veto," since the Constitution requires that the president must have ten days, during which Congress is in session, to sign legislation. If he does not sign or veto within ten days, then the legislation becomes law anyway. But lacking those ten days the bill lapses and has no more effect than vetoed legislation.

Though Lincoln was not required to provide written reasons for his action, as he would be in the case of a veto, in this instance he did so anyway. The already-outraged sponsors of the bill became even more furious after the pocket veto and began drafting what would become known as the Wade-Davis Manifesto. According to Lincoln's presidential secretaries John Nicolay and John Hay, it was "the most vigorous an attack that was ever directed against the President from his own party during his term." Its authors concluded the manifesto with the words: "A more studied outrage on the legislative authority of the people has never been perpetrated." Lincoln "must understand that our support is of a cause and not of a man; that the authority of Congress is paramount and must be respected." Appearing three months before the 1864 presidential election, and issued after more than three years of bloody, stalemated war, it had the potential to be very damaging, however much of the party leadership, the national press, and even a number of War Democrats took the side of the president. Likewise, General William T. Sherman's capture of Atlanta, Georgia, in September 1864 provided a significant morale boost that helped Lincoln gain reelection over his Democratic opponent, General George McClellan. The manifesto did not have nearly the effect that its authors had hoped it would. But Lincoln's assassination in April 1865 would reopen the door to congressional control of reconstruction.

See also *Reconstruction*

—DAVID E. LONG

BIBLIOGRAPHY

Goodwin, Doris Kearns. *Team of Rivals: The Political Genius of Abraham Lincoln.* New York: Simon and Schuster, 2005.

Long, David E. *The Jewel of Liberty: Abraham Lincoln's Re-election and the End of Slavery.* Mechanicsburg, Pa.: Stackpole, 1994.

McPherson, James M. *Battle Cry of Freedom: The Civil War Era.* New York: Oxford University Press, 1988.

War Democrats

The War Democrats were a faction of the Democratic Party that joined with Republicans at the outbreak of the Civil War in support of the war effort and the policies of the Lincoln administration. The group differed from "regular," "mainstream," or "legitimist" Democrats, who continued to oppose the Republicans on issues pertaining to civil liberties, economic policies, and emancipation, as well as Peace Democrats who called for an armistice and negotiated peace. Illinois senator Stephen A. Douglas, when he offered his support to Lincoln and the administration in the wake of Fort Sumter, became the natural leader of the group, and he declared that those who opposed the war were traitors. Essentially Douglas divided the Democratic Party into loyal and disloyal camps. When Douglas died on June 3, 1861, John J. Crittenden's resolution stating that the war was being fought to maintain the Union and not to interfere with slavery provided a foundation for the War Democrats' position throughout 1861.

At the state level, War Democrats joined with Republicans in fusion movements throughout the North in the fall of 1861. Under the "Union Party" or "People's Party" label, War Democrats' influence varied. In Massachusetts, for example, Republicans rebuffed War Democrats, and in Pennsylvania, War Democrats joined with Constitutional Unionists in opposition to Republicans. Yet in Ohio, War Democrat David Tod was elected governor on a Union Party ticket. In general, War Democrats added to Republican margins of victory across the North in 1861. Emancipation, however, divided the War Democrats as early as 1862, as did conflicts over civil liberties and opposition to the arrest of former congressman and Peace Democrat Clement Vallandigham. War Democrats throughout the North realigned themselves with the mainstream Democrats, even as their influence waned within the party.

From the first days of his administration, Lincoln recognized the importance of the War Democrats to his goals. Elected without a popular majority, Lincoln believed it was important to cultivate support for his administration and his party among this group. War Democrats' support was crucial to Lincoln's strategy for keeping the Border States in the Union. Consequently Lincoln appointed Democrats as generals, including George B. McClellan, Benjamin Butler, and William Rosecrans. He appointed Joseph Holt of Kentucky judge advocate general. Indeed, Lincoln's effort to build a broad base of moderate support came at the expense of radicals within his own party, many of whom chafed at the advance of Democrats and complained that Lincoln was altogether too slow to move toward emancipation and too conciliatory to the border slave states.

When Lincoln revoked General John C. Frémont's proclamation in the Department of the West that freed the slaves of those who aided the rebellion, Radical Republicans were outraged, but Lincoln was hailed by War Democrats and Kentucky remained in the Union. Even as War Democrats' influence declined steadily in their own party, they played a pivotal role in ending slavery. Lincoln's Preliminary Emancipation Proclamation undermined War Democrats in the elections of 1862 because it widened the breach between mainstream Democrats and Republicans, alienating racially conservative War Democrats who rejoined the mainstream Democrats. From 1862 through 1864, mainstream and Peace Democrats grew in influence, gaining victories in state and local elections. The influence of Peace Democrats was evident at the Democratic National Convention in 1864. General George B. McClellan, a War Democrat, was nominated for president, but Clement Vallandigham drafted the party platform that called for armistice and negotiated peace.

At their national convention, Republicans used the nomination of Tennessee War Democrat Andrew Johnson for vice president to strengthen Democrats' and Southerners' support for the National Union Party, as the Republicans labeled themselves in 1864. Yet when Lincoln issued his Niagara Letter in July 1864, which made emancipation a prerequisite for re-union, some War Democrats withdrew their support. Sen. Reverdy Johnson of Maryland, for example, opposed the administration because he believed only a constitutional amendment or state action could end slavery. War Democrats who continued to sustain Lincoln were crucial in the months after Lincoln's reelection, as the president exerted his influence to secure passage of the Thirteenth Amendment in Congress. As early as 1863, some War Democrats called for a constitutional amendment ending slavery. On January 31, 1865, Congress passed the measure 119–56; Democrats provided the necessary votes to send the amendment to the states for ratification.

—Christine Dee

BIBLIOGRAPHY

Dell, Christopher. *Lincoln and the War Democrats: The Grand Erosion of Conservative Tradition.* Rutherford, N.J.: Fairleigh Dickinson University Press, 1975.

Silbey, Joel H. *A Respectable Minority: The Democratic Party in the Civil War Era, 1860–1868.* New York: Norton, 1977.

Smith, Adam I. P. *No Party Now: Politics in the Civil War North.* New York: Oxford University Press, 2006.

Vorenberg, Michael. *Final Freedom: The Civil War, the Abolition of Slavery, and the Thirteenth Amendment.* New York: Cambridge University Press, 2001.

Weber, Jennifer L. *Copperheads: The Rise and Fall of Lincoln's Opponents in the North.* New York: Oxford University Press, 2006.

Washington, D.C.

The capital city of the United States, encompassing land from both Virginia and Maryland, was chosen in the early 1790s. French émigré engineer Pierre-Charles L'Enfant designed the city's layout and incorporated wide streets and grand views, with the Capitol perched conspicuously upon a hill. In 1800 the three branches of government moved from Philadelphia to Washington.

Abraham Lincoln first arrived in Washington on December 2, 1847, to begin his term as a United States congressman. He and his wife, Mary, took up residence in a boardinghouse near the Capitol, located on the present site of the Library of Congress. In 1847 Washington had a population of around 40,000, including 2,000 slaves and 8,000 free blacks. The District of Columbia was quite cosmopolitan, with people from all over the country and the world. Yet most of the streets were unpaved, and the city's proximity to the swampy lowlands of the Potomac River made the weather muggy and often unpleasant.

While Lincoln was in Congress, Washington was a focal point in the growing debate over slavery. Most people recognized that the institution was protected in the states. The District of Columbia, however, was federal property. Many antislavery advocates petitioned Congress for an end to the institution there. Lincoln agreed that Congress had the power to abolish slavery in Washington, and while in Congress he drafted a bill to gradually end slavery in the District. His proposal called for a referendum on slavery in Washington and recommended gradual and compensated emancipation. Despite early support among some colleagues, Lincoln's plan met fierce resistance when it was made public. Consequently he decided against introducing a bill.

Washington continued to grow between Lincoln's time as a congressman and his election to the presidency in 1860. Major additions were made to the Capitol in the 1850s, the first Smithsonian building was finished, and construction of a large obelisk monument to George Washington had begun. Despite this progress, the District and the nation faced a crisis when Lincoln returned as president in 1861. His election had sparked Southern secession and the likelihood of civil war. Washington, D.C., was surrounded by two slave states, Virginia and Maryland, and many people were hostile to the Union and Lincoln. Eventually, of course, Virginia would secede. Allan Pinkerton, head of a national detective agency, had warned Lincoln of an assassination plot on his inaugural trip to Washington. Lincoln grudgingly agreed to sneak into the capital city at night by train. He arrived in Washington without incident, but when word of the secret train ride became public, newspapers and critics mocked him.

Washington, D.C.

On April 12, 1861, just over a month after Lincoln's inauguration, Confederate forces captured the federal garrison at Fort Sumter, South Carolina. Following Lincoln's call for 75,000 volunteers to suppress the rebellion, Virginia seceded and joined the Confederacy. Maryland's future in the Union seemed tenuous. The safety of Washington became a great concern for Lincoln and the rest of the loyal states. Few soldiers were stationed in the District, leaving the seat of government vulnerable. A contingent of 120 westerners in Washington offered some military defense. Led in part by Kansas senator James H. Lane, the Frontier Guard served as Lincoln's personal bodyguard until reinforcements arrived. Getting more troops to the capital proved difficult. A mob in Baltimore attacked soldiers from Massachusetts on their way to Washington. Four soldiers and nine civilians were killed. Lincoln assured Maryland's governor, Thomas Hicks, that Union soldiers would go around Baltimore to avoid further problems. When angry Marylanders demanded that no federal troops cross through their state, Lincoln stood firm and declared his commitment to protect the capital.

Secessionists in Maryland burned bridges and cut telegraph lines. Officials in Washington expected an attack from Virginia at any point. Lincoln was seen pacing in the White House and wondering aloud when reinforcements would come. By the end of April, thousands of Union troops filed into Washington. Finding room for the soldiers was difficult, and some men even camped inside the Capitol.

The Confederacy established its capital at Richmond, Virginia, around 100 miles to the south. The close proximity of the two opposing governments guaranteed that northern Virginia would see some of the most brutal military battles of the war. Washington became a hub of military activity. By the end of the war, the District had sixteen hospitals for wounded and ailing soldiers. Five prisons were also established for Confederate captives. Lincoln not only faced the problem of leading a nation during wartime, but he was daily surrounded by the horrors and realities of war.

In 1864 General Jubal A. Early marched a force of 15,000 Confederates into Maryland and swung south to threaten the capital. Officials in Washington panicked, as the city seemed unprepared for an assault by a veteran Confederate army. A ragtag Union force stalled Early's men at the Monocacy River for a day, giving reinforcements time to arrive. Early's men assaulted Fort Stevens in the northern part of the District in mid-July. Lincoln observed some of the fighting at the fort, standing so close to the combat that bullets struck men near him on two different occasions. He seemed unconcerned with his own safety and only left his exposed position after General Horatio G. Wright threatened to forcibly remove him. Early's attack on Washington failed, and the Confederate army retreated into Virginia.

Lincoln accomplished his earlier goal of abolishing slavery in the District. On April 16, 1862, he signed a bill that ended the institution, provided compensation to slave owners, and authorized the government to partially fund the colonization of any blacks in the city who wanted to leave the country. In the end no one accepted the offer and the appropriation went unused.

On April 14, 1865, John Wilkes Booth shot Lincoln at Ford's Theatre. The president was carried across the street to a residence, where he died the following morning. Both locations now stand as museums and memorials to Lincoln. Washington, D.C., is also home to the Lincoln Memorial, a large monument that immortalizes the president in marble, on the western edge of the National Mall.

—Ian Michael Spurgeon

BIBLIOGRAPHY

Brooks, Noah. *Washington, D.C., in Lincoln's Time.* Chicago: Quadrangle, 1971.

Furgurson, Ernest B. *Freedom Rising: Washington in the Civil War.* New York: Knopf, 2004.

Kimmel, Stanley Preston. *Mr. Lincoln's Washington.* New York: Coward-McCann, 1957.

Leech, Margaret. *Reveille in Washington, 1860–1865.* New York: Harper, 1941.

Weed, Thurlow

Thurlow Weed (1797–1882) was a powerful Albany, New York, newspaperman and a confidant of William Henry Seward, secretary of state from 1861 to 1869. Like Lincoln, Weed was a longtime Whig who joined the Republican Party in 1856. At the Chicago Republican National Convention in 1860 Weed managed Seward's candidacy for president. Sensing that Seward's strength as the front-runner would decline after the first ballot, Weed, through a subordinate, approached William Butler, a Lincoln associate, offering the vice presidential nomination to Lincoln. Aware of Lincoln's position, Butler immediately replied that "under no circumstances could [Lincoln's] name be used in a second place on the ticket."

Though he was bitterly disappointed when Seward lost the nomination to Lincoln, after the convention Weed accepted an invitation to visit Lincoln in Springfield. The meeting went extremely well. Weed surprised Lincoln by making no demands upon him in exchange for the active support of the "Albany Regency" in the election. Lincoln promised that if elected he would pursue a policy of fair play in awarding patronage. Both men kept their promises. Weed worked diligently for Lincoln's success in the campaign and kept him informed of the political situation in the East. As the election approached, Weed flooded New York City and other vulnerable places in the state with speakers and "Wide Awake" party activists to beat back a late effort at fusion by anti-Lincoln candidates. Though New York City gave the fusion ticket a 30,000-vote majority, Lincoln won the Empire State by a margin of 50,000 votes.

After the election Lincoln chose Weed's friend Seward as his secretary of state. While Lincoln was considering the appointment, Weed again visited Springfield at Lincoln's invitation to discuss political matters. Weed hoped to influence the president-elect to Seward's way of thinking on the selection of appointees in the new administration. Weed also had a plan to check Southern secession and save the Union, a plan that he had printed in his *Albany Evening Journal* and shared with Seward before he left for Springfield. Weed proposed the revival of the Missouri Compromise line to separate slavery from freedom in the territories. In Springfield Lincoln made it clear to Weed that he opposed any deviation from the Republican platform against the extension of slavery in the territories. Weed also failed to persuade Lincoln to appoint a majority of former Whigs to his cabinet.

When the war began, Weed threw his support behind Lincoln's policies. In November 1861 Seward sent him to Europe to counter Confederate propaganda. After his return, Weed became alarmed at the rise of radicals in the Republican Party who demanded emancipation as a war aim. Weed opposed Lincoln's Emancipation Proclamation and became upset when the president appointed his political enemies, radical supporters of secretary of the Treasury Salmon P. Chase, to positions in the lucrative New York Custom House. When the war became stalemated during the summer of 1864 and Lincoln's popularity plummeted, Weed considered voting for George B. McClellan, the Democratic candidate for president. But he came over to Lincoln after the president replaced the radicals in the Custom House with men acceptable to him. Weed took charge of the Lincoln forces in the state and pressed officeholders for contributions to the campaign.

In early 1865 Lincoln sought Weed's assistance in securing the appointment of former New York governor Edwin D. Morgan as secretary of the Treasury. When the effort failed, Lincoln had Weed approach Hugh McCulloch about the position. McCulloch eventually accepted the post. Weed praised Lincoln's second inaugural address for its "magnanimous spirit" toward the South, and after the war he supported President Andrew Johnson's conservative reconstruction policy.

See also *Seward, William*

—WILLIAM C. HARRIS

BIBLIOGRAPHY

Basler, Roy P., ed. *The Collected Works of Abraham Lincoln.* New Brunswick, N.J.: Rutgers University Press, 1953–1955, 1974, 1990.

Harris, William C. *Lincoln's Last Months.* Cambridge, Mass.: Belknap Press of Harvard University Press, 2004.

Lincoln, Abraham. *Papers.* Manuscript Division, Library of Congress, Washington, D.C.

Van Deusen, Glyndon G. *Thurlow Weed: Wizard of the Lobby.* Boston: Little, Brown, 1947.

Weed, Thurlow. *Life of Thurlow Weed, Including His Autobiography and a Memoir.* 2 vols. Boston: Houghton, Mifflin, 1883.

Welles, Gideon

Gideon Welles (1802–1878) served as secretary of the navy in the Lincoln administration and beyond. Born at Glastonbury, Connecticut, on July 1, 1802, he was the son of Anne and Samuel Welles, the latter a successful merchant who pushed Gideon toward the law. During a trip to Pennsylvania in 1822, Gideon spent time with his uncles, lawyers themselves, who encouraged him to take up the profession. In 1825 he read law under Hartford attorney William W. Ellsworth. He also became editor of the *Hartford Times and Weekly Advertiser,* which brought him to the attention of local political groups as a staunch supporter of Jacksonian Democracy. Through political influence Welles became postmaster of Hartford in 1836. In 1846 he became the first civilian to head a bureau in the Department of the Navy, as chief of the Bureau for Provision and Clothing during and after the Mexican War.

During the 1850s Welles, an ardent abolitionist, broke with the Democratic Party and joined the Republican Party. In the presidential campaign of 1860 Welles campaigned vigorously for Abraham Lincoln, helping him to win Connecticut. In return Lincoln chose him to be the New Englander in his cabinet, appointing Welles secretary of the navy. Welles's Democratic background—he had served in the Department of the Navy under President James Polk—also helped balance the cabinet politically. When Welles took office, he had to contend with an almost nonexistent navy and a divided nation. Like Lincoln, Welles sought to bring the South back into the Union as rapidly as possible and fought the influence of hard-line Radical Republicans, who wished to punish the South for seceding by attacking slavery.

Almost immediately Welles had to prepare for General Winfield Scott's Operation Anaconda, which proposed a naval blockade of the South. To do so Welles first had to build a navy. Exercising judicious executive oversight, Welles set out to build dozens of ships and to convert merchant vessels for military purposes. Within months of the attack on Fort Sumter, the Union fleet's effort to assert control over the Southern coast was well under way. As the war progressed, Welles embraced technological innovations such as ironclad battleships, with the guidance and cooperation of assistant secretary of the navy Gustavus Fox. The ironclads proved a masterful achievement of the American navy.

Welles steadfastly supported Lincoln's vision of reconciliation with the South, and though he feared that it might steel the South's will to fight on, he quietly backed Lincoln's call for the emancipation of slaves in 1862. As the war dragged on, Welles remained true to the president's vision and proved himself a loyal and trusted confidant. During the cabinet crisis of late 1862 and early 1863, for instance, Welles led the way in rallying the cabinet and urging Lincoln to disregard the hue and cry for the removal of secretary of state William Seward, whom Senate Republicans had accused of undermining the president. Even as the war's end came into view, Welles continued to resist the radicals' calls for harsh punishment of the South, believing that Lincoln's more moderate message of reconciliation was the correct one. After Lincoln's assassination, Welles held firm to Lincoln's view and was one of the few members of Lincoln's cabinet to continue to serve in the Andrew Johnson administration, consistently advising Johnson to stay a course of reconciliation with the South and resist the demands of the radicals. After his time as secretary, Wells devoted his energy to revising his wartime diaries for publication. He died from a streptococcus infection in 1878.

See also *Cabinet, Lincoln's*

—CALEB KLINGLER

BIBLIOGRAPHY

Goodwin, Doris Kearns. *Team of Rivals: The Political Genius of Abraham Lincoln.* New York: Simon and Schuster, 2005.

Niven, John. *Gideon Welles: Lincoln's Secretary of the Navy.* New York: Oxford University Press, 1973.

Welles, Gideon. *Diary of Gideon Wells: Secretary of the Navy under Lincoln and Johnson.* Edited by Howard K. Beale and Alan W. Brownsword. New York: Norton, 1960.

Whig Party

The Whig Party was one of the two major political parties in the United States during most of Abraham Lincoln's adult life. It was formed in 1834 in the wake of the second straight loss of a National Republican candidate to the Democrats' Andrew Jackson, and largely in response to what many saw as Jackson's tyrannical exercise of presidential power, particularly his vetoes of legislation that was important to National Republicans. The Whig Party drew its name from the party in British politics that opposed monarchical tyranny (they dubbed Jackson "King Andrew I"). As did many other National Republicans, in 1834 Lincoln moved easily from his earlier allegiance into the Whig Party, where he stayed until its demise in the mid-1850s. The move was easy because the leadership, the political agenda, and much of the constituency of the earlier party rallied under the banner of the new Whig coalition.

Before the end of the decade the party had become organized in nearly every state in the Union, and although it was strongest in the North and East, it was a worthy competitor to the Democrats in every region of the country. Over the next two decades the Whigs elected two presidents (William Henry Harrison in 1840 and Zachary Taylor in 1848), and they occasionally won majorities in the House and/or Senate (1841–1845, 1847–1849). Though Lincoln's Illinois never elected a Whig to statewide office, Lincoln served four terms in the Illinois State House of Representatives (1834–1841) as a Whig and one term in the U.S. Congress (1847–1849).

The three greatest National Republicans, Henry Clay, Daniel Webster, and John Quincy Adams, became the leaders of the Whigs until their deaths at mid-century. Clay, the Kentucky senator and perennial Whig presidential contender (he was the party's official nominee only in 1844), was undoubtedly the greatest. Lincoln would declare that Clay was his "beau ideal of a statesman," the "man for whom he fought all his life." Webster contributed fierce political and rhetorical support for the party in New England. He ran for the presidency only once, in 1836, when the fledgling party ran three candidates in a vain attempt to stop Martin Van Buren, Jackson's handpicked successor, from attaining the presidency. Webster's reply to the nullifier Robert Y. Hayne (1830), defending "Liberty and Union," would be one of the few documents Lincoln drew on to write his first inaugural address in 1861. Lincoln briefly served with Adams in his lone congressional term in the 1840s. A later Whig leader, William Seward (New York governor and U.S. senator), became Lincoln's chief rival for the presidency in 1860 and his secretary of state for the duration of his administration.

In their first years the Whigs suffered some ideological confusion because in the transition from National Republican to Whig they picked up support from a coterie of states' rights Southerners, most notably John C. Calhoun of South Carolina, whom Jackson had angered by his opposition to nullification. By the early 1840s, however, when most of that group returned to their more natural affiliation with the Democratic Party, the Whigs expressed their inherent nationalism, embodied eloquently in the rhetoric of Webster and Clay. Lincoln would draw on both the ideas and the spirit of that Whiggish nationalism for the rest of his life.

Whig nationalism had both constitutional and developmental aspects. The Whig devotion to the Constitution and the laws can be seen in Lincoln's first really important speech, his address to the Young Men's Lyceum in Springfield in 1838. Like most Whigs he demonstrated a fear of violence and disorder in the republic. His cure for this disease was a dedication to the Constitution and the laws that was almost a political religion. This Whiggish constitutionalism guided Lincoln long after the party itself died, and it continued to shape his response to slavery and secession in particular. It helps account for his reluctance to pursue emancipation as rapidly as some of his Republican colleagues, and it shaped the legalistic language of the Emancipation Proclamation when he did move against the institution. Lincoln's sure-footed rejection of secession also grew out of his commitment to a nationalistic reading of the Constitution and a Whiggish fear of dissolution and anarchy if the momentous compromises of the past were too easily thrown aside.

Whigs also advocated a national plan of development, embodied in Henry Clay's American System. This plan called for the federal government to commit itself to the creation of a national bank, a protective tariff, and aid to internal improvements. It had been Andrew Jackson's opposition to the American System, in his vetoes of the Maysville Road project (1830) and the recharter of the National Bank (1832), that had led to the creation of the Whig Party in the first place. From his earliest days in politics Lincoln expressed loyal devotion to these Whig principles. His Speech on the Sub-Treasury (1839), though not one of his better efforts, was an attempt to tear down the Democrats' attempt to find a substitute for a national bank. His very first political speech (1832) advocated government aid for transportation improvements in his own central Illinois. When he prepared to enter Congress in 1846, he rehearsed reasons why reducing the tariff would bring ruin to the country.

Whigs were also social reformers, though they did not always ask for government support for their reform efforts. Whiggery was as much a political culture as it was a political party. It embodied a vision of the world that its members wanted to achieve, sometimes with the aid of government, sometimes by private effort. A great many Whigs had accepted some form of the evangelical Protestantism that swept over the country during the Second Great Awakening. Although Lincoln did not share this religious affiliation, he did share the general Whig commitment to many reforms that advocated individual development and self-control. Like most Whigs, Lincoln was a great advocate of education and readily expressed his desire that both government and individuals be committed to its advance. In a striking speech of 1842, Lincoln powerfully advocated temperance, the largest reform effort of the antebellum era and one that Whigs were known to promote much more than their Democratic opponents did. Lincoln did not advocate governmental support for this reform, about which Whigs were ambivalent, despite his—and their—strong belief in the necessity for temperance reform itself.

In the 1840s Whigs largely opposed the expansionist tendencies of the age, preferring to develop and reform the nation within its current boundaries. This stance appeared most strongly in Henry Clay's opposition to the annexation of Texas in the election of 1844 and in the party's opposition to the Mexican War, which the victory of Clay's expansionist opponent, James K. Polk, eventually precipitated. Lincoln's lone term in Congress was noteworthy only for his ill-fated effort to maintain a good Whig line by attacking Polk's heavy-handed pursuit of an imperialistic war with Mexico.

In the late 1840s and early 1850s the Whig Party began to lose some of its coherence and energy. New economic conditions had caused the old core issues of bank, tariff, and internal improvements to lose their force. New issues, particularly nativism and a rejuvenated political temperance movement, began to cause splits in the party. The result was a distinct lack of Whig zeal in the campaign for Winfield Scott in 1852. Lincoln, like many other Whigs, had lost some of his interest in politics and the fortunes of the Whig Party. He had immersed himself in his legal practice and played very little part in the presidential election.

The repeal of the Missouri Compromise, part of Steven Douglas's Kansas-Nebraska Act (1854), finally precipitated the breakup of the old Whig Party and its replacement over the next two years by a new Republican coalition. A remnant of the old party nominated Millard Fillmore for president in 1856, but most free-state Whigs had already moved into the new, antislavery Republican Party. The Republicans adopted most of the old Whig political agenda but added antislavery issues to its rhetoric and its platform, now that the Southern wing of the old Whigs had abandoned the party as the issue of slavery took center stage. Lincoln, though incensed and energized politically by Douglas's repeal of the Missouri Compromise, was reluctant to leave the Whigs. He hoped to attack the repeal—and the "Slave-Power conspiracy" that had caused it—from within the party that had always been his political home. By 1856, however, it was clear to him that Whiggery was no longer viable, and like most former Whigs from the free states, he campaigned vigorously for the Republican John C. Frémont for president.

The Whigs have often been seen as an ineffective political party, inasmuch as they elected only two presidents in more than twenty years and because they often resorted to nominating military heroes (William Henry Harrison, Zachary Taylor, and Winfield Scott) who seemed only nominally connected to the Whig political agenda. But this is a mistake. The Whigs' impact on antebellum politics cannot be measured only by presidential victories. They had a profound effect on the political culture of the era, and they influenced state politics and society far more than their national successes might suggest. Most of all, through Lincoln, who brought his Whig background into the White House, from 1861 to 1865 their ideas helped preserve the constitutional unity of the nation, effect national support for the development of its resources, and eradicate slavery.

See also *Clay, Henry*

—Lawrence Frederick Kohl

BIBLIOGRAPHY

Holt, Michael. *The Rise and Fall of the American Whig Party: Jacksonian Politics and the Onset of the Civil War.* New York: Oxford University Press, 2003.

Howe, Daniel Walker. *The Political Culture of the American Whigs.* Chicago and London: University of Chicago Press, 1979.

Whigs, Conscience

As President John Tyler pursued the annexation of Texas in 1844, a small band of Northern Whigs, soon to be known as "Conscience Whigs," bitterly opposed the addition of another slave state to the Union. In Massachusetts, the

Conscience Whigs unsuccessfully lobbied the state party to adopt a platform formally condemning annexation. In New York, a small number of Conscience Whigs bolted rather than support Henry Clay for the presidency after he moderated his own anti-annexation position so as to appeal to voters in the South. The small group of disgruntled Conscience Whigs in New York may have tipped the balance in the very close election to the Democratic candidate, James K. Polk. Polk carried New York by a scant 5,000 votes, while Birney received more than 15,000.

Prominent Conscience Whigs included Charles Francis Adams, Abbott Lawrence, Charles Sumner, and Henry Wilson of Massachusetts; Thurlow Weed, William Henry Seward, and Horace Greeley of New York; and Benjamin F. Wade of Ohio. While some of the Conscience Whigs remained steadfast to their party until the bitter end in 1854, others placed their antislavery ideology over partisan loyalty.

Following the Mexican War, political debate focused on how to integrate the newly acquired territories into the Union. In 1846 Democratic representative David Wilmot of Pennsylvania introduced a proviso stating that slavery would not be introduced into the territories gained from Mexico. Conscience Whigs supported the Wilmot Proviso and wanted the party to adopt it as official policy. Once again, the Conscience Whigs clashed with the larger party and lost. Sen. Henry Clay proposed as an alternative that no territory be added to the United States. While many Whigs, Abraham Lincoln of Illinois included, supported Clay's position, it was not a genuine policy but a device that allowed the Whigs to avoid taking a clear stand on the highly controversial Wilmot Proviso. Conscience Whigs saw it as shameless politicking.

When the Whigs nominated General Zachary Taylor for the presidency in 1848, many Conscience Whigs bolted. They objected to the fact that the candidate was a Southern slaveholder. Instead they voted for the Free Soil candidate, Martin Van Buren, who supported the Wilmot Proviso. Taylor won despite the Conscience Whig defection, as even more Democrats abandoned their party to support Van Buren.

In December 1848 Rep. Daniel Gott of New York introduced a bill to ban slavery in the District of Columbia, a long-standing objective of the Conscience Whigs. However, even the mention of it was divisive to the party. Abraham Lincoln joined other conservatives and moderates in thwarting Gott's effort. After 1848 many Conscience Whigs preferred to work on fusion efforts with Free Soil Democrats that emphasized antislavery issues instead of following a strictly partisan line. In one of the most successful fusion efforts, former Conscience Whig Charles Sumner of Massachusetts was elected to the U.S. Senate on the Free Soil Democrat ticket.

Conscience Whigs continued to defect from the party in the wake of the Compromise of 1850. They objected to several features of the compromise but directed most of their anger toward the Fugitive Slave Act because it placed the federal government at the disposal of slaveholders and undermined state personal liberty laws that protected free blacks as well as fugitive slaves.

By 1852 most Conscience Whigs had left the party. Some had drifted into the nativist movement, but most continued to work on fusion efforts with Free Soil Democrats. The remaining Conscience Whigs supported General Winfield Scott for president, but his dismal showing at the polls signaled the end of the Whig Party. By the 1856 presidential election the remaining Conscience Whigs had moved over to the new Republican Party with its strident antislavery-extension platform.

Abraham Lincoln was not a Conscience Whig. In the 1840s he considered their demands excessive and their hostility toward Texas annexation bordering on the irrational. Lincoln understood politics to be the art of compromise and had little patience for the radicals on either side who clung to unalterable, extreme positions. He also understood that the object of politics was to win office. He looked at the Conscience Whigs and concluded that their third-party maneuvering had only succeeded in aiding proslavery Democrats such as Polk. He thus considered the Conscience Whigs a threat to the national and party harmony that he believed was necessary for the survival of a constitutional republic. He also thought that the Conscience Whigs distracted from the economic agenda that was essential to the well-being of all American citizens.

But Lincoln's attitudes changed markedly after the passage of the Kansas-Nebraska Act in 1854. The repeal of the Missouri Compromise led him to adopt some of the precepts of the Conscience Whigs. Lincoln advocated free-soil doctrines and adhered to the concept that a small, undemocratic, slaveholding oligarchy of the South was seeking to subvert the republic and destroy the Constitution. As president, Lincoln, at the strong urging of former Conscience Whigs, achieved several objectives that the Conscience Whigs had been advocating for over a decade, and even some that he himself had earlier opposed, such as banning slavery in the District of Columbia. Lincoln also admitted Kansas as a free state, signed a treaty with Great Britain pledging American support to the suppression of the illegal slave trade, and later emancipated the slaves.

After the Civil War some leaders who had once been Conscience Whigs became Radical Republicans. They advocated a harsh reconstruction of the South and demanded the incorporation of the former slaves as citizens with all the constitutionally guaranteed rights of free white men.

—GREGORY J. DEHLER

BIBLIOGRAPHY

Blue, Frederick J. *The Free Soilers: Third Party Politics, 1848–1854*. Urbana: University of Illinois Press, 1973.

Carwardine, Richard. *Lincoln: A Life of Purpose and Power*. New York: Knopf, 2003.

Donald, David H. *Charles Sumner and the Coming of the Civil War*. New York: Knopf, 1960.

———. *Lincoln*. New York: Simon and Schuster, 1995.

Holt, Michael F. *The Rise and Fall of the American Whig Party: Jacksonian Politics and the Onset of the Civil War*. New York: Oxford University Press, 1999.

Howe, Daniel Walker. *The Political Culture of the American Whigs.* Chicago: University of Chicago Press, 1979.

Smith, Elbert B. *The Presidencies of Zachary Taylor and Millard Fillmore.* Lawrence: University Press of Kansas, 1988.

Whigs, Cotton

In the 1840s, when the issue of slavery in the territories divided the nation, a conservative faction of Northern Whigs known as "Cotton Whigs" advocated compromise and national reconciliation. Unlike the antislavery Conscience Whigs, who wanted to stress the immorality of slavery, the Cotton Whigs placed national harmony and national economic development as the supreme political objectives. Cotton Whigs wanted a harmonious Union to foster economic growth through a protective tariff, funding of internal improvements, and a national banking system. Rep. Robert Winthrop and Sen. Daniel Webster of Massachusetts and President Millard Fillmore of New York were important Cotton Whigs.

The zenith of the Cotton Whigs' influence came during the election of 1848. To many Cotton Whigs, General Zachary Taylor was a perfect candidate because he could unite the party, win votes in all sections, and run strongly in areas where the party historically had been weak. Abraham Lincoln of Illinois stood fully behind Taylor and campaigned vigorously on his behalf. Taylor's administration, however, was a disaster for the Cotton Whigs. He failed to dispense patronage in a manner that would have healed the party. During the sectional crisis of 1849 and 1850 Taylor used militant language to chastise the South and appeared unwilling to compromise with the South at all. Taylor's death in July 1851 put Millard Fillmore, a Cotton Whig, in the White House. Unlike Taylor, Fillmore negotiated with both parties and sections to fashion the Compromise of 1850.

Cotton Whigs supported the compromise as an act of principled statesmanship because they believed it would restore national harmony. However their eager support of the compromise drew strong criticism from some quarters in the North. Sen. Daniel Webster of Massachusetts, for example, demanded that his fellow Northerners support the Fugitive Slave Law, no matter how odious they personally considered it, out of respect for the law, the Constitution, and their fellow citizens of the South.

Although Abraham Lincoln can be more correctly identified as a moderate, rather than a Cotton Whig, he shared some similar views. He prized the cause of Union above all others and believed strongly in the economic platform. As president both of these elements would be central to his administration. He also was willing to put Union before the morality of slavery. As a congressman in 1848 and 1849 he worked with the Cotton Whigs to stop an attempt by the Conscience faction to outlaw slavery in the District of Columbia. An important difference between Lincoln and the Cotton Whigs, however, concerned the nativist movement. Following the nomination of General Winfield Scott as the Whig presidential candidate in 1852, many Cotton Whigs followed President Millard Fillmore into the anti-immigrant American Party, also called the "Know-Nothings." Lincoln refused to make that jump. Instead he had come to see that the slaveholding oligarchy was subverting the Constitution, and he joined other moderates, Conscience Whigs, and Free Soil Democrats in the new Republican Party.

—GREGORY J. DEHLER

BIBLIOGRAPHY

Carwardine, Richard. *Lincoln: A Life of Purpose and Power.* New York: Knopf, 2003.

Donald, David Herbert. *Lincoln.* New York: Simon and Schuster, 1995.

Holt, Michael F. *The Rise and Fall of the American Whig Party: Jacksonian Politics and the Onset of the Civil War.* New York: Oxford University Press, 1999.

Howe, Daniel Walker. *The Political Culture of the American Whigs.* Chicago: University of Chicago Press, 1979.

Whitman, Walt

Born on Long Island in West Hills, New York, Walt Whitman (1819–1892) left school in 1830 to help support his family as a printer's devil (or apprentice). He was largely self-taught when he became a schoolteacher on Long Island (1838–1839), and he chiefly worked as a printer, compositor, editor, and journalist while writing poetry and prose for New York newspapers. Whitman's interest in politics led to a position as editor of a Democratic newspaper, the *Brooklyn Daily Journal.* After working as a newspaper editor for the *New Orleans Crescent* in 1848, Whitman became an abolitionist when he returned to Brooklyn as a journalist for the *Brooklyn Freeman,* a Free Soil newspaper. His poetry collection *Leaves of Grass* (1855) was a commercial failure, despite praise from reviewers who included Ralph Waldo Emerson. Whitman wrote in free verse to re-create the rhythm of American vernacular speech. Larger editions published in 1856 and 1860 were also unpopular, but the undaunted Whitman prepared a ninth edition in 1892 shortly before his death.

When his brother George was wounded in the Battle of Fredericksburg in December 1862, Whitman visited him in a Union army field hospital in Falmouth, Virginia. The unattended misery he saw there inspired him to work for the next three years as a daily volunteer hospital visitor or missionary. He found a job as a clerk in the army paymaster's office in Washington to support himself but spent his free time visiting wounded soldiers. Donations from friends in New York provided his small gifts of fruit, candy, tobacco, and reading or writing materials, but more important, his cheerful nature assisted young wounded soldiers who were neglected, lonely, and homesick in overcrowded, unsanitary hospitals. In 1863 he sold four articles to the *New York Times*, including "The Great Army of the Sick," a report of February 26, 1863, about makeshift hospitals and convalescent camps in Washington housing more than fifty thousand casualties.

Walt Whitman's poems "When Lilacs Last in the Dooryard Bloom'd" and "O Captain! My Captain!" were inspired by Abraham Lincoln's death.

Source: Library of Congress

By January 1863 a recommendation from Emerson to secretary of the Treasury Salmon Chase led to Whitman's appointment as an Interior Department clerk. At the same time, Whitman was also appointed a soldiers' missionary for the Christian Commission, a wartime agency of the YMCA. This gave him official permission to spend his free time as a volunteer hospital visitor (1862–1865) in the fifty or more temporary military hospitals in Washington. More than six hundred hospital visits, in which he ministered to sick and wounded Union and Confederate soldiers, inspired Whitman's Civil War poetry, *Drum-Taps* (1865) and *Sequel to Drum Taps* (1866). These collections included the most celebrated poem about Lincoln, "When Lilacs Last in the Dooryard Bloom'd," and his most popular poem (though the one he liked least), "O Captain! My Captain!" one of the most memorable elegies in American literature. Since 1861 Whitman had seen Lincoln, often walking or riding, in Washington, and he came to love the president. His close friend Peter Doyle was an eyewitness to the assassination, and Whitman listened closely to Doyle's descriptions of the tragedy at Ford's Theatre.

In 1865 Whitman lost his position in the Department of the Interior because of charges that *Leaves of Grass* was an immoral book containing homosexual references. Whitman then moved to a clerkship in the attorney general's office. *Democratic Vistas,* his prose collection, appeared in 1871, but he suffered a paralytic stroke in 1873 while working late in his office in the Treasury Building. He moved to Camden, New Jersey, with his brother and became an international literary figure, considered one of the most influential poets in the United States. Walt Whitman lived as a semi-invalid in Camden until his death on March 26, 1892.

—Peter C. Holloran

BIBLIOGRAPHY

Kaplan, Justin. *Walt Whitman, A Life.* New York: Simon and Schuster, 1980.

Lowenfels, Walter, ed. *Walt Whitman's Civil War.* New York: Knopf, 1961.

McElroy, John Harmon. *The Sacrificial Years: A Chronicle of Walt Whitman's Experiences in the Civil War.* Boston: Godine, 1999.

Morris, Roy. *The Better Angel: Walt Whitman in the Civil War.* New York: Oxford University Press, 2000.

Whittier, John Greenleaf

John Greenleaf Whittier (1807–1892), abolitionist and poet, was born near Haverhill, Massachusetts, the son of Quaker farmers John Whittier and Abigail Hussey. Whittier demonstrated an early love of literature but had little formal education. His desire to write poetry sprang from his exposure to the works of Robert Burns. Whittier's first poem appeared in 1826 in the Newburyport *Free Press,* edited by William Lloyd Garrison. Garrison befriended the nineteen-year-old and mentored him in his career as a journalist and as an antislavery activist. By 1830 Whittier was editor of an influential Whig journal, the *New England Weekly Review.* His first antislavery pamphlet, *Justice and Expediency,* appeared in 1833 and launched his career as an antislavery writer and poet. His poems, such as "Our Countrymen in Chains," appeared regularly in Garrison's antislavery weekly, the *Liberator,* and were often reprinted as antislavery broadsides.

Unlike Garrison, Whittier sought a political means to end slavery. He campaigned for Whig politicians throughout the mid-1830s. By the time his most prominent poetry collection, *Voices of Freedom,* appeared in 1846, Whittier was widely read and quoted by abolitionists throughout the North. He also gained a reputation for his activism in the political movement to end slavery. By 1844 he strongly supported the Liberty Party candidate, James G. Birney. He was elected a delegate to the 1848 Buffalo Convention that formed the Free Soil Party but was unable to attend because of his health. Although somewhat in disagreement with the party's nomination of former president Martin Van Buren, Whittier campaigned heartily for his election. In addition to his political activism, Whittier remained a prolific author, and his publication of some 109 poems and 275 essays after 1847 gained increased readership throughout the 1850s. Whittier's voice garnered considerable influence inside and beyond antislavery circles.

As an immediate abolitionist, Whittier was somewhat ambivalent about the Republican Party's nomination of Abraham Lincoln in 1860. Nevertheless, following the return of Charles Sumner to the U.S. Senate Whittier canvassed his home town of Amesbury, Massachusetts, on Lincoln's behalf. After John Brown's 1859 raid on the federal arsenal at Harpers Ferry and other events that increased sectional tensions, Whittier came to believe that Lincoln offered the best hope for preserving the Union. In a letter to his friend Edward Gilman Frothingham, which was later published in the Amesbury *Villager,* Whittier celebrated Lincoln's integrity and patriotism but worried that he would not bring an end to slavery: "He stands pledged to follow the example of Washington and Jefferson, in preventing the extension of Slavery. That is all. He will leave the Slave States to the enjoyment or endurance of their peculiar institution."

Lincoln was also apparently aware of the writings of Whittier. The poet's adaptation of an old German hymn, "Ein Feste Burg Ist Unser Gott," was reportedly read before Lincoln's cabinet, and the president later told a journalist that the poem influenced his writing of the Emancipation Proclamation. Once the proclamation was announced, Whittier joined others in celebrating the end of slavery in the rebellious states, and he continued to write poems about the political climate of the nation. His Civil War poems were collected in the volume *In War Time and Other Poems,* published in 1863. Upon learning of Lincoln's assassination in April 1865, Whittier expressed grief and dismay. He wrote to a friend, "Under the horror and gloom of the sad news from Washington...I have no words for the occasion."

Whittier did find his poetic voice again. He wrote what is widely considered his masterpiece, "Snow Bound," in 1866. With his longtime goal of ending slavery finally achieved, Whittier spent the remainder of his life as an active author and supporter of racial and gender equality. He died in 1892.

See also *Garrison, William Lloyd*

—L. DIANE BARNES

BIBLIOGRAPHY

Blue, Frederick. *No Taint of Compromise: Crusaders in Antislavery Politics.* Baton Rouge: Louisiana State University Press, 2005.

Donald, David Herbert. *Lincoln.* New York: Simon and Schuster, 1995.

Pickard, John B., ed. *The Letters of John Greenleaf Whittier.* 3 vols. Cambridge, Mass.: Belknap Press of Harvard University Press, 1975.

Wide Awakes

On November 1, 1860, the *New York Tribune* wrote that the Wide Awakes were one of the greatest achievements of the "political revolution of 1860" and that their participation would become a "glowing chapter" in histories of the campaign. The second half of that prediction never became fact, probably because the Civil War overwhelmed much of the political cavalcade that immediately preceded it. Though most postwar monographs and treatises written about the 1860 presidential election largely overlook the Wide Awakes, other than to comment on their torchlight processions, conspicuous symbols, and quasi-military appearance, the organization actually played a very important role for at least several hundred thousand young Republicans energized by that year's presidential election campaign. Estimates of the number of members of Wide Awake clubs have been as high as several million, and even though that estimate is certainly too high, there may have been as many as 500,000 young men who in some manner participated. It was certainly a campaign phenomenon that exceeded in energy and activity any other election year organization of its kind in American history.

The history of the Wide Awake symbol itself is interesting. The large eyeball that adorned many of the banners and posters of the organization was a popular illustration of the early nineteenth century, representing somebody or something that was fully aware of the facts and circumstances of the community and world around them. It is a symbol that has been employed over the years to symbolize a government or police force that could see everything being done by the citizenry and thus has had something of a negative connotation. In the early nineteenth century, however, the symbol seems to have become associated with the First Great Awakening. Jonathan Edwards and other early American Christian preachers urged their followers to repent of the sins they had fallen into as a result of the Enlightenment and convert back, or "awaken," by some public act of humiliation and atonement. During this time religious services and revivals were often associated with an entire town or community, so that references to being "awakened" or "wide awake" often referred to entire towns. As it grew more common it became a familiar part of political meetings and gatherings as well. Probably the first use of it in a political campaign came in March 1840, when a political rally in Hartford, Connecticut, included one banner that read, "Old Milford, they call her 'Sleepy Hollow'—She's Wide Awake for Harrison and Reform."

During the 1840s and 1850s this concept was often associated with the rise of nativist sentiment in the United States, in response to the first large influx of Roman Catholics from Ireland. Anti-immigrant groups sought to "awaken" the country to the foreign invasion that was taking place, and as these local groups began to put their agendas into action and develop a national identity in the

In 1860, members of a Republican club, the Wide Awakes, marched for presidential candidate Abraham Lincoln. This membership certificate reflects the club's dedication to the Union and the nonextension of slavery.

Source: Library of Congress

American or "Know-Nothing" Party they also produced street gangs (a common part of nineteenth-century political parties) that were often referred to as Wide Awakes. This is entirely different from the Republican Wide Awakes of 1860.

Republican Wide Awake societies were formed across the North in early 1860. The term and the organization would have a decidedly antislavery cast, a primary difference from the Wide Awakes who were part of the Know-Nothing movement. On March 3, 1860, the Republican Wide Awakes of Hartford, Connecticut, adopted a constitution that was published in the *Hartford Courant* newspaper. This document almost seemed to become an operating manual for Wide Awake organizations across the country. Among its provisions were ones directing all members to obtain for themselves, at their own expense, a glazed cap and cape and to pay into the treasury seventy-five cents, which would entitle them to carry a gaslight torch for parade. The members would also be required to attend drill sessions and then participate in all parades called for by the association; to obey the orders of their captains on occasions; and to avoid any kind of "boisterous or disorderly conduct or unnecessary demonstration of any kind," subject to the penalty of expulsion from the organization. They adopted Hardee's *Tactics* as their drill book for military-style training, and in the case of the New York Wide Awakes they even included more advanced maneuvers such as the "Rail Fence Movement," in which the company marched in a zigzag pattern, diagonally from one side of the street to the other, intending to simulate a rail fence symbolic of Abraham Lincoln's campaign. Wide Awakes performed at parades every time important Republican speakers came to town, and apparently their marching and the brilliance of their many gaslight torches were quite entertaining.

The largest and most elaborate of the Wide Awake parades took place in New York City on October 3, 1860. At least 12,000 uniformed Wide Awakes marched for over two hours in a downtown procession that included bands and wagons full of fireworks that were set off at designated places along the parade route. Months of preparation had gone into the event, and it lived up to expectations. It was undoubtedly the biggest and most lavish political parade of the nineteenth century. On election day, November 6, the Wide Awakes took off their caps and cloaks and became witnesses at the polls to protect friendly voters and safeguard the victory that nearly everybody expected. Within a very few months many of the Wide Awakes would be responding to the president's call for volunteers after the firing on Fort Sumter. Undoubtedly most of them served in the Union army during the war, and undoubtedly many were killed and wounded, but for reasons difficult to explain, the Wide Awake phenomenon ended with the 1860 presidential election and was never seen again. It was a unique and important phenomenon that engendered the patriotism and idealism of young voters in the 1860 presidential election, and yet it has largely been forgotten by history.

—DAVID E. LONG

BIBLIOGRAPHY

DeWitt, J. Doyle. *Lincoln in Hartford.* Connecticut Civil War Centennial Commission. Rare Book Collection, Alfred Whital Stern Collection of Lincolniana. Library of Congress, Washington, D.C.

Rathbun, Julius G. "The Wide-Awakes: Great Political Organization of 1860." *Connecticut Quarterly,* October 1895.

Wilmot Proviso

On August 8, 1846, President James K. Polk sent a message to Congress expressing his desire to end the two-month-old war with Mexico on the basis of a peace that was just and honorable to both parties. To that end the president requested an appropriation of $2 million to pay for any territorial concessions that might be made by Mexico. That evening the House took up the request. After a handful of Whigs flayed the president for what they considered an unnecessary war, the chair recognized David Wilmot, a first-term Democrat from Pennsylvania. A loyal supporter of the administration, Wilmot praised the president for his readiness to negotiate an honorable peace. To ensure that goal, Wilmot offered an amendment to the appropriation bill prohibiting slavery in any territory acquired from Mexico. Although his proviso to the bill passed in the House, it failed in the Senate.

Wilmot spoke for a number of Northern Democrats who were dismayed by what they considered a Southern tilt in the Polk administration. Northern and eastern Democrats opposed the reductions in duties in the tariff of 1846. The president's veto of a rivers and harbors bill incensed western Democrats. And Polk's willingness to compromise on the Oregon dispute with England, ceding American claims north of the 49th parallel, outraged Democrats in the Old Northwest, who had insisted on a boundary of 54° 40'. Although these alienated Democrats supported the war, they and their constituents were troubled by this Southern president's plan for land acquired from Mexico. As Eric Foner has astutely argued, Wilmot's proviso was at one level an expression of alienation and frustration by Northern Democrats. At another, it was an attempt to quell growing free-state opposition to the war.

Political principles and ideology also informed the logic of the proviso. Strict-construction Democrats argued that the national government lacked the power to create a local institution such as slavery in the national domain. Adopting the language of the Northwest Ordinance, Wilmot also insisted that free territory would be devoted to the expansion of American free institutions. These restrictionists also insisted that the defense of individual liberty, which lay at the heart of the proviso, also motivated the Founding Fathers in their revolt against England. Just as the revolutionaries defended their autonomy from the despotic encroachments of a distant government, so too would supporters of the proviso defend western settlers from the evils of slavery and the pretensions of slaveholders.

Southerners responded that if individual liberty constituted one of the animating objects of the American political system so did the principle of equality: the equality of slaveholders under the Constitution and of the slave states within the Union. Restriction, they contended, would reduce Southern citizens—slaveholders and non-slaveholders alike—to a second-class, degraded status. Wilmot's proviso would be the means of their enslavement within the Union. Southerners would oppose this threat to their equality just as the Revolutionary generation had resisted British efforts to reduce the colonies to a condition of vassalage within the empire. The proviso, then, signaled an abandonment of that Revolutionary heritage and the resuscitation of the eternal struggle between tyrannical majorities and abused minorities.

Although Abraham Lincoln was not in the House at the time Wilmot's proviso was first introduced, he would later remember that he voted for the proviso, or for the principle on which it was based, "at least forty times." Lincoln and other restrictionists rejected a proposal that would have extended the Missouri Compromise line of 36° 30' through any cession of Mexican territory to the Pacific Ocean. The "Proviso men"—himself included—voted it down "because by implication it gave up the Southern part to slavery, while we were bent on having it *all* free."

Lincoln's personal views on the proviso are illustrative of the trajectory political antislavery activists followed from the mid-1840s to the 1860 campaign. The proviso, Lincoln observed, was "the best mode of preventing such extension of slavery, and at the same time as not endangering, any dearer object." But, he added, if adherence to the proviso "tended to endanger the Union, I would at once abandon it." Lincoln's position on the proviso confirms the argument that slavery restriction allowed antislavery Northerners to resolve the conflict between their hatred of slavery (and slaveholders) and their love of the Union under the Constitution. Agitating for the abolition of the institution in the slave states would threaten the Union. But by restricting the spread of slavery into territories already free, they believed, as Lincoln put it, that the institution would "be put in the course of ultimate extinction."

In the Treaty of Guadalupe Hidalgo, which brought an end to the Mexican-American War, Mexico ceded to the United States 525,000 square miles of territory, including California and New Mexico. Repeated attempts to organize the territories of Utah and New Mexico on the basis of slavery restriction failed. In the Compromise of 1850 they were given territorial status without any restriction on slavery. Although most Americans proclaimed this compromise to be final, the issue of slavery extension was reintroduced into politics in 1854 with the Kansas-Nebraska Act. Framed by Stephen Douglas, the act organized the territories on the basis of popular sovereignty and repealed the Missouri Compromise ban on slavery.

Douglas insisted that his act was consistent with the underlying principles of the Compromise of 1850; Lincoln strongly disagreed. In a speech in Bloomington, Illinois, in the fall of 1854 he asserted that nothing in the compromise measures of 1850 repudiated the Missouri Compromise. "The Wilmot Proviso had nothing to do with the Northwest Territory or the Louisiana purchase," he argued, "and the Missouri Compromise had nothing to do with New Mexico or Oregon, or with any other territory save that to which it was originally applied." But if the proviso signaled the continuing determination of antislavery activists like himself—and the Founding Fathers—to limit the spread and thus the existence of slavery, Douglas's Nebraska act betrayed that Revolutionary heritage. He charged that Douglas had deviated from the Founders' policy by creating a basis by which slavery would be national and perpetual.

In his debates with Douglas in 1858 Lincoln repeatedly insisted that the only way to end slavery agitation in national political discourse was to return to the intent of the Founders and place the institution "back upon the basis where our fathers put it. Restrict it forever to the old States where it exists." If we would arrest the spread of it, Lincoln contended, "if we would place it where Washington,

Jefferson, and Madison placed it...the public mind would be at rest in the belief of its ultimate extinction." In other words, free soil should be preserved for the free labor of free white men.

As Lincoln understood, the importance of the proviso to national politics and to his own career could not be overstated. The introduction of slavery restriction, in the form of Wilmot's proviso, began the sectionalization of American politics that would destroy Lincoln's Whig Party and usher in the creation of the Republican Party, which Lincoln would represent in the 1860 campaign. The sectional debates over the proviso, the Compromise of 1850, and the Kansas-Nebraska Act led antislavery Northerners to conclude that Southern slaveholders and Northern "doughfaces" like Douglas had departed from the Founders' intent to limit the scope and life of slavery. Lincoln and other antislavery activists denied that their support of the proviso and slavery restriction thereafter was aggressive. To the contrary, they insisted, they were preserving the essence of the Revolution and the intent of the framers of the Constitution.

In November 1837 an anti-abolition mob in Alton, Illinois, shot and killed Elijah Lovejoy, the editor of an abolitionist newspaper. In November 1860 Lincoln was elected president of the United States on a wholly sectional vote. The contrast is instructive. In 1860 Lincoln ran on a platform that endorsed a homestead act, a protective tariff, and observance of immigrants' rights. But the sectional issue in the form of slavery restriction—not abolition—lay at the heart of the Republican appeal. The party denounced Stephen Douglas's popular sovereignty solution as a fraud. And it pledged itself against opening the slave trade and for prohibiting the extension of slavery anywhere outside the slave states. In the canvass, party members insisted that they neither maintained any principle, nor proposed to carry into practice any policy, that had not been sanctioned by every administration from Washington to William Henry Harrison. In that contest, Lincoln prevailed. As he and other Republicans peered into the future, they concluded that the success of his administration would determine whether the principles of the Declaration of Independence would prevail or were to be changed into a semi-despotism of the few. The deaths of 600,000 combatants would prove their point.

See also *Mexican War; Polk, James K.*

—MICHAEL A. MORRISON

BIBLIOGRAPHY

Basler, Roy P., ed. *The Collected Works of Abraham Lincoln.* New Brunswick, N.J.: Rutgers University Press, 1955.

Foner, Eric. "The Wilmot Proviso Revisited." *Journal of American History* 56 (1969): 267–279.

Going, Charles Buxton. *David Wilmot, Free Soiler: A Biography of the Great Advocate of the Wilmot Proviso.* New York: D. Appleton, 1924.

Morrison, Chaplain. *Democratic Politics and Sectionalism: The Wilmot Proviso Controversy.* Chapel Hill: University of North Carolina Press, 1967.

Morrison, Michael A. *Slavery and the American West: The Eclipse of Manifest Destiny and the Civil War.* Chapel Hill: University of North Carolina Press, 1997.

Neeley, Mark E, Jr. "Lincoln's Theory of Representation: A Significant New Lincoln Document." *Lincoln Lore* 1683 (1978): 1–3.

Wood, Fernando

Born in Philadelphia, Fernando Wood (1812–1881) was a successful merchant on New York City's East River waterfront in 1836, when he joined the Tammany Hall organization as a Jacksonian Democrat. The votes of Irish longshoremen elected him to the House of Representatives (1841–1843) until secretary of state John C. Calhoun appointed him as a dispatch agent at the port of New York and secretary of state James Buchanan reappointed him (1844–1847). Wood ran unsuccessfully for mayor of New York City in 1850 but succeeded in 1854, despite opposition by Horace Greeley's *New York Tribune.* Wood was reelected in 1856, overcoming his disputes with Tammany leaders about patronage. Wood was a flamboyant and controversial character, allied with the Locofoco Democratic faction in 1835 and secretly allied with the nativists in the 1840s. Nonetheless immigrant German and Irish voters preferred him to the openly nativist candidates, and his colorful speeches against rich "nonproducers" won him many working-class supporters.

Wood's administration was dynamic but notoriously corrupt, with criminal gangs in the Five Points slum district battling each other. Rival police departments, the Democrats' Municipals and the Republicans' Metropolitans, rioted over control of City Hall when they attempted to arrest Mayor Wood in 1857. He challenged the Republican-sponsored state law creating the Metropolitan police force but lost in court, and his Municipal force disbanded in 1857.

The Republicans' new state laws on liquor licenses and Sunday closings led to riots by New York City gangs and German and Irish workers who supported Wood. The Panic of 1857 created much unemployment in the city. Wood promised relief in the form of unprecedented public works projects but could not deliver on the proposals. As a result, a combination of Republicans, Know-Nothings, and discontented Democrats defeated Wood in the 1857 election. Undeterred, he purchased the *New York Daily News* to promote his next campaign. After forming his own rival political machine, Mozart Hall, he was elected mayor for a third term in 1859 with a message of racial hatred, class warfare, and dire warnings that emancipation would flood Northern cities with African American workers. Like many so-called copperheads, Wood was a conservative Democrat who opposed the changes that the Republicans and the Civil War imposed on the country. Concerned more with his own political career than party principles or the national welfare, Wood cynically attempted to evade or straddle Civil War issues. After a divorce, his second wife's fortune helped him become wealthy through Manhattan real estate investments.

Like many merchants and Democrats in the city, Wood openly expressed sympathy for the South and concern that war would disrupt the city's profitable cotton trade with the Southern states. Wood supported proslavery candidate James Buchanan in 1856 and Stephen A. Douglas in 1860, advocated compromise with the South, and opposed the war. John Brown's raid on Harpers Ferry in 1859 prompted the *Daily News* to denounce Brown as a demagogue led by Republicans. His suggestion in January 1861 that New York City secede from the Union contributed to his defeat in the election that year. Wood also criticized the seizure of the *Monticello,* a steamer bringing muskets and ammunition from New York to Savannah.

When the newly elected president visited New York in February 1861, Mayor Wood was a gracious host at City Hall and urged Lincoln to avoid war, which Lincoln said he hoped to do. In January 1862 Wood wrote Lincoln praising the Union war effort, while in New York he urged peace negotiations with the Confederates. In 1863 he proposed a national referendum on continuing the war and recognition of the Confederacy. Although Republican critics blamed him for the July 1863 draft riots and stigmatized him as a traitor, Wood raised a regiment to fight for the Union during the war. He supported George McClellan for president in 1863 and remained a prominent ally of Clement L. Vallandigham and the Peace Democrats, or "copperheads," as Horace Greeley's *New York Tribune* dubbed them. Wood returned to the House of Representatives (1863–1865, 1867–1881), where he was an ardent critic of Radical Reconstruction and represented the city's financial interests until his death in Hot Springs, Arkansas, on February 14, 1881. Wood was buried in Trinity Cemetery in New York City.

—Peter C. Holloran

BIBLIOGRAPHY

Klement, Frank L. *Lincoln's Critics: The Copperheads of the North.* Shippensburg, Pa.: White Mane Books, 1999.

Mushkat, Jerome. *Fernando Wood: A Political Biography.* Kent, Ohio: Kent State University Press, 1990.

Pleasants, Samuel A. *Fernando Wood of New York.* New York: Columbia University Press, 1948.

Schecter, Barnet. *The Devil's Own Work: The Civil War Draft Riots and the Fight to Reconstruct America.* New York: Walker, 2005.

Yates, Richard

Richard Yates (1818–1873) was governor of Illinois for most of Abraham Lincoln's presidency, serving from January 1861 to January 1865. Kentucky born, Yates moved with his family to Illinois in 1831, the year after Lincoln did. He studied law in Jacksonville and was elected to the Illinois House of Representatives, where he served three terms as a Whig and a supporter of Henry Clay. Yates was known to be a good-natured, well-spoken orator, who was too often publicly inebriated. He was a strong supporter of women's rights, and was unquestionably antislavery, but was not vocal in his opposition until after he was elected to Congress in 1850. In Congress, Yates voted along with fellow Whigs against the Kansas-Nebraska Act. Accused of consorting with the Know-Nothings, he was defeated in his reelection bid. Yates was considered for the U.S. Senate in 1855 but yielded to Lincoln as an early candidate. The Republican Party looked to Yates in 1860 as the gubernatorial candidate most likely to win the important central Illinois counties. It was a wise move, and Yates won by nearly 13,000 votes. In that year's presidential election Yates initially withheld support for Lincoln, preferring Edward Bates of Missouri, but eventually campaigned for him.

The Yates-Lincoln relationship was not always smooth. Though he knew that his 1861 inaugural remarks would hold special significance in helping to set national policy, Yates still declined to consult with President-elect Lincoln before delivering his speech. Compared with Lincoln's moderate approach toward slavery and compromise to avert war, Yates was unmistakably more radical. After Fort Sumter, Yates responded energetically to Lincoln's call for troops. Then, after Illinois senator Stephen Douglas died in May, Governor Yates appointed Orville Browning—a tepid supporter of Lincoln—to complete his term. Yates was unwilling to endorse a draft to raise more troops, believing that Illinois had already responded generously and fearing an electoral backlash.

Yates chastised Lincoln for weak leadership and military inaction, demanding sterner measures to crush the rebellion and defeat the enemy. To Yates that meant arbitrarily arresting possible traitors and emancipating and arming blacks. Throughout the war Yates was particularly troubled by reports of possible Confederate invasion of southern Illinois, believing rumors of dangerous and disloyal secret societies fermenting there. To the frustration of Yates, the president refused to act upon that fear, judging such apprehensions unwarranted and exaggerated. The Yates administration faced fierce opposition from the Democratic state legislature, especially after 1862. That body accused the governor of unconstitutional use of power, called for investigations into Yates's use of state funds, and demanded a peace resolution. The governor was able to maneuver around the opposition.

Early in 1864 Yates hoped for someone more radical as a presidential candidate. When that did not come to pass he backed Lincoln as the best chance to unify the country. For his own part, Yates decided to run for the U.S. Senate, and he won the seat. In early 1865, in his last act as governor, Yates called on Illinois to repeal its black laws. As to Yates's opinion of Lincoln, it took the final Union victory in April 1865, followed closely by Lincoln's assassination, to convince him that he had judged the president too harshly and too quickly on emancipation and on his war measures. As a senator Yates effectively pushed for the Fourteenth and Fifteenth Amendments, remarking that such measures the country owed to Lincoln. He also voted for President Johnson's impeachment in 1869. Yates retired from the Senate after his single term and died in 1873.

See also *Illinois*

—RON J. KELLER

BIBLIOGRAPHY

Bailey, Blake. *A Tragic Honesty: The Life and Work of Richard Yates*. New York: St. Martin's, 2004.

Cole, Arthur. *Centennial History of Illinois, Volume 3: The Era of the Civil War, 1848–1870*. Springfield: Illinois Centennial Commission, 1919.

Hesseltine, William B. *Lincoln and the War Governors*. New York: Knopf, 1948.

Howard, Robert. *Mostly Good and Competent Men, Illinois Governors, 1818–1988*. Springfield: Illinois State Historical Society, 1988.

Lusk, D.W. *Eighty Years of Illinois Politics and Politicians, 1809–1889*. Springfield, Ill.: Rokker, 1889.

Young America

A popular expression of the 1840s and 1850s, "Young America" had multiple, related meanings. It was generally applied to informal movements defined by an exuberant, youthful, and aggressive romantic nationalism, support for territorial expansion, and liberal internationalism. The phrase was inspired by movements in Europe such as Young Italy, Young Ireland, and Young Hungary. In the area of culture "Young America" referred to writers and artists who actively sought to create or promote distinctive American art and literature. Much of this activity was centered in New York City in the 1840s.

In politics "Young America" referred to a rising generation of politicians who advocated support for democratic revolutions in Europe and aggressive territorial expansion of the young United States in the Americas. In the latter manifestation it was connected to a faction of the Democratic Party, in particular to partisan editor John L. O'Sullivan and Lincoln's political rival Stephen Douglas. Political Young America drew from the Jackson tradition, but it was more enthusiastic about economic development than the older generation of Jacksonian Democrats, supporting the passage of general incorporation laws and the development of railroads, with state aid if necessary. Young America Democrats condemned the more cautious members of their party as "old fogies." Many supported an aggressive theory of manifest destiny and would justify the annexation of Cuba, the acquisition of all of Mexico after the Mexican-American War, and other schemes for expanding the boundaries of the United States. Political Young America was generally an apologist for slavery, but it was otherwise of a liberal internationalist bent and embraced cultural differences. Although Young America's supporters often insisted on the innate inferiority of Africans, they were very open to incorporating non–Anglo Saxon European immigrants and the mestizo peoples of Mexico and the Gulf region into the American nation as equal citizens and rejected the anti-Catholic prejudice of the nativist Whigs.

By the mid-1850s the phrase "Young America" was used as a term of derision by its critics at least as frequently as it was proclaimed by supporters. Not surprisingly, because of the term's association with Stephen Douglas, Lincoln defined himself against Young America and was one of its frequent critics. In his "Second Lecture on Discoveries and Inventions," Lincoln mocked Young America from the first sentence: "We have all heard of 'Young America.' He is the most *current* youth of the age. Some think him conceited and arrogant; but has he not reason to entertain a rather extensive opinion of himself? Is he not the inventor and owner of the *present,* and the sole hope of the future?" Lincoln bridled at Young America's desire to discard the past, as well as its assumption that the current America had achieved perfect liberty and only needed to spread it to the rest of the world. Lincoln's Whiggish notions of freedom were in the humanitarian reform tradition, in contrast to the liberal internationalism of Young America. Lincoln's awareness of America's imperfections and shortcomings meant that he directed his energies to improving freedom internally, rather than extending it externally. In many ways the political contests between Douglas and Lincoln in the last years before the Civil War were a contest between the liberal internationalist vision of Young America and the humanitarian reform tradition of Lincoln and the Republicans.

WILLIAM THOMAS KERRIGAN

BIBLIOGRAPHY

Kerrigan, William Thomas. "Young America! Romantic Nationalism in Literature and Politics, 1843–1861." Ph.D. diss., University of Michigan, 1997.

Widmer, Edward L. *Young America: The Flowering of Democracy in New York City.* New York: Oxford University Press, 1999.

Winger, Stewart. *Lincoln, Religion, and Romantic Cultural Politics.* De Kalb: Northern Illinois University Press, 2003.

Zouaves

Both the Union and Confederate armies fielded Zouave regiments during the Civil War. These uniquely clothed fighting units wore colorful uniform combinations and enjoyed great popularity with the public.

Officers in both armies constantly looked for ways to improve their troops. Often they examined foreign armies and their methods of conducting warfare. The creation of Zouave regiments was one of the most vivid examples of borrowing strategies from those foreign armies. Officers hoped to attach the pride and prestige of these elite overseas fighting units to their volunteers.

Zouave regiments in the United States based their uniforms on the Zouave Battalions of France. The French borrowed their unusual style from the Algerian brigades that fought with them during the 1830s colonial wars in North Africa, and the Americans and Confederates followed suit. The French and Algerian uniforms consisted of a fez or turban, tassels, a sash, baggy pants or pantaloons, and a short, open jacket that was more suited for warmer climates and permitted a greater range of motion than standard uniforms. They varied in color and color combinations. During the Civil War these uniforms appeared more regularly in the North because of the Confederacy's lack of material and resources.

One of the most famous Zouave regiments was the Eleventh New York, commanded by Colonel Elmer Ellsworth. Composed of 1,100 New York firemen, Ellsworth's Zouave unit eventually became known as the "Fire Zouaves." They drilled in their exotic uniforms in front of large crowds in New York City and across the North before departing for Washington. Ellsworth was a close friend of President Lincoln and worked on both his senatorial and presidential campaigns. Notably he was also the first Union officer killed in the Civil War when he attempted to remove a Confederate flag from atop a hotel in Alexandria, Virginia. After his death, the Fire Zouaves fought at the Battle of Bull Run, where they faced General J. E. B. Stuart's cavalry and suffered heavy casualties, as Stuart's troopers cut the "white turbans to bits, and they retreated in confusion."

The New York Fire Zouaves also drew national attention in a political controversy for President Abraham Lincoln. The *New York Herald* reported that two members of the Seventy-ninth New York Militia and one Zouave from the Eleventh New York had been murdered in Richmond as prisoners of war. Their jailer accused them of "peeping out a window" and had all three men shot.

An artist's depiction of the uniform of a Zouave sentry at Gen. George Meade's tent near Petersburg, Virginia, in August 1864. The creation of Zouave regiments was one of the most vivid examples of how officers in both Union and Confederate armies borrowed strategies from foreign armies. Zouave regiments in the United States based their uniforms on the Zouave Battalions of France.

Source: Library of Congress

Reports of the alleged execution named a Confederate officer as the perpetrator: Lieutenant David Todd. The sensational headlines greatly affected the president, for Lieutenant David Todd's sister was Mary Todd Lincoln, the president's own wife. Lieutenant Todd used the notoriety created by this event to denounce his brother-in-law and the Union. Using his favorite phrase, "I'd like to cut out Old Abe's heart," he embarrassed the already beleaguered president.

These shocking revelations served to further remove the Lincolns from established Washington, D.C., political culture. Opponents of the president used the news to assert that Lincoln and the entire Todd family were nothing more than "provincials . . . monsters, and traitors." These accusations illustrated how deeply the war divided the president's extended family.

After the war ended, so too did the need for Zouave regiments. The U.S. Army disbanded all Zouave units, but their legacy lived through veterans' groups that celebrated the Franco-Algerian inspired uniform that made the Zouaves so popular.

See also *Ellsworth, Elmer Ephraim*

—PETER SMITH

BIBLIOGRAPHY

Berry, Steven. *House of Abraham: Lincoln and the Todds, a Family Divided by War.* New York: Houghton Mifflin, 2007.

Donald, David Herbert. *Lincoln.* New York: Simon and Schuster, 1996.

Foote, Shelby. *The Civil War: A Narrative—Fort Sumter to Perryville.* New York: Random House, 1958.

Linedecker, Clifford. *Civil War A to Z: A Complete Handbook of America's Bloodiest Conflict.* New York: Random House, 2002.

Troiani, Don. *Civil War: Zouaves, Chaussers, Special Branches, and Officers.* Mechanicsburg, Pa.: Stackpole Books, 2002.

Index

Bold page numbers indicate principal treatment; italic page numbers indicate illustrations.

Abbott, Lawrence, 711
Abolitionism, **1–5**, 113, 283–286, 334, 408, 535, 564, 565
"Abraham, Martin, and John" (song), 415, 447
Abraham Lincoln, 16th President of the United States (Marchant painting), 304
Abraham Lincoln: The War Years (Sandburg), 445
Abraham Lincoln Boyhood National Historic Site, Hodgenville, Kentucky, 440
"Abraham Lincoln Won 1936 Olympic Games" (headline), 416
Academy Awards, 445
ACS. *See* American Colonization Society
Adams, Charles Francis (1807–1886), **5–7**, 16, 252, 253, 273, 302, 639, 711
Adams, Henry, 614
Adams, John, 5, 170, 301
Adams, John Quincy, 5, 139, 301, 464, 465, 708
The Advance (Pullman car), 425
Aesop's *Fables*, 355, 403, 427
Africa, return of blacks to. *See* Colonization
African Americans, 2, **8–15**, *9*, *670*
  abolitionism and, 1–5
  Brown (John) and, 91
  colonization and, 20, 49, 352
  Confiscation Acts and, 157–158
  Douglass and, 219–220
  Dred Scott case and, 55
  emancipation and, 189, 234–236
  at end of war, 569
  Freedman's Memorial and, 304–305
  as fugitive slaves, 392
  Garrison and, 284
  Lincoln–Douglas debates and, 435–438
  military service of, 317, 336, 374, 542, 610, 669–672

  Order of Retaliation and, 503
  Reconstruction and, 368, 371
  rights of, 350, 513, 521, 545–548, 585, 612, 620, 645, 657–658
  scapegoating of, 169, 210, 224–226
  Thirteenth amendment and, 665
  U.S. Colored Troops (USCT), 220, 239, 548, 610, **669–673**, *670*
  Young America movement and, 729
"African Colonization Unveiled" (Ruffin), 574
Age of Jackson, 54
Alabama, CSS, 7, **15–18**, 253, 459
Alaska, 588
Albany Evening Journal, 560, 705
Albemarle, CSS, 15
Albert, Prince, 302, 614, 663
Aldrich, Cyrus, 329
Alexander, Archer, 235
"Almanac case" (1857), 441
Alton, Illinois, debate, 114, 389, 412, 438
Alton Weekly Courier, 110
American Anti-Slavery Society, 220, 283, 398, 516
American Colonization Society (ACS), 10, **18–20**, 28, 139, 147. *See also* Colonization
American Farmer (journal), 573
American Indians. *See also* Black Hawk War (1852)
  Lincoln's relations with, **356–358**
  Navajo removal (1864), 357–358, **455–456**
  Sioux uprising, 357, 358, **603–604**
"American Moses," 304
American Party. *See* Know-Nothing (American) Party
American Revolution, 45, 58, 164, 187, 308, 511, 532, 607

Index

American System, **20–22**, 54, 139, 361, 553, 709
Amesbury Villager (newspaper), 717
Amistad case (1841), 644
Amy Warwick, CSS, 538
Anaconda Plan, **22–25**, 23, 71, 580, 706
"An Act to Increase the pay of Privates and for other purposes." *See* Ratification Act
Anderson, Marian, 416
Anderson, Robert, 258, 260, 261–262, 263, 541, 618
Anderson Cottage, Soldiers' Home, 618
Andrew, John, 90, 91, 515, 549
Annual Messages to Congress
  (1861), 19, 135, 148, 580
  (1862), 11, 146, 151, 309, 359
  (1863), 46, 121, 557, 697
  (1864), 167, 597
Anthony, Susan B., 4
Anticipations of the Future, to Serve as Lessons for the Present Time (Ruffin), 574
Antietam Campaign, **25–27**, 30, 32, 83, 161, 194, 337, 373, 394, 413, 463, 656
Anti-Masonic Party, 465, 467
Anti-Nebraska Party, 110, 118, 379, 563, 564
Antislavery, **27–31**, 624. *See also* Abolitionism; *specific special interest groups*
"Apotheosis" (print), 415
"Appeal of the Independent Democrats," 379
"Appeal to Border State Representatives to Favor Compensated Emancipation" (1862), 19
Appomattox Courthouse, Virginia, 31, 157, 300, 371, 396, 414, 424, 596
Argus of Western America (newspaper), 63
Arizona Territory, 282, 357
Arlington Cemetery, 425
Armed Forces Retirement Home, President Lincoln's cottage. *See* Soldiers' Home
Armstrong, Fort, 227
Armstrong, Jack, 405, 490
Army, U.S., 31, 69, 70, 91, 152, 156, 160, 180, 181, 579
Army of Northern Virginia
  Antietam Campaign, 25
  Fredericksburg and Chancellorsville Battles, 269–270
  Gettysburg Battle, 291
  Grant's campaigns against, 300, 590
  Lee as commander of, 393, 394, 395
  Overland Campaign, 505
  Union Naval Blockade and, 73
Army of the Cumberland, 35
Army of the Gulf, 48
Army of the James River, 506
Army of the Ohio, 35, 601
Army of the Potomac
  Antietam Campaign, 25
  Ball's Bluffs Battle, 39, 41
  Fredericksburg and Chancellorsville Battles, 269, 270, 271
  Gettysburg Battle, 291–292
  Joint Committee on the Conduct of the War investigation of, 373, 374
  McClellan as commander of, 163, 189, 461, 462
  New York draft riots and, 226
Army of the Shenandoah, 337
Army of the Tennessee, 595, 598, 601
Army of Virginia, 25, 394
Army of Western Virginia, 287
Arnold, Samuel Bland, 76, 77
Arthur, Chester A., 618
Article of War (1862), 670
Ashley, James M., 122, 657
Assassination, **31–35**
  Booth's plot, 74, 77
  motivation for, 13
  Whitman poetry on, 715
  Whittier on, 717
Atchison, David, 377, 391
Atkinson, Henry, 56, 57
Atlanta Campaign, **35–37**, 156, 188, 300, 595
Atlantic Monthly (magazine), 576, 634
Atlantic Telegraph Company, 676
Atzerodt, George Andrew, 32, 76, 77

Bacon, Henry, 449
Bad Axe River massacre, 57
Badeau, Adam, 424
Bailey, Frederick Washington Augustus. *See* Douglass, Frederick
Bailey, Gamaliel, 399
Bailey v. Cromwell (1841), 175
Baker, Edward Dickinson, 39, 40, 406, 409, 417, 419, 432, 454
Baker, Reule C., 61
Balch, Thomas, 15
Ball, Thomas, 234
Ball's Bluff, Battle of, **39–41**, 163, 372, 417, 432
Baltimore Convention (1860). *See* Democratic Convention (1860)

Baltimore Convention (1864), 144
Baltimore mob, **42–44**, 242, 312, 328, 442, 692, 703
Banking and monetary policy, **45–47**, 182–183, 353–354. *See also* Currency; Greenbacks
Bank of Middletown (Pennsylvania), 107
Bank of the United States, 21, 45, 52, 54
Banks, Nathaniel Prentice (1816–1894), **47–48**, 101, 467, 515, 558, 589, 653, 688
"Bank War," 45, 54
Barboncito, Chief, 456
Barney, Charles D., 183
Barrancas, Fort, 255
Barry, John, 62
Bates, Edward (1793–1869), **48–50**, *237*
   Blair and, 63, 66, 106
   Browning and, 92
   Colfax and, 145
   on *habeas corpus* suspension, 313
   in Lincoln's cabinet, 79, 104, 302, 542
   New York Tribune endorsement of, 493
   as presidential candidate, 117, 205, 412, 560, 561, 562
   as president of Rivers and Harbors Convention, 572
   Yates and, 727
"The Battle Hymn of the Republic" (Howe), 91
The Battle of Gettysburg (film, 1913), 445
Beardstown Courthouse, Illinois, 441
Bear Flag Revolt, 280
"Beast Butler," 101
Beauregard, Pierre G.T., 97, 98, 102, 263, 602
Bedell, Grace (1848–1936), **50–51**, 555
Beecher, Henry Ward, 632
Beechwood plantation (Coggin's Point), 573
Bell, John (1797–1869), **51–53**, *116*
   as Constitutional Union Party candidate, 96, 119, 177, 241, 562
   Johnson and, 369
   Kentucky support for, 381
   Stuart support for, 636
Bell, Joshua F., 457
Bellevue Place Sanitarium, Batavia, Illinois, 421
Bennett, James Gordon, 143, 596
Bennett, John C., 477
Bennett, Lerone, 14, 416
Benton, Jessie, 280
Benton, Thomas Hart (1782–1858), **53–55**, 65, 142, 280, 366
Berger, Andrew, 451
Berlin Olympics, 416

Bermuda Hundred, Virginia, 102
Bernard, Simon, 254
Berry, William F., 406, 491, 685
The Bible, 355, 427, 524, 617
Bickley, George W.L., 385, 386
Big Bethel, assault on, 101, 372
Billings, George, 51
Billings, Harlow Drake, 51
Billy the Barber. *See* Florville, William
Birney, James G., 398, 399, 717
Bissell, William Henry, 110
Bixby, Widow, 320, 323
Black, Jeremiah, 627
"Black Easter," 35
Black Hawk, Chief, 56, 57, 406, 647
Black Hawk War (1852), **56–57**
   Illinois legislative election campaigns and, 491
   Indian relations and, 357
   Lincoln's military experience in, 286, 405–406
   Scott as Lincoln's commanding officer in, 580
   Zachary Taylor in, 647
"Black Jack" stamp, 626
Black Kettle, Chief, 357, 358
"Black Laws," 8, 9, 10
"Black Republicans," 210, 228
Blacks. *See* African Americans
Black Suffrage, **58–61**
Blair, Austin (1818–1894), **61–62**
Blair, Francis Preston, Sr. (1791–1876), **63–65**, 318, 394
Blair, Frank, Jr. (1821–1875), 55, 65, 146
Blair, Montgomery (1813–1883), **65–67**, *237*
   Benton and, 55
   on blockade of Southern ports, 542
   Dred Scott case and, 228
   as postmaster general, 79, 104, 105, 121
   resignation from Lincoln's cabinet, 106, 123, 510
   Sherman and, 594
"Bleeding Kansas," **67–71**, 216, 256, 392, 534
Blenker, Ludwig, 290
Blockade, Union Naval, *23*, **71–73**
   cabinet positions on, 542
   civil liberties and, 136
   Congress and, 162–163
   cotton exports and, 384
   Great Britain and, 301
   international law on, 155, 252
   Mason and, 459
   Supreme Court upholds constitutionality of, 538, 539, 540
   Taney on, 646

Index

Blood Tubs, 42
Bloomington, Illinois, speech, 532–533
Bloomington convention, 70
Blue Ridge Mountains, 588
Booth, Edwin, 32, 424
Booth, John Wilkes (1838–1865), **74–78**
  motivation of, 13
  plot and conspirators, 31, 32, 33, 587
Booth, Junius, 32, 74
Booth, Richard, 74
Border States, **78–82**
  African American soldiers and, 671
  congressional members from, 11
  conservatives in, 413
  Democratic Party and, 208
  emancipation, effect on, 30, 55, 158, 176, 608, 609, 617, 669
  Greeley on, 536
  habeas corpus suspension in, 121
  Hicks and, 327–328
  Lincoln's cabinet and, 104, 105
  National Union Party in, 487, 488
  patronage in, 510
  Preliminary Emancipation Proclamation and, 285
  slaveholding in, 131, 150–151, 179
  taxes in, 354
  Thirteenth Amendment and, 656, 657
  volunteer troops and, 693
  War Democrats and, 700
Border State Unionists, 65, 80, 81, 165, 281
Boritt, Gabor S., 46
Borroughs, Joseph "Peanuts," 33
Bosque Redondo, New Mexico, 357–358, 456
Boston Brahmins, 516
Boston Vigilance Committee, 516
Boyd, Linn, 457
Boyle, Jeremiah T., 382
Brady, Mathew (c.1823–1896), **82–84**, 184, 185, 419, 443, 451, 453
Bragg, Braxton, 85, 386–387, 474
Branson, Jacob, 391
The Breadwinners: A Social Study (Hay), 323
Breckinridge, John Cabell (1821–1875), **84–85**, *116*
  as Buchanan vice president, 117
  Cass support for, 125
  Johnson support for, 369
  Kentucky and, 381
  as presidential candidate, 95, 118, 205–206, 562
Breese, Sidney, 112, 437
Brenner, Victor David, 451, 453

Brilliante, CSS, 538. *See also Prize Cases (1863)*
Britain. *See* Great Britain
Broadside on murderers of Lincoln (War Department), 75
Brooklyn Daily Journal, 714
Brooklyn Freeman (newspaper), 714
Brooks, Noah, 496
Brooks, Preston (1819–1857), 69, **86–88**, 535, 638
Brooks, William H. T., 292
Brough, John, 684
Brown, Albert Gallatin, 279
Brown, Benjamin Gratz, 64
Brown, Frederick, 69, 70
Brown, John (1800–1859), **88–92**, *89*. *See also* Harper's Ferry raid (1859)
  Bleeding Kansas Battles, 69, 70, 534–535
  Buchanan on, 95
  congressional investigation of Harper's Ferry raid, 459
  Constitution and, 170
  election of 1860, impact on, 116
  Lee's capture of, 393
  Phillips on, 517
  Ruffin on, 574
  Seward on, 560
Brown, Joseph, 198
Brown, William, 44
Browning, Orville Hickman (1806–1881), 80, **92–93**, *161*, 281, 727
Brown resolution, 624
Brutus, Junius, 74
Buchanan, James (1791–1868), **94–97**, *116*
  in Anti-Masonic Party, 465
  Bleeding Kansas and, 70, 71
  Breckinridge as vice president for, 84
  Cameron support for, 107
  Cass as secretary of state for, 124, 125
  corruption in administration of, 190
  as doughface, 214
  Douglas and, 333
  Douglas supported by, 112
  election of, 109, 111
  election of 1856, 281
  Fort Sumter and, 259, 260
  Homestead Act veto by, 329
  Lincoln attacks on, 228, 229, 334, 335
  Morrill Act veto by, 478, 480
  Morrill tariff and, 482
  patronage and, 509
  on protection of slaveholders' property, 117
  as secretary of state, 614
  sends troops to Fort Pickens, 254

Sherman and, 591
slavocracy and, 606
Buckalew, Charles R., 372
Buckner, Simon B., 266
Buell, Don Carlos, 299, 601, 602
Buena Vista, Battle of, 197, 466, 648
Bulloch, James D., 253
Bull Run, First Battle of (First Manassas), **97–99**
  Brady photographs, 83
  congressional investigation of, 163, 372, 373
  Greeley and, 307
  Radical Republicans and, 550
  Scott's warnings on, 24, 580
  Union Army enlistments after, 168, 286, 693
  Zouave regiment in, 731
Bull Run, Second Battle of (Second Manassas), 25, 163, 337, 357, 394, 462, 628
Bunker Hill Monument, 654
Burbridge, Stephen G., 382
Burgess, Andrew, 83
Burial and tomb, Lincoln's, **99–100**
Burleigh, William, 4
Burlington, Vermont raid, 475
Burns, Robert, 490
Burnside, Ambrose E., 26, 270, 374, 387, 395, 474–475, 557, 683
Burton Historical Collection of the Detroit Public Library, 51
Butler, Andrew P., 86, 535
Butler, Benjamin Franklin (1818–1893), **100–102**
  appointment as general, 700
  confiscation of slaves by, 80, 158, 179–181
  at Democratic Convention of 1860, 204
  election of 1864, 121–122, 370
Butler, William, 704
Butt Enders, 42

Cabinet, Lincoln's, **103–106**, 247–248
Cadwalader, George, 243
Caldwell, Elias, 18, 147
Calhoun, John C., 21, 140, 155, 531, 708
"Calhoun of the South," 197
California, 280–281, 470
Calvinist theological doctrine, 274
Camden Street Station, Baltimore, 42, 43, 44
Cameron, Simon (1799–1889), **106–108**
  Curtin and, 292
  on Fort Sumter, 261
  as Lincoln supporter, 121
  on naval blockade, 542
  as presidential candidate, 49, 560, 561
  resignation of, 163, 190

as secretary of war, 80, 104, 105, 509
Stanton and, 627
Campaign of 1856. *See* Election of 1856, Presidential
Campaign of 1858. *See* Election of 1858, Lincoln's Senatorial
Campaign of 1860. *See* Election of 1860, Presidential
Campaign of 1864. *See* Election of 1864, Presidential
Campbell, John A., 318, 570, 690
Camp Butler, Springfield, 343
Camp Curtin, Pennsylvania, 194
Camp Douglas, Chicago, 343
Canada, 129, 210, 249
Can an Abolitionist Vote or Hold Office under the United States Constitution? (Phillips), 517
Canyon de Shelle, 456
Carey, M.B., 180
Caribbean territory, 66, 148, 193
Carleton, James H., 357–358, 455, 456
Carpenter, Francis Bicknell, 304, 340
Carrington, Henry B., 386
Carson, Kit, 357, 455, 456
Cartoons, political, *23, 116, 121, 187, 378, 493, 555, 662*
Cartwright, Peter, 409
Cass, Lewis (1782–1866), **124–126**, 152, 215, 273, 377, 471, 531–532, 605, 648
Catholic Church, 385, 388
Cedar Creek, Battle of, 590
Census of 1850, 115, 216
Central America, 12, 19, 148, 193, 385
Central Pacific Railroad (CP), **126–127**, 553, 667
Chambrun, Marquis de, 571
Chancellor's Tavern, 271
Chancellorsville, Battle of. *See* Fredericksburg and Chancellorsville, Battles of
Chandler, William, 121
Chandler, Zachariah (1813–1879), 40, 123, **127–129**, 163, 372, 374
Chappel, Alonzo, 83
Charles D. Barney and Company, 183
Charles River Bridge case (1837), 644
Charleston, Illinois, debate, 114, 437
Charleston Convention (1860). *See* Democratic Convention (1860)
Charleston Courier, 257
Charlestown, Virginia, 89
Chase, Salmon Portland (1808–1873), **129–132**, *237*
  abolitionist support for, 30

Index

Chase, Salmon Portland—*continued*
  Blair and, 64, 66
  Chief Justice appointment of, 658
  Colfax and, 146
  Confiscation Act and, 160
  Cooke and, 182
  criticisms of Lincoln, 122, 123
  Davis (Jefferson) and, 199
  endorsement of Lincoln as presidential candidate, 3
  federal bond sales and, 353, 354
  Fessenden and, 247
  "Free Soil, Free Labor, Free Men" slogan of, 674
  on Kansas-Nebraska Act, 379
  on Legal Tender Act of 1862, 396, 398
  in Liberty Party, 399
  as Lincoln supporter, 119
  on McClellan, 25
  on McLean, 466
  monetary policy of, 46, 309, 359
  on naval blockade, 542
  as Ohio governor, 109
  portrait on currency, 451–452
  as presidential candidate, 49, 117, 561, 562
  Radical Republican support for, 4, 317, 529, 530, 550
  resignation of, 106, 270
  as secretary of Treasury, 103, 104–105
  Sherman (John) and, 592
  Stanton and, 627
  Sumner and, 639
  Supreme Court appointment, 106, 452, 673, 676–677, 679
  Vallandigham and, 683
Chattanooga Campaign. *See* Chickamauga and Chattanooga Campaign
Chautauqua Association, 491
Cheever, George, 4
Cherokee Nation v. Georgia (1831), 365
Chestnut, James, 257
Cheyenne Indians, 357
Chicago Convention (1860). *See* Republican Convention (1860)
Chicago Telephone Company, 425
Chicago Times, 387, 684
Chicago Tribune, 386
Chickamauga and Chattanooga Campaign, 85, 395, 557, 595, 628
Chickasaw Bayou assault, 687
Chiriqui (Panama), 64
Christiana Slave Riot, 249
Christy, David, 383

Cincinnati Commercial (newspaper), 143, 204
Cincinnati platform of 1856, 204
Circuit Courts, Eighth Judicial, **133–135**, 409, 411, 420, 437
Circuit Courts, First Judicial, 408
"The Circumstances Favorable to Literary Improvement in America" (Everett), 241
City Point, Virginia, 570–571, 596, 690
Civil liberties, **135–138**
Civil Rights Act of 1875, 102, 551, 665
Civil Rights Movement, 305
Civil War. *See also* Confederate States of America; *specific battles and leaders*
  Alabama claims from, 17
  Anaconda Plan and, 22–24
  Brady as photographer in, 83
  Buchanan on, 96
  constitutional issues, 136, 172
  Democratic Party and, 207
  desertions and pardons, 211–212
  emancipation and, 3
  financing of, 397, 485, 486
  General War Order Number One, 286–288
  Gettysburg Address on, 202, 296, 413
  inaugural address on, 350–352
  Joint Committee on the Conduct of the War, 372–375
  Lincoln's political philosophy and, 523, 525
  Navajo attacks during, 456
  soldiers' voting rights, 618
Clary's Grove, Illinois, 405
Clay, Cassius Marcellus, 561, 562
Clay, Henry (1777–1852), **139–141**
  in American Colonization Society, 18, 19, 147
  Benton and, 53, 54
  Compromise of 1850 and, 153, 215, 249
  Conscience Whigs and, 711
  Curtin as supporter of, 194
  economic policy of, 20, 21, 553, 709
  Free Soil Party and, 273
  Lincoln as admirer of, 9, 29, 356, 361, 363, 381, 404
  Lincoln's political philosophy and, 521, 523
  Missouri Compromise and, 472
  as presidential candidate, 398–399, 466, 527
  Todd (Robert Smith) and, 419
  Whig Party and, 708
Cleveland, Grover, 463
Cleveland Convention (1864), **141–145**, 290, 317, 551
Cleveland Herald, 143
Clinton, Bill, 444, 618

Cobb, Howell, 207
Cochrane, John, 144
Cold Harbor, Virginia, 507
Coleman, Franklin M., 391
Coles County, Illinois, 437
Colfax, Schuyler (1823–1885), 33, **145–147**
The Collected Works of Abraham Lincoln (Basler, ed.), 577
Colonization, 49, 64, 66, **147–149**, 352, 547, 574, 644, 657. *See also* American Colonization Society (ACS)
Columbian Orator, 218
Commentaries on the Constitution (Story), 244
Committee of Thirteen, 192, 515
Committee on the Territories, 153, 377
Commonwealth Edison Company, 425
"Commutation" provision, 330
Compensated Emancipation, 2, **149–151**
Compromise of 1850, **152–154**
  Cass support for, 125, 532
  Clay as architect of, 140
  Conscience Whigs and, 711
  Douglas support for, 343, 605
  Fillmore support for, 249
  Seward and, 585
  Stephens support for, 630
  Taylor opposition to, 648
Compromise Tariff (1833), 21
Comptroller of the Currency, 485, 486
Confederate States of America, 23, 154–157. *See also specific battles and leaders*
  Booth and, 75–76, 77
  Border States and, 79, 151, 238–239, 609
  commerce raiding by, 15–16
  Confiscation Acts and, 158, 160, 180
  Constitution and, 176, 242–243
  cotton exports and, 384
  creation of, 96, 217, 259, 582
  Davis (Jefferson) as president of, 197–200
  diplomacy and, 252, 586, 587
  foreign government recognition of, 6, 302, 615
  habeas corpus suspension and, 311
  Hampton Roads Conference and, 318–319
  Indians and, 357
  inflation in, 46, 309
  legal status of, 646
  military forces of, 35–36, 37, 72, 85, 300, 386, 394, 459, 503, 506, 595, 597
  naval blockade of, 7, 71, 73, 538–539
  postage stamps in, 625, 626
  Richmond as capital of, 97, 569
  scrip, 570
  Stephens on, 268
  Todd family and, 660
  Trent affair and, 661–663
  Virginia Plan and, 690–691
Confiscation Act, First (1861), **157–159**, *180*
  Confederacy, impact on, 156
  Congress and, 164
  habeas corpus suspension under, 313
  Lincoln approval of, 80
  Radical Republicans and, 550
  slaves as contraband under, 181
  Trumbull and, 665
  U.S. Colored Troops and, 669–670
Confiscation Act, Second (1862), **160–162**
  Confederacy, impact on, 156
  Congress and, 164, 165
  Greeley on, 537
  martial law and, 136
  U.S. Colored Troops and, 670
Confiscation Cases, In re (1873), 161
Congress
  Lincoln's relationship with, 105, 108, **162–167**
  Thirtieth, 197, 409, **611–613**
  Thirty-seventh, 162, 163, 164, 165, 329–340, 372, 373, 375, 682, 697
  Thirty-eighth, 162, 164, 165, 166, 372, 373, 375, 657
Conscience Whigs, 549, **710–713**. *See also* Cotton Whigs; Whig Party
Conscription Act of 1863, 137, 165, **167–169**, 188, 295. *See also* Draft, military; Volunteers, Ninety-Day
Conservative Union Party, 637
Constitution, U.S. *See also specific amendments*
  Article I, 136, 170
  Article I, Section 2, 170
  Article I, Section 9, 170, 174, 311
  Article I, Section 10, 170
  Article IV, 170, 558
  Article IV, Section 2, 514
  Article V, 170
  abolition of slavery and, 657
  civil liberties and, 136, 313, 365
  Confiscation Acts and, 161
  Democratic Party and, 208, 296
  Dred Scott case and, 95, 227, 229
  Garrison on, 283, 516
  Lincoln's views on, 173–177, 334, 350, 524–525
  monetary policy and, 45

Constitution, U.S.—*continued*
  Polk on, 571–572
  protective tariffs and, 21
  secession and, 186, 583, 697
  slavery and, 28, **170–172**, 267, 380
  suffrage and, 60, 618
  Taney and, 645
  Taney on, 243–244
  Whig Party and, 708
The Constitution—A Proslavery Document (Phillips), 516
Constitutional Convention of 1787, 581, 604
Constitutional law, **173–177**
Constitutional Union Party, 51, 52, 96, **177–179**, 369, 381, 467, 472, 562, 579
A Constitutional View of the War Between the States (Stephens), 631
Continental Congress, 497, 581, 654
Continental dollar, 45, 359, 397
Contrabands, **179–182**
Cooke, Jay (1821–1905), 130, **182–183**
Cooper Union Address, 82, 90, 117–118, **183–186**, 268, 412, 493, 524, 565, 567
Copperheads (Peace Democrats), 165, **186–189**, *187,* 207, 208, 209, 210, 344, 475. See also Democrats, Peace
Cornell, Ezra, 478
"Cornerstone Speech" (Stephens), 630
Corning, Erastus, 413, 683
Cornish, Dudley T., 671
Corpus Christi, Texas army camp, *470*
Corruption in the Federal government, **190–191**
Cotton is King (Christy), 383
Cotton Whigs, 562, **713–714**. *See also* Conscience Whigs; Whig Party
Couch, Darius N., 292
Covode, John, 372
Cox, Samuel S., 207
Crampton's Gap, Battle of, 26
Crawford, Josiah, 400
Crawford, William, 18
Crédit Mobilier scandal, 146, 668
Crenshaw, CSS, 538. *See also Prize Cases* (1863)
"Crime against Kansas" speech (Sumner), 86, 638
Crimean War, 460
Crisis of 1850, 630
Crittenden, John J., 115, 191, 192, 515, 700
Crittenden Compromise, 85, **191–193**, 681
Crittenden–Johnson Resolution (1861), 179, 369, 556

Crocker, Charles, 126
Crook, William, 33, 570
Crystal Palace, London, 82
Cuba, 85, 94, 204
Cumberland Furnace Ironworks, 53
Currency, **451–452**, 453. *See also* Banking and monetary policy; Greenbacks
Currier and Ives, 341, 554
Curtin, Andrew Gregg (1817–1894), **194–195**, 291, 292
Curtis, Benjamin R., 492
Cushing, Caleb, 204
Cutler, Manasseh, 498

Daguerrean Miniature Gallery, 82
Dakota communities, 603
Dakota War. *See* Sioux Uprising
Dane, Nathan, 498
Dano–Prussian War (1864), 303
Daughters of the American Revolution's Constitution Hall, Washington, D.C., 416
Davis, David, 90, 561, 673, 674, 675, 676–677, 679, 683
Davis, Henry Winter, 67, 123, 166, 550, 653, 696–699
Davis, Jefferson (1808–1889), **197–200**
  Atlanta Campaign and, 36
  Blair (Francis) meetings with, 64, 318
  Butler support for, 101
  on captured black soldiers, 503–504
  as Confederacy president, 155, 156
  diplomacy of, 254
  Hampton Roads Conference and, 319
  Lee as military adviser to, 394
  in Mexican War, 469
  Missouri and, 368
  naval blockade and, 542
  portrait on postage stamps, 626
  Richmond home of, 569–570
  as secretary of war, 616
  as Senator, 117, 192, 203, 279
  Slidell and, 614
  Taylor (Zachary) and, 648
  Trent affair and, 661
Davis, Joseph Evan, 198
Dayton, William L., 70, 379, 411, 561, 562, 615
Dayton Empire (newspaper), 681
De Bow, J.D.B., 383
Debs, Eugene V., 666
Declaration of Independence, 10, **200–202**, 296, 438, 523–524, 568, 645
Delaware, 78, 79

Democratic Convention (1860), 84, 115, **203–206**, 278, 279, 560, 684
Democratic Convention (1864), 144, 701
Democratic Party, **206–209**
  Bell and, 47
  Breckinridge and, 84
  Buchanan and, 94, 95
  election of 1856, 109, 110
  election of 1860, 203–206, 366
  election of 1864, 124
  Hamlin and, 316
  Lincoln's senatorial campaign of 1858 and, 112–113
  McClellan and, 489
  McLean and, 467
  Taylor and, 54
Democratic Vistas (Whitman), 716
Democrats, Peace. **209–211**, 483, 683, 684, 701. *See also* Copperheads
Dennison, William, 106, 122
Department of the Gulf, 653
Department of the Kentucky, 382
Department of the Monongahela, 292
Department of the Navy, 706
Department of the Ohio, 387, 683
Department of the Susquehanna, 292
Department of the West, 55, 158, 336, 373, 701
Department of West Virginia, 290
Desertions, **211–213**
  "bounty jumpers" and, 222
  from Confederate armies, 598
  Vallandigham encouraging, 683
Devens, Charles, 39
Devil's Den photograph, 83
Dickey, T. Lyle, 29, 115
Dickinson, Anna, 4
Dickinson, Daniel S., 370, 531
DiLorenzo, Thomas, 416
Diplomacy, Lincoln's, **252–254**
District of Columbia, **702–704**
  abolition of slavery in, 3, 11, 29, 150, 158, 160, 161, 611, 612, 613, 711, 712
  Compromise of 1850 and, 153
  congressional power over, 149, 170, 175, 272
  Crittenden Compromise and, 192, 193
  Maryland and, 42–44
Divine Right of Kings, 524
Dodge, Augustus C., 377
Dodge, Grenville, 667
Dodge, Henry, 57
Dodge, Richard, 553
Donald, David Herbert, 577

Dondero, George A., 51
Donelson, Fort. *See* Fort Donelson, Tennessee
Dorsey, Sarah, 199
"Doughface," **213–214**, 216, 467, 519
Douglas, H. Ford, 10, 11, 66
Douglas, Stephen Arnold (1813–1861), *116*, **214–218**, *434*. *See also* Lincoln–Douglas debates
  in American Colonization Society, 19
  as attorney, 134
  on black suffrage, 58
  Breckinridge and, 85
  Compromise of 1850 and, 140–141, 153, 249, 343
  Crittenden Compromise and, 192
  in debates with Lincoln, 284, 433–439
  on Declaration of Independence, 201
  Democratic Convention of 1860 and, 203–206
  Democratic Party and, 207, 366
  as doughface, 214
  on *Dred Scott*, 229, 230, 334–335
  election of 1856, 110
  election of 1860, 116–117, 118
  Greeley support for, 306
  Illinois Central Railroad and, 344
  Johnson (Andrew) and, 369
  Kansas-Nebraska Act and, 2, 29, 30, 268, 379, 380, 411, 473, 511, 512, 518, 606
  Lecompton Constitution opposition by, 95, 333
  as Mary Todd suitor, 419
  McClellan support for, 460
  New York Tribune on, 492
  popular sovereignty policy and, 476, 477, 522, 532, 605
  race-baiting by, 547
  on racial equality, 10
  as Senator, 377
  senatorial campaign of 1858, 112, 113–114
  Shields support for, 600
  state banks and, 685
  Stephens support for, 630
  Sumner on, 86
  Vallandigham support for, 681
  War Democrats and, 700
  Young America movement and, 729
Douglass, Charles, 220
Douglass, Frederick (1818–1895), **218–221**, *219*
  Brown (John) and, 89
  on Confiscation Acts, 670
  on election of Lincoln, 656

Index

Douglass, Frederick—*continued*
  on Fort Pillow killings, 504
  on Freedmen's Memorial, 235–236, 304
  Garrison and, 284
  as Lincoln adviser, 548
  on Lincoln policies, 4, 11, 12, 13
  as Radical Republican, 549, 551
Douglass, Lewis, 220
Dow, Charles W., 391
Doyle, James, 535
Doyle, Mahala, 535
Doyle, Peter, 715
Draft, military, **221–223**. *See also* Conscription Act of 1863; Volunteers, Ninety-Day
Draft riots, New York City, 169, 188, 223, **224–226**, *225*, 295
Drayton, William, 6
Dred: A Tale of the Great Dismal Swamp (Stowe), 633
Dred Scott v. Sandford (1857), **227–231**
  Benton on, 55
  Buchanan on, 94, 95, 117
  as catalyst for war, 678
  Democratic Party on, 204
  Douglas on, 277–278, 436
  Lincoln disagreement with, 10, 173–174, 175
  McLean on, 467, 471
  Missouri Compromise and, 473
  New York Tribune on, 492
  popular sovereignty and, 533
  Republican Party and, 564
  slavocracy and, 606
  Taney and, 643, 645
Drum-Taps (Whitman), 715
DuBois, W. E. B., 13–14, 305
Dudley, Thomas Haines, 16, 253, 302
Dunker Church, 83
Du Pont, Lammot, 663
Durham Station, North Carolina, 596

Early, Jubal A., 395, 590, 591, 703
East Room, White House, 99
Eckert, Thomas, 33
Edwards, Elizabeth, 419, 421, 659, 660
Edwards, Ninian, 419, 659, 660
Egypt, 384
Eisenhower, Dwight, 443
Eisenhower Executive Office Building (old War Department), 443
Election of 1856, Presidential, **109–111**, 582
Election of 1858, Lincoln's Senatorial, **111–115**, 333

Election of 1860, Presidential, **115–120**, 177–178, *493*, 533
Election of 1864, Presidential, **120–124**, 487–489, 619
Electoral College, 123, 170, 178, 227, 605
Eleventh New York regiment (Fire Zouaves), 233, 731
Eliot, William Greenleaf, 235
Ellsworth, Elmer Ephraim (1837–1861), **233–234**, 731. *See also* Zouaves
Ellsworth Avengers (44th New York Volunteer Infantry Regiment), 234
Emancipation (mural), 449
Emancipation Day, *2*
Emancipation Monument, **234–236**
Emancipation Proclamation (1863), **236–240**. *See also* Preliminary Emancipation Proclamation (1862)
  black soldiers and, 669
  Blair (Austin) support for, 62
  Blair (Francis) support for, 64
  Chase support for, 103
  civil liberties and, 135
  Confederacy and, 156
  Confiscation Acts and, 165, 181
  Congress and, 697
  Copperheads and, 188
  Curtin support for, 292
  Davis (Jefferson) on, 503
  Democratic Party and, 208
  Douglass and, 12
  drafting of, 444
  Florville support for, 251
  Garrison support for, 285
  Great Britain support for Union and, 7, 302, 303–304, 385
  Greeley support for, 307, 537–538
  Hamlin support for, 317
  Johnson (Andrew) and, 370, 557
  jurisdiction of, 176, 609, 610
  opposition to, 705
  Radical Republicans and, 550
  Seward and, 587
  Speed on, 622
  Stowe on, 633
  Sumner and, 639
  Thirteenth Amendment and, 656
Emerson, Irene, 227
Emerson, Ralph Waldo, 240, 714
Emerson John, 645
Enabling Act, 437
England. *See* Great Britain
The Enlightenment, 1, 27, 524, 568

Index

Enrollment Act (1863), 222, 224, 226. *See also* Conscription Act (1863)
Enrollment Act (amended, 1864), 223
"Era of good feelings," 473
Erlanger bond issue, 459
Escott, Paul, 198
Essay on Calcareous Manures (Ruffin), 573
Etheridge, Emerson, 166
Europe/Europeans, 276, 289, 302–303, 384, 586, 587, 639, 729
Eustis, George, 615
Evans, W.A., 419
Everett, Edward (1794–1865), 19, 52, 119, 177, 195, **240–241**, 295, 562
Ewing, Thomas, Sr., 593
Ex parte. See *name of party*

Fairfax, Donald, 661
Fair Oaks, Battle of, 394
Farmer's Almanac, 441
Farmers' Register, 573
Farragut, David G., 123, 686
Fehrenbacher, Don E., 548
Fessenden, Samuel C., 316
Fessenden, William Pitt (1806–1869), 106, 183, **247–248**
Field, Cyrus West, 676
Field, David Dudley, 572, 675
Field, Stephen Johnson, 673, 674, 675–676, 679
Field Order No. 15 (Sherman's), 161
Fifteenth Amendment (1870), 60–61, 135, 551, 592, 684, 728
Fifth Amendment, 135, 150, 170, 172, 176, 313, 473, 645, 656
Fifth Massachusetts Cavalry, 671
Fillmore, Millard (1800–1874), **248–250**
  in American Colonization Society, 19
  colonization and, 148
  Compromise of 1850 and, 153
  as Cotton Whig, 713
  election of 1856, 109, 110–111, 379, 564, 710
  internal improvements legislation and, 572
  Stuart support for, 636, 637
  succeeds to presidency, 648
Films about Lincoln, **444–446**
Fine Arts Commission (1911), 448–449
Finley, Robert, 18, 147
"Fire Zouaves" (11th New York regiment), 233, 731
First Confiscation Act (1861), 369

First Inaugural Address. See Inaugural Address, First
First Kansas Colored Volunteers, 671, 672
First Manassas. *See* Bull Run, First Battle of
First Presbyterian Church, Springfield, Illinois, 418
The First Reading of the Emancipation Proclamation before the Cabinet (Carpenter painting), 304
First South Carolina Colored Troops (Union Army), *670*
First South Carolina Volunteers (African Descent), 336, 671
Fish, Hamilton, 17
Fisher, Fort, 72–73, 102
Fitzhugh, George, 522
Five Forks, Battle of, 396
Fleurville, William de. *See* Florville, William
Florida, CSS, 15, 16, 253, 459
Florville, William (1807–1868), 12, **250–251**
Floyd, John B., 266
Fonda, Henry, 445
Foote, Andrew H., 265, 266
Foote, Henry, 107
Foote, Shelby, 40
Forced into Glory: Abraham Lincoln's White Dream (Bennett), 416
Ford, Francis, 445
Ford's Theatre, 31, 32, 33, 34, 74, 77, 300, 317, 421, 424, 440, 628, 704
Ford's Theatre National Historic Site, 443
Foreign Relations and Diplomacy, Lincoln's, **252–254**
Forrest, Joseph K.C., 386
Forrest, Nathan Bedford, 266, 373, 504
Fort Armstrong, Illinois, 227
Fort Barrancas, Florida, 255
Fort Donelson, Tennessee, 238, **264–267**, 298, 343, 462, 601
Fort Fisher, North Carolina, 72–73, 102
Fort/Fortress Monroe, Virginia, 101, 102, 158, 179, 181, 442
Fort Heiman, Kentucky, 265
Fort Henry, Tennessee, 238, **264–267**, 298, 343, 462, 601
Fort Hindman, Arkansas, 688
Fort Johnson, South Carolina, 263
Fort Leavenworth, Kansas, 336
Fort McAllister, Georgia, 598
Fort McHenry, Baltimore, 137, 174, 242–243, 314
Fort McRee, Florida, 255
Fort Moultrie, South Carolina, 258, 262

Index

Fort Pickens, Florida, **254–256**, 261, 263, 541
Fort Pillow, Tennessee, 373, 504, 505
Fort Ridgely, Minnesota, 603
Fort Snelling, Wisconsin Territory, 227, 645
Fort Steadman, Virginia, 396
Fort Stevens, District of Columbia, 439–440, 443, 703
Fort Sumter, South Carolina, **256–264**, *257*
   Blair (Montgomery) as Lincoln adviser on, 65–66
   cabinet discord over, 105
   Congress and, 162
   Douglas on, 217
   Ruffin at, 574
   Scott as Lincoln adviser on, 579
Fort Texas, Brownsville, 623
Fort Warren, Boston, 615, 661
"Forty-Eighters," 289–290
Forty-fourth New York Volunteer Infantry Regiment (Ellsworth Avengers), 234
Foster, Charles W., 671
Founding Fathers, Lincoln's view of, **267–269**, 276, 411, 413, 438, 498, 513, 524, 533–534, 564–565, 567, 678
Fourteenth Amendment (1868), 135, 199, 551, 684, 728
Fox, Gustavus Vasa, 64, 261–262, 541
Framers of the Constitution. *See* Founding Fathers, Lincoln's view of
France, 64, 124, 252, 303, 318, 385, 459, 612, 638, 639, 731
Franco-Algerian uniforms, 732
Franklin, Benjamin, 268, 355, 626
Franklin, William B., 374
Frederick Douglass' Paper (previously *North Star*), 219
Fredericksburg and Chancellorsville, Battles of, **269–271**, 291, 373, 374, 395, 695, 715
"Free banking" laws, 486
Free Democrat, 467
Freedman's Bureau, 4, 161, 166, 639, 665
Freedman's Memorial Society, Washington, D.C., 304
Freedmen's Memorial to Abraham Lincoln, **234–236**
Freeport, Illinois, debate, 113–114, 279, 412, 435
Freeport Doctrine, 114, 204, **277–280**, 436, 533
"Free Soil, Free Labor, Free Men" slogan, **274–277**, 329
Free Soilers, 549, 574, 608
"Free soil" ideology, 564

Free Soil Party, **272–274**
   antislavery, 30, 608
   Blair (Austin) and, 62
   Blair (Francis) and, 63
   Chase and, 129, 676
   formation of, 471
   Garrison and, 284
   Hale and, 399
   McLean and, 466–467
   Sumner and, 638
   Van Buren and, 648, 711
   Whittier and, 717
"Free Speech, Free Press, Free Soil, Free Men" slogan, 564
Free-State Hotel, Lawrence, Kansas, 391
Frelinghuysen, Theodore, 466
Frémont, Jessie Benton, 55
Frémont, John Charles (1813–1890), **280–282**
   abolitionist support for, 4
   Benton and, 53–54, 55
   Blair (Montgomery) and, 66, 67
   Carson and, 455
   election of 1856, 47, 70, 94, 110–111, 250, 379, 471
   election of 1860, 561
   election of 1864, 122, 123, 142, 144, 488
   Emancipation proclamation in Missouri by, 3, 11, 80, 93, 131
   Joint Committee on the Conduct of the War and, 373
   Lincoln revocation of Emancipation proclamation of, 155, 158, 180
   Lincoln's removal of, 290, 372
   as Radical Republican, 550, 551
   Republican Party and, 564
   as Union general, 608
French, Daniel Chester, 449
French Revolution, 549
Frontier Guard, 703
Frothingham, Edward Gilman, 717
Fry, James Barnett, 222
Fugitive Slave Act/Law (1793), 110, 284, 514, 517, 644–645
Fugitive Slave Act/Law (1850)
   Breckinridge on, 85
   Brown (John) on, 88
   Chase on, 130
   Clay and, 140–141
   Confiscation Acts and, 158, 161, 180
   Conscience Whigs and, 711
   constitutionality of, 10, 514, 515
   Cotton Whigs and, 713
   Crittenden Compromise and, 192

Democratic Party and, 118, 204, 206
enforcement of, 11
Fillmore and, 249
Garrison on, 283
Lincoln on, 346, 435, 512
Mason and, 459
McLean and, 110
Phillips on, 516, 517
Radical Republicans and, 549
Seward on, 117
Stowe on, 632
Sumner and, 639
Vallandigham support for, 681
Fusion Party, 563, 591, 695, 704–705
"Fusion" ticket, 487

Gag Rule, 605
Galena, Illinois speech, 258
Galesburg, Illinois, debate, 114, 412, 437
Gamble, Hamilton, 367
Gardner, Alexander, 82, 83
Garfield, James A., 425, 592
Garrison, William Lloyd (1805–1879), **283–286**, *284*
  on American Colonization Society propaganda, 19
  on Blair, 66
  on colonization idea, 148
  on Emancipation Proclamation, 4
  Liberty Party and, 398
  Radical Republicans and, 549
  relationship with Douglass, 218, 219
  relationship with Phillips, 516
  secession and, 581
  Whittier and, 716
Gasparro, Frank, 453
Geary, John W., 70, 392
General Land Office, 464
General Order No. 11 (Hunter's), 159, 336
General Order No. 28 (Butler's), 101
General Order No. 38 (Burnside's), 387, 683
General War Order No. 1, 265, **286–288**
The Genius of Oblivion and Other Original Poems (Hale), 654
The Genius of Universal Emancipation, 283
Gentry, James and Allen, 403
George III, king of England, 187
German Americans, Lincoln and, 142–143, 186, **288–291**, 367, 650
Gettysburg, Battle of, 32, 83, 188, 195, 202, **291–294**, 373, 395, 557
Gettysburg Address, 120, 195, 202, 240, 269, **294–297**, 307, 355, 413, 442, 449, 567

Gettysburg Battlefield, 448
Gettysburg Cemetery Commission, 295
Gettysburg National Cemetery, 439
Giddings, Joshua, 3, 611, 612
Gilmer, John A., 510, 514
Gilmore, James R., 536
Gist, William Henry, 257
Gladstone, William, 16
Globe (newspaper), 63
Godey's Lady's Book, 632, 654
Godwin, Parke, 123
"Golden spike" ceremony, 667
Gooch, Daniel W., 372
Goosenest Prairie, Illinois, 437
Gott, Daniel, 612, 613, 711
Graham, Mentor, 490, 575
Grant, Julia, 32
Grant, Ulysses S. (1822–1885), **297–301**, *298, 506*
  absence from Lincoln assassination, 32
  amnesty for Confederate forces, discontinued by, 137
  appointment as general in chief, 121, 188, 395
  on black regiments, 670, 671
  Colfax as running mate, 146
  criticisms of, effectiveness of, 688
  Curtin and, 195
  diplomacy during presidency of, 385
  election of 1864, consideration as presidential candidate in, 143–144
  election of 1872, 308
  Forts Henry and Donelson, 266
  Hampton Roads Conference, 318
  Illinois Campaign, 343
  Indian relations, 358
  Johnson (Andrew) on surrender terms set by Grant, 371
  Lincoln (Robert Todd) and, 424
  Magoffin as governor of Kentucky and, 457
  on McClellan, 460
  in Mexican War, 469
  Overland Campaign, 505–508, 551
  relationship with Lincoln, 375, 413
  relationship with Sherman, 593, 594–595, 597, 602
  settling conflict between Stanton and Sherman, 628
  Shenandoah Valley Campaigns of 1862 and 1864, 590
  Sherman and Atlanta Campaign, 37
  Shiloh, Battle of, 601–602
  Supreme Court nomination of Stanton, 629

surrender of Lee to, 157, 396
tribunal to settle outstanding war claims, 17
Vicksburg, 295
Vicksburg Campaign and, 687–689
victories in Tennessee and Kentucky, 238, 265
Virginia Campaign, 122
Wilderness Campaign, 504
"Great Apostate," 52
"The Great Army of the Sick" (Whitman), 715
Great Britain, 301–303
   cotton supplied from South to, 383–384, 539
   Douglass' freedom purchased by British abolitionists, 218
   Lincoln's foreign relations with, 252–253
   Lincoln signing treaty with on suppression of illegal slave trade, 712
   Morrill Tariff, 482
   neutrality in Civil War, 73
   Pacific Northwest controversy with, 528
   relations with Union and Confederacy, 6, 16, 459, 586–587
   Trent incident and, 638, 661–663, *662*
   Union wheat embargo and, 385
"Great Compromise," 472
"Great Compromiser," 9, 18, 139, 521
Great Depression, 655
"Great Emancipator," 13, 235, **303–305**, 340, 416, 439, 545
"The great writ," 311
Greeley, Horace (1811–1872), **306–308**
   Anaconda plan and, 24
   Bates for presidential nominee, supporter of, 49
   critical of Union tactics, 39
   as Douglas supporter, 112, 145
   on *Dred Scott* decision, 228
   election of 1860 and opposition to Seward, 560–561
   favoring compromise peace with Confederacy, 188, 320
   "Forward to Richmond" opinion of, 97
   on Harper's Ferry raid, 90, 91
   Herndon correspondence with, 325
   homestead proposal of, 329
   on Lincoln oratory at Cooper Union, 185
   Lincoln public letter to, 239, 413, 537, 567, 669
   New York Tribune founded by, 492–494
   Nicolay and, 495
   "The Prayer of Twenty Millions" by, 536–538
   seeking to replace Lincoln as party nominee, 123
   urging Lincoln to free the slaves, 239, 413, 536–538
Greenbacks, 44–45, 247, **308–309**, 359, 397. *See also* Banking and monetary policy; Currency
Grier, Robert C., 95, 249, 539
Griffith, D.W., 445
Grigsby, Aaron, 403
Grigsby, Sarah Lincoln (1807–1828), 356, 401, 402, 403, 422, 428
Grow, Galusha A., 163
Gruber, Jacob, 644
Grundy, Felix, 52
Guerin, Jules, 449
Gulf of Mexico, 71

Habeas corpus, Lincoln's suspension of, **311–315**
   Booth and, 75
   campaign of 1864 and, 121
   civil liberties and, 136
   Congress, relations with Lincoln and, 162, 165
   constitutional law and, 173, 174, 176
   criticism of, 682
   defense of, 49
   draft cases and, 169, 223
   effect of, 80
   events leading to, 75
   Jackson, Andrew and, 365
   in Kentucky, 382
   McClellan and, 463
   Merryman and, 242–244
   military campaign and, 692
   personal liberty laws and, 514, 515, 523
   Prize Cases, 539
   Republicans and, 565
   second declaration of, 44
   Taney and, 645–646, 678, 679
   Trumbull and, 665
Habeas Corpus Act (1863), 137, 314, 683
Hahn, Michael, 13, 60, 558
"Hail to the Chief," 33
Haiti, 12, 148, 159, 160, 219, 639, 657
Hale, John P., 399, 467
Hale, Sarah Josepha, 654
Halleck, Henry W., 25, 265, 266, 293, 298, 300, 462, 550, 594, 601, 602
Halstead, Murat, 204
Hamilton, Alexander, 268, 322

Hamlin, Hannibal (1809–1891), 104, **315–318**, 370, 488, 510, 562
Hammond, James Henry, 383
Hampton Roads Conference (1865), 64, 300, **318–320**, 631
Hanks, Dennis (cousin), 402, 403, 426
Hanks, John (cousin), 405, 554, 555
Hansell, Emerick, 34
Hardee, William J., 598
Hardin, John J., 406, 409
Hardin County, Kentucky, 428
Harding, Benjamin F., 372
Harding, Warren G., 450
Harlan, James, 425
Harlem Renaissance, 416
Harpers Ferry, Battle of, 589, 590
Harpers Ferry raid (1859)
   Brown, John, role at, 89–91
   Buchanan on, 95
   Lee's capture of John Brown at, 393
   Mason investigation of, 459
   Phillips' praise of, 517
   Republican Party and, 561, 564
   Ruffin writing inspired by, 574
   Southern reaction to, 608
   Whittier's reaction to, 717
Harper's Weekly, 82, 83, 117
Harris, Clara, 32
Harris, Ira, 32
Harris, Isham, 542
Harris, James, 535
Harrison, Benjamin, 425
Harrison, George, 57
Harrison, William Henry, 45, 52, 56, 125, 140, 398, 408, 466, 554, 708, 710
Harrison's Landing, 462
Hart, James, 386
Hartford Convention, 581
Hartford Times and Weekly Advertiser, 706
Hatch, Ozias M., 495
Hawk, Harry, 33
Hay, John (1838–1905), 66, **320–323**, *321*, 497, 699
Hayes, Rutherford B., 129, 484, 592, 618
Hayne, Robert Y., 333, 708
Hazel, Caleb, 401
Hearst, William Randolph, 491
Hecker, Friedrich, 289
Heiman, Fort, 265
Henderson, John, 657
Henning, Fanny, 622
Henry, Anson G., 206

Henry, Fort. *See* Fort Henry, Tennessee
Henry, James, 57
Henry, Patrick, 28
"Henry Clay Whig," 206
Henry Ford Museum, Michigan, 441
Hepburn v. Griswold (1870), 398. *See also* Legal Tender Act (1862); *Legal Tender Cases*
Herald of Freedom (newspaper), 391
Herbert, John C., 18
Herndon, William Henry (1818–1891), **324–327**, 345, 409, 420, 423, 427, 429, 441, 491, 576, 577
Herndon law firm and Lincoln, 324, 441–442
Herndon's Lincoln: The True Story of a Great Life (Herndon), 326
Herold, David Edgar (Davy), 33, 34, 76, 77
Hiatt, James, 386
Hiawatha, CSS, 538. *See also* Prize Cases (1863)
Hicks, Thomas Holliday, **327–328**, 703
Hildene estate, Vermont, 425
Hill, A.P., 26
Hindman, Fort, 688
Hines, Thomas, 475
Hodgenville, Kentucky, 401, 440
Hodges, Albert G., 8, 176, 238
Hofstadter, Richard, 237, 239
Hollywood Cemetery, Richmond, 199
Holmes, Oliver Wendell, Jr., 40
Holt, Joseph, 700
Holt, Michael F., 190, 465
Homestead Act (1862), 22, 55, 104, 307, **328–331**, 361, 364, 459, 478, 565
"Honest Abe," 190, 220, **331–332**, 416, 509, 685
Hood, John Bell, 36, 595, 597, 598
Hooker, Joseph, 27, 271, 292, 374, 395
Hopkins, Mark, 126
Hosmer, Harriet, 235
House Committee on Agriculture, 479
"House Divided" speech (1858), 9–10, 112, 229, 258, **332–336**, 355, 380, 412, 435, 436, 606
House Select Committee on the Rebellious States, 653
Houston, Sam, 52
Howard, John Eager, 18
Howard, Joseph J., Jr., 43
Howard, Oliver O., 293
Howe, Julia Ward, 91
Howell, Varina, 198

Howells, William Dean, 119
Hughes, John, 615
Hughes, Langston, 416
Hunter, David (1802–1886), 3, 11, 80, 131, 159, 180, **336–338**, *337,* 537, 550, 590, 639
Hunter, Robert M.T., 318, 481
Huntington, Collis P., 126–127

IC. *See* Illinois Central Railroad
Iconography, **339–341**
"I Have a Dream" speech (King), 416, 450
Illinois, **341–344**
Illinois Central Railroad (IC), 343, **344–345**, 460, 553
Illinois Central Railroad v. County of Mclean (1856), 345
Illinois General Assembly, 407, 408, 410, 438, 512, 572
Illinois-Michigan canal, 344
Illinois politics, 727–728
Illinois Republican Party, 87, 92
Illinois Staats–Anzeiger (newspaper), 289
Illinois Supreme Court, 175, 345, 408, 409
Inaugural Address, First, 11, 173, 175, 219, **346–350**, *347,* 515, 555–556, 568, 608, 678, 708
Inaugural Address, Second, 12, 221, **350–353**, 355, 450, 558
Income Taxes, **353–355**
Independent (newspaper), 123
Independent Treasury system, 527
India, 384, 663
Indiana, **355–356**
Indiana Sanitary Commission, 483
Indian-head penny, 452
Indian relations, **356–358**. *See also* American Indians
Indian Territory (Oklahoma), 357
Inflation, **358–360**
In re. See name of party
Interior Department, 104, 129, 190
Interior Department Bureau for Colored Troops, 671
Internal Improvements, **360–361**
Internal Revenue Act of 1862, 160, 164
The Intimate World of Abraham Lincoln (Tripp), 623
In War Time and Other Poems (Whittier), 717
Ireland, 218
Irish immigrants, 186, 224–225, 289, 388
"Irrepressible conflict" speech (Seward), 117
Island Mound, Missouri skirmish, 672
Iuka and Corinth offensives, Tennessee, 299

Jackson, Andrew (1767–1845), **363–366**
  American System, opposition to, 21, 709
  banking policy of, 45, 52, 54, 527
  Black Hawk War, 56
  Buchanan as supporter of, 94
  Copperheads and, 186
  election of 1824, 139
  election of 1828, 464–465
  Polk and, 527
  Second Bank of United States and, 685
  Taney, appointment of, 643
  on two-cent stamp, 626
  Whig Party and, 707
  Young America movement and, 729
Jackson, Claiborne Fox (1806–1862), **366–368**
Jackson, Thomas J. (Stonewall), 48, 98, 270, 271, 281, 394, 589–590
Jacksonian Democracy/Democrats, 20, 21, 58, 363, 369, 406, 467, 523, 706
Jacobins, 549
Jay Cooke and Company, 182
Jayne, Julia, 600, 664
Jefferson, Thomas, 147, 170, 186, 268, 296, 301, 348, 498, 581, 626
Jefferson Davis Presidential Library, Biloxi, Mississippi, 200
Jeffersonian Republican Party, 21, 139
Jenifer, H.W., 40
The Jerry Rescue, 249
"John Brown Republicans," 91
"John Brown's Body" (song), 91
Johnson, Andrew (1808–1875), **368–371**, *488,* 555
  assassination plot against, 32, 77
  critics of, 127, 248, 592
  Davis, amnesty for, 199
  end of slavery and, 610
  Hamlin and, 317
  as military governor, 266, 372, 556–557, 602, 652
  National Union Party and, 489
  patronage and, 510
  Radical Republicans and, 530, 551
  Reconstruction and, 138, 566
  as senator, 372
  Stanton and, 629
  Trumbull and, 665
  as vice president, 122, 317, 488
  Wade and, 696
  as War Democrat, 701
  Yates and, 728
Johnson, Fort, 263

Johnson, Reverdy, 701
Johnston, Albert Sidney, 265, 299, 601
Johnston, Daniel, 426
Johnston, Elizabeth (Lincoln's stepsister), 426
Johnston, John D. (Lincoln's stepbrother), 405, 426
Johnston, Joseph E., 32, 35, 97, 98, 394, 396, 462, 596, 628
Johnston, Matilda (Lincoln's stepsister), 426
Johnston, Sarah Bush. *See* Lincoln, Sarah Bush Johnston
Joint Committee on Reconstruction, 247–248
Joint Committee on the Conduct of the War, 39, 41, 128, 163, 287, 293, 369, **372–375**, 504, 550, 690, 695
Joint High Commission, 17
Jomini, 292
Jominian military strategy concepts, 292
Jones, Samuel, 391
Jones, William, 363
Jonesboro, Illinois, debate, 114, 436
Jonesborough, Battle of, 36
Joy, James F., 345
Juarez, Benito, 253
Judd, Norman B., 411, 433, 664
Judiciary Committee, 160
Julian, George W., 372
Justice and Expediency (Whittier), 716

Kane, George P., 44
Kansas-Nebraska Act (1854), **377–380**
 author of, 112, 141, 153, 215, 268, 343
 backers of, 125
 campaign of 1860 and, 115
 Dred Scott decision and, 229, 230
 impact of, 67–68, 95, 215–216, 518–519, 608
 Lincoln-Douglas debates, 154, 436
 Lincoln's opposition to, 10, 70, 145, 201, 268, 296, 334, 411, 498, 510–513, 548
 Missouri Compromise and, 471, 473
 opposition to, 29, 55, 194, 247, 289, 483, 591, 727
 passage of, 86, 469
 popular sovereignty and, 532
 Republicans and, 87, 109, 563, 565
 slavery legalized in territories, 2
 Whig Party and, 52
Kansas Territory, 67, 201, 215, 333, 366, 377, 379, 386, 391, 435, *511*, 535. *See also* "Bleeding Kansas"
Kearsarge, USS, 15, 17
Keene, Laura, 31

Keim, William H., 242
Kellogg's Grove, Battle of, 56
Kelso, Jack, 490
Kendall, Amos, 63
Kennedy, John F., 415
Kennesaw Mountain, Battle of, 36
Kentucky, 78–79, 281, **381–383**, 457
Kentucky Resolutions, 581
Kentucky Unionists, 81
Kernstown, Battle of, 589
Key, Ann, 643
Key, Francis Scott, 18, 147, 643
Key, Philip Barton, 627
A Key to Uncle Tom's Cabin (Stowe), 633
Kickapoo Rangers, 70, *378*
King, Albert, 34
King, Martin Luther, Jr., 415, 416, 450
King, Rufus, 498
King, William R., 518
"King Andrew," 364, 707
King Cotton, 72, 73, **383–385**
King James Bible, 524, 567
Knights of the Golden Circle, **385–387**
Knobs Creek, Kentucky, 401, 428
Know-Nothing (American) Party, **388–389**
 anti-immigrant stance of, 719
 Banks as member of, 47
 Bates's affiliation with, 412
 Cameron as, 107
 Colfax and, 145
 Constitutional Union Party formed from, 119, 177, 468
 Crittenden and, 191
 Curtin and, 194
 Fillmore and, 249, 564
 Hicks and, 327
 Lincoln's criticism of, 289
 McLean and, 467
 Republican Party formation and, 87, 118, 379, 562
 Stuart and, 636
 Vallandigham and, 681
 Whig Party members joining, 52, 714
 Wood defeat in NYC and, 724
 Yates and, 727
Knox v. Lee (1871), 398. *See also* Legal Tender Act of 1862; *Legal Tender Cases*
Kramer, Larry, 416, 622
Ku Klux Klan, 596

Ladies Magazine and Literary Gazette, 654
Laird, J. R., 16
Lake Okeechobee, Battle of, 647

Lamon, Ward Hill, 4, 261, 326
Lane, Henry S., 483
Lane, James H., 69, 70, 703
Langston, John Mercer, 59
Larue County, Kentucky, 381
The Last Hours of Lincoln (Chappel painting), 83
Law practice, Lincoln's, 324, 407–410, 419, 441–442, 454
Lawrence, Amos, 391
Lawrence, Kansas, **391–393**, 535
 sacking of, 68, 69
League of Gileadites, 88
Leale, Charles, 34
Leavenworth, Fort, 336
Leaves of Grass (Whitman), 714, 716
Leavitt, Humphrey, 683
Leavitt, Joshua, 3
Lecompton Constitution, 216, 278, 333, 411, 437, 438, 564
Lecompton Convention, 95, 108, 112, 128
Lee, "Light Horse" Harry, 393
Lee, Robert E. (1807–1870), **393–396**
 Antietam Campaign, 25–27
 confiscation of home of, 160–161
 Fredericksburg (1862) and Chancellorsville (1863), Battles of, 269–271
 Gettysburg, Battle of (1863), 291–294, 295
 Harpers Ferry and capture of John Brown, 89
 McClellan and, 462, 463
 in Mexican War, 469
 as military adviser to Davis at start of war, 589, 590
 Overland Campaign, 505–508
 surrender of, 157, 300, 358
 Union seeking to enlist, 64
Lee, Samuel, 64
Leesburg, Virginia, 39
Legal Tender Act of 1862, 45, 164, 308–309, 364, **396–398**, 485, 592
Legal Tender Cases (1870, 1871), 398, 676
Lemmon Slave Case (pamphlet), 492
L'Enfant, Pierre-Charles, 702
"Let's Go See Old Abe" (Hughes), 416
Liberal Republican ticket, 308
Liberator, 66, 283–284, 285, 716
Liberia, West Africa, 9, 19, 148, 159, 160, 639, 657
Liberty Party, 1, 3, 30, 129, 219, 272, 273, 284, **398–399**, 549, 676
Library of Congress, 425
The Life of Washington (Weems), **400–401**
Lincoln (Spielberg, film), 417

Lincoln, Abraham (1809–1865), 9, 116, *121, 237, 321, 434, 461, 488, 493, 546, 555, 570, 626*
 African Americans and, **8–15**
 on amnesty, 697–698
 assassination of, **31–35**
 on black suffrage, 13
 burial and tomb of, **99–100**
 cabinet of, **103–106**, 247–248
 childhood and youth (1809-1831), **401–404**
 on colonization, 9, 11, 19, 20
 Congress, relations with, 105, 106, **162–167**
 constitutional law and, **173–177**
 on currency, **451–452**
 debates with Douglas, **433–439**
 Declaration of Independence, view of, **200–202**
 on equality of races, 10
 in films, **444–446**
 foreign relations and diplomacy of, **252–254**
 founding fathers, view of, **267–269**
 German Americans and, 142, 143, 186, **288–291**, 388
 Herndon law firm and, 324, 441–442
 historic sites, preservation, **439–444**
 Indian relations and, **356–358**
 Jackson, Andrew and, **363–366**
 Johnson, Andrew and, **368–371**
 legal and early political careers of, 324, **407–410**, 419, 441–442, 454, 678
 memory of, **414–417**
 in music, **446–448**
 as national figure (1854-1865), **410–413**
 patronage and, **509–510**
 penny and, **452–453**
 political culture and, **520–522**, 708–709
 political philosophy of, 264, **522–526**
 postage stamps and, **625–626**
 racism/racial thought and, **545–549**
 rail-splitter image of, 363, **554–555**
 reconstruction, Virginia plan for, **689–691**
 rhetoric in public speeches of, **566–568**
 Richmond, Virginia, arrival in, **569–571**
 senatorial campaign of 1858, **111–115**
 on slavery, 1, 28, 29
 on suffrage, 8
 U.S. Colored Troops (USCT) and, **669–672**
 Whig Party and, **707–710**
 on Young America movement, 729
 young manhood to eve of political career, **404–407**
Lincoln, Edward Baker (son, 1846–1850), 99, **417–418**, 419, 420, 424

Lincoln, Josiah (uncle), 428
Lincoln, Mary Todd (wife, 1818–1882), **418–422**, *419*
   at assassination of Lincoln, 32, 34
   broken engagement with Lincoln, 408
   burial of Lincoln, 99
   courtship of, 622, 660
   Douglass, memento sent to after death of Lincoln, 221
   grieving loss of child, 418
   Hay's dislike for, 322
   Kentucky origins of, 381
   letter exchange with Queen Victoria, 303
   living at Soldiers' Home, 616–617
   naming of son Thomas "Tad," 429
   in Richmond, 570
   rumored to be spy, 163
   on Rutledge's relationship with Lincoln, 576
   Shields and, 600
   social events and, 121, 551
   Todd family and, 659–660
   Trumbull and, 664
Lincoln, Mordecai (uncle), 428
Lincoln, Nancy Hanks (mother, 1784–1818), 356, 381, 401, 402, **422–423**, 426, 428
Lincoln, Robert Todd (son, 1843–1926), 100, 320, 417, 419, 420, 421, **424–426**, 430, 450, 451, 554, 576
Lincoln, Sarah (sister). *See* Grigsby, Sarah Lincoln
Lincoln, Sarah Bush Johnston (stepmother, 1788–1869), 402, **426–427**, 428
Lincoln, Tad (son, 1853–1871), 99, 419, 421, 425, **429–431**, 571, 616
Lincoln, Thomas (1812), 422, 428
Lincoln, Thomas (father, 1778–1851), 28, 326, 342, 381, 401, 402, 404, 405, 407, 426, 427, **428–429**
Lincoln, William "Willie" Wallace (son, 1850–1862), 92, 99, 251, 419, 420, 424, 430, **431–433**, 617, 660
Lincoln Bedroom, White House, 442
Lincoln Boyhood National Memorial, Lincoln City, Indiana, 423
Lincoln–Douglas debates, 19, 58, 66, 95, 113–114, 117, 154, 216, 277–278, 333, **433–439**, *434*, 441, 472, 606. *See also specific locations*
Lincoln five dollar note, 451
Lincoln Highway, 415
Lincoln historic sites, preservation of, **439–444**

Lincoln Home National Historic Site, Springfield, Illinois, 442
Lincoln in film, **444–446**
Lincoln in music, **446–448**
Lincoln Log Cabin State Historic Site, Lerna, Illinois, 441
Lincoln Memorial, Washington, D.C., 294, 415, 416, 425, **448–450**, 451, 453, 704
Lincoln Memorial Commission (1902), 448, 449
Lincoln on currency, **451–452**
Lincoln Park, Chicago, 425
Lincoln Park, Washington, D.C., 235
Lincoln penny, 415, 451, **452–453**
Lincoln–Rutledge engagement, 576
Lincoln Sitting Room, White House, 442
Lincoln Studies Center, Knox College, 326
Lincoln the Man (Masters), 416
Lincoln the President (Randall), 576–577
Lincoln Tomb, Springfield, Illinois, 425, 431, 432
Lincoln Trail Homestead State Historic Site, Decatur, Illinois, 441
Lincoln Unmasked: What You're Not Supposed to Know about Dishonest Abe (DiLorenzo), 416
Little Crow, Chief, 603
"Little Giant," 112, 113, 145, 215, 217, 436
Little Pigeon Creek Baptist Church, Indiana, 355, 403
Liverpool, England, 16, 253, 302
Loan, Benjamin F., 372
Locke, John, 27
Logan, David, 409
Logan, John, 343
Logan, Stephen Trigg (1800–1880), 409, **454–455**, 599, 636, 660
Logan and Lincoln law firm, 324, 454
"Log Cabin and Hard Cider" slogan, 554
Log cabin birthplace, 401, 439, *440*
"Long Nine," 408, 685–686
Longstreet, James, 270
"The Long Walk," 357–358, **455–456**. *See also* Indian relations
Longworth v. Lewis (1849), 678
Los Angeles Times, 416
"Lost Speech" (Lincoln's), 87
Lott, Trent, 200
Louisiana Native Guards (Union), 671
Louisiana Purchase, 139, 152, 377, 473, 563, 605
Lovejoy, Elijah, 324, 329, 342, 516, 686
Lovejoy, Owen, 110, 388, 433, 549
Lower Sioux Agency, 603

Loyal War Governors Conference (1862), 195, 292
Lundy, Benjamin, 283
Lyceum Address of 1838 (Clay), 523
Lyon, Nathaniel, 367
Lyons, Lord. *See* Pemell, Richard Bicketron

Macbeth, 571
MacDonald, John, 17
Macfarland, James E., 615
Macon County, Illinois, 405, 407
Macon County Historic Complex, Illinois, 441
Madison, James, 18, 21
Magoffin, Beriah (1815–1885), 80, 381, **457–458**
Maine Law, 649
Malin, James, 535
Mallory, Charles K., 180
Malvern, USS, 569, 570
Manassas. *See* Bull Run, First Battle of; Bull Run, Second Battle of
Manifest Destiny, 215, 357, 377, 469, 527
Maps, *23*, 511
Marble, Manton, 143
Marchant, Edward Dalton, 304, 340
March on Washington (1963), 450
March to the Sea, 37, 595–596, **597–599**
Marine and Fire Insurance Company lobby, Bank One, Springfield, 442
Marlbourne plantation, 573
Marshall, John, 365, 643
Marshall House, Alexandria, 233–234
Martin, Patrick C., 76
Marx, Karl, 237–238, 306
"Mary Had a Little Lamb" (Hale), 655
Maryland, 78, 79
Mason, James Murray (1798–1871), 66, 125, 252–253, 302, **458–460**, 614, 615, 639, 661–663
Mason, John, 18
Mason-Dixon line, 608
Massachusetts Anti-Slavery Society, 218
Massachusetts Volunteers, 54th and 55th regiments (black), 671
Massey, Raymond, 445
Masters, Edgar Lee, 416, 576
Matson, Robert, 409–410
Matson fugitive slave case, 285, 409
Matteson, Joel, 411
Maysville Road, 21
McAllister, Fort, 598
McCardle, Ex parte (1869), 676
McCleary, James, 448

McClellan, George B. (1826–1885), *121*, **460–464**, *461*
  Antietam Campaign, 25–27
  Ball's Bluff, Battle of, 39
  campaign of 1864 and, 36, 120, 122–123, 125, 144, 189, 209, 382, 489, 595, 620, 699
  Congress and, 163
  criticism of, 128, 183, 195, 374–375, 628
  Grant and, 298
  Lincoln, relations with, 40–41, 63, 266, 286–287, 394
  McClellan saddle, 460
  Mexican War and, 469
  Peninsula Campaign and, 288, 374
  Radical Republicans and, 550, 551
  removal of, 98, 105, 131, 270, 375
  runaway slaves and, 179
  Shenandoah Valley Campaign, 589
  Vallandigham and, 684
  as War Democrat, 700
McClellan's Own Story (Prime), 464
McClernand, John A., 83, 299, 329, 343, 594, 687–688
McClure, Alexander K., 299, 370, 496
McCormick reaper patent case, 627
McCulloch, Hugh, 106, 705
McDowell, Irvin, 97–98, 442, 461, 589, 693
McHenry, Fort. *See* Fort McHenry, Baltimore
McKinley, William, 481, 592
McLean, John (1785–1861), 109–110, 117, 205, **464–468**, 560
McNamar, John. *See* McNeil, John
McNeil, John, 575
McPherson, James B., 36, 255, 354
McRee, Fort, 255
Mdewakaton Dakota tribe, 603
Mdewakaton Soldier's Lodge, 603
Meade, George G., 291, 292, 293, 294, 295, 375, 395, 506, *506*, 507, 732
Medary, Samuel, 210
Medical Bureau, U.S. army, 635
Medill, Joseph, 279, 561
Meigs, Montgomery, 255
Menard Axis (newspaper), 576
Men of Our Times (Stowe), 634
Meridian Campaign, 595
Merryman, Ex parte (1861), 49, 137, **242–245**, 312, 539–540, 646, 679
Merryman, John, 137, 174, 242, 312, 314, 365, 645–646
Merwin, James B., 650
Metamora Courthouse State Historic Site, Illinois, 441

Metz, Karl, 414
Mexican–American War. *See* Mexican War
Mexican Cession, 527, 528, 531
Mexican War, **469–471**
  Benton on, 54
  Cameron on, 107
  Davis in, 197
  expansion of slavery into territories acquired in, 152, 272, 473, 531
  Frémont in, 142, 280
  Knights of the Golden Circle and, 386
  Lincoln in Congress and, 361, 436, 560, 624
  Pierce in, 518
  Polk and, 528
  provocation for, 624
  Scott in, 579
  Shields in, 600
  Taylor's victory in, 466
  Welles and, 706
  Whig Party opposition to, 709
  Wilmot Proviso and, 605, 720–723
Mexico City, 253, 393, 528
Mexico plan (Blair's), 319
Meyer, Gustavus, 690
Michigan and Erie Canal, 342
Michigan Territory, 124, 125
Military Division of the Mississippi, 595
Militia, **540–543**
Militia Act (1795), 692
Militia Act (1862), 168, 222, 670
Miller, Samuel, 673, 674–675, 677, 679
Miller v. United States (1871), 136
Milligan, Lamdin P., 315–316
Milligan, Ex parte (1866), 137, 314, 675, 676
Minor, Charles, 416
Mississippi River, 24, 48, 72, 107, 295, 342, 689
Mississippi Territory, 268
Missouri, 78, 79
Missouri Compromise (1820), **471–474**
  Benton's defense of, 55
  Clay and, 139
  Crittenden Compromise and, 192
  doughfaces and, 213
  Dred Scott and, 227, 229, 467
  election of 1856 and, 110
  election of 1860 and, 268
  Northern opposition to, 605
  unconstitutionality of, 467
  Weed and, 705
  Western territories, proposed extension to, 531
Missouri Compromise, repeal of (1854). *See also* Kansas-Nebraska Act (1854)
  Bell's vote against, 52
  Brooks and, 87
  Cass and, 125
  Conscience Whigs on, 712
  Douglas and, 29, 153, 215, 511, 532
  Lincoln on, 334, 392, 498, 512
  Whigs on, 512, 709, 710
Missouri Daily Republican, 572
Missouri Supreme Court, 227
"Mobtown" (Baltimore), 42
Monroe, Fort. *See* Fort/Fortress Monroe, Virginia
Monroe, James, 19, 139, 147, 301, 464, 466
Monroe Doctrine, 385, 489
Monterrey, Battle of, 197, 647
Montgomery, Alabama, 97, 155
Montgomery Mail, 257
Montreal, Canada, 75
"Moral suasion," 284, 649, 650
Morgan, Edwin D., 559, 705
Morgan, John Hunt, 392, 474
Morgan's Raid, 392, **474–476**, 484
Mormons, 136, **476–477**, 478
Morrill, Justin Smith (1810–1898), **478–479**, 481
Morrill Act, Second (1890), 136
Morrill Anti-Bigamy Act (1862), 136, 477
Morrill Land Grant Act (1862), 136, 164, 361, 478, **479–480**, 565
Morrill tariff, 478, **481–482**
Morris, Gouverneur, 604
Morris Island, South Carolina, 262
Morse, Samuel F.B., 82
Morton, Oliver P. (1823–1877), 386, 475, **482–484**
Mosby's Rangers, 76
Moton, Robert, 450
Moultrie, Fort. *See* Fort Moultrie, South Carolina
Mountain Department, 142, 374
Mount Rushmore, South Dakota, 415
"Mount Vernon of the West," 491
Movies and Lincoln, **444–446**
Mr. Buchanan's Administration on the Eve of the Rebellion (Buchanan), 96
Mudd, Samuel A., 76, 77
Mumford, William, 101
Murray, Anna, 218
Music about Lincoln, **446–448**

Napoleon III, 253, 615
Narrative of the Life of Frederick Douglass (Douglass), 218

Index

"Nashville Movement," 582
Nast, Thomas, 546
National Archives, 51
National Banking Act (1863), 46, 397, **485–487,** 565, 592
National Bank Note Company, 625
"National Confederate Anthem" (sheet music), 582
National Currency Act. *See* National Banking Act (1863)
National Democrats (Danites), 112, 437
National Era (newspaper), 399, 632
National Film Registry, 445
National Historic Landmark, 444, 618
National Intelligencer, 674
National Lincoln Monument Association, 99, 637
National Mall, 449
National Park Service, 356, 439, 440
National Photographic Art Gallery, 82
National Register of Historic Places, 491
National Republic, 432
National Road, 685
National Trust for Historic Preservation, 444, 618
National Union Party, 121, 122, 123, 165, 370, **487–490,** 551, 658, 700, 701
Native Americans, 377, 455, 456. *See also* American Indians
Nat Turner rebellion (1831), 170
Nauvoo, Illinois, 476, 477
Navajo Removal (1864), 357–358, **455–456**
Navy, U.S., 7, 15, 72
Navy Department, 190
Navy Yard, 33
Nebraska Territory, *511,* 606
Neely, Mark E., 311
Nell, William C., 284
Nelson, Samuel, 540
Newburyport Free Press, 716
Newburyport Herald, 283
"New Departure." *See* Democratic Party
New England Emigrant Aid Company, 391
New England Federalists, 581
New England Weekly Review, 716
New Jersey militia, 292
New Market, Battle of, 85, 337
New Mexico Territory, 153, 357, 377, 455, 456, 605
New Orleans, 72, 100, 101, 102, 107, 363, 403, 557, 558, 686
New Orleans Crescent (newspaper), 714
New Orleans Picayune (newspaper), 228

New Salem, Illinois, 403, 405, 407, 441, **490–491**
New Ulm, Minnesota, 603
New York Board of Supervisors, 226
New York City Council, 169, 224
New York City draft riots. *See* Draft riots, New York City
New York Court of Appeals, 492
New York Custom House, 705
New Yorker, 306
New York Evangelist, 632
New York Evening Post, 123
New York Herald, 143, 731
New York Historical Society, 83
New York Times, 415, 519, 715
New York Tribune, **492–495.** *See also* Greeley, Horace
  Colfax and, 145
  on Copperheads, 725
  on *Dred Scott,* 228
  Frémont investigation, 374
  Hay and, 323
  Lincoln public letter to, 239, 413, 537, 567, 669
  urging march to Richmond (1861), 24, 97
  Wade-Davis manifesto, 654
  on Wide Awakes, 718
New York World, 143, 208
"The Next Presidential Election" (1864 pamphlet), 530
Niagara Falls, Canada, 307, 320
Niagara Letter, 701
Nicolay, John G. (1832–1901), 66, 320, *321,* 323, 370, **495–497,** 699
Ninety-Day Volunteers. *See* Volunteers, Ninety-Day
North American Party, 467
North Anna River, Virginia, 507
Northcote, Stafford, 17
Northern Democrats, 117, 215, 471
Northern Pacific Railroad, 183
North Star (newspaper), 218
Northumberland Gazette, 107
Northwest Ordinance (1787), 175, 268, 472, **497–499,** 501
Northwest River and Harbor Convention, Chicago (1848), 306
Northwest Territory, 341, 355, 513, 565
Northwood: A Tale of New England (Hale), 654, 655
Notes on the State of Virginia (Jefferson), 147
"No Union with Slaveholders" slogan, 517

"Now he belongs to the ages" (Stanton), 628
Nueces River, 624
Nullification Crisis (1832), 364

Oak Ridge Cemetery, Springfield, 99, 251, 326
Odell, Moses Fowler, 372
Offett, Denton, 403, 405, 490
Office of Indian Affairs, 358
Oglesby, Richard J., 343, 554
"Oh, Captain! My Captain!" (Whitman, poem), 414, 715
Ohio and Mississippi Railroad, 460
Ohio Penitentiary, 475
Ohio River, 344, 472–473, 474, 475
Ojibwa people, 57
O'Laughlen, Michael, Jr., 76, 77
"Old Henry Clay Whig," 19
"Old Hickory," 363
Old Main Building, Knox College, Galesburg, 441
Old Northwest, 475, **501–503**
"Old Rough and Ready," 647
"Old Sacramento" (cannon), 70
Old Salem Chautauqua, 491
Onstott, T.G., 491
Opdyke, George, 224
Open Door Policy, 323
Operation Anaconda. *See* Anaconda Plan
Order of American Knights, 387
Order of Retaliation (1863), **503–505**
"An Ordinance for the Government of the Territory of the United States, North-West of the River Ohio." *See* Northwest Ordinance
Oregon boundary claim, 94, 527, 528, 661
Oregon Territory, 418
"Organization to make S. P. Chase President," 529
"Orphan Brigade," 85
Osawatomie, 69–70
O'Sullivan, John L., 729
O'Sullivan, Timothy, 83
Ottawa, Illinois, debate, 113, 278–279, 433
Our American Cousin (play), 31, 33, 421, 443
"Our Countrymen in Chains" (Whittier), 716
Overland Campaign, 188, 294, **505–508**, 551
Oxford Bible, 622

Pacific Northwest, 528
Pacific Railroad/Railway Acts (1862, 1864), 126–127, 164, 361, 480, 565, 667
Page, William, 82

Paley, William, 524
Palfrey, John G., 612
Palmerston, Henry, 7, 252, 253
Palmetto Guard, South Carolina forces, 574
Palmito Ranch, Texas skirmishes, 672
Palo Alto, Battle of, 647
Panic of 1837, 21, 128, 361, 408
Panic of 1857, 397
Parker, Ely Samuel (Do-He-No-Geh-Weh), 358
Parker, Theodore, 325
Pate, Henry Clay, 69
Patronage, **509–510**
Patterson, Robert, 98
Payne, Lewis. *See* Powell, Lewis
Peace Convention (1861), 193
Peace Democrats. *See* Democrats, Peace
Pea Ridge, Arkansas, 238
Pearl (ship) incident, 611–612
The Pearl of Orr's Island (Stowe), 634
Pemberton, John C., 688, 689
Pemell, Richard Bicketron, 6, 302, 663
Pendleton, George H., 123, 189, 209, 211, 463
Peninsula Campaign, 183, 287, 288, 374
Pennsylvania Canal, 107
Pennsylvania Quakers, 28
Penny. *See* Lincoln penny
Pennybacker, Isaac S., 459
Pensacola Naval Yard, 255
People v. See name of opposing party
People's Party, 194, 483, 563, 700
Peoria Speech (1854), 268, 498, **510–513**, 523–524, 545–546
Personal liberty laws, **514–516**
Personal Memoirs (Grant), 301
Petersburg, Battle of, 31, 36, 188, 395, 396, 507, 551, 590
Petersburg Benevolent Mechanic Association, 573
Petersen House, 421, 424, 440, 443
Peterson, William, 34
Phillips, Wendell (1811–1884), 2, 4, 285, 325, **516–517**, 549, 551, 653
Phillips, William, 18
Piccirilli Brothers, 449
Pickens, Fort. *See* Fort Pickens, Florida
Pickens, Francis W., 263, 541
Pickett's Charge, 291
Piedmont, Battle of, 337
Pierce, Franklin (1804–1869), **518–520**
  defeat of Buchanan, 94
  election of 1852, 532
  Kansas and, 71

Pierce, Franklin (1804–1869)—*continued*
  Kansas-Nebraska Act and, 606
  Lincoln's attack on for opening territories to slavery, 95
  Scott and, 579
  in Slave Power conspiracy, as charged by Lincoln, 214, 229, 334–335, 606
Pierpont, Francis H., 556, 690–691
Pigeon Creek Baptist Church, 428
Pilgrim's Progress, 403, 427
Pillow, Fort. *See* Fort Pillow, Tennessee
Pillow, Gideon, 266
Pinckney, Charles Cotesworth, 170
Pinkerton, Allan, 42, 43, 702
Pittsburgh Landing, Tennessee. *See* Shiloh, Battle of
Pittsfield Pike County Free Press, 495
Plains States, 330
Plug Uglies, 42
"Pocket veto," 699
Poganuc People (Stowe), 634
Poinsett, Joel R., 280
Political culture and Lincoln, **520–522**. *See also* Whig Party
"The Political Economy of Slavery" (Ruffin), 574
Political philosophy, Lincoln's, **522–526**
Polk, James Knox (1795–1849), **526–529**, *527*
  Benton and, 54
  Buchanan in administration of, 94
  Clay opposition to, 709
  election of 1844, 140, 398–399
  Lincoln's criticism of, 361, 560, 623–624, 638, 712
  Mexican War and, 207, 272, 470, 647
  rivers and harbors bill, veto of, 571–572
  on Taylor, 648
  Wilmot Proviso and, 720–721
Polk, Leonidas, 80, 457
Pollock, James, 194
Pomeroy, Samuel, 122
Pomeroy Circular, **529–531**
Pope, John, 25, 357, 394, 462
Pope, John Russell, 449
Popular sovereignty, **531–534**
  Cass and, 124–125, 152, 215, 605
  Democratic 1860 platform and, 203–204
  Douglas and, 112–113, 116–119, 153, 201, 473, 605
  Freeport Doctrine and, 278–279
  Kansas-Nebraska Act and, 68, 377, 379–380, 722

Lincoln's opposition to, 10, 71, 201, 207, 216–217, 268, 437, 474
  Mormons and, 476–477
  Republican Party and, 723
  slavery expansion and, 71, 88
Populist movement, 666
Porter, David Dixon, 255, 569, 570, 688
Porter, FitzJohn, 337, 374
Port Gibson, Mississippi, 688
"Porthole portrait," 451
Port Royal, Virginia, 77
Posse comitatus, 243
Postage stamps. *See* Stamps, Postage
Post Office, U.S., 625
Pottawatomie Creek Massacre (1856), 69, 89, 216, **534–536**
Potter, David M., 140, 198
Pottsville Courthouse State Historic Site, Illinois, 441
Powell, Lewis Thornton (aka Lewis Payne), 32, 33–34, 76, 77, 587–588
Powhattan, USS, 255
Prairie du Chien, surrender at, 57
Prairie State, 343
"The Prayer of Twenty Millions" (Greeley), 307, 413, 493, **536–538**
Preliminary Emancipation Proclamation (1862)
  Antietam victory and, 26, 463
  black troops and, 220, 239
  border states and, 80–81
  British reaction to, 253
  Chase and, 131
  civil liberties and, 135
  Confederate reaction to, 3, 670–671
  Copperheads and, 188
  Garrison reaction to, 285
  one-hundred-day warning of issuance of Emancipation Proclamation, 236, 656
  purpose of, 239, 382, 413
  Stowe and, 633
  War Democrats and, 701
Preservation of Lincoln historic sites, **439–444**
Presidential pardons, **211–213**
President Lincoln's Cottage, Soldiers' Home, 618
President's Street Station, Baltimore, 42, 43, 44
Price, Sterling, 70, 367, 368
Prigg v. Pennsylvania (1842), 284, 466, 514, 644
Primary Geography (Stowe), 632
Prime, William C., 464

Prize Cases (1863), 136, 137, **538–540**, 646
Proclamation Act, 542
Proclamation Calling Militia, **540–543**
Proclamation of Amnesty and Reconstruction (1863), 529, 557, 652, 657, 697–698
"Proclamation of Blockade against Southern Ports," 71
Proclamation of Insurrection (1861), 541
Promontory Summit, Utah Territory, 127, 667
Protestants, 186, 225, 274, 275, 388, 400
"Proving up" process, 330
Public works, **360–361**
Pugh, George, 204–205
Pulitzer Prize, 445
Pullman, George, 425
Pullman Palace Car Company, 425

"Quaker Gun" incident, 39, 462
Quakers, 223
Quantrill, William Clarke, 392
Quantrill's raid/raiders, 392
Quincy, Illinois, debate, 412, 438

Racism and racial thought, **545–549**
Radical Abolition Party, 3
"Radical Democracy," 144
Radical Republicans, **549–552**
  Bates's opposition to, 49
  Butler and, 102
  Chandler and, 128
  Colfax as, 145
  endorsement of Lincoln as presidential candidate, 3
  equality for African Americans and, 66
  Frémont and, 290
  Joint Commission on the Conduct of the War and, 504
  Lincoln considered to be one of, 4
  Morton and, 484
  opposition to Lincoln, 488
  Phillips, Wendell, and, 517
  reconstruction and, 559
  Wade-Davis bill and, 558
Railroads, **552–554**
Rail-splitter image, Lincoln's, 363, **554–555**
Ralston, Robert, 18
Ramsey, Alexander, 603, 604
Randall, James G., 576
Randall, Ruth Painter, 577
Randolph, John, 147, 213
Rapidan River, 271, 395

Rappahannock River, Fredericksburg, 270, 271
Rathbone, Henry, 32, 33, 34, 77
Ratification Act, 313–314
Raymond, Henry, 122, 143
Reagan, Ronald, 415
The Real Lincoln (Minor), 416
Reconstruction, **555–559**. *See also* Proclamation of Amnesty and Reconstruction; Wade-Davis Bill
  Butler and, 102
  Conscience Whigs and, 712
  cost of, 354
  Davis and, 199
  Fessenden and, 301
  Hay and, 320–321
  imagined under Lincoln, 14
  Johnson's policy for, 127, 368, 371, 588
  Lee and, 396
  peaceful reunification and, 156
  Radical Reconstruction and, 550–551
  Republicans and, 566
  Stephens and, 631
  support for, 628
  Supreme Court and, 673
  tariffs and, 482
  Ten Percent Plan, 320, 651–654
  Virginia Plan and, 689–691
  Weed and, 705
Red Necks, 42
Red River Campaign, 48
Red Square Toy Company Lincoln Logs, 416
Reeder, A.H., 69
Religious Poems (Stowe), 634
Republican Convention (1856), 47
Republican Convention (1860), 49, 104, 117, 118, 194, 306, 412, 455, 502, **559–562**, 704
Republican Party, **563–566**. *See also* Radical Republicans
  1860 platform of, 256
  1864 election, 4
  American System and, 21
  black suffrage and, 58, 60
  Blair's alienation from, 64
  "Bleeding Kansas" and, 535
  Brooks and, 86–87
  Confiscation Acts and, 164
  divisions within, 165
  Douglass and, 219
  draft of Lincoln, 1858, 343
  Dred Scott decision and, 228
  effect of debates and, 268

Republican Party—*continued*
  efforts to strengthen in Illinois, 111
  election of 1856, 70, 94
  election of 1860, 47
  elements of new party, 273
  formation of, 29–30, 52, 714
  free labor philosophy and, 276
  free soil philosophy and, 274
  Frémont and, 142
  fusion of other parties into, 109
  fusion within, 379
  Greeley and, 307
  growth in stature of, 71
  Hamlin, Harry and, 316
  Harpers Ferry raid and John Brown and, 90, 91, 95
  Herndon and, 325
  Homestead Act and, 22
  in Illinois, 437, 501
  Indian relations and, 456
  Lincoln as presidential nominee of, 3, 10
  Lincoln on fusion within, 388
  Lincoln's role in, 411
  McLean and, 467
  National Union Party and, 488
  in New York, 306
  New York Tribune and, 492
  in Pennsylvania, 103
  platform of 1860, 171, 553
  railroad bills and, 126
  slaveholding interests, resistance to, 333
  Slave Power and, 638
  slavery views of, 656
  soldiers' vote and, 619
  Supreme Court and, 673
  Trumbull and, 664–665
  Whigs and, 710
Resaca de la Palma, Battle of, 647
Revolutionary War, 397, 568, 659
Reynolds, John, 56, 405
Reynolds v. United States (1879), 136
Rhetoric in Lincoln's public speeches, 296–297, **566–568**
Richards, Leonard, 213
Richmond, Virginia
  Butler aim to attack, 102
  capture of, as goal, 292, 300, 394–395, 442, 505–506, 589
  as Confederate capital, 97, 703
  Davis burial in, 199–200
  evacuation of, 199, 396
  "Forward to Richmond" slogan, 23, 24, 307
  Lincoln's arrival in, 304, **569–571**, 690

  Lincoln statue unveiled in (2003), 416
  Sherman march toward, 596
  siege of, 36, 300, 395, 505, 590
Ridgely, Fort, 603
Riggs, George Washington, Jr., 616
Riney, Zachariah, 401
Rio Grande River, 71, 470, 528, 624, 647
Ripon, Earl of, 17
The Rise and Fall of the Confederate Government (Davis), 199
River Queen (Union steamboat), 300, 319, 571, 596, 631
Rivers and Harbors Convention (1847), 49, **571–573**
Rives, William C., 260
RMS *Trent. See* Trent (British mail steamship) affair
Robinson, Charles, 69
Robinson, George, 34
Robinson, James F., 457
Rockett's Landing, Virginia, 569
Roman Republic, 75
Roosevelt, Franklin Delano, 138, 330, 655
Roosevelt, Theodore, 452–453
Rosecrans, William, 700
Ross, Frederick, 522
Ruffin, Edmund (1794–1865), **573–575**, *574*
Rush, Richard, 18
Russell, John, 7, 16, 302, 663
Russia, 94, 108, 195, 252, 588
Rutgers, Henry, 18
Rutledge, Ann Mayes (1813–1835), 198, 326, 491, **575–577**, 685
Rutledge Tavern, New Salem, 403, 575

Sac and Fox tribal lands, 406
Sacramento, California, 667
Safford, Henry, 34
Saint-Gaudens, Augustus, 415
Santo Domingo, West Indies, 147
St. Joseph Valley Register (newspaper), 145
St. Louis arsenal, 366–367
Salisbury, William, 316
Sandburg, Carl, 445
Sand Creek massacre, Colorado Territory (1864), 357, 373
Sanford, John F. A., 227
Sangamon County, Illinois, 110, 215, 324, 331, 406, 408, 490, 491, 572, 659
Sangamon Journal, 491, 600
San Jacinto, USS, 66, 614, 661
Santa Anna, Antonio Lopez de, 648
Sartain, John, 304

Saukenuk tribal community, 56
Sauk people, 56, 57
Savannah, Georgia, 598
Schmidt, Ernst, 289
Schofield, John, 392
Schurz, Carl, 290
Scott, Charlotte, 235
Scott, Dred, 65, 104, 174
Scott, John Emerson, 227
Scott, Winfield (1786–1866), **579–581**, 706
　abandonment of Fort Sumter, 65
　advice to Lee, 394
　advice to Lincoln on Fort Sumter, 260
　advice to Lincoln on Virginia, 255
　Anaconda Plan and, 22–24
　arrest of saboteurs and, 242
　blockade of Southern ports, 71
　Bull Run (First) and, 97
　Conscience Whigs and, 712
　Lee and, 393
　Lincoln assassination attempt, investigation of, 42
　McClellan and, 461
　Merryman arrest and, 243
　suspension of *habeas corpus* order and, 312
　as Whig presidential candidate, 273, 518
"Scott's Great Snake," 23. *See also* Anaconda Plan
Scott v. Sandford. *See Dred Scott v. Sandford* (1857)
Scripps, John L., 555
Seaman's Aid Society, 654
Secession, **581–585,** 651–652, 708
Secession Convention, Virginia's, 542
Second American Party System, 21, 140
Second American Revolution, 269
Second Bank of the United States, 21, 45, 54, 139, 363, 527, 643, 685
Second Great Awakening, 709
Second Inaugural Address. *See* Inaugural Address, Second
"Second Lecture on Discoveries and Inventions" (Lincoln), 729
Second Legal Tender Case. *See Knox v. Lee* (1871)
Second Manassas, Battle of. *See* Bull Run, Second Battle of
Sedition Act of 1789, 581
Seminole War, Second, 647
Semmes, Raphael, 15
Senate Committee on Commerce, 128
Senate Committee on Foreign Relations, 252, 459, 638

Senate Committee on the Territories, 95
Seneca Indians, 358
Sequel to Drum-Taps (Whitman), 715
Sequestration Act (1861), 160
Seven Days Battles, 394, 462
Seventy-ninth New York militia, 292, 731
Seward, Fanny, 34, 588
Seward, Fred, 34
Seward, Gus, 34
Seward, William Henry (1801–1872), *237,* **585–588**
　Adams and, 7
　Anti-Masonic Party and, 465
　assassination attempt on, 34, 77
　blockades and, 542
　Brown, John and, 90
　call for resignation of, 270, 529
　Chase and, 130, 131
　colonization and, 148
　critics of, 75
　Crittenden Compromise, 192
　election of 1848, 249
　election of 1856, 109
　election of 1860, 3, 6, 30, 38, 117, 118, 119, 184, 185, 190, 203, 306, 412, 493, 560, 565
　election of 1864, 121, 502
　Fort Pickens and, 255
　Fort Sumter and, 261, 262
　Great Britain and, 30, 252, 253, 301, 302, 539, 615, 639, 661, 663
　Hampton Roads Conference and, 318, 319
　Inaugural Address and, 348–349
　Johnson and, 370
　Liberty Party and, 399
　personal liberties laws and, 515
　Ruffin and, 574
　as secretary of state, 49, 65, 66, 103, 104–105, 106, 247, 550
　slavery and, 167, 173, 412
　on Southern nationalism, 23
　Stanton and, 627
　Sumner and, 638, 639
　Weed and, 704
　Whig Party and, 708
Seymour, Horatio, 169, 207, 224
Shakespeare, William, 490, 567, 617
Shannon, Wilson, 69, 391, 519
Shaw, Lemuel, 515
Shenandoah, USS, 15
Shenandoah Valley Campaigns (1862, 1864), 48, 97, 189, 300, 337, 394, 395, 462, 507, 508, **588–591,** 600

Shepherdstown, Battle of, 26
Shepley, George F., 557
Sheridan, Philip H., 189, 300, 395, 508, 590, 591
Sherman, Charles Taylor, 591
Sherman, Henry "Dutch," 535
Sherman, John (1823–1900), 122, 130, 161, 481, **591–593**, 594
Sherman, William, 535
Sherman, William Tecumseh (1820–1891), **593–596**, *594*
   Atlanta Campaign and, 35–37, 699
   as brother of John, 591
   conflict with Stanton, 628
   Field Order No. 15 (confiscation of land) and, 161
   Long Walk and, 456
   march to the sea and, 156, **597–599**
   relationship with Grant, 602
   relationship with Lincoln, 375, 413
   soldiers' vote and, 620
   Vicksburg Campaign and, 687
Sherman Anti-Trust Act (1890), 592
Shields, James (1810–1879), 419, **599–600**
Shiloh, Battle of, 85, 298–299, 343, 594, **600–602**
Shiloh Cemetery, Coles County, Illinois, 427
Sibley, Henry, 603
Sierra Leone, 147
"Sifting the Ann Rutledge Evidence" (Randall), 576–577
Sigel, Franz, 290, 337, 367
Simon, John Y., 577
Sinking Spring Farm, Kentucky (birthplace), 428
Sioux Uprising, 357, 358, **603–604**. *See also* Indian Relations
Slaughterhouse Cases (1873), 674
"Slavehound of Illinois," 517
Slave Power, **604–607**
   Bleeding Kansas and, 70
   "doughfaces" and, 213–214
   Douglas, Stephen and, 710
   Douglass on, 219
   Free Soil Party and, 272
   Kansas-Nebraska Act and, 380
   Lincoln's opposition to in Illinois, 110
   Mexican War and, 638
   as political issue, 519
   as political weapon, 389, 608
   Republican party and, 563, 564
The Slave Power (Richards), 213
Slavery, **607–611**, 644
Slave Trade Act of 1819, 18

Slavocracy. *See* Slave Power
Slemmer, Adam J., 255
Slidell, John (1793–1871), 66, 125, 252–253, 302, 459, 528, **614–615**, 639, 661–663
Smith, Caleb B., 104, 146, 148, *237*, 542. *See also* Cabinet, Lincoln's
Smith, Charles F., 601
Smith, Edmund Kirby, 199
Smith, Gerrit, 3, 4
Smith, James, 418
Smith, Joseph, 476, 477
Smith, Samuel, 18
Smith, W. Dexter, Jr., 414
Smith-Barney, 183
Snelling, Fort. *See* Fort Snelling, Wisconsin Territory
"Snow Bound" (Whittier), 717
"Soldiers' Friend," 483
Soldiers' Home, 76, 444, **616–618**
Soldiers' National Cemetery, Gettysburg, 443
The Soldier's Right to Vote, Who Opposes It? Who Favors It?, 619
Soldiers' vote, **618–621**
"Some Thoughts for the President's Consideration" (Seward), 586
Sons of Liberty, 387
Sons of Temperance, 650
South Carolina, 258
South Carolina Sea Islands, 80
Southern Democrats, 113, 366, 436
Southern Pacific Railroad, 127
Southern Unionists, 156, 514, 583, 651
South Mountain, Battle of, 26, 463
Southwest Ordinance (1790), 473
Spain, 94, 252, 290
Spangler, Edman, 33, 77
Sparrow, Elizabeth and Thomas, 402
Special Order No. 1, 288
"Specie," 45, 308, 309, 359, 397, 486
Speed, James, 79, 80, 106, 571, 622
Speed, Joshua Fry, 79, 175, 303, 324, 381, 382, 388, 476, **621–623**
Speed, Lucy G., 622
Spencer County, Indiana, 404
Spielberg, Steven, 417, 446
"Spoons Butler," 101
"Spot resolutions," 272, 470, 528, **623–625**, 648
Spotsylvania, Virginia, 507
Spotsylvania National Military Park, Virginia, 442
Sprague, William, 465
Springfield, Illinois, 99, 250–251, 342, 408, 410, 414, 419, 686

Springfield Conservative, 636
Springfield Scott Club, 518
Springfield Young Men's Lyceum address, 568
Stamps, postage, **625–626,** *626*
Stanford, Leland, 126
Stanly, Edward, 557
Stanton, Edwin M. (1814–1869), *237,* **627–629**
  appointment to War Department, 163
  assassination of Lincoln, 32–33
  clashes with Lincoln, 292
  colonization efforts and, 148–149
  Indian relations and, 358
  on influence of Scott, Winfield, 580
  McClellan and, 25, 462
  opinion of Lincoln, 104
  relations with Blair, 66
  Sanitary Commission and, 635
  Shenandoah Valley strategy and, 589
  Vallandigham and, 683
  working relationship with Lincoln, 105
Stanton, Elizabeth Cady, 4
Stanton, Henry, 3
Star of the West (merchant vessel), 96, 259
The Stars and Stripes, 262, 263
State-Journal (newspaper), 442
State of the Union address (1852), 19, 148
Steadman, Fort, 396
Stephens, Alexander Hamilton (1812–1883), 154, 155, 201, 268, 318, 357, 471, **629–631**
Stevens, Fort. *See* Fort Stevens, District of Columbia
Stevens, Thaddeus, 163, 165, 166, 195, 465, 517, 549, 651, 697
Stillman's Run, Battle of, 56
Stoddard, William O., 496, 616
Stone, Charles P., 39, 40
Stones River, Battle of, 85
Storey, Wilbur F., 387
Story, Joseph, 277, 284, 637, 644–645
Stover, John, 345
Stowe, Calvin E., 632
Stowe, Harriet Beecher (1811–1896), 399, **632–634**
Strader v. Graham (1851), 645
Strong, George Templeton (1820–1875), **634–635**
Strozier, Charles, 577
Stuart, J. E. B., 731
Stuart, John Todd (1807–1885), 115, 406, 407, 409, 454, 476, 491, **636–637,** 659, 660
Stuart and Lincoln law firm, 419

Sumner, Charles (1811–1874), **637–640**
  abolition and, 665
  British relations and, 6, 16
  Brown, John and, 91
  caning of, 69, 86–87, 110, 216, 535, 564
  Civil Rights Acts, 102
  as Conscience Whig, 711
  on emancipation, 30
  endorsement of Lincoln as presidential candidate, 3
  foreign policy and, 252–253
  Free Soil Party and, 273
  Kansas-Nebraska Act and, 379
  McLean, John and, 466
  Radical Republicans and, 549, 551
  reconstruction and, 651, 697
  Wendell, Phillips and, 517
Sumner, Edwin, 69
Sumter, Fort. *See* Fort Sumter, South Carolina
Supreme Court. *See* U.S. Supreme Court
Surplus Distribution Act (1836), 21
Surratt, John Harrison, Jr., 76, 77, 430
Surratt, Mary, 76, 77, 443
Susquehanna River, 107, 291
Sutter's Mill, 593
Swayne, Noah, 673, 674, 676–677, 679
Swayne, Wager, 674
Swett, Leonard, 636
Sydney, Algernon, 74

Taft, Charles, 34
Taft, William Howard, 450
Tallmadge, James, 472
Taney, Roger Brooke (1777–1864), **643–647,** *644*
  death of, 123, 132, 658
  Dred Scott decision, 10, 94–95, 173–174, 228–229, 473, 523, 678
  Emancipation Proclamation, 237
  habeas corpus and, 49, 137, 243–244, 312, 365, 492, 539–540
  Lincoln on, 678
  McLean and, 465, 467
  slavery and, 112–113, 334, 335, 606
Tariff of 1828, 140
Taylor, John, 18
Taylor, Sara Knox, 198
Taylor, Zachary (1784–1850), **647–649**
  California and, 55, 152–153
  Cotton Whigs and, 713
  death of, 248, 532
  election of 1848, 124, 125, 152, 272–273, 466, 471, 532

Taylor, Zachary (1784–1850)—*continued*
 inauguration of, 82
 Mexican War and, 470, 624
 patronage and, 509
 Stephens and, 629–630
 Whigs and, 708, 710
 Wilmot Proviso and, 605
Temperance, 563, **649–651**
"Temporary insanity" defense, 627
Tennessee, 369–370
Ten Percent Plan, 320, **651–654**
Tenure of Office Act (1867), 629
Territorial Emancipation Act (1962), 160
Texas, Fort, 623
Texas annexation (1845). *See also* Mexican War; Wilmot Proviso
 Buchanan and, 94
 Clay and, 140
 Conscience Whigs and, 710, 712
 Free Soil Party and, 272
 growth of national domain and, 528
 Knights of the Golden Circle, 386
 Liberty Party and, 398
 Polk and, 527
 Tyler and, 54
 Whigs and, 709
Texas Revolution (1836), 527–528
Thanksgiving, **654–655**
Theodora (blockade runner), 614, 661
Third American Party System (1856–1896), 563
Thirteenth Amendment (1865), **656–658**, 657
 Congress and, 30, 166, 319
 Garrison and, 285
 Gettysburg Address and, 296
 implementation of, 631
 Kentucky and, 458
 Lincoln's role and, 4, 547
 National Union Party and, 489
 opposition to, 637
 Radical Republicans and, 550
 ratification of, 135, 151, 610, 665
 Republican Party, 610
 support for, 146, 684
 Trumbull and, 665
 War Democrats and, 701
Thirtieth Congress. *See* Congress
Thomas, Benjamin P., 577, 685
Thomas, George H., 598
Thompson, H.S., 414
Thornton, Seth, 623, 624
"Thunderbolt of the Confederacy," 474

Tilden, Samuel J., 484, 666
Tilton, Theodore, 4, 123
Titus, Henry, 70
Tod, David (governor of Ohio), 700
Todd, David (brother of Mary), 732
Todd, Levi (grandfather of Mary), 659
Todd, Robert Smith (father of Mary), 418–419, 424
Todd family, 78, **659–661**. *See also specific family members*
Toombs, Robert, 192, 263, 437
"Topeka movement," 68, 68–69
Transcendentalism, 240
Treasury, U.S., 45, 54, 103, 130, 182, 190, 308–309, 384, 397, 452, 486
Treasury bonds, U.S., 485, 486
Treaty of Guadalupe Hidalgo (1848), 471, 528, 531, 625
Treaty of Washington (1871), 15, 17
Trent (British mail steamship) affair, **661–664**
 Blair advice on, 66
 British relations and, 302
 Cass on, 125
 circumstances of, 6–7, 252–253, 586
 Mason and, 459
 Slidell and, 614–615
 Sumner and, 639
Tribunal of Arbitration, Geneva (1872), 15
"Tribune Tracts No. 4," 493
Tripp, C.A., 623
Trudeau, Noah Andre, 672
Trumbull, Lyman (1813–1896), **664–666**
 Confiscation Act and, 160
 conspiracy with Lincoln alleged by Douglas, 434–437
 defeat of Lincoln for Senate (1858), 111, 380, 411
 Democratic Convention (1860), 205–206
 Joint Committee on the Conduct of the War and, 40
 as Mary Todd suitor, 419
 Thirteenth Amendment and, 658
Turner, Nat, 170
Turner; People v. (1840), 134
Turner's Gap, Battle of, 26
Tyler, John, 21, 52, 54, 55, 140, 466, 710

Uncle Tom's Cabin (Stowe), 399, 632, 633
"Unconditional Surrender" Grant, 298
Underground Railroad, 128
The Union. *See also specific battles and leaders*
 abolitionism and, 4
 black soldiers in, 189

Blair (Austin) and, 62
Blair (Francis) and, 63, 64
Border States and, 79
Chase on, 131
Confederate states readmitted to, 13, 138, 550, 654
Confiscation Acts and, 158, 161, 537
conscription in, 168, 221
fugitive slaves in, 3, 179
Grant as military commander for, 188
Hampton Road Conference, 318–319
Lincoln's commitment to preservation of, 151, 173, 268, 412
Lincoln's political philosophy on, 524–525
McDowell as military commander for, 98
military strategy of, 287
monetary policy in, 46
naval blockade by, 71–73, 384
popular sovereignty and, 533
preservation of, 656
railroads and, 553
relations with Britain, 6, 7, 16
Stanton and, 628
Virginia Plan and, 690–691
war fought to maintain, 11
Whittier and, 717
Union army/armies, 22, 39, 80, 180–181, 186, 297, 382, 506, 589, 671. *See also specific field armies by name*
Unionist Democrats, 158, 189, 382, 384, 457, 488
Union League Club, 635
Union Pacific Railroad (UP), 126, 127, 146, 553, **667–668**
Union Party. *See* National Union Party
Union (Republican) Party Convention (1864), 144
United States Sanitary Commission, 634, 635
Upper South, 52, 582–583, 584
U.S. Army, 91, 475
U.S. Army Corps of Engineers, 280
U.S. arsenal, 95
U.S. Capitol, 340, *347,*414
U.S. Cavalry, Third, 336
U.S. Colored Troops (USCT), 220, 239, 548, 610, **669–673,** *670*
U.S. Military Academy, West Point, New York. *See* West Point
U.S. Supreme Court. *See also specific cases and justices*
  Browning wanting appointment to, 93
  Chase appointment to, 106, 452, 673, 676–677, 679

on civil liberties, 136–137
on Civil Rights Act of 1875, 551
constitutional law and, 173–174
Emancipation Proclamation and, 237, 239
habeas corpus writ and, 243, 312. *See also Habeas corpus,* Lincoln's suspension of
on Legal Tender Act, 397–398
Lincoln's appointments to, 327, **673–677**
Lincoln's view of, **677–679**
McLean appointment to, 464–465, 467
on *Prize Cases,* 538–540
on Second Confiscation Act, 161
Taney and, 644–646
on territorial government's ability to pass slavery legislation, 203, 278–279
Usher, John, 104, 106. *See also* Cabinet, Lincoln's
Utah Territory, 153, 377, 477, 605

Vallandigham, Clement Laird (1820–1871), 174, *187,* 189, 208, 210, 307, 387, 413, **681–684,** *682,* 700, 701. *See also* Copperheads
Vallandigham, Ex parte (1863), 679
Van Buren, Martin, 8, 54, 94, 107, 140, 273, 398, 408, 466, 527, 648
Vance, Zebulon, 198
Vandalia, Illinois, **685–686**
Vandiver, Frank E., 199
Vicksburg Campaign, 48, 188, 202, 291, 295, 299, 343, 395, 475, 557, 594, **686–689,** *687*
Victoria, queen of England, 6, 303
Virginia, Restored Government of, 556, 690–691
Virginia Central Railroad, 337
Virginia Convention, 574
Virginia Military Institute, 337, 590
Virginia Plan, **689–691.** *See also* Reconstruction
Virginia Unionists, 556
Voices of Freedom (Whittier), 716
Volunteers, Ninety-Day, 24, 97, 167, 168, 541, **692–694.** *See also* Conscription Act (1863); Draft, military

Wade, Benjamin Franklin (1800–1878), 40, 123, 163, 166, 192, 372, 549, 653–654, **695–696,** *696,* 711
Wade-Davis Bill (1864), 550, 558, 653, 689, **696–699.** *See also* Reconstruction
Wade-Davis Manifesto, 654, 699
Wadsworth, James S., 672
Wakarusa War, 69, 391

Walker Tariff (1846), 527
Wallace, Frances Todd, 431, 659
Wallace, William, 431, 659
War Democrats, 186, 207, 290, 317, 368, 510, 547, 656, 658, **700–701**
War Department
  appointment of Stanton to, 163, 627
  Bureau for Colored Troops and, 671
  corruption in, 190
  firing of Cameron from, 108
  leniency toward Quakers, 233
  militia quotas and, 168
  response to assassination, 75
  slaves as contraband question, 181
  soldiers' vote and, 619
  transcontinental railroad survey and, 553
  USCT, status of, 672
"War Hawk," 139
War of 1812, 20, 21, 124, 139, 254, 312, 472, 552, 581, 647
Warren, Fort. *See* Fort Warren, Boston
"Was Abe Lincoln a White Supremacist?" (Bennett), 14
Washburne, Elihu B., 146, 206, 298, 300, 579
Washington, Booker T., 305
Washington, Bushrod, 147
Washington, D.C., **702–704**. *See also* District of Columbia
Washington, George, 74, 268, 322, 355, 415, 626
Washington Conference (1871), 17
Washington Globe, 318
Watch Night—or, Waiting for the Hour (painting), 285
Wayland, Francis, 524
Wayne, James Moore, 540
Ways and Means Committee, 163, 166, 481
Webster, Daniel, 19, 82, 153, 241, 249, 333, 523, 524, 708, 713
Webster Whig, 478
Weed, Thurlow (1797–1882), 306, 465, 560, 561, **704–705**, 711
Weems, Mason Locke (Parson), **400–401**
Weik, Jesse W., 326
Weitzel, Godfrey, 569–570, 690
Welles, Gideon (1802–1878), 6, 104–106, 121, 237, 316, 542, **706–707**
Wells, Robert, 227–228
Western Department, 142
Western Female Academy, 632
Western Sanitary Commission, 235
Western Theater of the Civil War, 85
West Indies, 147

West Point, 198, 374, 393, 460, 593
West Virginia, 556
Wheeler, Joseph, 597
"When Lilacs Last in the Dooryard Bloom'd" (Whitman), 714
Whig Party, **707–710**. *See also* Conscience Whigs; Cotton Whigs
  American System, 21
  Bell and, 52
  break by Lincoln with, 87
  campaign of 1856, 109–111
  campaign of 1860, 118
  capitalism and, 521–522
  Chandler and, 128
  Clay and, 139–141, 381, 404
  Compromise of 1850, 152
  constitutional ideology of Lincoln and, 172
  Democrats and, 207
  end of, 29
  expansion and, 54
  Fillmore and, 249–250
  Free Soil Party and, 272–273
  Greeley and, 306
  homesteading and, 329
  in Illinois, 125, 130, 206, 215, 331, 659, 685
  internal improvements and, 36, 360
  Jackson and, 363–364
  Kansas-Nebraska Act and, 52, 379
  Lincoln-Douglas debates, 433–434
  Lincoln in agreement with, 9
  McClean and, 465–467
  path to Republicanism and, 564
  political philosophy and, 523
  slavery and, 606
Whipple, Henry, 358, 603
Whitman, George, 715
Whitman, Walt (1819–1892), 414, **714–716**, *715*
Whittier, John Greenleaf (1807–1892), **716–717**
"Wide Awakes," 119, 389, 704, **718–720**, *719*
The Wigwam, Chicago, 343, 559–560
Wilderness Campaign, 504
Wilkes, Charles D., 66, 252, 614, 615, 661
Wilkes, John, 74
Wilkinson, Allen, 535
Willard Hotel, Washington, D.C., 442
Willich, August, 290
Wills, David, 195
Wilmot, David, 152, 215, 531, 711
Wilmot Proviso, 2, 125, 150, 272, 531, 532, 605, 611, 638, 711, **720–724**
Wilson, Henry, 517, 633, 711

Wilson, James F., 658
Wilson, Woodrow, 138, 482
Wilson's Creek, Missouri, Battle of, 281, 372
Winnebago Indians of Wisconsin Territory, 107
Winslow, John A., 15
Winthrop, Robert, 713
Wisconsin Heights, Battle of, 57
Wisconsin Territory, 227
Wood, Fernando (1812–1881), 210, **724–725**
Wood Lake, Battle of, 603
Woodson, Daniel, 69
Woodward, George W., 463
World War I, 138
World War II, 138, 453
Wright, Elizur, 3
Wright, Henry, 4
Wright, Horatio G., 703
Wright, Joseph, 372

Yancey, William Lowndes, 204
Yankees, 98
Yates, Richard (1818–1873), 298, 386, 387, 411, 512, **727–728**
Yeatman, James, 235
YMCA Christian Commission agency, 715
Young, Brigham, 477
Young, John Russell, 322, 496
"Young America," **728–730**
"Young Indians," 629
Young Men's Lyceum speech, 568, 708
Youngstown Sheet and Tube v. Sawyer (1952), 138

Zouave Battalions of France, 731, *732*
Zouaves, 233, 234, **731–732**, *732*. *See also* Ellsworth, Elmer Ephraim